The Push Guide to WHICH UNIVERSITY 2006

Edited by: Ruth Bushi and Johnny Rich

Written by: Dan Jones, Anthony Leyton and Johnny Rich

11th Edition
Head Honcho: Johnny Rich
Project Editor: Ruth Bushi
Deputy Editor: Michelle S H Ho
Editorial Assistant: Richard Simm

Investigators: Sarah Ackling, Guy Atkinson, Tom Ashton, Alistair Baker, Guy Bingley, Donna-Louise Bishop, Clare Bunting, Liz Cremona, Amisha Desai, Caroline Dundas, Leanne Franklin, Sarah Hamilton, Anne Hurst, Jo Kidd, Gloria Lin, Jenna Lloyd, Emma McGuire, Huw Rees, Gillian Salmon, Kathryn Skegg, Dan Sim, Richard Simm, Heather Thomas, Esther Webber, Jessica Williams-Chadwick.

Thanks to: Calum Bartlett, David Jones, Andy Varley.

Special thanks to: Paul Farnworth, Nicole Linhardt-Rich, Adrian Moss, Peter Oates, Clare Wheelwright.

Published by: Nelson Thornes

Push Online: www.nelsonthornes.com/push

Push
...like it is

First published in 1992 as *PUSH 93* (*The Polytechnic and University Students' Handbook*)

Eleventh edition published in 2005 by:
Nelson Thornes Ltd
Delta Place
27 Bath Road
CHELTENHAM
GL53 7TH
United Kingdom

05 06 07 08 09 / 10 9 8 7 6 5 4 3 2 1

A catalogue record for this book is available from the British Library

ISBN 0 7487 9489 1

Page make-up by Pantek Arts Ltd, Maidstone

Printed and bound in Spain by GraphyCems

Flunk rates are calculated by Push from data published by the Higher Education Statistics Agency, who produce Performance Indicators in Higher Education on behalf of the four UK funding bodies.

Source of data: HESA Performance Indicators in Higher Education in the UK 2002/03, Table T5. Data used by permission of the Higher Education Statistics Agency. HESA cannot accept responsibility for any inferences or conclusions derived from the data by third parties.

Note from *Push*
The *Push Guides* have just about the best research methods you could hope for. We visit every university and produce more pages of research than is healthy for the world's rainforests. Yet, even the best make mistakes occasionally. We do everything in our power to avoid it (including checking everything at least three times), but if we've got something wrong or it's changed since we went to press, then we're really sorry, but, basically, bite me – it's not our fault. Go stew. But do let us know first, okay? Not only will we put it right, we'll give you a credit for it, too.
Text in the university profiles in italics is *Push's* opinion – take it or leave it.

Push on

CONTENTS

University profiles

Push power

Push is an independent organisation that collects the largest ever resource of information about student life in the UK.

Push distributes that information through five services:

The Push Guide to Which University. The best-selling guidebook (tip: you're reading it) with essential facts, figures and opinions on every university in the UK.

The Push Guide to Choosing a University. Top advice about choosing the right university for you.

The Push Guide to Money: Student Survival. The lowdown on what you'll have to spend, what you'll have to spend it on and how the cost varies at each of the UK's universities.

Push Online (www.nelsonthornes.com/push). Regularly up-dated information, advice and links about student life and choosing a university.

Push Visits. The personal touch: *Push* experts visit schools and colleges to give specialist advice.

DID YOU KNOW?

Push has employed more than 500 researchers, photographers and writers over the past 12 years.
Push researchers visit every university in the UK.
Push's research probes the universities themselves, students' unions, public and Government bodies and thousands of students.
Each year *Push* generates over 15,000 pages of exclusive research.
Push's entire database of information is fully updated every year.
Push information has all been checked at least three times.
Push researchers and staff are high-flying students and recent graduates.
Push is the UK's most widely used resource about student life, used by students, teachers, careers advisers, parents, universities, Government bodies, political parties, media organisations and many others.
Push always strives to provide the most up-to-date information in the most accessible style and at an affordable cost.

Everything we do is by students for students.

We love hearing glowing praise. We shed a tear over harsh criticism. If you have the former, or, if you must, the latter or just want to be involved with life in the *Push* lane and think you cut the mustard, drop us a line at:

The Push Guides
Nelson Thornes
Delta Place
27 Bath Road
Cheltenham
Gloucestershire
GL53 7TH
Tel: (01242) 267 943

Or by e-mail to editor@push.co.uk

Push start

Foreword by Kat Fletcher, President of the National Union of Students

Choosing the right university and course for the next three years of your life can feel like a daunting process; however *Push* is a comprehensive resource to help you make the right choices for you.

University is a fantastic experience with innumerable opportunities. As well as the obvious benefits that a degree provides, you'll have the chance to get involved in countless projects for often the first, and sometimes only, time in your life. And university communities can be an eclectic mix of personalities, with people from all sorts of different backgrounds working, living and socialising together.

The factors that will influence your decision are varied. Distance, nightlife, entertainment, halls of residence, extra-curricular activities, graduate employment and beer prices may be reasons for and against choosing a particular course, location and university.

This year, the decision is made much harder for prospective students as a result of top-up fees. Universities should offer a range of bursaries to their prospective students so it is vital that you speak to institutions and find out what support is on offer and about the level of fees you will be expected to pay.

Make a shortlist of your favourite places and take advantage of the open days on offer. This will give you a great opportunity to meet real students and find out if you really want to go there. You may have older siblings, parents or friends who have already been to university and can give you advice on what university and course to choose, but remember it's your future and your choice.

As soon as you arrive on campus, make a beeline to the students' union to collect your NUS card and check out all the activities on offer. You may want to join a club or society, try out for the sports teams, join a voluntary project in your local community, write for the union newspaper or find a part-time job. The SU will be able to advise you on all these opportunities. As well as being the best days of your life, university will help you develop skills that will be invaluable once you go out into the world of full-time work. Whatever your interests and experience you can be sure student life will be as diverse and cosmopolitan as you make it.

Don't forget that NUS represents over 5 million students in the UK and your SU will be able to support you on campus during your studies.

Good luck in making your choices and I wish you all the best for your time at university.

Kat Fletcher
NUS President
www.nusonline.co.uk

Pushover

Using *The Push Guide* is a pushover. A 5-year-old child could understand it, but before you rush out to find a 5-year-old child because you can't make head nor tail of it, here's the idiots' guide to *The Push Guide* – also invaluable for gifted 5-year-olds, vastly over-qualified academics and you...

The Push Guide has been designed and devised to make it as easy to use as possible, whatever you want to do with it.

Well, maybe if you want to use it as a pet, you're probably better off with a goldfish, but as a guide to real life at the UK's universities and colleges, it's the best there is.

The Push Guide isn't trying to replace UCAS or the colleges' own prospectuses. We're just lending a hand in what is frankly the sort of decision that has most people reaching for the pin cushion. *The Push Guide* provides the sort of information you really want to know in order to decide, not all that stuff about course codes and quotas which appears everywhere else.

And don't let anyone tell you your decision doesn't matter. Manchester Metropolitan, Warwick and Cambridge Universities may each do a Maths course, but students are letting themselves in for more than algebra and calculus. Differentiation and integration mean something quite different when your chosen college becomes your home for the next few years.

Push tells you the real story and tells it straight. But there's no point just telling you that one university is the best and that everyone should go there. Everyone wants something different and every university offers something unique. What *The Push Guide* does is match you with the university of your dreams ... or near enough.

The Push Guide backs up nearly everything with facts, figures and statistics and when nothing tells it better than an honest opinion, we're not ashamed to admit that it's a personal view – even if it is the best-informed opinion available anywhere. In fact, we slap it in italics just so you know. Although our judgements are scrupulously researched and representative, we still advise a pretty hefty accompanying dose of salt. After all, even *Push's* opinion is still only an opinion.

With *The Push Guide* you can make comparisons and pin-point the features that you're looking for. The symbols, charts and maps give a quick and easy reference to the sort of factors that might really sway your decision, not just courses. The profiles for each college make it possible to check out whether they make the grade in the important parts other colleges cannot reach.

For help getting to grips with *Push's* icons, ratings and other features, read on.

WHEN TO USE THE PUSH GUIDE:

Choosing a course is obviously one of the first things to do and *The Push Guide* provides a table of all courses on offer (see '*Push*, of course', page 705). Since you don't want to see essentially the same course listed under 93 different names in 203 different places, *Push* has standardised the names and listed them alphabetically by subject areas.

This means that you don't have to wade through pages of different institutions to find the few that offer the course you're looking for. A word of warning: the standardisation of nearly 10,000 degree courses means that some get grouped together in a way which would perhaps be objectionable to those who appreciate the finer differences between Phonic Linguistics and Linguistic Phonemics. For exact details of any course, its contents and with which other courses it may be combined, check availability with the institutions themselves, their prospectuses or UCAS's listings.

If you know more or less what course you want to study and that course is not unusual – like Maths or English Literature, but not Cartesian Astrophysics with a side order of Sewage Management – then, no problem, you can choose entirely on the strength of other factors as outlined in each college's *Push* profile. However, if the course is only offered at a few universities, you should make a shortlist from the '*Push*, of course' lists (page 705) and then turn to the profiles for the clinching factors: Where is it? Is there any social life beyond a non-alcoholic cocktail bar and regular bus-spotting conventions? Is there a croquet club? Will it be possible to buy cigarettes at 3 in the morning?

Even for quite unusual courses, there are so many institutions to choose from that you should take the opportunity to get pushy – to demand exactly what you want or as near as damn it.

But maybe you don't know what course you want to study, don't care or just haven't quite finalised it yet (it's still a toss up between Fine Art or Chemical Engineering, for example). Well, then there are no constraints – you can choose entirely on the basis of where you'd like to study and in what environment, rather than what you'd like to study. Either way, *The Push Guide* is the best key to all the vital factors students have to put up with on a day-to-day basis.

To make life a bit easier, we've used icons (explained a bit further on) to give you an at-a-glance feel for accommodation and booze prices, facilities for welfare and sports provisions, and for academic rankings. Mostly, the icons are based on official statistics – which can't possibly tell the whole story. *Push* knows tht only a fool would decide where to spend three years of their life based on a thumb – so do yourself a favour and read the text in each profile for the bigger picture.

NAMES AND CROSS-REFERENCING:

When all the old polytechnics became universities way back at the start of the 90s, we suddenly found ourselves with lorry-loads of universities with wacky names like De Montfort University (formerly Leicester Poly) and Liverpool John Moores University (formerly Liverpool Poly) which is named after the bloke who founded the Littlewoods Pools. However, since old habits die hard, if you look up a college under the old name you will find it cross-referenced to its new name anyway.

All the profiles are arranged alphabetically (ignoring the words 'University' or 'University of'), but some places like UEA (University of East Anglia) are sent simply to try the brains behind *Push*. Should it be U for 'UEA'? E for 'East'? Or A for 'Ah, we're in Norwich'? Well, if you can't beat 'em ... put it under all three. However you try to look up even the most awkward of names you should find it cross-referenced.

THE PUSH SYMBOLS:

On the last page you'll find the key to the *Push* symbols – handy and at hand.

GLOSSARY & ABBREVIATIONS:

It's a jargon jungle out there. Everything in higher education would be so easy to understand if the colleges didn't insist on using acrid acronyms and tedious terminology all the time. In fact, it's a plot to stop the unemployed from becoming professors, but that's another (paranoid) story. *Push* unleashes the lingo in its 'Short, sharp *Push*' (Abbreviations, page 762) and 'When *Push* comes to shove' (Glossary, page 753).

OTHER OPTIONS:

Even though all the old polytechnics are now universities, you should still remember that higher education doesn't begin and end there. The choice for prospective students is bigger than Victoria Beckham's wardrobe allowance. There's thousands more universities abroad. And how about vocational training, rather than a degree? Free your mind, and your pants will follow.

The Push Guide can't include all the options – it would be thousands of pages long, years out of date, cost the earth and be impossible to pick up, let alone read. Apart from that, we like the idea.

GETTING IN TOUCH:

We crave feedback. We love it. We would crawl naked over splintered glass to hear what you have to say about *Push*. Unless, that is, you just want to slag us off or sue us for libel. Assuming you have some worthwhile and constructive response, not necessarily positive, please feel free to write to *The Push Guides*, Nelson Thornes Ltd, Delta Place, 27 Bath Road, Cheltenham, Gloucestershire, GL53 7TH, or e-mail us at editor@push.co.uk.

For next year's edition, we will again need researchers with an unassailable sense of duty and a streak of masochism – if you think we might not slam the door in your face while doubling up in fits of giggles, please drop us a line with reasons why you meet *Push's* exacting standards.

Making the most of the university profiles

NAMES:

As a headline, *The Push Guide* uses the name most students use or the most convenient title. So, for example, LSE is LSE, not the London School of Economics & Political Science. The institutions's exact name is used in the address, in case you really need to know.

ADDRESSES:

For each university, *The Push Guide* lists the address and telephone number of the administration and of the students' unions, as well as any e-mail or web addresses there might be. We've given the address of the main site, or if there is more than one main site, we say, what the hey, and give them all.

GENERAL

STATISTICS:

All statistics were right up to the minute of going to press and *Push* is really, really cut up if they're wrong later, but, hell, that's the way it goes. To keep that to a minimum though, where possible we've used official, nationally comparative figures from HESA (the Higher Education Statistics Agency). Some institutions, for various reasons, don't release certain statistics. Although we are not known for willingly taking 'no' for an answer, *Push* follows the old journalistic maxim: 'If in doubt, leave it out'. We suggest readers should follow the cynics' maxim: 'What are they trying to hide?' We've used 'n/a' where figures weren't relevant to an institution, or we just couldn't get hold of them.

Founded: Many institutions have hazy histories either too deep in the clouds of time or involving too many complicated mergers and changes of name to have just one founding year. Some newer institutions, desperate to appear venerable and ivy-covered, prefer to give the founding date of an obscure technical college on the other side of town that eventually morphed into the current institution after 14 name changes and multiple mergers. *Push*, however, has used the latest techniques (a step beyond the 'Eeny-Meeny-Miny-Mo Principle') to select just one year and, if further clarification is worthwhile, it's explained elsewhere in the profile.

Full-time u'grads: This includes students on sandwich courses, which are nothing to do with learning what to put between slices of bread, but courses where some time is spent not actually studying but on a work placement.

Part-time: Those on undergraduate courses only. Official figures from HESA include students writing theses or career folk doing short, full-time courses. *Push* has used this figure too because it can give you a feel of what being on campus – the atmosphere, facilities and student make-up – is like. But, statistics being the pesky buggers that they are can complicate things. For instance, while HESA's part-time figure at, say Oxford University, is rather high, you can't actually apply to do an undergrad degree there. Don't blame *Push*, we don't make this stuff up you know.

Postgrads: Full-time postgraduate students (who've already taken a degree).

Non-degree: Often HND (Higher National Diploma) students but all sorts of vocational, access and pre-degree courses might be offered, especially at newer universities. Again, figures are for full-time students.

Ave course: Strictly speaking, for the pedantic statisticians out there, this is the modal length of courses. Or, in English, the most common course length.

Ethnic: Some institutions prefer not to ask their students to classify themselves into one racial box or another; others are concerned to keep tabs on the ethnic origins of students, in order to ensure no bias or discrimination is occurring. Criteria for definition will vary but this figure should give a pretty good idea of the cultural mix at a particular institution. Oxbridge colleges in particular can be a bit cagey about giving this figure; we leave it up to you to decide what to make of that.

State:private school: The ratio of undergraduates educated at state schools to those from privately-funded secondary schools. Nationally (across the UK) the proportion of students from private schools is about 13%.

Flunk rate: This is an indication of the percentage of full-time undergraduates who, for one reason or another, don't successfully complete their course by being awarded a degree. The national average is 14% (around 1 in 7) with figures for individual institutions ranging from 1% to 37% – which means that well over a third of students come away with nothing. Nada. Not even a cuddly toy or Blankety Blank cheque book and pen.

Our flunk rates use data supplied by HESA. These figures project how many students who started in the academic year 2001-02 will neither gain a degree nor transfer to another university or course.

Mature students: Those aged 21 or over at the time of starting their courses. Postgrads aren't included in this figure.

International students: Includes EU students from outside the UK.

Disabled students: Colleges, if they keep records at all, often define 'disabled' differently. Some include only registered disabled students, others extend the definition to students with dyslexia, asthma or any students who, for whatever reason, choose to define themselves as disabled. So, for a bit of consistency, *Push*'s figures come from HESA, and refer to the number of full and part-time students in receipt of the Disabled Students' Allowance. Not all disabled students have to tell the university they're receiving this, or even classify themselves as disabled. However, it can be a useful guide to how well your needs may be catered for and whether there may be others in the same dinghy as you.

Local: Students who were resident within 30 miles of the institution when they applied. A higher percentage of local students can affect the atmosphere, from giving it a more independent spirit to meaning that the campus is a ghost town at weekends.

Academic ranking: (Oxbridge colleges) Based on the Norrington (Oxford) and Tompkins (Cambridge) tables, which rank colleges according to students' end-of-year or final exam results. Rankings are relative to other colleges in the same university, and were correct at the time of going to press.

ATMOSPHERE:

This section in the profiles, more than any other, gives the real feel of the place.

TOWN DETAILS:

As well as describing what the nearest city or town is like, we've given a breakdown of population, distance from the city centre to the university and weather details. Do you need to pack a sun hat or a shower cap? This is the place to look. High and low temperatures are given in centigrade. Rainfall is given in millimetres.

TRAVEL:

Trains and buses: Fares given are the best we've been able to find at the time of writing (though it can be beyond even *Push* to get a straight answer out of National Rail Enquiries at times). That means the cheapest possible return journey with a student discount card or apex ticket. Some of these don't apply at certain times of the day and apex tickets have to be bought at least 2 weeks in advance.

Hitching: *Push* would like to warn readers that if they don't know that hitching can be dangerous, then there is something wrong with them. *Push* accepts no responsibility for students who have bad experiences when thumbing it, such as waiting 6 hours in the rain for a lift, being picked up by Capri-driving 'X-Files' obsessives or being made to listen to the Cheeky Girls on the car stereo.

College: Transport listed here is that which the institution lays on, sometimes free, sometimes not.

CAREER PROSPECTS:

What kind of careers facilities there are, including how many full- and part-time staff there are. You'll also find the graduate unemployment rate listed here – that's the number of students who don't go on to employment or futher study within six months of graduating.

FAMOUS ALUMNI:

A bit of celebrity gossip – who went where. Just so students can boast that they're going to the same college as that famous 1920s Swiss serial killer or whoever.

FURTHER INFORMATION:

Prospectuses are absolutely essential if you're seriously considering applying to an institution and invaluable for seeing what the college would like you to think of them. However, they are sales documents and whilst almost every word will be true, it will not be the truth, the whole truth and nothing but the truth. They are available from the address at the top of each profile.

On the other hand, some students' unions publish 'alternative' prospectuses, which present the point of view of students at the college. Also worth getting, although the views contained are almost exclusively biased and, since the writers have rarely visited a representative number of colleges, not very comparative.

We've also listed any videos, CD-Roms, websites or other sources of information. Some are just prospectuses dumped on the net – others are more revealing. Where possible we give the address for the SU website, as well as the official university one. If you've got the time and the facilities, check them out.

A C A D E M I C

The teaching standard is:

 barely hovering

 flying

 soaring high

ACADEMIC STATS:

Range of points required for entrance: You'll need to know whether you're likely to be able to get in and so here's the top and bottom benchmarks that the college uses based on the UCAS points tariff (see Entrance requirements', page 725). Not every course requires the same points though. You may need 300 points to get into a university's law degree, for instance, but be able to get into the same place to do catering and tourism with just 80. But it's not as cut and dried as some people make out. It depends how you gather your points – what qualifications and in what subjects. For example, AS Levels aren't always as enticing to Universities as A Levels. Or, you can have 360 points in English, French and History A Levels, but it won't get you in to study Physics even if they claim to only want 200 points. In the end, you'll have to double check with the university anyway about what points they'd want from you for an individual course but, for what it's worth, we've also given the average points students have on entry.

Applicants per place: The average number of students battling it out for a place in Toenail Biology, or whatever.

Clearing: The percentage of students who entered through the UCAS clearing system. Some institutions have (sometimes undeserved) reputations as UCAS dumping grounds. This figure should give an idea of the number of students whose presence isn't entirely by choice. UCAS don't release figures for individual institutions and, understandably, some universities are a little coy about revealing this figure.

Number/length of terms: Different colleges split up the year differently. Some have three short terms, others have two long ones (semesters). It may not seem all that important, but, apart from anything else, if the vacations are shorter, odds are you won't be earning as much money during them.

Staff/student ratios: This isn't as straightforward as it may appear. Part-time staff and students can muddy the statistical waters. But it gives you a rough idea of whether tutorials are going to be cosy little sherry sessions a deux, or rugby scrums with the tutor as the ball.

Study addicts: The percentage of students who stay on for further helpings after a first degree.

Teaching: Based on assessments made by the Quality Assurance Agency for Higher Education (QAA). The teaching rating summarises departments' QAA scoring of various criteria including teaching and students' progress. The more stars, the higher the average QAA score, relative to other universities.

Research: The average figure for the college based on the last Government-funded Research Assessment Exercise. For undergrads, the level of research isn't as directly important as colleges would like you to think, but it is a good general indicator of a top-notch department. *Push* represents the teaching and research figures by 1-5 stars, where more stars means higher scores relative to the other institutions. Bear in mind though that these are average scores. Those particularly interested in how a particular department or subject rates would do well to investigate further.

ADMISSIONS:

Whether applications should be made through UCAS, GTTR etc., or whether the institutions can be approached directly, for example, for part-time or mature study.

SUBJECTS:

We've given an indication of the main subjects studied. Where courses scored more than 20 out of 24 in the last QAA assessment we've named them in this section (which means that the QAA thought provisions and teaching for those courses were particularly good).

LIBRARIES:

Unless otherwise stated, we give the total number of books and study places in all the college libraries, not just the main library. The spend per student is shown as a five-level rating where more pound signs means a higher spend.

COMPUTERS:

We give the number of computer workstations available for general use and don't include places or terminals set aside exclusively for students on a particular course. Spend per student is again shown as a five-level rating, where more pound signs means a higher spend.

ENTERTAINMENT

Beer is:

 expensive

 average

 cheap

BEER, WINE AND SOFT DRINKS:

Prices of beer, wine and soft drinks are given as the average at student bars and in towns.

SOCIAL & POLITICAL

The SU's activities and facilities are:

 frozen stiff

 lukewarm

 hot, hot, hot

CLUBS AND SOCS:

Clubs and societies have been split into sporting and non-sporting, which isn't always easy. *Push* puts them under whichever heading the college uses and you'd be well advised to check under both headings if the existence of a certain club is really important to you. Since it would get a bit repetitive otherwise, we've missed out the ones which crop up just about everywhere in the college profiles, but to be sure that the club you want is at the college you're looking at, turn to the 'clubs' tables at the back (page 736). The only ones usually missed out are the course-related societies (for sucking up to tutors).

Of course, if you've decided that somewhere is perfect apart from the fact that it doesn't have a 'South Park' Fan Club, you shouldn't dismiss it out of hand. At most colleges it's fairly easy to start a society – you only need to find between 20 and 50 others to say they want to join and the SU may well give you a packet to spend on parkas, overpriced merchandising and that vital sight-seeing trip to Colorado.

SPORTS

Student sport is:

 slobbish

 average

 active and triumphant

Text in italics is Push's point of view – take it or leave it.

ACCOMMODATION

The average rent is:

  cheap

  average

  expensive

Push's icons tell you how expensive accommodation is, both living out (on the left) and in college (on the right).

ACCOMMODATION:

Colleges tend to transform mysteriously into conference centres the moment vacations start, so if you're in halls you may well get turfed out with all your belongings to allow some pantyhose salesman to attend a corporate beerfest. *The Push Guide* gives a weekly cost and how many weeks you're going to be paying. Also given are the percentages of full-time undergraduates living in catered and self-catered accommodation. Bear in mind that 'catered' can mean anything from the full-board of three square meals a day and a Harrods hamper for your picnics, to a single 'pay-as-you-eat' canteen which you have to catch a bus to get to and which serves cockroaches in the soup.

As well as costs, *The Push Guide* also gives you details of the availability and standard of college accommodation and the kinds of security arrangements you can expect. As if that weren't enough there's even information on local housing. We even give you a rough idea of what contents insurance might set you back (the quotes we got were based on £2,000-worth of possessions, without any fancy gubbins like mobile phones and computer extras). More £ signs means more expensive.

WELFARE

The welfare provision is:

 poor

passable

pampering

Crime rate: The crime rate comes from figures published by the Home Office. They're not based on incidents on campus or university property, but are a general idea of what goes on in the town or city. The rating ranges from one (low) to five (high) exclamation marks.

FINANCIAL:

Access funds: When student loans were introduced in 1990, the Government made some money available to colleges to help avoid the problems that were likely to arise for students who were less able to pay. The figures given are the total amount each college is currently allocated. Students who want a slice of the cake should apply annually to their college, but not until they get there. Other sources of available income are listed below this figure.

Successful applications: The number of students who get a slice of the cake gives an indication of how large a slice they each got. Some colleges were only willing or able to provide figures as a percentage. Others couldn't give us any figures at all, or wouldn't because they're 'orrible.

There's more to student life than poverty and fun ... see the clubs tables at the back of the book.

Push links: Other services from *Push*

Push is an independent organisation that does more annual research into UK student life than anyone else.

The Push Guide to Which University is just one of the services we provide to university applicants. Since all of our services are designed to work together to help you make the best decision and to support you once you've made it, we might as well take this opportunity to plug the others.

THE PUSH GUIDE TO CHOOSING A UNIVERSITY

What's the point of half the information contained in *The Push Guide to Which University*? Stuff like the price of beer – that's obviously important, but why, for instance, should anyone care how many staff the careers service has or whether the accommodation is catered or self-catering?

These are the very things that really affect student life and mean that no two universities are the same. They differ radically, with strengths and weaknesses, quirks and habits.

The Push Guide to Choosing a University explains all those differences, why they matter and how they affect life as a student. It's also jam-packed with tips about choosing and it dissects the application process, student funding and, perhaps best of all, has *Push's* unique Choose Your Top University Questionnaire to help design your ideal institution and match which comes closest.

PUSH ONLINE (www.push.co.uk)

The ultimate online guide to UK universities.

For members, our interactive tools take the guesswork out of finding the perfect university, including the Choose Your Top University Questionnaire. Want to be close enough to home to take your washing home but don't want the folks popping over for tea? No problem – punch in your preferences and let *Push* do the searching for you.

Once you've got your shortlist, go check out your top choices to compare entertainment, accommodation, sport, travel and every other aspect of student life with *Push's* in-depth university profiles.

There's plenty of free stuff too, from short, sharp university profiles to articles about everything student-related, plus extra goodies for subscribers.

THE PUSH GUIDE TO MONEY: STUDENT SURVIVAL

Perhaps the biggest issue for students today is the cost of it all. In *Push's* unique tell-it-like-it-is-style, we explain what you'll have to spend, what you'll have to spend it on and how to get by.

The Push Guide to Money also gives unique details of how important costs differ at every university in the UK.

MORE COMING SOON...

Push's ongoing commitment to applicants means we'll not rest until we've provided every goddamn thing we can think of to help you pick the right university.

Already our experts give talks in schools and colleges throughout the country and we'll be launching yet more new books and services soon. Watch this space.

*Push*ing in: Getting into university

So. How do you get into university? Some say you need a degree to understand how to apply for a degree. *Push* cuts through the jargon and tells you how it really works.

The first acronym to learn is UCAS (pron 'you-cass'), the Universities and Colleges Admissions Service. They manage the application process for most universities and colleges in the UK for first degrees, foundation degrees and some diplomas, though they don't have anything to do with deciding who actually goes where.

UCAS applications used to involve a forest of paper forms, and therefore a lot of worry about whether your handwriting might make you look like a psycho. Nowadays, like pop music, pornography and *Push*, UCAS applications are embracing the net.

Schools still get paper forms sent to them from May, and courses and requirements can be checked in UCAS's Big Book (no, that's what it's called, not just what it looks like). However, the web-savvy will spend the early summer feverishly clicking their way through the online process at www.ucas.com/apply. Eventually, everyone who applies will have to do so online.

For now, whichever way you choose, there are spaces on the application to apply to up to six courses, but you don't have to use them all. You can apply to the same course at up to six different universities, six different courses at the same university or, indeed, six different courses at six different universities. The first technique is usually the one to go for, as universities like to feel you've got at least some idea of what you want to do. If you're applying for some medicine-related or Art & Design courses, you may not get the full six bites of the cherry – you may only have three or four choices.

Next you need to answer all sorts of questions about your past grades, what exams you're taking in the future and how you justify your existence to date. It's the main chance to convince the universities how committed you are to the course you've chosen, how brilliant you'll be at it and what a generally happening person you'd be to have around. You can get useful tips in filling in your personal statement, and on the application process in general from *Push* Online (www.nelsonthornes.com/push).

There's also a section that the school fills in where they either sing your praises or *diss you like a wrong 'un*. They'll also say what they think you're likely to get in your A Levels, Highers or other exams. Unfortunately, you don't get to see what they've said about you because they add their comments last, before sending the form straight back to UCAS. (However, under the Data Protection Act, you can ask to be shown your reference, which is handy if you think you've been given a tabloid smear job.)

If you apply on the web and as an individual, you'll be responsible for pasting your reference in yourself. You should give your referee the UCAS how-to guidelines on what they should be bigging up, and ask them to send it back to you electronically so that you don't have to type it all out again yourself. Needless to say, don't be tempted to add a few literary flourishes of your own – it'll stick out like George Bush at a peace rally and the universities you're applying to won't be impressed.

UCAS starts accepting applications from the end of September. If you're applying for Oxbridge, or to do medicine, dentistry or veterinary science it'll need to be in by 15th October, otherwise you've got till 15th January to get your act together. And for Route B Art & Design courses, it's 24th March.

If your application arrives after those dates, UCAS will still process your application, but universities will probably only consider your application if they've got places left. And if you don't get your application in until after 30th June (12th June for those Route B Art & Design courses), you'll be in Clearing (see below), which is a bit like one of Dante's circles of hell. Whatever deadline you're aiming for, there could potentially be hundreds of other students applying for the same course at the same university. The early bird gets the worm in the bush. You know what we're saying.

You should get an acknowledgement fairly quickly that UCAS have received the form and another within the next six weeks giving you an application number and a record of what UCAS thinks you've applied for. If you apply online, you'll get this acknowledgement electronically. If you apply by post, don't forget to complete the acknowledgement card that's part of the application pack.

Meanwhile the universities get copies of the form and write to you direct with their decisions.

They'll either make a conditional offer, effectively saying that if you get certain grades in your A Levels or other forthcoming exams, then they'll take you.

Or they might make an unconditional offer, saying they'll take you whatever your grades, but this isn't likely unless you've already done some A Levels, Highers or equivalent.

Or they might turn you down outright.

Or they'll ask you for interview. In which case it's a good opportunity to check out the place. If you get an interview, be prepared. Be keen. Be enthusiastic. Above all, be yourself. If you're worried about it, grab your careers adviser or nearest friendly teacher and insist they help you. Remind them that they chose their atrociously paid profession for love rather than money.

After the interview, the university will either make you a conditional or unconditional offer or they'll reject you. If you don't get in, console yourself with the fact that thousands of other hopeful students also got turned down and, besides, you didn't want to go to that nasty dump anyway.

UCAS will send you a note of the universities' decisions as they make them. Whatever they say, you don't have to respond until you've got a full set of replies from all the universities you applied to. You should hear from them all, one way or another by, at the latest, the end of April and, when you hear from the last one, UCAS will send you a summary of all the responses.

If you've got any unconditional offers, you can reject them right away or accept one, go away, relax and prepare to start that course at the beginning of the next year.

If you've got more than two conditional offers, then you've got to dump some. You've also got to say which is your favourite and firmly accept it. That means that if you manage to meet whatever conditions they've made, then that's where you're off to. You're allowed to keep a back up (or 'insurance') offer by provisionally accepting another offer with easier conditions. That means if you don't make the grades for your first choice, you've still got somewhere to go.

It is possible that none of your choices will make you an offer, or maybe that you'll decide after an interview or visit that you don't like the place. Alternatively, maybe you just won't make the grade for either of the two offers you've kept. In this case, you've got two choices. Either take a year out and go through the whole process again. Or try to go through Clearing.

Clearing is the mad scramble that takes place between the day the exam results come out and the first day of the universities' new terms, where students without a university place try to get matched up with university courses that don't have enough students. Although it's all masterminded by UCAS in theory, in practice they don't have much to do with it and this time you get to approach universities directly.

Be careful, though, if you do end up in Clearing, not just to jump at the first place you get offered. Clearing gets even the coolest cats hot and bothered and it's easy to end up on a course you don't like at a university you hate.

It's important to pick a course and a university that suit you as an individual – if you don't, you may live to regret it. Nearly 1 in 7 students doesn't successfully complete the course they start and the proportion is highest among those who get in through Clearing.

If you're not at school or college in the UK, you can get a paper UCAS form and courses listings from UCAS, Rosehill, New Barn Lane, Cheltenham, Glos., GL52 3LZ, Tel: (0870) 112 2211. Or, have a look at www.ucas.com.

Hard *Push*ed: Student finance

Nowadays, being a student is almost the same as being in debt, but there are ways of stashing the cash and diverting the debts.

If you're thinking about embarking on a course of study at a UK university or college, you should be thinking about debt at the same time. The two go together like cream cheese and bagels (only less tastily). Debt has become such a fact of life for most students that some fall into a state of paralysis about the whole thing and never really deal with the problem. *Push* can't wave a magic cliché and make debts disappear, but we can come up with a few ideas to help students make the best out of a situation roughly equivalent to swimming the Atlantic with John Prescott strapped to your knees.

At the brink of a promising career, starting with being accepted to university or college, most students don't want to think of the poverty they're going to have to put up with until they land that cushy job in merchant banking, marketing or medicine. Still less, if they are looking forward to a career where the greatest reward will be the warm glow of job satisfaction, such as teaching, social work or even acting.

However, there's little point starting a course you're not going to be able to afford to finish. Students have to ask themselves how they're going to make ends meet.

If the answer is that your parents are so phenomenally wealthy and indulgent that they'll give you all the cash you need, then your problems are over. But, for those on this side of the rainbow, there are a number of issues to consider.

In fact, there are so many that we've produced a book all about it – **The Push Guide to Money: Student Survival**. It covers everything to do with student finance – what you'll have to spend, what you'll have to spend it on and how to put the fun back into funding. Rush out and steal a copy now (it's only £9.95, but you might as well start saving now).

If you didn't take that advice and you're still reading, the following brief guide may help till you realise you need that truly excellent publication.

ECONOMISE

Whatever other options you take, economy is always the one that puts shoes on your feet. Decide what's important and pay for that. Then see how much money you have left and decide what else you'd like if possible. Plan expenditure – on a weekly basis, if your income's tight – and stick to your plan.

Be pessimistic. Optimistic students don't check their balance when they shove their cards in the cash machine and sooner or later their card gets swallowed. Realists check their balance and then get out half the amount they wanted. Pessimists don't bother going to the cashpoint because they know it was only ever created in order to swallow cards. That way, they preserve enough readies to live a miserly, but not miserable existence.

As with many things, sensible moderation is the key. Students who are so desperate to economise that they never set foot in the SU bar and don't buy anything not directly related to food, shelter or academic survival may come out the other end with a first-class degree and a bank balance not too far out of the black. Chances are, though, they'll also have missed out on much of the stuff that makes a degree course worthwhile. Students may have to accept that Maserati and Armani aren't going to be on the shopping list for the next few years, but the odd pint of beer or the next Coldplay CD aren't going to cast you into the fiery furnace of debt hell.

GOVERNMENT FUNDING

Few things in life get quite so confusing as the student funding situation over the last few years. *Push*, as ever, is here to help you tell the wood from the deforestation trucks and find out how you'll be affected.

First off, although top-up fees (see below) are moving the balance towards students, the Government still pays most of the tuition fees for most first-degree students. What students themselves have to pay is a portion of the wad that's needed to pay for all those libraries, loos and lecturers. Unfortunately, however, that money's paid direct to the university by the Local Education Authorities (LEAs) and the like. Students don't even get so much as a sniff of it, but they shouldn't forget to apply for it – or they could end up paying out themselves.

Poorly *Push*: Welfare

Student life has its ups and downs and welfare – the support system provided by universities and colleges to help students with their health and happiness – is the safety net for the down times. *Push* seeks out a friendly ear.

Universities do worry about students beyond whether they get their essays in and pay their tuition fees on time. They worry about their welfare. After all, if students aren't healthy, wealthy (or solvent) and happy, they're hardly likely to get their essays in or pay their tuition fees on time.

Some care more than others. However, most do provide services to look after students including some, if not all the following:

Health: doctors, nurses and, sometimes, physiotherapists, chiropractors, psychiatrists and so on.

Well-being and happiness: counsellors and advisers trained to deal with all the problems likely to be faced by students, including exam stress, depression and sexual problems. There may also be access to groups and advisers with specific concerns, such as for lesbian, gay, bisexual and transgender students; those with disabilities; women and so on.

Finance: debt counsellors, hardship funds, emergency loans, bursaries and some scholarships.

Others: help finding housing and dealing with accommodation problems, legal advice, chaplains, help landing a job (part-time, temporary or a career), crèches and nurseries and so on.

Often some or even all of these services are provided by the students' union or they provide complementary services, such as academic appeals representation, financial help and nightline – a Samaritans-style free and confidential phone service, staffed by trained students.

As well as the provisions from the universities and unions (found in the Welfare section of each college profile), here are some other helpful contacts:

The National Bisexual Helpline: (0845) 450 1264 (Tues and Wed 7.30-9.30pm; Sat 10.30am-12.30am).

Eating Disorders Association (EDA): Offers support and mutual care to those suffering from Anorexia or Bulimia Nervosa, binge eating, and other eating-related problems. (0845) 634 7650 (callers 18 and under Mon-Fri 4-6.30pm and Sat 1-4.30pm) or e-mail talkback@edauk.com. See also www.edauk.com

Get Connected: A free confidential helpline for young people that will put them in touch with the right help they need. (0808) 808 4994 (every day from 1pm-11pm), or e-mail help@getconnected.org.uk

London Lesbian and Gay Switchboard: A national service for lesbians, gays and anyone needing support regarding their sexuality. Information, advice, listening and referral. (020) 7837 7324 (24 hours) or www.llgs.org.uk

National AIDS Helpline: For anyone concerned about HIV/AIDS. Offers information and advice, can make referrals: (0800) 567 123 (24 hours). See also www.playingsafely.co.uk for general links on matters sexual.

Talk to Frank: Resources for anyone concerned about drug misuse, including users, families, friends and carers – (0800) 77 66 00 (24 hours). See www.talktofrank.com

The Samaritans: Providing confidential, emotional support to anyone in need: (08457) 90 90 90 (UK) or (1850) 60 90 90 (ROI). E-mail: jo@samaritans.org

Sexwise: Information, advice and guidance for young people on sexual health and sexuality. See the website (www.ruthinking.co.uk) or call (0800) 28 29 30 (7am-midnight every day).

National Debtline: Exactly what it says on the tin. (0800) 808 4000 or see www.nationaldebtline.co.uk

*Push*ing back the frontiers: Students with disabilities

Having a disability doesn't mean your needs can't be met at University. Skill (the National Bureau for Students with Disabilities) points the way...

Being disabled doesn't mean going to higher education will be different for you – the other information in *The Push Guide* is as relevant to you as anyone else – but if you do have a disability, medical condition or specific learning difficulty, you may have a few more things to think about before you apply.

The Disability Discrimination Act is in force to ensure disabled students aren't treated any less favourably than non-disabled students. Universities have to make reasonable adjustments to make sure you're not at a disadvantage because of a disability. While you'll need to know if your disability-related needs can be met by the college or university, don't be tempted to make disability the only criteria you use when making choices – remember that the subject you're going to study, the social life, where provisions are geographically located and so on are all just as important to you as to a non-disabled student.

Skill produces a guide, Into Higher Education, which gives advice about applying. It includes contact details of all institutions offering higher education courses, with details of some of the facilities they offer disabled students. You can also find out information from prospectuses, the SU, internet, league tables and by talking to other disabled students. Don't be afraid to contact institutions before applying. If you're not sure what's available, never be afraid to ask.

It's also a good idea to visit before applying. Open days are a good way for you to check out the university's facilities and attitude. Consider all areas of student life – it may be just as important for you socially to get into the bar and meet other students as it is for you academically to get into the library and find books.

As long as you meet eligibility criteria there's a Disabled Students' Allowance to help with disability-related costs in studying. Skill produces a lot of information about these allowances and how to apply for them.

Skill's Information Service is available for telephone enquiries (Tuesday 11.30am-1.30pm and Thursday 1.30pm-3.30pm) on (0800) 328 5050, textphone (0800) 068 2422 or e-mail at info@skill.org.uk. You can also post messages for other students and access a range of information booklets at Skill's website, www.skill.org.uk

There's no need for you to do everything on your own. Most colleges have disability advisers/co-ordinators and union welfare officers to help make sure your experience at university is of great benefit to you both academically and socially, and there may be disabled students' groups. Skill also has a membership scheme and a newsletter for students called 'Notes and Quotes'. So if you have any questions, hit any problems or if you would like to be involved in Skill's work, why not get in touch?

*Push*grads: Postgraduates

Some students become addicted to student life and think, what the hell, I'll do another degree. But life as a postgrad is very different from the lazy, hazy daze of undergrad life and it can be just as troubled financially. Here are some of the pitfalls for postgrads.

There are a whopping half a million postgrad students in UK universities at the moment, including those who stayed on after graduating or returned to take postgraduate courses. The reasons vary greatly, from putting off the 9-5 grind, worries about getting employment at all, sheer love of particle physics (it happens) or pure love of student life.

But those simply expecting an extension of undergrad life are sorely misled. Postgrads study all year round with no long holidays to recharge batteries or bank accounts.

Funding, too, is harder to come by – very few postgrads are guaranteed financial support for any course (trainee teachers are one notable exception). This applies not just to maintenance costs (postgrads aren't allowed to apply for student loans), but also to tuition costs, all of which postgrads have to meet themselves, regardless of income. What grants are available are awarded on a competitive basis and so it's a good idea to have a pretty damn impressive first degree (even a good 2:1 may be cutting it fine for humanities and arts subjects because there's less funding about). It also helps if you're able to apply to a funding council who're more generous with grants.

There are also Government-subsidised Career Development Loans mostly for courses which can claim some kind of vocational element (translating obscure Abyssinian limericks probably doesn't count) and which pay out between £300 and £8,000. See www.lifelonglearning.co.uk/cdl for the fine print.

At the end of the day, a postgrad qualification may solve the financial problems it creates. Postgrads stand out from the crowd to potential employers and can expect to earn more. However, some employers prefer to train recent undergraduates and postgrads can find themselves overqualified. Some postgrads become professional academics, but the financial rewards alone are not likely to be a temptation.

Postgraduate courses split into two broad types – those that centre on research and those that are mainly taught.

Researchers study for 1 or 2 years to get a Masters degree or MPhil, or 3 years for a Doctorate (PhD). However, these are minimum periods – many students take a bit longer, sometimes up to twice as long. That extra time, including the costs of living, eating and socialising, also racks up the final bill.

Funding for research is available from Research Councils, charities or on research contracts from the institutions themselves – see www.rcuk.ac.uk Commercially valuable research can often attract industrial sponsorship so delving into new types of plastic is likely to be less financially fraught than examining the philology of Philo.

Although there's no teaching in a research degree, postgrads' work is supervised and it's important the supervisor is appropriately clued up. Postgrads should interview whoever will be supervising them before accepting a place – it's important not only that supervisors are able to appreciate the subtleties of their postgrads' work, but also that they get on well.

As for taught courses, they are usually part of an extended career ladder or a stepping stone to a research degree. They are either for students who want to specialise in a particular field or want to convert their qualifications to a different area. Conversion courses in particular vary greatly in what they offer, so students should be sure not just that it's suitable, but also why it is. Awards for these courses are available from the same sources as for research degrees.

United we *Push*: Students' unions

Call them talking shops, bop shops, shopping centres or advice centres, what are students' unions? Who are they? Over to the NUS...

Inescapable, unavoidable and absolutely essential. Within minutes of arriving at university you'll find yourself in your students' union (SU).

SUs form the collective voice of the student body. Each student is automatically a member of the SU and each will be involved in running the union through general meetings and electing executive officers. It costs you zero and you can't get much cheaper than that. The union represents you and your interests and whatever you want to do, you can, because you own and run your union and you can make it happen.

SUs work in different ways. If you want to know where to find accommodation, contraception, more money, even how to get a job, they have trained staff and student officers to help. If you want to disco till dawn, eat, drink and be merry, this is the place to be. But it's more than top bands, cheap drink, decent food and good advice. If you want to join any one of the thousands of different student sporting, social, political, cultural or special interest clubs and societies, from the flat cap society to Alan Partridge appreciation, then get down to the union.

If you've a particular gripe – if there aren't enough books in the library, minibuses for the hockey teams or you've got problems in your halls of residence – union officers will take on the university administration and sort it out by representing your views at meetings and making sure that the student voice is heard.

Your union will also probably be a member of the National Union of Students. NUS is a confederation of unions representing over 5 million students in the UK and gives you national representation, letting Parliament and the press know exactly what you think and lobbying for change. NUS also provides back-up and training for all your individual elected union officers.

*Push*ing the pennies: Charity Rags

Today's Rag is all things to all people. Whatever you want out of student life, Rag can provide it. The Rag network is an instant and no-hassle social life. At the same time Rag exists to raise thousands of pounds for needy causes. UKRag explains the ins and outs of being a good Samaritan.

So, what exactly do Rags do? Each one's different, but overall they exist to raise funds for charity through student activity. It might mean organising Rag balls, concerts, pantos, clubnights, sponsored runs, bungee jumps … pretty much anything. They also offer the chance to travel the UK, for free, so you could find yourself spending a Saturday collecting for charity in some far flung city. One of the most fun parts of Rag is the chance to go to Megaraids, where loads of Rags collect in one place, and have a massive party afterwards.

While beer and parties are good, when it comes after a long day when you've achieved something for other people, when you've had a laugh with some of the best mates you will ever meet – then it's absolutely priceless.

Not only that, but it'll give you those extra-curricular skills employers always seem to harp on about. If you want a good job you need more than just your degree: interpersonal skills; team experience; ICT; project-management. By joining Rag, and putting in as much or as little time as you want, you'll get back much more than you could possibly want out of your time at Uni.

If you want to get involved get in touch with your Rag, as soon as you get to campus, if not before. Of course, some universities/colleges won't have a Rag group set up yet but there are plenty of resources and help out there if you have the nouse to start one yourself. www.UKRag.net has the gen on the best way to go about it.

Everyone brings something unique to the mix – business skills, leadership, a love of money, computer skills – so don't assume that 'warm and fuzzy' is all that's required. Last year Rags all over the UK raised several million pounds for charity, beating cancer, feeding the starving, housing the homeless, fighting AIDS, helping kids, as well as caring for the sick, desperate and deserving. It's a serious mission, but in return for your time and effort you'll be part of the biggest, most fun and most useful student network the UK's ever seen.

Rag is a tradition that spans centuries as an essential part of UK university life. It was even the inspiration behind Comic Relief and Red Nose Day. There's a massive community of us out here, and plenty of help and support is always available, especially on www.UKRag.net, a community of Raggies, Rags, and charity reps and we'd love to see you there.

University of Aberdeen
....
University of Abertay Dundee
....
Aberystwyth, University of Wales
....

APU
Chelmsford Campus
....

Anglia Polytechnic see APU
....

University of the Arts, London
....

Aston University
....

University of Aberdeen

The University of Aberdeen, University Office, King's College, Aberdeen, AB24 3FX
Tel: (01224) 272 090 E-mail: sras@abdn.ac.uk Website: www.abdn.ac.uk
University Students' Association, Luthuli House, 50/52 College Bounds, Old Aberdeen, AB24 3DS
Tel: (01224) 272 965 E-mail: ausa@abdn.ac.uk Website: www.ausa.org.uk

GENERAL

The first university the alphabet has to offer is way, way up north in the *affectionately named* Granite City. Aberdeen lies on the east coast of Scotland, suitably placed to be the oil capital of Europe and *spanned all round by spectacular castles, coastline, beaches and lochs* and *the majesty of the Grampian Highlands – even Push gets poetic at the thought of it*. The city itself's a *pretty place* too with flowers, parks and *great* architecture. The University is based on three sites which once made up two separate universities. In fact, Aberdeen had two universities back when that was the total number in the whole of England. The larger, main site is King's College in Old Aberdeen, *a satisfying eyeful* of 15th-century buildings, modern blocks, green space and cobbled streets, 1,200m north of the city centre. The Medical School at Foresterhill is a mile and a half from the main campus. The *concretey* Hilton campus houses the School of Education, a theatre, a library and various accommodation blocks.

Sex ratio (M:F): 46:54	Founded: 1495
Full-time u'grads: 9,200	Part-time: 1,060
Postgrads: 1,460	Non-degree: 466
Ave course: 4yrs	Ethnic: n/a
State:private school: 85:15	Flunk rate: 13%
Mature: 19%	International: 18%
Disabled: 142	Local: 33%

ATMOSPHERE:
Most Aberdonian students enjoy the beautiful and relaxed environment for their four years of study. A strong sporting ethos and an exciting nightlife complement the academic end of the tunnel and town/gown relations couldn't be cosier.

ABERDEEN:

- Population: 211,250 • City centre: 1 mile • London: 410 miles
- Dundee: 67 miles • Edinburgh: 126 miles
- High temp: 17 • Low temp: 0 • Rainfall: 61

Aberdeen is a very old city made prosperous over the past century thanks to its strong associations with the North Sea oil industry. The flammable black ooze from the dawn of time has brought the city *a varied cultural cocktail from all over the UK, a predictable industrial presence and a lot of tankers. The fishing trade that once dominated is headed to Davy Jones's locker as a result,* but the salty scent of sea-life still swirls the streets. The city centre's *gorgeous* architecture and *ample* amenities *are contrasted by the outskirts, which contain some of the grimmer aspects of 70s civil engineering.* Just outside the city, swathes of countryside continue on and on and on and on before arriving at anywhere vaguely urban. *It's a self-contained town and it has to be – it's bloody miles from anywhere.*

TRAVEL:

Trains: *Despite being so far north* (the same latitude as St Petersburg), rail connections are *quite good, if expensive.* Among others, services are offered to London (£62.70), Glasgow (£22.40) and Birmingham (£29.00).
Buses: National Express coach services to London (£40.00), Glasgow (£27.70), Birmingham (£37.50) and others. For coach journeys within Scotland there's Scottish Citylink; Stagecoach also run services.
Car: A92, A93, A94 and A96. Two miles to the nearest junction.
Air: Inland flights around the UK and to some European cities.
Ferries: There's a ferry service to Lerwick in the Shetlands.
Hitching: *The A92 is fairly major and once hitchers have got to the M90, it's plain sailing. But the hitch of hitching is that it's a long, long road and going west inland is nigh impossible.*
Local: *Good* bus services run anywhere in the city from 35p, *useful for getting into the centre from King's.*
Taxis: *Useful late at night, but expensive* – £5 from the station to King's, £10 from the airport.
Bicycles: *Despite the heavy traffic and the cold winds, many students take to cycling.* Some halls are only 1,200m from the campuses so pedal power can be just the ticket. Bike theft is as rare as any other crime in Aberdeen.

CAREER PROSPECTS:

- Careers Service • No. of staff: 9 full • Unemployed after 6mths: 6%

The Careers & Appointments Service organises seminars and workshops, sends weekly job update emails and performs *that fave corporate fad* – psychometric testing. Also newsletters, bulletin boards, interview training and job fairs ago-go.

FAMOUS ALUMNI:

Nicky Campbell (DJ); Iain Crichton-Smith (poet); Iain Cuthbertson (actor); Alistair Darling MP (Lab); Sandy Gall (ITV newsreader); Denys Henderson (Chair of ICI); Kenneth McKellar (singer); David McLean MP (Con); James Naughtie (BBC Radio 4 'Today' presenter).

FURTHER INFO:

- Prospectuses: undergrad; postgrad; some departmental; international • Open days

Applicants receive a guidance pack containing advice, accommodation info and a pamphlet for parents to pore over. The admissions website is www.abdn.ac.uk/sras.

A C A D E M I C

Since many academic staff are involved in national and international level research staff/student relations are fairly cosy – *a sort of 'we're all in this learning thing together'.* Teaching comprises lectures and compulsory tutorials, with the odd one-to-one session thrown in here and there. 4th year brings with it the *perils* of dissertation.

Entry points: 200-320	Ave points: n/a
Applns per place: 6	Clearing: 9%
No. of terms: 3	Length of terms: 12wks
Staff/student ratio: n/a	Study addicts: 97%
Teaching: ***	Research: ***
Year abroad: 2%	Sandwich students: <1%
Firsts: 7%	2.2s: 19%
2.1s: 37%	3rds: 2%

200-320   POINTS

ADMISSIONS:

- Apply via UCAS

SUBJECTS:

Unusual: Belgian Law.

LIBRARIES:

- 1,141,603 books • 1,548 study places
- 24-hr access • Spend per student: ££££

There's *oodles* of shelf-space spread over four large libraries and some smaller departmental libraries and archives. The main Queen Mother library has self-service issue and return facilities and it (along with the Taylor and Medical libraries) has wireless facilities – *so students can play minesweeper while they work*. Members of the public are allowed into all libraries on a 'look don't touch' basis.

COMPUTERS:

- 1,133 workstations • 24-hr access • Spend per student: ££

PCs in the libraries, halls and the main IT centre in the Edward Wright Building. All PCs have CD readers and writers and all students have a page on the University's network, which contains exam results, library loans, tuition and hall fees and other *useful but Big Brotherish* info.

OTHER LEARNING FACILITIES:

Aberdeen houses the European Documentation Centre as well as language labs, drama studio, rehearsal rooms, CAD lab, audio/TV centre and practice courtroom. *All together now: 'You can't handle the truth!'*

ENTERTAINMENT

THE CITY:

- Price of a pint of beer: £2 • Glass of wine: £2.50 • Can of Red Bull: £1

Cinemas: Vue and the UGC are there for *brainless popcorn-guzzling*. The Belmont provides artier flicks.

Theatres: His Majesty's Theatre attracts big-time ballet and opera on tour as well as less elite delights like pantos. Its biggest seller is the Student Charities Campaign show. The Aberdeen Arts Centre is smaller and hosts more fringe theatre, am dram and some student productions.

Pubs: *A mixture of old men's pubs and pretentious glittery bars with little dance floors. Pushplugs: the Illicit Still; the Bobbin; Machar Bar.*

Clubbing: *Aberdeen has enough clubs to keep hip hips moving. Liquid, Espionage, Priory and Ministry around Belmont Street are good for movers and shakers.*

Music venues: Folk music *infests* most pubs at some point. The Music Hall does a mixture of classical, rock, pop, jazz and more folk. The Lemon Tree is a 'concept' venue, *meaning it's quite small, has a stage and that Radiohead once played here.*

Other: Bundles of museums and galleries. *Worthy of note* are the Zoology Museum, Aberdeen Art Gallery and Stratosphere – where you can play with the exhibits like some kind of *crazy child*.

Eating out: *A bit pricey. Pushplugs: Café 52 and The Olive Tree for French; Buffet King for Oriental nibbling; Blue Elephant Tandoori for the best Aberdeen has to offer in Indian; and Lamba for boozed-up Mexican dishes and dancing on chairs.*

UNIVERSITY:

• <u>Price of a pint of beer: £1.60</u> • <u>Glass of wine: £1.50</u>

The sword of Damocles is currently hanging over the Aberdeen entertainment scene. Poor turnover at Union bars and clubs has led the SA to threaten closure of several venues and possibly create one giant uber-bar to rule the world of ents. The outcome is uncertain... Will the students start drinking again? Will the SA find the cash to keep its babies alive? Tune in next week...

Bars: Six bars in the Union: the Dungeon (home to free entertainment throughout the week); Sivell's (large, airy, domed, art deco with murals); Factory (*industrial look*, main venue); Associates (non-smoking bar); the Seasons Café bar; the Loft (club/comedy/film venue). With looser licensing laws than England and Wales, students can quaff away till 2 or 3am.

Theatres: The theatre at the Hilton campus gets an airing now and then, as do some of the town venues (see above). *Despite the Centre Stage Society's attempts to thesp up their fellow students, it's sport not soliloquising that appeals to most.*

Film: The Loft turns into a screening room a few times a week when the Cinema Club gets its paws on a new DVD.

Music venues: The Elf, the Factory and Liquid Loft host live bands: Toploader, Tailgunner, Michael Kilkie. Folk music free in the Union on Wednesdays.

Clubbing: The Elf, the Factory, the Dungeon and Liquid Loft pump up the disco jam several nights a week.

Comedy/Cabaret: Comedy night every other Wednesday in the Loft.

Food: The Refectory has three floors of *good value chow*, the Dining Room restaurant goes down the pasta/curry/veggie avenue. *Balcony Lounge serves junk to wash down with beer and Zeste Cafe is a relaxing 70s style joint that does everything to be found in motorway services plus takeaways.*

Other: Quiz nights and bingo *aren't just for grannies.* There are Departmental balls throughout the year as well.

SOCIAL & POLITICAL

ABERDEEN UNIVERSITY STUDENTS' ASSOCIATION

• <u>6 sabbaticals</u> • <u>NUS member</u> • <u>Turnout at last ballot: 57%</u>

AUSA has Union offices at Hilton and Gallowgate from where it extends its tendrils into the lives of every Aberdeen student. *The student body are by and large political animals and AUSA regularly herds them into protests and strikes against hiked up tuition fees and is showing no sign of giving up any time soon.*

SU FACILITIES:

The *lively* Union Building (the second largest in Scotland) is in the city centre near Marischal, although it also has a mini-market at Hillhead Halls and a general shop. The SA runs six bars and four clubs – two of each in the Union building. Other than that: restaurant; cafeteria; snack bar; fast food joint; games room (with pool tables, video games and table football); meeting rooms; minibus; showers; photocopiers; photo booth; advice centre; vending machines; ATMs; secondhand bookshop; launderette; dark room.

CLUBS (NON-SPORTING):

LLM and Law PhD Student; Student Community Action; Students Charities Campaign; Student Show; Agricultural; Women's Bird Club; Cantonese; Celtic; Centre Stage; Chemical; Choral; Cinergi Film Association; Student Concert Band Dance; Scottish Dance; Drumming; Economics; Elphinstone Fiddlers; Engineering; English Studies & Contemporary Arts Society (ESCA); Finance & Investment; First Aid; Forestry; Geography; Gilbert & Sullivan; Gliding; Grand Prix; Hellenic; Hispanic; Law; Mooting; Life Saving; Malt Whisky; Marine Mammal; Medic; Muslim; OTC; Philosophy; Physics; Politics & International Relations; Psychology; Red Cross; Revelation Rock Gospel Choir; Roleplaying; Roadtrip; Samuel Beckett; Scandinavian; SciFi & Fantasy; Scottish Nationalist Association; Scout & Guide; Singapore; Street Entertainers; Treading The Boards; Wilderness Medical; Wine; Zoology. **See also Clubs tables.**

OTHER ORGANISATIONS:

Debater: As well as AUSA students become members (free and automatically) of Debater, one of the country's oldest mooting societies that does nothing but host discussions on topics of every breed and flavour and come to conclusions (or not) about them. *It's popular, fun and not as pompous and Toryfied as the Oxbridge debating unions.*

Others: Weekly paper Gaudi is a *geriatric* 70 years old and, *unusually for a student newspaper, actually contains news.* As part of the Charities Campaign, the annual Torcher Parade – *not as medieval or painful as it sounds* – is the largest torchlit parade in Europe. Students have 16 hours to design and make their own float and then process through the streets with folks throwing money at them. SCA (Student Community Action) is the energetic local help organisation run by student volunteers.

RELIGIOUS:

• <u>11 chaplains (CofE, CofS, Methodist, Quaker, RC, Greek Orthodox, Mormon) plus an imam and a rabbi</u>

Two chapels and a small mosque in the University. Locally, apart from St Mary's Cathedral (Catholic), St Andrew's Cathedral (Episcopal) and St Machar's Cathedral (Presbyterian), there are places of worship for most faiths.

PAID WORK:

• <u>Job bureau</u>

Union-run JobLink helps find part-time, vacation and temp work (see www.ausa.org.uk/joblink for job ads). Students can sometimes find work in the oil industry, particularly those with studies in a relevant field. *If not, it's time to get out the rod and go fish.*

SPORTS

• <u>Recent success: skiing</u> • <u>BUSA Ranking: 18</u>
AUSA runs and sails a tight sporting ship. Sporting success is highly regarded and consequently highly frequent. Instructional classes are available in various things, including yoga, boxercise, Pilates, dance and sports conditioning. Fitness consultations and therapy services are also available to tone those flagging muscles.

SPORTS FACILITIES:

Most facilities available on both sites. The Butchart Recreation Centre (King's) has been refurbished and contains a sports hall, gym, cardiovascular equipment, fitness and testing room, weights room, four squash courts and a climbing wall. Also two more squash courts, playing fields, three all-weather tennis courts (or sometimes an all-weather pitch instead) and a swimming pool. The main sports fields are at Balgowery, 2 miles north, where there are more playing fields for football, rugby, hockey and cricket (bringing the total to just under 20 acres), a running track, golf course and dry ski slope. Elsewhere, the University has a boathouse on the River Dee, a glider at Aboyne and a mountain hut at Lochnagar. All facilities and fitness classes cost a *nice, round* £1 per session.

SPORTING CLUBS:

Boat; Boxing; Curling; Field Sports; Gaelic Football; Gliding; Gymnastics; Ju-Jitsu; Lacrosse; Life Saving; Mountain Biking; Potholing & Caving; Powerkite; Rifle; Rollerhockey; Shinty; Sky diving; Surf; Table Tennis; T'ai Chi; Triathlon; Ultimate Frisbee; Underwater Hockey; Waterpolo. **See also Clubs tables.**

ATTRACTIONS:

The local football team is one-time Scottish giants Aberdeen FC – alias 'the Dons'.

ACCOMMODATION

IN COLLEGE:

• <u>Catered: 11%</u> • <u>Cost: £75-94 (32wks)</u>
• <u>Self-catering: 15%</u> • <u>Cost: £50-64 (32-48wks)</u>

• First years living in: 15% • Insurance premium: £
Availability: All 1st years can be housed, but most students find themselves living out for at least 2 years. The *bog standard 70s and 80s style* halls are spread over the city. The Hillhead Halls are the largest, about 1,200m north of King's, a mixture of halls (*with tiny rooms*) and flats. *Popular Hillhead is the most spirited hangout, as well as the cheapest. Dunbar and Crombie-Johnston Halls are closer and dearer.* Corridors and floors tend to be single-sexed. Most halls have launderettes, study spaces, TV rooms and gaming facilities, some have an on-site bar. The self-catering accommodation is split between blocks of flats, shared between six to eight students, and local flats and houses either owned or leased by the University, a few of which are available for married couples. The University has a deal with Aberdeen Student Village, which manages four halls of residence in the city centre.
Car parking: Parking *isn't too much of a problem* with a permit, but the city's green policy means the authorities are attempting to discourage students bringing cars.

EXTERNALLY:

• Ave rent: £65 • Living at home: 5%
Availability: 61% of Aberdeen's students have gone off to seek their domestic fortunes alone, which can be a tricky affair given that most local landlords are trying to pipe into the oil industry for tenants. *Sandilands is cheap (and rough), house-hunters are better off trying their luck in Ferryhill, Seaton, King St, George St, Urquhart Rd and Rosemount, for example.*
Housing help: The Union accommodation service advertises widely and offers advice on living out. The University sticks to advising on its owned or managed flats.

WELFARE

SERVICES:

• Lesbian/Gay/Bisexual Society • Ethnic Minorities Society • Women's Society
• Mature Students' Society • International Students' Officer & Society
• Postgrad Officer & Society • Disabilities Officer & Society • Self-defence classes
• Nightline • Taxi fund • College counsellors: 3 full • Crime rating: !!
For a university once renowned for being the student suicide capital of the UK, Aberdeen's welfare safety net has few holes. The SA has a welfare sabbatical officer as well as a finance adviser.
Health: Four GPs and two nurses staff the University's *comprehensive* medical practice which has a full range of NHS services. King's campus has a dental health unit.
Crèches/Nursery: 47 places are available for littluns up to 5yrs.
Disabilities: It's a very old city with a very old university built in times when disabilities were symptoms of witchcraft, so *wheelchair access is none too hot.* Improvements are being made, and the SA's *pretty determined* they should be. Ramps have been added, doors widened and induction loops fitted. The University's prepared to re-schedule lectures and all departments have a disabilities co-ordinator. Accommodation is adapted as needed.

FINANCE:

• Ave debt per year: £1,065
Fees: The SA will have chained itself to a good many gates before top-up fees hit home. International fees range from £7,560–18,570.
• Access fund: £250,000 • Successful applications/yr: 1,031 • Ave payment: £200
Support: There are about 150 endowments, bursaries, external grants and trusts available for school leavers coming to Aberdeen University. *Some are very obscure:* for one, applicants must be from Cabrach (a *tiny* village 40 miles away) and promise not to drink or smoke throughout their degree. *As if.*

University of Abertay Dundee

- *Formerly Dundee Institute of Technology.*
University of Abertay Dundee, Bell Street, Dundee, DD1 1HG
Tel: (01382) 308 000 E-mail: sro@abertay.ac.uk Website: www.abertay.ac.uk
University of Abertay Dundee Students' Association, 158 Marketgait, Dundee, DD1 1NJ
Tel: (01382) 227 477 E-mail: j.weir@abertay.ac.uk Website: www.abertayunion.com

GENERAL

Abertay, Dundee's newest university, divides itself among five main blocks ranging from a Victorian former textile mill to the 90s library. The main site, set around a *green and pleasant* quad, is *like a warren* inside. All the buildings are a *couple of mins walk* from the middle of town, including the *all-singing, all-dancing* new student centre (2004). The University has been *in the middle of a facelift* for the last five or six years, and whilst that means there are parts of it that look like *Joan Collins in the morning*, there are others that resemble a *radiant and freshly-botoxed Catherine Zeta Jones.*

Sex ratio (M:F): 54:46	**Founded: 1888**
Full-time u'grads: 3,485	**Part-time: 330**
Postgrads: 365	**Non-degree: 435**
Ave course: 4yrs	**Ethnic: 7%**
State:private school: 87:13	**Flunk rate: 30%**
Mature: 32%	**International: 15%**
Disabled: 79	**Local: 62%**

ATMOSPHERE:

There's a *fondness* for Abertay that stems *largely* from the *high proportion* of local students. *That can spell homesickness for Sassenachs and international students*, but overall it's a *friendly, techie* kind of place with more of a *chip on the shoulder* about Dundee University than the local residents, *most of whom put up with students without too much fuss.*

DUNDEE: see Dundee University
- City centre: 0 miles

TRAVEL: see Dundee University
Dundee station is 10 mins walk from the University. There's an *extensive* local bus service, which ferries between halls and campus for 80p.

CAREER PROSPECTS:
- Careers Service • No. of staff: 2 full/3 part • Unemployed after 6mths: 10%
Newsletters, bulletin boards and job fairs. The new student centre has online careers resources.

FAMOUS ALUMNI:

David Jones (inventor of the Lemmings computer game); Maurice Malpass (Dundee Utd); Andy Nicoll, Craig Redpath, Tom Smith (rugby internationals); George Simpson (former Chief Executive, GEC); Brian Souter (Stagecoach Chairman).

FURTHER INFO:
- Prospectuses: undergrad; postgrad • Open days • Video

ACADEMIC

Abertay's a techie university split into four schools: contemporary science, the Business School, computing and advanced technology and social/health sciences. *Not a layabout English student in sight.*

Entry points: 168-264	Ave points: n/a
Applns per place: 5	Clearing: 3%
No. of terms: 2	Length of terms: 15wks
Staff/student ratio: 1:20	Study addicts: 15%
Teaching: *	Research: ***
Year abroad: <1%	Sandwich students: 3%
Firsts: 7%	2.2s: 35%
2.1s: 36%	3rds: 11%

168-264 **POINTS**

ADMISSIONS:

• Apply via UCAS
A Wider Access University, so there's active recruitment of varying ages, abilities and nationalities. Postgrads and part-timers can apply direct.

SUBJECTS:

Business School: 25%   Contemporary Sciences: 15%
Computing: 30%   Social & Health Sciences: 30%

LIBRARIES:

• 158,437 books • 725 study places • Spend per student: ££££

COMPUTERS:

• 632 workstations • 1,082 internet access points
• 24-hr access • Spend per student: ££££

OTHER LEARNING FACILITIES:

The new crime scene for the Forensic sciences department was opened by Inspector Rebus creator Ian Rankin. There's also a fully-equipped language learning centre.

ENTERTAINMENT

THE CITY: see Dundee University

UNIVERSITY:

• Price of a pint of beer: £1.40 • Can of Red Bull: £1
Bars: The main bar opens six days a week, with *occasional* happy hours, karaoke, DJs and food. Decked out in royal blue velour, it *looks a bit like an airport lounge.* The sports bar has, *unsurprisingly*, a big screen for daily Sky sports viewing.
Clubbing: There's a *popular* 80s night and the Untouchables have been tempted into playing recently, but overall ents are *pretty flaccid.*
Food: The University refectory in the Kydd building is open mornings and lunchtimes. The Union bar does lunch, dinner and snacks. *Nothing special but it's cheap and does the job.*

SOCIAL & POLITICAL

UNIVERSITY OF ABERTAY DUNDEE STUDENTS' ASSOCIATION:

• 3 sabbaticals • Turnout at last ballot: 10% • NUS member
Relations between the SU, the college suits and the students are pretty snug, helped by the small size of the place.

SA FACILITIES:

The new student centre planned for late 2004 will include: bars and nightclub facilities; study spaces and meeting rooms for clubs and societies; gym; family areas and children's play areas; advice and support services; open plan office space for students and support staff; online careers support; cinema; theatre; exhibition space; food court; debating chamber. The SA also has: pool tables; minibus hire; photocopying/fax/printing services; TV lounge; juke boxes; stationery shop; vending machines; bookshop; launderette.

CLUBS (NON-SPORTING):
Celtic Supporters; Liverpool Supporters; Role Play; Friendz of the Union. **See also Clubs tables.**

OTHER ORGANISATIONS:
Focus magazine is free every month. There are occasional charity bashes (Halloween etc.).

RELIGIOUS:
• 5 chaplains (RC, CofS, Episcopalian)
A chaplaincy centre is available for those of 'all faiths and none'. There's also a Muslim Prayer Room.

PAID WORK: see Dundee University
• Job bureau
Work is easiest to find outside term. The careers service can help find work during term.

SPORTS

• Recent successes: Gaelic women's/men's football • BUSA Ranking: 48
Abertay are *plucky overachievers*, given the size of the place. Facilities *aren't anything to write home about*, but students *bound for sporting immortality* can make use of the Elite athletics programme (golf, athletics, swimming etc.), which gives advice on diet and coaching. Special deals for students at local facilities.

SPORTS FACILITIES:
Football, hockey and all-weather pitches; tennis, squash, basketball and netball courts; sports hall; swimming pool; running track; athletics field; multigym; aerobics studio; golf course. Dundee has a leisure centre, athletics field, squash and tennis courts, ice rink and another golf course. Then there's the *rugged* Scottish countryside, with mountains and rivers to *climb, jump off and plunge into*.

SPORTING CLUBS:
Waterpolo. **See also Clubs tables.**

ATTRACTIONS: see Dundee University

ACCOMMODATION

IN COLLEGE:
• Self-catering: 21% • Cost: £38-58 (36-52wks)
• Insurance premium: £
Availability: Livers-in forage for themselves but halls are *reasonably kitted* out. Some even have dishwashers, *which cuts down on the numbers of rotting sinks*. All first years are offered rooms, but some may have to share. Corso Street and Meadowside Hill halls are *in vogue* with mature and European students. Alloway and Hillside *are the halls of choice for gregarious* first-years. A 500-room student village should be ready for 2005.
Car parking: *Ridiculously easy*.

EXTERNALLY: see Dundee University
• Ave rent: £45
Availability: Many local students save rent by staying at home. Those who live out can expect to have *a fairly easy time* finding semi-furnished flats *close* to university. Perth Road is *popular, but getting quite expensive*. Most try to avoid *slumming it* on the city's east side.
Housing help: *Not much to set students on their way, only an approved landlord list*.

ACADEMIC

Highly rated teaching in most subjects. International Politics, History and Welsh History among others are particularly strong. Courses are credit-based and modular, with students taking 120 credits per year. Modularisation varies: some courses have relatively few optional modules, others are less rigid.

150-300

Entry points: 150-300	Ave points: 303
Applns per place: 5	Clearing: 7%
No. of terms: 2	Length of terms: 15wks
Staff/student ratio: 1:24	Study addicts: 91%
Firsts & 2.1s: 20%	Research: ***

POINTS

ADMISSIONS:

• Apply via UCAS
Aber caters for applicants from non-traditional academic backgrounds and has a relaxed attitude to mature students without formal qualifications.

SUBJECTS:

Art & Design: 38%   Sciences: 30%
Humanities & Social Sciences: 32%
Best: Accounting & Finance; Bio Sciences; Celtic Studies; Computer Studies; English; Environmental Science; Geography; Information Studies; Information & Library Studies; International Politics; Irish.
Unusual: Aber's International Politics course was the first of its kind in the galaxy.

LIBRARIES:

• 720,000 books • 1,400 study places • Spend per student: ££££
The Hugh Owen library and its three baby brothers are backed up by the *humungous* National Library of Wales, free to Aber students.

COMPUTERS:

• 700 workstations • 24-hr access
The number of computers ain't such a drag as all student rooms can jack into the net.

OTHER LEARNING FACILITIES:

Language labs; rehearsal rooms; CAD lab; Audio/TV centre and *an astonishing* five drama studios. Aber provides web-posting space to all who want it so hundreds of student web pages are accessible from the main site, ranging from extensive drunken photo galleries to detailed analyses of different types of peat. *Whatever clicks your button, eh?*

ENTERTAINMENT

THE CITY:

• Price of a pint of beer: £2.00 • Glass of wine: £1.90 • Can of Red Bull: £1.90
Cinemas: The Commodore is *crumbly but cosy* and right in the town centre.
Theatres: A small theatre by the harbour hosts touring productions (everything from cabaret to Brecht). Performances by professional groups also appear at the University's Arts Centre.
Pubs: *Warm, cosy and somewhat pricey.* Pushplugs: Rummers, Glengower, Varsity, Lord Beechings, The Cambrian. There's a new Wetherspoons – *Starbucks of the pub world* – for cut-price liquids. Students *tend to avoid the Nag's Head.*
Clubbing: *Not exactly cutting edge.* Pier Pressure, K2 and the Footie *are all pretty run-of-the mill.* The Bay has occasional indie/grunge aspirations.
Music venues: Local bands play at a couple of the pubs and, in the true Welsh spirit, Aber has its own male voice choir. There's also annual Jazz and world music festivals.

Eating out: An *excellent* variety of local restaurants, especially for fresh fish. *Harry's is top choice for special occasions – it's too expensive for more regular visits. Rumbletums promises an affordable Sunday lunch. Serendipity and Gannets are both popular bistros.* Other Pushplugs: Agra and The Light of Asia (curry), Little Italy (guess), Le Café Noir (guess again), Mandarin (no, not oranges) and the pubilicious Varsity, Bar Essential and the Brasserie on the Pier.

> Brunel's maths block was the setting for Alex deLarge's re-education in Stanley Kubrick's A Clockwork Orange.

UNIVERSITY:
• Price of a pint of beer: £1.70 • Glass of wine: £1.70 • Can of Red Bull: £1.60
Bars: The Joint keeps the beer flowing till 1 or 2am (not Sundays) *and is rush-hour busy most nights.* Cwrt Mawr Bar by one of the halls juggles Pound-a-Pint nights, TV sports events and, *oh Lord*, karaoke. The wee Outback in Llanbadarn is open till 1am on Thursdays. *The Rosser draws in quite a crowd.*
Theatres: The Arts Centre is *proper swish* and hosts productions by both students and *real people. The Theatre, Film & TV Studies department is particularly mighty* and spawns its drama-babies in several studios.
Film: *Two films a day ensure distraction is always available. Varied cocktail of mainstream, arthouse and world cinema.*
Music venues: The Union's main venue pumps out warbles from ickle indie and rock bands nearly every week. Bigger noises have come from the likes of Electric Six, Shed Seven and Idlewild. The Arts Centre has a *cluttered calendar of all kinds of musical events throughout the year.*
Clubbing: Reload (Wed) and Wired (Fri) are the Union's biggest nights. Visiting DJs have included Shaun Ryder and Tim Burgess.
Comedy/Cabaret: Fortnightly Tuesday Comedy Network nights at the Union. The Arts Centre has *laughable musings* every so often too.
Food: Aber's 'food loyalty card' functions a bit like a phone top-up card and can be spent in any of the many catering outlets. *The system has saved more than a few from budget-related starvation.* Dining rooms in halls of residence operate on a pay-as-you-eat basis. Food is available till 1am.
Other: The Union-hosted May Ball is the biggest black-tie bonanza of the year.

SOCIAL & POLITICAL

ABERYSTWYTH GUILD OF STUDENTS:
• 6 sabbaticals • Turnout at last ballot: 28% • NUS member
The Guild is subdivided into the UMCA (Welsh Speakers Students Union – *the acronym works in Welsh*), which has its own sabbatical officer and looks after the Welsh contingent. Relations between the Guild and University bigwigs *are smooth and co-operative. Politics comes in a fairly left-wing form, although round these parts PC means Plaid Cymru rather than Political Correctness.*

SU FACILITIES:
Four bars (two union-run); three cafeterias; snack bar; fast food joint; pool tables; meeting rooms; Endsleigh Insurance Office; Abbey National and HSBC ATMs; general store; stationery shop; post office; new and secondhand bookshops; gaming and vending machines; travel agency; launderette; fax and printing services; photocopier; photo booth; payphones; advice centre; TV lounge.

CLUBS (NON-SPORTING):

Natural History; Singers; Amateur Radio; Elizabethan Madrigal Singers; Meditation; Art; Asia-Pacific; Bell-ringing; Biological & Environmental; Computer; English; Environmental Earth Science; Erasmus; European; Expedition; Film & TV; Gentlemen's Society; Geography; German; Global Politics; Anime; Hip Hop; History; Indiesoc; Aber Journal of World Affairs; Jive; Juggling and Circus Skills; Law; MUG (Mac Users Group); Methodist; Musicians; La Société Française; Philosophy; Aber Osgars; Physics; Warpsoc; Wine. **See also Clubs tables.**

OTHER ORGANISATIONS:

The Courier is Aber's award-nominated student mag. There's also Yr Utgorn for Welsh-speakers. Bay Radio broadcasts four programmes a day in the Union building. Aber Rag is one of Europe's biggest and regularly raises five-figure sums, but then, they do have four minibuses which shoot off round the country every weekend to hassle strangers for cash. The excellent Community Action group is called 'Dim Prob' (which is not a reflection on the Aberystwyth intellect of the participants, but Welsh for 'No Problem'), spends its selfless time gardening for the elderly, giving parties for disabled kids *and generally being nice to everyone.*

RELIGIOUS:

The College has its own chapel and several chaplains. Town has churches for most Christian denominations as well as a mosque.

PAID WORK:

- Job bureau • Paid work: term-time 40%: hols 60%
Bar, cleaning and supermarket work are all available, especially in the summer when the tourists are in town. Aber's Job Link service *does its best* to find work for those who need it – bar and cleaning gigs are common.

S P O R T S

- Recent successes: fencing, basketball • BUSA Ranking: 48
Despite some national triumphs, *the Aber attitude to sport is friendly and open to even the most wimpish athlete. There's a good many water-based sports and Aber is nearly top of the list when it comes to getting wet and sweaty.* About half the students are members of the Athletics Union, which is run by a sabbatical officer.

SPORTS FACILITIES:

A mighty selection: 12 football, four rugby, four hockey, an all-weather and two cricket pitches; 13 squash, eight tennis, two basketball and four netball courts; two sports halls; swimming pool; athletics field; gym; multigym; aerobics studio; climbing wall; golf course; lake and river (Rheidol) access and a boathouse for larking about on the Irish Sea *or watching bronzed bikinied beauties or speedoed studs splashing around – you sick puppy.* Costs £25 a year for full access, *which is better value than any luxury 'gym'.* Locally: golf course; swimming pool; bowling green.

SPORTING CLUBS:

American Football; Aikido; Cheerleaders; Bodyboarding; Boxercise; Canoeing; Caving; Clay Pigeon; Expedition; Lacrosse; Sky-diving; Surfing; Ultimate Frisbee; Walking; Water polo; Wind-surfing. **See also Clubs tables.**

A C C O M M O D A T I O N

IN COLLEGE:

- Catered: 18% • Cost: £76 (30wks)
- Self-catering: 43% • Cost: £33-63 (36wks)
- First years living in: 100% • Insurance premium: £
Availability: All 1st years can live in (less than 2% sharing) and the majority of finalists return to halls in their 3rd year. Most 2nd years live out. There's a wide selection of accommodation from larger halls on campus to the *enormous* Pentre Jane Morgan Student Village and *adorable little places* on the seafront. All rooms are *good quality and well*

looked-after and secure – CCTV, hall wardens and blokes tend to be put on the ground floor *so murderers can get them first*. Student rooms come complete with insurance cover, *which is handy*. Neuadd Pantycelyn hall houses a treasury of old Welsh stuff (paintings and musical instruments). There's a bring-your-own bedding policy but bedding-packs are available *for a reasonable price – just don't expect satin sheets*. Insurance is included in residence fees.

Car parking: *Easy* at Penglais campus (permits required, £20/yr), less so in the town. The seafront pads have no facilities for cars.

EXTERNALLY:

• Ave rent: £58 • Living at home: 1%
Availability: Aber's too small to fit all its eggs in one basket so some have to go elsewhere to seek their bed. *It's not too tricky and accommodation in the area is on the cheap side and far from scummy. Unsurprisingly, the seafront is popular.*
Housing help: *The proactive Accommodation Service is dedicated to domestic well being – no one gets left out in the cold.* They approve and blacklist landlords, publish vacancy lists and bulletin boards, offer legal/contract advice, hold safety seminars and will intervene in domestic disputes – *that's wrangles with landlords, not The Great I'm Not Making The Tea War of 2006.*

WELFARE

SERVICES:

• Lesbian/Gay/Bisexual Society • International Students' Society • Postgrad Society
• Nightline • College counsellors: 2 full/3 part • Crime rating: !
There's a Welsh language group. Town provides a rape crisis line. All students have personal tutors they are required to see three times a term.
Health: Students Health Centre with doctors and nurse, but students are also asked to register with a local GP and dentist.
Women: Attack alarms available for £2.50.
Crèches/Nursery: The University runs a crèche facility with 63 places, 6mths–4yrs.
Disabilities: *Though improving, wheelchair access is problematic for geographical reasons. The University has a welcoming attitude, but short of flattening the whole town, there's not much they can do.* Disabled applicants are encouraged to get in touch for an individual assessment. *Facilities for sight-impaired students are good and dyslexia is well supported with assessment, academic assistance and weekly group meetings.*
Crime: *'Lowest crime rate in Britain'* echoes through the valleys.

FINANCE:

• Ave debt per year: £2,728
Fees: International students pay between £7,375 and £9,775 depending on whether it's an arts or science degree, postgrads between £3,010 and £9,950 (full-time). Aber won't be charging top-up fees in 2006–7, but the jury's still out for what will be happening after that.
• Access fund: £450,000 • Successful applications/yr: 800 • Ave payment: £600
Support: The Student Financial Support Office provides help and advice for all matters fiscal. There are a good many scholarships available (up to £3,450), plus hardship funds and bursaries for students from low-income families.

APU

• *Formerly Anglia Polytechnic.*
Anglia Polytechnic University, East Road, Cambridge, CB1 1PT
Tel: (0845) 271 3333 E-mail: answers@apu.ac.uk Website: www.apu.ac.uk
APUSU, Victoria Road South, Chelmsford, Essex, CM1 1LL
Tel: (01245) 258 178 E-mail: info@apusu.com
See below for details of other sites.

GENERAL

Along with Ulster, De Montfort and Cranfield, *this is as close as a university's different sites get to being separate colleges.* In fact, Anglia Polytechnic University's two main campuses were once separate colleges – Cambridge College of Art & Technology (CCAT) and the Essex Institute of Higher Education in Chelmsford – until they merged in 1989, became a poly in 1991 and a university in 1992. *All in the time it takes to get a degree.* They're merged in the loosest sense, because they're still *geographically and socially quite distinct.* It's the last institution in the UK to retain the dreaded 'P' word in its name although most people refer to it as Anglia or APU.
See below for details of each site.

Sex ratio (M:F): 35:65	**Founded: 1989**
Full-time u'grads: 9,985	**Part-time: 11,755**
Postgrads: 710	**Non-degree: n/a**
Ave course: 3yrs	**Ethnic: 11%**
State:private school: 95:5	**Flunk rate: 17%**
Mature: 60%	**International: 13%**
Disabled: 107	**Local: 80%**

65%
35%

ATMOSPHERE:
The spirit at each site varies as much as the place names on the train tickets and there's no common overtone. The Cambridge site's about as far removed from its illustrious neighbour as it's possible to get, both in distance from the historic town centre and in attitude: there's a definite defiance at being part of APU rather than Cambridge. Chelmsford (see below for fuller description) has more mature students and part-timers, so it's not as self-consciously studenty as the Fens-based campus.

CAMBRIDGE: see University of Cambridge
• City centre: 800m
See below for details of the Chelmsford site.

TRAVEL: see University of Cambridge

CAREER PROSPECTS:
• Careers Service • No. of staff: 2 full/2 part • Unemployed after 6mths: 7%

Aston University

Aston University, The Triangle, Birmingham, B4 7ET
Tel: (0121) 204 300 E-mail: admissions@aston.ac.uk Website: www.aston.ac.uk
Aston Students Guild, Aston University, Aston Triangle, Gosta Green, Birmingham, B4 7ES
Tel: (0121) 359 6531 E-mail: guild.liaison@aston.ac.uk Website: www.astonguild.org.uk

GENERAL

Just 5 mins leg action from the centre of Birmingham is the *not-quite-triangular* Aston Triangle – *a modern, green, landscaped campus of brown, brick buildings*. Within them lie over 3 miles of corridors and the oldest public swimming pool in the country (1860). And a University. A pair of *intimidating* sky lifts slide up and down the main building, *which although 'futuristic' in appearance, is beginning to look a bit dated, paradoxically enough. It's what the 60s thought the future would look like – watching Buck Rogers has the same effect. Despite the campus's compact size there's also the Vice-Chancellor's Lake – work, play and hangovers all mix on the lakeside lawns when the sunshine hits.* **For general info about Birmingham: see University of Birmingham**.

Sex ratio (M:F): 49:51	Founded: 1895
Full-time u'grads: 5,260	Part-time: 160
Postgrads: 595	Non-degree: 0
Ave course: 4yrs	Ethnic: 24%
State:private school: 89:11	Flunk rate: 10%
Mature: 8%	International: 19%
Disabled: 74	Local: 23%

51%
49%

ATMOSPHERE:

Aston's an unusual kettle of squid in that it's never been a polytechnic yet places a hefty emphasis on vocational degrees and career-based learning. Students are more than keen for the complete fun-fuelled, drink-drenched package, but make sure they gather a few precious CV points on the way. The placement year of most courses is central to this and many students spend time on additional summer placements, tutoring and voluntary work. The small campus setting means everyone knows everyone else – the law of the Aston Loop means that everyone can be linked, like Kevin Bacon, to everyone else by six people. It's cosy enough but the bright lights of Brum are all around if things get claustrophobic.

BIRMINGHAM: see University of Birmingham

TRAVEL: see University of Birmingham
Trains: New Street Station is 15 mins walk away.
Coaches: Digbeth is a National Express station, 5 mins taxi-ride from the campus.
Cars: There's no parking on campus and the nearby streets are limited. There are several pay & displays in walking distance – but *not many students bother with cars.*
College: The Residents' Association (ACRA) runs a minibus service to local supermarkets *so there's no excuse to go hungry.* Coaches and minibuses also go to the recreation site.
Bicycles: Bikes are more and more common thanks to Birmingham's improved cycle network. *Locked shelters on campus help deter wandering hacksaws.*

CAREER PROSPECTS:

• Careers Service • No. of staff: 9 full/1 part • Unemployed after 6mths: 8%
Aston is top of the job pops when it comes to graduate employment. The Careers Service is a part of student life from the word 'matriculate'. It offers the usual careers shebang (library, newsletters etc.) plus e-mail updates, visiting employers, mock interviews, Microsoft courses, placement support and tutorials.

FAMOUS ALUMNI:

Gregor Townsend (Rugby); Laura Jones (BBC reporter); Lord Rooker MP (Lab); Jasper Carrott has an honorary degree.

FURTHER INFO:

• Prospectuses: undergrad; postgrad; departmental • Open days • DVD
Alternative and international prospectuses also available.

ACADEMIC

Whilst not a 'vocational' university, teaching could be considered more career-training than knowledge-gathering. The University pioneered the sandwich course and the year-long work placements are common. Overall grades are a combination of 1st year results, placement year performance, dissertations and final year marks. The Business school is *highly esteemed* and Aston's *strong in languages, health sciences and engineering*, too.

240-340		POINTS
Entry points: 240-340	**Ave points: 312**	
Applns per place: 8	**Clearing: 8%**	
No. of terms: 3	**Length of terms: 10wks**	
Staff/student ratio: 1:15	**Study addicts: 10%**	
Teaching: ***	**Research: ******	
Year abroad: 9%	**Sandwich students: 72%**	
Firsts: 11%	**2.2s: 30%**	
2.1s: 54%	**3rds: 3%**	

ADMISSIONS:

• Apply via UCAS

SUBJECTS:

Art & Design: 4%
Business/Management: 30%
Engineering: 15%
Medical Sciences: 20%
Modern Languages: 8%
Sciences: 13%
Social Sciences: 10%

Best: Accounting; Biology; Business Computing & IT; Business & Management; Electronic Engineering; European Studies; French; German; International Business & Economics; Languages; Marketing; Optometry; Pharmacy; Psychology; Politics.
Unusual: Audiology; Logistics; Optometry; Translation Studies.

LIBRARIES:

• 320,000 books • 500 study places
Aston's main library is open seven days and although *it's not quite a literary powerhouse*, intranet facilities are extensive, with searchable online catalogues and reservations.

COMPUTERS:

• 950 workstations • 24-hr access • Spend per student: £££££
Wireless internet access across campus, including in all student bedrooms for £10 a month.

The Prince William Effect: 2001 was the first year in 20 that St Andrew's filled all of its courses without clearing.

OTHER LEARNING FACILITIES:

A Maths Drop-in centre is available to all those who *forget how to count*. Rehearsal rooms, CAD lab, audio/TV centre, and *top-notch* labs for neurosciences and optometry. Tons of language labs and not restricted to those on language courses. There are also some *sketchy* online resources.

ENTERTAINMENT

THE CITY: see University of Birmingham
Aston students *favour* city-centre bars like Bar Med, Zinc and the Glee Comedy Club. Other areas for *a good night out in Brum* are Moseley, Harborne and Digbeth (lots of Irish pubs). For gigging there's the National Indoor Arena and Birmingham Academy (100m from campus).
Clubs: Air, Apt and the Works – big student nights. *Loads* of eats across the city, and *not just limited to balti*. The new Bull Ring shopping centre is massive and has a far few diversions (and is a good source for part-time work).

UNIVERSITY:
• Price of a pint of beer: £1.60 • Glass of wine: £1.60 • Can of Red Bull: £1.40
Bars: Einstein's is a *pubby, popular* affair that keeps the liquor swilling till 2am on ent nights. The Loft is the sportsman's choice, while the Blue Room is a coffee bar by day which gets boozy in the evenings with the adjoining Guild Hall till 2am. Café Astons has a more *mature* air – it's postgrads and staff only. Thursday night is Larryoke, named in honour of Larry the Eternal Barman, *supposedly a student who never got round to leaving*. This is honoured by karaoke and play-your-cards-right. *Naturally.*
Theatre: The Great Hall draws in student and professional thesps.
Film: One free indiscriminate blockbuster shown every week.
Clubbing/Music venues: The Guild Hall (940) crams dancers in four nights a week: School Days – *uniform fetishes and Rick Astley – is the biggest heel-clicker*. Rag organises Freakers, which has a *sexual fantasies theme – nurses, bored housewives, llama farmers etc*. Tony Blackburn, Trevor Nelson, Jamelia, Big Brovaz and Miss Dynamite are among those who've spun or crooned a few tunes recently.
Comedy/Cabaret: The Blue Room hosts comedy nights where *80s relics* Timmy Mallett, the cast of Rainbow, Keith Harris & Orville and the like up the comedy kitsch factor.
Food: Cafélogo offers refectory-style dining and made-to-order pizzas three times a day. La Serre does *cheap* takeaway sarnies, and there's a Costa Coffee on campus. Grub can be had from bars and the Guild Hall till 11pm most nights.
Other: *Lavish May Ball and Graduation Ball and a mean Fresher's Week.*

SOCIAL & POLITICAL

ASTON STUDENTS' GUILD:
• 5 sabbaticals • Turnout at last ballot: 24% • NUS member
The Union is a massive part of student life – socially and sportingly at least. They're not the most political banana in the bowl but they did rustle up 98 protestors for the anti-top-up fees march in London which shows they are prepared to show willing when politics gets too close to home.

SU FACILITIES:

Purpose-built nightclub and music venue; five bars; two cafeterias; pool/snooker tables; loads of meeting rooms; three minibuses for hire; NatWest, HSBC and Lloyds banks with ATMs; photocopiers; photo booth; fax and printing service; payphones; advice centre; games room; hairdresser; vending machines; general store; stationery shop; bookshop; ticket agency; launderette.

CLUBS (NON-SPORTING):
Alternative Music; Ballroom & Latin American; Drinking; Extreme Ironing; Fusion; Hellenic; Live Music; Irish; Juggling; Krishna Consciousness; Links (St John Ambulance); Mary Jane; Moflava; Plastic Dreams (urban culture); Racing; Rock; Singaporean; Turkey. **See also Clubs tables.**

OTHER ORGANISATIONS:
There's a student mag five times a term. Rag *is a busy little beaver,* raising hefty sums through a *crammed calendar* of pub crawls, slave auctions, *colossal piss-ups and the usual tomfoolery. There's gazillions of different community groups* who do a mixture of conservation work, coaching in local schools and community stuff.

RELIGIOUS:
• 3 chaplains: (FC, CofE, RC)
The multi-faith chaplaincy and variety of prayer rooms cater for Christian, Sikh, Hindu, Jewish and Islamic faiths. Birmingham city centre has many more.

PAID WORK: see University of Birmingham
• Job bureau • Paid work: term-time 60%: hols 85%
The Guild's job shop advertises local jobs (bars, pubs, clubs, shops and restaurants) and the Union also employs a few itself. There's also a vacation work placement scheme which helps find course-related positions with decent wages.

SPORTS

• Recent successes: women's football, women's netball • BUSA Ranking: 48
The ladies may be in the lead but sport is popular across the student body. The University takes it seriously too, having spent 200 thou on a new fitness suite and redeveloping the gym (including personal trainers). They may be followed by a new sports centre within the next few years.

SPORTS FACILITIES:
No shirking on the facilities front: nine football/rugby pitches; one cricket, four hockey and two all-weather pitches. Five squash, four tennis and two basketball courts; two sports halls; swimming pool; multigym; gym; aerobics studio; climbing wall; snooker and table tennis tables; solarium; large pavilion with three bars. Fitness centre membership costs £40 for three months, sports hall hire £12 an hour.

SPORTING CLUBS:
10-pin bowling; Aikido; Canoeing; Caving; Dance; Handball; Ice Skating; Ju-Jitsu; Lacrosse; Mountaineering; Sky-diving; Snooker; Surfing; Thai boxing. **See also Clubs tables.**

ATTRACTIONS: see University of Birmingham

ACCOMMODATION

IN COLLEGE:
• Self-catering: 40% • Cost: £53-81 (39 wks)
• First years living in: 80% • Insurance premium: £££
Availability: Aston accommodation comes in en-suite or standard. All halls and flats are on campus and *consequently over-subscribed* but first years are guaranteed a place. About 30% of those living in have a toilet to call their throne and the en-suite rooms are in *sexy, modern lakeside low-rises. The standard variety is older, built when comfort wasn't a priority and plumbing was just a few steps ahead of some straw in the corner. It's not all that grim though* – there are postcard views across Birmingham from the high-rises. All 1st years can be housed and are given the option of single-sexed/mixed and smoking/non-smoking. Although there's no catered accommodation, students can buy a meal deal pass for £250 a term that gives them ten refectory meals a week. Halls are swipe card entry and porters are on duty day and night.
Car parking: *Don't even go there.*

EXTERNALLY: see University of Birmingham
• Ave rent: £45 • Living at home: 20%
Availability: The 2nd-year campus exodus *usually winds up in* Erdington or Aston Brook Green, which are *relatively* cheap and campus-accessible. New developments by people like UNITE are springing up in the city and are *proving popular*.
Housing help: Vacancies, approved landlord lists, contract and legal assistance from the Housing Office.

WELFARE

SERVICES:

• Lesbian/Gay/Bisexual Officer & Society • Ethnic Minorities Officer & Society
• Women's Society • Mature Students' Officer & Society
• International Students' Officer & Society • Postgrad Officer & Society
• Disabilities Officer & Society • Self-defence classes • Nightline
• College counsellors: 4 full/3 part • SU counsellors: 3 full • Crime rating: !!!!
Health: The campus health service has three doctors, four nurses, a dentist and an optometrist.
Women: Some single-sex flats for women as well as women-only pool and gym sessions.
Crèches/Nursery: 50 places on campus for kids 6wks–5yrs.
Disabilities: Campus is *compact, flat and self-contained* and there are ramps and lifts in most buildings for wheelchair users. There's a small number of adapted bedrooms and parking permits are free to disabled students. Hearing loops and dyslexia support tutor.
Crime: Two rozzers patrol the campus. There are the usual town crime concerns but *they don't encroach on campus*.
Drugs: There's an annual safe drinking campaign and a zero tolerance policy on drug users.

FINANCE:

• Ave debt per year: £2,771
Fees: Postgrad fees are £6,000–17,000. International students pay up to £10,000.
• Access fund: £300,000 • Successful applications/yr: 700
Support: Hardship funds, travel bursaries and an assortment of other prizes, including the Aston bursary (£2,000), are available to those who need them.

Bangor, University of Wales

University of Bath

Bath Spa University College

Bath College of Higher Education see Bath Spa University College

Belfast, Queen's University see Queen's University of Belfast

Birkbeck, University of London

University of Birmingham

Birmingham Conservatoire see University of Central England

Birmingham Poly see University of Central England

Birmingham Polytechnic see University of Central England

Bolton Institute for Higher Education see University of Bolton

University of Bolton

Bournemouth University

Bournemouth Polytechnic, Dorset Institute see Bournemouth University

University of Bradford

University of Brighton

Brighton Polytechnic see University of Brighton

University of Bristol

Bristol, University of the West of England

Bristol Polytechnic see Bristol, University of the West of England

Bristol Poly see Bristol, University of the West of England

Brookes University see Oxford Brookes University

Brunel University

University of Buckingham

Buckinghamshire Chilterns University College

Bangor, University of Wales

- **Part of the *University of Wales***
(1) University of Wales, Bangor, Gwynedd, LL57 2DG
  Tel: (01248) 351 151 E-mail: admissions@bangor.ac.uk Website: www.bangor.ac.uk
  Undeb Myfyrwyr Bangor Student's Union, Deiniol Road, Bangor, Gwynedd, LL57 2TH
  Tel: (01248) 388 000 E-mail: undeb@undeb.bangor.ac.uk Website:
  www.undeb.bangor.ac.uk
(2) School of Education, University of Wales, Bangor, Gwynedd, LL57 2PX
  Tel: (01978) 316 316
(3) Faculty of Health Studies, Wrexham Technology Park, Wrexham, LL13 7YP

GENERAL

'Didn't we have a lovely time the day we went to Bangor?' Probably not if it was pouring with rain and we were after a big night out. Bangor is a *small* city to be found between the *rugged beauty* of Snowdonia and the Menai Strait, which divides Anglesey from the rest of Britain. That's Wales, *for the geographically hazy*, and *deepest rural Wales at that*. The city is *unmistakably pretty* with *gorgeous* scenic views, and a *modest* crop of high street chains. It's surrounded by *quaint* little towns with their own castles – places like Beaumaris, Conwy and Caernarfon. The main University building is a *cathedral-esque creation*, though some others on the College Road *resemble old country hotels*.

Sex ratio (M:F): 36:64		Founded: 1884
Full-time u'grads: 5,430		Part-time: 1,995
Postgrads: 1,185		Non-degree: n/a
Ave course: 3-4yrs		Ethnic: 5%
State:private school: 94:6		Flunk rate: 14%
Mature: 30%		International: 10%
Disabled: 268		Local: 20%

ATMOSPHERE:

This is cagoule and sensible footwear country rather than planet party, but if it's the peaceful life that appeals, there are probably few better places. Bangor is laid-back, comfortingly small and pretty close knit. Students almost double the city population during term-time and relations with the locals are largely easy. The University is a hit with native Welsh speakers and there's a sizeable Irish population, attracted by the close quarters of Holyhead.

SITES:

School of Education: (1,528 students – Education, Sport Science) *Welcome to north Walian suburbia. The community is extraordinarily close, with plenty of curtain twitching and gossip mongering.* The central college buildings are about a mile away and buses stop outside the department.

Wrexham: (Radiography, Nursing & Midwifery) 60 miles from Bangor, the Wrexham site is actually on a science park on the edge of town. Chester, 12 miles further, is the *focus* of student attention. It's a *tourist trap*, with plenty of *worthy* historic sites to *yawn* around, as well as a *far more exciting* set of bars, pubs, clubs and theatres.

BANGOR:

- Population: 116,800 • London: 236 miles • Cardiff: 180 miles • Manchester: 85 miles
- High temp: 19 • Low temp: 3 • Rainfall: 70

The sea breeze *blows squalls of tourists* into the city, to marvel at the *admittedly marvellous* views. *There are lots of shops – though not much in the way of variety – as well as a reasonable night scene.*

TRAVEL:

Trains: The station is 800m from the main University buildings. Trains take about 4 hours direct to London (from £40 return). Just about everywhere else involves a change at Crewe (£17).
Coaches: National Express to London (£33) takes between 9-12 hours. Birmingham (£18.25), Cardiff (£35.75) and other destinations are also available.
Car: *An increasingly necessary student accessory, although they're more for getting out of Bangor than around the city, which is almost entirely walkable.*
Local: Buses run around town and all across Gwynedd. Day trips on the ferry to Ireland cost £9, and there's an *incredible* single carriage steam train ride up Snowdon.
Taxis: *Not too costly as there's nowhere far to go in the city.*
Bicycles: *Bangor is hillsville, and pedalling demands thighs of steel. Still, sporty Bangorites seem to get a kick out it and cycling's surprisingly popular.*

CAREER PROSPECTS:

- Careers Service • No. of staff: 13 full/8 part • Unemployed after 6mths: 10%

The careers service is involved in the GO Wales/Cymru Prosper Wales work exprerience project, promoting employment for students who live in Wales.

FAMOUS ALUMNI:

Danny Boyle (film director); Tim Haines (Producer, BBC's Walking with Dinosaurs); Mark Hughes (former Wales football team manager), Richard Attenborough and Carol Vorderman are honorary fellows.

FURTHER INFO:

- Prospectuses: undergrad; postgrad; departmental; video; CD-Rom • Open days

Bilingual prospectuses. SU a so does an info pack – see the web.

A *magnet* for sport and exercise science students, *Bangor has an increasingly bitchin' psychology department*. Also runs a *respected* Welsh degree, which lures a lot of local students.

POINTS 220-300		
Entry points: 220–300	**Ave points: 280**	
Applns per place: 4	**Clearing: 8%**	
No. of terms: 2	**Length of terms: 15wks**	
Staff/student ratio: 1:14	**Study addicts: 29%**	
Teaching: n/a	**Research: *****	
Year abroad: 5%	**Sandwich students: 1%**	
Firsts: 9%	**2.2s: 36%**	
2.1s: 46%	**3rds: 7%**	

ADMISSIONS:

- Apply via UCAS

SUBJECTS:

Arts & Social Sciences: 39%   Health Studies: 9%
Education: 8%   Science & Engineering: 44%
Best: Biological Sciences; Chemistry; Forestry: Music; Ocean Sciences; Psychology; Theology & Religious Studies; Welsh.
Unusual: Environmental Forensics; Marine Chemistry; Ocean Informatics; Three-Language Honours.

LIBRARIES:

• 672,500 books • 1,104 study places • Spend per student: £
Two main faculty and five smaller departmental libraries

COMPUTERS:

• 575 workstations • 24-hr access • Spend per student: ££

OTHER LEARNING FACILITIES:

The Ocean Sciences department has a multi-million pound research ship *to probe the depths of the high seas.*

ENTERTAINMENT

THE CITY:

• Price of a pint of beer: £2.10 • Glass of wine: £1.90 • Can of Red Bull: £1.60
Cinemas: The Apollo has a couple of screens. Those with wheels make the trip to the Cineworld multiplex in Llandudno Junction (20 mins drive).
Theatres: Theatre Gwynedd has its own production company and also hosts touring shows.
Pubs: *The quayside pubs are small and personable. Pushplugs: Patricks (aka Paddy's, small, cheap, cosy); Y Glob (Welsh pub); Joott (late licence, obligatory dancefloor); O'Shea's (chirpy, chirpy, cheap, cheap); Fat Cats (pricey but good food).*
Clubbing: The University *bears the clubbing brunt*, but Octagon *draws a crowd* on student nights.
Eating out: *Pub grub ago-go. Wetherspoons is predictably popular. Pushplugs: The Pizza House; Mike's Bites; Late Stop; the Kebab House.*

UNIVERSITY:

• Price of a pint of beer: £1.65 • Glass of wine: £1.50 • Can of Red Bull: £1
Bars: NUS only, unlike the University club. Saturday night cheese in the Main Bar is a *crowd puller*. The Basement Bar holds indie and rock nights. University-owned Ffriddoedd Bar does a full bar menu. *Space is at a premium. The Main Bar is often stuffed to the ceiling by 8pm.*
Theatres: There's a *small but committed* thesp set made up of three societies: Rostra (am dram); BEDS (English drama); Soda (musicals). All use the Theatr Gwynedd next door to the SU.
Film: Theatr Gwynedd doubles up as a screen for arty films.
Music venues: Recent visitors have included Lemar, Lisa Maffia and Goldie Lookin Chain.
Clubbing: *In a strange reversal of normal affairs* the town looks to the University for thrills. Time/Amser is a *ferry-shaped yet curiously barn-like sort of place* open to the public as well. It's the *most happening* place in Bangor on a Friday night, *for what that's worth*. Trevor Nelson and Tim Westwood have both diddled their decks there.
Comedy/Cabaret: Monthly gigs at the Main Bar from up-and-coming gag merchants.
Food: Freddy's, the SU fast-food place, *provides the grease*. Y Glan Newydd does more *wholesome* lunches and the University runs self-service joint Bistro 1. There's also Dylans; Mrs P's (deli); Ceri's Diner.
Other: Summer, Christmas and plenty of Halls' balls to boot.

SOCIAL & POLITICAL

BANGOR STUDENTS' UNION/UNDEB MYFYRWYR BANGOR:

• 5 sabbaticals • Turnout at last ballot: 8% • NUS member
The SU *gets along well* with the University suits. *They tend to concentrate on welfare and services over party politicking.*

SU FACILITIES:

Union building; two bars; café; snack bar and deli; meeting room; minibus hire; bank (Natwest) and ATMs; photcopier/fax/printing; pool and snooker tables; general store; stationery shop; vending machine; games room; crèche; photo booth.

CLUBS (NON-SPORTING):

Archaeology, BEDS (Drama); BUMS (Mountaineering); BUGS (Guides & Scouts); BWRPS (Wargaming & Roleplay); Concert Band; Christians in Sport; Duke of Edinburgh; Hellenic (Greek); Indian; Japanese; Latino; Stage Crew; Rostra (Drama); SODA (Drama), Yoga. **See also Clubs tables.**

OTHER ORGANISATIONS:

Monthly student newspapers in English (Seren) and Welsh (Y Ddraenen) and a student radio station (Storm).

RELIGIOUS:

• Team of chaplains (CofE, RC)
The CofE chaplaincy centre also has 28 self-catered rooms *for the really keen* and an ecumenical centre where followers of all faiths can drop in. Locally, there's a Cathedral as well as Catholic, Methodist, Church of Wales and Baptist churches, a Quaker house and a mosque.

PAID WORK:

• Job bureau • Paid work: term-time 80%: hols 65%
Jobs can be *hard to come by*, although Welsh speakers are *at an advantage* for office/admin work. GoWales provides 97 paid placements in north-west Wales during vacations and after graduation. The Portfolio Worker Project helps develop freelancing abilities.

SPORTS

• Recent successes: football, basketball, trampolining, swimming • BUSA Ranking: 48
Poor pitches are *holding back* otherwise-successful outdoor sports teams.

SPORTS FACILITIES:

Six football pitches; hockey pitch; two rugby pitches; all-weather pitch; cricket ground; four squash courts; two tennis courts; four basketball courts; three netball courts; three sports halls; running track; athletics field; gym; aerobics studio; multigym; climbing wall. In town, the JJB Fitness Centre does student discounts.

SPORTING CLUBS:

Gaelic Football; Gymnastics; Ki-aikido; Mountain Walking; Octopush; Surfing; Rowing; Thai Kick-Boxing; Ultimate Frisbee. **See also Clubs tables.**

ATTRACTIONS:

Bangor FC *barely raise a cheer* but local facilities are *pretty good*. There's a leisure centre, swimming pool, athletics field, squash and tennis courts, a *sporty* sort of river, pot-holing caves, and mile upon mile of *glorious* mountainside. Llandudno has a dry ski slope. The national centres for watersports and mountaineering are accessible from Bangor.

ACCOMMODATION

IN COLLEGE:

• Catered: 7% • Cost: £74-85 (30wks)
• Self-catering: 5% • Cost: £49-66 (30-36wks)
• First years living in: 100% • Others living in: 25%
• Insurance premium: £
Availability: Accomodation is *widely available*, with some women-only blocks and rooms for disabled students. The Ffriddoedd site is Bangor's *finest*, with *box-fresh* en-suite rooms. There's one hall for Welsh-speaking students, *which proves popular for the close-spun community*.
Car parking: Cheap and easy. A year-long permit costs £8.40.

EXTERNALLY:

• Ave rent: £40 • Living at home: 10%
Availability: Standard *varies enormously*, from the *decidedly decent* to the *dangerous and dodgy*. Rent is *much more wallet-friendly* than in halls.
Housing help: The Accommodation Office advertises vacancies and provides a code of standards for landlords to sign up to.

WELFARE

SERVICES:

- Lesbian/Gay/Bisexual Officer & Society • Women's Officer
- International Students' Officer & Society • Postgrad Officer & Society
- Disabilities Officer • Self-defence classes • Nightline
- College counsellors: 1 full/2 part • Crime rating: !

Health: Student nurse on campus. A nearby surgery has five GPs on the books.
Crèches/Nursery: 35 places, 3mths-5yrs.
Disabilities: Accommodation for wheelchair users, but some of the older college buildings have *very poor* access. The Dyslexia Student Service provides *internationally-renowned* support.

FINANCE:

- Ave debt per year: £4,277 • Access fund: £500,000
- Successful applications/yr: 500 • Ave payment: £800-2,000

Support: *Dosh-happy* academic scholarships, various departmental awards and sports opportunity bursaries of £1,000.

University of Bath

The University of Bath, Claverton Down, Bath, BA2 7AY
Tel: (01225) 383 019 E-mail: admissions@bath.ac.uk Website: www.bath.ac.uk
University of Bath Students' Union, Claverton Down, Bath, BA2 7AY
Tel: (01225) 386 612 E-mail: union@bath.ac.uk Website: www.bathstudent.com

GENERAL

At the foot of the Cotswolds, an energetic stone's throw south-east of Bristol, is Bath – one of England's most *beautiful and unspoilt cities*. The Celts sniffed around the springs and the Romans built the first settlement here, but it was in Georgian times that it became the *pretty place* we know today – *although, as all tight-trouser fans will be aware, Jane Austen called it 'a monstrosity of epic proportion', but then set half her novels there, so what did she know?*
The many tourists don't come just to see the Roman Baths and the golden stones of the historic city but also the local countryside, the Mendip Hills and the Severn Estuary. *Unfortunately, the University, being on a small 60s campus 2 miles from the city centre, shares very little of this elegance. It's a disorienting place at first, with no immediately apparent focus or entry point. The buildings, with all the concrete charm of a shopping precinct, are definitely not the best feature. Still, there's loads of grassy and leafy bits to frolic in as well as the itsy bitsy University lake – perfect for those Mr Darcy moments – compensating a bit for the windy location.*

Sex ratio (M:F): 51:49	Founded: 1966
Full-time u'grads: 7,155	Part-time: 2,425
Postgrads: 1,330	Non-degree: 400
Ave course: 3/4yrs	Ethnic: n/a
State:private school: 80:20	Flunk rate: 3%
Mature: 10%	International: 14%
Disabled: 179	Local: n/a

(49% ♀ ... 51% ♂)

ATMOSPHERE:

Bath babies may be a touch isolated from the city (which isn't exactly Shangri-La to begin with) but they don't mind too much. Although serious about studies, both the library and the bars bustle merrily away throughout the day and students find plenty of time for sports, other activities, and then some more sports. Many are rather well-off – they'd have to be to live in Bath – but there's no real snobbery or pretentiousness, more a generous helping of community spirit, topped with lashings of charity work and garnished with a volunteering side salad. Delicious.

BATH:

• Population: 169,040 • City centre: 1.5 miles • London: 100 miles • Bristol: 11 miles • High temp: 21 • Low temp: 2 • Rainfall: 72

Bath's a *strikingly beautiful* c ty and one of only three on the planet to win a place on UNESCO's World Heritage list. Its most distinguishing feature is the hot water spring that produces a quarter of a million gallons of hot liquid a day, giving the city its name. The Roman Baths are a *necessary touristy* stop off. So too will be the Bath Spa public baths – *when and if they ever open* – which will draw on the same thermal water source and allow visitors to see what the Romans were on about. The spa resort heritage and *gorgeous* surroundings flood the city with tourists and their associated cash, but the *flipside is the wealth of amenities and cultural attractions can leave the humble student significantly out of pocket*. The two institutions (see also Bath Spa) bring some *much-needed* youth to the city, and the atmosphere car get lively and interesting for those who know where to go. Outside the city there's Bristol for urban thrills, Stonehenge, Salisbury Plain and Glastonbury *if you like your culture served quasi-mystical* and Claverton Cats & Dogs Home (close to the University) – always appreciative of volunteer dog-walkers and cat-cuddlers.

TRAVEL:

Trains: Bath Spa Station roughly 2 miles away has services to London Paddington, Bristol, Birmingham and beyond.
Coaches: Bath Coach Station has several National Express and First Group services, including London and Bristol.
Car: Bath's 9 miles off the M4 down the A46 and on the A4. The city centre's bus gate makes it *pretty much unnavigable*. The Council is planning to introduce a parking scheme to stop students and staff clogging residential streets with cars. Students living on campus or living privately in BA1 or BA2 postcodes are not eligible for annual permits. For others, they cost between £103 and £155 depending on location.
Air: Bristol Airport 18 miles away has flights inland and to main European destinations.
Hitching: *Many students cadge lifts up the hill to the University and the M4's good for thumbing down to London.*
Local: The SU has negotiated with First Bus to bring about the 'Bright Orange' bus service (No. 18) which operates between the city and Bath University every 6 mins during term. The Union shop sells books of 20 tickets (£9.40).
Taxis: Well stocked for cabs. A ride from the station to campus is around a fiver.
Bicycles: Some of the more energetic students and staff do cycle to campus *but the distance is prohibitive to, well, norma' people. Bathwick and Widcombe Hills are definitely not for the faint-hearted or unfit.* There's a cycle shed at the bottom of Bathwick for those who prefer the bus up the hill, plus sheds on campus.

CAREER PROSPECTS:

• <u>Careers Service</u> • <u>No. of staff: 8 full/2 part</u> • <u>Unemployed after 6mths: 7%</u>
The *ass-kicking* one careers service runs a variety of aids for all students including personal skills workshops, aptitude testing, computer-aided guidance systems (*nothing to do with controlling missiles*), job fairs and employer presentations. A lot of Bath students do vacation placements while studying, arranged by the careers folk.

FAMOUS ALUMNI:

Don Foster (Lib Dem spokesman); Jon Sleightholme (rugby player); Russell Senior (formerly of Pulp); Charles Lewington (ex-Tory Director of Communications); 'Dr' Neil Fox (Capital Radio DJ, Pop Idol judge and *utter pillock*).

FURTHER INFO:

• <u>Prospectuses: undergrad; postgrad; international</u> • <u>Open days</u>
The International Office produces an International Students' Handbook – see www.bath.ac.uk/international-office. Other prospectuses can be ordered online (www.bath.ac.uk/admissions) or by phone. Open days in June and September.

ACADEMIC

Apart from having one of the most meaningless Latin mottos – 'Generatim discite cultus' ('Learn each field of study according to its kind') – Bath has a strong record of providing professional courses, particularly in sciences, engineering and management. It's a *firm believer* in the powers of the placement year and study years abroad and three in five students pack their bags for industrial placements or a year studying abroad during their degree courses. There's no institutional assessment scheme as many courses are accredited by external, professional bodies. *On the one hand students can be sure of learning up-to-date professional skills, on the other some may feel a tad uneasy spending several years being moulded into cogs for the industrial machine.* Students can opt to take a learning unit outside their main course – *most opt for career-bolsterers like languages or management.*

280-360	
Entry points: 280-360	Ave points: 315
Applns per place: 8	Clearing: 2%
No. of terms: 2	Length of terms: 15wks
Staff/student ratio: 1:14	Study addicts: 16%
Teaching: ****	Research: *****
Year abroad: n/a	Sandwich students: 60%
Firsts: 18%	2.2s: 21%
2.1s: 58%	3rds: 4%

ADMISSIONS:

• <u>Apply via UCAS</u>
Bath operates a student-centred admissions policy, meaning that, *in theory at least*, they judge applications by whether the student will benefit intellectually *rather than how much money they can make out of them. Quite sweet really.*

SUBJECTS:

Engineering & Design: 24%	Management: 9%
Humanities & Social Sciences: 28%	Science: 39%

Best: Architecture; Business & Management Studies; Chemical Engineering; Civil Engineering; Economics; Education; Electronic & Electrical Engineering; Materials Technology; Maths; Organismal & Molecular Biosciences; Pharmacy & Pharmacology; Physics; Politics; Social & Policy Administration; Sports Sciences & Leisure Management; Statistics & Operational Research.

LIBRARIES:

• <u>535,000 books</u> • <u>1,005 study places</u> • <u>24-hr access</u> • <u>Spend per student: £££££</u>
The single multi-level library has three rooms with specialist equipment for special needs and disabled students. It gets new books every week and keeps a number of special collections.

COMPUTERS:

- 2,000 workstations • 24-hr access • Spend per student: £££££

There are several computer rooms and a PC suite. A new wireless environment around the Central Parade is in the process of being created. All bedrooms have intranet access.

OTHER LEARNING FACILITIES:

There's a self-access language centre on level 5 of the library with audio-visual resources. The Arts Theatre has rehearsal space for dance and drama, and there are music rehearsal rooms, a design lab and a TV centre.

ENTERTAINMENT

BATH:

- Price of a pint of beer: £2.40 • Glass of wine: £2.60 • Can of Red Bull: £1.70

Cinemas: The ABC's *an old school town-centre cinema with character*, showing major releases one by one. *The locally cherished Little Theatre Cinema has two screens for mainstream/arthouse flicks* and there's a new Odeon about. There's also a film festival.

Theatres: The *popular* Georgian Theatre Royal shows musicals and West End stuff with the occasional B-list celebrity appearance. The smaller Ustinov Studio attached to it is a good place to catch quirky fare like puppet shows, local am dram and one-man events. Rondo Theatre's an *intimate* studio spot with a *diverse* line-up. All offer student deals.

Pubs: *Quaint and plentiful with many a potent pint, but expensive. Many are designed purely to part the tourist trade from their money, but most are welcoming enough. Pushplugs (or maybe Bathplugs):* The Boater; the Huntsman; the Pulteney Arms; the Porter; the Pig & Fiddle.

Clubbing: *Not a huge deal going on, but things are more lively than the staid, touristy image might suggest. Pushplugs:* Cadillacs *(very pink, Monday is student night);* Po Na Na; Moles *(live music and DJs).*

Music venues: *Up-coming indie rockers congregate in Moles on a Saturday night. Porter Butt is also good for guitar-based rockeries.*

Eating out: The dozens of *chintzy* tea rooms aimed at tourists have been replaced by various chain coffee outlets, *but they go down just as well with visiting parents (and their wallets). Other, more student-friendly Pushplugs:* Café Retro *(lively and cheap);* Porter Bar *(homemade veggie);* Eastern Eye *and* Pria *do good curries;* Schwartz Bros *(non-plastic fast food);* Café Cadbury *(food made from chocolate). Try* Sally Lunn's – *totally touristy, but everything comes with a traditional Bath bun.*

Other: *Brilliant for museums and art galleries: the Holborne Museum, Victoria Art Gallery, Royal Photographic Centre and the museums of Costume, Native Art and East Asian Art are all worth spending pennies in (actual pennies, not weeing).*

UNIVERSITY:

- Price of a pint of beer: £1.80 • Glass of wine: £1.95

Bars: The Plug Bar attached to the Venue club is the *classic student boozer, stuffed* with arcade machines (including giant Jenga and Connect 4). The Parade bar is pricier *and a bit more pretentious* with wooden floors *and an older crowd. Opening hours are erratic, although it does have a late licence. Warning to quiet-lovers: the volume gets turned up big style around 9pm.* The Sports café's also licensed.

Theatres: The Arts Theatre is the home of BUST (Bath University Student Theatre), which puts on 3-5 shows a year. Professional companies also visit.

Film: Membership of the film society gets varied regular filmic fare, screened in a stereoequipped lecture theatre.

Clubbing: The Venue does its bit for the disco dollies and sets the stage for karaoke, dance, cheese etc. *Horny is the popular Friday night meat market.* Sports clubs take over on Wednesdays. There's a cocktail bar – *but it's not Tom Cruise-quality.*

Food: The *dull-looking but cheap* Choices food court has a *shopping-mall style* selection of oriental, pizza, market and traditional foodstuffs and is backed up by fast food Pitstop, Munchies (free pizza delivery around campus), the bars, and several delis, cafés and snack-stops.

Other: At least two balls a year (Rag and Graduation) and occasional comedy nights.

SOCIAL & POLICITAL

UNIVERSITY OF BATH STUDENTS' UNION:

• 6 sabbaticals • NUS member • Turnout at last ballot: 13%
They may not be the most powerful political force in the galaxy but BUSU is quietly confident when it comes to matters like welfare support, commercial enterprise, ents, societies and community-polishing volunteer projects. Most importantly, the University actually makes a point of listening to them and representatives' views go straight to the highest echelons of command. 98% of Bath students are involved in some form of club or soc.

SU FACILITIES:

BUSU's based at Norwood House, where it offers: two bars; nightclub; cafeterias; snack bars; the Pitstop; pool tables; Barclays, NatWest and HSBC banks and ATMs; general shop; convenience store; travel agency; new and secondhand bookshops; hairdressers; vending and gaming machines; photocopiers; payphones; fax and printing service; advice centre; launderette.

CLUBS (NON-SPORTING):

A Capella; Astronomy; Break Dancing; Buddhist; Chinese; Chamber Choir; Circus Skills; Clubbing; Comedy; Creative Writing; Curry Appreciation; Ethical; Gospel; Guides & Scouts; Japanese; Live Action Role Play; Malaysian & Singaporean; Mandarin; Motorcycle; Musicals; Newspaper; Impact; Orthodox; Salsa; Scandinavian; Soul & Popular; Technical Services (theatre staging); Television; Visual Arts; Wine. **See also Clubs tables.**

OTHER ORGANISATIONS:

The Union publishes Impact every fortnight. University radio Bath can be heard all over campus and has been highly successful at the Student Radio Awards – five award nominations and one win, in Best Speech-Based Non-Factual Show. *Never-resting* Rag has a sabbatical coordinator and sucked £85,000 out of the public last year, through a series of ridiculous stunts and events, including the annual duck race – where several thousand rubber ducks are deposited into the river Avon from a crane-suspended 15ft egg. *And, Push promises, they've done much crazier things than that.* BUSCA – Bath University Students' Community Action – *is very active* in arranging volunteer initiatives and events on local and international levels.

RELIGIOUS:

• 9 chaplains (CofE, RC, URC, Orthodox, Quaker, Methodist, Baptist)
The Chaplaincy Centre provides a non-denominational meeting place for the faithful. There's a Muslim prayer room with washing facilities on campus. Bath has plenty of churches, a mosque and Buddhist groups. The nearest synagogues and Sikh Gurdwaras are in Bristol.

PAID WORK:

• Job bureau
Bath's ever-flowing stream of tourists provides plenty of seasonal work. SU-run JobLink *is a far cry from the typical tatty Union notice board* and operates similarly to a council job centre, advertising casual part-time work and keeping to a strict Code of Practice. On-campus there's work available in shops, bars and admin.

SPORTS

• Recent successes: football, bob skeleton • BUSA Ranking: 2
Sport takes a high priority at Bath – none of this wimpy crap about it only being a game. Facilities are world class, tuition is expert and there's also a sports training village. In 2002 the elite Team Bath became the first student team to reach the first round of the FA cup in 100 years. Bath Uni's been declared a Regional Centre for Sporting Excellence and facilities are being extended and improved all the time. *Everybody's favourite loser Tim Henman got very excited by the new tennis courts a while back.*

SPORTS FACILITIES:

The excellent amenities are all on campus: two sports halls; 95 acres of playing fields; 50m pool; four squash courts; two all-weather pitches; eight indoor/ten outdoor tennis courts; two Astroturf hockey pitches; three netball courts; two basketball courts; athletics field; 132m indoor running straight; climbing wall; weights room; multigym; sauna; bobsleigh push-start track; fencing salle; judo dojo; indoor shooting range. *The best thing* is it's all as free as sunshine to students, except the members-only fitness suite. Next door there's a golf course and in town further facilities like a bowling green, river and so on.

SPORTING CLUBS:

American Football; Ballroom Dancing; Gliding; Gymnastics; Hot Air Ballooning; Ice Club; Ju-Jitsu; Lacrosse; Life Saving; Motor Club; Mountain Biking; Parachute; Paragliding; Rifle Club; Boat Club; Skater Hockey; Sky-diving; Surfing; Table Tennis; T'ai Chi Chuan; Triathlon; Ultimate Frisbee; Wakeboard & Waterski; Waterpolo; Windsurfing.
See also Clubs tables.

ATTRACTIONS:

Bath Rugby Club for the cauliflower-eared. Bath City FC is in the Nationwide Conference League.

ACCOMMODATION

IN COLLEGE:

- Catered: 1% • Cost: £83 (35-38wks)
- Self-catering: 34% • Cost: £52-77 (35-38wks)
- First years living in: 98%
- Insurance premium: £

Availability: All 1st years and international students are offered a place in the University housing, mostly on campus, though Bath also has some complexes in town, generally used by locals, matures and late-comers. Few others live in. The *limited* catered halls provide ten meals a week. Launderettes are plentiful. *Some of Eastwood's a bit basic and a shade shabby but the low rents make it ideal for scrimpers and savers* and parts were recently refurbished. *Malborough and Solsbury Court are at the glamorous and expensive end.* Some off-site family flats for those with children and single-sex accommodation available upon request. There are no curfews, *but heavy metal gigs or atom bomb testing after 11.30pm are frowned upon.* CCTV, entry phones and 24-hour security office *fight the forces of evil. No tuck-in service though.*

EXTERNALLY:

- Ave rent: £63 • Living at home: 2%

Availability: *Bath's a wealthy town and house prices reflect it* but it's still possible to find the odd habitable hovel. Provided students put any thought of the gracious Regency terraces out of their minds and concentrate on the less central areas, living out is manageable. *Oldfield Park and Coombe Down are good bets, but avoid smeggy Twerton and Fairfield Park.*
Housing help: The five accommodation office staff maintain a private lettings database and a notice board. It works in conjunction with the Union's AWARE housing office to provide contractual advice. No property vetting, but Bath Council has an accreditation scheme.

WELFARE

SERVICES:

- Lesbian/Gay/Bisexual Officer & Society • Ethnic Minorities Officer
- Women's Officer & Society • Mature Students' Officer & Society
- International Students' Officer & Society • Postgrad Officer
- Disabilities Officer & Society • Nightline
- College counsellors: 1 full/2 part/3 voluntary • Crime rating: !

The SU AWARE centre is the focal point of student support and holds a weekly solicitor's surgery.

Health: On-campus Medical Centre with three medical officers and three nurses, as well as a Dental Centre with real live dentist.

Crèches/Nursery: The award-winning Westwood Nursery *is one of the best in the country* and has 48 places for kids 6mths to school age.

Disabilities: Access around the compact campus is *generally good*: all major buildings have ramps and lifts, *but some areas can be limiting*. There's an *extensive* range of support services for students with dyslexia, including weekly workshops, specialist library equipment and software, plus laptop/tape-recorder loans. The Bath Assessment Centre gives students the choice of 'high tech', 'low tech' or 'no tech' levels of support – *good for students who resent special treatment*.

Crime: *A notoriously crime-free city*.

FINANCE:

• Ave debt per year: £7,471

Fees: The common or garden postgrad fee is £3,400 but it varies. International students pay £10,100 for lab courses, £7,900 for others. The top-up fees sting will be softened by bursaries of up to £1,500 for those on all or part of the maintenance grant.

Support: Students who have to do vacation and field study can apply for special awards. There's a sports scholarship scheme where exceptional students can take an extra year for their degrees combined with intensive training. Hardship fund also available.

Bath Spa University College

• *Formerly Bath College of Higher Education.*

(1) Bath Spa University College, Newton St Loe, Bath, BA2 9BN
Tel: (01225) 875 875 E-mail: enquiries@bathspa.ac.uk Website: www.bathspa.ac.uk
Bath Spa University College Students' Union, Newton Park Campus, Newton St Loe, Bath, BA2 9BN Tel: (01225) 875 588 E-mail: bathspasu@bathspa.ac.uk Website: www.bathspasu.co.uk

(2) Bath Spa University College, Sion Hill, Lansdown, BA1 5SF Tel: (01225) 875 875
Bath Spa Students Union, Somerset Place, Lansdown, BA1 5SF Tel: (01225) 875 684

GENERAL

Like the University of Bath, the main site of Bath Spa isn't actually in Bath, nor even in the town of Keynsham nearby, but around 5 miles away, with *the main Newton Park site amidst hilly countryside more National Trust than NUS. The buildings themselves are, for the most part, built with golden-coloured Bath stone in the classic Regency style that can make every day feel like an episode of Pride and Prejudice. The unwritten rule obeyed by all the students, that no one drops litter, preserves the beauty of the place (unless you're into post-modern garbage collages, that is). The buildings of the Newton Park campus are caked in history* – the chandeliered administrative centre is a former manor house, complete with trapdoor in what was the master bedroom for the maid to do some after hours 'room service'.

Sex ratio (M:F): 34:66	**Founded: 1983**
Full-time u'grads: 3,220	**Part-time: 270**
Postgrads: 630	**Non-degree: 195**
Ave course: 3yrs	**Ethnic: 2%**
State:private school: 80:20	**Flunk rate: 12%**
Mature: 32%	**International: 5%**
Disabled: 181	**Local: n/a**

66%
34%

ATMOSPHERE:

The high number of female and mature students has a significant effect, shifting the focus from traditional alcoholic boisterousness towards a quieter and more friendly little college, where everyone knows everyone else and staff seem to genuinely care about their charges. It's the sort of place that you wouldn't mind having in your own backyard, if you had a backyard big enough. The students are generally quietly wealthy and content with their lot. The main party nights are on weekdays, and the campus has a tendency to empty faster than bowels after a vindaloo come the weekend, meaning that those who live there can feel isolated. Contact with Bath locals is at a minimum, thanks to the remoteness of the location.

OTHER SITES:

Sion Hill: (Bath School of Art & Design) Exclusively for Arts students to frolic in, the *peaceful and pretty* Sion Hill Campus is sat atop a *sizeable* hill in a *quiet* residential area within walking distance of Bath town centre. It has computing facilities, refectory, bar, purpose-built sculpture studio and accommodation. Somerset Place, the main bit of the campus, is the longest stretch of Georgian Crescent with a single owner in the galaxy. *Or something.*

BATH: see University of Bath

TRAVEL: see University of Bath

Car: *A motor is very handy given the remoteness of the college*, although 1st years living in halls aren't allowed them on campus. Others require free permits *but parking isn't a worry.*
Local: *Buses are far and away best for the Newton Park-Bath journey*, two an hour, *quite reliably*, until around 2.30am. Badgerline 418 runs between town, Bath Spa and Bath University for £2.10 rtn and does season tickets. A bus also runs between Newton Park and Sion Hill.
Taxis: The College has a deal with a local firm – it's a flat £7.50 into town.
Bicycles: *Strictly for recreational use since it's just too darned far to pedal anywhere useful.*

CAREER PROSPECTS:

• Careers Service • No. of staff: 1 full/4 part • Unemployed after 6mths: 5%
Bulletin board, careers library, workshops, and a host of online resources, including computer guidance software and a job database that the careers staff have just blasted into cyberspace.

FAMOUS ALUMNI:

Andy Bradshaw (novelist); Howard Hodgkin (Turner Prize painter); Anita Roddick (Body Shop); Jason Gardner (athlete); Clive Deamer (musician, Portishead); Andy David (musician, Goldfrapp). William Harbutt, the inventor of plasticine, lectured here.

SPECIAL FEATURES:

• The Newton Park campus is built on Duchy of Cornwall land (meaning Prince Charles is the landlord), so although there's plenty of space, *getting planning permission for new buildings is nearly impossible.*
• The grounds were originally designed by 17th-century landscaping revolutionary, Capability Brown.

FURTHER INFO:

• Prospectuses: undergrad; postgrad; CD-Rom • Open days
Ring the College to get hold of any prospectus or check out the detailed one that lives on the web. In addition to open days, there are visit afternoons on the last Wednesday of every month.

Having won the University Challenge chapionship in 2004, Magdalen College Oxford became the only institution to win the trophy three times.

ACADEMIC

Degree programmes are spread between seven academic schools and are *thoroughly* modular. Students take six modules a year and flexibility of course options increases in the 2nd and 3rd years. Over 200 Bath Spa students take their 1st year at associated FE colleges around Wessex.

Entry points: 160-200	Ave points: 180
Applns per place: 5	Clearing: 7%
No. of terms: 2	Length of terms: 15wks
Staff/student ratio: 1:23	Study addicts: 15%
Teaching: ***	Research: **
Year abroad: 0%	Sandwich students: 0%
Firsts: 7%	2.2s: 56%
2.1s: 35%	3rds: 2%

ADMISSIONS:

• Apply via UCAS/direct for part-time

The University *laps up* applications from mature students and from those with non-traditional backgrounds.

SUBJECTS:

Art & Design: 14%
Education: 23%
English & Creative Studies: 13%
Historical & Cultural Studies: 13%

Music & Performing Arts: 13%
Social Sciences: 14%
Science & Environment: 11%

Best: Art & Design; Business & Management; Education; Environmental Biology; Psychology; Sociology; Study of Religions.
Unusual: The Remote Sensing course (studying satellite/aircraft surveillance of Earth) is part of the Geographic Information Systems qualification and is unique to Bath Spa; Writing for Young People (MA).

LIBRARIES:

• 172,663 books • 268 study places

Libraries at Newton Park and Sion Hill stock course-relevant material, DVDs and other handy audio-visual paraphernalia.

COMPUTERS:

• 570 workstations

Both libraries have workstations and there are several other open-access computer rooms, available till about 10pm.

OTHER LEARNING FACILITIES:

A drama studio and music rehearsal rooms. Sion Hill has some specialised art, design and sculpture rooms.

ENTERTAINMENT

THE TOWN: see University of Bath

UNIVERSITY:

• Price of a pint of beer: £1.80 • Bottle of wine: £5 • Can of Red Bull: £1.20
Bars: The Newton Park bar is the biggest and *most popular, with three late nights a week (winding down around 12.30am),* and comedy, salsa and karaoke. The Sion Hill Bar *is less of a favourite, and the SU have resorted to begging people to go to make it worthwhile cashwise.*
Music venues: The bar at Newton Park has live, generally student bands every other Monday. The Michael Tippets Centre catches bigger birds.

Clubbing: Three nights a week at Newton Park bar, including the *unnaturally cheesy* Flex on Fridays.
Comedy/Cabaret: Comedy Network acts alternate with live music on Mondays.
Food: The Refectory's basically a *school dinner hall with school dinner food and rather limp and cringeworthy* attempts at themed days for Divali, Chinese New Year and the like. Small snackages sold by the SU shop.
Other: Big summer ball every year, sporadic quiz nights, visiting hypnotists and other *nearly entertaining shenanigans.*

SOCIAL & POLITICAL

BATH SPA UNIVERSITY COLLEGE STUDENTS' UNION:
• 3 sabbaticals • Turnout at last ballot: 12% • NUS member
The SU has facilities on both sites. *Political opinions are treated as thought-crime at Bath Spa. The students themselves know little and care less about the Union's existence – to the extent that the SU shut down all its facilities for two days in 2003 to prove that it was a useful organisation and spark up some interest in getting involved. Apathy still reigns supreme.*

SU FACILITIES:
Spread between the sites: two bars; shop; two cafeterias; canteen; three pool tables; juke box; two meeting rooms; minibus for hire; NatWest ATMs; photocopier; fax and printing service; payphones; photo booth; advice centre; post office; new and secondhand bookshops; vending and gaming machines; launderette.

CLUBS (NON-SPORTING):
BogSoc (environment & drinking); Higher Learning (DJ); History; Poetry; Spatial Brew (geography & drinking); 3rd Year Degree Show. **See also Clubs tables.**

OTHER ORGANISATIONS:
The SU produces the *eminently readable* H2O fortnightly. There's a Rag organised in conjunction with the University of Bath, which successfully raises several grand a year. A Student Community Action group organises environmental and art projects, and goes into local schools doing nice things to children.

RELIGIOUS:
• 5 chaplains (CofE, RC, URC, Orthodox, Methodist)
A small chaplaincy runs a drop-in centre on campus. See University of Bath for local worship info.

PAID WORK: see University of Bath
• Job bureau
The job shop provides part-time work for students – quite literally, since it employs three students itself – and maintains an online job database.

SPORTS

• Recent successes: rugby • BUSA Ranking: 48
Although they've recently entered a moderately triumphant rugby team into the BUSA leagues, sport remains a forgettable diversion to the majority. The Sports Hall is so underused it effectively doubles as a meditation centre and there are plans to scrap it completely and turn it into an enhanced Student Union Centre.

SPORTS FACILITIES:
2 hectares of playing fields; sports hall; gym; multigym. Use of the facilities costs £8 a term.

SPORTING CLUBS:
Five-a-side; Health & Fitness; Pedal; Surf. **See also Clubs tables.**

ATTRACTIONS: see University of Bath

IN COLLEGE:

* Self-catering: 20% • Cost: £57-84 (38wks) • First years living in: 90%
* Insurance premium: £
Availability: Priority goes to 1st years coming from over 30 miles away but 10% still end up without a room. *No one else has a hope in hell.* 7% share. The accommodation is grouped into a village right on the campus doorstep and *while the more basic rooms are small, they're also well equipped and modern.* At Sion Hill, the *beautiful* converted Georgian Crescent has room for 100. No catered accommodation. 24-hour security.
Car parking: No livers-in can park, but commuters can register for a free permit.

EXTERNALLY: see University of Bath
* Ave rent: £60
Availability: Oldfield Park is a *popular option. Whiteway and Twerton are on the rougher side of inhabitable but some students end up landing there regardless.*
Housing help: The College and SU Accommodation Offices employ two full-time staff that can help with finding vacancies, emergency housing and warn of blacklisted landlords & properties.

WELFARE

SERVICES:

* Lesbian/Gay/Bisexual Officer & Society • Women's Officer
* International Students' Officer • Nightline • College counsellors: 3 part
* Crime rating: !
Health: A doctors' surgery visits the campus twice a week *so injuries have to be carefully scheduled.*
Women: £1 attack alarms from the SU.
Crèches/Nursery: Nursery service with 30 places for crawlers to toddlers.
Disabilities: *Listed buildings don't help matters,* but BSUC has undertaken a major works programme to improve access on both campuses. *The $1\frac{1}{2}$-mile spread of teaching rooms will still cause problems.* Both campuses have ramps, hearing loops, stair lifts, automatic doors and adapted accommodation. There's a full-time Disability Officer who assesses individual needs.

FINANCE:

* Ave debt per year: £5,528
* Access fund: £312,000 • Successful applications/yr: 727 • Ave payment: £293
Support: Hardship loans and grants available.

Bath College of Higher Education

see Bath Spa University College

Birkbeck, University of London

• **The College is part of the <u>University of London</u> and students are entitled to use its facilities.**
Birkbeck University of London, Malet Street, Bloomsbury, London, WC1E 7HX
Tel: (020) 7631 6000
E-mail: admissions@bbk.ac.uk Website: www.bbk.ac.uk
Birkbeck Student's Union, Malet St, Bloomsbury, London, WC1E 7HX
Tel: (020) 7631 6335
E-mail: president@bcsu.bbk.ac.uk Website: www.bbk.ac.uk/su

GENERAL

For general information about London: see <u>University of London</u>. The College was originally founded as the London Mechanics' Institution in a pub on the Strand. It's changed a bit since then – *no more lectures over a pint or ten, Push supposes.* Specialising in courses for mature students with jobs, people otherwise occupied during the day or the unemployed, most Birkbeck teaching occurs in the twilight hours between 6 and 9. Almost all Birkbeck students are part time and courses have an excellent reputation. The main building is a *stark redbrick construction* close to Trafalgar Square and handy for ULU.

Sex ratio (M:F): 35:65	**Founded: 1823**
Full-time u'grads: 15	**Part-time: 17,920**
Postgrads: 860	**Non-degree: 10,576**
Ave course: 4yrs	**Ethnic: 25%**
State:private school: n/a	**Flunk rate: n/a**
Mature: 99%	**International: 5%**
Disabled: 37	**Local: n/a**

65%
35%

ATMOSPHERE:
What with *heavy* commitments, it's not the average student scenario. *There's an industrious vibe and while people are friendly, they're busy and are often mid-rush, so laid-back chat is rare.* The majority are adults hoping to change careers or improve themselves professionally and *there's a great deal of respect for the college and the life-changing opportunities it affords.*

LONDON: see <u>University of London</u>

TRAVEL: see <u>University of London</u>
Trains: Euston Station and Kings Cross (for national and local travel) are within walking distance.
Coaches: Kings Cross has services from National Express and most major companies.
Local: Buses *a-plenty* serve the site (10, 24 29, 73 and 134 from Gower Street; 7 and 188 from Russell Square; 10, 24, 29, 73, 13 from Tottenham Court Road). Euston and Goodge Street stations are both close by for Victoria line tube travel.
Bicycles: *No problems cycling with parking spaces provided.*

CAREER PROSPECTS:

• <u>Careers Service</u>
Birkbeck uses the <u>University of London</u> careers service (ULCS). It offers facilities from drop-in services to longer advisory interviews. The Graduate Career Resource Centre, the largest in London, is also accessible to students and graduates.

FAMOUS ALUMNI:

Dido (singer); Phillipa Forester (TV presenter); Ramsay Mcdonald (former PM); Laurie Taylor (media sociologist); Tracy Thorn (Everything but the Girl); Helen Sharman (first British astronaut); Sandy Shaw (barefooted 60s babe); Jah Wobble (80s punk rocker).

FURTHER INFO:

• Prospectuses: undergrad; postgrad • Open days

ACADEMIC

Study's what Birkbeck's all about, *everything else is just icing.* It's one of a handful of universities specialising in part-time study, courses are often vocational and mostly taught by formal lecture. Those over 21 (most students) can apply without formal qualifications.

ADMISSIONS:

• Apply direct/via UCAS for certain courses

SUBJECTS:

Birkbeck has four faculties (Arts, Science, Social Science and Continuing Education) with 16 schools teaching a number of different courses.

LIBRARIES:

• 235,000 books • 316 study places
The main and Gresse Street libraries are open seven days a week and there are several others locally. The college runs UK Libraries Plus, which lets borrowers access 120 higher education libraries in the UK.

COMPUTERS:

• 150 workstations • 24-hr access
Got the essentials (printers, PCs), helpdesk and some special needs provision.

ENTERTAINMENT

THE CITY: see University of London

UNIVERSITY:

• Price of a pint of beer: £1.70 • Glass of wine: £2 • Can of Red Bull: £0.95
When half the busy students have to leg it home to feed the plant, water the cat and put the kids out for the night (or whatever), demand is low. Bigger things come from the shared University of London facilities.
Bars: *The SU bar is more of a convenience than a social hangout, but students can at least enjoy a sneaky tipple after lectures.*
Food: Malet Street and Gordon Square have the normal refuelling stops.

SOCIAL & POLITICAL

BIRKBECK STUDENTS' UNION:

• 1 sabbatical • NUS member
Politically dud, sportingly non-existent, socially lacklustre, the SU is there for essentials alone.
SU Facilities
Common room; TV lounge; pool table; photocopier; shop; Lamp & Owl magazine. The University also has a crèche, payphone, advice centre and post office. There's also an independent stationers, printing service and general store.

PAID WORK: see also <u>University of London</u>
• <u>Job bureau</u> • <u>Paid work: term-time 90%: hols 90%</u>
Since students generally have work already, there's only ULU's (*admittedly massive*) jobshop and careers service.

SPORTS

Sport's purely recreational. There are sports clubs, but the Birks have to use ULU's facilities.

ACCOMMODATION

IN COLLEGE:

• <u>First years living in: 0</u> • <u>Insurance premium: £££</u>
If required places are available in London's inter-collegiate accommodation. The <u>University of London</u> accommodation office is there for students to use and abuse.

EXTERNALLY: see <u>University of London</u>

WELFARE

SERVICES:

• <u>Disabilities Officer & Society</u> • <u>Nightline</u> • <u>Crime rating: !!!!!</u>
Advice available through the SU, but the age range of the students means a lot of help comes via academic tutors. While there's a crèche, everything else comes from the <u>University of London</u>.
Disabled: The Disabilities Office supports students with special needs, a disabled students allowance is available for special equipment, software, orthopaedic chairs, induction loops for the hard-of-hearing and so on. Ramps and rails have been installed in the old buildings.

FINANCE:

• <u>Ave debt per year: £125</u>
• <u>Access fund: £500,000</u> • <u>Successful applications: n/a</u> • <u>Ave payment: n/a</u>
Support: Hardship funds, college research funds (which can cover fees and/or maintenance).

University of Birmingham

University of Birmingham, Edgbaston, Birmingham, B15 2TT
Tel: (0121) 414 6727 E-mail: admissions@bham.ac.uk Website: www.bham.ac.uk
Birmingham University Guild of Students (Bugs), The University of Birmingham, Edgbaston
Park Road, B15 2TU Tel: (0121) 251 2300
E-mail: enquiries@bugs.bham.ac.uk Website: www.bugs.bham.ac.uk

GENERAL

Forget everything you think you know about Birmingham. Well, not quite everything: this is
still the UK's second-biggest city, an old *industrial splurge* of a conurbation *in the dead-eye
centre* of England. And yes, that Black Country accent still has *acres of comic potential for
plummy southern types. But that's as far as it goes*: Birmingham's *had a fuller facelift than
Wacko Jacko*. Built around a Bull Ring centre, the city has *just everything a student could
hanker after*: a *swanky* Selfridges and a smaller Harvey Nicks for Sloanes and *trendies,
every* high street chain *imaginable* and a jewellery quarter. Then there's the entertainment:
IMAX cinema, NEC for big gigs, a 60m big wheel imported from Paris, *loads* of bars and
restaurants, an *infamous* clubbing scene and several miles of Balti houses, selling Brum's
very own Indian invention.
  The University, $2\frac{1}{2}$ miles from the town centre and *an island of greenery* amid the bustle
of Edgbaston, is *self-consciously* redbrick, although the central area of the campus is
grandly traditional. Many students are pretty *focused* on their degrees, although a *lot* of
them *aren't* (sport is the main distraction).

Sex ratio (M:F): 43:57	**Founded: 1900**
Full-time u'grads: 15,975	**Part-time: 4,280**
Postgrads: 5,140	**Non-degree: 1,713**
Ave course: 3yrs	**Ethnic: 20%**
State:private school: 80:20	**Flunk rate: 7%**
Mature: 11%	**International: 25%**
Disabled: 240	**Local: 26%**

(57% / 43%)

ATMOSPHERE:

Cheery, chummy, varied and accommodating. Birmingham is a *welcoming* place to study,
although relations with the locals can be *fraught, particularly in student-heavy areas of
town, where traffic cone battles at 3am can fray tempers*. Students are *proud* of the
University's topflight status for study and sport. *As with many* of the redbrick places, it's
pretty middle class, with *big smiles* and *brownie points* for achievement in the sports hall
and the exam hall. The student concentration at Selly Oak means that it's *hard to go
anywhere* without bumping into a familiar face, but the city's size means that it's *easy to
disappear into the shadows if necessary.*

Birmingham:

• Population: 977,087 • City centre: 2.5 miles • London: 105 miles
• Manchester: 75 miles • Coventry: 20 miles
• High temp: 20 • Low temp: 2 • Rainfall: 64
Shopping trollies have been hooked out of canals, concrete has been cobbled or paved,
some of the worst architectural monsters have been slain and the whole place is revamped,
spruced up and ready to entertain.

TRAVEL:

Trains: Uniquely, there's a station on campus, connecting to Birmingham New Street for mainline links from London (£8.50 adv single), Manchester (£6.50 adv single), Edinburgh (£15.50 adv single) and *just about every other city in the country.*

Coaches: £18.50 rtn to London on National Express. Also Manchester (£8.20), Edinburgh (£26) and all over. West Midlands Travel and London Liner are on hand too.

Car: A38, M5, M6, M42 are the best roads to get to the University. *Avoid rush-hour unless staring at motionless bumpers sounds like a fun day out.*

Air: My Travel Lite, Duo, Ryanair, FlyBe and other budget airlines jet out of Birmingham International Airport, 9 miles east from the campus, with flights to the USA, Europe, Ireland and domestic routes.

Hitching: *Birmingham is the motorway Mecca of England. Pick a junction and get thumbing.*

Local: Bus services are late-night-running and *abundant* but *busy*. It's also easy to get into town, but *hard* to get around the edge. Overground trains run around the city – *they're faster than buses, but more expensive and unreliable. Possibly useful for those in Selly Oak.*

College: The University lays on a free bus between Edgbaston and Selly Oak (pass needed), and another from halls to various places around campus with uni ID.

Taxis: About £6 from town to college. *As usual*, minicabs undercut the black cabs.

Bicycles: Bikes are *commonplace* on campus and there are cycle lanes and *plenty* of places to lock them up.

CAREER PROSPECTS:

• Careers Service • No. of staff: 12 full/5 part • Unemployed after 6mths: 6%
Accessible and *helpful* service with bulletin boards, vacancy lists, employer contacts, website, skills training and other events.

FAMOUS ALUMNI:

Hilary Armstrong MP (Lab); Tim Curry (Rocky Horror star); Philippa Forrester (TV presenter); Jeff Green (writer, comedian); Simon Le Bon (Duran Duran); Desmond Morris (zoologist); Sir Paul Nurse (Cancer Research, Nobel winner); Chris Tarrant (TV and radio presenter); Victor Ubogu (rugby player); Ann Widdecombe MP (Con); Victoria Wood (comedian).

FURTHER INFO:

• Prospectuses: undergrad; postgrad; some departments • Open days
See www.marketing.bham.ac.uk/admissions/ for more info.

 A C A D E M I C

Good library and academic staff and a strong reputation in subjects including medicine, European languages, psychology, sport science, engineering, history and social sciences. Workload is *fairly high* – students have to put in about 40 hours a week during the 15-week semesters. Assessment is a mixture of essays, multiple choice questions, presentations, class tests, practical/laboratory work and formal written exams with some group work involved too.

ADMISSIONS:

Entry points: 160-360	Ave points: 300
Applns per place: 9	Clearing: 3%
No. of terms: 2	Length of terms: 15wks
Staff/student ratio: 1:15	Study addicts: 26%
Year abroad: 4%	Sandwich students: 1%
Teaching: ****	Reseaarch: *****
Firsts: 12%	2.2s: 28%
2.1s: 56%	3rds: 4%

• Apply via UCAS/GTTR/direct for postgrad

SUBJECTS:

Art & Social Sciences: 46%   Life & Health Sciences: 28%
Engineering & Physical Sciences: 26%
Best: Classics; Education; Philosphy; Political Science; Sport & Exercise Sciences; Theology.

LIBRARIES:

• 2,600,000 books • 2,280 study places • Spend per student: ££
Even with a gigantic library and nine smaller ones, there's still pressure on spaces.

COMPUTERS:

• 2,402 workstations • Spend per student: ££££
Students are *chuffed* with the techie *wizardry* on offer. There's free broadband in 80% of rooms and wireless facilities for laptops, video editing suites and assistive technology booths for special needs students around campus.

ENTERTAINMENT

THE CITY:

• Price of a pint of beer: £1.90 • Glass of wine: £2.00 • Can of Red Bull: £1.70
The town is *jam-packed* with temptations and opportunities. The shopping is *superior*, there's booze and Balti galore and the cinemas, theatres, clubs and music venues *would make a Londoner jealous*. If boredom sets in, Alton Towers, Cadbury's World and Stratford-upon-Avon are all on tap nearby.
Cinemas: The blockbusting UGC multiplex does student discounts and there are three others if that doesn't appeal. Push counted 38 screens in the big cinemas alone and there are various smaller cinemas, including specialist Indian ones and the arty Electric.
Theatres: The Birmingham Rep is *one of the best* in the country. There's also the Alexandra Theatre and the Hippodrome for ballet as well as loads of smaller operations.
Pubs: Brum pubs come in handfuls, but not all are student-friendly. *Pushplugs: Three Horseshoes; Gun Barrels. The Station, the Goose and Soak are best avoided.*
Clubbing: An *awesome* club scene has developed recently. *Pushplugs: Renaissance; God's Kitchen (Fridays); Miss Moneypenny's; Babooshka; Sundissential.*
Music venues: Stadium stars rock the NEC and NIA, but the *best* venue is Birmingham Academy, whose recent guests have included Primal Scream, Starsailor, The Coral, Athlete, Kings of Leon, Basement Jaxx, Ocean Colour Scene, The Flaming Lips and Black Rebel Motorcycle Club. There's also Ronnie Scott's (jazz) and the Symphony Hall (classical).
Other: There's the Silver Blades Ice Rink and Merry Hill, which is one of the largest shopping centres in Europe and houses a multiplex cinema and bowling alley. There's also the *eye-catching* Bullring shopping centre, home to Selfridges and Harvey Nicks.
Eating out: Whatever tickles the tastebuds is somewhere in Birmingham. *Pushplugs: Polaris; Kushi; Livingroom; Magic Bean (cheap veggie); the Mud Café (good value Italian); Selly Sausage (huge portions); House of Phoenix (Persian). Otherwise it's local curry houses in Selly Oak.*

UNIVERSITY:

• Price of a pint of beer: £1.65 • Glass of wine: £1.20 • Can of Red Bull: £1.70
Bars: Joe's (cap 700) is the main hangout and gets pretty *raucous*. There's also the Underground, a recently refurbished club-cum-pub that fits 400. *For pubbier traditionalists*, the Beorma bar does real ale and sofas. There are also bars in all the halls.
Theatres: Brum is *thesp central – a serious number* of theatre groups all put on three plays a year. The Allardyce Nicholl Theatre within the guild raises the curtain on many of them.
Film: Various film groups hold screenings around campus.
Clubbing: Fab and Fresh (£3) takes over Joes and The Underground every Saturday night for garage, house, cheese and disco classics. Stomp is the Friday night indie/cheese session and, just to warm up, Villy Vodkas Vodka Factory takes over Joes every Thursday.
Food: The University has a *clutch* of culinary options: Café Connections (pasta, paninis, coffee) is *pleasant*; Food Court (kebabs, jackets, fry ups and pasta) is *cheap but busy*; Avanti (baguettes, pasta, spuds, curries etc.) also gets *hectic*; Go (sandwich bar); Cafego (deli bar); Go2 and Cybergo (variations on the theme); and loads of other sandwich bars.
Other: Balls ago-go provide OTT celebrations for freshers, graduates, departments and others.

BIRMINGHAM UNIVERSITY GUILD OF STUDENTS (BUGS):

• <u>7 sabbaticals</u> • <u>Turnout at last ballot: 10%</u> • <u>NUS member</u>
Birmingham isn't much of a political hotspot and there was a *shockingly bad* turnout for the top-up fees demo. The 14-strong SU executive look after welfare and ents and *cosy up nicely* to the University suits.

SU FACILITIES:

The Guild building provides: three bars; nightclub; two canteens; four snack bars; a fast-food outlet; pool tables; meeting rooms; minibus/car/van hire; Endsleigh Insurance; HSBC banks and ATMs; photocopiers; fax; printing; photo booth; payphones; advice centre; crèche; TV/video games; jukeboxes; general store; stationery shop; post office; vending machines; bookshop; STA travel; ticket agency; launderette; CD shop.

CLUBS (NON-SPORTING):

Choirs; Big Band; Symphonic Wind Band; Brass Ensemble; A Partridge Amongst the Pigeons (Steve Coogan appreciation); Adventist Christian Society; Alpha; Alternative Performing Arts; American & Canadian Studies; Angsoc (Anglican Society); Art Society; Article 19 (GTG); Astronomical Society; Ballroom & Latin; American Dance; Beatz n Pieces; Before and After Lectures Drinking (BALD SOC); Bengali; Buddhist; BUNAC; BURN FM; BUST the WAR (Birmingham University againST the WAR); Carnival; Centre for West African Studies Society; Change Ringers; Cheerleading (Pussycats); Chinese Students; Circus; Club Latino; COGS (Computer Science Dept Society); Community Action; Computer & Video Games Society; Conservation Volunteers; Culture & Civilisation; Duke of Edinburgh; Egyptian; Ethical Trade; European Studies; Evangelical Christian Union; Far East Connections; Filmsoc; Fishtank Productions; Free Tibet; French; Fun Bus Productions; Fusion; German; Ghanaian Students; Guild Musical Theatre Group; Guild Television (GTV); Hellenic Society; Hindu; Hispanic (Circulo Hispanico); History of Art; Hitch; Home Students Society; Indian Cultural Society; Indian Overseas Students & Scholars; Indie Society; Indonesian Students Society; International Students Association; International Students Welcome Committee; InterVol; Italian; Japan Society; Korean Students; Krishna Consciousness; Liberal Democrats; LINKS (St John Ambulance); Local Leagues Volunteers Assoc; Malaysian Society; Maple Bank Residents Association; Marketing Mix; Maths Society (Mathsoc); Mature Students Committee; Medsin; MethSoc (Methodist Student Christian Society); Mexican; Modern Languages; Multi-Cultural Week; Navigators; New Theatre (NTS); NEXON (Nigerian Students Association); Niteline; Nursing & Physiotherapy; nVision; Pagan; Pakistan Cultural; People & Planet; Postgraduate Students Committee; Quran and Sunnah Society; Real Ale; Recycling; Redbrick; Scottish Country Dancing; Selly Oak Campus Committee; Sikh; Singaporean Students; Special Technology; Square Circle; St Silovan Orthodox Christian; Student Action for Refugees (STAR); Student Advice; Student Industrial Society; Student Reps; Student Staff; Student with Disabilities; Taiwanese Students; Talking Hands; Thai Students; Turkish Students; Twelve-Ten; United Nations (UBUNA); University House; Watch This (Society of Orginal Theatre); Welsh; Women's Association. **See also Clubs tables.**

OTHER ORGANISATIONS:

Free student paper Redbrick is published regularly by Bugs. Burn FM broadcasts on the airwaves and the web. There's also a very active Rag group, Carnival, which raised £70,000 for charity at last year's count. A couple of community action groups help out around Brum.

RELIGIOUS:

• <u>University chaplaincy (multi-faith)</u>
The University's St Francis Hall is a multi-denominational centre, catering for all Jewish and Christian hues. There's also a Muslim prayer room. Birmingham itself is a multicultural city and has cathedrals and churches of all types, as well as mosques, temples and synagogues.

PAID WORK:

• <u>Job bureau</u> • <u>Paid work: term-time 30%: hols 30%</u>
The Job Zone arranges jobs and placements with the help of the careers centre's services. Loads of opportunities around campus in the kitchens, libraries, bars, alumni office, careers service and so on.

SPORTS

• Recent successes: football, hockey rugby • BUSA Ranking: 4
Birmingham think of Loughborough in roughly the same way that Oxford think about Cambridge: horrid little upstarts who need to be taught a lesson (but who usually win). The rivalry is intense and Brum are pretty proud of their sporting record.

SPORTS FACILITIES:

Five multi-purpose pitches for football, rugby and hockey; cricket pitch; squash court; tennis court; basketball court; netball court; sports hall; swimming pool; running track; athletics field; gym; aerobics studio; sauna/steam room; lake at Edgbaston; river at Worcester; gymnastics centre; climbing wall; martial arts centre; sports shop. Courses are £11 for a term of ten classes; gym membership is £95 a year (off peak), £131 peak. Club membership £60 a year. In the city: a sports centre; running track; tennis and squash courts; swimming pool; ice rink; croquet/bowling green; golf course; and a dry ski slope. *Pushplugs: Fitness First does a very competitive student membership rate.*

SPORTING CLUBS:

10-pin bowling; American Football; Gliding; Gymnastics; Hangliding; Ice Hockey; Ju-Jitsu; Kayak; Korfball; Kung Fu; Lacrosse; Life Saving; Mountain Biking; Mountaineering; Nimpo-budo; Paintball; Rafting; Rowing; Snowboarding; Surfing; Table Tennis; Triathlon; Ultimate Frizbee; Waterpolo; Wayfarers; Windsurfing. **See also Clubs tables.**

ATTRACTIONS:

The national golf centre has hosted the Davis Cup, the NEC held the 2003 world indoor athletics championships. Edgbaston is a Test cricket ground and home to Warwickshire CCC. Local football teams are Aston Villa and Birmingham (*decent*), Wolves (*less decent*), West Brom (*middling*) and Walsall (*dire*).

ACCOMMODATION

IN COLLEGE:

• Catered: 11% • Cost: £85-112 (30-42wks)
• Self-catering: 23% • Cost: £66-76 (42-50wks)
• First years living in: 90%
• Insurance premium: £££
Availability: Most 1st years are guaranteed accommodation, although those who make it to Brum through clearing or live locally aren't always lucky. Accommodation is *fiercely expensive*, although much has been refurbished and caters for disabled students. Most halls are in one of three student villages, the Vale village is the latest to get a facelift. 80% of accommodation is within 25 mins hot-foot from college. *None are heinously awful.* Shackleton Hall, in the Vale, *is the address of choice.* Cleaners only look after communal areas, although in the summer vacation rooms are cleaned and *cleared of any students buried by their own overflowing ash-trays.*
Car parking: Available but *strictly rationed.* A (free) permit is needed.

EXTERNALLY:

• Ave rent: £48
Availability: *It's tough to find a decent pad at a pretty price.* But as just about everyone descends on the same neighbourhood – Selly Oak – *they're all in the same boat.*
Housing help: Housing services runs a property registration scheme, checking out houses before they're advertised. There's also advice for those *plagued by dodgy private landlords.* The Guild's advice and representation centre also offers advice on housing issues.

WELFARE

SERVICES:

- Lesbian/Gay/Bisexual Society • Women's Officer & Society • Mature Students' Officer
- International Students' Officer & Society • Postgrad Officer & Society
- Disabilities Officer & Society • Nightline • College counsellors: 3 full/7 part
- Crime rating: !!!!

Brum *knows how to look after students*. There are University welfare and Guild services and students have welfare tutors.

Health: On-campus NHS practice with eight GPs, five nurses, an osteopath, a part-time health visitor and a part-time midwife. On-campus dental practice with three dentists and dental nurses.

Women: Women's association runs welfare drop-ins and has a women's room with advice leaflets, books and chill out space. There are harrassment advisers at the University for all students.

Crèches/Nursery: Two nurseries with 124 places (3mths-5yrs).

Disabilities: Campus is *large and hilly* with several listed buildings that can't be properly adapted, although the newer buildings are *a bit better*. Sports facilities are adapted for access. There's also dyslexia tuition, note-taking, assisted technology (kurzweil, jaws, texthelp, inspiration) and extended loans in the libraries.

Crime: Burglary can be a bit of a problem in *PlayStation-heavy* student areas.

Drugs: *Guild membership is whisked away if they find your stash.*

FINANCE:

- Ave debt per year: £3,480
- Access fund: £902,155 • Successful applications/yr: 1,413 • Ave payment: £100-3,500

Support: A range of bursaries is offered by both University and Guild, for academic success and financial hardship. Amounts vary from £1,000 to full payment of fees and maintenance payments at ESRC rate.

Birmingham Conservatoire

see University of Central England

Birmingham Poly

see University of Central England

Birmingham Polytechnic

see University of Central England

Ricky Gervais was inspired to write The Office while ents officer at London University Union.

University of Bolton

• *Formerly Bolton Institute for Higher Education.*
The University of Bolton, Deane Road, Bolton, Lancashire, BL3 5AB
Tel: (012904) 900 600 E-mail: enquiries@bolton.ac.uk Website: www.bolton.ac.uk
The University of Bolton Students' Union, Deane Road, Bolton, Lancashire, BL3 5AB
Tel: (01204) 900 850 E-mail: bisu@bolton.ac.uk Website: www.bisu.co.uk

GENERAL

Growing up amongst the likes of Liverpool, Manchester and Preston wouldn't do much for a smaller industrial town's confidence, but Bolton is big and hard enough to stand its ground as a major Northern civic centre. Of eight universities in the North West, Bolton is the newest (it changed its name to reflect its university status in 2005), although its origins as a centre for vocational and educational training date back to the early 19th century. Just outside the town centre the main Deane campus is a child of the 60s, dominated by the new £6m glass-fronted Design Studio. This isn't the place to get back to nature – the only green bits are hungover students – but there's the Lake District, moors and dales not too far away for communing with Mother Earth.

Sex ratio (M:F): 54:46	Founded: 1982
Full-time u'grads: 3,190	Part-time: 2,630
Postgrads: 500	Non-degree: 2,040
Ave course: 3yrs	Ethnic: 13%
State:private school: 96:4	Flunk rate: 36%
Mature: 86%	International: 15%
Disabled: 45	Local: 80%

46%
54%

ATMOSPHERE:
Studying at Bolton can be a quiet experience – except for the noise of traffic from the surrounding roads. Large numbers of mature students and locals means that the University is more of a drop-in lecture centre than a cosy student bubble, although that's not to say there's nothing in the way of ribaldry and frolicking – just on a smaller scale than at other places.

SITES:
Deane Campus: The largest campus with most of the students and facilities, including the SU, sports hall, the Design Studio and a range of cafés. Prone to building work.
Chadwick Campus: (Arts, Education and Cultural & Creative Studies) 800m from the Deane Campus, Chadwick holds a theatre, refectory and shop as well as teaching facilities. *Students are a little more laid back and there's more evidence of pleasant greenery.*

BOLTON:
• Population: 261,037 • City centre: 800m • London: 182 miles
• Manchester: 10 miles • Blackpool: 35 miles
• High temp: 20 • Low temp: 1 • Rainfall: 68
Bolton is a busy industrial town and *the area around the University is something of a strip mall – thick with roads, supermarkets and drive-thru burger joints. The upside of the setting is the number of modern amenities (malls). The downside is it looks a bit grim.* Relics of the cloth industry include the Tonge Moor Textile Museum. The Last Drop Village is *Bolton's answer to the theme park*, an 18th-century converted farmhouse extended to create a

picturesque village with cottages, pub, restaurant, hotel, craft shops and other would-be tourist traps (if there were any tourists). *The world is waiting for Bolton Council to formally apologise for Sara Cox.*

TRAVEL:

Trains: Bolton mainline station is 800m from the University and offers connections to Manchester every 15 mins.
Coaches: The coach station (next to the railway) has National Express services to most major cities.
Car: The *devilish* A666, M61, M62 and A679 all serve Bolton. *Parking is as easy as a drunken hooker* with plenty of free space on campus for student cars. The town is *cheapish* for parking too.
Air: Manchester Airport (EasyJet) takes 30 mins by car.
Hitching: *The network of main roads means hitching isn't a crazy option.*
Local: Buses *are refreshingly regular*, with many using the *inexpensive* services to get to and from halls until 11.30pm. A nightbus from Manchester chugs in at 1am, 2.30am at weekends.
Taxis: *More than enough.* Town to halls costs about 2 or 3 quid.
Bicycles: Even with cycle lanes, busy roads mean *cycling in Bolton can seem like running a gauntlet of death. That doesn't stop people nicking bikes though. They probably use them for car parts.*

CAREER PROSPECTS:

• Careers Service • No. of staff: 1 full/3 part • Unemployed after 6mths: 15%
The Student Centre *looks weedy* but punches well above its weight: newsletters, bulletin boards, careers library, interview training and CV surgery sessions.

FAMOUS ALUMNI:

Stephen Blyth (Gregory award poet); Peter White (former Coates Viyella); Josie Cichockyi (paralympic champion and first female in a wheelchair to break 3-hour barrier in the London marathon).

SPECIAL FEATURES:

Bolton has two student intakes a year, accepting applications for February and September entry.

FURTHER INFO:

• Prospectuses: undergrad; postgrad; some departmental • Open days
There are nine open days a year – see website for all admission details.

ACADEMIC

Bolton the town is big on industry. Bolton the University is big on industrial courses. *Business and materials-based courses are big boomers* and the textiles department gets brownie points for designing the material for Man U football shirts. It also does a lot of design work for the Ministry of Defence (*all a bit hush hush*). Courses are modular, *meaning if a student bails before three years are up they'll still take home a certificate in something.* Teaching is spread throughout the day (9am-9pm) so there's a good deal of flexibility in learning (*or drinking*) schedules.

140-180		POINTS
Entry points: 140-180	**Ave points: 140**	
Applns per place: n/a	**Clearing: n/a**	
No. of terms: 2	**Length of terms: 18 wks**	
Staff/student ratio: 1:5	**Study addicts: n/a**	
Teaching: *	**Research: ***	
Year abroad: 8%	**Sandwich students: 15%**	

ADMISSIONS:

• Apply via UCAS

The admissions policy is geared towards roping in what they call 'non-traditional students', *although that's a bit of a meaningless umbrella.*

SUBJECTS:

Art & Design: 7%
Built Environment: 10.1%
Business Logistics & Information: 2.5%
Business Studies: 14.7%
Computing & Electronic Technology: 16.2%
Cultural & Creative Studies: 16.2%
Education: 8.3%

Engineering & Safety: 5.5%
Health & Social Science: 13.7%
Management: 1.6%
Product Design & Development: 2.3%
Psychology & Life Science: 8.7%
Sport, Leisure and Tourism Management: 2.9%

Best: Communications, Education, Materials Technology, Media Studies, Nursing, Organismal Biosciences (Biology); Philosophy, Psychology.

LIBRARIES:

• 170,000 books • 510 study places

Libraries at Deane Street and Eagle Mall. *Not really enough books.*

COMPUTERS:

• 550 workstations • 24-hr access

Or enough computers, for that matter. There's a 24-hour PC lab with more computers stashed in various departments.

OTHER LEARNING FACILITIES:

Chadwick has a drama studio and a CAD lab for budding e-designers. A £17m redevelopment of Deane campus completed in summer 2004 includes a new design centre and a face-lift for the textile labs. There's an incubator unit for business start-ups (*not baby chickens*).

ENTERTAINMENT

BOLTON:

• Price of a pint of beer: £1.49 • Glass of wine: £2 • Can of Red Bull: £2

Bolton makes up for the SU's deficiencies. Nearby Manchester makes up for Bolton's.
Pubs: *Plenty of liver-curdling possibilities.* 'The drunken mile' is a row of about 20 bars – *the bar-boom has hit Bolton hard and new ones are opening all the time. Some town centre pubs can get a bit grumpy at students but many are amiable enough. Malloney's is popular during cocktail hour for those at the posher end. Pushplugs: J2 (four floors of mainstream music); BL1 (cheap); Cattle Market (near halls).*
Cinemas: 3 miles away, the ten-screen UGC *is a bit of a hike.*
Theatres: The Octagon hands out free student tickets for a mix of modern plays, Shakespeare and panto at Xmas.
Clubbing: *Recent refurbs all over the shop. J2 has the variety to keep punters keen.* The Ritzy and the Crown & Cushion do student nights and Hawthorn's is an indie hang-out. *Atlantis & IKON are worth notice too.*
Music venues: Various venues with anything from rock to Ravel. *Pushplugs: Oscar's Café (jazz, blues, rock); Gypsy's Tent (alternative); Albert Hall Complex (classical, blues).*
Eating out: *Kentucky fried creatures and various McNibbles can be caught and eaten over the road but there's not much doing for the dedicated epicure.* Tiggi's (pizza) is *cheap*; Cook in the Books is veggie.

UNIVERSITY:

• Price of a pint of beer: £1.50 • Glass of wine: £1.50 • Can of Red Bull: £1.20

The SU makes a token effort but generally all is quiet on the entertainment front.
Bars: The Venue bar in the *freakin' ugly* Union building opens 10am-11pm and shows *loads of sport on the permanently playing big screen TV.*
Theatres: Chadwick's Pavilion theatre lets drama students tread the boards regularly.
Film: Small facilities and the odd free film.

Clubbing/Music venues: Lesser known visiting bands and guest DJs use the Venue as a venue (*so that's why...*). Several club nights go on but most clubland fun is based around the SU's Macauley's sponsorship deal.
Food: *The Deane Deli is a bit of a roadside caff from films about murderous hitchhikers.* The Venue dishes up till 6pm with pizza and a pint deals *seemingly every other day.*
Other: Black-tie balls for Christmas, Spring, Graduation and various sports.

S O C I A L   &   P O L I T I C A L

THE UNIVERSITY OF BOLTON STUDENT'S UNION:
• 3 sabbaticals
Not one for the politicos, the SU concentrates on running its various drinking societies (sorry, 'sporting clubs') and keeping its ents afloat. The building is currently looking to relocate somewhere less architecturally offensive on Deane campus, so it's (hopefully) new facilities ahoy.

SU FACILITIES:
One bar; one café; pool room; three meeting rooms; juke box; gaming machines; general store; stationery shop; photocopier, printing and fax services; photo booth; advice centre.

CLUBS (NON-SPORTING):
Beer & Crisps; Friends of Palestine; Games; Irish; Music; Roleplay. **See also Clubs tables.**

OTHER ORGANISATIONS:
Bolton has eight proud pages in Student Direct – the *ad-laden* free weekly mag run jointly with Salford and UMIST. Rag *provides excuses for pub crawls.* A group on Chadwick campus does work on sexing-up the local area.

RELIGIOUS:
• 1 chaplain (CofE)
The University also has four volunteer chaplains for Muslim, Hindu and other Christian faiths. There's a multi-faith prayer room on campus and facilities in town for Muslims, Hindu, RC, CofE, Baptist, URC, Methodist, Quaker and Scientologist practitioners.

PAID WORK:
• Job bureau
The job shop at the Student Centre posts part-time vacancies. Bar, restaurant and supermarket work is fairly common.

S P O R T S

• BUSA Ranking: 48
The SU runs all sports clubs and arrangements and keeps costs to a minimum to preserve sports for all levels of involvement. *Team competitions occur more in the pub than in the field. Boat races at Bolton are more likely to entail beer and bar stools than boats.*

SPORTS FACILITIES:
Two football pitches; rugby, hockey and all-weather pitches; cricket wicket; basketball, squash and netball courts; sports hall, gym, multigym; running track; croquet lawn/bowling green; climbing hall; health and fitness centre and sporting lake available.

SPORTING CLUBS:
10-pin Bowling; Gaelic Football; Hung Kuen; Shaolin Kung Fu; Snowboarding; Surfing. **See also Clubs & Socs tables.**

ATTRACTIONS:
Bolton Wanderers FC are kicking around nearby.

IN COLLEGE:

• Self-catering: 34% • Cost: £47 (40 wks)
• First years living in: 100% • Insurance premium: £££££
Availability: *1st years have guaranteed accommodation on campus to look forward to and, bearing in mind that most mature students look after themselves and many others are local, few are left in the lurch.* Orlando village houses 380 in a collection of flats 10 mins walk from the Deane campus. *Internet access* is a big draw for Hollins Halls (*or perhaps it's the red-light area location...*). Kitchens have fridges, freezers and ovens but have bring-your-own policy on kettles and toasters. Beefy security guards fend off intruders and throw out guests come midnight – *pyjama parties not allowed.*
Car parking: Extensive free parking *makes Bolton a parking-lover's dream come true.*

EXTERNALLY:

• Ave rent: £40
Availability: *Accommodation is reasonably easy to find but some have to live further out than they might have hoped. In the Great Home Quest, the first task is to look for a shared house preferably in Chorley Old Road, Chorley New Road, Heaton Park Road, Queen's Park Road or just Park Road. Rough Darcy Leaver and the crime-ridden Mencroft Avenue area are best avoided – otherwise speak softly and carry a large dog.*
Housing help: The Student Centre helps vet contracts, gives legal advice and publishes vacancy lists.

SERVICES:

• Women's Officer • Mature Students' Society • International Students' Society
• Self-defence Classes • Nightline• College counsellors: 2 full • SU counsellors: 2 full
• Crime rating: !!!!
Disabilities: A University Disabilities Officer provides support on all campuses. Wheelchair access is generally very good, especially in the SU. Braille, ramps, adapted accommodation and large print signs for the visually impaired (*medically or alcoholically*).

FINANCE:

• Ave debt per year: £3,435
Fees: Non-UK students pay £6,025.
• Access fund: £600,000 • Successful applications/yr: 391
Support: Budget advice, hardship funds, emergency loans and some bursaries available.

Bournemouth University

• *Formerly Bournemouth Polytechnic and Dorset Institute.*
(1) Bournemouth University, Talbot Campus, Fern Barrow, Bournemouth, BH12 5BB
   Tel: (01202) 524 111 E-mail: enquiries@bournemouth.ac.uk Website:
   www.bournemouth.ac.uk

The Students' Union at Bournemouth University, Talbot Campus, Fern Barrow, Bournemouth, BH12 5BB
Tel: (01202) 965 765 E-mail: subu@bournemouth.ac.uk Website: www.subu.org.uk
(2) Bournemouth University, Lansdowne Campus, Christchurch Road and Holdenhurst Road, Bournemouth, BH1 3LT

GENERAL

Bournemouth is the largest of three towns rolled into one, with Poole to the west and Christchurch to the east and 350,000 people shared out between them. Following the coast east, the New Forest stretches inland. The main Talbot Campus of the University is technically in Poole, $2\frac{1}{2}$ miles north of Bournemouth town centre. It's a modern campus, *resembling beige Lego linked by brick pathways*. This is reflected in its *single-minded*, career-oriented philosophy.

Sex ratio (M:F): 42:58	**Founded: 1976**
Full-time u'grads: 9,045	**Part-time: 3,455**
Postgrads: 1,285	**Non-degree: 0**
Ave course: 4yrs	**Ethnic: 9%**
State:private school: 93:7	**Flunk rate: 14%**
Mature: 18%	**International: 13%**
Disabled: 380	**Local: n/a**

58%
42%

ATMOSPHERE:

The student body tends to be middle-class, clean-cut and car-owning. It's a high spec world with teeth gritted for the free market, a more economic, plastic substitute for the original ivory tower. The focus is getting a return on the investment of time and money, rather than a 4-year holiday. Having said that, in the last few years, the expansion of the University has made Bournemouth less of an undertaker's waiting room and more of a happening funville, full of eager students.

SITES:

Lansdowne Campus: (4,500 students – Health, Community Studies, postgrad Business School) Lansdowne is *less of a campus and more a collection of buildings* in Bournemouth's town centre, near the bus and train stations and less than a mile from the sea. SUBU's nightspot, the Old Fire Station, is based here.

BOURNEMOUTH/POOLE:

- Population: 138,400 • City centre: $2\frac{1}{2}$ miles • London: 100 miles
- Southampton: 26 miles • Bristol: 60 miles
- High temp: 22 • Low temp: 2 • Rainfall: 67

In summer, Bournemouth's a bristling, bustling town full of tourists, little hotels, sandy beaches, sea and ice-cream melting down your wrist. It doesn't totally close in winter, but there's a little less fun to be had. It does have 2,000 acres of parks in town though and has enough shops to keep students kitted out, although true shopaholics may start to feel faint and shaky after a while. The urban village of Winton, less than a mile from the campus, has shops for mundane necessities. Not far away, just to the west of Poole/Bournemouth, is the World Heritage Site – the Jurassic Coast – which is now a *major* tourist attraction and area of interest to naturalists and Alan Titchmarsh fans.

TRAVEL:

Trains: From Bournemouth station, 2 miles from the campus, to London (£21.80), Brighton (£17.65) and all over.
Coaches: Megabus run twice daily to and from London (from £1 each way) – *third world transport at third world prices*. National Express also run.
Air: Bournemouth International Airport is about 5 miles away. Ryanair fly from there to Dublin, Glasgow and Barcelona. Rockhopper fly to the Channel Islands. Budget flights include various European destinations from Thomsonfly and Belfast (Jet2).

Car: The A38, A31 and A35. *Many Bournemouth students have cars, despite parking shortages, particularly at Lansdowne Campus.*
Ferries: From Poole's *busy* port to the Channel Islands and France.
University: Wilts and Dorset provide a subsidised bus service, 35p between the Lansdowne and Talbot campuses every 10 mins.
Taxis: Taxis are *frequent and easy to pick up* from the town centre and other locations. Average cost varies but between £2.50 and £7 will take you most places around town. Some firms offer discounts or frequent-user deals. It's often cheaper to book ahead.
Bicycles: *Top notch* cycle routes lead to and from the University's Talbot Campus. The local area is *fairly bike-friendly* (some hills, but also paths that follow former railway lines into the towns and out into the countryside). Bike lock-ups/sheds on both campuses. *The aptly named Cemetery Junction roundabout is deadly.*

CAREER PROSPECTS:

• Careers Service • No. of staff: 6 full-time • Unemployed after 6mths: 8%
Workshops in CV writing, interview skills, assistance with finding placements, links with local business.

FAMOUS ALUMNI:

Paul Clarke (who hooked up with Helen on Big Brother); Bella Crane (presenter, C4's A Place in the Sun); Toby Farrow (playwright); Michael Jackson (*not that one*, the former big cheese at C4); Paul Kavanagh (computer animator, The Phantom Menace); Tom Lawton (inventor); Tommy Sandhu (presenter, UK Living's Strip Search).

FURTHER INFO:

• Prospectuses: undergrad; postgrad • Open days
Also a CD-Rom for international students.

A C A D E M I C

Bournemouth's *best known* for its media school with courses in PR, computer animation and scriptwriting – *just take a look at the alumni*. Most are sandwich courses involving work placements for a year. *The record of getting into these cut-throat industries at the end is impressive.*

180-300		POINTS
Entry points: 180-300	Ave points: 239	
Applns per place: 6	Clearing: 11%	
No. of terms: 3	Length of terms: 11wks	
Staff/student ratio: 1:12	Study addicts: 7%	
Teaching: *	Research: ***	
Year abroad: 2%	Sandwich students: 62%	

ADMISSIONS:

• Apply via UCAS/direct for part-time courses/NMAS for nursing

SUBJECTS:

Business & Law: 27%	Health & Community Studies: 3%
Conservation Sciences: 6%	Media: 21%
Design, Engineering & Computing: 24%	Services Management: 20%

Best: Advertising & Marketing Communications; Archaeology; Clinical Nursing; Communication; Financial Services; International Marketing Management; Media Production; Multi-Media Journalism; Midwifery; Public Relations; Scriptwriting for Film & TV; TV & Video Production.
Unusual: Forensic Archaeology; Sports Management (golf); Food Marketing.

LIBRARIES:

• 400,000 books • 1,000 study places
The library has a network of tutor librarians specialising in each of the University's academic areas.

COMPUTERS:

• 1,000 workstations• 24-hr access
Many lecturers put lecture notes online (*usually after lectures have been given – they still want students to turn up*). Some of the IT equipment is flashy stuff, such as the UK's National Centre for Computer Animation and a CAD lab modelling facility (*that's computer modelling, not the other kind*). Not everyone gets to play with them though.

OTHER LEARNING FACILITIES:

Music rehearsal studio; audio and TV editing suites including fully working TV studio.

ENTERTAINMENT

BOURNEMOUTH/POOLE:

• Price of a pint of beer: £2 • Glass of wine: £2.50 • Can of Red Bull: £2
Cinemas: Bournemouth has an IMAX, ABC and Odeon and Poole, a UCI and the refurbed Lighthouse Arts Centre.
Theatres: The Pavilion *for 'shows', in the spangly-costumed sense of the word*, eg Holiday On Ice, as well as appearances from *headliners* like Elvis Costello and *rodent munchers* like Freddie Starr. The Lighthouse is for *serious* plays and musicals (with student discounts).
Pubs: Around Old Christchurch Road there's a *popular* strip of pubs. Walkabouts, Bliss, Toko (*trendy, bit expensive*), the Inferno (next to SUBU's Old Fire Station), Consortium (*alternative feel*) and Slam (£1 a drink).
Clubbing: Alcatraz is a *home-from-home* for many international students with Latin sounds and Eurohits. *Most prefer Union-run theme nights at the Old Fire Station.* Berlins offers cheap nights and a foam party. The *hugely popular but slightly townie* Opera House offers 'Slinky' at weekends and 'Hot And Horny' on Thursdays. The Great Escape provides R'n'B, house and breakbeats.
Music venues: The Lighthouse is the home of the Bournemouth Symphony Orchestra – one of the UK's major orchestras. BIC has big rock names (Coldplay, Travis, etc). The Villa is a step down in size from that with The Thrills, Biffy Clyro etc. Mr Smiths *is a scuzzy, fun little place if you like rock, punk and metal ska*. The Gander and O'Neills host local bands.
Eating out: Charminster Road is *good* for curry at Coriander and *appetising* Middle Eastern bites at the Baraca Café and Restaurant. The Caribbean Café Bar on Old Christchurch Road has a student night Mondays with special promos, plus Salsa and Reggae nights and an allday eat-as-much-as-you-like buffet for £5 on Sundays.

UNIVERSITY:

• Price of a pint of beer: £1.50 • Glass of wine: £2.25 • Can of Red Bull: £1.50
Bars: Dylan's is a pub-style bar with the odd live band playing, quiz nights and *good value* food during the day. D2 is a café bar with *more pretensions* (*less grease*, table service). Bar Heat is a *stylish* place in the town centre where students fire themselves up for a night at the nearby Old Fire Station.
Theatres: *Drama isn't strong but the Allsebrook Lecture Theatre is there for thesps.*
Film: There's the Good Film Club.
Music venues: Bands like Electric Six and Eighties Matchbox B-Line Disaster have *stormed* through the Old Fire Station (cap 1,200) on a Wednesday.
Clubbing: *The hugely popular* Old Fire Station tries to cover all bases and *mostly succeeds* with Fancy Dress Mondays – from chavs to Playboy bunnies. Wednesday nights alternate between the Comedy factory and Rock City. Friday is Lollipop (pop anthems), Also: Loveshack (Sat, retro and contemporary) and other parties. Dylan's has club nights at the weekend.
Comedy/Cabaret: Every 2 weeks at the Old Fire Station and Dylan's.
Food: All the bars do food. Dylan's and D2 do *great* pizzas for £2.50 and *the best wedges in the world*. The Student Refectory (8.30am-3.30pm) *is very busy at lunchtimes but quiet earlier, when they do a fab brekkie*. Jumbucks is an 'Australian Pie Bar' franchised into the University (£2.75 a meal, *possibly kangeroo meat or possum kidneys*). Studio Café Bar is a cyber café with muffins, danish etc.
Other: The largest SU summer ball in the country (6,000 students) as well as Freshers' and Graduation Balls.

SOCIAL & POLITICAL

STUDENTS' UNION AT BOURNEMOUTH UNIVERSITY (SUBU):

• 3 sabbaticals • Turnout at last ballot: 12% • NUS member
Bournemouth never used to be a hotbed of radicalism, Trotskyism or any kind of -ism. Except maybe careerism. And yet over 1,000 students went to protest about top-up fees at the Labour Party Conference, *so maybe a wind of change is sweeping through Dorset.*

SU FACILITIES:

Endsleigh Insurance; cafeteria; hall; bar; video games; photocopier and fax service; four pool tables; three minibuses; a general store; stationery shop; new and secondhand bookshops; launderette; Barclays Bank with cashpoint; the Old Fire Station Bar in town.

CLUBS (NON-SPORTING):

ANSA Norway; Archaeology; Bollywood Film; Duke of Edinburgh; Forensic; Indian; Law; Performing Arts; St John Ambulance; SciFi & Film; See Live Centre (trips to see live bands); Street Dance. **See also Clubs tables.**

OTHER ORGANISATIONS:

The Nerve Media Network *is Bournemouth students' answer to Rupert Murdoch.* It consists of a radio station and a TV station, which has won more than twice as many awards as any other student TV station in the country *despite (or because)* of the latter's recent Big Brother-style show, featuring students locked in together for the weekend. Nerve Magazine was nominated in the 2004 Guardian Media Awards and, increasingly, content is going on the web with Nerve Online. Newspaper Student Press isn't part of the Union but has a high student readership and a *leftwing slant only slightly at odds with their 'student page-3 girls'* (not topless, *Push* should point out). Rag Week raised £20,000 last year through the usual Rag raids, fancy dress parties, skydiving etc.

RELIGIOUS:

• 3 chaplains (FC, CofE, RC)
The inter-faith chaplaincy has a central meeting area on the Talbot Campus which includes a quiet room and a Muslim prayer room. Two rabbis (Reform, Orthodox) and an imam are available.

PAID WORK:

• Job bureau • Paid work: term-time 54%: hols 87%
There's a *steady demand* for students in local hotels, bars, clubs etc. B&Q and Asda *also lick their lips eagerly* at the start of every academic year.

SPORTS

• BUSA Ranking: 48
Bournemouth's *clawing its way* up the BUSA rankings. The University's insistence on scheduling lectures on Wednesday afternoons *hampers activity. What do they think this is, an educational institution?*

SPORTS FACILITIES:

Football, rugby, hockey and all-weather pitches; squash, tennis, basketball and netball courts; sports hall; climbing wall; gym; multigym. For a joining fee of £10 students can use all these facilities and get discounts at the swimming pool and other facilities in town.

SPORTING CLUBS:

Motorsports; Rowing; Surfing; Ultimate Frisbee. **See also Clubs tables.**

ATTRACTIONS:

Bournemouth FC have found a *comfortable niche* at the upper end of the Coca-Cola league.

IN COLLEGE:
- Self-catering: 25% • Cost: £64-76 (41/50wks)
- First years living in: 65% • Others living in: 3% • Insurance premium: £

Availability: The non-smoking student village on the Talbot campus only has places for 250 1st years (ie. not a lot), with 1 in 4 sharing rooms. The houses *look like the set of Brookside and are shared between four, five or seven students. They're not cheap and a bit far from shops – a bit far from anything except the campus for that matter, but they've got en-suite showers and internet sockets in each room.* The *extremely lively* Cranborne (499 students) and Hurn House (152 students) are based near the Lansdowne Campus and are *more popular* than the student village, despite being 2 miles from the main site. There's £50 a year in extras (admin and insurance) and a £365 returnable deposit. A new development will be available from autumn 2005.
Car parking: All students based in University housing can get a parking permit (£50/yr), *but space is limited everywhere.*

EXTERNALLY:
- Ave rent: £64 • Living at home: 20%

Availability: After the summer, there's plenty of housing in the Winton and Charminster areas near all the *studenty* pubs and clubs. The University manages 250 private houses through the Unilet scheme (£61-70) and there's a private hall (Glenfern House, 120 places, £61-71 plus bills) in the centre of town. The University also make arrangements with hotels and guest houses from £70/wk (sharing) to £92 (single) including breakfast and evening meal.
Housing help: The Accommodation Service manages and lets the local housing mentioned above. They can also help find other options if needed.

SERVICES:
- Lesbian/Gay/Bisexual Society • Ethnic Minorities Officer
- Mature Students' Officer & Society • International Students' Society
- Postgrad Officer & Society • Disabilities Officer & Society
- Late-night/Women's minibus • College counsellors: 4 full • Crime rating: !

Counselling and advice services are contracted out to the local authority.
Health/Crèches/Nursery: The medical centre in Talbot House has a doctor and nurses and is also home to the Talbot Woods Day Nursery for babies 3-30mths and nursery school rugrats 2-5. Also a half-term play scheme for 5-12 yrs.
Disabilities: All buildings have ramps and automatic doors, lifts are fitted with voice instructions and Braille keypads. The learning support unit assists students with dyslexia and other special needs.

FINANCE:
- Ave debt per year: £6,945 • Home student fees: £3,000/yr
Fees: Bursaries of between £1,500-£2,700/yr for low-income students.
- Access fund: £448,490 • Ave payment: £850
Support: A few scholarships, but more bursaries.

Bournemouth Polytechnic, Dorset Institute
see Bournemouth University

University of Bradford

(1) University of Bradford, Richmond Road, Bradford, West Yorkshire, BD7 1DP
Tel: (01274) 233 081 E-mail: course-enquiries@bradford.ac.uk Website:
www.bradford.ac.uk
University of Bradford Union, Longside Lane, Bradford, West Yorkshire, BD7 1DP
Tel: (01274) 233 300 E-mail: ubu-communications@bradford.ac.uk
Website: www.ubuonline.co.uk
(2) The School of Management, Emm Lane, Bradford, BD9 4JL
Tel: (01274) 234 393 E-mail: management@bradford.ac.uk

GENERAL

Bradford was built on woolly sheep, *which is better than being built by woolly sheep*, but means it's historically a *dense, industry-driven* town. Despite being one of the ten largest cities in the UK, Bradford *doesn't have much to shout about* in terms of architecture or atmosphere. It's a *typically grim, gritty city, full of* 60s concrete architecture and traffic – the £1.5m being pumped into a city regeneration fund should help. The Brontë sisters painted their pictures of passionate and idyllic English country life from Haworth (8 miles outside town). The campus is close to the city centre, and is *compact, modern* and *high-rise*, with plenty of room to park cars – assuming students can get them through Bradford's *linguine-like* web of roads and roundabouts.

Sex ratio (M:F): 43:57	Founded: 1966
Full-time u'grads: 6,670	Part-time: 1,705
Postgrads: 1,020	Non-degree: 638
Ave course: 3yrs	Ethnic: 48%
State:private school: 94:6	Flunk rate: 15%
Mature: 33%	International: 19%
Disabled: 155	Local: 27%

ATMOSPHERE:

The campus springs to life on a Monday morning, although by the weekend it's drained of it – probably because of the large number of local and mature students. It's a laid-back ethnic melting pot with a decent social scene that leans heavy on Manchester and Leeds for fireworks. There's a strong sporting scene and a pumped-up political atmosphere railing against the war, racism, the BNP and the accursed top-up fees.

SITES:

The School of Management: (1,000 students) The 14-acre parkland site is about 3 miles from the main campus, which is connected via a shuttle bus. *And given the level of excitement on offer out in Bradford's 'burbs, students will need it.*
School of Health Studies: Situated in the Unity Building on Trinity Road, 5 mins walk from the main campus.

BRADFORD:

• Population: 467,665 • City centre: 800m • London: 180 miles
• Leeds: 9 miles • Manchester: 30 miles
• High temp: 19 • Low temp: 1 • Rainfall: 73

Bradford's a scrimping student's paradise – it's rumoured to be the cheapest place to study in the whole of these fair isles. In fact it has been rated as one of the few places where the cost of living is actually less than the maximum student loan. *And there are enough ways to blow cash, too,* with plenty of bars, cinemas, theatres and curry houses. There's even *a cursory nod towards culture* with the *fabulous* National Museum of Photography and the Alhambra Theatre.

TRAVEL:

Trains: National Rail trains to Leeds (£1.45 sgl), London King's Cross (£33), Manchester (£8 rtn), York (£7.55) and Sheffield (£4.60 sgl).
Coaches: National Express from Bradford Interchange to Leeds (£2.50), London Victoria (£22.50), Manchester (£8 rtn), York (£5) and Sheffield (£6.25).
Car: Just a few minutes off the M62 down the M606, on the A58, A658 and A650. Be warned: *the one-way system around town is bad enough, but Bradford also has some of the worst drivers in the country.*
Air: Leeds & Bradford Airport ($6\frac{1}{2}$ miles away) operates flights inland and to Europe, Ireland and North America.
University: A *nippy* shuttlebus runs between the main campus and the School of Management. The SU's free weeknightly safety bus drops students at home (within 2 miles of campus).
Local: Buses are *cheap* and *convenient* for campus, town and the Emm Lane site. West Yorkshire DayRover: a one-day leisure ticket for unlimited travel in West Yorkshire. £3.80 bus only, £4.50 bus and train. £6 family DayRover (covers bus and train).
Taxis: *Not too expensive,* costing £4 from the campus to the station. Bradford's compact and local journeys are *cheap.*
Bicycles: *Bradford and the campus are a bit hilly so students need to be riding something with as many gears as spokes.*

CAREER PROSPECTS:

• Careers Service • No. of staff: 9 ful/10 part • Unemployed after 6mths: 7%
Lots of vocational courses, much-touted collaboration with industry employers, *a well-stocked* careers service with online vacancies and an e-mail advice service to make job-hunting *a little less stressful.*

FAMOUS ALUMNI:

David Bailey (photographer); Brian Blessed (actor, honorary graduate); The Rt Hon Betty Boothroyd (former Speaker of the House of Commons, H DLitt); Lord Melvyn Bragg (Member of the House of Lords and TV presenter); Roland Boyes, David Hinchliffe, Alice Mahon, Ann Taylor (all Lab MPs); John Hegley (poet); David Hockney (artist); Tom Ingall (BBC Look North presenter); Al Kelly (radio presenter); Stephen McCabe (MP); Jon McGregor (writer); Sir Tony O'Reilly (Irish millionaire tycoon). Lord David Puttnam has an honorary scroll. Duncan Preston (actor) is an honorary graduate.

FURTHER INFO:

• Prospectuses: undergrad; postgrad; departmental • Open days
For open day info: www.bradford.ac.uk/openday or call (01274) 233 081. A Mature Students' Guide can be had from course-enquiries@bradford.ac.uk or call (01274) 233 081.

ACADEMIC

Bradford's always been big on vocationally driven courses and has recently been beefing up its academic arsenal with meaty development plans. Placements and sandwich courses are commonplace, particularly in Health Studies, commerce and industry. There's a lot of investment in the pharmaceutical department, funding *brainy types in white coats* to work on *potentially mind-altering* drugs.

The Liverpool Students' Union specialised sport is Leg Wrestling.

200-320

POINTS

Entry points: 200-320	Ave points: 268
Applns per place: 7	Clearing: 18%
No. of terms: 2	Length of terms: 15wks
Staff/student ratio: 1:12	Study addicts: 11%
Teaching: **	Research: ****
Year abroad: 1%	Sandwich students: 23%
Firsts: 11%	2.2s: 36%
2.1s: 49%	3rds: 4%

ADMISSIONS:

• Apply via UCAS/NMAS for nursing/direct for part-time
They're keener than mustard on mature students and big believers in recruiting from the local area.

SUBJECTS:

Archaeological, Geographical and Environmental Sciences: 4%
Engineering, Design and Technology: 11%
Health Studies: 16%
Informatics: 16%
Lifelong Education and Development: 1%
Life Sciences: 26%
Management: 11%
Social and International Studies: 15%
Best: Archaeological Sciences; Biomedical Sciences; Bradford Centre for International Development; Chemical Engineering; Civil & Environmental Engineering; Electronics & Digital Media; Industrial Technology; Interdisciplinary Human Studies; Midwifery; Nursing; Optometry; Peace Studies; Pharmacy; Physiotherapy; Radiophy.
Unusual: Cancer Biology; Creative Writing & Identity; Design for Computer Games; Economics & Development Studies; Forensic & Archaeological Sciences; Mechatronics; Media Studies with Cinematics; Psychology & Crime; Robotics with Artificial Intelligence.

LIBRARIES:

• 548,000 books • 975 study places • 24-hr access • Spend per student: ££££
One *big* bookstack at JB Priestley library and a couple of smaller ones at the Management and Health sites.

COMPUTERS:

• 750 workstations • 24-hr access
Commendable cyber-credentials all round – halls are 100% jacked in to (free) broadband and a wireless network has been set up on campus so *Hungarian fetish porn is never far away if that's your (brown paper) bag.* Discounted laptops are available to students.

OTHER LEARNING FACILITIES:

A recent £130m's worth of 'corporate initiative' is intended to *sex up the campus no end*, with new lecture theatres, a digital arts studio and an Institute of Cancer Therapeutics on the horizon.

E N T E R T A I N M E N T

THE CITY:

• Price of a pint of beer: £1.90 • Glass of wine: £2.10 • Can of Red Bull: £2
Cinemas: A 16-screen Cineworld shows *everything* from Hollywood to Bollywood. Also an IMAX with a *behemoth* of a screen and the Cubby Broccoli Cinema in the National Museum of Film and Photography for *anything with subtitles or sex.*
Theatres: Alhambra is Bradford's answer to the West End and shows *suitably showy shows* – musicals, opera, ballet and pantos with *washed-up* soap stars. The Studio Theatre next door does *smaller-scale* touring pieces and new writing.
Pubs: The 'West End' area has several *enormous* chain pubs (Wetherspoons, Firkin, Varsity) with cheap drinks offers. *Any cheaper and they'd be giving away tenners as beer mats.* There are some quality alehouses and whisky dens if you're prepared to explore. Push plugs: The Beehive, if you can find it.
Clubbing: *Loads of cheesy clubs with student nights, but nothing for the more discerning clubber – try Leeds.*

Music venues: St George's Hall for *biggish* bands (Franz Ferdinand, Stereophonic-style *dirge*; Morrissey, Jools Holland), comedy and spoken tours (eg. Tony Benn). Rio's *thrashes out* rock & metal *to drunken students, which is eased along* by even more cheap booze. MacRory's bar (Irish) on Easby Road has live bands and a *much-needed* bit of atmosphere. **Eating out:** *Curry houses and kebab shops to die for (rather than after). Pushplugs: Raja's (takeaway); Royal Balti (curries and kebabs); Tariq's (best pizzas in Bradford); Flying Dragon (Chinese); The International (posh curry); Angelo's (Italian). Also Lunch Box (breakfasts, sandwiches) and Cafe Bleu (coffee & panini).*

UNIVERSITY:

• Price of a pint of beer: £1.45 • Glass of wine: £1.75 • Can of Red Bull: £1.50
Bars: The *picks* of the pack are the Courtyard Bar and the *cavernous* Basement, which runs some of the biggest club nights in town.
Theatres: *Thesp-ville. Drama-minded* students put plays on *all the time* at the Theatre in the Mill on Shearbridge Road.
Film: The 9m-wide biggest student cinema screen in the world (*...ever?*) shows the latest blockbusters and old classics every fortnight and all for free. *Bonus.*
Clubbing: *There's plenty going on most weeknights, but the big, stonking cheese-fest has to be* the evergreen FND (Friday Night Disco). AllSorts is the LGBT night, *while Tuesday's Club Soda is poptastic.*
Music venues: The Tamsin Little Music Centre *deals with the respectable, classical side of things*, while The Basement hosts DJs (eg. Westwood) and *ironic student favourites* (*the eternal* Chesney). There are also *less well-known* rock bands at Stoned, the indie *mope or mosh night.*
Comedy/Cabaret: Monthly gigs at the Biko Bar.
Food: *Plenty of options:* The Mondiale Refectory on the main campus does three hot meals a day. *Posher* fodder on offer at the Toscana cafe. Jazzman's serves sandwiches and snacks until the early evening and the Biko Bar *keeps mouths watering* until 11pm.

SOCIAL & POLITICAL

UNIVERSITY OF BRADFORD UNION:

• 6 sabbaticals • Turnout at last ballot: 13% • NUS member
Way more political than most places, UBU campaigns on *all sorts of leftie platforms*, from boycotting Nestlé, Bacardi and Esso to *berating* MPs about fees, through to a lecture walk-out over Israeli occupation of Palestine. UBU also runs the Commie (shorthand for the Communal Building), and is *heavily involved* with the University's decision-making.

SU FACILITIES:

The Commie – three-storey building with five bars; two canteens; coffee bar; eight pool tables; meeting rooms; minibus hire; Endsleigh Insurance; Natwest bank & ATMs; photocopying/printing/fax services; photo booth; payphones; advice centre; crèche; juke boxes; video games; general store and post office; new and secondhand bookshops; travel agency; launderette.

CLUBS (NON-SPORTING):

Arch Soc; Bowling; BURPS – Bradford Role Playing Society; BUSOMS – Bradford University Society of Operetta's & Musicals; Chinese Students; Cocktails; Computing; Cult TV; Cyber Society; Egyptian; Forensic Chemistry; Friends of Palestine; Hellenic; Mature Students; Muslim Women's Forum; Optometry; Peace Studies; Persian Pride; Pharmacy; Real Ale Society; Sikh Society; Speak; Vamp; Student CND; Student Action for Refugees; Twirling (circus skills). **See also Clubs tables.**

OTHER ORGANISATIONS:

Scrapie is the monthly Union paper with an award-winning website. Campus News is a joint University/UBU e-newsletter. Ramair (www.ramairfm.co.uk) broadcasts on AM across the campus. 'What's On' is the fortnightly newsletter. There's also the UCAN volunteering project.

RELIGIOUS:

• <u>Team of chaplains (RC, CofE, Methodist) and Muslim advisers</u>
The University has a quiet room and a Muslim prayer room. The city has an Anglican cathedral and other places of worship for Christians, Jews, Muslims, Sikhs and Hindus.

PAID WORK:

• <u>Job bureau</u>
The JobShop helps students find part-time work, which many do in cinemas, theatres, SU bars & shops and pubs & restaurants in town.

SPORTS

• <u>Recent successes: rugby, weightlifting</u> • <u>BUSA Ranking: 48</u>
Students are *generally sporty and active* and facilities are *decent enough*. But there's a *hefty* fee for student membership: £35-210 a year depending on which bits users want unlimited access to. Otherwise around £1.20 a visit for most activities.

SPORTS FACILITIES:

22 acres of sports grounds including: four footie, three rugby, hockey, astroturf and cricket pitches; squash, tennis, basketball and netball courts; sports hall, swimming pool; gym/multigym, sauna and spanking new solarium; aerobics studio; river. In Bradford there's a leisure centre; squash and tennis courts; swimming pool; ice rink; golf course; hills for walking/climbing/hang-gliding etc.; artificial snow ski slope; and pot-holing caves.

SPORTING CLUBS:

Katana; Ju-Jitsu; Tae Qwon-do; Twirling Society; Ultimate Frisbee; Waterpolo; Weights. **See also Clubs tables.**

ATTRACTIONS:

The Bradford Bulls play with an oval ball, Bradford FC with a round one.

ACCOMMODATION

IN COLLEGE:

• <u>Self-catering: 27%</u> • <u>Cost: £46-72 (39 or 51wks)</u> • <u>First years living in: 100%</u>
• <u>Insurance premium: ££££</u>
Availability: All 1st years can be accommodated and the University tries to give them the halls they ask for. No one has to share. Most accommodation is on campus, and the rest is only 5 mins walk away. *Trinity halls are the nicest, but some rooms come with a hefty price tag* (£72/wk for en-suite) *and the stigma of being posh.* University halls and Bradford halls are dead in the centre of campus, *but they've seen some hard times and they're starting to creak.* Plans are afoot for a new student village to be built on campus.
Car parking: Parking's available everywhere except for Wardley House, although it's *limited* at all halls. There's some free parking around campus and in nearby residential bits of town. A campus permit costs undergrads £19, £25 for grads.

EXTERNALLY:

• <u>Ave rent: £38</u> • <u>Living at home: 41%</u>
Availability: Rent is *rock-bottom* and there's *tons* of choice – *although some students share rather grotty hovels with mice.* Housing a short walk from campus can cost as little as £25 a week. Great Horton is popular with bed-addicts as it's near campus. *Not everyone likes Manningham* (former red light district).
Housing help: Unipol on campus helps students find a room of their own in the local area.

SERVICES:
- Lesbian/Gay/Bisexual Officer & Society • Ethnic Minorities Officer
- Women's Officer & Society • Mature Students' Officer & Society
- International Students' Officer • Disabilities Officer • Late-night minibus
- College counsellors: 1 full/16 part • SU counsellors: 2 • Crime rating: !!!!

Health: Health service and eye clinic. Good medical centre with four GPs and a few nurses.
Women: Attack alarms free from the SU.
Crèches/Nursery: 48 places for 6 mths-5 yrs.
Disabilities: Access is reasonable although the campus *is rather hilly*. There's a disability officer.

FINANCE:
- Ave debt per year: £5,898
- Access fund: £420,000 • Successful applications/yr: 969 • Ave payment: £500

Support: Hardship loans (£500); 20 postgrad bursaries (£1,000); travel awards.

University of Brighton

- *Formerly Brighton Polytechnic.*
(1) University of Brighton, Mithras House, Lewes Road, Brighton, BN2 4AT
   Tel: (01273) 600 900 E-mail: admissions@brighton.ac.uk Website: www.brighton.ac.uk
   University of Brighton Students' Union, Cockcroft Building, Lewes Road, Brighton, BN2 4GJ
   Tel: (01273) 642 870 E-mail: ubsu@brighton.ac.uk Website: www.ubsu.net
(2) Grand Parade Campus, Grand Parade, Brighton, BN2 0JY
   University of Brighton Students' Union, Main Building, 58-67 Grand Parade, Brighton,
   BN2 0JY
   Tel: (01273) 643 190
(3) Falmer Campus, Falmer, Brighton, BN1 9PH
   University of Brighton Students' Union, Village Way, Brighton, BN1 9PH
   Tel: (01273) 643 328
(4) Eastbourne Campus, Trevin Towers, Gaudick Road, Eastbourne, BN20 7SP
   University of Brighton Students' Union, Bishopsbourne, 32 Carlisle Road, Eastbourne,
   BN20 7SP
   Tel: (01273) 643 816
(5) University Centre Hastings, Havelock Road, Hastings, TN34 1DQ Tel: (08456) 020 607

GENERAL

Brighton enjoyed its heyday in the late 90s, when the sun was always out and it was okay to like Tony Blair. A few things have changed, but the city (including its more staid Siamese sibling, Hove) is still a south-coast hotspot driven by drinking, dancing and lounging around on the beach. The University is spread over four campuses, one of which isn't even in Brighton – in fact it's some way east along the south coast in Eastbourne. Each of the sites is noticeably different and only a fool would apply without making sure exactly which campus they were heading for.

Sex ratio (M:F): 37:63	**Founded: 1976**
Full-time u'grads: 10,705	**Part-time: 4,460**
Postgrads: 1,170	**Non-degree: 1,423**
Ave course: 3yrs	**Ethnic: 13%**
State:private school: 92:8	**Flunk rate: 14%**
Mature: 40%	**International: 17%**
Disabled: 356	

ATMOSPHERE:

Brighton is a youthful, fast-paced city – a bit like the better bits of London, set by the sea. There's top shopping, with loads of cool boutiques and psychedelic bazaars scattered around a healthy dose of high-street names. Plus of course enough clubbing action to scare seals witless. A couple of festivals come to town in the summer, including a mammoth arts fest (mammoth as in big, not hairy, tusky and extinct) in May, as do droves of sun-seekers on bank holiday weekends. There's plenty of greenery in the centre of town, which adds to the chilled-out feel. The atmosphere varies at each site, but it's generally creative and cosmopolitan.

SITES:

Moulsecoomb: The main admin hub. Two miles from the seafront, it even has its own train station.
Grand Parade Campus: (1,852 students – Art & Design, Fashion, Humanities) Slap in the middle of town, *easy enough on the eyes and chock-full of arts students doing their best to be radical.*
Falmer Campus: (6,014 students – Education, Social Sciences, Languages) Three miles out of town and *feels a bit isolated* even though there's an easy rail link with the city centre. The new medical school – a joint venture with <u>Sussex University</u> – lives here too.
Eastbourne Campus: (2,250 students – Sport & Leisure, Nursing, Leisure Management & Marketing) Dotted across the centre of Eastbourne, a town *with a reputation for being full of things on sticks – that's lollipops and geriatrics, not cocktail sausages.*
University Centre Hastings: (500 students – Education, Business, Tourism, Computing, Health) Not just a Brightonian baby but managed by the University and run in partnership with other institutions in the region to give access to higher education for all.

BRIGHTON:

- <u>Population: 247,817</u> • <u>City centre: 0–3 miles</u> • <u>London: 55 miles</u>
- <u>Southampton: 56 miles</u> • <u>Eastbourne: 26 miles</u>
- <u>High temp: 20</u> • <u>Low temp: 2</u> • <u>Rainfall: 61</u>

Brighton's eclectic population rubs shoulders without too many problems. It's posher than the average kiss-me-quick coastal town with craft shops rather than candy floss and fashion boutiques in place of bawdy-postcard hawkers. North Laines is hipsterville, rammed to the hilt with trendy clothes, jewellery and antique shops. The lavish excesses don't mask a serious problem with homelessness, though.

Eastbourne, long the butt of oldie jokes, really is dominated by Mr Burns types. But that leaves the nightlife to the students, which is no bad thing. It's not nearly as eye-catching as Brighton and the shopping isn't really up to scratch – it's possible to buy more than just hair nets and dog food, but not a lot more.

TRAVEL:

Trains: Connections to London (£6.60), Bristol (£23.75), Sheffield (£38.30) and beyond.
Coaches: National Express routes to London (£10.50), Bristol (£32), Sheffield (£25).
Car: A23 connects to London (M25) via the M23. *Parking is a nightmare,* and complicated by a pre-pay voucher system.
Air: 23 miles from Gatwick on the A23.
Local: The south coast is *better travelled by train than the timely but sluggish bus services.*
College: Free minibus between Varley Halls of Residence and Falmer campus.

Taxis: Lots of taxi firms, all charging *extortionate* prices (£10 for 3 miles).
Bicycles: Campuses have bike racks and sheds and cycle lanes are on the increase, but traffic is chaotic and the hills thigh-busting.

CAREER PROSPECTS:

• Careers Service • No. of staff: 7 full/8 part • Unemployed after 6mths: 8%

FAMOUS ALUMNI:

Kate Allenby (Olympic bronze – Modern Pentathlon); Helen Chadwick (late artist); Norman Cook aka Fatboy Slim (DJ); Harvey Goldsmith (promoter); Julien McDonald (designer); Helen Rollason (late BBC sports reporter); Tanya Streeter (world champion freediver); Keith Tyson (Turner Prize winner); Jo Whiley (Radio 1 DJ); Rachel Whiteread (*plaster-mad* artist).

FURTHER INFO:

• Prospectuses: undergrad; postgrad • Open days
The SU's alternative prospectus is available online.

Brighton runs some *fairly outlandish-sounding courses*, such as Editorial Photography, Horse Studies and Podiatry. Arts students typically have around ten hours a week in college.

180-320		**POINTS**
Entry points: 180-320	Ave points: 240	
Applns per place: 6	Clearing: 10%	
No. of terms: 2	Length of terms: 16wks	
Staff/student ratio: 1:22	Study addicts: 70%	
Teaching: ***	Research: *	
Year abroad: 18%	Sandwich students: 20%	
Firsts: 9%	2.2s: 43%	
2.1s: 38%	3rds: 6%	

ADMISSIONS:

• Apply via UCAS/NMAS for nursing/GTTR for PGCE

SUBJECTS:

Art & Architecture: 12% Management & Information Services: 22%
Education & Sport: 21% Partner Colleges: 6%
Health: 24% Science & Engineering: 13%
Best: Architecture & Design; Art & Design; Building; Civil Engineering; Education; Electrical Engineering; History of Art; Hospitality, Leisure, Recreation, Sport & Tourism; Librarianship & Information Management; Maths; Modern Languages; Molecular & Organismal Biosciences; Nursing; Pharmacology & Pharmacy; Philosophy.
Unusual: Criminology; Oriental Medicine; Sports Journalism (BA); Wine Studies.

LIBRARIES:

• 588,424 books • 1,403 study places • Spend per student: ££
A large main library is bolstered by smaller departmental ones on each campus. A brand new learning resource centre includes a library and IT facilities at University Centre Hastings.

COMPUTERS:

• 3,300 workstations • 1,429 internet access points
• Spend per student: ££
Every room in halls has internet access. The Computer Pool rooms have PCs, Macs, printing and scanning.

ENTERTAINMENT

THE CITY:

• Price of a pint of beer: £2.50 • Glass of wine: £3.50 • Can of Red Bull: £2
Brighton's not cheap. In fact it's positively pocket-sorry so students tend to stick to the cheaper chain pubs. Luckily, the beach is free. It's a friendly and liberal-minded place, so there are few no-go areas. It's also one of the UK's most prominent (not to mention flamboyant) *gay scenes.*

Cinemas: Three cinemas including the *arty* Duke of York Picturehouse, UCG (week-long student discount) and Odeon multiplexes.

Theatres: Theatre Royal caters for mainstream West End-style tastes. The out-of-town Gardner Arts centre is *lower-key and lefter-field.*

Pubs: *Expensive. Pushplugs: Hector's Horse; The Bear; AliCats; Zanzibar; The Marlborough* (gay).

Clubbing: Brighton's clubs are *legendary,* led by The Beach (home to Big Beat Boutique). *Pushplugs: Honey Club; Atlantis* (student nights); *Boogie Knights* (regular theme nights).

Music venues: A *varied* music scene with summer showpiece festivals. The Brighton Dome, the Event and the Brighton Centre host big names. Others include: Joogleberry (Latin, jazz); the Portland Rock Bar (rock); Prince Albert (dance, acoustic, Latin).

Eating out: *Anything and everything edible abounds. Push can plug a few: Picasso's* (pizza/ pasta for £2.50); *Bombay Mix* (Indian all-you-can-eat for £5.95); *Market Diner* (24-hour greasehouse).

UNIVERSITY:

• Price of a pint of beer: £1.80 • Glass of wine: £2.00 • Can of Red Bull: £1.75

Bars: Falmer's is currently being re-vamped, which means no bar for the next two years, but students can avail themselves of the bars at Sussex Uni (bus service laid on).

Theatres: The drama society organises trips, but the thesp scene *isn't exactly thriving –* students look to town to tread the boards, *and we don't mean the pier.*

Film: The Falmer bar shows free films on a Sunday night.

Music venues: The Sallis Benney theatre for occasional world music and jazz.

Clubbing: *SU facilities verge on the non-existent, but the town more than makes up for it.*

Comedy/Cabaret: Brighton's a stop on the circuit travelled by comedy folk such as Adam Bloom and Sean Collins.

Food: *Loads* of snack bars, coffee bars and refectories at all sites.

Other: Regular balls in Eastbourne and Brighton. *Tickets can be hard to lay hands on.*

SOCIAL & POLITICAL

UNIVERSITY OF BRIGHTON STUDENTS UNION:

• 5 sabbaticals • Turnout at last ballot: 5% • NUS member
So-so facilities are spread across the sites. UBSU is as political as a brained squid.

CLUBS (NON-SPORTING):

Believers Loveworld Fellowship (Christian group); Bob's Bits (swap shop); Breakdance/Street dance; BUGGED (Brighton University Geography, Geology and Environmental Department); Chess; Investment & Trading (finance society with Bloomberg training and trips to the stock exchange); Podiatry Society (foot fetishists go footloose and fancy free); Rehabilitation Science Society (scientists); Women's Group. **See also Clubs tables.**

OTHER ORGANISATIONS:

A new glossy mag is just being launched, and there's also the UBSU newsletter. The University runs @ctive Student, which is both an initiative to get students involved in community work *and an example of gratuitous typographical brand-imaging.*

RELIGIOUS:

Prayer rooms for all denominations. Town has places of worship for all the major faiths.

PAID WORK:

• Job bureau • Paid work: term-time 37%

There are *plenty* of jobs going in bars, shops and restaurants around town, *although most of them are during the summer vacation.*

S P O R T S

• BUSA Ranking: 36

Facilities at Eastbourne are *good*, thanks to sports degrees.

SPORTS FACILITIES:

Three sports halls; playing fields; athletics track; swimming pool (at Eastbourne) – for something bigger try the sea, 50+miles to France; floodlit tennis courts, 5-a-side football pitch and netball court; climbing wall; gyms; multigym; putting green; sauna; cardiovascular gym (Moulsecoomb); Sport & Racquet club (£10 membership for students at Falmer).

SPORTING CLUBS:

Boxing; Circuit Training; Gaelic Football; Ju-Jitsu; Kickboxing; Lacrosse; Rowing; Table Tennis; Triathon. **See also Clubs tables.**

ATTRACTIONS:

Portsmouth and Southampton are the south coast's *footballing heavyweights.* Brighton and Hove Albion are *less impressive.*

A C C O M M O D A T I O N

IN COLLEGE:

• Self-catering: 15% • Cost: £56.50-85 (39/50 wks) • First years living in: 40%
• Insurance premium: £

Availability: *Basic but functional halls.* Those who defer places or accept unconditional offers before the end of June are guaranteed places, as are most international students. There's a limited number of couples' flats. Most halls have disabled facilities. Insurance is included in the rent.

Car parking: Falmer and Mouslecoomb have a few parking spaces, but *traffic in Brighton is horrendous. Adding to the congestion is not a great idea.*

EXTERNALLY:

• Ave rent: £65-75 • Living at home: 11%

Availability: Most choose to live between Mouslecoomb and Falmer, along the main bus route. *Central Brighton and Hove are out of most students' leagues and nowhere is especially cheap. Digs in Eastbourne cost a bit less and Hastings is the cheapest of the lot.*

Housing help: The University has a list of registered properties and manages some private sector accomodation.

W E L F A R E

SERVICES:

• Lesbian/Gay/Bisexual/Transgender Society • Mature Students' Society
• International Students' Society • Postgrad Society • Late-night minibus • Nightline
• College counsellors: 3 full/3 part • SU counsellors: 4 full • Crime rating: !!

Health: Each site has a medical centre, but students tend to register with local practices to take the pressure off.

Crèches/Nursery: Crèches at Moulsecoomb, Grand Parade and Eastbourne. 70 places for children aged 2-5yrs.

Disabilities: Ramps and hearing loops. Special accommodation is provided on all sites. The University's welfare office has a dedicated dyslexia support department.

Drugs: *There's no denying Ecstasy and other drugs are widely available* in city clubs.

FINANCE:

• <u>Ave debt per year: £2,114</u>
• <u>Access fund: £750,000</u> • <u>Successful applications/yr: 2,000</u> • <u>Ave payment: £100-3,500</u>
Support: Bursary top-ups and scholarships for international students. Fees are temporarily waived for low-income postgrads.

Brighton Polytechnic

see <u>University of Brighton</u>

University of Bristol, Senate House, Tyndall Avenue, BS8 1TH
Tel: (0117) 928 9000 E-mail: admissions@bristol.ac.uk Website: www.bristol.ac.uk
University of Bristol Students' Union, Queens Road, Clifton, BS8 1LN
Tel: (0117) 954 5800 E-mail: communications-ubu@bris.ac.uk Website: www.ubu.org.uk

Bristol sits on the river Avon, by the mouth of the Severn, in the armpit of Wales and south-west England. *That's about as close to an armpit as it gets, though, as Bristol is actually quite scenic and pleasant. The countryside that surrounds the town is lush and lovely.* There's an *attractive* hotch-potch of old and new buildings, *the best of the lot* being in Clifton, the *posh* and *quite exclusive* home to the main University. University Precinct is *imposing –* the *splendid* Gothic tower of the Wills Memorial Building *dominates the cityscape.* Converted Victorian houses form the Arts departments, and the 18th-century mansion Royal Fort House adds *a little decadent splendour. Unfortunately,* there's *a large and unlovely maggot in the apple –* the Union building is an *ugly* concrete block that's *out for demolition.*

Sex ratio (M:F): 47:53	**Founded: 1876**
Full-time u'grads: 10,575	**Part-time: 3,895**
Postgrads: 2,615	**Non-degree: n/a**
Ave course: 3/4yrs	**Ethnic: 12%**
State:private school: 61:39	**Flunk rate: 3%**
Mature: 10%	**International: 21%**
Disabled: 193	**Local: 7%**

ATMOSPHERE:

They're not exactly happy about it, but Bristol students have a reputation as Sloaney Oxbridge rejects. The Trustafarian, faux boho image is one the University would sooner kick loose, and the SU's doing its best to play up a state school slant in admissions. Whatever, Bristol's a serious academic university in a buzzing city, still enjoying the cachet of its late-90s trip-hop cool. The SU comes to life at night, with loads of facilities and enough to occupy the most committed of work-shirkers.

BRISTOL:

- Population: 380,615 • City centre: 0 miles • London: 111 miles
- Birmingham: 77 miles • Cardiff: 29 miles
- High temp: 21 • Low temp: 2 • Rainfall: 72

Bristol's *effectively* the capital of the south-west. It was, until the 19th century, as important as London, Brum or Manchester, but the old maritime industry has gone now and the docks have been redeveloped with offices *for yuppies*. Bristol's *highlights* include: the Cabot Tower (which, from below, can be seen from almost anywhere and, from the top of which, almost anything can be seen) and the *outrageous* Clifton Suspension Bridge, designed by Brunel. Also designed by Brunel in 1843 is the SS Great Britain, now in dry dock at the Maritime Heritage Museum. For science *with knobs on*, try @bristol on the waterfront, for art and nature, the City Museum & Art Gallery and for caged animals *slowly losing their minds*, Bristol Zoo. In some ways, Bristol is the British San Francisco: *beautiful, quirky, culturally thriving, but with a few too many hippies and hills.*

TRAVEL:

Trains: Bristol Temple Meads is one of the country's centres for mainline routes: London (£27.15), Birmingham (£20.45) and elsewhere. Bristol Parkway for Wales.

Coaches: Similarly well served by coach services, including National Express buses to, among other places, London (£15), Birmingham (£12.75) and Cardiff (£6.50). Arrow and Bakers Dolphin also offer cheap return trips to London.

Car: On the way to the Severn Bridge, the M4 bypasses Bristol with the M32 going into the city. The M5 comes down from the Midlands, and the A38, A4 and A37 also all visit Bristol.

Air: Bristol Airport, 7 miles outside the city centre, has flights inland and to Europe.

Local: There are several British Rail stops in and around the city providing a reliable, frequent and comprehensive service without staggering cost. Local buses fill in where trains can't go, costing £1 from Temple Meads Station to the Union.

College: The UBU Bus services run in the evening between Stoke Bishop, via Clifton and the Union, down to the city centre, and back. It's £1 a trip and several services visit halls of residence. Buses run till 11.30pm.

Taxis: *Useful for students who go home when the kebab vans close. But it's about a fiver a trip – about a large doner and chips.*

Bicycles: Cycle lanes are appearing around the city. *They'll keep the nuttier drivers at bay, but not the thigh-busting hills.*

CAREER PROSPECTS:

- Careers Service • No. of staff: 12 full/15 part • Unemployed after 6mths: 6%

FAMOUS ALUMNI:

David Bamber (actor); Paloma Baeza (actress); Paul Boateng (MP); Josh Lewsey (England rugby player); Derren Brown (magician/mindreader/*charlatan*); Alex Cox (film director); Dominik Diamond (one-time Gamesmaster presenter); Judy Finnegan (daytime TV's *greatest old soak*); Caroline Goodall (actress); Sahar Hashemi (founder of Coffee Republic); Will Hutton (TV journalist/producer); Sue Lawley, Sarah Montague (ex- and current Radio 4 Today presenters); Matt Lucas, David Walliams (comedians, Little Britain); Caron Keating (late TV presenter), Dick King Smith (writer of *The Sheep Pig*, on which the film Babe was based); Chris Langham (writer/actor/director); Sheena McDonald (TV presenter/newsreader); Chris Morris (Brass Eye); Lembit Opik, MP (Lib Dem); Simon Pegg (actor); Iain Percy (Olympic gold medallist, sailing, 2000); Timothy Pigott-Smith (actor); Colin Sell (pianist in Radio 4's I'm Sorry I Haven't A Clue); Alastair Stewart (news presenter).

FURTHER INFO:

- Prospectuses: undergrad; postgrad • Open days • Video

UBU's alternative prospectus available online.

ACADEMIC

Strong reputation and pretty successful across the board. Especially good for engineering.

160-360 POINTS

Entry points: 160-360	Ave points: 280
Applns per place: 12	Clearing: 1%
No. of terms: 3	Length of terms: 10wks
Staff/student ratio: 1:13	Study addicts: 25%
Teaching: ****	Research: *****
Year abroad: 3%	Sandwich students: 6%
Firsts: 16%	2.2s: 55%
2.1s: 14%	3rds: 15%

ADMISSIONS:

• Apply via UCAS/GTTR for teaching

SUBJECTS:

Faculty of Arts: 21%   Faculty of Medical & Veterinary Sciences: 11%
Faculty of Dentistry & Medicine: 12%   Faculty of Science: 22%
Faculty of Engineering: 14%   Faculty of Social Sciences & Law: 20%
Best: Anatomy & Physiology; Archaeology; Biological Sciences; Classics & Ancient History; Drama: Economics; Experimental Psychology; Film & Television; Graduate School of Education; Maths & Engineering Mathematics; Medicine; Molecular Biosciences; Pharmacology; Philosophy; Politics; Theatre, Theology & Religious Studies; Veterinary Science.
Unusual: Engineering Design.

LIBRARIES:

• 1,400,000 books • 2,100 study places
One large Arts & Social Sciences library and *lots* of smaller departmental ones.

COMPUTERS:

• 1,200 workstations • 24-hr access
Internet points in most halls.

ENTERTAINMENT

THE CITY:

• Price of a pint of beer: £2.50 • Glass of wine: £2.50 • Can of Red Bull: £2
Cinemas: A *wide* range of flicks in all kinds of picture palaces. Try the Arts Centre Cinema, the Watershed and the Arthouse Cinema at the city's *superlative* dockside arts complex, the Arnolfini. There's also a Vue at the Cribbs Causeway shopping complex.
Theatres: The Old Vic is England's oldest working theatre and hosts *high-brow, high-minded shows*. The Hippodrome holds West End re-runs.
Pubs: Whiteladies Road has a *ridiculous* number of pubs lining it. *Pushplugs: The Black Boy Inn, Penny Farthing and Vittoria (in Bohemia); trendier venues are Sloanes, Henry J Beans and Henry Africa's Hot House (cocktails); Roo Bar for sports; more sedate environments in Browns or Bar Ha Ha.*
Clubbing: *A few to tickle the fancy. Pushplugs: Warehouse (student-only cheese and RnB); Dojo (hip-hop); Thekla (underground); Blue Mountain (breakbeat and hip-hop).*
Music venues: Bristol built a *cutting-edge* reputation by *churning out* artists like Roni Size, Portishead, Tricky and Massive Attack. *That golden age has passed*, but there are lots of good venues in town. *Pushplugs: Colston Hall (eclectic, rock to orchestra); Victoria Rooms (classical); Anson Rooms (rock, alternative); Bierkeller (unsigned bands of a Tuesday). The Carling Academy and the Fleece and Firkin are rated for gig line-ups.*
Eating out: *Lots of nice places close to campus including: Chandos Deli (sarnies); Boston Tea Party (late breakfasts); Saha (Moroccan).*

UNIVERSITY:

• Price of a pint of beer: £1.30 • Glass of wine: £1.50 • Can of Red Bull: £0.70

Bars: The Epicurean ('The Epi', cap 650) on the 3rd floor of the Union Building is the *gravitational centre* of student social life. The Avon Gorge Bar is on the 5th floor with roof garden and events. The University runs a number of other bars in the halls.

Theatres: Bristol's *one of the strongest* for student drama. Winston Theatre and Lady Windsor Studio are both run by the Union. The drama department uses the Glynn Wickham Studio and the Victoria Rooms (700) are used for *large-scale* productions. Bristol usually sends something to the Edinburgh Fringe.

Film: The Fine Film society shows the best of modern and classic flicks.

Music venues: Epi showcases student bands and *their heroes*. Recent visitors include Franz Ferdinand, the Von Bondies and Keane.

Clubbing: *Occasional* club nights at the Union, Anson Room and the Epi. The *regular repairs* for clubbers are student nights in the city's clubs.

Food: Café Zuma has a *famous* all-day breakfast at a famously friendly price (£2).

SOCIAL & POLITICAL

UNIVERSITY OF BRISTOL UNION:

• 7 sabbaticals • Turnout at last ballot: 17% • NUS member

UBU's building is *one of the largest and best equipped in the country*. The Union has a significant say in the University but still *doesn't attract much interest* from students. Campaigns include trying to get the Union moved, *which would require a very big crane*.

SU FACILITIES:

At the Union building: three bars; restaurant; snack bar; vending machines; travel agent; huge new general shop; secondhand bookshop; NatWest cash machines; video arcade; market stalls; swimming pool; two dark-rooms; music rooms; pottery workshop; art studio; pool; two theatres; launderette; hairdresser and barber; study rooms; photo booth.

CLUBS (NON-SPORTING):

Aixel Syd (Dyslexia); Alexander Technique; Artofficial; Ballroom Dancing; Bristol Exotic and Wild Animal Society (BEWAS); Bridge; Bristol Information Technology Society (BITS); Boarding; Bristol Volunteers for Development Abroad (BVDA); Capoeira; Challenges Worldwide; Change Ringers; Chocolate; CircuSoc (Circus Society); Classical; Club Italia; Coalition For Tibet; Computer Gaming (COGS); Conservation Group; Duke Of Edinburgh Award; Expeditions Society; Fair Trade Society; Film; Football Supporters Club; Flat Caps and Ferrets; Folk; GameSoc; Geology; German; Guide & Scout; Hot Air Ballooning (BUHABS); Hung Kuen School of Shaolin Kung Fu; Inventors (CDT Society); Jazz Funk Soul; Jungle; Lesbian, Gay, Bisexual, Transgender (LGBT); Madrigal Ensemble; Marrow; Massage; MedSIN; Model United Nations (MUN); Movida Latina; Motorclub; Navigators; Opera; Pottery; Power Kite; Red Cross; Restaurant; Rock; RUBBERecords; Sahaja Yoga; Save the Children; SIGGRAPH (Computer Graphics); SignSoc; Spelaeological (Caving); St John Ambulance; Stage Technicians; Stop Aids Society; Students Supporting Street Kids (SSSK); Student Security; T'ai Chi; Vegetarian & Vegan Society; Wine Circle; Wing Tsun Kung Fu. **See also Clubs tables.**

OTHER ORGANISATIONS:

UBU's regular Epigram is the *excellent* fortnightly newspaper. Burst FM is the student radio station. Do-gooders do good through the Bristol-wide charity Rag and the active Students Community Action, involved in over 29 local projects.

RELIGIOUS:

• 8 chaplains (FC; CofE; Lutheran; RC; Methodist; Orthodox; URC)

The Ecumenical Chaplaincy Centre houses meetings and services. Also a quiet room for prayer and reflection. In town, worshippers of every species have everything from Sikh temples and the Salvation Army to the Vedanta Movement and synagogues.

PAID WORK:

• Job bureau • Paid work: term-time 18%: hols 20%

There's always go-go dancing, but otherwise just the *normal limited* selection of bar work and restaurants. The SU runs a student employment office.

SPORTS

• Recent successes: waterpolo, skiing, sailing, hockey • BUSA Ranking: 8
Pull on your boots, flex those pecs – this is one of those places where students are *as likely to be carrying Deep Heat as they are dope*. Bristol are clawing their way back up the BUSA league and the emphasis is *firmly* on sports for the sporty, and *even slobby couchers can turn into Mr Motivator in this environment*. There's also a high performance squad for top international players, fancy that.

SPORTS FACILITIES:

If a sport's worth playing, facilities are probably slotted in for it somewhere around the University. The sports centre by the main University buildings houses a gym and facilities for many indoor sports. Under the Union building is a swimming pool and further out, by the halls of residence at Stoke Bishop and at Coombe Dingle, there are 38 acres of playing fields, a floodlit artificial pitch and 16 grass tennis courts. Hockey's played on an Astroturf pitch and there's an indoor tennis centre (also to be used by the LTA). There are further sports provisions at the halls including squash and tennis courts. Sailors swing their booms down at Chew Valley sailing club and rowers use the boathouses on the Avon. A Sportspass costs £150 (2 years) or £225 (for 3). In Bristol there's a sports hall, running track, squash and tennis courts, croquet/bowling green, golf course, lake and river and mountains and caves for potholing.

SPORTING CLUBS:

Aikido; Boat Club; Clay Pigeon; Combat Karate; Explorers; Hang Gliding; Ju-Jitsu; Korfball; Kuro Hebi; Lacrosse; Mountain Bike; Mountaineering; Polo; Riding; Rifle; Shorinji Kempo; Sky Diving; Snooker; Snowboarding; Surf; Waterpolo; Triathlon; Ultimate Frisbee; Waterski; Weightlifting; Windsurfing; X-Games. **See also Clubs tables.**

ATTRACTIONS:

Bristol Rugby Club, Bristol Packers, local American Football team and, with round balls, Bristol Rovers and Bristol City FCs. Gloucestershire County and Cricket Club. Yellow balls fly at the Redland Lawn Tennis Championship.

ACCOMMODATION

IN COLLEGE:

• Catered: 17% • Cost: £79-111 (30-38wks)
• Self-catering: 14% • Cost: £37-78 (38wks)
• First years living in: 91% • Insurance premium: ££
Availability: Most 1st years live in halls (a few latecomers can't, *even if they beg*), but they're out on their ears after that. Halls are based in three areas: six large halls at Stoke Bishop (just under 2 miles north of the University Precinct); three halls near the *gorgeous* gorge in Clifton (less than a mile west); and student houses in and around the Precinct itself, which are all self-catering and scarce. There are five catered halls (*with food to die from, rather than for*), four self-catering halls (two of which are blocks of shared flats) and 19 houses for 9-25 students. *Stoke Bishop may be cut off, but the cameraderie's a real seller.*
Car parking: Cars only allowed with a permit and *there's more chance of selling a salad to Rik Waller than getting hold of one.*

EXTERNALLY:

• Ave rent: £65 • Living at home: 4%
Availability: *Finding a pad should be easy, although prices are ever on the up.* Although local relations are *quite good*, some areas of Bristol are *rough as it comes*. St Paul's and

In 1613 James VI made a gift of books to St Andrews. Then refused to pay for them.

Knowle *have crackheads and dealers on the corners but some students live there for the gutter cred. Avoid South Bristol in favour of Bishopston, Cotham, Clifton and Redland. Wherever students lay their nat, they find it hard to park their car.*
Housing help: The University accommodation office keeps a vacancies register and database and provide general help, landlord blacklist and advice.

WELFARE

SERVICES:

- Lesbian/Gay/Bisexual Society • Ethnic Minorities Society
- Women's Officer • Mature Students' Society
- International Students' Officer & Society • Men's Officer
- Minibus • Nightline • College counsellors: 4 full
- SU counsellors: 8 part • Crime rating: !!!!!

Health: Sickly students can drag themeselves to the health service at University Precinct. Up to nine doctors and medical officers and ten nurses dole out the drugs, bandages and bedside sympathy.
Crèches/Nursery: Two nurseries. University Day nursery has 34 places for kids aged 2-5yrs & 22 places for babies from 3mths. Langford Nursery at the School of Clinical Veterinary Science has 15 places for children aged 2-5yrs and five places for babies from 3mths.
Disabilities: Old buildings and hilly terrain make access *tricky* despite the University's efforts.
Drugs: *Bristol's a major port for weed smuggling. Drugs of all sorts are easy to come by.*

FINANCE:

- Ave debt per year: £5,767 • Access fund: £500,000
- Successful applications/yr: 676 • Ave payment: £100-4,500

Support: Convocation bursaries (£1,000) to low-income students from schools in Avon. Sports scholarships for the talented, plus the usual compulsory top-up-related bursaries for those receiving the maintenance grant.

Bristol, University of the West of England

- *Formerly Bristol Polytechnic.*
(1) UWE, Frenchay Campus, Coldharbour Lane, Bristol, BS16 1QY
    Tel: (0117) 328 3333 E-mail: admissions@uwe.ac.uk Website: www.uwe.ac.uk
    UWE Students' Union, Frenchay Campus, Coldharbour Lane, Bristol, BS16 1QY
    Tel: (0117) 328 2577 E-mail: union@uwe.ac.uk Website: www.uwesu.net
(2) Glenside Campus, Blackberry Hill, Bristol, BS16 1DD Tel: (0117) 328 8534
    SU Tel: (0117) 328 8514
(3) St Matthias Campus, Oldbury Court Road, Fishponds, Bristol, BS16 2JP
    Tel: (0117) 965 5384
    SU Tel: (0117) 328 4435
(4) Bower Ashton Campus, Kennel Lodge Road, Bristol, BS3 2JT Tel: (0117) 328 4716
    SU Tel: (0117) 328 4725

For general information about Bristol: see <u>University of Bristol</u>. UWE is divided into four campuses with a main campus 5 miles north of the city centre at Frenchay. It's been facelift central since the late 90s with new lecture theatres, a five-floor library, a new Education facility, new Architecture studios, a £1m Genomics lab and a £1m Revolutionary Machining lab. The other campuses, described below, are spread out around Bristol. They have their own courses and are *roughly* self-contained, although all students are allowed to use facilities at the main campus. A new student village with sports facilities plus living space for 2,000 students is due in 2006.

Sex ratio (M:F): 41:59	Founded: 1992
Full-time u'grads: 15,940	Part-time: 4,995
Postgrads: 1,540	Non-degree: 3,279
Ave course: 3yrs	Ethnic: 9%
State:private school: 84:16	Flunk rate: 21%
Mature: 24%	International: 8%
Disabled: 201	Local: 48%

ATMOSPHERE:
The University's a bit fragmented, with the subsidiary sites feeling a bit lonely. The city, though, lends itself to student shenanigans. There's a safe, middle-class feel about, although the SU has been known to raise up some political agitation in the past. There's occasional tension with locals, though no more than at other student cities.

SITES:
Glenside Campus: (2,762 full-time students – Faculty of Health & Social Care). An imposing Victorian edifice, $1\frac{1}{2}$ miles from Frenchay, with refectory, bar and so on.
St Matthias Campus: (2,300 – Schools of Cultural Studies, English, History) $2\frac{1}{2}$ miles from Frenchay with two halls of residence. *By far the best-looking site* with a Gothic-style listed building and sunken lawn. *It feels more like Hogwarts than a University.* A tight-knit community and *almost a college in its own right.*
Bower Ashton Campus: (1,500 – Bristol School of Art, Media & Design) 2 miles from the city centre near the Clifton Suspension Bridge, but with the advantage of being in a *studenty* area. $7\frac{1}{2}$ miles from Frenchay, this is an overwhelmingly white concrete and glass oblong, *not built to appeal to the aesthetic nature of students based here*. Surrounded by *pleasant* fields, and again almost entirely separate from the main campus.

BRISTOL: see <u>University of Bristol</u>

TRAVEL: see <u>University of Bristol</u>
University: There's a free inter-campus bus every 30 mins. Hourly student shuttle bus to/from city centre student accomodation to Frenchay campus for £1 (sgl).

CAREER PROSPECTS:
• <u>Careers Service</u> • <u>No. of staff: 8 full/4 part</u> • <u>Unemployed after 6mths: 7%</u>

FAMOUS ALUMNI:
Kyran Bracken, Simon Shaw (England World Cup rugby players); David Hempleman-Adams (adventurer); Dawn Primarolo MP (Lab); Geoff Twentyman (ex-footballer now BBC sports presenter).

FURTHER INFO:
• <u>Prospectuses: undergrad; postgrad; some departmental</u> • <u>Open days</u> • <u>CD-Rom</u>

ACADEMIC

UWE has a *slight techie bias*, although it's *pretty competent* for arts and humanities.

Entry points: 180-220	Ave points: 250
Applns per place: 6	Clearing: 9%
No. of terms: 3	Length of terms: 11wks
Staff/student ratio: 1:20	Study addicts: 10%
Teaching: ****	Research: **
Year abroad: 2%	Sandwich students: 15%
Firsts: 10%	2.2s: 36%
2.1s: 46%	3rds: 3%

180-220 **POINTS**

ADMISSIONS:

• Apply via UCAS/NMAS (nursing)/GTTR (teaching)

SUBJECTS:

Applied Sciences: 8%
Art, Media & Design: 6%
Built Environment: 9%
Bristol Business School: 13%
Computing, Engineering & Mathematical Sciences: 11%

Education: 3%
Health & Social Care: 20%
Humanities, Languages & Social Sciences: 21%
Law: 5%

Best: Art, Media & Design; Biological & Biomedical Sciences; Building & Quantity Surveying; Business & Management; Cultural & Media Studies; Economics; Education; Electronic Engineering; English; French, German, Spanish & Linguistics; Land & Property Management; Law; Maths, Statistics & Operational Research; Nursing & Midwifery; Physiotherapy, Occupational Therapy, Radiography; Politics; Psychology; Sociology; Town & Country Planning & Housing.

LIBRARIES:

• 593,105 books • 2,334 study places • Spend per student: £
There are libraries on all campuses relating to the studies based there.

COMPUTERS:

• 1,820 workstations • 24-hr access • Spend per student: ££
Internet access all over the University, with cyber kiosks in two bars on Frenchay campus.

ENTERTAINMENT

THE CITY: see University of Bristol

UNIVERSITY:

• Price of a pint of beer: £1.60 • Glass of wine: £1.80 • Can of Red Bull: £1.50
Bars: Frenchay's Core 24 has recently been refitted and is the *poshest, most exciting joint* on campus. The Escape bar's *a social hub* but the Venue hosts events and St Matts is *popular*. The Bower's *gaining ground* as a venue.
Music venues: The Venue at Venue bar (cap 500). Recent visits from Athlete, the Scratch Perverts and Naked Apes.
Clubs/Discos: Crunchie (cheese/RnB) is the Friday night spectacular. Saturday night's Escapism (hip hop, funk, soul, metal) at the Escape bar is *a refuge against cheese*.
Food: The SU's main food stop in the Merchant Refectory sells *just about anything and everything*. Cribs Coffee Shop is *popular* too. There's also a Traders coffee bar on every campus.
Other: Four black tie balls a year.

SOCIAL & POLITICAL

UNIVERSITY OF THE WEST OF ENGLAND STUDENTS' UNION:

• 4 sabbaticals • Turnout at last ballot: 5% • NUS member
UWESU has at least an office on each campus and usually a bar and common room as well, but the *main centre's* at the Frenchay campus. Relations with the University are *generally lovey*, bar when 10,000 students rallied to demand a new sports complex, which will be in place by 2006.

SU FACILITIES:

Bars on each campus; meeting and training rooms; computing facilities; shop; photocopying/printing/fax services; games and vending machines; pool table; juke box; nursery; launderette.

CLUBS (NON-SPORTING):

Buddhist Meditation; Chinese; Drum 'n' Bass; Exhibition; Finance; Hellenic; Malaysian Students; Nigerian Students; Rocsoc; Scandinavian; Sign; Sri Lankan; St Matts Drama; Urban; Yoga. **See also Clubs tables.**

OTHER ORGANISATIONS:

Western Eye is the fortnightly union paper. *It's got a tough act to follow if it wants to live up to* the monthly Westworld magazine, which won a Guardian student media award in 2002.

RELIGIOUS:

• 6 religious advisors (CofE, RC, Methodist, URC, Eastern Orthodox, Quaker), rabbi
The Octagon houses the University's multi-faith chaplaincy centre. There's also a separate Islamic prayer room.

PAID WORK: also see University of Bristol

• Job bureau • Paid work: term-time 60%: hols 80%
Two staff and *reasonable* facilities to get students lining their own pockets.

SPORTS

• Recent successes: rugby, rowing, football, hockey, netball • BUSA Ranking: 48
UWE has a *fearsome urge* to put one over on its *notoriously sporty* neighbour (Bristol). They've even hired three sporting development officers. *Sports facilites* aren't great at the mo' but a new Sports Hall (badminton, basketball, footie and aerobics facilities) is due to be ready by the end of 2006. It'll feature a whole host of courts, pitches, nets and studios.

SPORTS FACILITIES:

9 acres of *shabby* pitches include: two football, one all-weather and one cricket pitch. Also two squash courts and gym/multigym. For facilities in Bristol: see University of Bristol.

SPORTING CLUBS:

Aikido, American Football; Cheerleading; Duke of Edinburgh; Gliding; Kickboxing; KITEuwe; Motorclub; Paintball; Polo; Shorinjkempo; Shotokan Karate; SkydiveUWE; SSAGO; Ultimate Frisbee; Waterpolo. **See also Clubs tables.**

ATTRACTIONS: see University of Bristol

A C C O M M O D A T I O N G E N E R A L

IN COLLEGE:
- Self-catering: 13% • Cost: £50-60 (46wks)
- Head tenancy cost: £41-61 (46wks)
- First years living in: 70% • Insurance premium: £

Availability: 1st years get priority, as long as they apply on time, most will get places. There are halls at Glenside and St Matthias, a student village at Frenchay and some new developments in the city centre (*better for all the fun of Bristol, worse for making that 9am lecture*). A student village (housing 2,000) is due to be completed by September 2006 and will complement the 17 existing halls. There are strict rules for those in halls regarding 'guests'. Insurance is included in fees.

Car parking: Not in city centre accommodation and *it's pretty tight everywhere else too.*

EXTERNALLY: see University of Bristol
- Ave rent: £60 • Living at home: 10%

Housing help: Advisers in the accommodation office keep a register of properties and lists of vacancies and dodgy landlords.

W E L F A R E

SERVICES:
- Lesbian/Gay/Bisexual Officer • Ethnic Minorities Officer
- Women's Officer • Mature Students' Officer
- International Students' Society • Postgrad Officer
- Disabilities Officer • Late-night minibus
- Self-defence classes • Nightline (8pm-8am) • Drop-in advice centre (10am-4pm)
- College counsellors: 9 full/1 part • Crime rating: !!!!!

Health: Local doctor holds a surgery at Frenchay every lunchtime for students living on campus.

Crèches/Nursery: Halley Nursery at St Matthias campus takes more than 20 children (6mths-5yrs).

Disabilities: *Good* access at Frenchay, but at the older buildings, especially St Matthias, it's *not the best.* Special accommodation is available, full details on the website.

Crime: A police crackdown was needed following a spate of stabbings in the city.

Drugs: *Bristol's a druggy city – weed, speed and ecstasy are all widely available.* If it becomes a problem, the student-run nightline has a non-judgemental ear.

FINANCE:
- Ave debt per year: £5,215
- Access fund: £1,045,826 • Successful applications/yr: 1,276
- Ave payment: £100-3,500

Support: Hardship and NHS bursaries, LEA/NHS allowances, pre-entry bursaries and short-term loans all available to help out if things get tight.

As far as fees go, UWE estimates that more than half of all students will receive a cash sweetener – up to £1,250 a year for students from low-income families – and the money doesn't have to be spent on university facilities.

Bristol Polytechnic

see Bristol, University of the West of England

Bristol Poly

see Bristol, University of the West of England

Brookes University

see Oxford Brookes University

Brunel University

(1) Brunel University, Uxbridge, Middlesex, UB8 3PH
   Tel: (01895) 274 000 E-mail: courses@brunel.ac.uk Website: www.brunel.ac.uk
   Union of Brunel Students, Cleveland Road, Uxbridge, Middlesex, UB8 3PH
   Tel: (01895) 462 300. E-mail: vp.communications@brunel.ac.uk
   Website: www.brunelstudents.com
(2) Osterley campus, Borough Road, Isleworth, Middlesex TW7 5DU Tel: (020) 8891 0121

GENERAL

Uxbridge is *a metallic satellite-town on the western end of the Metropolitan and Piccadilly Lines with space-age offices, a slick, spick'n'span shopping mall and a few quaint streets.* A mile south of Uxbridge proper are the redbrick and grey concrete buildings of the main campus of Brunel University. *They were designed to be more practical than sexy, although grassy patches and a stream (the optimistically titled 'River' Pinn) help create a feeling of space.* There's also a smaller site at Osterley (half of the former Brunel University College), 11 miles from Uxbridge.

Sex ratio (M:F): 50:50	**Founded: 1966**
Full-time u'grads: 9,715	**Part-time: 1,050**
Postgrads: 1,625	**Non-degree: 202**
Ave course: 3 or 4yrs	**Ethnic: 52%**
State:private school: 79:8	**Flunk rate: 11%**
Mature: 24%	**International: 17%**
Disabled: 187	**Local: 66%**

ATMOSPHERE:

Brunel used to be overrun with geeks who told maths jokes that could make hyenas look glum. This image is no longer accurate as in recent years more students are studying humanities (though they can tell pretty dodgy jokes too). However, students still tend to be focused on careers rather than careering through student scrapes, and though it is a fun place to study, the work ethic is strong and the research ethic stronger.

LONDON: see University of London

UXBRIDGE

Uxbridge is a modern town with all the required boxes ticked – supermarkets, banks and so on. It's been gradually face-lifted and tummy-tucked over the past few years and now has a look of a modern town about it, including a new cinema, bars and malls to loiter menacingly in. It's still quite a trek from the centre of London though (40 mins by tube) and the Uxbridge site is 20 mins walk from the town centre, but this does mean that the site has a leafy, rural feel to it. Thankfully, London is just about accessible, which is necessary for any serious stimulation.

TRAVEL: see University of London
Trains: West Drayton and Hayes are the stations nearest to the Uxbridge site both a short bus ride away (Uxbridge tube station is closer). There are trains to Bristol, Cardiff, Slough and other cities in the south-west served by trains out of London Paddington (at least 45 mins away, £8.30 return from Uxbridge). For other services, the *quickest route is usually* via London mainline stations.

Buses: National Express and London Country coach services bypass Uxbridge. The nearest stop is Heathrow Airport (25 mins by bus).
Car: Brunel is on the London escape route to the west, near the M25 (2 miles), and on the M4, M40, A4, A40 and A30.
Air: Heathrow is 4 miles from the Uxbridge campus.
Hitching: *No shortage of main roads (although hitchers have to get on to them to start with), but drivers aren't too enthusiastic.*
Local: Uxbridge is still within London's local transport network, *which is convenient but expensive.* It's served by buses 207, 222, U1, U3, U4, U7, Express Coach 607 and Night Bus N89 (which goes right into London's West End, though it can take a while).
Underground: Uxbridge station (a mile from campus) is the last stop on the Metropolitan and Piccadilly Lines *and offers a fast but expensive service into London (£5.40 off-peak one day travel card).*
Taxis: Cabs charge London and Heathrow prices. *Town centre to campus is £5.*
Bicycles: *Bikes are useful for local trips although the busy roads can make it hell.* Increased security and installation of bike sheds has made the bikes safer, *if not their owners.*

CAREER PROSPECTS:

• Careers Service • No. of staff: 9 full/4 part • Unemployed after 6mths: 11%

FAMOUS ALUMNI:

Tony Adams (ex-Arsenal and England); Linford Crawford (first black barrister on the Bar Council); Jo Brand (comedienne); James Cracknell (Olympic gold coxless 4s); Audley Harrison (boxing Olympic gold medallist); Richard Hill (member of England's Rugby World Cup-winning team); Patricia Hodge (actress); Lee Mark (comedian); Alan Pascoe, Marcia Richardson, Kathy Smallwood (athletics); Iwan Thomas (British 400m record-holder).

FURTHER INFO:

• Prospectuses: undergrad; postgrad; departmental • Open days

A C A D E M I C

Brunel has traditionally taught sciences, social sciences and engineering, but in more recent years has been *dabbling* in arts and humanities. Half the students study 'thin sandwich' courses, comprising a chunk of industrial placement for two terms in the first three years of study and a *lumpy spread* of academic study for the rest of the time. Performance in work placements is taken into account by the examiners, *bless 'em.*

Entry points: 240-320	Ave points: 260
Applns per place: 12	Clearing: 23%
No. of terms: 3	Length of terms: 12wks
Staff/student ratio: 1:19	Study addicts: 16%
Teaching: ***	Research: ****
Year abroad: 6%	Sandwich students: 37%
Firsts: 13%	2.2s: 30%
2.1s: 51%	3rds: 4%

240-320 **POINTS**

ADMISSIONS:

• Apply via UCAS

SUBJECTS:

Art & Design 11%   Engineering: 11%
Arts/Humanities: 11%   Sciences: 14%
Business/Management: 15% Social Sciences: 13%
Best: American Studies; Biological Sciences; Design; Drama; Economics; Education; Electrical Engineering; Film & TV; General Engineering; Health; History; Maths; Politics; Psychology; Sociology; Sports Sciences.

LIBRARIES:

• 428,464 books • 1,049 study places • Spend per student: ££££

The library at Uxbridge has doubled in size in the past few years and is now the proud owner of an Assistive Technology Centre.

COMPUTERS:

• 500 workstations • 436 internet access points • 24-hr access

OTHER LEARNING FACILITIES:

Free classes in photography, ceramics, painting, drawing and drama. Free weekly rehearsals for choirs, orchestra and chamber groups.

ENTERTAINMENT

THE CITY: see University of London

UXBRIDGE:

Cinemas: The nine-screen Odeon does a 10% student discount.

Theatres: The Beck Theatre in Hayes *can't compete* with the West End but it has regular plays, musicals, jazz and classical music.

Pubs: *Lots of traditional pubs, which get packed out by business lunchers. The Hogshead is colourful, big and student-friendly. A crop of new openings (bars, DJ bars, coffee bars) have increased the number of places to flash cash.*

Music venues: *Royale's is a cheap and tacky pick-up joint. Most students prefer to hit London's expensive and tacky pick-up joints.*

Eating out: *Pub grub is usually a good deal. Pushplugs: the Three Tuns; the Metropolitan; Auberge (pricey, but big portions of, er, mussels and chips).*

UNIVERSITY:

• Price of a pint of beer: £1.50 • Glass of wine: £1.80 • Can of Red Bull: £2

Bars: The main Union bar, Loco (cap 400) at Uxbridge is *perky enough* with weekly quizzes and occasional music nights; Bishops Bar *looks like an airport lounge*; Sports Bar is *more relaxed*.

Theatres: Several productions every year at the Howell Theatre in conjunction with the University's arts centre.

Music venues: The Academy (600) is the University's largest site for sounds.

Clubbing: The Academy sees *cool, underground* names like Killa Kela and Scratch Perverts. The weekly flagship night is 'Decades' on Wednesday; Elements spins commercial dance on Fridays.

Cabaret: Brunel is a *serious spot* on the alternative comedy circuit, with recent *mirthsters* including Jimmy Carr, Hattie Hayridge and Norman Lovett.

Food: The Uni-run Refectory and Café Quick provide decent snacks, Café Direct for a coffee hit, Locos Kitchen for table service and proper meals; Chicken Joes for fast food. The University canteen, the Stephenson Room, does affordable meals.

SOCIAL & POLITICAL

UNION OF BRUNEL STUDENTS:

• 4 sabbaticals • Turnout at last ballot: 12% • NUS member

Emphasis and energy is devoted to clubs and societies, which maintain a broad involvement in the Union's gamut of goings on. Politically speaking, Brunel students are notoriously uninterested.

SU FACILITIES:

Two bars; two catering outlets; the Academy nightclub; information and advice centre; Endsleigh Insurance office; launderette; four minibuses; photo booth; vending and games machines; juke box; pool tables; conference and function rooms; mini supermarket; Waterstones bookshop; HSBC bank/ATM. Osterly has: information and advice service; three minibuses.

CLUBS (NON-SPORTING):

Anglo Saxon & Norse; Brunel Links (First Aid); Brunel University Law Society; Celtic; Chinese Society; Computing; Drum'n'bass; Electronics; Everyone Link; Film, TV & Literature; Fire Juggling; Gaming; Great Wall Chinese Society; Hellenic; Hindu; His People Society; House & Garage; International Students; Krishna Conscious; Latin; LGBT; Mature Students; Motor; Music of Black Origin; Music; Muslim Unity; Occupational Therapy Society (BOTS); Pagan; Persian; Photographic; Planet 21st; Postgrad; R'n'B & Hip Hop; Rock; Seeds of Palestine; Sikh; Sinhalese; Socialist Students; Society Presidents; Somali; Taiwanese; Tamil; The Design Society; The Paintball Society; The Penfold Society. **See also Clubs tables.**

OTHER ORGANISATIONS:

The SU's Route 66 is a slick monthly mag. There's also B1000 Radio. The community action group is funded by the SU, and concentrates on helping the very old or the very young.

RELIGIOUS:

• 6 chaplains

The Meeting House chaplaincy at Uxbridge welcomes believers of all faiths and there's also a small mosque, plus a counselling room at Osterley. There are local churches for most flavours of Christianity.

PAID WORK: see University of London
• Job bureau

S P O R T S

• Recent successes: rugby, trampolining, super heavyweight boxing • BUSA Ranking: 26
For a small university, Brunel has some big-time facilities – including a new £6.5m outdoor complex and a £7m athletics and netball centre – and has had several successes in recent years.

SPORTS FACILITIES:

Two large and one small multi-purpose sports hall; facilities and support for elite athletes; all-weather facilities (including a flood it 6-lane track); pavilion; five football, one all-weather hockey, and two rugby pitches; two synthetic playing fields; four squash courts; climbing wall, fitness suite; weights room; sports bar; boathouse on the Thames; sailors make use of the Queen Mother Reservoir. Scholarships are available to students who aren't taking sports academically, but who are particularly nifty at them.

SPORTING CLUBS:

10-Pin Bowling; Chinese Boxing; Club Chairs; Dance; Gaelic Football; Ju-Jitsu; Karting; Lacrosse; Riding; Rowing; Skydiving; Snow Club; Surfing; Table Tennis; TFOGS; Ultimate Frisbee. **See also Clubs tables.**

ATTRACTIONS: see University of London
The MCC's second cricket ground is in Uxbridge and Queen's Park Rangers are the local football team. For a flutter on the nags, there's nearby Kempton and Sandown.

ACCOMMODATION

IN COLLEGE:

• Self-catering: 27% • Cost: £62-76 (38/51wks)
• First years living in: 74% • Insurance premium: ££££
Availability: Only 1st years and postgrads have the *luxury of* living in; everyone else has to try their luck elsewhere. Faraday and Fleming Hall are the *most sought after*, with big en-suite rooms. 127 self-catering bed spaces are available at the Osterly campus and new accomodation is being built at Uxbridge *as part of the University's 40th anniversary celebratory blowout*.
Car parking: Permit parking (£36-130pa). Clamping in operation.

EXTERNALLY: see University of London
• Ave rent: £70 • Living at home: 15%
Availability: Many students set up camp in Hayes, within 3 miles of the campus, mostly in shared houses and flats. *There are enough vacancies for students to have some choice in the matter.*
Housing help: There's a University-run accommodation office to get home-hunters off to a good start.

WELFARE

SERVICES:

• Lesbian/Gay/Bisexual Officer & Society • Mature Students' Officer & Society
• International Students' Officer & Society • Postgrad Officer & Society
• Disabilities Officer & Society • Late-night/women's minibus
• University counsellors: 4 full/3 part • Crime rating: !!!
Health: NHS practice on campus.
Disabilities: Disability and dyslexia service provide *good* support and Brunel tells us all buildings are now adapted for wheelchairs.

FINANCE:

• Ave debt per year: £2,866
• Access fund: £604,405 • Successful applications/yr: 794 • Ave payment: £722
Support: Hardship loans, and some new bursaries available.

University of Buckingham

University of Buckingham, Hunter Street, Buckingham, MK18 1EG
Tel: (01280) 814 080 E-mail: admissions@buckingham.ac.uk
Website: www.buckingham.ac.uk
University of Buckingham Students' Union, Tanlaw Mill, University of Buckingham, MK18 1EG
Tel: (01280) 822 522 E-mail: student.union@buckingham.ac.uk

GENERAL

Naming Buckinghamshire after Buckingham is every bit as daft as calling Greater London Tootingshire, but at least it's got a nice ring to it. Stretching from the north-west of London, the jewel of the Home Counties contains many bigger towns – the great urban experiment Milton Keynes, for one. For over 1,000 years Buckingham has been a quiet market town and shows no signs of stopping. Just on the edge of town are the University's two 8-acre sites: Hunter Street (Business & Humanities) and Verney Park (Law & Sciences). The buildings are mostly modern and attractive – although a converted mill, milk factory and chapel date back a century or so and the River Ouse wanders through the Hunter Street site. The surrounding fields, trees and old stone buildings make it seem completely cut off from the outside world – and in one sense, it is. Buckingham is a unique university; the only private institution of its kind in Britain. This means no government funding and almost £10,000 a year in fees alone. Ouch.

Sex ratio (M:F): 45:55	Founded: 1974
Full-time u'grads: 553	Part-time: 48
Postgrads: 87	Non-degree: 48
Ave course: 2yrs	Ethnic: 72%
State:private school: n/a	Flunk rate: n/a
Mature: 30%	International: 79%

ATMOSPHERE:

Bucking the general HE trend and dumping the Government has worked so far, although the full fee whammy has given Buckingham an élitist image which it's eager to shed – ditching Maggie Thatcher as Chancellor was a start. Those who can afford to come here for two-year fast track degrees fall into three broad categories: international students (they'd probably pay more in the long run doing a three-year course elsewhere); rich students; and mature students who see it as the quickest, easiest way of acquiring employable qualifications. Aware that many take a gamble in coming here, the University is very customer-driven and strives to provide good service and value for money. Naturally, the condensed degree course means the workload is heavy and there's very little time for extra-curricular activities or drunken shenanigans. Life here isn't just like riding the assembly line of a degree factory – the small size and campus ethos make for a strong sense of community: everyone's in the same canoe. Couple that with the huge number of international students – harking from over 80 different countries – and you have what may be the most self-contained and multicultural village on the planet, with all the positive (open-minded and cosmopolitan) and negative (nationalist cliquiness) aspects that entails.

BUCKINGHAM:

- Population: 13,000 • City centre: 400m • London: 50 miles
- Oxford: 21 miles • Milton Keynes: 14 miles
- High temp: 20 • Low temp: 0 • Rainfall: 54

Buckingham's a pretty town, but as Meatloaf might say, it sure has a helluva lot to learn about rock and roll. It's got everything necessary to keep its inhabitants alive – banks, bookshops, beauticians and boutiques – but not a lot to keep them lively. The closest thing to an all-night party is the fish counter at the 24-hour Tesco's. Milton Keynes is fun-o-rama by comparison, but even its giant multiplex pales in comparison to the entertainment available in every other major city in the world. And in most large boxes, come to mention it.

TRAVEL:

Trains: The nearest stations are at Bicester and Milton Keynes (London to MK £8.20 day rtn).
Buses/Coaches: Buses take 20 mins to get to MK and National Express services go from there all over the country. The X5 hourly Stagecoach Express goes between Oxford and Cambridge, taking in Buckingham, Bedford and MK en route. Also two coaches daily to Northampton and Leicester, one a day to Nottingham.

Car: *Students who can afford Buckingham's fees can often afford a car as well – there's a thriving used-car sale scene in the Union – more free enterprise. Parking presents few problems and permits are free if students ask nicely.* Routes include the M1, which bypasses MK, the A5, going straight through it, or the A43. Direct roads include A413, A421 and A422.

Air: London Luton is the closest international airport (36 miles), with hangars *stuffed* with easyjet planes.

Hitching: *Hitching in the home counties is like carving a roast with chopsticks – it's just about possible, but it takes a long time, you end up covered in meat, and there are easier ways.*

Local: The No. 40 bus meanders around Buckingham and calls at Tesco's.

College: The University runs a shuttle service weekdays between the main Hunter Street site and the law school at Verney Park for those who find a 10-min walk too demanding.

Taxis: Some firms offer student discounts but *since the town is so small and long-distance travel too expensive, taxi rides are extravagant luxuries and also largely pointless.*

Bicycles: *What with the quality and quantity of fresh air, the rural rarity of traffic and the 800m between the sites a bike is a handy asset indeed – if hills aren't too off-putting.*

CAREER PROSPECTS:

• Careers Service • No. of staff: 3 full • Unemployed after 6mths: 12%

The careers service has a library, publishes a newsletter, arranges job fairs and practice interviews. It's also open to the public, for a small charge *of course (all in the best free market tradition).*

FAMOUS ALUMNI:

Marc Gene (Formula 1 driver); Leopold Mills II (Secretary to the Cabinet, Government of Bermuda); Alex Jovy (film director).

SPECIAL FEATURES:

Many courses start in the beginning of the calendar year, leaving what would be an autumn term free for travel – frequently on University-arranged programmes in Europe and Japan. This gives international students opportunity to take a top-up course in English before their courses start. It also means that students can graduate six months before students at other universities, giving them a head start in the race for employment. *Sly.*

FURTHER INFO:

• Prospectuses: undergrad; postgrad; some departmental; international • Open days

A C A D E M I C

Cramming three years of study into two years is a bit like trying to swallow a beach ball. The four intense ten-week terms give students less vacation time, but when they're paying so much to be there, too much holiday seems like poor value for money. Contact teaching hours fill about 24 hours a week, and a good many more are taken up with private study. It's only the last 18 months of study that influence the final grade, so students have 6 months to get *in the swing before the panic sets in.* Being a private university, Buckingham is largely left to its own devices when it comes to academic inspection from outside bodies and *pesky* Government interference. Exams, however, are externally graded, so a degree from here is just as valid as one from any other university – *the Law School in particular is getting itself a good rep.*

> Rupert Murdoch had to buy the copyright for the Sun from Aston University - it was the name of their first Student Union Newspaper.

Entry points: 180-240	Ave points: 220
Applns per place: 10	Clearing: 38%
No. of terms: 4	Length of terms: 10wks
Staff/student ratio: 1:10	Study addicts: 27%
Year abroad: 0	Sandwich students: 0
First: 11%	2.1s: 31%
2.2s: 40%	3rds: 11%

180-240 **POINTS**

ADMISSIONS:

• Apply via UCAS/direct for part-time or postgrad

SUBJECTS:

Business: 19%	International Studies: 14%
Humanities: 10%	Law: 49%
Information Systems: 3%	Psychology: 2%

Unusual: Marketing with Psychology.

LIBRARIES:

• 93,234 books • 215 study places
The Hunter Street Library spans three floors of Business and Humanities books and was once the barracks of the Royal Bucks Hussars – some 19th-century bits remain. The Franciscan Library at Verney Park houses Law and Science volumes. Student computers are available in both. 24-hour access during exams.

COMPUTERS:

• 130 workstations • 24-hr access
Computer rooms are spread around both sites. All student rooms have internet access points.

OTHER LEARNING FACILITIES:

Language lab with Audio/Video and computer-based learning facilities; CAD lab and Satellite TV room with channels from all over the globe.

ENTERTAINMENT

THE TOWN:

• Price of a pint of beer: £2.50 • Glass of wine: £2.50 • Can of Red Bull: £1.80
For a fix of fun or culture, Buckingham is as happening as a pork chop in a synagogue. Students either have to tone down their entertainment requirements or leg it to Oxford, MK or London.
Cinemas/Theatres: There is a local am dram group, but MK is the only option for sit-down entertainment.
Pubs: There are several traditional-style pubs within walking distance of the campus but many are fairly expensive. *Pushplugs: the Mitre (pool tables and snuggly log fires); the New Inn (Sri Lankan food, live music); the Woolpack (riverside beer garden); the King's Head (cocktails) and the White Hart (regular karaoke and themed nights).*
Music venues: A few pubs host local bands (eg. the New Inn, the Woolpack). The White Hart and Grand Junction have DJ nights and late licences at weekends.
Eating out: *Not a great deal to tempt the discerning budget diner but 'budget' isn't always a relevant concept here.* There are quite a few Indians offering discounts, like Buckingham Fort & Dipalee Tandooris. *Beijing, the China Cottage and Cheng Du are the places to go for Chinese; Prego is popular for Italian.* Most of these also do student discounts.

UNIVERSITY:

• Price of a pint of beer: £1.60 • Glass of wine: £1.80 • Can of Red Bull: £1.50
Bars: George's Bar opens lunchtimes and evenings – *all-day benders don't seem to be the done thing. George is a busy man when he's open though.* The bar shows big screen sport and MTV and has special events/quizzes towards the weekend.

Theatres: The Radcliffe Centre for student productions, some of which come from the pulsing pens of the Buckingham Arts & Theatre Society (BATS).

Clubbing/Music venues: The Refectory occasionally clears out the crockery to host student and local bands. It also runs themed nights and societies' parties and *gets the dance floor humming on weekend nights.*

Food: The Refectory's big enough to feed all Buckingham students, which it does for around £2 a meal. BBQs and themed days crop up every so often. The Verney Park Coffee Bar dishes out hot meals, snacks and cakes.

Other: The Graduation Swan Ball every February.

SOCIAL & POLITICAL

UNIVERSITY OF BUCKINGHAM STUDENTS' UNION:

• 1 sabbatical • Turnout at last ballot: 30%

A dead gerbil in a tutu makes more of a political statement than Buckingham SU ever have – but since many students are only spending a short time in the UK, politics isn't a priority. With the restricted amount of leisure time and the exec being changed twice a year rather than annually, there's not a lot the SU can do. It provides services, co-ordinates clubs and runs the annual Rag week and Ball, but beyond that, students aren't aware of its existence except when they need embassy details, train times or party booking.

SU FACILITIES:

The SU's based on the Hunter Street site in the converted Tanlaw Mill, which also houses the refectory and some indoor sports amenities. The SU runs: bar; cafeteria; Sky TV, games machines; three pool tables; snack bar; fax service and juke box. Other facilities: photocopiers; post office; new and secondhand bookshops; TV lounge; launderette; stationery shop; vending machines.

CLUBS (NON-SPORTING):

Bahamian; BATS; British; Bulgarian; Film; International; Korean; Law; Music; Nigerian; Wine & Dine. **See also Clubs tables.**

RELIGIOUS:

A Muslim prayer room is available. There are CofE, RC and Methodist churches in town.

PAID WORK:

There are few opportunities, needs or time for moonlight occupations. *There are a couple of restaurants, pubs or shops in the town that recruit students, and the Union bar and library night shifts are student-staffed.* The University's careers department lends a hand finding temporary jobs and things like the Grand Prix or mayoral elections crop up and need workers from time to time.

SPORTS

• Recent successes: none • BUSA Ranking: 48

Many don't find time to hit the pitch, but this means that those who play sports can do so for fun without suffering any serious competitive urges (racket rage etc.). Or any major successes for that matter.

SPORTS FACILITIES:

In the Tanlaw Mill: fitness centre (£40/year); aerobics and martial arts room; a snooker room. There are also table tennis tables, basketball, netball and tennis courts, an all-weather 5-a-side pitch, a floodlit training area and 32 acres of playing fields for football, rugby and cricket. Local sports centres cost cash, but provide a broader choice of provisions including a swimming pool.

SPORTING CLUBS:

See Clubs tables.

ACCOMMODATION

IN COLLEGE:

- Self-catering: 69% • Cost: £69-110 (52wks)
- First years living in: 95%
- Insurance premium: £

Availability: All 1st years and a fair few 2nd years are given rooms in the various halls on campus. No one has to share but most accommodation divides kitchen/bathroom facilities between two to eight people. Most rooms have their own washbasin and a baby fridgelet, phone/internet connections and TV aerial sockets. The smaller rooms are in corridor-style halls; others take the form of shared flats. Hunter Street has the refectory and bar on its doorstep and Mitre Court and Hunter Street halls are popular for larger rooms and en-suite facilities, *but there's no truly shameful housing.* Mature and postgrad students have their own block. Blokes get plonked on ground floors and there are some women-only corridors.

EXTERNALLY:

- Ave rent: £100+ • Living at home: 1%

Availability: Buckingham itself offers *limited and expensive housing,* which can be a problem given that the University requires all students live within 10 miles. Parental purchasing power is a plus point for many students, however, and prices *aren't prohibitive to the majority,* who find themselves living all over Buckingham and local villages.

Housing help: The Accommodation Officer keeps a list of agencies in the area.

WELFARE

SERVICES:

- Disabilities Society • College counsellors: 1 full/1 part • Crime rating: !

The small student body and good staff relations means most students have good contact with personal tutors.

Health: The town's North End Surgery has five GPs available Mon-Fri.

Disabilities: *The converted buildings are lacking on the access front but they're trying to change that.* The Disability Support Department offers support for most physical and mental disabilities including ramps, hearing loops, note-takers and special academic arrangements for dyslexics.

FINANCE:

- Home student fees: £9,295

Fees: Debt figures vary enormously. Some students owe nothing; some have £22 grand to pay back to the bank. It's the only university where postgrad fees can be less than undergrad's – although they range from £8,000-12,000. *As far as top-up fees go – they couldn't give a flying French frig.*

Support: With no government support there's also no access fund, although there are fee discounts of £4,040 for local students, some hardship funds and sponsorship deals available for certain subjects and from some local organisations. The Rotary Club, for example, has sponsored students in the past. Graduates get discounts on further study based on academic results. For more on scholarships (including for local, mature and marketing/media/journalism students) see the website.

Buckinghamshire Chilterns University College

(1) Buckinghamshire Chilterns University College, Queen Alexandra Road, High Wycombe, HP11 2JZ Tel: (01494) 522 141 Website: www.bcuc.ac.uk
Buckinghamshire Chilterns Students' Union, Queen Alexandra Road, High Wycombe, HP11 2JZ Tel: (01494) 446 330 Website: www.bcsu.net
(2) Wellesbourne Campus, Kinghill Road, High Wycombe, HP13 5BB
(3) Chalfont Campus, Gorelands Lane, Chalfont St Giles, HP8 4AD

GENERAL

Halfway down Buckinghamshire, *within whistling distance* of the M40, is a *densely populated* commuter belt, home to people *rich enough to live this close to London and still see trees*. It's called High Wycombe, *not because of the house prices*, but because it's set amidst the rolling Chiltern Hills. *But what's in a name? Well, Buckinghamshire Chilterns shouldn't be confused with the University of Buckingham, which is in, er, Buckingham.* And it's not a university *in the strictest sense*, although it's been dealing in degrees since 1996. One of the sites is in Chalfont St Giles, *which is great rhyming slang, but no bustling metropolis. But then again, maybe long country walks and lungfuls of unpolluted air are more your bag.*

Sex ratio (M:F): 43:57	**Founded: 1893**
Full-time u'grads: 6,020	**Part-time: 3,140**
Postgrads: 140	**Non-degree: 844**
Ave course: 3yrs	**Ethnic: 10%**
State:private school: n/a	**Flunk rate: 12%**
Mature: 30%	**International: 13%**
Disabled: 208	**Local: n/a**

ATMOSPHERE:
Abandon hope of thumping party action all ye who enter Wycombe. It's a pleasant but drowsy market town whose main tourist attraction is a chair museum. True, the concrete labyrinth of the University site isn't going to be bringing home architectural awards, but it's not going to frighten babies either. Stumbling into the bar is light relief – funky Ministry of Sound décor and chill-out gas in the air add to the all-round feeling of warm, unassuming community.

SITES:
Wellesbourne Campus: (Leisure & Tourism) Wellesbourne is a collection of *nondescript* 60s buildings a couple of miles from the main campus. It's connected by a regular bus service (£1).
Chalfont Campus: (1,900 students – Business School, Health Studies) The Chalfont campus is a *self-contained* 18th-century mansion in Chalfont St Giles – about 9 miles from Wycombe. Minibuses take students to and from the main campus, although the *only call* to go there is for SU events.

HIGH WYCOMBE:
• Population: 162,000 • City centre: 0 miles • London: 40 miles
• Oxford: 35 miles • Birmingham: 122 miles
• High temp: 22 • Low temp: 1 • Rainfall: 48
Wycombe is your average, everyday, friendly neighbourhood market town – identikit shops, Daily Mail readers, and a handful of diverting amenities. There's a cinema, a scattering of student-friendly pubs and a club, but that's about the lot. Unless it's chairs that tickle your fancy.

TRAVEL:

Trains: The station is 400m from main campus; services go direct to London Marylebone (£6, 40 mins) and Birmingham.
Coaches: National Express coaches go to London, Oxford, Reading and all over.
Car: Wycombe is right next to the M40 and Chalfont is close to the M25. No student parking at college though.
Air: Heathrow is 40 miles away.
Hitching: *Junction 4 of the M40 is the closest hitch pitch but it might be a long, long wait.*
Local: Buses have the surrounding countryside covered *but there's not much to travel for.*
Taxis: Station to campus costs 3 quid.
Bicycles: The town's *not huge, but it's hilly. Not exactly bikers' paradise.*

CAREER PROSPECTS:

• Careers Service • No. of staff: 2 full/1 part • Unemployed after 6mths: 10%

FAMOUS ALUMNI:

Howard Jones (80s teen idol); Zandra Rhodes (fashion designer).

FURTHER INFO:

• Prospectuses: undergrad; postgrad; departmental • Open days
E-mail marketing@bucuc.ac.uk for more info.

A C A D E M I C

Business, health and design are the *major* degrees, taught by *the usual combination* of lectures, seminars and tutorials. *Less run-of-the-mill* is the choice of courses, ranging from equine management to jewellery studies. The music department is *a mini-Motown* with its very own record label.

Entry points: 130-220	**Ave points: n/a**
No. of terms: 3	**Length of terms: 12wks**
Staff/student ratio: 1:10	**Clearing: 19%**
Teaching: *	**Research: ***
Sandwich students: 1%	

ADMISSIONS:

• Apply via UCAS

SUBJECTS:

Applied Social Sciences & Humanities: 10%	Health Studies: 20%
Business: 19%	Leisure & Tourism: 10%
Design: 24%	Technology: 17%

Unusual: Equine Industry Management; Equine Sports Performance; International Music Management; Jewellery (BA).

LIBRARIES:

• 1,770,000 books
The main library opens late most days *to accomodate the dreaded essay crises.*

COMPUTERS:

• 150 workstations

E N T E R T A I N M E N T

THE TOWN:

• Price of a pint of beer: £2 • Glass of wine: £3.50 • Can of Red Bull: £1.80

Cinemas: A six-screen UCI in town does student discounts. There's another one at Gerrard's Cross, *just a quick hop* on the train.

Theatres: The Wycombe Swan is the thespy outlet, *but it's not exactly highbrow fare.*

Pubs: Mainly *traditional towny* pubs, but a couple are *student-savvy. Pushplugs: Antelope, Firkin, Hobgoblin. Avoid the Saracen's Head and White Horse or risk a healthy portion of shoe supper.*

Clubbing: Club Eden does a student night on Wednesdays.

Music venues: There's a *stunted* sort of indie scene in the Nag's Head *but London's a better bet and not too far.*

Eating out: *Hardly Cordon Bleu territory. Pushplugs: Bella Pasta; Francesco's (Italian); Pizza Hut gorge-yourself-for-a-fiver deal.*

UNIVERSITY:

• Price of a pint of beer: £1.80 • Glass of wine: £2 • Can of Red Bull: £1.90

Bars: The White Room (cap 800) in the Union has regular nights including a *cheesefest* at Club Tropicana. Bar Two in Chalfont (cap 600) also does regular nights *to try and shake the cabin fever.*

Film: The SU shows an *arty* flick once a week.

Food: Every site has a refectory. The White Room in Wycombe does sandwiches and snacks. Bar Two serves *pubbier grub.*

Other: The May Ball summons *a few big names,* such as Goldie, Trevor Nelson and *student favourite* Chesney *'Omnipresent'* Hawkes.

S O C I A L & P O L I T I C A L

BUCKINGHAMSHIRE CHILTERNS STUDENTS' UNION:

• 8 sabbaticals • NUS member • Turnout at last ballot: 7%

The SU concentrates on ents rather than political foment.

SU FACILITIES:

Bars; nightclub; photocopier; payphone; video games; fax; juke box; sandwich bar; late-night minibus; vending machines; photo booth; pool tables.

CLUBS (NON-SPORTING):

Anime; Chalfont Acoustic Music; Clubbing; Creative (writing, mainly); Feast (international cooking); Fine Wine; Internet Radio; Law; Poker. **See also Clubs tables.**

OTHER ORGANISATIONS:

Magazine the Noise comes out five times a year. A radio station *is clogged up in the pipeline somewhere.* Student Volunteering is *active* in the local community, helping out at schools, running talent shows etc.

RELIGIOUS:

• 1 chaplain (CofE)

Places of worship for Christians, Muslims and Sikhs.

PAID WORK:

• Job bureau

SU bars employ students, as do bars, restaurants, call centres and temping agencies in town.

- BUSA Ranking: 48
Sport isn't really the thing here. It's more for fun than shiny cups and trophies.

SPORTS FACILITIES:

Wycombe campus: fitness, aerobics and weights room; gym; tennis courts; football pitches. Wycombe town: leisure centre; golf course; sauna and solarium; dry ski slope. Chalfont campus: sports hall; swimming pool; multigym; tennis courts; athletics field; all-weather pitch; gym. There are outdoor facilities at Wellesbourne. An annual membership card (£35) gives access to everything and a discount at the swimming pool.

SPORTING CLUBS:

Cheerleading; Outdoor Pursuits; Polo; Snowboarding. **See also Clubs tables.**

ATTRACTIONS:

Wycombe Wanderers is the local football club. *They're a good deal less entertaining than* Wasps, the rugby union side. *And a good deal less entertaining than the stinging insects too, come to think of it.*

IN COLLEGE:

- Self-catering: 19% • Cost: £64 (38wks) • Insurance premium: £
- First years living in: 90%
Availability: Pressure on space at halls is *pretty intense.* Newland Park is the largest hall, with 700 places. Another 500 are divvied between Brook Street Hall and John North Hall, both in the centre of Wycombe. St Peter and St Giles Halls are both on Chalfont campus.
Car parking: *Ludicrous* on campus in Wycombe, although it's *not too silly* in halls and *an entirely rational prospect* at Chalfont.

EXTERNALLY:

- Ave rent: £50
Availability: *There for the taking. The best bits are Wycombe town, Desborough, Green Street and Upper Street. West Wycombe should be given a similar berth to a colony of leprous mormons.*
Housing help: The accommodation office *does its best to help students set up shop nearby.*

SERVICES:

- Lesbian/Gay/Bisexual Society • International Students' Society • Late-night minibus
- College counsellors: 4 full • SU counsellors: 2 full • Crime rating: !!
Health: Three GPs at Wycombe, three at Chalfont.
Disabilities: Wheelchair access on campus is *passable.*

FINANCE:

- Ave debt per year: £4,164 • Access fund: £160,000
Support: There's a hardship fund for emergency loans and *a few* scholarships. Bursaries of between £300–£1,000 per year will be available to students coming from linked local schools and those enrolling on particular degrees.

University of Cambridge
Christ's College, Cambridge
Churchill College, Cambridge
Clare College, Cambridge
Corpus Christi College, Cambridge
Downing College, Cambridge
Emmanuel College, Cambridge
Fitzwilliam College, Cambridge
Girton College, Cambridge
Gonville & Caius College, Cambridge
Homerton College, Cambridge
Jesus College, Cambridge
King's College, Cambridge
Lucy Cavendish College, Cambridge
Magdalene College, Cambridge
New Hall College, Cambridge
Newnham College, Cambridge
Pembroke College, Cambridge
Peterhouse, Cambridge
Queens' College, Cambridge
Robinson College, Cambridge
Selwyn College, Cambridge
Sidney Sussex College, Cambridge
St Catharine's College, Cambridge
St Edmund's College, Cambridge
St John's College, Cambridge
Trinity College, Cambridge
Trinity Hall, Cambridge
Wolfson College, Cambridge

Canterbury see The University of Kent

Canterbury Christ Church University College

Cardiff University

Cardiff Institute (UWIC)

Caythorpe see De Montfort University

Cambridgeshire College of Arts & Technology (CCAT) see APU

University of Central England

University of Central Lancashire

Central London Poly see University of Westminster

Central St Martins College of Art & Design see University of the Arts, London

Charing Cross & Westminster Hospital see Imperial College, London

Charlotte Mason see Lancaster University

Chelsea College of Art see University of the Arts, London

Cheltenham & Gloucester College of Higher Education see University of Gloucestershire

Chester College see Liverpool University

University College Chester see <u>Liverpool University</u>

Chichester College see <u>University College Chichester</u>

University College Chichester
Bognor Regis

Cirencester see <u>Royal Agricultural College</u>

City of London Poly see <u>London Metropolitan University</u>

City University

Coleraine see <u>University of Ulster</u>

Courtauld Institute of Art, London

Coventry University

Coventry Polytechnic see <u>Coventry University</u>

University of Cambridge

University of Cambridge, Admissions Office, Fitzwilliam House, 32 Trumpington Street,
Cambridge, CB2 1QJ
Tel: (01223) 333 308 E-mail: admissions@cam.ac.uk Website: www.cam.ac.uk
Cambridge University Students' Union, 11/12 Trumpington Street, Cambridge, CB2 1QA
Tel: (01223) 356 454 E-mail: info@cusu.cam.ac.uk Website: www.cusu.cam.ac.uk

GENERAL

Surrounded by the flat and marshy Fenlands, the ancient city of Cambridge sits smugly on
the edge of East Anglia, bulging arse-end of England – *geographically speaking, no offence
to East Anglians*. The reason for the city's smugness lies in the sprawl of colleges, faculties
and departments that make up the University. About a century after the trend started in
Oxford, higher education sprouted in Cambridge and now, nearly 800 years later, these are
among the *most famous, most highly revered and possibly the most extraordinary
universities in the world*. The University remains (much more than at Oxford) the focal point
of the *stunning* city, *which is largely composed of attractive buildings* in light golden stone.
The University buildings are its colleges – 31 in all – and they are as attractive examples of
English architecture spanning eight centuries as are likely to be found anywhere. *The area
they cover is remarkably compact and to the outsider has a slightly surreal feeling hanging
in the air, aided and abetted by the bizarre language students use* – 'backs', 'cuppers',
'bedders', 'bumps'.
*These words are part of the world inhabited by the elite – a controversial word to which
the University objects. They can pretend all they want that they're firmly grounded in the real
world – and, don't get us wrong, there are plenty of 'normal' people here – but the truth is
that, from the moment you sign in at the Porter's Lodge to the day you graduate at Senate
House, you're really not in Kansas any more.*

Sex ratio (M:F): 46:54	Founded: 1284
Full-time u'grads: 11,955	Part-time: 4,595
Postgrads: 5,210	Non-degree: 0
Ave course: 3yrs	Ethnic: 16%
State:private school: 55:45	Flunk rate: 1%
Mature: 6%	International: 28%
Disabled: 42	Local: n/a

54%
46%

ATMOSPHERE:

Okay, so Cambridge and Oxford are more similar than Kylie's arse and a ripe melon and only their prospectuses would claim they're completely different. Like Oxford, most of the students' social concerns and the intense academic life revolve around the colleges, which run themselves, arrange their own admissions and are fiercely competitive with each other. However, unlike Oxford, there are plenty of opportunities to switch courses and an even stronger sense that this is a student city.

Cambridge's picturesque façade hides a rigorous work ethic – three years' studying here is one of the most intense educational experiences anyone can hope to have with their clothes on. In this compact and University-dominated city, there is virtually no escape. It can be challenging, it can be claustrophobic and it can be compared to being locked in a prison cell with 50 double-glazing salesmen. That's just the work side of things though – those who know all work and no play makes Jack reach for the Kalashnikov try to cram every waking hour with extra-curricular activity: sport; drama; journalism; music; politics; archaic drinking clubs; whatever. Cambridge students do a lot of whatever. They need to have good time management skills or learn them pretty quick.

Life in the colleges is even more cosseted, closeted and all-consuming and range in size from Lucy Cavendish *(120 undergrads) to* Trinity College *(over 700). Most colleges have around 400 undergraduates and many students experience a little shock when they emerge into the big, bad real world ('What do you mean "make my own bed?"'). The colleges themselves do vary more than Kylie's arse and a ripe melon, however, and it's a foolhardy fool who uses the pinprick picking method. Odd ceremonies and traditions persist, and it remains the case that students from 'non-Cambridge' backgrounds (state schools, women, ethnic minorities) may take longer to adjust than others, whatever the prospectuses may say. The following Push entries expose the naked truth and the neatly garbed falsehoods about the undergrad colleges. Push doesn't cover Darwin or Clare Hall, which are postgrad colleges. We suggest you write to the above address or the colleges themselves if this upsets you (letters of complaint to Push will be duly noted and used as coffee filters).*

CAMBRIDGE:

- Population: 108,863 • London: 58 miles • Oxford: 77 miles • Norwich: 57 miles
- High temp: 22 • Low temp: 1 • Rainfall: 46

The Romans didn't know what they were letting the world in for when they first settled here. If the University hadn't come to town at the end of the Middle Ages, the city would most likely have remained as the legionaries left it – a small, insignificant fenland village of eel fishers. Now, of course the city bustles all year round with snap-happy tourists, students and a number of bemused locals who don't see what all the fuss is about. All the basic ingredients are here – although a single city-centre Sainsbury's can't feed everybody, and the club scene is lame if not legless. There's tons of traditional real ale pubs, bookstores ago-go, a fabulous daily market, Kettles Yard Art Gallery and a mass of museums. The wheels of commercialism are grinding on though, and some central streets are in danger of being swamped by chain stores and restaurants – although several quirky and trendy one-offs are fighting the flood. The River Cam is the summertime highlight, littered with ducks and drunken punters at every lazy meander. Locals don't have much problem with the students – the primary civic moneyspinners – but they do have their quibbles with the University and its colleges which own most of the land in the city and plague planning permission applications. Everyone, however, hates the tourists. More or less, the centre point of Cambridge (for the purpose of measuring distances to the colleges in Push entries, at any rate) is the breath-stoppingly beautiful King's Parade.

TRAVEL:

Trains: Cambridge's *smallish* station connects to London King's Cross (three an hour), Liverpool Street, Liverpool Lime Street, Birmingham, Bristol and more. Incidentally, the station is some way beyond the city centre because the *University authorities didn't want rough common London folk coming too close to the sensitive young undergraduates – they might catch cockney diseases.*

Coaches: The *shabby* outdoor bus station on Drummond Street runs plenty of competitive services. Greenline, Premier Travel and National Express run to London, Bristol, Oxford and elsewhere.

Car: Circled by the A14 and just a few minutes off the M11 from London. Also the A428 and A10. *The city centre's practically devoid of cars and the limited multi-storey parking costs more than a night with Julia Roberts.* Students aren't allowed to keep cars without good reason.

Air: Cambridge Airport for private jets. London Stansted, 23 miles down the M11, is on a direct train link and has loads of budget flights.

Hitching: Variable – *aim towards M11 junctions, or A10/Trumpington Road for London.*

Local: Stagecoach runs bus services as *regular as prunes* to the surrounding villages, Ely, Huntingdon, the station and the outer colleges.

Taxis: *The short distances between places means cab companies are comfortable hiking up prices – similar length journeys would be cheaper in larger cities – but there are always plenty of black cabs around.* Some colleges have free taxi arrangements at night – see separate entries.

Bicycles: *Bikes are virtually a prerequisite for living in Cambridge – and it's not just the student stereotype of books in a basket, scarf flapping in the breeze – many locals push pedals too.* There are *ample* racks around town and in the colleges, *though there's also a lucrative trade in bike-napping and cycle skeletons are to be seen on railings across the city.*

CAREER PROSPECTS:

• Careers Service • No. of staff: 10 full/20 part • Unemployed after 6mths: 6%
Although '(Cantab)' after your name might not be the sure-fire guarantee of a top job it once was, a Cambridge education rarely does harm on a CV and, supposedly, employers find Cambridge students more down-to-earth than those from Oxford (who must surely then be abject space cadets). The careers people operate a load of facilities, including a substantial library, one-on-one CV/interview/advice sessions, job fairs, weekly e-mail bulletins *from the moment a student signs up till the day they die,* employer presentations and a GradLink service – which puts starry-eyed hopefuls in touch with graduates in their chosen professions.

FAMOUS ALUMNI:

See individual colleges. *Cambridge seems particularly strong on spies, Tory MPs and comedians. Draw your own conclusions.*

SPECIAL FEATURES:

Undergrads have to 'keep term', which means that they may not live more than 3 miles from the church of St Mary's in the centre of the city and they must get permission before going away during term time.

FURTHER INFO:

• Prospectuses: undergrad; postgrad; departmentals; alternative • Open days
Get online or contact the Cambridge Admissions office for prospectuses. Postgrads should contact the Board of Graduate Studies (01223) 766 606. The Colleges have their own prospectuses and open days.

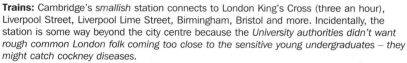

The Rathmell Building at Newport's thought to be on the site of an old Roman road, which might explain why ghostly centurions have been seen wandering the corridors.

Eight-week terms may sound cushy, but Cambridge students have anything but an easy academic ride – the constant pressure and unrelenting deadlines ruin all hopes of long vacations watching Trisha. The actual cushy part is that, three years after graduating, students get handed an MA on a plate, simply for still being alive (the University wanted to give MAs immediately upon graduation simply because they figured the gruelling study merited them, but, understandably, other universities argued them down).

340-360

POINTS

Entry points: 340-360
No. of terms: 3
Staff/student ratio: 1:12
Teaching: *****
Firsts: 24%
2.1s: 60%

Ave points: n/a
Length of terms: 8wks
Study addicts: n/a
Research: *****
2.2s: 13%
3rds: 2%

ADMISSIONS:

• Apply via UCAS
Some courses require tests in addition to interviews, namely: the National Admission Test for Law; Sixth Term Examination Papers in Maths (STEP); the Bio-Medical Admissions Test (BMAT); and the Thinking Skills Assessment Test (TSA). Several colleges and courses require a portfolio of essays to be submitted in addition to UCAS forms and the Cambridge Application Form (CAF).

At the end of the day, it's down to the colleges to say who's in or out and there's also the 'pooling' system – *sort of like a baby version of clearing. Naturally, all the pitfalls of clearing apply to pooling too.*

Cambridge has never been free from accusations of snobbery when it comes to admissions although it has a programme of widening participation in state schools.

SUBJECTS:

Best: Anatomy & Physiology; Anglo-Saxon, Norse & Celtic Studies; Archaeology; Chemical Engineering; Classics & Ancient History; Clinical Medicine; Clinical Veterinary Medicine; Economics; Education; Engineering; History of Art; Land Economy; Materials Science; Maths; Modern & Mediaeval Languages; Molecular & Organismal Biosciences; Oriental Studies; Pharmacology; Philosophy; Physics & Astronomy; Politics & Sociology; Psychology; Theology & Religious Studies.

LIBRARIES:

• 6,300,000 books • 988 study places
The *great 60s phallus* that is the University Library (www.lib.cam.ac.uk) is one of five copyright libraries in the country and as such has the right to claim a copy of every new book published in the UK. Every year, the number of new additions, if laid end to end, would extend the collection by a mile. The library attracts loads of top academics and intellectual celebrities like Germaine Greer can regularly be spotted perusing its endless shelves. *As if the UL weren't enough*, every college has its own library and there are more than 30 libraries devoted to individual subjects – *quite a few books, then.*

COMPUTERS:

• 2,800 workstations • Spend per student: £££££
Most colleges have their own *variable* computing facilities but the central computing service has a number of cutting edge IT suites for student use.

OTHER LEARNING FACILITIES:

There are more specialised facilities and labs than most students will ever realise exist, including astronomy observatory, open-access language labs, music rehearsal rooms and the ADC theatre.

CAMBRIDGE:

• Price of a pint of beer: £2.50 • Glass of wine: £2.50 • Can of Red Bull: £1.80

Cinemas: The *massive mall-style multiplex* at the Grafton Centre gets all the big movies, but the Arts Picturehouse on St Andrews Street does a range of new releases, art house, world cinema, cult classics, *good beer and really great crêpes.*

Theatres: The Arts Theatre shows popular mainstream drama and the *annual Christopher Biggins panto.* The Junction shows more eclectic material.

Pubs: *Cambridge has many a quality alehouse, although the prices seem attached to London's. Riverside pubs are popular student haunts. In particular: The Mill, which spills onto 'Beer Island' – a summertime barbecue oasis circled by the Cam; The Anchor (watch fat American tourists fall off their punts). The King's Street Run is a legendary alternative hangout, whilst quieter, quainter pubs like the Pickerel, the Castle, the Eagle (where Watson & Crick discovered DNA) provide pleasant inebriation. Other Pushplugs: The Cow (ultratrendy, cocktail deals); the Vaults; the St Radegund (smallest pub in town). Students would do better staying at home and sticking pins in their faces than going into Wetherspoons or the Rat & Parrot on weekends.*

Clubbing: *It is possible to have a good night out with the aid of large amounts of malted hops, but college ents are by far the most popular nights. Nonetheless Pushplugs: Ballare (still known by its ten years out-of-date title 'Cindy's'); the Junction (Dot Cotton gay night once a month, Boogie Wonderland on Fridays); Mondays at The Fez.*

Music venues: The Corn Exchange has big name bands, *seemingly alternating weekly with The Levellers,* while pub venues like the Man on the Moon and the Portland Arms have respectable local giggers.

Other: Mainstream comedy comes to the Corn Exchange. CAMRA (Campaign for Real Ale) hits town in summer and winter for beer festivals and the annual Strawberry Fair on Midsummer Common is a *fun hippy festival of moozic and booze. Let's not forget punting on the Cam, the archetypal Cambridge pastime* – there are punt stations at Quayside and by the Anchor, the requisite strawberries and champagne are available in Sainsbury's.

Eating out: *It's customary to take out one's parents or at least their credit cards. Many cafés are just pricey tourist traps, but there are a few pubs and restaurants that do good value, good quality food. Pushplugs: The Castle (Thai); Eraina Taverna (Greekish); the Bun Shop (tapas); Teriyaki (Japanese); Dojo's (Oriental). The burgers at the Alma are possibly divine in origin.*

UNIVERSITY:

Bars: The University has no central bar of its own but the individual colleges have at least one, *varying from airport lounges like* Trinity *to opium dens like* King's *and cutesy pubbettes like* Pembroke. *Some are for college members and their guests only, but it's never too hard to crash.*

Theatres: The newly refurbished, fully equipped and student-run ADC theatre shows two productions four nights a week, year-round, *ranging from the inspired to the despised.* There's also the *tiny* Playroom for more intimate performances and many colleges have their own performance spaces, notably Queens' Fitzpatrick Hall. In May Week, almost every college offers some kind of drama in its gardens, usually Shakespeare. Cantabrian thespians hit Edinburgh by the dozen every year.

Film: Most colleges have their own film club, which usually amounts to rented videos in the JCR, although some are more professional (especially at St John's, Queens', Peterhouse and the Cambridge Union Society). Being run by students, these, of course, show just about anything students might want to see and *often just what the projectionist wants to.*

Music venues: The University Concert Hall hosts mainly classical concerts including the University's many orchestras, choirs and chapel music groups. *The college JCRs are prepared to use almost any room available for more contemporary noises.*

Clubbing: In-college ents are the biggest nights going – *no one minds how loud, dingy and sweaty they can be.* CUSU tries to organise a big out-of-town event every year – *it's always a failure.*

Comedy/Cabaret: The Cambridge Footlights Revue has given birth to *some of the world's best chuckle-mongers* including half the Monty Python Team, Peter Cook & Dudley Moore, Smith & Jones, Fry & Laurie, Clive Anderson, Clive James, Emma Thompson, Tony Slattery and so on ad ridiculum, *although the talent scouts haven't been so ready with their chequebooks in recent years. Cambridge Comedy is unkillable, though, and the Footlights show goes on (and on and...).* Occasional comedy nights in the Colleges *often surpass them in the hilarity stakes.*

Food: Livers-in (ie. the vast majority) eat in college dining halls, but there are also cafeterias and sandwich bars in some departments and the University Library. *Meals are cheap* but that's because they're subsidised by the Kitchen Fixed Charge that all students pay at the beginning of term. So even if you go out for the other kind of KFC, you've paid for your meal already. All colleges hold 'formal halls' at least once a week – some of the larger ones daily – which are generally formal table-service affairs with *better than average food. For many students they're a good excuse to get trashed on cheap wine and the traditional practice of 'pennying' (putting a penny in someone's glass, obliging them to down the contents in order to stop the queen from drowning, or something equally ridiculous).* Big, candle-lit, roast-pig-with-fruit-rammed-up-every-orifice dinners still go on, just not every day.

Balls: *Wild parties in penguin suits and ball frocks which usually end up covered in strawberries and vomit. Most colleges have one (or share one with another college) and some are huge (such as <u>Trinity's</u>). The one thing they almost all have in common is a discussion with the bank manager – a double ticket can cost in excess of £180 (plus the dry-cleaning bill) for 11 hours of all-inclusive extravagance and big-name bands. Some colleges have cheaper versions with fewer thrills and frills. The odd thing is the balls are almost all in June and yet are called May Balls. May Week also includes 'Suicide Sunday' – nothing to do with exam pressure but a day to begin alcoholic consumption at 9am and carry on until oblivion.*

Others: *Terribly civilised entertainments flourish, especially in the last few weeks of the summer term when exams are over and all students have to do is hang around sipping Pimms during the annual college/society/faculty garden party crawl.*

SOCIAL & POLITICAL

CAMBRIDGE UNIVERSITY STUDENTS' UNION:

• 6 sabbaticals • NUS member

The colleges' JCRs and MCRs have really plugged the gap that students' unions usually fill and CUSU (which, to be fair, is good at what it does) doesn't have much of a profile – in part due to the continuing non-existence of a central SU building, for which it's been fighting for years. CUSU co-ordinates many campaigns (Target Schools, Green and so on) and concentrates on keeping the wheels of student admin turning. *Amazingly,* it's one of the poorest student unions in the country and its sabbaticals are amongst the poorest paid – *its facilities are also a poor reflection of Cambridge's stature.* CUSU publishes various (*largely unread*) handbooks (Societies Guide, Diary, Alternative Prospectus, termly paper, Sex Guide – 'wear gloves, use lube' – and Green Guide) *and lashings of political hackery. However, the politics is limited, because most students get all the (non-party) politics they need through their own JCR. On the quiet, CUSU does all sorts of valiant representation and welfare work in the University*, trains and advises JCR officers and co-ordinates more societies than there are days in the academic year.

SU FACILITIES:

Facilities at the CUSU Offices include: *cheap* photocopier, shop, fax, stationery, condoms; minibus hire. Practically speaking, it aims at providing for JCRs who then provide amenities for individual students.

CLUBS (NON-SPORTING):

This list doesn't include college-based societies. What do you want, the moon on a stick? Abacus; Action Aid; Air Squadron; Anglo-Japanese; Anti-Bloodsports; Archimideans; Art; Assassin's Guild; Baby Milk Action; Backgammon; Baha'i; Ballet; Bangladesh; Birders; Black & Asian Caucus; Bone Marrow; Brass Band; Bridge (community); Buddhist; Campus Children's Holidays; Canadian; Canal; Cannabis Legalisation; Ceilidh; Chamber Choir; Chocolate; Christian Music; Christian Science; Cobblers; Cognitive Science; Comic (the paper variety not stand-up); Community Church; Computer; Contact (helping the elderly); Cuba; Cycle Safety; Dance; Detective Fiction; Diamond Way; Diplomacy (game); Disabilities; Dr Who; Duke of Edinburgh Award; Early Music; Eating Disorders; Enterprise (Star Trek); Environment Action; Esperanto; Essex; European; European Theatre Group (international touring company); Excitium; Explorers & Travellers; Field Sports; Film & TV; First Aid; Fisher Society (Catholic); Footlights; Freaky Comics; Free (libertarian); Freemasonry; French; Friends of the Earth; Gamelan (gongs); German; Go (game); Greenlink; Grimsoc (professional Northerners); Hellenic; Heraldic; Hillwalking; Hindu; Hispanic; Holistic Medicine; Hong Kong & China; Hungarian; Imfundo (South African Educational Trust); India; International; Iran; Israel; Italian; Jews & Christians; Jomborg the New (fantasy); Jugglers; Kettle's Yard (visual arts); Light Entertainment; Link Africa; Linkline; Literary; Madhouse Theatre; Mah-Jong; Malaysia & Singapore; Marlowe Dramatic; Massage; Medical Action; Methodist; Middle East; Mummers; Mystical; Officers' Training Corps; Opera; Orthodox; Overlanders (rough travel); Oxfam; Pakistan; Poetry; Pottery; Progressive Jewish; Punjabi; Quorum; Radio; Railway; Raleigh; Revolver & Pistol; Roleplaying; RN; Science Fiction; Scientists for the Earth; Scottish & Irish; Scouts & Guides; Seres (Chinese magazine); Sheila & Her Dog (relapse into childhood); Slavonic & East European; Sri Lanka; Strathsprey & Reel (Scottish dancing); Student Christian Movement; Support for the Homeless; Survival (tribal rights); Tibet Support; Tolkien; Transcendence; Troubadours; Ugandan Children; Underwater Exploration; Union Society; Union Society Boycott; United Nations; Up Shit Creek Without a Paddle (ignore exams); Visual Arts; Welsh; West End; Wine; Young Friends (Quakers). **See also Clubs tables.**

OTHER ORGANISATIONS:

Media: *Proper papers* Varsity and the Cambridge Student (TCS) vie for the attention of both students and locals on a weekly basis. Varsity is the elder – the 1st student paper to go full colour – *but has become more tabloidy in recent years.* Other publications come and go, but *Arsity* the satirical online mag *is worth a glance.* Cambridge University Radio (CUR) broadcasts from <u>Churchill</u> to nowhere in particular. A few *unfortunate* local cable-owners unintentionally pick up the programmes produced by Cambridge University Television (CUTE).

Rag: Colleges compete in raising money for the University's charity Rag. With competition spurring them on, they raise vast sums every year. The biggest event of the year is the Rag Blind Date where students are assigned dates based on how fit the Rag reps think they are, *then spend an entire evening failing to sleep with a stranger.*

Student Community Action: As shown by the list above, there are a number of Cambridge clubs with a conscience. Some of these and other organisations – in all about 50 – do voluntary work in all sectors of the community.

Music: Cambridge offers *the perfect opportunity to get together and make sweet music,* mostly of the classical variety with the Chamber Orchestra (CUCO), the Music Society (CUMS), the *dangerously acronymed* Cambridge University Musical Theatre Society or in any of the many college orchestras, choirs, etc. Contemporary musicians either form bands the usual way or use the Musicians Directory to find each other. Basically, whatever toots your flute, there'll be a society, club or association devoted to it.

RELIGIOUS:

Every denomination of Christianity is here and virtually no religion is unrepresented (including a few religious orders started by students wanting to avoid poll tax in the 90s). Most colleges have a CofE or multi-faith chapel/chaplain, <u>Corpus Christi</u> has a mosque. Try the following for some *communal God-squadding*: the Christian Union (Anglican); the Fisher Society (Catholic); the Methodists; the Islamic Society (linked to local mosque); not one, but two Jewish societies, Progressive and Orthodox (with a synagogue, rabbi and kosher restaurant of their own) and so on. There are local places of worship for Hindus, Sikhs and Buddhists.

PAID WORK:

• <u>Paid work: term-time 10%; hols 50%</u>

Cambridge University authorities officially debar their students from working more than six hours a week. As a result, many students ignore them and get bar or baby-sitting jobs around town, and most take on temporary holiday work. Life-modelling opportunities for local artists are common and can provide some quick cash for those who don't mind getting their kit off.

SPORTS

• Recent successes: rowing • BUSA Ranking: 7

Face it, Cambridge breeds many more than its fair share of sporting deities. Many of the rulers of rugby, captains of cricket and angels of athletics have come running from Cambridge's sporting fields. However even the weediest wimps are encouraged to exert themselves in anything from tiddlywinks to boxing, but most often, rowing. Intercollegiate rivalries perk up the sporting calendar no end, as do Varsity fixtures with the <u>University of Oxford</u> – the annual boat race is still a huge national event. Whatever the game it's probably played in a college society or team and, if not there, in the University as a whole.

SPORTS FACILITIES:

Each College has its own facilities to a varying degree, but the University as a whole doesn't have all that much to call its own, except for *endless* playing fields, a squash centre, three new indoor cricket lanes, a gym and one of the country's few real tennis clubs – *a cross between tennis and extreme violence.* There's funding galore for redressing deficiencies, however, and the city itself offers several important amenities. Kelsey Kerridge Sports Centre has a swimming pool, climbing wall and sports courts, and the River Cam offers the rowing teams, canoeists and inadvertent swimmers plenty of moist recreation.

SPORTING CLUBS:

See individual college entries for the bigger picture. American Football; Boxing; Caving; Clay Pigeon Shooting; Croquet; Drag Hunt; Eton Fives; Field Sports; Gymnastics; Hang Gliding; Hill Walking; Korfball; Lacrosse; Life Saving; Parachuting; Pétanque; Polo; Power Lifting; Rambling; Real Tennis; Revolvers & Pistols; Rifles; Rugby League; Surf Squad; Trampoline; Ultimate Frisbee; Windsurfing. **See also Clubs tables.**

ATTRACTIONS:

As if the University's own sports didn't satisfy every possible desire to spectate, there's always Cambridge United & City Football and Rugby Clubs. *The more Sloaney set can don their toff hats and pop off to Newmarket for the races and lose all daddy's money.*

ACCOMMODATION

IN COLLEGE:

• Catered: 95% • Insurance premium: £

Availability: *One of Cambridge's best features* is being able to live in college accommodation. Most colleges have room for all 1st years and finalists, and 2nd years who can't be squeezed into the college itself will usually be offered some kind of college-owned housing nearby. *The rooms vary from palatial suites to pokey cupboards without central heating, although most are fairly impressive.* Older rooms around the college courts can look spectacular from the outside, *but the more modern tend to offer better living conditions. Sharing a room is rare, but sets (two linked rooms with lounge/study area) are fairly common. On the flipside, there can be a reality-shock when students graduate after having been shielded for three years from the unpleasantness of cooking, cleaning and domestic budgeting.* There's limited availability for couples and even less for students with children. At many colleges, the best rooms are reserved for Scholars – those who get firsts in exams. Each college makes its own arrangements so check the college entries.

Car parking: *Students aren't technically allowed to bring cars to their colleges, but some outer colleges (where parking is less impossible) aren't as staunch sticklers for policy.*

EXTERNALLY:

• Ave rent: £66

Availability: Accommodation can be tough to source. *The hand-me-down housing method has kept the severest problems at bay but students do have to keep an eye open for a few landlords who're willing to make a fast buck from a student's bad luck.* Usually livers-out share houses but digs (a room in a landlord's house) are not uncommon. *Relations with the* local community are generally pretty good and there are no student ghettos, although quirky, cosmopolitan Mill Road and, although rarely from choice, Milton Road are popular. The only place students should rule out is the north of the city, because it's easy enough to find something closer. Students who choose to live out have to find somewhere within 3 miles of the city centre.

Housing help: For fast relief students can refer to the Accommodation Syndicate (18 Silver Street) who keep a list of suitable accommodation, *often a little pricier than those on the open market but always up to scratch.*

WELFARE

SERVICES:
- Lesbian/Gay/Bisexual Officer • Women's Officer • Mature Students' Officer
- International Students' Officer • Disabilities Officer • Nightline
- College counsellors: 4 full/7 part • Crime rating: !!!

CUSU has no full-time welfare staff – that's another job for the colleges – but there is the University Counselling Service, which many students turn to at some point during their time here: academic pressure is high. There are support groups of every flavour, including HIV/AIDS, and most colleges have a society of some description for postgrads.

Health: Most colleges have their own nurses or doctors and the University operates a dental service for students' teething troubles.

Women: Several colleges have only started to allow women students over the last two decades and *some are still reeling from the shock. As female numbers grow the situation and the facilities improve,* but the academic staff of some departments and colleges are still ominously predominantly male. *The prevailing chauvinism is that of a previous generation and some women end up pedalling on a lower gear just to show they can. The most blatant m-c-piggery rears its head in some college bars where the tone can border on the oppressive.* But, in the face of aggression, women have taken steps. There's a Women's Council, Women's Executive, Women's Handbook, free rape alarms and so on.

Crèches/Nursery: Queens' has run a University-wide staff & student crèche for some years and Gonville & Caius is now following suit. The University nursery has 88 places for staff and students' kids.

Lesbian/Gay/Bisexual: Cambridge has the largest LGB Society in the UK and *there's a long tradition of relative sexual tolerance in the University.* Gay icons such as E M Forster, Sir Ian McKellen and Stephen Fry have passed through its portals.

Disabilities: Cambridge was not originally built with wheelchairs in mind, although it is blessed with a lack of hills. However, a fair amount of building has been going on over the last 20 years and there has been a genuine attempt to make these new buildings accessible at least. Individual colleges have provisions for disabled students. The Disability Resource Centre (DRC) has a number of advisers and resources. For sight-impaired students, large print or Braille exam papers are available. *Access in the colleges varies, but students with motor disabilities should look at Robinson, Fitzwilliam and New Hall first.*

Crime: Not a huge problem in the city, *but trouble lurks on open spaces like Jesus Green and Parker's Piece should be avoided at night.*

Drugs: The colleges officially have a zero tolerance policy, *but cannabis possession isn't a hanging offence (walk on the roof however, and you're out). Harder drugs, particularly cocaine, aren't uncommon among male sloanes – but then, they can get away with anything, really.*

FINANCE:
- Ave debt per year: £1,488

Fees: Cambridge will charge the whole three grand for tuition fees from 2006, but bursaries dependent on parental income will cover the full whack. There'll be up to £5,000 a year for mature students.

Support: Most financial assistance comes from the colleges and takes the form of hardship funds, academic prizes or *archaic* bursaries (cash for Catholic girls whose parents converted from Judaism, for instance).

Christ's College, Cambridge

• *This College is part of the <u>University of Cambridge</u> and students are entitled to use its facilities.*
Christ's College, Cambridge, CB2 3BU Tel: (01223) 334 953
E-mail: admissions@christs.cam.ac.uk Website: www.christs.cam.ac.uk
Christ's College Student Union, Cambridge, CB2 3BU Tel: (01223) 465 545
E-mail: christs-jcr@lists.cam.ac.uk Website: www.christs.cam.ac.uk/ccsu

Christ's is only 300 metres from King's Parade and is slap bang in the middle of the city, right by the shops and the bus station (and Burger King). It is one of the older and most beautiful colleges, built around four courts (with some parts dating back to the 15th century), except for 'the Typewriter', the 1970s accommodation block, *which, visually, is a poke in the eye, but, socially, a pat on the back. Academic standards are very high which can cause pressure (there are showers in the library for students working a little too hard). The bar used to shut at 8.30pm until a recent campaign to keep it open, and there's a cheerful, supportive, sociable atmosphere.*

Sex ratio (M:F): 58:42	Founded: 1448
Full-time u'grads: 440	Part-time: 0
Postgrads: 120	Mature: n/a
State:private school: 47:41	Disabled: n/a
Academic ranking: 2	International: 12%

Smallish Buttery Bar; two bops/term, biennial balls; theatre/venue (200); film soc; Plumb auditorium for recitals; music rehearsal rooms; drama *strong* at the purpose built New Court Theatre; audio/tv centre. Christ's Pieces termly newspaper (£1); Milton Society for dining/debating. Three libraries (120,000 books); 40 computers, 24-hr; internet access points in all rooms. *Strong* Christian Union; CofE chapel. JCR taxi reimbursement scheme with College; vending machines. Successes in men's football and hockey; squash courts on site, but most sports facilities (four football, one cricket and two rugby pitches, two squash courts) a mile away; new boats in the boat club; active societies for table tennis, pool and, erm, tiddlywinks. All live in College or in Jesus Lane hostels; *nice rooms let down a little by lack of oven in kitchens.* Canteen and formal meals. CCTV; college sick bay; nurse; late-night taxi service; free rape alarms; LGB officer; international students officer; women's officer (and men's officer if welfare officer isn't a bloke). GBT and International reps. Means-tested bursaries and academic scholarships.

FAMOUS ALUMNI:

John Milton (poet, loser of Paradise); Charles Darwin (revolutionary evolutionary); Lord Mountbatten of Burma; Sacha Baron-Cohen (aka Ali G, *booyakasha*); C P Snow (writer); Richard Whiteley (Countdown *love-God*).

Churchill College, Cambridge

• *This College is part of the <u>University of Cambridge</u> and students are entitled to use its facilities.*
Churchill College, Storey's Way, Cambridge, CB3 ODS Tel: (01223) 336202
E-mail: admissions@chu.cam.ac.uk Website: www.chu.cam.ac.uk
Churchill JCR, Storey's Way, Cambridge, CB3 ODS
E-mail: jcr-president@chu.cam.ac.uk Website: http://jcr.chu.cam.ac.uk

A mile from King's Parade *and looking rather prison-like, Churchill isn't the most attractive or best located of colleges. It is however one of the more modern, progressive and larger, and home of the University radio. Its newness offers other advantages over more traditional Cambridge colleges in terms of facilities and space. More students come from state schools and there are more scientists, so pretensions and stereotypes get funny looks rather than approval.*

Sex ratio (M:F): 67:33	**Founded: 1960**
Full-time u'grads: 479	**Part-time: 0**
Postgrads: 319	**Mature: 1%**
State:private school: 63:35	**Disabled: 48**
Academic ranking: 19	**International: 15%**

Two bars; bops on Friday; happy hours at weekends; termly event with Fitzwilliam's; spring ball; film theatre (cap 300); GODS theatre group; jazz; professional recitals; orchestra; soundproof rooms; party room. Winston mag for goss; University radio. Four libraries (45,000 books); 37 computers, 24-hr; free language and computer courses offered to all students. Chapel. Sports pitches; squash courts; multigym. All 1st/2nd years and 50% of finalists live in; biggest dining hall in Cambridge, non-formal; some smoking areas; phone & computer sockets in all rooms; cafeteria, access to self-catering; veggie options; kitchens *reasonable*; CCTV; swipe cards. Nurse; counselling; *some disabled facilities*; scholarship; travel grants; hardship fund.

Clare College, Cambridge

• **This College is part of the University of Cambridge and students are entitled to use its facilities.**
Clare College, Trinity Lane, Cambridge, CB2 1TL Tel: (01223) 333 200
E-mail: admissions@clare.cam.ac.uk Website: www.clare.cam.ac.uk
Union of Clare Students, Memorial Court, Queens Road, Cambridge, CB2 1TL

Tel: (01223) 333 200 E-mail: ucs@clare.cam.ac.uk Website: http://ucs.clare.cam.ac.uk

Clare's *proud* of its history – it's the second oldest college in Cambridge, with the oldest bridge, which links the parts of the college that sit on either bank of the Cam. It's a *gorgeous and gleaming* riverside college with an *unpretentious* attitude and a *healthy* social mix. Clare Cellars hosts bands and DJs a couple of times a week and has a strong rep for jazz. *Students from other colleges (Push will let them remain anonymous) have been heard to say that, if they had their time over again, they'd put Clare at the top of their list for applications.*

Sex ratio (M:F): 50:50	**Founded: 1326**
Full-time u'grads: 469	**Part-time: 0**
Postgrads: 191	**Mature: 1%**
State:private school: 60:40	**Disabled: 9**
Academic ranking: 4	**International: 8%**

Atmospheric cellars (bar cap 200) have a University-wide ents reputation; two venues – bar and a chill-out room; pool table, juke box; weekly theme nights, DJs, jazz; comedy; extensive gardens used for annual May Ball attended by 950 students (*most romantic in Cambridge*). College paper, Clareification. Two libraries (33,000 books); 24-hr law reading room *for reading law, natch*; 40 computers; all rooms have internet access. CofE chapel used for classical recitals; semi-professional choir. Sports fields (4 acres) $1\frac{1}{2}$ miles away; football and rowing strong. 1st, 2nd and 3rd years are guaranteed rooms but a few 2nd years live out. Secure bike compound. Most students eat in the dining hall (Italian bias with veggie option). CCTV;SU welfare officers, nurse; counselling; hardship fund, travel and book grants.

FAMOUS ALUMNI:

Sir David Attenborough (TV naturalist); Chris Kelly (ex Food and Drink); Peter Lilley MP (Con); Paul Mellon (philanthropist); Matthew Parris (ex-MP, Times sketch writer); Siegfried Sassoon (war poet); Cecil Sharp (folk music historian); Richard Stilgoe (entertainer/lyricist); James Watson (discovered DNA); Andrew Wiles (proved Fermat's Last Theorem).

Corpus Christi College, Cambridge

• *This College is part of the* <u>University of Cambridge</u> *and students are entitled to use its facilities.*
Corpus Christi College, Cambridge, CB2 1RH Tel:(01223) 338 000
E-mail: admissions@corpus.cam.ac.uk Website: www.corpus.cam.ac.uk
Corpus Christi JCR, Corpus Christi College, Cambridge, CB2 1RH
Website: www.corpus.cam.ac.uk/jcr

Corpus Christi, founded by the townsfolk to train priests, is found downtown (on King's Parade), more or less opposite <u>St Catharine's</u>. *The dark stone of many of its buildings can appear daunting at first glance but after a while the shadowy gatehouse becomes warm and welcoming – like the students inside.* The Old Court is mid-14th century; its *hardly modern* equivalent New Court was completed in 1827 by the designer of the National Gallery. It's one of the smallest colleges and *retains a tight community and a strong identity as a consequence.*

Sex ratio (M:F): 62:38	**Founded: 1352**
Full-time u'grads: 257	**Part-time: 0**
Postgrads: 182	**Mature: 1%**
State:private school: 58:42	**Disabled: 3**
Academic ranking: 10	**International: 15%**

Bar with regular 'slacks' – live music – and bops; *enthusiastic* drama, owns the experimental Playroom theatre in town; two or three concerts in the Master's Lodge each term; May Ball every year. Two libraries – a third is being built that will more than double the book stock (over 100,000 books including the largest collection of medieval manuscripts in the UK); 15 PCs/Macs; Ethernet in all rooms. Weekly newsletter (Corporeal); CofE chapel; *involved* JCR. *Good rowers and ruggers*; 3 acres of sports fields 10 mins away; squash courts, bowling green, snooker room. Everyone lives in; gates closed at 11pm but students have keys; thrice weekly candlelit dinner with waiter service; cafeteria. Three rooms for mobility-impaired students; *access not brilliant.* Finance tutor to help with money worries; bursaries, scholarships, hardship fund.

FAMOUS ALUMNI:

Christopher Isherwood (writer); Christopher Marlowe (playwright); Lord Sieff (M&S); E P Thompson (historian).

Downing College, Cambridge

• *This College is part of the* <u>University of Cambridge</u> *and students are entitled to use its facilities.*
Downing College, Cambridge, CB2 1DQ Tel: (01223) 334 826
E-mail: admissions@dow.cam.ac.uk Website: www.dow.cam.ac.uk
Junior Common Room, Downing College, Cambridge, CB2 1DQ
Tel: (01223) 334 825 E-mail: jcrofficers@dow.cam.ac.uk Website: www.downingjcr.co.uk

A little over 500 metres from King's Parade is the *elegant* Downing College, a *welcoming* expanse of *spacious* lawns and neoclassical architecture from the last 200 years. *It's sat roughly where town meets gown geographically speaking, a tad further out than the other city centre colleges – perhaps this is why its students are more down-to-earth. The College is noted for sporting achievements, but there's plenty of opportunity at a lower level if your idea of exertion is feeding the vast squirrel population. Social indulgence can take precedence over banner-waving, but Downing students are active on the University-wide hack scene as well. Music is also strong.*

Sex ratio (M:F): 56:44	Founded: 1800
Full-time u'grads: 440	Part-time: 0
Postgrads: 250	Mature: 1%
State:private school: 51:49	Disabled: 180
Academic ranking: 17	International: 6%

Large, *plush* bar, longest hours in the University – *historic Fountain pub close by*; student bands, cabaret, films and drama in Howard Building (theatre, cap 120), *luvvie-ed up* drama soc shows in the Dining Hall; weekly bops in Party Room – cheesy/jazz/theme discos and karaoke; music practice rooms; annual June Event for 1,200 partygoers. Bi-termly college mag, Griffin; library (47,000 books); 40 computers, 24-hr; intranet sockets in most bedrooms (*small* charge). CofE chapel; Student community action group. *Sportilicious – strong on rowing, football, rugby and hockey*; new boathouse plus 9 acres of playing fields a mile away, gym on-site. Everyone lives in (£43-83); *quality* rooms; CCTV, entry phones; two flats for couples; pay-as-you-eat meals; three candlelit formals a week; LGB, women's, men's, mature, international, postgrad and ethnic minorities officers; nurse, physio and nearby medical practice; free pregnancy tests and attack alarms; fortnightly women's council meeting; *good access*, adapted rooms; hardship fund, travel grants.

FAMOUS ALUMNI:

Michael Apted (director, James Bond); Mike Atherton (former England cricket captain); Quentin Blake (illustrator); John Cleese (comedian); Andy Hamilton (comedian & script writer); Thandie Newton (actress); Trevor Nunn (theatre director); Michael Winner (*bad* film director/restaurant critic).

Emmanuel College, Cambridge

• **This College is part of the University of Cambridge and students are entitled to use its facilities.**
Emmanuel College, Cambridge, CB2 3AP Tel: (01223) 334 290
E-mail: admissions@emma.cam.ac.uk Website: www.emma.cam.ac.uk
Junior Common Room, Emmanuel College, Cambridge, CB2 3AP
E-mail: online@ecsu.org.uk Website: http://ecsu.org.uk

Emma (as Emmanuel's affectionately known), 500 metres from King's Parade, is a collection of *dignified* 16th-century buildings, 60s accommodation blocks, *elegant* gardens and a duck pond, replete with 50 resident ducks and *cute but stupid* ducklings every spring. *Emmanuel's perceived by other students as unpretentious and approachable, and its students are well represented in University activities.*

Sex ratio (M:F): 49:51	Founded: 1584
Full-time u'grads: 494	Part-time: n/a
Postgrads: 176	Mature: n/a
State:private school: 56:44	Disabled: 20
Academic ranking: 1	International: 4%

Refurbed bar (cap 200); ball/event every year; theatre in new Queen's building; films, DJ nights, quizzes, live funk, indie and jazz nights; college music and drama societies. Weekly Roar mag. Library (60,000 books); 30 computers, 24-hr. Chapel designed by Christopher Wren. Sports fields ($2\frac{1}{2}$ acres) 20 mins away; squash courts; swimming pool; boats; cricket, volleyball, hockey and rowing *success*. Most undergrads live in; internet connections in most rooms. Optional formals; veggie and vegan options. CCTV; part-time nurse; part-time counsellor; free condoms and pregnancy tests; exam-time stressbusters (yoga, study skills workshops and bouncy castles); women's group & officer; disabilities and access officers.

FAMOUS ALUMNI:

Graham Chapman (Monty Python's Brian); Michael Frayn (playwright); Eddie George (ex-Gov, Bank of England); Griff Rhys Jones (comic); F R Leavis (lit crit); Lord Cecil Parkinson (Tory); Rory McGrath (TV *personality*).

Fitzwilliam College, Cambridge

• *This College is part of the* <u>*University of Cambridge*</u> *and students are entitled to use its facilities.*

Fitzwilliam College, Huntingdon Road, Cambridge, CB3 ODG
Tel: (01223) 332 000 E-mail: admissions@fitz.cam.ac.uk Website: www.fitz.cam.ac.uk
Junior Members' Association, Fitzwilliam College, Huntingdon Road, Cambridge, CB3 ODG

Fitz isn't a typical Cambridge college. For a start, its main buildings are modern and redbrick. It admits more state school students than most. *It's friendly, down to earth and not at all claustrophobic or overwhelming.* It's also set apart from the other colleges, a mile from King's Parade at the top of Cambridge's only hill (*well, a shallow slope*) next to <u>New Hall</u> in the city's *businessy area*. The location may contribute to its *sociable atmosphere* – students have to make more of an effort than most to meet people outside the college walls.

Sex ratio (M:F): 61:39	**Founded: 1869**
Full-time u'grads: 468	**Part-time: n/a**
Postgrads: 202	**Mature: 1%**
State:private school: 70:30	**Disabled: 15**
Academic ranking: 15	**International: 8%**

Large *departure-loungey* bar host quizzes and karaoke; Fitz Entz (£6) twice a term, *big and very popular*; concerts in chapel; Fitz Barbershop swing band; regular theatre; brand new 250-cap venue for theatre, cinema, concerts and sports; termly Events (miniballs); annual ball. *Good JCR facilities*; 'Fitz News' newsletter. Library (38,000 books); 40 computers, 24-hr; cyber café. Chapel; chaplain. Good sports fields (7 acres) including a boathouse 600m away plus facilities on site; tennis and squash courts, multigym; football *success*. All years can live in College or College-owned houses; internet points in rooms. CCTV, swipe cards; shared nurse, welfare officers; free taxis and attack alarms; Linkline listening service. Two en-suite disabled rooms; chairlift access; extra exam time for dyslexic students; ramps.

FAMOUS ALUMNI:

Nick Clarke (broadcaster); Norman Lamont (ex-Chancellor); Christopher Martin-Jenkins (cricket commentator); Derek Pringle (cricketer); Dr David Starkey (historian).

Girton College, Cambridge

• *This College is part of the* <u>*University of Cambridge*</u> *and students are entitled to use its facilities.*

Girton College, Huntingdon Road, Cambridge, CB3 OJG Tel: (01223) 338 972
E-mail: admissions@girton.cam.ac.uk Website: www.girton.cam.ac.uk
Girton College JCR, Girton College, Huntingdon Road, Cambridge, CB3 OJG
Tel: (01223) 338 898 E-mail: president@girtonjcr.cam Website: www.girtonjcr.com

Girton is $2\frac{1}{2}$ miles from King's Parade and the city centre (*a bike is pretty much compulsory*). It started life as a women-only college, before going mixed in 1979. *Nowadays, it's one of Cambridge's most liberal, relaxed and actively fun colleges.* Being out of town gives it over 50 acres of grounds with Gothic redbrick buildings. *The distance means integration with the rest of the University is rare, although Girtonians seem quite proud of their distinctive lifestyle.*

Sex ratio (M:F): 50:50	**Founded: 1869**
Full-time u'grads: 539	**Part-time: 0**
Postgrads: 182	**Mature: 2%**
State:private school: 50:50	**Disabled: 4**
Academic ranking: 25	**International: 15%**

College bar, darts, pool and table football tournaments; regular ents; film nights, annual garden party; annual revue; *successful and comparatively cheap* spring ball; dramatic society; the prestigious choir tours and records choral CDs, frequent classical performances. JCR newsletters: termly Angle and *anarchic* fortnightly bogsheet; *vivacious but apolitical* JCR with *staunch green* policies. JCR provides common rooms, vending machines, photocopying, laminating and binding facility. One *massive and new-smelling* library (100,000 books); 35 24-hr computers; net access in most rooms; JCR computer reps. Chapel. *Well-funded sports* facilities on site (the only college with an indoor heated swimming pool) and the bike ride into town *keeps Girtonians fit; good record in football and rugby*. All students live in (£73/32wks); *rents on the up; full* kitchens; weekly formal meals – *less rowdy thanks to iron-fisted porters, revolution imminent;* reciprocal dining rights with <u>Clare</u>, <u>Pembroke</u> and <u>Downing</u>. Car park. Free taxis at weekends and to exams; self-defence classes; CCTV; card-operated entry; night porter. International students', Ethnic Minorities', Women's & LGBT officers; ethnic minorities shadowing scheme; free condoms *galore*, pregancy tests. Prizes for firsts, hardship scholarships, travel grants.

FAMOUS ALUMNI:

Lady Brenda Hale (first woman lawlord); Axman Luge (journalist); Queen Margarethe of Denmark; Joan Robinson (economist); David Starkey (TV historian); Arianna Stassinopoulos (writer); Angela Tilby (writer and TV producer); Sandi Toksvig (*dinky* comedian).

Gonville & Caius College, Cambridge

• This College is part of the <u>University of Cambridge</u> and students are entitled to use its facilities.
Gonville & Caius College, Cambridge, CB2 1TA Tel: (01223) 332 447
E-mail: admissions@cai.cam.ac.uk Website: www.cai.cam.ac.uk

Gonville & Caius Students' Union, Gonville & Caius College, Cambridge, CB2 1TA
Tel: (01223) 332 447

The most important thing about Gonville & Caius is to pronounce its name correctly. Gonville's okay, apart from sounding like a Muppet character and most people drop that bit anyway, but Caius is pronounced 'keys'. Caius is based on two sites, 8 mins walk apart. The main building's at one end of King's Parade and is centred on the fine *old renaissance Caius Court, next to* French-Chateau-style *Tree Court, the only college court in Cambridge with, er, trees. The other site is Harvey Court, the 1st year accommodation block, designed in the 60s in concrete and grey brick (*and the worse for it*), and situated on the other side of the river on the Backs (meadow banks). It's known for having the worst hall in Cambridge, but there's a friendly enough atmosphere and a good social mix.*

Sex ratio (M:F): 57:43	**Founded: 1348**
Full-time u'grads: 562	**Part-time: n/a**
Postgrads: 226	**Mature: 1%**
State:private school: 55:45	**Disabled: 0**
Academic ranking: 5	**International: 15%**

One bar; Bateman concert room; annual ball. Caiustone newsletter; many drinking/dining clubs; *active* music soc. Working library and old library (90,000 books); 52 PCs, some 24-hr. Chapel; CofE chaplain. *Good* sports facilities in College and 400m away (3 acres and a bar). All 1st and 3rd years live in hall, 2nd years in *crummier* College hostels; almost all rooms have internet points; *was worst food in Cambridge, getting better*; occasional formal meals; some accommodation for married students. Swipe cards; nurse, pregnancy tests, free condoms; ethnic minorities' officer; women's officer; access officer; bursaries; scholarships; grants and book grants. Ground floor accommodation and ramps for disabled students; lift access to Cockerell Library.

FAMOUS ALUMNI:

Harold Abrahams (Olympic runner, featured in Chariots of Fire); Kenneth Clark MP (Late Con MP); Francis Crick (Nobel prize-winning geneticist); David Frost (broadcaster); William Harvey (discovered circulation of blood); Stephen Hawking (scientist); Sir Nevill Mott (Nobel prizewinning physicist); Titus Oates (of Popish plot fame); Dr Venn (as in Venn diagram).

> The oldest student to graduate from the University of Kent was over 80.

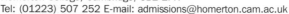

Homerton College, Cambridge

• *This College is part of the University of Cambridge and students are entitled to use its facilities.*
Homerton College, Cambridge, CB2 2PH
Tel: (01223) 507 252 E-mail: admissions@homerton.cam.ac.uk
Website: www.homerton.cam.ac.uk
Homerton Union of Students, Homerton College, Cambridge, CB2 2PH
Tel: (01223) 507 236 Website: www.hus.org.uk

Homerton's probably the least Cambridgey Cambridge college, because of its location (2 miles out of town) and its academic set-up (formerly education, though most subjects are now available). It's less wealthy than some other colleges so has to court the conference trade. It's an outgoing, enterprising place filled with 'can-do' types who make the most of what's on offer. Students tend to socialise in College, but Homerton types have made their University-level mark in sport, journalism and more.

Sex ratio (M:F): 30:70	Founded: 1695
Full-time u'grads: 550	Part-time: n/a
Postgrads: 617	Mature: 6%
State:private school: 77:23	Disabled: 33
Academic ranking: 24	International: 7%

Bar; live bands in the Main Hall (300); dance/drama studio; steel band; choirs; chamber orchestra; wind band; annual ball; art room; politically active JCR. Hush, College mag. Library (60,000 books); 70 computers, 24-hr. Sports fields (25 acres) on site; squash courts. All-day buttery; dining hall; *food can still get better*. Accommodation for all 1st yrs, and those finalists that want it; *very expensive but good quality*; internet access in rooms. Nurse; half-term crèche. Mature, international, LGB, women's, ethnic minorities' and skills training officers. Travel and choral scholarships; hardship fund; mature student bursaries. All accommodation has disabled access.

FAMOUS ALUMNI:

Julie Covington (actress/singer); Nick Hancock (They Think It's All Over – *wish he were*); Cherie Lunghi (actress); Ben Oakley (British windsurfing coach).

Jesus College, Cambridge

• *This College is part of the University of Cambridge and students are entitled to use its facilities.*
Jesus College, Jesus Lane, Cambridge, CB5 8BL Tel: (01223) 339 339
E-mail: undergraduate-admissions@jesus.cam.ac.uk Website: www.jesus.cam.ac.uk
Jesus College Student Union, Jesus College, Cambridge, CB5 8BL
Tel: (01223) 507 223 E-mail: jcsu_president@jesus.cam.ac.uk
Website: www.jcsu.jesus.cam.ac.uk

Jesus College, built around an old convent with buildings dating from the 12th century, is 5 mins walk from King's Parade. Its chapel (built 1140) is the oldest building in Cambridge. *It's seen as a posh, trendy college and combines sporting enthusiasm with a liberal, if not radical, ethos. It makes a genuine effort to recruit more women and students from state schools. The bar is the social suction point and is usually full by nightfall.*

Sex ratio (M:F): 56:44	Founded: 1496
Full-time u'grads: 542	Part-time: n/a
Postgrads: 229	Mature: <1%
State:private school: 59:41	Disabled: n/a
Academic ranking: 9	International: 4%

Bar, *cliquey but well-equipped* with TV screen, pool table, games machines; classical concerts in the Chapel (250); active choir; annual May Ball; music practice room. College mags: Red & Blackmail and Peripheral Vision. Two libraries (25,000 books); 26 computers, 24-hr. CofE chapel. *Excellent* sports; sports fields (4 acres) and facilities on site; football, hockey and cricket *especially strong*. All students can live in; 2nd & 3rd years in *desirable* converted houses on College perimeter; eat in dining hall; formal meals five times weekly; self-catering facilities; net connections in rooms. Night porter; CCTV, entry-phones; nurse; physiotherapist; subsidised rape alarms; women's and welfare officers; bursaries, hardship fund and travel grants.

FAMOUS ALUMNI:

S T Coleridge (poet); Alistair Cooke (late broadcaster); Thomas Cranmer (former Archbishop of Canterbury); Ted Dexter (cricketer); Prince Edward (*showbiz impresario*); Wilfred Hadfield (invented double yellow lines); Nick Hornby (writer); Richard Lacey (food safety *guru*); Thomas Malthus (economist).

King's College, Cambridge

• *This College is part of the University of Cambridge and students are entitled to use its facilities.*
King's College, King's Parade, Cambridge, CB2 1ST Tel: (01223) 331 100
E-mail: undergraduate.admissions@kings.cam.ac.uk Website: www.kings.cam.ac.uk
JCR, King's College, King's Parade, Cambridge, CB2 1ST
Tel: (01223) 331 454 Website: www.kcsu.org.uk

King's College, on King's Parade, has many a dreaming spire and the famous King's chapel (started in 1446). *There's a good mix of all Cambridge's different types and awe-inspiringly ancient surroundings. King's has a somewhat leftist tradition, relaxed and down to earth with an unusually high proportion of state school students. Its porters are reputed to be the nicest in Cambridge.*

Sex ratio (M:F): 55:45	Founded: 1441
Full-time u'grads: 413	Part-time: n/a
Postgrads: 200	Mature: <1%
State:private school: 87:13	Disabled: 4
Academic ranking: 20	International: 5%

College bar open lunchtimes and four evenings a week. Every term there's a Mingle (mini ball); June Event is a deluxe Mingle. Red Dragon Pie student mag; Ecumenical chapel. Two libraries (130,000 books); 33 computers, 24-hr. Sports fields (6 acres) 15 mins walk; multigym; squash courts; boats and canoes. All students can live in and eat in the dining hall; self-catering provision; weekly formal meals during Michaelmas and Lent terms. Entry-phones; nurse; LGB, ethnic minorities and access officers; a few rooms for wheelchair users.

FAMOUS ALUMNI:

David Baddiel (comedian); Martin Bell MP (Ind); Rupert Brooke (poet); Zadie Smith (novelist); Alan Turing (computers); Johns Bird & Fortune (comedians); E M Forster (writer); John Maynard Keynes (economist); Michael Mates MP (Con); Salman Rushdie (writer).

Lucy Cavendish College, Cambridge

• *This College is part of the <u>University of Cambridge</u> and students are entitled to use its facilities.*
Lucy Cavendish College, Lady Margaret Road, Cambridge, CB3 0BU
Tel: (01223) 332 190 E-mail: lcc-admission@list.cam.ac.uk Website: www.lucy-cav.cam.ac.uk
The Student's Union, Lucy Cavendish College, Cambridge, CB3 0BU

Four of the buildings of Lucy Cavendish College (600 metres from King's Parade) date from the end of the 19th century, the rest are modern, including the library. The site's full of trees, *tranquil and quite beautiful*, complete with a tiny Anglo-Saxon herb garden – *perfect for peaceful study*. Only women over 21 years old are admitted and the average age is 30. There's no bitchy boarding school atmosphere though – *it's a refreshingly diverse and progressive college with dedication, creativity and flexibility rated higher than early educational success. There's a healthy dose of partying along with the intellectual exertions, though, and students are increasingly making their mark on the wider University stage.*

Sex ratio (M:F): 0:100		Founded: 1965
Full-time u'grads: 115		Part-time: n/a
Postgrads: 85		Mature: 100%
State:private school: 60:40		Disabled: 3
Academic ranking: 26		International: 45%

Magdalene College, Cambridge

• *This College is part of the <u>University of Cambridge</u> and students are entitled to use its facilities.*
Magdalene College, Cambridge, CB3 0AG
Tel: (01223) 332 135 E-mail: admissions@magd.cam.ac.uk Website: www.magd.cam.ac.uk
Magdalene JCR, Magdalene College, Cambridge, CB3 0AG
E-mail: jcr.access@magd.cam.ac.uk Website: http://jcr.magd.cam.ac.uk

If you want to cause a sudden embarrassed hush at parties say 'Maggdalleen'. To flow with wit and wisdom pronounce it correctly as 'Maudlin' – to be in the in-crowd, call it 'The Village'. The atmosphere at this college, 700 metres from King's Parade and with more river frontage than any other, is far from maudlin and the lively social scene revolves around the bar. Magdalene's one of the smaller colleges and tradition and camaraderie pervade. An international flavour lends an air of culture to the atmosphere and the location gives students barely rivalled ease-of-access to pubs and eateries. The College features medieval and 15th- and 16th-century courts and Pepys' Library, but unfortunately, it hasn't escaped clumsy postwar architecture at some residential blocks.

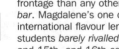

Sex ratio (M:F): 51:49	Founded: 1542
Full-time u'grads: 360	Part-time: 0
Postgrads: 165	Mature: 1%
State:private school: 50:50	Disabled: 3
Academic ranking: 22	International: n/a

Bland bar; common room with widescreen Sky TV, pool table, ents; termly karaoke and quizzes; classical and jazz concerts in Benson Hall (cap 100); annual musical and freshers' play; annual garden party; biennial ball (*one of the best, very posh*). Ars Magna termly College mag and biweekly Magd In and Magd Out e-mail newsletters. Three libraries (30,000 books in main one); 23 computers, 24-hr. CofE chapel. Good sports fields (8 acres) 500 metres away shared with St John's; boathouse shared with Queens'; hockey and waterpolo successes. All students live in; accommodation varies – new building due in 2005; canteen and self-catering facilities; nightly formal meals among Cambridge's *finest*; all rooms networked. CCTV; nurse; free rape alarms. International and LGB officers; Equal Opps Rep. Scholarships.

FAMOUS ALUMNI:

William Cash (journalist); Katie Dereham (Classic FM); Bamber Gascoigne (quizmaster, writer); Gavin Hastings (former Scottish rugby captain); Anthony Jay (writer, Yes Minister); Charles Kingsley, C S Lewis (authors); Charles Stewart Parnell (19th-C Irish nationalist); Samuel Pepys (diarist); Alan Rusbridger (editor, The Guardian); John Simpson (TV reporter).

New Hall, Cambridge

• *This College is part of the* <u>University of Cambridge</u> *and students are entitled to use its facilities.*
New Hall, Cambridge, CB3 0DF Tel: (01223) 762 100
E-mail: admissions@newhall.cam.ac.uk Website: www.newhall.cam.ac.uk
New Hall Union, Cambridge, CB3 0DF E-mail: jcr-president@newhall.cam.ac.uk
Website: www.newhall.cam.ac.uk/students/jcr

Founded in 1954 to up Cambridge's female population, New Hall's situated 1,200 metres from King's Parade and is capped with a *striking* dome roof – the only college dome in Oxbridge. Free from excess history, tradition or accumulated wealth, New Hall concentrates on supporting its students in their academic pursuits. *It can take itself too seriously sometimes, but the youth of the college means it's constantly evolving and can be an exciting place to study.* New Hall has remained resolutely single-sex and while students are *perky enough about this, they tend to socialise elsewhere.*

Sex ratio (M:F): 0:100	Founded: 1954
Full-time u'grads: 393	Part-time: 4
Postgrads: 90	Mature: <1%
State:private school: 60:40	Disabled: 21
Academic ranking: 23	International: 13%

Bar (cap 100, open four times a week), giant TV, film, jazz nights; pool table; concerts, drama soc, student bands and events at the Dome (cap 300), Vivien Stewart Room (60), Fellows' Drawing Room (45 and a Steinway) or the Long Room (200); vending machines. Library (60,000 books); 24 computers, 24-hr access; art room (largest collection of contemporary women's art in Europe); darkroom. 39% turnout last ballot; JCR newsletter, New-S Worthy. *Successful* boat club; multigym; squash and tennis courts. 96% of undergrads live in; wide price range, *good* quality, most with internet connections; pay-as-you-eat-canteen (*could be better but good for veggies*); formals once a week; permit parking; some CCTV; swipe cards; nurse; LBG, international and women's officers; various support funds, including interesting expeditions *but New Hall's not rich.*

FAMOUS ALUMNI:

Jocelyn Bell Burnell (discovered Pulsars); Frances Edmonds (writer); Joanna MacGregor (pianist); Sue Perkins (of Mel & Sue); Tilda Swinton (actress); Claudia Winkleman (TV presenter).

Newnham College, Cambridge

• *This College is part of the <u>University of Cambridge</u> and students are entitled to use its facilities.*
Newnham College, Sidgwick Avenue, Cambridge, CB3 9DF
Tel: (01223) 335 700 E-mail: admissions@newn.cam.ac.uk Website: www.newn.cam.ac.uk
Newnham JCR, Newnham College, Sidgwick Avenue, Cambridge, CB3 9DF
Tel: (01223) 335 700 E-mail: jcr.access@newn.cam.ac.uk Website: www.newnhamjcr.co.uk

In 1870 lectures for ladies was a new and dangerous idea. In 1871 Newnham college *gave the establishment the finger* and started life as a house for young women who had to travel to learn. Only 1,200 metres from King's Parade, *Newnham's a distinctive Victorian building set in huge gardens. The College now buzzes with enthusiasm and, ahem, love of learning.* Students have some of the most diverse backgrounds of the colleges and a determination to get involved in and everything out of the Cambridge experience – which includes enjoying the second longest corridor in Europe. Wowsers.

Sex ratio (M:F): 0:100	**Founded: 1871**
Full-time u'grads: 422	**Part-time: 0**
Postgrads: 135	**Mature: <1%**
State:private school: 55:45	**Disabled: 4**
Academic ranking: 13	**International: 10%**

Boilerhouse bar (*nice and cheap*), regular live bands, comedy nights, quizzes and pool/table football tournaments; classical concerts and clubbing in the College Hall (cap 250); performing arts studio; choir; orchestra; film nights; biennial ball; garden parties; plays performed in theatre studio, hall or garden. JCR provides TV, video and DVD, vending machines, photocopier. Observatory; improved library (90,000 books, 50 study places with net access points); 35 computers, 24-hr access; art room. N-Vie mag; JCR supports remaining single sex and campaigns financial issues. *Strong* photographic, politics and Bollywood societies; *almighty* Rag. Rowing; footie; rugby; sports field on site; multigym; tennis and netball courts; successes in rowing, football, netball. Vast majority live in; *assortment of room standards*, some with antiques. Food is *non-fatal*, self-catering facilities are *good*, all rooms have network points; six student parking spaces. Nurse; rooms for wheelchair users; free rape alarms; self-defence classes; special finance tutor; Women's, LGB, International and Ethnic Minorities Officers; £600 scholarships for firsts, book, room and travel grants, various bursaries and hardship funds.

FAMOUS ALUMNI:

Dianne Abbot MP (Lab); Clare Balding (sports commentator); Joan Bakewell (broadcaster); Eleanor Bron, A S Byatt, Margaret Drabble, Katherine Whitehorn (writers); Germaine Greer (*female eunuch* & academic); Patricia Hewitt MP (Lab); Dorothy Hodgkin (Chemistry Nobel laureate); Sarah Rowland Jones (medical researcher); Ann Mallalieu (Labour peer); Miriam Margolyes (actress); Susie Menkes (fashion consultant); Julia Neuberger (female rabbi); Sylvia Plath (poet); Emma Thompson, Olivia Williams (actresses); Shirley Williams (Lib Dem peer).

Pembroke College, Cambridge

• *This College is part of the* <u>*University of Cambridge*</u> *and students are entitled to use its facilities.*
Pembroke College, Cambridge, CB2 1RF Tel: (01223) 338 100
E-mail: admissions@pem.cam.ac.uk Website: www.pem.cam.ac.uk
Junior Parlour, Pembroke College, Cambridge, CB2 1RF
E-mail: jp-president@pem.cam.ac.uk

14th-century spires and *beautiful* gardens mingle with redbrick buildings and 90s constructions: just off King's Parade but away from most of the tourists, Pembroke College is *an attractive place to study*. The place has a rep of academic excellence and a host of extracurricular activity. Plays are put on in the grounds and *the place is bursting with enthusiasm and life. Students are well integrated with university existence, but things can get a bit insular. Sport and partying blow off steam.*

Sex ratio (M:F): 55:45	**Founded: 1347**
Full-time u'grads: 441	**Part-time: 0**
Postgrads: 195	**Mature: 2%**
State:private school: 55:45	**Disabled: 12**
Academic ranking: 6	**International: 10%**

Bar; Old Reader (cap 50, theatre); concerts in Old Library (90); student bands in Junior Parlour (80) and New Cellars (cap 80); twice termly bops and events; library (60,000 books); music room; 38 computers; all rooms have internet connection. CofE chapel. Pembroke St newsletter; Pem arts mag. Pembroke runs a community centre in South London (where students can also stay). Rowing; sports fields and courts; gym; aerobics; athletics; multigym; oldest bowling green in Europe. All students live in college or college houses; students eat in canteen; optional formal every night; *good food and veggie options*; *limited* self-catering in college; night porters; nurse; grants and scholarships; attack alarms and self-defence classes for women; equal opportunities; LGB and women's officers.

FAMOUS ALUMNI:

Tim Brooke-Taylor, Bill Oddie ('Goodies'); Peter Cook (comedy *god*); Raymond Dolby (audio inventor); Thomas Gray, Edmund Spenser (poets); Ted Hughes (late poet laureate); Eric Idle (Monty Python); Clive James (writer, presenter); Jonathan Lynn (writer, director); Pitt the Younger (PM); Tom Sharpe (writer); Chris Smith MP (Lab); Sir John Sulston (Genome project).

Peterhouse, Cambridge

• *This College is part of the* <u>*University of Cambridge*</u> *and students are entitled to use its facilities.*
Peterhouse, Cambridge, CB2 1RD Tel: (01223) 338 223
E-mail: admissions@pet.cam.ac.uk Website: www.pet.cam.ac.uk
Peterhouse JCR, Cambridge, CB2 1RD Website: www.thesexclub.tk

The smallest and oldest of the Cambridge colleges, with *beautiful* and well-kept gardens. High standards and fierce competition for places, even for Cambridge, Peterhouse *sucks in the academic elite and spits them out into top jobs. It's rich and well-respected. Being so small, energetic movers and shakers play on the wider University stage. Alcohol, sport, drama and alcohol are the more popular pastimes.*

Sex ratio (M:F): 60:40	**Founded: 1284**
Full-time u'grads: 276	**Part-time: n/a**
Postgrads: 128	**Mature: 2%**
State:private school: 56:44	**Disabled: 22**
Academic ranking: 21	**International: 10%**

Bar; Music Room (cap 100) for clubbing and student bands, *but college tutors disapprove if it gets too boisterous*; theatre (180) for drama and classical concerts; biennial ball; drinking and debating societies; termly mag, the Sex. Library (45,000 books), 16 computers. CofE chapel. Sports facilities (8 acres shared with <u>Clare College</u>); squash court; gym. All students live in College maintained or arranged housing; most eat in the *gorgeous* dining hall; *limited self-catering (best at Parkside, off-site housing)*. Nurse; women's advisers; hardship fund; prizes and scholarships.

FAMOUS ALUMNI:

Charles Babbage (computing pioneer); Thomas Campion (poet); Stephanie Cook (Olympic gold medallist); Richard Crashaw (poet); Sir Christopher Cockerel (invented the hovercraft); Colin Greenwood (Radiohead); Michael Howard MP (Con leader); James Mason (actor); Sam Mendes (director); Max Perutz (Nobel Prize winner); Michael Portillo MP (Con); Frank Whittle (invented the jet engine).

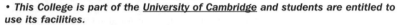

Queens' College, Cambridge

• **This College is part of the <u>University of Cambridge</u> and students are entitled to use its facilities.**
Queens' College, Cambridge, CB3 9ET Tel: (01223) 335 511
E-mail: admissions@quns.cam.ac.uk Website: www.quns.cam.ac.uk
Queens' College JCR, Cambridge, CB3 9ET Tel: (01223) 335 511
E-mail: jcr_ctte@quns.cam.ac.uk Website: http://jcrwww.quns.cam.ac.uk

Queens' is halfway along Silver Street, a *major* student pipeline to the main arts faculties. It's a mixture of *beautiful* Elizabethan courts, a *passable* redbrick thing and one of Cambridge's many *vile* Cripps Court *concrete monsters*. It's right opposite the Anchor, a *favourite* student and tourist hang-out so close to the river that it frequently floods. It has a *friendly, laid-back charm*, *a sort of bastion of innocent fun*, and a *healthier* state/private mix than some colleges. It's *notoriously thespy* and holds a *high-profile* drama competition every year.

40%		
Sex ratio (M:F): 60:40	**Founded: 1448**	
Full-time u'grads: 494	**Part-time: n/a**	
Postgrads: 288	**Mature: 0**	
State:private school: 55:45	**Disabled: 0**	
Academic ranking: 8	**International: 8%**	
60%		

Bar; Fitzpatrick Hall (380, theatre) for student bands and the *best* college club nights in Cambridge as well as Jingles (*cheese*); films; biennial ball; three music rooms. The Drain student mag; JCR newsletter. Successful Rag raised £10,000. Two libraries (70,000 books); 13 computers, 24-hr. CofE chapel. Multigym and squash courts on-site; big sports fields (15 acres shared with <u>Robinson</u>) 800m away; *very modern* boathouse; success in male and female footie. All undergraduates can live in, except a few 4th years; eat in dining hall; *very limited* self-catering. Nurse; crèche; hardship fund (usually pays crèche fees); scholarships.

FAMOUS ALUMNI:

Erasmus (Renaissance scholar); Mike Foale (first Brit in space); Stephen Fry (the *inimitable* writer, actor and comedian); Michael Gibson, John Spencer (rugby players); Tom Holland (Bond's Q 1986-89); Graham Swift, T H White (writers).

Robinson College, Cambridge

• **This College is part of the <u>University of Cambridge</u> and students are entitled to use its facilities.**
Robinson College, Grange Road, Cambridge, CB3 9AN Tel: (01223) 339 100
E-mail: undergraduate-admissions@robinson.cam.ac.uk Website: www.robinson.cam.ac.uk
Robinson College Students' Association, Grange Road, Cambridge, CB3 9AN
Website: www-stud.robinson.cam.ac.uk/rcsa

Looks aren't everything, which in Robinson's case is just as well. It's a bit of a car park. As so often in life, though, the college makes up for pug-ugly features with a nice personality. It's modern, the only historically mixed-sex place in Cambridge and it's handy for the University library and arts faculties. Anywhere more than 5 mins walk from King's Parade is a world away in Cambridge, so Robinson, at about 15 mins brisk stroll, is considered far out. There's a friendly community between the years, who mingle along the living corridors. Most unusually of all, they don't mind people walking on the grass.

Sex ratio (M:F): 61:39	**Founded: 1979**
Full-time u'grads: 417	**Part-time: 0**
Postgrads: 80	**Mature: 3%**
State:private school: 61:39	**Disabled: 4**
Academic ranking: 16	**International: 8%**

Two bars; bands, concerts and plays in the Auditorium (cap 250); frequent club nights. Fortnightly newsletter, termly mag. Two libraries (48,000 volumes); 30 computers, 24-hr. Chapel with *famous* organ. Sports fields (15 acres shared with Queens') 1,200m away; some facilities on-site. All students live in; most rooms en-suite with phone and net connections, *good* self-catering. Doctor and nurse; *good* JCR welfare; free rape alarms and taxis for the stranded; financial tutor; various funds and scholarships; *excellent* disabled access.

FAMOUS ALUMNI:

Morwenna Banks (comedian); Adrian Davies (Welsh rugby); Charles Hart (lyricist); Gary Sinyor (film director).

Selwyn College, Cambridge

• **This College is part of the University of Cambridge and students are entitled to use its facilities.**
Selwyn College, Grange Road, Cambridge, CB3 9DQ Tel: (01223) 335 896
E-mail: admissions@sel.cam.ac.uk Website: www.sel.cam.ac.uk
Selwyn JCR, Grange Road, Cambridge, CB3 9DQ Tel: (01223) 335 846
E-mail: jcrpresident@sel.cam.ac.uk Website: www.jcr.sel.cam.ac.uk

Selwyn's been called Cambridge's best-kept secret. *It's a bit of an exaggeration*, but the cluster of *pretty* neo-Gothic buildings behind the arts faculties and across the road from Newnham College is certainly *low-profile* compared with the *more raucous* river colleges. Like most of Cambridge, it's *scarred* with a Cripps building. *Nevertheless*, it's one of the *friendly* colleges (rather like Pembroke, Robinson or Queens'), with a *lively* bar scene and *not much in the way of any sort of attitude.*

Sex ratio (M:F): 59:41	**Founded: 1882**
Full-time u'grads: 396	**Part-time: 0**
Postgrads: 165	**Mature: 1%**
State:private school: 45:55	**Disabled: 7**
Academic ranking: 11	**International: 7%**

Three bars (two for events only); theatre and weekly bops in Selwyn Diamond (cap 600), also live music in Main Hall (200) and JCR (100); themed events; Snowball at Xmas. 1 college mag, Kiwi. Library (48,000 books); 23 computers, internet points in all rooms. CofE chapel. Two drama societies, *strong* music scene, sports facilities 200m away shared with other colleges; rowing's *especially strong*. Most live in; very *limited* self-catering; three formals a week (non-compulsory). *Decent* college food and renowned formal hall. Nurse; sickbay; bursaries, scholarships, prizes; free attack alarms; parenting; some disabled facilities.

FAMOUS ALUMNI:

Clive Anderson (TV host, lawyer); John Gummer MP (Con); Simon Hughes MP (Lib Dem); Hugh Laurie (comedian, actor); Malcolm Muggeridge (journalist); Rob Newman (comedian, novelist).

Sidney Sussex College, Cambridge

• *This College is part of the <u>University of Cambridge</u> and students are entitled to use its facilities.*
Sidney Sussex College, Sidney Street, Cambridge, CB2 3HU Tel: (01223) 338 800
E-mail: admissions@sid.cam.ac.uk Website: www.sid.cam.ac.uk
Sidney Sussex College JCR, Sidney Street, Cambridge, CB2 3HU
Tel: (01223) 338 800
E-mail: sscsu.president@sid.cam.ac.uk Website: www.srcf.ucam.org/sidneyjcr

Sidney's *one of the prettier* colleges, with red-brick *just about complementing the grander* late 16th-century stuff. *It's small enough to be undaunting, but big enough to avoid stifling. And best of all,* Sainsbury's is about 20 metres away. There's an *active* JCR, some of the *best* sports grounds in Cambridge and students have a *high profile* in University drama and Rag. It's also one of the *least stuffy* places in town – around 10% of students are Asian, it was one of the first colleges to let girls in and the Master is a mistress.

Sex ratio (M:F): 48:52	Founded: 1596
Full-time u'grads: 340	Part-time: 0
Postgrads: 190	Mature: 2%
State:private school: 63:37	Disabled: 4
Academic ranking: 18	International: 6%

Only student-run bar in Cambridge (cap 175) used for fortnightly bops; Knox Shaw Room (40 seated); biennial ball. Sid News and El Sid mags, Yearbook and their own Rag mag. Library (40,000 books); 36 computers, 24-hr. Chapel. Sports fields (22 acres) $1\frac{1}{2}$ miles away. All live in (£50-70/week); eat in dining hall (food *improving*, veggie option); adequate self-catering. CCTV; chaplain; nurse; hardship fund; bursaries; book grants; prizes. One room for a disabled student, some lifts.

FAMOUS ALUMNI:

Asa Briggs (historian); Oliver Cromwell (Lord Protector); Lord Owen (ex-SDP leader); Carol Vorderman (*fawning* daytime telly mathmo).

St Catharine's College, Cambridge

• *This College is part of the <u>University of Cambridge</u> and students are entitled to use its facilities.*
St Catharine's College, Cambridge, CB2 1RL Tel: (01223) 338 300
E-mail: undergraduate.admissions@caths.cam.ac.uk
Website: www.caths.cam.ac.uk/admissions
Saint Catharine's College JCR, Cambridge, CB2 1RL
Website: www.caths.cam.ac.uk/jcr

Catz, as St Catharine's is known to *those in the know*, is set back from the beginning of King's Parade opposite Corpus Christi and bears witness to more than five centuries of building. *It's strong on sporty and musical pursuits and big enough to be diverse, small enough to be intimate. Its self-sufficiency isn't complete, however: in order to take competition to a higher level and for more frequent ents, students can't ignore the rest of the University altogether. Like so much of Cambridge, it's mobbed by tourists in the summer, although most are more interested in* <u>King's</u> *next door and the porters do their best to keep out the hordes.*

Sex ratio (M:F): 53:47	Founded: 1473
Full-time u'grads: 467	Part-time: 0
Postgrads: 145	Mature: <1%
State:private school: 48:46	Disabled: 2
Academic ranking: 7	International: 11%

Bar (*centre of life* for most of the college); bops every three weeks; Octagon theatre (cap 150) and chapel (100) used for concerts; biennial ball. Catzeyes magazine. Two libraries (70,000 books); 38 computers, scanning, printing; internet access in all rooms; record library. CofE chapel. Sports fields (3 acres, new pavilion) 1,200m; only Astroturf pitch in a Cambridge college; success in rowing. All students live in (all 2nd years in the octagonal St Chad's building); eat in dining halls; self-catering limited. CCTV; nurse; sick bay; five rooms for wheelchair users; *good* access; some financial support; academic scholarships and prizes.

FAMOUS ALUMNI:

Peter Boizot (founded Pizza Express); Kevin Greening (Radio 5 Live); Sir Peter Hall (theatre director); Malcolm Lowry (writer); Sir Ian McKellen (actor); Jeremy Paxman (BBC *bulldog*).

St Edmund's College, Cambridge

• *This College is part of the University of Cambridge and students are entitled to use its facilities.*
St Edmund's College, Cambridge, CB3 0BN Tel: (01223) 336 250
E-mail: admissions@st-edmunds.cam.ac.uk Website: www.st-edmunds.cam.ac.uk
St Edmund's College Combination Room, Cambridge, CB3 0BN
Website: www.st-edmunds.cam.ac.uk/student/

Students at St Edmund's (*Eddies to those in the know*) are either mature (*in age, not necessarily attitude*) or affiliated, so *work takes precedence over binge drinking. It's friendly, with a close community and a bop that attracts Cambridge's more discerning college ent socialites*. While it's been around since the end of the 19th century, it's only been a full college of the University since 1965. It's one of the University's six graduate colleges but also teaches around 100 mature undergrads.

Sex ratio (M:F): 62:38	Founded: 1896
Full-time u'grads: 126	Part-time: n/a
Postgrads: 182	Mature: 100%
State:private school: n/a	Disabled: 1
Academic ranking: 29	International: 50%

Prospectuses from college; open day; library; bar; active music society; May Ball; success at bumps (intercollegiate rowing competition); rooms for 130 single students (some family maisonettes for two adults, two children); ethernet in all rooms; limited cooking facilities – most accommodation is catered. Daily worship, RC chapel. Academic prizes and scholarships; hardship fund.

St John's College, Cambridge

• *This College is part of the University of Cambridge and students are entitled to use its facilities.*
St John's College, Cambridge, CB2 1TP Tel: (01223) 338 703
E-mail: admissions@joh.cam.ac.uk Website: www.joh.cam.ac.uk
Junior Combination Room, St John's College, Cambridge, CB2 1TP
Tel: (01223) 338 685 Website: http://jcr.joh.cam.ac.uk

This is as good as life in an Oxbridge College gets – think 'Brideshead Revisited'. John's is a posh, sporty, wealthy riverside college large enough to cater for most types although so big that some students can feel lost. Tourists flock to see the Gothic splendour of New Court and the beautiful Bridge of Sighs, and tickets for the May Ball (rivalled only by Trinity's extravaganza) are like gold dust.

Sex ratio (M:F): 59:41	Founded: 1511
Full-time u'grads: 559	Part-time: 0
Postgrads: 324	Mature: 1.5%
State:private school: 50:50	Disabled: 14
Academic ranking: 14	International: 13%

Bar; Pythagoras Building (theatre); art and music rooms; Palmerston Room (cap 350) for bands; Old Music Room (100) for concerts; Boiler Room (120) for fortnightly bops; annual ball. Lady Margaret Players (*major* drama society); weekly JCR newsletter and twice termly Cripptic mag; cable TV. Two libraries (120,000 books); 45 computers, 24-hr. Large cathedral-like CofE chapel. Large on-site sports hall, *superb* hockey club and extensive sports fields 200m away; cardiovascular gym. Everyone lives in or in hostels; *good* self-catering. CCTV, swipe cards; nurse; *very good* disabled access and provisions. *Excellent* financial support: book grants and assistance for students suffering unexpected hardship.

FAMOUS ALUMNI:

Douglas Adams (late author, Hitch Hiker's Guide to the Galaxy); Rob Andrew (former England rugby player); Thomas Clarkson, William Wilberforce (anti-slavery campaigners); Derek Jacobi (actor); Lord Palmerston (PM); William Wordsworth (poet).

Trinity College, Cambridge

• **This College is part of the University of Cambridge and students are entitled to use its facilities.**
Trinity College, Cambridge, CB2 1TQ Tel: (01223) 338 400
E-mail: admissions@trin.cam.ac.uk Website: www.trin.cam.ac.uk
Trinity College Students' Union, Trinity College, Cambridge, CB2 1TQ
Tel: (01223) 367424 E-mail: tcsu-president@trin.cam.ac.uk
Website: http://tcsu.trin.cam.ac.uk

Trinity, *which sprawls laconically* between the backs and the centre of town, is Cambridge's largest and *arguably grandest* college. It has an *enormous* Great Court and pictures of the portly founder Henry VIII bedeck the walls. Its students fight with tourists to get across Great Court, home of the largest covered fountain in Europe, *for whatever that's worth*. Insanely wealthy, Trinity is the third largest landowner in the country, after the Crown and the Church – there's some very pissed-off tenant villages in Suffolk. Almost bottomless pockets are generously dipped into to help less well-off students, and College is slowly redressing its white public-schoolboy image and *freaks, geeks, sloanes, jocks, hacks and downright normal folk now co-exist in relative harmony. Emphasis on the 'relative'.*

Sex ratio (M:F): 58:42	Founded: 1546
Full-time u'grads: 738	Part-time: 0
Postgrads: 364	Mature: 2%
State:private school: 44:56	Disabled: 13
Academic ranking: 3	International: 17%

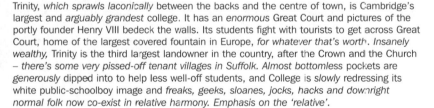

Airport-lounge bar with juke box, pool, quiz machine and table football; Chapel (200) and Combination Room (100) for live music (prestigious choir) and fortnightly sweaty bops in Wolfson Party Room (150); biggest annual ball (2,000 tickets); regular jazz, fortnightly Magpie & Stump comedy debating and theatre in gardens or Great Hall. JCR with TV, Playstation 2, DVD player. *Countless ever-changing societies.* SU newsletter three times a term, *in theory*.

Widespread political disinterest, with pockets of arch-conservatism. Two libraries, one for law, *imposing* (Christopher) Wren Library (300,000 books); 70 24-hr computers in three computer rooms; internet access in most rooms. CofE chapel; three chaplains; charity fund-raising. Extensive sports fields 800m from College; success in rowing and rugby. Everyone lives in; rooms vary (attics with oak beams, grand rooms with high ceilings, modern with en-suite facilities); mixed sex couples can choose to share; eat in *dark and moody* Great Hall; popular and *riotous* formal hall every night); *varied kitchen facilities*; booze-dispensing buttery, *vast* wine cellar. CCTV, swipe cards; nurse; Women's and Access Officers, LGB rep; *wheelchair access dreadful*, some adapted rooms; *generous* financial support, usually in the form of *bizarre* prizes; choral and organ scholarships.

FAMOUS ALUMNI:

Francis Bacon (artist); Lord Byron (*mad, bad* poet); Prince Charles; Lord Hurd (Con, former Foreign Secretary); Lord Macaulay (historian); Vladimir Nabokov (writer, Lolita); Isaac Newton (scientist); Enoch Powell (late MP); Bertrand Russell, Ludwig Wittgenstein (philosophers); Alfred, Lord Tennyson (*less mad* poet); Lord Whitelaw (ex Tory minister).

Trinity Hall, Cambridge

• **This College is part of the <u>University of Cambridge</u> and students are entitled to use its facilities.**
Trinity Hall, Cambridge, CB2 1TJ
Tel: (01223) 332 500 E-mail: admissions@trinhall.cam.ac.uk
Website: www.trinhall@cam.ac.uk
Trinity Hall JCR, Cambridge, CB2 1TJ
Tel: (01223) 332 500

Tit Hall (*the nickname's only amiably abusive*) is a river college that *nestles* behind <u>Clare</u>, <u>Caius</u> and <u>Trinity</u> colleges, tucked away just off King's Parade. It's the fourth smallest in Cambridge, *which means it's friendly and intimate, or stifling and incestuous, depending on who you ask*. It has a *rather pretty* Georgian courtyard *although the new academic spirit might mean you won't spend all your time dossing in it*.

Sex ratio (M:F): 52:48	**Founded: 1350**
Full-time u'grads: 359	**Part-time: 0**
Postgrads: 236	**Mature: 1%**
State:private school: 58:42	**Disabled: 3**
Academic ranking: 12	**International: 10%**

Bar; indie and dance bands; fortnightly Global nights with London DJs; lecture theatre for drama and music (cap 270). Hallmark weekly newsletter; active Rag. Two libraries (85,000 books); 20 computers, 24-hr. CofE chapel. Sports fields (3 acres) a mile away; 'boaty' rep. Most live in; accommodation split between college and Huntingdon Road, a mile away. Nurse; hardship fund (£50,000), book loans, scholarships.

FAMOUS ALUMNI:

Lord Howe (Con, former Cabinet Minister); Nicholas Hytner (theatre/film director); Donald Maclean (spy); J B Priestley (writer); Tony Slattery (comedian); Terry Waite (former church envoy held hostage in Beirut).

Sir Bobby Robson, then manager of Newcastle United, was awarded an honorary degree from Newcastle University. The robes he was given consisted of red and white stripes – the colours of arch-rivals Sunderland.

Wolfson College, Cambridge

• *This College is part of the* <u>*University of Cambridge*</u> *and students are entitled to use its facilities.*
Wolfson College, Barton Road, Cambridge, CB3 9BB
Tel: (01223) 335 900 Website: www.wolfson.cam.ac.uk
Wolfson College Student Association, Cambridge, CB3 9BB
Website: www.wolfson.cam.ac.uk/wcsa

Wolfson's a graduate and mature college, which takes affiliated medical students as well as students for all the rest of the University's degrees. *It's less champagne and hierarchy-driven than most of the other colleges,* with no JCR/SCR division and a serious approach to work. *They like to think of themselves as modern, cosmopolitan and lively, and given it's such a young college, that's fairly true.*

Sex ratio (M:F): n/a	Founded: 1965
Full-time u'grads: 129	Part-time: 120
Postgrads: 530	Mature: 20%
State:private school: n/a	Academic ranking: 28

Bar; meeting rooms; boat club; college paper (Wolfhound); snooker tables; formal dinners; library (24-hr access); music rooms; multigym, tennis courts and aerobics society; 12 overseas scholarships; hardship trust; disabled facilities.

Canterbury

see <u>University of Kent at Canterbury</u>

Canterbury Christ Church University College

(1) Canterbury Christ Church University College, North Holmes Road, Canterbury, Kent, CT1 1QU Tel: (01227) 767 700 E-mail: admissions@canterbury.ac.uk
Website: www.canterbury.ac.uk
Christ Church Students' Union, North Holmes Road, Canterbury, Kent, CT1 1QU
Tel: (01227) 782 416 E-mail: president@canterbury.ac.uk Website: www.c4online.net
(2) Broadstairs Campus, Canterbury Christ Church University College, Northwood Road, Broadstairs, Kent, CT10 2WA
Tel: (01843) 280 600 Website: http://thanet.canterbury.ac.uk
Canterbury's Students' Union, Room CG13, Northwood Road, Broadstairs, Kent, CT10 2WA Tel: (01843) 280 600

GENERAL

CCCUC, *as absolutely no one but lazy typists call it,* is mostly found in Canterbury, but three other little pieces of it are scattered around Kent – namely: Broadstairs, Chatham and Tunbridge Wells. It's been handing out degrees ever since the Church of England set it up as a teacher training college in 1962 and is now *waiting patiently for someone to notice its good work and promote it to full university status.* With the main site only 10 mins from the centre of one of England's *most visited* cities (see University of Kent), *it's pretty popular. The main campus at Canterbury blends in nicely with its leafy, Kodak-moment surroundings, but once inside it's also modern and well-equipped.*

Sex ratio (M:F): 26:74	**Founded: 1962**
Full-time u'grads: 5,692	**Part-time: 7,024**
Postgrads: 870	**Non-degree: 2,763**
Ave course: 3yrs	**Ethnic: 10%**
State:private school: 96:4	**Flunk rate: 14%**
Mature: 61%	**International: 6%**
Disabled: 151	**Local: 87%**

ATMOSPHERE:

The main campus is surprisingly self-contained, considering nearly nine out of every ten of students come from the local area. There's a warm, friendly atmosphere that's only slightly soured by occasional disputes about noise with the local residents and some alleged hassle from the lager-fuelled townie youths who aren't actually studying here.

SITES:

Broadstairs Campus: (1,000 students – Business, Education, Nursing, Media, Music, Policing) Thanet's 18 miles from Canterbury, not far from the Kent coast and Margate and Ramsgate. It's *not as pretty* as the main site but *those into aesthetics can always head over to the beaches and watersports, or pop into Horizons bar and the refectory.* Most students are local and/or mature.
Chatham, Medway: (Health, Education, Policing) CCCUC has just shipped its first batch of students over to the *fancy new* Medway site, which is part of the Universities at Medway partnership (jointly with University of Kent and Greenwich University).
Salomons Campus, Tunbridge Wells: CCUC's associate campus 40 miles from Canterbury is a training centre for public sector professionals, *so most students will never even know it exists.*

CANTERBURY: see University of Kent

TRAVEL: see University of Kent

Local: A minibus shuttles between sites.

CAREER PROSPECTS:

• Careers Service • No. of staff: 4 full/3 part • Unemployed after 6mths: 4%
2nd year BA/BSc students undergo a Career Development Programme during the last three weeks of the academic year which involves advice and work placements or short courses. Career seminars cover a variety of *useful* subjects.

FAMOUS ALUMNI:

Kate Blewett (award-laden documentarian); Jane Carter (Classical honcho, BBC Music); Jonathan Holmes (writer and presenter); Geraldine McCaughrean (author).

FURTHER INFO:

• Prospectuses: undergrad; postgrad; international; alternative; video • Open days

ACADEMIC

The University's one of the top three providers of teacher training in the country and specialises in churning out graduates for useful jobs in the public services: nurses, social care, policing and the like. The media and sports science programmes are *fairly rammed*, too.

Entry points: 160-180
Applns per place: 5
No. of terms: 3
Staff/student ratio: n/a
Teaching: **
Year abroad: 0%
Firsts: 7%
2.1s: 38%

Ave points: 180
Clearing: 10%
Length of terms: 12wks
Study addicts: 11%
Research: *
Sandwich students: <1%
2.2s: 41%
3rds: 13%

ADMISSIONS:

• Apply via UCAS
Widening participation is the name of the game at the admissions office (Monopoly got boring after a while), and they encourage applications from international, mature and part-time students with or without formal qualifications, so long as they can show they're up to the job. Cranially well-endowed candidates can occasionally leapfrog the first year and go straight into the second.

SUBJECTS:

Arts/Humanities: 27%   Education: 30%
Business & Science: 11%   Health: 21%
Best: Drama, Dance & Cinematics; Maths, Statistics & Operational Research; Nursing; Subjects allied to Medicine.

LIBRARIES:

• 226,500 books • 625 study places • Spend per student: ££
There are libraries at all sites, although the one at Broadstairs is the dwarf of the fellowship.

COMPUTERS:

• 720+ workstations • 24-hr access • Spend per student: £
Although students have their quibbles every now and then, the IT people at Canterbury are doing their best to improve matters. Most halls at Canterbury have net access and all do at Broadstairs. There are internet cafés at Canterbury and Chatham.

OTHER LEARNING FACILITIES:

Language labs; open-access drama studio; CAD lab; media centre; courtroom; sports science lab; nursing lab.

E N T E R T A I N M E N T

THE CITY: see University of Kent

UNIVERSITY:

• Price of a pint of beer: £1.55 • Glass of wine: £1.25 • Can of Red Bull: £1.75
Bars: Unusually, the bar in the Union building at Canterbury is actually run by the University. It offers all the usual bar essentials and a bit more (quizzes, three lounges, two TV rooms, a coffee shop, two club nights a week and, obviously, booze). Broadstairs students also have the intimate Horizons bar.
Theatres: With all the media students around you'd expect a bit of thesping. Student productions are quite well known in the area.
Film: £2 membership of the Film Society provides access to regular film screenings here and at the nearby University of Kent.
Music venues: The SU runs an unplugged evening every Thursday and there have been visits from Lisa Maffia and the Appletons. The University-run main hall (cap 400) has seen acts ranging from Blue to the Bluetones as well as Liberty X, Space and Republica.
Clubbing: Funky Fridays runs on, yes, a Friday and provides a mountain of cheesy pop for fans to slalom down. On Wednesday nights the University's sports teams run their own party.

Food: The canteen-style Food Court is the *prime* munchery and keeps a ladlin' till 7pm. The South Room café and the Union Bar also do snacks and there are other outlets on all sites. **Other:** CCCUC *is ball heaven (or ball hell)* with six of the things throughout the year including the *legendary* summer ball, known in these parts as The Big One. Usually 4,000 students attend with big (*but not necessarily good*) acts like Blue in the main hall and tribute bands like the Bandit Beatles and Coolplay nearby. There are also beer tents and games across the whole campus till 6am.

SOCIAL & POLITICAL

CHRIST CHURCH STUDENTS' UNION:
• 4 sabbaticals • Turnout at last ballot: 5% • NUS member
The Union's *refreshingly active* considering its location in the *smugly affluent* end of Kent. In 2004 the Union Council *grandly* agreed on a Bill of Rights for students. They hold regular rallies and *enthusiastically* joined the NUS campaign against top-up fees. *They don't shirk on the ents front either, arranging distractions every night of the week.*

SU FACILITIES:
Most facilities are run by the University (bars, cafés etc.) but the Union also has two pool tables, a minibus, a TV lounge, an advice centre, gaming machines, and a new and secondhand bookshop. *Facilities are still relatively limited.*

CLUBS (NON-SPORTING):
Ents; History & Debating; New Life Group; Pagan; Rock. **See also Clubs tables.**

OTHER ORGANISATIONS:
The free fortnightly student newspaper has the *uncharacteristically bloodthirsty* title of Bluebeard. There's also C4 Radio (nothing to do with Channel Four), which was the first student radio station to be broadcast on the net (www.c4radio.com) and there's C4TV, which is even less to do with Channel 4. A charity Rag *helps the helpless.*

RELIGIOUS:
• 2 chaplains (CofE)

PAID WORK:
see University of Kent
• Job bureau • Paid work: term-time 70%: hols 75%
The Jobshop's vacancy board and e-bulletins can help find part-time work during studies, including the possibility of doing up to 15 hours a week for the SU, as well as relevant vacation opportunities. Hospitality, retailing and clerical support are the *front runners* in the local area.

SPORTS

• Recent successes: rugby; netball; women's football; men's hockey • BUSA Ranking: 48
The University spends *a fair few notes* on sport and they get *good value for money from consistent success across the board. It's not all about the sweet smell of stonking triumph and the humiliating agony of defeat, however – students can be involved to whatever level they wish (as long as they're prepared to schlepp off-campus to the facilities).*

SPORTS FACILITIES:
Very little on site, but students can use: four football pitches; rugby pitch; three tennis courts; two sports halls with one netball and four basketball courts; gym. For £29 a year (plus user fee) students can go for the burn at the St George's Fitness Centre, 5 mins away from the College, where there are weights and *everything else you need to become as ripped as a Metallica track.* The Kent Coast is a *top spot* for watersports.

SPORTING CLUBS:

Canoe; Cheerleading; Lacrosse. **See also Clubs tables.**

ATTRACTIONS:

Kent County Cricket Club and Gillingham FC are the local teams. See <u>University of Kent</u>.

A C C O M M O D A T I O N

IN COLLEGE:

- <u>Catered: 3%</u> • <u>Cost: £62 (39wks)</u>
- <u>Self-catering: 9%</u> • <u>Cost: £75 (39wks)</u>
- <u>First years living in: 28%</u> • <u>Insurance premium: £</u>

Availability: All 1st years who want to can live in. Priority goes to students younger than 24 who live further away, but all younger international and all disabled students are guaranteed a bed. *For the majority who make it into the ivory tower, standards are pretty high.* Weirdly, the catered halls operate on a 'pay as you eat' system, so food costs extra. The halls vary from blocks of 20 rooms to a 300-room student village (Parnham Road) and are at most a 25-min walk from the College. About a third are en-suite. Quibble-wise, *it can sometimes take the powers that be a while to deal with problems.* The village at Parham Road is furthest away from campus, located in a *less well turned-out* area of Canterbury, and there have been reports of theft. Christ Church campus is right in the middle of town, *which is great*, but it means locals use it as a short cut, *inevitably* leading to some vandalism and bike theft. Porter patrols try to prevent this and security has been *beefed up*. There's nothing available for couples and all accomodation is single sex where possible.
Car parking: *Difficult. Scarce parking facilities on campus and not much around it.* Parnham Road has a few spaces, as does Pin Hill, but at a charge of £1 a day.

EXTERNALLY: see <u>University of Kent</u>

- <u>Ave rent: £70</u>

Housing help: The Accommodation Office lists private sector landlords and operates a housemate matching scheme.

W E L F A R E

SERVICES:

- <u>Lesbian/Gay/Bisexual Officer & Society</u> • <u>Ethnic Minorities Officer</u>
- <u>Women's Officer & Society</u> • <u>Mature Students' Officer</u>
- <u>International Students' Officer</u> • <u>Postgrad Officer</u>
- <u>Disabilities Officer</u> • <u>Nightline</u> • <u>College counsellors: 2 full</u> • <u>Crime rating: !</u>

The University provides *generally okay* support services although the NUS has advised against using the nightline because operators haven't had enough training.
Health: Contracted GP services, providing a range of NHS specialists.
Women: The Student Union provides attack alarms for £2.
Crèches/Nursery: 20 places at the nursery on Havelock Street by the main campus for kids aged 3mths-4yrs.
Disabilities: Recent work has meant most campus buildings are now accessible, *although there are still obstacles here and there.* Induction loops, ramps, lifts, Braille facilities, note-takers, adapted rooms and dyslexia support are all on-hand.
Crime: North Holmes Road down the side of the College is one of five local roads that've been identified as problem areas by local police. A few foreign students have come in for harassment from an *in-bred* minority in the town.

FINANCE:

- Ave debt per year: £3,733
- Access fund: £712,521 • Successful applications/yr: 1,581 • Ave payment: £549

Support: A hundred £300 Young Student Bursaries for those under 21 when starting their course. Mature students can grab up to £500.

Cardiff University

- *Includes the former Wales College of Medicine.*
- (1) Cardiff University, PO Box 921, Cardiff, CF10 3XQ Tel: (029) 2087 4839
  E-mail: prospectus@cardiff.ac.uk Website: www.cardiff.ac.uk
  Cardiff University Students' Union, Park Place, Cardiff, CF10 3QN
  Tel: (029) 2078 1400 E-mail: studentsunion@cf.ac.uk Website:
  www.cardiffstudents.com

GENERAL

Cardiff's been *spruced up* in the last few years and is now a *giant, sparkly gem in the country's crown*. It's the *biggest, brightest* city in Wales and has been the capital city since 1955. It's *green and pleasant* by day, *bright and raucous* by night. The University is *dead in the middle* of town, 5 mins from the main shopping centre. It's spread along a single street, *so it feels like a little town of its own*. The buildings are *pretty fancy* and even the newer ones have lots of green space *to lounge about in* (*although Push wouldn't in mid-January when things get nippy*). Wales College of Medicine has been part of the package since 2004, adding an extra campus at Heath Park and making Cardiff the biggest university in Wales as a consequence.

Sex ratio (M:F): 43:57	**Founded:** 1883
Full-time u'grads: 13,035	**Part-time:** 4,005
Postgrads: 3,845	**Non-degree:** 846
Ave course: 3yrs	**Flunk rate:** 8%
Mature: 18%	**International:** 20%
Disabled: 296	**Local:** 23%

57%
43%

ATMOSPHERE:

'Human Traffic' has given Cardiff something of a reputation as a 24-hr party city, which isn't too far from the truth. Cash keeps rolling into the city and it feels like a young, fast-paced kind of place. Partying is on a par with hitting the books and the sports pitch.

OTHER SITES:

Heath Park Campus: (3,200 students – Schools of Medicine, Dentistry, Healthcare Studies, Nursing & Midwifery Studies) A *short bus ride* (or *20 mins beating the streets*) from the main University buildings. It's *quietish* with a few cafes, bars and libraries to call its own. *But it's very much in the orbit* of the main deal, especially since the College of Medicine became officially hitched.

CARDIFF:

- Population: 305,200 • City centre: 0 miles • London: 143 miles
- Bristol: 30 miles • Swansea: 40 miles
- High temp: 21 • Low temp: 2 • Rainfall: 87

Massive redevelopment has made Cardiff a *proper 21st-century city*. The *most obvious bit* is the Millennium Stadium, which is *mighty impressive outside and breathtaking inside*. The Millennium Centre is the next part of it, and will house lots of Wales's *arty stuff*. Cardiff's *sorted for lower-brow culture*, too, with *lots of bars in the mix. Like most big cities, though, it can get a bit hairy on Saturday night.*

TRAVEL:

Trains: Direct trains from Cardiff Central: London (£17.15); Birmingham (£13.20); Manchester (£25.10).
Coaches: National Express to most places including London (£18) and Birmingham (£14.50).
Car: To get to Cardiff there's the M4, A470 and A48. *There's not much call for a car in the city* and parts of the city centre are pedestrianised *but they can be handy for exploring the South Wales countryside*, just 5 miles away.
Air: Cardiff International Airport has flights to the Channel Islands, Ireland and even the USA, as well as inland trips.
Hitching: *The A48's a bonus – only 5 mins walk from the campus – and the Welsh are willing.*
Local: Local bus services run every 20–30 mins all round town: *reliable* with an average trip costing 50p.
Taxis: Lots of firms will *happily rip off* anyone that can't, or can't be bothered, to walk home.
Bicycles: *Everything's within pedalling distance* and there are sheds at all the halls. Bike-rustling is a bit of problem, though.

CAREER PROSPECTS:

- Careers Service • No. of staff: 7 full • Unemployed after 6mths: 5%

A *huge* range of services, including help for *budding Bransons and media-wannabes*. There's also participation in Cymru Prosper Wales, which includes paid summer placements for graduates with Welsh businesses.

FAMOUS ALUMNI:

Huw Edwards (BBC TV newsreader); Arwel Hughes (conductor); Karl Hyde, Rick Smith (Underworld); Neil and Glenys Kinnock; Professor Bernard Knight (ret'd Home Office Pathologist, crime writer); Sian Lloyd (weatherwoman); Philip Madoc (actor); Sian Philips (actress); Tim Sebastian (BBC reporter).

FURTHER INFO:

- Prospectuses: undergrad; postgrad; some departments • Open days

A C A D E M I C

Like tabasco sauce, Cardiff's a good *all-rounder and pretty hot on lots of courses*. The science departments have had *lots of money chucked at them*, including from the merger with the College of Medicine, and *posh* new schools of chemistry, optometry and life sciences.

240-360		POINTS
Entry points: 240-360	Ave points: 350	
Applns per place: 6	Clearing: 3%	
No. of terms: 2	Length of terms: 15wks	
Staff/student ratio: 1:6	Study addicts: 24%	
Teaching: n/a	Research: *****	
Firsts: 14%	2.1s: 56%	
2.2s: 26%	3rds: 3%	

ADMISSIONS:

• Apply via UCAS

There are a *brain-boggling* 28 academic schools – everything from the School of Architechture to the School of Welsh.

SUBJECTS:

Business & Law: 17%   Health/Life Sciences: 20%
Engineering/Planning: 10%   Humanities: 28%
Healthcare: 15%   Physical Sciences: 10%

Best: Accounting; Ancient History & Archaeology; Anatomy & Physiology; Architecture; Bio-chemistry; Biology Chemistry; City & Regional Planning; Civil Engineering; Dentistry; Education; Electrical, Electronic & Systems Engineering; Enviromental Engineering; Language & Communication; Mechanical Engineering; Medicine; Optometry; Pharmacy; Philosophy; Psychology.

Unusual: The joint Cardiff-Bordeaux scheme offers a Cardiff degree in Politics and a diploma from the institute of Political science in Bordeaux. Students study for two years in each country.

LIBRARIES:

• 1,170,219 books • 3,404 study places • Spend per student: ££

Ten libraries in all with three main: Arts & Social Studies, the Aberconway and Science.

COMPUTERS:

• 5,500 workstations • 24-hr access • Spend per student: ££££

The University is kitting out student rooms with internet points.

E N T E R T A I N M E N T

THE CITY:

• Price of a pint of beer: £1.90 • Glass of wine: £1.40

Cinemas: The Chapter Arts Centre's arthouse screen adds more *refined/pretentious* culture to the several mainstream multiplexes in the city.

Theatres: Five theatres, including the Chapter Arts Centre (which also has a dance studio and exhibition centres), the New Theatre (home of the Welsh National Opera), the Sherman Theatre and the new Wales Millennium Centre, which houses art exhibitions as well as stage productions.

Pubs: *Some excellent boozers and some very average theme pubs that aren't worth the effort. Pushplugs: Clancey's (Irish); Rat & Carrot; The Woodville Arms (aka the Woody – a student haven); Sam's Bar; Macintosh (skittles in the summer). The redeveloped docks are full of pubs and clubs, which are generally student-supporting.*

Clubbing: *Tons of clubs to choose from, some with stickier carpets than others. Pushplugs: Liquid (Mondays); The Philly (medics night on Thurs); Sunday Service at Jumpin Jaks; Emporium and Blah Blah's (cheese); Club Ifor Bach (aka the Welsh Club) is popular on Wednesdays; the Square.*

Music venues: *Megastars call at International Arena and the Millennium Stadium when on tours. Mere musical mortals make do with St David's Hall or the Jazz bar.*

Other: For *culture-hounds*, there's the Museum of Welsh Life and Techniquest, a *big* hands-on science exhibition.

Eating out: *Cardiff boasts an entire street (Caroline Street) of kebab shops, which gets literally hidden under a carpet of polystyrene wrappers and semi-masticated donkey/doner meat on a Friday night. Pushplugs: Ethnic Deli (£10 for five dishes); Las Iguanas and Old Orleans (Tex-Mex); Ramone's (greasy spoon); Bistro 116; The Pear Tree (Cathays community centre); Taurus (steakhouse).*

LIBRARIES:

• 280,000 books • 650 study places
Four libraries, one on each of the main sites, and open till around 9pm Mon-Thu during term (earlier closing at weekends and completely on a Sunday). There's a slide library at Howard Gardens but this is a one-man-show *and its hours and facilities are as predictable as a monkey with a chainsaw.*

COMPUTERS:

• 1,000 workstations • 24-hr access
Computer facilities at Llandaff and Colchester Avenue are available through the small hours. The libraries all have networked workstations for students.

OTHER LEARNING FACILITIES:

Language labs; drama studio; CAD lab; media centre.

ENTERTAINMENT

CARDIFF: see Cardiff University
UNIVERSITY:

• Price of a pint of beer: £1.05 • Glass of wine: £1.30 • Can of Red Bull: £1.30
Bars: The Union runs five: one's a nightclub bar in Cardiff city centre; there are others on each site. Cyncoed's is the *fattest* of these and is *particularly sexy to sporty types.* Howard Gardens is a testing-ground for student bands, Llandaff's is a pre-club DJ promo spot, and *Colchester Avenue's isn't much use to anyone since it closes at 3pm.*
Theatres: Drama's *almost unheard of* outside the teaching course.
Music venues: A few student bands gig in Howard Gardens, *but only if the Union can convince them to put their dignity at stake.*
Clubbing: The Union club in the centre of Cardiff hosts a few club nights a week (often with free bus from halls), the most remarkable being Saturday's The Amp – a rocky, indie night marketed as 'the alternative to shit music' – *simple and to the point. We like it.*
Comedy/Cabaret: Fortnightly comedy network.
Food: *Nowt to shout about.* There's a cafeteria on each campus, plus a snack bar on the Cyncoed site.
Other: The Christmas Ball at the Cardiff International Arena induces all-night queuing when tickets go on sale and sell out in hours. Wheatus, Space, Cast and The Dum Dums are past headliners.

SOCIAL & POLITICAL

UNIVERSITY OF WALES INSTITUTE, CARDIFF STUDENTS' UNION:

• 3 sabbaticals • Turnout at last ballot: 15% • NUS member
Aside from running bars and shops, *UWICSU doesn't really have all that much to do politically.* Sports and welfare are its *biggest* hitters, with *rather lacklustre efforts* at keeping the kids in the halls entertained and at arranging the epic Freshers' Fortnight.

SU FACILITIES:

Spread over the four sites and managed by either University or Union: five bars; four cafeterias; two snack bars; three minibuses; ATMs; nursery; advice centre; three general/stationery/clothes shops; vending machines; launderette.

CLUBS (NON-SPORTING):

Alternative Music; American Football; Humanities. **See also Clubs tables.**

OTHER ORGANISATIONS:

Retro is the free monthly '*newspaper*', backed up by a weekly What's On? e-zine which students can subscribe to.

RELIGIOUS:

• 1 chaplain (CofE)
UWIC has a chapel and Cardiff is well stocked with mosques and churches.

PAID WORK: see Cardiff University

• Job bureau
Many UWIC students work during term and the Careers Service runs a job shop to help. The SU employs bar staff and shop assistants.

S P O R T S

• Recent successes: rugby union, squash, athletics, women's hockey • BUSA Ranking: 48
UWIC's Athletics Union copes well with limited funding – *students may need to fork out the cash to participate in national events* – and the facilities it uses are modern and *impressive for such a relatively new, small and disparate institution.*

SPORTS FACILITIES:

Football, rugby and Astroturf pitches; tennis centre; squash courts; indoor athletics centre; basketball court; gym; swimming pool. There's also the river for those who like their sport moist. Membership costs £15/yr, on top of which it's £1 per use. Cardiff's ice rink, dry ski slope and assorted leisure centres are accessible too.

SPORTING CLUBS:

Aquatics; Canoe; Ju-Jitsu; Lacrosse; Triathlon. **See Clubs tables**.

ATTRACTIONS: see Cardiff University

A C C O M M O A T I O N

IN COLLEGE:

• Catered: 1% • Catered cost: £81 (39wks) • Self-catering: 5%
• Self-catering cost: £53-90 (39wks) • First years living in: 90% • Insurance premium: £
Availability: Halls are available at the Cyncoed Campus, the Plas Gwyn Residential Campus (within walking distance of Llandaff) and at Evelian Court (a mile from Llandaff). All campuses, the city centre and popular areas for private student accommodation are served by the UWIC Rider. Most students loiter in the halls closest to the campus in which they're based. CCTV and 24-hr security patrols keep the peace.
Car parking: Permits aren't required, *but camels and eyes of needles spring to mind*.

EXTERNALLY: see Cardiff University

• Ave rent: £40 • Living at home: 20%
Availability: Most students manage to wrangle a shared house within reach of campus. *Quality of accommodation, however, is like a box of chocolates – some are lovely, others are just stinky brown goo.*
Housing help: The Accommodation Service publishes a vacancy list. *But that's it.*

Manchester University were banned from taking part in University Challenge in the 70s for answering every question 'Lenin' or 'Marx'. They were protesting against Oxbridge colleges being allowed to enter as separate institutions.

WELFARE

SERVICES:
- Lesbian/Gay/Bisexual Officer & Society • Nightline
- SU counsellors: 1 • Crime rating: !!!

Health: There are nurses on each campus and a drop-in doctor's surgery on the Cyncoed campus, weekdays.
Crèches/Nursery: Places for 40 kids aged up to 5.
Disabilities: Some adapted bedrooms and a dyslexia support centre. Contact the Disability Department before applying.

FINANCE:
- Ave debt per year: £3,061

Support: Hardship funds and sports scholarships have *a wee bit o' cash in them*.

Caythorpe

see De Montfort University

Cambridgeshire College of Arts and Technology (CCAT)

see APU

University of Central England

- *Formerly Birmingham Polytechnic*
University of Central England, Perry Barr, Birmingham, B42 2SU
Tel: (0121) 331 5000 E-mail: info@ucechoices.com
Website: www.ucechoices.com or www.uce.ac.uk
UCE Union of Students, Perry Barr, Birmingham, B42 2SU
Tel: (0121) 331 6802 E-mail: union.president@uce.ac.uk Website: www.uceunion.com

GENERAL

Birmingham, the pug-ugly duckling that got silicone implants and a face lift, is home to the nine very different campuses of UCE. Most of the sites are close to the city centre, except Bournville which is away on its own, *being arty and mysterious, but secretly just eating chocolate.* Perry Barr is the main site, catering for at least half of the students and it's only 3 miles from the centre. *Today's Birmingham is a culturally varied, exciting and modern city despite its mass of council housing and factories.* See also: University of Birmingham

Sex ratio (M:F): 39:61	Founded: 1971
Full-time u'grads: 11,915	Part-time: 6,660
Postgrads: 1,540	Non-degree: 1,892
Ave course: 3yrs	Ethnic: 40%
State:private school: 97:3	Flunk rate: 20%
Mature: 37%	International: 10%
Disabled: 309	Local: 65%

61%

39%

ATMOSPHERE:

Students have picked up on the determined, easy-going cheerfulness common to people in less than perfect surroundings and have a business-like attitude to work. UCE offers many FE courses and free courses for the unemployed, so the social mix isn't just the usual bunch of undergrads. The city's got plenty to do so boredom's rarely an issue.

SITES:

Perry Barr: (Most courses) Despite being the main site, Perry's not too big. Students stride *around purposefully*, getting an education. *Perry Barr is a fairly grubby part of the city (although the campus itself is a large and pleasant enough island). Its best features are a good number of local shops, a greyhound stadium opposite the campus and a station to get the hell out of there.*

Westbourne Road/Edgbaston: (Education and Nursing) 6 miles from Perry Barr, the main advantage of the site is the social scene offered at Broad St, 5 mins away. It attracts students from all around, *the nurses have nothing to do with it.*

Bournville: (Art & Design) 4 miles from the city centre, near the choccy factory, Bournville is one of four sites housing art and design courses. *Unsurprisingly, students are arty, and like a good, boozy laugh.*

Others: Gosta Green (Art & Design); Margaret Street (Art & Design); The Birmingham Conservatoire (Music); The Jewellery School (*Maths?*) in the city's Jewellery Quarter, *which is turning touristy.* There's also the Technology Innovation Centre at Millennium Point.

BIRMINGHAM: see University of Birmingham

TRAVEL: see University of Birmingham
With no inter-site transport laid on by the University, cars are handy.

CAREER PROSPECTS:

• Careers Service • No. of staff: 11 full/1 part • Unemployed after 6mths: 13%
Careers advice; interview training; jobs fairs and the *ever-useful* bulletin board are on hand for job needs.

FAMOUS ALUMNI:

Jim Crace (novelist); Alfred Bestall (creator, Rupert the Bear); Apache Indian (singer); Betty Jackson (fashion designer); Larry (cartoonist); Nigel Mansell (ex-F1 driver); Jas Mann (Babylon Zoo); Judy Simpson (Nightshade in Gladiators); Frank Skinner (comedian).

FURTHER INFO:

• Prospectuses: undergrad; postgrad • Open days

A C A D E M I C

UCE's got a *stonking* range of courses, grouped into serveral faculties: The Birmingham Conservatoire; The Birmingham Insititute of Art & Design; Business School; Innovation Centre; Health & Community Care; Law, Humanities & Social Sciences. Many of the courses are career-related, nurses especially tend to go straight into work, and many part-time and sandwich courses are up for grabs.

Entry points: 40–280	Ave points: n/a
Clearing: 10%	Applns per place: n/a
No. of terms: 3	Length of terms: 11wks
Staff/student ratio: 1:15	Study addicts: 16%
Teaching: **	Research: *
Year abroad: <1%	Sandwich students: 3%
Firsts: 16%	2.2s: 37%
2.1s: 52%	3rds: 5%

ADMISSIONS:

• Apply via UCAS

SUBJECTS:

Birmingham Institute of Art & Design: 15%
Business School: 14%
Computing: 9%
Education: 7%
Health: 27%
Unusual: Gemmology; Horology.

Law, Humanities & Social Sciences: 6%
Music: 2%
Property & Construction and Planning & Housing: 6%
Technology Innovation Centre: 11%

LIBRARIES:

• 691,316 books • 897 study places • Spend per student: £
Perry Barr has the main Kenrick Library and there are seven more specialist libraries on the different sites for the courses based there. *A good variety of books, but competition can be fierce.*

COMPUTERS:

• 900 workstations
Each site has its own computer rooms, not all have internet access.

ENTERTAINMENT

CITY: see University of Birmingham

UNIVERSITY:

• Price of a pint of beer: £1.50 • Glass of wine: £1.25
Bars: Including the Union bar, Bar 42 (cap 600); the Edge at Westbourne Road (350); the Village Inn (200). There are also bars at Moor Lane and the Conservatoire.
Theatres/Film: A drama group has been *relentlessly* doing stuff like Grease for the past few years, but people love it. The film club shows blockbusters, world cinema and old favourites twice a week.
Music venues/Clubbing: Big name bands are a rare sight, but Birmingham itself is always on the route of famous musicians passing through. Clubbing can be had at Perry Barr; Bar 42; the Edge and the Union Club (600).
Comedy/Cabaret: Funsters pop in fortnightly.
Food: Every site has an eatery; kosher and vegan meals are now on the menu.
Other: Two sports balls a year and various faculties and societies like to put on a bit of a do.

SOCIAL & POLITICAL

UNIVERSITY OF CENTRAL ENGLAND STUDENTS' UNION (UCESU):

• Turnout at last ballot: 9% • NUS member
UCESU was the first SU to become a limited company. *Split sites, limited facilities and downright disorganisation don't inspire confidence. They're good with awareness campaigns though.*

SU FACILITIES:

The Union has facilities on five sites. At the SU's main centre at Perry Barr, there's a *cheap* bar, shop, advice centre, Endsleigh Insurance office, games machines, photo booth and photocopier. There's also a NatWest bank.

CLUBS (NON-SPORTING):

Archaos (architecture); Cedd House (religious & secular forum); Podiatry (feet). **See also Clubs tables.**

58%	
Sex ratio (M:F): 42:58	Founded: 1828
Full-time u'grads: 15,490	Part-time: 9,312
Postgrads: 680	Non-degree: 11,088
Ave course: 3yrs	Ethnic: 14%
State:private school: 96:4	Flunk rate: 26%
Mature: 21%	International: 15%
Disabled: 427	Local: 27%
42%	

ATMOSPHERE:

There are two types of students in Preston: level-headed bookish types with a thirst for learning but not much more beyond; and their racier colleagues, with a taste for life's thrills, who tack the learning bit on as an inconvenient extra. They don't mix much, though both keep out of the way of the locals, who see students as fair game for Saturday night target practice.

PRESTON:

• Population: 129,600 • City centre: 500m • London: 202 miles
• Blackpool: 15 miles • Manchester: 25 miles
• High temp: 19 • Low temp: 1 • Rainfall: 71

Preston gets a *double thumbs-up*: one for cost and one for quality of life. It's *not really a student city*, but there are *enough* cheap drinks promos to *keep the pub-bound in pocket*. The Lancashire countryside is beautiful, as are some of the north-west's seaside towns (Southport, Morecambe etc.).

TRAVEL:

Trains: Preston Station, 400m from campus, runs direct trains to London (£28.40), Manchester (£6.55) and beyond.
Coaches: National Express services to, among other places, London (£18.50) and Manchester (£3.40).
Car: Preston is on the A6, A49, A59 and A677, and just off the M6, M55 and M61. The town centre can get congested, although there's a new park and ride in the 'burbs.
Air: Manchester International is the closest for cheap international and domestic flights.
Hitching: *North or south by the A6 or M6.*
Local: Local buses keep to a persnickety fare system (no change given). Discounted Rambler tickets (anywhere in town, £5.20/week) are available.
Taxis: *Cheap and plentiful – like a chav's jewellery.*
Bicycles: Bikes are *popular* for getting around the campus *sprawl*, but it's *not much fun* humping them around the hills.

CAREER PROSPECTS:

• Careers Service • No. of staff: 2 full/4 part • Unemployed after 6mths: 6%
Bulletin boards, jobs fairs, careers library and interview training to help repay those *mountainous* overdrafts.

FAMOUS ALUMNI:

Mark Beaumont (NME hack); Victoria Darbyshire, Ian Payne (BBC Radio 5 LIve); Simon Kelner (Editor, the Independent); Joe Lydon (rugby league); Phil MacIntyre (pop promoter); Vicky Marsden (DJ); Tjinder Singh, Ben Ayres (Cornershop).

FURTHER INFO:

• Prospectuses: undergrad; postgrad; some depts • Open days
For open day and campus tour information call (01772) 892 700.

A C A D E M I C

Lots of vocational and practical subjects *boosted by cosy links with local industries*. The NCTJ journalism course is *pretty well respected* and oversubscribed as a result. Some courses offer a year out or sandwich placements.

Entry points: 90-300
Applns per place: n/a
No. of terms: 2
Staff/student ratio: 1:18
Teaching: **
Firsts: 8%
2.1s: 40%

Ave points: 220
Clearing: 21%
Length of terms: 15wks
Study addicts: 18%
Research: ***
2.2s: 39%
3rds: 6%

ADMISSIONS:

• Apply via UCAS/NMAS for nursing

SUBJECTS:

Business School: 13%
Cultural Legal & Social Studies: 26%
Design & Technology: 22%

Health: 24%
Science: 14%

Best: American Studies; Art & Design; Biological Sciences; Built Environment; Business & Management; Drama; Education; Hospitality, Leisure, Recreation & Sport; Joint Languages; Journalism; Linguistics; Nursing & Midwifery; Politics; Psychology; Subjects allied to Medicine.
Unusual: Motor Sports (students actually get to race).

LIBRARIES:

• 692,864 books • 1,240 study places • 24-hr access • Spend per student: ££
The main library's housed in one of the campus's *more modern* buildings. In addition to the folding paper variety, there are 10,000 e-books to scroll through. The library's open till 2am on school nights, for *post-pub essay crises*.

COMPUTERS:

• 991 workstations • 24-hr access

OTHER LEARNING FACILITIES:

Language labs; music rooms; CAD lab; audio/TV centre; 3D visualisation lab; practice courtroom; TV/radio studios; crime scene house; clinical skills lab.

ENTERTAINMENT

THE CITY:

• Price of a pint of beer: £1.60 • Glass of wine: £2 • Can of Red Bull: £2
Cinemas: Two, with 17 screens between them.
Theatres: The Charter Theatre, 15 mins walk from campus, serves up a diet of Shakespeare and mainstream *modern* stuff.
Pubs: *Generally student-hardened*, although, *as Elton says, Saturday night's alright for fighing*. Pushplugs: Roper Hall; O'Neill's; the Adelphi; the Ship.
Clubbing: *Pushplugs: the Mill (alternative, free bus service); Squires (Mondays); Tokyo Jo's (Wednesdays).*
Music venues: The Guild Hall is the place for *lots of mainstream* stuff. The Adelphi is an indie-fan's *home from home*. Prest Fest is the University's autumn extravaganza.
Eating out: *Varied, cheap and open well after McDonald's has turfed out. Pushplugs: Isis Café bar; ultimate student friendly Chill-Out Zone; Tiggi's (50% student discount); Bella Pasta (half-price on Wednesdays).*

UNIVERSITY:

• Price of a pint of beer: £1.80 • Glass of wine: £2 • Can of Red Bull: £1.80
Bars: Source is the latest boozer to land in 53 Degrees, the new Union building with a late weekend licence, wine and cocktails, plasma-screen for sport and telly, and more.
Theatres: Semi-official alt drama scene uses St Peter's Arts Centre for *all sorts* of productions.

Film: The film society shows one a week and organises jaunts to the local cinemas. Membership is £3, with a £1.50 entry fee for every film. Also *regular* trips to European cities (Paris, Amsterdam, Dublin, Barcelona).

Clubbing: 'Preston Biggest Bender' and 'Pop Shack' are the *most popular* nights. Trevor Nelson has stopped by recently, as have Feel, Eddie Halliwell and Scott Bond.

Music venues: The new Union building brings UCLan its first major live venue (capacity 1,200) and one of the biggest in the local area. Confirmed acts include Goldie Lookin' Chain and *pint-sized* Trevor Nelson.

Comedy/Cabaret: *Hugely popular* comedy nights feature acts like Rob Deering and Kerry Marks, as well as twice-yearly comedy weekends at the SU amphitheatre.

Food: Three refectories open all day. The SU eateries (Mr Nibbles for sarnies, Polygon for pub lunch and Union Square for all-day breakfasts) are also foodie *favourites*.

SOCIAL & POLITICAL

UNIVERSITY OF CENTRAL LANCASHIRE STUDENTS' UNION:

• 7 sabbaticals • Turnout at last ballot: 7% • NUS member

The SU are pretty close to the University authorities and although election turn-outs have picked up in recent years, *there's not a lot of politicking* to be done in Preston.

SU FACILITIES:

53 Degrees – the new SU building – is so new *the paint's still wet*. New facilities *have bumped up the entertainment X-factor* – there's space for live music, concerts and clubbing, and two new bars. Meanwhile, the old SU building is being given *the botox treatment* and should emerge with new retail facilities supplying student essentials (*paperclips and Pot Noodle, then*), a café and an offie.

CLUBS (NON-SPORTING):

Campanology (bell-ringing); Musical Theatre; Paintball; Poker. **See also Clubs tables.**

OTHER ORGANISATIONS:

The weekly paper, Pluto, isn't a Disney comic, but an award-winning student newspaper staffed by *keenos* from the journo department. Their companions on the airwaves are Frequency 1350AM.

RELIGIOUS:

• 2 chaplains (RC, multi-faith)

Multi-faith centre for prayer worship and quiet reflection. The city has a cathedral, churches and places of worship for Muslims, Hindus, Sikhs, Buddhists and Jews.

PAID WORK:

• Job bureau

Jobshop ('the Bridge'). *Loads* of vacancies round college and in Preston for part-timers.

SPORTS

• Recent successes: none • BUSA Ranking: 48

Sports facilities are *pretty extensive* and students *take advantage of everything they can find* in the city. There's an annual Lancashire Cup competition against Lancaster University.

SPORTS FACILITIES:

65 acres of sports fields including: 12 football, four hockey, six rugby and four cricket pitches; squash, tennis, netball and basketball courts; sports halls; running track and athletics field; gym/multigym; aerobics studio; climbing wall. The Foster Sports Centre has

studios for health and fitness, martial arts and fencing, as well as a weights room and courts for a variety of ball sports. The local area has athletics and running space; squash and tennis courts; swimming pool, ice rink; bowling green; golf course; dry and artificial snow ski slopes; pot-holing caves, lakes and rivers for splashing about in. Joint membership of Preston Sports Arena and University facilities costs £28/term or £45/yr.

SPORTING CLUBS:
See Clubs tables.

ATTRACTIONS:
Preston's home to the National Museum of Football. Preston North End are the *less glamorous* local team.

ACCOMMODATION

IN COLLEGE:
- Catered: 1% • Cost: £51 (37wks)
- Self-catering: 8% • Cost: £59-66 (37wks)
- First years living in: 50% • Insurance premium: £££

Availability: Accommodation's reserved for 1st years. Everyone who wants a room – normally about half the fresher population – can get one. It's *bog-standard* student digs, with shared kitchens and bathrooms. A few rooms are adapted for disabled students and all are on campus. The catered rooms are a *bit schooly*, with school dinners to boot, but there's *more camaraderie* than in the self-catered flats. Roeburn Hall is *the address of choice – luxurious and expensive* with en-suite facilities. 24-hour security's *tight* and there's a free internal phone system in all college rooms.
Car parking: *Easy enough* with a permit.

EXTERNALLY:
- Ave rent: £58

Availability: *Hardly a hassle* to find a house in Preston, the standard's *decent*, too. Students *prefer* to live in Plungington and Broadgate rather than Deepdale or Ashton. Lots of private halls have sprung up in the last few years. It's a *small city*, so students *don't tend to worry* about *long* and *tedious* commutes into college.
Housing help: Eight staff in the accommodation office *spread their net* all over town.

WELFARE

SERVICES:
- Lesbian/Gay/Bisexual Officer & Society • Ethnic Minorities Officer & Society
- Women's Officer & Society • Mature Students' Officer & Society
- International Students' Officer & Society • Postgrad Officer & Society
- Disabilities Officer & Society • Late-night minibus • Self-defence classes • Taxi fund
- University counsellors: 1 full/8 part • Crime rating: !!!

The 'i' Student Advice Centre does student support and answers enquiries on most issues, from Council tax to accommodation quibbles via specific support for international and disabled students, and anyone else who needs a hand.
Health: A health centre on campus has five GPs and two nurses.
Crèches/Nursery: 70 places for ages 1-5yrs.
Disabilities: *Good* access all across campus with wheelchair access, hearing loops and special accommodation.

Dundee University staff and students rehearsed and produced 7 Brides for 7 Brothers in 23 hours and 30 mins and now hold the world record for the fastest ever staging of a musical.

FINANCE:
- Ave debt per year: £5,178
- Access fund: £1,387,020 • Successful applications/yr: 1,130
- Ave payment: £100-3,500

Support: A small hardship fund is available to international and some part-time students and emergency loans of up to £250 *can keep the more desperate in baked beans and Wotsits for as long as necessary*. 'Ones to Watch' scholarships offer a grand to full-time undergrads who come from mid-income families.

Central London Poly
see University of Westminster

Central St Martins College of Art
see University of the Arts, London

Charing Cross & Westminster Hospital
see Imperial College, London

Charlotte Mason
see Lancaster University

Chelsea College of Art
see University of the Arts, London

Cheltenham & Gloucester College of Higher Education
see University of Gloucestershire

Chester College
see Liverpool University

University College Chester
see Liverpool University

University College Chichester, Bishop Otter Campus, College Lane, Chichester, West Sussex, PO19 6PE Tel: (01243) 816 000 E-mail: admissions@ucc.ac.uk Website: www.ucc.ac.uk
University College Chichester's Students' Union, Bishop Otter Campus, College Lane, Chichester, West Sussex, PO19 6PE Tel: (01243) 816 390
E-mail: studentsunion@ucc.ac.uk Website: www.uccsu.org.uk
See below for details of other sites.

Despite the name, only one of this college's three sites is in Chichester itself. The Bishop Otter Campus, named after the 19th-century religious leader *and aquatic mammal*, is a 38-acre site just outside the centre of this *pretty* cathedral city, 20 miles from Portsmouth. It was founded in 1839 as Bishop Otter College. They merged in 1977 and both sites (see below for details of the Bognor Regis site) have several modern additions. A high proportion of students are on teaching-related or sports courses. The College now validates its own degrees and has started to offer degrees off the mainland in association with the Isle of Wight College.

Sex ratio (M:F): 30:70	**Founded: 1839**
Full-time u'grads: 2,435	**Part-time: 735**
Postgrads: 240	**Non-degree: 413**
Ave course: 3yrs	**Ethnic: 5%**
State:private school: 87:2	**Flunk rate: 14%**
Mature: 46%	**International: 6%**
Disabled: 116	**Local: 29%**

ATMOSPHERE:

Given the size of the campuses, it's not surprising that there's a close-knit, friendly atmosphere. It feels as though everyone knows everyone else, but luckily, the students are laid back and lively enough to keep things from getting too claustrophobic. Half sports students half everyone else can sometimes lead to a bit of a culture clash, but nothing bad tempered. The two main campuses are 6 miles apart and free buses run between them.

MINOR SITES:

Crawley: (Education & English) This *small, friendly* satellite campus in Crawley was originally set up for mature students. Most Crawley students also spend a day a week at one of the main campuses. **See below for details of the Bognor Regis site.**

CHICHESTER:

• Population: 106,450 • City centre: 800m • London: 75 miles • Portsmouth: 20 miles • Brighton: 32 miles • High temp: 21 • Low temp: 2 • Rainfall: 75
The Bishop Otter campus is set in parkland on the outskirts of Chichester, a historic cathedral city known to the locals as 'Chi' (pronounced to rhyme with 'eye'). *It's a cream tea and antiques kind of place. Although four Georgian shopping streets add a bit of bustle to the centre, quaintness is never far away.* **See below for details of Bognor Regis.**

TRAVEL:

Trains: Chichester Station (15 mins walk from campus) has direct services to London Victoria (90 mins, £14.55); Portsmouth (45 mins, £4.90 sgl); Brighton (55 mins, £5.50); Southampton (50 mins, £13.95).
Coaches: The coach station (15 mins walk from campus) has services to London Victoria (£18.40, 5 hrs); Portsmouth and Brighton ($2\frac{1}{2}$ hrs, £6.40); Southampton ($2\frac{1}{2}$ hrs, £10.40).
Car: *Decent* road links to London including M25 London orbital ($1\frac{1}{4}$ hr via A27/A3); Bristol (3 hrs via A27/M27/A36); Birmingham ($3\frac{1}{2}$ hrs via A27(M)/A34/M40). Parking *isn't a nightmare, and should be even sweeter when the promised park & ride scheme gets off the ground.*
Air: Flights from Southampton (34 miles), Gatwick (43 miles) and Heathrow.
Local: Buses and trains from/to campuses cost £5 and £3.40 return respectively.
College: Free coaches *nip* between sites, though they're not suitable for wheelchairs or those with mobility problems. They run weekdays, hourly during the day, latest service 9.20pm.
Bicycles: Pedal pushers can get between campuses in 30-40 mins. *And why not, with plenty of bike spaces and no major theft problem?*

CAREER PROSPECTS:

• Careers Service • No. of staff: 2 full/1 part • Unemployed after 6mths: 6%
Bulletin boards, library, teaching fair, job fairs, one-to-one guidance and interview training.

FAMOUS ALUMNI:

Jason Merrills (actor, Casualty/Cutting It).

FURTHER INFO:

• Prospectuses: undergrad; postgrad; departmental; part-time/int'l • Open days
Mature student evenings and taster days in some depts where applicants can sample lectures or workshops.

ACADEMIC

Modular undergrad courses, *with a cosy, friendly touch to them*. Teaching is based on seminars, workshops, syndicates and small group learning rather than lectures. Most courses involve about 12 hrs a week, 20 for teaching, visual and performing arts courses. Assessment methods range from seminar presentations to exams, dissertations in the final year. *Teaching and Sports Science are the traditional high flyers.*

Entry points: 160-300	Ave points: 217
Applns per place: 5	Clearing: <1%
No. of terms: 2	Length of terms: 15wks
Staff/student ratio: 1:20	Study addicts: 11%
Teaching: *	Research: *
Year abroad: 1%	Sandwich students: 1%
Firsts: 5%	2.2s: 47%
2.1s: 40%	3rds: 8%

160-300   POINTS

ADMISSIONS:

• Apply via UCAS
The College considers applicants from non-traditional backgrounds (*so good for mature students without formal qualifications*). International students need equivalent qualifications.

SUBJECTS:

Cultural Studies: 15%	Sport Sciences: 19%
Performing Arts: 16%	Teacher Education: 21%
Physical Education: 13%	Visual Arts: 5%
Social Studies: 8%	

Best: Dance; Fine Art; Media; Theology; Sports Science.
Unusual: Adventure Education.

LIBRARIES:

• 260,000 books • 480 study places • Spend per student: ££
Library on each campus (Bishop Otter's is *the bigger*, with 160,000 books and 410 study spaces). An integrated system means students can borrow, request and return books from either library. CDs, DVDs and videos can be also used in either library. *With headphones, natch.*

COMPUTERS:

• 155 workstations • Spend per student: £££££
IT provisions at Bishop Otter are housed in the library, where there are also three laptop points. *Computer rooms don't open late enough to suit nocturnal candle-burners.*

OTHER LEARNING FACILITIES:

Drama facilities; media centre; music rooms; art gallery.

ENTERTAINMENT

THE TOWN:

CHICHESTER

See below for details of other sites.
- Price of a pint of beer: £2.30 • Glass of wine: £2.30 • Can of Red Bull: £1.70

Cinemas: The New Park Centre (within walking distance of campus) has a bar and shows up to five arthouse films and new releases a day (one screen), as well as hosting an annual 18-day film festival. Student discounts here and at the nearby six-screen Cineworld.

Theatres: Next door to campus the *famous* Chichester Festival Theatre and its extension, the Minerva Theatre, put on a wide variety of shows.

Pubs: *Several are student-friendly including the Swan, Hogshead and the Chichester. Pushplugs: Weatherspoons (cheap); the Hope (near-by); and the Nag's Head (good nosh). Best avoided: the Cross (boring); the George & Dragon (pretentious); the Slug & Lettuce (soulless).*

Clubbing: Drayton has an 80s-style student night on Tuesdays and 90s, Garage and RnB occasions the rest of the week.

Music venues: Local bands across the musical spectrum play at pubs like the Four Chestnuts, the Fountain, the Swan and the Chichester Inn.

Eating out: *Weatherspoons is typically popular, and there's KFC and McDonald's in the new Southgate complex. There are truckloads of sandwich shops and tea rooms around the town, but some can be expensive. For evening eating, the Charcoal Grill offers drunken punters salvation in the form of their kebabs, and Perfect Pizza is also open till midnight.*

Other: Aside from the rolling serenity of the South Downs and the Sussex coast, culture and calm can be found in Chichester Cathedral, Arundel Castle, the Pallant House Gallery and Goodwood Sculpture Park.

THE COLLEGE:
- Price of a pint of beer: £1.80 • Glass of wine: £1.70 • Can of Red Bull: £1.70

Bars: The new Zeebar building has space for 600 *boozy* girls and boys but those not boozing are well-up for the *varied* ents including karaoke and quizzes. A kitchen is expected in the near future.

Theatres: The Showroom Theatre hosts professional and student performances.

Clubbing/Music venues: Local and unsigned bands make a beeline for the Zeebar. There's *a bit more to get excited about* in the nightclub (also in the Zeebar) with the likes of Shaggy and DJ Spoony putting in appearances. Wednesday night is cheesy, but at two quid to get in it's *as cheap as chips*.

Food: The College-run canteen can hold 150 *munchers*. Holts Coffee Bar is more expensive *but unbeatable when it comes to a biscuit and a bit of a sit down*.

Other: Five balls a year – Freshers, Graduation, Christmas, Valentines and, *best-of-all*, the all-night Valedictory Ball.

SOCIAL & POLITICAL

UNIVERSITY COLLEGE CHICHESTER'S STUDENTS' UNION:
- 2 sabbaticals • Turnout at last ballot: 13% • NUS member

Politics isn't the name of the SU's game, but it does organise ents, sports clubs/teams and socs and *sticks up for its members whenever necessary*. The new SU building, Zeebar, is *£1.6m well spent* – it's a multi-purpose bar/meeting area that's open all day and usually *buzzing*. Relations with the College are *warm and toasty*.

SU FACILITIES:

Two bars; two canteens; pool tables; two minibuses for hire; cashpoint; photocopier; fax; photo booth; phone; games machine; vending machine; shop; launderette.

CLUBS (NON-SPORTING):

Art; Board Riders; Cinema; Drama; Literature Society; Mature Students; Music Society; Rock/Indie Music. **See also Clubs Table.**

OTHER ORGANISATIONS:

The Clash is the SU paper (free, twice termly). Rag *did well* in raising three grand last year for good causes.

RELIGIOUS:

• 1 chaplain (CofE)

Chapel on site. There are CofE, RC and Baptist churches in and around Chichester. Other faiths might have to look a little harder.

PAID WORK:

• Job bureau

Jobshop for internal and external jobs and vacancies board. The careers service *does what it can* to help students find vocational/vacation work. The College employs a number of students in catering, marketing, accomodation etc., and the city itself has a few retail opportunities.

• Recent successes: basketball; hockey; netball; rugby • BUSA Ranking: 48

A healthy contingent of sports students and decent facilities keep sporting success high on the agenda. The SU organises recreational sporting shenanigans and the PE Department looks after the academic side of things. *A bit of internal wrangling goes on over whether the College provides competitive sport or sport for all – it tries its best to do both.* The College's sports staff were heavily involved with some of the 2004 Olympics' athletes.

SPORTS FACILITIES:

9 acres of sports fields; lacrosse pitch. The sports centre at Bishop Otter includes a sports hall, indoor and outdoor climbing walls, fitness suite, Astro pitch, tennis/netball courts and two gyms. Sports clubs train free; other students get membership at a maximum of £90 a year. The *large* Westgate Leisure Centre in town has courts, swimming, gym, classes, sauna and jacuzzi. The Chichester Lawn Tennis & Squash Club offers a yearly subscription.

SPORTING CLUBS:

Frisbee; Lacrosse; Land Boarding; Rock Climbing; Surfing. **See also Clubs table.**

IN COLLEGE:

• Catered: 19% • Cost: £85-110(30wks)
• First years living in: 90% • Insurance premium: £

Availability: 458 places in catered accommodation are allocated on a first-come, first-served basis, *which leaves one in ten 1st years disappointed.* 5% share. More than half the rooms are en-suite and launderette, TV lounge and common room facilities are available to all. Two rooms are adapted for disabled students Insurance is included in the rent.

Car parking: By £10 permit. 1st years living on campus aren't allowed parking. About 70% of students have wheels. *Some have cars too.*

EXTERNALLY (CHICHESTER):

• Ave rent: £60 • Living at home: 40%

Availability: The influx of summer visitors means 9-month contracts are pretty common – *these are a handy way of keeping costs low over the long vacation.* Most students live in privately rented houses, flats or homestays (ie. with a landlord or family, perhaps including meals). *Lodgings are cheaper further away from campus.*

Housing help: The accommodation office (three staff) has: vacancy list; approved landlord list; property vetting; fire/gas certificate checks; bulletin board.

WELFARE

SERVICES:
- Lesbian/Gay/Bisexual Society • Ethnic Minorities Officer & Society
- International Students' Officer • Disabilities Officer • Taxi fund
- College counsellors: 1 full/2 part • SU counsellors: 1 full/8 part • Crime rating: !

Health: Full-time nurse; GP surgeries twice a week.
Women: Cheap attack alarms supplied by the SU.
Disabilities: Access *isn't comprehensive, but the campus is flat and most central buildings and two teaching buildings are accessible.* The disability support team helps with technical stuff like note-taking, readers, communicators and non-medical helpers. There are taping, Braille and large screen computer facilities and plans for a guide dog pen.

FINANCE:
- Ave debt per year: £4,015

Fees: Part-time students pay £145 a module. An MA costs £2,500, as does an MSc. International students cough up £6,300 for classroom-based courses, £7,000 for lab-based ones.
- Access fund: £281,000 • Successful applications/yr: 120 • Ave payment: £500-3,500

Various scholarships are available from various departments.

Bognor Regis

University College Chichester, Bognor Regis Campus, Upper Bognor Road, Bognor Regis, West Sussex, PO21 1HR
Tel: (01243) 816 000
The site dates from 1947 and is centred on a Georgian mansion terrace in the seaside resort of Bognor Regis. Its 1,200-odd students create a *buzzing atmosphere similar to that found 6 miles away at the Chichester site.*

BOGNOR REGIS:

A traditional seaside resort with plenty of easily-accessible coastline to pull in watersports lovers. It's popular with tourists, particularly in the summer.
Travel: Bognor has its own mainline railway station within walking distance of the site ($1\frac{3}{4}$ hrs direct to London Victoria) and good road links to the rest of the country. Driving times to the Bognor Regis Campus are 15 mins longer than those given above for Chichester. Disabled parking spaces are available.

ACADEMIC:

Teacher Education; Business Studies; Tourism Management; IT and Maths are all based at Bognor. A Learning Resource Centre provides 70 study spaces, 100,000 books and 70 computers, all with internet access.

ENTERTAINMENT:

The town: *All the fun of the seaside. Pushplugs: Hatters/Wetherspoons (cheap, heaving and unhampered by anything unpleasant like atmosphere); The Beach House (mad atmosphere, DJs like the Minestrone of Sound or the Chemistry Brothers); the Waiting Room (live music, very student-friendly); The Prom/Bottle bar (weekend DJs, late-opening); William Hardwick (pricey but quiet and comfy).* As well as the usual range of fast food outlets there are a few *reasonable restaurants.* The Alexandra Theatre has plays and films, and the *old-fashioned* Picturedrome shows *recent releases.* Clubwise, there's Vision (student nights on Tuesdays and Thursdays) and Oceans 11 (alternative music on Wednesdays).
Site: The Macklin Bar has a main bar upstairs and a cocktail affair below. Entertainment of the open mic or karaoke variety is laid on nearly every night. There's also free Playstation 2 as well as pool tables and arcade machines to *while the hours away.* The refectory is run by the same company as the main site, *so don't expect Bognor delicacies.*

CAREER PROSPECTS:

• Careers Service • No. of staff: 6 full • Unemployed after 6mths: 6%
The vocational nature of many courses means most students are *highly employable* on graduation.

FAMOUS ALUMNI:

Brendan Barber (TUC president); Michael Fish (weatherman); Stelios Haji-Ionnau (Easy group); Ruby Hammer (Ruby & Millie make-up); Dermot Murnaghan (newsreader); Sophie Raworth (BBC newsreader); Jack Warner (Dixon of Dock Green – *ask your gran*).

FURTHER INFO:

• Prospectuses: undergrad; postgrad; departmental • Open days
Open days can be arranged by schools.

A C A D E M I C

City has made vocational business and technology courses its niche and has an *impressive* reputation, notably in the journalism department, whose postgraduate diploma is *world-renowned*.

Entry points: 80-320	Ave points: n/a
No. of terms: 3	Length of terms: 10wks
Staff/student ratio: 1:18	Study addicts: 15%
Teaching: **	Research: **
Year abroad: 2%	Sandwich students: 7%

ADMISSIONS:

• Apply via UCAS/NMAS

SUBJECTS:

Arts/Humanities: 4%	Business/Management: 16%
Medical Sciences: 34%	Sciences: 4%
Social Sciences: 14%	IT: 15%

Best:
Art & Design; Business & Management; Economics; Electrical & Electronic Engineering; Librarianship & Information Management; Maths/Statistics; Nursing; Other studies allied to Medicine; Psychology.

LIBRARIES:

• 250,000 books • 1,274 study places • Spend per student: £
Two main libraries are supplemented by several departmental ones. The Cass Business library is *ultra-modern and sorted* for everything students need.

COMPUTERS:

• 400 workstations • 24-hr access
Despite a *reasonable* spread of computers across the site there can be *a lot of pressure on* places.

E N T E R T A I N M E N T

THE CITY: see University of London

• Price of a pint of beer: £2.50 • Glass of wine: £2.80 • Can of Red Bull: £2
Islington, Shoreditch and the City have their share of *diverse* entertainments including pubs, clubs, bars, a welter of restaurants and snack bars, galleries, theatres, cinemas and more.
Cinemas: The Screen on the Green and a Warner Village cater for cult and mainstream tastes.

Theatres: Sadler's Wells is just across the road, and shows ballet, contemporary dance and international theatre.

Pubs: A trip from lectures to the Bull *is like staggering out of the back door and finding a raucous party in the shed. The Peasant's rather upmarket* and has a *reputation as a hip gastropub. Neither could be described as cheap, even though the Bull feels as though it should be.* Nevertheless, they're *popular* with students, despite rivalry from Islington and Clerkenwell's other boozers.

Clubbing: Fabric and Turnmills (Clerkenwell/Farringdon) are within easy stomping distance.

Music venues: The Carling Academy in Islington's N1 centre hosts a lot of hot young indie bands – Franz Ferdinand were recent visitors

Eating out: Kebab houses and chip shops are *ten a penny* almost anywhere in London, but in Islington so are bistros, gastropubs, sandwich/coffee shops and *credit-card-busting posher* places.

UNIVERSITY:

• Price of a pint of beer: £1.50 • Glass of wine: £2 • Can of Red Bull: £1.50

There are regular *cheap and cheerful* nights in the University bars, with prominent TVs and computer games to help idle away the hours. The *regulation cheese-fests* play second fiddle to a *more bling* brand of ents which attract *big names* from the UK urban scene.

Bars: The Wonderbar is a *clubby, hectic, humid sort of place*, while Saddlers bar is a *little more refined, if only a very little more.*

Clubbing: Pressure Cooker at the Wonderbar is the *most aptly named, not to mention popular* night. DJ Nicky Smood (Kiss FM), MC Klakie (Ministry of Sound) and Rampage (Radio 1Xtra) are recent bookings.

Comedy/Cabaret: Occasional comedy nights *provide a break* from the drinks and dancing.

Food: The University runs two refectories – *pricey but convenient*, and the Wonderbar does Mexican food. Saddlers bar serves snacks and sandwiches. As university fodder goes, *nowhere's particularly cheap, but readjust to London prices, and it's not criminally costly.*

Other: The Freshers Ball is *a chance to pull on the penguin suit.*

SOCIAL & POLITICAL

CITY UNIVERSITY STUDENTS' UNION

• 7 sabbaticals • NUS member

CUSU did a *canny* bit of business in turning the social scene management over to university hands, but it has left the student rep body *without a great amount to do*. Facilities are *lightweight* in comparison to ULU, which City students are not entitled to use (*although many do*).

SU FACILITIES:

Two bars; committee room; general shop; games area; minibus hire; snooker and pool tables; vending machines and video games; travel shops; secondhand book stall.

CLUBS (NON-SPORTING):

Finance & Investment, Chinese, Cypriot, Economics, Hellenic, Hindu, Law, Malaysian, Mauritian, Nordic, Optometry, Sikh. **See also Clubs tables.**

OTHER ORGANISATIONS:

The CUSU-run student paper, Massive, is published two or three times a term and Divercity radio can be caught on the net, in the SU foyer and from time to time in the Wonderbar. City has a *long tradition* of charity rag, and has held events ranging from the *sexy* (World's largest Ann Summers Party, erotic dance nights) to the *stupid* (life sized carrot costumes).

RELIGIOUS:

• 5 chaplains (Methodist/FC; CofE; RC; Greek Orthodox), rabbi

There's a Muslim prayer room on site, but London provides well for all faiths.

PAID WORK: see University of London

• Job bureau • Paid work: term-time 18%: hols 30%
There are *plenty* of opportunities for students to find work and the university job bureau helps students on their way after graduation.

SPORTS

• BUSA Ranking: 48
City is *decidedly sluggish, with study and partying higher on most agendas.*

SPORTS FACILITIES:

City owns a *modest* sports centre, providing: aerobics; basketball courts; gym; martial arts; netball courts; squash courts; sports hall; sauna and steam room. Membership costs £20 per month. Shared rugby, hockey, football, tennis and cricket grounds are dotted around north London and the rowing club has a boathouse at Chiswick. Surfers can use the Queen Mary Sailing Club.

SPORTING CLUBS:
See Clubs tables.

ATTRACTIONS: see University of London

Arsenal are the local football team, although chances of getting tickets are *slim. Otherwise there's the pick of London's plethora of teams across just about every possible sport.*

ACCOMMODATION

IN COLLEGE:

• Self-catering: 12% • Cost: £89-96 (35-48wks) • Insurance premium: £££
Availability: Accomodation is generally *good, secure and close to university.* The prices may seem *steep* but a quick look at the private rental market in the area says students are getting *a bit of a steal.* Francis Rowley Court is the *address of choice.* Walter Sickert Hall is *less desirable.* Most accomodation has shared kitchens and laundrette facilities; cleaners are also on hand in some locations.

EXTERNALLY: see University of London

• Ave rent: £80 • Living at home: 20%
Availability: Finding *affordable* digs anywhere this near the centre of London is a *nightmare,* particularly if you can't pay more than £80 a week. *Hackney, Camden and Stoke Newington are all good bets with easy* bus routes into Islington.
Housing help: The University-run accomodation service has an approved landlord list, vacancy list and property vetting.

WELFARE

SERVICES:

• Lesbian/Gay/Bisexual Officer & Society • Ethnic Minorities Officer • Women's Officer
• Mature Students' Officer • International Students' Officer • Disabilities Officer
• Self-defence classes • Nightline• College counsellors: 2 full/4 part • Crime rating: !!!!!
Health: There's close contact with a GP service, as well as a nurse advisory service and University optometry clinics.
Women: The women's officer is the *main port of call.*
Crèches/Nursery: No crèche on site, but the University has an established relationship with a local nursery for 2-5-year-olds.
Disabilities: T-loops, some special accomodation, lifts and note-takers.

FINANCE:

• Ave debt per year: £1,683

Fees: Fees vary for international, postgraduate and EU students.

Support: The Sir John Cass Foundation offers 14 scholarships a year to undergraduates from London studying Computing, Engineering, Mathematics and Actuarial Science or Nursing and Midwifery. Awarded to 2nd and 3rd year students, they're worth £1,000 per year for up to 3 years. The Reeves Foundation and Finsbury Educational Trust offer scholarships to Greater London students.

Coleraine

see University of Ulster

Courtauld Institute of Art, London

• **The College is part of University of London and students are entitled to use its facilities.**

The Courtauld Institute of Art, Somerset House, Strand, London, WC2R 0RN

Tel: (020) 7848 2645 E-mail: ugadmissions@courtauld.ac.uk Website: www.courtauld.ac.uk

Courtauld Student's Union, Somerset House, Strand, London, WC2R 0RN

Tel: (020) 7848 2717

GENERAL

For general information about London: see University of London.

The Courtauld is *appropriately* housed in one of Europe's *most elegant* 18th-century public buildings, Somerset House, located on a huge site between the north bank of the Thames and the Strand. Formerly the public record office, the building's been opened up to the public and is now chocka with cafés, restaurants and art, including the Courtauld Collection. The Institute's the UK's only college specialising solely in the history of art. Somerset House is plastered with paintings, sculptures, architectural features and the Institute's own *remarkable collection*. Only 500m from Trafalgar Square and the rest of central London, *it's extremely well served for entertainments, culture and other disturbingly expensive activities.*

Sex ratio (M:F): 35:65	Founded: 1932
Full-time u'grads: 115	Part-time: 0
Postgrads: 210	Non-degree: 30
Ave course: 3yrs	Ethnic: n/a
State:private school: 40:60	Flunk rate: n/a
Mature: 10%	International: 37%
Disabled: 3	Local: 30%

ATMOSPHERE:

A high proportion of students come from public schools, leaving a faint aroma of Swiss finishing school about the place. Quite a few are relatively well-off and happy to have London licking their wallets clean every weekend. As the Institute has no sports or

entertainments facilities of its own, the focus is on work. Occasionally someone reminds students they can use the University of London's *sports facilities and when everyone stops laughing they get back to work again.*

LONDON: see University of London

TRAVEL: see University of London
Trains: Waterloo, Charing Cross and Blackfriars are a 10-min stomp away.
Buses: Students are spoilt for choice: 1, 4, 25, 59, 68, X68, 76, 168, 171, 176, 188, 341, 501, 505, 521, N1, N175, N176 stop nearby.
Underground: Covent Garden, Temple, Holborn and Charing Cross are all close.
Bicycles: A *popular* way of getting around with bike facilities on campus.

CAREER PROSPECTS:

• Careers Service • Unemployed after 6 mths: 5%
See University of London.

FAMOUS ALUMNI:

Anthony Blunt (former director of the Institute and Russian spy, *the rotter*); Anita Brookner (writer); Andrew Graham-Dixon (art historian); Neil MacGregor (National Gallery); Vincent Price (*creepy* actor); Nicholas Serota (Tate); Brian Sewell (*sickeningly posh art critic*).

FURTHER INFO:

• Prospectuses: undergrad; postgrad • Open days

A C A D E M I C

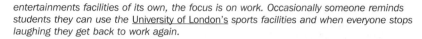

The Institute has the distinct advantage of having many of the subjects of their subjects in the Gallery. Focus is on seminar-based small-group teaching, though there are also lectures. Assessment's based on course work and end of year exams.

Entry points: 270-290	Ave points: n/a
Applns per place: 3	Clearing: n/a
No. of terms: 3	Length of terms: 10wks
Staff/student ratio: 1:5	Study addicts: n/a
Teaching: *****	Research: *****
Firsts: 10%	2.2s: 80%
2.1s: 10%	3rds: 0

ADMISSIONS:

• Apply via UCAS
Candidates with no qualifications but who actually know something about the history of art are encouraged to give it a go.

SUBJECTS:

Arts: 100%
Best: History of Art.

LIBRARIES:

• 180,000 books • 65 study places • Spend per student: £££££
The libraries are among the country's best sources for art history with 1,600,000 reproductions. 800,000 photographs, but they're only open till 9pm *and students aren't known for keeping sensible hours.*

COMPUTERS:

• 32 workstations • Spend per student: £

All 'puters have web access, but inaccessible after 9pm. Students can also use facilities at King's College, next door.

OTHER LEARNING FACILITIES:

Good links with public lectures at places like the National Gallery, which the Institute encourages students to attend.

ENTERTAINMENT

THE CITY: see University of London

UNIVERSITY:

• Price of a pint of beer: £1.30 • Glass of wine: £1.80

Your average art historian could probably outdrink an entire rugby tour, yet there are no bars at the Institute. Still, students have access to King's College and University of London bars and the rest of ULU's stuff.

Food: There's a refectory (cap 100). *It's quite nice.*

Other: A bit of a mass knees-up once a term.

SOCIAL & POLITICAL

COURTAULD STUDENT'S UNION:

• NUS member

The SU (no sabbs, but *they're working on it*) is, *in theory, an ents-based organisation, but in practice does bugger all.*

SU FACILITIES:

A lounge and very popular pool table (with a long queue).

CLUBS (NON-SPORTING):

See Clubs tables.

RELIGIOUS:

• 1 chaplain (CofE)

See University of London

PAID WORK: see University of London

• Job bureau

Normal London chances of getting a job, slightly improved with the help of University of London's *epic* job shop.

SPORTS

No sports facilities of their own, *but also no real inclination to do anything sportier than running to the loo. There've been sporadic attempts to set up mixed-sex football teams that might one day come to fruition.* University of London's facilities are, as ever, available.

SPORTING CLUBS:

See Clubs tables.

ATTRACTIONS: see University of London

ACCOMMODATION

IN COLLEGE:
• Insurance premium: £££
Availability: No facilities of their own but University of London's inter-collegiate housing can be applied for.

EXTERNALLY: see University of London
• Ave rent: £85
Availability: *London has many a cheap and quality student house, but, as they're hidden behind the masses of expensive or seriously dodgy ones, a note of caution is advised.*

WELFARE

SERVICES:
• Crime rating: !!!!!
All of the University of London's vast services are at available, and there's an NHS practice in Gower Street.
Disabled: Ramps/lifts, *good* wheelchair access. The Institute tries to make adjustments and provide necessary facilities for any disabled students to attend courses.

FINANCE:
• Ave debt per year: £2,728 • Access fund: £20,000
• Successful applications/yr: 18 • Ave payment: £500
Support: Postgrad scholarships and disability support through the hardship fund.

Coventry University

• *Formerly Coventry Polytechnic.*
Coventry University, Priory Street, CV1 5FB
Tel: (0845) 055 5850 E-mail: rao.cor@coventry.ac.uk Website: www.coventry.ac.uk
Coventry University Students' Union, Priory Street, Coventry, CV1 5FT
Tel: (024) 7657 1200 E-mail: suexec@coventry.ac.uk Website: www.cusu.org

GENERAL

Old Coventry, one of the Midland's *most historical* cities, was completely destroyed during a single night's bombing in WWII. The locals disapproved and rebuilt it again almost as quickly – and it kind of shows. *The inner city resembles a huge futuristic machine with giant chimneys and intestinal roads wound between buildings.* In the middle there's a *sprawling* shopping centre and, *handily,* the University. Near *grander* civic buildings (the sports centre, art gallery, museum and *famous* glass cathedral) the redbrick campus has *been tarted up* with sculptures, flowerbeds, paved squares and, *bizarrely,* gravestones. A recent *shopping spree* has endowed the University with an eclectic collection of additions: a performing arts & media centre; a design and modelling facility; and an aerospace lab, complete with Harrit Jump Jet and Scout helicopter.

Sex ratio (M:F): 50:50	Founded: 1843
Full-time u'grads: 10,920	Part-time: 4,605
Postgrads: 1,235	Non-degree: 3,212
Ave course: 3yrs	Ethnic: 37%
State:private school: 96:4	Flunk rate: 15%
Mature: 21%	International: 18%
Disabled: 306	Local: 29%

ATMOSPHERE:

Coventry students like a giggle. Priority-wise, politics comes behind sport, which comes far behind both having a good time and bagging a good job at the end of it all. Students are friendly and largely from state schools. While the locals can get territorial, town/gown relations aren't too strained.

COVENTRY:

• Population: 300,700 • London: 88 miles • Birmingham: 16 miles
• High temp: 20 • Low temp: 2 • Rainfall: 55

Coventry's past is flaunted, like Lady Godiva's buttocks, in a number of museums, galleries and tourist attractions. Some outer areas look like they were inspired by a breezeblock, but most have been built with consideration, often for practicality. A mile-long pedestrianised shopping centre has enough shops to *suck at the most carefully guarded loan.* The city is constantly being renovated for the future under such ongoing plans as the Millennium Initiative. A growing number of festivals also *liven things up a bit.*

TRAVEL:

Trains: The main station's about a mile from campus and on the main line to London (£11.80) and Birmingham (£2.30).

Coaches: National Express Bharat and Harry Shaw run loads of services, including London (£12), Birmingham (£4) and Manchester (£11).

Car: *Being slap-bang in the middle of the country, it's easy to get to (via the M6, M69, M45 and A45 and it's close to the M1, M40, M42 and A5), but once there the one-way streets are bad for the blood pressure.*

Air: Birmingham Airport is under 10 miles away.

Taxis: *The town's snug so for £2 you can go far.*

Bicycles: *A nice, flat landscape but roads are busy and bikes go walkies.*

CAREER PROSPECTS:

• Careers Service • No. of staff: 3 full/2 part • Unemployed after 6mths: 8%

FAMOUS ALUMNI:

John Kettley (weatherman); Steve Mattin (Mercedes designer); Andrea Mclean (TV presenter); Michael Rodber (designed Eurostar); Alison Snowden (Oscar-winning animator); Chris Stevenson & Piere Webster (Ford Ka designers); David Yelland (Talk Radio owner).

FURTHER INFO:

• Prospectuses: undergrad; postgrad; part-time • Open days

A C A D E M I C

Six academic schools. Strong in Engineering, Automotive Design, Health and Disaster Mangement. They're pretty proud of their online learning tool, Web CT, too.

Entry points: 170-300	Ave points: n/a
No. of terms: 3	Length of terms: 8-12wks
Teaching: **	Research: **
Year abroad: <1%	Sandwich students: 2%
Staff/student ratio: 1:15	Study addicts: 13%
Firsts: 10%	2.2s: 38%
2.1s: 48%	3rds: 4%

ADMISSIONS:
• Apply via UCAS

SUBJECTS:

Art & Design: 13%
Business school: 24%
Maths & Information Sciences: 13%

Health and Social Sciences: 26%
Science & Environment: 11%
Engineering: 13%

Unusual: Avionics Technology; Motorsport Engineering; Wine Studies.
Best: Economics; Art & Design; Sociology; Languages; Psychology.

LIBRARIES:
• 350,000 books • 1,200 study places • Spend per student: £££
The library has a café, but would do better with a few more books. A well-placed bookshop takes up the slack for those with the dough.

COMPUTERS:
• 2,000 workstations • 749 internet access points • 24-hr access

ENTERTAINMENT

THE CITY:
• Price of a pint of beer: £1.80 • Glass of wine: £1.80
For what Coventry lacks, proximity to Birmingham, Wolverhampton and other cities means alternatives can be hunted down.
Cinemas: Three ten-screeners, two on the edge of town and the Skydome complex in the centre.
Theatres: *Belgrade Theatre for run-of-the-mill dramatic fayre.*
Pubs: *Some local pubs aren't all that student-friendly, but Push plugs: Oak Inn; the Phoenix; the Lanes; Gringoes; Old Orleans; the Golden Cross.*
Clubbing: *A thriving Drum 'n' Bass scene. Pushplugs: Colosseum (mainstream); Diva; Icon; Scholars (towny); Dog & Trumpet.*
Music venues: *There's more variety in Birmingham and Wolverhampton, but try: West Indian Centre (world music); Dog & Trumpet; Colosseum; Hand & Heart.*
Eating out: *Something cheap and cheerful for everyone, except possibly those blokes who eat lightbulbs: Browns; Pizza Express; TGI Friday's; Varsity's; Yates's; The Litten Tree (more upmarket – take the wrinklies).*
Balls: Coventry students hold their balls annually.

UNIVERSITY:
• Price of a pint of beer: £1.45 • Glass of wine: £1.30
Bars: The Cox Street venue houses Casbar, the main Union bar, as well as 'Chiller' (chill-out lounge) and, *cruelly*, an alcohol-free bar, Universe.
Music venues: *Old Britpop doesn't die, it just gets sent to Coventry.*
Clubbing: Weekly club nights include Phase (the *big* student night) and Trollied (*for all your Edam requirements*).
Food: Reunion serves *standard* eats. Hot and cold scoffs available in Casbar and Universe, and hidden round campus are the Best Cellar; Fads; the Pavilion Bar; the Lanchester Restaurant; and The William Morris Bistro.

SOCIAL & POLITICAL

COVENTRY UNIVERSITY STUDENTS' UNION:
• 5 sabbaticals • Turnout at last ballot: 19% • NUS member
CUSU has been making a real effort to stir the student body from its cryogenically frozen attitude to politics. Now they're just apathetic and uninformed, which is an improvement.

SU FACILITIES:

The SU building provides: general shop; bars; four minibuses for hire; photo booth; video games; hairdresser; vending machines; pool tables; juke boxes; two meeting rooms. The Junction has a music rehearsal room, print and copy shop, meeting rooms, IT and printing and fax facilities.

CLUBS (NON-SPORTING):

Ba'hai; Choir; Clubbing; Palestine (friends of Palestine); Pacific Soul. **See also Clubs tables.**

OTHER ORGANISATIONS:

There's monthly magazine Source as well as Source Radio. The community action group raises money for and participates in local voluntary work.

RELIGIOUS:

• 3 (CofE, RC, FC)

There's a Muslim prayer room on campus. Locally there are *pious palaces of prayer* for many faiths, *most notably*, the Anglican Cathedral.

PAID WORK:

• Job bureau

Coventry Bureau for Employment (CUBE) is run by students, who help each other find all sorts of work from bar work to phone monkeying.

S P O R T S

• BUSA Ranking: 13

Students are more interested in sports than politics – but what does that say? Facilities are good, though.

SPORTS FACILITIES:

A brand new facility on campus has: a four-court sports hall and a two-court minor hall; dance/martial arts studio; large fitness suite; sports injury clinic. Otherwise, Westwood Heath has: three football pitches; three rugby pitches; cricket pitch; floodlit hockey pitch; 9-hole golf course; four tennis courts. Generous bursaries and scholarships for elite athletes. The local sports centre has an Olympic sized swimming pool, squash courts and student discounts. Warwick has two council-owned golf courses. The Millennium development will eventually add a new arena and leisure complex.

SPORTING CLUBS:

American Football; Handball; Ju-Jitsu. **See also Clubs tables.**

ATTRACTIONS:

Coventry FC's the local side. Warwick has horse racing.

A C C O M M O D A T I O N

IN COLLEGE:

• Catered: 5% • Cost: £86 (40wks) • Self-catering: 18%
• Cost: £53-63 (40/50wks) • Insurance premium: £££££
• First years living in: 98%

Availability: Four halls of residence and 1,000 places in head tenancy schemes – 1st years get priority but 5% *get nothing*. Lots of mature and local students are already sorted. A minority have to share and most accommodation is single sex. The rent for most rooms is inclusive of internet access and membership at the University's sports centre. Most places are in Priory Hall on campus but *Singer Hall is the nicest* (600). Caradoc Hall (64 single bedsits and 62 twin flats) is 3 miles away and there are also 350 places in University-owned houses in town, though *some get grumpy about living so far out.* A security service is shared between the halls.

Car parking: Rare but some availability at Singer Hall (priority to residents there) at an extra cost.

EXTERNALLY:

• Ave rent: £50
Availability: Previously students have been snagging cheap gaffs, but *landlords are starting to catch on. Best areas: Earlsdon, Stoke, Cheylesmore, Radford and Chapelfields. Hillfields is Coventry's Bronx. Parking is so rare and costly, it's not worth trying.*
Housing help: The Accommodation Office checks out every place on its books, offers a handbook and contract advice.

WELFARE

SERVICES:

• Lesbian/Gay/Bisexual Officer & Society • Ethnic Minorities Officer & Society
• Women's Officer & Society • Mature Students' Officer & Society
• International Students' Officer & Society • Postgrad Officer & Society
• Disabilities Officer & Society • Late-night/Women's minibus • Self-defence classes
• Nightline • College counsellors: 5 part • Crime rating: !!!
There's an advice centre for soul-baring of any kind. The campus's medical centre has eight doctors, both male and female, and nurses.
Women: The SU produces a women's rights booklet. Women get priority on the free minibus, *though it can be irregular.*
Crèches/Nursery: There's a crèche but *demand is high and places not guaranteed.*
Disabilities: Disabled Students' Forum. The Disabilities Office has staff and facilities for students with various forms of disability, especially sight impairments. The University will try to adapt courses, assignments or venues as needed.
Crime/drugs: The city *has had a bit of a rep for drugs* but things are improving and, anyway, the University seems unaffected.

FINANCE:

• Ave debt per year: £3,372
• Access fund: £667,310 • Successful applications/yr: 668 • Ave payment: £840
Support: There's also a small welfare fund for the desperate, short-term loans and arts and sports bursaries, the latter worth up to £750 a piece.

Coventry Polytechnic

see Coventry University

De Montfort University
....
De Montfort University, Bedford
....

University of Derby
....

Derbyshire College of Higher Education see University of Derby
....

Distributive Trades see University of the Arts, London
....

DIT see University of Abertay Dundee
....

Dorset Institute see Bournemouth University
....

Dundee University
....

Dundee Institute of Technology see University of Abertay Dundee
....

University of Durham
....

De Montfort University

• *Formerly Leicester Polytechnic*.
De Montfort University Leicester, The Gateway, Leicester, LE1 9BH
Tel: (08459) 454 647 Email: enquiries@dmu.ac.uk Website: www.dmu.ac.uk
De Montfort University Students' Union, 1st Floor, Campus Centre Building, Mill Lane,
Leicester, LE2 7DR Tel: (0116) 255 5576 Website: www.mydsu.com
See below for details about other sites.

GENERAL

De Montfort University is a curious beast. When Leicester Polytechnic stopped being
Leicester Polytechnic in 1992, the powers-that-be began a colonisation project almost
imperialist in scope, setting up academic outposts in Bedford, Lincoln and Milton Keynes.
Ten or so years later, the empire began to crumble and DMU is withdrawing its troops and
consolidating power at home. The Milton Keynes site was closed in 2003 and the Scraptoft
site in Leicester has also been, er, scrapped. Bedford's twin campuses are in the process of
combining and an ambitious ten-year redevelopment project in both Bedford and Leicester
will concentrate on domestic expansion *rather than national conquest. DMU's 'distributed'*
status has been a bit of a double-edged sword: on the one hand, it can offer one of the
widest ranges of courses in the UK; on the other, there's no sense of a central university
identity except in name. Hopefully, the forthcoming changes will alter that, but it's still likely
that the palpable Bedford/Leicester division will remain. The main Leicester City campus in
the groovy bit of town has recently realised the error of its 60s architectural ways,
demolished all the brutalist blocks, flung up some more appealing modern buildings and
created an intriguing (and much less depressing) gathering of architectural styles, including
the medieval Trinity building.
See below for details at Bedford.

Sex ratio (M:F): 42:58	Founded: 1969
Full-time u'grads: 13,910	Part-time: 4,280
Postgrads: 1,205	Non-degree: 5,187
Ave course: 3yrs	Ethnic: 34%
State: private school: 96:4	Flunk rate: 18%
Mature: 28%	International: 9%
Disabled: 319	Local: 39%

ATMOSPHERE:

Students tend to be committed to having a good time, getting a good degree then going on to a good job. The University is simply too spread out to make generalisations about atmosphere, however – it'd be like comparing Australia to Canada – so see details for the Bedford campus, town and travel at the end.

LEICESTER SITES:

Charles Frears Campus: (Nursing & Midwifery) Just outside the city centre, *briskly walkable and even more briskly busable* from the main City site, Charlie Frears has his own medical library and teaching facilities *in a pleasant enough setting.*

LEICESTER: see Leicester University

• City centre: 0 miles

TRAVEL: see Leicester University

University: A shuttlebus service connects both Leicester sites with the city centre and the train station. It's used by the public too, but DMU students get *hefty* discounts.
Cars: There's no student parking at the main campus, but a *limited* number of spaces at Charles Frears.

CAREER PROSPECTS:

• Careers Service • No. of staff: 8 full • Unemployed after 6mths: 9%
Careers DMU is highly focused on shifting graduates into business. It has a contract with the local adult guidance network and provides newsletters, bulletin boards, e-mail updates and job fairs in addition to interview training, workshops, presentations, career-selection software, workshops, CV writing guidance, psychometric testing and assessment preparation.

FAMOUS ALUMNI:

Charles Dance (actor); Eddie 'the Eagle' Edwards; Engelbert Humperdinck (60s singer); Prolapse (indie band); Janet Reger (*nice knickers*); Kendra Slawinski, OBE (netball); Liz Tilberis (late editor, Vogue); Simon Wells (director); Debra Veal (Atlantic rower). Jimmy Choo (the shoe man) holds an honorary doctorate in Design.

SPECIAL FEATURES:

De Montfort takes its name from Simon De Montfort, the 13th-century Earl of Leicester. The earl banned Jews from the city, tried to overthrow the king, led the baronial revolt, kidnapped Henry III and his son, all before he finally got his head chopped off and put on a spike. His father, also called Simon, fought in the Fourth Crusade. His son, er, also called Simon, may or may not have fornicated his way through Kent. None of them, however, had any firm policies on lifelong education, the rights of all to get academic and professional qualifications or indeed the merits of charity shop clothing.

FURTHER INFO:

• Prospectuses: undergrad; postgrad; some departments • Open days
Prospectuses can be ordered online or by calling (08457) 443 311. A guide for international students is published annually. Faculty open days held throughout the year.

ACADEMIC

DMU offers a *jaw-dropping* variety of courses, most with an intensely vocational bent – *let's face it, no one is going to take a BA in Adventure Recreation out of idle curiosity* – and teaching methods/hours vary widely from course to course. All undergrad degree courses are modular, with students taking four to six modules over the course of each year. Degree grades are based on performance in the 2nd and 3rd years, with the final year doubly weighted.

160-300	**POINTS**

Entry points: 160-300
Applns per place: 5
No. of terms: 3
Staff/student ratio: 1:19
Teaching: *
Firsts: 6%
2.1s: 38%

Ave points: 232
Clearing: 17%
Length of terms: 12wks
Study addicts: 12%
Research: ***
2.2s: 43%
3rds: 6%

ADMISSIONS:

• Apply via UCAS
DMU is *especially friendly* towards local and mature applicants, under-represented groups and those with alternative experience and non-traditional backgrounds. Research-wise, DMU has been praised for being the best post-1992 research institute in the UK, *which sceptics might call a 'Very Good, Considering...' type accolade.*

SUBJECTS:

Art & Design: 20%
Business & Law: 22%
Computing Sciences & Engineering 20%

Education & Contemporary Studies (Bedford): 13%
Health & Life Sciences: 14%
Humanities: 11%

Best: Accounting & Finance; Art & Design; Communication & Media Studies; Dance, Drama & Cinematics; Education; History; History of Art; Hospitality, Leisure & Recreation; Nursing; Politics; Psychology; Pharmacology & Pharmacy; Other subjects allied to Medicine.
Unusual: Adventure Recreation; Audiology (NHS pays course fees); Broadcast Technology; Contour Fashion; Criminology; Footwear Design; Globalisation; Pharmaceutical & Cosmetic Sciences; Radio Production; Retail Buying.

LIBRARIES:

• 531,772 books • 1,521 study places • Spend per student: £££
The Leicester site has a library on each of its two campuses. The Kimberlin library (city campus) is the largest and is open till 10pm. The Charles Frears Library is a tenth of the size and stocks books on nursing and midwifery. *Which is handy for nurses and midwives.*

COMPUTERS:

• 2,000 workstations • Spend per student: £££££
The number of workstations is for DMU as a whole. All libraries have web-enabled workstations and there are 30 laptops *kicking around* too. Each faculty has their own IT suites and 1,125 first year rooms now have network points.

OTHER LEARNING FACILITIES:

Since there are a lot of specialist courses, there's also a lot of specialist facilities: language labs; drama studios; music technology studio; pharmacy practice suite; working newsroom.

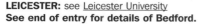

E N T E R T A I N M E N T

LEICESTER: see <u>Leicester University</u>
See end of entry for details of Bedford.

UNIVERSITY:

• <u>Price of a pint of beer: £1.30</u> • <u>Glass of wine: £1.50</u>
Bars: At Leicester the main lunchtime boozer is the Lava Lounge but Level 1 takes over for events.
Theatres: The De Montfort Theatre Company put on performances in the Y Theatre and often take shows to Edinburgh.
Film: There's a VCR in the bar.
Clubbing: Level 1 flashes its lasers at weekly regulars ranging from the Big Cheese (Saturdays: 70s, 80s & 90s cheese) to Kinky (70s, 80s, & 90s cheese) to Bump (Fridays, urban). Tickets sold from SU reception throughout the week.
Music venues: The SU has pulled in big names of the calibre of Atomic Kitten (*RIP*), Coldplay and the Cream tour.
Food: The Lava Lounge and the Servery *fulfil most hot and cold requirements*. Level 1 does sandwiches, toasties and – *after an embittered battle with the authorities* – cheesy chips. *Oh glory.*
Other: Festive Snow Ball at Christmas time. A summer ball is stuck somewhere in the pipeline.

S O C I A L & P O L I T I C A L

DE MONTFORT UNIVERSITY STUDENTS' UNION:

• <u>7 sabbaticals</u> • <u>NUS member</u> • <u>Turnout at last ballot: 5%</u>
The Global Union (*which sounds more like something created to fight the Dark Side*) represents all sites but is based in Leicester, but there are also site-specific officers responsible for Bedford's SU branch. *They're fairly political and ethically minded, boycotting Nestlé and so on.*

SU FACILITIES:

Two bars; purpose-built nightclub/venue; cafeteria; fast food outlet; two pool tables; meeting room; minibus hire; NatWest bank with ATM; HSBC ATM; photocopier; fax service; photo booth; payphones; general store with dry cleaning, alterations and photo-developing service; stationery shop; vending and gaming machines; new bookshop.

CLUBS (NON-SPORTING):

Adventist Students; Chinese; Dynamite Dance; Games; Hindu; History; Krishna Consciousness; Malaysian; Music; Pagan; Public Policy; Prock; Sikh; Singers; Street Law; De Montfort Theatre Company (DTC). **See also Clubs tables.**

OTHER ORGANISATIONS:

Student paper the Demon speaks out monthly while award-winning radio station Demon FM broadcasts daily through the Leicester airwaves. There's also a TV station called – *guess what* – Demon TV. *A shame-faced Rag is struggling to maintain students' flagging interest.*

RELIGIOUS:

• <u>Team of chaplains (RC, CofE)</u>
Muslim prayer room at City campus. See <u>Leicester University</u> for details of provisions in the city.

PAID WORK: see <u>Leicester University</u>

• <u>Job bureau</u>

Work Bank is a privately run company that caters for all DMU sites and matches local jobs with student needs. Jobs Live is an online vacancy database that allows CV posting so potential employers can *check out the talent*. The SU employs students in bars and shops.

SPORTS

• <u>Recent successes: men's football</u> • <u>BUSA Ranking: 48</u>

The distance between Bedford and Leicester makes it difficult to generate University-wide enthusiasm or a sense of sporting identity, but DMU are regulars in the BUSA leagues, and students at the Leicester site *enjoy a kickabout as much as the next man and his dog*.

SPORTS FACILITIES:

At Leicester City Campus the John Sandford Sports Centre has: fitness studio; weight training suite; courts for badminton, tennis, 4-a-side football, squash and basketball; solarium; sauna; table tennis tables . Access to the centre is either by day pass or yearly Leisure Card (£36). There's also: football, rugby, cricket, hockey and all-weather pitches; swimming pool; climbing wall; athletics field; aerobics studio. The lake and the River Soar near the campus *are handy for a paddle*. See <u>Leicester University</u> for local facilities.

SPORTING CLUBS:

Aikido; American Football; Caving; Ju-Jitsu; Rowing; Shoot Fighting; Tae Kwon Do. **See also Clubs tables**.

ATTRACTIONS: see <u>Leicester University</u>

The John Sandford Sports Centre is also home to British Basketball league team, the Leicester Riders.

ACCOMMODATION

IN COLLEGE:

• <u>Self-catering: 18%</u> • <u>Cost: £73 (39-43wks)</u>
• <u>First years living in: 63%</u> • <u>Insurance premium: £££££</u>

Availability: More than half of all 1st years are accommodated at Leicester, and none have to share. Students are given five preferences when it comes to choosing halls. No one has more than a 10-min walk and five *sexy* new halls sprang up a couple of years ago, all with en-suite facilities and network points. Buildings are fitted with secure entry systems, CCTV and night porters. Lockable cycle pods in all halls. Single sex flats available.
Car parking: Permits at halls are only for the disabled.

EXTERNALLY: see <u>Leicester University</u>

• <u>Ave rent: £50</u> • <u>Living at home: 25%</u>

Availability: The majority of 2nd and 3rd years live out, generally sharing houses around Leicester, which are *pretty cheap on the whole. Finding a place is quite a hassle-free process as long as it's started early.*
Housing help: The University Accommodation Office (has a presence at all sites) has a bulletin board and newsletter. It works with Leicester City Council and the Leicester Landlords Association on an accredited housing scheme.

Senate House, headquarters of London University, was rumoured to be where Hitler planned to set up his UK headquarters if he invaded UK. Supposedly that's the reason it was never bombed.

WELFARE

SERVICES:

* Lesbian/Gay/Bisexual Society • Women's Officer • Mature Students' Society
* International Students' Society • Late-night minibus • Self-defence classes
* University counsellors: 2 full/3 part • Crime rating: !!!!

There are University and Union welfare services on all sites. A mental health co-ordinator is on hand to support students with histories of mental illness, raise awareness and reduce social stigma.

Health: The City campus health centre houses five GPs, four nurses, physio, health visitor and a midwife.

Disabilities: There's an on-going programme of access improvement – all buildings now have ramps and/or lift access and pushpad/automatic doors. There are a few adapted study bedrooms and there's a dyslexia support worker.

FINANCE:

* Ave debt per year: £2,726

Fees: International undergrads are charged from £7,990. Individual modules cost £147 each. Top-up fees *all the way*, with a bursary or several *to ease the pain*.

* Access fund: £1,300,000 • Successful applications/yr: 1,350 • Ave payment: £900

Support: Hardship funds are available to cover childcare, travel, accommodation etc. Academic awards of up to £3,500 *dangle invitingly* too.

DE MONTFORT UNIVERSITY, BEDFORD

De Montfort University, Bedford, 37 Lansdowne Road, Bedford, MK40 2BZ
Tel: (01234) 793 484 Fax: (01234) 350 833
E-mail: bed-admissions@dmu.ac.uk Website: www.dmu.ac.uk/ecs
De Montfort University Students' Union (Bedford), 37 Lansdowne Road, Bedford, MK40 2BZ
Tel: (01234) 793 012 E-mail: suenquiries@dmu.ac.uk

40 miles from the much larger Leicester site, De Montfort's *baby brother* Bedford is home to around 2,500 students (Humanities, Performing Arts, Education, Sports Science, Business and Social & Cultural Studies). There are two sites: the Lansdowne (*sporty*) and Polhill (*arty*) campuses, 2 miles apart on the outskirts of the town. Students have little or no contact with their counterparts at Leicester, so *it can feel like an entirely separate institution*. DMU's extensive redevelopment programme is running full steam ahead and it won't be long before all Lansdowne operations are transferred to a new and improved Polhill. Plans include: swathes more land, 500 new student rooms, teaching facility extensions, and a new campus central building with bar and catering facilities, and a 350-seat theatre.

BEDFORD:

* Population: 147,911 • London: 50 miles • Leicester: 40 miles • Cambridge: 30 miles

Bedford is a quiet county town – founded by Beda, an 8th-century Saxon chief for those who aren't yet boring enough in the pub – impaled by a pretty stretch of the River Ouse and surrounded by what people insist on calling 'unspoilt countryside', diddy villages and signposts with delusions of grandeur: 'Bedford – A Progressive County'. Quite what a regressive county would involve, Push can't say. It's got the usual gamut of shops, pubs and the odd club (that's 'odd' in both senses of the word) but its more vivacious inhabitants thank their lucky stars that London is less than an hour away.

Travel: London 40 mins away by train from Bedford station, ditto Leicester. Luton Airport a *mere* 17 mins, for quick getaways. The A1, M1 and M25 are *easily accessible*. DMU runs a shuttlebus between campuses, the town and station. Some on-site student parking.

ACADEMIC:

The Bedford library facilities are smaller than Leicester's with 128,868 books, 361 study places and 137 web-enabled workstations for student use. The £6m Polhill Library and Information Centre boasts a state-of-the-art IT suite. There are also biochemistry and physiology labs.

ENTERTAINMENT:

Local: Bedford *is less of a studenty, cosmopolitan city than Leicester* but it has *a fair few ye olde ale houses* and a couple of *passable* night spots. *Student pubby, clubby, grubby faves include the Bankers Draft, The Rose, Enigma, Foresters, Chicago's clubs and Gulshan's Tandoori*. Also: Aspects Complex near Polhill with a six-screen cinema and 10-pin bowling; an annual regatta; and the *notoriously dangerous* beer festival.
University: The Bowen West Theatre *is a little more dynamic than its Leicester counterpart – probably because the performing arts courses are based here*. Many contemporary dance and drama shows are put on throughout the year. Food can be grabbed from all-day refectories at both Lansdowne and Polhill. Bars on each campus.

SOCIAL & POLITICAL:

Two sabbatical SU officers liase with the larger Union body in Leicester and offer social and welfare support to Bedford-bound students. There's a performing arts society to add to the socs list and the campus has its own chaplain.

SPORTS:

One of Bedford's students currently lays claim to the world championship title for Korean martial art, Tang Soo Do. The Alexander Sports Hall is *huge* and has: courts for basketball, volleyball, tennis and badminton; a climbing wall; sauna and solarium; and a health and fitness suite. The Lansdowne campus has a swimming pool, dance studios and a gym. Astroturf, cricket, football and rugby pitches are there for the tramping. Charges are the same as at the Leicester campus. Two new gym buildings are in the planning stages as part of the Polhill redevelopment. Locally there's a large leisure complex with pool, athletics stadium and a hockey centre.

ACCOMMODATION:

On site:
• Catered cost: £64-74 (35 wks) • Self-catering cost: £50-61 (39wks)
Bedford's three halls offer 350 rooms – meaning that 18% of students based here can be accommodated, usually 1st years. The halls are a combination of converted Victorian houses and purpose-built blocks. Most places at Bedford are catered and usually only people with special dietary requirements will get into a self-catered hall. *Not liking the canteen food probably doesn't count*. Things are about to change, however, and soon all accomodation will be self-catered. 24/7 security patrols and lockable cycle pods. Parking is disabled only. Limited head tenancy schemes.

EXTERNALLY:

• Ave rent: £45-55 • Living out: 66%
Living costs and rents in Bedford are cheaper than Leicester and below the national average. *Bonus*.

WELFARE:

Health: Lansdowne and Polhill have a medical centre each. Physiotherapy's also available.
Crèches/Nursery: There's a crèche on the Polhill campus providing day care for 2-5-yr-olds.
Disabilities: The new Polhill library and info centre is *riddled* with lifts, and has adapted desks on each of its four floors.

University of Derby

* **Formerly Derbyshire College of Higher Education.**
University of Derby, Kedleston Road, Derby, DE22 1GB
Tel: (01332) 590 500 E-mail: admissions@derby.ac.uk Website: www.derby.ac.uk
University of Derby Students' Union, Kedleston Road, Derby, DE22 1GB
Tel: (01332) 591 507 E-mail: info@udsu.co.uk Website: www.udsu-online.co.uk

GENERAL

At the southern tip of the *beautiful* Derbyshire Peak District is the *not-quite-so-stunning* city of Derby, in the north of the Midlands. The University is based at eight sites around the city *and can be something of a labyrinth to navigate.* The main site is the Kedleston Road campus just outside town to the north-west, amidst *rather pleasant* open countryside. *Modern, brightly coloured and welcoming – the authorities haven't ignored the feng shui effects of a good water feature.* Having taken the leap from a College of Higher Education to University in 1992, Derby now offers a wide range of subjects, many of which are vocational. The University of Derby College, Buxton, attached to Derby University, has recently moved to the town centre and offers a variety of Degree-level/FE courses: A Levels, HNDs, NVQs *and several alphabets' worth of other acronyms.*

Sex ratio (M:F): 46:54	Founded: 1851
Full-time u'grads: 8,360	Part-time: 2.505
Postgrads: 490	Non-degree: 8,141
Ave course: 3yrs	Ethnic: n/a
State:private school: 97:3	Flunk rate: 21%
Mature: 51%	International: 8%
Disabled: 239	Local: 53%

54%
46%

ATMOSPHERE:

The Kedleston campus is a friendly, buzzing environment and its inhabitants are largely a casual, down-to-earth crew, many of them from the local area. The big fashion department polarises students into those who look cool and those who wear anoraks. But even among those who still think Terylene is trendy, there's a generally good vibe.

SITES:

An inter-site bus service makes getting around easy.
Kedleston Road: The largest site, containing most of the students and University admin blocks.
Mickleover: (1,000 students – Health & Community Studies, Education, Social Science) Mainly concrete site, 2 miles from the city centre, with some halls of residence.
Green Lane: (100 – Film & TV) Bang in the city centre, 3 miles from Kedleston, is this listed Victorian building – a purpose-built art college.
Britannia Mill: (800 – Art & Design) Arty atmosphere in a converted mill, also in the city centre.
Cedars: (400 – Occupational Therapy) An Edwardian building juxtaposed with *modernist chunks*, 3 miles from the main site.

Jackson's Mill: (200 – Art & Design) Close to the halls of residence at Bridge Street but 20 mins walk to the main campus for books, food and beer.
Derby Royal Infirmary (DRI): 300 students – Radiography.
Markeaton Campus: (50 students – Motorsports) 10 mins from Kedlestone Road, this site is being developed in anticipation of Derby becoming a 2-hub campus with Kedlestone Road.

DERBY:

- Population: 221,700 • City centre: 2 miles • London: 128 miles
- Nottingham: 15 miles • Birmingham: 41 miles
- High temp: 20 • Low temp: 1 • Rainfall: 59

Those who dismiss Derby as being as ugly as a warthog with eczema are missing the historical significance of the place (if not the general appearance). After all, Derby played an important role in the Jacobite Rebellion and a crucial part in the Industrial Revolution. *So there.* Like many small cities it's growing rapidly, and as new shops appear, the old ones get more upmarket. It has 600 listed buildings, a good number of parks, lots of *useful* shops and amenities and three museums: the Derby Museum, Industrial Museum and Pickford House, as well as attractions like the Arboretum Park and, outside town, Elvaston Castle, Shipley Country Park and Chatsworth House – *most of which are essentially large old houses with gardens.*

TRAVEL:

Trains: Derby station is $2\frac{1}{2}$ miles from Kedleston Road: London (£23.10), Sheffield (£4.75) and beyond.
Coaches: National Express and other services operate to London (£15.75) and Sheffield (£5), among other places.
Car: Derby is 8 miles from the M1 and on the A6, A38, A50, A52.
Air: East Midlands is the closest airport, 8 miles south-east of town, with flights inland and to Europe.
Hitching: *Kindly motorists on long hauls on the main roads. Some lard-guzzling truckers too, but that's the way it goes in this game.*
Local: *Reliable* buses run every 10 mins to the town centre from the main campus. Multi-ride passes offer a 50% discount. *Regular* buses between sites.
Taxis: £2-3 between sites and city centre – several companies offer 10% student discounts.
Bicycles: Plans for a bike link between city and sites are still plans: *roads are too busy for all but the most stubborn or suicidal cyclist.*

CAREER PROSPECTS:

- Careers Service • No. of staff: 5 full/4 part • Unemployed after 6 mths: 7%

The Career Development Centre emails fortnightly vacancy and careers information bulletins, offers free online psychometric testing, arranges seminars, workshops and job fairs and keeps a physical and online library of careers resources. See www.derby.ac.uk/careers for resources for staff, students and graduates, prospective students and employers.

FAMOUS ALUMNI:

Cedric Brown (former British Gas fatcat); Jyoti Mishra (White Town).

FURTHER INFO:

- Prospectuses: undergrad; postgrad; alternative • Open days • Video

Around four open days a year, info hotline: (08701) 202330. Successful applicants are invited to attend course-specific visit days to view the campus and facilities. Prospectuses can be ordered at www.derby.ac.uk/prospectus

 ACADEMIC

Derby's five sites have *a wealth of courses stashed in them ranging from the mundane to the implausible*, at degree, HND and Further Education levels. There are a *mind-boggling* number of part-time options – hence a sizeable part-time student body – and a wide-ranging Combined Subject and Joint Honours degree programme, meaning that subjects *as different as chalk and chinchillas* can often be studied together. Derby's acknowledged strong points include business, design and technology-related courses.

Entry points: 140-260	Ave points: n/a
No. of terms: 3	Length of terms: 12wks
Staff/student ratio: 1:22	Study addicts: 88%
Teaching: *	Research: *
Year abroad: 1%	Sandwich students: 15%

140-260 · **POINTS**

ADMISSIONS:

• Apply via UCAS

SUBJECTS:

Best: Art & Design; Biology; Business & Management; Education; Maths & Computing; Pharmacy; Psychology; Subjects allied to Medicine; Tourism & Hospitality Management.
Unusual: 3D Design; Aseptic Services; Beauty & Spa Services; Complementary Therapies; Early Childhood Studies; Events Management; Forensic Science; Global Hazards; Illustration for Animation; International Spa Management; Sex, Sexuality & Gender; Third World Development.

LIBRARIES:

• 323,000 books • 1,680 study places
Five libraries – *obtusely known as 'Learning Centres'* – one at each site, all course-specific. Study space is pretty cramped but the Learning Centre at Kedleston has added more space. Buxton and Cedars Libraries are closed at weekends.

COMPUTERS:

• 850 workstations
There are IT rooms at all sites except Cedars. All halls of residence are networked to the University.

OTHER LEARNING FACILITIES:

Language labs (for undergrads and the wider community); drama studio; rehearsal rooms; CAD lab; audio/TV centre; a practice courtroom for budding Perry Masons. A Virtual Campus is up and humming, so students can access online modules, assessments and subject message boards.

ENTERTAINMENT

THE CITY:

• Price of a pint of beer: £1.80 • Glass of wine: £2.60
Cinemas: There are two multiplexes with 22 screens between them, as well as the *artier* Metro.
Theatres: The Derby Playhouse has its own repertory company and offers 10% discounts.
Pubs: Nearby Burton is the brewing capital of England. *Pushplugs: the Friary; the Ram (cheap and friendly); Varisty; Revolution. The Ashbourne Mile is a renowned bar crawl.*
Clubbing: Derby is picking up speed on the club front. *Other Pushplugs: Blue Note; Gatehouse; McCluskys.*
Music venues: *No massive venues, but several large enough to attract more than local strummers and drummers.* Victoria Inn and the Flower Pot and the Loft host live muzak. The Assembly Rooms has major bands *but they charge the earth.*
Eating out: The pizza chains do student discounts. *The Ram near halls does a tasty burger for a couple of quid.* Curzon Street and Normanton Road embody the curry nexus. *Pushplugs: Friargate (Cantonese); Excelsior (Chinese); Moghul (Indian); Plug Tonic (posh); Antibo's (Italian); Cactus Café (Mexican); New Normanton, 10 mins from city centre, is good for all sorts of restaurants.*

UNIVERSITY:

• Price of a pint of beer: £1 60 • Glass of wine: £2

Bars: The Union runs three bars. Blends on Kedleston Road is a *relaxed* booze-plying café-style affair that shuts at 6pm. The Arms (also at Kedleston) is a multi-level 'Gothic' joint with *appealing pre-tiles* happy hours – but *equally frustratingly* closes at 6pm most nights. Lonsdale bar *has the most life in it*, stretching to proper pub hours and featuring aspiring record-riders.

Theatres: The drama and performing arts students stuff a show or two into the University's theatre.

Clubbing/Music venues: Wednesday night at the Gatehouse is an NUS cheese-fest indieshrine called Spank.

Food: The Atrium in the large entrance hangar at Kedleston does *inexpensive* snacks and meals, and there are other cutlets at most sites.

Other: The Graduation Ball and the May Ball are a *truly massive pair* that often have A-listers headlining.

SOCIAL & POLITICAL

UNIVERSITY OF DERBY STUDENTS' UNION:

• 4 sabbaticals • NUS member

Links between the SU and the University are much better than previously. The good vibes are also showing in imported sports facilities and the new radio station. A bigger and better bar is due to be developed on campus soon.

SU FACILITIES:

Three bars; cafeteria; snack bar; six pool tables; meeting room; minibus for hire; Endsleigh Insurance branch; Natwest bank and Lloyd's ATM; fax and printing service; photocopier; photo booth; advice centre; payphones; general and stationery stores at Kedleston, Britannia Mill and Buxton; Waterstone's; juke boxes; gaming machines.

CLUBS (NON-SPORTING):

Chinese; Expressive, Caring, Therapeutic Arts; Geology; Kids Team; Law; Photography; R&B/Hip Hop; Radio. **See also Clubs tables**.

OTHER ORGANISATIONS:

Dusted is the monthly mag and D1 is the campus radio station. There's now a permanent member of staff in charge of Rag so the figures are growing. The Community Development Area also *gets up to a lot of good*.

RELIGIOUS:

• 5 chaplains (CofE, RC, Russian Orthodox, FC)

Hindu, Muslim, Sikh, Jewish, Baha'i and Buddhist faith advisers are also available. The Religious Resource & Research Centre has prayer facilities at both Kedleston and Mickleover and there's a Muslim prayer room at Kedleston. In Derby, there's an Anglican cathedral and provisions for Christians of every hue, Hindus, Muslims, Sikhs and Jews.

PAID WORK:

• Job bureau

The Career Development Centre doubles as a part-time piggy bank filler, maintaining the online jobs@hand database as well as running the Student Employment Agency. UDSU has a number of ongoing positions available in bars, shops, admin, gyms etc. All are minimum wage.

SPORTS

- Recent successes: women's hockey/badminton, rugby union • BUSA Ranking: 48
There isn't exactly a sporty slant but occasional smudges of athletic achievement and not inconsiderable facilities mean bats and balls do collide regularly.

SPORTS FACILITIES:

Facilities are based at Mickleover. Fizeek Fitness Studio; five football and two rugby pitches; swimming pool; all-weather pitch; climbing wall; multigym; running track; badminton court; American football pitch. Derbyshire adds various other goodies like golf courses, cricket facilities, the river and, of course, the Peak District.

SPORTING CLUBS:

American Football; Canoe; Cheerleading; Dance; Ju-Jitsu; Kick Boxing; Rowing; Tae Kwon Do. **See also Clubs tables.**

ATTRACTIONS:

Derby County FC and Derbyshire Cricket Club. As for the Derby horse race – that's in Epsom. *We know, it's confusing.*

ACCOMMODATION

IN COLLEGE:

- Self-catering: 28% • Cost: £38-71 (39wks) • First years living in: 75%
- Insurance premium: £££
Availability: 1st years are *pretty much guaranteed* hall accommodation and provisions aren't overly stretched thanks to the number of local students living at home. Residences are all modern, purpose-built jobs but *there's a hefty walk (15 mins or more)* to get to campus. Peak Court has en-suite rooms and is *nearish* the main site, so *demand tends to be higher. Mickleover halls, on the other hand, are a tad cramped and a smidgen further away.* CCTV, entry phones, and a 24-hour watch scheme stop most things going bump in the night. Less than 1% have to share a room.
Car parking: Most halls have car parks, although places are *limited*. A permit costs £25.

EXTERNALLY:

- Ave rent: £53
Availability: *Generally, rental accommodation is fairly bog standard – although if a student has specific needs for a grime-infested rathole, they'll have no trouble finding one. Most of studentville is on direct bus routes to the University. The West End, Ashbourne Road and Kedleston Road are the main pockets of student habitation. Normanton and Peartree are the red-light districts – if that's of any interest one way or the other.*
Housing help: The six staff in Derby Student Residences post vacancies and offer advice and assistance, as can the SU.

WELFARE

SERVICES:

- Lesbian/Gay/Bisexual Society • Ethnic Minorities Society
- Mature (& Postgrad) Students' Officer & Society
- International Students' Officer & Society
- Disabilities Officer & Society • Women's Officer
- College counsellors: 4 full • Crime rating: !!!!

Health: GP practice and nurse surgeries on campus.
Crèches/Nursery: The private Discovery Day Nursery can take in students' kids 3mths-14yrs.
Disabilities: Wheelchair access is *variable* according to site – *all new developments are excellent*. The University is rightly proud of its Deafness Studies Unit – there are BSL signers available, as well as enlarged texts, Braille signs and tape recordings available for the visually impaired. Also help for dyslexic students.

FINANCE:
• <u>Ave debt per year: £3,272</u> • <u>Home student fees: £3,000</u> • <u>Access fund: £800,000</u>
• <u>Successful applications/yr: 1,000</u>
Support: Under 21s can apply for an opportunities bursary. Means-tested bursaries to ease the new fees, including help for local (Derby) students.

Derbyshire College of Higher Education
see <u>University of Derby</u>

Distributive Trades
see <u>University of the Arts, London</u>

DIT
see <u>University of Abertay Dundee</u>

Dorset Institute
see <u>Bournemouth University</u>

Dundee University

(1) University of Dundee, Dundee, DD1 4HN
Tel: (01382) 344 160 E-mail: srs@dundee.ac.uk Website: www.dundee.ac.uk
Dundee University Students' Association, Airlie Place, Dundee, DD1 4HE
Tel: (01382) 221 841 E-mail: dusa@dusa.co.uk Website: www.dusa.co.uk
(2) University of Dundee, Kirkcaldy Campus, Forth Avenue, Kirkcaldy, KY2 5YS
Tel: (01592) 268 888

GENERAL

Tucked onto the northern side of the Firth of Tay and a trundle down the east coast of Scotland from Aberdeen, is Dundee. The Tay estuary, the surrounding expanse of sandy shore and the highlands rising inland are *very picturesque – although, the same can't really be said for the city*. A mile west of the city centre, in an area of town *scenically overlooking the river*, is the self-contained main campus of Dundee University. It's gone *redevelopment crazy* in the last few years and whole chunks of the campus are being dug up, added to, taken from and generally diddled with in a major revamp scheduled to finish in 2007. So, *while there may be workers drilling through walls for a while, the facilities should be vastly improved soon, if not sooner.* This is in keeping with the University's history of buildings *sprouting in spurts* throughout the last century or so, which explains its *jumbled* architecture. *Despite the campus's spaciousness, greenery is, literally, thin on the ground.*

Following a cluster of mergers over the past decade, the University has spread over various other campuses around the city, notably the medical departments at Ninewells Hospital and Gardyne Campus (social work and education). There's also the Kirkcaldy Campus in *the scenic (and touristy)* town of Kirkcaldy, Fife, 30 miles away.

Sex ratio (M:F): 32:68	**Founded: 1967**
Full-time u'grads: 8,685	**Part-time: 3,650**
Postgrads: 940	**Non-degree: 0**
Ave course: 4yrs	**Flunk rate: 17%**
Mature: 23%	**International: 20%**
Disabled: 139	**Local: n/a**

ATMOSPHERE:

The main campus is compact and the University untraditional. The mix of students on campus is broad – more than two-thirds from Scotland, one in five from elsewhere in the UK (especially Northern Ireland). It's full of normal, unpretentious people and, although there's fun to be had, the joint is hardly rocking.

SITES:

Kircaldy Campus: (Nursing & Midwifery) Based about 30 miles away in a *dinky* Fife town (pop: 47,000), about 15 miles from Edinburgh.

DUNDEE:

- Population: 142,700 • City centre: <1 mile • London: 384 miles
- Edinburgh: 50 miles • Aberdeen: 60 miles
- High temp: 19 • Low temp: 0 • Rainfall: 55

Nowhere near as ugly as it used to be, Dundee has settled comfortable into modern townhood (ie. it's got a big shopping complex). The Tay, Riverside and the port area have certain attractions and there are 1,300 acres of parkland including golf courses, a zoo and nature trail. Two bridges span the Tay, both of which are more successful than the first bridge which collapsed in 1879 shortly after it was built, killing 75 people (as described in the world's worst poem by William McGonagall). The people are friendly enough too. The city has the requisite bunch of museums, galleries and historic buildings to keep residents from boredom-inspired killing sprees, including Bonar Hall (a University-owned exhibition centre). Worth an ogle are the Observatory on Balgay Hill and Captain Scott's ship 'Discovery'.

TRAVEL:

Train: Dundee station has services to London (£54.90), Glasgow (£14.40) and routes to most parts of Scotland and England.
Coaches: National Express, Stagecoach and Citylink services including London (£32), Glasgow (£11) and Edinburgh (£10).
Car: From the south, the M90 goes up to Perth (19 miles west) from where there's the A90, or the A914 which crosses the Tay. From the north, there's the A92, A929 and A923.
Air: Dundee (Riverside Park) Airport serves UK destinations and the odd international.
Hitching: *Not easy. Too many roundabouts around Dundee where hitchers can get stuck all day. The best bet is to get a lift on the A92 along the coast and try to swing by Edinburgh.*
Local: The *good* bus service *is fairly cheap* (80p across town, exact fare only), but the last is at around 11.15pm.
University: The Students' Association provides a night bus that takes, *erm, tired and emotional* students back to halls after a night at the Union.
Taxis: *Cheapest in Scotland.*

Bicycles: *Not too hilly and theft isn't a major problem, but bikes aren't really that necessary.*

CAREER PROSPECTS:

• Careers Service • 3 staff • Unemployed after 6mths: 6%
The usual gamut of interview prep, bulletin boards and career fairs.

SPECIAL FEATURES:

• The late Queen Mother was Dundee's first Chancellor and Lorraine Kelly is the current Rector.

FAMOUS ALUMNI:

Kate Atkinson (novelist); Sir James Black (Nobel laureate, medicine; current Chancellor); Stewart Campbell (rugby); Lynda Clark (Scottish Advocate General); Brian Cox (actor); Fred MacAulay (comedian); Lord Robertson of Port Ellen (Secretary General, NATO); Albert Watson (photographer).

FURTHER INFO:

• Prospectuses: undergrad; postgrad; all departments; alternative; international; video • Open days
The website *is one of the most applicant-friendly going* and the SA provides a *dirt-dishing* guide for freshers and prospective students.

ACADEMIC

Medicine, Life Sciences and Art & Design all *raise studious eyebrows* and Dundee maintains strong links with industry, especially pharmaceuticals. Courses are modular, meaning students pick'n'mix subjects and many of the courses run continual assessment. 20 *lucky* students each year get to take part in the Transatlantic Student Exchange programme and jet off to the States to go to toga parties – we mean study – in America or Canada for a year.

Entry points: 150-348	Ave points: 330
Applns per place: n/a	Clearing: 10%
No. of terms: 2	Length of terms: 15
Staff/student ratio: 1:10	Study addicts: 21%
Teaching: ****	Research: ****
Firsts: 9%	2.2s: 22%
2.1s: 36%	3rds: n/a

ADMISSIONS:

• Apply via UCAS/CATCH for Nursing and Midwifery

SUBJECTS:

Arts & Social Sciences: 17%	Law & Accountancy: 9%
Duncan of Jordanstone: 13%	Life Sciences: 8%
Education & Social Work: 6%	Medicine, Dentistry & Nursing: 41%
Engineering & Physical Science: 6%	

Best: Biology; Computing; Economics; English; Finance & Accounting; Geography; Graphic Design & Textile Design; History; Law; Medicine; Psychology.

LIBRARIES:

• 690,000 books • 930 study places
More than half the books are in the Main Library, but there are eight other various book stashes across the campuses and departments, reflecting their subjects.

COMPUTERS:

• 156 workstations
16 separate IT suites and various other PC places, *which sounds dandy, till you hear the number of machines, which ain't so impressive.*

ENTERTAINMENT

THE CITY:

• Price of a pint of beer: £1.95 • Glass of wine: £2 • Can of Red Bull: £1.50
Cinemas: The UGC and Odeon multiplexes (10 screens each) *see to students' cravings for bangs, gags and fluffy endings. Or the arty, 2-screen DCA for subtitled films and soul-destroying endings.*
Theatres: The Dundee Rep for *more hardcore* theatre. Caird Hall for ballet, opera and pantos.
Pubs: *Being Scotland, pubs are open virtually all the time. Pushplugs: The Globe (friendly, good food); Tally-Ho (beer yard). Avoid the Speedwell and the Taybridge – old men alert.*
Clubbing: *Dundee's clubs may not be world-renowned, nor indeed cheap, but that doesn't scare off desperate students. There's certainly no shortage.* Fat Sam's and The Social are the main alternative for students bored with DUSA.
Music venues: Gigs at Fat Sam's. Caird Hall hosts classical and pop while the West Port pub *swings* to Cajun and Mexican rhythms.
Eating out: *Pubs are usually a good starting point – most of the student favourites do food beyond pork scratchings in cider sauce. Pushplugs: Braes; Visocchi's.*
Other: *For fun before nightfall,* there are the zoo and wildlife sanctuary and the beaches.

UNIVERSITY:

• Price of a pint of beer: £1.50 • Glass of wine: £1.50 • Can of Red Bull: £1.20
Bars: £4.8m has been spent refurbishing the Union. *Alternative* Pete's Bar *has sadly lost its uniquely rough and grimy ambience and is now more habitable.* The *relaxed* Tav Bar hosts bar-type thrills like karaoke, sports quizzes and *tacky, snacky* food in shiny, glassy surroundings. The Liar Bar draws the DJs for big club nights. The balcony attached to Mono & Mono *is a vomit-related accident waiting to happen.*
Theatres: LIP Theatre Company pulls on the hose and doublets at the Dundee Rep Theatre.
Film: The film society shows one movie a week, *normally mainstream.* Also weekly viewings at the local cinema.
Music venues: The Thrills, Mark Owen and Kym Marsh have played Mono & Mono.
Clubbing: *Mono holds the funkiest club nights.* Trevor Nelson, Sister Bliss and UNKLE have all swabbed the decks.
Food: The Tav Bar does the *best nosh for very reasonable* prices but you can get a cheap coffee in the Student Association cantina.
Other: Graduation ball, sports ball and *diddier* faculty bashes.

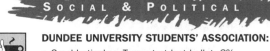

SOCIAL & POLITICAL

DUNDEE UNIVERSITY STUDENTS' ASSOCIATION:

• 3 sabbaticals • Turnout at last ballot: 8%
New students could be forgiven for blinking at the sight of the modernist mirrored glass visual assault of a building where DUSA is based. The students can also be a bit whingy about the services they get out of the SA, but to be fair, they do a good job of keeping the ents boat afloat. Politically though, most students don't care if they're right, left or hanging from the ceiling by their ankles (DUSA's not affiliated to NUS), so long as the beer doesn't run out.

SA FACILITIES:

The SA provides: five bars; canteen; coffee bar; fast food place; two meeting rooms; three minibuses and a van; RBS bank with ATM; Clydesdale ATMs; photo booth; crèche; general store; stationery shop; vending machines; new & secondhand bookshops; advice centre; TV lounge; post office.

CLUBS (NON-SPORTING):

American Studies; Bands; DUBAPS (Biology, Anatomy & Physiology); Chinese; Cumbrian Roads (history); English; Geography & Environmental; Hellen c; Lip Theatre; Music; Operatic & Musical; Roleplaying; Young Entrepreneurs. **See also Clubs tables.**

OTHER ORGANISATIONS:

Blunt Instrument, the free student paper, comes out once a term. Radio station, Vertigo, broadcasts across the city and on the internet. DUMS does raggish charity stuff.

RELIGIOUS:

• 9 chaplains (RC, CofE, Methodist, Baptist, CofE, FCofS, Congregational, Orthodox)
Only one chaplain is full-time, but the others are found often enough at the chaplaincy, which also caters for other flavours of faith (quite literally, actually – they've got a coffee bar). Also a Muslim prayer room.

PAID WORK:

Most people who want work can get it – there's no end of part-time McJobs in the city centre. Apart from listing these on its website, DUSA hires quite a few people itself and holds recruitment fairs to entice the next generation of ent, security and bar staff into its clutches.

SPORTS

• Recent success: skiing • BUSA ranking: 30
Interest's not as hot as the facilities.

SPORTS FACILITIES:

Six football pitches; four rugby pitches; three hockey pitches; three all-weather fields; cricket pitch; four tennis courts; four netball courts; swimming pool; gym; climbing wall; running track; aerobics studio; four squash courts; four basketball courts; sports hall; sauna ... *you work up a sweat just listing them.*

SPORTING CLUBS:

Boating; Boxing; Curling; Harriers; Ju-Jitsu; Sunday League; Waterpolo; Women's Football; Women's Rugby. **See also Clubs tables**.

ATTRACTIONS:

Dundee United and Dundee FC *bicker on and off the pitch*.

ACCOMMODATION

IN COLLEGE:

• Catered: 2% • Cost: £85 • Self-catered: 8% • Cost: £65
• First years living in: 100% • Insurance premium: £
Availability: In theory, 1st years are guaranteed a place in halls if they want one, although this will be easier in practice when the building work is finished in 2007, by which time all rooms will be en-suite. Self-caterers try to get elbow-room at the cooker with five other students on average (*not a bad sharing rate*). The University *is in cahoots* with the police which, coupled with CCTV and night porters, ensures beauty sleep is normally undisturbed.
Car parking: £60 gets a parking permit and there's usually room to stash bikes in the entrances to halls.

Pembroke College, Cambridge has the oldest bowling green in Europe.

EXTERNALLY:
• Ave rent: £55 • Living at home: 23%
Availability: Over 70% live out (nearly $\frac{1}{4}$ are mature students), many in their parents' or their own homes. *So they're alright, Jack. There's enough choice around for students to be able to pick somewhere near where they study. Choice pitches include Perth Road, but even this is getting to be quite expensive and students are moving further and further out. The east side and city centre are a bit too rough for more sensitive souls.*
Housing help: The University Residences Office, apart from allocating University places, offers bulletin boards, advice and booklets, provided by eight staff. DUSA runs an online service.

WELFARE

SERVICES:
• Lesbian/Gay/Bisexual Society • Ethnic Minorities Officer
• Postgrad Society • International Students' Officer & Society • Disabilities Officer
• Late-night minibus • College counsellors: 4 part
• SU counsellors: 1 • Crime rating: !
DUSA's Information & Support Service offers drop-in lunchtime sessions and arranges police and solicitor's clinics. A student support worker helps with anything from landlords to loneliness and co-ordinates 'Peer Connections', a mentoring scheme for students to look after each other.
Health: The Student Health Service has a part-time doctor and two nurses.
Crèches/Nursery: 40 places for kids over 2yrs.
Disabled: Disability Support Officers in each department are there to see students get what they need. There's also a special IT suite and dyslexia service.

FINANCE:
• Ave debt per year: £3,482
Support: Through the Student Money Adviser and assistant, the SAS (*that's the Student Advisory Service, not the balaclava-headed crack assassins*) provides financial advice and there are bursaries for mature students.

Dundee Institute of Technology
see University of Abertay Dundee

University of Durham

(1) University of Durham, University Office, Durham, DH1 3HP
  Tel: (0191) 334 2000 E-mail: admissions@durham.ac.uk Website: www.durham.ac.uk
  Durham Students' Union, Dunelm House, New Elvet, Durham, DH1 3AN
  Tel: (0191) 334 1777 E-mail: enquiries@dsu.org.uk Website: www.dsu.org.uk
(2) The University of Durham, Queen's Campus, Stockton, University Boulevard, Thornaby, Stockton-on-Tees, TS17 6BH Tel: (0191) 334 2000

Durham City, laced by the River Wear, lies in the heart of the Geordie-speaking North-East, near the Northumbrian Moors, 10 miles from the North Sea and 52 miles south of the Scottish border. The University is *planted* in the middle of the ancient, small city and on weekdays during term students dominate it socially as much as the cathedral and castle do physically. The castle is actually one of the University's 16 colleges, which spread out in three main groups across the city *giving the advantages of a collegiate, civic and campus university as well as a handy defence against invading Vikings*.

The University has two branches outside Durham itself: a small Catholic college 4 miles outside the city, and the Queen's Campus, an entirely modern and separate site in Stockton, 21 miles away, and *a mini university in itself, that could hardly be more different from Durham's quiet and old-world charm if it tried.*

Sex ratio (M:F): 45:55	**Founded: 1832**
Full-time u'grads: 10,380	**Part-time: 385**
Postgrads 2,190	**Non-degree: 156**
Ave course: 3yrs	**Ethnic: 7%**
State:private school: 61:33	**Flunk rate: 2%**
Mature: 8%	**International: 15%**
Disabled: 61	**Local: 18%**

(Left margin: 55% ... 45%)

ATMOSPHERE:

As England's third oldest university, there's something of the Oxbridge about Durham with its traditions, its formal dinners and balls (of the black-tie variety). One major difference though is the strength of its central SU. Although the weather's chilly, the hearts are warm. The college system and the size of the city create a communal atmosphere that some find claustrophobic, but the city's becoming more student-friendly, so there's more chance to escape.

THE COLLEGES:

Much of a student's social life is centred on the college where they eat, sleep and drink. Students remain members of their college even if they don't live there. However, unlike Oxbridge, teaching is not college-based. The main colleges are grouped into three areas *and each group has a flavour of its own. So it's important to pick the right college – each one tastes different.*

The Peninsular: The oldest colleges are on 'the Peninsula', along 'the Bailey', *and they appeal particularly to those who admire their architecture and tradition (if not their facilities) and to raging Sloanes. These colleges are:*

University College or 'Castle': (650) The first college and one of the most over-subscribed (16 applications per place). *Students sacrifice a few creature comforts to live in a castle in their third year (if they're lucky).* Founded in 1072, the castle is the oldest building used for student accommodation in the country.

Hatfield: (746) *Rugby and beer. Not the place for shy, retiring, sensitive types.*

St Chad's: (323) *Croquet and Pimms. Very small but with character.*

St John's: (356) Small, quaint and in cahoots with the Church. *Predominantly Christian. First years get to live next to the cathedral, the jammy beggars.*

St Cuthbert's Society: (1,093) 80% live out of college. Many mature students, *but this is balancing out.*

The Hill Colleges, near the science departments, were mostly built in the 60s *and tend to be more progressive. These colleges are:*

St Aidan's: (781) *Motivated and progressive students. They have to be to climb that hill and still party.*

Van Mildert: (881) *Like Aidan's but less motivated and not on a hill. The most cosmopolitan college.*

Trevelyan: (559) *'Trevs' has honeycomb maze architecture and, for no special reason, rather arty students.*

St Mary's: (622) After many years as an all-female bastion, Mary's is now mixed. *The atmosphere (a strange mix of the knitting and nighties brigade and sporty party monsters) is likely to change for good. Possibly the most attractive buildings of the hill colleges.*
Grey: (899) *Slightly more character than its name suggests.*
Collingwood: (1,046) The youngest college is *media hacksville but unpretentious.*
The third area isn't really a group. It's the hilly north bank of the Wear where the largest college, **St Hild & St Bede** (1,100), stands alone on a 16-acre site. *Its students are a mixture of all sorts, variously accused of being too insular or too dominant.*
There's also **Ustinov College** (1,200) for postgrads only and **Ushaw College**, a Catholic seminary 4 miles out of the city. A new 400-bed self-catering college looms on the horizon, and is being built about a mile from Durham centre.
Two colleges, **John Snow College** (9841) and **George Stephenson College** (935), are based at the Queen's Campus at Stockton, *which is completely unlike Durham in terms of atmosphere, history, geography and absence of pomp. It feels like a completely separate university*, with its own union and ents, but maintains the same infrastructure.

DURHAM:

• Population: 87,709 • City centre: 0 miles • London: 240 miles • Newcastle: 15 miles
• High temp: 19 • Low temp: 0 • Rainfall: 54
Durham used to be the epicentre of the North-East's mining tradition. *Nowadays there's not much in Durham not connected to the University or the cathedral.* It does have a shopping mall, an open-air and a covered market, lots of quaint *shoppes*, army and arts museums and certainly *carries an air of its own history but, well, there's no buzz. Things are picking up but thrill-seekers and hardened shoppers sneak into Newcastle when Durham's not looking.*
Stockton, 21 miles south of Durham, but only 3 miles out of Middlesbrough, is the birthplace of the steam engine and the Industrial Revolution, *but don't expect it still to be so cutting edge. Manufacturing industries went out with Maggie Thatcher and left Stockton in need of the kind of rejuvenation that Durham's Queen's Campus was intended to bring.*
See University of Teesside *for local details.*

TRAVEL:

Trains: Mainline connections from Durham to London King's Cross (£47.50) and *handy trains to Newcastle (£2.60). Stockton is near Darlington train station, on the London-Edinburgh line.*
Coaches: National Express and Blue Line services to many destinations: London (£25.50), Newcastle (£3) and so on.
Car: 5 mins off the A1, but the city operates a congestion charge in the centre and around town, *walking is easy enough (and the riverside paths are blissful)*. Stockton connects to the A1 via the A66.
Air: Newcastle and Teesside Airports are close to both campuses – flights to London, Northern Ireland and Europe.
Hitching: *Not bad from the A1.*
Local: Good bus services *that lazy students use to get up the hills* in Durham. Fares from 32p. A service runs between Durham and Queen's Campus.
Taxis: *Some of Britain's cheapest taxis* (min fare £1, £15 Durham-Newcastle) make it *a worthwhile share.*
Bicycles: *A bit hilly for bikes.*

CAREER PROSPECTS:

• Careers Service • No. of staff: 20 • Unemployed after 6mths: 7%

SPECIAL FEATURES:

• Teikyo University, a Japanese college, has set up an outpost at Durham University, where its students can *come for a year, get a taste of English students and go home all the wiser.* It includes two small halls of residence, but some students also stay at the neighbouring St Mary's College.

FAMOUS ALUMNI:

George Alagiah, Jeremy Vine (BBC reporters); Biddy Baxter (ex-producer of Blue Peter); Will Carling, Phil de Glanville (England rugby captains); Jack Cunningham MP (Lab); Hunter Davies (journalist); Jonathan Edwards (triple jumper); Harold Evans (ex-Sunday Times ed); Will Greenwood (England rugby centre); Nasser Hussain (ex-England cricket captain); Cmdr Tim Lawrence (Princess Anne's hubby); Edward Leigh MP (Con); James Wilby (actor).

FURTHER INFO:

• Prospectuses: undergrad; postgrad; alternative; mature; international

ACADEMIC

250-350

Entry points: 250–350	**Ave points: 382**
Applns per place: 9	**Clearing: 7%**
No. of terms: 3	**Length of terms: 9wks**
Staff/student ratio: 1:19	**Study addicts: 24%**
Teaching: *****	**Research: *******
Year abroad: 3%	**Sandwich students: 1%**
Firsts: 15%	**2.2s: 24%**
2.1s: 57%	**3rds: 3%**

POINTS

ADMISSIONS:

• Apply via UCAS

SUBJECTS:

Arts/Humanities: 27%   Social Sciences: 40%
Faculty of Science: 33%
Best: Archaeology; Biological Sciences; Biomedical Sciences; Business Finance; Classics & Ancient History; Education; Economics; Engineering; French; German; Maths; Philosophy; Physics; Psychology; Sport; Theology.
Worst: Spanish.

LIBRARIES:

• 1,300,000 books • 1,200 study places
As well as the main library, there are four other libraries (including education, ecclesiastical and special collections). Each college and many departments also have their own libraries.

COMPUTERS:

• 1,300 workstations • 24-hr access
Despite six classrooms, several computer rooms, 24-hr access and all colleges having net capabilities, *getting at a computer can still occasionally prove tricky*. Around 5,000 student rooms have high-speed net access. Introductory courses in web design, spreadsheets and general *techno guff* are available.

ENTERTAINMENT

DURHAM:

• Price of a pint of beer: £2.40 • Glass of wine: £2 • Can of Red Bull: £2.10
Durham's a bit dinky and still can't fully quench the student thirst. Many sidle off to Newcastle in search of good times – see Newcastle University *for further info.*
Cinemas: The Gala Cinema in Durham has one screen but boasts an IMAX and occasional theatre too.
Theatres: The Gala, er, Theatre. One stage, but boasts a cinema and, *oh never mind…*
Pubs: *A few, not all are student-friendly but some serve real ale if that's your cup of tea: Pushplugs: Swan & 3 Cygnets; Walkabout (late licence); Colpitts; The Shakespeare; Dun Cow (here be ale); Market Tavern; New Inn; Saints (internet café); Scruffy Murphy's. Probably best avoided are Yates' and the Fighting Cocks.*

Clubbing: *Klute is a Durham institution, in that it's rubbish, but like a much beloved but lame dog, you can't bring yourself to shoot it through the head, despite it being named 'n' shamed as 2nd Worst Club in Europe. There's also DH1 and Studio, but Newcastle has better options.*

Music venues: The Jug has regular bands. The Fishtank is *tiny*, but hosts *decent* alternative music and comedy.

Eating out: *Little choice really, but one or two to help students recover from beans on toast and Pot Noodle overdoses. Pushplugs: La Spaghetatta (Chinese, only kidding, Italian); Market Tavern (top pies); The Court Inn (good grub).*

UNIVERSITY:

• Price of a pint of beer: £1.30 • Glass of wine: £1.50

Bars: Kingsgate is the SU's main bar. It's open regularly and *cruelly painted orange to distract students from the service. Each college has its own bar too, where most of the serious drinking gets done and around which a lot of college life revolves (that's what happens when you drink too much).* The Queen's campus has the Rocket Union.

Theatres: Student drama is well represented, with regular shows at The Asssembly Room theatre and some going on to the Fringe. *Beware though, levels of theatre-ness can change dramatically from year to year.*

Film: No cinema, but there are film societies and Hild/Bede students are liberal with the use of DVDs on their OHP.

Clubbing/Music venues: The Ballroom (cap 750), Riverside Café (150) in Dunelm House are used along with a smaller room and Stockton's Rocket Union. The colleges have smaller facilities that they don't bother using much. *Friday night's Planet of Sound cums on and feels the noize all over campus. Big-name acts think Durham is what you do with drumsticks but that didn't stop Chesney. Nothing can stop Chesney.*

Comedy/Cabaret: Termly comedy nights at the Riverside Café.

Food: Kingsgate and Riverside and Rocket do *pretty standard stuff.*

Balls: Each college puts on at least one a year, costing from a few quid to £130+ for a double ticket at Castle's *elitist* June Bash. There's also the Freshers' Ball where *Durham's posh kids (easily spotted, they're the ones whose over-bite appears to have swallowed their chin) get a bit squiffy and embarrass the family name.*

SOCIAL & POLITICAL

DURHAM STUDENTS' UNION/(DUSU):

• 5 sabbaticals • Turnout at last ballot: 27% • NUS member

DSU doesn't just keep the students quiet with booze. *It's a politically shrewd union with a representative voice in the University and a tendency to grab headlines, appear on television and launch political careers. Less-political students sometimes complain that this is at the expense of other aspects of the Union's responsibilities.* Regardless, the students rally together for one of the country's largest *(and occasionally silliest)* collections of clubs and societies at any university.

SU FACILITIES:

The large Union building, Dunelm House, is placed right in the middle of Durham where it offers: three bars; a ballroom; Riverside Room Cafeteria; small hall; shop; travel agency; launderette; stationery shop; secondhand bookshop; advice centre; ticket agency; pool tables; minibus; car and van hire; fax, print and photocopier services; meeting room; games and vending machines; juke box; public phone; photo booth.

CLUBS (NON-SPORTING):

All Good Music; Alternative Music; Anglo-Japanese; Anthropology; Anti-Sweatshop; Applied Psychology; Archaeology; Arthur Holmes Geological; Arts Society; Assassins; Astronomical; Belly Dancing; Big Band; Biological; Boris Johnson Fan Club; Brass Band; Breakbeat; Business; Caledonian (wearing kilts and dancing); Capoeira Senzala; Cerinus; Chamber Choir; Change Ringers; Chemical; Chinese; Choral; Classics; Combined Social; Computing; Concert Band; Creative Arts; Creative Writing; Cultural Exchange; Duke of Edinburgh; Economics; Egg & Spoon; English; European; Expedition; Fabians; Fine Arts; First Aid; Folk; Football Supporters; French; Games; German; Heckling; Hellenic; Hill Orchestra; History; Hong Kong; Improv Comedy; Industrial; Inner Temple; Instep

Dance Company; Jazz; Journalism; Kendo; Latin Dance; Law; Light Opera Group; Linguistic; Local Asylum Support; Mad Soc; Mah-jong; Malaysian; Management Consultancy; Manga & Anime; Mathematical; Meditation; Merhaba; Methodist; Model United Nations; Mornington Crescent Club; Motor Sports; Music; Natural Sciences; Network Gaming Society; New Music; Orthodox; Pagan; Paintball; Palestine; Philosophy; Real Ale; Recording Studio; Red Cross; Religious & Theological; Relation; Ridiculously Good-looking Society; Rock; Scandinavian; Science; Scout & Guides; Shakers (cocktails); Shorinji Kempo (martial art); Singapore; Sociology; Spanish; SPEAK (faith); Student Action for Refugees; Tenteleni Travel (volunteers); Theatre; Tough Guy; Treasure Trap (live action roleplay); Unicef; Urban & Underground; Welsh; Wine Tasting; Young Federal Union. **See also Clubs tables.**

OTHER ORGANISATIONS:

Palatinate, the student newspaper, has won awards recently. LIP (Level Information Project) is a national mag aimed at a pro-multicultural student readership. www.durham21.co.uk (three times NUS website of the year) is a not-for-profit online newspaper, with all proceeds going to Durham University Charity Week (aka DUCK). DUCK, incidentally, is what they call their active charity Rag (following the ban of Rag after, reputedly, students broke *in* to Durham Top Security Prison). Student Community Action acts as an umbrella for projects including SPARK, which promotes work with local youngsters. The Durham Union Society (DUS) is the long-standing debating society, which offers more than just debating – *often seen as a right-wing alternative to DSU or as a refuge for the sophisticated Sloane* – either way it costs £35 to get in, runs a bar, TV room, café and a range of events.

RELIGIOUS:

There's a 1,500 year-old Christian heritage, *so finding a church is easy.* As well as the cathedral, there are Anglican, Catholic, Methodist, Quaker and United Reformed churches. Most colleges have their own chapel. For Muslims a prayer-room is provided, but the nearest mosque is in Sunderland. Everyone else has to go to Newcastle to find a *worship shop.*

PAID WORK:

• Job bureau
Work can be found in the University bars, libraries or locally and there's a *comprehensive* jobshop to find folk work, *but jobs are still hard to come by.*

S P O R T S

• Recent successes: rowings, cricket, rugby • BUSA Ranking: 8
Durham tends to wow when it comes to sports, possibly because they pump so much money into it or, in the case of rowing, hire ex-Olympian alumni to coach the team. Or maybe it's the fresh air. Whatever, they take it seriously.

SPORTS FACILITIES:

Sports hall; 60 acres of playing fields; all-weather pitch; multigym; athletics and running track; gym; croquet lawn and bowling green; tennis and squash courts; the River Wear. Outdoor pitches are floodlit. Durham City also has a public baths. Stockton will have all-weather floodlit pitches and there's a public sports centre nearby with watersports facilities.

SPORTING CLUBS:

Aerobics; Aikido; Boardriders; Boats; Boxing; Bridge; Clay Pigeon; Fives; Freefall; Gliding; Hapkido; Hill Walking; Kung Fu; Lacrosse; Polo; Rifles; Speleological; Ultimate Frisbee; Waterpolo. **See also Clubs tables.**

ATTRACTIONS:

The Durham Regatta is one of the top annual university rowing events. Durham University doesn't actually run it though, *but does do well in it.* Durham city has a *strong* cricket team. Newcastle, Sunderland and Middlesbrough FCs are nearby.

ACCOMMODATION

IN COLLEGE:

- Catered: 48% • Cost: £121 (28wks) • Self-catered: 5% • Cost: £84 (29/40wks)
- First years living in: 100% • Insurance premium: ££

Availability: Almost all first years live in and some colleges can provide accommodation for a further year. Housing is mixed and disabled facilities are available. *With so many different colleges, what students call home varies big time, from cold but atmospheric chambers in the Castle with limited facilities to en-suite modern rooms at most of the hill colleges. University College's housing is the worst, Collingwood's the best. Most shared kitchens, being pants, make it hard to create anything more substantial than toast and a cuppa, especially in the catered rooms.* Stockton's two colleges are self-catering (shared kitchens).
Car parking: A permit is required to get at the few spaces available. *What with the congestion charge too there's little point having a car if living in.* Stockton has a bit more space for cars, though.

EXTERNALLY:

- Ave rent: £54 • Living at home: 3%

Availability: *Housing is expensive and rare in the local area,* so many students resort to the surrounding villages, *which aren't too far away.* In the city there are Victorian terraced houses that tend to share between three and five. *The Viaduct is a sought-after spot, closely followed by Bowburn and Langley Moor. The pit villages should be avoided. Cars are unnecessary and the cause of much local tension, but people still bring them.*
Housing help: There's a web-based house search for all students. St Cuthbert's Society helps its own guys.

WELFARE

SERVICES:

- Lesbian/Gay/Bisexual/Transgender Officer & Association • Mature Students' Officer & Association • International Students' Officer & Association • Postgrad Officer & Association • Disabilities Officer & Association • Self-defence Classes • Nightline
- Counsellors: 4 full/9 part • Crime rating: !

Welfare provision is *very good*: union reps cover most areas as well as professionally-trained staff, so-called 'moral tutors' in the colleges and a student health centre (colleges also allocate their students to local NHS practices). There's even free legal advice and an 85-capacity crèche.
Disabled students: Durham University Service for Students with Disabilities (DUSSD) offers help to get around the fact that, being old, Durham wasn't designed with any kind of disability in mind. *Modern, purpose-built Stockton is much more accessible.*

FINANCE:

- Ave debt per year: £2,722

Fees: The top-up fight has been fought and lost. Durham's one of the *Holy Trinity* of universities (along with Oxford and Cambridge, *natch*) offering the full three grand of support to students from families with less than £16,000 yearly income.
- Access fund: £518,284 • Successful applications/yr: 795 • Ave payment: £100-3,500

The hardship fund also gives out £50,000 a year, shared out last year between 49 overseas students. *Although it's not unheard of, to get more than £2,000 from the hardship or access fund requires exceptional circumstances (being 'thirsty' doesn't count).* The Union tells students how to get money out of the University, but doesn't offer any itself. Academic prizes are up for grabs, as are awards for students who want to do some worthy extra-curricular stuff but can't afford it.

Ealing College see Thames Valley University

University of East Anglia

University of East London

Economics see LSE

University of Edinburgh

Edinburgh College of Art see Heriot-Watt University

University of Essex

Essex IHE see APU

Exeter University

Ealing College

see Thames Valley University

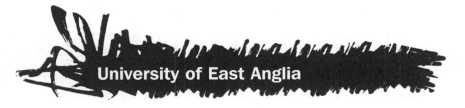

University of East Anglia

University of East Anglia, Norwich, NR4 7TJ
Tel: (01603) 591 515 E-mail: admissions@uea.ac.uk Website: www.uea.ac.uk
Union of UEA Students, Union House, University of East Anglia, Norwich, NR4 7TJ
Tel: (01603) 593 272 E-mail: su.comms@uea.ac.uk Website: www.stu.uea.ac.uk

GENERAL

Things that are flat: *still water, car parks and East Anglia. East Anglia's* northern bit is also soggy because of the Broads – miles of lakes, waterways and fenlands *which also means tourists.* When Norwich was Britain's second biggest city, the Broads were full of traders instead of Americans, but times change. During the Industrial Revolution other cities cottoned on to cotton or cashed in on coal, Norwich made it with mustard and still has a thriving industry. Nowadays Norwich, *a rather hilly market town considering its surrounding topography,* is a tourist attraction, administrative centre for Norfolk and home to 270 acres of premium university known as the 'University Plain' (*seeing herds of students moving across it at sunset can be quite emotional*). $2\frac{1}{2}$ miles out of town, between a 40s council estate and a conservation area, UEA is a concrete complex surrounded by greenery and its very own lake.

Sex ratio (M:F): 35:65	**Founded: 1963**
Full-time u'grads: 6,903	**Part-time: 3,805**
Postgrads: 2,010	**Non-degree: 197**
Ave course: 3yrs	**Ethnic: 14%**
State:private school: 90:10	**Flunk rate: 7%**
Mature: 30%	**International: 16%**
Disabled: 34	**Local: 23%**

ATMOSPHERE:

An easy going, informal but sometimes cliquey atmosphere in a largely white, middle-class environment. Those who can cope with this, lousy weather and the tumbleweed at the weekends (despite good ents) will enjoy themselves. When the claustrophobia's too much to bear, the town's only a short bus or bike trip away. UEA's a true greenfield site, so don't expect cutting-edge style or busting rhymes on street corners.

NORWICH:

• Population: 121,700 • City centre: 2 miles • London: 103 miles
• Birmingham: 139 miles • Cambridge: 62 miles
• High temp: 20 • Low temp: 1 • Rainfall: 55

Locals like to remind students that Norwich is a city, not a town. It does, after all, have not one but two cathedrals and contains all the amenities such as a *whole bunch* of supermarkets, late-night shops, bookshops, banks and *cunningly-located* cashpoints. Apart from the cathedral glut, tourists *quite like* the Norman castle, which has been converted into two museums and an art gallery. The area between the University and the town is known as 'the Golden Triangle', with lots of students and amenities and a *community feel. For UEA students, Norwich is like a favourite grandparent, warm and friendly, but unlikely to offer much in the way of high-octane excitement.*

TRAVEL:

Trains: Nearest station is Norwich, 3 miles from campus. Direct services to London (£19.95), change there for other destinations or via Peterborough for the North.
Coaches: Various services include London (£15.25) and Glasgow (£42.50).
Car: The A11, A47, A140 and A146 go via Norwich.
Air: Flights inland and to about 200 cities worldwide from Norwich Airport.
Local: Buses 25, 26, 27 and 502 regularly run from nearby St Stephen's Meadow and St Stephen's Street in town to the main campus. Taxis can work out cheaper than taking a bus if in a group and most firms give a special rate to/from UEA. If heading into the city, make sure you ask for 'the city' and not 'the town'; *locals are particular.*
Bicycles: *Some cycle lanes near UEA, but it's advisable to wear a gas mask on the ring road. Otherwise it's good territory for two wheelers.*

CAREER PROSPECTS:

• Careers Service • No. of staff: 5 full • Unemployed after 6mths: 8%
Interview training, jobs fairs, careers library and Matrix, an online training service.

FAMOUS ALUMNI:

Jenny Abramsky (Radio 5 Live); Trezzo Azopardi, Martyn Bedford, Kazuo Ishiguro, Toby Litt, Ian McEwan, Clive Sinclair, Rose Tremain (writers); Jack Davenport (actor); Charlie Higson, Arthur Smith (comedians).

FURTHER INFO:

• Prospectuses: undergrad; postgrad • Open days

ACADEMIC

UEA is particularly renowned in two areas. The first is English and American Studies, including *the world-famous MA in writing* (check out the alumni). The other is Environmental Studies, which although it contains meteorology and the like, *isn't quite as green as it sounds.* A fair amount of genetic *meddling* goes on at the John Innes Centre. Students are allowed to take a module in something unrelated to their course – most opt for Creative Writing or a language.

200-360 POINTS

Entry points: 200-360	Ave points: 300
Applns per place: n/a	Clearing: 14%
No. of terms: 3	Length of terms: 12wks
Staff/student ratio: 1:12	Study addicts: 19%
Teaching: ****	Research: ****
Year abroad: 2%	Sandwich students: 0
Firsts: 10%	2.2s: 28%
2.1s: 54%	3rds: 5%

ADMISSIONS:

• Apply via UCAS

SUBJECTS:

Arts & Humanities: 25%   Sciences: 25%
Medical Sciences: 20%   Social Sciences: 30%
Best: American Studies; Art History; Biological Sciences; Drama; Economics; Film Studies; Management; Maths; Philosophy; Physiotherapy; Politics; Subjects allied to Medicine.

LIBRARIES:

• 750,000 books • 1,200 study places
Adequate opening hours and a *good* range of different materials.

COMPUTERS:

• 2,000 workstations • 24-hr access
Lots of computers. All students are cleared out of the IT centre when the library closes and let back in with their swipe cards. *Which is odd*.

OTHER LEARNING FACILITIES:

Most students can take part in an exchange year which counts towards their final degree.

ENTERTAINMENT

THE CITY:

• Price of a pint of beer: £2.10 • Glass of wine: £2.60 • Can of Red Bull: £1.10
Discounting holidays, a student could get drunk in a different pub every night of the year (and die of acute alcohol poisoning but that's by the by). Food and music aside, there's a pretty decent representation of fun in Norwich that should keep all but the most picky occupied.
Cinemas: The *arty* Playhouse, as well as Ster Century and UCI multiplexes.
Theatres: The Theatre Royal is the largest (cap 2,000), providing mainstream fare, opera and Shakespeare. *The Norwich Playhouse is a bit more radical and Norwich Arts Centre yet more so.*
Pubs: Norwich has a massive amount of pubs, over 300 in all. The best are clustered in the Golden Triangle. *Pushplugs: Garden House; Unthank Arms; Belle Vue; Café Da (vodka bar); Mad Moose (rugger buggers). Best to avoid pubs on certain estates like West Earlham and the Larkman.*
Clubbing: *A varied selection which has nurtured Norwich's hitherto lame nightlife. Pushplugs: Mercy (cap 2,000); Liquid (Tuesday student night, free entry); Zoom (indie/garage); Marvel (hip hop/acid jazz) and Gas Station (soul/funk) at The Loft; Ikon (student nights); Mojo's Club (trip hop/drum 'n' bass); Optic; Time.*
Music/comedy: The Arts Centre (cap 350) offers an eclectic selection of music and even comedy, though the University is still probably the best venue in East Anglia.
Eating out: *The worryingly titled 'Tombland' is a restaurant-heavy part of town that boasts a variety of eaterie ethnicities, often with student discounts. Pushplugs: Tree House (wholefood); Anchor Quay; Pedro's (Mexican); Earlham Café, Unthank Kitchen (greasy spoons).*

UNIVERSITY:

• Price of a pint of beer: £1.70 • Glass of wine: £2.10 • Can of Red Bull: £1.50
As the town is for pubs, UEA is for music. Most of its entertainments are decent; UEA's music, however, borders on the legendary. The arts centre is pretty stonking too.
Bars: The Union Pub is the main watering hole, offering pool tables, quizzes and assorted drinky bargains. The Blue Bar is similar, but with big screen sport comin' atcha.
Theatres: The UEA Drama Studio is the site of some *fine* work by dram and non-dram students alike, who've also taken shows to the Fringe. Touring companies like to stop by too.
Film: The Union show two films a week, ranging from blockbuster to arthouse and back again.
Music venues: Two Union venues, LCR and Waterfront, are among East Anglia's biggest music venues and see a *huge variety of top acts* including, among many others: Groove Armada, Gomez and The Thrills. For more classical tastes the site for sound is the small concert hall (150).
Clubbing: LCR hosts the week's big clubbing event (Thurs). The SU's Waterfront sees some less mainstream nights and has cred. *On the whole, they lean more towards alternative and retro sounds than pappy chart R&B, but that hasn't stopped Trevor Nelson, Fatboy Slim and Lisa Pin-Up putting in appearances.*
Comedy/Cabaret: Monthly in the LCR. Big names like Nina Conti, Danny Bhoy and Will Smith *have been braving the giggle-hungry mobs*.
Food: Campus has eight face-stufferies, from the cheap fast food in the Diner to the SASSAF sandwich bar, where all profits go to charity. The Hive Coffee Bar in the Union is an *essential* snack stop.
Other: The *incredible* Sainsbury Centre for Visual Arts on campus has a *very impressive* array of tribal, modern and other art. It was built for a collection owned by the supermarket bloke and has pieces by Francis Bacon, Henry Moore and Giacometti. There are also Latin parties, and balls every summer, Christmas and graduation.

SOCIAL & POLITICAL

UNION OF UEA STUDENTS:

• 4 sabbaticals • Turnout at last ballot: 12% • NUS member
UEA is working on restoring its rep as a left-wing hotbed. Relations with the administration are a bit on the Alaskan side. A portion of the student body are uninterested in politics, another part wave banners like they were surgically attached. Apart from a *comprehensive* voicing of objections to top-up fees and keeping the drama department up and running, campaigns have been run for drugs, alcohol and tobacco awareness, Environment Week, Safe Sex Week and Fairtrade Fortnight.

SU FACILITIES:

In Union House and elsewhere on campus: five bars; shop; newsagent; post office; travel shop; secondhand bookshop; Waterstones; games room; common room; print room; photocopying; advice; women's room; snack bar; vending machines; minibus hire; snooker tables; launderette; ticket agency; Barclays and Lloyds banks and ATMs.

CLUBS (NON-SPORTING):

Arnarchist Students; Anime; Arts; Ballroom & Latin American Dancing; Buddhist; Cocktail; Contemporary Music; Deviant (alt music); East Asian; Football Supporters; French; Games; History; Juggling; Latin; Law; Malaysian; Management Social; Maths; Medsin; Medical; Mexican; Middle Eastern; Music; Pub Crawl; Speak (social justice); STAR (student action for refugees); Streetjazz. **See also Clubs tables.**

OTHER ORGANISATIONS:

Weekly newsletter (the Rabbit), and an independent fortnightly newspaper (Concrete, winner of national awards) let the student body know what's going on. Student Media Award nominated Livewire radio broadcasts upstairs in the Union pub, while Nexus TV screens downstairs. A volunteer co-ordinator helps students find work with voluntary organisations and *Rag throws together* theme nights.

```
The last Inspector Morse episode was filmed on the front quad of
Exeter College, Oxford.
```

RELIGIOUS:

Non-denominational chaplaincy on campus and a worship room for Muslims. In the city there's a *splendid* Anglican cathedral and another for Catholics, as well as prayer areas for Jews, Muslims and Buddhists.

PAID WORK:

• Job bureau

The jobshop is jointly run by the SU and the University. There's less unemployment in East Anglia than most of the country and apart from the usual bar work, students can get better paid jobs in local government and other areas.

SPORTS

• BUSA Ranking: 36

The campus is big enough to sport sports facilities of a size that stretches eyes as well as limbs. Athletic activity is a mass participation thing and the SU has a 'sports-for-all' policy, but some people are put off by the cliqueiness of the sports clubs.

SPORTS FACILITIES:

Most facilities are on campus, including: sports hall; gym; badminton courts; multigym/gym; indoor football pitches; swimming pool; baseball diamond; squash courts (charged); tennis courts; cricket nets; artificial pitch; county athletic track; climbing wall; aerobics studio; rugby pitch; hockey pitches. On the edge of University Plain are 30 acres of playing fields; locally there are the Norfolk Broads for water sports and the city for swimming pool and golf course.

SPORTING CLUBS:

10-Pin Bowling; American Football; Baseball; Cheerleading; Duke of Edinburgh; Futsal (Brazilian football); Kayak; Korfball; Lacrosse; Pool; Ski & Snowboarding; Snooker; Surf; Table Tennis; Ultimate Frisbee; Windsurfing; Yoga. **See also Clubs tables.**

ATTRACTIONS:

A few miles from the University is the massive Norwich Sports Village – a multi-million squid sports centre. There's a dry ski slope at Trowse (4 miles away), an indoor kart club, snooker hall, 10-pin bowling and Quasar laser skirmishes to be had in the city. Norwich FC has Delia Smith on the board.

ACCOMMODATION

IN COLLEGE:

• Self-catering: 43% • Cost: £45-70 (34/38wks) • Insurance premium: £

Availability: 1st years who come from 12 miles or more away are guaranteed a place, disabled students get priority and non-EU students are guaranteed accomodation throughout their course. Most rooms on campus are in mixed halls and *are on the small side*. Norfolk and Suffolk Terraces have *good* views of the Broads. 24-hr security, emergency phones and CCTV on all campuses. All halls are self-catering.

Car parking: For 1st years who have to travel and the disabled only.

EXTERNALLY:

• Ave rent: £40-£50

Availability: *It's not too hard to find rooms in Norwich.* The Golden Triangle is full of them – try Unthank, Earlham and Dereham Roads. *It's a bit of a yuppie ghetto but that's where the good pubs and the 24-hr shops are so, funnily enough, it's where the students go too. Avoid Larkham and West Earlham like they were really dodgy estates.*

Housing help: Homerun's the SU's online housing bureau, which vets properties and offers advice. There's also the standard housing bueau, who do the same thing face-to-face.

SERVICES:

• International Students' Officer • Disabilities Officer & Society • Women's Officer
• Nightline • College counsellors: 3 full/1 part • Crime rating: !!!!

UEA's health and welfare services are *comprehensive*, there are *reasonable* considerations made for *pretty much anything happening short of alien experimentation* and the health centre even has a midwife.

Health: 24-hr health centre on campus with nurses, GP service, dentist and psychiatrist.

Women: Personal alarms and a women's group, and a delayed fare system in late-night taxis.

Crèche: Nursery on campus for 6wks to school-age kids.

Disabilities: *Wheelchair access is pretty good, mainly because the campus is so flat, but there are also plenty of lifts, ramps and all that good stuff, as well as a special needs awareness society. There's a dyslexia support society and HEFCE funding for students with dyslexia and hearing problems.*

FINANCE:

• Ave debt per year: £2,407 • Access fund: £306,755
• Successful applications/yr: 405

Support: Hardship funds and loans, temporary assistance in the event of financial emergencies and grant aid. Guidance also available from the advice centre in the SU.

University of East London

• *Formerly Polytechnic of East London, North East London Polytechnic.*

(1) University of East London, Longbridge Road, Dagenham, Essex, RM8 2AS
    Tel: (020) 8223 3000 E-mail: admiss@uel.ac.uk Website: www.uel.ac.uk
    University of London Student's Union, Longbridge Road, Dagenham, Essex, RM8 2AS
    Tel: (020) 8223 2420 Website: www.uelsu.net

(2) University of East London, Stratford Campus, Romford Road, London, E15 4LZ

(3) University of East London, Docklands Campus, Royal Albert Way, London, E16 2RD
    Tel: (020) 8223 3000

For general information about London: see University of London. The University of East London (UEL) isn't just in east London. In fact, it's in on three main sites, 4 miles from each other, *sprawling from the reclaimed wasteland* that is the Docklands to the suburbia of Ilford and Barking. The Stratford Campus (nothing to do with Shakespeare), $5\frac{1}{2}$ miles north-east of Trafalgar Square, has the main building, a *grand chunk of listed Victorian* architecture that doesn't exactly fit the surroundings (imagine it in Albert Square). The Barking campus (nothing to do with dogs) *looks like an over-sized sixth form college* set in Goodmayes Park (*an oasis in this part of Essex*). The Docklands Campus is made of *strangely shaped, brightly coloured, waterside* buildings, which is *all very modern, but a bit like the set of a TV programme for 3-year-olds*. Stratford and Docklands maintain close links, but both ignore the Barking Campus as if hoping it'll go away, which it will at some point in the near future.

Sex ratio (M:F): 45:55	**Founded: 1970**
Full-time u'grads: 7,540	**Part-time: 2,625**
Postgrads: 1,410	**Non-degree: 3,354**
Ave course: 3yrs	**Ethnic: 59%**
State:private school: 96:2	**Flunk rate: 28%**
Mature: 75%	**International: 25%**
Disabled: 442	**Local: 80%**

(55% / 45% pictogram in left margin)

ATMOSPHERE:
Go to UEL to quietly get on with the studious part of being a student. Despite being on the edge of London between its notorious East End and the more recently notorious Essex, crazy student antics (like gangster-baiting and drink-your-loan-dry days) just don't happen. This is gutting for some, but great for the high proportion of study-minded mature students. While facilities may be wanting, the interesting cultural cocktail – many students are local and/or from ethnic minority backgrounds – makes for a tolerant and friendly atmosphere in which to study (more than a platform for politics).

LONDON: see <u>University of London</u>

THE EAST END, DOCKLANDS AND DAGENHAM
Stratford and the rest of London's East End are traditionally the home of London's dispossessed: first, Jews; nowadays Asians, yuppies and the occasional unfortunate but accurate stereotype (wearing a shellsuit, calling some bird a 'shlaaag'). The lively community atmosphere though is hard to find elsewhere. Petticoat Lane market may be a bit more gimmicky than it used to be, but Brick Lane is an overdose for the shopaholic, even late night.
   Docklands is a strangely soulless mix of warehouses converted into loft apartments for rich city brokers, Barratt homes, business parks, out of town shopping centres, dual carriageways and the Thames Barrier. Floating above are the small trains of the Docklands Light Railway monorail and the small planes landing at London City Airport.
   Barking and Ilford are the natural habitat of the Essex Bloke and Bird. There are shops and pubs, but the variety and culture pale beside Stratford.

TRAVEL: see <u>University of London</u>
Buses: There are a few buses running between sites, but it requires lots of changing and waiting. Plenty of services run into central London (particularly the City) and back.
Trains: For Stratford the nearest rail station is Maryland (10 mins from London Liverpool Street) Barking station is 13 mins from London Fenchurch Street Station. The Docklands Light Railway Cyprus Station is right at the entrance of the Docklands Campus.
Car: *It's London, so expect traffic trickiness. Parking can cause friction with the locals.*
Air: London City Airport is so near the Docklands Campus, *students almost have to duck and although it's mostly business flyers, there are occasional budget deals.*
Hitching: *Usually impossible inside London, hitchers have to get to the outskirts and, as a rule of thumb, Essex is a no-go. However, some of the dual carriageways around the Docklands campus (such as the A13) might be worth a try.*
Underground: Stratford is on the Central Line; Barking (District and Hammersmith & City during peak times) and Plaistow are good for some buildings.
Bicycles: *If black nostrils cause no concern, biking is the cheap option for students, until their bike gets nicked. Some decent bike lanes around the area.*

CAREER PROSPECTS:
• <u>Careers Service</u> • <u>No. of staff: 3 full/4 part</u> • <u>Unemployed after 6mths: 17%</u>
Lots of potentially useful vocational courses and a standard job shop for part-time term-time work.

FAMOUS ALUMNI:
Jake Chapman (Young British Artist™ and Chapman Brother); Daljit Dhaliwal (TV presenter); Ian MacAlister (Chair of Network Rail); Terence Stamp (actor); Lord Trotman (Chair of ICI); Sam Taylor-Wood (artist). Honorary degrees for Trevor Brooking and Billy Bragg.

FURTHER INFO:
• <u>Prospectuses: undergrad; postgrad</u> • <u>Open days</u>

ACADEMIC

Heavy emphasis on vocational studies, particularly when it comes to psychology, teaching and law.

120-300

Entry points: 120-300	**Ave points: 210**
Applns per place: 4	**Clearing: 46%**
No. of terms: 2	**Length of terms: 15wks**
Staff/student ratio: 1:19	**Study addicts: 86%**
Teaching: *	**Research: ***
Year abroad: 0	**Sandwich students: 5%**
Firsts: 6%	**2.2s: 45%**
2.1s: 36%	**3rds: 13%**

POINTS

ADMISSIONS:

• Apply via UCAS
Mature students who don't have typical entry requirements are encouraged to apply and normally get an interview. They're told about short courses to help them qualify and the mature student advisers can give further advice.

SUBJECTS:

Architecture: 7%
Art & Design: 10 %
Arts/Humanities: 15%
Business/Management: 15%
Computing and Technology: 12%
Education: 8%

Law: 8%
Psychology: 7%
Sciences: 12%
Social Sciences: 8%

Best: Architecture; Art & Design; Civil Engineering; Politics; Psychology.
Unusual: Complimentary Therapy; Computer Games & Interactive Entertainment; Digital Journalism; Forensic Science.

LIBRARIES:

• 297,056 books • 24-hr access
Four libraries, all with 24-hr access Mon–Thurs in term.

COMPUTERS:

• 1,000 workstations
Computers are spread across the campuses, *but with terminals shared between thousands of students who work instead of getting sozzled, expect difficulties.*

ENTERTAINMENT

THE CITY: see University of London

EAST LONDON

• Price of a pint of beer: £1.90 • Glass of wine: £2 • Can of Red Bull: £1.80
Apart from the occasional Spearmint Rhino strip joint, The Docklands are a bit of an entertainments abyss. Stratford's a lot more lively.
Cinemas: Multiplexes at Romford and Gant's Hill, Ilford (ten screens in all), a four-screener at Stratford and Warner Bros in Dagenham who sponsor the student mag and do freebies.
Theatres: The Theatre Royal Stratford East do shows that transfer to the West End where they're more expensive, so *use your noggin.*
Pubs: Many a *cheerful* boozer keeps the East Enders warm at night and TV/film clichés are made up from little bits of all of them. *Common sense suggests avoiding the dodgy gaffs (people flying through windows: bad. Happy, unbloodied clientele: good). Most places are cheaper but less varied than central London. Pushplugs: The Spotted Dog; The Golden Grove; King Edward; Princess Alice; The Pigeons.*
Clubbing: *East End clubs; nature's way of culling the student population. Go to London, Benjies on Mile End Road (indie nights); The Rex; The Pigeons Club (complements SU events) and Fabric (trendy, has beds).*

Eating out: The diversity of food stops matches the diversity of people and *the best stuff is on the ethnic end of the foodometer. Try: Sombrero Steak House (Ilford); Raj (Barking); Galleria (Barking good veggie option).*

UNIVERSITY:
• Price of a pint of beer: £1.80 • Glass of wine: £1.80 • Can of Red Bull: £1.60
Bars: Each campus has its own bars (Duel 1, 2 and 3), *with Docklands being the most studenty, Barking the most ents-based and Stratford the most popular. The student bars are an alternative to the not-always pukka local options.*
Clubbing/Music: Regular nights at Stratford and Barking, including 'Back to the Old School', 'Fusion' and *the more worrying* 'Abomination'. Bands are rare but do happen.
Comedy/Cabaret: Comedy nights several times a year.
Food: Eight cafeterias exist across the three campuses, *varying from swish to friendly to bog standard at best. No shortage, but not much excitement.*
Other: Two balls a year, for freshers and in summer.

SOCIAL & POLITICAL

UNIVERSITY OF EAST LONDON STUDENTS' UNION:
• 6 sabbaticals • Turnout at last ballot: 7% • NUS member
Despite the laughable turnouts, the mostly dingy-looking unions have overtly political ambitions. Even the graffiti is political ('Did Blair pay tuition fees? No! Do you pay tuition fees? Yes!'). Hot on race and welfare issues.

SU FACILITIES:
Collectively, the sites offer: four bars; three cafeterias; three coffee bars; seven pool tables; meeting rooms; a minibus; insurance; Barclays and Natwest banks and ATMs; photocopier/fax/printing; photo booth; payphones; advice; a crèche; women's room; juke box; bookshops; launderette; games machines; vending machines; stationers; internet café.

CLUBS (NON-SPORTING):
Botswanan; Computer Games; Entrepreneurship; Exclusive; Fashion; Friends of Palestine; Gratis Cinema; Hellenic; High Sensation; Hip-Hop; International Development; Kegites, Malaysian; Oriental; Poetry; Radio (Cr:uel); Samba, Sikh; Socialist Resistance; Tamil. **See also Clubs tables**.

OTHER ORGANISATIONS:
Refuel, the student paper, won an award for Best Low Budget Newspaper. The student radio station broadcasts over the net only. Plots are being hatched for a TV station too. Watch this space.

RELIGIOUS:
• 1 chaplain (CofE)
Muslim prayer room availible in the T Block at Barking, Catholic church literally next door and most religions are catered for in the area.

PAID WORK: see University of London
• Job bureau
Limited work to be had in the various bars and cafés, but the Job Shop helps students to scour locally. Workbank helps students find work, the Enterprise Zone helps 'em develop skills and CV-bigging-up prowess.

SPORTS

• Recent successes: Ju-Jitsu, football
The Ju-Jitsu club are regional superstars, respected as far as, er, Norwich. Apart from that, the sporting spirit is decidedly diluted and facilities are limited.

SPORTS FACILITIES:
Four tennis courts; squash courts; swimming pool; two gyms; sauna/steam room; sunbeds.

SPORTING CLUBS:
Hotsteppers; Ju-Jitsu; Rowing; Yoga. **See also Clubs tables**.

ATTRACTIONS: see University of London
Newham Sports Centre is well-stocked. Nearby is a dry ski slope, athletics track and amenities for most sports. If London gets its 2012 Olympic bid, an Olympic stadium will turn up on UEL's doorstep. West Ham (say 'Wess Tam' to blend in) is local footie side. Leyton Orient's close by too.

ACCOMMODATION

• Self-catering cost: £49-78 (30wks) • Insurance premium: £££
Availability: Accommodation varies quite a lot in price (from £51–78 a week in Park Village, £82 at Docklands and around £72 at Barking), *but with so many local and mature students, there's no serious shortage*. There are 1,068 places in all, including purpose-built rooms for disabled people.
Car parking: *Quite a distance from London's parking purgatory, so not too bad*, but a permit is needed.

EXTERNALLY: see University of London
• Ave rent: £45-80
Availability: Most mature students have their homes already sorted. *East London is cheaper than many other parts of the capital. It's possible to live quite far out and still be on the doorstep*. Students don't even try to live in the Docklands area unless they're rich enough to clean their teeth with caviar. *Stratford is a likely local as are Leyton, Becton, Goodmayes, Ilford, Dagenham, Forest Gate and East Ham. Also Leytonstone and Walthamstow, but they're a bit of a trek*. It depends which campus students are based at.
Housing help: The three accommodation offices employ six full- and three part-time staff.

WELFARE

SERVICES:
• Lesbian/Gay/Bisexual Officer & Society • Ethnic Minorities Officer • Women's Officer
• Mature Students' Officer • International Students' Officer • Postgrad Officer
• Disabilities Officer • Self-defence classes • Nightline
• College counsellors: 6 full time • SU counsellors: 2 • Crime rating: !!!
Advice on a variety of issues comes from Student Services and the sabbatical officers of the Union are *keen* to help with personal and academic problems.
Health: Medical centres on two sites are staffed by nurses.
Women & Ethnic Minorities: UEL has a *crusading* equal opportunities policy, reflected in the high proportion of students from ethnic minorities, *which is particularly important given local social and racial tensions*. The Black Mentor Scheme pairs up black students with successful black mentors in their chosen field.
Crèches/Nursery: Barking Campus has a daytime nursery for children *that don't poo everywhere when the staff's backs are turned*.
Disabilities: Newer buildings, like Docklands, are designed with disabled access in mind. Meanwhile, there are also a disabilities adviser, Arkenstone readers for the sight-impaired in the main library, a Minicom for the hearing-impaired, specialist tutors and workshops for dyslexia sufferers on all campuses.

FINANCE:

• Ave debt per year: £4,443 • Access fund: £300,000 • Successful applications/yr: 1,000
Support: Loans of up to £500 and payments of £700 to £1,500 are available in cases of hardship, as are bursaries (apply to the Student Finance Department), *but the criteria are pretty tough.* Also scholarships for part-time unwaged students and partial fee-remission schemes.

Economics

see LSE

University of Edinburgh

University of Edinburgh, Old College, South Bridge, Edinburgh, EH8 9YL
Tel: (0131) 650 1000 E-mail: rals.enquiries@ed.ac.uk Website: www.ed.ac.uk
Edinburgh University Students' Association, EUSA, The Potterow, 5/2 Bristo Square,
Edinburgh, EH8 9AL Tel: (0131) 650 2656 E-mail: eusa.enquiry@ed.ac.uk
Website: www.ed.eusa.ac.uk

GENERAL

Scotland's capital, Edinburgh, sits on the Firth of Forth on the east coast. *Anyone who's read any Irvine Welsh might think they've a fairly good idea what to expect: scag, hoorin', fitba and so on. Then there's the festival clichés: a lot of arty types descend for a month and block the streets with performance art and mime shows.* The reality is somewhere between the two, although *Push* reckons there's *more chance of bumping into a juggling unicyclist on the Royal Mile than Franco Begbie down Easter Road.* Like most cities there are some *darker* streets, but student life mainly revolves around *gorgeous, historic* buildings and *beautifully* planned gardens. There are four universities in town: Napier, Heriot-Watt, Queen Margaret College and the University of Edinburgh itself, which is the sixth oldest in Britain. The three main sites are at George Square/Old College (city centre), King's Buildings (science and engineering campus, 2 miles south) and the residential Pollock Halls site (east, near Holyrood Park). Even the more modern buildings are *attractive,* built in local stone with *concern for the city's beauty.*

Sex ratio (M:F): 44:56	**Founded: 1582**
Full-time u'grads: 15,095	**Part-time: 1,055**
Postgrads: 3,275	**Non-degree: n/a**
Ave course: 4yrs	**Ethnic: n/a**
State:private school: n/a	**Flunk rate: 7%**
Mature: 13%	**International: 18%**
Disabled: 374	**Local: 50%**

(56% / 44%)

ATMOSPHERE:

With 50,000 students at the four universities there's a *large and visible presence* in the city and *just as the buildings are integrated throughout the city, so are the students.* Edinburgh's *arguably more anglicised* than Glasgow (there's a 40% Sassenach population). Relations with the locals are *good,* bars and books are *hit with equal vigour* and the city has a *lively feel* about it.

EDINBURGH:

- Population: 435,430 • City centre: 1.5 miles • London: 391 miles
- Glasgow: 44 miles • Newcastle: 93 miles
- High temp: 18 • Low temp: 1 • Rainfall: 53

Edinburgh's built on seven hills, with mini-mountain (and recently active volcano) Arthur's Seat topped by the castle in the middle. The architecture *reflects some rich history*, with a medieval city centre and the New Town to the north. There are three main streets running parallel: Queen Street, George Street and Princes Street. The Royal Mile, a series of small interlinked streets, runs through the centre of town. It's a *major* stop on the tourist track: Holyrood Palace, the Museum of Scotland, the National Gallery, the castle and *much more*. The nightlife is *famous, particularly for late licensing*. Of course there are *rougher* areas, but staying safe *isn't a huge problem*.

TRAVEL:

Trains: Edinburgh Waverley Station is the most central with a direct line to Glasgow (£4.95) and others north and south including (via Newcastle and York) London (£50.80). Connections also to Birmingham and Bristol.

Coaches: National Express, Stagecoach and Citylink services to London (£27.25), Glasgow (£5) and others.

Car: The M8 and M9 connect with the A8 to the west. There are also the A1, A7, A68, A70, A71, A702, A703 and A90. Coming into Edinburgh through Biggar can be a *bit of a slow process, but at least the scenery is spectacular.*

Air: Edinburgh (Turnhouse) Airport, $5\frac{1}{2}$ miles west of the city centre, has a range of international and internal flights (from £69 return to London).

Hitching: *The A1 is good for getting into the city, but not so hot for getting out. The M8 and M9 are good for Glasgow and Perth.*

Local: Bus services are good all round the city and quite cheap (from 50p). A frequent night bus runs all over the town.

Taxis: £3 across town. *A happy luxury.*

Bicycles: *Useful, but remember those hills. And bikes that aren't chained down get ghosted off.*

CAREER PROSPECTS:

- Careers Service • No. of staff: 23 full/9 part • Unemployed after 6mths: 8%

A *pretty comprehensive service*: careers consultations; information centres; skills development workshops; online vacancies. See www.careers.ed.ac.uk.

FAMOUS ALUMNI:

James Barrie, Arthur Conan Doyle, Walter Scott, Robert Louis Stevenson (authors); Dr Barry (world's first qualified woman doctor – she impersonated a man to study and practise); David Brewster (invented the kaleidoscope); Gordon Brown MP, Robin Cook MP (Lab); Thomas Carlyle (historian/philosopher); Charles Darwin (revolutionary evolutionary); David Hume (philosopher); Eric Liddell (Chariots of Fire runner) and Ian Charleson, who played him; Lord Mackay of Clashfern; Julius Nyerere (ex-President, Tanzania); Malcolm Rifkind (Con, ex-minister, ex-MP); Peter Roget (of Thesaurus fame); Kirsty Wark (TV presenter, Newsnight); James Watt (engineer/inventor).

SPECIAL FEATURES:

Rectors are elected every three years by students. Previous post holders have included Magnus Magnusson, Winston Churchill, Muriel Gray, Donnie Munro (of Runrig), Sir David Steel and James Robertson Justice.

FURTHER INFO:

- Prospectuses: undergrad; postgrad • Open days

EUSA produces an alternative prospectus and an essential guide to househunting etc. See the websites for more info.

ACADEMIC

Scotland's leading research university, with a *top-flight reputation* across a wide range of subjects. Some four-year degrees have the option to pursue several different options during the course. *Heavy* emphasis is placed on personal study and self-motivation.

120-290		POINTS
Entry points: 120-290	**Ave points: 240**	
Applns per place: n/a	**Clearing: 5%**	
No. of terms: 2	**Length of terms: 11wks**	
Teaching: ***	**Research: *******	
Year abroad <1%	**Sandwich students: 1%**	

ADMISSIONS:

• Apply via UCAS

SUBJECTS:

Best: Accounting; Cellular & Molecular Biology; Chemistry; Computer Studies; Electrical & Electronic Engineering; European Languages; Finance; Geology; History; Maths; Organismal Biology; Physics; Social Policy; Social Work; Sociology; Statistics; Veterinary Medicine;

LIBRARIES:

• 2,700,000 books • 3,500 study places

There's an *enormous* Main Library and six other *more specialised* ones (Divinity; Law; the Europa Institute; Medicine; Music; Science & Veterinary Medicine).

COMPUTERS:

• 1,500 workstations

ENTERTAINMENT

THE CITY:

• Price of a pint of beer: £2.50 • Glass of wine: £2.30 • Can of Red Bull: £2

Edinburgh is a *party city* all year round, but *it really kicks off* in August when the festivals come to town. The Edinburgh Festival is the world's biggest arts bash, and the fringe (hundreds of student and low-budget shows) turns *almost any space imaginable* into a theatre. At the same time there are film, dance, jazz, TV and book festivals and *a lot of drinking and shagging goes on, too*. Of course, this is outside term time, but *it would be bordering on the criminal* not to make the most of the time at Edinburgh to get involved.

Cinemas: Seven cinemas with 40 screens between them.

Theatres: 13 theatres, but of course the festivals bump this up to the hundreds. *Things are arty all year round*. The *grandest* theatres are the Festival Theatre (*what else?*), The Royal Lyceum, King's Theatre and the Traverse.

Pubs: Most don't chuck out till 1am and it's *a good idea* to get a taste for Scotch. *Try the Grassmarke area for the best boozers*. Pushplugs: Maggie Dicksons (*good grub*); Sneaky Pete's and Whistlebinkies (*for the serious quaffer*); Iguana; Bar Kohl (*studenty*); Black Bo's (*cheap*); The Kitchen (*funky music*); Jekyll & Hyde (*in the New Town*).

Clubbing: *A decent, if not quite legendary clubbing scene*. Pushplugs: Pure (*hardcore, at The Venue, £6-£7*); Mercado (*dance of all sorts*); Joy (*gay*) and Bound To Please (*house*) at the New Calton Studios; Café Graffiti; JP's.

Music venues: Pubs and clubs are *hot* for live music, but there is a *glut of other venues all scraping by*. Pushplugs: Usher Hall (*classical, including the Scottish National Opera*); Queen's Hall (*indie and more*); Playhouse (*AOR*); The Venue (*indie*); Rocking Horse (*metal mayhem*).

Other: *Lots for tourists, who come to see kilts, bagpipes and funny hats*. There's cabaret *everywhere* and the Tattoo, a military parade at the castle.

Eating out: Edinburgh eateries are *among the best* in Scotland. As such, they're *among the most fearsomely expensive* too. *Them's the breaks*. Pushplugs: Henderson's (*veggie hangout*); Pierre Victoire and Chez Jules (*bistro*); Mamma's (*value Italian*); Kalpna (*gorgeous Indian veggie*).

UNIVERSITY:

• Price of a pint of beer: £1.55

With the University so spread out, there are *plenty of options* for the *footloose reveller*.

Bars: Dotted across the main sites. The main ones are the Teviot Row House, with five bars, and a 400 capacity club, the Potterow union bars and the Pleasance bar, which is *rather pubby*.

Theatres: The drama scene is, *unsurprisingly*, *very strong*. The Bedlam Theatre Company runs its very own theatre.

Film: The Film Society has scooped the Best Student Film Society award recently. *Not quite an Oscar, but good going nonetheless*. Films are screened throughout the week. Members can buy a £15 pass to see more than 60 films a year.

Music venues: The Union at Potterow features *popular* acts like Chikane, Mark Owen and local favourites Big Hand. It also features *godawful abominations of the airwaves* like the Cheeky Girls. *Shame*.

Clubbing: Pleasuredome (dance) is the *big night*, but indie, funk, soul and cheese are all catered for. The Bristo Square experience links up Teviot Row and Potterow for a *huge* Friday night bash.

Comedy/Cabaret: The Pleasance is a *major* stop on the comedy circuit, featuring names like Dave Gorman, Miles Jupp and Andy Zeltsman.

Food: 13 EUSA outlets *feed the famished* until 10pm.

Other: Balls throughout the year. The *glittering* night of the social calendar is the Societies Ball in February.

SOCIAL & POLITICAL

EDINBURGH UNIVERSITY STUDENTS' ASSOCIATION (EUSA):

• 4 sabbaticals • Turnout at last ballot: 9%

Far from following the herd, Edinburgh is *wilfully independent* not to mention *brain-achingly complicated* in student representation. EUSA is an umbrella for the SRC (Student Representative Council) which does political and representative work, and The Union which provides student services. There's also a Sports Union (free, automatic membership) and an Advice Place – EUSA isn't an NUS member so provides its own welfare stuff.

SU FACILITIES:

Teviot Row: five bars; jukeboxes; snack bar; two cafeterias; restaurant; games room; music room; satellite TV; shop; launderette; free showers.

King's Buildings House: sports facilities; mature, international and postgrad students' lounge; welfare advice; shop; bar; the University's largest catering outlet.

Potterow: 1,200-capacity nightclub and music venue; games room; eateries. A popular lunchtime meeting place and has the biggest and busiest EUSA shop.

The Pleasance: bar; Societies Centre; catering; technical equipment hire; theatre (cap 270); meeting/function rooms.

Also: print service; five shops; crèche; NatWest, Halifax and Royal Bank of Scotland cashpoints; library; photo booths; pool tables; games and vending machines; travel agency; TV lounges; meeting rooms; launderettes.

CLUBS (NON-SPORTING):

A-ha Revival; American; Asylum & Immigration Bill; Celtic Supporters; Chess; Children's Holiday Venture; Chinese Cultural; Cyborg; Duke of Edinburgh Award; European; Fabian; Folk Song; Football Supporters; Footlights (revue); Friends of Edinburgh Direct Aid; Games & Recreational; GEAS (role-playing); Goth & Rock; Hearts Supporters; Hellenic; Help (Scotland); Highland; Hispanic; Huggabugga Jaffa Cake Appreciation; Hungarian; Indonesian; Japanese; Jazz Orchestra; Juggling; Korean; Malaysian Students; Methodist; Mooting; Motorcycle; New Philosophy; New Scotland Country Dance; Norwegian Students; Opera; Perfidious Albion; Pie-Eaters; Piping; Poetry; Politics; Rajayoga Meditation; Red Cross; Reel; Renaissance Singers; Revelation; Savoy Opera; Scottish Militant; Sign Language; Singaporean; SNP; Sri Chimnoy; Student Action for Refugees; Student Christian Movement; Suave; Tibet Support; Turf; Unicef; Untapped Talent; Up the Kilt Productions; Virtual Trading & Investment; Wargames; Water of Life (whisky appreciation); Wind Ensemble; Wind (kite-flying); Wine; Yoga. **See also Clubs tables.**

OTHER ORGANISATIONS:

Student is a weekly independent paper, Hype is the fortnightly EUSA rag. Fresh Air *occasionally* broadcasts on FM and can be heard in the EUSA buildings. ESCA's a *really wild* Rag organisation and SCAG helps out in the community, as does Settlement. The Debates Committee is more like the Unions of Oxford and Cambridge than a run-of-the-mill debating club.

RELIGIOUS:

• 1 chaplain
Local places of worship include all sorts of churches as well as places for Sikhs and Jews.

PAID WORK:

• Job bureau • Paid work: term-time 40%: hols 80%
Loads of opportunities to work in the thriving city centre, especially showing tourists round in the summer. The University/Union-run Student Employment Service helps out with adverts for part-time and vacation work.

S P O R T S

• BUSA Ranking: 30
Students are *far from duffers* on the field (the attractions of the city *help prise back the blinkers a little*) but there isn't *the same sporting fever* as at some other universities (*think Birmingham, Loughborough*).

SPORTS FACILITIES:

Outdoor facilities at Peffermill Sports Ground (including 25 acres of playing fields and three clay tennis courts); playing fields with a floodlit synthetic grass pitch; tennis courts; golfing facilities. At the Uni Sports Centre (10 mins from Pollock Halls) there's a sports hall, a small hall, fitness room, ten squash courts, table tennis studios, a combat salle, a rifle and archery range. At the Firbush Point Field Centre 80 miles from Edinburgh: sailing, canoeing, skiing and hills to walk. The city has many golf courses, a large swimming pool, ice rink and the Meadowbank Stadium. Half the city is made of parks and open spaces (including Queen's Park and Arthur's Seat).

SPORTING CLUBS:

Curling; Hot-Air Ballooning; Korfball; Lacrosse; Motorsports; Rifle; Shinty; Skater; Ultimate Frisbee; Weight-lifting; Windsurfing and Surfing; **See also Clubs tables.**

ATTRACTIONS:

Hibs and Hearts divide the city across similar partisan lines as Celtic and Rangers in Glasgow. But the teams are *nowhere near as wealthy, entertaining or high profile* and there's *a lot less* of *the sectarian sentiment about their supporters*. Murrayfield is the home of the *currently woeful* Scottish rugby team. Edinburgh, the club rugby side, are *a bit more successful*. There's also athletics at Meadowbank.

A C C O M M O D A T I O N

IN COLLEGE:

• Catered: 13% • Cost: £101-116 (33wks)
• Self-catering: 25% • Cost: £60-77 (38/52wks)
• First years living in: 90% • Others living in: 8% • Insurance premium: ££
Availability: All 1st years who want to live in can, although a *minority* have to share. There are mixed and single-sex flats, some fitted out for wheelchair access. The standard is *pretty good*, and all halls are within 10 mins *trot* of the main campus. About a quarter of rooms have en-suite facilities. Kitchens are basic (microwave, kettle, toaster, fridge) and they, along with other communal areas, *are kept from festering* by University cleaners.
Car parking: Okay in halls, although a pass is needed (free for disabled students, then £50-80 depending on location). But it's a *horrorshow* trying to park on campus.

EXTERNALLY:

• Ave rent: £60-70 • Living at home: 16%

Availability: Accommodation is *easy to find*, as long as you avoid August (festivals) and September (last-minute panics). *Enterprising* students with an *eye for a quick buck* rent a flat at the beginning of the summer and sub-let it at an *extortionate* price to visiting thesps with a budget to blow. *Hey presto – no overdraft. The best areas are Marchmont, Bruntsfield and Newington: studenty, quite central and homely. Avoid Niddrie, Pilton and Wester Hailes.*

Housing help: The Accommodation Service helps out with registered landlords, property vetting, a bulletin board, contract approval and legal advice.

WELFARE

SERVICES:

• Lesbian/Gay/Bisexual Society • Equal Opportunities Officer • Women's Society
• International Students' Society • Postgrad Officer • Disabilities Officer & Society
• Nightline (6pm-8am) • College counsellors: 6 full/2 part • Crime rating: !

EUSA's Advice Place is responsible for welfare and acts as a drop-in centre for all sorts of problems.

Health: The Student Health Centre has six doctors as well as nurses, a psychologist, physiotherapist, pharmacist and family planning unit.

Crèches/Nursery: 39 places for kids 5wks-6yrs.

Disabilities: Access isn't great, thanks to the University's age and locations. But the disability office and Special Needs Committee do their best to be accommodating, even up to making building improvements, if given early notice. There's also a dyslexia adviser available to help.

FINANCE:

• Ave debt per year: £3,360 • Access fund: £742,308
• Successful applications/yr: 750 • Ave payment: £300-2,000

Support: 100 bursaries for undergrads in financial trouble. Also postgrad scholarships available to Chinese, Canadian, Indian and American students.

Edinburgh College of Art

see Heriot-Watt University

University of Essex

(1) University of Essex, Wivenhoe Park, Colchester, Essex, CO4 3SQ
Tel: (01206) 873333 E-mail: admit@essex.ac.uk Website: www.essex.ac.uk
University of Essex Students' Union, Wivenhoe Park, Colchester, Essex, CO4 3SQ
Tel: (01206) 863211 E-mail: su@essex.ac.uk Website: www.essexstudent.com
(2) East 15 Acting School, Hatfields, Rectory Lane, Loughton, Essex, IG10 3RY
Tel: (020) 8508 5983 Website: www.east15.ac.uk

Forget the Essex Girl jokes – the University isn't in the famously maligned part of Essex that's *full of parked Ford Capris and peroxide blondes*. It's $2\frac{1}{2}$ miles from Colchester, a thoroughly modern Roman town located a bit further from London. It's one of the *dinkiest* fully-fledged universities according to student numbers, but it's set amid three large lakes in 200 acres of *scenic* parkland, designed to hold a much larger institution – the University slowed its ambitious expansion a few years after it was founded (*although it's done some catching up lately*). It has remnants of the big plans, though: the campus contains shops, eating places and facilities *which betray the grander designs*. They're all arranged in a *confusing* series of interlinked courtyards and modern concrete buildings, flanked by towering multi-storey residential blocks.

Sex ratio (M:F): 48:52	Founded: 1964
Full-time u'grads: 5,480	Part-time: 1,815
Postgrads: 1,840	Non-degree: n/a
Ave course: 3yrs	Ethnic: 20%
State:private school: 96:4	Flunk rate: 15%
Mature: 18%	International: 45%
Disabled: 102	Local: n/a

ATMOSPHERE:
Being such a small University, based in a big campus (if you include the parkland), there's quite a sense of community. This can either be seen as friendly solidarity or as busy-body nosiness, close-knit groups or cliques. Whatever, most of the atmosphere is tightly focused on the bars and things are particularly, er, vibrant at weekends. Less gregarious students can have a hard time and relations with the locals aren't particularly warm, particularly the large contingent from the nearby barracks. While run-ins with pissed-up squaddies can happen, students should remain unscathed as long as they steer clear of enemy territory (the Hippodrome on a Saturday night – which should be treated as No Man's Land in any case.)

SITES:
East 15 Acting School: (253 students – acting) The drama department's based on the Hatfields campus on the outskirts of London, 50 miles from the main University campus. It's set in the residential area of Loughton near Epping Forest. Specialist facilities include 14 rehearsal rooms, music room, dance and radio studio, purpose-built theatre and screening room, with £1.3m new facility with a costume department and rehearsal rooms. The University tries to help students find accommodation locally.

COLCHESTER:
• Population: 155,796 • City centre: 2 miles • London: 40 miles • Ipswich: 17 miles
• High temp: 20 • Low temp: 0 • Rainfall: 67
Like we said, the Romans started Colchester, although they went home some time ago. It's the oldest recorded town in the country – *and the town plan hasn't been greatly changed since*. But, as when all the bits of a car have been replaced so many times you have a new car (*in these parts, usually with wooden spoilers and neon under-lighting*), Colchester has established many modern pockets: shopping centres and light industry, busy roads and modern architecture and Leisureworld (*possibly the bastard relation of skate rink Rollerworld) – an alternative universe of slidy, splashy fun*. There are still many pretty parts, old houses and ancient buildings, not least the original Roman Wall and the castle (built by William the Conquerer) which houses the town's museum. *The area's most recent claims to fame, ex-Mods/reborn slackers Blur, have left less of an impression on the town. As has Jodie Marsh and the scruffy one from Fame Academy.*

During the 2003 season, the Beaufort Polo Club, where the Royal Agricultural College students train, teamed up with production company RDF Media to produce a programme for the Channel 4 series Faking It.

TRAVEL:

Trains: The nearest mainline station to the campus is Colchester North, 3 miles away. Colchester Town station is nearest the town centre, but with fewer services. Direct services run into London Liverpool Street. Connections via London are possible all over the country including Birmingham, Bristol and Edinburgh.

Coaches: National Express services to London, Birmingham and more.

Car: Colchester is visited by the A120, A12, A133 and the A604.

Ferries: To the Hook of Holland from Harwich and Felixstowe, 22 and 27 miles away, respectively.

Air: Stansted is 32 miles west on the A120.

Hitching: *The slip roads of the A12 are the best bet, but trying to get a lift in Essex is basically the same as simply waving a thumb at passing cars.*

Local: *Buses are expensive, but they're reliable and* tour the local villages *which is useful for those living there*. A new line serves University Quays, the new accommodation development. University: *Night owls can hop on the late-night minibus.*

Taxis: Some firms are less expensive than others, *but Push wouldn't use the word 'cheap' for any of them*. Luckily, the SU has done a wheeler deal with a local company that means the SU will stump up the fare if a student can't foot the bill. *To be repaid, obviously.*

Bicycles: There's a cycle network around Colchester and *Essex is quite flat*.

CAREER PROSPECTS:

• <u>Careers Service</u> • <u>No. of staff: 8 full/6 part</u> • <u>Unemployed after 6mths: 9%</u>
Services include: newsletters; bulletin boards; careers library; job fairs; interview training.

FAMOUS ALUMNI:

Oscar Arias (former President of Costa Rica & Nobel Prize winner); John Bercow (MP); Virginia Bottomley MP (Con); Brian Hanrahan (BBC reporter); Rodolfo Neri Vela (Mexico's first astronaut); Ben Okri (writer, Booker Prize winner); Chandra Sonic (Asian Dub Foundation); Mike Todd (Chief Constable of Greater Manchester Police).

SPECIAL FEATURES:

• There are a lot of ducks on the three lakes, and around the campus there are more rabbits than students. Each year, much to the distress of the students, the University carries out a bunny cull (*to weed out myxomatosis not for the sheer hell of it*).

• The University has a collection of Sigmund Freud's letters and Europe's only public collection dedicated exclusively to modern and contemporary Latin American art.

FURTHER INFO:

• <u>Prospectuses: undergrad; postgrad; all departments; alternative; international</u> • <u>Open days</u>
The alternative prospectus can be found at www.essexfirst.co.uk and postgrads can e-mail pgadmit@essex.ac.uk

A C A D E M I C

Essex hits above its size in terms of academic reputation. Courses are flexible and it's possible to switch courses at the end of the 1st year.

Entry points: 240-340	Ave points: 299
Applns per place: 5-21	Clearing: 10%
No. of terms: 3	Length of terms: 10wks
Staff/student ratio: 1:13	Study addicts: 14%
Teaching: ****	Research: ****
Year abroad: 2%	Sandwich students: n/a
Firsts: 10%	2.2s: 33%
2.1s: 46%	3rds: 10%

240-340 **POINTS**

ADMISSIONS:

• Apply via UCAS

SUBJECTS:

Humanities and Comparative Studies: 25%   Science and Engineering: 29%
Law: 10%   Social sciences: 34%
Best: Art History & Theory; Biological Sciences; Economics; Electronic System Engineering; Language & Linguistics; Maths; Philosophy; Politics; Psychology; Sports Science; Sociology.
Unusual: English & French Law LLB (taught jointly at Essex and the University of Paris); Human Rights; Marine & Freshwater Biology (which includes field trips to the Honduras and remote islands of Indonesia).

LIBRARIES:

• 880,000 books • 1,134 study places
As well as your average bookshelf, the Library has pamphlets, microfilms and special collections of international importance. A large reading room is open 24-hrs during term.

COMPUTERS:

• 522 workstations
Networked computers *whirr* in open-access labs on campus. There's an IT helpdesk and, in halls, internet points in bedrooms. Essex also run IT courses for *repentant Luddites*.

OTHER LEARNING FACILITIES:

Language lab; drama studio; music rehearsal rooms; audio/TV centre; multimedia lab.

ENTERTAINMENT

COLCHESTER:

• Price of a pint of beer: £1.50 • Glass of wine: £2 • Can of Red Bull: £1.60
Cinemas: Students can grab a discount at the ten-screen Odeon multiplex.
Theatres: The Mercury Theatre hosts a rep company.
Pubs: *Students more usually stick to their own bars or the pubs close by, since the local pubs are full of soldiers. A few Pushplugs: The Lamb (noisy); Hole in the Wall (goth/indie); Wig & Pen; Horse & Groom (aka the Doom & Gloom). Avoid Wetherspoons and the larger town centre chains unless you appreciate velour tracksuits and brainless violence.*
Clubbing: *The real stiletto-heeled, mini-skirted cattle markets are in Southend (40 miles away) and Chelmsford (24 miles). Colchester's clubs are slower lane, more down-to-earth, but still tacky. Students don't often bother. Terrace (student DJs, but no student groovers, sadly); Hippodrome (large, sweaty, crowded). The Route is popular.*
Music venues: *The Hippodrome has naff PAs. Better stick to The Twist (blues, rock and teeniemetal), The Arts Centre (indie, reggae) and the Charterhall (various). Better still, go up to London.*
Eating out: Colchester has restaurants of every description – *worth checking out those with student discounts* – and junkyards of fast food. *Pushplugs: The Red Lion (historic hotel with an expensive but reliable menu); Food on the Hill (veggie); Jade Garden (cheap Chinese); Granata's; The Lemon Tree (pricey); Thai Dragon; Rose & Crown for parental purchasing; Playhouse; Wig & Pen (cheap pub grub); Sloppy Joe's (Tex-Mex). The famous Talbooth in Dedham is a good choice for those with rich parents and cars; ditto The Barn Brasserie.* Some kebab shops and the like are open till 4am.

UNIVERSITY:

• Price of a pint of beer: £1.50 • Glass of wine: £2 • Can of Red Bull: £1.60
Bars: The SU's Main Bar is, *unsurprisingly, the chief quaffing spot*, holding 1,000 thirsty people when it's chocka. This and *the Level 2 bar, which hosts society, quiz and karaoke nights, were recently refurbished. The Underground is open late for club-style events. The newest and smallest kid on the block is Café Mondo, a swish affair famed for its salsa nights.* The University runs Top Bar, which holds 300.
Theatres: The University is *well-equipped* and the Lakeside Theatre has many visits from national companies. Student shows are also *enthusiastically* produced – some make it to the Edinburgh Fringe.

Film: The Filmsoc (mainstream) and Art Film Soc (arthouse) organise three showings a week in lecture theatres. The International Film Club also shows one flick a week.
Music venues: The Underground (cap 1,000) gets the headline acts. Local and up-and coming bands appear at Level 2.
Clubbing: Regular clubnights and specialist dance acts at The Underground.
Comedy/Cabaret: Weekly comedy nights at Level 2.
Food: *The snacks in the Blues Cafe, SX Express and the Top Bar are beyond the pockets of many students, who tend to stock up on eats in the main SU bar.*
Other: The Law Soc, Christmas and Summer Balls are big events. The University has a purpose-built exhibition gallery.

SOCIAL & POLITICAL

UNIVERSITY OF ESSEX STUDENTS' UNION:

• 5 sabbaticals • NUS member • Turnout at last ballot: 16%
Essex had a radical reputation as a red-hot hot-bed, then became known for a few blue-eyed Thatcherites, but the students are somewhat more apathetic nowadays. However, UESU was a major player in the campaign against tuition fees, so maybe politics isn't dead.

SU FACILITIES:

In SU building: four bars; six nosh places; minibus hire; printing services; general shop; pool tables; Barclays and Lloyds banks; NatWest ATM; Endsleigh Insurance office; function room (cap 100); TV room; three meeting rooms; secondhand bookshop.

CLUBS (NON-SPORTING):

Loads, including: American Society; Amnesty International; Art Film; Art Society; Asian Soc; Chess Club; Chinese Christian Fellowship; Choir; Christian Union; Clubbing Society; CMS; Comedy Society; Computer Society; CSSA; Cypriot Society; Da Fonk; Dance Hall Corner; Debating Society; Democracy in Burma; Discordian; DJ Society; Drum and Bass; Essex Marine Conservation; Essex University Complementary Therapies Society (E.U.C.T.S); European Society; Explore UK Society; Fashion Art and Beauty (FAB); Film Making; Flamenco; Gig Soc; Goth Society; Gregorian Soc; Hellenic Society; Hong Kong Chinese; Human Rights Society; Indian Cultural Society; Indie Soc; Italian Society; Japan International; Jesus Alive Fellowship; Juggling; Korean; Latin American; Latin American Womens Society (SOMLEI); Law; LGB Society; Malaysian; Mature Students Society; Media; Metal Soc; Mexican; Multiplayer Gaming; MUSOC; Nordic; Pakistani Cultural Society; Peace Campaign; Philosophy; Photographic; Politics; Psychic; Psychology; RnB; Rocky Horror; Roleplaying; Sikh; Silly; Sisters Society; Sociology; Socrates-Erasmas; Spanish Fiesta; St Johns LINKS; Student Action for Refugees (STAR); SWD (Students with Disabilities); Taiwanese; Thai; The Punk Society; Theatre Arts; Turkish; Urban Society. **See also Clubs tables.**

OTHER ORGANISATIONS:

The student media includes the fortnightly newspaper Rabbit, mag Parklife and Red AM 1404, which broadcasts 24 hours. V-Team, the Community Action group, gets students stuck into projects such as sports coaching, mentoring young offenders and conservation work and was recently awarded £80,000 by the Home Office for group volunteer work. Rag raised £2,000 last year for local charities.

RELIGIOUS:

• Chaplains (CofE, RC, URC, Unitarian, Quaker, Baptist, Congregational, Orthodox)
There's a worship area in the University Chaplaincy centre for use by all religions. During term, there are Anglican services each Sunday and Mass three times a week. There are religious provisions for *all colours of the spiritual rainbow*, including Jewish, Muslim, Buddhist and Chinese Christian Fellowship. The Islamic Society organises a prayer schedule and has a deep freeze with Halal meat. A kosher kitchen supplies the general shop.

PAID WORK:

• Job bureau
The University and SU give students paid shop, bar and office work. The Jobshop helps students find work on- or off-campus. It has vacancy boards, a regularly-updated website and it advises on CVs and employment-related issues such as tax and National Insurance.

SPORTS

• Recent successes: rugby, judo, athletics, swimming • BUSA Ranking: 41
As with many other things, the University has sports facilities that were intended for somewhere much larger. But who's complaining? The number of students means that the University is less likely to boast as many bionic men and women as larger colleges, but it still holds its own (and sometimes other people's) in competitions, while maintaining a good overall level of participation.

SPORTS FACILITIES:

A purpose-built sports science laboratory currently takes pride of place while 40 acres of the parkland are used for sports including: playing fields; a grass athletics track; a floodlit synthetic sports pitch; three all-weather tennis courts; four squash courts; fitness room; archery range; an exercise circuit ('the Squirrel Run') and the only 18-hole frisbee golf course in the country. Also a gym and sports hall including six badminton courts, another tennis court, a climbing wall (largest in the south-east), six squash courts (four elsewhere on campus), weights and other indoor sports facilities. Students get special rates on University sport facilities, eg. a quid for the fitness room, £3.20 for netball courts, £1.50 for aerobics. Colchester also provides swimming pools and a roller rink.

SPORTING CLUBS:

10-Pin Bowling; Aikido; American Football; Capoeira; Cheerleading; Women's Football; Gliding;; Ju-Jitsu; Kung Fu; Pool; Women's Rugby; Watersports. **See also Clubs tables**.

ATTRACTIONS:

Colchester United is the local football team. There's also Essex County Cricket Club.

ACCOMMODATION

IN COLLEGE:

• Self-catering: 44% • Cost: £45-75 (39/50wks) • First years living in: 78%
• Insurance premium: £
Availability: There are six tower blocks on campus *which are reckoned to provide a good social life for the undergrads who inhabit them. Apparently*, the architect was a bit *eccentric* and based the campus design on an Italian hill town. Avon Way house is *less popular because of its location* (10 mins walk). A newish development, University Quays, has given 760 more students a place to rest their heads. *Not a bad selection, meaning that the University is able to guarantee accommodation* (usually on the campus) to all 1st years who apply in time, and house an *impressive* 44% of all undergrads. All international students are housed by the university unless they don't want to be. Rooms are all single, mostly in shared flats for between four and six students. *Many are quite spacious and well-equipped. Students' main gripe is the lack of common or TV rooms.* Most flats are mixed, although some single-sex flats are available.
Car parking: Automotive students living on or near campus have to pay and display.

EXTERNALLY:

• Ave rent: £55 • Living at home: 15%
Availability: *Finding suitable accommodation in Colchester, Wivenhoe (peaceful), Greenstead (cheap) or other surrounding villages presents few problems. Students should avoid Lexden (too expensive) and Tollgate is just too far. If living out, a car is handy, but the cost of parking should be brought into the reckoning.*
Housing help: The University Accommodation Office provides general help, approves some houses and flats and can fix students up in lodgings (with live-in landlord/lady).

SERVICES:

- Lesbian/Gay/Bisexual Society • Mature Students' Officer & Society
- International Students' Officer & Society • Postgrad Officer & Society
- Disabilities Officer & Society • Late-night minibus • Nightline
- College counsellors: 13 full • Crime rating: !!

The SU Advice Centre provides help and referral for students with all manner of difficulties. It's staffed by student volunteers, trained and supported by professional staff. The University has a welfare adviser in the Student Support Office. *In general, the welfare provision is extensive and well-structured at every level.*

Health: The campus health centre provides one full- and two part-time counsellors, three nurses, five doctors, two physios and an administrator.

Women: There's a late night minibus and women's officer. Attack alarms available from Nightline.

Crèches/Nursery: 100 places for littl'uns (aged 0-5).

Disabilities: There's a disability support team and departmental liaison officers. Special provisions and representative channels for students with all forms of special needs, including a Braille map of the campus, induction loops in lecture theatres and adapted housing for wheelchair users in the houses on campus. *Accessibility and provisions are among the best in the country.*

FINANCE:

- Ave debt per year: £3,395

Fees: Postgrads pay around £3,010, less for part-timers. Non-EU students get charged £8,240–10,595, depending on the course.

- Access fund: £290,0000 • Successful applications/yr: 419 • Ave payment: £640

Support: There are a few things in place to ease financial pain. The Foundation Bursary for Refugees and the Children of Refugees support the students as their name suggests. The Sports Bursary scheme is open to athletes who compete at national and international level. It includes financial support, free access to University and local sports facilities (and a bunch of other non-financial perks). The J P Morgan Fleming Bursary is meant for mature students from the local area.

Essex IHE

see Anglia Polytechnic University

Exeter University

University of Exeter, Northcote House, The Queen's Drive, Exeter, EX4 4QJ
Tel: (01392) 661 000 E-mail: admissions@exeter.ac.uk Website: www.exeter.ac.uk
University of Exeter Guild of Students, Devonshire House, Stocker Road, EX4 4PZ
Tel: (01392) 263 540 E-mail: ask@guild.exeter.ac.uk Website: www.guild.ex.ac.uk or www.xnet.ex.ac.uk
University of Exeter in Cornwall, Tremough Campus, Penryn, Cornwall, TR10 9EZ
Tel: (01326) 371 801 Email: cornwall@exeter.ac.uk

GENERAL

The River Exe flows out into the English Channel in a wide estuary with the golden, sandy beaches of south Devon all around. The river springs inland amidst the windy wilds of Exmoor, in the heart of the West Country, 9 miles from the coast. Where the river starts to widen, there's Exeter, not a big city, but a *pretty* one. Although the place was almost wiped out by a single night's bombing in World War II, the Luftwaffe didn't manage to destroy any major landmarks, such as the ancient cathedral (built in 1050), the city walls (built by the Romans) or the Guild Hall. Among the other things not destroyed by bombing was the University – mainly because it wasn't built until 1955. Some of its buildings date from the last century though, but most were built in the 50s and 60s and are *low-rise blocks* in light stone. The University's about a mile from the city centre in a *particularly hilly* and green area. *The setting is stunning, perfect for both town and country*, with two streams and ponds dotted about the campus.

Sex ratio (M:F): 47:53	**Founded: 1955**
Full-time u'grads: 7,715	**Part-time: 1,655**
Postgrads: 2,010	**Non-degree: 1,351**
Ave course: 3 yrs	**Ethnic: 3%**
State:private school: 71:29	**Flunk rate: 5%**
Mature: 7%	**International: 15%**
Disabled: 261	**Local: 15%**

53% ♀♀♀♀ ♂♂♂♂♂ 47%

ATMOSPHERE:

Exeter once had a reputation for attracting rich kids who couldn't make it to Oxbridge though things are a bit more mixed these days. It's a very friendly place and the gorgeous setting is more than enough compensation for the odd bit of social friction. Lots of student houses are spread across the city and relations with locals are pretty good generally.

SITES:

St Luke's Campus: (1,500 students – Education, Sports Science) Although it's only $1\frac{1}{2}$ miles from the main campus this site feels a *bit like a separate institution* and there's a constant battle to include the 'Lukies' in Guild activities, *though it does have a community spirit all of its own.* St Luke's Hall has housing for 209 students.
Tremough Campus, Cornwall: (Earth & Environment Science, Conservation Biology, Geography, English) 50 million smackers worth of *hot* new campus action, Tremough may be *billions* of miles from Exeter (*that's right, billions*), and shared with *the far more geographically qualified* Falmouth College of Arts, but *the University is particularly pleased* with its new outpost by the surf-lashed Cornish shores. It's the proud centrepiece of the Combined Universities in Cornwall Initiative and the home of Exeter's *favourite toy* – its mineral analysis machine used in forensic investigation. *Push prefers its Tracy Island.* 500 en-suite self-catering bedrooms are available in Glasney Parc, the student village, together with bars, restaurant and sports centre.

EXETER:

• Population: 111,200 • City centre: 1 mile • London: 170 miles
• Bristol: 69 miles • Plymouth: 46 miles
• High temp: 21 • Low temp: 2 • Rainfall: 64
While it's never going to be a party in a tin, according to the EC the *cute and cuddly* city of Exeter has the highest quality of life of any English city *and is far from devoid of zesty perks.* In part, this must be due to the *ample* selection of high street shops, supermarkets and banks, and to *numerous, wholesome cafés.* There's even a half-decent club or three lying around. Tourist attractions include the ancient cathedral, the historic Guild Hall and various museums, including the Royal Albert Museum and Art Gallery, with its *amusing* giraffe. *Devon at large has its own appeal – spooky Dartmoor,* for one thing, as well as a *staggering* number of breweries, cider presses and Buckfast Abbey, where generations of monks have made what they call 'tonic wine' *and Push calls 'liquid tar'.* A few miles away there's the Jurassic Coast with various fossilised mini-dinosaurs and, of course, the sea.

TRAVEL:

Trains: Exeter St David's Station is $\frac{1}{2}$ mile from the University. There are direct lines to London, Bristol, Birmingham and connections all over.

Buses: National Express services all over the country. The new Megabus (www.megabus.com) takes 5 hours to get to London and there's nowhere to put your stuff, *but at £1.50 each way, that's forgivable.*

Car: Exeter is at the southern end of the M5, or there's the A30, A377 and A38.

Air: Exeter Airport (6 miles) offers inland and European flights with FlyBe.

Hitching: *The M5 is good for heading north.*

Local: *Local buses are reliable and quite comprehensive, but not cheap. The same can be said of local trains – there are four stations around the city, but they're not very usefully placed.*

College: Free buses from St David's Station to Streatham campus at peak travelling times morning and late afternoon.

Taxis: £2.50-3 from Streatham campus to city centre; Hackney cabs can be hailed in the street.

Bicycles: Bikes are *frequently* used by students, despite the hills. The campus has numerous places to lock up bikes on campus and there are cycle paths around the city.

CAREER PROSPECTS:

• Careers Service • No. of staff: 6 full/8 part • Unemployed after 6mths: 7%

There's a databank of 500 alumni willing to offer careers advice to current students (*but probably none of those listed below*). There's also plenty of careers *gumpf* like business placements, Earn & Learn jobshop, guidance interviews and so on.

FAMOUS ALUMNI:

Toby Amies (MTV); Emma B (Radio 1 presenter); Felix Buxton (Basement Jaxx); Anastasia Cooke (TV presenter); Paul Downton, Richard Ellison (England cricketers); Richard Hill (former England rugby captain); Paul Jackson (TV producer); John O'Farrell (comic author/columnist); Stewart Purvis (former ITN chief exec); J K Rowling (writer, Harry Potter); Sam Smith (tennis player); David Sole (former Scotland rugby captain); Matthew Wright (TV presenter); Will Young (*lantern-jawed* Pop Idol); Thom Yorke (Radiohead).

FURTHER INFO:

• Prospectuses; undergrad; postgrad; departmental; CD Rom • Open days • Video

ACADEMIC

There are 26 academic departments spread across 13 Schools, including the Peninsula Medical School, run with the University of Plymouth, and another joint initiative with Exeter University in Cornwall (Conservation Biology, Earth & Environmental Sciences, Geography, English).

240-420		POINTS
Entry points: 240-420	Ave points: 360	
Applns per place: 9	Clearing: 5%	
No. of terms: 2	Length of terms: 12wks	
Staff/student ratio: 1:14	Study addicts: 19%	
Teaching: ***	Research: *****	
Year abroad: 2%	Sandwich students: 0	
Firsts: 12%	2.2s: 28%	
2.1s: 58%	3rds: 2%	

ADMISSIONS:

• Apply via UCAS or direct for part-time

SUBJECTS:

Arab & Islamic Studies: <1%
Biosciences: 6%
Business & Economics: 11%
Classics, Ancient History & Theology: 4%
Education & Lifelong Learning: 2%
Engineering, Computer Science & Mathematics: 13%
English: 7%
Geography, Archaeology & Earth Resources: 10%

Historical, Political & Sociological Studies: 13%
Law: 7%
Modern Languages: 11%
Performance Arts: 3%
Physics: 3%
Psychology: 4%
Sport & Health Sciences: 5%

Best: Archaeology; Arabic; Business & Management; Classics & Ancient History; Drama; Economics; Education; Engineering; Materials Technology; Mathematical Sciences; Physics; Politics; Psychology; Sports Sciences; Theology.
Unusual: Arab & Islamic Studies; Conservation Biology & Ecology; (at Cornwall campus); International Relations; Internet Computing; Renewable Energy (Cornwall again); European Law (4-year dual qualification combining both UK & French/German law degree).

LIBRARIES:

• 1.1 million books • 1,733 study places • Spend per student: ££££
The library includes an Arab World Documentation Unit. Their Special Collections include an *impressive* amount of works by, and material relating to, Agatha Christie, Daphne du Maurier and John Betjeman.

COMPUTERS:

• 1,000 workstations • 24-hr access
The majority of rooms in halls have internet access (annual fee £60 but no usage charge).

OTHER LEARNING FACILITIES:

Specialist financial and stockmarket software (Bloomberg, Micropal, Datastream).

ENTERTAINMENT

THE CITY:

• Price of a pint of beer: £2.20 • Glass of wine: £2
Cinemas: There's a three-screen Odeon; one-screen Phoenix Arts Centre (students £1 off) and the *friendly, sophisticated* Exeter Picture House (two-screen) for arthouse stuff.
Theatres: The Northcott on campus is the main regional theatre, but the Barnfield and the Arts Centre *encourage less commercial fare.*
Pubs: *Pushplugs: Fermat's Number (Part of the Scream chain, discounts for NUS); the Red Cow's got a basketball hoop out back; Victoria Inn's good for watching the footie; Henry's Bar is in the middle of studentsville. Jolly Porter; Mount Radford (for Lukies); Double Locks (a bit far, but worth it in summer); and the Black Horse are all worth a mention. Avoid the Turk's Head (a Royal Marines pub).*
Clubbing: Most clubs, such as Warehouse, Arena, Club Rococo's and Volts, are mainstream; *Pushplugs: Rococco's; The Cavern; Timepiece (eclectic indie).*
Music venues: The Cavern *provides a more intimate, less mainstream alternative to the University.* Phoenix Arts Centre also puts on bands.
Food: *Not a huge selection of cheap eats but you won't starve either. Late night food can be hard to come by unless you're near a 24-hr garage. Pushplugs: Jyanti and Chadni for Indian; Mad Meg's (supposedly haunted by a medieval cook); Harry's (pizza, Mexican, steaks); Double Locks (pub lunches by the river).*

UNIVERSITY:

• Price of a pint of beer: £1.50 • Glass of wine: £1.50 • Can of Red Bull: £1.60
Bars: The Ram's *hugely popular throughout the day, maybe because it looks like a proper pub, albeit one that does fantastic white hot chocolate and posh coffees.* There are two Union bars and four non-Union ones. The Lemon Grove (Lemmy) has a varied programme of events including big screen sport and games evenings. The halls have their own bars, only open to residents of that hall and their guests. Cross Keys at St Luke's (cap 700) turns into a club at weekends and shows sports in the week. Clydes House at the postgraduate centre does food and theme nights. Cornwall campus has a bar too.

Theatres: Northcott Theatre (cap 433) is based on campus and student companies put on occasional productions there, as well as jaunts up to Edinburgh and other parts of the country. **Film:** CinSoc shows three a week. *Excellent* mixture of mainstream and world cinema, £1.50 members, £3 non-members.

Music venues: The Lemon Grove (cap 1,300) hosts varied club nights twice a week. Live sounds *pound* there and in the Great Hall (cap 1,700), which doesn't actually belong to the Guild, but is regularly borrowed from the University and is one of the biggest venues in the South West with top indie and rock acts – Franz Ferdinand, The Thrills, Joss Stone and Feeder played last year.

Clubbing: The Lemmy for R'n'B, hip-hop, drum'n'bass and chart stuff.

Food: The Refectory opens for lunch and dinner and the *good-value* Coffee Bar *is popular all day*. The Ram bar does *good*, freshly-cooked food and snacks in the evenings. The Coffee Bar serves *awesome* breakfasts – £2 for ten items all day long.

Other: Many big balls, the highlight being summer's.

SOCIAL & POLITICAL

UNIVERSITY OF EXETER GUILD OF STUDENTS:

• 7 sabbaticals • NUS member • Turnout at last ballot: 17%

The Guild's facilities are based in Devonshire House and are shared with various University activities. Both St Luke's and Tremough campuses have Guild representatives *who communicate with the mothership and keep everybody nicely represented*.

SU FACILITIES:

Advice centre; two bar/clubs; shop; crèche; coffee shop; fast food; meeting rooms; minibus; Natwest Bank; launderette; post office; new and secondhand bookshop; travel agency; ticket agency; launderette; fax and printing service.

CLUBS (NON-SPORTING):

Aerobics; Arabic; BeerSoc; Biking; Bands (rock bands); Breakdancing; Caledonian; Change Ringing (hand-bell ringers); Choir; Circus; Creative Writing; Duke of Edinburgh; Egg & Spoon; Expedition; Flute Choir; Folk; Footlights; German; Gilbert & Sullivan; Games Soc; Roleplay (boardgames); French; International; LARP; (Live Action Roleplay); Meditation & Buddhist; Motorsoc; Motor Club; NetGamer; NOB Soc (*more wacky stunts*); EU Opera Society; RocSoc (rock); Sky Diving; Jazz; Lib Dem; Korean; Italian; Japanese; Malaysian; Spanish; Turkish; Vegetarian; Wine. **See also Clubs tables.**

OTHER ORGANISATIONS:

Impressive newspaper, Exeposé; Xpression radio; XTV which pumps award-winning drama plus comedy, news and music into bars. There is also a charity Rag, which raises *loads* – £65K last year – and organises the Safer Sex Ball, the largest World AIDS Day event in the country. The major league community action organisation manages 36,000 hours of voluntary work a year, including work with kids' camps.

RELIGIOUS:

• 7 chaplains

Worship shops for the major faiths in town.

PAID WORK:

• Job bureau • Paid work: term-time 35%: hols 90%

A few local jobs for students in the tourist trade and some bar and clerical work in the Guild. Earn & Learn, the online jobshop, finds part-time and vacation work, and students can sign up to be campus tour guides, outreach ambassadors and *general PR monkeys* to bring in some pennies.

S PORTS

- Recent successes: climbing, snooker, karate, sailing, wind-surfing • BUSA Ranking: 20

SPORTS FACILITIES:

16 football pitches; three rugby, two hockey, four all-weather and two cricket pitches; 18 tennis, three basketball and five netball courts; two gyms (St Luke's); running track; climbing wall; indoor cricket nets; eight squash courts; golf course; multigym; two aerobics studios; indoor swimming pool (St Luke's); physiotherapy clinic; new indoor LTA standard tennis courts. Annual membership for £20 plus participation fee or £100 for annual Gold membership (unlimited gym use) and £190 for Platinum (unlimited everything). The sea, the River Dart and the moors *are also assets*.

SPORTING CLUBS:

Aikido; Gliding; Kick-boxing & Self-Defence; Lacrosse; Ninjitsu; Polo; Rifle; Rowing; Snooker; Snowboarding; Speleology; Surfing; Ultimate Frisbee; Water Polo; Waterski & Wakeboard; Windsurf & Kitesurf.
See also Clubs tables.

ATTRACTIONS:

Exeter FC is the local footy team and there are rugby and hockey outfits as well. The races are also popular round here – horses at Newton Abbot, speedway, dogs and people in town.

A CCOMMODATION

IN COLLEGE:

- Catered: 25% • Cost: £87-115 (30wks)
- Self-catered: 25% • Cost: £55-86 (34/39/50 wks)
- First years living in: 100% • Insurance premium: £

Availability: All 1st years can be housed and there's still space for many from other years. The majority of 1st years choose to live in the catered halls, which, with the exception of St Luke's Hall, are right next to the campus and vary in style from 19th-century buildings to new *very plush* halls. Most students who live in after their 1st year are housed in the self-catering flats. *Prices are steep but standards, especially in the newer accommodation, are very high.* There are also 142 places in a head tenancy system.

Car parking: Permit parking available for students living more than $1\frac{1}{2}$ miles from campus or with a *convincingly forged doctor's note*.

EXTERNALLY:

- Ave rent: £55

Availability: *Finding private accommodation in Exeter doesn't present a major problem.* Some car-owners travel quite a way into the countryside (*but find beautiful country homes there*). *The best places are St James and Pennsylvania near the campus and Newtown nearer the St Luke's site.*

Housing help: The accommodation office keeps a list of possible lodgings.

W ELFARE

SERVICES:

- Lesbian/Gay/Bisexual Officer & Society • Ethnic Minorities Officer
- Postgrad Association Representative • Women's Officer & Society
- Mature Students' Officer & Society • International Students' Officer & Society
- Disabilities Officer & Society • College counsellors: 2 full/2 part • Crime rating: !!

Health: Two GPs, nurse.
Crèches/Nursery: 53 place nursery for 6wks-5yr-olds. Half-term playschemes for 5-14-yr-olds.
Disabilities: The campus is *hilly and difficult to get around by wheelchair* but all buildings offer disabled access. Disability Resource Centre helps students with study problems or other difficulties.

FINANCE:

• Ave debt per year: £3,988 • Access fund: £391,985 • Successful applications/yr: 694
• Ave payment: £469
Support: Sports bursaries (free accomodation and £1,000 a year), Science scholarships (£4,000 over 3 or 4 years), a variety of Access bursaries (up to £4,000 for locals) and short-term Guild loans of £50 are all available. Access to Exeter bursaries ensure that students from any background with an inkling to come here can.

George's Hospital see St George's Hospital Medical School

Glamorgan University

Polytechnic of Wales see Glamorgan University

University of Glasgow

Glasgow Caledonian University

Glasgow Polytechnic see Glasgow Caledonian University

University of Gloucestershire

Goldsmiths College, London

Gordon University see Robert Gordon University

Greenwich University

Guy's Hospital see King's College London

George's Hospital
see St George's Hospital Medical School

Glamorgan University

• *Formerly Polytechnic of Wales.*
(1) University of Glamorgan, Treforest, Pontypridd, Wales, CF37 1DL
  Tel: 0800 716 925 E-mail: enquiries@glam.ac.uk Website: www.glam.ac.uk
  University of Glamorgan Union, Forest Grove, Treforest, Mid Glamorgan, Wales, CF37 1UF
  Tel: 01443 483500 E-mail: studunion@glam.ac.uk Website: www.glamsu.com
(2) Glyntaff Campus, University of Glamorgan, Cemetery Road, Glyntaff, Pontypridd, Wales, CF37 4BL

GENERAL

In South Wales, up the Taff Valley from Cardiff, is the market town of Pontypridd. A mile away is the terraced, ex-mining village of Treforest and overlooking it on a steep hillside are the 70 acres of the University of Glamorgan. It's a mix of different buildings, old Welsh stone, demountables and redbrick with a *squat, white and controversially expensive block* in the middle. When the sun comes out students get dazzled by the *extraordinary* views over the valleys *and remember why they went there in the first place. Then the sun goes in again and they go to the pub.*

Cardiff's a *mere* 15 miles away – *handy for those craving a bit of Big City Action.* Adventurous types *are happy to make-do with stunning* local countryside, which is *perfect* for everthing from walking to rock-climbing and from swimming to surfing.

Sex ratio (M:F): 48:52	Founded: 1913
Full-time u'grads: 9,380	Part-time: 7,240
Postgrads: 845	Non-degree: 1,842
Ave course: 3yrs	Ethnic: n/a
State:private school: 97:3	Flunk rate: 25%
Mature: 53%	International: 13%
Disabled: 280	Local: 48%

ATMOSPHERE:

Small and weather-dependent, Glamorgan can feel nigh on perfect in the summer when the students are scattered over the grass with their books and pints, drinking in the view. On other days it's clear that a valley is essentially just a big hole in the ground and in this case a soggy one. 'Glam' students have gained a bit of a rep as drinkers, but they know how to work when it counts. Most people are friendly and robustly cheerful and everyone who frequents the small Union knows each other, often biblically.

OTHER SITE:

Glyntaff Campus: (Law, Care Sciences, Welsh Institute of Health & Social Care) 15 mins walk from the main campus. *It's not so much a campus as a bunch of lecture rooms and a lounge, but they had to call it something.*
The new VC has big plans for more than just a paint job on the main campus – watch this space.

PONTYPRIDD:

- Population: 231,900 • City centre: 1 mile • London: 145 miles • Cardiff: 15 miles
- Birmingham: 90 miles • High temp: 21 • Low temp: 2 • Rainfall: 87

Pontypridd, or Ponty, *is rather cramped. It's mostly a single road with shops on it.* There's an indoor market and an outdoor one once a week, *and a large park that takes people by surprise (not by jumping out and demanding their valuables, but because it's hidden down a side street).* Ponty and Treforest together have all the basic amenities and Cardiff is a short train journey away. It's Cardiff most students will go to for a big night out, see Cardiff University.

TRAVEL:

Trains: From Treforest station, right outside campus, trains go to Cardiff every 20 mins (£1.60). Change there for London (£24.60), Swansea (£8.80) and Manchester (£24.60). Buy tickets in advance or the price can double. The last train back from Cardiff is at 11.20pm.
Coaches: National Express return to London is £18.
Car: Treforest is on the A470 and about 8 miles off the M4.
Hitching: *The Welsh take pity on hitchers and once on the M4 prospects are good, but remember it's pronounced 'Pontypreeth'.*
Local: Bus services go every 20 mins to Ponty and every 25 to Cardiff. A free student shuttle within a 10-mile radius of campus runs after 10.30pm.
Taxis: About £1.50 into Ponty and £20 back from Cardiff.
Bicycles: *The hills put people off and bikes can disappear. Positively though,* the Taff Trail is a straight and *exceptionally scenic* cycle route straight into Cardiff.

CAREER PROSPECTS:

- Careers Service • No. of staff: 12 full/1 part • Unemployed after 6mths: 6%

There's a job shop and Cymru Prosper Wales are active in the area. They find relevant work experience for students and also help graduates

FAMOUS ALUMNI:

Max Boyce (entertainer); Ian Hamer (Olympic athlete); Jonathan Humphreys (rugby player); Rupert Moon (rugby player and broadcaster); Michael Owen (the rugby player, not the footballer). Patrick Moore is an honorary fellow.

FURTHER INFO:

- Prospectuses: undergrad; postgrad; departmental • Open days

ACADEMIC

A big emphasis on links with 'real' work and getting hands-on experience.

Entry points: 80-280	Ave. points: 200
Applns per place: 4	Clearing: 20%
No. of terms: 3	Length of terms: 12-15wks
Staff/student ratio: 1:20	Study addicts: 18%
Teaching: n/a	Research: *
Firsts: 14%	2.2s: 35%
2.1s: 36%	3rds: 15%

ADMISSIONS:

• Apply via UCAS

SUBJECTS:

Art Design & Performing Arts: 14%	Engineering & Technology: 15%
Arts/Humanities: 13%	Maths, Science, IT and Computing: 13%
Built Environment: 3%	Sciences: 19%
Business/Management: 23%	Social Sciences: 14%

Best: Accounting & Finance; Applied Science: Mineral Surveying Programme; Business & Management; Creative Writing; Electrical & Electronic Engineering; Public Sector Schemes; Theatre & Media Studies.
Unusual: Animation; Live Entertainment; Police Sciences; Science and Science Fiction.

LIBRARIES:

• 247,255 books • 785 study places • Spend per student: £
The Learning Resource Centre (LRC) offers all the usual library stuff plus 24-hr book return. *It's not that big though and students sometimes go to Cardiff to get the books they need.*

COMPUTERS:

• 1,220 workstations • 24-hr access
Computer access can be irksome as the rooms are often clogged by students and lectures.

OTHER LEARNING FACILITIES:

The LRC doubles as the media centre, with TV and audio studios and equipment hire.

ENTERTAINMENT

PONTYPRIDD: For Cardiff, see Cardiff University
• Price of a pint of beer: £2.00 • Glass of wine: £1.50 • Can of Red Bull: £1.50
Ponty, being small and imperfectly formed for nightlife, sends students to Cardiff in droves. Students learn to do a lot of socialising at home.
Cinemas: Nant Gawr has a 12-screen cinema, a quick drive away or 20-min walk. Ponty itself has the Muni, which shows *arty and popular* films. *Locals go there to shout advice at the characters and have sex.*
Theatres: The Muni again. Cardiff has a couple though.
Pubs: *Treforest has the more student-friendly pubs: the Otley; the Forest; the Pick and Shovel; Raffles (the only place that could be called trendy).*
Clubbing: *Raffles is popular* and Ponty has a club or two *with entertaining fights at the weekend. Best go to Cardiff.*
Music venues: Raffles does acoustic nights and other pubs very occasionally have bands stop by, often mates of the owners.
Eating out: *All of the pubs do serviceable nosh, Raffles being easily the best of the bunch. Also numerous take-aways, grease-joints or, for Italian, Jack and Maria's in Ponty.*

UNIVERSITY:

• Price of a pint of beer: £1.75 • Glass of wine: £2 • Can of Red Bull: £1.90
The Union's facilities may be small and cute but it manages to get an impressive amount of things to happen. It's at the top of a hill – *difficult going up, painful rolling down.*
Bars: The three Union bars are right next to each other *but pleasantly different* and students can stick to one or two most of the time. The Baa Bar *has been Ikea'd,* Smiths downstairs has the pool table, computer games and booths to sit in, and Shafts turns into the nightclub halfway through the night.
Theatres: An *enthusiastic* drama contingent uses the theatre and shows often go to Edinburgh, but not recently.
Music venues: Shafts is where most music happens. *Glamorgan has had a knack of having small bands play who go on to make it big.*
Clubbing: Shafts is the mainstay nightclub and the doors open into the Baa Bar to increase the capacity. *The novelty wears off though* and buses ship students to Creation in Cardiff on a Monday.
Comedy/Cabaret: They manage to squeeze in about 15 a year, usually top comedians doing the university circuit.
Food: All three bars serve pub food that's *cheap, hot and often nice.* A mobile van lurks on the campus, foisting fast food on the unwary. *The Gallery Restaurant is the slightly posher option with a pricing scheme that defies the laws of mathematics.* The Courtyard has two coffee shops.

SOCIAL & POLITICAL

UNIVERSITY OF GLAMORGAN UNION:

• 6 sabbaticals • Turnout at last ballot: 7% • NUS member
The Union campaigns a lot for local charities and issues close to home, like keeping Wednesday afternoons free. *Tending not to be too political, it keep its head down on improving its own students' lot.*

UNION FACILITIES:

The building is small but crammed with goodness. The Union is responsible for three bars, one of which becomes the nightclub; cafeteria; media training centre; restaurant; minibuses; travel agency; general shop; cashpoints; insurance office; photocopier; photo/phone booths; gaming and vending machines; pool tables; juke box; launderette; fax machine; printing service; advice centre.

CLUBS (NON-SPORTING):

Cheerleading; Chiropractic; Hellenic (Greek); Law; Live Music; Pagan; Police Sciences; War Games & Roleplaying.
See also Clubs tables.

OTHER ORGANISATIONS:

Leek, the student newspaper, and the popular GTFM, the FM/net radio, which has won Radio One/Lee Jeans Radio Station of the year.

RELIGIOUS:

• 3 chaplains (CofE, FC, RC)
The mosque on campus has facilities for ablutions and male and female prayer rooms.

PAID WORK:

• Job bureau • Paid work: term-time 60%: hols 85%
A handful of jobs available on campus and locally, more for those willing to go to Cardiff or sell their body to medical science. Jobshop, open days and Cymru Prosper Wales (see above).

SPORTS

• BUSA Ranking: 30
Glamorgan haven't won anything recently but in many sports, rugby league, football, Women's hockey, squash, cheerleading, they're near the top of the leagues. *They also have high hopes for boxing, karate and 400m atheltics. Saying, of course, ain't doing.*

SPORTS FACILITIES:

30 acres of playing fields (some flood-lit); all-weather pitch; flood-lit trim trail; sports hall; four squash courts; climbing wall; fitness room; multigym; sauna/solarium/steam room; two gyms; golf practice area; archery range; boules, bowls and croquet lawns; flood-lit tennis court and a sports injury clinic. Membership ranges between £29-40 a year.

SPORTING CLUBS:

Football (inc women's); GAA (Gaelic Athletic Association); Ju-Jitsu; Rugby (inc women's, union and league); Scientific Diving; Swimming & Waterpolo. **See also Clubs tables.**

ATTRACTIONS:

Rugby Union in Ponty and mountains, lakes, caves, the River Taff, a golf course and a swimming pool locally.

ACCOMMODATION

IN COLLEGE:

• Catered: 2% • Cost: £81 (37wks) • Self-catering: 12% • Cost: £51-64 (37wks)
• First years living in: 75% • Insurance premium: £
Availability: Preference is given to first years, but not all of them can get in halls. *This isn't a great loss, as even the best and largest set of housing, Glamorgan Court (en-suite single rooms), is up a very steep hill and the rest is 20 mins walk away and often cramped and slightly scuzzy.*
Car parking: *Parking's really tough.* Students have missed lectures because they can't find spaces.

EXTERNALLY:

• Ave rent: £40
Availability: Most available houses in the immediate area are taken by students. *Houses aren't hard to find. However, nice houses and honest landlords are. Ponty and Merthyr can be particularly dodgy. Every house should be thoroughly scrutinised before signing anything.*
Housing help: The University runs an accommodation service and a *vital* list of reputable landlords.

WELFARE

SERVICES:

• Lesbian/Gay/Bisexual Society • Ethnic Minorities Officer & Society
• Women's Officer & Society • Mature Students' Officer • International Students' Officer
• Postgrad Officer • Disabilities Officer & Society • Late-night/Women's minibus
• Self-defence classes • Nightline • Taxi fund • College counsellors: 6 • Crime rating: !

The building in which most freshers at Christ's College Cambridge live was designed by Jørn Utzon, who also designed the Sydney Opera House.

The Student Support centre helps with careers, counselling and advice, health, student finance, disability and dyslexia. It also has resident personal tutors and an international support unit.

Disabled: *Effort has been made for disabled students.* The newer buildings have been purpose-designed but it's on a hill – not easy for wheelchair users, who also have to go outside to go downstairs at the Union. Otherwise Glamorgan has tactile maps, guide dog pens, Braille facilities, dyslexia considerations and support workers. Accomodation can be adapted to suit needs.

FINANCE:
• Ave debt per year: £4,568
• Access fund: £860,806 • Successful applications/yr: 1,256 • Ave payment: £774
Support: The Union provides short-term hardship loans of £50 in exchange for a post-dated cheque. Help with applications to the Financial Contingency Funds (Welsh Access Fund). There are a number of scholarships and bursaries available, including for sports.

Polytechnic of Wales
see Glamorgan University

University of Glasgow

(1) The University of Glasgow, University Avenue, Glasgow, G12 8QQ
    Tel: (0141) 330 2000 E-mail: prospectus@gla.ac.uk Website: www.gla.ac.uk
    Student Representative Council, University Avenue, Glasgow, G12 8QQ
    Tel: (0141) 339 8541 E-mail: enquiries@src.gla.ac.uk Website: www.glasgowstudent.net
(2) Crichton Campus, University of Glasgow, Rutherford McCowan Buildings, Dumfries, DG1 4ZL
    Tel: (01387) 702 001 E-mail: information@crichton.gla.ac.uk Website: www.cc.gla.ac.uk

GENERAL

Glasgwegians have endured enough jokes about Irn Bru, deep-fried Mars Bars and incomprehensible men in kilts head-butting one another to last anyone a lifetime. These days they're desperate *to convince* anyone who'll listen that Glasgae is the Scottish Florence, which is just about true, although it says more about Scotland than Italy. The old industrial town now has an *upmarket* shopping centre, some *pretty impressive* parks, cinemas, museums, galleries and a *pleasantly laid-back* West End cafe district. One thing they're not going to change, though, is the weather. *Cold, wet, wet, cold and wet. And cold.* The University's the UK's fourth oldest, founded by Papal Bull (*that's an ordinance, not an animal*) in 1451. It's been on Gilmorehill, in the West End, since 1870, although many of the buildings date from the 50s and 60s. There's a *splendid* chapel, some *peaceful secluded* quads, the academic centre in the Landmark Gilbert Scott Building and the Hunterian Museum.

Sex ratio (M:F): 42:58	Founded: 1451
Full-time u'grads: 14,815	Part-time: 4,565
Postgrads: 2,510	Non-degree: 4,536
Ave course: 4yrs	Ethnic: n/a
State:private school: 86:14	Flunk rate: 15%
Mature: 11%	International: 11%
Disabled: 188	Local: 42%

58%
42%

ATMOSPHERE:

Big Brother 4's Federico, *wannabe head boy* of the Students' Representative Council, once described his fellow students as abhorrent, egotistical, self-absorbed, class-obsessed cretins. It's *a harsh view, but* some Glasgow students *definitely consider themselves a cut above the rabble*. Within the University there's a *liberal, cosmopolitan* feel, *but it stems from a high-trendy middle-class insecure sort of safety in numbers. Most of the insecurity focuses* on the townies, known as neds, who (*unwittingly*) receive a regular slagging in the *stuck-up* University newspaper. Still, students are *well in* with the locals, *partly because many of them actually* are *locals.*

SITES:

Crichton Campus: (275 students – Faculty of Arts & Engineering) In Dumfries, about 80 miles from Glasgow and with its own accommodation block, swimming pool, gym and 9-hole golf course. Video links to the main campus supplement on-site teaching.

GLASGOW:

• Population: 609,370 • City centre: 1 mile • London: 367 miles • Edinburgh: 52 miles • High temp: 19 • Low temp: 0 • Rainfall: 79
The city sits on the banks of the Clyde, which flows out towards the Isle of Arran to the west. The Strathclyde hills *yaw off to the east and the skeletons of the once-mighty* steel and shipping industries *rattle their chains* all around. Glasgow's been *dragging itself out of recession* and is now a *modern, cultured* European city. There are 35 museums and galleries, an IMAX cinema, *some big* music venues and the *best* upmarket shopping this side of Knightsbridge. But the underbelly is *dark, dangerous* and *druggy.* Some areas have *serious* drug problems with crime figures *to match.*

TRAVEL:

Trains: Queen's Street and Central Stations are the main ones, with regular services to London (£40 sleeper), Birmingham, Inverness, Fort William, Aberdeen, Dundee and more. Sail and Rail services go to Ireland (£29 return). Partick Station's closest to the University, though the main stations are *only* a 5-min subway ride away.
Coaches: Eurolines coaches go to Paris, Amsterdam and Brussels. Silverchoice Express goes to London (£24 return sleeper), National Express goes to Birmingham (£32.50), Cardiff (£44) and on. Buchanan Bus station is the main terminus, again 5 mins by subway.
Car: *Good* connections all over the country including the M74, A8/M8, A80/M80, A82, A77 and A736. Parking's fairly restricted; students need permits on University property.
Air: Glasgow International Airport (£5 by bus) is the main airport. Glasgow Prestwick (£5 train ride) offers Ryanair flights to Paris Beauvais, Brussels and Belfast.
Local: Buses around the city centre (55p/£1) are *frequent and cheap.* Local rail services are *pretty good too*, stopping all over the city. A termly (10-week) pass is £339. The subway, known locally as the Clockwork Orange, is 90p a trip. Strathclyde Public Transport issues a travelcard (£12.10/week) for unlimited weekly travel.
College: Free Campus-to-Halls Minibus Service until 10.30pm. The bus is driven by student drivers and stops at residences including Murano Street, Queen Margaret Residence, Winton Drive, Wolfson Hall, Cairncross House, Kelvinhaugh Street and Maclay Hall/Park Circus. *Not wheelchair friendly, though.*
Taxis: Black hackneys and privates *charge like the Light Brigade. Worth it for the very rich or very drunk.*
Bicycles: Hills, *snarly* traffic and *decent* public transport mean bikers are in a minority, but cycle routes between campus and residences ensure those that choose pedal power are provided for.

CAREER PROSPECTS:

• Careers Service • No. of staff: 17 full • Unemployed after 6mths: 7%
The service participates in the Club 21 scheme, which places students with big graduate employers like AMEC and Deutsche Bank.

FAMOUS ALUMNI:

John Boyd Orr (nutritionist); William Boyd, A J Cronin (writers); Gerard Butler (actor and 007 hopeful); Menzies Campbell MP (Lib Dem); Donald Dewar (Scotland's late First Minister); the Delgados; James Herriot (vet, writer); Shell Jubin (Big Brother 5's nude gardener); Pat Kane (Hue & Cry); Lord Kelvin (of the temperature scale); Charles Kennedy (Lib Dem leader); Dr Kamal Ketuly (Deputy Minister for Human Rights in Iraq); Joseph Lister (pioneer of antiseptics); John Logie Baird (invented TV); Anne Louise McIlroy (pioneering woman in medicine); Professor Macquorn Rankine (wrote first engineering textbook); Shereen Nanjiani (TV presenter); Emma Richards (yachtswoman); Adam Smith (economist); John Smith (late Labour leader); Frederick Soddy (scientist); James Watt (inventor).

FURTHER INFO:

• Prospectuses: undergrad; postgrad; some depts • Open days

ACADEMIC

The University's got a *proud* reputation and has churned out *lots of eminent* inventors, politicians and so on. Degrees are *quite* flexible, and some students can mix and match bits from other courses and faculties. Arts, Science and Social Science students choose three subjects to study in their first year.

200-340		POINTS
Entry points: 200-340	**Clearing: 2%**	
No. of terms: 2	**Length of terms: 12/14wks**	
Staff/student ratio: 1:13	**Study addicts: 28%**	
Teaching: ***	**Research: *******	
Year abroad: <1%	**Sandwich students: 7%**	
Firsts: 8%	**2.2s: 20%**	
2.1s: 42%	**3rds: 4%**	

ADMISSIONS:

• Apply via UCAS

SUBJECTS:

Adult Education: 9%	Law & Financial Studies: 6%
Award in Continuing Education: 9%	Medical Sciences: 10%
Education: 4%	Science: 21%
Engineering: 7%	Social Science: 9%
Faculty of Arts: 21%	Veterinary Medicine: 3%

Best: Cellular & Molecular Biology; Chemistry; Classics & Ancient History; Computing Science; Economics; English; European Languages; French Studies; Geography; Geography & Topographic Science; Geology; History; Medicine; Organismal Biology; Philosophy; Physics; Psychology; Social & Urban Policy; Sociology; Veterinary Medicine.
Unusual: Astronomy; Avionics; Countryside Management; Neuroinformatics; Parasitology; Virology.

LIBRARIES:

• 2,000,000+ books • 3,200 study places • Spend per student: ££££
The University Library also stocks periodicals and manuscripts, as well as *lots of dusty rooms full of specialist books and scholars gathering cobwebs. Slack-jawed window-gazing over the city is best done on the 11th floor.*

COMPUTERS:

• 663 workstations
There are computers all over the University Library and faculties. The facilities *aren't brilliant* but there's *not much* money to buy any new kit either. All students are required to pass a Basic IT Competence test *to ensure they don't pour coffee in the keyboards or chew floppy disks*. All rooms are networked.

OTHER LEARNING FACILITIES:

Media Centre; theatre; language labs; CAD studio; rehearsal rooms; practice courtroom.

ENTERTAINMENT

THE CITY:

• Price of a pint of beer: £2.20 • Glass of wine: £2.50 • Can of Red Bull: £1.50
There's *loads* to do in Glasgow, but thanks to council *killjoys*, happy-hour bingeing's no longer one of them. Bars can only serve *cheap* booze if they agree that the *cheap* prices will be permanent. *So it can be pricey.*
Cinemas: 35 screens in the city, including a *collossal* UCG multiplex, an IMAX 3D screen, the arty Glasgow Film Theatre and the *plush* independent Grosvenor (serves *cheap* beer all day).
Theatres: A *few to choose from*, including the King's Theatre (*mainstream* family musicals), the Tramway in Pollokshields (*lefty* performance art), the Theatre Royal (*posh* ballet and opera) and the Pavilion (Xmas pantos and music hall).
Pubs: *Pubbers paradise*. Sauchiehall Street in the city centre is a *major* pub crawl with Firewater, the Hall, Driftwood and Nice 'n' Sleazy playing commercial pop and indie. The Brunswick Cellars, Babooshka, Buddha and the Local cater to *more expensive tastes – mostly not those of students*. The Merchant City area has Bargo (*perfect in summer but pricey*) and Blackfriars (live music, *popular on Sundays*). Princes Square's October (*cheap vodka/Red Bull*) is *popular pre-club*. Off the little side lanes from Buchanan Street there are cosy bars with DJs: Bar 10; Bar Soba; or the Lab. *Keep well away from the Rangers and Celtic pubs in Paisley Road West and Gallowgate.*
Clubbing: A *fast-moving and fast-changing* scene is beloved by Glasgow students. *Pushplugs:* Subclub (tech house, Sunday spectaculars); Buff Club (gay); Liquid Lounge; The Arches (*cool with some student promos but costs up to £25 to get in at weekends*). Student prices and cheese are at Garage, Jumpin Jack's and the Shed. There's also the Cathouse (goth) and Blanket (cheese/R&B). The Tunnel (once legendary) is now best avoided.
Music venues: *Lots of variety*, including the Barrowlands and Carling Academy for international acts and club nights; the Centre for Contemporary Arts (CCA) for almost everything; King Tut's Wah Wah Hut for up-and-coming indie acts; and the *gargantuan* SECC.
Eating out: *Chainy and cheap. Pushplugs:* Driftwood (2-for-1 fajitas); Nice 'n' Sleazy (massive burgers); Counting House (£3 for beer and burger); Mini Bar (massive portions); Bloc (pasta and pizza); Modern India (£5 lunch buffet); Buffet King (Chinese buffet).

UNIVERSITY:

• Price of a pint of beer: £1.25 • Glass of wine: £1.25 • Can of Red Bull: £1.50
Bars: Ten bars are split between two Glasgow SUS (see below for more details on Unions). At Glasgow University Union (GUU) there's the Beer Bar (*pubby refuge*); Deep 6 (sports and bands); the Playing Fields (sports); Altitude (chilled out with pool tables); the Cocktail Bar (cocktails, *duh*); and the Billiard Hall (snooker). At Queen Margaret Union (QMU) there's Jim's Bar (*great* acoustic open mic night); Qudos (*legendary* club nights) and the Coffee Bar (*relaxed, eco-conscious hippy chill-out*).
Theatres: The Gilmorehill Centre has a theatre space for student groups' public performances.
Film: Shown one night a week, veering from arthouse to mainstream.
Music venues: QMU *takes music seriously*. It *prides* itself on the acts it attracts and even has its own record label. Nirvana and Red Hot Chili Peppers have both appeared. These days they still catch the *coolest* acts around, like Franz Ferdinand, Scissor Sisters and Roni Size.
Clubbing: Qudos is *the place to be seen*. Cheesy Pop's *an old fave*, Revolution (nu-metal/alternative) *a young pretender*. GUU's Hive club is *regarded as the best in town*.
Comedy/Cabaret: Monthly nights at Qudos with funnymen like Alex Horne, Alun Cochrane and Ray Peacock.

Food: QMU has the Food Factory (sarnies and soup) and a fairtrade coffee bar, as well as a Delice de France cafe (toasties and bagels). The GUU Servery does hot and cold food all day, and is *easy on the pocket*.

Other: The QMU Christmas extravaganza is the 12-hr Cheesy – *the name sums it up*. For *more civilised* sporting types, the GUSA Annual Awards celebrates those who've *run, jumped and sweated the best* during the year. GUU's annual Daft Friday is a *ginormous* black tie ball.

S O C I A L & P O L I T I C A L

STUDENT REPRESENTATIVE COUNCIL/GLASGOW UNIVERSITY UNION/QUEEN MARGARET UNION:

• 4 sabbaticals • Turnout at last ballot: 6%

Take a deep breath – this is complicated. There are five SUs in Glasgow, with two in competition. First, there's the Student Representative Council (all students get automatic membership), which organises student representation, welfare, clubs and societies. *It's gently left-wing and not very high profile.*

Next come the two services unions. A student can be a member of only one of these and they must choose in their first few weeks. The rivalries are *not too distinct* and students can use the facilities at both most of the time, but can only vote in their own union. Not joining either means no use of facilities at either. *So there.* Glasgow University Union, originally a men-only affair, has a large centre in a listed building near the centre of the campus. It organises debates, as well as services, and *rates with the Oxbridge Unions* for the speakers it attracts. Fans of QMU (formerly the Women's union) would argue that, despite its size, theirs *is where the cool people who don't like rugby hang out and ents are given priority over laddish drinking games.*

The fourth union is the Sports Association (GUSA). Finally, there's the Postgraduate Research Club, GUSA. None of the unions is a member of NUS, but they're members of Northern Services, a 'buying consortium', *ie. cheap beer*.

SU FACILITIES:

SRC: Printing; secondhand bookshop; vending machines.

GUU: Seven bars; cafeteria; restaurant; minibus; travel agency; six pool tables; ten snooker tables; canteen shop; 24-hr student facilities; print shop; photocopying; games machines; pool; juke box; vending machines; two libraries; meeting and conference rooms; launderette; Bank of Scotland ATMs.

QMU: Three bars; cafeteria; restaurant; sandwich bar; print shop; photocopying; shop; games and vending machines; two pool tables; study rooms; juke box; snooker room (members only); TV lounge; meeting rooms; customised nightclub; launderette; Bank of Scotland ATM.

CLUBS (NON-SPORTING):

Caribou House Canadian Society; European; East Timor & Indonesia; Hindu; Hellenic; Indian; International; Japanese; Malaysia; Muslim; Singapore; Slavonic Society; Turkish Student Society; Alchemist Society; Astronomical Society; Beta 2002; Cecilian (Musical & Operatic); Chamber Choir; Chinese; College Club; Cuckoo's Nest (Live roleplaying society); Delta 2004 Yearclub; Design; Dialectic (debating); Exploration; Gaming (roleplaying); Glasgow Go; GUARDS World of Darkness Role Playing; Glasgow Health & Society Seminar; GUST (Glasgow University Student Television); Humanist; Jewish; Kelvin Ensemble; Korean; Ladies' Club; Linux; Living Marxism; Ossianic (Celtic); Physical Society; Potholing; Scottish Nationalist Association (GUSNA); Shorinji Kempo; Singapore; Slavonic; STAR (Student Action for Refugees); Student Volunteers Abroad (SVA); Student Theatre; Travel; UNISON; Visual Art Club; Young European Movement. **See also Clubs tables.**

OTHER ORGANISATIONS:

The Guardian (not that one) is an award-winning newspaper whose journos regularly scoop the Herald Student Journalist of the Year awards. Glasgow University Magazine is the oldest student publication in Scotland and mixes lighthearted and serious content *pretty effectively*. There's a bi-weekly read in the Independent newsletter. SubCity broadcasts on FM for a month of every year across the West End; GUST TV wins regular awards for the hour of original broadcasts it shows every week. Rag raises cash for causes all year, and there are *countless* opportunities for *conscience-led* volunteers.

RELIGIOUS:

CofE, Methodist, Free Church, Baptist, RC and CofS chaplaincies on campus. In town there's Glasgow (CofS) and St Andrew's (RC) Cathedrals. Also places of worship locally for Muslims, Jews, Buddhists, Hindus and Sikhs.

PAID WORK:

• Job bureau

Loads of information and training, student advisers try to lend a hand. The GU Templine places candidates in temporary jobs, and the Jobcentre in Partick's also *geared* towards students. The SRC posts vacancies too. *Glasgow's a busy, bustly place and there are plenty of pubs, clubs and shops that actively seek out students to do the gruntwork.*

SPORTS

• Recent successes: football, hockey, lacrosse, netball, rugby, squash, swimming
• BUSA Ranking: 26

There's a *well-organised* sporting scene with *okay – and getting okayer by the year –* facilities.

SPORTS FACILITIES:

92 acres of sports fields; two rugby pitches; grass shinty/lacrosse pitch; squash and tennis courts; sports halls; two basketball courts; swimming pool; gym/multigym; aerobics studio; sauna. In and around Glasgow: leisure centre; running track; squash and tennis courts; swimming pool; ice rink; croquet lawn/bowling green; golf course. Use of the facilities costs £30 a year. A new development at the Garscube outdoor site will house another swimming pool, eight badminton courts, a gym and a health suite. The river, mountains and dry and artificial snow ski slopes *give further amusement*

SPORTING CLUBS:

Aikido; Boat Clubs (mens & ladies); Curling; Far Flung; Gaelic Football; Lacrosse; Motor Sports; Mountaineering; Network Gaming; Paintball; Parachuting; Pussycat Cheerleading Squad; Rifle; Scottish Country Dancing; Staff Bowling Club; Ultimate Frisbee; Women's Rugby. **See also Clubs tables.**

ATTRACTIONS:

Celtic and Rangers are the *bitterest* of rivals, as well as the *only teams in Scotland worth watching.*

ACCOMMODATION

IN COLLEGE:

• Catered: 2% • Cost: £103 (32wks)
• Self-catering: 20% • Cost: £58-79 (39wks)
• First years living in: 28% • Insurance premium: ££££

Availability: Priority in halls goes to non-Weedgies though the University usually finds space for everyone who needs it – around 15% have to share (they do try to avoid sticking chalk with cheese though). Most 1st years who want to can live in, and 25% of rooms are reserved each year for returning students. Standards and facilities vary from *passable to plush, and unsavoury to en-suite.* All are within 25 mins walk of campus. Wardens *ward off evildoers* 24/7. Disabled and family accommodation also available.

Car parking: *Not too hard* at most halls with a permit (£15).

EXTERNALLY:

• Ave rent: £70 • Living at home: 58%

Availability: Rent in the West End is *reasonable* and standards *pleasantly high*. There are *cheaper* bits of Glasgow, but *none so convenient.*

Housing help: Vacancy database, annual housing help day, and access to the Private Accommodation Database (Pad) which covers all five Glasgow institutions and accredits *decent* private housing.

WELFARE

SERVICES:

- Lesbian/Gay/Bisexual Society • Women's Officer & Society • Mature Students' Society
- International Students' Officer & Society • Postgrad Society • Disabilities Officer & Society
- Late-night minibus • Nightline • College counsellors: 6 full/2 part • Crime rating: !!

Health: Free University health service with GPs, psychiatrist, clinical psychologist, opthamologist and nursing sister.

Crèches/Nursery: 74 places for newborns up to 5yrs.

Disabilities: Facilities in newer halls of residence are *okay* and there's a specially adapted learning centre in the library, but *even the best intentions can't stop the main building being old and inaccessible.*

Drugs: *An ugly druggy scene in the city. Proceed with caution.*

Crime: Car theft's *a problem* around campus, *but there's little else to cry about.*

FINANCE:

- Ave debt per year: £3,330

Fees: Scottish Universities don't charge top-up fees – to Scottish Students, at least.

- Access fund: £774,550 • Successful applications/yr: 1,335 • Ave payment: £100-£2,000

Support: The Carnegie Trust pays tuition fees, the mature students' bursary helps with childcare costs. The University has a scholarship programme for *talented* athletes, which pays bursaries of £300-1,500 and the Beaton Scholarship has £1,500 up for grabs for the best sob story.

Glasgow Caledonian University

- *Formerly Glasgow Polytechnic.*

Glasgow Caledonian University, Cowcaddens Road, Glasgow, G4 0BA
Tel: (0141) 331 3000 E-mail: rhu@gcal.ac.uk Website: www.caledonian.ac.uk
Glasgow Caledonian University Students' Association, 70 Cowcaddens Road, Glasgow, G4 0BA
Tel: (0141) 332 0681 E-mail: gcusagcal.ac.uk Website: www.caledonianstudent.com

GENERAL

For general information on Glasgow: see University of Glasgow. Glasgow Caledonian's a modern-faced institution with a historical background. It began in 1875 as a small college with a *mere* 100 students. These days it's a *much bigger, hearty* University with a load more students and is moored in the heart of Glasgow's city centre. Recent cash-splashing means that *facilities are good*, especially for healthcare students.

Sex ratio (M:F): 39:61	**Founded:** 1875
Full-time u'grads: 10,610	**Part-time:** 2,305
Postgrads: 905	**Non-degree:** n/a
Ave course: 4yrs	**Ethnic:** n/a
State:private school: 96:4	**Flunk rate:** 18%
Mature: 38%	**International:** 6%
Disabled: 105	**Local:** 90%

61%
39%

ATMOSPHERE:

The student population is overwhelmingly local and/or mature. It's a *functional* sort of place that teaches degrees and *not a lot more*, something *most* of the students *appreciate*. *They're happy to get on with studying and leave the student capers to the trendies at the posher* University of Glasgow.

GLASGOW: see University of Glasgow
• City centre: 0 miles

TRAVEL: see University of Glasgow
Trains: Queen Street station's 10 mins walk from the City campus.

CAREER PROSPECTS:

• Careers Service • No. of staff: 7 full • Unemployed after 6mths: 10%

FAMOUS ALUMNI:

Cathy Jamieson (Scottish Executive Justice Minister); Andy Kerr (Scottish Executive Finance Minister); Rhona Martin MBE (Olympic gold medal winning curler).

FURTHER INFO:

• Prospectuses: undergrad; postgrad • Open days

ACADEMIC

The business school's the *glittery trinket* in Caledonian's *tiara*. It's the biggest one in Scotland and was opened by Michelle Mone, businesswoman and creator of the gel-filled bra (madam, we salute you). There's a *healthy medical rep*, with 1 in 5 of Scotland's nurses and healthcare professionals training here. Teaching-wise, lectures and tutorials are the norm. Engineering, Science and Computing students have their own labs with specialist equipment. There's also a clinical simulation lab (mock hospital) for *Florence Nightingale types*.

Entry points: 140-300	Ave points: n/a
No. of terms: 2	Length of terms: 15wks
Staff/student ratio: 1:10	Study addicts: 92%
Teaching: *	Research: **
Year abroad: 1%	Sandwich students: 17%

ADMISSIONS:

• Apply via UCAS/CATCH for Nursing & Midwifery

SUBJECTS:

Built & Natural Environment	Health & Social Care
Caledonian Business School	Law & Social Sciences
Computing & Mathematical	Life Sciences
Engineering, Science & Design	Nursing, Midwifery & Community Health

Best: Biomedical Sciences; Computing; Engineering; Nursing; Optometry.

LIBRARIES:

• 335,100 books • 1,367 study places
The Library & Information Centre houses the library (books, journals, internet access, e-mail and e-information services) and the Learning Café which gives students the option to study in a more relaxed atmosphere, check e-mail or just grab a coffee. *Nice.* The centre also houses the Careers Service and the Effective Learning Service.

COMPUTERS:

• 1,550 workstations
All 1st year rooms have internet points.

ENTERTAINMENT

THE CITY: see <u>University of Glasgow</u>

UNIVERSITY:

• <u>Price of a pint of beer: £1.75</u> • <u>Glass of wine: £1.30</u>

A new SA building's pencilled in for a grand opening (*perhaps by another lingerie designer*) in 2006. It should have two bars, an internet cafe, games room and more. *As things stand, though, ents are at a sorry ebb. Students look to the city for kicks.*

Bars: The Bedsit contains three bars: the Lounge, the Games Room and the Back Bar. *They're nothing spectacular. The entertainment only goes as far as the occasional quiz and karaoke session.*

Food: The City campus refectory is pretty expensive, although the coffee shop *isn't too bad.*

Other: Two graduation balls and a sports ball fill the frill quota every year.

SOCIAL & POLITICAL

GLASGOW CALEDONIAN UNIVERSITY STUDENTS' ASSOCIATION:

• <u>4 sabbaticals</u> • <u>NUS member</u> • <u>Turnout at last ballot: 13%</u>

The SA have *vague* ambitions to political agitation, *especially* if it involves the Scottish end of the Free Education Movement.

SA FACILITIES:

SA building (the Bedsit): three bars; canteen and pizza cafe; pool tables; meeting room; Bank of Scotland ATM; photocopying/printing services; photo booth; payphones; advice centre; crèche; video games; stationery shop; new book shop and book-trading service.

CLUBS (NON-SPORTING):

Chinese; CUMSA (Muslim society); Hellenic; International; Psychsoc; Scottish Socialists; SSOS; TTH (Travel, Tourism & Hospitality); Wig & Gown (lawyers). **See also Clubs tables.**

OTHER ORGANISATIONS:

Re:Union's the monthly student paper, run and paid for by the SA. Rag week bundles most of the University's charity work into seven *frenzied days* once a year.

RELIGIOUS:

• <u>1 chaplain</u>

Chaplaincy room and Muslim prayer room.

PAID WORK:

• <u>Job bureau</u>

SPORTS

• <u>Recent successes: men's hockey</u> • <u>BUSA Ranking: 48</u>

SPORTS FACILITIES:

With no outdoor faciltes to call its own, the University makes do with its new(*ish*) sports complex which has: gym; massage service; various yoga/pilates/aerobic classes; trampolining; netball; karate; judo; basketball; table tennis; Muay Thai boxing; handball; volleyball.

SPORTING CLUBS:

Adventure Club; American Football; Handball; Muay Thai Boxing; Sailplane & Gliding; Snowboarding; Table Tennis; Target Shooting & Paintballing (*hopefully the two are kept separate*); Tei Karate. **See also Clubs tables.**

ATTRACTIONS: see <u>University of Glasgow</u>

ACCOMMODATION

IN COLLEGE:
• Catered 6% • Cost: £70 (38wks)
• Self-catering: 5% • Cost: £65-75 (38wks) • First years living in: 80%
• Insurance premium: £££££
Availability: Facilities in Caledonian Court are *far from ideal*. There's not room for *anything like* the whole fresher intake, and anyone outside the 1st year can *dream on*. The accommodation that's there is *okay – modern* and *close to town* – about half of all rooms are en-suite and there are flats adapted for disabled students.
Car parking: *Limited* in halls. Most student drivers leave cars in local car parks.

EXTERNALLY: see University of Glasgow
• Ave rent: £50
Availability: Students who look early find the *top* property. Those who leave it until September can end up in some *pretty miserable dives*.
Housing help: The University accommodation office vets landlords and posts vacancies.

WELFARE

SERVICES:
• Lesbian/Gay/Bisexual Society • Ethnic Minorities Society • Women's Society
• Mature Students' Society • International Students' Officer • Postgrad Society
• Disabilities Society • College counsellors: 7 full • SA counsellors: 1 • Crime rating: !!

Nursery: The Beechwood Nursery looks after kids while mum/dad hits the books.
Disabilities: *Good* facilities in the modern buildings, with all the necessary ramps, lifts, loops and so on.

FINANCE:
• Ave debt per year: £2,516
Fees: It's Scotland, so no top-up fees. *Hooray for Scotland*!
• Access fund: £240,000 • Successful applications/yr: 1,000 • Ave payment: £20-500
Support: Emergency loans (£20-50) are available and the hardship fund will shell out £400-500 at a throw. Scholarships are available for undergrads and grads studying travel and tourism. The University helps with some students' childcare costs.

Glasgow Polytechnic
see Glasgow Caledonian University

University of Gloucestershire

• *Formerly Cheltenham and Gloucester College of Higher Education.*
(1) University of Gloucestershire, Park Campus, The Park, Cheltenham, GL50 2RH
Tel: (01242) 532 700 Email: admissions@glos.ac.uk Website: www.glos.ac.uk
University of Gloucestershire Students' Union (Park Campus), The Park, Cheltenham GL50 2RH
Tel: (01242) 532 848 E-mail: pksu@glos.ac.uk Website: www.ugsu.org

(2) Francis Close Hall Campus, Swindon Road, Cheltenham, GL50 4AZ
Tel: (01242) 532 900
University of Goucestershire Students' Union (FCH Campus), Swindon Road,
Cheltenham, GL50 4AZ
Tel: (01242) 543 439 E-mail: fchsu@glos.ac.uk
(3) Pittville Campus, Albert Road, Cheltenham, GL52 3JG
Tel: (01242) 532 210
University of Gloucestershire Students' Union (Pittville Campus), Albert Road,
Cheltenham, GL52 3JG
Tel: (01242) 532 219
(4) Oxstalls Campus, Oxstalls Lane, Longlevens, Gloucester, GL2 9HW
Tel: (01452) 876 600 University of Gloucestershire Students' Union (Oxstalls Campus),
Oxstalls Lane, Gloucester, GL2 9HW
Tel: (01452) 876 659

GENERAL

The two towns of Cheltenham and Gloucester are less than 7 miles apart amidst the
genteel hills of Gloucestershire, beyond the end of the Bristol Channel, where it gives up
being the Severn Estuary and becomes the River Severn. The main site at Park Campus
(originally a botanic and zoological garden, note the Africa-shaped lake) is a *leafy retreat*
$1\frac{1}{2}$ miles from Cheltenham town centre, with *elderly* buildings, *elegant* grounds and an
extraordinary garden. Among the tennis courts and the large pond where the ducks
occasionally allow students to row, it's one of the few places in England where Wellingtonia
trees can be found. *They have very soft bark, which can be punched or head-butted without
fear of pain – it's not good for the trees but handy for students wandering home drunk.*
Gloucestershire University has *reinvented itself more times than Madonna* – beginning life
as the Mechanics' Institutes in Cheltenham and Gloucester in the early 1800s, then
dabbling in the waters of teacher training for just under a century before various separations
and mergers morphed it into an Arts and Technology College and finally, in 2001, a
university. A new site opened in Gloucester in 2002, which meant that the University's
previous name was briefly accurate, before they immediately changed it. Nowadays, the
University spreads its talents over four sites.

Sex ratio (M:F): 46:54		Founded: 1834	
Full-time u'grads: 5,815		Part-time: 1,865	
Postgrads: 525		Non-degree: n/a	
Ave course: 3-4yrs		Ethnic: 4%	
State:private school: 94:6		Flunk rate: 22%	
Mature: 30%		International: 5%	
Disabled: 220		Local: 30%	

ATMOSPHERE:

*With its spotlessly clean white walls and soothing ambience, the Park Campus in
Cheltenham would make a great rehab centre for drug-pickled celebs. Like the town, the
student body is mostly middle-England and middle-class, with just a pinch of eccentricity
and vague aspirations towards something a bit cooler. Students don't have much contact
with locals and, if they did, the pronounced age difference would mean they had nothing to
talk about anyway.*

OTHER SITES:

Francis Close Hall: Teachers have been trained at the Francis Close Hall Campus for over
150 years. Social Sciences, Theology, Religious Studies, Environmental Programmes and
Humanities are more recent additions. FCH is picturesque and classically *academic-looking
with an Oxbridge-style gothic quadrangle and clock tower*. Notable facilities include the
Gloucester Suite training restaurant for Hospitality students and a studio and lab for
environmentalists. SU rep on site.

Pittville Campus: (2,500 students – Art & Design, Media) Just outside Cheltenham town
centre, near the racecourse, overlooking the *beautiful* Cotswolds, the most modern of the

campuses is *peaceful and laid-back* – a home to sculpture, painting and print-making studios, a graphics editing suite and an art gallery, multi-media suites and a broadcast journalism studio.

Oxstalls Campus: (Sport & Leisure) Five mins from the centre of Gloucester (9 miles from Cheltenham) is a newish £19m campus with two halls of residence housing 308 students. Gloucester itself is *riddled with history* and chunks of Roman paraphernalia are scattered around. The city possesses a *stunning* medieval cathedral (which was used for corridor scenes in the Harry Potter films).

CHELTENHAM:

* Population: 110,000 • City centre: 1 mile • London: 95 miles
* Bristol: 40 miles • Birmingham: 43 miles
* High temp: 22 • Low temp: 1 • Rainfall: 60

Cheltenham became a fashionable resort in the 18th century when the famously demented George III decided that its spring water would be good for him. The result can still be seen in the elegant Regency architecture that sprang up at the time. However, the spa ran dry in 2003 and these days it's probably horses and spies which are the town's main claims to fame. GCHQ, the top-secret-in-a-very-British-way (ie. everybody knows about it but officially it doesn't exist) snoop centre is just up the road. Despite its staid appearance, the town does manage to attract well-respected jazz and literary festivals every year.

TRAVEL:

CHELTENHAM

Trains: Cheltenham Spa station is a mile from Park Campus, offering direct links to London (£27 rtn), Birmingham (£10.30 rtn), Manchester (£10 sgl) and elsewhere.
Coaches: National Express, Marchants and Swanbrook operate coach services from Cheltenham's Royal Well bus station: a return trip to London costs around £21.50, but advance fares on National Express start at a quid.
Car: Main road links to the A40, M5 and M40. Cheltenham has a *tricky* one-way system to master.
University: The colourful Unimotion bus service shuttles between campuses every 10 mins and hops from Cheltenham station to the Park Campus in 5 mins.
Air: Heathrow's less than 2 hrs away but Birmingham International, Staverton and Bristol airports are closer by for *less ambitious* flights.
Bicycles: The University offers a subsidy to students who want to buy bikes.

GLOUCESTER

Trains: Gloucester to London Paddington for around £22 rtn, day rtn to Bristol Parkway for under 6 quid.
Coaches: The National Express service runs between Gloucester and London Victoria (prices as Cheltenham), and elsewhere.
Cars: The M5 runs close by.

CAREER PROSPECTS:

* Careers Service • No. of staff: 1 full/6 part • Unemployed after 6mths: 8%

25-min drop-in sessions on a first-come-first-served basis during term or by appointment during the summer.

FAMOUS ALUMNI:

Chris Beardshaw (TV gardener); Chris Broad and Sarah Potter (cricketers); David Bryant (bowls champion); Adam Buxton (the Adam & Joe show); Jonathan Callard (rugby international); Peter Edwards (artist); Beverley Knight (R&B diva); Roger Lovegrove (wildlife broadcaster); P H Newby (writer).

FURTHER INFO:

* Prospectuses: undergrad; postgrad; some departments; DVD; international newsletter
* Open days

The *snazzy* DVD 'brochure' was made by former students and follows seven finalists at the end of summer term. International students should contact the international office – intoffice@glos.ac.uk

ACADEMIC

There are seven schools, one each for Art, Design & Media, Education, Environment, Health & Social Sciences, Humanities, Sports & Leisure and the Business School. The University's long tradition of teacher training has made it something of a *hot spot* for education courses. Assessment is flexible – final marks are calculated either from final grades or average results over the previous two years, whichever's better, *helping students breathe more easily*. Courses lean towards the vocational and are modular, allowing joint and major/minor subject combinations. 1st years face compulsory modules in study skills and personal development (leadership, teamwork etc.).

Entry points: 100-280
Applns per place: 5
No. of terms: 2
Staff/student ratio: 1:19
Teaching: **
Year abroad: 3%
Firsts: 6%
2.1s: 35%

Ave points: 200
Clearing: 6%
Length of terms: 15wks
Study addicts: 13%
Research: ***
Sandwich students: 20%
2.2s: 36%
3rds: 21%

ADMISSIONS:

• <u>Apply via UCAS or direct for part-time</u>
The University welcomes applications from mature students on Access courses and works in partnership with local education colleges and the Gloucestershire Open College Network to help plan and approve Access programmes. International students can get help with obtaining and completing application forms from their local British Council office.

SUBJECTS:

Art, Media & Design: 14%
Business: 31%
Education: 5%
Environment: 8%

Health & Social Sciences: 12%
Humanities: 12%
Sport & Leisure: 18%

Best: Art & Design; Communication & Media; Hospitality; Leisure, Sport & Tourism; Psychology; Sociology; Town & Country Planning/Landscape.
Unusual: Adventure Leisure Management; Media and Music Management.

LIBRARIES:

• <u>242,512 books</u> • <u>821 study places</u> • <u>Spend per student: £££</u>
There are subject-specific libraries on each site. Park Campus is the largest, with nearly half the University's book provision.

COMPUTERS:

• <u>470 workstations</u> • <u>Spend per student: £££££</u>
Each campus has an IT-equipped Learning Centre, open 70 hours a week during term but also has some 24-hr provision. Student rooms at Oxstalls, FCH and Park have broadband.

OTHER LEARNING FACILITIES:

Language labs; CAD labs; media centre and specialised facilities on each campus.

The original Alice in Wonderland was the daughter of the Dean of Christ Church, Oxford.

ENTERTAINMENT

CHELTENHAM & GLOUCESTER:
• Price of a pint of beer: £2.40 • Glass of wine: £2.40 • Can of Red Bull: £1.50
Cinemas: A seven-screen Odeon in Cheltenham, *but more discerning hit the Blue Room at Gloucester's Guildhall for cult films.*
Theatres: The *high-brow* Everyman is half price for students. The Bacon offers 10% off its many musicals and concerts. The Playhouse stages over 20 amateur productions a year.
Pubs: *A fairly typical* mix of pubs and wine bars, most of which at least tolerate students. *Pushplugs: Norwood; Restoration; Slug & Lettuce; Frog & Fiddle; Pepper's. Try the Montpellier Run – a string of good pubs close-ish by.*
Clubbing: *Moda is charty/dancy; Chemistry is more indie.* Both are in Cheltenham, both do student nights.
Music venues: Cheltenham Town Hall hosts symphony orchestras, opera, folk festivals and the Cheltenham International Jazz festival every spring, as well as the Fringe Music Festival. In Gloucester, the Guildhall *is a haven for the artily weird,* with African drum classes, belly dance lessons, cult movies and gigs.
Eating out: There are the usual fast food chains and plenty of pubs do *better than average grub. Cheltenham Pushplugs: The Balti Walla (quality BYOB curry house); Franco's (mainly for Franco's comedy value); Joe's Café; Munchie's Baguette Bar; Gianni's (don't let the bus station surroundings put you off); The Daffodil (the converted cinema setting holds more appeal than the food, though). Gloucester Pushplugs: Pizza Piazza; Burger Star; The Orchard, Longford Inn and Twelve Bells (pub grub); Balti Hut; Berry's; Comfy Pew; Seasons; Siam Thai; Shanghai.*
Other: The annual Cheltenham Literary Festival draws oodles of bookish types down to talk, workshop and *bitch about each other.* There are also Science and Music festivals to get excited about.

UNIVERSITY:
• Price of a pint of beer: £1.70 • Glass of wine: £1.30 • Can of Red Bull: £1.05
Bars: Most of the Union's main events (karaoke, pool comps, quizzes, bands, cocktail parties and so on) kick off at the *colossal* Park Bar in Cheltenham which is *nicely laid-back* during the day, *loud and vibrant* by night. Pittville and the Francis Close (big screen sports) both have *more mellow* hang-outs. Gloucester's got the newer Oxtalls bar *where all the sports posse pose after a hard day learning how to break people like match-sticks.*
Theatre: The Chapel hosts music and drama *once every month of blue moons.*
Film: Every Tuesday the Film Society (membership £5) screens new releases at Francis Close.
Music venues: The Park campus bar attracts local and not-so-local bands, mostly hopefuls.
Comedy/Cabaret: *Once a month lucky comics get huge mileage out of the name Pittville at the Union* and there's weekly stand up at the Francis Close bar.
Clubbing: Try Open Mic Night or Sub:mission, £3, at the Union, which has a themed night every month.
Food: Refectory on each campus, open 8am-7pm Mon-Fri. Francis Close students can have their peers cook for them in the Gloucester Suite training restaurant – *go in summer, they know what they're doing by then.*
Other: Five balls a year. The Summer Ball's held at Cheltenham Racecourse and keeps going till a *comparatively wussy* 2am. Big (*but not necessarily clever*) names are persuaded to drop by, including the likes of Trevor Nelson, Girls Aloud and the Fun Lovin' Criminals. In 2004 the SU had a poll to decide who played. It was won by Busted, with Jules Holland in second place but, *tragically,* both were either too pricey or unavailable.

SOCIAL & POLITICAL

UNIVERSITY OF GLOUCESTERSHIRE STUDENTS' UNION
• 4 sabbaticals • Turnout at last ballot: 14% • NUS member
The bright and welcoming SU is on a mission to entertain – politics would just be a hindrance – and jealously protects its members from the lures of town entertainments by keeping the ents calendar stuffed to bust.

SU FACILITIES:

Most facilities are based at Hardwick, near Francis Close: club, four bars; four canteens; four snack bars; 12 pool/snooker tables; a whole load of meeting rooms; Alliance & Leicester ATM; photocopier, fax and printing service; photo booth; payphones; advice centre; juke box; games machines; general store; stationery shop; vending machines; launderette.

CLUBS (NON-SPORTING):

Chinese; English; Iranian; Live Music; Marketing; Music, Acting & Dancing; Open Source Computing; Pool; Pro Wrestling; Real Ale; Spooky; The Other Society. **See also Clubs tables.**

OTHER ORGANISATIONS:

The free SU paper is called Space. Rag *is pretty eager*, arranging frequent (*and frequently ridiculous*) events in the name of charity. Student Community Action is about the only student group that really mixes with the local population and gathers a fair few CV points as it does.

RELIGIOUS:

• 2 chaplains (CofE)
The 1908 Chapel at Francis Close is the University's god spot. *Other faiths aren't so lucky* although a prayer room for all faiths is being developed at Park. There are also world faith advisors.

PAID WORK:

• Job bureau • Paid work: term-time 65%
The SU hires over 100 students and has its own employment agency. UCAS is based in Cheltenham and often employs students, as do other local head offices for Kraft Foods, Bird's Eye Walls, British Energy and many others – including *Push*. Failing that there's sometimes £6.50 an hour on offer at the Betting Terminal at Cheltenham Racecourse. Gold Cup organisers recruit temporary staff at the twice yearly Jobs Fayre, where an assortment of local companies put in appearances.

S P O R T S

• Recent successes: trampolining • BUSA Ranking: 48
They may never crack the Olympics, but Gloucestershire jocks are launching a determined attack on the BUSA leagues.

SPORTS FACILITIES:

Football, hockey, cricket, rugby and all-weather pitches; squash, netball, basketball and three tennis courts; sports hall; multigym; swimming pool; gym; aerobics studio; boathouse. Free gym membership. Cheltenham town's facilities include: the Balcarras Sports Centre, Chapel Rock Gymnasium, Cloud 9 Ladies' Health Club; squash courts; running track; pool; lake and river. Gloucester offers a couple of leisure centres.

SPORTING CLUBS:

Cheerleading; Karting; Kendo; Kickboxing; Lacrosse; Snow; Swimming & Water Polo; Watersports. **See also Clubs tables.**

ATTRACTIONS:

Cheltenham Town FC are the local team. There's also Beaufort Sports & Polo Centre (as seen on C4's 'Faking It') for *horsey types*.

A C C O M M O D A T I O N

IN COLLEGE:

• Self-catering: 20% • Cost: £61-77 (41wks)
• First years living in: 60%
• Insurance premium: £

Availability: Up to 95% of 1st years can be housed in mainly en-suite rooms with shared kitchens. Park Campus has an award-winning student village with its own refectory, bar and shop. The *most popular* halls are Eildon and Merrowdown as they're *attractive* Regency buildings near the campus and the town centre; *Challinor Hall is cheaper but to be avoided if possible*. Shaftesbury Hall at Francis Close is the latest addition and is *pretty special*. New accommodation has been completed at Francis Close Hall and at Upper Quay in Gloucester.
Car parking: Parking on the streets round campus is free but *spaces are scarce* during term. Campus parking's reserved for students living outside halls (with a £30 permit).

EXTERNALLY:

• Ave rent: £50 • Living at home: 33%
Availability: Standards *vary wildly* but there's plenty of accommodation in both Cheltenham and Gloucester.
Housing help: The accommodation offices at Francis Close and Oxstalls maintain a database of registered flats and houses.

WELFARE

SERVICES:

• Lesbian/Gay/Bisexual Officer & Society • Mature Students' Officer & Society
• Postgrad Officer • International Students' Officer • Disabilities Officer & Society
• College counsellors: 3 full/1 part • Crime rating: !!
The Unimotion shuttle bus runs from 5pm to midnight.
Health: Park Campus has a medical centre with GP surgeries, information and advice. Physiotherapy sessions are available for those sporting sporting injuries.
Crèches/Nursery: 50 places for 6mths-5yrs, 8am-6pm. Also a Pre-School Centre for those too young to ship off to school (*quite a waiting list*) and an after-school club for 4-11-year-olds.
Disabilities: *Competent* Student Disability Advisers will help with access or study problems. Note-takers and sign interpreters are available.

FINANCE:

• Ave debt per year: £4,015
• Access fund: £450,000 • Successful applications/yr: 650 • Ave payment: £300
Support: There's a Student Finance Officer offering guidance on money matters and hardship assistance– *all the fun of a bank manager with none of the guilt*. In addition to subject-specific bursaries, a disabled students' allowance provides help buying specialist equipment and with other costs.

Goldsmiths College

• *The College is part of the* University of London *and students are entitled to use its facilities.*
Goldsmiths College, University of London, New Cross, London, SE14 6NW
Tel: (020) 7919 7171 E-mail: admissions@gold.ac.uk Website: www.goldsmiths.ac.uk
Goldsmiths College Students' Union, Dixon Road, New Cross, London, SE14 6NW
Tel: (020) 8692 1406 E-mail: gcsu@gold.ac.uk Website: www.gcsu.org.uk

GENERAL

The *main* sight that greets anyone arriving in New Cross Gate by train is a giant scrapyard, *and it's a pretty good symbol of this chunk of south-east London – rather tatty, careworn and in need of a good seeing to. But that's inner-city life and the good news is that Goldsmiths is a bit of a beacon in the gloom. The surroundings have inspired some seriously big names in the arts, from Lucien Freud to Damien Hirst, Malcolm McLaren and most of Blur.* The main college building is a *(relatively) clean, attractive* three-storey affair with a patch of green space at the back. *Most of the college buildings don't exactly leap out of the landscape, but they're modern and house a lively, diverse, creative bunch of students.* If there's one landmark addition, it's the Ben Pimlott Building, which features a sculptural 'scribble' – *so it's a bit more 'urban scrawl' than 'urban sprawl'.* New Cross is docklands territory, and the Dome is just visible from the library – *whether that's an inspiring sight is a matter of opinion.*

Sex ratio (M:F): 34:66	**Founded: 1891**
Full-time u'grads: 3,560	**Part-time: 1,255**
Postgrads: 1,375	**Non-degree: 1,243**
Ave course: 3yrs	**Ethnic: 52%**
State:private school: 91:9	**Flunk rate: 14%**
Mature: 68%	**International: 21%**
Disabled: 582	**Local: 49%**

ATMOSPHERE:

If the London colleges are like Friends, then Goldsmiths is Phoebe – artsy, conscience bound and decked out with big earrings and plastic jewellery. The emphasis on the creative arts adds to a laid-back attitude and students get on well with the locals, helped hugely by close community links. It's absolutely not City-slick suit-and-boot-land – breadheads beware. The Brand Council have, er, branded Goldsmiths 'cool' several times in recent years, which is a source of much pride for the college authorities and of faint embarrassment for the students – a bit like mum developing an interest in hip-hop.

LONDON: see University of London
• City centre: 6 miles
New Cross and Lewisham are *pretty dingy* and *at 6 miles away* are *removed from the frantic bustle of central London.* But the Docklands redevelopment has *rubbed off in spots,* particularly in Greenwich, where the famous Observatory and Maritime museum lend culture. It's *cheap, too, for London.*

TRAVEL: see University of London
Trains: New Cross and New Cross Gate have direct services into London Bridge and Charing Cross.
Buses: *Loads* including numbers: 21, 36, 53, 136, 171 (to the West End) and night-buses too.
Car: Just off the south circular and outside the congestion zone, both of which help. But finding a parking spot *isn't much fun. Road-rage sufferers be warned.*
Underground: New Cross and New Cross Gate are on the East London line. DLR and Jubilee lines pass through the area, but the *quickest* route into town is by train.
Bicycles: *Two wheels are better than four, and students know it.* Bike facilities in college help.

CAREER PROSPECTS:
• Careers Service • No. of staff: 2 full/2 part • Unemployed after 6mths: 7%
The careers service provides an e-mail service with vacancies, discussion forums and careers advice.

FAMOUS ALUMNI:
Most of Blur; Martin Brabbins (conductor); John Cale (Velvet Underground); Vic Charles (karate champ); Julian Clary (comedian); Wendy Cope (poet); Lucien Freud, Damien Hirst,

Tom Keating, Bridget Riley (artists); Tessa Jowell MP (Lab); Linton Kwesi Johnson (dub poet); Malcolm McLaren (Sex Pistols creator); Brian Molko (Placebo); Molly Parkin (writer); Mary Quant (designer); Lord Melvyn-Rees (former Home Secretary); Gillian Wearing (Turner prizewinner 1997); Colin Welland (playwright/actor); Vivienne Westwood (fashion designer).

FURTHER INFO:

• Prospectuses: undergrad; postgrad • Open Days • Video
Prospectuses also available for study-abroad, PGCE and part-time students.

ACADEMIC

A *big name* in the artistic field, Goldsmiths's end of term exhibitions and degree shows generally *excite a lot of interest. They may or may not have invented the word 'interdisciplinarity' but,* either way, it describes the ideas frequently exchanged between their departments and, *if well positioned, scores highly in Scrabble.* Work is assessed by a mix of exams, dissertations, shows, exhibitions, coursework, performances and, *of course,* more exams.

Entry points: 190–300	**Ave points: 287**
Applns per place: 7	**Clearing: 17%**
No. of terms: 3	**Length of terms: 10wks**
Staff/student ratio: 1:10	**Study addicts: 13%**
Teaching: **	**Research: *****
Year abroad: <1%	**Sandwich students: <1%**
Firsts: 10%	**2.2s: 33%**
2.1s: 51%	**3rds: 6%**

ADMISSIONS:

• Apply via UCAS

SUBJECTS:

Art & Design: 8%	Languages: 5%
Arts/Humanities: 25%	Maths, Statistics & Operations Research: 1%
Computing: 4%	Music: 8%
Drama & Perfoming Arts: 4%	Social Sciences: 30%
Education: 11%	Social Work: 4%

Best: Anthropology; Art & Design; Drama; Mathematics; Media & Communications; Politics/Economics; Psychology; Sociology.

LIBRARIES:

• 221,000 books • 942 study places
The Rutherford Information Services Building houses a *modern* library.

COMPUTERS:

• 241 workstations
Online learning is in place for some subjects so *students can go to college without getting out of bed*.

OTHER LEARNING FACILITIES:

The glossy new Ben Pimlott building opened in 2005 with *up-to-date* studios and facilities for budding Damien Hirsts – *dead sheep and formaldehyde not included*.

ENTERTAINMENT

THE CITY: see University of London
• Price of a pint of beer: £2.50 • Glass of wine: £2.50
Cinemas: Multiplexes at Greenwich, Peckham and Surrey Quays are *cheaper, plusher and newer* than some in the West End.
Theatres: Provisions in Greenwich but again *the West End is the best bet*.

Pubs: *Pushplugs: New Cross Inn, Marquis of Granby, Rosemary Branch, Paradise Bar, Goldsmiths Tavern*.

Clubbing: *Pick of the tunes* are to be found at the Rivioli Ballroom, Jes Suis Music and The Venue.

Eating out: *Lots of good, easy-on-the-pocket* ethnic restaurants. *Pushplugs: The Thailand (one of the best in London); Moonbow Jakes; Marie's Cafe, Gem's; Mr Cheung; Raj Bhujan*.

COLLEGE:

• Price of a pint of beer: £1.90 • Glass of wine: £1.60

Bars: The Green Room is the *main bar, with all the usual trimmings*: bar snacks, karaoke, cheap booze, cheesy music and a pub quiz.

Theatres: *With all these arty types*, there's a *strong* thesp scene, which is boosted by a *huge* stage and *active* drama group.

Film: The film society has a screen of its own and shows *appropriately leftfield* films, with the occasional blockbuster thrown in *for good measure*. The Stretch Bar has a weekly film night.

Music venues: Old boys Blur get back for the occasional low-key gig, and other *biggish* indie/alternative acts (eg. Athlete) also turn up *from time to time*.

Clubbing: Club Sandwich is a *popular* weekly cheese-fest. Drum and bass names (Fabio, Grooverider) crop up *fairly regularly*, too.

Comedy/Cabaret: The Stretch Bar's comedy nights attract comedic *heavyweights* like Lee Mack and Noel Fielding.

Food: *Healthier-than-average fare* at Loafer's Corner and the Refectory, and *pleasant enough* dining at the newly revamped Stretch. *But pocket-friendly greasy booze-sops are best found at Revolution*.

Other: Four balls a year and regular hall and society events.

SOCIAL & POLITICAL

GOLDSMITHS COLLEGE STUDENTS' UNION (GCSU):

• 5 sabbaticals • NUS member • Turnout at last ballot: 16%

GCSU has a reputation as a *vocal, lefty* kind of student body, and uses links with the College's *more celebrated* old boys to good effect. Campaigning issues are *many and various* with a *wider world-view* than just top-up fees and student access.

SU FACILITIES:

Advice centre; two bars; bank and ATM (Natwest); bookshop (Waterstone's); canteen; three snack/coffee bars; general store; juke-box; laundrette; minibus hire; photo booth; three pool tables; vending machines; video games.

CLUBS (NON-SPORTING):

Chinese; Hellenic; Hip Hop; Japanese; International; Chiaroscuro (film). **See also Clubs tables.**

OTHER ORGANISATIONS:

Guardian award-winning monthly student mag Smiths, student radio station Wired.

RELIGIOUS:

• 4 chaplains (CofE, RC, Methodist, URC) and an imam

PAID WORK: see University of London

• Job bureau

Part-time jobs are *easily had* in London, and there are *plenty* on campus.

SPORTS

• Recent successes: football • BUSA Ranking: 46

Students are *generally a bit more Brecht than Beckenbauer*, but the SU has an increasing sports agenda and offers classes in yoga, circuit training etc.

SPORTS FACILITIES:
Twenty one acres of playing fields 8 miles away in Sidcup. Students are entitled to use ULU facilities, *which are a bit better*. A £10 Student Activities Card allows students to dip into clubs and societies without paying full membership fees. The College is looking into getting an on-campus fitness centre up and running by autumn 2005.

SPORTING CLUBS:
Aerobics; Aikido & other Martial Arts; Kickboxing; Women's Self-Defence. **See also Clubs tables**.

ATTRACTIONS: see University of London
Local football team Millwall have cleaned up their act *since the bad old days*, while Crystal Palace *are currently unsteadily standing smug (and a tad surprised), having made the Premiership*. Charlton Athletic are *currently having a whale of a time*, and have a *high-flying* ladies football side.

ACCOMMODATION

IN COLLEGE:
• Self-catering: 30% • Cost: £66-90 (39wks)
• First years living in: 95% • Insurance premium: £££
Availability: All accommodation is *near* campus and around ¾ of rooms have en-suite facilities. Nobody needs to share, and all 1st years who want accommodation can get it.
Car parking: Two halls have parking (registration with college required); disabled students have priority.

EXTERNALLY: see University of London
• Ave rent: £70
Availability: House-hunting is *easier and cheaper south of the river, which just about makes up for relatively poor transport links*. Brockley and Lewisham *prove popular despite being a bit shabby*. Brixton's *still tarred with the 'cool' brush* and has *more than its fair share of trustafarians getting all ghetto-fabulous as a result*.
Housing help: The college and GCSU provide a *hands-on* service and help students through every stage of finding a new place.

WELFARE

SERVICES:
• Lesbian/Gay/Bisexual Officer • Ethnic Minorities Officer • Women's Officer
• Mature Students' Officer • International Students' Officer • Postgrad Officer
• Disabilities Officer • Self-defence classes
• Nightline • College counsellors: 1 full/4 part • Crime rating: !!!!
The college looks out for its students, has *good* facilities and welfare provisions by the bucket. *Some of the older college buildings are tricky for disabled students, though*.
Health: Medical centre on campus with two full-time GPs and two practice nurses.
Crèches/Nursery: Crèche with 20 places for 3mths-5yrs.
Disabilities: Newer buildings have *decent* access and facilities (ramps, lifts, hearing loops, Braille signs) but sharp corners and stairs make older parts *difficult*. There's also a full-time dyslexia tutor on hand.

FINANCE:
• Ave debt per year: £3,652 • Access fund: £396,548
• Successful applications/yr: 757 • Ave payment: 750
Support: A postgrad scholarship scheme makes payments of up to £1,000. The alumni discounts scheme grants £500 at a time and there's an accommodation bursary with a total fund of £30,000.

Gordon University

see Robert Gordon University

Greenwich University

- *Formerly Woolwich Polytechnic, Thames Polytechnic.*
(1) The University of Greenwich, Old Royal Naval College, Park Row, Greenwich, London, SE10 9LS
Tel: (020) 8331 8000 E-mail: courseinfo@gre.ac.uk Website: www.gre.ac.uk
University of Greenwich Students' Union, Cooper Building, King William Walk, Greenwich, London, SE10 9JH
Tel: (020) 8331 7629 Website: www.suug.co.uk
(2) Avery Hill Campus, Avery Hill Road, Eltham, London, SE9 2UG
Students' Union, 1 Boleyn Court, Avery Hill Road, Eltham, London, SE9 2UG
Tel: (020) 8331 9596
(3) Medway Campus, Medway, Kent, ME4 4AW
Students' Union, Jellicoe Building, Chatham Maritime, ME4 4AW
Tel: (020) 8331 8053

GENERAL

Greenwich University comprises a *stately* threesome of campuses, two of which live up to their name by being in the borough of Greenwich – *where the time comes from*. The main site, Maritime Greenwich, revolves around the *stunning*, partly Wren-designed Old Royal Naval College, birthplace of kings and a *firm filmic favourite*. Avery Hill, a few miles away, is a combination of Victorian mansion and more modern buildings, swathed in parkland *and generally very pleasant all over*. Then there's Chatham in Kent, a former naval barracks on the historic dockyard, *and the feeling here is much more rural*. The different sites offer different courses and students considering applying should check where they'd be based, *since, despite strong transport links, they're largely self-contained and as different as chalk and chutney.*

Sex ratio (M:F): 46:54	Founded: 1890
Full-time u'grads: 10,605	Part-time: 4,070
Postgrads: 2,285	Non-degree: n/a
Ave course: 3yrs	Ethnic: 42%
State:private school: 95:5	Flunk rate: 23%
Mature: 83%	International: 23%
Disabled: 253	Local: n/a

ATMOSPHERE:

The University's far enough away from the city centre to feel relaxed, but plenty of student activity means life is far from dull. The two major SU venues, particularly Bar Latitude in Greenwich and the Dome at Avery Hill, provide a social focus which would otherwise be lost in the distances between sites. This and the social melting pot of many ethnic groups help to provide a sense of fun and an extra-curricular buzz that's missing at some of the other 'new' universities.

OTHER SITES:

Avery Hill: (6,000 students – Education & Training, Health & Social Care, Architecture & Construction) An *attractive site*, 3 miles south of Woolwich, set in an 86-acre park with a listed mansion as the main building and *gorgeous* Winter Gardens. The nearest major shopping area is Eltham, a mile away.

Medway: (2,000 students – Engineering, Natural Resources Institute, Science, Pharmacy) Based at Chatham and in association with the Natural Resources Institute. It has a robotics centre, computer-aided design studio and satellite technology base. *Swanky*. It's also currently being developed as an integrated campus with the University of Kent and Canterbury Christ Church University College.

LONDON: see University of London
The London borough of Greenwich, which hugs the south bank of the river at the eastern end of the Thames, is firmly a tourist top-spot, thanks in part to features like the Cutty Sark and the Royal Observatory. Meanwhile, residents and students are kept happy with enough shops, bars and clubs to shake several sticks at. The *ever-ailing* Dome is no longer open, but current plans are to transform it into a waterfront sports, leisure and entertainment complex. *Woo hoo. It's easy enough* to get into central London on the DLR railway – the *absence of the tube proper means Greenwich is a bit of a respite from the maddening crowds, and outside of tourist-hunting season has a chilled, laid-back air.*

TRAVEL: see University of London
Trains: For Avery Hill, Falconwood or New Eltham stations (both 30 mins travel and 15 mins walk). Chatham station for Medway. There's a DLR station (Cutty Sark) at Greenwich. London Bridge is the nearest tube and mainline train station, 15 mins from Greenwich, 20 mins from Avery Hill and just over an hour from Medway.
Buses: All sites are served by a wide range of regular London bus services.
Underground: London Bridge (Northern, Jubilee) is the nearest tube.
University: Free inter-site shuttlebuses run twice a day – timetables available from the SU.
Car: Local parking permits are needed. There are student spaces at Avery Hill and Medway, but not Greenwich.
Bicycles: *Your life in the hands of juggernaut drivers.*

CAREER PROSPECTS:
• Careers Service • Unemployed after 6mths: 12%
The University's service has a *poorly advertised but pretty comprehensive package* to students and recent graduates. Services include: online key skills training; mentoring for ethnic minority students; job shop; job fairs; interview training; careers library; bulletin boards.

FAMOUS ALUMNI:

Hale & Pace (*unamusing* double act); Rachel Heyhoe Flint (cricketer); Graham Ingham (BBC TV reporter); Brian Jacks (former judo champ); Matt James (Gene drummer); Prof Charles Kao (inventor of fibre optics); William G Stewart (Fifteen to One).

FURTHER INFO:
• Prospectuses: undergrad; postgrad; some departments; international students
• Open days
Visit the admissions website for open day details, course introductions, student testimonials and virtual tours.

 A C A D E M I C

Research, scientific and technical-based studies *are what Greenwich does best, academically speaking.* Teaching is getting in on the technology act with innovations like web CT and an online campus. Some distance learning options are offered. Final grades are *the bastard children of* 2nd and final year exams and coursework.

120-260			
Entry points: 120-260		Ave points: n/a	
Applns per place: n/a		Clearing: 38%	
No. of terms: 2		Length of terms: 15wks	
Staff/student ratio: 1:15		Study addicts: n/a	
Teaching: **		Research: **	**POINTS**

ADMISSIONS:
• Apply via UCAS

SUBJECTS:

Agricultural: 1%	Engineering: 7%
Architecture: 7%	Law: 3%
Art & Design: 1%	Mathematical: <1%
Arts/Humanities: 1%	Medical Sciences: 13%
Business/Management: 18%	(Modern) Languages: 3%
Computer Science: 14%	Sciences: 9%
Education: 15%	Social Sciences: 5%

Best: Business & Management; Economics; Education; Hospitality, Leisure, Recreation, Sport & Tourism; Nursing; Pharmacology & Pharmacy; Philosophy; Psychology; Politics; Theology & Religious Studies.

LIBRARIES:
• 505,000 books • 920 study places • Spend per student: ££
Students aren't exactly jumping over the moon about library facilities, given the scrums over primary texts and the fact that they're closed on Sundays. The good news though is that each site has at least one library open until 9pm.

COMPUTERS:
• 1,400 workstations • No. of internet access points 1,200 • Spend per student: £
Computers are based in the libraries at all three sites, *so all the same opening hour quibbles apply.*

OTHER LEARNING FACILITIES:
Language laboratory; media centre.

ENTERTAINMENT

LONDON: see University of London
Except Greenwich itself, there is little to do outside college as the sites aren't exactly in London's most jumping joints.
Cinemas: Students get discounted tickets at Greenwich Film Works and the *heaving* Bluewater.
Theatres: The Greenwich Playhouse and the Greenwich Theatre have both had students tread their boards.
Pubs: *Pushplugs: The Ordnance; the Trafalgar in Greenwich.* There's a newish Wetherspoon next to Greenwich DLR Station which proves *popular when desparate.*
Music venues: Various late night bars offer live tunes. *Try Up The Creek (also good for comedy) or the late-opening St Christophers or Live Bar.*
Eating out: Budget-conscious students grab a cheap bite at Goddard's, Tae Won Mein and Noodle Time. *Pubs along the river are a pricier alternative.*
Other: The *vibrant and thrilling* Greenwich and Docklands International Festival invades the borough each June.

UNIVERSITY:
• Price of a pint of beer: £1.70 • Glass of wine: £1.30
Bars: The main ones are happy-hour-fuelled Bar Latitude at Greenwich, the Dome at Avery Hill (made up of Jester's and Mazey's bars and open til 2am twice a week), the more traditional Drunken Sailor, and the Sparrows Farm Sports Bar, *where drunken football nuts go karaoke crazy.*
Theatres: *Nothing on campus – student thesps get involved in productions at local theatres.*
Film: There's a film society, though no screenings at present – this may change.
Music venues: The Dome at Avery Hill can hold 1,000 punters. Recent offerings include Jamelia, Big Brovaz and Lamarr. There's also a jazz night at Bar Latitude.
Clubbing: Three or four club nights a week, *usually serving up commercial, cheese or RnB grooves.* The likes of Trevor Nelson and Tim Westwood have appeared. *Pushplugs: Dizzy at the Dome, a Friday night delight for many.*

Comedy/Cabaret: The Dome hosts a regular comedy night, which features chuckle monsters from the Up the Creek comedy circuit.

Food: A range of eateries across the expanse, notably Greengages and Pembroke canteen-style restaurants and the smaller, nibblier Queen Anne coffee shop. Halal food available. Some club nights are catered.

Other: Summer ball and sports and societies award dinner.

SOCIAL & POLITICAL

UNIVERSITY OF GREENWICH STUDENTS' UNION:
• 5 sabbaticals • Turnout at last ballot: 4% • NUS member
The concentration of SU facilities at Greenwich and Avery Hill tends to leave the further-flung members somewhat out of the equation, although representation at Medway has improved in recent years. The entertainment facilities are well used, but politics is a cold potato – the Socialist Worker Society bit the dust after a lack of support. Instead, the SU plays it safe and stays politically neutral, which could be why its relationship with the University is warm and back-slappy.

SU FACILITIES:
Four main and three smaller bars; three minibuses; three shops; post office; vending and games machines; pool tables; juke box; photocopying; fax; printing; photo booth; payphone; advice centre; STA travel; Endsleigh Insurance; launderette; TV lounge; three meeting rooms.

CLUBS (NON-SPORTING):
Arabic; Asian; Business Club; Chinese; Computing; Drama; Economics; Explore UK; Happy Here *(for people who are happy to be here)*; Hindu; Hellenic; International; Iranian; Law; Mobo; Photography; Pub Crawl; Salsa; Sikh; Travel. **See also Clubs tables.**

OTHER ORGANISATIONS:
The student magazine, Sarky Cutt, is published every 6 weeks. There's an active Rag and Community Projects bursaries for voluntary groups. *Plans for a TV and radio station are under way.*

RELIGIOUS:
• 5 chaplains (CofE, RC, Chinese, Associate Chaplains for other faiths)
The Maritime campus chapel is open to the public every day. Muslim prayer rooms available at each site. All faiths are represented in London at large, but around Greenwich it can vary.

PAID WORK: see University of London
• Job bureau

SPORTS

• Recent successes: men's football; rugby; hockey; boat club; athletics; tae kwon do
• BUSA Ranking: 48
For a University mostly inside the M25, Greenwich has some pretty good sports facilities, but only a certain proportion of the students get into the spirit. Successes tend to be individual rather than team efforts. Sports facilities are concentrated at the Avery Hill site.

SPORTS FACILITIES:
Avery Hill: Sports centre with multigym, squash courts, snooker tables; gym; football, rugby, hockey pitches; tennis courts; running track.
Medway: Sports hall.

SPORTING CLUBS:
Mountain Climbing; Table Tennis. **See also Clubs tables.**

ATTRACTIONS: see University of London
Charlton Athletic, Millwall and Gillingham are the respective local football teams.

ACCOMMODATION

IN COLLEGE:
• Self-catering: 21% • Cost: £66-96 (40wks) • First years living in: 50%
• Insurance premium: £
Availability: The University guarantees to house all 1st years who request it, although this might mean private accommodation (head tenancy or housing association schemes). The majority of University-owned housing is at Avery Hill but there's something at each site. All sites have disabled facilities, CCTV, entry-phones and 24-hr security. There's one hall just for postgrads. 75% of rooms are en-suite. There are also 50 places in *pricier* studio flats (£120-150), *a few of which* are suitable for couples.
Car parking: Parking is by permit sticker only. *There's plenty of room for motors at Avery Hill and Medway, less so at Greenwich.*

EXTERNALLY: see University of London

LOCAL:
• Ave rent: £80
Availability: *East and South-East London, especially Woolwich and Plumstead, are cheaper than north of the river, but you get what you pay for. Some parts, such as Thamesmead, are a bit deficient on the safety front.*
Housing help: The University runs a housing office on each site. Bulletin boards, vacancy lists and approved landlord lists keep students in the know. Advisers can check contracts and help with legal stuff.

WELFARE

SERVICES:
• Lesbian/Gay/Bisexual Officer & Society • Women's Officer • Mature Students' Officer
• International Students' Officer • Postgrad Officer • Disabilities Officer & Society
• College counsellors: 3 full • Crime rating: !!!!
The SU runs a welfare and advice department and the University runs a counselling service, *easily accessible on the larger sites only*. They organise workshops for coping with stress, anxiety and so on. *Sadly*, the minibus doesn't run late.
Health: Greenwich: two off-campus NHS practices with four GPs and three nurses. Avery Hill: practice with five GPs and three nurses. Medway: practice with three GPs and one nurse.
Women: There's a women's officer (non-sabbatical).
Crèches/Nursery: 30 places are available for children aged 6mths-5yrs (term only).
Disabilities: Disabled parking and wheelchair access to the campuses are *pretty good, although the 18th-century buildings at Maritime Greenwich can be tiring to navigate*. Facilities for taping lectures, portable word processors, portable loops and conversers and disabled parking are all in place. The Disability and Dyslexia Service *does oodles* to help people with learning difficulties, offering software advice, special exam arrangements, software advice, study skills workshops and more. Disabled students get priority when it comes to allocating accommodation and the University have *a bit of cash set aside to make any individual adaptations that might be needed*. Incidentally, Greenwich topped the league table in employing disabled professors.

FINANCE:
• Ave debt per year: £3,652 • Access fund: £1.7m • Successful applications/yr: 2,100
• Ave payment: £100-2,500
Fees: Greenwich is one of the handful of places not going the whole top-up fees hog. For further info about bursaries, check 'em out online.

Guy's Hospital
see King's College London

> Royal College of music students have been banned from practising in the disabled toilets.

Hallam see <u>Sheffield Hallam University</u>

Harper Adams University College

Hatfield Polytechnic see <u>University of Hertfordshire</u>

Heriot-Watt University

University of Hertfordshire

Heythrop College, University of London

Holloway see <u>Royal Holloway, University of London</u>

Hope University see <u>Liverpool Hope University College</u>

University of Huddersfield

Huddersfield Polytechnic see <u>University of Huddersfield</u>

University of Hull

Humberside University see <u>Lincoln University</u>

Hallam
see <u>Sheffield Hallam University</u>

Harper Adams University College

Harper Adams University College, Newport, Shropshire, TF10 8NB
Tel: (01952) 815 000 E-mail: admissions@harper-adams.ac.uk
Website: www.harper-adams.ac.uk
Harper Adams Students' Union Tel: (01952) 815 313 E-mail: su@harper-adams.ac.uk
Website: www.harper-adams.ac.uk/studentunion

GENERAL

Welcome to the countryside. Harper Adams isn't just a rural campus – it lives, breathes and exists for the sticks. The small, self-contained college is set in 700 acres of *ruralest* Shropshire. It specialises in agricultural topics and has its own 236-acre working farm. It's cut off from urban civilisation by *distance* and *limited* transport links, *but that's part of the charm.*

Sex ratio (M:F): 65:35	Founded: 1901
Full-time u'grads: 1,340	Part-time: 100
Postgrads: 70	Non-degree: 689
Ave course: 4yrs	Ethnic: 8%
State:private school: 15:85	Flunk rate: 17%
Mature: 16%	International: 10%
Disabled: 97	Local: 10%

ATMOSPHERE:

Friendly and intense. Everyone knows everyone else and there's not much getting away from the intimate social scene. Of course that's not for everybody – cabin fever sufferers might be best to steer clear – for others it's a welcome safety net. At the end of the day, the specialised nature of the syllabus means that everyone knows why they're there and most of them are pretty happy about it.

NEWPORT:

• Population: 158,500 • Town centre: 3 miles • London: 146 miles • Telford: 10 miles
• Birmingham: 36 miles
• High temp: 20 • Low temp: 0 • Rainfall: 58

Newport is a one-horse town, so it's lucky there's a lot more livestock to hand at college. The beautiful Shropshire countryside can only be stared at admiringly for so long so it's fortunate that Telford and Shrewsbury are nearby, though neither could be called mindblowing. Luckily it takes less than an hour to get to Birmingham, so urban fun is not out of the question.

TRAVEL:

Trains: The nearest stations are in Telford (10 miles) and Stafford (16 miles).
Coaches: National Express services run from Telford to London, Birmingham and all over.
Car: M6, M54, A41. Parking on campus is *free* and *easy which is just as well as cars are quite heavily relied upon*.
Air: Birmingham International (45 miles) for low-cost internal and international flights (Ryanair, FlyBe, Mytravel).
Local: Buses are *infrequent and unreliable*. Cars, bikes or – oh horrors – walking are better options.
College: Beer bus (free all night) run by local landlords *ferries revellers around* on Wednesdays, Fridays and Saturdays from town to the University.
Taxis: Easy to get and run £1 to town deals on Wednesday nights. They're *very popular*, and *cheap* at any other time (£2 into town), *but there's more chance of hitching a lift on a Friesian than hailing one in the street.*
Bicycles: A cycle lane connects town and campus. There are also pods and racks at college.

CAREER PROSPECTS:

• Careers Service • No. of staff: 2 full • Unemployed after 6mths: 4%
Bulletin boards, newsletters, vacancy lists, job fairs etc.

FURTHER INFO:

• Prospectuses: undergrad; postgrad; departmental; short course brochures • Open days

ACADEMIC

The College runs a *highly specialised* set of subjects concentrating on land and agricultural studies. There are five main subject groups: Animals, Business & Agri-food, Rural Affairs & Environment, Engineering and Crops. *Teaching Quality is a College buzzphrase and the obligatory placement year is a significant boon when it comes to graduate employability.* Agriculture and Forestry merit a special mention.

Entry points: 210-350
No. of terms: 3
Staff/student ratio: 1:14
Teaching: n/a
Year abroad: 18%
Firsts: 7%
2.1s: 45%

Clearing: 21%
Length of terms: 10/11wks
Study addicts: 10%
Research: *
Sandwich students: 100%
2.2s: 43
3rds: 5%

210-350

POINTS

ADMISSIONS:

• Apply via UCAS

SUBJECTS:

Animals: 16%
Business & Agri-foods: 10%
Crops: 29%
Engineering: 14%
Rural Affairs & Environment: 31%
Best: Agriculture; Animal Health & Welfare; Business & Agfri-food; Rural Affairs & Environment.
Unusual: Dairy Herd Management; Off-road vehicle Design.

LIBRARIES:

• 45,600 books • 143 study places • Spend per student: ££
The Bamford Library is a recent addition, comprising a two-storey library, a JCB Engineering Design Centre, an exhibition hall and the Kaldi Café. Its *impressive* eco-credentials include a rainwater harvesting system unit and a natural ventilation system – *which is not another word for 'draughty' apparently.*

COMPUTERS:

• 200 workstations
Halls and the library have wireless access.

OTHER LEARNING FACILITIES:

Language labs; drama studio; CAD lab; rehearsal rooms; Engineering Design Centre.

ENTERTAINMENT

THE TOWN:

• Price of a pint of beer: £1.90 • Glass of wine: £2.00 • Can of Red Bull: £1.50
Cinemas: There's a UCI multiplex in Telford.
Pubs: 17 waterholes in town, and students *sometimes venture into local territory.* Ozzey's Wine Bar (promotions a-plenty) and the Phez are *popular.*
Clubbing: *Cheesier than a sweaty foot in a Wotsits factory.* Zanzibar, Athena and Barley all provide some groove action.
Music venues: Weston Park, 15 mins from campus, is the host site for the annual V festival.
Eating out: Sunday carvery at the Swan is *about as adventurous as it gets. If students can be bothered to go there, nearish-by* Ludlow is the British capital of Michelin-starred restaurants, barring London.

UNIVERSITY:

• Price of a pint of beer: £1.80 • Glass of wine: £1.25 • Can of Red Bull: £1.10
With the town *bottoming out* on entertainment, the *bulk* of the fun has to come from the Uni. Thankfully, the SU do a *sterling* job.
Bars: The main bar's big night is Wednesday (sporty types' *big night out*) and it opens till late on weekends. The daily haunt is the *less rustically named* Lounge.
Theatre: The QMH drama society *thesps about the place a bit.*
Film: There's a film on once a week in the Lounge bar.
Music venues: Live bands in the main bar every Wednesday night, *but this isn't TOTP territory.*
Food: The dining hall is a *school-dinnery* kind of canteen, while the Cafeteria and LRC do cafe snacks. *Hardy fare, but hardly tantalising.*
Others: Big Summer all-night ball, plus Christmas Ball and Paddies Ball, organised for St Patrick's Day by the, *you guessed it,* Irish society, Harper Ireland.

SOCIAL & POLITICAL

HARPER ADAMS STUDENTS' UNION:

• 1 sabbatical
The 15-strong executive *gets on pretty well* with the University powers that be. Its *main* role is to look after welfare and provide ents to *distract from the rural plod*.

SU FACILITIES:

Bar/club/music venue; lounge bar; three canteens; two pool tables; meeting room; photocopier/fax/printing service; payphones; late-night minibus; TV lounge; general store; stationery shop; vending machines; bookshop; launderette.

CLUBS (NON-SPORTING):
See Clubs tables.

OTHER ORGANISATIONS:

Rag does the *usual* stuff to raise money for charidee.

RELIGIOUS:

• 4 chaplains (CofE, Methodist, RC)
Prayer room on campus. *Most Christian denominations have godstops in the local area. Everyone else will have a job on their hands.*

PAID WORK:

• Job bureau • Vacancies board • Paid work: hols 90%
Careers Service, intranet job postings and summer jobs bulletin board.

SPORTS

• Recent successes: rugby, hockey • BUSA Ranking: 48
A strong reputation, especially at rugby, where the college punches way above its weight. Everyone's encouraged to get involved in sport of some kind.

SPORTS FACILITIES:

Two football pitches; three rugby pitches; hockey pitch; cricket pitch; tennis courts; netball court; sports hall; swimming pool; croquet lawn; gym; new multigym; climbing wall; shooting ground. There's a golf course and driving range in the vicinity. The nearby mountains are great for climbing, hang gliding, *falling off* and so on. Gym membership costs £25 per semester.

SPORTING CLUBS:
See Clubs tables.

ACCOMMODATION

IN COLLEGE:

• Catered: 28% • Cost: £95 (32wks)
• Self-catering: 4% • Cost: £50 (32wks)
• First years living in: 95% • Insurance premium: £
Availability: Almost all the livers-in are 1st years, who are guaranteed accommodation. *Some of them live like lords and ladies of the manor* – en-suite facilities, cleaners and a laundry service (returning cleaned and ironed clothes to the door), and three meals a day. All halls are on campus and security is tight. There are a few self-catering rooms, with basic cooking facilities. One hall is all male and what was intended to be an all-female hall is currently a collection of single-sex floors.

Car parking: *This deep into the countryside, cars are useful.* There's parking for all students but a (free) permit is required.

EXTERNALLY:

• Ave rent: £55 • Living at home: 5%

Availability: Accommodation in Newport is *easy enough to find* and it caters for the *essentials – close to campus and clean.*

Housing help: A student adviser helps find housing. The office keeps a vacancy list and blacklist of unscrupulous landlords, helps out with safety checks etc.

WELFARE

SERVICES:

• Disabilities Officer • International Students' Officer • Late-night minibus
• College counsellors: 1 part • Crime rating: !!

Student wardens are available to help with personal problems, as are the part-time counsellor, personal tutors and student services staff.

Health: An on-campus NHS practice runs five days a week with a nurse available on Wednesdays. There's also a surgery in town.

Disabilities: The old building has *poor access*, although some of the accommodation is a *bit better* and more alterations are under way. *Good* dyslexia support.

FINANCE:

• Ave debt per year: £1,173

Fees: Courses include a sandwich year in which fees are £550.

• Access fund: £50,000 • Successful applications/yr: 122 • Ave payment: £500

Support: An *extensive* range of scholarships and bursaries for new students each year. Prizes are awarded by key employers to outstanding students. There are rugby scholarships available to students from the Republic of Ireland.

Hatfield Polytechnic

see University of Hertfordshire

Heriot-Watt University

Heriot-Watt University, Edinburgh, EH14 4AS
Tel: (0131) 449 5111 E-mail: enquiries@hw.ac.uk Website: www.hw.ac.uk
Heriot-Watt University Students' Association, Edinburgh, EH14 4AS
Tel: (0131) 451 5333 E-mail: HWUSA@hw.ac.uk Website: www.hwusa.org

GENERAL

For general information about Edinburh, see University of Edinburgh.

$6\frac{1}{2}$ miles from the ancient stones of Edinburgh University sit *the much less geriatric bricks* of Heriot-Watt University's Edinburgh Campus. 380 acres of parkland provide an *almost soporific* natural backdrop to what was once the site of an old mansion house and is now the wooded home of HWU, which has been expanding for the past 50 years – the campus was completed in 1992 – and merged with the Scottish College of Textiles, 37 miles away, along the way. The Edinburgh Conference Centre was developed by the University and more recently the School of Planning and Housing at Edinburgh College of Art became part of HW's School of the Built Environment. *It's not the most exciting place in the world, but the woodland and the artificial lake make for a pleasantly uneventful afternoon's wandering.*

Sex ratio (M:F): 61:39	**Founded: 1821**
Full-time u'grads: 4,905	**Part-time: 225**
Postgrads: 1,200	**Non-degree: 215**
Ave course: 4yrs	**Ethnic: 29%**
State:private school: 61:8	**Flunk rate: 18%**
Mature: 21%	**International: 26%**
Disabled: 96	**Local: 40%**

ATMOSPHERE:

The self-contained Edinburgh campus is a serene, relaxed, 9-to-5 kind of place and most students who live off campus don't hang around come tea-time, leaving the place a bit bleak, except for the lesser-spotted fresher who can be observed, flitting nervously through his (and the male is the dominant gender here) brick habitat. There's little contact with other local species except in Edinburgh, where students are such a common breed that trouble is rare.

SITES:

Scottish Borders Campus: (600 students – Textiles, Design and some Management) SBC (as it's abbreviated) is the campus formerly known as the Scottish College of Textiles. It's in the *small but attractive* town of Galashiels, 37 miles from the main campus at Edinburgh (a shuttle-bus runs between the two). *There's not a lot to do around here – especially since the outpost of the SA closes throughout the weekend but students can bus it to the Edinburgh campus to catch some top gigs.* Many students spend some of their time studying on both campuses.

Orkney Campus: (Marine and Environment-related courses) Situated in Stromness (the second largest town in the Orkney islands – *not that that says much*), the campus consists of The International Centre for Island Technology *where they concentrate a marine energy and the environment.*

EDINBURGH: see <u>University of Edinburgh</u>
• <u>City centre: $6\frac{1}{2}$ miles</u>

TRAVEL: see <u>University of Edinburgh</u>

Car: The Edinburgh campus is about a mile outside the A720 Edinburgh ring road, just off the A71 on its way out of the city. There are parking spaces on the campus.

Local: Buses run in and out of Edinburgh town centre from 5.30am till 4am. The N25 night service runs every hour from 12.15am to 4.15am and costs £2. Daytime service to the town cost £1.

University: There's a shuttle bus running to the Scottish Borders Campus and back again. It's free but places must be pre-booked.

Taxis: 20-min rides to Waverley Station are convenient, but prices climb to £13 at night.

Bicycles: *A bit far to the city centre, but the union canal and other cycle paths improve access to the town. Cycling is popular despite the hills.*

CAREER PROSPECTS:

• <u>Careers Service</u> • <u>No. of staff: 7 full</u> • <u>Unemployed after 6mths: 10%</u>

The Careers Advisory Service's calendar is *chock-full of* job fairs, recruitment programmes, CV clinics and talks. Short and long-term vacancies are posted in online and printed newsletters. There's also a *helpful* Alumni Mentoring Programme whereby graduates offer phone and e-mail advice to current students – *particularly useful for international students.*

FAMOUS ALUMNI:

Nigel Brockton (World Championship Speed Skier); Adam Crozier (CE, Royal Mail); Craig Joiner (rugby player); Archy Kirkwood MP (Lib Dem); Henry McLeish (former First Minister of Scotland); Martin O'Neill MP (Lab); Jim Telfer (Director, Rugby, Scottish Rugby Union plc); Irvine Welsh (Trainspotting author).

SPECIAL FEATURES:

The name Heriot-Watt has nothing to do with cow-invading TV vet James Heriott. James Watt (1736-1819) was one of the innovators of the Industrial Revolution with his work on steam engines. George Heriot (1563-1623), known as 'Jinglin' Geordie', was a jeweller and financier to James VI of Scotland (James I of England).

FURTHER INFO:

• Prospectuses: undergrad; postgrad; alternative • Open days
Fresh, the alternative prospectus, is a collaboration between students and staff. A brief prospectus is also available in Braille. A Scholar Programme that goes into high schools is intended to ease the transition between school and university. See www.hw.ac.uk/recruitment for more info.

A C A D E M I C

The courses on offer at Heriot-Watt broadly cover the interests of its two namesakes: science, industry, engineering and textiles. It has strong links with modern industry and has one of the UK's two specialised centres in actuarial maths and statistics. Logistics, Photonics and Petroleum Engineering are among its poster-subjects.

180-280			POINTS
Entry points: 180-280		Ave points: n/a	
Applns per place: 5		Clearing: 7%	
No. of terms: 3		Length of terms: 10wks	
Staff: student ratio: 1:14		Study addicts: 16%	
Teaching: ****		Research: ****	
Year abroad: 3%		Sandwich students: <1%	
Firsts: 12%		2.2s: 33%	
2.1s: 43%		3rds: 7%	

ADMISSIONS:

• Apply via UCAS
HWU has a policy of pulling in under-represented groups and broadening participation – especially when it comes to mature, local and disabled students.

SUBJECTS:

Built Environment: 14%	Management & Languages 24%
Engineering & Physical Sciences: 25%	Maths & Computer Sciences: 18%
Life Sciences: 9%	Textiles & Design: 8%

Best: Engineering & Computing; European Languages.
Unusual: Brewing & Distilling.

LIBRARIES:

• 156,500 books • 780 study places • Spend per student: ££££
There's a main library at the Edinburgh campus, where Irvine Welsh allegedly wrote most of Trainspotting. *Which can only be worrying.* There are also collections in some departments and at least one library at each of the other sites.

COMPUTERS:

• 460 workstations • 24-hr access

Most University residences have networked workstations with 24-hour access. Some buildings now have wireless laptop connection points. The Scott Russell Building has 48 PCs available all night; other computer centres on both campuses close comfortably before midnight.

OTHER LEARNING FACILITIES:

Language labs, a design lab and an audio/TV centre.

ENTERTAINMENT

THE CITY: see University of Edinburgh

UNIVERSITY:

• Price of a pint of beer: £1.30 • Glass of wine: £1.14

Bars: Three in the Union: Liberty's (a daytime snack-café that gets more alcoholic at night), Zero Degrees (more of a nightclub/event venue) and Jinglin' Geordies (*pubby* with a gaming area – pool, video games and juke box). An external company runs the bar in the conference centre.

Film: £5 a year gets the pleasure of viewing one *mainstream or cultish* film per week in Zero Degrees.

Clubbing/Music venues: Jam Fridays *(on Fridays, surprisingly) draws the biggest crowd into the cheese'n'chart-filled Zero Degrees* with its 80p spirit and mixer deals. Dancephobes can escape to the chillout room in Liberty's. Regular karaoke and live music events.

Comedy/Cabaret: The Hairy Watt Comedy Club at the Union showcases gagmeisters every fortnight (admission £3).

Food: The University Refectory dishes out three meals a day. All the bars provide food of some description. Jinglin' Geordies Tea Time Special has full meals from £1.50 and keeps the platters coming till midnight.

Other: Weekly pub quizzes and the odd ball.

SOCIAL & POLITICAL

HERIOT-WATT UNIVERSITY STUDENTS' ASSOCIATION:

• 4 sabbaticals • NUS member • Turnout at last ballot: 6%

Politics is generally a bigger turn-off for Heriot-Watt students than Chris Moyles in a tutu smeared in Marmite, but this was one of the first unions to campaign against top-up fees and admin charges on tuition fees and the fight is far from over. *As far as most are concerned, however, the Student Association is first and foremost a services organisation.*

SA FACILITIES:

The Association's building, named The Union, contains: three bars; disco; cafeteria; shop; travel agency; PA hire; welfare library; meeting rooms. The Scottish Borders Campus has a union building designed by SBC students.

CLUBS (NON-SPORTING):

Aussie Travellers; Brewing (biggest beer fest in Scotland); Bookworm; Celtic Supporters; Collectable Card Players; Clubbing; Distortion; Film; Freedom for Fish; Four-by-Four Club; French Students; German Theatre; Hong Kong Students; International Banking & Finance; Orkney; Parthenon Hellenic; Vegetarian; Venture Scouts. **See also Clubs tables**.

OTHER ORGANISATIONS:

Watts On is the free paper three times a term. No radio station but there's been some talk of getting one started, so watch this space (*or listen to it*).

RELIGIOUS:

• 1 chaplain (CofS)
The multi-faith chaplaincy has several honorary chaplains (CofE, RC, Methodist, Greek, Orthodox, Free Church of Scotland) and there's a Muslim prayer room.

PAID WORK: see University of Edinburgh

• Job bureau • Paid work: term-time 75%: hols 85%
Jobs on campus are posted by the University jobshop (an offshoot of the Careers Advisory Service).

S P O R T S

• Recent successes: rugby, tennis, hockey • BUSA Ranking: 48
With such large grounds, the University has provided some *excellent* sporting facilities *that have attracted a fair number of muscle-bound Olympians – not least two Canadian ice hockey players who get to go to University for free, so long as they keep chasing that puck.* The Sports Union co-ordinates all sports activities and remains entirely independent of the SA. Scholarships are available for badminton, golf and squash.

SPORTS FACILITIES:

The Edinburgh campus boasts the *impressive* National Squash Centre, but also has a number of large playing fields (five football, two rugby, one cricket), a floodlit training area, jogging track, three tennis courts, three sports halls, climbing wall, two multigyms, golf driving nets, weights and fitness rooms and indoor sports courts. Membership is spilt into Gold, Silver and Bronze tariffs (year, academic year and term), ranging from £18-60. A Sports Academy opened recently and includes pro-quality facilities and floodlit and indoor synthetic pitches. See also University of Edinburgh.

SPORTING CLUBS:

Aikido; Boat; Curling; Gaelic Football; Mountaineering; Rifle; Snowsports; Table Tennis. **See also Clubs tables.**

ATTRACTIONS: see University of Edinburgh

A C C O M M O D A T I O N

IN COLLEGE:

• Catered: 6% • Cost: £81 (33wks)
• Self-catering: 11% • Cost: £45-60 (39wks)
• First years living in: 60% • Insurance premium: ££
Availability: All 1st years get a room (*that's not a euphemism for getting frisky*), if they want one. All halls are on campus (1,800 beds) and consist of single study bedrooms with small shared kitchen in catered and bathroom (although many self-catered halls have en-suites). The University houses 240 students in a head tenancy scheme based in town centre flats. *There's not much to choose between halls. However the catered halls are older, do more unpleasant things with concrete and are beginning to look run-down.* Security patrols hunt down bogeymen at night.
Car parking: Free permits.

EXTERNALLY: see University of Edinburgh

• Ave rent: £55-70
Availability: Students tend to remain close to campus in areas like West Side, Slateford, Grogie and Morningside.
Housing help: The Accommodation Office has three staff providing a bulletin board and advice. *Many homeless students find the Student Pad website run by* University of Edinburgh *helpful.*

WELFARE

SERVICES:

- Lesbian/Gay/Bisexual Officer & Society • Mature Students' Officer & Society
- International Students' Officer & Society • Postgrad Officer & Society
- Disabilities Officer & Society • Self-defence classes • Taxi fund
- College counsellors: 1 full • SU counsellors: 3 full • Crime rating !

The SA Vice-President is responsible for student welfare on the Scottish Borders Campus.

Health: The main campus has a medical centre with four GPs, three nurses, a dentist and a physio.

Crèches/Nursery: The University nursery on the Edinburgh campus has full-day or part-day places (birth upwards).

Disabilities: *Access to some departments and buildings is just great and awareness is good, but considering how modern a campus this is, there have been some omissions.* The Union has been refurbished to improve access. There are 22 specially adapted rooms and there's a Special Needs Adviser.

FINANCE:

- Ave debt per year: £4,355

Fees: International undergrads pay £7,350–9,600, postgrads £3,200 (home) or up to £9,700 (int'l). Distance learning modules are available – costs vary.

- Access fund: £360,000 • Successful applications/yr: 569 • Ave payment: £400

Support: In addition to the access fund, several bursaries and scholarships can be plundered, including a fee waiver for part-timers, living support for students under 25 from low-income families, hardship loans, a hardship fund, sports scholarships and mature students bursary scheme (for married students over 25 who have been self-supporting for 3 years).

University of Hertfordshire

- ***Formerly Hatfield Polytechnic.***

(1) University of Hertfordshire, College Lane, Hatfield, Hertfordshire, AL10 9AB
Tel: (01707) 284 800 E-mail: admissions@herts.ac.uk Website: www.herts.ac.uk
University of Hertfordshire Students' Union, College Lane, Hatfield, Hertfordshire, AL10 9AB
Tel: (01707) 285 004 E-mail: ushu@herts.ac.uk Website: www.ushu.herts.ac.uk
(2) Faculty of Law, St Albans Campus, University of Hertfordshire, 7 Hatfield Road, St Albans, Hertfordshire, AL1 3RS

GENERAL

Barely 8 miles from the outskirts of London, Hatfield is the University of Hertfordshire's centre of operations. *Being a commuter town, it's a sleeping satellite and a fairly uninteresting one at that, although it's aware of its failings and has been attempting a makeover for some time now.* Hertfordshire is one of the *less trite* Home Counties with *sprinklings of pretty rural villages* and the *attractive* St Albans. *The main campus seems divorced from everything but the A1, which runs right along one edge.* It's a couple of miles away from the train station in Hatfield – and *in Hatfield, the station is the most appealing feature, at least until the town's revamp kicks in. The 30-year architectural history of uninspiring blocks that made up most of the campus is thankfully being phased out, with the brighter and more modern buildings of the new de Havilland campus leading the way into the future.*

Sex ratio (M:F): 45:55	**Founded: 1952**
Full-time u'grads: 13,465	**Part-time: 3,545**
Postgrads: 1,655	**Non-degree: 760**
Ave course: 3yrs	**Ethnic: 39%**
State:private school: 95:5	**Flunk rate: 16%**
Mature: 55%	**International: 19%**
Disabled: 281	**Local: 59%**

The fact that the immediate vicinity isn't the most socially happening slab of commuter-land hasn't dampened students' spirits. In fact, it galvanises them to build fun factories of their own. This doesn't, however, distract them from their main purpose in coming to Herts – the old 'choose university, choose degree, choose career' mantra. Town/gown relations aren't exactly hugs and bunnies, particularly when it comes to parking. There are, however, plans for a new car park at Angerland Common, so there's another 800 reasons to be cheerful on the way. Local youths have been a problem in the past, particularly towards the University's substantial Chinese population (probably because, living in Hatfield, they haven't got anything better to do). Insularity is an issue on campus too – locals and internationals tend to stick to their own kind rather than integrate and the significant part-time contingent coming and going scuppers any continuous sense of community. The SU are working on it and a number of community initiatives and Rag projects are oiling the joints somewhat.

SITES:

College Lane Campus: (All subjects not based at other sites) This 93-acre site is the main campus, but *the least attractive – it's the sort of place that will take over the world when the Orwellian nightmare begins. Sadly, a few colourful drainpipes don't do enough to redeem the overall aesthetic.*

Faculty of Law, St Albans: (1,100 students – Law) About 6 miles from Hatfield in the *pretty* Roman town of St Albans is the heart of the local legal community and the University's law faculty lives right in the middle of it. *It's a much pleasanter, more exciting town than Hatfield, which is why it's a bit of a drag there's no student accommodation on or near this site.*

De Havilland Campus: (Humanities & Education) Just a mile across Hatfield from College Lane perches the £120m phoenix that rose from the ashes of Watford and Hertford campuses. It's an *ultra-modern, glassy arrangement of* giant auditorium, giant learning resource centre (LRC), giant blocks of student accommodation and not-so-giant refectory that *somehow manages to look a bit flimsy.* There's no SU bar, so the University Bus Service *is a must* to get to College Lane for a beer, but there is the Sports and Social club for a quieter night close to home.

HATFIELD:

- Population: 97,600 • Town centre: 1 mile • London: 8 miles • St Albans: 5 miles
- High temp: 21 • Low temp: 1 • Rainfall: 49

Hatfield's essentially a springboard into London and has thus never really bothered to acquire much personality of its own. Having said that, there are some historical gems – Old Hatfield is the nice bit, home to Hatfield House, a *charming* Jacobean mansion where Queen Bessie I used to hang out. The newer bit of town is *nondescript, bordering on drab. Architectural magnificence or fun stuff have never been of much interest to the pharmaceutical and computing industries that Hatfield is at the centre of – useful for sandwich placements though. The massive Galleria shopping centre on the outskirts has distracted a few, but St Albans is far and away friendlier, prettier and more popular with students.*

TRAVEL:

Trains: Hatfield station is $1\frac{1}{2}$ miles from the main campus, useful for the direct service to London King's Cross to the south and Stevenage to the north. From these stations there are also direct services all the way to York, Newcastle and Edinburgh and connections to the rest of the country. Hertford station is about $\frac{1}{2}$ hour from London (£5.10).

Coaches: No National Express service to Hatfield. The nearest stops are London's Victoria Coach Station and Luton (12 miles away). London Country and Greenline buses run services to and from London.

Car: The A1(M) runs right by the campus. The A1000 passes through Hatfield, as does the A414 which also goes to Hertford. All sites are within 5 miles of the M25. The Galleria shopping centre has free parking, and there are pay & displays around College Lane (50p/day) – but there's no parking at all on the de Havilland site. The University has established a car-sharing policy.

Air: Luton Airport, offering international and inland flights, is 11 miles north-east.

Hitching: *The Home Counties as a rule aren't good for picking up lifts but the A1 is just about the best road to be on. Try the junction with the M25, 6 miles down the road.*

Local: *Buses aren't the cheapest in the country, but are useful for quick trips into Hatfield.* Also routes to St Albans, Stevenage, Watford and Welwyn Garden City.

College: The Universities Uno bus service does subsidised student fares.

Taxis: Numerous firms, *but prices rocket beyond any of the town boundaries.*

Bicycles: *A bike's a useful way of rolling around the campuses.*

CAREER PROSPECTS:

• Careers Service • No. of staff: 1 full/4 part • Unemployed after 6mths: 9%
The Careers Advisory Service provides vacancy newsletters, bulletin boards, a programme of talks, workshops, mock interviews and aptitude testing.

FAMOUS ALUMNI:

Sanjeev Bhaskar (Goodness Gracious Me, The Kumars); Ian Dowie (footballer); Helen Lederer (comedian); Lady Parkinson (wife of Cecil); Jayne Zito (mental health campaigner).

FURTHER INFO:

• Prospectuses: undergrad; postgrad; departmental; alternative • Open days • Video
There are three general open days annually, although mid-week campus tours occur throughout the year. There a specific open days for Art & Design and Nursing & Midwifery. See website for prospectuses and details.

ACADEMIC

Hertfordshire's six faculties have undergone rapid expansion in recent years *and the academic balloon ain't gonna stop inflating any time soon.* The University's also responsible for a number of students in the local college consortium: Hertford Regional, Oaklands, North Hertfordshire and West Herts colleges. Weekly lectures are backed up by weekly tutorials. *Forget any notion of cosy fireside chats over cherry brandy, however –* most tutorials contain 20-25 students. Most courses divide into four modules each term, assessment for some is 100% coursework-based. The *techno-savvy* StudyNet system allows online access to module materials, lecture notes, message boards and LRC resources.

140-340	POINTS	
Entry points: 140-340	Ave points: 220	
Applns per place: 4	Clearing: 15%	
No. of terms: 2	Length of terms: 15wks	
Staff/student ratio: 1:18	Study addicts: 18%	
Teaching: *	Research: **	
Firsts: 10%	2.2s: 41%	
2.1s: 37%	3rds: 12%	

ADMISSIONS:

• Apply via UCAS/NMAS for Nursing/GTTR for PGCE

Herts is beefing up its Equal Opps policy to encourage minority groups, including those with no formal qualifications. Mature Students and those working while studying can use the Credit & Accumulation Transfer Service (CATS), which allows students to choose their own pace of study. Application packs for Counselling courses available from (01707) 284 800.

SUBJECTS:

Art & Design: 7%
Business/Management: 12%
Consortium Colleges: 5%
Engineering & Information Sciences: 20%
Health & Human Sciences: 35%
Humanities, Languages & Education: 9%
Interdisciplinary Studies: 7%
Law: 5%

Best: Art & Design; Business & Management; Economics & Tourism; Education; Electrical & Electronic Engineering; General Engineering; Linguistics; Maths; Mechanical, Aero & Manufacturing Engineering; Molecular Biosciences; Nursing; Philosophy; Physics & Astronomy; Psychology.
Unusual: Paramedic Science.

LIBRARIES:

• 300,000 books • 2,940 study places • 24-hr access

The de Havilland and College Lane LRCs keep going through the night and cover all subjects except Law – the smaller library at St Albans is *stuffed with weighty* legal tomes. *Lawyers need their sleep apparently:* their library shuts at 10pm most nights.

COMPUTERS:

• 1,540 workstations • 24-hr access

Staffed computer rooms on all sites and magic laptop sockets for web access in the libraries. The 1,600-room halls of residence at de Havilland come complete with broadband access included in their rent. *Technophobes beware.*

OTHER LEARNING FACILITIES:

Language labs are annexed to the LRCs. There's also a CAD lab, music rehearsal rooms and a media centre. The practice courtroom at St Albans was donated to the University by Hatfield Magistrates Court. *Presumably they'd finished with it.*

ENTERTAINMENT

HATFIELD & ST ALBANS:

• Price of a pint of beer: £2.20 • Glass of wine: £1.90

The sheer nocturnal dullness of Hatfield has obliged many students to throw themselves wholeheartedly into the Union ents scene. Or in front of a train. Or onto a train bound for London. The pubs scene doesn't exactly embrace students open-armed so much as stare at them open-mouthed. Luckier lawyers enjoy St Albans, which is bigger, more cosmopolitan, and densely stuffed with pubs.

Cinemas: The nine-screen UCI in the Galleria complex has reduced student tickets (£4.50-5.50). Watford and Stevenage have similar celluloid centres.

Theatres: The Gordon Craig Theatre offers everything from films to tribute bands. And plays, obviously.

Pubs: *Mai Tai's (which changes its name with alarming frequency) in the Galleria is really the only place students bother with – probably because of the boozy deals on offer. The Philanthropist & Firkin may stretch punchy alliteration to its limits but it's good enough for the lawyers. Hatfield's The Cavendish and the aptly-named Harrier aren't exactly student-friendly.*

Clubbing: Batchwoods (chart, cheese, urban, dance) based in a converted manor in St Albans is gaining momentum thanks to the Pub2Club Thursday night deal with the Union. £3 gets entry, a drink, and return bus travel to and from funkytown.

Music venues: Knebworth and Wembley are a 30-min drive.

Eating out: The Galleria's many eateries include MacDonald's and other *plastic food* in plastic packs. Hatfield has a few restaurants (Indian, Italian, Greek and Chinese) and snack shops, such as burger bars, chippies and spud places. Celeb chef Jean-Christophe Novelli's lakeside restaurant Auberge du Lac is one for gourmets and those with bulging wallets.
St Albans, Hertford and Watford also have tasty but somewhat expensive eateries.

UNIVERSITY:
• <u>Price of a pint of beer: £1.80</u> • <u>Glass of wine: £2.50</u> • <u>Can of Red Bull: £2.75</u>
Bars: The biggest, *loudest, busiest* bar is the Font Bar on the main campus, with different entertainments and open doors till 1am every night. Hutton Hall bar's got live music events and the Elephant House bar is blessed with karaoke, film and sports nights.
Theatres: The new Auditorium at de Havilland seats 450 and shows both student and touring shows. The dedicated University Arts Programme is responsible for over 60 productions a year, including drama, dance, music and other cultural events.
Film: The Ele House shows a weekly mainstream film, £2.
Clubbing/Music venues: The Font Bar is the most popular venue, kicking off the Pub2Club event and holding the *thumping* Uni-t urban night. Nicky Snood, Adam F and Charlie Angel have all hit the decks. Guest crooners have included Big Brovaz, David Sneddon and former Take That member Mark *'not dead after all'* Owen.
Comedy/Cabaret: Fortnighly comedy at the Ele House. Chucklemeisters include Jarred Christmas, Gordon Southern, Nick Wilty.
Food: The Font Bar spoons out a mixture of *lovely junk* and Oriental goodies till midnight. Elephant House has all manner of speedy snacks on offer, which are usually cheaper than refectory food.
Other: The June Ball's held jointly with Luton University – *that's the official line anyway. Luton can't afford their own so have hijacked Hertfordshire's – it's a grand affair*, with live bands, casino, fairground rides, food court and gallons and gallons of fermented goodness.

S O C I A L   &   P O L I T I C A L

UNIVERSITY OF HERTFORDSHIRE STUDENTS' UNION:
• <u>5 sabbaticals</u> • <u>NUS member</u> • <u>Turnout at last ballot: 12%</u>
The Elephant House is the SU's own building, but it also has offices in the University's Hutton Block. *It's strictly a leave-your-politics-at-the-door affair,* and political societies are banned out of policy – *not that that's a bone of contention, many students are more interested in playing massive message board games of Mallett's Mallet than in following a cause.* The focus is on immediate issues (namely rent and parking), and *the exec do a pretty good job of representing student views to the powers above.* The SU elections tend to be highly contested, *although there's not much evidence of international student involvement.*

SU FACILITIES:
Bars; nightclub; two snack bars; canteen; two fast food outlets; two pool tables; meeting room; minibus hire; car for hire; Endsleigh Insurance office; Lloyd's and NatWest ATMs; general store; stationary shop; bookshop; travel agency; vending & gaming machines; fax & printing services; photocopiers; payphones; photo booth; advice centre; launderette.

CLUBS (NON-SPORTING):
Alternative Music; Chinese; Greek Cypriot; Hindu; Kenyan; Krishna Consciousness; Morpheus Project; Philosophy; Psifa; Sikh; St John Ambulance. **See also Clubs tables.**

OTHER ORGANISATIONS:
Newsletter University comes out five times a year, also online. Horizon, the University paper, is monthly. There's also Solar, a weekly e-mail newsletter mainly containing events listings. Radio station Crush is well over 20 years old and broadcasts online and around campus and bars till 1am. The Hertfordshire Rag *has been raking it in* (in the region of £10,000 a year) and is introducing a year-round calendar of charity stunts instead of its previous one-off Rag Week.

> The Birkbeck College was founded in 1823 by George Birkbeck who believed that workers should be entitled to an education. He was criticised by the London Mechanics' Institution, who accused him of 'scattering the seeds of evil'.

RELIGIOUS:

• **1 chaplain (multi-faith)**

On campus facilities for Muslim and Christian worship, including an ecumenical chaplaincy and a Muslim prayer room. Also Anglican, Catholic and Evangelical churches in Hatfield.

PAID WORK:

• Job bureau • Paid work: term-time 55%: hols 55%

Vacancy boards are posted and updated by the recruitment office. There are plenty of term-time and vacation pocket-lining opportunities at the Galleria complex and in local supermarkets. The Union has casual work available in bars and shops and an online vacancy notice board. The University Student Ambassador Scheme helps find casual local jobs.

SPORTS

• Recent successes: American football • BUSA Ranking: 48

Hertfordshire Sports Village has become one of the University's top selling points – *the standard of sporting success is still lagging behind the variety and quality of the facilities, but it's early days.* There are links with Saracens rugby, Watford football and Arsenal ladies football team.

SPORTS FACILITIES:

Hertfordshire Sports Village at de Havilland has an indoor cricket hall, eight-lane swimming pool, climbing and bouldering wall, 100-station fitness suite, 12 badminton courts, two floodlit Astroturf pitches and extra outdoor sports fields. Students get massive discounts on season passes or per session.

SPORTING CLUBS:

Aikido; American Football; Cheerleading; Exploration; Ju-Jitsu; Kickboxing; Rowing; Wu Shu Kwan. **See also Clubs tables**.

ATTRACTIONS:

Hatfield Town FC's nearby. Milton Keynes now has Wimbledon FC and the Snowdome.

ACCOMMODATION

IN COLLEGE:

• Self-catering: 21% • Cost: £49-80 (32wks)
• First years living in: 94% • Insurance premium: £

Availability: 1st years are guaranteed accommodation if application deadlines are met but few others get a look-in. The de Havilland campus has 1,600 *luxury* rooms – with en-suite and broadband – and is *popular as a result*, despite being in the most expensive price band. Accommodation takes the form of clustered flats, *so there's a sense of community. The halls on the far edge of College Lane are a bit on the dreary side but affordability makes them popular regardless.* Mixed sex couples are *easily* housed, single sex accommodation is also available. There's no catered accommodation, *and the kitchens can have up to 11 students trying to microwave lasagne simultaneously.* There are plans to add another 1,400 *high quality* rooms at some point in the future.
Car parking: Free permits are up for grabs at College Lane and St Albans. De Havilland is strictly car-free.

EXTERNALLY:

• Ave rent: £65

Availability: Since the closure of the Watford and Hertford campuses, the number of students trying to find external housing in Hatfield at the same time has caused problems. The January house-hunt is *competitive*, with losers forced out of the town centre and into suburbs or nearby villages. The University's head tenancy scheme and 'digs' arrangements with local families help, *but not enough to keep everyone happy*. Hazel Grove is close to College Lane *and is therefore the most convenient place to be for many students. Fat chance of finding a place to live there, though*.

Housing help: The Accommodation Office run the head tenancy scheme and offer advice. The Union-run advice service posts vacancies *and is handy for finding hassle-free accommodation that is actually habitable. By humans.*

WELFARE

SERVICES:

- Lesbian/Gay/Bisexual Officer & Society • Mature Students' Officer
- International Students' Officer & Society • Postgrad Society • Disabilities Officer & Society
- Nightline • College counsellors: 10 full • Crime rating: !!

Health: On-campus NHS practice with GPs and nurses.

Crèches/Nursery: The campus nursery has places for children up to 5yrs.

Disabilities: Despite some steep slopes between buildings the Hatfield campus has *comparatively excellent access* and special accommodation provisions including rooms for carers. Also various amenities for hearing- and sight-impaired students. Many lecture theatres have hearing loops, all main switchboards are equipped with minicoms and *there's good support for dyslexics* in conjunction with the local Access Centres.

Crime: Campus crime is low – partly thanks to a University Watch scheme run jointly with the police and Unisecure. Off-campus there've been spates of burglary (made more painful by a lack of contents insurance in some cases). A few idiotic local youths have caused problems for students in the past, with racially motivated crime *not unheard of*. The University liaises with police to deal with this kind of *small-town bigotry* – the appointment of a community Liaison Officer should help matters.

Drugs: The Union operates a zero tolerance policy and there's often random sniffer dog testing at venue entrances. *Needless to say, drug abuse is not common as a consequence.*

FINANCE:

- Ave debt per year: £4,970

Fees: Postgrads pay *a relatively gentle* £2,870 tuition. Internationals shell out £7,600.
- Access fund: £727,393 • Successful applications/yr: 1,974 • Ave payment: £500

Support: Engineering and some Science students with over 280 UCS points can bag £3,000 scholarships.

Heythrop College, University of London

- **The College is part of the University of London and students are entitled to use its facilities.**

Heythrop College, University of London, Kensington Square, London, W8 5HQ
Tel: (020) 7795 6600 E-mail: enquiries@heythrop.ac.uk Website: www.heythrop.ac.uk
Heythrop College Students Union, Kensington Square, London, W8 5HQ
Tel: (020) 7795 4255 E-mail: hsupresident@heythrop.ac.uk

Right next door to Kensington Tube is one of London's smallest and oldest institutions. Over the centuries Heythrop has been on an international pilgrimage, starting off in Louvain, Belgium, in 1614, pausing for breath at Liège, and moving on through Stonyhurst, North Wales and Oxford before landing in this *appealing* little Victorian campus in the *poshest part* of London. Originally a breeding-ground for Jesuit priests (*if they're allowed to breed, that is*) it offers courses in philosophy and theology. It's still a Catholic institution though – *this is not the place to look for Shaolin kung fu monks, devil worshippers or Ian Paisley. The charmingly eccentric campus shares its space with a number of other institutions, including an American college and an assortment of religious groups, all of which add different flavours to the social stew pot.*

Sex ratio (M:F): 40:60	**Founded: 1614**
Full-time u'grads: 184	**Part-time: 350**
Postgrads: 438	**Non-degree: 17**
Ave course: 3yrs	**Ethnic: n/a**
State:private school: 80:20	**Flunk rate: 17%**
Mature: 20%	**International: 6%**
Disabled: 1%	**Local: 15%**

ATMOSPHERE:

Kensington High Street may be frighteningly busy and jammed with braying trustafarians, bemused tourists looking for Harrods and largely ignored Big Issue sellers, but the air surrounding Heythrop College couldn't be more tranquil if you filled it with cannabis fumes. Many students and staff are members of religious orders or wannabes, which gives it a very close-knit, cosy feel with no 'them & us' divide between the two (lots of matures help). Many students fall in love with the Escher-esque curio of a campus and the atmosphere of quiet reflection at first sight. Others find the aura of reverence and deathly hush of the common room suffocating. There are a fair few more lively attractions in the locale though, including a number of snug old pubs, achingly trendy bars and the Royal Court Theatre. Kensington Palace, Britain's loveliest council flat, is nearby too.

LONDON: see University of London

TRAVEL: see University of London
Local:
Trains: Kensington Olympia is the nearest mainline station.
Buses: 9, 10, 27, 28, 31, 49, 52 are the lucky numbers for this bus route lottery.
Underground: High Street Kensington tube is next-door.
Bicycles: Kensington's generally quite flat and bike-able, and many Heythropians find it the best way to get around.

CAREER PROSPECTS:

• Careers Service • Unemployed after 6mths: 8%
See University of London

FAMOUS ALUMNI:

Frederick Copleston (philosopher); Gerard Manley Hopkins (poet); Nick Stuart (TV presenter).

FURTHER INFO:

• Prospectuses: undergrad, postgrad, departmental • Open days • Video

ACADEMIC

The sheer diddiness means small class sizes, with one-to-one tutorials for undergrads, but a fair share of more conventional lectures and seminars are thrown in. There are two schools, one for each discipline. Two terms are 12 weeks long, the other a mere six.

Entry points: 240-260	Ave points: 250
Applns per place: n/a	Clearing: 8%
No. of terms: 3	Length of terms: 12/6 wks
Staff/student ratio: 1:20	Study addicts: 5%
Teaching: *****	Research: n/a
Sandwich students: 0	Year abroad: 0
Firsts: 6%	2.2s: 40%
2.1s: 42%	3rds: 12%

ADMISSIONS:

• Apply via UCAS

SUBJECTS:

Arts/Humanities: 100%
Best: Philosophy, Theology.
Unusual: Philosophy, Religion & Ethics.

LIBRARIES:

• 250,000 books • 60 study places
Heythrop keeps one of the largest specialist philosophy libraries *in the known universe. No Danielle Steele, then?*

COMPUTERS:

• No. of workstations 20
The main library has networked 'puters – an odd juxtaposition with 500-year-old manuscripts. There's also campus-wide wireless.

ENTERTAINMENT

LONDON: see University of London

UNIVERSITY:

With very few entertainment facilities on campus, most venture into Kensington to find the fun.
Theatres: *There's a fully teched-up stage space that doesn't get much use.*
Film: *Free sporadic screenings of big budget chart-toppers.*
Food: The Maria Assumpta Canteen doles out cheap nosh till 7pm.
Other: Two black-tie balls a year, including the Summer Ball at the *uber-posh.* Institute of Directors on Pall Mall.

SOCIAL & POLITICAL

HEYTHROP STUDENTS UNION:

• Turnout at last ballot: 37% • NUS member
There's very little to argue about in Heythrop, so the SU isn't the most political pea in the pod, mainly focusing on the events calendar. Positions are available on the College governing body and various committees for some subjects.

SU FACILITIES:

Pool table; meeting room; photocopier; stationery shop; new and secondhand bookshops; table football; DVD player; widescreen TV and personal lockers (£5/yr). College-run TV lounge; snack bar; cafeteria; payphones; advice centre; vending machines also available.

CLUBS (NON-SPORTING):

Chapel Singers; Salsa; Liturgy; Justice & Peace. **See also Clubs tables.**

OTHER ORGANISATIONS:

Heythrop Rag bagged nearly £3,500 last year – more than King's, *to the rather ungodly delight of the Union. The highlight of the frolics was an attempt to break the record for world's largest three-legged pub-crawl. Ambitious for an institution with fewer than 200 undergrads and no bar.*

RELIGIOUS:

• 2 chaplains (RC, Baptist)

Heythrop's *Jesuit past doesn't have the stranglehold on faith that it once did. The college makes provisions for a variety of religious beliefs (or non-beliefs), although Christianity is still big daddy.* Mass is celebrated daily in the chapel and there's a college-wide mass (or *extended lunch break*) on Thursdays. A Muslim prayer room is available.

PAID WORK: see University of London

• Paid work: term-time 50%: hols 80%

Kensington High Street has plenty of shops, bars and restaurants *for gruntwork.*

• Recent successes: none

SPORTS FACILITIES:

One all-weather, all-purpose pitch – *though finding anything resembling a ball might be tricky.* The football team kicks around the London intercollegiate league *but students' minds are generally on more spiritual goals.*

SPORTING CLUBS:

See Clubs tables.

ATTRACTIONS: see University of London

Chelsea, Fulham and QPR football grounds are close by.

IN COLLEGE:

• Catered: 10% • Cost: £100 (30 wks) • Self-catered: 16% • Cost: £100
• First years living in: 100% • Insurance premium: £££

Availability: Also access to the UoL Intercollegiate halls as required. *Kitchens in the catered halls are utility-laden.* The Maria Assumpta Halls are women-only.

Car parking: Few spaces on campus (by arrangement with the College) *but cars aren't popular anyway.*

EXTERNALLY: see University of London

• Ave rent: £100

Availability: *Living conditions are rarely anything but plush in Kensington. House-rents are rarely anything but satanic.*

Housing help: see University of London

WELFARE

SERVICES:

• Welfare Officer • Nightline • College counsellors: 1 full-time • Crime rating: !!!
One of the chaplains is a trained counsellor. The Equality & Welfare Officer holds responsibility for the mixed bag of international, disabled and women students.
Health: UoL's health service is on Gower Street.
Disabilities: Chair-lifts, stair-lifts and ramps have been fitted where possible, but *the staircrazy college buildings make access damned difficult.* Signings in lectures have been arranged in the past and UoL offers dyslexia support.
Crime: *Not generally a Christian pastime. Kensington is about as safe as large, expensive, security-conscious houses.*

FINANCE:

• Ave debt per year: £3,681 • Home student fees: £3,265
Fees: Home student fees for undergrads are almost three times the average, *probably because the college is more excited about postgraduate study,* for which students pay a *relatively gentle £2,905.*
Support: Limited access fund and a few small bursaries.

Holloway

see Royal Holloway, University of London

Hope University

see Liverpool Hope University College

University of Huddersfield

• *Formerly Huddersfield Polytechnic.*
University of Huddersfield, Queensgate, Huddersfield, HD1 3DH
Tel: (01484) 422 288 E-mail: prospectus@hud.ac.uk Website: www.hud.ac.uk
Huddersfield University Union, University of Huddersfield, Queensgate, Huddersfield, HD1 3DH
Tel: (01484) 538 156 E-mail: president@hud.ac.uk Website: www.huddersfieldstudent.com

GENERAL

First-time visitors are forgiven a double take. If the area around Huddersfield looks strangely familiar it's because it provided the setting for Last of the Summer Wine and more recently The League of Gentlemen. Huddersfield's just east of the Pennines in the middle of northern England, not too far from Leeds and Manchester. Millions of quids of recent development into campus buildings have been like much-needed botox shots.

Sex ratio (M:F): 43:57	Founded: 1992
Full-time u'grads: 9,600	Part-time: 5,150
Postgrads: 1,030	Non-degree: 468
Ave course: 3-4yrs	Ethnic: 18%
State:private school: 97:3	Flunk rate: 21%
Mature: 55%	International: 8%
Disabled: 113	Local: 45%

ATMOSPHERE:

There's a bluff heartiness to both town and gown – welcoming and friendly without any nancying around. It's a multicultural society with a 'work hard, play hard' attitude. The University powers that be are still gloating about having enticed new Chancellor and local luvvie Patrick 'Make it so' Stewart to the helm.

HUDDERSFIELD:

• Population: 388,900 • City centre: 0 miles • London: 174 miles • Leeds: 14 miles • Manchester: 23 miles • High temp: 19 • Low temp: 1 • Rainfall: 73

Recent years have brought *much-needed* regeneration to the town, which was *badly hit* by recession and the swift demise of native manufacturing. Now there's a *whopping great* shopping centre, a *glut* of trendy bars and a *few more jobs* to go around. *Someone forgot to turn on the bright lights though,* so fun-seekers tend to hop on the train to Leeds or Manchester.

TRAVEL:

Trains: The station is 10 mins walk from campus. Services go direct to Leeds (£2.80) and Manchester (5.80) several times an hour. London trains (£29.60) are via Wakefield.
Coaches: National Express to London (£16.75), Birmingham (£13.75) and elsewhere.
Car: A few minutes from the M62 via the A62, A642, A629 and A616.
Air: Manchester airport for low-cost national airlines.
Hitching: *A62 or a short hop on a bus to Junction 24 of the M62.*
College: There is a *regular* shuttle bus service to Storthes Hall Park student village.
Taxis: *Taxis are plentiful and plenty cheap.*
Bicycles: Only *a true glutton for punishment* would take on Huddersfield's hills.

CAREER PROSPECTS:

• Careers Service • No. of staff: 9 full/3 part • Unemployed after 6mths: 10%

FAMOUS ALUMNI:

Gordon Kaye (Rene in 'Allo 'Allo); Wilf Lunn (eccentric inventor); George Buckley (CEO of the $60bn Brunswick corporation).

FURTHER INFO:

• Prospectuses: undergrad; postgrad; some departments • Open days
A CD-Rom is available. More info online.

ACADEMIC

Sandwich courses are Huddersfield's thing, and the vocational edge they give to the courses *helps keep the grad employment rate up.* The University's *worked hard at getting tight* with local industry and health service providers. The business incubator programme hatches an *admirable* number of young entrepreneurs every year.

Entry points: 260-300	Clearing: 20%
No. of terms: 3	Length of terms: 12wks
Staff/student ratio: 1:19	Study addicts: 17%
Teaching: **	Research: **
Sandwich students: 20%	

ADMISSIONS:

• Apply via UCAS/NMAS for nursing

SUBJECTS:

Art & Design: 9%   Computing & Engineering: 13%
Arts/Humanities: 9%   Education & Professional Development: 17%
Business: 18% Sciences: 9%   Human & Health Sciences: 25%

Best: Art Design & Materials Technology; Education; Electrical & Electronic Engineering; Food Science; Hospitality Management & Transport and Logistics; Maths; Medicine-related subjects; Molecular Biosciences & Organismal Biologies; Nursing; Psychology & Sociology; Politics; Statistics & Operational Research.
Unusual: Computer Games Programming; Podiatry (walking and corrective walking studies); Smart Design (architecture).

LIBRARIES:

• 400,000 books • 996 study places • 24-hr access • Spend per student: £££
The library runs a delivery system for part-timers.

COMPUTERS:

• 1,622 workstations • 24-hr access • Spend per student: £££
Resources include electronic journals and audio-visual study aids. Broadband connections in all halls.

OTHER LEARNING FACILITIES:

Part of the old SU facility has been *magically transformed* into drama studios, where Chancellor Patrick Stewart plies his trade leading theatrical workshops. There are also media studios at the town centre Queensgate campus.

ENTERTAINMENT

THE TOWN:

Huddersfield is racing with (and lagging behind) neighbouring Leeds when it comes to trendying up. The social culture is more pubby than clubby, but sexy new independent shops, bars and cafés are adding to the urban hum.
• Price of a pint of beer: £2 • Glass of wine: £2 • Can of Red Bull: £1.50
Cinemas: The UCI 12-screen multiplex is 10 mins bus ride from college.
Theatres: The Lawrence Batley Theatre for mainstream productions and musicals.
Pubs: *Real ale country*, though traditional pubs now rub shoulders with *ubiquitous* chain bars. Most pubs are student-friendly. *Pushplugs: Revolution; Vox; College Arms; Zephyr.*
Clubbing: *Howlingly awful club scene requires swallowing pride along with a few stiff drinks. Heavy-hearted Pushplugs: Heaven and Hell (Monday night is student night); Camel Club (two student nights a week); Session.*
Music venues: Zephyr runs a *half-decent* indie acoustic night.
Eating out: *Varied and cheap. Pushplugs: Mensahib (Indian); Shamus O'Donnell's (pub-grub); Blue Rooms (veggie).*

UNIVERSITY:

• Price of a pint of beer: £1.50 • Glass of wine: £1.50 • Can of Red Bull: £1.10
Bars: Bar action is dominated by the new SU building, which has social facilities for boozers and non-boozers alike.
Film: The film society shows a couple a week.
Music venues: *The new Union development has made room for a 600-capacity gig den.*
Comedy/Cabaret: The SU are members of the Paramount comedy network and have hosted visitors like Daniel Kitson.
Food: *Loads* of places to graze, mainly *cheap and cheerful* coffee shops and canteens.

SOCIAL & POLITICAL

UNIVERSITY OF HUDDERSFIELD STUDENTS' UNION:

• 5 sabbaticals • Turnout at last ballot: 6% • NUS member
UHSU aren't the most active of student bodies and though they put the effort into welfare, they border on the apolitical. 2005 saw a new Union facility enter the world, with bars and facilities for live music and comedy gigs.

SU FACILITIES:

Bars and coffee bars; social areas; cafeteria; music/comedy venue; printing service; general shop; photocopying; pool room; games and vending machines; juke box; function rooms.

CLUBS (NON-SPORTING):

Boardriding (surfing, snowboarding, skating); Chess; Caving; Climbing Gaming (roleplay/wargames); Juggling; Medieval Re-enactment; Outdoor Pursuits (outward bound); Scat Man John (tribute to *motormouth singer 'popular'* in the early 90s); Sikh. **See also Clubs tables.**

OTHER ORGANISATIONS:

Budding hacks at the Huddersfield Student have scooped 'Best on a Small Budget' Guardian award. Ultra FM broadcasts for one month a term within 5 miles of Milton Hall. The SU has a dedicated sabbatical officer to raise money for good causes.

RELIGIOUS:

• 3 chaplains (RC, CofE, FC)
The interdenominational chaplaincy and Muslim prayer room are bonuses in a town *well-provided* for most faiths.

PAID WORK:

• Job bureau • Paid work: term-time 69%; hols 87%
The job shop helps local businesses find student employees. The University also employs 400 students during vacations.

SPORTS

• BUSA Ranking: 48
The *town is better kitted out than the University* for sporting satisfaction and success. A Kirklees Passport (£6/year) gives discounted rates at local facilities.

SPORTS FACILITIES:

15 acres of playing fields 2 miles from campus; sports hall; athletics field; Astroturf pitch; squash courts; multigym; fitness gym. The town doubles up on all of these and also has a croquet lawn, bowling green, running track, swimming pool, golf courses, tennis courts, saunas and an all-weather pitch. There's a lake, river and hills nearby.

SPORTING CLUBS:

Boxing; Gaelic Football. **See also Clubs tables.**

ATTRACTIONS:

Galpharm Stadium is home to Huddersfield FC and their *more successful* rugby league counterparts, the Huddersfield Giants (who are sponsored by the University, doncha know).

IN COLLEGE:

• <u>Self-catering: 15%</u> • <u>Cost: £68 (41/42wks)</u>
• <u>First years living in: 90%</u> • <u>Insurance premium: £££££</u>
Availability: The University has deals with various private halls (run by Digs – see www.campusdigs.com) including Storthes Hall (4 miles from campus, with shuttle bus, minimarket, café, DVD library, TV lounge, launderette, gym and bars) and Ashenhurst (less than a mile away but at the top of a *near-vertical* hill). There's also Snow Island (*on the doorstep and plush enough*). Applicants with Huddersfield as their 1st choice are guaranteed accommodation (dependent on deadlines and deposits, *yadi yada yada*).
Parking: Free parking at Ashenhurst.

EXTERNALLY:

• Ave rent: £45
Availability: There's *no shortage* of digs and the *quality increases further out*. Bradford Road, Springrove, Newsome, Birkby and Lockwood are all good. Sheepridge, Deighton and Fartown are a bit rough and maybe worth avoiding.
Housing help: The Accommodation Office is on call to allocate halls and help liver-outers find a roof to go over their heads.

SERVICES:

• <u>Lesbian/Gay/Bisexual Society</u> • <u>Women's Officer</u> • <u>International Students' Society</u>
• <u>Postgrad Society</u> • <u>Late-night minibus</u> • <u>Nightline</u> • <u>Taxi fund</u>
• <u>College counsellors: 6 full/1 part</u> • <u>SU counsellors: 3 full/1 part</u> • <u>Crime rating: !!!</u>
The University Advice centre is *well-run, efficient and helpful*.
Health: On-campus NHS practice has 20 staff including three GPs.
Crèches/Nursery: 24 places for children aged 6wks-5yrs.
Disabilities: Access problems are being tackled in older buildings. Hearing loops, note-takers and specialist help for dyslexics are available. There are adapted rooms in Storthes Hall.
Drugs: The University has a zero tolerance approach to drugs.

FINANCE:

• <u>Ave debt per year: £4,175</u> • <u>Access fund: £799,000</u>
• <u>Successful applications/yr: 505</u> • <u>Ave payment: £1,582</u>
Support: Local student bursaries for West Yorkshire students who are the first in their family to go to university. Some individual course bursaries.

Huddersfield Polytechnic

see <u>University of Huddersfield</u>

University of Hull

University of Hull, Hull, HU6 7RX
Tel: (0870) 126 2000 E-mail: admissions@hull.ac.uk Website: www.hull.ac.uk
Hull University Union, University House, Cottingham Road, Hull, HU6 7RX
Tel: (01482) 445 361 E-mail: hullstudent@union.hull.ac.uk Website: www.hullstudent.com
Scarborough Campus, Filey Road, Scarborough, YO11 3AZ
Hull University Union – Scarborough Campus, Filey Road, Scarborough, YO11 3AZ
Tel: (01723) 367 258

GENERAL

'There are only three universities in Britain,' brayed Blackadder's General Melchett, 'Oxford, Cambridge and Hull. And Oxford's a complete dump!' Hull (full title Kingston upon Hull) has long been the butt of rather unkind jokes, *associated with turd-coloured Ford Cortinas and was recently voted Britain's Crappest Town.* In reality, the less industrialised bits of this north-eastern city are rather *pretty* and the nearby coastline is *stunning.* The campus is *large, leafy, low-lying and modern-ish* (mostly built within the last 80 years). It's *spoiled* only by some *ugly* 60s architecture. It's a couple of miles from the town centre and since 2001 has incorporated University College Scarborough, though *beware* – this is 40 miles from the main site.

Sex ratio (M:F): 40:60	**Founded: 1927**
Full-time u'grads: 9,615	**Part-time: 8,110**
Postgrads: 1,775	**Non-degree: 4,700**
Ave course: 3yrs	**Ethnic: 13%**
State:private school: 93:7	**Flunk rate: 13%**
Mature: 52%	**International: 21%**
Disabled: 362	**Local: 56%**

ATMOSPHERE:

Hull is a classic civic campus: integrated with the town, but far enough removed to provide a haven of dirt-cheap beer, student accomodation and even learning. The town, by turn, provides a pleasant escape should campus life begin to stifle. It punches above its weight in the nightlife stakes, although cynics might suggest that's no great achievement. Overall, Hull lacks a certain je ne sais quoi. Perhaps it's joie de vivre.

SITES:

Scarborough Campus: (1,400 students – Creative Music, Technology, Drama & Dance, Coastal/Marine Sciences) Scarborough campus is, perhaps not surprisingly, in Scarborough, 40 miles from Hull. The town has the *bare essentials* – a few shops and pubs, but the nearest *shiny lights* can be found in York. *Scarborough has a great reputation for its creative technology subjects.* Scarborough students are *fiercely protective of their own campus,* although it doesn't offer any*thing like the souped-up student microcosm* to be found in Hull.

HULL:

• Population: 243,400 • City centre: 2 miles • London: 165 miles • York: 34 miles
• Leeds: 50 miles • High temp: 21 • Low temp: 1 • Rainfall: 54

Hull was built on fish and is now driven by large-scale industries, particularly chemical manufacture. *Neither are particularly fancy-dan trades* and the town's boasts of having its own telephone system, suspension bridge and record-sized submarium *are unlikely to set student hearts a-flutter.* The *glamourless* reputation puts off the tourists, but Hull is *perfectly adequate* for the essentials of daily life. Shops, banks, bookshops, art galleries and so forth are all present *and correct* and, for the town's size, there's a *decent* range of drinking dens. Hull employs a *large* number of students and this eases relations between town and gown, *although Saturday-night boozing often stirs things up again.*

TRAVEL:

Trains: Newcastle costs a *hefty* £28, London £38.30 and Birmingham £24.40 as standard returns with a young person's railcard.
Coaches: Clipper and National Express services all over the country including London (£22.50), Birmingham (£17.75) and Newcastle (£16.75).
Car: From the south the M18 connects the M1 with the local Hull motorway, the M62. From the north, take the M1 then M62 which leads into the A63, then look out for the A1079.
Air: Humberside Airport, 12 miles south across the Humber is mainly for inland flights, although it has some to Europe.
Hitching: *There's a semi-official hitch pitch on the A63 that all traffic has to pass.*
Local: There are two *fiercely competitive* bus companies running until midnight-ish.
Taxis: *Sharing taxis is often cheaper than catching a bus or train.*
Bicycles: Hull is very flat with straight wide roads and cycle lanes between the residential and functional parts of the University. *Buy a bike lock – theft is rife.*

CAREER PROSPECTS:

• Careers Service • No. of staff: 2 full/4 part • Unemployed after 6mths: 6%

FAMOUS ALUMNI:

Lord Dearing (of Dearing Report fame); Sarah Greene (TV ex-sex goddess and Mrs Mike Smith); Jonathan Harvey (playwright); Lord Hattersley; Philip Larkin (poet); John McCarthy (former hostage) & Jill Morrell (his campaigning ex-partner); Roger McGough (poet); Anthony Minghella ('English Patient' director); Juliet Morris, Jenni Murray (broadcasters); Sinead O'Quinn (pop 'star'); Tom Paulin (TV arts critic); John Prescott MP (Lab); Michael Stock (S****, Aitken & Waterman); Ben Watt & Tracey Thorn (Everything But The Girl).

FURTHER INFO:

• Prospectuses: undergrad; postgrad; all depts • Open days • Video
DVD/CD-ROM for prospective students.

ACADEMIC

The University has a *good reputation* for the sciences, particularly chemistry, and is *well supported* by local industry. Both sites are good for drama and the digital arts. Teaching centres around seminars (compulsory) and lectures (optional, but *useful*) and the workload on most courses is *about average.* The University is doing *its best to embrace the new millennium* and invests in modern learning methods, while the medical school pools resources with York.

Entry points: 20-340
Applns per place: 4
No. of terms: 2
Teaching: **
Staff/student ratio: 1:15
Firsts: 7%
2.1s: 48%

Ave points: 253
Clearing: 20%
Length of terms: 15 wks
Research: **
2.2s: 35%
3rds: 3%

ADMISSIONS:

• Apply via UCAS
Local students can apply for University bursaries *but with only 40 to go around it's pretty competitive.*

SUBJECTS:

Arts/Humanities: 9.6%
Business/Management: 15.2%
Computer Science: 4.7%
Drama & Music: 4%
Faculty of Arts & Social Science: 41.8%

Law: 6%
(Modern) Languages: 10%
Nursing: 13.1%
Psychology: 5.3%
Sciences: 29.8%

LIBRARIES:

• 1,031,000 books • 1,500 study places • Spend per student: £££
A large collection of books *is all well and good, but Hull really trumps its rivals in the staring out-of-the-window department.* The view from the Brynmor Jones library over the Humber estuary is *awesome.* This is where Phillip Larkin was a librarian (and, supposedly, masturbated in his office). It's *pretty up-to-speed* in terms of technology and opens till 10pm on weekdays. It also offers a free bus service to the British Library. *Assignment-shirkers beware.*

COMPUTERS:

• 1,120 workstations • 24-hr access • Spend per student: £
Brynmor Jones is well kitted out with 24-hr access, Bluetooth wireless access and computers on every floor.

OTHER LEARNING FACILITIES:

A 21st-century playground with CAD-labs, language labs, music rehearsal rooms and a drama studio.

E N T E R T A I N M E N T

HULL:

• Price of a pint of beer: £1.80 • Glass of wine: £2 • Can of Red Bull: £2
Hull *conforms precisely to the stereotype* of a port town: awash with pubs, *many with dubious nautical themes, if not genuine 17th-century salty sea-dogs. There's a good range and most are student-friendly. Enough to provide relief from campus life when required.*
Cinemas: All multi-screen, two offering student discounts.
Theatres: *The more highbrow is the* New Theatre for *posh* plays, opera and ballet. Spring Street Theatre is a rep base, the home of the *excellent* Hull Truck Theatre company and also hosts cabaret nights.
Pubs: *Watch out for those with* stuffed fish on the walls and glass balls in nets and you won't go far wrong. *Pushplugs:* Gardener's Arms (definitely a student haven); Haworth Arms (sponsors sports teams); Canon Junction; the Piper. The Bev Road Run, a 12-pub crawl, is *a good bet for the hollow-legged. Stay away from the* Tiger in Cottingham *on pain of … well, pain.*

There are rumours of mysterious tunnels and chambers under Glamorgan University.

Clubbing: Currently in vogue are Pozition, V-Bar (cheese) and Spiders (goth). *There's little to satisfy the diehard clubber though.*

Music venues: *A decent indie scene and Hull City FC's shiny new KC stadium hosts the occasional megastar, although that may mean Elton John. Pushplugs: the Room, the Adelphi (small-scale gigs); City Hall, Tower Ballroom (bigger draws); Hull Arena.*

Eating out: *Hull's well-provisioned, if lacking late-night grease spots. The eaterie of choice is Mimosa (Turkish, good atmosphere, nicely priced). Push also plugs: Mason's Café and Wine Bar (bistro); Hitchcock (veggie); Zoo Café (hippy); Old Grey Mare (good value pub grub).*

UNIVERSITY:

• Price of a pint of beer: £1.65 • Glass of wine: £1.50 • Can of Red Bull: £1.50
Students are spoilt with a *large and varied* range of bars and even a purpose-built and *pretty successful* club.

Bars: Something for everyone here – from the *busy* Reskinov bar, with pool and games, to the *slightly misleadingly-titled* Continental, which is *more relaxed and suited to those with the taste for a slower pace.* A massive bar is due to open at the end of 2005.

Theatres: The chest-pounding, board-treadingly popular student drama scene, which puts on over 100 plays a year and sends numerous starry-eyed thesps off to Edinburgh every summer.

Film: Two film societies regularly show cult films.

Music venues: Asylum features mainstream acts like Girls Aloud and Lemar.

Clubbing: Asylum is a *well-named, tailor-made social hub of a superclub*, which can cram in 1,200 sweaty revellers, occasionally to the beats of names as big as L T J Bukem, Goldie and, er, Frank Bruno. *It's cheap, cheerful and hugely popular.*

Comedy/Cabaret: Weekly gags at the union from established circuit funnymen, such as Daniel Kitson and Dan Antopolski.

Food: Campus food ranges from the *cultured* (Continental snacks at the Reskinov bar) to the *congealing* (fried stuff in the main hall), all at *reasonable* prices.

Other: Posh-frocks donned for the end of year mega-bash ball and throughout the year for individual department knees-ups.

SOCIAL & POLITICAL

HULL UNIVERSITY UNION:

• 8 sabbaticals • Turnout at last ballot: 11% • NUS member
Besides the ubiquitous Nestlé boycott, there's a notable absence of firebrand student politics. But the Union does an okay job of maintaining its facilities, and generally keeps University authorities sweet, too.

SU FACILITIES:

Union facilities are *top-notch. Pride of place goes to* Asylum (see above), but facilities include: ATM (HSBC and Natwest); bank (HSBC); three bars; canteen; crèche; insurance sales; general store; eight meeting rooms; four minibuses for hire; payphones; photo booth; eight pool tables; printing service; new/secondhand bookshop; two snack bars; sports and fitness centre; stationery shop; ticket agency; travel agency; TV lounge; video games; women's room.

CLUBS (NON-SPORTING):

AIDEC; Backfire (motorbikes); Ballroom Dancing; Beatroot (DJ); Big Band; Buddhist; Change Ringing (bells); Chinese; Cock (cocktails); CRAIC (Ceilidh, Rave & Irish Culture); Drum'n'Bass; Dutch/Flemish; European Football Supporters; Evangelical; Gilbert & Sullivan; Hellenic; Hempology; Italianissima; Jazz; Kabbadi; Links First Aid; Malaysian; Mediterranean; Methodist; Music. **See also Clubs tables.**

OTHER ORGANISATIONS:

Hullfire is the self-financing student paper, run by the students themselves and published monthly. A history of award-winning journalistic quality *has deserted it recently*. The student radio station JAM1575 broadcasts daily on an AM frequency. HUSSO (Hull University Social Services Organisation) is a Union-run charity which does community projects like refugee aid, mental health-care and prison education. *All very worthwhile and great CV brownie points.*

RELIGIOUS:

• 9 chaplains (CofE, RC, Orthodox, Methodist, Baptist, URC, Friends), rabbi
The University is close to a number of Christian churches, although there's no local mosque. University facilities are *limited*, but a non-denominational prayer room is planned.

PAID WORK:

• Job bureau • Paid work: term-time 50%: hols 80%
The town employs *large numbers* of students and the Union has a job exchange with facilities for helping students find work: e-mail service; links with local businesses; jobs fairs; NASE membership; vacancy board.

SPORTS

• BUSA Ranking: 19
Despite a *full roster* of sports facilities – the university is a *premier* coaching centre – Hull students remain *duffers on the pitch*, with no recent successes to sing of. *Keen but unconvincing.*

SPORTS FACILITIES:

At the Sports & Fitness Centre: indoor sports; fitness and weight training; two multigyms; sauna and solarium; jacuzzi. At the Sports Centre (close to the Union): gym; two sports halls; badminton and seven squash courts; all-weather pitch; climbing wall. 11 playing fields on the campus and near the Lawns Halls, an athletics and running track, 11 tennis courts and a boathouse at Beresford Avenue. Netball/5-a-side courts. The city also has a swimming pool and an ice rink.

SPORTING CLUBS:

See Clubs tables.

ATTRACTIONS:

Hull City FC have a new ground and have started pulling in *whopping crowds*, given their size. Also two *major* rugby league clubs.

ACCOMMODATION

IN COLLEGE:

• Catered: 13% • Cost: £75-95 (31wks)
• Self-catering: 16% • Cost: £56-73 (31-50wks)
• First years living in: 56% • Insurance premium: £££
Availability: All 1st years can live in University accomodation – the *location of choice* is The Lawns, 3 miles from campus and the *hub of fresher life*. There is more expensive accomodation at Taylor Court, *better suited to mature students and postgrads*. Single and mixed-sex digs are available and the overall standard is *basic but functional*. Halls are kitted out with launderettes, TV common rooms and network internet access. Accommodation is *secure* and university cleaners *keep it habitable*.
Car parking: By permit only – free in halls, £75 per year at Taylor Court.

EXTERNALLY:
• Ave rent: £40 • Living at home: 10%
Availability: Housing is easy to come by, and relatively cheap – £40 per week keeps students *living in comfort. Students could do worse than Beverley Road, Cottingham Road, Newland Avenue and Prince's Avenue.*
Housing help: Information on private housing is available from the SU's Advice Centre. The University has close links with private landlords.

WELFARE

SERVICES:
• Lesbian/Gay/Bisexual Officer & Society • Women's Officer & Society
• Mature Students' Officer & Society • International Students' Officer & Society
• Postgrad Officer & Society • Disabilities Officer
• Late-night/Women's minibus • Self-defence classes • Nightline
• Taxi fund • College counsellors: 2 full/4 part • Crime rating: !!!!!
Welfare support comes with the housing: residential pastoral staff in halls and non-resident staff for houses and flats. Also advice centres for personal and legal problems.
Health: *Not brilliant.* No health facilities on campus and local practices are *unwelcoming and inaccessible.*
Women: Attack alarms are available, as are appointments with the equal opportunities officer.
Crèches/Nursery: A crèche has *limited* places for children from 3mths-5yrs.
Disabilities: T-loops, ramps and note-takers are in place, although access in the central administration building is pretty *shabby.*

FINANCE:
• Ave debt per year: £3,917
• Access fund: £902,513 • Successful applications/yr: 718 • Ave payment: £1,125
Support: Financial assistance is available in the form of hardship funds, emergency funds, bursaries for books and a postgrad teaching support scheme.

Humberside University

see University of Lincoln

Imperial College, London

Imperial College, London

• **The College is part of the _University of London_ and students are entitled to use its facilities.**
Imperial College London, South Kensington Campus, London, SW7 2AZ
Tel: (020) 7594 8014 E-mail: info@imperial.ac.uk
Website: www.imperial.ac.uk
Imperial College Union, Prince Consort Road, London, SW7 2BB
Tel: (020) 7594 8060 E-mail: presicent@imperial.ac.uk
Website: www.union.imperial.ac.uk

GENERAL

Jam sandwiched between the Natural History Museum and the Royal Albert Hall in South Kensington, $1\frac{1}{2}$ miles from Trafalgar Square, is Imperial College. It was formed in 1907, when the Royal School of Mines, City & Guilds College and the Royal College of Science merged. The Medical School joined the party in the late 80s and Wye College (which specialised in farming and environmental courses) in 2000. *The main building is what Prince Chas would call a 'carbuncle' – a towering, oversized portakabin of aluminium, smoked glass and concrete.* The two new buildings, the Sir Alexander Fleming and the Tanaka Business School (which will provide a new entrance to the campus), were designed by top architects Foster & Partners. Inside, *it's well ordered* – echoing walkways with glass displays and cabinets full of scientific paraphernalia, *all adding to the sense of awesome thinkology*. Overshadowing all this is the Queen's Tower, which has now been locked off. *Allegedly, too many frustrated finalists were flinging themselves from the parapet, knowing at least enough physics to realise it was a sure-fire way of getting out of exams.* Apart from the campus at South Kensington and the various hospital campuses, Imperial has a campus at Wye in Kent and a 260-acre site at Silwood Park, near Ascot, mainly for scientific fieldwork.

Sex ratio (M:F): 63:37	Founded: 1907
Full-time u'grads: 7,365	Part-time: 0
Postgrads: 3,165	Non-degree: n/a
Ave course: 4yrs	Ethnic: 40%
State:private school: 59:41	Flunk rate: 4%
Mature: 13%	International: 33%
Disabled: 23	Local: 24%

ATMOSPHERE:

Just because Imperial's students are overwhelmingly male and all studying science, technology or medicine, doesn't mean they're all geeks. There are a few nerds, spods, boffins and dweebs as well. No, that's not really fair, but they do work very hard, on a 9-to 5 basis mostly and academic standards are world-renowned. Outside hours, they know how to chug a pint and there's a substantial sporty set as well. Relations with the immediate locals (posh Kensingtonians) are next to non-existent. With the sex ratio at two-to-one, the main problem for Imperial's (straight) males is, of course, intense sexual frustration.

SITES:

Wye Campus: (400 students) Formerly Wye College, 50 miles from the main campus in the quiet little village of Wye (*surprise, surprise*). *The setting – a 300-hectare estate in an Area of Outstanding Natural Beauty – feels a world away from the metropolitan bustle of South Kensington.* Students are associate members of University of Kent's SU. Their own Union organises events every couple of days, an end-of-year ball and clubs and societies ranging from salsa to squash. *Most students live on or near campus (there's College accommodation for 370) and have little reason to venture to the bright lights. This keeps life cheap, at least compared to London, but the connection with the main site is skinny to say the least.*

Medical students spend most of their first two years at the main South Kensington site, after which they study at one of the other four sites in West London:

St Mary's: (190 students) 2 miles from Imperial, in Paddington, and part of the faculty of Medicine. *If you thought the scientists worked hard, the doctors-to-be do even more. Despite this, they have time to use* the recreation centre on site, as well as the swimming pool and bar.

Royal Brompton: (140 students) What used to be known as the National Heart and Lung Institute is now the Royal Brompton site in Chelsea, a mile from the main site. *Apart from academic facilities, fun-time is restricted to a sarnie shop.*

Charing Cross: (225 students) Not, despite its name, anywhere near Charing Cross, this site is 3 miles from the main site, in Hammersmith. There's a bar and a café.

Hammersmith: (347 students) Formerly the Royal Postgraduate Medical School, this site is mostly for postgraduates.

Silwood Park: 81 postgrad students.

LONDON: see University of London

The area immediately surrounding the College is a *prim quad* with privet hedges in the *relative peace* of South Kensington ('South Ken', to his friends). Kensington itself is *a well-to-do area* with Harrod's just round the corner in Knightsbridge (*although we don't recommend students use it for their weekly shop*). The area's full of expensive boutiques and delicatessens. *Even the kebab joints have French names round here.* It's also an *erudite* part of London, brimming with museums and libraries and educational institutions. It's *way too pricey* to live in South Ken itself. *Shepherd's Bush or Earl's Court are a likelier bet.* However, it's well connected for the West End and ULU only takes 20 mins by tube or slightly longer by bus.

TRAVEL: see University of London

Trains: The nearest mainline BR stations are Paddington and Victoria, each about $1\frac{1}{2}$ miles away, but on direct bus routes.

Buses: 9, 10, 14, 51, 74 and C1. Night buses: N14 and N97.

Car: Parking at the college is limited to those with disabilities. The congestion charging zone is not far away and *it might swallow South Ken in the future*.

Underground: Gloucester Road and South Kensington (both on the District, Circle and Piccadilly Lines).

CAREER PROSPECTS:

• Careers Service • No. of staff: 6 full/1 part • Unemployed after 6mths: 9%

The careers service offers *just about everything you could want (bar a foot massage)*: psychometric testing, internship and market trends info, careers events, employer presentations and drop-in sessions, and interview training. *Potential employers, particularly in scientific and technical areas, regard Imperial as a goldmine of bright bods.*

FAMOUS ALUMNI:

Mary Archer (bigwig scientist, no really, she is, even though her husband Lord Jeff says so too); Sir Roger Bannister (4-minute miler); Sir Alexander Fleming (discovered penicillin); Rajiv Gandhi (late Indian Prime Minister); W G Grace (cricketer); David Irving (revisionist 'historian'); David Livingstone (explorer); Brian May (large-haired Queen guitar hero); Trevor Phillips (Chair of the Commission for Racial Equality); Joan Ruddock MP (Lab); Simon Singh (author, Fermat's Last Theorem); H G Wells (writer); J P R Williams (rugby player); Francis Wilson (weatherman).

SPECIAL FEATURES:

Imperial's mascot is a 185lb micrometer, *which avoids the trend among London colleges of stealing each other's mascots.*

FURTHER INFO:

• Prospectuses: undergrad; postgrad; some departments • Open days
International students get a special guide once they receive an offer.

A C A D E M I C

Imperial's academic standards are renowned worldwide and 25% of students get 1st-class degrees. Although it's famous for its science and technology work, a few arts and language courses are also on offer. Most courses offer a year abroad or in industry. Some graduates end up with unusual letters after their names (such as ARCS, ARSM and ACGI) showing they're now associates of Imperial's constituent colleges.

99% of the teaching staff have PhDs and students can get their hands dirty with real research too through the Undergraduate Research Opportunities Programme (UROP) where they can help out postgrads and staff with their work and maybe get credited on scientific publications even before graduating. Students can also follow up their own interests *(no bombs and stuff though)*. In addition, they may get their name on scientific publications before they even graduate *(impressive for sure)*. Things don't quieten down too much outside term either. In the summer vacation, some students get a bursary based on the level of those paid to postgrads for helping out. These are particularly popular with international students who don't need work permits for UROP projects. See www.imperial.ac.uk/urop.

Entry points: 274-353	Ave points: 341
Applns per place: 5	Clearing: 3%
Staff/student ratio: 1:9	Study addicts: 31%
Teaching: *****	Research: *****
Year abroad: 6%	Sandwich students: 3%
Firsts: 23%	2.2s: 17%
2.1s: 44%	3rds: 3%

ADMISSIONS:

• Apply via UCAS

SUBJECTS:

Engineering: 39%   Medical Sciences: 26%
Life Sciences: 12%   Physical Sciences: 23%
Best: Aeronautics; Biochemistry; Biology; Chemical Engineering & Chemical Technology; Chemistry; Civil Engineering; Composite Materials; Computing; Earth Science & Engineering; Electrical & Electronic Engineering; Environmental Science & Technology; Geology; Materials; Management; Mathematics; Medicine; Physics.
Unusual: Biomedical Engineering; Physics with Studies in Musical Performance (joint with the Royal College of Music).

LIBRARIES:

• 950,000 books • 2,400 study places • Spend per student: £££££
There are 17 libraries in all, including the Central Library, the Science Museum Library, six medical libraries and eight departmental libraries. These house 13,000 full text electronic journals as well as nearly a million books. *Not bad, eh?*

COMPUTERS:

• 2,000 workstations • Spend per student: £££
There are workstations in every department and 450 general access workstations in the Central Library. The College has a high speed, wireless network so students can access onsite and off-site resources.

OTHER LEARNING FACILITIES:
Language lab; drama studio; music rooms; computer-aided design lab; audio/TV centre. If so inclined, most students can take a language, humanities or management course.

ENTERTAINMENT

THE CITY: see University of London
South Ken has a fair level of entertainments of its own, but it's mainly wine bars and posh clubs, although the Queen's Arms is popular. The West End is within an energetic stroll's distance and many of the areas around Kensington offer some thrills and spills (Notting Hill, Earl's Court, Hammersmith, Chelsea, Fulham, Putney). Other local pubs worthy of a Pushplug: Rat & Parrot and Finnegan's Wake.

UNIVERSITY:
• Price of a pint of beer: £1.50 • Glass of wine: £1.60
Bars: The five bars at the main site include Da Vinci's *(still looks like a Butlin's leisure lounge despite having been done up)*, Southside *(pipe 'n' slippers pub)*, Union Bar *(also pubby, popular with rugby gorillas)* and dBs *(womb-like venue bar)*.
Theatres: Imperial has two halls, *which are both eminently suitable as theatres for the strangely strong dramatic contingent*, including medical opera and drama societies (for medics, not medical operas and dramas). Not only do they take shows to the Edinburgh Fringe, they rent a whole theatre there and sub-let it to other groups.
Film: Imperial has the largest student cinema screen in the country and shows two mainstream films a week.
Music venues: The Great Hall has a capacity of 600 and there's also the Concert Hall (cap 450) and dBs (450).
Clubbing: Several club nights every week: the mainstream Pop Tarts; Common People (indie); Hedonizm (dub); Shaft (70s) and more.
Comedy/Cabaret: Once a fortnight, in the Union building, there's a comic on the bill.
Food: The JCR does a self-service all-day breakfast bar, which gets *chocka* at lunchtimes. QT in the Sherfield Building sells snacks in the daytime as well as the Main Dining Hall which serves slightly more substantial scoff. dBs does baguettes. There are also cafés in several department buildings, including the Sir Alexander Fleming building *(watch out for the penicillin experiments – it's a type of mould, don't you know?)*
Other: Two big balls a year, occasionally in posh London hotels. Also Christmas and departmental *binges* and three carnivals a year.

SOCIAL & POLITICAL

IMPERIAL COLLEGE STUDENTS UNION:
• 6 sabbaticals • Turnout at last ballot: 13%
The Union is politically independent, even of the NUS. *It exists to provide services to its members, who lap them up when they can tear themselves away from work. Urging the students into any political activity is harder than learning Gujurati from a Martian.*
Also ULU: see University of London

SU FACILITIES:
The Union has facilities at the main site, St Mary's, Wye and Charing Cross. At South Ken, the Union building, called Beit Quad, is on the other side of the road. In all, the Union offers bars, a cafeteria, sandwich bar, travel agency, resources centre, two shops, minibus hire, photo booth, video and games machines, juke boxes, cinema and fax service. There's a new centre housing advice, welfare, chaplaincy services, a media centre, store and library.

CLUBS (NON-SPORTING):

Amateur Radio; Arabic; Best; Book; Cypriot; Exploration; Finance; ICUWWW; Indian; Italian; Japanese; Junior Enterprise; Korean; Latin American; Lebanese; Newspaper; Persian Gulf; Quiz; Radio Modellers; St John Ambulance; Scandinavian; Sikh; Singapore; Spanish; Sri Lankan; Thai; Turkish; Wargames. **See also Clubs tables.**

OTHER ORGANISATIONS:

Felix is the Union's weekly newspaper and there's also a radio station (Imperial College Radio) and a TV station (STOIC – Student Television of Imperial College). *Imperial College's Rag is very energetic, although as much energy goes into oh-so-wacky stunts as into actual fund-raising.* There's the annual tiddlywink race down Oxford Street and legends abound of the naked parachute leap which ended in nude students being bundled out of a van at Harrod's. Felix claims to have photos.

RELIGIOUS:

• 2 full-time chaplains (CofE, RC); 2 part-time (CofE)
The College has links with Methodist, Free Church and Lutheran chaplains. There's an Islamic Prayer room and the Regent's Park Mosque (one of the country's largest) is nearby. The Chaplaincy Centre can point other believers in the right direction and has a prayer room for use by individual Christians and Buddhists.
Religion in London: see University of London

PAID WORK: see University of London
Imperial students can appeal to the firms constantly vying for their talents for vacation work or there's Imperial's UROP scheme (see above) where they help lecturers with their research work and can expect to earn cash *and many brownie points.* The Careers Service advertises *any part-time job opportunities that come its way.*

• Recent successes: plenty • BUSA Ranking: 22
Bearing in mind that Imperial students are entitled to use ULU and the University's facilities as well as their own *excellent* amenities, *they've got the world at their feet like a football.* Imperial is top of the London colleges in the student sports league.

SPORTS FACILITIES:

Imperial has 60 acres of playing fields at Harlington (15 miles from Kensington), and $12\frac{1}{2}$ acres at Teddington with four tennis courts. The College lays on buses two days a week to get to Harlington so that students can use the pavilion and pitches (including an all-weather pitch). Meanwhile, over the road from the South Ken ranch, Imperial has a new sports centre which has squash courts, a large studio for classes, a larger fitness gym, climbing wall, sports injuries service and, *for couch potatoes with good intentions*, a juice bar. There's also a mountain hut in Snowdonia *for hardy types.*

SPORTING CLUBS:

Billiards; Ju-Jitsu; Rowing; Snooker. **See also Clubs tables.**

ATTRACTIONS: see University of London

IN COLLEGE:

• Catered: 10% • Cost: £85-115 (30/34/38wks)
• Self-catering: 36% • Cost: £55-127 (34/38/51wks)
• First years living in: 94% • Insurance premium: ££
Availability: Imperial accommodates all its 1st years either in their own halls or intercollegiate halls, but College housing is limited for other students. There are 11 halls in all and five *so-called* student houses, the largest of which, *Bernard Sunley House, we'd call*

large enough to be a hall. Women have to apply to the University for intercollegiate rooms if they want all-female housing. *A whopping 50% of students in College accommodation have to share rooms, sometimes even in triple rooms, but they are charged less.* The halls are mostly around South Ken, but also spread throughout west London. Some self-catered places are in flats in South Ealing. Swipe card entry and security guards in all halls. There are 60 flats available to couples, 16 of which are suitable for families.
Car parking: *Very tricky* in South Kensington (permit required); *easier* at Wye and Silwood Park.

EXTERNALLY: see University of London
• Ave rent: £125
Availability: Hammersmith is the closest location *for those who haven't struck lucky on the scratch cards.*
Housing help: The Union has a housing advice scheme and the University Private Housing Office provides housing lists, legal advice and a bulletin board.

SERVICES:
• Lesbian/Gay/Bisexual Society • Mature Students' Officer & Society
• International Students' Officer & Society • Postgrad Officer & Society
• Disabilities Officer • Self-defence classes • Nightline • Taxi fund
• College counsellors: 1 full/3 part • Crime rating: !!!!!
Health: The Health Centre is home to five doctors, two nurses, NHS dentists, psychotherapists, physiotherapists and one full-time and three part-time counsellors. There's also a visiting psychiatrist, weekly sports medicine physician and private alternative therapists.
Women: *With less than one woman to every two men, the most severe problem is solitude, although the increasing number of medical students is levelling the figures out.*
Crèches/Nursery: Space for 54 tots aged 6mths-5yrs.

Disabilities: The South Kensington campus is fairly compact, but *access could still be improved in places.* To this end, the College is refurbishing older buildings and newer ones have *good* facilities. There's specially designed accommodation for wheelchair users and hearing- and sight-impaired students. The College employs a Disabilities Officer, and anyone thinking of studying is encouraged to get in touch. There are hearing loops in some lecture theatres and lifts around the main building.

FINANCE:
• Ave debt per year: £5,582
Fees: International students have to cough up five figures – £14,050 is standard, but some courses charge premium *sell-your-granny* rates.
• Access fund: £440,721 • Successful applications/yr: 403
Support: *Many, many scholarships and sponsorships are available.* As for tuition fees, help will be particularly good for those studying science, engineering and medicine. Those on the full maintenance grant who meet the UCAS deadline for accepting an offer AND get top grades in at least three A-levels are up for an *astonishing* four grand's worth of bursary booty.

KCL see King's College London

Keele University

University of Kent

King's College London

Kingston University

Kingston Polytechnic see Kingston University

KCL

see King's College London

Keele University

Keele University, Keele University, Keele, Staffordshire, ST5 5BG
Tel: (01782) 621 111 E-mail: undergraduate@keele.ac.uk Website: www.keele.ac.uk
Keele University Students' Union (KUSU), Keele, Staffs, ST5 5BJ
Tel: (01782) 583 700 E-mail: sta15@kusu.keele.ac.uk Website: www.kusu.net

GENERAL

Keele University is situated near the 'Potteries' towns of Stoke-on-Trent and Newcastle under Lyme in the north Midlands, *but at the same time manages to feel a million miles from anywhere. It's an arrangement of geometric blocks in a square mile of parkland, mostly modern but including the bootylicious Keele Hall, the oldest building (19th-century) on the estate.* It gained a bit of a rep in the post-war higher education expansion for its flexibility of study, *which many institutions have since stolen – sorry, emulated,* and its communal atmosphere.

Sex ratio (M:F): 34:66	**Founded: 1962**
Full-time u'grads: 4,905	**Part-time: 4,795**
Postgrads: 1,055	**Non-degree: 1,000**
Ave course: 3yrs	**Ethnic: 9**
State:private school: 83:9	**Flunk rate: 4%**
Mature: 11%	**International: 12%**
Disabled: 92	**Local: 26%**

(66% female / 34% male)

ATMOSPHERE:
Keele is a small, busy but friendly university, with 70% of students and many of the staff and their families living on campus. Newcastle under Lyme and Stoke offer some respite if the atmosphere starts to cloy, but even they don't have much to offer the discerning thrill-seeker. Whether the familiar community feel is relished or resented is a matter of taste, but the bustling campus could never be called 'humdrum', and Push won't even try.

KEELE: for Stoke, see _Staffordshire University_
- Population: 122,000 • City centre: $3\frac{1}{2}$ miles • London: 147 miles
- Manchester: 34 miles • Birmingham: 43 miles
- High temp: 20 • Low temp: 0 • Rainfall: 56

Keele only just makes it to village status. The surrounding area was built on the 19th-century pottery industry, hence the name The Potteries. Wedgwood, Spode and Royal Doulton pottery all came from round here. _Habitat and Tupperware didn't._ Local facilities in the old market town of Newcastle are _a tad limited, however, there's more than enough to get by_ – all the major banks and _a fair few_ shops. For more commercial trappings, Hanley (one of the six towns that make up the city of Stoke-on-Trent) _is better equipped and The Potteries Shopping Centre could just about support a spending spree._ Local attractions include all the various Pottery Museums, the once industrial, but now leisure canals, Festival Park (shops, cinema, dry ski slope), the Stoke City Museum & Art Gallery and Alton Towers, the _theme park-cum-vomit factory,_ $\frac{1}{2}$hr down the road.

TRAVEL:

Trains: The nearest train station is 5 miles away at Stoke (London £28.70; Manchester £7.20).
Coaches: London to Stoke by National Express takes 5 hrs (£21.50).
Car: From the south, leave the M6 at Junction 15 and follow the signs for Newcastle under Lyme. From the north, leave the M6 at Junction 16 and take the A500 for Crewe and Nantwich.
Local: From Stoke-on-Trent station the No. 29 bus heads for campus every 15 mins.
College: Safety bus runs between campus, halls and the area.
Taxis: Takes about 15-20 mins from Stoke Station, costs about a fiver.
Bicycles: _Handy on campus but everything else is too far away and too darn hilly._

CAREER PROSPECTS:

• Careers Service • No. of staff: 3 full/2 part • Unemployed after 6mths: 5%
The careers service website has vacancies and news plus the Windmills Programme, a virtual career coach.

FAMOUS ALUMNI:

Don Foster MP (Lib Dem); Michael Mansfield QC (Barrister); Lord Melchett (of Greenpeace, not Blackadder); Alun Michael MP (Secretary of State for Wales); Nick Partridge (AIDS campaigner); Clare Short MP (Lab); Phil Soar (author); Jack Straw MP (Foreign Secretary); Adelaide Tambo (MP, African National Congress).

FURTHER INFO:

• Prospectuses: undergrad; postgrad; departments • Open days

ACADEMIC

Flexibility's the name of the game – 90% of students do joint honours degrees, so arts students find themselves dabbling in science and vice versa. _The upside is students get an insight into matters they might have otherwise ignored, but some might find it a travesty of the natural order._ Keele recently stuck the European Quality Label for Mobility on its correspondence, owing to the fact that almost every student has the chance to spend a semester at a sister institution in America, Australia, South Africa or Europe. The Keele University School of Medicine recently opened at the City General Hospital. _Would-be doctors and won't-be patients rejoiced._

80-340		POINTS
Entry points: 80-340	Ave points: 240	
Applns per place: 7	Clearing: 14%	
No. of terms: 2	Length of terms: 15wks	
Staff/student ratio: 1:11	Study addicts: 14%	
Teaching: ***	Research: ***	
Year abroad: 2%	Sandwich students: <1%	
Firsts: 9%	2.2s: 41%	
2.1s: 45%	3rds: 3%	

ADMISSIONS:

• Apply via UCAS/NMAS

SUBJECTS:

Humanities: 20%   Natural Sciences: 22%
Health: 11%   Social Sciences: 47%
Best: American Studies, Economics, Education, Life Sciences (biology and neuroscience), Life Sciences (biochemistry and biomedicine), Management, Maths & Statistics, Nursing & Midwifery, Philosophy, Physics & Astrophysics, Psychology, Sociology, SPIRE (Politics, International Relations & Philosophy).

LIBRARIES:

• 500,000 books • 554 study places • Spend per student: ££££
A big push on the electronic journal front has made essay research maybe not a breeze, but at least a light gust.

COMPUTERS:

• 3,500 workstations
All bedrooms on campus have network access. Most systems now have Windows XP *and all the trimmings.*

OTHER LEARNING FACILITIES:

Language lab, music rehearsal rooms.

ENTERTAINMENT

NEWCASTLE UNDER LYME/HANLEY: for Stoke, see Staffordshire University
• Price of a pint of beer: £2.10 • Glass of wine: £1.75 • Can of Red Bull: £2
Cinemas: 8-screen Vue in Newcastle under Lyme and 10-screen Odeon in nearby Festival Park.
Theatres: The New Vic in Newcastle and the Regent in Hanley both offer NUS discounts.
Pubs: *There's no shortage of pubs in Newcastle under Lyme. Even the old town hall has been converted into one. Wetherspoons is popular (because it's cheap).* In Keele Village, the Sneyd Arms *is good for food but expensive.* The Old Brown Jug does *great* cider and live music.
Clubbing: Fluid, Creation and Liquid in Hanley all offer student nights. In Newcastle there's Zanzibar, Maxim's and Metropolis for poppy dance, the Sutherland Arms for rockers and Longton's for all kinds of dancefloor tunes.
Music venues: Three rock pubs in Newcastle, the Rigger, Full Moon and the Black Friar, all support live bands.
Eating out: George Street in Newcastle *has something for everyone in possession of a mouth, teeth and digestive tract* with four kebab houses, a French restaurant, three Chinese, a couple of Indians, a Thai, a chippy and a burger stall to tempt starved revellers tumbling out of the Zanzibar.

UNIVERSITY:

• Price of a pint of beer: £1.60 • Glass of wine: £1.90 • Can of Red Bull: £1.60
The Students' Union is the largest purpose-built entertainment venue in Staffordshire, *which may not be as impressive as it sounds when you think about what the rest of Staffordshire is like, but it's still something to say to those who think of Keele as a sleepy backwater.*
Bars: With nine different bars, from the *deeply cool* Gallery Bar, with its umpteen games machines and appearances from top underground DJs like Scratch Perverts, to the Union Lounge Bar – *the new HQ in swank and sophistication* – Keele makes a stronger claim to a *happening nightlife than many urban campuses.*
Theatres: Most summers there's outdoor Shakespeare from the Drama Society in the Clockhouse Courtyard, indoors *boards are trodden with moderate exuberance throughout the year.*
Film: Free films are shown every fortnight in the Union (usually alternative). Twice-weekly flicks at the University cost £2 a pop.

Music venues: A *good selection of bands hit the extremely impressive* 1,200-capacity Ballroom, from Embrace and The Darkness to Girls Aloud and Liberty-X. K2 has smaller, *but no less perfectly formed* gigs now and then.

Clubbing: The usual super-DJ suspects Carl Cox, Paul Oakenfold and Judge Jules have taken a spin on the decks at The Ballroom as well as Steve Lamacq, Trevor Nelson and others. Friday nights is 'Loaded', Wednesdays it's 'Retro Rooms'. K2 does its share of club-hosting for the smaller nights.

Comedy/Cabaret: Paramount Comedy Club acts every fortnight.

Food: Harvey's Sandwich bar is *good for the healthy option, swiftly nullified* by a trip to the Diner for a fry-up, or Wednesday's kebab and curry night (*surely that should be kebab OR curry night?*). The University offers Comus Restaurant with *cheap* daily specials, the award winning – for design, not food, *sadly* – Le Café, Vite & Eat, The Italian Job for *dining in style*, Union Square for pizzas, burgers etc. and Hawthorn's Restaurant for Sunday roasts.

Other: Six balls a year, including Grad, Christmas and Athletics. Six months after the Freshers Fair, the Refreshers Fair *doesn't distribute fizzy sweets* but rather reminds students of clubs and societies they might have missed.

Social & Political

KEELE UNIVERSITY STUDENTS' UNION (KUSU):

• 4 sabbaticals • Turnout at last ballot: 20% • NUS member

This is almost an old-fashioned banner-waving, barricade-building political Union, but not quite. *Politically, it's full of wide-eyed interest, but very few party affiliations. The SU's a source of pride to students, who're not afraid to stand up to the University on welfare and other issues.* KUSU recently launched a safety campaign that won them swipe card access to halls. *Welfare is the SU's forte.*

SU FACILITIES:

The Union Building in the middle of campus has: eight bars; three cafés; two snack bars; fast food outlet; ten pool/snooker tables; meeting rooms; four minibuses; Endsleigh Insurance office; Natwest Bank; two cashpoints (Lloyds, Co-op); photocopier; fax & printing service; photo booth; payphone; advice centre; TV lounge; and a secondhand book exchange.

CLUBS (NON-SPORTING):

Anti-Capitalist; Bar; Chinese Students & Scholars; Critical Legal; Eco; England; French; Global Education; Globalise Resistance; International Students; Japanese; KRAP (Keele Rock Appreciation Posse); Philosophers; Psychology; Revelation Rock-Gospel Choir; Snooker; Social Progress; Sword & Sorcery; T'ai Chi; War Games & Board Games; Writers. **See also Clubs tables.**

OTHER ORGANISATIONS:

Free Union newspaper Concourse comes out fortnightly. KUBE FM radio-station broadcasts across campus during term. *Rag scrapes pennies together. A voluntary group, Active, lives up to its name.*

RELIGIOUS:

• 3 chaplains (RC, CofE, visiting Orthodox)

The big inter-denominational Christian chapel is a *bizarre* grey, brick structure, rectangular with two cylindrical turrets at one end. Muslim prayer room provided on campus. In Newcastle and Stoke, apart from various churches, there are places of worship for Muslims, Sikhs and Buddhists.

PAID WORK:

• Job bureau

The SU pretty much has a monopoly on employment; *everything else is too far away. Luckily,* it employs about 500 students.

SPORTS

• Recent successes: men's rugby • BUSA Ranking: 48
A fairly good level of facilities and involvement, both competitive and recreational. There's a small charge for some facilities if not organised through the sporting clubs.

SPORTS FACILITIES:
Close to the principal parts of the University (halls of residence, the SU and the main teaching areas), the sports facilities spread over 50 acres including eight football pitches, a hockey pitch, two cricket pitches, three rugby pitches, all-weather pitch, six squash courts, two basketball courts, three sports halls, 12 tennis courts, four netball courts, running track, gym, climbing wall, running track, aerobics studio, sunbeds and 5-a-side football in the Leisure Centre.

SPORTING CLUBS:
Ju-Jitsu; Judo; Korfball; Lacrosse; Table Tennis. **See also Clubs tables.**

ATTRACTIONS:
Locally, there's Stoke City and Port Vale Football Clubs, Uttoxeter Race Course, the Potteries Marathon and, most years, the Lombard Rally. Keele also hosts the National Karate Championships.

ACCOMMODATION

IN COLLEGE:
• Self-catering: 65% • Cost: £52-85 (33/37/42wks)
• First years living in: 90% • Others living in: 56% • Insurance premium: ££
Availability: Living in is the norm. *It's one of the big pluses about Keele as far as Keele is concerned.* 1st years actually have to apply to live out rather than to live in. As a result, almost all are housed in the University's five halls on campus. *Conditions vary depending on how much you pay – in the cheaper halls you might have to share a kitchen with 30 people.* All halls are self-catering (some have pay-as-you-eat refectories and snack bars), vary in size from 400 to 800 places and some offer single-sex blocks. Two halls are blocks of flats for four students sharing a kitchen and bathroom, although these are mainly for finalists, 95% of whom live in. More than a third of 2nd years and postgrads live in too. Some space is available on campus for mature students and single parents. All the halls have bars and *Hawthorns is especially popular despite* being the furthest away (about 15 mins walk).
Car parking: Permits cost £15 but spaces are *limited*.

EXTERNALLY:
• Ave rent: £35-40 • Living at home: 5%
Availability: *It's pretty easy to find cheap rooms a bus ride away from campus, but there's nothing close. Newcastle or Silverdale are the preferred options, being on a handy bus route, although Hanley and parts of Stoke are also on the house-hunter's checklist. Knutton and Cobridge are a bit rough and Parkside is getting worse. If living out, a car wouldn't go unused.*
Housing help: The University's Accommodation Office has three full-time officers, a vacancies newsletter and a housing approval scheme.

SERVICES:

- Lesbian/Gay/Bisexual Officer & Society • Ethnic Minorities Officer
- Women's Officer • Mature Students' Officer
- International Students' Officer & Society • Postgrad Officer & Society
- Disabilities Officer • Late-night/Women's minibus • Nightline
- College counsellors: 2 full/2 part • SU counsellors: 4 • Crime rating: !!

The University's Counselling Service, assisted by the chaplains, *keeps emotions on an even keel (geddit?)*. The Union runs an independent Advice Unit which offers a free and confidential listening service, financial and legal advice, help for international students, drugs info and support for lesbian and gay students. Freshers are assigned a resident tutor.
Health: The Keele General Practice is based on campus and employs a male and a female doctor, two nurses and a dentist. As well as normal health care, it offers a psychiatry clinic.
Crèches/Nursery: 124 places for 12wks-5yrs. Links with local schools provide three after-school clubs for 5-11-yr-olds.
Disabilities: *The sprawling campus is difficult to get around by wheelchair* but support for deaf, blind and dyslexic students is *commendable*.
Crime: 32 burglaries were reported in 2003 and *students are pressuring the University to improve security.*

FINANCE:

- Ave debt per year: £4,653 • Access fund: 287,076
- Successful applications/yr: 561 • Ave payment: £100-£3,500

Support: Hardship loans and opportunity bursaries (for students from low-income families) and mature student bursaries are available, as well as other help for students with children. The SU and chaplaincy have further arrangements for small emergency loans and grants.

University of Kent

University of Kent, The Registry, Canterbury, Kent, CT2 7NZ Tel: (01227) 764 000
E-mail: recruitment@kent.ac.uk Website: www.kent.ac.uk
University of Kent Students' Union, Mandela Building, University of Kent, Canterbury, Kent, CT2 7NW Tel: (01227) 824 200 E-mail: union-president@kent.ac.uk
Website: www.kentunion.co.uk

The county of Kent *may be the Garden of England or its compost heap* depending on how you look at it – or how you react to the smell of the hops that it grows and brews. Canterbury, despite its idyllic old England countryside setting and wealth of medieval stonework, *is more than a slice of ye olde heritage industrie – it's a modern city with a six-century history*. The University it's home to *doesn't share* its ornate architecture, being *largely 60s redbrick, but with nothing like as much concrete as could be expected.* The 300 acres of campus land are $1\frac{1}{2}$ miles from the city centre and are set in *a lovely patch of green space and landscaped garden. The University overlooks the city and cathedral, making the view beautiful but the air blustery.* It's split into four distinct colleges and also lays claim to the University of Kent at Medway in Chatham, *but not much goes on there.*

Sex ratio (M:F): 45:55	Founded: 1965
Full-time u'grads: 8,165	Part-time: 3,370
Postgrads: 1,075	Non-degree: 546
Ave course: 3yrs	Ethnic: n/a
State:private school: 88:12	Flunk rate: 12%
Mature: 16%	International: 24%
Disabled: 119	

ATMOSPHERE:

Kent's collegiate system is a double-edged sword. On the one blade, it's created a real sense of loyalty, community and competition within the colleges. On the other, cliques form and there's little reason to mix between colleges that well, especially as each has its own mini Union and ents. There's little remarkable difference in life at the colleges (about 1,500 undergrads in each) and students rarely express a preference when applying (nor is it necessarily a good idea to do so). Since a fair few students are from the Home Counties, weekends bring a small but noticeable exodus from campus. Those that stay pile into the Venue and have fun behind their backs.

SITES:

The University of Kent at Medway: Together with the University of Greenwich and Canterbury Christ Church University College, Kent has a presence on a Medway campus in Chatham – an industrial, residential and *not exactly beautiful* town. The experiment is only just under way, *and facilities are still on the annoyingly inadequate side*, but so far Bridgewardens and Horsted Colleges are little more than academic outposts of Kent University, 30 miles away. *This will all change, however, when Kent moves in with its partner institutions on the more permanent Pembroke Campus.* Canteen, bar and 90 rooms are currently available. Rent is *cheap* in the surrounding town – *but travel costs balance this out*.

CANTERBURY:

- Population: 135,278 • City centre: 1 mile • London: 60 miles
- Dover: 30 miles • Ramsgate: 30 miles
- High temp: 22 • Low temp: 1 • Rainfall: 63

Canterbury has most of the amenities of a large city with the added treasures that come with being a small town in a beautiful place. Most people head straight for the grand and imposing cathedral – effectively the centre of the Anglican universe. The medieval city walls are still standing firm and historical buildings litter the city. Old lanes intertwine with newer streets, making simply wandering around a leisure activity in itself. More modern developments and giant chain stores are encroaching from the outskirts, and it does have a slightly shoddy underbelly, but who'd hold that against a place that has managed to stay so pretty for so long? It's not most people's idea of a student town, let alone a party animal's paradise, but there's fun to be had – just not the crazy, pulsing 24-hour kind.

TRAVEL:

Trains: Although Canterbury West is closer, Canterbury East is the station for London (£17.30 single) and Dover and connections to Edinburgh, Birmingham and Bristol.
Coaches: Canterbury Bus Station in the town centre has National Express services running all over the country, including London Victoria (£9.90 rtn).
Car: The A2 and M2 connect London with Canterbury while the A28 runs to the south coast. *The M20 can be handy.* Although the centre of town is pedestrianised, there are plenty of car parks around the University, and a few around town. The student car park costs £2 a day for those who don't have a £20 permit – available to students who live over a mile away.
Hitching: *Enough busy roads to make it seem a possibility – especially the A2 and the A28 – but Kentish drivers are surprisingly keen on travelling alone.*
Local: Useful Stagecoach buses 4a and 4u run through the campus every 15 mins during the day (every 30 mins evenings and weekends) until around midnight. Students can splash out on an annual bus pass (£170-290) or supersaver ticket if they're keen on public transport.

University: A late-night minibus trundles to and from the town centre in term.
Taxis: Two ranks on campus. Cabs are private hire only and can cost anything from £4-7 from campus to town, depending on time of day.
Bicycles: *Common sights around University even though campus is on a big hill.* There are loads of cycle lanes in the city and around the campus.

CAREER PROSPECTS:

• Careers Service • Unemployed after 6mths: 5%
The Careers Advisory Service caters for Kent students as well as a variety of smaller local colleges. It offers a full library, application advice and Carousel, a skills analysis programme.

FAMOUS ALUMNI:

Paul Ackford (rugby player and journalist); Alan Davies (frizzy-haired comedian); Gavin Esler (journalist); Anna Hill (broadcaster); Kazuo Ishiguro (writer); Wayne Otto (karate champ); Paul Ross (TV presenter); Ramon Tikaram (actor, played Ferdie in This Life); David Walsh (historian); Charles Wigoder (mobile phone entrepreneur); Tom Wilkinson (actor).

FURTHER INFO:

• Prospectuses: undergrad; postgrad; international; alternative • Open days
Prospectuses can be ordered online or from (01227) 827 272. Open days are held twice a year though visitors are welcome any time – contact the Admission & Recruitment Office for more information.

ACADEMIC

Three faculties comprising 18 departments with courses in humanities, science, technology and medical studies, social sciences and other *bits n' bobs*. The modular courses are flexible and up to 25% of a degree can be taken in another subject. There's also a law clinic that handles real cases and enables law students to gain some practical experience of casework. Humanities and social sciences courses often incorporate learning a foreign language and the opportunity for a year abroad. Sandwich years in industry are common choices.

Entry points: 160-320	**Ave points: n/a**
Applns per place: n/a	**Clearing: n/a**
No. of terms: 3	**Length of terms: 12wks**
Staff/student ratio: 1:10	**Study addicts: n/a**
Teaching: ***	**Research: ******
Year abroad: 1%	**Sandwich students: 5%**

ADMISSIONS:

• Apply via UCAS
'Widening Access' is a University committee buzz-phrase, especially as far as the Medway campus is concerned.

SUBJECTS:

Humanities: 33%	Social Sciences: 36%
Science, Technology & Medical Studies: 18%	Other courses: 13%

Unusual: Internet & Multimedia Communications; Sports Therapy; Health & Fitness; War Studies.

LIBRARIES:

• 1,000,000 books • 1,500 study places
The main Templeman library has a bundle of special collections. The Centre for the Study of Cartoons & Caricature has 90,000 cartoons, *of the satirical type, not Ren & Stimpy's Greatest Hits.* There's a smaller library at the Medway campus *but not many need to use it.* The colleges have their own *baby* collections and the cathedral library has shelf upon shelf of dusty tomes – *not for the likes of plebby undergrads, mind.* The University buys 16,000 new books a year.

COMPUTERS:
• 600 workstations • 24-hr access
70% of student rooms are networked.

OTHER LEARNING FACILITIES:
There's a design lab and language labs for students doing languages as part of their course.

ENTERTAINMENT

THE CITY:

• Price of a pint of beer: £1.70 • Glass of wine: £2.50 • Can of Red Bull: £2
Cinemas: The Odeon has two screens, and can shave off a couple of pounds for students.
Theatres: The Marlowe Theatre is the city's main venue for touring drama and sex-soap pretty boy panto. *Literary types might like to know* T S Eliot's play Murder in the Cathedral was written for and performed in Canterbury Cathedral.
Pubs: The city has *firkinfuls* of traditional ale pubs, largely thanks to the hop-soaked beer factories that populate the county. *Students don't just drink 'Manky Brian's Famous Whippleweasel' though: trendy joints like Alberry's Wine Bar pull in a fair few, the Scream pub is popular for its cheap prices and the Cherry Tree's range of flavoured vodkas has titillated a taste bud or two in its time.*
Clubbing: *Canterbury isn't Club City but it's occasionally worth ignoring that the Works is a dirt-cheap cheesy dive and that the Chicago Rock Café's horrendously overpriced during the week.*
Music venues: Classical concerts are held in the cathedral, the Marlowe Theatre has a few big names (and mouths) warbling now and then (Van Morrison, Vonda Shepherd). Several pubs provide local bands with excuses to perform.
Eating out: Local scoff shops are geared to the student and tourist trade and there are plentiful Indian, Italian, Mexican, Chinese, French and vegetarian restaurants, as well as various fish'n'chip shops and other takeaways. *Pushplugs: Café Naz (Indian with discounts); Café des Amis (Mexican, natch); Ask (pizza).*

UNIVERSITY:

• Price of a pint of beer: £1.20 • Glass of wine: £1.50 • Can of Red Bull: £1.80
Bars: In addition to the four college bars, the Union has three larger boozeries. The Lighthouse does tons of food and opens its 2nd room for club nights. Woody's serves the main halls of residence and *has a buzzing atmosphere.* The Venue is the biggest and the busiest (on campus and in Canterbury), juggling promotions every night. The University runs four other bars, *which tend to be cosy but more low key.*
Theatres: The Gulbenkian Theatre on campus *is very well kitted out* but is shared with the wider community. It hosts touring productions, concerts and the annual Canterbury festival, as well as a good many plays put on by the student drama society. Kent has one of the largest drama departments in the country.
Film: Cinema 3 is another shared venue that shows several *mainstream-ish* films a week for £3.50. Kent Student Cinema stock their own DVD library and produce a termly magazine.
Music venues: The Gulbenkian Theatre runs a number of live performances, usually world music, classical and jazz-orientated.
Clubbing: The Venue *is well-named given it's pretty much the only club option going in Canterbury. Wednesday and Saturday nights tend to be the most sweat-soaked.* DJ Spoony, Judge Jules, Trevor Nelson, Artful Dodger and Dan from Big Brother have filled the 1,400-capacity club. There are open mic nights too.
Comedy/Cabaret: The drama department run one comedy show weekly and the Union brings in the professionals *when that falls flat.*
Food: Catering is mainly centred in individual college refectories *but the bars dish out till late evening.* The Lighthouse has a Costa Coffee franchise that dishes out paninis.
Other: Apart from college and society dos, there's at least one major event a term, culminating in the Grand Summer Ball.

SOCIAL & POLITICAL

UNIVERSITY OF KENT STUDENTS' UNION:
• 5 sabbaticals • NUS member • Turnout at last ballot: 11%
From Mandela House, the financially-beleaguered Union battles for dominance over the smaller Junior College Committees (JCCs, baby-unions for the individual colleges and organisers of a fair bit of college social life). The main SU isn't out of the picture by any means, though; it's established a strong relationship with the University and is engaged in all the hot political topics: top-up fees; Britney or Christina? etc.

SU FACILITIES:
The SU owns three buildings: Mandela House, the Virginia Woolf Building and the Venue, er, venue. Seven bars; a nightclub. The Virginia Woolf Building contains the jobshop and the campus shop. Mandela House has: travel agency; fax and printing service; minibus hire; Endsleigh Insurance office; payphones; general shop; secondhand bookshop; five pool tables; juke box; vending machines; TV lounge; two meeting rooms; launderette; stationery shop; photocopier; photo booth; van hire. Also HSBC, NatWest and Lloyds banks with ATMs on campus.

CLUBS (NON-SPORTING):
Adventure Gaming; Anime; Art; Anthropology; Ballroom Dancing; Buddhist; Chinese; Christian Fellowship; Christian Performing Arts; Creative Writing; Critical Lawyers Group; Current Affairs; DJ & Clubbing; Drum & Bass; East African; Erasmus; Focus (academic); French; German; Girl Guiding; Global Kind; Hellenic; Hip Hop; Hong Kong; Indie/Alternative Music; Japanese; Kink; Latin American; Latin American Dancing; Live Music; Musical Theatre; Pagan; Philosophy; Photography; Poker; Pro-life; Shiatsu & Earth Healing; Space; Stage Spiders (kids' theatre); Subtext; Temple (barristers); Theme Park; Thursday Club; United East; Yoga. **See also Clubs tables.**

OTHER ORGANISATIONS:
The Union produces Kred every month, the *cringingly-named* student paper. The film society churns out the monthly film-making mag, Big Lens. UKCR's the 24-hr campus radio station that has aspirations of gaining a community radio licence (which will change its name to CSR). Rag raises a *fair amount* of cash through its annual Snow Ball, auctions and other *deranged* events, for local and national charities.

RELIGIOUS:
• 2 chaplains (CofE, RC)
Ten part-time chaplains cover most Christian denominations and Jewish, Islamic, Buddhist and Baha'i faiths. The Eliot Chapel is the campus prayer place although there are various makeshift worship shops in colleges as well as a Muslim prayer room. In town, there's the cathedral, of course, *but Christians who fancy something a little less lofty don't have to worry about any kind of theological drought. Non-Christians may get a bit more spiritually thirsty.*

PAID WORK:
• Job bureau • Paid work: term-time 20%; hols 75%
The Union jobshop has vacancy boards, newsletters, advice *and a good rep with local employers.* In the summertime, the Garden of England needs harvesting, and there are hop and fruit picking jobs going. *A foreign language can be helpful for getting a job dog-walking some of the millions of tourists.* There's bar and admin work in the Union and similar stuff in the city.

SPORTS

• Recent successes: cricket, skiing, snowboarding, volleyball • BUSA Ranking: 48
Intercollegiate rivalry gets pretty heated on the pitch, if a little lukewarm on the national level. Outstanding athletes can receive awards of up to £1,500.

SPORTS FACILITIES:
Three football, two rugby, hockey, all-weather and two cricket pitches; six squash, 12 tennis, three basketball, six badminton and netball courts; sports centre with multigym, dance studio, archery range, boxing ring, sunbeds, sauna and café. £60 annual membership gives free use of the facilities plus concessions for fitness tests and sauna use. Sports club members are obliged to buy membership to cover training costs. The centre's also open to the public. The local area has: leisure centre; pool; bowling green; dry ski slope; golf course; more racket sport courts and caves; the river and a lake are available for those who like to take it outside.

SPORTING CLUBS:
10-Pin Bowling; American Football; Capoeira Handball; Karting; Kendo; Kickboxing; Korfball; Lacrosse; T'ai Chi; Ultimate Frisbee. **See also Clubs tables.**

ATTRACTIONS:
Gillingham FC (*who?*) and Kent County Cricket Club practise their art nearby. Dog racing and windsurfing at Whitstable.

ACCOMMODATION

IN COLLEGE:
• Catered: 17% • Cost: £65-90 (32wks) • Self-catering: 1% • Cost: £63 (34wks)
• First years living in: 100% • Insurance premium: £
Availability: There are a total of 3,200 rooms available so in theory just under half of undergraduates can be accommodated – 1st years are guaranteed if they apply by August. Whether or not they live in, students remain members of their colleges throughout their courses. Living on campus is undoubtedly convenient, *but those in college halls can finish the year more out of pocket than they'd expected.* No cooking facilities means eating in the college refectories or dining on micro-filth, *which quickly adds up.* Come the witching hour, hall access is only for keycard-equipped residents. Most halls have a JCR (*basically a communal chill-out zone*). Self-catering University houses like Beckett Court *are popular with 2nd and 3rd years*, as is *Park Wood*, a little village of student houses with its own bar and shop set in *charming* woodland. Launderettes are available to all.
Car parking: Not too much of a problem for those living at Park Wood, but you'll need a good reason to keep one anywhere else – *needing 'The Lovemobile' close to you at all times isn't one.*

EXTERNALLY:
• Ave rent: £68 • Living at home: 2%
Availability: *Finding somewhere to live in Canterbury is like rooting for truffles (easy enough if you keep your nose to the ground) and the January house-hunt isn't as frenetic as it might be. An increasing number are moving out to Herne Bay and Whitstable (5-7 miles north), where rents are cheaper, places more plentiful and life more dull. For those who are bed-wettingly keen for something closer to the action, Wincheap and Downs Road are the places to aim for.*
Housing help: The four guys in the Accommodation Office place 1st years on campus, manage an off-campus vacancy list and help with legal wrangles. *The SU is much more hands-on in its advice-giving.*

WELFARE

SERVICES:
• Lesbian/Gay/Bisexual Officer & Society • Women's Officer & Society • Mature Students' Officer &Society • Ethnic Minorities Officer & Society • International Students' Officer & Society • Postgrad Officer & Society • Disabilities Officer & Society • Late-night minibus • Self-defence classes • College counsellors: 4 full/1 part • Crime rating: !

The *unfeasibly caring* Union also appoints a Men's Officer and a Students with Dependants' Officer. The taxi fund is for SU staff only.

Health: The University Medical Centre comes complete with six doctors, four nurses and a residential sick bay.

Women: Free attack alarms for anyone who wants one.

Crèches/Nursery: The University crèche looks after up to 50 children between 6wks-4yrs.

Disabilities: Priority parking, lifts and ramps for all buildings. The Disability Support Unit provides support and information for all disabled students, including screening and exam arrangements for dyslexics.

Crime: The SU is wrestling with a slight anti-social behaviour issue between campus and town. *Let's hope their 70s public information film-inspired 'Silent Students, Happy Homes' campaign smoothes ruffled feathers.*

FINANCE:

• Ave debt per year: £3,608
• Access fund: £160,000

Support: Some academic, music, art and sport bursaries available to those with talent, plus a range of bursaries to help top-up afflicted students. The Master of each college has £200 or so kicking around for anyone who really needs it and emergency loans are available.

King's College, London

• **The College is part of the <u>University of London</u> and students are entitled to use its facilities.**

(1) King's College London, University of London, The Strand, London, WC2R 2LS
Tel: (020) 7836 5454 E-mail: ceu@kcl.ac.uk Website: www.kcl.ac.uk
King's College London Students' Union, Macadam Building, Surrey Street, London, WC2R 2NS Tel: (020) 7836 7132 E-mail: enquiries@kclsu.org Website: www.kclsu.org

(2) Guy's Campus: King's College London, Guy's, King's and St Thomas's Schools of Medicine, Dentistry & Biomedical Sciences, London, SE1 1UL Tel: (020) 7848 6000
Guy's Campus Student Union, Boland House, London, SE1 1UL Tel: (020) 7955 5000

GENERAL

For general information about London: see <u>University of London</u>. In 1829 King George IV and the Duke of Wellington got together and came up with King's College as their gift to Higher Education *('Duke's College' somehow isn't as punchy)*. It's the second oldest college of the University of London and its *genteel rivalry with the top-spot holder, UCL, remains intense*. Its biggest site is situated at one end of the Strand, *which places it roughly where 'Chance' is on the Monopoly board*. The Thames is a boulder's throw away, as are Fleet Street, the <u>Courtauld Institute of Art</u>, <u>LSE</u> and Aldwych (a five-lane crescent curving round Bush House, the HQ of the BBC World Service). *King's also edges on to the West End so it's a prime entry point into London's social and cultural hub. The 70s front of the King's College main building is in stark contrast to the more traditional buildings that surround it.* It's made of various shades of grey, concrete, glass and even has a giant internet screen in reception. *Hidden away at the back of the building, overlooking the Thames, is much finer Georgian architecture, but that far into the building it's hard to find your way out again.* The Waterloo, Guy's and St Thomas's campus sites are just across the river; there's also Denmark Hill campus in Camberwell.

Sex ratio (M:F): 35:65	Founded: 1829
Full-time u'grads: 11,915	Part-time: 2,430
Postgrads: 2,910	Non-degree: 340
Ave course: 3yrs	Ethnic: 53%
State:private school: 71:21	Flunk rate: 7%
Mature: 29%	International: 22%
Disabled: 120	Local: 36%

ATMOSPHERE:

Like London at large, KCL is a heady, cosmopolitan jumble. The college pulses with life and academic rigour. Strand, Guy's and Waterloo are the focus of studying and social life although there's also the University of London central Union and the legion of local venues. The Strand in particular is at the heart of it all, so some of the more distant sites can end up feeling more like the kidneys. The college's medical departments are renowned, and the hospital campuses have an air of professionalism about them – but there are very few students in any department who don't take their course seriously. No time-wasters, please.

SITES:

The Strand: (6,250 students – Humanities, Law, Physical Sciences, Engineering, Social Sciences) This is the eastern end of the West End. *There's a million ways to spend money but nowhere to live, or many places to do the weekly shopping without your daily bread costing more than your dough.* The SU's based at this site and the nearest college halls are just 10 mins walk away.

Guy's Campus: (6,000 students – Medicine, Dentistry and Biomedical Sciences) A collection of *Georgian style* buildings close to London Bridge. From the top of Guy's Tower *there's an incredible view across the city.* It's 2 miles from the Strand site on the Thames's South Bank. There's also a fairly new teaching base and facilities to match at Guy's campus as well as a new SU and welfare provisions.

Waterloo Campus: (3,000 students – Health & Life Sciences, Nursing, Social Sciences) Half a mile from the Strand, *slap bang in the cultural strip that is the South Bank,* the site has a more subdued atmosphere, probably because it's the centre of college administration.

St Thomas's Hospital: (aka *Tommy's*) 1,200m from Trafalgar Square, opposite the Houses of Parliament on the south side of the Thames, is *Tommy's modern 70s open-plan development with bright, clean, inter-connected buildings.*

Denmark Hill Campus: (1,000 students – Psychiatry, Medicine, Dentistry). King's College Hospital in Camberwell. *A different kettle of cod altogether, Camberwell's in South London and, almost necessarily, shabbier as a result. It's not London's safest area (or its worst – London gets much worse), but it's cheap, residential and good for shopping. Camberwell's getting better for entertainment though still a bit old-men's-pubville but it's very well connected for the West End.* The campus has its own social life anyway.

LONDON: see University of London

TRAVEL: see University of London

Trains: Charing Cross is the most accessible mainline station for the Strand site. Waterloo station for (ahem) Waterloo, Denmark Hill for King's Hospital and London Bridge for Guy's.

Buses: Strand: 1, 4, 6, 9, 11, 13, 15, 23, 26, 59, 68, 76, 77a, 91, 168, 171 *(mathematicians may want to calculate the sequence there).* Denmark Hill: 12, 35, 40, 45 and others. 108, 501 and 133 go near Guy's and Waterloo; 77 and 507 go to Tommy's. The Riverside bus RV1 connects the Strand, Guy's and Waterloo. *Plenty* of night-buses cover all bases.

Underground: Temple (District & Circle) or Holborn (Piccadilly & Central) for the Strand site. Northern and Bakerloo lines for Waterloo; London Bridge (Northern) for Guy's; Lambeth North (Bakerloo) for Tommy's. The Jubilee line serves students based at both Guy's and Waterloo.

College: A bus is provided for medical students travelling between Guy's and Tommy's.

Bicycles: *Chances of being mown down by cars are slim since most vehicles in the area tend to be stationary, although choking to death on exhaust fumes is no one's idea of a giggle. Still the fastest way of getting around though.*

CAREER PROSPECTS:

• <u>Careers Service</u> • <u>No. of staff: 11 full/1 part</u> • <u>Unemployed after 6mths: 5%</u>
The Grad Club, as they call it, provides the Full Monty: newsletters, bulletin boards, vacancy lists, interview training, job fairs, seminar programmes and career consultations on each campus.

FAMOUS ALUMNI:

W S Gilbert (Sullivan's other half); Thomas Hardy (*depressing novelist, miserable poet*); Rory Bremner (impressionist); Anita Brookner, Susan Hill, Hanif Kureishi (novelists); George Carey (Archbishop of Canterbury); Arthur C Clarke (sci-fi writer); John Eliot Gardner (composer/conductor); Njongonkulu Winston Ndungane (Archbishop of Cape Town); Chapman Pincher (writer/journalist); Ian Shaw (jazz singer); Desmond Tutu (Archbishop and source of student rhyming slang); Maurice Wilkins (Nobel Laureate DNA Scientist).

SPECIAL FEATURES:

With a £400m refurb under its belt, *KCL is pretty smug*. It's also $\frac{1}{4}$ of SIMFONEC (with the RVC, City University and St Mary's), a *ginormous* scientific business enterprise specialising in teaching entrepreneurship and encouraging business innovation in the London universities.

FURTHER INFO:

• <u>Prospectuses: undergrad; postgrad; some departmental</u> • <u>Open days</u>
All info from admissions. KCL website has an online prospectus, virtual tour and allows cyberchat with current students. E-mail for international applicants: international@kcl.ac.uk.

ACADEMIC

Over 200 courses available, ranging from traditional core subjects to *ludicrously innovative fields*. The college is split not quite down the middle into medical sciences on one side and everything else on the other. *Biomedical Sciences on Guy's campus are particularly cutting-edge*. Most departments (especially Humanities) offer modular study and coursework as opposed to exams, and students can choose how much weight is given to either in the final assessment.

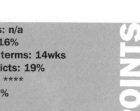

Entry points: 120-170	**Ave points: n/a**
Applns per place: 10	**Clearing: 16%**
No. of terms: 2	**Length of terms: 14wks**
Staff/student ratio: 1:9	**Study addicts: 19%**
Teaching: ****	**Research: ******
Year abroad: <1%	**Ethnic: 42%**
Firsts: 10%	**2.2s: 59%**
2.1s: 25%	**3rds: 6%**

ADMISSIONS:

• <u>Apply via UCAS</u>
Not a stickler for A levels, KCL also considers Access courses, BTEC or other vocational courses. Relevant work experience can be counted rather than quals for courses like nursing.

SUBJECTS:

Arts/Humanities: 14.8%   Social Sciences: 12.1%
Law: 8.4%   Sciences: 16.5%
Medical Sciences: 37.8%
Best: Biomedical Sciences; Classics; Computer Science; Dentistry; Education; French; German; Maths; Medicine; Midwifery & Gerontology; Molecular Biosciences; Nursing; Nutrition & Dietetics; Philosophy; Pharmacy; Physics; Portuguese; Psychiatry; Spanish; Theology; War Studies.
Unusual: Portuguese & Brazilian Studies; Turkish & Greek.

LIBRARIES:
• 900,000 books • 2,800 study places
As well as the *vast* University of London library at Senate House, KCL students have several libraries at their disposal. The main Maughan Library used to be the Public Record Office and is now the largest new university library in Britain since WWII. It's also got the only remaining Victorian zinc ceilings. Open till 10pm weekdays.

COMPUTERS:
• 1,600 workstations • 24-hr access
PAWs (Public Access Workstations – *otherwise known as 'computers'*) are sprinkled across campus, including in the libraries. Assorted opening times, but there's also wireless access, for *essential e-mail checking on the go*, as well as college-network access in a number of buildings.

OTHER LEARNING FACILITIES:
Language labs offer seven levels of teaching in various foreign languages. Music rehearsal rooms are available; there's also access to teaching at the Royal Academy of Music. The 'Virtual Campus' allows some online learning.

ENTERTAINMENT

THE CITY: see University of London

COLLEGE:
• Price of a pint of beer: £1.60 • Glass of wine: £1.30 • Can of Red Bull: £1.25
KCL's ents are dwarfed by the larger social scene at the University of London Union. The proximity of London's West End is also an issue, drawing King's students out of the campus and into the glittering nightlife of the city.
Bars: Three bars at the Strand, including The Waterfront *which can get packed,* and Tutu's (the flagship venue), *offers a great view of the Thames and a reasonable cocktail menu.* Denmark Hill, Guy's and Waterloo have bars too.
Theatres: The Greenwood Theatre has Question Time, Jackanory, Countdown and Jo Brand on its CV and it's been tarted it up even more since its TV glory days. 20+ productions each year with regular jaunts to Edinburgh. *King's Players rule the dramatic roost but other societies and departments get a look-in too.*
Clubbing/Music venues: Tutu's holds regular cheesy club nights, as does The Penthouse Bar at Denmark Hill. *The truth is, ULU's far better at doing this sort of thing.*
Comedy/Cabaret: Fortnightly comic capers in The Comedy Basement at Guy's. *In theory anyway – they're notoriously irregular.*
Food: King's restaurant in the Strand site flogs *cheap* pie 'n' chips concoctions. Tutu's and its sibling bars sell food late into the night, the hospitals have canteens and there are *cheap, chirpy* cafés on most sites.
Other: Yearly bevy of black-tie balls. The Summer Ball is the biggest and ULU schedules some top formal nights as well.

SOCIAL & POLITICAL

KING'S COLLEGE LONDON STUDENTS' UNION:
• 5 sabbaticals • Turnout at last ballot: 15% • NUS member
KCLSU is the oldest union in London *but it certainly ain't the most political. The ballot turnouts are impressive but the overall feel is businesslike rather than Bolshevik and the focus is on events and facilities rather than revolution.*

SU FACILITIES:
Five bars; four cafeterias; nightclub; four coffee/snack bars; two fast food outlets; eight pool tables; Endsleigh Insurance branch; at least two ATMs on each site; payphones; crèche; two bookshops (one Blackwells); STA travel branch; general store; vending machines; stationery shop; juke boxes; TV lounge; meeting rooms; photocopier; fax service; printing service; photo booth; advice centre. There's a new student centre at Waterloo.

CLUBS (NON-SPORTING):

Abacus (British & Chinese Students); Chinese; Ahlul Bayt (Islam); Arabic; Contemporary Music; European; Gilbert & Sullivan; General Practice; German; Hellenic; Hindu; Hip Hop; Hispanic; History; Japan; King's Players; King's Traditional Music & Dance; Krishna; Links (St John Ambulance); Malaysian Singaporean; Maths; Maxwell; Medsin; Model UN; Paediatrics; Pakistan; Persian; Quality Stuff (self-proclaimed Geeks with a fondness for Thundercats and all things 'Ho'); Sexpression (sex education); Sikh; SIS; Sri Lankan; Surgical; Thai; War Studies; Wind Band. **See also Clubs tables.**

OTHER ORGANISATIONS:

Roar is the SU mag (includes listings) and there's talk of a radio station. *The Rag's beer races with UCL go down well and London colleges have a penchant for pinching each other's mascots. King's mascot was Reggie, a $\frac{1}{4}$-ton red copper lion, until he was stolen by City & Guilds who castrated him. The new mascot was filled with concrete and was quickly stolen with the aid of trucks and winches. Now they've got a copper lion again, which is just asking for it.*

RELIGIOUS:

• 4 chaplains (CofE, RC, Orthodox, FC)
Chapels at the Strand and Guy's, Muslim prayer rooms are located on various sites.
PAID WORK: see University of London
Some paid work is available with the SU, mainly bar work.

SPORTS

• Recent successes: athletics, ju jitsu • BUSA Ranking: 47
Things are surprisingly sporty considering the outdoor facilities are divided around Cobham, New Malden, Dulwich and Honour Oak Park – all more than a light jog away. 40% of University of London team members are King's students.

SPORTS FACILITIES:

13 football pitches; six rugby pitches; hockey pitch; six cricket wickets; two squash courts; 19 tennis courts; two basketball courts; eight netball courts; sports hall; two swimming pools; running track; athletics field; K4 fitness gym; multigym; aerobics studio; four rounders pitches; shooting range. *Most of which are bloody miles away, but at least they're free to use.* There's a shooting range at Strand, while Guy's has a swimming pool. Locally there are public facilities and the courtyard of the Courtauld Institute becomes an ice rink at Xmas time.

SPORTING CLUBS:

Aerobics; Aerosports; Boat; Boxing; Bujinkan; Capoira; Ju Jitsu; Kickboxing; Kung Fu; Lacrosse; Polo; Ladies' Sports; Rifle & Pistol; Shaolin Kung Fu; Thai Boxing; Ultimate Frisbee; Waterpolo; Windsurfing; Yoga. **See also Clubs tables.**

ATTRACTIONS: see University of London

ACCOMMODATION

IN COLLEGE:

• Catered: 4% • Cost: £98 (40wks) • Self-catering: 22% • Cost: £56-99 (40wks)
• First years living in: 73% • Insurance premium: £££
Availability: Eight halls of residences dotted around London, most within a 4-mile radius of the Strand. The Hampstead Halls are *in demand for their posh, leafy looks,* even though they're at the other end of town, while Stamford Street is *the most luxurious, with swanky en-suites* and basement fitness centre. There are single-sex halls as well as some provision for couples. All halls have launderette facilities, and most have common rooms and TV lounges. Self-catered kitchens have *plenty of appliance goodies.*
Car parking: Almost *impossible* at almost all halls. *Permits are trickier to get hold of than epileptic eels,* but the Residence Office has a few for special cases.

EXTERNALLY: see University of London

Housing help: The accommodation office works in conjunction with the University of London to help those living out. Bulletin boards and legal advice are available from KCL, otherwise see the University of London's facilities.

WELFARE

SERVICES:
- Lesbian/Gay/Bisexual Officer • Postgrad Officer • Self-defence classes
- College counsellors: 17 full • Crime rating: !!!!!

Health: The College runs a Counselling and Medical Centre with four doctors, three nurses, a counsellor and a psychotherapist. Full dental service available in the College Hospitals.

Crèches/Nursery: King's offers subsidised places with a private local nursery.

Disabilities: *Good intentions, but old buildings don't lend themselves easily to wheelchair use. There are a number of Disability Advisers and a guide for disabled students, but accommodation is limited to a handful of adapted rooms.*

Crime/Drugs: *Denmark Hill is a bit rougher around the edges than the others and drug-related crime is a concern.*

FINANCE:
- Ave debt per year: £4,703

Fees: International students can pay up to £23,070 for clinically based degrees. For postgrads, it's between £2,940 (Arts) and £4,298 (Nursing)
- Access fund: £675,594 • Successful applications/yr: 713 • Ave payment: £1,000

Support: 100 bursaries are available for applicants in addition to other scholarships, bursaries and hardship funds for internationals.

Kingston University

- *Formerly Kingston Polytechnic.*

Kingston University, River House,
53-57 High Street, Kingston upon Thames, Surrey, KT1 1LQ
Tel: (020) 8547 2000 E-mail: admissions-info@kingston.ac.uk Website: www.kingston.ac.uk
Kingston University Students Union, Penrhyn Road, Kingston upon Thames, Surrey, KT1 2EE
Tel: 020 8547 8868 E-mail: studentsunion@kingston.ac.uk Website: www.kingstonsu.com

GENERAL

Kingston didn't used to be in London, but the city's swell means that King Henry VIII's one-time country retreat is now a part of the big smoke, *even if there's a lot less smoke and a lot more greenery than the rest of the capital.* It's south-west London, some 10 miles from

Swansea University's in a city that's the site of the world's only commercial leech farm, and the invention of instant custard.

Trafalgar Square and *still retains some of the character of its historical glory*. Hampton Court Palace is the obvious highlight, surrounded by acres of deer-parks. Across the *handsome* Kingston Bridge sit the four sites of the university, *all of which lack palatial splendour, to say the least*. The buildings are within 4 miles of one another and vary from whitewashed *charm to new-fangled mangle*.

Sex ratio (M:F): 49:51	**Founded: 1971**
Full-time u'grads: 12,675	**Part-time: 1,880**
Postgrads: 1,215	**Non-degree: 1,956**
Ave course: 3yrs	**Ethnic: 47%**
State:private school: 92:8	**Flunk rate: 19%**
Mature: 38%	**International: 15%**
Disabled: 197	**Local: n/a**

51%
49%

ATMOSPHERE:
Students have a *strong* affinity for their college, *which isn't diluted* by the multiple sites or the *occasionally depressing* architecture. The main site at Penrhyn Road (7,500 students) is a *hive of activity*, with campaigning, drinking, dressing up and *general riotousness in full show*. Knight's Park (2,000) has *more of a thoughtful, arty feel* to it, whereas Roehampton Vale (500) is *a bit nerdier* – lots of engineers either engineering or *keeping things low-key*. The halls site at Kingston Hill (6,000) has a *strong sense of community* and a *healthy (or possibly unhealthy) dose of Sloaney types*.

LONDON: see University of London
- Population: 147,600 • Town centre: $\frac{1}{2}$ mile • London: 10 miles
- Birmingham: 106 miles • Edinburgh: 423 miles
- High temp: 22 • Low temp: 4 • Rainfall: 49

KINGSTON:
A *lively* town centre focuses on the 700-year-old marketplace. There's a *village-like* character *which stops just short of buxom milkmaids with a glint in their eye*. Development has installed a quayside redevelopment with courtyards, walkways, bars and shops. There's also a *high-profile* bluechip industry presence, where *serious men in suits* and *geeks in labcoats* make *stacks of cash* for companies like Nikon, Sitel and Unichem.

TRAVEL: see University of London
Trains: A standard single from Waterloo to Kingston costs £3.40.
Car: *Acres* of car parking space but unfortunately also thousands upon thousands of cars too, *so balancing the two isn't always easy*.
Air: Kingston's *quite convenient* for Gatwick and Heathrow.
College: Free buses cover the different sites and run every 15 mins, 9am-6pm Mon-Fri.
Taxis: £8 from station to student residence. There's *a lot of competition*, which *can only be a good thing* for students who can be bothered to haggle.
Bicycles: Students make *full* use of a good cycle lane network.

CAREER PROSPECTS:
- Careers Service • No. of staff: 5 full/4 part • Unemployed after 6mths: 11%

FAMOUS ALUMNI:
Glenda Bailey (editor, US Marie Claire); Angie Bowie (Dave's 1st wife); Lawrence Dallaglio (former England rugby captain); Trevor Eve (actor); Patrick Forge (DJ); Caryn Franklin (TV presenter); Richard James (the Aphex Twin); Graeme Le Saux (footballer); Steve Mason (Gene guitarist); John Richmond, Helen Storey (fashion designers); Stella Tennant (posh model). Sir Gulam Noon (*one-man chiken tikka masala empire*) has an honorary doctorate.

FURTHER INFO:
- Prospectuses: undergrad; departmental; audio; video • Open days

 A**CADEMIC**

A broad range of subjects on offer and decent module-based teaching. Kingston's at the forefront of the online learning revolution – the vast majority of course modules are now online.

POINTS

90-360

Entry points: 90-360
No. of terms: 3
Staff/student ratio: 1:9
Teaching: ***
Year abroad 3%
Firsts: 9%
2.1s: 39%

Ave points: 200
Length of terms: 12wks
Study addicts: 19%
Research: ***
Sandwich students: 3%
2.2s: 36%
3rds: 3%

ADMISSIONS:

• Apply via UCAS

SUBJECTS:

Best: Architecture & Design; Art & Design; Built Environment & Manufacturing Engineering; Civil Engineering; Economics; History of Art; Maths, Statistics & Operational Research; Modern Languages; Molecular Biosciences; Nursing & Midwifery; Politics; Radiography; Sociology; Sports Science.
Unusual: The only Aircraft Engineering Foundation course in the country.

LIBRARIES:

• 431,293 books • 1,359 study places
Four main libraries, one on each site, devoted to the faculties based there. Weekend opening hours (10.45am-3.45pm) clash with long pub lunching though.

COMPUTERS:

• 1,600 workstations

OTHER LEARNING FACILITIES:

Students on the Aircraft Engineering foundation degree get a real-live Learjet *to play with*.

E**NTERTAINMENT**

LONDON: see University of London

KINGSTON UPON THAMES:

• Price of a pint of beer: £2.20 • Glass of wine: £2.50 • Can of Red Bull: £1.75
Cinemas: A 14-screen Odeon in the *fatly-named* Rotunda centre does a neat 20% student discount.
Theatres: The Kingston Theatre is in the *swish* Quays development.
Pubs: About 20 to choose from so *ideal for pub golf*. They include the *very nice, very classy and very expensive*. *Pushplugs: Bar Casa, Ha Ha's, Kingston Mill (it's a Scream chain)*.
Clubbing: Oceania is a *whooping* eight-room club on the site of the old bus station. Monday and Wednesday are student nights. Otherwise, The Works is a student den, Bacchus *somehow makes a dingy cellar seem like a decent venue* and Bar Euissa plays all sorts.
Music venues: The Peel and The Grey Horse have indie and alternative bands. *Useless trivia*: the Lost Prophets played one of their first gigs in Kingston.
Eating out: *Lots of chains*. *Pushplugs: Wagamama, Nando's, Blue Hawaii, Little Italy, Pizza Express, Frango*.

UNIVERSITY:

• Price of a pint of beer: £1.65 • Glass of wine: £2.25 • Can of Red Bull: £1.65

Bars: Bar Zen is the biggest and does theme nights. The *slightly more leftfield* Knight's Park bar has DJ nights, indie rock evening, events and live bands. It *somehow manages to achieve a laid-back ambience while being packed tighter than Linford Christie's shorts.* Hannafords, on the Kingston Hill campus, is a community boozer and the Tolworth Court sports bar is *jocksville,* especially on a Wednesday.

Theatres: The drama course has *vamped up the thesp levels.* Kingston now sends productions to the Edinburgh Fringe and has its own studio theatre.

Film: The society *sticks up a screen whenever it finds a room spare* and shows cult classics.

Music venues: Bar Zen and Knight's Park both host live bands. Idlewild, Boxer Rebellion and Seachange have all dropped by.

Clubbing: KUSU has sorted out a deal with Oceania and The Works for cheap student nights. Students can hop the queues and get discounted tickets.

Comedy/Cabaret: Paramount Comedy network visitors crack gags twice a month.

Food: There's a Subway sandwich bar and a *canteeny* sort of place called Avenance as well as smaller *trougheries* on all the sites.

Other: Plans for three *glitzy* balls a year from 2005.

S O C I A L & P O L I T I C A L

KINGSTON UNIVERSITY STUDENTS UNION:

• 4 sabbaticals • Turnout at last ballot: 9% • NUS member

Left-leaning and *usually at loggerheads* with the University over cash – *they've got it, KUSU want it.*

SU FACILITIES:

The *portacabinesque* Union Building is based at Penrhyn Road and offers bars with TVs, pool tables and games machines, a travel office, bookshop, photocopying and printing. Each site has its own Union office and bar (except Roehampton).

CLUBS (NON-SPORTING):

Alternative Music; Ahmadiyya Muslim; Arabic Architecture; Arts & Social; Asian Entertainments; Believers Loveworld; FACT (Film & Cult TV); Fore Crime; French; Hindu; Engineering; KUSEDS (Students for the Exploration & Development of Space); Law; Music & Design; Oriental; Oriental Sport; Politics; Research Students; Rock; Sikh; Writer's Circle. **See also Clubs tables.**

OTHER ORGANISATIONS:

The weekly Union-run broadsheet SUblime (*not bad at all*) is filled with student contributions. STONE Radio is *battling with bureacracy to get itself set up.* Students and staff do a fair deal of community work painting schools, working with kids and so on.

RELIGIOUS:

There are a number of churches, mosques, temples and synagogues in the local area and an interdenominational prayer room provided by the University.

For religion in London: see University of London

PAID WORK: see University of London

• Paid work: term-time 60%: hols 90%

There's *no need* to go job-hunting in central London when there are *plenty of opportunities* on the doorstep. Shopping centres, Union bars, Uni admin, tutoring, office temping, bar work are *all there for the taking.*

SPORTS

• Recent successes: hockey, badminton, rowing, swimming • BUSA Ranking: 26
Excellent sporting facilities as the University runs a Talented Athlete Scheme to help top sportsmen and women compete nationally and internationally. Talented athletes get bursaries, free use of the Uni's fitness centre, free sports massage, professional office backup and 'flexible' workload – ie. *not too much of it.*

SPORTS FACILITIES:
The University owns a *whole lot* of pitches at Tolworth Court, including ten football pitches, two hockey pitches, tennis courts, a gym at Kingston Hill; and a fitness centre and aerobics studio at Penrhyn Road. Also a local public leisure centre and swimming pool.

SPORTING CLUBS:
American Football; Boxing; Cance; Ju-Jitsu; Karate Goju Rhu; Karate Shotokar; Karting; Motorcycle; Mountaineering & Caving. **See also Clubs tables.**

ATTRACTIONS: see University of London
World class rugby at Twickenham is *close by* and there's racing at Sandown Park. Wimbledon for the tennis – and strawberries at a pound each – after summer exams.

ACCOMMODATION

IN COLLEGE:
• Self-catering: 19% • Cost: £85 (32wks)
• First years living in: 33% • Insurance premium: ££££
Availability: Halls are *generally* of a *pretty decent* standard, although some are a *bit of a trek* from campus. Clayhill Hall has had a major refurb and is no longer referred to by students as 'Clayhell'. Middlemill Halls, near the campus, are the *most popular.* Some rooms are modified for wheelchair access.
Car parking: *Fine* in halls, *forbidden* in Uni.

EXTERNALLY: see University of London
• Ave rent: £85 • Living at home: 30%
Availability: Most accommodation is to be found 2 miles from campus in Surbiton (*of The Good Life fame*) but many letting agents *run a mile* at the sniff of a student. *It's not cheap, either.*
Housing help: The University accommodation office *does its best* to try and help out.

WELFARE

SERVICES:
• Lesbian & Gay Society • International Students' Society • Ethnic Minorities Officer
• Women's Society • Late-night minibus • College counsellors: 6 full
• SU counsellors: 2 part • Crime rating: !!
There's a Citizens' Advice Bureau on campus that deals with all sorts of welfare issues.
Health: There are three GPs, a nurse and two counsellors at the on-campus NHS practice.
Crèches/Nursery: A few places in the nursery for kids up to 5yrs.
Disabilities: Disabled parking, a technical support centre and decent access in the main bulidings. There's also a dyslexia support officer.

FINANCE:
- Ave debt per year: £3,457
- Access fund: £627,000 • Successful applications/yr: 627
- Ave payment: £1,200-1,500

Support: Hardship loans are available.

Kingston Polytechnic

see Kingston University

La Sainte Union see <u>University of Southampton</u>

Lampeter, University of Wales

Lancashire Polytechnic see <u>University of Central Lancashire</u>

Lancaster University

Leeds University

Leeds Metropolitan University

Leeds Polytechnic see <u>Leeds Metropolitan University</u>

Leicester University

Leicester Poly see <u>De Montfort University</u>

Leicester Polytechnic see <u>De Montfort University</u>

University of Lincoln

University of Lincolnshire and Humberside see <u>University of Lincoln</u>

University of Liverpool

Liverpool Hope University College

Liverpool John Moores University

Liverpool Poly see <u>Liverpool John Moores University</u>

Liverpool Polytechnic see <u>Liverpool John Moores University</u>

The London Institute see <u>University of the Arts, London</u>

London Metropolitan University

London South Bank see <u>South Bank University</u>

University of London

London College of Fashion see <u>University of the Arts, London</u>

London College of Printing see <u>University of the Arts, London</u>

London Guildhall University see <u>London Metropolitan University</u>

Loughborough University

LSE

University of Luton

Luton College of Higher Education see <u>University of Luton</u>

La Sainte Union

see <u>University of Southampton</u>

Lampeter, University of Wales

• *Formerly St David's College.*
• *Part of the University of Wales.*
University of Wales, Lampeter, Ceredigion, SA48 7ED
Tel: (01570) 422 351 E-mail: recruit@lamp.ac.uk Website: www.lamp.ac.uk
University of Wales, Lampeter, Students' Union, Lampeter, Ceredigion, SA48 7ED
Tel: (01570) 422 619 E-mail: ents@lamp.ac.uk Website: www.lamp.ac.uk/su

GENERAL

Deep in the hills of south-west Wales, where valleys and leylines meet, is the *tiny* market town of Lampeter. In this virtual village, *around the corner from nowhere, is the correspondingly small* University – the oldest degree-awarding institution in Wales and the third oldest in Britain. Modelled on an Oxbridge college, *its elegant stone buildings, which engulf the town, are quietly impressive, with none of the pomp and grandeur of their Oxbridge counterparts. For the wiccans of the world, the whole area is a channelling point for mystical energy. Beyond the borders of the town are the beautiful, rugged hills from which Stonehenge was cut – then lugged 300-odd miles for some twisted, druidic reason.* The red kite soars above the valleys and, around the coast, dolphins frolic. *Aw.*

Sex ratio (M:F): 36:64	Founded: 1822
Full-time u'grads: 875	Part-time: 5,185
Postgrads: 180	Non-degree: 84
Ave course: 3yrs	Ethnic: 5%
State:private school: 60:40	Flunk rate: 10%
Mature: 45%	International: 18%
Disabled: 92	Local: 18%

ATMOSPHERE:

Lampeter has one of the smallest campuses in Britain and can be a very quiet place when students are buried in the bar/library. The student body is a mixture of sensible country folk and happy hippies who manage to perk things up in a laidback sort of way. Staff/student closeness is one of the plus points and social and academic life combine in a strong sense of community where it's well-nigh impossible not to know everyone else. Because of the size of the town and the age of the University, locals are more of a clique than the dominant community and relations are friendly as a result.

Some, particularly those who've woken up here after clearing, can find the remoteness tricky to adjust to, but doing a degree here is not entirely unlike spending 3 years in the chillout tent at Glastonbury – with all the ancient spookiness both places share. Hauntings and possessions have been reported, but then there are lots of mushrooms growing on them there hills.

LAMPETER:

• Population: 3,000 • Town centre: 0 miles • London: 220 miles
• Carmarthen: 23 miles • Aberystwyth: 27 miles
• High temp: 18 • Low temp: 2 • Rainfall: 71

To call Lampeter a town would be *stretching things* – it's got about 20 shops, a pub for each night of the week *and that's it. Lampeter has a remote and forgotten feel to it, as though it's been hidden away from the world.* There's no station – the nearest is in Carmarthen which is about three times the size, relatively good for shopping but still a far cry from a buzzing metropolis. Students head to Aberystwyth for the *comparatively* big noise. *The local area is dripping with history, natural beauty and sheep.* There's a Roman goldmine; plenty of ruins; Talley Abbey; Pembrokeshire National Park; the National Botanical Garden of Wales, Aberglasney; and the famous Devil's Bridge. For those into literary research, Lampeter town and campus got a significant (and somewhat satirical) mention in Malcolm Pryce's recent novel Last Tango in Aberystwyth.

TRAVEL:

Trains: From Carmarthen you can get mainline trains to London (£27.70), Cardiff (£10.30) and Birmingham (£24.25). Aberystwyth station is better for northbound journeys.
Coaches: Lampeter is on a National Express route to London via Cardiff (£30.60), Cardiff (£12.10) and Birmingham via Swansea (£26.15).
Car: *A car – or failing that, a rocket pack – makes a big difference to the quality of life. Day trips and shopping become feasible for a start.* 18 miles off the A40.
Air: Cardiff International or Birmingham are the closest – *which is to say they're both several inconvenient hours away.*
Hitching: *Without any major roads, it ain't easy. Allow a day to get anywhere and take a sleeping bag just in case. To make things a little easier – bring a car with you too.*
Local: The buses stick to the timetables, hourly till about 5.30pm. It's £3.50 return to Carmarthen with a similar service to Aberystwyth.
University: Occasionally organise trips to Swansea, Cardiff and Aberystwyth.
Taxis: *Sure, there are taxis, but frankly, students can't afford them – about £20 to Carmarthen. Maybe worth it to have a night out in town if sharing the ride back.*
Bicycles: There are sheds, not too many hills and virtually no theft, *but without motorised legs, most places are out of cycle reach.*

CAREER PROSPECTS:

• <u>Careers Service</u> • <u>No. of staff: 4 full</u> • <u>Unemployed after 6mths: 9%</u>
The Employability Unit is a job centre and career guidance facility, sending newsletters, sorting out job fairs, distributing all sorts of useful booklets and giving interview practice.

FAMOUS ALUMNI:

Jack Higgins (thriller writer); Anthony Hopkins (actor); T E Lawrence (of Arabia fame).

SPECIAL FEATURES:

• Single honours degrees may be started in January as well as the more usual late September.

FURTHER INFO:

• <u>Prospectuses: undergrad; postgrad; some departments</u> • <u>Open days</u>
There's an online overseas guide offering practical information for international students, as well as a mature students' guide, both via the main website. Lampeter attracts a large number of long distance learners – *understandable since it's such an effort to actually get there.* E-mail the SU for alternative info.

ACADEMIC

Lampeter specialises in Arts, Humanities and Social Sciences. *Its small size means that seminars and tutorials can be intimate affairs and students have a clearer vision of the academic staff as actual people rather than talking books.* With no science subjects to complicate the schedules, all students can expect between 10-20 contact hours per week, less in the 3rd year. The modular credit-based system is flexible, so units from other department can also be studied.

Entry points: 160-260	Ave points: 200
Applns per place: 4	Clearing: 8%
No. of terms: 3	Length of terms: 11/8wks
Staff/student ratio: 1:8	Study addicts: 27%
Teaching: n/a	Research: ***
Year abroad: 3%	Sandwich students: 0
Firsts: 7%	2.2s: 34%
2.1s: 52%	3rds: 7%

ADMISSIONS:

• Apply via UCAS
Lampeter has a good record for widening access and considers applications on individual merits.

SUBJECTS:

Arts/Humanities: 94%   Business: 6%
Unusual: Australian Studies; Chinese Studies; English with Creative Writing; Islamic Studies; Jewish Studies.

LIBRARIES:

• 230,000 books • 200 study places
Two libraries: the Founder's (20,000 historical books, documents and manuscripts) and the Main Library. *Both adhere to slightly archaic hours*, closing early at weekends and blink-and-you'll-miss-it opening on Sundays.

COMPUTERS:

• 200 workstations
Five labs, including one in the Main Library. One lab has 24-hr access.

OTHER LEARNING FACILITIES:

The *ultra-sexy* Media Centre is open 9-5 and has a range of facilities, including a film and TV studio, video editing/conferencing suite, digital printing and scanning, subtitling, digital camera and web streaming equipment – all for free.

ENTERTAINMENT

LAMPETER:

• Price of a pint of beer: £2 • Glass of wine: £2 • Can of Red Bull: £2
It's a tiny place, but it's got all the basics and one or two unexpected luxuries. Boredom isn't much of a problem – there's enough to do to keep all but the most fundamentalist clubthumper amused.
Theatres: Theatr Felinfach: theatr fach fywiog yn werth ymweld a hi. *If you don't understand that, don't bother.*
Pubs: 14 pubs within a $1\frac{1}{2}$ mile radius, *of which the most popular are the Black Lion (attractive and fun) and the Cwmanne Tavern (cheaper, friendly and sociable). There are no 'locals-only' haunts, but best leave your sheep jokes at home.*
Eating out: There's a few eateries including an Indian, *but the Ram Inn's food is tasty, cheap and big.*

UNIVERSITY:

• Price of a pint of beer: £1.70 • Glass of wine: £1.50 • Can of Red Bull: £1.50
Bars: *Students and staff mix in the Old Bar, which has a late licence when it needs one and holds regular karaoke, music and talent events. The Extension acts as bar-cum-club.*
Theatres: The Arts Hall's a multimedia performance venue, *which means it's essentially a large room with no specialist equipment.* The drama society puts two or three plays on a year, sometimes more.
Film: The Arts Hall becomes a cinema for five or six films a week. There are three different film societies so the schedule is wildly varied from Disney to Polanski to George A Romero.

Music venues: The Old Bar and the Extension combine to create one giant venue that reaches places the Arts Hall can't. Both host bands, from the local groups to megastars like, *ahem, Timmy Mallett and The Foundations.* There are also classical music events.
Clubbing: Saturday is Team-Up Night when two clubs or associations pool their collective musical juices and stage a club night. DJ Cash Money, Ainsley Burrows and Scratch Perverts have performed.
Food: The Refectory offers basic school dinnery stuff, but the portions are generous. Pooh's Corner and the Pizza Bar in the SU are more likely to tempt jaded palates. The shop offers the *three nutritional staples:* the pasty, the sandwich and the packet of crisps.
Other: The President's Ball is *a typical marquis job (big name + bar + dance tent x alcohol = wasted). Apparently they also mud wrestle.*

SOCIAL & POLITICAL

LAMPETER, UNIVERSITY OF WALES, STUDENTS' UNION:

• 3 sabbaticals • Turnout at last ballot: 35% • NUS member
The small size of the University makes it hard to escape SU involvement and *although party politics doesn't often go beyond discussions on the ethical status of Twiglets – a single firebrand can make a huge difference. The Union Exec prides itself on being completely unbiased and there's an overall feeling of tolerance and liberalism. The new Vice Chancellor has a pro-student stance, so relations with the authorities are harmonious.*

SU FACILITIES:

The Union building has a bar; cafeteria; restaurant; advice centre; printing and photocopying; payphones; general shop; pool tables; juke box; TV room; function room; bookshop; gaming and vending machines and minibus hire. The Union Extension provides a dance floor, bar, nightclub facilities and a conference suite.

CLUBS (NON-SPORTING):

Battle Re-enactment (*also good at first aid*); Geek (campaigning for geek rights to sit in a room and do nothing); Live Action Role Play; Pagan (particularly large, due to the area); Pudding. **See also Clubs tables.**

OTHER ORGANISATIONS:

1822 is the University's satirical magazine, four times a term. Lazarus radio broadcasts permanently online. Rag organises the customary three-legged pub-crawl, and reeled in a *respectable £5,000 last year.*

RELIGIOUS:

• 1 chaplain (CofE)
There's a *dinky little* chapel, a mosque and a Buddhist shrine. *The pagan society's adventures take them off into the woods. Other faiths will have further to travel.*

PAID WORK:

• Job bureau
The Employability Unit helps find local vacancies. Some jobs are up for grabs in the Union and the bar. Local pub and shop work isn't out of the question but besides that and the organic food packing centre, there's not a lot about.

SPORTS

• Recent successes: rugby • BUSA Ranking: 48
Lampeter's the oldest rugby-playing institution in Wales. Considering it's such a weeny place, sporting success is surprisingly frequent but the emphasis is on fun and the attitude is encouraging to all.

SPORTS FACILITIES:
There's a *stark* modern sports hall, 5 acres of playing fields, squash and tennis courts, an all-weather pitch, basketball/netball court; swimming pool, multigym (£25/year). The river (Afon Teifi) is *useful for some sports but not large enough for any aquatic Olympics.* Around town, there's a golf course and pony trekking and the mountains *are excellent* for rambling, climbing, hang-gliding *and getting cold*.

SPORTING CLUBS:
See also Clubs tables.

ACCOMMODATION

IN COLLEGE:
• Self-catering: 53% • Cost: £49 (36wks)
• First years living in: 85% • Insurance premium: £
Availability: The majority of undergrads live in, 1st years are guaranteed accommodation and about half who live in have en-suite facilities. All accommodation is on campus and *no one gets turfed out when it comes to vacation – which is popular with finalists.* Kitchens are shared with around seven others. *There are a few dodgy digs and damp is a problem but most students swallow their pride and are content with the basics.* Mixed-sex couples are accommodated as are those sharing, with twin beds, larger rooms and a reduction (a tenner per person per week). There are all-night porters *but that's more of a token gesture than a security measure as crime in halls is uncommon to say the least.*
Car parking: Not a problem.

EXTERNALLY:
• Ave rent: £37 • Living at home: 10%
Availability: Many students can find something suitably cheap close to the University. Those that can't opt for seaside locations like Newquay and Aberaeron.

WELFARE

SERVICES:
• Lesbian/Gay/Bisexual Officer & Society • Women's Officer & Society
• Mature Students' Officer & Society • International Students' Officer & Society
• Postgrad Officer & Society • Disabilities Officer & Society • Nightline
• College counsellors: 1 full/4 part • Crime rating: !
Health: The University shares the town GP service which has four doctors and a nurse.
Women: Free attack alarms and a walk-home service from *chivalrous* security staff.
Crèches/Nursery: 30 places for kids between newborn (*ish*) and 5yrs. There's a playscheme during vacations.
Disabilities: *The age of the buildings can present some access problems but the campus itself is compact and largely doable.* Ramps, hearing loops and adapted accommodation all feature.
Crime: *Lowest in the UK, so the police say.*
Drugs: *Arts & Humanities students, mushrooms growing locally – go figure.* The University has a zero tolerance policy and *a few blind spots.*

FINANCE:
• Ave debt per year: £2,608
Fees: International undergrads are looking at £6,700, postgrads at £3,010. It'll be 2007 before top-up fees hit, but *the Union is steadily mounting a strong defence.*
• Access fund: £185,241 • Successful applications/yr: 420 • Ave payment: £500
Support: Aside from the rugby scholarships, there are accommodation bursaries and awards for mature students and an assortment of cash pots available via application or academic achievement, from £20–£2,000.

Lancashire Polytechnic

see University of Central Lancashire

Lancaster University

Lancaster University, Bailrigg, Lancaster, LA1 4YW
Tel: (01524) 65201 E-mail: ugadmissions@lancs.ac.uk Website: www.lancs.ac.uk
Lancaster University Students' Union, Bailrigg, Lancaster, LA1 4YW
Tel: (01524) 593 765 Website: www.lusu.co.uk

GENERAL

A few miles south of the *lovely* Lake District, the county town of Lancaster dates from Roman days *and still has plenty of honey-coloured Georgian buildings left to show off at parties*. Flanked by countryside in most directions, with *lumpy* Cumbria beckoning to the north, it reaches out to Morecambe and Heysham 4 miles away on the north-west coast, as well as to the treeless Forest of Bowland – *starter for ten: 'forest' means crown property for hunting, trees are an added feature*. 2 miles from the city centre and perched on a hill, the University of Lancaster is comprised of nine colleges that form the *large Greenfield* campus. Many of the 60s buildings are *beginning to look uglier than Jerry Springer in fishnets* but the University has forked out *squillions on* a number of redevelopments and extensions. The campus centre is Alexandra Square, a large paved area surrounded by light brick buildings and filled with students walking, chatting, working, sleeping and putting up posters. Circling the campus 250 acres of landscaped woods, parklands and fields provide a *serene* rural backdrop to the college buildings and the *bustling* University atmosphere.

59% ♀ / 41% ♂

Sex ratio (M:F): 41:59	**Founded: 1964**
Full-time u'grads: 7,510	**Part-time: 6,005**
Postgrads: 1,510	**Non-degree: 1,447**
Ave course: 3yrs	**Ethnic: 5%**
State:private school: 85:15	**Flunk rate: 6%**
Mature: 11%	**International: 19%**
Disabled: 142	**Local: 16%**

ATMOSPHERE:

The most pronounced influence on the University's atmosphere is the collegiate system (although nowhere near the extent of Oxbridge) which gives a 'community within a community' air. Although the colleges are little more than glorified halls of residence, most teaching is college-orientated and the social life tends to hang itself around college bars. The colleges themselves don't conduct admissions, although students can express a preference when applying – not that there's that much to prefer since the only obvious difference is in size, varying between 500 and 800-odd students. There's a varied crowd, with all sorts of different backgrounds mingling nicely. Despite the lack of a major ents venue on site, students are keen to keep the fun on campus, with the occasional jaunt into town for big nights out. The local population in turn is largely relieved that the University's a safe distance from the city centre and that students don't overrun the place as a result.

LANCASTER:

- Population: 133,914 • City centre: 2$\frac{1}{2}$ miles • London: 250 miles
- Preston: 26 miles • Manchester: 48 miles
- High temp: 19 • Low temp: 1 • Rainfall: 71

Lancaster's a rather sweet and quaint city, with tourist-fuls of history oozing down its winding little streets. The Ashton memorial dominates the skyline on one hill while the castle and the priory gaze down from another. The castle's dual function as tourist attraction and prison neatly mirrors the atmosphere of the city and its people: ancient architecture and English-rose beauty compete with a whiff of small-town bigotry and a fashion sense reliant on baseball caps and excessive gold jewellery. Lancaster has the usual deck of amenities: supermarkets, late-opening shops, bookstores and libraries, as well as the Maritime Museum. *Marketgate and the St Nicholas arcade are good for tipping mothballs from the purse.*

TRAVEL:

Trains: Lancaster station, 3 miles from the campus, has direct connections to London, Manchester, Birmingham and other places, *some nice, some nasty. So it goes.*
Coaches: *The considerate people at* National Express *have plonked a coach stop on the campus with passing routes to a number of major cities – dangerously tempting after a tankard or eight.*
Car: The M6 bypasses Lancaster from north to south, slicing past the edge of the campus. The A6 and A683 go right into the centre. *Parking's okay, though the University isn't keen on students having cars and buses are very accessible.*
Air: Manchester Airport 50 miles away has most major budget airlines.
Hitching: *There's a special shelter on campus and an established point in town for pick-ups for trips to and from the University although most students don't use it since the University and the Union have been telling hitching horror stories. For longer journeys the M6 is a good option. There are also offers of lifts and car-pooling on notice boards.*
Local: There's a big bus stop right in the middle of the campus. Trips into town are £1.10 (rtn), although students can fork out £120 for a yearly pass. *Check online first, though: there are discounts aplenty lurking in cyberspace.*
Taxis: *Taxis tend towards the wallet-emptying:* £5 between town and the campus. *Pre-booking with one of the local firms is advisable – flagging them down is a bad idea.*
Bicycles: There's a cycle path running from the campus to the city centre and Morecambe. *Hills are good for you, apparently, so the students are in luck there.*

CAREER PROSPECTS:

- Careers Service • No. of staff: 10 • Unemployed after 6mths: 6%

Vacancy newsletters, a library, interview training and job fairs. The online resources at http://careers.lancs.ac.uk are *pretty damn comprehensive.*

FAMOUS ALUMNI:

Richard Allinson (DJ); Anna Lawson (actor); Oly Marsden (skier); Alan Milburn MP (Lab); Jason Queally (Olympic cycling gold medallist); Andy Serkis (Gollum); Simon Smith (rugby player); Gary Waller MP (Tory); Peter Whalley and Marvin Close (Coronation Street writers).

SPECIAL FEATURES:

- There's the new Infolab 21 – not a secret Government alien-probing pod but a £15m communication and IT centre. It looks like a *gigantic lego brick*, but it's packed to the gills with research expertise, training and skills-learning facilities and, er, 'business incubation'.
- The new Lancaster Environment Centre will house the largest group of environmental scientists in Europe. *The Guinness Book of Records is yet to show interest.*

FURTHER INFO:

• Prospectuses: undergrad; postgrad; alternative • Open days • Video

Two open days a year, plus conducted campus visits on the 1st and 3rd Wednesday of every month. Places can be booked by phoning up or completing the form in the prospectus. www.lancs.ac.uk/depts/schools/visit.htm has the relevant dates for your diary.

A C A D E M I C

Undergraduate teaching at Lancaster has reaped an award or two and its sociology, statistics and management departments *have a few feathers stuffed* in their research caps. Learning is very flexible in the 1st year – *by the time they reach 2nd year students can find themselves doing a completely different course than the one they applied for.* The Management School is undergoing a £9.5m extension and facelift that will add two *massive* lecture theatres and the Leadership Centre, an entrepreneurial institute working with regional businesses.

140-340

Entry points: 140-340	Ave points: n/a
Applns per place: n/a	Clearing: 4%
No. of terms: 3	Length of terms: 10wks
Staff/student ratio: 1:9	Study addicts: 25%
Teaching: *****	Research: *****

POINTS

ADMISSIONS:

• Apply via UCAS

Lancaster *likes* mature students, who need a minimum of two A levels or equivalent to apply.

SUBJECTS:

Art & Design: 4%	Engineering & Technology: 4%
Arts/Humanities: 16%	Maths, Sciences & IT: 5%
Business/Management: 2.5%	Sciences: 19%
Combined Studies: 5%	Social Sciences: 24%

Best: Art; Biological Sciences; Educational Research; Engineering; Linguistics; Philosophy; Physic; Politics & International Relations; Psychology; Pure Maths; Religious Studies; Sociology; Statistics; Theatre Studies.

LIBRARIES:

• 1,000,000 books • 900 study places

The University Library at the centre of the campus contains audio and visual playback equipment, 140 PC workstations, microfilm reading and a rare books room. *And books of course.* The Ruskin Library has an *extensive* collection of books, letters and manuscripts centred around Pre-Raphaelite art critic and *priggish paedophile*, John Ruskin.

COMPUTERS:

• 1,500 workstations • 24-hr access

Several computer clusters around campus, the largest being in the main library. Students get their mitts on some *respectable kit*, including a *wide variety* of course-specific software.

OTHER LEARNING FACILITIES:

Lancaster has rehearsal rooms, drama studio, language labs, practice courtroom, design lab and a TV centre with digital video editing suite.

> Dundee University staff and students rehearsed and produced 7 Brides for 7 Brothers in 23 hours and 30 mins and now hold the world record for the fastest ever staging of a musical.

ENTERTAINMENT

THE CITY:

• Price of a pint of beer: £1.70 • Glass of wine: £1.50 • Can of Red Bull: £2

Cinemas: The 2-screen Regal offers blockbusters in response to The Dukes Theatre Arts Centre's avant garde efforts. Both offer NUS discounts.

Theatres: The Grand shows a variety of mainly amateur drama and other events. Dukes covers the touring circuit. Open-air 'Promenade plays' (there's no stage – the audience follows the action around the grounds) are put on, again by the Dukes, at the *stunning Williamson Park every summer.*

Pubs: *Chain bars are springing up like chicken pox in Lancaster, as in most cities,* but there are still loads of traditional real ale pubs in the city. *Toast and Santa are favoured vodka bars. The Water Witch is a canal-side summertime frolic-spot. There's nowhere that's unwelcoming to students as such, but that doesn't mean that stomping around the pubs plastered, playing 'pin the tracksuit on the townie' is a good – or indeed survivable – idea.*

Clubbing/Music venues: The Sugarhouse is the main venue – owned and run by the SU but situated in the city centre – and it draws in the bigger gigs. Otherwise, there's Brookes and the Warehouse (mainstream), the Carleton (indie/dance), Springs, Elemental (trendy bar), the Alex (rock) and Club Liquid (mainstream).

Eating out: *Not a vast selection, but all bar the pickiest palates will be satisfied. Pushplugs: Nawaab Tandoori (excellent value balti); Sultan's (Indian, in a converted church); Paulo Gianni's (Italian, student discounts); Whaletale Café (veggie); Marco's; Icky's; Bodrums.*

UNIVERSITY

• Price of a pint of beer: £1.47 • Glass of wine: £1.40 • Can of Red Bull: £1.50

Bars: Each college has a bar, *popular* with its own students. Cross-fertilisation only usually happens when there's an event on somewhere or students play 'Bar Golf' (a pint in each college bar in turn, doubling back for an 18-hole course).

Theatres: The Theatre Society is the most active in the University and stages regular productions in the *flexible* Nuffield Theatre, sending a few up to Edinburgh for the summer thesp-fest.

Film: Blockbusters and more are shown five times a week *by one of the biggest and bestequipped student film clubs in the country* (admission £2.50).

Music venues: The Sugarhouse rules: The Thrills, the Fun Lovin' Criminals and The Inspiral Carpets have been lured in for Union ents.

Clubbing: Fridays are Frisky in the Union's newly refurbed Sugarhouse *and so are most of the students who flock to the cheese-barn. Saturday's* Scandalous night is *popular too.* There are club events three nights a week, ranging from indie to hard house *but lingering on charty pop and kitsch.* Serious DJs like Hannif, Lick MTV and the Dream Team have called by.

Comedy/Cabaret: *Laugh-a-minute* every fortnight in the Sugarhouse.

Food: *Students are spoiled for choice:* there's the Wibbly Wobbly Burger Bar (*we kid you not*) open till midnight, plus Pizzetta Republica, Moonlight's Kebabs, Diggles sandwiches, curries, chips and *even real food* on the go all day.

Other: Two or three balls a year, including Christmas and Graduation.

SOCIAL & POLITICAL

LANCASTER UNIVERSITY STUDENTS' UNION:

• 6 sabbaticals • Turnout at last ballot: 18% • NUS member

LUSU has the ground floor of the *plush* Slaidburn House to administer *its little empire.* Representation, ents and services are also provided on a college level through Junior Common Rooms (JCRs). *Students here are more politically aware than some we could mention and the SU rouses rabbles on their behalf.*

SU FACILITIES:
Nine college bars; Sugarhouse venue; cafeteria; snack bars; pool tables; meeting rooms; Barclays and HSBC ATMs; photocopiers; printing service; payphones; advice centre; travel agent; new bookshop. Also around the campus there are banks, a post office, petrol station, bookshops (new and secondhand), hairdresser, chemist, newsagent, supermarket, bakery, ticket agency and a few smaller shops.

CLUBS (NON-SPORTING):
Buddhist; Chinese; Finnish; Jugglers; Motoring; Poetry. **See also Clubs tables.**

OTHER ORGANISATIONS:
SCAN (Student Comment & News) is the fortnightly Union-issue toilet roll. Bailrigg FM keeps going 24-hrs a day, broadcasting on 87.7FM and online. *Either the charity Rag will survive a forthcoming stab at the world record in aftershock-downing and continue to raise money for local charities, or they won't. In which case it was nice knowing them.* LUVU is a voluntary group that works in the local community.

RELIGIOUS:
• 3 chaplains (CofE, RC, Methodist)
Two chapels (Anglican and Roman Catholic) as well as rooms for the Jewish community with a Kosher kitchen. There's a non-denominational Chaplaincy Centre on campus, which hosts visits from ministers of most religions, and a Muslim prayer room. There are various places of worship in town, including a number of different churches and a mosque.

PAID WORK:
• Job bureau
The SU keeps a notebook of term-time vacancies and runs a jobshop. Some local shops and bars help put the pennies in, and tourist-related jobs *abound* in the summer.

SPORTS
• BUSA Ranking: 13
College rivalries emerge in tussles for the Carter Shield. When they gang up to take on other universities ... well, they lose. They do have a good record of snatching the annual Roses Cup from the hands of York University however, so all is not lost.

SPORTS FACILITIES:
18 acres of playing fields *(which allegedly provide a fine harvest of magic mushrooms in season)*; all-weather pitches; sports hall; eight tennis and eight squash courts; croquet lawn; bowling green; 25m swimming pool; climbing wall; multi gym; sauna and solarium; gym; weights rooms (male and female); dance studio; athletics area; golf practice area; archery range; floodlit hard playing area; and the University's Lake Carter. Locally, a golf course and the River Lune (where the University has a boat house). The Sailing Club uses the Glasson Dock marina.

SPORTING CLUBS:
American Football; Korfball; Lacrosse; Snowboarding; Table Tennis; Riding. **See also Clubs tables.**

ACCOMMODATION

IN COLLEGE:
• Self-catering: 83% • Cost: £50-90 (31/51wks)
• First years living in: 92% • Insurance premium: £
Availability: All 1st years get rooms if Lancaster's their first choice. Students returning from sandwich placements or years abroad get accommodation guaranteed as well, but 2nd years are largely out on their own. Lancaster's colleges use self-catering halls (single rooms,

some en-suite, with shared kitchen) and a number of furnished houses as part of their head tenancy scheme. *Porters keep a close eye on things overnight.* Some colleges have single-sex floors and flats whilst couples *can get down to it* in some of the flatlets and twin rooms available. Cos of the college thang, students in halls have access to bars, study areas, games rooms and TV lounges. At the moment, County College's friendly atmosphere gets *the thumbs up,* but Lancaster's in the middle of a *massive* residence redevelopment plan that should add another 1,750+ rooms to the ballot.

Car parking: *Limited* free parking 5-10 mins from the colleges. *Even more limited permit parking nearer,* but 1st years aren't allowed to bring cars.

EXTERNALLY:

• Ave rent: £40–60

Availability: Living costs in Lancaster are at the lower end, so students can afford to shop around for a decent pad. *Places are fairly easy to find – Bowerham is the most convenient, but Galgate, Dale Street and Blade Street are worth considering. Skerton is to be avoided, no questions asked.*

Housing help: The Union runs a house-finding service, backed up by the University Accommodation Office. They post vacancies, keep a list of accredited landlords and *make sure that money-grabbing opportunists with outhouses* for rent don't get a look in.

W E L F A R E

SERVICES:

• Women's Officer • Mature Students' Society • International Students' Society
• Late-night women's minibus • Nightline • College counsellors: 10
• SU counsellors: 1 full • Crime rating: !!

LUSU's Welfare Officer works in close cahoots with the University Welfare staff advising and supporting all types of tear-jerking trauma.

Health: The Bailrigg Medical Centre contains a practice staffed with male and female GPs. There's a 24-nurse unit, a dentist and an alternative therapies centre.

Women: Attack alarms are available and there are minibus runs home from the Sugarhouse on club nights for women only, 7pm-2am.

Crèches/Nursery: The paying pre-school centre has 30 places for under-2s and 82 for older children.

Disabilities: *Lancaster gets kudos for making almost the whole of its compact campus accessible.* Several adapted bedrooms are available and the library has a Kurzweil text-reading machine and Braille embosser. Hearing loops in lecture theatres. Dyslexic students get extra support, including extended time in exams.

FINANCE:

• Ave debt per year: £3,920

Fees: International students pay £8,000.

• Access fund: £448,323 • Successful applications/yr: 558 • Ave payment: £100-3,500

Support: Nearly £75,000 in bursaries, mainly aimed at mature students, students with kids, and postgrads.

Leeds University

The University of Leeds, Leeds, LS2 9JT
Tel: (0113) 243 1751 E-mail: prospectus@leeds.ac.uk Website: www.leeds.ac.uk
Leeds University Union, PO Box 157, Leeds, LS1 1UH
Tel: (0113) 231 4254 E-mail: comms@union.leeds.ac.uk Website: www.luuonline.com

GENERAL

Leeds University celebrated its centenary in 2004 but in the last hundred years it's gone from being the cloistered academic institution represented by the *virginally white* clock tower of Parkinson House to an institution which *sprawls* across the city. About 13% of Leeds residents are students and together with neighbouring <u>Leeds Metropolitan University</u> they occupy a massive *studentland* conurbation of lecture theatres, halls and *Victorian terraced houses decorated with badly blu-tacked posters.*

Sex ratio (M:F): 43:57	Founded: 1904
Full-time u'grads: 21,130	Part-time: 4,555
Postgrads: 5,920	Non-degree: 3,713
Ave course: 3yrs	Ethnic: 8%
State:private school: 73:27	Flunk rate: 6
Mature: 19%	International: 18%
Disabled: 462	Local: 20%

(57% ♀ / 43% ♂)

ATMOSPHERE:

The sheer number of students and the variety of entertainment available might mean frantic hedonism and furious activity – but scepticism and apathy have a pretty palpable presence too. An observer crueller than Push would say few consider anything more deeply than the bottom of their glass – the Union Bar's always busy, of course. In a city this size with a social scene rivalling Manchester and London, there's fun to be had for those that want it – and many that don't.

LEEDS:

• <u>Population: 715,500</u> • <u>City centre: 0 miles</u> • <u>London: 189 miles</u> • <u>Manchester: 40 miles</u>
• <u>High temp: 19</u> • <u>Low temp: 1</u> • <u>Rainfall: 58</u>
Although the bombs of WWII missed Leeds, the 60s developers and town planners didn't. At the top of Parkinson House there's amusement to be had watching hapless drivers trying to navigate the spaghetti-tangle of bypasses and one-way systems. Of course it's not quite so much fun for the people doing the driving but at least they might see the glorious Victorian buildings of the Town Hall, City Museum, Henry Moore Gallery and Opera North's home at the Grand Theatre. The semi-pedestrianised main street, Briggate, has every local amenity a student could possibly want and many they couldn't, including a branch of Ab-Fab favourite Harvey Nicks.

TRAVEL:

Trains: Leeds station is the centre of the *very efficient* West Yorkshire metro train network serving all the local Yorkshire towns (Bradford, Wakefield, Sheffield and York). There are also direct services to London (£38.30), Manchester (£9.10), Edinburgh and elsewhere.
Coaches: National Express to London (£16.75), Manchester (£7), Edinburgh (£22.50) and other destinations. Also served by Blueline.
Car: 10 mins off the M1 and on the M62 to Manchester. *Cars aren't necessary for local travel – public transport's pretty good and most places you'd want to be in staggering distance of are.*
Air: Leeds/Bradford Airport for inland and European flights. Manchester Airport's $1\frac{1}{2}$ hrs away for international trips.
Hitching: *Chances of a lift are good on the M1 or M62, but obviously there are safer ways of getting around.*
Local: *Very reliable and frequent* trains and buses (maximum off-peak fare is 80p). A monthly student Metrocard (bus and train) is £39.50, the Student First travel card (£34 a month) is valid on bus routes from the University to the city centre.
Taxis: Local taxi firms will accept student cards in place of a fare for those caught short. They then claim the money off the University who return the card on repayment. *Handy, huh?*
Bicycles: There are plenty of cycle paths (and hills) but also a need for state-of-the-art security to protect your bike from certain light-fingered locals.

CAREER PROSPECTS:

• Careers Service • No. of staff: 27 full/19 part • Unemployed after 6mths: 5%
The careers service is *highly efficient – but it'd have to be with the legions of staff.* Performing Arts students get an in-house casting service and those interested in becoming self-employed have a dedicated service, Spark.

FAMOUS ALUMNI:

Steve Bell (cartoonist); Mark Byford (ex-BBC boss); Barry Cryer (writer/comedian); Paul Dacre (editor, Daily Mail); Jeremy Dyson (League of Gentlemen); Andrew Eldritch (Sisters of Mercy); David Gedge (singer, Wedding Present); Mystic Meg (*who only got a 2:2 so obviously didn't foresee her exam questions*); Alastair McGowan (funnyman impressionist); Mark Knopfler (Dire Straits); Gerald Ratner (*crap* jeweller); Claire Short MP; Jack Straw (Foreign Secretary and ex-SU president); Wole Soyinka (poet & playright); Nicholas Witchell (BBC newsreader, ex-editor of Leeds Student); Alan Yentob (BBC *big cheese*).

FURTHER INFO:

• Prospectuses: undergrad; postgrad; some departments • Open days
Alternative prospectuses and a guide for mature students are also available. Open days in June and September.

ACADEMIC

Leeds is strong on research and traditional subject areas.

Entry points: 190-360	Ave points: 202
Applns per place: 7	Clearing: 5%
No. of terms: 2	Length of terms: 12wks
Staff/student ratio: 1:15	Study addicts: n/a
Teaching: ****	Research: *****
Year abroad: 4%	Sandwich students: 16%
Firsts: 12%	2.2s: 27%
2.1s: 56%	3rds: 6%

190-360   POINTS

ADMISSIONS:

• Apply via UCAS

SUBJECTS:

Arts/Humanities: 12%
Biological Sciences: 8%
Business/Management: 4%
Earth & Environment: 5%
Engineering: 9%
Unusual: Bsc Colour & Polymer Chemistry.

Maths/Physical Sciences: 5%
Medical Sciences: 16%
Performance, Visual Arts & Communications: 16%
Social Sciences: 16%

LIBRARIES:

• 2,712,000 books • 4,000 study places • Spend per student: £££££
Two main libraries and seven departmental. Librarians are subject specialists, *not just droning 'Sssh'-machines.*

COMPUTERS:

• 9,000 workstations • 24-hr access
Despite the stonking general provision, only some halls enjoy the pleasures of networking.

OTHER LEARNING FACILITIES:

Language labs; drama studio; rehearsal rooms; media centre.

ENTERTAINMENT

THE CITY:

• Price of a pint of beer: £2.50 • Glass of wine: £2.60 • Can of Red Bull: £1.50
Leed's rapidly developing nightlife has more than cottoned on to the possibilities of the student market. Headingley in particular, where many students live, has morphed from scraggy city centre satellite to sparkly student boozing heaven.
Cinemas: Two independent single-screen *flea pits*, three multiplex.
Theatres: *Everything* from opera at the Grand to Alan Ayckbourn and am dram. The West Yorkshire Playhouse is a world-renowned modern repertory theatre complex. The City Varieties may be the oldest surviving music hall in the country, *but that's no excuse for bankrolling Ken Dodd.*
Pubs: This is the home of Yorkshire bitter *and there are few local pubs that don't serve a decent pint. Serious imbibers should contemplate the Otley Run, a 14-pub crawl of mythical proportions, including the Eldon, the Skyrack, the Original Oak and the Dry Dock (on a boat). Or try the Royal Park, the Arc and Headingley Taps. City centre waterholes worth draining a firkin in: North Bar (European beers); Fab Café (built by cult TV geeks for cult TV geeks); Velvet (gay-friendly); Arts Café.*
Clubbing: Leeds is an all-night city thanks to a tolerant council licensing policy. It's also home to some great clubs, if you can squeeze past the queues. *The Push posse would want to be on the guest-list for: Funky Mule at the Warehouse; the Hi Fi Club; Majestyk. The Cockpit has seen more misspent youths pass through it than a juvenile detention centre.*
Music venues: *Leeds is a compulsory stop for touring bands from big names to the biggest and there's a thriving live scene. Pushplugs: the Cockpit; Joseph's Well Irish Centre (all indie).*
Eating out: *Grubstops to satisfy all palates and pockets. Pushplugs: Theo's (kebabs and the best lentil burgers in the world); Zacks (pizza/pasta buffet £4); Sala (good value Thai); Salvos (Italian); Baraka (Moroccan); Original Oak (pub lunches); Clock Café; Grove Café; Manuela's; Dino's; Fujihiro and Little Tokyo (cheap Japanese food).*
Other: For those who don't drink, eat, dance or watch stuff, Leeds has a fair few afternoon-fillers – the Royal Armouries, Tropical World and Kirkstall Abbey being three of them.

UNIVERSITY:

• Price of a pint of beer: £1.50 • Glass of wine: £1.60 • Can of Red Bull: £1.10
Bars: With five bars in the Union and at least one in most of the other halls students *are in little danger of dying of thirst.*

Theatres: One workshop theatre (the Bretton Hall Performance Centre) and two other potential destinations where Leeds students hone their shows for the yearly jaunt to the Edinburgh Fringe.
Film: Two mainstream films a week.
Music venues: The Union is home to Leeds' largest live music venue with recent acts like Ash, Groove Armada and Blue.
Clubbing: Stylus and Bar Coda are the Union's *premier party nights.*
Comedy/Cabaret: The likes of Mark Lamarr, Rhona Cameron and, er, Rolf Harris have braved Harvey's Milk Bar *(which doesn't serve milk).*
Food: *The refectory's best for fuelling-up before lectures. MJ's coffee bar deals with snacks and the bars all serve up a good range of eats.* The Union's supermarket is good for food on the move.
Other: One of the biggest graduation balls in the country with 5,000 people. A freshers' do in October.

S O C I A L & P O L I T I C A L

LEEDS UNIVERSITY UNION:

• 13 sabbaticals • Turnout at last ballot: 12%
Most other student bodies would be delighted to have an operation on the scale of LUU to represent them but size brings its own problems. When the executive tried to remove the sabbatical posts at the Nightline and Student Radio, they were overwhelmingly voted down. So they don't rule the roost. Most of the time as long as the beer's cheap and the ents are up to scratch most people are happy. There's a fair bit of politicking going down, too.

SU FACILITIES:

Bars; coffee bar; darkroom; opticians; travel agency; book shop; ATMs; hair salon; photo booth; gaming/video machines; newsagent; insurance broker; off-licence; meeting rooms; launderette and dry-cleaning. A recent £5m spent on new nightclub and supermarket as well as sports clubs and societes facilities.

CLUBS (NON-SPORTING):

Advertising; AIESEC; Animal Rights; Arts; Asian; Anime; Arabic & Middle Eastern; Aviation; Backstage; Baha'I; Ballet; Band; Bangladeshi; Biochemistry; Biology; Biomedical Sciences; British Born Chinese; Buddhist Meditation; Business; Café Babel; Change Ringers; Chemical Engineers; Chemistry; Chinese Physical Culture; Chinese; Civic Engineering; Colour Chemistry; Comedy; Communications; Computer; Creative Writing; Cutting Edge; Cocktail; Dance Band; Dance Exposé; Dental; Design Management; DJ; Duke of Edinburgh; Earth Sciences; East Asian Research; Egyptian; Engineers Without Borders; English; Envy; Erasmus; Folk & Traditional Music; French; Fresh Funk; Fire; Game Development; Geography; German; Globalise Resistance; Hellenic; History; Hong Kong; Indian; Indonesian; Investors; Iranian; Irish Dancing; ISKCON; Italian; Japanese; Joint Honours; Juggling & Circus Skills; Kabal; Korean; Law; Lippy Magazine; Live Action Roleplay; Live Music Appreciation; Luso Brazilian; LUST; Lybian; Malaysian & Singaporean; Maths; Mauritian; Medical; Medsin; Mexican; Microbiology; Modern Dance; Musical Theatre; Omani; Orthodox; Pakistani; Palestinian; Panzer Attack; Philosophy; Physics; Playbus; Poker; Politics; Politics & Parliamentary; Pre Clin CMF; Psychology; Punk; Real Ale; Record Lending Library; Revelation Rock Gospel Choir; Rock; Role Playing, Wargames & Card Games; Sikh; Scottish Dancing; Scout & Guide; Singaporean; SIS; SLAP; Stage Musical; Speak; Speleology; Sports Science; Sri Lankan; St John's Links; STAR; Student Stop AIDS; Sudanese; Sketch Show; Soulcity; Thai UN; Vietnamese; Wine; Yoga; Zoot (40s dance). **See also Clubs tables.**

OTHER ORGANISATIONS:

Leeds Student (weekly paper) is produced jointly with Leeds Metropolitan University with a readership of 50,000. The radio station (LSR FM) is also a joint venture. LS:TV shows an hour a day throughout the Union. Rag raises several grand for worthwhile causes each year. CALM (another joint operation) runs 60 *effective* local help projects.

RELIGIOUS:

• 9 chaplains (CofE, Baptist, RC, Lutheran, Methodist, Orthodox, Quaker, Salvation Army, URC), plus imam and rabbi
Ecumenical Chaplaincy Centre with the above Christian churches working together. Prayer rooms and other facilities for Jews, Hindus, Muslims and Sikhs. The Islamic Society says

daily prayers on campus. The city offers places of worship for all strains of god-fearer; Hindus, Muslims and Sikhs are *particularly well-catered for.* Leeds has the largest Jewish student population outside Manchester.

PAID WORK:

• Job Bureau

The *usual* bar work and stewarding at Union ents and joblink run by the SU with the emphasis on safe employment practices. Leeds as a city is *teeming* with bar and retail opportunities.

S P O R T S

• Recent successes: frisbee, cheerleading • BUSA Ranking: 6

Facilities and precedents are there for sporting success and *there are no end of hopefuls but last year the trophy cabinet remained mysteriously bare.*

SPORTS FACILITIES:

Locally a sports centre provides facilities for everything from weight training to ballet. The Weetwood playing ground 4 miles away has football, hockey, rugby, American football, lacrosse and cricket pitches. Also an Astroturf football pitch, three squash courts and four tennis courts. With a £40 a year sport user card many facilities are free and some only cost 50p-£1. The sports centre also has a climbing wall, although the University's Yorkshire Dales and Lake District outdoor centres offer the real thing. The solarium, however, *is the most reliable source of sun round these parts.*

SPORTING CLUBS:

10-Pin Bowling; Aikido; American Football; Boarders; Boxercise; Boxing; Break Dance; Bridge; Canoe & Kayak; Capoeira Heranca; Cheerleading; Cross Country; Dancesport; Gliding; Gymnastics; Handball; Hiking; Kickboxing; Korfball; Lacrosse; Motor Sports; Mountaineering; Rifle; Roller Hockey; Rounders; Samurai Ju Jitsu; Ski & Snowboarding; Skydiving; Surfing; Swimming & Waterpolo; Table Tennis; Tai Chi Hsing Yi; Thai Boxing; Ultimate Frisbee; Volleyball; Wind Surfing. **See also Clubs tables**.

ATTRACTIONS:

This is *the heartland* of rugby league and with Leeds United *not waving but drowning* at Elland Road, international cricket at Headingley and Olympic swimming facilities *only a paddle away,* there's something to see all year round.

A C C O M M O D A T I O N

IN COLLEGE:

• Catered: 10% • Cost: £65-119 (31wks)

• Self-catering: 25% • Cost: £51-101 (40wks)• Insurance premium: £££££

Availability: All 1st years who want to can live in a variety of *highly comfortsome* halls. The older ones, such as Bodington and Devonshire (both catered), require 10% of students to share but that does keep the rent down. The self-catering flats hold anything from four to 14 students. *There are complaints about restrictions (on sticking posters up, for example) and about cleaners arriving at what they coyly describe as 'inopportune' moments.*
Car parking: *Expensive, unnecessary and in short supply.*

EXTERNALLY:

• Ave rent: £43

Availability: *Most students stick to the large quantity of late 19th-century back-to-back terraced housing. Conditions vary but the UniPol code of practice has sorted out a few problems with unscrupulous landlords. Favourite areas for students are Headingley, Woodhouse and Hyde Park. Most choose not to live in Chapeltown, which can get a bit rough.*

Housing help: UniPol, the joint University and Leeds Metropolitan University SUs' housing service provides *lots* of help and advice with a code of standards and an *excellent* internet search service. It also keeps tabs on the worst landlords. *Watch out for local letting agents (of the devil) announcing a housing shortage and pressuring students into renting before the Unipol list goes up.*

WELFARE

SERVICES:

- Lesbian, Gay, Bisexual & Transgender Officer & Society
- Ethnic Minorities Officer & Society • Mature Students' Officer & Society
- International Students' Officer & Society • Postgrad Officer & Society
- Disabilities Officer & Society • Women's Officer & Society
- Late-night/Women's minibus • Nightline • Taxi fund
- College counsellors: 7 full/9 part • Crime rating: !!!!

Nightline is one of only two in the country with a sabbatical officer at the helm. Self-defence classes cost £1 per session.

Health: The student health service has its very own mini-hospital with doctors, a seven-bed sickbay and even a minor operation suite. In total there are 13 GPs, eight nurses and eight sickbay attendants.

Crèches/Nursery: 60 places for kids 6mths-5yrs.

Disabilities: The University and the Union are making efforts to improve access and have adapted the entire Union building. Campus has *middling* wheelchair access, but key buildings have been fitted with automatic doors and card entry – a map's available that shows wheelchair-friendly routes. Also 35 designated disabled parking bays. *Solid* dyslexia support.

FINANCE:

- Ave debt per year: £4,188

Fees: Part-time students pay £570 for arts programmes, £774 for science programmes. Postgrads pay £2,940, international undergrads between £7,765 and £9,035.

- Access fund: £875,000 • Successful applications: 1,000 • Ave payment: £875

Support: Scholarships are available for students from less affluent Leeds suburbs like Ogden and Skipton. There's the usual bursaries/welfare funds and a range of budgeting advice, debt counselling and even – *a sign of the times* – help with bankruptcy. The Union offers emergency loans of up to £100.

Leeds Metropolitan University

- *Formerly Leeds Polytechnic.*

Leeds Metropolitan University, Calvery Street, Leeds. LS1 3HE
Tel: (0113) 283 3113 E-mail: course-enquiries@leedsmet.ac.uk Website: www.lmu.ac.uk
Leeds Metropolitan University Students Union, Calvery Street, Leeds, LS1 3HE
Tel: (0113) 2098400 E-mail: enquiries@lmusu.ac.uk Website: www.lmusu.org.uk

GENERAL

Right in the middle of Leeds there's a university. Right next-door is another one. *Somewhere one ends and the next begins, but it's not easy to tell where.* Like its more elderly neighbour, the Met's buildings are a jumble of old and new, but it centres on seven *brooding* concrete tower blocks, *from which the Metropolitan proudly reminds us that Leeds hasn't gone entirely soft since the arrival of Harvey Nicks and the rest. It's a sobbing shame that* the site cannot be shifted en masse to the Beckett Park Campus, 3 miles out in a *chocolate box* wooded site arranged *tastefully* around a cricket square.

Sex ratio (M:F): 47:53	Founded: 1970
Full-time u'grads: 14,280	Part-time: 8,180
Postgrads: 1,195	Non-degree: 2,711
Ave course: 3yrs	Ethnic: 12%
State:private school: 93:7	Flunk rate: 17%
Mature: 19%	International: 13%
Disabled: 428	Local: 70%

(53% ♀ / 47% ♂)

ATMOSPHERE:
Leeds Met has a hefty helping of part-time students but this hasn't affected the atmosphere. In fact, grumbly locals would probably suggest that all the students seem to be part-time, judging by the numbers of them out and about every night. That's a bit unfair, though. In such a friendly, sociable town there are bound to be temptations. Leeds fully deserves its reputation as Party Central and Leeds Met students are more than happy to play their central part in keeping it so.

SITES:
Headingly Campus: 3 miles from the city campus, Beckett Park is in 100 acres of woods and parkland, affording panoramic views across Leeds and based round a main building dating back to 1913. It's home to various departments (including Business, Education, IT, Law, Sports Sciences and Languages) and the main sports facilities.

LEEDS: see Leeds University

TRAVEL: see Leeds University
College: A bus service runs between the sites every 6 to 10 mins.
Taxis: Students finding themselves short at the end of the night, can give the taxi driver their student card instead of paying. The University then pays and students get their card back when they pay the University. *Cunning, eh?*

CAREER PROSPECTS:
• Careers Service • No. of staff: 5 full/4 part • Unemployed after 6mths: 9%
The Careers Service runs development workshops and lends a hand with job applications and laying hands on work experience.

FAMOUS ALUMNI:
Marc Almond (singer); Glen Baxter (cartoonist); Betty Boothroyd (former Speaker of the Commons); Peter Cattaneo (film director); Sir Henry Moore (sculptor); Ron Pickering (late sports commentator); Eric Pickles MP (Con); Keith Waterhouse (writer).

FURTHER INFO:
• Prospectuses: undergrad; postgrad

ACADEMIC

Leeds Met is strong on vocational degrees, particularly those that involve fun: Hospitality, Sport, Leisure and Tourism. The Business School, Events Management and PR courses also have a good reputation.

Entry points: 120-300	**Ave points: 128**
Applns per place: 6	**Clearing: 15%**
No. of terms: 3	**Length of terms: 11wks**
Staff/student ratio: 1:18	**Study addicts: 9%**
Teaching: **	**Research: ****
Year abroad: <1%	**Sandwich students: 0**

ADMISSIONS:
• Apply via UCAS/GTTR for PGCE
They're flexible in their recruitment policy and will take experience into account as much as bits of paper.

SUBJECTS:
Unusual: Creative Music & Sound Technology combine both the creative and technical sides of melody making. *Most techie courses don't teach anything about writing a decent tune.* Events Management; Public Relations.

LIBRARIES:
• 400,000 books • 2,300 study places
Opening hours at the main library and learning centre *aren't bad* and they go 24-hr at peak times (ie. for exams), albeit with no staff *bar a few bored security guards.* They've even given up the beep-beep battle and designated certain small areas mobile-friendly.

COMPUTERS:
• 1,578 workstations • 24-hr
It's open round the clock as exams loom closer.

OTHER LEARNING FACILITIES:
Some students get to hang their masterpieces in the University's *groovy* gallery.

ENTERTAINMENT

THE CITY: see Leeds University

UNIVERSITY:
• Price of a pint of beer: £1.70 • Glass of wine: £1.25 • Can of Red Bull: £1.10
Bars: The Met Bar is heaving throughout term thanks to the cheap food during the day and solid sounds three nights a week. It's got the biggest TV screen in the town, *so Leeds Utd's triumphs and travesties can be scrutinised in magnified detail.* The Becketts Sports Bar is also generally packed.
Theatre: The University runs a studio theatre, *but very little student drama ever goes on on campus.*
Clubbing: The Met Bar hosts club nights on Wednesdays (OTT – R&B, chart), Fridays (Star – indie) and Saturdays (the Bop), many of which drag in young locals and Leeds University students.
Music venues: *Leeds Met has a become a major venue on national tours, completely overshadowing its more staid neighbour.* The Lost Prophets, the Darkness, Damien Rice, Athlete, New Found Glory, Coldplay, Doves, Oasis and the Thrills have all popped into the Met Bar recently. Local bands play free gigs at Beckett Park.

Cabaret: Nothing regular, but Craig Charles and Rob Newman have both appeared at the Met Bar, as well as Mark & Lard and student hero dope-fiend (and now Leeds resident) Howard Marks.

Food: The main refectory, the Depot, offers *good value* for limited dosh. *The Grapevine is a posher affair where the lecturers hang out.* The refectory at Beckett Park is *confusingly* also called the Depot and Costa Coffee has somehow infiltrated the main University building.

SOCIAL & POLITICAL

LEEDS METROPOLITAN UNIVERSITY STUDENTS' UNION (LMUSU):

• 5 sabbaticals • Turnout at last ballot: 4% • NUS member

Politics isn't exactly cut-throat. Students aren't really bothered who's running things. They're more concerned about who scored the winning try, what's gone wrong this week at Leeds Utd and whose round it is.

SU FACILITIES:

The main facilities are at the City Campus where there are: two bars; five coffee bars; two print rooms; Endsleigh Insurance; games & vending machines; a health and fitness suite; general and stationery shops; bookstore. At Beckett Park, there's not only another bar, but also a café, bank, photo booth, games machines, pool tables, TV lounge, a disco and a juke-box.

CLUBS (NON-SPORTING):

Asian; Friends of India; Juggling & Circus Skills; Law; Sikh; The Socia (politics & current affairs); Walking.
See also Clubs tables.

OTHER ORGANISATIONS:

The SU produces a free fortnightly newsletter, Headliner, as well as, jointly with Leeds University, the award-winning weekly Leeds Student newspaper. Leeds Student Radio (www.lsrfm.com), also run jointly, broadcasts locally 24-hrs a day from September 2005. One-off volunteering events happen occasionally.

RELIGIOUS:

Six chaplains are shared with Leeds University. Meanwhile, there's an adviser and not one, but two prayer rooms for Muslims. Jews make do with just an adviser and, *Push presumes,* pray wherever the mood takes them.

PAID WORK: see Leeds University

• Job bureau

The *excellent* job shop has filled well over 2,000 vacancies and is available online. Students on the Retailing BA can gather academic credits from working for a range of retail chains (Asda, IKEA, Debenhams etc.).

SPORTS

• BUSA Ranking: 48

To use the facilities, student must stump up £25 a year, which also buys them access to a *heavily subsidised* physiotherapy department should they play a little too hard.

SPORTS FACILITIES:

The facilities at Beckett Park include: the new Centre of Excellence for Tennis; the Carnegie Regional Gymnastics Centre; swimming pool; squash courts; athletics and playing fields (including 12 football pitches, four rugby, one lacrosse, two synthetic floodlit and one 5-a-side pitch); a multigym; weights room; running track; tennis courts and regular aerobics classes. These facilities were acquired through lottery funding, which means that the public also get to use them. The city has its own leisure centre, pool, sauna, ski slope, a lake and river, a bowling green and golf course. See Leeds University for local facilities.

SPORTING CLUBS:

Boxing; Gaelic Football; Handball; Ju Jitsu; Kayaking; Lacrosse; Shaolin Kung Fu; Snowbaord; Tai Jutsu; Triathlon; Water Polo. **See also Clubs tables.**

ATTRACTIONS: see Leeds University

ACCOMMODATION

IN COLLEGE:

• Catered cost: £79-89 (32wks) • Self catering: 18% • Cost: £45-59 (41/43wks)
• First years living in: 60% • Insurance premium: £££££
Availability: Just over half of 1st years live in (non-locals have priority), either at the *popular and evocatively named* Kirkwall Brewery complex in the centre of town or the *less popular* Sugarwell Court a mile or so further out. The rest are handled by UniPol, not an international crime-fighting agency, but the Leeds universities' *first-rate* joint student property management scheme. The Met's halls are placed at *quite a distance from each other*, although most are close to the University. 20% of rooms are en-suite and about six students *jostle* for use of each kitchen. CCTV and keycard entry systems *help them sleep soundly.* See also Leeds University
Car parking: *Very limited at Beckett Park and non-existent at the city campus.*

EXTERNALLY: see Leeds University

• Ave rent: £43
Availability: *Most students stick to the large quantity of late 19th-century back-to-back terraced housing. Conditions vary but* the UniPol code of practice has sorted out a few problems with unscrupulous landlords. *Favourite areas for students are Headingley (a massive student enclave), Woodhouse and Hyde Park. Most choose not to live in somewhat rough and druggy Chapeltown.*
Housing help: UniPol *to the rescue once again. Certain unscrupulous local letting agents try to tell newbies there's a housing shortage to get them to sign contracts before the UniPol list is up.* Leeds Met also has its own Accommodation Office and, so far, nobody's ended up sleeping on the gym floor. 1st years who don't get into halls are invited to meet and get to know each other with a view to house-sharing with people who won't end up killing each other over the washing-up.

WELFARE

SERVICES:

• Lesbian/Gay/Bisexual Society • Mature Students' Society • Self-defence classes
• Nightline • Taxi fund • Crèche• College counsellors: 5 full/2 part • Crime rating: !!!!
Health: Health centre at Beckett Park.
Disabilities: Some buildings can't be adapted for wheelchair users. UniPol (see above) makes an extra effort to accommodate students with disabilities. There's a full-time dyslexia support officer and induction loops at Beckett Park.

FINANCE:

• Ave debt per year: £4,339
• Access fund: £990,000 • Successful applications/yr: 800
Support: Debt counselling is available from the Budget Adviser and two part-timers. There's an emergency fund for international students and top musclers can apply for a sports scholarship.

Led Zeppelin played their first gig at Surrey University.

Leeds Polytechnic

see Leeds Metropolitan University

Leicester University

University of Leicester, University Road, Leicester, LE1 7RH
Tel: (0116) 252 5281 E-mail: admissions@le.ac.uk Website: www.le.ac.uk
University of Leicester Students' Union, Percy Gee Building, University Road, Leicester, LE1 7RH
Tel: (0116) 223 1111 E-mail: lusu@le.ac.uk Website: www.leicesterstudent.org

GENERAL

Leicester (along with Nottingham to the north and Northampton to the south) is one of the principal cities of the East Midlands. *But it doesn't really feel all that big. It's something about the attitude of the people, which is generally full of small-town small-talk friendliness. The suburbs are attractive,* but the centre, tarred and feathered with history, has a few dodgy areas. Parts have been pedestrianised, mainly the shopping areas. A mile from the centre, opposite a large cemetery and the *rather pretty* Victoria Park, is the city's older University – bigger sibling of De Montfort. It's a mixture of *pleasant* old architecture, such as the original Georgian and Edwardian buildings, and *new-fangled* post-war bits 'n' bobs. Three of these are particularly prominent on the skyline: the Attenborough Building, 18 storeys high, which won a design award (but then, France won the 1998 World Cup); the ten-storey Charles Wilson Building; and the Engineering block, which is Grade II listed, having won an award in the 1960s for its use of aluminium – *although, today, it's about as sexy as a non-stick frying pan.*

Sex ratio (M:F): 47:53	Founded: 1921
Full-time u'grads: 7,575	Part-time: 1,635
Postgrads: 1,870	Non-degree: n/a
Ave course: 3yrs	Ethnic: n/a
State:private school: 88:12	Flunk rate: 8%
Mature: 11%	International: 29%
Disabled: 212	Local: 17%

ATMOSPHERE:

Leicester's scholarly types are into having a good time, whether on the playing fields or in the bars. They're a very friendly and welcoming crowd and the substantial international contingent offers a multicultural mix that the more staid student can find somewhat intimidating. The huge amount of greenery surrounding the campus promises plenty of frolicking, but heightens the impression that the University is slightly divorced from the rest of town, physically as well as socially.

LEICESTER:

- Population: 279,800 • City centre: 1 mile • London: 98 miles
- Birmingham: 33 miles • Nottingham: 28 miles
- High temp: 21 • Low temp: 0 • Rainfall: 49

The city of Leicester is a *fairly* thriving commercial centre with the odd throwback to Roman times dotted about – as any visitor to the Jewry Wall and its attached museum will no doubt be told. The Guildhall in the centre of the city is medieval and, nearby, the discerning tourist finds the 700-year-old covered market – still one of the largest in Europe. *The castle and cathedral are worth a look-in, but let's stop dwelling in the past and enjoy the place as it is now – a heady cosmopolitan* mixture of people with *a huge* Asian population and *a full deck* of modern amenities like restaurants, curry houses, shops, pubs, curry houses, galleries, more curry houses and Gary Lineker's dad's fruit stall. For those not satisfied with what's on offer in town, Bradgate Park – former home of Lady Jane Grey (who was queen for nine days) – has *lovely, rolling* greenery and lots of deer, while Rutland Water – the biggest man-made reservoir this side of the Orient Express – *offers everything worth getting wet for.*

TRAVEL:

Trains: Leicester Station operates many services direct all over the Midlands and the rest of the country, including London, Sheffield, Edinburgh, Leeds and beyond.
Coaches: National Express and other services to London, Sheffield, Edinburgh and elsewhere.
Car: The M1 skirts the edge of Leicester and the M69 connects with the A5 from the city's outskirts. Also the A6, A46, A47, A50 and A607.
Air: Flights from East Midlands Airport (16 miles away) inland and to Europe. Birmingham International – a 45-min drive – offers more exotic destinations.
Hitching: *Excellent for London or Birmingham. Catch a bus out to near the M1 or M69 motorway junctions.*
Local: *Buses are reliable, cheap (60p from campus to town),* well used and run until 11pm.
Taxis: £3 for an average journey from halls to town.
Bicycles: Leicester, 'Britain's First Environmental City', has introduced cycle ways and there are racks on campus.

CAREER PROSPECTS:

- Careers Service • No. of staff: 13 full • Unemployed after 6mths: 6%

The *thorough* careers service gives careers a good servicing which means sending out regular newsletters and e-mail vacancy updates, throwing job fairs and employer presentations, giving CV, application, interview and assessment assistance and offering advice on starting a business – *anything from double-glazing to porn empires.*

FAMOUS ALUMNI:

Sir Malcolm Bradbury (writer); Sue Cook (TV presenter); Sue Campbell (sportswoman); Heather Couper (TV astronomer); Carol Galley (City whizz kid); Michael Jack MP (Con); Bob Mortimer (comedian, Vic's other half); Pete McCarthy (late comedian, TV presenter); Michael Nicholson (ITN newscaster); Andrew Taylor (chief exec McDonald's); Tony Underwood (rugby player); Sir Alan Walters (economist); Sir John Stevens (Comissioner of the Met Police).

FURTHER INFO:

- Prospectuses: undergrad; postgrad • Open days

Prospective undergrads and postgrads get the choice of two open days a year each, as well as one just for the medical school.

A C A D E M I C

A range of *traditional, but forward-thinking* courses with tons of combined honours and joint degree options. Every subject is modular, with students taking 120 credits a year. *Physics and Space Science have always had a bit of a reputation – which contributed in part to the arrival of the National Space Science Centre in Leicester.* The University is keen to teach key skills along with the subject in question, so even a student of Medieval Baking should come out of it with basic numerical and IT ability. (NB. *Sad to say, Medieval Baking is not actually on offer.*)

Entry points: 240-340	Ave points: 371
Applns per place: 8	Clearing: 5%
No. of terms: 2	Length of terms: 16wks
Staff/student ratio: 1:9	Study addicts: 30%
Teaching: ****	Research: ***
Year abroad: 15%	Sandwich students: 1%
Firsts: 11%	2.2s: 30%
2.1s: 53%	3rds: 5%

240-340 **POINTS**

ADMISSIONS:

• Apply via UCAS

Leicester relishes applications from mature and international students as well as those from schools with little record of sending students on to university. Applicants with 'suitable advanced qualifications' can fast-track straight into the 2nd year.

SUBJECTS:

Arts/Humanities: 19%	Medical Sciences: 20%
Business/Management: 3%	(Modern) Languages: 3%
Education: 3%	Sciences: 20%
Law: 10%	Social Sciences: 22%

Best: American Studies; Ancient History; Archaeology; Economics; Education; History of Art; Maths; Medicine; Museum Studies; Molecular & Organismal Biosciences; Physics & Astronomy; Politics; Psychology.
Unusual: Genetics.

LIBRARIES:

• 1,100,000 books • 1,100 study places • Spend per student: £££££

In addition to the *fatly stocked* main library, there are smaller, specialised libraries for Education and Clinical Sciences. The main library opens till midnight on weekdays and has squirrelled away some *impressive* special stuff, including a collection of early kids' books and the letters and manuscripts of *barmy* farce playwright, Joe Orton.

COMPUTERS:

• 628 workstations • Spend per student: £££££

Computer clusters are, er, clustered around the campus including in the libraries. Some rooms are open till 2am and most have printer access. There are NTL network points in all bedrooms.

OTHER LEARNING FACILITIES:

Leicester students have access to language labs (open to all, not just linguists), rehearsal rooms, a theatre for drama, a media centre and a room to practise mooting (*that's debating to you and me*).

E N T E R T A I N M E N T

LEICESTER:

• Price of a pint of beer: £2 • Glass of wine: £2.80 • Can of Red Bull: £1.90

Cinemas: The eight-screen Odeon and the Cannon (for mainstream movies and the occasional Indian film), a Warner multiplex, the Phoenix Arts centre (for arthouse flicks) and Capital Cinema (for Asian epics).

Theatres: The Haymarket hosts populist productions and touring companies and, again, the Phoenix for fringe and cult dramatic fodder.

Pubs: *Pushplugs: Varsity; the Dry Dock; the Loaded Dog; Fullback & Firkin; and Bar Gaudi for cocktails. The Old Horse is far from knackered, but does offer a more traditional pubular feel. Don't bother with the Braunstone (anti-student) or the Angel (unless you support Leicester City).*

Clubbing: *Leicester has enough clubs to suit all but the most pernickety of tail-feather shakers, although some aren't up to much. Pushplugs: Planet (trance/acid, big queues); SHAG at Zanzibar (which the SU has a hand in); Attik (ambient/drum'n'bass); the Fan Club and Alcatraz (indie); Streetlife (gay); Junction 21 (hip hop, dub); Mosquito Coast (NUS night indie/retro). Po Na Na's is good for guest DJs.*

Music venues: De Montfort Hall, *an important indie venue,* shouldn't be confused with De Montfort University, which is also *not too bad for gigs.* The Charlotte, Half Time Orange and the Shed have smaller indie bands.

Comedy: *The comedy scene here is funtastic – check out Club Jongleurs and the Leicester Comedy Festival which is the biggest in Britain, attracting over 40,000 people a year.*

Other: *Leicester's numerous ethnic communities add to the party calendar with annual Caribbean and Mela (Asian) carnivals and Diwali (Hindu) celebrations.*

Eating out: *Leicester's curry scene almost, but not quite, rivals Bradford's. Among the dozens of options, Akash, Shireen and Manzel's stand out, but there are plenty more. Other Pushplugs: Que Pasa (Mexican); the Good Earth (veggie); Lynn's Café (greasy spoon); Café Brussels; Bread & Roses (veggie); Dino's (Italian); Fat Cat Café.*

UNIVERSITY:

• Price of a pint of beer: £1.40 • Glass of wine: £1.50

Bars: *The Red Fearn's mix of alternative music, pub food and amber nectar make it the most popular bar, but there's back-up boozery at Elements and the Global Café which does international nights.*

Theatres: Leicester's assorted drama groups share the thesping in Queen's Hall several times a year.

Film: A haphazard schedule and selection of weekly cinematic treats. *Nothing revolutionary.*

Music venues: The Venue draws some class acts, who've included Terry Walker and Aqualung.

Clubbing: Wednesday's cheesy retro-fest, Reagan's, always packs the Venue. Friday's 'Madfer-it' has some *cracking* drinks offers and party anthem nostalgia – *the Vengaboys live on. Unfortunately.* Brighton Beach (Classic Soul, R'n'B, alternative) pays a visit one Saturday a month.

Food: The University offers a discount card for food bought on campus. Scoff stops include: Snappers Diner; Loafer's for fast food at lunchtimes; Piazza 2 go (pizza); the Venue Food Court *does cheap and chompable fare* while the Café Piazza has a *pricey continental style.*

Other: The Venue hosts the Summer Ball. Girls Aloud, Jools Holland and the Scratch Perverts made the line-up last year. The Union lays on other events as and when it feels like it.

SOCIAL & POLITICAL

UNIVERSITY OF LEICESTER STUDENT'S UNION:

• 5 sabbaticals • Turnout at last ballot: 17% • NUS member

The SU enjoys a good relationship with the University administration and with the students. It concentrates on organising successful ents and advisory services and on keeping the money machine in motion (not that they print their own or anything). Issues revolve around awareness and information and, rarely get overly political – that's the societies' business.

SU FACILITIES:

Three bars; nightclub; cafeteria; snack bar; fast food outlet; three pool tables; meeting room; three minibuses for hire; NatWest and HSBC banks with ATMs; photocopier; fax service; payphones; advice centre; TV lounge; vending and gaming machines; general store; print shop; travel agency; secondhand bookshop.

CLUBS (NON-SPORTING):

Academia; Arab; Archaeology; AstroSoc; Ballroom & Latin American Dance; Band; Big Band; CAMRA; Changeringers; Chemistry; Chess; Chinese; Choral; Classical; Cyprus; Duke of Edinburgh; Economics; Engineering; English; Football Supporters; Free Tibet; Friends of Falun Gong; Games; Geography; Geology; Hindu; History; Ideological; Italian; Investors; Japanese Animation; Jedi; Law; LeSEDS (space science); Let Us Play; Malaysian;

Mass Communications; Maths & Computing; MedBioGen; MedSIN; Modern Dance; Modern Languages; Museum Studies; PC; Poetry; Politics; Psychology; PsyNeuro; Saudi; Scandinavian; Sikh; Singapore; SLUGS (Scout & Guides); Small Black Flowers (alternative music); Sociology; Street Jazz; Student Action for Refugees; Style Council (design); Taiwanese; Turkish; Travel; Umoja Gospel Choir; Viking. **See also Clubs tables.**

OTHER ORGANISATIONS:

Apart from Ripple, the independent student newspaper (fortnightly), there's also Leicester University Student Television or LUST for short and LUSH FM – which recently got back on air and can be heard at www.lushfm.org The charity Rag has a full-time sabbatical organiser and sets its sights on raising 50 grand a year through parachute jumps, beer festivals and the ilk. 'Contact' is the student community group, which runs about ten local help projects with up to 400 student volunteers.

RELIGIOUS:

• 7 chaplains (CofE, RC, Methodist, URC, Quaker, Salvation Army, International students)
The Gatehouse Chaplaincy Centre welcomes students of all denominations and maintains links with Jewish, Hindu, Buddhist, Muslim and Sikh faith representatives. It has a TV lounge and offers cheap lunches – *so it's not all about God*. There's a Muslim prayer room on campus. Locally, there are churches and places of worship for every brand of god-fearer including a Jain Centre, unique outside the Indian subcontinent.

PAID WORK:

• Job bureau • Paid work: term-time 45%
The Union-run jobshop matches students with casual jobs and, failing that, there's always the Walkers Crisps factory. The University runs a student employment centre allowing local companies to recruit directly from the student body.

S P O R T S

• Recent successes: football, hockey • BUSA Ranking: 48
The Athletics Union is one of the best-funded around and *although they're no champs (Loughborough University takes most of the trophies in this neck of the Midlands), the Leicester lot haven't thrown in any towels just yet. Rugby Union is getting quite militant.*

SPORTS FACILITIES:

The Manor Road Sports Hall plays host to 5-a-side, volleyball, netball, four badminton courts, two cricket nets, tennis, table tennis and runs fitness programmes. The Charles Wilson Sports Hall is the main onsite facility, offering all of the above plus frisbee, judo, fencing, karate and a sports shop. Three squash courts are sited near the School of Education. Leicester has 25 acres of playing fields, including an all-weather pitch, athletics track and nine tennis courts, plus Greenhouse 1 & 2, its *well-equipped* health and fitness suites. Facilities are free with a Sports Card for £45 a year. Leicester itself adds a croquet lawn/bowling green, seven swimming pools, four squash courts, hockey pitch, sports injury clinic, snooker and pool facilities, roller-blading rink, health and fitness club, golf course, basketball centre, dry ski slope, sauna and solarium, and the River Soar.

SPORTING CLUBS:

Fell Walking; Ju-Jitsu; Rifle; Ultimate Frisbee. **See also Clubs tables.**

ATTRACTIONS:

Apart from Leicester City FC, there are the Tigers (rugby), the Riders (basketball), the Panthers (American Football), Leicestershire Cricket Club, Cannons sports complex *(very expensive though)* and the Cycling Stadium.

ACCOMMODATION

IN COLLEGE:
- Catered: 9% • Cost: £75-104 (30wks)
- Self-catering: 62% • Cost: £52-95 (39/52wks)
- First years living in: 90% • Insurance premium: £££££

Availability: 1st years are guaranteed a place in University accommodation if they want it, and international students and returning finalists have priority too. The choice is between the five catered halls at Oadby, $2\frac{1}{2}$ miles from the campus (60s blocks and Edwardian houses *beautifully* set in the University's Botanical Gardens), the hall at Knighton (halfway to Oadby) or the five self-catering student houses and blocks, mainly at Knighton, but some nearer the campus. Gilbert Murray Hall is non-smoking only. *Plush* Opal Court apartment complex appeared in 2003 and offers 669 self-catered places very near campus – mainly sought after by returning postgrads – *the University is a bit precious about its new baby, however, and demands a £200 damage deposit in case students burn it down or poo on the walls.* 9% of students in halls have to share rooms and all halls are mixed, although sexes are split into corridors. The rooms themselves are a decent size – some are very new and have en-suite facilities (Beaumont and Stamford for example) and the halls *are well kitted-out* with most having bars, JCRs and, about half, computing facilities. The houses have single rooms and each is single sex but groups of houses are mixed. Some halls have night porters, wardens or postgrads that live on site.

Car parking: Plenty of spaces at most halls – with a £35 permit required for two of them.

EXTERNALLY:
- Ave rent: £38 • Living at home: 12%

Availability: *A decent standard at pretty reasonable prices for those prepared to look. The best places to hunt are the Tudor Road and Narborough Road areas, Clarendon, Knighton and the cosmo-trendy Evington with its cultural mix. The city centre is also good. Highfields is the dodgy district, so only those who enjoy being stalked at night should try it. Parking is about as difficult as getting a needle through the eye of a camel without the RSPCA complaining.*

Housing help: The University has the obligatory accommodation service that gives legal help and contract approval while the Union-run Accommodation Office provides a vacancy board and help and advice in the great home-hunt.

WELFARE

SERVICES:
- Lesbian/Gay/Bisexual Officer & Society • Ethnic Minorities Officer • Women's Officer
- Mature Students' Officer • International Students' Officer • Disabilities Officer
- Late-night minibus • Self-defence classes • College counsellors: 5 full
- Crime rating: !!!!

The Welfare Advisory Centre mops up the tears and the Union runs a minibus back to halls on Wednesdays and Fridays after club nights at 1.40am and 2.15am (£1).

Health: The Freemen's Common Health centre offers six doctors and three nurses.

Disabilities: There's the Richard Attenborough Centre for Disability and the Arts, a disability co-ordinator and an Accessibility Centre for students with specific difficulties. The University publishes its prospectus in Braille *and the campus is easily accessible to wheelchair users.*

FINANCE:
- Ave debt per year: £3,747
- Access fund: £415,119 • Successful applications: 1,000+

Support: Numerous hardship funds exist, some for specific groups (mature students, overseas students etc.), scholarships for physics, engineering and sports bursaries. The SU gives hardship loans up to £100 and special needs students are given priority.

Leicester Poly

see De Montfort University

Leicester Polytechnic

see De Montfort University

University of Lincoln

• *Formerly University of Lincolnshire and Humberside.*
University of Lincoln, Brayford Pool, Lincoln, LN6 7TS
Tel: (01522) 882 000 E-mail: enquiries@lincoln.ac.uk Website: www.lincoln.ac.uk
SU Office (Lincoln): ULSU Co-operative, Brayford Pool, Lincoln, LN6 7TS
Tel: (01522) 886 142 E-mail: sureception@lincoln.ac.uk Website: www.lincolnsu.com

GENERAL

Lincoln's a young University that's *traditionally* had strong links with Humberside. The town's *pretty, although when the most notable feature is a cathedral, the party-free alarm bells should start clanging.* Since emerging from the University of Lincolnshire and Humberside, Lincoln's *flexing its muscles and trying to prove it can stand on its own two feet* and has recently opened an *impressive* £5.4m science facility.

Sex ratio (M:F): 43:57	**Founded: 1861**
Full-time u'grads: 7,875	**Part-time: 5,235**
Postgrads: 985	**Non-degree: 1,200**
Ave course: 3yrs	**Ethnic: 7%**
State:private school: 97:3	**Flunk rate: 22%**
Mature: 40%	**International: 24%**
Disabled: 289	

(57% / 43%)

ATMOSPHERE:
This modern (but not gruesomely so) £70m development on the edge of an ancient harbour in the historic city of Lincoln is primed for continued expansion. Recent additions include the £10m school of Architecture. Lincoln has lots of eager types, keen to better themselves in a development that looks more like a conference centre than an academic facility. There are several sites in Lincoln itself, the main one being the marina-side Brayford campus. Students at Hull, an hour away, might feel like they're at a different university. University of Hull, *possibly.*

SITES:
Brayford Campus: (5,568 students) Home to the main teaching building, Learning Resource Centre, Architecture and Media Communications. There's also the main library and *most importantly*, the SU bar. The campus is in the city centre, so there's no need for a car. The newish science building houses all the science courses and has all the usual technical mcgubbins.

Riseholme Campus: (378 students) 5 miles from Lincoln's city centre and in a rural setting – which is just as well, really, as it's home to the countryside and animal-related courses. There are over 1,000 acres of farmed land and nearby there's woodland, deer parks and golfing. *Campus or holiday park, Push wonders.*
Cathedral Campus: (929 students – Arts, Design, Conservation & Crafts)
Hull Campus: (2,073 students – Health & Social Care; Art & Design; Media Technologies) An hour from Lincoln, 45 mins from Leeds or Scarborough. The University's invested £4m into the City Centre Campus, as it's known, which means a new Learning Resource Centre and lecture theatres.

HULL: see University of Hull

LINCOLN:
• Population: 85,600 • City centre: 0 miles • London: 132 miles • Hull: 44 miles • High temp: 20 • Low temp: 1 • Rainfall: 58
Lincoln's a *beautiful* cathedral city surrounded by flat, *peaceful, boring* countryside. Despite the long tradition of students in the area local amenity providers are only just waking up to the (*allegedly lucrative*) student market.

TRAVEL:

HULL: see University of Hull

LINCOLN:
Trains: The station, a few mins walk from the campus, has services to London (£27.70), Birmingham (£16.65), Edinburgh (£51.30) and more.
Car: The A1 runs nearby, intersecting with the A46 at Newark and the A57 near Retford. Lincolnshire has no motorways.
Bicycles: *Flat beyond your dreams. Get pedalling.*

CAREER PROSPECTS:
• Careers Service • No. of staff: 4 full • Unemployed after 6mths: 12%

FAMOUS ALUMNI:
Elliott Morley MP (Lab); Mary Parkinson (TV presenter).

FURTHER INFO:
• Prospectuses: undergrad; postgrad • Open days • Video
Magazine and newsletter also available on request.

A C A D E M I C

There are now five faculties: Art, Architecture & Design; Applied Computing Sciences; Business & Law; Media & Humanities; Health, Life & Social Sciences. There are also institutes of Medical Science and Educational Leadership. The Lincolnshire School of Agriculture is *one of the country's best*, for, er, learning about agriculture.

240-299		POINTS
Entry points: 240-299	Ave points: 240	
Applns per place: 5	Clearing: 5%	
No. of terms: 2	Length of terms: 9wks	
Staff/student ratio: 1:18	Study addicts: n/a	
Teaching: *	Research: ***	
Year abroad: 10%	Sandwich students: 10%	

ADMISSIONS:
- Apply via UCAS

SUBJECTS:
Best: Art & Design; Education Leadership; Health Studies; Political & International Relations; Psychology; Tourism.
Unusual: Conservation & Restoration; Museum & Exhibition Design.

LIBRARIES:
- 250,000 books • 1,541 study places

Provisions have improved following the recent expansions. Problems are inevitable though, what with the sites sharing books and not having had all that long to build up a collection.

COMPUTERS:
- 1,510 workstations

ENTERTAINMENT

THE TOWN: see University of Hull

LINCOLN:
- Price of a pint of beer: £1.90 • Glass of wine: £2

Cinemas: There's a new multiplex cinema *almost within popcorn throwing* distance of the campus.
Theatres: Board-treading *in abundance* at the Theatre Royal and Bishop's Palace.
Pubs/Clubs: The high street and Marina area have seen an explosion in student haunts, among them Revolution, Yate's, Edward's, Walkabont, the Annexe, Orgasmic and Dogma. Pulse, Ritzy, Jumpin Jaks and Po Na Na are *the most popular clubs.*
Music venues: Grafton House and O'Rourke's host local indie wannabes and O'Rourke's also has jazz nights.
Eating out: Indian restaurants on the High Street, French, Thai, Mexican and traditional food in the Bailgate and many other restaurants dotted around the city.

UNIVERSITY:
- Price of a pint of beer: £0.99 • Glass of wine: £1.40

Bars: Delph, the new bar at Lincoln (cap 360) has DJ nights and live bands.
Music venues: Thursday nights showcase Lincoln's finest stage-strutters.
Clubbing: High Voltage is the Friday night club at Delph. The Clublife society organises trips to cities like Nottingham and Sheffield.
Food: The main Refectory *is usually packed* and everyday nosh is *pretty good*.
Other: Occasional balls. The Hull Music & Drama Soc do productions, to much acclaim. Fancy a bit of Little Women? – well, these are your guys.

SOCIAL & POLITICAL

LINCOLN STUDENTS' UNION:
- 3 sabbaticals • Turnout at last ballot: 30% • NUS member

The SU has suffered over the years from a bad case of spreading themselves too thin over different sites. Recent campaigns have included an anti-tuition fees demo which attracted 500 protesters.

CLUBS (NON-SPORTING):
Alternative Music; Air Max Breakdance Crew ; Breakdancing; Bullet Magazine; Chinese; DJ; Film; Freshers Helpers; Gaian; International; Reputation; Social Policy; Socialist Students; Urban Society. **See also Clubs tables.**

OTHER ORGANISATIONS:

SU mag is Bullet and there's an indie Student paper, the Defender. Siren FM broadcasts for a month every year. Annual Rag week in April.

RELIGIOUS:

• 2 chaplains

PAID WORK:

• Job bureau

SU-run Job Exchange provides details of sits vac for those trying to get into the job queue.

• Recent successes: none • BUSA Ranking: 48

A recently added £5m sports facility should make its mark soon. *Ish.*

SPORTS FACILITIES:

Football, all-weather and hockey pitches; squash, basketball and netball courts; sports hall; gym, multigym, sauna; aerobics studio; climbing wall; golf course; lake. There's also a *popular* canoeing club and two public pools in Lincoln.

SPORTING CLUBS:

American Football; Equestrian; Lincoln Ladybirds; Motor Racing; South West Coastal Path Walkers Club; Surf Club; Ultimate Frisbee. **See also Clubs tables.**

IN COLLEGE:

• Catered: 2% • Cost: £60-£65 (38wks)
• Self-catering: 15% • Cost: £74 (38wks) • Insurance premium: £

Availability: Rooms on a first come, first served basis, though the University tries to house as many non-local 1st years as possible. There are 984 study bedrooms on campus at Lincoln, most are en-suite and there are facilities for disabled students too. Rooms in one of the five buildings on Hull campus average £57 a week: each hall has a Hall Assistant. There are also accommodation staff on site to give support where needed.
Car parking: Free permit parking, *but insufficient.*

EXTERNALLY: see University of Hull

LINCOLN:

• Ave rent: £57

Availability: *Because Lincoln isn't yet swamped with house-hungry students there's enough private accommodation going, especially the relatively cheap Victorian houses around Monks Road and West Parade. The areas near the football ground are somewhat grimmer.*
Housing help: Information on private housing is available from the SU. The University has close links with private landlords and there's a code of practice.

SERVICES:

• Lesbian/Gay/Bisexual Officer • Mature Students' Officer • Women's Officer
• Disabilities Officer • Nightline • College counsellors: 3 full • Crime rating: !!!
The University advice office, with three full-time counselling staff, deal with most problems that life can throw up. There are also new welfare drop-in sessions on both campuses.
Health: The student health service is staffed by three nurses.

Disabilities: The University's Disability Access, Resources & Technology service (DART) gives info on allowance payments, arranges dyslexia assessments and equipment or facilities (notetakers, readers and so on). Facilities are available at both campuses.

FINANCE:

• Ave debt per year: £4,157• Access fund: £500,000
• Successful applications/yr: 1,500
Support: The University waives fees for part-time undergraduates on income support.

University of Lincolnshire and Humberside
see University of Lincoln

University of Liverpool

University of Liverpool, 150 Mount Pleasant, Liverpool, L69 3GD
Tel: (0151) 794 2000 E-mail: ugrecriutment@liv.ac.uk Website: www.liv.ac.uk
The University of Liverpool Guild of Students, 160 Mount Pleasant, Liverpool, L69 7BR
Tel: (0151) 794 4128 E-mail: gensec@liv.ac.uk Website: wwww.liverpoolguild.org.uk

GENERAL

From Gerry and his Pacemakers and the cast of Bread, to the dearly departed Brookside and the mostly dead legends that were the Beatles, Liverpool has always dipped its toes in the waters of youth culture. Merseyside's sliced in two by the River Mersey, dividing Liverpool from the Wirral. The city began as the primary seaway of the North-West and is still a bustling port. *Lucky Northerners get two major cities for the price of one* as Manchester is only 28 miles away. A major programme of redevelopment has been underway for some years now, and investors are still pouring their cash in, so *attractive* modern buildings are springing up amongst the art deco and post-industrialist architecture.

Liverpool's first university (joined by Liverpool John Moores University in 1992) is the original 'redbrick' institution. The word was coined to describe the University's Victoria Building on Brownlow Hill. Many of the other buildings are redbrick too but others are more modern – *well, 60s and 70s* – based on a 100-acre site (big for an inner city campus) in the Mount Pleasant area of town, gazing out on the city from the brow of a hill.

ATMOSPHERE:

Sex ratio (M:F): 45:55	Founded: 1881
Full-time u'grads: 12,500	Part-time: 4,265
Postgrads: 2,225	Non-degree: 3,829
Ave course: 3yrs	Ethnic: n/a
State:private school: 93:7	Flunk rate: 9%
Mature: 18%	International: 16%
Disabled: 121	Local: n/a

Liverpool students tend to be enveloped by the atmosphere of the city: down-to-earth, unpretentious and with a deeply ingrained sense of fun. Like the locals, the students have a strong sense of loyalty to their town that extends beyond a passing appreciation of its musical and footballing history through to its cultural, social and academic possibilities. They know they're here to work and they enjoy some excellent academic facilities, but with one of the best-equipped Unions in the country and some of the most stomping club venues, partying and studying mix together as smoothly as a double vodka and Red Bull.

LIVERPOOL:

* Population: 439,473 • City centre: 800m • London: 201 miles
* Chester: 26 miles • Manchester: 28 miles
* High temp: 21 • Low temp: 2 • Rainfall: 63

Having snatched the prestigious title of European Capital of Culture 2008 from under Newcastle's nose, Liverpool's come a long way from its roots as a prosperous mercantile port and is now recognised for its *thriving social scene and city-wide cultural infusion*. The sense of history still pervades, however – grand Victorian houses are still dotted around and ancient streets built for carriages still wind their way throughout the town. *It's not all glitzy olde worlde glamour though – there are still some areas that put the 'void' in 'avoidable'. But avoid the rough edges and there's oodles of fun to be had –* Liverpool's bar scene and nightlife are buzzing and the musical heritage – largely thanks to Lennon and Co. – is still a source of intense civic pride, as testified by the mind-boggling quantity of Beatles tours and paraphernalia available to the discerning musical tourist. The Albert Dock drags in droves of sightseers eager to check out the unmistakable Liverpudlian waterfront, with its vast array of shops, bars, restaurants, museums and galleries (and, of course, This Morning's floating weather map).

TRAVEL:

Trains: Liverpool Lime Street is about 10 mins walk down the road, offering mainline services to London, Manchester, Leeds, Birmingham and loads of other cities, big and small.
Coaches: The National Express station on Norton Street is 800m from campus and runs regular coaches to Leeds, Birmingham, London and hourly to Manchester (£6 rtn).
Car: M53, M56, M57, M58 and M62 (good for North-West and Wales). There's a multi-storey car park sat beside the campus, £3 a day. *Parking on University premises is not an encouraging prospect.*
Air: Liverpool Airport is 8 miles from the city. It covers national and international destinations and runs cheap flights through Easyjet and Keen.
Ferry: Liverpool's the main port for Belfast and there are other regular ferries to Ireland. *And, of course, there's the famous ferry 'cross the Mersey.*
Hitching: *Good connections are a boon when it comes to lift-scrounging. Edge Lane is a top spot to pick up lifts just before it hits the motorway and the M57's not a bad option either. The University's dead against hitching.*
Local: Arriva buses 86 and 26 are *useful, reliable* services for getting to and from the University. Student fares cost £1 or so, but yearly or termly passes are *cheaper and less faffy* – check the Arriva website for discount deals. The train station in the city centre sends passengers off to local towns and nearby cities like Southport (£2 rtn).
University: Passes are available for the University bus service which runs between the Guild and halls of residence.
Taxis: Plenty of black cabs crawl the kerbs – *complete with proud-to-be-Scouse, seen-it-all cabbies* – but pre-booking with local companies Delta or Botanics often works out cheaper.
Bicycles: *It's not a hilly city, but Liverpool's a bit large and car-orientated for cycling to be the best transport choice.*

CAREER PROSPECTS:

* Careers Service • No. of staff: 25 full • Unemployed after 6mths: 8%

The *excellent* Careers Service is a subdivision of the Centre for Lifelong Learning and offers students job alert e-mails, a fortnightly job bulletin, career fairs, employer presentations, work seminars and *a wealth of* application, CV and interview guidance.

FAMOUS ALUMNI:

Steve Coppell (footballer and manager); Barry Horne (footballer, Everton and Wales); Maurice Colclough, Tony Neary (rugby union); Hugh Jones (marathon runner); Chris Lowe (Pet Shop Boy); Alison Mowbray (Olympic rower); Phil Redmond (TV mogul and the brains behind Brookside, Grange Hill and Hollyoaks); Prof. Joseph Rotblat CBE (Nobel prize winning physicist); Patricia Routledge (actress); Jon Snow (ITN reporter).

FURTHER INFO:

• Prospectuses: undergrad; postgrad; international; alternative • Open days
In addition to the annual open days independent visits can be arranged by contacting lstewart@liverpool.ac.uk. Prospectuses can be ordered via the main website which also offers a *comprehensive but plug-heavy* virtual tour of the campus.

ACADEMIC

Liverpool's rather hot stuff academically, with a wide range of professionally directed, forward thinking courses up for the taking. It was the first place in the UK to open up departments in Architecture, Biochemistry, Civic Design and Oceanography and its English department was one of the first to admit that Science Fiction might be worth a second academic glance. Eight Nobel Prize winners have come and gone – it was here the link was made between mosquitoes and malaria – so there must be something good going on. Thirty-three departments are grouped into six faculties – students are allocated a personal tutor from their faculty's staff, whom they check-in with twice a term. Teaching is a mix of seminars, compulsory lectures and practicals (as necessary). Courses are accessed through coursework, exams, presentations and projects; final grades are totted up as a combo of exam results over the course.

Entry points: 240-390	Ave points: n/a
No. of terms: 2	Length of terms: 19wks
Staff/student ratio: 1:15	Study addicts: n/a
Teaching: ****	Research: ***
Firsts: 12%	2.2s: 28%
2.1s: 43%	3rds: 4%
Year abroad: <1%	Sandwich students: 6%

240-390 *POINTS*

ADMISSIONS:

• Apply via UCAS
Liverpool has an open door policy when it comes to providing Higher Education for people of all ages and backgrounds. Those with non-traditional qualifications or experience *need not be scared to apply.*

SUBJECTS:

Arts: 21%	Science: 23%
Engineering: 7%	SES: 28%
Medicine: 17%	Veterinary Medicine: 4%

LIBRARIES:

• 1,700,000 books • 1,678 study places • Spend per student: £££££
Of the four biggest libraries, the Sydney Jones Library is the daddy, but the Harold Coen Library alone would be big enough for most universities. The Law and Education Libraries are fairly chunky too, and there a large number of smaller, departmental book stashes.

There was a University in Northampton in 1261 but it only lasted 3 years.

COMPUTERS:

• 1,200 workstations • 24-hr access • Spend per student: ££

Brownlow Hill computer lab is 24-hr access – as long as students cough up £10 a year for the privilege. Workstations are available in the libraries and departmental labs. Study bedrooms now all have broadband facilities.

OTHER LEARNING FACILITIES:

Drama studio to prance in; rehearsal rooms to dance in.

ENTERTAINMENT

THE CITY:

• Price of a pint of beer: £1.50 • Glass of wine: £1.50 • Can of Red Bull: £1.50

Cinemas: Six in the city centre, mostly big blockbuster bonanzas with the exception of Fact – the first purpose-built arts project in Liverpool for 60 years. The £10m complex houses three cinema screens (old, new and arty films) – one of which has comfy sofas – two galleries, a media lounge and *the trendiest of trendy bars.*

Theatres: The Empire is a pre-West End stopover for touring shows. The smaller and *more daring* Everyman Theatre has an *innovative and unconventional slant, while the tiny Neptune is a cross between a cabaret hall and a proud palace of panto.* The Royal Court is primarily a music venue, but comedy, drama and opera share the stage on occasion. The Liverpool Playhouse in the centre hosts some major productions and there's also the *small but perfectly formed Unity Theatre for an appealing array of comedy, dance and drama.*

Pubs: *The boom in swish trend-setting bars and national chain pubs has hit Liverpool with all the force of the fifth tequila slammer. There are now lots of new places worthy of student attention,* including the *very sophisticated* Tea Factory, *the funky but cheesy* Baa Bar – which does loads of £1 shooters – and Baby Cream on Albert Dock. Brook House is a *popular* pub in the middle of a student housing area and has the added bonus of drawing in the *unfeasibly attractive* stars of Hollyoaks. *There are too many other places to mention, but Modo, Blue Bar, Revolution, Walkabout and Tru Bar & Grill are all good places to start.*

Clubbing: *More choice than any dedicated dance-fiend could ever deserve. Medication at Cream (Wed) piles the punters into its three rooms – a mix of urban, dance and cheese. Vodka Nation at Garlands (Thurs) is student night but's better at the weekends for those not into dance and Scouse House. The Razz could be cleaner but there's something so seductive about its relentless onslaught of cheesy pop every night of the week.*

Music venues: *The Royal Court is the big 'un for chart-toppers and classical tunes. The new Carling Academy is one of the few places in the world where it's still acceptable to shout 'Let's Rock!' without being ironic. There's loads of other smaller venues, like the Empire and The Flying Picket next to John Moores.*

Eating out: *It's entirely possibly to live without a kitchen in Liverpool – although only the supremely minted would consider dining out all the time. There are some good value eateries though:* Shere Khan is close to being the finest curry house in the world – or at least Liverpool – *with funky décor and extensive menu.* Kimos has a *half-hearted Mexican theme but does divine kebabs.* Caesar's Palace is the venue for posh dates without posh prices and Tabac, Magnet and Ask are also popular. *Check out China Town for eat-till-you-puke buffets.*

UNIVERSITY:

• Price of a pint of beer: £1 • Glass of wine: £1.25 • Can of Red Bull: £1.45

Bars: There are ten bars in and around the Guild and University. The Liver Bar is an *art deco-style haven of purple, pink* and pound-a-pint offers all day every day. The Gilmour Bar is *highly ornate,* with a listed ceiling. The Ken Saro Wiwa bar (named after the executed Nigerian political prisoner) is a modern place that's a good spot for a cheap lunch. The other lounge, basement and balcony bars get an airing on club nights.

Theatres: The Stanley Theatre in the Guild and the University Theatre. The two active drama societies put quite a few shows on each year, usually one up in Edinburgh too.

Film: The large screen in the Guild shows films fairly regularly.

Music venues: The Liverpool Academy 1, 2, 3 and 4 are major venues both for the University and the rest of the city. The year-round programme of gigs has featured The Darkness, Coldplay, Goldie Lookin' Chain, the Killers and Keane.

Clubbing: Monday's Double Vision at the Guild is now *one of the largest nights going in the UK* featuring pop, indie, dance, R&B – *everything really* – in three rooms, including the Live Lounge where upcoming talent is showcased. Time Tunnel, the Saturday retro night, is now over ten years old and hasn't yet lost its sense of kitsch. Trevor Nelson, Tim Westwood and Mr Scruff have DJed their socks off in the past.

Comedy/cabaret: Weekly comedy in Academy 1 has brought in Johnny Vegas, Daniel Kitson and Lee Mack.

Food: The bars all serve some kind of food or other, and the Reilly and Courtyard Cafés are good for working lunches. The 700-seat Courtyard *makes the Guild the culinary and social centre of the campus and completely eliminates the need for a main University refectory.* Several departments have *itty bitty* snack bars.

Other: All major departments arrange balls *which pale in comparison to the enormous Graduation Ball in July.*

SOCIAL & POLITICAL

THE UNIVERSITY OF LIVERPOOL GUILD OF STUDENTS:

• 4 sabbaticals • Turnout at last ballot: 12% • NUS member

With the second-largest Union building in Europe (Paris holds the top spot), *Liverpool students are a lucky bunch, especially when it comes to entertainment – which the ents officer lays on thick and fast. The exec is a slick, professional organisation with a number of commercial interests that help to stock its ample piggybank. Relations with the University are co-operative – both the Guild and Uni authorities are prepared to listen to each other and the SU is represented on most University committees. Although not overly political, students have launched a few volleys against 'Top-Up' Tony's tuition fee proposals.*

SU FACILITIES:

Ten bars; five cafeterias; print shop; general shop; photographers; optician; Little Cohen library with study area; travel agency; ticket agency; advice centre; Royal Bank of Scotland with ATMs; prayer room; international lounge; launderette; hairdresser; table tennis; snooker/pool tables; Mountford Hall; Monday market (clothes, CDs, plants etc.); theatre; new bookshop; dark room; band practice room; function rooms; photo booth; post office; games and vending machines; film-making facilities; minibus hire; photocopying.

CLUBS (NON-SPORTING):

AIESEC (arranges student work placements); Anime; Archaeology; Classics & Egyptology; Band; Basement Film Unit; Body Soc (dance); Break Dancing; Chemistry; Chinese Sports; CND; Cocktail; Computing; Dance Music; Drum & Bass; English; Enter Liverpool (business enterprise); French; Friends of Palestine; Fusion; Geographical; Herdman Earth; American; Chinese; Links (St John Ambulance); LMSS (medics); LUVS (vets); LUVZV (veterinary zoologists); Malay Speaking Circle; Meditation; Mexican; Music; Open Air Club; Physoc (physics); Pol Soc (politics); Real Ale; Roleplay & Gaming; Sikh; Singapore; SLAGS (Scouts & Guides); Socialist; Sociology; Sri Lankan; STAR (refugee action); Stop the War Coalition; Thai; Vegetarians & Vegans; Wing Tsun Kung Fu; Young Greens. **See also Clubs tables.**

OTHER ORGANISATIONS:

Liverpool Student is a city-wide publication that John Moores and Liverpool Hope also have hands in. It and its hacks have been noticed several times by the Student Media Awards. Icon radio broadcasts daily on the net. Liverpool Rag is *lively* and bagged £50,000 for charity last year, while Liverpool Student Community Action goes forth and does good works.

RELIGIOUS:

• 2 chaplains (CofE, RC) rabbi

There's a Muslim prayer room in the Union and an Anglican chaplaincy on campus. Two cathedrals in town, Catholic and Anglican, in *strongly contrasting* architectural styles, and both within praying distance of the Union. There are plenty of churches, more synagogues than in any other English town this size and a few mosques, as well as temples for Hindus, Buddhists and Hare Krishnas.

PAID WORK:

• Job bureau • Paid work: term-time 65%: hols 90%
PULSE is run through the Careers Service and sources part-time and temporary vacancies which it advertises through e-mail and text alerts. The Business Bridge scheme can help with finding placements in local companies. Liverpool itself has a high unemployment rate, but the tenacious job-seeker should be able to find bar, shop or restaurant work.

SPORTS

• Recent successes: women's basketball, triathlon • BUSA Ranking: 22
Only three years younger than the University itself the Athletics Union lures around a third of the student body into *its oiled and muscular grip. Facilities are among the best of any university in the country, and include a 4-court sports hall, changing facilities, state-of-the art dance and fitness centre and disabled facilties in the pool. Sporting successes of the past couple of years have lifted competitive spirits.*

SPORTS FACILITIES:

Strewth: over 70 acres of playing fields for athletics, football, rugby, hockey, lacrosse and cricket spread over the area around halls of residence. There are more playing fields at Maryton Grange and Widnes (served by University minibuses). Two sports centres on campus include: swimming pool; climbing wall; dance studio; multigym; basketball/netball courts. Thrown into the bundle are the boathouse at Knowsley Park and the outdoor activity centre all the way over in Snowdonia. Membership of the AU costs £24/year. Liverpool itself adds extra facilities into the mix, including the River Mersey, a dry ski slope, a golf course and a number of *high quality* leisure centres (Toxteth, Everton and Kirby, for example).

SPORTING CLUBS:

10-Pin Bowling; Ballroom Dancing; Boat; Diving; Frisbee; Ju-Jitsu; Kung Fu; Lacrosse; Rifle & Pistol; Surf; Table Tennis; Waterpolo; Windsufing; Wu Shu. **See also Clubs tables.**

ATTRACTIONS:

Liverpool FC are still legendary in the world of football and have kept one of the most impressive records in English club history. That's not to say that their neighbours Everton haven't done pretty damn well for themselves though – ditto their *less famous but still feisty friends* the Tranmere Rovers. The Grand National venue Aintree Race Course is around and about, as well as some other *diamond* spectator-spots.

ACCOMMODATION

IN COLLEGE:

• Catered: 17% • Cost: £88-100 (32wks)
• Self-catering: 10% • Cost: £66 (38/40wks)
• First years living in: 81% • Insurance premium: £
Availability: Liverpool's halls are almost exclusively stocked with 1st years, who are guaranteed a room if they apply in time. Rent prices include insurance (*a relatively unusual bonus*), cleaning of communal areas and, in catered accommodation, two *entirely edible* meals a day. Melville and Mulberry Halls *are popular by virtue of their closeness to campus,* but Greenbank and Carnatic – both on *pleasant green sites* 3 miles away – *have strong social atmospheres* and are served by a University bus service morning and evening. Most halls have laundry facilities, TV lounge, sports facilities on hand, computers and a bar.
Car parking: Limited permit-only parking.

EXTERNALLY:

• Ave rent: £55
Availability: *Generally no problem* finding somewhere to live, but the crème de la caramel is always gone by mid-February so – *as when showering in prisons* – it pays to be vigilant. The biggest problem students face is finding somewhere close to their place of study, but

few end up miles away. *Smithdown Road is popular for its easy bus routes and Garsten is also getting some attention. Some areas have developed as decidedly studenty, such as Wavertree (a veritable student ghetto), Sefton Park (more expensive, but arty, converted flats), Allerton, Mossley Hill, Aigburth, Old Swan and the famous Penny Lane. Some areas are less appealing, such as Toxteth and Walton, but students do live there quite happily. Kensington is also worth a mention – many choose to live there for the cheapness despite bad press.*

Housing help: Liverpool University and John Moores joined forces to create Liverpool Student Homes – an accommodation-finding service that has branches on campus, at Mount Pleasant and on Edge Lane. Contract approval, safety checks and vacancy posting are all within its remit.

WELFARE

SERVICES:

- Lesbian/Gay/Bisexual Officer & Society • Ethnic Minorities Officer
- Women's Officer & Society • Mature Students' Officer & Society
- International Students' Officer & Society • Postgrad Society • Disabilities Officer & Society
- Late-night/Women's minibus • Nightline • College counsellors: 5 • Crime rating: !!!!

The Student Advice Centre and the sabbatical Welfare Officer act as first points of contact for troubled students – they either dole out advice or refer to one of the University's specialist support services. As well as the above there are nine associate volunteer counsellors (professionally trained). Student Health Services and the Medial Faculty have a part-time clinical psychologist each.

Health: The Brownlow Group Practice based at the Student Services Centre offers full-time surgeries all year round, as well as emergency treatment and medical services at halls.

Women: Women-only swimming lessons and priority on the University bus service.

Crèches/Nursery: 68 places for kiddies younger than 5.

Disabilities: *Access isn't entirely peachy*, but there's been *serious* investment towards ramps and lifts in some campus buildings. There's a Disabled Students' Working Party as well as particular provisions for hearing-impaired and students with dyslexia.

Crime: *Not much of a problem*, but minor thefts are common enough to warrant caution.

Drugs: There's a help service on campus for students with drug problems, but these are few and far between. There are the usual drug issues in the city.

FINANCE:

- Ave debt per year: £3,583

Fees: The University and the Union are both opposed to top-up fees.

- Access fund: £66,883 • Successful applications/yr: 996 • Ave payment: £640

Support: The University offers financial advice and assistance to students with holes in their piggy banks. A large number of bursaries and scholarships are available, including the Alumni Scholarship (which pays out £2,000 for academic achievement), the John Lennon Memorial Scholarship (£1,200) for Merseyside residents with environmental interests and several hardship funds.

Liverpool Hope University

- **Formerly Liverpool Institute for Higher Education.**
(1) Liverpool Hope University College, Hope Park, Liverpool, L16 9JD
   Tel. (0151) 291 3000 E-mail: admissions@hope.ac.uk Website: www.hope.ac.uk
   Liverpool Hope Students' Union Website: www.hopesu.ac.uk
(2) Hope at Everton, Haigh Street, Liverpool, L3 8QB Tel. (0151) 291 3578

GENERAL

Five miles from the centre of Liverpool sits the *calm and collected* world of Liverpool Hope. It began its life by linking St Katherine's and Notre Dame Colleges of Teacher Education for Women, annexed their male equivalent, Christ Church, spent a brief spell as the Liverpool Institute for Higher Education in 1980, then pupated into its current incarnation in 1995. It's always had *strong godly leanings* and maintains *a firmly* religious outlook – although it's by no means as Christian-centric as it once was. The campus itself is a compact collection of *drab* bricks and glass, which conceal some of the *much more exciting* architecture of the original buildings and chapels at the campus's centre. It'll achieve full university status *any day now.* **For general info about Liverpool: see <u>University of Liverpool</u>.**

Sex ratio (M:F): 30:70	Founded: 1844
Full-time u'grads: 5,280	Part-time: 2,139
Postgrads: n/a	Non-degree: n/a
Ave course: 3 yrs	Ethnic: n/a
State:private school: n/a	Flunk rate: n/a
Mature: n/a	International: n/a
Disabled: n/a	Local: n/a

ATMOSPHERE:

The Hope community is cosy almost to the point of claustrophobia – even woollen airlocks couldn't be this close-knit. Most students treat their workload with relaxed determination, intent on getting the job done then getting a job, without too much excitement en route. In fact, 'University life' is a bit of an oxymoron here. Students drain from the campus at weekends – even the cafés close – but the SU musters enough enthusiasm for an ent or two midweek. The bulk of the party action, however, is orientated around Smithdown Road, where many students live out. Relations with locals have moments of tension due to noise and parking, but no one gets hurt.

SITES:

Everton: (1,000 students – Creative Arts) 4 miles from Hope Park and closer to the city centre, this site is situated in a newly-developed residential area and provides accommodation blocks and some of the *artier* facilities, plus the Great Hall theatre venue, a bar and a café.

LIVERPOOL: see University of Liverpool

TRAVEL: see University of Liverpool
Trains: Mossley Hill, about 3 miles away, is the nearest station, but Liverpool Lime Street, $5\frac{1}{2}$ miles away, is *a better bet* for national journey-making.
Coaches: National Express Coaches trundle out of Edge Lane Drive, $1\frac{1}{2}$ miles from campus.
Car: *Like a whalebone corset, parking regulations on campus are both morally controversial and restrictive* – there are very few spaces and visitors have to book in advance. The neighbourhood is residential, so on-street parking is a possibility, *but this isn't going down too well with the residents themselves.*
Local: Buses 75 and 78 make the half-hour journey into the city centre every 10 mins for 90p.
College: A free hourly shuttlebus runs between both main sites. Students living in Aigburth or Everton halls get a discounted bus pass in deference to their distance.
Bicycles: *Barely any bike theft on or around campus, largely because there's barely any bikes to thieve.*

CAREER PROSPECTS:

• Careers Service • No. of staff: 8 full/1 part • Unemployed after 6mths: 7%

The Career Development Service provides guidance, e-guidance (*we don't mean drugs advice*), a library, interview training, vacancy lists and arranges job fairs. Someone is always available out of hours *to deal with career emergencies – of the 'Help! My professional development is swerving dangerously off course' type.*

FAMOUS ALUMNI:

Willy Russell (playwright, Shirley Valentine).

FURTHER INFO:

• Prospectuses: undergrad; postgrad; departmental; international; PGCE; video • Open days

ACADEMIC

The College's strong ecumenical background means that even the academic side of life has a strong religious aftertaste – instead of faculties or departments, students study in 'deaneries'. Courses are modular and very flexible, particularly in the 2nd and 3rd years, when students can find themselves studying several diverse subjects as part of the same course. There's no scheduled one-to-one lecturer contact as such, *but since everyone's so darned friendly and accessible,* individual help is always available. Course-wise, teacher training is probably its *biggest hitter.*

Entry points: n/a	Ave points: 200
No. of terms: 3	Length of terms: 10wks
Teaching: *****	Research: n/a
Year Abroad: n/a	Sandwich students: n/a
Firsts: n/a	2.2s: n/a
2.1s: n/a	3rds: n/a

ADMISSIONS:

• Apply via UCAS/direct for part-time courses

LHUC is predisposed to applicants with some sort of religious conviction and also looks positively on hopefuls who are mature, disabled, international or who need to remain in the North West for any reason *(except maybe house arrest).*

SUBJECTS:

Best: Art & Design; Management & Business; Maths, Organismal Bioscience; Psychology; Sociology; Statistics & Operational Research; Theology & Religious Studies.
Unusual: Computer Gaming.

LIBRARIES:

• 250,000 books • 750 study places • 24-hr access

The *arcane-sounding* Sheppard-Worlock Library is open all day, every day and has substantial collections of child education books (and toys) and, *unsurprisingly enough,* theology. Fans of *soft porn chav-soap* Hollyoaks may find the library eerily familiar – it's used as the set for courtroom scenes.

COMPUTERS:

• 1,400 workstations

No workstation is more than 4 years old as a matter of policy, *although that's still pretty geriatric by today's standards.*

OTHER LEARNING FACILITIES:

Drama studio; music rooms; media centre with video recording and editing facilities; radio studio.

E N T E R T A I N M E N T

The CITY: see <u>University of Liverpool</u>

There are very few pubs in the local area, so students have to venture city-wards *to quench their thirst/get blind stinking trollied*. As far as clubbing goes, Blue Angel (Tues) is the *unofficial Hope night out*, with 95% of the punters being Hope students enjoying the any-drink-for-a-pound-promotion.

COLLEGE:

• <u>Price of a pint of beer: £1</u> • <u>Glass of wine: £1.50</u> • <u>Can of Red Bull: £2</u>

Bars: Two boozers at Hope Park. Derwent is *so laid back it's upside down, but buzzes on Friday nights*. Wednesday is sports night and Thursday's open mic night is like *Russian Roulette with talent*. D2 is bigger and gets used for more special events – comedy nights, big screen sports etc. There's a third bar at Everton *but no one gets very excited about it*.

Theatres: The *arty* sorts at Everton put on a couple of shows in the Great Hall each year, but the big event is the Cornerstone drama, music and poetry festival which attracts visiting professionals.

Film: The film society shows one free film a week, usually of an offbeat bent.

Music venues: Great Hall hosts classical concerts; D2 has a band on each term, and there's the open mike/decks in Derwent each week.

Clubbing: CRUNCH is D2's Friday night free cheesy chart extravaganza. God's Kitchen in Derwent is *all about the trance, baby*. Drag queen DJ, Miss Carmen Storm, pays regular visits. Comedy/Cabaret: Twice termly comedy in D2 from the Avalon Comedy Network (Chris Addison, Natalie Haynes, Hugh Lennon & his Hypno-Dog). At £3-4, this is the only event the *generous* SU charges for.

Food: *Not many people bother with the Derwent Kitchen in the Union; most opt for the canteen-style Refectory or the Fresh Hope café*. All three are closed at weekends.

Other: The Graduation and Christmas Balls are held at the *swanktastic* Adelphi Hotel in town.

S O C I A L & P O L I T I C A L

LiVERPOOL HOPE STUDENTS' UNION:

• <u>2 sabbaticals</u> • <u>NUS member</u> • <u>Turnout at last ballot: 10%</u>

Although it dresses slightly to the right, a pickled badger is more actively political than LHSU, which concentrates on welfare and providing free ents to its members, though it does get involved in national NUS campaigns and is currently fighting to free up Wednesday afternoons for sporty activities. The College *lovingly* nurtures the SU with helpful cash handouts where necessary, so relationships are *pretty sound*.

SU FACILITIES:

Derwent House Union Building has: two bars; canteen; four pool/snooker tables; meeting room; Endsleigh Insurance; hairdressers; NatWest bank & ATM; photocopier, fax & printing service; photo booth; payphones; advice centre; crèche; TV lounge; juke box; gaming machines; general store; stationery shop; vending machines; bookshop; computer shop; launderette.

CLUBS (NON-SPORTING):

Black & Asian; Funky House; Gospel Choir; Nyeusi & Moindi. **See also Clubs tables.**

OTHER ORGANISATIONS:

Liverpool Student is the free city-wide fortnightly newspaper run jointly with the <u>University of Liverpool</u> and <u>Liverpool John Moores</u> – a Hope student is still polishing his Student Journalist of the Year award. Radio Hope has just celebrated its first birthday and broadcasts across the city 4pm-12am daily. Rag raises *a quid or two* for good causes and Hope One World sends do-gooders out to Nepal, India, Sri Lanka and Africa to, er, do good.

RELIGIOUS:
• 3 chaplains: (CofE; RC; Methodist)
LHSU is a *deeply* religious institution so most brands of Christian are well-provided for by the two chapels – one's Anglican, the other Catholic, and *despite historical precedents, they work closely together.*
Religion in Liverpool: see University of Liverpool

PAID WORK:
• Job Bureau • Paid work: term-time: 50%; hols 95%
Jobzone at the Career Development Service allows browsing of vacancies. Teacherzone does the same for the more vocationally-minded. The Business Bridge scheme ships 200-300 students into local companies each year.

 • Recent successes: men's rugby league • BUSA Ranking: 48
They may not punch the hardest in the sports ring, but LHSU has an admirable 'have a go' attitude and tries to cater for as many different sports as it feasibly can.

SPORTS FACILITIES:
The Sports Hall is independent from the College and self-financing. Students have access to: four pitches (football, rugby, hockey, all-weather); two tennis courts; sports hall; gym; aerobics studio; dance studio; multigym. £12 a year covers usage costs. See University of Liverpool for local facilities.

SPORTING CLUBS:
Gaelic Football; Hurling. **See also Clubs tables.**

ATTRACTIONS: see University of Liverpool

IN COLLEGE:
• Catered: 5% • Cost: £79-83 (31wks) • Self-catered: 19% • Cost: £66-74 (36wks)
• First years living in: 80%
Availability: Almost all 1st years have a room if they want one, given the usual deadline and application criteria. Halls are mainly on campus, with one at the Everton site and another at Aigburth (both about 4 miles away). *They're spick and span alright, but there have been a few trashings at Everton* due to security lapses (in theory, it's watched 24 hrs a day). No smoking in communal areas and some halls. Just over half the rooms are en-suite. Vending machines, telephones, launderettes and plasma/widescreen/Sky TV lounges are available on all sites.
Car parking: *They'd really rather you didn't, and definitely not permanently.*

EXTERNALLY:
Availability: see University of Liverpool
Housing help: LHSU provides a list of postcodes that might be worth a glance. See University of Liverpool for services provided by Liverpool Student Homes.

SERVICES:
• Lesbian/Gay/Bisexual Officer • Women's Officer • Mature Students' Officer
• Ethnic Minorities' Officer • Postgraduate Students' Officer

• International Students' Officer & Society • Disabilities Officer & Society
• Women's Officer • Nightline • College counsellors: 1 full/ 2 part
Compass the Student Services organisation, has a *friendly and competent* welfare arm.
Health: Two visiting doctors look after students in College accommodation every Tues and Wed and there's a full-time College Nurse. Those living out have to register at a recommended GP surgery.
Crèches/Nursery: The SU-run nursery has places for 24 kidlings 3mths-5yrs.
Disabilities: Access and support for disabled students is *very good*, with specialised study bedrooms, support workers, note-takers and technological resources for the deaf and blind. An outside agency runs a Study Skills support service.
Crime: Campus *is considered very safe*. A copshop on campus *helps, as do the links the College fosters with local police.*

FINANCE:

• Access fund: £450,000 • Successful applications: 576 • Ave payment: £100-3,500
Support: The International Students' Bursary provides several scholarships for Middle Eastern students. A Crisis Loan *is just what it sounds like.*

Liverpool John Moores University

• *Formerly Liverpool Polytechnic.*
Liverpool John Moores University, Roscoe Court, 4 Rodney Street,
Liverpool, Merseyside, L1 2TZ Tel: (0151) 231 5090 E-mail: recruitment@ljmu.ac.uk
Website: www.ljmu.ac.uk
The Liverpool Students' Union, The Haigh Building, Maryland Street, Liverpool,
Merseyside, L1 9DE Tel: (0151) 231 4000 E-mail: STUDENTSUNION@livjm.ac.uk
Website: www.l-s-u.com

GENERAL

A *colossal Merseyside explosion seems to have scattered pieces of LJMU across the city.* Or rather, the merging of four separate colleges in the 60s resulted in a glut of disparate sites and buildings uniting under the name of the bloke who invented the Littlewoods pools. While it's *almost impossible* to say where the University's main site actually is, many are like self-contained colonies, with most students living at their chosen subject's site. Some University buildings are modern, purpose-built constructions while others, such as the Fine Art Department, are *fine* examples of Georgian and Victorian architecture. The sites are clustered in the city centre, near Liverpool University, and further out around the city's edges. **For general information about Liverpool: See University of Liverpool.**

Sex ratio (M:F): 45:55	**Founded: 1970**
Full-time u'grads: 13,500	**Part-time: 4,160**
Postgrads: 1,170	**Non-degree: 4,231**
Ave course: 3yrs	**Ethnic: 8%**
State:private school: 95:5	**Flunk rate: 22%**
Mature: 46%	**International: 11%**
Disabled: 40	**Local: 68%**

ATMOSPHERE:

Being smeared across such a lively, fun-stuffed city, LJMU hums with energy. The vibes are more sporty than political since such a huge number of students take sports-related degrees. Academic life can be fairly laidback, but more intense when the pressure's on. Town/gown animosities have been almost entirely resolved thanks to a number of community projects and although students may be on the receiving end of a local's sharp tongue from time to time, there are enough scouser jokes for them to have a comeback at the ready.

SITES:

Although LJMU can be divided into four main chunks, Mount Pleasant and Byrom Street each have many smaller annexes. There are also associated institutions throughout Merseyside and Cheshire.
Mount Pleasant: (4,000 students) The main building sports an impressive number of gargoyles outside and a huge, new Learning Resources Centre (*aka 'library'*) inside.
Byrom Street: (8,000 students) A 60s *carbuncle* 2 mins from the centre.
I M Marsh: (1,000 students) 3 miles from the city centre on the *ruralish* outskirts of Aigburth. *Usually swarming with sporty types.*

LIVERPOOL: see University of Liverpool

TRAVEL: see University of Liverpool
Car: Permits are required to park on any of the sites.
College: LJMU operates a shuttle bus between the various sites.

CAREER PROSPECTS:

• Careers Service • No. of staff: 8 full/5 part • Unemployed after 6mths: 8%
The Career Development Service provides bulletin boards, interview training, a careers library and arranges job fairs, as well as running skills training programmes for graduate jobseekers.

FAMOUS ALUMNI:

Caroline Aherne (The Royle Family); Stephen Byers (MP and *truth-deficient* ex-transport secretary); Julian Cope (80s musician); Bill Drummond (KLF); Phil Gayle (C4 newsreader); Debbie Greenwood (ex-Miss England and TV presenter); Jim King (Cream club runner); John Lennon; Martin 'Chariots' Offiah (rugby league); Phil Selway (Radiohead's drummer); Stu Sutcliffe (5th Beatle). Liverpool and Everton FCs have honorary degrees.

FURTHER INFO:

• Prospectuses: undergrad; postgrad; departmental; alternative; DVD • Open days
Prospectuses can be requested from the main website. Also guides for mature students and student finance. For info on open days, hit the net, cyberdude.

ACADEMIC

Astrophysics and Sports Science both have international reputations for progress in their fields. Varied teaching methods *keep things fresh* in the classroom: lectures, tutorials, seminars, visiting high profile specialists (including Steven Speilberg, and Phil Redmond of Brookside fame) and even a 'marine simulator' for practical sessions. *No, Push isn't sure what that is either.* Courses are modular, with students taking a set of modules each year (in theory up to 120 hours of study each). Entry to the 2nd year depends on 1st year performance. After that, everything counts towards the final grade.

POINTS **120-300**

Entry points: 120-300	Clearing: 15%
No. of terms: 2	Length of terms: 15wks
Staff/student ratio: 1:22	Study addicts: 15%
Teaching: **	Research: **
Firsts: 8%	2.2s: 42%
2.1s: 40%	3rds: 10%

ADMISSIONS:

• Apply via UCAS/direct/NMAS for nursing diplomas/GTTR for PGCE
LJMU welcomes applications from mature students and those without formal qualifications but with ability – apply to get special consideration.

SUBJECTS:

Business & Law: 20%	Media: 13%
Education & Community & Leisure: 10%	Science: 20%
Health: 16%	Technology: 18%

Best: American Studies; Building, Land & Property Management; Business & Management; Civil Engineering; Communication & Media Studies; Drama, Dance & Cinematics; Economics; Education; Hospitality, Recreation, Leisure & Sport; Land & Property Management; Maths, Statistics & Operational Research; Molecular Biological Science; Nursing; Organismal Biological Science; Other subjects allied to Medicine; Pharmocology & Pharmacy; Physics & Astronomy; Politics.

LIBRARIES:

• 684,812 books • 1,622 study places • 24-hr access • Spend per student: ££££
Of the three libraries, the main Aldham Robarts LRC is open 24 hrs, the others *wuss out* at 11pm weekdays. They're called 'Learning Resource Centres' to emphasise services other than books on offer, like the 16,000 e-books and 5,000 e-journals for example. All the LRCs have wireless internet access.

COMPUTERS:

• 1,600 workstations • 24-hr access

OTHER LEARNING FACILITIES:

The 'Blackboard' system allows students to access resources and course materials from the comfort of their own modems. Extra-curricular language teaching also available, as well as a drama studio, CAD lab, rehearsal rooms, media centre, sports science labs, practice courtroom and 360-degree ship simulator.

ENTERTAINMENT

CITY: see University of Liverpool

UNIVERSITY:

• Price of a pint of beer: £1.60 • Glass of wine: £2.25 • Can of Red Bull: £1.80
Bars: The SU building (The Haigh) houses three bars, all of which are alive and throbbing till 2am. I M Marsh and Byrom Street have watering holes too.
Theatres: *Drama ain't big business here* with only a pocketful of plays performed each year. The theatre's mainly used by drama students, although the Beautiful South recorded a music promo here recently – *check Woolworth's bargain bin if interested.*
Film: No cinema on campus but the Cooler in The Haigh pulls down its big screen for free weekly showings of 'out nows'.
Clubbing/Music venues: The Cooler has club nights most nights, including Saturdays 'Loveshack' (40 years' worth of student anthems). *The dance scene is flirty and fun* with Ann Summers nights, shag tag events, Greek nights and Doctors & Nurses dos. Gigs have included such unlikely bedfellows as Judge Jules, Elvis Costello and Chesney 'the one and only, *thank God*' Hawkes.

Comedy/Cabaret: You guessed it, the Cooler again. Sporadic samplings of up-and-coming but-not-got-there-yet talent.

Food: Nearly all sites have a refectory and all bars have chompable goodies available till 8ish. Scholars and The Cooler *are popular for pub food*, and the latter's evening curry club.

Other: Several black tie balls a year: Sportsman's, Graduation and the Snowball (in winter – natch).

SOCIAL & POLITICAL

THE LIVERPOOL STUDENTS' UNION:
• 6 sabbaticals • Turnout at last ballot: 11% • NUS member

LSU claims to be the most popular SU in the country, probably because of its largely free club nights and abolition of joining fees for all societies. For LJMU students, The Haigh is the main social hub and they get active politically too. The University itself enjoys good relations with LSU. The campaign against top-up fees drummed up a record number of students. *Nice to know someone is fighting the power.*

SU FACILITIES:
The Haigh contains most of the facilities, which include: three bars; two cafeterias; eight pool tables; Link ATMs; photo booths; payphones; photocopier; fax services; juke boxes; advice centre; late-night minibus; vending machines; post office; and a general store. Other sites contain bars and some smaller shops (including an art supply store).

CLUBS (NON-SPORTING):
Engineers without Borders; Fusion (Christian); Pagan; German; Chinese; Circus; Debating; DJ & Dance Music; Real Ale; Role Play; St John Ambulance; Welsh; Wine Tasting. **See also Clubs tables.**

OTHER ORGANISATIONS:
Reload is the *fort-and-a-half-nightly* student *hackrag* (every three weeks, that is). Shout FM hits a few of the SU bars and can be accessed on the web. The Rag committee raises money *and blisters* with hot coal walks, abseiling stunts and the like. There's *good* community action (*and karma*) through charity projects, conservation and work with the elderly.

RELIGIOUS:
• 3 chaplains (CofE, RC, Methodist)

There are two prayer rooms for use by Muslims and a multi-faith chaplaincy (which includes atheists). City centre locations mean places of worship are *easily accessible to most faiths – ever-fond of producing guides,* LJMU also do one on faith services in the city.

PAID WORK: see University of Liverpool
• Job bureau • Paid work: term-time 68%; hols 98%

Two-thirds of students work for their dosh during term. Workbank in the SU is run by an independent company and helps find work during or between terms and 'Business Bridge' helps find work relevant to studies.

SPORTS

• Recent successes: men's rugby • BUSA Ranking: 48

Lycra and studs tend to be donned more for pleasure than for glory, although students at I M Marsh take it all more seriously than those at other sites.

SPORTS FACILITIES:

Football pitch; two rugby pitches; four tennis courts; basketball court; sauna/steam room. At the I M Marsh site: two gyms; two dance studios; renovated sports hall; indoor swimming pool; five playing fields; all-weather athletics track. Students at other sites can trek to I M Marsh or use The B2 at the St Nicholas Building near the city centre, which has various fitness programmes and classes, a gym, sports hall and massage facilities. Otherwise, it's public facilities (£15 student discount pass) or those at University of Liverpool.

SPORTING CLUBS:

Funky Dance; Gaelic Football; Hang Gliding; Kickboxing; Mountaineering; Mountain Biking; Nippon Kempo; Parachuting; Rowing; Waterpolo; Windsurfing. **See also Clubs tables.**

ATTRACTIONS: see University of Liverpool

ACCOMMODATION

IN COLLEGE:

- Self-catering: 20% • Cost: £53-78 (36/42wks)
- First years living in: 100% • Insurance premium: ££££

Availability: Most accommodation is in the city centre and consists of modern purpose-built halls of residence and flats which are *well laid out and comfortable*. About two-thirds of rooms are en-suite. 1st year students are generally posted near their faculty. Cleaning rooms is up to students and *woe betide* anyone caught festering in a pile of pants. Failing the random inspections results in a visit from the cleaners (*actual cleaners, not hitmen*) at your own expense. Most halls have on-site amenities like vending machines and a convenience store, sometimes a bar.

Car parking: *Shedloads of space on the city streets* but LMJU *doesn't take kindly* to cars stopping for too long on its land. Some sites and halls require parking permits.

EXTERNALLY: see University of Liverpool

- Ave rent: £43 • Living at home: 20%

Housing help: LJMU and University of Liverpool jointly run Liverpool Student Homes. It offers advice, legal help, landlord blacklists and vacancy lists *and pledges to find a bed for every wandering urchin who needs one.*

WELFARE

SERVICES:

- Lesbian/Gay/Bisexual Officer & Society • Ethnic Minorities Officer & Society
- Women's Officer • Mature Students' Officer & Society
- International Students' Officer & Society • Postgrad Officer & Society
- Disabilities Officer & Society • Self-defence classes • Nightline
- College counsellors: 5 full • SU counsellors: 4 full • Crime rating: !!!!

Each student has an academic 'counsellor' and the SU has four welfare and three financial advisers.

FINANCE:

- Ave debt per year: £5,225

Fees: Tuition costs for EU students and those from further afield average out at £7,000.
Support: Some local businesses sponsor students through their courses. Various bursaries, scholarships, hardship fund and emergency loans are kicking around, including £2,000 scholarships for local Merseyside students from low-income families.

Liverpool Poly

see Liverpool John Moores University

Liverpool Polytechnic

see Liverpool John Moores University

The London Institute

see University of the Arts, London

London Metropolitan University

• *Formerly University of North London and London Guildhall University.*
London Metropolitan University, 166-220 Holloway Road, London, N7 8DB
Tel: (020) 7133 4200 E-mail: admissions@londonmet.ac.uk
Website: www.londonmet.ac.uk
London Metropolitan University Students' Union, MG48, Tower Building,
166-220 Holloway Road, London, N7 8DB Tel: (020) 7133 2769
E-mail: su@londonmet.ac.uk Website: www.londonmetsu.org.uk

GENERAL

2002 saw the *teenage wedding* of London Guildhall University and the University of North London under the new name of London Metropolitan. They're *still in a bit of a honeymoon period*, but all signs *suggest that the merger might give birth to something special*. City campus sits on the outskirts of the financial and business headquarters of the UK and is surrounded by an *enormous wealth* of architectural variety (and money, of course). 16th- and 17th-century buildings give way to Victorian landmarks which give way in turn to the *daunting phalluses* of modern design. Norman Foster's *tremendous todger* of a tower ('The Gherkin') dominates the skyline. To the east *the suits get a bit raggier and the buildings a bit shabbier*: the infamous East End. The area around the London North campus has become *terribly fashionable in recent years, darling, and celeb-infested* Islington and Camden are bustling with bars and shops – *expect to find the 3am Girls plying their salubrious trade*. A *wander up the road to Finsbury Park should put things in perspective though.*

Sex ratio (M:F): 46:54	Founded: 2002
Full-time u'grads: 16,460	Part-time: 8,565
Postgrads: 2,430	Non-degree: 2,330
Ave course: 3yrs	Ethnic: 57%
State:private school: 95:5	Flunk rate: 28%
Mature: 53%	International: 25%
Disabled: 203	Local: 44%

ATMOSPHERE:

Lots of part-timers, locals and matures make London Met feel more like a community resource centre than a university. There's very little sense of 'young people away from home' and a corresponding lack of silly, drunken tomfoolery but despite this no one takes themselves or their institution too seriously. Many students have no family history of university attendance and set their sights on vocational courses rather than BAs in Post-Feminist Albanian Mythology Studies. Businesslike determination is the order of the day, but the campus becomes the village of the damned at weekends.

SITES:

Departments are spread between sites so students *rarely feel the need to cross from one campus to the other. This had led to something of an internal City/North divide and with so little interaction apparent between the two one wonders why they bothered merging in the first place.*
City Campus: The chunk that used to be London Guildhall.
North Campus: The chunk that used to be the University of North London.

LONDON: see <u>University of London</u>
• <u>City centre: 2 miles</u>

TRAVEL: see <u>University of London</u>
Trains: Liverpool Street and Fenchurch Street for City campus. King's Cross for North.
Car: *Both sites are pretty much unparkable and smack in the middle of Congestion Charge Central. Even clamping can work out cheaper and less painful.*
Local: A huge number of bus routes, so both sites *are very well serviced.* 15, 25, 40, 253 are just a few numbers for City's SU. 4, 19, 43, 153, 236, 271, 279 for North campus. Plenty of night-buses too.
Underground: City: Moorgate (Northern, Metropolitan, Circle, Hammersmith & City); Aldgate (Metropolitan, Circle); Aldgate East (Hammersmith & City, District); Tower Hill (District, Circle). **North:** Holloway Road (Piccadilly); Caledonian Road (Piccadilly); Highbury and Islington (Victoria).
Bicycles: *Cheap and green on one hand, difficult and dangerous on the other.*
Other: Tower Gateway (Docklands Light Railway) is opposite City's Tower Hill site.

CAREER PROSPECTS:

• <u>Careers Service</u> • <u>No. of staff: 14 full/4 part</u> • <u>Unemployed after 6mths: 17%</u>
Careers library, newsletters, one-to-one guidance, interview practice, workshop training, bulletin boards and job fairs.

FAMOUS ALUMNI:

Celebrities and world-changers are yet to emerge from London Met but from the former institutions: Sonya Aurora Madan (Echobelly); Joy Gardner (*victim of extradition procedures*); Kate Hoey MP (Lab, ex-Spurs physio); Jools Holland (*the prince* of piano); Michael Jackson (TV executive rather than '*troubled*' pop monkey); Nick Leeson (the bloke who broke the bank at Barings); Terry Marsh (former boxing champ); Alison Moyet (singer); Vic Reeves; Mark Thatcher (*Maggie's pride and joy*); Miki Berenyi (Lush); Jake Chapman (sex and death artist); Garth Crooks (journalist, ex-Spurs star); David Kossof (actor); Martyn Lewis (newsreader); Stephen Platt (editor, New Statesman & Society); Sinead O'Connor (singer); Pete Tatchell (gay activist); Neil Tennant (Pet Shop Boy); Jamie Theakston (TV and radio presenter).

SPECIAL FEATURES:

The fresh-faced University's still in a period of gestation with a number of buildings taking shape around its two main sites, including North's Graduate Centre, designed by *top set square user* Daniel Libeskind. There are hopes for a new science centre at North campus in the near future.

FURTHER INFO:

• Prospectuses: undergrad; postgrad; some departmental • Open days • Video

Extensive provisions for non-EU students. The University has offices in Chennai, New Delhi and Lahore, among others, and *international students get extra-nice treatment*, including a special welcome programme and guaranteed accommodation.

A C A D E M I C

Modular courses. Those taking four modules per term can expect to spend 40 hours a week on their studies. If that sounds too daunting, students can switch between full and part-time studying, take a break altogether, or benefit from daytime and evening teaching – handy for those with family or jobs. Many courses involve work placements. The many industrial and career-orientated subjects are *among the University's strongest courses.*

Entry points: 80-240	Ave points: n/a
Applns per place: n/a	Clearing: 28%
No. of terms: 2	Length of terms: 15wks
Staff/student ratio: 1:10	Study addicts: n/a%
Teaching: *	Research: **
Year abroad: 1%	Sandwich students: 3%
Firsts: 5%	2.2s: 42%
2.1s: 29%	3rds: 24%

80-240

POINTS

ADMISSIONS:

• Apply via UCAS/GTTR for teaching

London Met attracts a large number of mature students partly because it bases admissions on commitment and experience as much as formal qualifications (unless the particular course requires a basic level of knowledge, eg. biological sciences). International students need an English Language qualification – the minimum is IELTS 5.5.

SUBJECTS:

Architecture, Building, Planning: 2%
Art & Design: 5%
Arts/Humanities: 1%
Biological Sciences: 4%
Business/Management: 29%
Combined: 17%
Computer Science: 10%

Education: 6%
Law: 7%
Librarianship & Information Studies: 2%
Mathematical Sciences: 2%
Medical Sciences: 2%
Social Sciences: 7%

Best: Art & Design; Business & Management; Dance & Cinematics; Economics; Education; Electrical & Electronic Engineering; Hospitality & Leisure; Materials Technology; Maths & Statistics; Modern Languages. Nursing; Other Medicine; Drama, Philosophy; Politics; Psychology;
Unusual: Polymer Technology.

LIBRARIES:

• 801,300 books • 2,000 study places

The merger means there are now seven libraries with *an immense volume of volumes* as well as an assortment of multimedia learning resources (DVDs, videos, tapes, online resources).

COMPUTERS:

• 2,600 workstations

Four computing centres support course-tailored software programs (including DTP, CAD, statistical analysis and programming languages). North campus boasts an IT technology tower with seven floors of open-access computing facilities and printing.

OTHER LEARNING FACILITIES:

City has two new language labs in Moorgate. North's Language Centre is an open-access study area and there's a practice courtroom at the new Goulston Street building. The TV studio and editing suite is set to be complemented by a radio station.

ENTERTAINMENT

LONDON: see University of London

CAMDEN, ISLINGTON AND EAST END:

• Price of a pint of beer: £2 • Glass of wine: £2.90 • Can of Red Bull: £1.20
Many local students have their own personal pub preferences peppered across London and don't care for venues near campus. Likewise, few pubs in the area bother with the student market and some are positively unfriendly. North campus has all the shabby delights of Camden and Islington within reach. City has a lot of trendy wine bars jammed with besuited financiers, but the East End is worth venturing into for Queen Vic style pubbage.
Cinemas: The Barbican Cinema is a *luxurious* arthouse flickbox, while *the more mainstream* Lux Cinema in Hoxton Square shows a *wide range of popcorn fodder.* Both offer 10% NUS discounts.
Theatres: Islington has the Almeida Theatre (new drama, touring opera) and the *wonderful* pub theatre, the King's Head (top names, quality drama). The Barbican Arts Centre on the South Bank *plays second fiddle to the National but does so at a consistently impressive standard. Good for standbys.*
Pubs: Just north of City campus are the *extremely popular* Bricklayer's Arms, the Fox in Paul Street and the *cosy snughole that is the* Griffin. *Pubs in the City tend to go crazy on weekday nights – stuffed with wideboys toasting guzzilion dollar deals. North campus is better off with the Camden Head (alcocool), the Albion (rural and beer-gardened), the York (bar stool football commentary), the Duke of Cambridge (upmarket gastro-pub) and the unmistakably Irish Filthy McNasty's.*
Music venues: *Tons of local bands in Islington and Camden's pubs and on the streets.*
Eating out: For the City campus, two words suffice: Brick and Lane. *Enough restaurants to give Egon Ronay stress-rashes, most with an Indian flavour. Pushplugs: Bengal Cuisine, Preem, and Viet Hoa (great Vietnamese for under a tenner).* Islington Green has the Afghan Kitchen, *which is cheap and quirky.* La Porchetta's *pizzas can get pricey but Italy itself would be hard pressed to top them.*

UNIVERSITY:

• Price of a pint of beer: £1.50 • Glass of wine: £1.80 • Can of Red Bull: £1
Bars: Of seven bars, two are *fighting for supremacy.* City's Sub Bar is two floors *and heaving.* North's The Rocket Complex *is most students' choice for nights of crazy, frolicsome fun.*
Theatres: *Drama students* churn out 15-odd shows a year.
Film: *Strong culture of film and cinema* but no purpose-built venue. Film showings alternate between the two main bars: 2-3 a week (£2 admission). The Film Society arranges occasional screenings in the video studies. There's also a deal with Islington's Warner Village which has a few freebies for Met students.
Clubbing/Music venues: The main bars are big enough to accommodate bands and the weekly calendar *is usually jammed with entertainments and club nights.* Jools Holland has returned to his roots to play here. Other visitors include Ms Dynamite, Asian Dub Foundation, Punjabi Hit Squad, Trevor Nelson and Artful Dodger.
Comedy/Cabaret: Weekly comic events hit the Rocket Complex and Sub Bar. Norman Lovett has aired his Northern musings here.
Food: All but one of the food outlets are run by an external catering company *so prices are hiked up at the expense of popularity.* The Diner in Goulston Street *may feel like a greasy spoon full of builders, but at least it's cheap.*
Other: *Big-assed May Ball and Winter Ball each year. Formal Sports Awards dinner.*

LONDON METROPOLITAN UNIVERSITY STUDENTS' UNION:
• 5 sabbaticals • Turnout at last ballot: 1-2% • NUS member
The newly-formed SU's still finding its feet. Unlike many other universities, the Union, or 'MetSU', is involved in no commercial operations whatsoever – the University runs the bars – so focuses instead on services and welfare. Guildhall's SU was fairly strong, North London's as limp as lettuce – MetSU looks like settling somewhere in between. Its biggest task at present is to overcome the palpable City/North divide.

SU FACILITIES:
Seven bars; four cafeterias; three snack bars; pool tables; Barclays bank; ATMs (Barclays, NatWest, Nationwide); Endsleigh Insurance branch; minibus hire for sporting societies; loads of meeting rooms; photocopiers; fax and printing services; payphones; advice centre; gaming and vending machines; new and secondhand bookshops (Waterstone's, Blackwells); stationery shops; three advice centres.

CLUBS (NON-SPORTING):
Bangladeshi; Bouncy Castle Appreciation (*oh, the wags*); Chinese; Conservative Futures; Hellenic; Law; Paintball; Pan African; Persian; Roleplaying; Russian; Salsa; Sikh; University Challenge; Utopia (Politics & Modern History). **See also Clubs tables.**

OTHER ORGANISATIONS:
SU paper Student Metro *hits the litterbins* monthly. The FM-licensed radio station is now ready to roll again – online broadcasts. Rag was born recently, *but is yet to develop motor skills.*

RELIGIOUS:
• 3 chaplains (CofE), imam
A prayer room is available for Muslim women.

PAID WORK:
• Job bureau
The Careers Development and Employment Service advertises part-time temp/vacation work, work experience and placements. Lots of Met students are employed during term time and the University itself has a large number of clerical positions. Employment Service vacancies are exclusive to Met students.

• Recent successes: tennis, hockey, basketball • BUSA Ranking: 30
The University Sports Department takes its responsibilities very seriously. *Eager* to establish a sporting rep for themselves *they're splashing the cash all over their teams and facilities.*

SPORTS FACILITIES:
The facilities shared with Arsenal and Essex Cricket Club include: five football, one rugby and three cricket pitches; two basketball and one netball court; two sports halls; gym; multigym; aerobics studio. Various sports cards allow varying access to facilities (£30-42). There's access to a swimming pool, ice rink, squash and tennis courts and the River Thames from both campuses.

Films including The Mummy Returns and Four Weddings and a Funeral used Greenwich's Old Royal Naval College as a location.

SPORTING CLUBS:
See Clubs tables.

ATTRACTIONS: see University of London
Arsenal and Tottenham are the local teams for North, *but it's considered bad manners to support them both.*

A C C O M M O D A T I O N

IN COLLEGE:
• Catered: 1% • Cost: £90 (40wks)
• Self-catering: 7% • Cost: £76 (40wks) • Insurance premium: ££££
Availability: Anyone hailing from more than 25 miles away is guaranteed a place in halls in their 1st year, but with so many local students there's not much call for University accommodation. Many halls are aimed at international students. All North's halls are within walking distance, but City's can be as far as 3 miles from campus (*a good 40 mins walk*). *They're not the last word in luxury, but they're comfy enough.* Many have on-site launderettes, sat TV, common rooms and pool tables and few have on-site bars. Security is tight: entry phones; 24-hr CCTV; 24-hr reception. Single-sex floors available.
Car parking: Permits from the council.

EXTERNALLY: see University of London
• Ave rent: £95
Availability: Lots of students live at home – many are matures after all. *Standards vary depending on proximity to the campus. City's expensive because it's the City – and it's not all that nice in any case. Islington is trendylicious and there are good, roomy student apartments for the taking at the higher prices. But overall, the further away you go, the cheaper it gets.*
Housing help: The Accommodation Service (three full-time staff) lists vacancies and approved landlords and offers legal/contract advice.

W E L F A R E

SERVICES:
• Lesbian/Gay/Bisexual Officer & Society • Ethnic Minorities Officer
• Women's Officer • International Students' Officer & Society
• Disabilities Officer & Society • College counsellors: 5 full/3 part
• Crime rating: !!!!!
With no bars to run and half a million squids set aside for welfare this has become the priority. The SU has two sabbatical officers and a squad of volunteers.
Health: Health centre at Calcutta House.
Women: The Women's Library at City has study places for the girls and only for the girls.
Crèches/Nursery: 83 places available in three nurseries for sprogs aged 2-5yrs. Subsidised fees.
Disabilities: Newer buildings have been built with disabled access in mind so ramps and lifts abound. There's a Dyslexia Resource Centre at City and The Independent Learning Unit at North. The University publishes a handbook for disabled students.
Crime: City campus is *in one of the poorest areas of central London so crime is a very real possibility. North campus's Islington backdrop is safer, although Finsbury Park can get a bit hairy.*

FINANCE:
• Ave debt per year: 4,475
Fees: International students pay £6,840. Postgrads pay £3,000-3,400 depending on course.
• Access fund: £2.5m • Successful applications/yr: 3,000 • Ave payment: £750
Support: A range of bursaries and scholarships is available.

London South Bank

see South Bank University

University of London

• *The information, which follows, refers to the University of London as an amorphous blob. The services described are those provided centrally by the University and by ULU, the Students' Union. The colleges and individual unions of the University provide services themselves, and Push covers these in individual entries. Similarly, the general comments about London apply on the whole to the central area, close to ULU itself, and these are of equal relevance to the many institutions which are in the city but not part of London University itself. For more specific discussion of the differences between Norf 'n' Sarf or Hackney 'n' Hampstead, see the individual entries.*

University of London, Senate House, Malet Street, London, WC1E 7HU
Tel: (020) 7862 8000 E-mail: enquiries@lon.ac.uk Website: www.lon.ac.uk
University of London Union, Malet Street, London, WC1E 7HY
Tel: (020) 7664 2000 E-mail: general@ulu.ucl.ac.uk Website: www.ulucube.com

GENERAL

London's far too big to be summed up even in one of Push's beautifully succinct epigrams. Something like eight million people live within the boundaries of the M25 (*150 miles of eight-lane car park*). Students who don't know the place, but are serious about studying here should get hold of one of the less touristy guides. Most years, Time Out magazine does a London Students' Guide (about £3). Since the days of the little Roman village of Londinium on the banks of the Thames, London has come a long way, becoming the country's centre of politics, finance, arts, heritage, tourism, media, pornography, crime, bagel production and so on. Appropriately, the University of London is also big. One in ten of the country's entire higher education population is at one of London University's 19 colleges and 11 institutions. *However, students rarely get a sense of the University as a whole*, especially since some of the larger constituent colleges, such as King's, Imperial and UCL, are big enough to be fairly sizeable universities on their own. The University's headquarters are in the *magnificent* art deco Senate House in Bloomsbury about a mile from Trafalgar Square. *Push* features entries for most of the undergraduate colleges, so read this and then read the separate colleges' entries too *because they vary as much as if they were different universities*. We don't cover postgraduate-only institutions; we do feature under individual colleges any medical schools or other institutions that are part of particular colleges (eg. King's College Hospital). For the record, these are the London colleges covered by Push:

Birkbeck College
Goldsmiths College
Imperial College
LSE (London School of Economics)
Royal Academy of Music
Royal Veterinary College
SOAS (School of Oriental & African Studies)
University College London

Courtauld Institute of Art
Heythrop College
King's College London
Queen Mary
Royal Holloway
St George's Hospital Medical School
School of Pharmacy

Sex ratio (M:F): 33:67	Founded: 1836
Full-time u'grads: 58,000	Part-time: 16,000
Postgrads: 37,000	Non-degree: n/a
Ave course: 3yrs	State:private school: 43:57
Ethnic: n/a	Flunk rate: 2%

LONDON:

- Population: 7,172,091 • City centre: 1 mile • Birmingham: 106 miles
- Manchester 172 miles • Edinburgh 423 miles
- High temp: 22 • Low temp: 2 • Rainfall: 67

It's easy to feel that you're not making the most of London if you're not spending every waking minute at the theatre, ballet, opera or cinema, in clubs or fashionable markets, in museums and galleries, sports grounds and parks. It's a bit like the salad counter in Pizza Hut – it's up to you to make a selection from the vast selection of goodies and pile them on your plate however you like, but you might end up face-down in a puddle of sweetcorn and Thousand Island dressing, while the waiters have a good laugh. In practice most students, and indeed most people who live in London, end up spending most of their time honing in on one particular, um, pizza slice – that being the area in which they live. Even locals often have a hazy area of what's going on in different areas of town outside the centre and their own immediate hangouts. The mutual suspicion beneath north and south of the river is well known. Less well known is the new rivalry between west (traditionally cool) and east (new, silly-haircut cool). The good news is that, whereas in other parts of the country you have to be brought up on centuries of distrust to achieve these levels of local rivalry, in London as soon as people move in they start to feel that wherever they happen to live is the centre of the universe. This might be because it's just way too expensive to go anywhere else. There are a number of responses to the high cost of living in London: (1) burst into tears; (2) mug someone; (3) live on credit; (4) ask daddy for lashings of cash. Alternatively, if these don't appeal, you can always use the following methods: (1) limit your spending by only going out when and where you can afford it (ULU fits the bill, offering cheap events for students); (2) buy secondhand – for books, there's ULU, Charing Cross Road and Waterloo and, for clothes, try Camden Market, Greenwich, Brick Lane and Portobello Road; (3) get a job – more London students have part-time jobs than anywhere else.

TRAVEL:

Trains: London is the centre of the network: Birmingham (£24.30 rtn, 1hr 45); Manchester (£34.40 rtn, 2hr 40); Leeds (£43.70 rtn, 2hr 45); Bristol Parkway (£28.50 1hr 25); Glasgow (£57.50 rtn, 6hrs).

Coaches: London's also the centre of the National Express system and a whole variety of other national bus services (Green Line, Blue Line and so on) letting you ride to Birmingham (from £33, £2hr 45) Manchester and so on.

Air: Served by four airports – Gatwick, Stansted, Luton and Heathrow, the world's busiest. Regular flights to Paris, Belfast, Prague, New York, Timbuktu, anywhere else you care to pluck out of your WH Smith School Atlas *for, often, ridiculously low prices.*

Hitching: *Not possible from Central London, but get out a little way on to the city's escape routes or beyond the M25 and a thumb's a first class ticket.*

LOCAL:

London's population swells by over a million every day thanks to commuters, tourists *and those bucket-shaking charity collectors. Unsurprisingly, this can put quite a strain on transport at peak hours.*

Trains: Local overground trains are *a speedy and sometimes pleasant way to travel and are moderately efficient. The main problems are ease of use, the high fares (although Travelcards keep costs down a tad) and the early closing (last trains between 11pm and 1am). Trains are often the best bet south of the river. The east of the city is covered by the tube/train hybrid, the DLR (Docklands Light Railway) which covers places like Canary Wharf, Mile End and East Ham.*

Underground: The 'Tube' is the largest underground train system in the world and, generally, *it's okay and takes you just about anywhere you want to go (though not always in east/south-east London). On the down side, it's often crowded, shuts down around midnight during the week, is often disrupted by strikes and breakdowns, and it's expensive. Talking to other tube passengers is tantamount to threatening to slaughter their pets – the only people who do it are tourists, mentalists and people who want to talk to you about Jesus.* Nearest tube to Senate House/ULU Building: Goodge Street (Northern Line), Warren Street (Victoria) or Russell Square (Piccadilly) – all zone 1.

Local buses: *Buses are just as efficient as tubes, offer even more destinations and are slightly cheaper (just over a quid for anywhere within central London). But buses are slow and, until you know your way around, it's difficult to know which ones take you where.* After midnight, buses come into their own – night-buses are London's only form of all-night public transport and *if you don't mind how long it takes,* you can go almost anywhere within 10 miles of the centre. They congregate at Trafalgar Square, which is a *handy central spot to head for post-club/pub/grub.*

Travelcards: The system's split into six zones, with central travel being more expensive than in the outer zones. *Students in full-time education are entitled to a discount on travelcards for bus/local rail/tube travel. If you can stump up the readies, it often works out cheaper to pay in advance – a year's zone 1 & 2 travel card costs from £596. Ouch. But still nearly £200 cheaper than paying for weekly (£14.90) travel cards year-round, which in turn is cheaper than paying for daily tickets or single journeys. Budgeting ahead for travel minimises end-of-loan solitary confinement.* Getting about in general is cheaper the more you can avoid passing through the central zones, ie. *where the most popular cinemas, museums, shops and Starbucks are located.* A yearly pass for any two consecutive zones other than 1 & 2 costs a *mere £364.* Equivalent fares are also often cheaper if you buy them on the Oyster Card, a kind of top-up travelcard, or if you shun the tubes and trains altogether in favour of the buses. See www.tfl.gov.uk for the low-down on the big spend. For details of other concessions to students, check with the relevant union.

Taxis: Two types: the classic black cabs, *which are well regulated and enormously expensive; and dodgy merchants in Ford Escorts, which are as regulated as Basra on a bad day and are just as expensive as the official ones anyway.* There are now also some run by and for women. *Basically though, forget all taxis, except late at night when all else fails and/or you're in a party of four or more. Far be it from Push to preach, but if you don't know the dangers of using unlicensed cabs when you're on your own, well, you probably haven't evolved opposable thumbs yet either.*

Car: *Parking in Central London is impossible, and although there is only one rush hour every day, it lasts from 6am till midnight (and until club-closing time at the weekend). The introduction of the congestion charge also now means paying to bring a car into central London during office hours, from £5 a day. Disabled drivers get some discounts; students don't.*

Bicycles: *A popular form of student travel given the pros: it's cheap and you zip through traffic jams. But there are the cons: London is big and full of exhaust fumes and bike thieves. The cycle network is making things slightly better all the time, though.*

CAREER PROSPECTS:

• Careers Service • No. of staff: 70

See www.careers.lon.ac.uk for vacancies and general information. The main office is at Gorden Square in Bloomsbury, but there are also facilities at nine colleges which vary according to subject/professions. Non-London students can also use the service, at a price, naturally.

FURTHER INFO

• Prospectuses: undergrad; postgrad

The University publishes a guide which covers all its colleges, a guide to student life and an *essential* accomodation pamphlet. Contact individual colleges, or see the University's website for other general info.

ACADEMIC

ADMISSIONS:

• Apply via UCAS to individual colleges

LIBRARIES:

• 2,000,000 books • 650 study places

The statistics refer to the vast central library at Senate House but individual colleges have their own facilities – see www.ull.ac.uk

COMPUTERS:

• 950 workstations

All computers have net access. Colleges also provide their own computers.

ENTERTAINMENT

LONDON:

• Price of a pint of beer: £2.50 • Glass of wine: £2.50

New bars, restaurants, clubs, exhibitions and shows come and go more often than adolescent boy bands. Time Out is compulsory kit for every wannabe London-savvy student. Its weekly listings detail pretty much everything going on around town.

Cinemas: *Many repertory cinemas offer student discounts and the Prince Charles Cinema just off Leicester Square shows a cool mix of Hollywood, cult and independent films, tix from £1.50. By contrast, the Square's also home to red-carpet-and-premier venues where tickets will cost at least ten times as much. Once again, the further from central London, the cheaper. Wood Green's Showcase cinema shows flicks from £3.50. Some fleapits charge a tenner at weekends, but most do student discounts. Pushplugs: Ritzy (Brixton); Everyman (Hampstead); Riverside (Hammersmith); NFT (South Bank, £5.50); the Gate (Notting Hill).*

Theatres: *Student standby tickets are sometimes available for West End shows, but they're still around £12. The National Theatre on the South Bank and the RSC at the Barbican are cheaper and feature some of the country's top talent. Also, don't forget the Fringe (the collective title for all the smaller theatres around town, ranging from back rooms at pubs to full-size auditoria) where you can often see high quality at low cost.*

Pubs: *The Jeremy Bentham, Marlborough Arms, University Tavern and Rising Sun are just a few pubs near ULU that are student friendly. Some other London pubs water down their ridiculously expensive beer, but you can often find a decent pint of Young's or Fuller's, or a good selection of guest ales (the Wetherspoon chain is a reliable if characterless starting point). Beyond that, every variety of drinking den, from Irish to Jamaican, from sports bars to wine bars, from plush chrome extravaganzas serving Belgian banana beer with a free half-hour on the net to rough dives that serve phlegmy Carlsberg and a filthy look to outsiders. Many pubs around the City business district, unlike almost anywhere else in the world, close at weekends.*

Clubbing: *London has just about every kind of club imaginable and a lot that aren't. Fabric, 333 and Heaven have all survived the downturn in dance music's fortunes. There are school discos by the dozen for those feeling prematurely nostalgic; hip DJ bars like the Embassy in Islington; Soho's Gossips for heavy metal/the plain vampiric; and GAY night at Astoria is legendary. If you can't find something to move to, you might ask yourself whether you've left your legs on the bus.*

Music venues: *Somewhere in London there's a band worth checking out every night of the week, it's just a question of finding them. There are the monster venues like Earl's Court, the hip 'n' happening like Brixton Academy, and the un-intimidating, like the Mean Fiddler. But the best place to see up-and-coming bands for a tenth of the price is the local boozer – some are occasionally host to impromptu performances by local s'lebs.*

Comedy/Cabaret: *London's a hot-bed of alternative laugh-mongers. Pushplugs: the Comedy Store near Piccadilly Circus or, more cheaply, Jongleurs (Camden, Battersea, Shepherds Bush); Balham Banana; Hackney Empire. Also, keep a look out for free tickets to TV and radio show recordings – start with the Beeb's website, www.bbc.co.uk. Pubs are also great places to catch funny business* – Jimmy Carr used to do a regular spot at the Hen & Chicken in Highbury.

Eating out: *Nowhere in the country, possibly the world, has a broader choice of eateries. There is every kind of café, restaurant and fast food and then some. Not everywhere is bank-busting either. Head for Soho and Chinatown for affordable food and late night nibbles. For budget fare in the West End, Pushplugs: Pollo's (madhouse Italian); Stockpot (school dinners, but superb value); Gaby's (friendly deli); Poon's (Chinese); Wagamama (Japanese noodles); Pret à Manger (imaginative sarnie chain); Food for Thought (veggie without stodge). If you run out of places to eat, you probably need to go on a diet.*

UNIVERSITY:

• Price of a pint of beer: £1.80 • Glass of wine: £2 • Can of Red Bull: £1.50
Individual College bars are the first port of call for students. At ULU:
Bars: Gallery Bar/Diner *(very popular all day)*; Duck & Dive *(café bar)*; Bar 101 *(chrome design, for clubs and big-name gigs).*
Music venues: *ULU can hold its own next to any of London's sticky-floored, mid-sized caverns.* Bands like Athlete, Death in Vegas, Coldplay, the Foo Fighters and many others have passed through.
Clubbing: *Beano on Saturday nights is the place for uncomplicated pop thrills.*
Food: The Gallery provides *cheap and (relatively) cheerful fodder* until 11pm.

S O C I A L & P O L I T I C A L

UNIVERSITY OF LONDON UNION:

• 5 sabbaticals • Turnout at last ballot: 1%
The individual colleges' SUs affiliate separately to NUS and are automatically part of ULU (which isn't a member of NUS) which offers *the most extraordinary level* of facilities at the building in Bloomsbury – open until 11pm or later when hosting an event. ULU (pronounced 'yooloo') is also the students' central representative body and has *effective* officers on most of the University's important committees. They're *a very cosmopolitan crowd* with a large percentage of mature and parttime students. Recent campaigns have included lobbying against the proposed amendment to the rate of the London Student Loan, the anti-fees protests and a continuing Voter Registration Campaign.

SU FACILITIES:

At ULU: three bars; two cafeterias; coffee bar, general shop; print shop; photocopying; travel agent; Barclays and Halifax banks/ATMs; Endsleigh Insurance office; opticians; minibus; vending machines; five pool and snooker tables; games and gambling machines; fax service; snack bar; sandwich shop; full-size swimming pool; fitness centre; gymnasium; theatre hall; offices and 20 meeting rooms; *and a partridge in a pear tree.* ULU also provides training for staff and student officers of all the member colleges' SUs and handbooks and publications about all aspects of London student life.

CLUBS (NON-SPORTING):

As well as at colleges, there's: AEGEE; Arabic; Arts; Ballroom & Latin Dance; Bridge; Campaign for Free Education; Caving; Chamber Choir; Chinese; Chorus; Debating; French Jive; Games; Hindu; Indian Dance; Jidokwan Taekwondo; Krishna; Lifesaving; Marxist; Meditation; Methodist; Muslim Women; Opera; Refugee Support; Salsa; Scandinavian; Shaolin; Singapore; Slavonic; Starfleet; T'ai Chi; Zhuan Shu Kuan. **See also individual Colleges and Clubs tables.**

OTHER ORGANISATIONS:

The free fortnightly London Student is Europe's largest student newspaper, and even features a column by Mayor Ken Livingstone *getting down with the yoofs.*

RELIGIOUS:

• 6 chaplains (CofE, RC, FC, Lutheran, Greek Othodox, Jewish)

London has religious groups for every denomination from Muslims to Moonies, Jews to Jains. *If you can't find spiritual solace here, please direct your complaint upwards.*

PAID WORK:

• Job bureau

Vacancy lists are posted up in the Union and ULU usually has vacancies itself. There are more opportunities in London for part-time work than anywhere else, but there are also more people trying to get those jobs. Students find work *quite easily* in all the usual places like bars and restaurants and also in theatres, offices and shops.

SPORTS

• Recent successes: rowing; karate; lacrosse; rifle • BUSA Ranking: 10

The basement of ULU has been converted into one of the *best gyms in London*, including an international-sized swimming pool. There is an inter-college league and all the accompanying rivalry.

SPORTS FACILITIES:

At the ULU Building, there are all the amenities mentioned above as well as an aerobics studio and sports hall. Students can join the University Health Club for £25 a month. There's also a boathouse at Chiswick on the Thames and sailing facilities at the Welsh Harp reservoir in North London. Not many Colleges have sports fields on site, owing to the sheer urban congestion of the city, *but, like elaphants in a mini, it's surprising how much pitch-space can fit it one tightly packed conurbation.*

SPORTING CLUBS:

See individual Colleges and Clubs tables.

ATTRACTIONS:

Depending on promotion and relegation, London generally has about six premiership football teams, plus all the others scuffling around in the lower divisions. Then there's cricket at Lords and the Oval, rugby at Twickenham, tennis at Wimbledon, athletics at Crystal Palace, *plus whatever miracles that may or may not happen as the Olympics bid gets closer.*

ACCOMMODATION

IN COLLEGE:

• Catered: 3% • Cost: £80 (32wks)
• Insurance premium: £££

Availability: The percentage of London students living in college accommodation varies enormously from college to college, but for those that the colleges don't accommodate, there's a limited number of catered places in the University's eight intercollegiate halls and 500 places in self-catered flats and houses. Halls are mainly mixed.

Amenities: Conditions in each hall are different but, it's mostly single rooms with showers and minimal cooking facilities. There is also a selection of other amenities including bars, TV rooms, telephones in every room, function, meeting and study rooms, libraries, launderettes, payphones and so on. Depending on the hall, students may be able to enjoy the *delights* of a squash court, darkroom, music room, bike sheds, gardens, videos and in College Hall there's also a hairdressing salon.

EXTERNALLY:

Availability: *Contrary to popular belief, it's really not that difficult to find accommodation in London. Thanks to the explosion in buy-to-let in recent years rents have actually been falling by 10-30% in many areas, so it could even be worth haggling with your prospective landlord. Before looking in Loot or the Evening Standard try checking out the excellent www.moveflat.com website or www.findaproperty.com (good for groups in search of houses). There's very little housing in Zone 1 even for yuppies, and students come a lot lower in the pecking order. Zone 2 is a bit better, particularly for single rooms in shared flats or houses in places like Wandsworth, Putney and Fulham and wherever the tube system is lacking. Zone 3 is relatively promising, but the catch is that it can take an hour to get to the centre. Zone 4 and beyond are not popular for the same reason, but, as they say, homeless students can't be choosers. Although there are many thousands of people living in cardboard boxes on London's streets, they aren't students. In fact, many students manage to find very comfortable flats for almost reasonable rents. There are also a number living in squats. To be safe, students coming to London should work out where they're going to stay first. Hammersmith, Shoreditch, Islington, Camberwell and Finsbury Park all have student ghettos but it obviously depends where in the city you need to get to every day.*

Housing help: The University's accommodation office bolsters college facilities and includes a register of 4,500 private landlords, lists of available properties, advice and a series of talks in March-April.

WELFARE

SERVICES:
- Mature Students' Officer • Postgrad Students' Officer & Society
- International Students' Officer • LBG Officer • Ethnic Minorities' Officer
- Women's Officer & Society • Disabilities Officer • Nightline • Crime rating: !!!!!

The London Student Centre is planned for 2005/6 and will provide a mass welfare service open to all students in London (not just those at London University). Currently most welfare services are provided at college-level.

Health: There's a health service facility with five counsellors as well as GPs and nurses.

Women: ULU's self-defence classes are *well-worth signing up for. Free attack alarms also available.*

Lesbian, Gay and Bisexual: *London's gay community is sizeable and proud, and has marked out a large chunk of Soho as pretty much its own. As a result, there are plenty of entertainments which don't conform to heterosexist stereotypes and a few London boroughs make special housing provisions. Many of the best clubs have gay nights or even, for a change, straight nights. And don't forget the Pride March & Festival, every summer.*

Disabilities: Some rooms are inaccessible to wheelchairs but there are ramps and lifts elsewhere, most lecture theatres have hearing loops and most colleges have a Special Educational Needs Department.

Crime: *London isn't as bad for crime as sensationalists would believe. Bloomsbury is one of the safest areas of central London due to high police presence and CCTV.*

Drugs: *Many Londoners live for years in the capital without ever encountering them. Having said that, every drug you've heard of and a great many beside are readily available on the streets and in the pubs and clubs of London. Cannabis is perpetually prevalent and ecstasy is still around, although not quite as popular as it has been. Cocaine is common currency amongst City and media types. Heroin is more common than in most English cities and the abuse/use of crack is spreading, especially in the South. They're often more expensive than elsewhere, but that shouldn't be regarded as any guarantee of quality – dangerous mixtures are common and the risks are your own. There are a number of help centres (including Narcotics Anonymous (020) 7351 6066) and the authorities usually take a progressive but firm attitude. The University, however, will automatically expel anyone found using illegal drugs.*

FINANCE:

Support: Any cash going is distributed by the colleges.

London College of Fashion
see University of the Arts, London

London College of Printing
see University of the Arts, London

London Guildhall University
see London Metropolitan University

Loughborough University

Loughborough University, Loughborough, Leics, LE11 3TU
Tel: (01509) 223 522 E-mail: admissions@lboro.ac.uk Website: www.lboro.ac.uk
Loughborough Students' Union, Loughborough, Leics, LE11 3TT
Tel: (01509) 635 000 E-mail: union@lufbra.net Website: www.lufbra.net

G ENERAL

Loughborough, pronounced 'Lufbra' by the locals and 'Loogabarooga' by the crazy and/or drunk, is a *middleweight* market town, set among the wandering countryside and small suburban villages of the East Midlands. Loughborough University sits about a mile west of the town centre in *green and pleasant* parkland. The campus buildings are *largely inoffensive*, low-rise blocks on a landscaped, 410-acre site. It's *perfect* for the various playing fields and sporting facilities – sport being *the University's favourite hobby horse* – and, by Jiminy, do they ride it well.

38% ♀	
Sex ratio (M:F): 62:38	**Founded: 1908**
Full-time u'grads: 10,165	**Part-time: 185**
Postgrads: 2,375	**Non-degree: 150**
Ave course: 3/4yrs	**Ethnic: 15%**
State:private school: 86:14	**Flunk rate: 7%**
Mature: 7%	**International: 17%**
Disabled: 166	**Local: 10%**
62%	

ATMOSPHERE:
Someone once said 'It's not the winning, but the taking part that counts.' We can promise you, they didn't go to Loughborough. Here, it's the winning that matters, along with the training beforehand and the celebration, analysis, recriminations and loud and liver-bothering drinking games afterwards. If you're not particularly interested in sport one way or another, don't be dismayed – there's plenty else to do, plus the influx of new arty types in the wake of the merger with Loughborough College of Art & Design. However, for those who are allergic to track suits and become apoplectic at the hint of exertion, applying here could be construed as a little perverse.

LOUGHBOROUGH:

- Population: 153,600 • London: 100 miles • Leicester: 13 miles • Nottingham: 17 miles
- High temp: 20 • Low temp: 1 • Rainfall: 59

Loughborough's not big enough to fit in more than a few sites of historic interest, but it gives its tuppence worth, including a few old churches and museums (eg. the Bell Foundry, Military and the Ancient Monuments museums). Apart from all the usual shops and public amenities, there's a twice-weekly street market, some *good* independent record stores and some ethnic jewellery shops. The town is surrounded by the ancient Charnwood Forest – *so ancient that there's not much forest left* – and various waterways flow through the area. Of local note is the Great Central Railway, still steaming its way cross-country.

TRAVEL:

Trains: Loughborough station, 2 miles from the campus, is on the mainline north from London St Pancras (90 mins, from £20.45 rtn) to Edinburgh (around £61.45 rtn, 5-hr journey, non-direct).

Coaches: Served by local coach company Paul Winson and National Express to Nottingham and London and beyond.

Car: The A6 goes straight through Loughborough and the M1 is less than 2 miles west of the campus.

Air: Nottingham East Midlands Airport (inland and European flights) is $5\frac{1}{2}$ miles from campus.

Hitching: *The M1's good, but it's a bus ride to the junction.*

Local: Local buses run between campus and town.

Bicycles: *Useful for getting into town (and the campus and its sports fields). The theft situation is improving, but it helps not to bring the most expensive, designer mountain bike.*

CAREER PROSPECTS:

- Careers Service • No. of staff: 7 full/8 part • Unemployed after 6mths: 7%

FAMOUS ALUMNI:

Steve Backley (javelin chucker); Sebastian Coe (former runner, ex-MP, now Lord in charge of London's Olympic bid); Michael Fabricant MP (Con); Lorna Fitzsimons MP (Lab, former NUS pres); Tanni Grey-Thompson (Para Olympic athlete); Barry Hines (writer, Kes); Jason Lee (England hockey player); David Moorcroft (athlete); Carole Tongue MEP (Lab); Bob Wilson (commentator, ex-Arsenal goalie).

FURTHER INFO:

- Prospectuses; undergrad; postgrad; all depts • Open days

A C A D E M I C

Originating as a technical college, which got full university status in 1966, the University continues to evolve and, since the merger with Loughborough College of Art & Design in 1998, has been offering Humanities/Arts courses. Business & Management, Design & Technology, Engineering, Social Sciences & Sports Science *can all hold their own in an academic showdown.*

260-360 POINTS

Entry points: 260-360	Ave points: 310
Applns per place: 7	Clearing: 5%
No. of terms: 2	Length of terms: 15wks
Staff/student ratio: 1:18	Study addicts: 23%
Teaching: *****	Research: *****
Year abroad: 6%	Sandwich students: 39%
Firsts: 12%	2.2s: 30%
2.1s: 54%	3rds: 3%

ADMISSIONS:
• Apply via UCAS

SUBJECTS:

Engineering: 26%   Social Sciences & Humanities: 57%
Science: 23%
Best: Aeronautical Engineering; Art & Design; Automotive Engineering; Building; Chemical Engineering; Civil Engineering; Drama; Economics; Electrical Engineering; Human Sciences; Information Sciences; Manufacturing Engineering; Materials Engineering; Maths; Mechanical Engineering; Physics; Sports Science.
Unusual: BSc Ergonomics (Applied Human Sciences).

LIBRARIES:
• 600,000 books • 760 study places • Spend per student: ££££

COMPUTERS:
• 387 workstations • 24-hr access • Spend per student: ££
All rooms in Halls are connected for phones and t'internet.

ENTERTAINMENT

THE TOWN:
• Price of a pint of beer: £1.65
Cinemas: The five-screen Curzon is one of the oldest cinemas in the country.
Theatres: Amateur and touring shows in the Town Hall.
Pubs: *Local pubs are popular with students who live out or want to get off campus. Pushplugs: The Griffin and the Paget (as studenty as any round here); Orange Tree; Hobgoblin; Barracuda; @the Office; Amber Rooms.*
Clubbing/Music venues: *Check out Pulse on a Tuesday or Thursday, Echos on a weekend.*
Eating out: *Again, it's necessary to go out of town for serious tastebud tingles but a few establishments are worth a look. Pushplugs: Mugals and the Far Pavillion are the most popular curry houses. Moomba is Australian themed. The Loco Lounge and Momentos for Mediteranean, big student discounts at the latter on Mondays and Tuesdays. Cactus Café (Mexican); Mr Chans (cheap Chinese). There are numerous Indian, Chinese and takeaway places, some open till at least 2am.*

UNIVERSITY:
• Price of a pint of beer: £1.20 • Glass of wine: £1.75 • Can of Red Bull: £1.60
Bars: 14 bars: three in residential halls, two on campus and nine in the Union Building, *which are always lively, especially when there's yet another sporting victory to celebrate.*
Theatres: Regular presentations in the Arts Centre and a Union-funded troupe in the Sir Robert Martin Theatre.
Cinemas: The film society shows pics and flicks twice a week (arthouse and blockbuster) in the Union's refurbed auditorium.
Clubbing: Five club nights a week *but students tend to shake their butts on the fields more than on the dance floor.* For those who need some ents-style exercise, FND is the most popular club night. UK Garage names like Spoony and Romeo have passed through.
Music venues: The main auditorium tempts up-and-coming acts as well as the likes of Liberty X, Girls Aloud and Daniel Bedingfield.
Cabaret: Weekly cabaret in the Union building. Dance/comedy night on Saturday nights *(as opposed to comedy dancing every other night of the week).*
Food: In the SU and student village students can find something edible to put in their mouths from 10am to 3am. There's an *imaginative* selection, including the University's own pizza delivery service.
Other: Freshers' week is a blur of ents from surf simulators to bucking broncos. At the other end of a student's stint is the Graduation Ball.

SOCIAL & POLITICAL

LOUGHBOROUGH UNIVERSITY STUDENT UNION

• NUS member • Turnout at last ballot: 25%
Politics is a non-issue for most students but the few who take it seriously are very committed indeed. Awareness campaigns go down well. LSU represents students from the University, Loughborough College and the RNIB Vocational College. Although the Union remains part of NUS, *it holds the national body at arm's length.*

SU FACILITIES:

A general shop (complete, of course, with sports gear section); nine bars; three catering outlets; travel agency; printing facilities; bookshop (Blackwells); market stalls; three banks (HSBC, Barclays, Natwest) plus other ATMs; Employment Exchange; Endsleigh Insurance office; photocopier; photo booth; games and vending machines; pool tables; juke box; meeting rooms; auditorium; optician; dentist; hairdresser; accommodation letting agency, taxi hire; seven minibuses; recording studio; gallery.

CLUBS (NON-SPORTING):

Anime; Asian; Black Students; Bollywood; Brass Society; Breakdance; Cedd House; Cheerleaders; Chess; Hindu; Live Music; Nigerian; R 'n' B; Roc-Soc; Scout and Guide Group; Sikh; Summit4 (hardcore and house); TIC; UCE Student TV. **See also Clubs tables.**

OTHER ORGANISATIONS:

The remarkable Rag is about the only thing that distracts anyone from sporting pursuits. The Bonfire organised last year was attended by 8,000 local residents and there's a successful Rag Week in Feb. The Student Community Action group runs other publicly-spirited activities. The student media includes the Label weekly paper, financed by the SU but run independently and the round-the-clock radio station, LCR, which is over 25 years old. LSUTV can be seen in the Union Building and on the web.

RELIGIOUS:

• 5 chaplains (CofE, RC, FC)
There's an ecumenical Christian chaplaincy, a Muslim prayer room and an Islamic library.

PAID WORK:

• Job bureau
There's a *very successful* employment exchange with a job database for students.

> The registrar and finance director of Hull University agreed to live on £10 each for a week to see what life was like for hard-pressed students

SPORTS

• Recent successes: hockey, rugby league, lacrosse • BUSA Ranking: 1
Did we mention that Loughborough University is big on sport? Applicants who think that running around a field in shorts, chasing/catching/kicking/throwing a ball is stupid should keep quite quiet about it if they go to Loughborough, unless they want to see grown men and women cry. The University enjoys a vast range of sporting facilities, virtually unmatched by any other, let alone by a university this size. Success in most sports has been phenomenal – they've won the British Universities Sports Association women's championship for the last 26 consecutive years and the men's version for the last 24. (Perhaps they're all bionic or clones, has anybody actually checked?)

SPORTS FACILITIES:

All sports clubs are fully insured against accidents, *which makes them relatively pricey to join, but the facilities are worth it.* Eight football pitches, five rugby, two hockey, two cricket and three all-weather pitches, five squash, 16 tennis, five basketball and five netball courts, two sports halls, swimming pool, running track, athletics field, croquet lawn, gym, aerobics studio, multigym, sauna, climbing wall, golf course, indoor gymnastics centre. The town doesn't really need to add anything, but the surrounding area does make outdoor sports, such as fell-walking and water-sports, possible. Loughborough is now the regional Centre of Excellence for the English Institute of Sport and to the England and Wales Cricket Board's ECB Academy.

SPORTING CLUBS:

Boardriders; Boxing; Jitsu; Kick Boxing; Snooker. **See also Clubs tables.**

ATTRACTIONS:

Formula 3 motor racing and motorcycle racing at Donnington.

ACCOMMODATION

IN COLLEGE:

• Catered: 28% • Cost: £85-120 (34/38wks)
• Self-catering: 19% • Cost: £52-72 (34/38wks)
• First years living in: 98% • Insurance premium: £
Availability: There are ten catered and six self-catering halls. They are all mixed (although some blocks or corridors are single sex) and accommodate between 150-650 students. This is enough to house almost all 1st years who request it and a good number of finalists. 11% of rooms are shared. They are all on or adjacent to campus except one en route to town 1/2 mile away. All halls are now networked. There are also self-catering flats arranged in courts or in the student village. Between six and eight students share each kitchen.
Car parking: Limited permit parking for 2nd and 3rd years (£48).

EXTERNALLY:

• Ave rent: £55
Availability: *It's a renter's market and you're unlikely to be left on the pavement. The best places, plucked by the early birds, are around Ashby Road and Storer Road, between the campus and Sainsbury's.*
Housing help: The Union runs an advice service and the University's student accommodation service holds an accommodation list and offers handy suggestions to new and bemused students. Also see the letting agency in the SU.

WELFARE

SERVICES:
- Lesbian/Gay/Bisexual Officer & Society • Mature Students' Officer & Society
- International Students' Officer & Society • Postgrad Officer & Society
- Disabilities Officer & Society • Late-night minibus
- College counsellors: 4 full/4part • Crime rating: !!

Health: *Comprehensive* medical centre with three doctors, 11 nurses and, *naturally, one of the best* university physiotherapy and sports injury clinics in the country.
Crèches/Nursery: 100 places for 6mths-5yrs.
Disabilities: Modern buildings pose *few access problems*. Support available for students with studying difficulties from the University disabilities and additional needs service.

FINANCE:
- Ave debt per year: £3,767 • Access fund: £400,000
- Successful applications/yr: 673 • Ave payment: £650

Fees: *Their top-up policy is still having its 't's dotted and 'i's crossed so watch this space.*
Support: International scholarships; music tuition scholarships and bursaries; some dept scholarships; student prizes; some sponsored courses.

LSE

• *The School is part of the* <u>University of London</u> *and students are entitled to use its facilities.*
The London School of Economics and Political Science, Houghton Street, London, WC2A 2AE
Tel: (020) 7405 7686 E-mail: stu.rec@lse.ac.uk Website: www.lse.ac.uk
LSE Students Union, East Building, LSE, Houghton Street, London, WC2A 2AE
Tel: (020) 7955 7158 E-mail: su.gensec@lse.ac.uk Website: www.lsesu.com

GENERAL

London's vim and vigour don't get very much more frantic than where the Strand hits Fleet Street. That's where LSE resides, and they couldn't have found a much better spot to set up one of the world's leading economics schools. It's not all E though – other social sciences are strong too. The buildings play sardines opposite BBC Bush House, a mile or so down the road from Trafalgar Square, just round the corner from <u>King's College London</u> *and the* <u>Courtauld Institute</u>. *It's cramped and busy with a mixture of grand old buildings and modern blocks.* **For general information about London see** <u>University of London</u>.

Sex ratio (M:F): 54:46	Founded: 1895
Full-time u'grads: 3,405	Part-time: 130
Postgrads: 3,585	Non-degree: n/a
Ave course: 3yrs	Ethnic: 41%
State:private school: 64:36	Flunk rate: 3%
Mature: 10%	International: 72%
Disabled: 49	Local: n/a

ATMOSPHERE:

LSE's a multicultural intellectual pressure-cooker, which means it's hot with ideas and action, but stay too long and there's a risk of your head exploding. It attracts the most intelligent, the most ambitious and the most jealously competitive from 152 countries, if not flocks of tanked-up party types. There are still traces of the radical spirit that the college was famed for during the 1960s, but there's more chance of bumping into a young Patrick Bateman than a young Tony Benn.

LONDON: see <u>University of London</u>

ALDWYCH:

Aldwych is *a stone's throw* from the City in the east, the West End in, *er*, the west and the legal fields and *hobos' hang-out* of Lincoln's Inn in the north. Chuck a stone south, and it'll plop gently into the Thames. *Push can't recommend actually hurling stones around the capital, as the Met don't tend to be very sympathetic.*

TRAVEL: see <u>University of London</u>

Trains: Charing Cross is about 500m down the Strand, for trains to London's 'burbs and the South-East. Waterloo and Blackfriars are within *sneezing range* too.
Car: *Don't even think about driving around this bit of town.* It's C-Charge central and jampacked with traffic. And there's nowhere to park at LSE.
Local: Buses 1, 4, 6, 9, 11, 13, 15, 23, 26, 59, 68, 76, 77a, 91, 16b, 171, 172, 176, 188, 341, 501, 505, 521, X68 and RV1 swing by. Nearest tubes are Temple, Holborn and Charing X.
College: Free late-night minibus to halls after hours.
Bicycles: *Bikes are predictably popular in this bit of town, but the college could do with more cycle racks.*

CAREER PROSPECTS:

• <u>Careers Service</u> • <u>No. of staff: 8 full</u> • <u>Unemployed after 6mths: 5%</u>
Lots of LSE's graduates go on to further training or another degree – *more through naked ambition than addiction to the lie-in lifestyle.*

FAMOUS ALUMNI:

Pat Barker (author); Cherie Booth QC (wife of you-know-who); Carlos the Jackal (terrorist); Ekow Eshun (editor, Arena mag); Clare Francis (yachtswoman, author); Lloyd Grossman (*absurd* foodie TV presenter); Mick Jagger ('Stone); Judge Jules (DJ); John F Kennedy (US president); Jomo Kenyatta, Mwai Kibaki (first and current presidents of Kenya); Robert Kilroy-Silk (*permatanned, Arab-baiting* ex-chat-show host); Bernard Levin (journalist); Beatriz Merino (Peru's first female PM); Mat Osman (Suede); Romano Prodi (ex-President, European Commission); Maurice Saatchi (advertising guru); George Soros (financier).

FURTHER INFO:

• <u>Prospectuses: undergrad; postgrad</u> • <u>Open days</u>
See www.lse.ac.uk/collections/undergraduateadmissions or /collections/studentRecruitment for admissions info. The alternative prospectus is at www.lsesu.com

ACADEMIC

Deserved reputation for excellence in its fields. Prestigious academic staff, great resources and prestigious guest speakers. Regular flirtations with the upper echelons of the league tables.

Entry points: 300-360	Ave points: 340
Applns per place: 13	Clearing: 0
No. of terms: 3	Length of terms: 10wks
Staff/student ratio: 1:8	Study addicts: 31%
Teaching: *****	Research: *****
Year abroad: 1%	Sandwich students: 0
Firsts: 17%	2.2s: 55%
2.1s: 24%	3rds: 4%

300-360 **POINTS**

ADMISSIONS:

• Apply via UCAS

LSE insists on two *proper A Levels (definitely not Business Studies). Don't even dream about getting a place through clearing.*

SUBJECTS:

Arts/Humanities: 7%   Sciences: 5%

Business/Management: 20%   Social Sciences: 68%

Best: Business & Management; Economics; Government; Industrial Relations; International Relations; Maths; Philosophy; Politics; Social Psychology; Sociology; Statistics; Statistics & Operational Research.

Unusual: Anthropology & Law; Economic History; Economic History with Population Studies; Industrial Relations; International Relations.

LIBRARIES:

• 4,000,000 books • 1,600 books • Spend per student: £££££

LSE's *huge* main library goes under the *appropriately grand* title of the British Library of Political & Economic Science. There are also several small departmental libraries. The main one has 24-hr access during exam term – *take a sleeping bag.*

COMPUTERS:

• 900 workstations • 24-hr access • Spend per student: ££££

All rooms in halls have internet access.

ENTERTAINMENT

THE CITY: see University of London

• Price of a pint of beer: £2 • Glass of wine: £2 • Can of Red Bull: £2

Aldwych is *convenient* for the bright lights *(and breathtaking prices)* of Leicester Square and Covent Garden. Pubs, theatres, ritzy cinemas and posh restaurants *a-go-go.*

UNIVERSITY:

• Price of a pint of beer: £1.20 • Glass of wine: £2 • Can of Red Bull: £1.50

Bars: The Three Tuns Bar (cap 700) is *pretty popular.* The Underground (120) is primarily an events venue and the Beaver's Retreat, which looks as if it's been furnished courtesy of MFI, *is expensive and only really popular with the academics.*

Theatres: The drama society won an award in 2004, but *they concentrate on quality over quantity,* putting on around four shows a year.

Film: A *mainstream* film a week. The film society charges a quid for the privilege. *Compared to a tenner a go at the Empire in Leicester Square, that's a snip.*

Clubbing: The Underground *goes overboard* for its Friday night disco Crush (sets by Jimmy Baker, Rowan Harvey, Judge Jules) and the Quad is used for student bands and the *very occasional* professional act.

Comedy/cabaret: Weekly shows at the Three Tuns from pros like Will Smith and *wet-nosed amateurs* like the Cambridge Footlights.

Food: The Union runs a café, which is *unusually good* for vegetarian and vegan grub, with furniture from the next decade and *trendy* murals. It also runs a pizzeria and restaurant.

SOCIAL & POLITICAL

LSE STUDENTS' UNION:
• 4 sabbaticals • Turnout at last ballot: 24% • NUS member

SU FACILITIES:
Three bars; four canteens; snack bar and fast food joint; pool table; meeting rooms; Natwest bank/ATM; printing/fax/photocopying services; payphones; photo booth; crèche; late-night minibus; juke box and games machines; stationery shop; post office; new and secondhand bookshops; travel agent.

CLUBS (NON-SPORTING):
More than 130, including: Aid for Bosnia; Animal Aid; Arabic; Bridge; Central/Eastern European; Chinese; Conservative; Cypriot; Dr Bike; European; Grimshaw Club; Hayek; Hellenic; Historical Materialism; Human Rights of Women; Indian; Italian; Jelly Baby; Mauritian; Mexican; Music; Modern Dance; Peace; Pakistan; Pyschology; Scandinavian; Schapiro Government Club; Stop the Fees; Student Industrial; Theatre Appreciation; Vedic. **See also Clubs tables.**

OTHER ORGANISATIONS:
SU-published the Beaver is the weekly read. The Script magazine comes out three times a year and PuLSE radio sporadically broadcasts on the internet.

RELIGIOUS:
• 4 chaplains (CofE, RC, Orthodox, FC)
Also Buddhist & Muslim facilities.

PAID WORK: see University of London
• Job bureau • Paid work: term-time 50%; hols 70%
Work going in the SU services and some opportunities within the University. Part-time jobshop tries to set students up with employers online.

SPORTS

• Recent successes: football • BUSA Ranking: 48
Most of LSE's greatest sporting moments are reserved for the Rugby Club Ball. Aldwych's *obviously* not the place for vast playing fields but *a hardy few* make the 40-min train journey to the School's 25 acres of playing fields at Berrylands near New Malden *way out* west. Students can, of course, use ULU's facilities.

SPORTS FACILITIES:
20 acres of grounds at Berrylands including playing fields, tennis courts, a croquet lawn, pavilion, bar and restaurant. On-site there are netball and squash courts; gym, multigym, aerobics studio; badminton court; snooker table and circuit room.

SPORTING CLUBS:
Aerobics; Extreme Sports; Muay Thai Boxing; Rowing; Running; Table Tennis; Yoga. **See also Clubs tables.**

ATTRACTIONS: see University of London

ACCOMMODATION

IN COLLEGE:
- Catered: 38% • Cost: £57-£120 (30wks)
- Self-catering: 13% • Cost: £86-£122 (30wks)
- First years living in: 95% • Insurance premium: £££

Availability: About $\frac{1}{3}$ of LSE's students live in University of London intercollegiate halls. 1st years are guaranteed accommodation, and *most* of them take it. Those who can't afford to pay £100+ for a *pleasant but pokey* college room can pay a little less and share. Passfield Hall's cheapest, with a *good community atmosphere*, whereas Bankside's *pricey and impersonal*. Most halls have bars and the communal areas are *kept from rotting* by college cleaners.

Car parking: *Horrendously difficult to get a permit, which costs a small fortune.*

EXTERNALLY: see University of London
- Ave rent: £100 • Living at home: 10%

Housing help: LSE has a web-based vacancy system with online waiting lists. There's also the UoL services (see University of London).

WELFARE

SERVICES:
- Lesbian/Gay/Bisexual Officer & Society • Ethnic Minorities Officer • Women's Officer
- Mature Students' Officer & Society • International Students' Officer • Postgrad Officer
- Disabilities Officer & Society • Late-night minibus (priority for women)
- Self-defence classes • Nightline • College counsellors: 3 full/6 part • Crime rating: !!!!!

Health: On-campus NHS practice with four GPs and two nurses *to mop feverish brows.*
Women: Free attack alarms and family planning advice.
Crèches/Nursery: 30 places for students' kids.
Disabilities: Access to everything but the main lecture theatres are *really poor* but there's lots of useful info at www.lse.ac.uk/collections/disabilityOffice on what else is available.

FINANCE:
- Ave debt per year: £2,763

Fees: Fees for postgrads are rising above the rate of inflation.
- Access fund: £108,611 • Successful applications/yr: 112 • Ave payment: £1,200

Support: Around £4.7m in financial assistance awarded every year (undergrads and postgrads), mostly on academic merit of financial hardship.

University of Luton

- *Formerly Luton College of Higher Education.*

University of Luton, Park Street, Luton, Bedfordshire, LU1 3JU
Tel: (01582) 734 111 E-mail: admissions@luton.ac.uk Website: www.luton.ac.uk
University of Luton Students' Union, Europa House, V carage Street, Luton, Bedfordshire, LU1 3HZ Tel: (01582) 743 286 Website: www.ulsu.co.uk

GENERAL

For years Luton's had a hard time living down the image of dropped aitches and having a local Vauxhall car factory as its most interesting feature. It's an outdated perception – Luton is metamorphosing into a lively, growing place with 150 acres of pleasantish greenery (winner of Britain in Bloom '97, *the highest accolade in the world, ever*) and it's not far from the Chiltern Hills. An International Carnival held every May packs more than 140,000 visitors into the town. The University is now one of the *kinkiest* features and *is going hell for leather on the expansion front*. It's grown *unrecognisably* since 1976 when it became a college of higher education. It gained university status in '93 and is getting bigger and more facility-stuffed by the year.

Sex ratio (M:F): 37:63	**Founded: 1993**
Full-time u'grads: 6,225	**Part-time: 3,620**
Postgrads: 1,015	**Non-degree: 4,300**
Ave course: 3yrs	**Ethnic: 30%**
State:private school: 99:1	**Flunk rate: 25%**
Mature: 45%	**International: 37%**
Disabled: 82	**Local: 53%**

ATMOSPHERE:

Many local students come here because it's on their doorstep. Of the rest not many have much choice in the matter, with a third coming here through clearing. But courses are career-focused and the work ethic is dedicated – an attitude the University likes to foster as it keeps up the graduate employability record. Lots of international students add a cosmopolitan feel and with the local element campus *is a friendly, happy place – just don't expect life-changing political moments or to achieve nirvana.*

SITES:

Park Square: (Main site) The *harsh architecture* of Park Square is *rather appropriate* to the utilitarian philosophy of the courses, although it's balanced by the *swish* Learning Resources Centre and the new Media Arts Centre.

Putteridge Bury: (500 students – Postgrad Business School) The *plush, tranquil* country mansion and landscaped gardens are exclusively a postgrad stomping ground 4 miles from Park Square. *Being the prettiest part* of the University, it's also hired out for conferences. See www.putteridgebury.com for other details.

LUTON:

- Population: 184,300 • City centre: 0 miles • London: 30 miles
- Milton Keynes: 21 miles • Bedford: 25 miles • Birmingham: 80 miles
- High temp: 21 • Low temp: 1 • Rainfall: 63

Luton started life as the centre of the hat and lace industry but is now a *busy* business town with *pretty good employment figures. It's the largest town in Bedfordshire, which doesn't say much as Bedford is the only competition.* Shops, libraries, banks, markets and the rest exist in *plentiful* supply but despite the significant ethnic population *it's still a bit small town in mentality. At least its residents were cosmopolitan enough to vote it 'Crappest UK Town' in 2004 – narrowly beating Kingston upon Hull to the coveted accolade. Worth a particular mention* are the *massive* modern Arndale Shopping Centre right by the University and the Galaxy Centre, which offers music, TV and multimedia facilities, cinema, art gallery, restaurant and café. *Nothing worth changing your trousers for though.*

TRAVEL:

Trains: Luton station is 5 mins walk from the University with trains to London King's Cross (£13.50), Bedford, Milton Keynes and east coast mainline services all the way to Edinburgh (£42).

Coaches: Green Line and National Express services (London £8, Birmingham £12).

Car: M1, A6 (straight through town), A1 and A5. Multi-storey parking is available in the Arndale Centre and there's pay & display near Park Street.

Air: Luton Airport is the home of budget airline easyJet and offers inland and international services to Europe, Ireland and the USA.

Hitching: *Despite good connections it's easier to pick up the white lines on the road than pick up a lift in the Home Counties. It's none too safe either and few try it.*

Local: 'Hopper' buses scuttle round the town every 30 mins till 11pm, around 60p a trip from the outskirts to Park Square. No local trains around town, but an excellent link into London and good for day-tripping. *However, the last train's too early and all too easy to miss.*

College: Free shuttle bus from Park Square to Putteridge Bury and back again (9am-5pm daily).

Taxis: *Not cheap, but worth using at night when the buses go to bed.*

Bicycles: *Although Luton's flat, few bike it. Maybe because three heavy padlocks and a cattle prod are needed to hang on to a bike for more than a week. They're useful for those who live off-site, though.*

CAREER PROSPECTS:

• Careers Service • No. of staff: 8 full • Unemployed after 6mths: 12%

The Student Centre Careers Service has a careers library with interview training, job fairs, bulletin boards, newsletters and website. Several big businesses in the area offer Graduate Apprenticeship Schemes to Luton students.

FAMOUS ALUMNI:

Gemma Hunt (CBBC presenter); Becky Jago (Capital Radio presenter); Ian Dury (Blockhead); Sir David Plastow (industrialist).

FURTHER INFO:

• Prospectuses: undergrad; postgrad • Open days • Video

Prospectuses come with *funky* free lifestyle mag, the Experience (*of the airline seat-pocket type*). Open days are formally held throughout the year, *but impromptu tours by 'student ambassadors' can be thrown together at a moment's notice.*

A C A D E M I C

Since promotion from HE college to university Luton has gained a reputation as a highly-rated new institution. This has been accompanied by a large influx of degree students and an even larger increase in expenditure on buildings and facilities. The focus is decidedly on employment-related skills and *nice things have been said about its teaching by a lot of people.* Charles Clarke (Home Secretary and former Secretary of State for Education & Skills) told Vice-Chancellor Les Ebdon over dinner that Luton's teaching was 'bloody brilliant'. *Booyakasha.*

Entry points: 160-240	Ave points: n/a	
Applns per place: 7	Clearing: 30%	
No. of terms: 2	Length of terms: 15wks	
Staff/student ratio: 1:20	Study addicts: 27%	
Teaching: *	Research: *	
Year abroad: 5%	Sandwich students: 5%	
Firsts: 9%	2.2s: 43%	
2.1s: 42%	3rds: 5%	

ADMISSIONS:

• Apply via UCAS

Luton takes work and life experience as seriously as academic records, so *it's good news for mature students. A Levels aren't the be all and end all* – Advanced GNVQs, Access courses, foundation degrees and equivalent foreign qualifications all go into the admissions cooking pot. There are international links and regular recruitment from 140 countries worldwide, ranging from China to Estonia.

SUBJECTS:

Creative Arts, Technologies & Sciences: 20% Luton Business School: 34%
Health & Social Sciences: 46%
Best: Anatomy & Physiology; Art & Design; Building; Communication & Media Studies; Molecular Biosciences; Nursing; Organismal Biosciences; Other subjects allied to Medicine; Pharmacology & Pharmacy; Psychology.
Unusual: BSc Computer Games Development; BA Contemporary Islamic Art.

LIBRARIES:

• 206,422 books • 979 study places • Spend per student: £
Two Learning Resource Centres and four much smaller hospital libraries spread Luton's collection between them. 24-hr access is available as exams approach at the main Park Square LRC, *which has somehow wound its way on to the Borough Council's must-see tourist itinerary.*

COMPUTERS:

• 1,210 workstations • Spend per student: ££
If Luton's IT improvement programme continues in the same vein, there'll soon be as many workstations as books. The new Media Arts facility more than doubled the computer provision, adding a legion of high-spec Macs and PCs. *There have been complaints about inadequate access at peak time, but the introdution of network points into all student rooms has all but quelled the rebellion.*

OTHER LEARNING FACILITIES:

As well as the drama studio, CAD lab, rehearsal rooms and new psychology lab, the University has splooged £5.5m on *a state-of-the-art* Media Arts facility in Park Square, including broadcast TV studio, indoor and outdoor performance spaces, digital radio studios and editing suites – *one of the most impressive (and expensive) facilities of its kind in the country.*

ENTERTAINMENT

THE TOWN:

• Price of a pint of beer: £2 • Glass of wine: £2.50 • Can of Red Bull: £1.50
Cinemas: Cineworld at the Galaxy Centre has 11 big, mainstream screens with weekday student discount. The smaller Library Theatre shows new and cult releases at NUS discount prices.
Theatres: The Hat Factory is a *lively* council-run arts and media venue in Bute Street just behind the main site, while the Library Theatre produces old favourites, kiddies' theatre and original material.
Pubs: *Red Red Red is a sultry chill-out zone with pints and pints of drinks promos. The Park on Park Street may be as dingy as a stoner's kitchen but hefty discounts make it a loud and larking hangout. Pushplugs: Bellini on Chapel Street (recently benefited from an extensive funk-over).*
Clubbing: Edge offers funky, punky, metallic fun for *alternative* types. Liquid (Gordon Street) and Space (Chapel Street) do a *fine line* in mainstream dance and charty cheese washed down with cheap booze. Monday is student night – known as 'Fresh Fish' for some *off-putting* reason.
Music venues: Liquid's probably Luton's *most popular* club and there's also Space in the town centre. Bellini and Brookes are both smaller but open late and offer an alternative to the full-on club scene.
Other: Ten-pin bowling at the Galaxy Centre. *Acne-encrusted 13-year-olds abound. An annual Beer Festival in studenty High Town is the highlight of the calendar for many hopoholics.*

Eating out: *Brookes on Castle Street does posh all-day brekkie; a cheaper version is to be had at The Caff down the road. Bellini's is the place to take relatives for Italian. Pushplugs: the lunchtime student menu at the Cork & Bull and Balti Nights (curry house).*

UNIVERSITY:

• <u>Price of a pint of beer: £1.60</u> • <u>Glass of wine: £2.20</u> • <u>Can of Red Bull: £1.50</u>

Bars: *The SU Bar's a modern and cosy daytime stop-off and a busy night-time drink-up with regular quiz nights and society events. The underground Sub Club (open till 2am club nights) is looking less dingy after a bit of a spit and polish and remains popular and bouncy.*
Clubbing: *Sporty 'Sin' night in the Sub Club draws the biggest and sweatiest crowd, but there's a wide-ranging weekly calendar. Local DJs get scratchy at Luton more than big name CD spinners. The Urban club scene's popular with local fly boys 'n gals.*
Food: *The SU toasts paninis and less posh sarnies and plenty of meat gets tossed at summertime bbqs. Local restaurant the Temple has hijacked some counter-space in the SU bar to peddle cheap and tasty Afro-Caribbean nibbles.*
Other: *A lack of Union funds has shaved Luton's balls somewhat the past couple of years. Students now relocate to Hertfordshire University for the annual piss-up. It remains to be seen whether the Union's own balls will be banging again or if they'll be cut off altogether. (Okay, we'll stop now.)*

SOCIAL & POLITICAL

UNIVERSITY OF LUTON STUDENTS' UNION:

• <u>4 sabbaticals</u> • <u>Turnout at last ballot: 14%</u> • <u>NUS member</u>

ULSU is apolitical (except when it comes to top-up fees, of course) and takes more care over its societies, ents and advice centre than anything else though the purse ain't overflowing. There's an Infonet service online: gripes about library hours; books for sale; suicide threats; adverts for swingers parties – whatever really.

SU FACILITIES:

The SU building (Europa House, next to Park Square) has: nightclub; bar; coffee bar; pool table; meeting room; club and society area; non-alcoholic area; photocopier; fax and printing service; payphones; advice centre; juke box; gaming and vending machines; secondhand bookshop; launderette.

CLUBS (NON-SPORTING):

Aylesbury Student Nursing; B-Boy Dance; Believers Love Word; Creative Writing; Gaming; Indian Students; Nigerian; Japanese; Law; Muslim Medila Forum; Nigerian Students; Pakistani; Quran & Sunnah; Sikh. **See also Clubs tables.**

OTHER ORGANISATIONS:

SU publications have an *indecent exposure theme*: Flasher is the free paper; Streaker is a free monthly magazine. The University publishes a more official and less risqué newspaper, Life. Luton FM broadcasts for one month each May. Despite the existence of an elected Rag Officer *Luton's charity efforts would make Scrooge blush with shame, although there are seasonal, sponsored events.* The University runs a Student Community Exchange programme which send students off *to be helpful* in the surrounding area.

RELIGIOUS:

• <u>1 chaplain (CofE)</u>

Prayer rooms for Muslims, meditation-space available upon request. The town has places of worship for most faiths including mosques, synagogue, several Sikh and Buddhist temples and churches for Jehovah's Witnesses, Catholics, Methodists, Anglicans, Baptists and United Reformists.

PAID WORK:

• <u>Job bureau</u> • <u>Paid work: term-time 90%; hols 95%</u>

Job shop posts vacancies, gives CV advice and finds voluntary work for *selfless do-gooders*. Several companies in Luton (the Airport, the council) employ students.

SPORTS

• <u>Recent successes: football, women's rugby league</u> • <u>BUSA Ranking: 48</u>
It matters not who wins or loses but whether there's a bar. The emphasis is on taking part and pecs are flexed by a good few and admired from the sidelines by a few more. The University's own facilities are, in a word, piffling, but deals have been done with neighbouring sports centres *and* Luton is now slowly climbing the student sports league.

SPORTS FACILITIES:

The Vauxhall Recreation Centre gives students access to football and hockey pitches, tennis courts, sports hall, gym, multigym and sauna (£60 a year or on a per session basis). Sports Therapy students get their hands on Luton's wounded warriors at the sports massage clinic. The town has a golf course nearby, plus a swimming pool and leisure centre. There are also the hills nearby for those who enjoy being vertically challenged.

SPORTING CLUBS:

Aerobics; Boxing; Cheerleading; Gaelic Football; Kick Boxing; Surf; Terra Firma (sky diving); Weight Training; Women's Rugby League; Wind Surfing. **See also Clubs tables.**

ATTRACTIONS:

Luton's biggest sporting non-attraction are 'the Hatters' (Luton FC).

ACCOMMODATION

IN COLLEGE:

• <u>Self-catering: 26%</u> • <u>Cost: £45-66 (30wks)</u>
• <u>First years living in: 100%</u> • <u>Insurance premium: £</u>
Availability: 20 halls, ranging from terraced houses to tower blocks. All new undergrads and postgrads are guaranteed a room, priced according to location/distance. *Cheaper halls are a little basic but while most tend to be poky, the single study bedrooms are kitted out with all the necessities (ie. beds and desks). The biggest, most central hall is on Bute Street and most 1st years are drawn to its promise of a pulsing social life.* Single-sex flats are available.
Car parking: Fairly easy, free permits at some halls. Town central Bute Street charges £50/year.

EXTERNALLY:

• <u>Ave rent: £48</u>
Availability: *There's no real shortage of appropriate housing, although the beginning of the year panic is becoming a regular 'mare. The best areas are High Town, Farley Hill, Park Town, New Town and the Town Centre, all within walking distance of the University. Bury Park is popular with local Asian students, but some regard it as unsafe.*
Housing help: Eight full-time advisers at the University Accommodation Office provide vacancy lists and give advice, but are reluctant to blacklist landlords – the SU does this instead.

WELFARE

SERVICES:

• <u>Lesbian/Gay/Bisexual Officer & Society</u> • <u>Ethnic Minorities Officer</u> • <u>Women's Officer</u>
• <u>Mature Students' Officer</u> • <u>International Students' Officer & Society</u>
• <u>University counsellors: 3 full</u> • <u>SU counsellors: 3</u> • <u>Crime rating: !!!!</u>

Health: No provision on campus, but there's a NHS practice 5 mins walk away.
Disabilities: The new buildings have been considerately built and all teaching buildings are wheelchair-friendly. There are adapted study bedrooms and induction loops in most lecture theatres. The LRC has a range of software for the use of all disabled students that includes mind-mapping and text-reading programs. Assessment-based provisions for unseen disabilities.
Crime/Drugs: *Burglaries are not unknown* during the moving-in period in halls. There's a Campus Watch safety scheme to combat this. The SU runs drugs and safe drinking campaigns.

FINANCE:
• Ave debt per year: £4,127
Fees: International undergrads pay £6,700-7,400. UK postgrads pay around £4,000. Luton will *be charging top-ups in 2006, gamely offset by a smattering of bursary packages.*
• Access fund: £497,588 • Successful applications/yr: 853 • Ave payment: £583
Support: Some funding from local businesses (£500 handouts). Specific funds are available for members of specific groups: locals, ethnic minorities, matures etc.

Luton College of Higher Education
see University of Luton

Newcastle SU produced a caricature of Liz Hurley saying 'Please Don't Suck My Grant' for their anti-poverty campaign. The actress asked for it to be withdrawn but she was so nice about it that the Union is pushing for her to have an honorary degree.

Magee see <u>University of Ulster</u>

University of Manchester

University of Manchester Insitute of Science & Technology see <u>University of Manchester</u>

Manchester Metropolitan University

Manchester Polytechnic see <u>Manchester Metropolitan University</u>

Metropolitan University see <u>Leeds Metropolitan University</u>

Middlesex University

Middlesex Polytechnic see <u>Middlesex University</u>

Milton Keynes see <u>De Montfort University</u>

Moores University see <u>Liverpool John Moores University</u>

Moray House see <u>University of Edinburgh</u>

Magee
see <u>University of Ulster</u>

University of Manchester

University of Manchester, Oxford Road, Manchester, M13 9PL Tel: (0161) 275 2077
E-mail: ug.admissions@man.ac.uk Website: www.manchester.ac.uk
University of Manchester Union, Steve Biko Building, Oxford Road, Manchester, M13 9PR
Tel: (0161) 275 2930 Website: www.umu.man.ac.uk

GENERAL

Welcome to the 25-hr party town, the battered but mad-for-it sprawl of Britain's second-largest city and the capital of the north-west. The tail-end of the Pennines divides Manchester's Lancashire setting from the posse of Yorkshire counties, and Liverpool's only 30 mins drive. It's a big place with over a quarter of a million students *loitering* in the Greater Manchester area, including surrounding Salford and Oldham. Most of them – the students, not the towns – belong to the University. The neighbouring UMIST (University of Manchester Institute of Science & Technology) was formally swallowed up in October 2004, cementing the University's status as one of the biggest in the country and bolstering both the number of students and the number and quality of learning facilities available. The campus is divided into North and South and is spread across the city centre. Factor in <u>Manchester Metropolitan University</u> and the other institutions and teaching hospitals and you've got the largest educational complex in Western Europe. *The buildings themselves are a hodgepodge of drab 60s concrete, art nouveau redbrick, Victorian grandeur and stark Thatcherite mingled among more modern offerings.*

Sex ratio (M:F): 39:61	**Founded: 1824**
Full-time u'grads: 17,795	**Part-time: 2,385**
Postgrads: 4,065	**Non-degree: 0**
Ave course: 3/4yrs	**Ethnic: 11%**
State:private school: 48:52	**Flunk rate: 7%**
Mature: 7%	**International: 19%**
Disabled: 451	**Local: n/a**

ATMOSPHERE:

Although it's always been a big University and has just got even bigger, Manchester's developed a surprisingly close-knit student community. The two halves of the campus are compact and close-by so no one gets isolated. Having said that, the size and constant bustle of the place – particularly the Union building – can put all but the most confident or loudmouthed students into the shade. They're a diverse bunch (students from about 150 countries). Mancunian businesses are heavily dependent on the student population, meaning lots of cheap bars and student discounts.

MANCHESTER:

- Population: 392,900 • City centre: 1 mile • London: 167 miles
- Liverpool: 28 miles • Birmingham: 72 miles
- High temp: 20 • Low temp: 1 • Rainfall: 68

Although it's been around since Caesar invented salad, Manchester (as a *superpower* rather than a settlement) was really built out of cotton during the Industrial Revolution – out of the money from cotton, to be more precise. *Industry flooded it and the canals drained it, making the city one of the all-time boomtowns. But it didn't last and Manchester found depression pretty depressing, scarring the city with slums. Some of these, such as Moss Side and Burnage, remain pretty bleak, but many areas have been redeveloped and its chequered history has left Manchester rich in culture. Everything a student could want is here (except perhaps quiet, rural countryside), from shops to galleries to pubs to clubs and back again. It may have lost its 90s title of youth culture capital of the universe, but Manchester can still go a few rounds in the ring with London or any other urban giant. Music still pulses through its veins as the vodka trickles down its throat. Life ain't cheap here, though, and many will need either a job or a trust fund just to get by. Manchester has little of the crowded loneliness or impersonality of London and its sons and daughters are by and large a proud and friendly people – traits which rub off on its students.*

TRAVEL:

Trains: Not one but two mainline stations, Manchester Piccadilly for London and the south, and Manchester Victoria for just about everywhere else. Routes go all over, including London, Birmingham, Edinburgh and more.

Coaches: All sorts of coach services to, among most other places, London, Birmingham, Edinburgh and beyond.

Car: From the north, M6 (then M61 or M62), A6 or M66; from the east, M62, A58, A62; from the south, M6, A6, A523, A34; and from Wales, the M56. *Parking may well be a problem in central Manchester, but, for the lazy and environmentally feckless, a car doesn't go amiss.*

Air: Manchester Airport's one of the UK's big ones – flights all over the world as well as inland.

Hitching: *Not possible from central Manchester, but quite good on arterial routes out of the city.*

Local: Manchester has a major bus network, running all over town, especially up and down Oxford Road. Trains are a *quicker alternative, especially for the outskirts*. The Metrolink tram service trundles around helpfully.

Taxis: *Manchester's centre, being relatively small, means taxi trips are a viable resort.* The black cabs that screech to a halt as you hail them are a lot more expensive than the private traders who are only supposed to pick up phone callers and drop-ins.

Bicycles: *Manchester's quite bike-friendly (flat with a fair few cycle lanes), but theft is rife.*

CAREER PROSPECTS:

• <u>Careers Service</u> • <u>No. of staff: 12 full</u> • <u>Unemployed after 6mths: 7%</u>
Manchester has the 2nd biggest careers service in the country. It has over 50 staff in all, *and is accordingly rather brilliant*. Services on offer include the *usual* caboodle of vacancy lists, bulletins, library and *tons of* job fairs, plus interview training (available on video), CV-polishing, psychometric testing, mentoring schemes with professionals and Careers Skills Training courses. They help students find both work placements and life-long careers, arranging around 120 companies-worth of employer presentations. See the dedicated website: www.graduatecareersonline.com

FAMOUS ALUMNI:

Sir Rhodes Boyson (ex-Con MP); Nick Brown MP (Lab); Anthony Burgess (writer); Louis de Bernières (author of Captain Corelli's Mandolin); Ben Elton, Rik Mayall, Ade Edmondson, (comedians); Anna Ford (BBC newsreader); Alex Garland (writer, The Beach); Peter Maxwell Davies (composer); Austin Mitchell MP (Lab); Sir Maurice Oldfield (MI6); Christabel Pankhurst (suffragette); Ernest Rutherford (Nobel Prize winner and atom-splitter); Mark Radcliffe (DJ); Justin Robertson (DJ); Meera Syal (comedian and actress); Louise Wener (Sleeper); Phil Woolas MP.
From UMIST: Margaret Beckett MP, David Clark MP (Lab cabinet ministers); Sir John Cockcroft (scientist); John Dalton (chemist – *not the condoms and hairspray variety*); Keith Edelman (Chief Executive, Storehouse); Ian Gibson (Chief Executive, Nissan); Sophie Grigson (TV cook); Sir Terry Leahy (Chief Executive, Tesco); Geoff Mulcahy (Chief Executive, Kingfisher Group); Keith Oates (Chief Executive, M&S); Sir Arthur Whitten-Brown (transatlantic pilot).

SPECIAL FEATURES:

• Manchester degrees are also awarded at the Institute of Advanced Nursing Education in London, Stockport College of Further & Higher Education and University College, Warrington.
• The newly refurbished and extended Manchester Museum is part of the University.

FURTHER INFO:

• <u>Prospectuses: undergrad; postgrad; some depts; alternative; international</u> • <u>Open days</u>
Undergrad and postgrad prospectuses can be ordered via the main website, the alternative prospectus's distributed by the SU. The University runs four open days a year – one of which is exclusively devoted to Medicine. For those who can't make open days, there are guided campus tours every 1st and 3rd Wednesday of the month.

ACADEMIC

Manchester's diamond 'ard when it comes to research and academia – both the University and UMIST were fairly solid as separate bodies, so it's no surprise they're good together. Several scholarly folk have changed the world from within its walls: Rutherford did a lot of his work on splitting the atom here and the world's first computer was built here in 1948 – *okay, it was about as sophisticated as an abacus by today's standards but you've got to start somewhere. The University's four faculties are still emitting bright sparks today* and its biomedical research is world-renowned. There's a *huge* variety of joint honours programmes available and *particular undergraduate strengths include: English, Drama, Engineering, Politics, Law and Medicine.*

Entry points: 240-340	**Ave points: 404**
Appins per place: 8	**Clearing: 8%**
No. of terms: 3	**Length of terms: 10wks**
Study addicts: 20%	**Research: *******
Teaching: ****	

ADMISSIONS:

• <u>Apply via UCAS</u>
Manchester considers a wide variety of qualifications when sorting the wheat from the chaff so *everyone* gets a look-in.

SUBJECTS:

Best: Anatomy & Physiology; Anthropology; Archaeology; Business & Management; Chemistry; Civil Engineering; Classics & Ancient History; Computer Science; Dentistry; Drama, Dance & Cinematics; Economics; Education; Electrical & Electronic Engineering; Geography; Geology; German; History of Art, Architecture & Design; Hospitality, Land & Property Management; Leisure, Recreation, Sport & Tourism; Iberian Studies; Materials Technology; Mathematics, Statistics & Operational Research; Mechanical Engineering; Mechanical, Aeronautical & Manufacturing Engineering; Medicine; Middle Eastern & African Studies; Molecular Biosciences; Music; Nursing; Organismal Biosciences; Other subjects allied to Medicine; Pharmacology & Pharmacy; Philosophy; Physics & Astronomy; Politics; Psychology; Social Policy & Administration; Sociology; Theology & Religious Studies; Town & Country Planning & Landscape.

LIBRARIES:

• 4,000,000 books • 3,200 study places • Spend per student: £££££

The *dullish* brick affair that is John Rylands University Library is much more interesting on the inside. It's second to Oxbridge on size, *but that's still pretty massive*. The range of electronic resources available rivals any other institution and *the sheer number of books can be quite daunting*. It closes at 9.30pm every day. In addition, there are ten smaller faculty libraries, including the original John Rylands Library at Deansgate which houses the University's special collections and – *sod the books* – *is probably the most gorgeous example of neo-Gothic architecture the city has to offer.*

COMPUTERS:

• 7,000 workstations • 24-hr access

The merger with UMIST has increased the number and quality of most facilities, but computing benefited in particular. There are four main computer clusters (the main library, Owen's Park, the Arts building and the Manchester Computing Centre) with a range of Pentium PCs, printing facilities and scanners. Other workstations are spread around the faculties. *Only in the unlikely event that more than half the students want to use a public computer at the same time would the facilities fall short.*

OTHER LEARNING FACILITIES:

The Language Centre has an extensive library and range of audio-visual material (*loads of arty films*) and allows anyone to learn a foreign tongue. Manchester's science labs are *impressive stuff* and include the famous Jodrell Bank Observatory astronomy research centre. A £35m Interdisciplinary Biocentre has just opened – *we're still trying to figure out what exactly it is*. The new music and drama building's *pretty special too*, housing a studio theatre, concert hall, rehearsal rooms, a library and audio-visual facilities.

ENTERTAINMENT

THE CITY:

• Price of a pint of beer: £1.90 • Glass of wine: £2.20 • Can of Red Bull: £2

Manchester's a *cultural jamboree*, bringing together the *brightest and the best* in theatre, food, nightlife and, *most recently, music to this corner of the country. The Steve Coogan film 24 Hour Party People is essential nostalgic viewing both for a lesson in musical history and for tips for a night on the tiles. Apart from the bit with the hooker.*

Cinemas: A multiplicity of multiplexes and sundry cinemas, everything from the eight-screen Salford Quays multiplex and the cool Cornerhouse (three screens) which shows many an arty flick. With a gallery and café thrown in, *it's a poser's paradise.*

Theatres: *A very thespy city*, with more theatres per head than anywhere else in Europe. The old Cotton Exchange is now the nationally renowned Royal Exchange Theatre – *some of the country's best shows* for under a fiver on student standbys. The Palace and Opera House *do good* pantos while the Green Room is more experimental.

Pubs: *Manchester has historic pubs in the truest tradition of the workingman's dive but there's everything from real ales to obscure cocktails to turpentine in a paper bag. If you must be a poseur, pose in Manto and Dry 201 but, for those living somewhere in reality, Pushplugs go to the central Rocket Bar, Revolution on Oxford Road, Jabez Clegg, Baa Baa on Deansgate, the Queen Of Hearts (Fallowfield), Retro Bar and Joshua Brooks.*

Clubbing: *The music is alive but the clubs come and go – The Hacienda, alas, continues only in spirit. Read City Life for the latest. Pushplugs: Vodka Island at Tiger Tiger (Mon) Temptation at Home (Weds); the Rock 'n' Roll Bar (indie); Hallelujah at the Paradise Factory; indescribably sticky The Bop at Jabes Clegg; Thursday night is student night at the hysterically tacky Royale. Brutus Gold's Love Train at Ritz (Weds) is a national treasure of tacky 70s retro. Check for the cheaper NUS-only nights and watch out for flyers for the alighting points of fly-by-night clubs.*

Music venues: The Manchester Evening News Arena lures the hugest names, *for those into binocular-rock. The Apollo, by most towns' standards, would be a best bet; however, all over town there are live venues of every size. Among the many others: The Academy (run by Manchester University SU); Boardwalk (indie); Jilly's (rock); Band on the Wall (rootsy); Chorlton Irish Club (folk); P J Bells (jazz); The Bridgewater Hall and the Royal Northern College of Music (classical). Many of these clubs also stage live bands.*

Other: *A breeding ground for stand-up talent. Live comedy is usually high-octane fun.* Bernard Manning is a local boy – *the world awaits a formal apology. Millionaire students, or at least lucky or stupid ones, will, no doubt, not want to miss Manchester's many casinos. The more cultured will find many a fond hour to spend in some of the city's splendid galleries (The City Gallery, The Cornerhouse and The Whitworth). The Lowry Centre has a theatre and gallery with some of L S Lowry's most famous paintings. As for shopping, head for the Trafford Centre (the mega-mall of the north-west).*

Eating out: *Okay, there may not be many places in the running for the Michelin Guide but if you want it good, quick, tasty, cheap and slightly dirty you've come to the right place. Chinatown (the oldest in Europe) is stacked with noodleries and Rusholme has half-a-mile of end-to-end Indian restaurants. There's the usual artery-assault of kebab and burger dens but Pushplugs go to: Generation X; Amigo's (Oxford Road, Mexican); Barca (tapas); Sangam, Shezan (Indian); Green Room (hip veggie with slack service); Dalton Cafe (greasy spoon and then some).*

UNIVERSITY:

• Price of a pint of beer: £1.35 • Glass of wine: £2 • Can of Red Bull: £1.65
The Union's Academy is one of Manchester's main entertainment venues – no mean feat round here.

Bars: The Hop & Grape at the top of the Union building's also a music venue, and there's the Solem Bar, Lunar Bar, the Cellar and, of course, the Academy for beer-shooping.

Theatres: *The University's a honeypot for luvvies and dahlings,* staging close to 30 shows a year as well as some Fringe Festival triumphs. The Contact Theatre has its own resident professional company but also provides a versatile space for student shows. The John Thaw drama studio provides back-up; several black box spaces in the Union building get an airing too. There's an annual month-long student drama festival and competition.

Film: The *huge* film society shows four free films a week to its members, from megabuck thrill-rides to moodily lit, subtitled *ponce-a-thons.*

Music venues: In addition to the Academy rooms 1, 2 and 3 – which have recently held The Darkness, Kelly Osbourne, The Levellers, The Von Bondies, Franz Ferdinand, Space, Keane and Amy Winehouse among many, many others – live bands also play the Hop & Grape and some of the other bars. Imagine 100 gigs a semester. *Awesome.*

Clubbing: Two or three nights a week, chart and nostalgia efforts such as Tuesdays' Club Tropicana (80s not orange juice) and Horny, with occasional guest nights (eg. Megadog, Paul Oakenfold and the *near-legendary* Gatecrasher) *for more serious clubbers.*

Food: The University Food Court and the SU coffee bar provide an *unimaginative* selection of burgers, sandwiches and chips *but portions are substantial and no one complains about poor value for money.* The Cafe Express in the Union does light lunches. The bars also do grub. Food's available 24 hrs a day.

Other: The University officially advises students to bring black-tie with them – *the regularity of events can make hiring expensive.* Highlights include the Fresher's Ball and the Graduation Ball but there are departmental shindigs and hall events all year round.

In 1994 students at Portsmouth were housed temporarily in a naval barracks and subjected to naval discipline.

SOCIAL & POLITICAL

UNIVERSITY OF MANCHESTER UNION:

• 6 sabbaticals • Turnout at last ballot: 7% • NUS member

UMU is as political and inflammatory as a Thatcher sculpture made of turds – and they're damn proud of it, being eager to rouse a rabble or two for all sorts of ethical, equal opportunity and higher education issues. Although some students might be deterred by their zealous left-wing energy, most bask in glee at the awesome ents and flabbergasting facilities that the Union provides.

SU FACILITIES:

In the *impressively big* Union Building there are: general shop; secondhand bookshop; opticians; travel agency; advice centre; Endsleigh Insurance office; hairdresser; ticket agency; customised nightclubs; photocopiers; coffee and snack bar; two burger bars; four bars and a pub (with satellite TV); Barclays and Halifax ATMs; minibus hire; taxi freephone; video, vending and games machines; TV room; meeting and function rooms; societies resource centre; showers; sauna and solarium; photo booth.

CLUBS (NON-SPORTING):

Alpha Kappa Psi (business training); Anthropology; Arab League; Architecture; Bangladesh Students; Biological Sciences; Blade (surgery); Bob Dylan; Brechtian; Buddhist; Chess; Chinese; Choir & Orchestra; Circus Skills; Classics; Cocktail; Combined Studies; Cuba Solidarity; Drinking; Egyptian; English; First (international student integration); French; Friends of Palestine; Geographical; Geological; German; Gilbert & Sullivan; Cypriot; Heavy & Alternative Rock Music; Hindu; Hispanic; History; ILAM (Institute of Leisure & Amenity Management); Indian; Italian; Japanese; Japanimation; Jazz Funk Soul Coalition; Jazz Orchestra; Jeff Forshaw Appreciation; Korean; Laugh Out Loud; Linguistics; MSSA (architecture again); Muslim Social Scientists; MUSTV; Malaysian; Manseds Space; Marrow; Mauritian; Mediconcern (Islam & medicine); Medsin; Megalomaniacs; Middle Eastern; Nigerian; Omani; Pakistani; Panto; PG Law; Pharmaceutical; Reachout; Russian-speaking; Samba; Scout & Guide; Seventh Day Adventist; Sikh; Singapore; Sofab (accountancy & finance); Speech, Language Therapy & Audiology; Spotlights; Stop AIDS; Stop the War Coalition; Syrian; Recordings; Rock; Unisex; Warped (sci-fi); Wilderness Medicine; Wine; Young Jain Students. **See also Clubs tables.**

OTHER ORGANISATIONS:

Student Direct comes direct once a week, although there's a bundle of other papers and newsletters coming and going. Pout, for example, is a monthly women's mag. Fuse FM fills two six-week slots a year and airs all over the city – it's bagged 'Best Student Radio Station' at the National Student Awards. MUSTV gives wannabe Richards & Judys a place to parade their presenting skills. Manchester charity Rag banked a *whopping* £230,000 last year and a couple of community action groups do nice things with young kiddies and old biddies.

RELIGIOUS:

• 3 chaplains

There's a multi-faith chaplaincy and Muslim prayer room on campus. *The big Jewish Society is as much social as spiritual and is a strong political force.* The city caters for most creeds' needs: local cathedrals, churches, temples, mosques, synagogues and almost all the usual places of worship.

PAID WORK:

• Job bureau

The University runs a fully-staffed job shop in the foyer of the Union building, the Careers service posts part-time and vacation vacancies. *Because Manchester's such a big centre for entertainment there are lots of part-time jobs in bars, clubs, shops and restaurants – but, of course, there are lots of people chasing them. Still, the situation's better than in some other parts of the north-west.*

SPORTS

• Recent successes: rugby, football, hockey • BUSA Ranking: 12

Both *extensive and plush* facilities and the sheer size of the student body *mean heavy helpings of sporting stardom*. The Athletics Union offers a vast choice of muscle-stretching pastimes so *even the slobbiest slob in slobland should find something sporty to do*. In preparation for Manchester hosting the 2002 Commonwealth Games the University *buffed up its facilities something chronic, but charges also went up*.

SPORTS FACILITIES:

There's a variety of sporting spots spread around the University sites. The Wythenshawe Ground is the largest: 60 acres of playing fields (10 acres more are within 4 miles of campus), totalling 28 pitches for football, rugby and cricket, six tennis courts and a pavilion. Firs Athletic Ground at Fallowfield in South Manchester has 31 acres of playing fields, eight tennis courts, an all-weather pitch and a large pavilion, all near the main student halls of residence. Nearby, the Fallowfield Stadium has amenities for track and field events and a soccer pitch. The Armitage Centre provides a sports hall for indoor ball sports, a climbing room, sauna and solarium, two martial arts dojos, table tennis and a fitness room. The Sugden Sports Centre holds more indoor courts, plus a fitness suite and free weights training area, as well as tennis courts and more outdoor pitches. The new Commonwealth pool (the Manchester Aquatics Centre) is in the middle of Oxford Road and is home to the swimming teams. The city offers *everything the discerning* sportsperson could wish for, including the canal for rowing and canoeing, an ice rink, golf course, dry ski slope, a lake, lots of leisure centres and the surrounding hills and caves for those who like to take it outside.

SPORTING CLUBS:

Aikido; Capoeira; Dance; Darts; Falun Gong; Free Fall Parachute; Hiking; Hung Kuen Kung Fu; Table Football; T'ai Chi Chuan; Wakeboard & Waterski; Wing Tsun Kung Fu. **See also Clubs tables.**

ATTRACTIONS:

Three football teams have swear-words in their names: Arsenal, Scunthorpe and *F***in' Manchester United. Real Mancunians (like the brothers Gallagher) tend to back the underdogs and chant for the less successful, but less-despised Man City*. For Test & County Cricket, there's Old Trafford; basketball (The Giants) and ice hockey (The Storm) at the Manchester Evening News Arena; speedway at Broadhurst Park; rugby at Swinton, Salford and Trafford Borough; volleyball at Sale.

ACCOMMODATION

IN COLLEGE:

• Catered: 15% • Cost: £80 (38wks)
• Self-catering: 19% • Cost: £77 (35/38/51wks)
• First years living in: 76% • Insurance premium: £££££

Availability: With more than 9,700 accommodation places, Manchester can afford to house just under half its undergraduates and guarantees 1st years and international students a roof for a year or two. Most accommodation is within 2 miles of the campuses and is *immensely varied in size, style, catering and cleaning arrangements*. From traditional and modern halls of residence to smart, modern flats through to small suburban Victorian houses, *there's something to suit all domestic tastes*. Several halls are like little colleges and have their own JCRs (*like mini students' unions*), so there's a strong community spirit. Catered Hulme Hall is the oldest, *sexiest and comfiest* – with larger than average rooms – *so it attracts a lot of attention*. St Anselm's may be all-male but it does formal dinners every night of the week *and is the top choice for returning students. Oak House and Moberly Tower, by contrast, are regarded as lonely*. 243 residences are available for couples and families and the University also leases a fair few private houses for 2nd, 3rd and 4th years, postgrads and families (£40-65 a week).

EXTERNALLY:

• Ave rent: £48

Availability: *Finding a decent, non-extortionately priced house in Manchester is even easier than a Sunday morning. There's a huge supply of housing and quality goes up because of the competition. Fallowfield, Victoria Park and Withington are the student ghettos. Didsbury is a bit more suburban but quite accessible. Rusholme can be quite rough but is improving. Levenshulme, Hulme and Moss Side should be treated with caution, although some hardy souls do settle there. There's a whole clutch of decent rooms in private halls of residence –* check out www.manchesterstudenthomes.com

Housing help: Manchester Student Housing nudges homemakers in the right direction. They list vacancies, approve landlords and vet properties.

WELFARE

SERVICES:

• Lesbian/Gay/Bisexual Officer & Society • Ethnic Minorities Officer & Society
• Women's Officer & Society • Mature Students' Officer & Society
• International Students' Society • Postgrad Officer & Society • Disabilities Officer & Society
• Late-night minibus • Self-defence classes • Nightline • University Counsellors: 9
• Crime rating: !!!!!

Half the SU's sabbs have welfare responsibilities and, *overall, the service – centred on the Union Advice Centre – is very good. A night-bus runs students home between 6pm and midnight. The Union is particularly pro-lesbian, gay and bisexual students, who are a powerfully vocal force amongst the students (and, indeed, in Manchester generally).*

Health: A student health centre for broken bones and scabbed knees.

Disabilities: *Access is improving steadily,* with ramps and lifts for wheelchair users and a study skill room with specialist dyslexia software and support materials.

Drugs: *The hard core of the Manchester scene is ecstasy. This and harder drugs are readily available in the clubs, pubs and on the streets of Manchester. Students' attitudes to drugs vary enormously between individuals and although use of E, acid (LSD), cocaine and cannabis is perhaps more widespread than the norm, the pressure to partake is small. Needless to say, the University comes down hard on anyone it catches.*

FINANCE:

• Ave debt per year: £1,454

Fees: For international students, fees are £8,300 a year for Arts courses, £10,750 for scientists and almost 20 grand for wannabe doctors and dentists.

Support: Some short-term loans and helpful handouts from both the Union and the University. *A range of supportive bursaries will help take the sting off top-up fees – see their website for the full breakdown.*

University of Manchester, Institute of Science & Technology

see University of Manchester

Manchester Metropolitan University

- *Formerly Manchester Polytechnic.*
Manchester Metropolitan University, All Saints, Oxford Road, Manchester, M15 6BH
Tel: (0161) 247 2000 E-mail: enquiries@mmu.ac.uk Website: www.mmu.ac.uk
Manchester Metropolitan Students' Union, 99 Oxford Road, Manchester,M1 7EL
Tel: (0161) 247 1162 E-mail: mmsu@mmu.ac.uk Website: www.mmsu.com

GENERAL

The main bit of Manchester Metropolitan at All Saints is part of the biggest educational complex in Western Europe, along with its neighbour the University of Manchester. There are also sites further up the A34 in the Didsbury area and even further away in Cheshire. *This critical mass of students is one reason why Manchester is such a vibrant, artistic place. It's also why so many rock bands from the city have gone in for student favourites like wearing long overcoats and writing songs about topping yourself.* The University's other claim to fame is that they were banned from University Challenge for many years in the 70s after a team answered every question 'Lenin' or 'Marx' as a protest against Oxbridge teams being allowed to enter as individual colleges. Since being allowed back in the 90s they've done very well and, under Paxman's iron rule, no such society-threatening anarchy has occurred. **For general info about Manchester: see University of Manchester.**

Sex ratio (M:F): 43:57	**Founded: 1970**
Full-time u'grads: 20,725	**Part-time: 4,060**
Postgrads: 2,275	**Non-degree: 4,748**
Ave course: 3yrs	**Ethnic: 20%**
State:private school: 95:5	**Flunk rate: 17%**
Mature: 45%	**International: 7%**
Disabled: 380	**Local: n/a**

(left margin: 57% ... 43%)

ATMOSPHERE:
Ever since the so-called Madchester scene at the end of the 80s Manchester Met has gained students attracted by the party-till-you-puke atmosphere. However, nearly half of them are mature students who might feel that the entertainment is aimed too specifically at the young, groovy and beautiful.

SITES:
Business School: (5,000) $\frac{1}{2}$ mile from All Saints and one of the largest business schools in the UK.
John Dalton: (5,200) Based in Chester Street, 100 metres from All Saints. Students in the science, engineering and technology departments get to play with petri dishes and capacitors *(whatever they are).*
Hollings: (1,700 students – Clothing, Food, Hospitality & Tourism) 3 miles (give or take) from All Saints in Fallowfield. Linked with the main campus by *the busiest bus route in Europe.*
Didsbury: (4,000 – Health, Social Care, Education) About 5 miles from All Saints. *A leafy site with lively restaurants, bars and good transport links to the centre.*
Elizabeth Gaskell: (3,500) About a mile from the main site. Psychology, Speech Pathology and Health Care students, as well as Law and Community Studies.

Crewe: (3,300) 28 miles south of Manchester. Home to trainee teachers and research degrees. **Alsager:** (1,592) 34 miles from Manchester in a *leafy* country suburb near Stoke-on-Trent. A variety of arts and sports science courses. *Good sports facilities. Despite coach trips to Manchester, some students feel excluded from the MMU experience and those applying to University for the bright lights should check where they're going to be based. Crewe and Alsager are less than dazzling.*

MANCHESTER: see University of Manchester

TRAVEL: see University of Manchester

CAREER PROSPECTS:
• Careers Service • No. of staff: 15 full-time • Unemployed after 6mths: 8%

FAMOUS ALUMNI:
Terry Christian (ex-Word presenter and Oasis biographer); Steve Coogan, John Thompson (comedians); Bernard Hill, David Threlfall, Julie Walters (actors); Sarah Hardy (MP); Mick Hucknall (Simply Red *soul dwarf*); L S Lowry (painter); Min Patel (cricketer); Bryan Robson (ex-footballer, pundit and *deeply unsuccessful* manager).

FURTHER INFO:
• Prospectuses: undergrad; postgrad • Open days

ACADEMIC

Entry points: 60-300	Ave points: n/a
Applns per place: n/a	Clearing: n/a
No. of terms: 3	Length of terms: 12wks
Staff/student ratio: 1:21	Study addicts: 8%
Teaching: **	Research: ***

ADMISSIONS:
• Apply via UCAS

SUBJECTS:
Best: Acting.

LIBRARIES:
• 850,000 books • 3,285 study places
Seven libraries in all.

COMPUTERS:
• 3,000 workstations • 24-hr access
There are drop-in 'puters at most University sites, and all bedrooms in halls have internet access.

ENTERTAINMENT

THE CITY: see University of Manchester

UNIVERSITY:
• Price of a pint of beer: £1.50 • Glass of wine: £1.30 • Can of Red Bull: £1.65
Bars: The bars in the Union building are large, noisy, *popular* and open from 11.30am till chucking-out/falling-over time. There's a *smaller, quieter* affair at Didsbury, as well as Alsager's Brandies.

Theatres: The acting course has *great* facilities at the Capitol Theatre but the drama society's *not particularly strong*. Performance Art students at Crewe have their own studio.
Film: The University shows three films a week at the Horniman Theatre, free to members.
Clubbing: Three or four club nights a week in the K-Two bar in the Union's main building. Revamped to the tune of £500k, charges £3-4 and plays mainly indie, chart and retro. Friday's Double Vision *packs in the biggest crowd and there's more snakebites at Wednesday's sporty back-slap night than a camping trip in the Everglades.*
Music venues: K-Two's the site for gigs. Eagle Eye Cherrie, Trevor Nelson, Phats and Small, the Chemical Brothers, Dreem Team and Space have appeared in the last few years. MMU students also slope off to the University of Manchester for even bigger names.
Food: The University Refectory's open 11am-3pm *but the SU coffee bar has a more interesting selection* and is open round the clock. Blue, the SU sandwich shop, *does exciting things with bread* for less than £2.
Other: Departmental balls and the annual Athletic Union bash is *popular*.

SOCIAL & POLITICAL

MANCHESTER METROPOLITAN STUDENTS' UNION
• 7 sabbaticals • Turnout at last ballot: 5% • NUS member
The Union's main building on Oxford Road has variously been named after Nelson Mandela, Martin Luther King and Bruce Forsyth, which *gives some idea of the level of political commitment round these parts.* Party political allegiances aren't that strong and *the only thing that gets the students really worked* up is money (or lack of it).

SU FACILITIES:

Main building: two bars; two cafés; travel agency; shop; Barclays and Link ATMs; sandwich shop; vending/games machines; pool tables; photo booth; TV lounge; function rooms; recycling facilities.

CLUBS (NON-SPORTING):

Arts & Galleries; Capital; Dechen Buddhist; Muslim Heritage; Role-playing; Sikh. **See also Clubs tables.**

OTHER ORGANISATIONS:

Free student paper Pulp comes out fortnightly.

RELIGIOUS:

Multi-faith chaplaincy.
Religion in Manchester: see University of Manchester

PAID WORK: see University of Manchester
Steam, the University jobshop, has close links with local job networks.

SPORTS

• BUSA Ranking: 48
Keeping up with course work and having a quick half in the bar *takes precedence* over busting a gut on the track, but there are a *few* brave souls prepared to strain the odd ligament in pursuit of glory.

SPORTS FACILITIES:

Sports halls and the Sugden Sports Centre at All Saints. Didsbury has a sports hall too, as well as squash and tennis courts and weight training. There's also a sports hall and Astroturf at Alsager. The *best* outdoor facilities are at the MMU Cheshire sites, where there are 32 acres of playing fields and an outdoor swimming pool. Manchester Canal *comes in handy* for rowing, canoeing etc.

SPORTING CLUBS:

See Clubs tables.

ATTRACTIONS: see University of Manchester

ACCOMMODATION

IN COLLEGE:
- Catered: 3% • Cost: £80 (34wks)
- Self-catering: 20% • Cost: £49-80 (40-44wks)
- Insurance premium: £££££

Availability: All 1st years are guaranteed accommodation. Rents include insurance. Halls are at All Saints, Victoria Park, Whalley Range and further out in Didsbury. *They're all friendly places with cleaners fighting the good fight against botulism, cholera etc.*
Car parking: Some halls provide parking although permits may be necessary.

EXTERNALLY: see University of Manchester
The Accommodation & Welfare Service keep vacancy lists, check properties/contracts and attempts to resolve disputes. A joint housing service is run in conjunction with the University of Manchester.

WELFARE

SERVICES:
- Lesbian/Gay/Bisexual Officer & Society
- Women's Officer & Society • Mature Students' Officer & Society
- Disabilities Officer & Society
- Nightline • Crime rating: !!!!!

Health: The University has St Augustine's doctors' surgery at All Saints which deals with most minor, and even the odd major, health issues.
Disabilities: Ramps and lifts are provided in most places.

FINANCE:
- Ave debt per year: £3,654
- Access fund: £1,449,561 • Successful applications/yr: 2,431

Support: The SU can give loans of up to £50. Access to Learning funds are available from the University.

Manchester Polytechnic
see Manchester Metropolitan University

Metropolitan University
see Leeds Metropolitan University

Middlesex University

• *Formerly Middlesex Polytechnic.*
Middlesex University, North London Business Park, Oakleigh Road South, London, N11 1QS
Tel: (020) 8411 5000 E-mail: admissions@mdx.ac.uk Website: www.mdx.ac.uk
Middlesex University Students' Union, Trent Park, Bramley Road, London, N14 4YZ
Tel: (020) 8362 6450 Website: www.musu.mdx.ac.uk

GENERAL

Middlesex used to be a county, *now it only really exists as a postal district, a cricket team and an abstract band down the western side of London. The location of Middlesex University is equally non-specific.* It's based on four major campuses and four hospitals. The London sites range from Trent Park 15 miles from Central London to the Hendon Campus (centre for Business & IT) set in a residential area of North West London. Another campus has just opened in Dubai – *that's how widely dispersed this place is.*

Sex ratio (M:F): 41:59	Founded: 1973
Full-time u'grads: 13,625	Part-time: 4,490
Postgrads: 2,605	Non-degree: 507
Ave course: 3yrs	Ethnic: 40%
State:private school: 80:20	Flunk rate: 27%
Mature: 45%	International: 27%
Disabled: 309	Local: 57%

(left margin: 59% ... 41%)

ATMOSPHERE:
The glut of mature students puts a different emphasis on things and being so spread out means that many students can feel as though they're not exactly cheering for the same team. Students, especially Hendon kids, are loyal to their own campus rather than to the University as a whole. Being so far north of the river means it doesn't really feel like a London university – the bright lights are a long way away – but then, so is the bustle, the smog and the other chaotic hassles of the city centre. With facilities all over the place, it's hard to know what's available and, once discovered, it can be rather an expedition getting there.

SITES:
Cat Hill: (1,931 students – Textiles, Product Design, Electronic Arts) In Barnet, where facilities include a multigym. *Its only bar closed down, leaving students feeling a bit miffed that there's not really anywhere to go.*
Enfield: (3,084 students – Social Science, Health Studies) Includes ents venue the Forum.
Health Campus: (3,118 students – Nursing) Teaching facilities spread across four North London hospitals (*so it can hardly be called a campus*).
Hendon: (5,708 students – Business, Computing & IT) The largest site in terms of numbers, 13 miles from Tottenham. Now boasts The Sheppard Library – a *pant-moisteningly* £12m new Learning Resource Centre.
Trent Park: (3,520 students – Performing Arts, Product Design and Engineering, Computing Science, and others). A 60-acre country campus set amid woodland and meadows – the main building is an 18th-century style mansion. *Which is nice.*

LONDON: see University of London

TRAVEL: see University of London
Trains: Nearest rail/tube stations are Finsbury Park, Seven Sisters and Tottenham Hale (all Victoria line), Oakwood for the Piccadilly line. The University sites are in zones 3-5.

Car: Free and paid-for parking at or near most sites, *but finding a space can mean a bit of bunfight*. Permits are required to park on campus and 1st years aren't allowed to at all anymore.
Local: The 299, 298 buses run to Cat Hill roundabout. At Enfield, Southbury station or buses 121, 149, 191, 259, 307, 310A, 310B, 313 (to Ponders End bus garage) or 279, 363, 517 to Ponders End High Street. For Hendon campus use Hendon Central stop (Northern line) then bus 183 or walk. Tottenham's well-connected by bus and tube.
College: The University minibus runs from Oakwood station to Trent Park campus every 10 mins in term-time (useful for Cat Hill and Trent Park).
Bicycles: Some cycle lanes at most campuses.

CAREER PROSPECTS:

• Careers Service • No. of staff: 4 full/3 part • Unemployed after 6mths: 13%
All the usual gubbins including alumni mentors, computer-based guidance and seminars.

FAMOUS ALUMNI:

Adam Ant (singer); Ray Davies (Kinks mainman); Nick Harvey MP (LibDem); James Herbert (novelist); Alison Lloyd (Ally Capellino fashion house); Anish Kapoor (artist); Matthew Marsden (ex-Corrie actor); Helen Mirren (actress); Omar (singer); Stephen Seargeant (sailor); Rianna Scipio (TV presenter); Vivienne Westwood (designer); Johnny Vegas (funny man); Arabella Weir (writer of Does My Bum Look Big In This?, comedian).

FURTHER INFO:

• Prospectuses: undergrad; postgrad; some departments • Open days
Two booklets – Somewhere To Live and Welcome to Middlesex – are also available. E-mail openday@mdx.ac.uk for open day information.

ACADEMIC

Academic strengths are training and research in Science, Engineering, Medicine (Middlesex was first to offer a degree in Herbal Medicine), Law, Arts, Languages, Linguistics and Politics. Language teaching is available to any student who fancies dropping into the lab. Some students go for the easy life, but a strong contingent of studious types match the workload of a more traditional university. The work-ethic in the Art & Design Department is particularly hectic.

Entry points: 120-280	Ave points: 220
Applns per place: 8	Clearing: 30%
No. of terms: 2	Length of terms: 12wks
Staff/student ratio: 1:18	Study addicts: 14%
Teaching: **	Research: ***
Year abroad: n/a	Sandwich students: 6%
Firsts: 9%	2.2s: 39%
2.1s: 38%	3rds: 8%

ADMISSIONS:

• Apply via UCAS/GTTR for PGCE/NMAS for nursing

SUBJECTS:

Arts: 25%
Business School: 27%
Computing Sciences: 21%
Health & Social Science: 20%
Lifelong Learning & Education: 5%

Best: Art & Design; Dance, Drama & Cinematics; Education; History of Art, Architecture & Design; Maths, Statistics & Operational Research; Nursing; Other subjects allied to Medicine; Politics; Psychology; Philosophy.
Unusual: Games Design; International Business for China; Psychoanalysis (MA); TV Production.

LIBRARIES:

• 725,000 books • 2,600 study places • Spend per student: £££

COMPUTERS:
• 2,000 workstations • Spend per student: ££££
Courses are supported online by the OASIS intranet learning material resource.

OTHER LEARNING FACILITIES:
Language labs; drama studio; music rehearsal rooms; CAD lab; media centre; dance studios.

ENTERTAINMENT

THE CITY: see University of London

UNIVERSITY:

• Price of a pint of beer: £1.70 • Glass of wine: £2 • Can of Red Bull: £1.60
Bars: Four are run by the SU on separate campuses, three others by the University. The Enfield set-up is the biggest, but there are others at Trent Park and Hendon. Entertainments range from weekly club events to talent shows – *expect a lot of drag.*
Theatres: The Simmonds Theatre on the Trent Park campus hosts student productions.
Food: Most catering outlets are now operated by an external contractor.
Other: *Middlesex is big on balls.* The Summer extravaganza usually lasts 36 hours and there's a big freshers' do. Lures to lubrication in the *often under-used* bars include Bar FTSE where the beer prices fluctuate with demand.

SOCIAL & POLITICAL

MIDDLESEX UNIVERSITY STUDENTS' UNION:
• 6 sabbaticals • NUS member • Turnout at last ballot: 3%
In the past, the SU has been all about services, representation and ents, rather than tearing down barricades and guillotining the University administration. The (largely left-of-centre) students are becoming more politically active. The SU works hard on behalf of a very varied student body, but things can seem a bit disorganised and the facilities leave a lot to be desired.

SU FACILITIES:
The SU has facilities on all campuses. There are bars, shops, snack bars, a printing service, fax service, photocopier, cashpoints, launderette, games machines, photo booths, meeting rooms, TV lounges and a minibus for hire. *What's there isn't bad, but students would dearly love more events and more places to chill out.*

CLUBS (NON-SPORTING):
Life-drawing; Malaysian; Millenium; Poetry; Traditional Chinese Medicine. **See also Clubs table.**

OTHER ORGANISATIONS:
Mud, the SU mag, is *better than the previous efforts.*

RELIGIOUS:
At Hendon there's a Jewish society and a large Jewish community. See University of London for other places of worship around the city.

PAID WORK: see University of London
• Job bureau
There's some work to be found at the University and SU, which employ students to marshal car parks, steward at balls, help at Open Days and suchlike.The JobsOnline website has an online vacancy service.

SPORTS

- Recent successes: men's trampolining, table tennis, basketball, karate
- BUSA Ranking: 48

BUSA wins a-plenty, including the national shield for men's basketball. Long-running karate champions, *apparently*. *No arguments.*

SPORTS FACILITIES:

The University has five sports halls and three playing fields. There are indoor and outdoor tennis courts, a sauna and steamroom, six multigyms, swimming pools, a hockey and an all-weather pitch. There are real tennis courts at Hendon. Recent expansion has been helped by Lottery funding.

SPORTING CLUBS:

Table Tennis. **See also Clubs tables.**

ATTRACTIONS: see University of London

ACCOMMODATION

IN COLLEGE:

- Self-catering: 14% • Cost: £68-82 (40wks)
- First years living in: 55% • Insurance premium: £££

Availability: There's *not particularly lovable* accommodation for 95% of 1st years who want it, in one of the seven halls on separate campuses *a hop, skip and a tumble* from most of the teaching sites. Kitchens are shared between 14 or so students. There have been cases where students have had to live at one site when their course is taught at another. *Doh.* CCTV watches over the entry-phones and night porters watch over the CCTV.

Car parking: First years can't park on site, but later years can get their mitts on the few permits.

EXTERNALLY: see University of London

- Ave rent: £65

Availability: *Most students must find their own housing and a lot live at home. It's not difficult to find somewhere decent since the sites are far enough from the city centre. Palmers Green is popular and convenient. Wood Green and Turnpike Lane are also handy.*

Housing help: The University runs an accommodation service which helps students find places in shared or self-contained house and flats. It vets properties and keeps an approved landlord list. There's also an online housing service.

WELFARE

SERVICES:

- Lesbian/Gay/Bisexual Society • International Students' Officer • Postgrad Officer
- University counsellors: 2 full/6 part • SU counsellors: 1 full/9 part • Crime rating: !!!

The SU's responsible for welfare provision, *but hasn't really got the hang of advertising what's on offer*. University-run website www.mdx.ac.uk/24-7 is a *comprehensive hub of useful student info, welfare-based or otherwise. Poor provision for bewildered overseas students has left some feeling a bit lost.*

Health: Parents' group and first aiders on all campuses.

Crèches/Nursery: The University's crèche of choice caters for sprogs aged 6wks-5yrs.

Disabilities: *Major improvements in access over the last few years, mainly facilitated by the very impressive Able Centre. Induction loops installed, dyslexia support.*

FINANCE:
* Ave debt per year: £4,193
* Access fund: £1,200,000 • Successful applications/yr: 1,616 • Ave payment: £200-3,500

Support: Chancellor's scholarships are awarded for academic, sporting, community or cultural achievements. In addition, undergrads with 300 or more UCAS points are entitled to a substantial yearly cash carrot to keep up the donkeywork. Short-term loans are available to those in dire straits.

Middlesex Polytechnic

see Middlesex University

Milton Keynes

see De Montfort University

Moores University

see Liverpool John Moores University

Moray House

see University of Edinburgh

> The Guild Buildings at Liverpool house Europe's largest toilet complex.

Napier University

Napier Polytechnic see <u>Napier University</u>

Nene University College see <u>University College Northampton</u>

Newcastle University

Newcastle Poly see <u>Northumbria University</u>

Newcastle Polytechnic see <u>Northumbria University</u>

Newport, University of Wales

North East London Poly see <u>University of East London</u>

North East London Polytechnic see <u>University of East London</u>

University of North London (UNL) see <u>London Metropolitan University</u>

University College Northampton

Northumbria University

University of Northumbria at Newcastle see <u>Northumbria University</u>

Norwich see <u>University of East Anglia</u>

University of Nottingham

Nottingham Trent University

Nottingham Polytechnic see <u>Nottingham Trent University</u>

Napier University

• *Formerly Napier Polytechnic.*
(1) Napier University, Craighouse Campus, Craighouse Road, Edinburgh, EH10 5LG
Tel: (0500) 35 35 70 E-mail: info@napier.ac.uk Website: www.napier.ac.uk
Napier Students' Association (NSA), 12 Merchiston Place, Edinburgh, EH10 4NR
Tel: (0131) 229 8791 E-mail: nsa@napier.ac.uk Website: www.napierstudents.com
(2) Merchiston Campus, 10 Colinton Road, Edinburgh, EH10 5DT
Tel: (0500) 35 35 70
(3) Craiglockhart Campus, 219 Colinton Road, Edinburgh, EH14 1DG
(4) Canaan Lane Campus, 74 Canaan Lane, Edinburgh, EH10 4TB
(5) Comely Bank Campus, Crewe Road South, Edinburgh, EH14 2LD
(6) Sighthill Campus, Sighthill Court, Edinburgh, EH11 4BN

Napier is one of the *young upstarts*, growing at *a healthy lick*. Four of its five sites (the exception being Sighthill Court) are dotted around a *pleasant, mainly middle-class* area out in the west of the city. The Merchiston campus is home to the majority of students and is built around the 15th-century Tower of Merchiston, where logarithm inventor (and University namesake) John Napier was born in 1550. Over 5,250 Science, Engineering and Arts students are based in the modern building and there's a converted house for the Students' Association (NSA). **For general info on Edinburgh see** <u>**University of Edinburgh**</u>.

Sex ratio (M:F): 44:56	**Founded: 1992**
Full-time u'grads: 8,635	**Part-time: 2,446**
Postgrads: 1,095	**Non-degree: 150**
Ave course: 4yrs	**Ethnic: 6%**
State:private school: 86:5	**Flunk rate: 37%**
Mature: 53%	**International: 17%**
Disabled: 31	**Local: 60%**

ATMOSPHERE:

This is definitely not back-scratching old-boy territory. Students are practical and pragmatic: they're here to get a job rather than chucking themselves headlong into the social scene. Social bonds are even looser thanks to the disjointed nature of the University – there's a lot of pressure on resources and students spend a lot of their time dashing between the different sites, not really knowing where they're supposed to be. Relations with the surrounding community are cuddly as custard though, thanks to large proportion of local students and the University's policy of keeping local residents informed of any plans that might affect them and accepting feedback. *Not every university is that considerate.*

SITES:

Craighouse Campus: (1,828 students – Music, Communication Arts, Psychology and Sociology) A one-time Victorian loony-bin on top of one of the city's seven hills and a couple of miles from Merchiston in *trendy* Morningside. *Great views over the city.*

Craiglockhart Campus: (3,200 students – Central Services, Electrical Engineering, Maths, Computing) The 19th-century hospital building houses the main admin centre, a bit of accommodation and a few sports facilities. Following a spot of post-millennial redevelopment, the site acquired what may be a contender for *'Weirdest University Building in Britain'* – a 200-seat lecture theatre inside a giant titanium-clad egg. The Craiglockhart Nature Trail makes getting from here to Craighouse a particularly *pleasant* prospect.

Canaan Lane Campus: (1,651 students – School of Acute & Continuing Care Nursing and some courses from the School of Community Health, eg. Complementary Therapy, Herbal Medicine) Within the grounds of Astley Ainslie Hospital near Morningside.

Comely Bank: (1,038 students) Situated in the north of the city and is an additional base for the Faculty of Health & Life Sciences.

Sighthill: This *behemoth of a building* – a six-storey tower block with a few extra bits (sports dome, NSA centre) tacked on the sides – is 3 miles east of Merchiston at the city limits and is mainly the home of Student Support Services.

EDINBURGH: see <u>University of Edinburgh</u>

TRAVEL: see <u>University of Edinburgh</u>

Trains: The closest stations are Haymarket (Merchiston, Redwood House); Waverley (Marchmont); Slateford (Craiglockhart); Wester Hailes or South Gyle (Sighthill).

Cars: A small number of permits are available to park on University premises, although the spaces available vary from site to site.

College: The college buses might be described as *compact and relaxed*. *Small and late* is closer to the truth.

Bicycles: Lockable bike racks at all campuses. *Be warned, though, hills are hilly.*

CAREER PROSPECTS:

• Careers Service • No. of staff: 10 full • Unemployed after 6mths: 11%
The Careers Advisory Service keeps an *arsenal* of job-hunter's resources, hosts job fairs, offers practice interview sessions and one-on-one guidance, and provides vacancy updates by bulletin board, e-mail and newsletter.

FAMOUS ALUMNI:

Colin Baxter (photographer); Jane Franchi, Bill McFarlan, Malcolm Wilson, Cathy McDonald and Jim White (all Scottish TV presenters); Mark Goodier (radio DJ); Greg Kane (of *has-beens* Hue & Cry); Derrick Lee (Scottish rugby player); Kenny MacAlpine (Superr aturals); Alison Paton (Siren the Gladiator); Lynne Ramsay (film director).

FURTHER INFO:

• Prospectuses: undergrad; postgrad; international; part time; some departments • Open days
Napier produces a range of other publications and pamphlets, including the *straight to the point* Show Me the Money finance guide and a guide to accommodation.

A C A D E M I C

The courses are *generally* geared towards the vocational (*lots* of placements and work experience) and *towards turning students into 9-5ers. Students doing less than 21 hours of study a week may have forgotten to turn over their timetables.*

Entry points: 200-240	Ave points: 200
Applns per place: 4	Clearing: 15%
No. of terms: 3	Length of terms: 15wks
Staff/student ratio: 1:15	Study addicts: 89%
Teaching: ***	Research: ***
Year abroad: 1%	Sandwich students: 25%
Firsts: 10%	2.2s: 44%
2.1s: 44%	3rds: 3%

ADMISSIONS:

• Apply via UCAS/CATCH for nursing
The University judges each application individually *and isn't a stickler for published requirements.*

SUBJECTS:

Arts & Social Sciences: 15%	Engineering & Computing: 23%
Business School: 36%	Health & Life Sciences: 25%

Best: Building; Cellular & Molecular Biology; Civil Engineering; Hospitality; Mass Communications; Maths; Organisational Biology; Statistics.

LIBRARIES:

• 220,320 books • 1,300 study places • Spend per student: £
Eight libraries. The *biggest* are at Merchiston (which has an *interesting* war poetry special collection) and Craiglockhart.

COMPUTERS:

• 1,034 workstations • 24-hr access • Spend per student: ££££
The Jack Kilby Computing Centre at Merchiston, *which bags architectural accolades by the hatful has the bulk of 'puters.*

OTHER LEARNING FACILITIES:
Digital language learning facilities at Craiglockhart; Sports Science labs, Adaptive Technology Centre and CAD labs at Merchiston; music studio and IT labs at Craighouse. There are several media centres *dotted around too.*

ENTERTAINMENT

THE CITY: see University of Edinburgh

UNIVERSITY:

• Price of a pint of beer: £1.75 • Glass of wine: £1.70 • Can of Red Bull: £1
Bars: Bar Twelve at Merchiston has pool, karaoke, quizzes, games, satellite TV and regular DJ sets every weeknight *(but not all at once)*. BaseRate at Craiglockhart is primarily a daytime stop-off *but will roll out the barrels of an evening if asked very nicely.* Bars shut at weekends, except for Twelve (open during the day on Saturdays).
Theatres: The drama society puts on a few productions and strolls over to the Fringe each year.
Film: There's a film society but it relies on local screens for entertainment.
Clubbing: Thursday (Hijack) and Friday (Logarhythms) nights at Twelve are the major party nights.
Food: There's food on offer in Twelve, BaseRate and from the refectories across all the other sites.
Other: Sports and society balls light up the social calendar *every so often.*

SOCIAL & POLITICAL

NAPIER STUDENTS' ASSOCIATION (NSA):
• NUS member

SA FACILITIES:
NSA's converted house and corporate headquarters at Merchiston Avenue has a bar/snack bar, common room, print shop, job shop, general shop, photocopier, DTP facilities, games rooms, pool table, juke box, games machines, vending machine, function room and car park. Also shops, pool tables and bars at Sighthill. There's another purpose-built SU with bar at Craiglockhart.

CLUBS (NON-SPORTING):
Arts & Culture; Celtic Supporters; Design; Duke of Edinburgh; Film Society. **See also Clubs tables.**

OTHER ORGANISATIONS:
Veritas is the *high-minded (in name at least)* student paper.

RELIGIOUS:
• 12 chaplains (multi-faith)
Two prayer rooms.
Religion in Edinburgh: see University of Edinburgh

PAID WORK: see University of Edinburgh
• Job bureau
NSA runs a net-based job bank and the Careers Advisory Service lends a hand by posting temporary or course-related vacancies.

SPORTS

• Recent successes: none • BUSA Ranking: 63
Sports facilities *aren't much cop and the University doesn't seem too bothered – it's only a game, innit? – although there's still a ripple of enthusiasm across the campuses.*

SPORTS FACILITIES:
Sports Centre at Sighthill with: two sports halls; multigym; a netball and two basketball courts; aerobics studio; squash courts. Special discount deals with Edinburgh Leisure for those who join a sports un on club. For Edinburgh's attractions see University of Edinburgh

SPORTING CLUBS:
American Football; Clay Pigeon; Ju-Jitsu; Kayak; Shooting; Sub-aqua; Waterpolo. **See also Clubs tables.**

ATTRACTIONS: see University of Edinburgh

ACCOMMODATION

IN COLLEGE:
• Self-catering: 8% • Cost: £65 (38wks)
• First years living in: 75% • Insurance premium: ££
Availability: 1st years living outside Edinburgh get preference for accommodation – if they apply before the deadline. That means that about 10% of students who want accommodation can't get it. All flats are single-sex and there are six developed for disabled use. Everything's *within walking distance* of the city and University or has *good* public transport links. *It's not the lap of luxury,* though – none of the rooms have en-suite facilities.
Car parking: Parking requires a permit but *that doesn't guarantee a spot.*

EXTERNALLY: see University of Edinburgh
• Ave rent: £70
Housing help: Three accommodation advisers do their best to match students with pads, warn them off dodgy landlords and offer legal advice.

WELFARE

SERVICES:
• Lesbian/Gay/Bisexual Society • University counsellors: 3 part • Crime rating: !
NSA, University counsellors and chaplains are available to help with any welfare problems. Counselling service for international and minority ethnic women students.
Health: Students are encouraged to register with a local practice when they arrive. The Health & Life Science campus has sessions on aromatherapy, reflexology, alternative medicine and herbal clinics.
Disabilities: *Although some buildings were built before disabilities were invented, the University keeps an eye on potential access problems and does a bit to overcome them.* Six rooms have been adapted and there are ramps, loops and the Adaptive Technology Centre, which provides specialist equipment, training, software and advice. There's a special needs co-ordinator and a dyslexia support adviser.

FINANCE:
• Ave debt per year: £1,040
• Access fund: £300,000 • Successful applications/yr: 2,000 • Ave payment: £100-1,200
Support: Scottish students can also apply for the young student's bursary (a grant of £2,100/yr for under-25s from low-income families). Also: a mature student's bursary (means-tested, up to £2,000/yr), hardship loans (up to £500/year) and a childcare fund, which grants up to £200 per child per month towards registered childcare costs.

Napier Polytechnic
see Napier University

Nene University College
see University College Northampton

Newcastle University

University of Newcastle upon Tyne, 6 Kensington Terrace, Newcastle upon Tyne, NE1 7RU
Tel: (0191) 222 5594 E-mail: enquiries@ncl.ac.uk Website: www.ncl.ac.uk
The Union Society, King's Walk, Newcastle upon Tyne, NE1 8QB
Tel: (0191) 239 3900 E-mail: union.society@ncl.ac.uk Website: www.unionsociety.co.uk

GENERAL

No, the Angel of the North isn't Alan Shearer. It's the giant, rusty winged sculpture that gazes over the A1 as it hurtles past Newcastle upon Tyne, the unofficial capital of the North East and, *as far as many Geordies are concerned, the world*. It's the biggest city on offer between Leeds and Edinburgh and *like most cities (and indeed most coins), it has two sides: fond memories of Sting & The Police on one, ambivalent feelings toward Ant & Dec on the other. It's magnificent, cosmopolitan and happening but, like any city this beefy, it has its poverty-stricken, shabbier areas too*. Its outer areas include the *run-down, like Byker* (of 'Bykah Groahve' fame) and the *luscious and leafy, like Jesmond, known for its nightlife*. The heart of the city is peppered with *inspiring* Georgian and Victorian architecture amid *nauseating* 60s shopping centres. There are two universities in town: Northumbria University and the University of Newcastle upon Tyne, a classic redbrick campus on a 45-acre site in the city centre. The buildings are mostly 19th-century, formed into *attractive* blocks arranged around paved squares, but there are also some *drab* concrete additions that, *while not quite turning the stomach, certainly give it a bit of a jolt.*

Sex ratio (M:F): 48:52	**Founded: 1834**
Full-time u'grads: 11,680	**Part-time: 1,170**
Postgrads: 3,770	**Non-degree: n/a**
Ave course: 3yrs	**Ethnic: 6%**
State:private school: 67:33	**Flunk rate: 7%**
Mature: 11%	**International: 22%**
Disabled: 379	**Local: 23%**

ATMOSPHERE:

The campus is buzzing and friendly but prone to cliquey-ness. Despite the city's rough diamond image, the student body is predominantly middle-class, leading to a bit of a 'posh rich kid' label, especially as far as students at Northumbria University *are concerned, and a traditional rivalry with other posh rich kid* University of Durham *nearby. Mixing between universities and, in turn, with locals isn't uncommon though – partly due to the large number of community action schemes operating from the Union – but the weekend is still largely ruled by locals when it comes to nightlife. The cost of living is quite low, so students can almost afford to enjoy Newcastle like real people do.*

NEWCASTLE UPON TYNE:
- Population: 259,600 • City centre: 0 miles • London: 255 miles
- Edinburgh: 94 miles • Manchester: 112 miles
- High temp: 19 • Low temp: 0 • Rainfall: 54

Newcastle's spirits are far from being moistened by the city's failure to scoop the title 'City of Culture 2008' – not that it means much anyway – and are continuing their thriving cultural renaissance regardless. It's appeared on more than one 'world's best party city' top tens and *its reputation for a kicking nightlife is growing fast.* The past few years of development – bringing with them the *great* glass armadillo that is The Sage musical centre, the iconic Millennium Bridge, a *growing* theatre scene, the *Tate-rivalling* Baltic art gallery and the imminent Dancehouse – *have helped drag the city from the shadows of the black and white stripes. The fog on the Tyne no longer belongs to Paul Gascoigne, thank God. It's now trendy, funky, artistic, musical and all the other nice things people usually say when being nice about London. And those who believe that the only way to judge a city is by the strength of its gay scene should stroll across Times Square in the heart of the Centre for Life. This city may be packing the pink, but not everything is rosy.* Crime and unemployment still feature on the urban landscape, although they no longer dominate and even in the dodgiest areas the atmosphere is much less Irvine Walsh than it used to be. The Metro Centre at nearby Gateshead is still *pretty humungous, if no longer* Europe's largest shopping centre. *Most people have yet to care.*

TRAVEL:
Trains: The station's about 10 mins walk from the city centre, 2 by Metro. Direct lines to London, Sheffield, Edinburgh and all over the country.
Coaches: Several coach companies, including Clipper, Blue Line and National Express, offer services to the above destinations and many more.
Car: The A1 hooks round the edge of the city. The A69, A692, A696, A189 and A19 *are all useful.* There's on-street meter parking around campus.
Air: Newcastle Airport, 6 miles from the centre, has inland and European flights.
Hitching: *Good prospects on routes out of the city, especially the A1.*
Local: Bus routes through the city are regular, *reliable and cheap, although travelling the compact city centre can be more of a lurch than a breeze. Walking is the easiest way to get around.*
University: A minibus (priority for women) takes students home from the library, school and Union building, 70p a trip. There's also a public transport discount scheme available to students.
Underground: *The world's best underground system may be Tokyo's, but Newcastle's Metro is right up there – clean, cheap, reliable and easy to use. It serves all the essential* student areas and has now been extended to Sunderland (£4 rtn).
Bicycles: *The city's hilly and full of traffic. There aren't many places to leave bikes off-campus without the danger of finding it smaller and with fewer wheels than when you left it, but things are steadily improving.*

CAREER PROSPECTS:
- Careers Service • No. of staff: 28 full/2 part • Unemployed after 6mths: 4%

Newcastle attracts some *fairly big* employers to *sift through its graduate output.* The careers service has an online database and e-mails vacancies. Regular CV and application form workshops.

FAMOUS ALUMNI:

Kate Adie (BBC flak-jacketed *überbabe*); Rowan Atkinson (comedian, who reportedly spent three years in his room); Ed Coode (Olympic rower); Bryan Ferry (Roxy Music); Richard Hamilton (artist); Debbie Horsfield (TV writer); Miriam Stoppard (TV doctor); Paul Tucker (Lighthouse Family).

SPECIAL FEATURES:
- The Enterprise Centre puts entrepreneurial students in touch with mentoring companies, who also provide the odd lecture, seminar or workshop.

• The University has *ambitious* blueprints for a 'cultural quarter' – a £40m project with a museum, art gallery and playhouse.
• *World-renowned architect* Sir Terry Farrell has planned the redesign of the University's main entrance.

FURTHER INFO:

• Prospectuses: undergrad; postgrad; departmental; international; alternative; video
• Open days
Personalised prospectus can be downloaded from the web. Printed copies can also be ordered from the main e-mail address. Two Visit Days a year and subject area open days after application.

ACADEMIC

Newcastle acquits itself admirably in the majority of its 200+ degree programmes, although things go particularly swimmingly in English, Maths and Sciences. It's also been commended for 'technology transfer within businesses' (whatever that means). A recent departmental restructure has spread the 27 schools into three faculties as opposed to the previous seven – whether this makes any practical difference to anyone is a different matter.

Entry points: 260-360	Ave points: n/a
Applns per place: 6	Clearing: 6%
No. of terms: 2	Length of terms: 15wks
Staff/student ratio: 1:7	Study addicts: 20%
Teaching: ****	Research: *****
Year abroad: 1%	Sandwich students: n/a
Firsts & 2.1s: 69%	2.2s & 3rds: 31%

260-360 *POINTS*

ADMISSIONS:

• Apply via UCAS
Applications for Medicine or Dentistry should be sent off early, usually by the preceding October. Mature students without recognised qualifications are assessed on an individual basis.

SUBJECTS:

Humanities & Social Science: 54%   Science, Agriculture & Engineering: 28%
Medical Science: 18%
Best: Agriculture; Archaeology; Biology; Chemical Engineering; Civil Engineering; Classics & Ancient History; Dentistry; Economics; Education; Electrical & Electronic Engineering; Fine Art; Linguistics; Marine Technology; Maths & Statistics; Medicine; Modern Language; Molecular Biosciences; Physics; Physiology; Politics; Psychology; Town & Country Planning & Landscape.

LIBRARIES:

• 1,000,000+ books • 3,000 study places • Spend per student: £££££
The comfy, well-stocked Robinson Library has a Relative Humidity of around 50%, *which may be part of the reason* Newcastle's library services have three charter marks for excellence. *Who knows?* Anyhow, it's the only UK university library that does. There's also the Walton Library for Law. *We can't tell you the humidity there. Sorry.*

COMPUTERS:

• 1,500 workstations • 24-hr access • Spend per student: £££££
45 computer clusters around the University, not all 24-hr. Some halls have IT clusters too, *but there's a general feeling that more workstations and a designated computing centre wouldn't go amiss.* A wireless network is on the technocards and laptops have started appearing on the grass.

OTHER LEARNING FACILITIES:
Aside from the 55 – *yes*, 55 – language labs (40 languages available for anyone and their dog to learn), rehearsal rooms, photo studio and darkroom, TV centre, art gallery and drama studio, Newcastle has several subject-specific facilities, including a marine laboratory, a biology field station, its own farms and 'Bernicia', a research boat on the Tyne. Most recently landed are the £11m cancer research centre and the *eco-licious* £19m environment and e-science institute. Currently in construction is the £4m Culture Lab – nothing to do with growing mould in petri dishes – it's a *swanky* new multimedia facility, and will be *digitised up to the eyeballs.*

ENTERTAINMENT

NEWCASTLE:
• Price of a pint of beer: £1.90 • Glass of wine: £2.50 • Can of Red Bull: £2
Newcastle is as stuff-stuffed a city as the next and rivals Leeds, Manchester and almost London when it comes to music, clubs, pubs and restaurants. Any bar worth its salt, tequila and lemon will have a free 'listings mag or six on the counter.

Cinemas: There's a ten-screener in the Gate Complex (NUS discounts), 5 mins from the city centre, the *excellent* Tyneside Arts Cinema (four screens) and the *diddy wee* Side Cinema on the Quayside – *all within walking distance of the University*. There's also a multiplex at the Metro Centre, *though this isn't used much by students as it's further out*.
Theatres: Newcastle has plenty of theatres *ranging from great stages to smaller poncing-boards. Pushplugs: The Theatre Royal (touring RSC and West End shows); The Playhouse (RSC seasons, local prods); and The Live Theatre, which has been pumped full of cash to produce innovative new writing.*
Pubs: Many, many pubs, some *rougher than students might like*, but plenty serve a welcome brew, not least a pint of the ubiquitous Newcastle Brown (aka 'Newky Brown' or 'Dog'). *The Hancock opposite campus gets points for convenience but medics prefer their traditional haunt, North Terrace. Diverse and atmospheric, Trent House is the coolest pub in Newcastle – it's official. Revolution's range of flavoured vodkas is a big draw, and the Cluny in Byker provides live music and a welcoming atmosphere. Bar 55 and the Attic are the places to go to feel important after lottery wins. Quayside has plenty of sexy quaff-houses.*
Clubbing: *A huge part of Geordie life and, accordingly, there's enough clubs to make seals extinct. Pushplugs (among others): Tiger Tiger; Foundation; Blue Bambu; Mood; World HQ; Sea; Baja Beach Club. Visitors to Legends, Planet Earth or the Riverside should leave pride, dignity and motor skills at home.*
Music venues: *The Metro Radio Arena has big names on its posters, but the Cluny gets a few cult heroes.* The new Norman Foster-designed Sage Gateshead Music Centre on the South Bank houses the Northern Sinfonia and the Folkworks programme (involved with the University's BA Folk & Traditional Music course). *Sneaking into* <u>Northumbria University</u>'s *Union isn't unheard of, either.*
Other: Comedy is common in various bars and pubs. *Try the Hyena Café for starters.*
Eating out: *Newcastle's got everything from classy bistros to bacterial blubber in a bun. Somewhere in between, Pushplugs: Rumpolis; Marco Polo's & Don Vito's (Italian); Cradlewell (all-day breakfasts); King Lau (Chinese). The Playhouse and the Tyneside Coffee Rooms are the places to pose and Stowell Street is good for Chinese food.*

UNIVERSITY:
• Price of a pint of beer: £1.60 • Glass of wine: £1.80 • Can of Red Bull: £1.50
Bars: The Union Building houses six bars, all open six days a week. The Mens Bar is not for men only, but named after the University motto, 'Mens agitat molem' *('subterranean rodents create havoc in the gents')*. However, it does retain a pretty laddish, sporty atmosphere. The Cochrane Lounge is *quieter, comfy* and smoke-free. The Global has a continental café style and doubles as a small-gig venue. The Green Room, Beats and the Bassment are mainly for weekend clubs and gigs. *They're all dark.*
Theatres: The drama group, NUTS, does lots of plays and is frequently to be found at the Edinburgh Fringe or in the campus Playhouse theatre.

Film: The film society (£4 membership) shows two weekly flicks, *generally recent arthouse hits (if that's not an oxymoron).*

Music venues: The Global and the Bassment have brought in some *huge hitsters:* The Darkness, Keane, Damien Rice, The Zutons and Snow Patrol have all paid a visit.

Clubbing: The Bassment's big enough to bring in the big guns, including Groove Armada, Groove Rider and DJ Yoda. Friday's Solution *is the cream of Union club nights.* Top national nights also get monthly outings, including: Brighton Beach (indie, non-cheesy retro); Turbulence (drum'n'bass); and Universal (*straight-friendly* gay night).

Comedy/Cabaret: The Global has fortnightly comedy. Highlights have been Perrier-darling Daniel Kitson, Andre Vincent and Eddie Brimson.

Food: The Bassment looks *like a prison canteen but is actually quite hot stuff with the, um, hot stuff.* The Martin Luther King is *small, bright,* smokeless and veggie. The other bars all do their share of the cooking too, but the Cochrane Lounge boasts the cheapest coffee going.

Other: At least four balls a year plus a five-day Freshers' binge and a Christmas Ball for each department. The Cochrane Lounge's regular quiz night *gets busy.* Arcane, the termly charity extravaganza, burns the midnight oil well beyond midnight.

SOCIAL & POLITICAL

THE UNION SOCIETY:

• 6 sabbaticals • Turnout at last ballot: 20% • NUS member

Newcastle's SU is as active and frantic as its bar staff on a Friday night. The colossal Union building is buzzing with entertainments and facilities and the ever-growing society lists offer something for everyone, no matter how twisted a fun fetish they may have. Relations with the University are good, but that doesn't matter one jot really since the SU is completely independent in every way and stands firmly on its own two feet, jumping up and down on its substantial piles of cash. Politics rarely goes beyond the awareness campaign stage, but who cares? Look! Another party! Woohoo!

SU FACILITIES:

An entire floor of the Union building's devoted to franchise outlets, including bookshops and a ticket agency. In addition: six bars; café bar; eight pool tables; four meeting rooms; minibus hire; van hire; Endsleigh Insurance office; ATMs; photocopiers; fax and printing services; photo booth; payphones; advice centre; TV lounge; juke boxes; gaming and vending machines; dry cleaning.

CLUBS (NON-SPORTING):

Accountancy; Acoustic Music; Anglo-Japanese; Agricultural; Archaeology; Architectural; Backgammon; Bioscience; Breakfast Club (break-dancing); Buddhist Meditation; Cat (catwalk society); Changeringers (bell-ringing); Chemical Enginering; Civil Engineering; Chinese; Clubbing; Combined Honours; Computing & LAN Gaming; Culture Club (museum visits and such, not Karma Chameleons); Drivers; Europe; Expedition; Friends of Palestine; Fringe (Edinburgh drama); Gilbert & Sullivan; Guinness & Real Ale; Ibero (Latin American); Indonesian; Jazz; Latin & Ballroom Dancing; Link (St John's Ambulance); MAD (adventure holidays); Malaysian; Mauritian; Maypole; Mechanical Engineering; Music; Nomad; Norwegian; Pakistan; Questlands (role play); Russian; Singapore; Scottish Dance; Socrates; South Asian; STAR (Student Action for Refugees); Stop the War Coalition; Swing Dance; Thai; Traditional Music; Wilderness Medics; Wind Band. **See also Clubs tables.**

OTHER ORGANISATIONS:

The weekly paper, The Courier, has the free Pulp entertainment and listings magazine tucked into it. Newcastle Student Radio's run jointly with Northumbria University and echoes around the city on FM twice a year for a month at a time. The charity Rag *regularly endangers lives for cash,* netting £8,000 in 2004, but SCAN (Student Community Action Newcastle) maintains *a much higher profile.* With around 5,000 members, it has its own fundraising shop and about 60 do-gooding projects on the go. Additionally, there's the university 'Students into Schools' programme, *where student tutors help local schoolkids become as clever as them.*

RELIGIOUS:

• 5 chaplains (CofE, RC, Baptist, Methodist, URC), 2 rabbis

The chaplaincy maintains links with various Christian churches in the city, as well as appointing visiting Orthodox and Reform Jewish, Muslim and Buddhist worship-leaders. The building has a common room, quiet room and a kitchen. There's a mosque on campus. Most faiths will find a *godshop* in Newcastle. If not, the Tyne & Wear conurbation will have something.

PAID WORK:

• Job bureau

The Union runs a jobshop which also monitors conditions and pay. Last year, it posted over 1,000 vacation and term-time vacancies. Registering students receive an induction on job-related issues. There are opportunities to stock the coffers in bars, shops, the theatres and *no end of soul-destroying* work at the Metro Centre.

S P O R T S

• Recent successes: volleyball, men's & women's rugby, football, badminton, canoe polo, fencing, skiing • BUSA Ranking: 17

Newcastle's no stranger to the BUSA league tables and the Athletics Union (which has its own sabbatical officer) *pumps hundreds of thousands into University sport each year. The downside is that, while the ethos is supposedly 'sports for all', there can be a bit of an elitist streak in the more popular sports which discourages wide participation. A new £5.5m indoor sports and dance facility is now up and running /sweating, and is part of the cunning plan* to make Newcastle one of the country's best universities for sports.

SPORTS FACILITIES:

On campus, there are facilities in the Claremont Sports Hall (sports hall, four squash courts). There are outdoor amenities on five sites: Heaton (medic's playing fields); Close House (10 miles out, 18-hole golf course, hockey pitches); Cochrane Park (playing fields); Longbenton (more playing fields); and Newburn Boat House on the Tyne for rowers. *There are 50 acres of playing fields in total, covering everything it's possible to do on grass except croquet.* Basic membership of the sports facilities costs £28, £44 including use of the local pool, £61 including health and fitness, and towering to £83 for use of the golf course. The city has many other leisure facilities, including an ice rink, dry ski slope and a lake. The Northumbrian countryside has enough caves and hills to keep outdoor-types exhausted.

SPORTING CLUBS:

10-Pin Bowling; Aikido; American Football; Boxing; Canoe Polo; Caving; Cheerleading; Clay Pigeon Shooting; Ice Hockey; Ju-Jitsu; Kick Boxing; Lacrosse; Life Saving; Mountain Biking; Parachute; Polo; Rifle; Rowing; Surf; Table Tennis; Thai Boxing; Ultimate Frisbee; Water Polo; Windsurfing. **See also Clubs tables.**

ATTRACTIONS:

Newcastle United's Toon Army of fans aren't the most self-effacing in the country and chances are even the most unsporty will recognise the stripy soldiers. The Falcons Rugby Club were much more low-profile – until people became aware that HRH Jonny Wilkinson, lord of the drop-kick, plays for them. The Newcastle Eagles basketball squad and the Vipers ice hockey team have dedicated followers too.

A C C O M M O D A T I O N

IN COLLEGE:

• Catered: 13% • Cost: £82 (38wks)
• Self-catering: 19% • Cost: £45-75 (38wks)
• First years living in: 79% • Insurance premium: £££

Availability: Housing's guaranteed to all 1st years coming from outside the city (and who meet the deadline) and there's usually enough left to cram in some locals and latecomers. Most halls are close to the University, but Henderson Hall (catered) is 3 miles away and *pretty quiet with it.* St Mary's is *way out* in Fenham, *which is a bit of a bummer if your flatmates turn out to be knobheads. The large and inescapably 60s Castle Leazes catered halls are the most popular and sociable, thanks to the on-site bar. Leazes Parade is similar, but smaller.* The self-catered flats on Richardson Road *aren't going to win architecture awards and can get a little claustrophobic, but at least they're only a short walk away from campus.* Most halls have launderettes and TV rooms, and computing facilities. The catered housing generally has a bar, shop, snooker and table tennis rooms, *although the kitchen facilities are unlikely to result in anything more gourmet than tea and toast.* No one has to share a room, and there's no single-sex accommodation. Some flats are available for couples and families.

Car parking: Parking's free, *space is tight* and some sites require permits. *More distant halls have better parking.*

EXTERNALLY:
• Ave rent: £53 • Living at home: 6%

Availability: *There's not much problem finding housing in Newcastle and students can afford to be choosy – as well as cautious since plenty of rip-off merchants are all too happy to take advantage of virgin house-hunters. Stick to accredited channels. Jesmond has the advantage of proximity to bars and fun, but its prices are inflating faster than Jordan's boobs.*

Heaton's cheaper but doesn't have much going on except for takeaway fans. Sandyford's small, but somewhere between the two when it comes to balancing the rent/nightlife ratio. Fenham isn't too bad, though its houses aren't as safe as the proverb says and Benwell and Scotswood shimmer in the twilight with the light from burning cars, so students try to avoid. Parking's restricted around the city centre and many find it too much effort keeping a car.

Housing help: The University Accommodation Service lists approved houses and flats, runs a landlord accreditation scheme and provides help, advice and contract guidance.

W ELFARE

SERVICES:
• Lesbian/Gay/Bisexual Officer & Society • Women's Officer & Society
• Mature Students' Officer & Society • International Students' Officer & Society
• Postgrad Officer & Society • Disabilities Officer & Society • Late-night/Women's minibus
• Nightline • University counsellors: 5 full • Crime rating: !!!

The Union has two welfare sabbaticals and *numerous* officers with specific responsibilities. All advice comes from trained personnel.

Health: On campus there are NHS doctors, a dentist and optician. Medical and dental practices abound throughout Newcastle, in particular in student suburbs like Jesmond and Heaton.

Women: Free alarms, condoms and sanitary products are available from the Union Welfare Officer, who also has responsibility for Women's Welfare.

Disabilities: Many Victorian buildings limit access, but there have been a number of *useful* adaptations, especially in the Union Building, which is now accessible on every level. Adapted housing's available for mobility- and hearing-impaired students. The University's disabilities unit has a trained dyslexia adviser who provides study skills support.

FINANCE:
• Ave debt per year: £1,362
• Access fund: £598,166

Support: There are up to 200 £2,000 bursaries for financially disadvantaged but academically talented students. The South African Scholarship provides funds for a South African student to study at Newcastle.

Newcastle Poly

see Northumbria University

Newcastle Polytechnic

see Northumbria University

Newport, University of Wales

- *Formerly University of Wales College, Newport.*
- *Part of the University of Wales.*

University of Wales, Newport, Caerleon Campus, PO Box 179, Newport, NP18 3YG
Tel: (01633) 432 432 E-mail: uic@newport.ac.uk Website: www.newport.ac.uk
Students' Union, Caerleon Campus, College Crescent, Caerleon, NP18 3YG
Tel: (01633) 432 076 E-mail: students.union@newport.ac.uk
Website: www.newportunion.com

GENERAL

In the south-east of Wales, not far from the Severn, is the *industrial* city of Newport, home
to the University's two sites. The main site's near the pre-Roman village of Caerleon, which
many historians and mythologists believe to have been the site of Camelot (*where King
Arthur kept his Round Table before IKEA even thought of selling them*). Nowadays, it's
more notable for the University, which began its life as a Mechanics Institute, became a
University College in 1996 and finally succeeded in its quest for the grail of full University
status in 2003.

The main building's dominated by an *impressive* clock tower and fronted by lawns where
students play football when the sun shines – *much to the annoyance of the Vice-chancellor,
whose windows overlook them. Campus is a quiet, attractive place in the summer, filled with
barbecuing and picnicking in the halls' courtyard and sunbathers on the grass.*

56%				
	Sex ratio (M:F): 44:56		Founded: 1841	
	Full-time u'grads: 2,535		Part-time: 4,700	
	Postgrads: 365		Non-degree: 567	
	Ave course: 3yrs		Ethnic: 10%	
	State:private school: 99:1		Flunk rate: 22%	
	Mature: 41%		International: 6%	
44%	Disabled: 32		Local: 72%	

ATMOSPHERE:

*Newport's still in limbo between technical college and full-flung University, at least as far as
atmosphere goes. The students are happy to be here, though, get on with things
academically and make their own fun as they go. A large proportion are local/from
surrounding towns, so keep to their own social lives as a result, missing out on the quiet,
friendly campus society livers-in enjoy. There's a strong work ethic – employability is the goal
for many – so friends and fun along the way are bonuses.*

SITES:

Allt yr Yn Campus: (830 students – Business & Management, Computing & Engineering, Social Studies & Art Foundation) The smaller campus is 10 mins walk from the city centre in one of Newport's *affluent, leafy* suburbs and much better placed for travel links and city nightlife. It houses specialist learning facilities for computing and engineering; two refectories; an art supply shop; LRC; Student Services office; careers service and ACES – Newport university's commercial arm.

NEWPORT:

• <u>Population: 137,000</u> • <u>City centre: 4 miles</u> • <u>London: 140 miles</u> • <u>Cardiff: 17 miles</u>
• <u>High temp: 21</u> • <u>Low temp: 2</u> • <u>Rainfall: 87</u>

Many people could be forgiven for thinking that Newport is an industrial wasteland with occasional bouts of remission. It's certainly not a pretty place, but despite losing core industries in past decades, re-investment and redevelopment is smoothing over the cracks and making the city less depressing to look at. Crime's going down, but unemployment's still high and there are remnants of everything that was bad about the Industrial Revolution loitering about the place. The centre is compact and navigable with a Norman castle floundering on the banks of the Usk. High street and trendy label shops sit amongst ex-catalogue discount stores and the enormous Transporter Bridge dominates the skyline. Postcards for parents tend to come from Caerleon village, however – which is small but a pleasant mix of ancient and funky. Newport's notable neighbouring attractions include the Big Pit mining museum, the Brecon Beacons and Cardiff.

TRAVEL:

Trains: Newport station is on the Cardiff–Birmingham line and is directly linked to London.
Coaches: The station's right in the city centre and has local and National Express services, including coaches to Gatwick and Heathrow.
Car: The M4's *handiest*.
Air: Cardiff International Airport is 30 miles away and has cheap flights (RyanAir and (BMIBaby).
Hitching: *A bad idea from the city centre. The M4 offers glimmers of hope.*
Local: From stand 25 at the bus station, 2a, 2B, C, D, E, X, 7 and 7D make the 15–20-min trip past campus (£1.65 rtn, no change given).
University: An hourly shuttle bus between the Caerleon Campus and Allt yr Yn campus 20 mins away.
Taxis: £5–6 from Newport centre to Caerleon Campus.
Bicycles: A hilly area and narrow roads, *so cycling can be tiring and dangerous.* Cycle bays and areas to lock bikes are provided on campus.

CAREER PROSPECTS:

• <u>Careers Service</u> • <u>No. of staff: 4 full/3 part</u> • <u>Unemployed after 6mths: 14%</u>
Part of the *admirable* Student Services department: vacancy updates; newsletters; interview practice; job fairs.

FAMOUS ALUMNI:

Asif Kapadia (film director with a BAFTA or two), Justin Kerrigan (writer and director of cult clubber movie Human Traffic); Terry Matthews (industrialist and Wales's richest man); Ian Watkins (Lost Prophet).

Students from Bangor Rag once 'closed' the island of Anglesey by erecting an 'Anglesey Full' sign.

FURTHER INFO:

• Prospectus: undergrad; postgrad; part-time • Open days
International students should contact the International Office (international@newport.ac.uk) for admissions enquiries.

 ACADEMIC

The six schools have a range of highly innovative course options, many vocational. The *highly-subscribed* Newport School of Art, Media & Design *has proved its mettle on many occasions, particularly when it comes to animation, photography, film and graphics. Newport Business School's pretty hot too and the University's been voted best in Wales for Entrepreneurship Action – but then, it did produce the country's most minted industrialist, so not really a surprise.*

Entry points: 140-200	Ave points: 180
Applns per place: 3	Clearing: 20%
No. of terms: 2	Length of terms: 12wks
Teaching: n/a	Research: ***
Staff/student ratio: 1:10	Sandwich students: 0
Firsts: 7%	2.2s: 38%
2.1s: 46%	3rds: 13%

ADMISSIONS:

• Apply via UCAS/GTTR for teaching

SUBJECTS:

Art, Media & Design: 37% Education: 16%
Business & Management: 7% Humanities & Sciences: 15%
Computing & Engineering: 9% Social Studies: 11%
Best: Business & Management.
Unusual: Documentary Photography; Global Citizenship.

LIBRARIES:

• 212,354 books • 317 study places • Spend per student: ££
Both campuses have libraries with self-service photocopying and dissertation-binding facilities. *The availability of books has rattled a few cages and the five-volume loan limit prompts the occasional four-letter outburst at the issue desk.*

COMPUTERS:

• 838 workstations • 24-hr access
Caerleon site's computer rooms hum through the wee hours; Allt yr Yn's close at 9pm most evenings. 100 Macs are spread between campuses in addition to the PCs, and video conferencing equipment is available.

OTHER LEARNING FACILITIES:

There are language labs on the Allt yr Yn campus (which any student can use for free) and music rehearsal rooms on both. Study Zone is a learning skills initiative that helps with things like revision planning and essay writing. A Distance Learning Centre provides IT support and general assistance for those off-campus.

NEWPORT:

- Price of a pint of beer: £2 • Glass of wine: £1.80 • Can of Red Bull: £2

Cinemas: The new-release City Cinema in Newport has the largest screen in Wales and offers £3 student tickets. The *fancy new* retail park UGC has *four million screens (or many, at least) and a complicated concessions arrangement.*

Theatres: The Dolman Theatre is invaded by touring productions, pantos and youth theatre. Otherwise, Cardiff offers more boards for the treading.

Pubs: The old town of Caerleon has about ten pubs, all of which are student-friendly. *The Dovers Arms, Minstrels and The Olde Bull have the advantage of being closest to campus. A drinking outing in some of Newport's shabbier areas has a 30% chance of resulting in minor injury or hurt pride.*

Clubbing: Several *ever-changing* student nights in the city *but Wednesday is 'the big night out'. The Union has discount deals with Walkabout and Vodka bar – both good weekday venues. Breeze and Chicago are good studenty bets too.* A bus runs from campus to *dancers' paradise* Cardiff Creation every Monday (£4).

Music venues: *The near-legendary TJ's is the premier live music venue, having had the likes of Oasis and the Stone Roses passing out in its dressing rooms.* Newport City Live Arena does some large-scale touring events.

Eating out: *Caerleon can be a bit pricey when it comes to wining and dining, but the Priory is just about worth it, The Olde Bull does good pub grub and Curo's is a top Spanish restaurant. There are takeaways open till 12.30am, but there's always food to be had for those who know where to look.*

UNIVERSITY:

- Price of a pint of beer: £1.70 • Glass of wine: £1.40 • Can of Red Bull: £1.70

A large number of students living out and a good many matures mean the Union has a tricky job of arranging an events schedule to keep everyone happy – some feel campus entertainment's a little lame.

Bars: The newly refurbed Clarence Bar is the only place to drown your studies on campus and is *very busy as a result – probably only because it's very small –* with plenty of quizzes, plasma screens and live bands. The Main Hall Bar is only open for balls, parties or comedy nights etc.

Music venues: The Main Hall regularly showcases local talent and – *often enough –* the Lost Prophets. Indie/rock is the big thing. *Just like in Twin Town.*

Clubbing: Occasional clubbing collaborations with Cardiff University on Fridays.

Food: The refectory at Caerleon ladles out main meals and *bitty* snacks from 9am. The Clarence Buttery *is quicker and junkier* but closed weekends. Bar snacks can be got from Clarence Bar and there are other outlets on the Allt yr Yn campus.

Other: The May Ball's an al fresco springtime *extravaganza*. There's also a Christmas Ball, held in a local hotel.

UNIVERSITY OF WALES, NEWPORT STUDENTS' UNION:

- 4 sabbaticals • NUS member

Politics is beaten out of the two Union offices with a big stick of neutrality – even though the Socialist Worker Society is the most active on campus. The student body quibbles with the Union's entertainment schedule and level of representation, but is generally too indifferent to get actively involved. They threw in their two cents' worth at the anti top-up rally in London, but generally SU concerns are much closer to home: parking restrictions and keeping Wednesday afternoons free for sport are top of the list. The sabbs have a drop-in centre, but they generally refer to Student Services who are in a much better position to offer help. The upcoming addition of an Education & Welfare officer might improve matters.

SU FACILITIES:

Bar; all-purpose venue; cyber café; two pool tables; two minibuses for hire; Link ATM (it charges); photocopiers; printing and binding service; photo booth; payphones; TV lounge; juke box; general store; stationery shop; gaming and vending machines; launderette.

CLUBS (NON-SPORTING):

Animation; Archaeology; Fashion; Photo 2000; South Asian; Wing-ed Monkeys. **See also Clubs tables.**

OTHER ORGANISATIONS:

The Grapevine is the newborn bi-termly newsletter sponsored by the Territorial Army. *Which is weird.* Newport Rag is *frankly pathetic.* It scraped £600 together last year – *mainly through sponsored hair dyeing.* There's a Newport Student Volunteering Group which does work in the local community but is independent of the University/Union.

RELIGIOUS:

• 1 chaplain (Methodist)
A prayer room's open to all denominations and Newport has a wide range of places of worship. Cardiff's is wider still.

PAID WORK:

• Job bureau
Many work part-time both in term and out. The University job bureau is essentially the Careers Service in a different hat. Acorn Recruitment visits the Fresher's Fayre each year *to hunt down fresh temping meat.* Some SU work's to be had – bar, library, shop, IT suites, marketing – and in the local area, mainly in shops, pubs, clubs and call centres.

SPORTS

• Recent successes: football, basketball • BUSA Ranking: 48
The state-of-the-art sports centre's shared by University and locals – it does beauty treatments, personal training and kiddy parties. There's a swimming pool in the pipeline. *Sport is open to all, and there are also some impressive* victories from dedicated athletes. *The University's keen to attract the sporty to its hallowed halls* and offers six £1,000 scholarships to prospective students of professional standard. In addition, £500 bursaries can be awarded to cover training and competition costs for national- or international-level jocks. Last year's BUSA football West Division was stormed by the Newport boys.

SPORTS FACILITIES:

The University borrow football and all-weather pitches from a local school, and make use of Newport city's athletics field. Their own facilities include a rugby pitch, two tennis courts, a basketball/netball court and the sports centre. Membership is £40/year with charges of £1.10 per session/£1.20 equipment hire (sporting clubs and teams are exempt). There's also a golf course. The Velodrome is 2 miles away, and there are a dry ski slope, swimming pool, lake and other facilities in the immediate area.

SPORTING CLUBS:

Ju-Jitsu; Kayaking; Mountain Sports; Surf & Skate. **See also Clubs tables.**

ATTRACTIONS:

The Newport Gwent Dragons rugby team play nearby. The Millennium Stadium is 20 mins by train. The Celtic Manor Golf Course – owned by Terry Matthews – will be hosting the 2010 Ryder Cup.

ACCOMMODATION

IN COLLEGE:

• Self-catering: 16% • Cost: £50 (39wks)
• First years living in: 70% • Insurance premium: £

Availability: 1st years are guaranteed a place in the self-catered campus halls, which are divided between $\frac{2}{3}$ en-suite and $\frac{1}{3}$ 'traditional' accommodation – *the tradition presumably being some ancient toilet-sharing custom.* Fully equipped kitchens are shared between either five or 15 people. Halls are grouped close to the main campus building, forming a cosy student village but there's an 11pm curfew. A 24-hr reception close to the student village co-ordinates security. Single and mixed-couple accommodation is available in special cases, although the University *keeps this fact to itself where possible.*

Car parking: The Union's trying to overturn restrictions on student parking as many have cars but anyway there are *too few* spaces. *Cars parked in the nearby village are open to vandalism if left too long.* There's a pay & display on campus and a permit-only car park (£40/yr or £10 if car-sharing).

EXTERNALLY:

• Ave rent: £50 • Living at home: 31%

Availability: Caerleon's not big enough to house everyone so many end up living in Newport itself or the smaller towns surrounding it. With such varying proximity, a car – *or an obliging friend with one* – are almost prerequisites. *Some areas of Newport are not the most habitable.*

Housing help: Accommodation Services provide regularly updated housing lists and various leaflets. They will help with looking over contracts, *but reserve the right to have no responsibility if everything goes tits up.*

WELFARE

SERVICES:

• Lesbian/Gay/Bisexual Officer • Women's Officer • Mature Students' Officer
• Postgrad Officer • Disabilities Officer • Self-defence classes • Nightline
• College counsellors: 2 part • Crime rating !!!!

Student Services are the first point of contact for anyone in difficulty. The SU sabbs are there to listen when needed but some women may find three men – which the sabbs generally are – off-putting.

Health: The University Medical Centre has a doctor and two nurses to plaster scraped knees.

Crèches/Nursery: The Tiny Tots Day-Care Nursery on the Caerleon site can take kids between 18mths-5yrs. *Students are frustrated with crèche facilities.*

Disabilities: Once the steep hill that leads to the campus is out of the way, access is *rather good* with lifts, ramps and electronic doors throughout the main building. There are some problems with narrow doorways and cramped teaching rooms. One-to-one tuition's available for dyslexics, plus extended loans and specialist software programs. Hearing loops are in many lecture theatres.

Crime: The University itself is a secure place to be. The city's *a different story* and although Newport's *climbing down from the No. 1 spot for violent crime thanks to more police beating the streets, pick-pocketing and other social disturbances are fairly common.*

Drugs: Smoking's only permitted in Clarence Bar and designated areas outside. Harder drugs aren't a problem on campus but Newport itself *has a bit of a rep.*

FINANCE:

• <u>Ave debt per year</u>: £4,362
Fees: Postgrads pay around £3,300 a year in tuition fees, internationals closer to £6,700. The University has a firm policy of widening access and is strongly opposed to the financial restrictions top-up fees will impose on prospective applicants.
• <u>Access fund: £461,442</u> • <u>Successful applications/yr: 624</u> • <u>Ave payment: £200-2,000</u>
Support: Total of £33,000 in bursary funding available each year (68 awarded in 2003). An emergency loan scheme slips skint students a few notes in sticky situations.

North East London Poly
see <u>University of East London</u>

North East London Polytechnic
see <u>University of East London</u>

University of North London (UNL)
see <u>London Metropolitan University</u>

University College Northampton

• *Formerly Nene College.*
University College Northampton, Park Campus, Boughton Green Road, Northampton, NN2 7AL
Tel: (0800) 358 2232 E-mail: study@northampton.ac.uk Website: www.northampton.ac.uk
University College Northampton Students' Union, Park Campus,
Bougton Green Road, Northampton, NN2 7AL Tel: (01604) 892 818
Website: www.ucnu.org

G E N E R A L

800-year-old Northampton's a *large, pleasant and unassuming* market town, slap bang between Brum and London, *a bit too far east to be properly in the Midlands and too far north to be in the Home Counties*. Its nearest neighbour is the *much maligned* Milton Keynes, but there's some *lovely* countryside nearby to get lost in. Historically, *there's no business like shoe business* and Northampton has been British footwear capital in past decades – the leather industry still has a strong *foothold*. UCN is about $2\frac{1}{2}$ miles away on two landscaped campuses – Park and Avenue (*the Manhattan-based pun isn't entirely coincidental*) – with modern developments *tastefully arranged around lovely rolling lawns*. Since 1999 it's had 'university college' status, meaning that while it's got a way to go before becoming a fully-feathered University (*one of its strongest aspirations*), it can hand out its own degrees.

Sex ratio (M:F): 37:63
Full-time u'grads: 7,230
Postgrads: 275
Ave course: 3yrs
State:private school: 98:2
Mature: 29%
Disabled: 220

Founded: 1999
Part-time: 2,625
Non-degree: n/a
Ethnic: 18%
Flunk rate: 25%
International: 7%
Local: 25%

ATMOSPHERE:

UCN is home to a broadly blended bunch of all ages and accents. They're friendly, far from pretentious and there's a strong sense of community, particularly amongst those who live in. The University's small enough not to get lost, but large enough to dissuade exclusive cliques from forming. The academic atmosphere at Park Campus errs on the sensible and serious side, while the number of arts students based at Avenue gives that campus a more trendy and flamboyant air.

SITES:

Park Campus: The main campus, just outside the town centre, housing Science and Humanities students, as well as the Business School and School of Healthcare (complete with on-site 'ward'). The newest kid on the block is 2005's Student Centre, giving space to, among other things, Student Services, more student housing and a GP surgery.
Avenue Campus: (Art, Design, Fashion, Performing Arts & Technology) $2\frac{1}{2}$ miles from Park Campus, the *pleasant* Avenue has all the facilities to function independently: drama and dance studios, a CAD lab, computer suite and bar and catering facilities. It's linked with Park via a free shuttle service.

NORTHAMPTON:

• Population: 194,458 • Town centre: 2 miles • London: 63 miles
• Birmingham: 52 miles • Manchester: 137 miles
• High temp: 21 • Low temp: 0 • Rainfall: 49
As big as a town can get without becoming a city, Northampton has managed to maintain its ancient market square (the largest in Britain) in *something approaching good nick* and there are some *admirable* examples of Georgian and Victorian architecture around the centre. *Some of the outer reaches are closer to prefab hell, however.* In among the urban planning exercise there's the Sol Central entertainment complex and the *usual array* of banks, malls, supermarkets, bookshops, galleries and museums, *although the Leather Museum isn't as much fun as it could be.* Other attractions include regular hot-air balloon festivals and one of the *best-preserved* Norman round churches in the country.

TRAVEL:

Trains: Northampton station is 4 miles from the Park campus and offers mainline services to London, Birmingham, Edinburgh and others.
Coaches: The coach station about 4 miles from Park runs National Express, Midland Fox and local services to various towns and cities, including London and Birmingham.
Car: The M1 zooms past the town – although there's at least 3 wiggly miles between it and the College. The A45, A50 and A43 also come in handy. *At College, permits are needed and overnight stays are charged.*
Air: Luton Airport is closest, *though if it's of use is another matter.* Some of the budget airlines use it though. Rail links to Birmingham Airport.
Hitching: *M1 junctions are good pick-up spots and there are enough major roads to make hitching possible.*
Local: The bus station is *utterly horrid, but services are reliable enough.* Trips between town and College cost 90p each way.
College: There's a free bus service for students and staff between the main campus and the town's bus and train stations.
Taxis: *Not too expensive and not too hard to get hold of.*
Bicycles: There are some cycle lanes but the constantly busy roads make traffic dodging *something of a bloodsport.*

CAREER PROSPECTS:

• Careers Service • Unemployed after 6mths: 6%
Students are treated to interview assistance, CV-writing lessons, psychometric and aptitude tests, bulletin boards and cne-on-one advice sessions. Facilities are available until three years after graduation.

FAMOUS ALUMNI:

Andrew Collins (BBC 6 DJ); David J (Bauhaus/Love & Rockets); Lord Hesketh (Formula 1 team manager); Jonn (Ned s Atomic Dustbin); Des O'Connor (*the poor man's Michael Parkinson*); Derek Redmond (athlete); Jonathon Waller (artist).

SPECIAL FEATURES:

• The School of Leather Technology has on display a *fine* specimen of a blue whale's foreskin.

FURTHER INFO:

• Prospectuses: undergrad; postgrad; international; part time • Open days
All prospectuses except international can be downloaded or ordered from the main website. UCN runs open days in spring and autumn tel. (0800) 3582232 or e-mail study@northampton.ac.uk for info). Tours can be booked online.

A C A D E M I C

Gold stars for Healthcare, Education, business-related courses and the Art & Design department. The Park Campus is a 9-5 affair; things are a little looser at Avenue.

40-240		**POINTS**
Entry points: 40-240	Ave points: 210	
Applns per place: n/a	Clearing: 10%	
No. of terms: 3	Length of terms: 12wks	
Staff/student ratio: 1:17	Study addicts: n/a	
Teaching: *	Research: *	
Year abroad: 1%	Sandwich students: 3%	

ADMISSIONS:

• Apply via UCAS/NMAS for nursing and midwifery/GTTR for teaching

SUBJECTS:

Applied Science: 9%	Health: 21%
Arts: 18%	Northampton Business School: 23%
Education: 12%	Social Science: 17%

COMPUTERS:

• 24-hr access
Each campus has an IT centre offering Broadband net access, available 24-hrs all week long. Free IT courses are available for the technologically backward and there's a plug-in area for student laptops.

OTHER LEARNING FACILITIES:

Drama studio, audio/TV centre. The Centre for Academic Practice on the Avenue Campus (*unmanageably acronymed CfAP*) offers courses in study skills.

ENTERTAINMENT

THE TOWN:

• Price of a pint of beer: £2 • Glass of wine: £2 • Can of Red Bull: £2

Cinemas: The Sol Central development has a Vue multiplex in the town centre. Also a UGC multiplex just outside town.

Theatres: The Royal puts on traditional stuff, mainly rep. The Derngate is a flexible, multi-purpose venue with lots of touring productions and the Roadmender puts on experimental stuff.

Pubs: Northampton now has three Wetherspoons *and, for some reason, they're proud of it. Big cheap chains have been colonising, although small independent places still get their share of student custom. Pushplugs: The White Elephant and Picturedrome near the Avenue Campus; The Charles Bradlaugh (massive mixing pot for students and staff).*

Clubbing: *Northampton's nightspots are on the up, but slowly. Monday night at Time & Envy is the big student dance hole – sponsored by the Union. Chicago Rock is also okay for aboozin' and a-boogyin'.*

Music venues: The Roadmender is a *fair-to-middling* indie stop-off and sells tickets via the Union.

Eating out: Northampton has the usual range of eateries, including burgers and pizzas till 4am. *Wellingborough Road is the best bet for value and variety. Pushplugs: Buddles (American diner. Legend has it no one has managed to finish a meal they're so big); Giggling Sausage; Papa Luigi.*

UNIVERSITY:

• Price of a pint of beer: £1.50 • Bottle of wine: £5.20 • Can of Red Bull: £1.40

Bars: Laidback is the only place to escape the campus's *stringent* anti-smoking policy and even then only in the evenings, *when it lives up to its name a bit more. Just because it's got 'sophisticated European-style café bar' written all over its décor doesn't stop it being a class A piss-up venue, and it's also got big screen sport, pool, open mic nights and karaoke to offer. George's at Avenue has a theme night or two, including the legendary Friday 13th night (£13 entry, drink the bar dry). The Pavilion's more chilled out, and the NN2 club spot has theme nights.*

Film: Laidback has a film night every Monday.

Music venues: NN2 is used to pamper local bands.

Clubbing: Weekend nights keep NN2 open till 2am. *Unlike every other Union in the country, Northampton students have protested against cheesy pop and the ents people are providing more diverse music.*

Comedy/Cabaret: Fortnightly comedy in Laidback.

Food: *Grubby grub at Laidback. The University refectory is more expensive, though the food's far from great.*

Other: The Xmas Ball is popular but the Freshers' Ball hasn't been drawing in the punters – *most of them are too busy and bleary-eyed to attend.*

SOCIAL & POLITICAL

UNIVERSITY COLLEGE NORTHAMPTON STUDENTS' UNION:

• 3 sabbaticals • Turnout at last ballot: 14%

Lucky UCNU has not one but three buildings, two at Park and one on Avenue, but the facilities at Avenue have a cloud over their heads and risk closure unless there's enough money down the back of the sofa to keep them afloat. *Meanwhile, UCNU doesn't attract much attention from the student body except as an ents and services provider. As suggested by their disaffiliation from NUS, when it comes to politics, UCNU doesn't give a flying monkey's, really. It gets on all right with the University itself now that they've started talking to each other.*

SU FACILITIES:

Three bars; café; three pool tables; minibus hire; advice centre; payphones; photocopiers; fax and printing service; photo booth; Endsleigh Insurance office; NatWest and Co-op ATMs.

CLUBS (NON-SPORTING):

African Students; Alternative; Asian; Chinese; Ethnic Roots; History; Irish; Law; Philosophy; Rock Music; Sick of Sectarianism. **See also Clubs tables.**

OTHER ORGANISATIONS:

Xpress is the regular e-newsletter from the Union; Wave is the printed one. Rag rakes in some cash relief for a different charity each month. Volunteers is an organisation that visits people in need of visiting, and smoothes things over with the locals.

RELIGIOUS:

• 2 chaplains (ecumenical, multi-faith)
The chaplaincy centre on campus is open to all faiths on the Avenue campus, *mainly for chatting and coffee.* There's a Muslim prayer room on each campus. Northampton is big enough to support all but the most esoteric spiritual requirements.

PAID WORK:

• Job bureau • Paid work: term-time 75%; hols 80%
Between them, the SU and University's Student Services unit run Jobs Junction which links up with local employers and posts a vacancy notice board. The Union and local bars and shops often have jobs going. Students can make extra pennies acting as student ambassadors, *or, in English, tour guides.*

SPORTS

• Recent successes: rugby league • BUSA Ranking: 48
Enthusiasm outstrips the facilities and trophy collection. Outside sponsorship has perked things up, though successes are mostly down to the women.

SPORTS FACILITIES:

The Park Campus has: sports hall with fitness suite; 25 acres of fields; pavilion. Nothing exclusively for the University at Avenue but it's close to the town's rugby/football pitches and has access to the swimming pool in the school next door and to the River Nene (not for swimming though). Use of the facilities costs £20 per year. There are leisure centres in Northampton and Milton Keynes Snowdome is 20 mins away.

SPORTING CLUBS:

Jogging; Lacrosse. **See also Clubs tables.**

ATTRACTIONS:

Northampton Rugby Club (aka the Saints) *are local heroes.* There's also Northampton Town FC (*known, not entirely inaccurately, as the Cobblers*) and not far away, the Silverstone Formula 1 circuit, home of the British Grand Prix. The Nene Whitewater Centre is within splashing distance. The County Cricket Club is a ball's throw from Avenue.

ACCOMMODATION

IN COLLEGE:

• Self-catering: 23% • Cost £45-65 (40wks)
• First years living in: 81% • Insurance premium: £
Availability: UCN has around 1,600 places in seven halls of residence, all but 250 of which are reserved for 1st years, meaning everyone can have a room on arrival. Very few in successive years live in. Halls are on campus, *so lie-ins are a regular feature of life here.*

The en-suite facilities at West Hall and Spencer Perceval put them in demand. Bassett Lowke – the only hall at the Avenue Campus – is a *popular* en-suite complex of generally single-sex flats. *Charles Bradlaugh Hall has been kicking around a good many years and is beginning to look it.* Accommodation for couples is available on application. CCTV, scan keys and night porters conquer the forces of evil.
Car parking: *Not exactly a piece of Battenburg.* Permits are around £120 yearly (not needed for day-parking).

EXTERNALLY:
• Ave rent: £48
Availability: *Local housing is pretty good and reasonable, although the hike between town and campus can get a little wearisome. Nearby Kingsthorpe and Abington are the best bets. Semilong can be a bit rough though a clean-up operation's in progress.*
Housing help: Student Services keep vacancy lists, approve landlords and offer a placement service. All 1st years are guaranteed a local home address at the beginning of the year.

WELFARE

SERVICES:
• Mature Students' Society • International Students' Society • Nightline
• College counsellors: 1 full/4 part • Crime rating: !!!!

The Union runs a drop-in Welfare & Advice Service that lends an ear. A PAL (Partners in Academic Life) scheme has been set up, whereby eight students act as points of contact for academic concerns. Nightline is open four nights a week – *so don't get suicidal on a Wednesday.*
Health: There's a GP surgery on the Park Campus and plenty of doctors and dentists available in the town.
Disabilities: Renovation has made most buildings *very accessible.* Both campuses have relief pens for guide dogs and induction loops have been installed in several lecture theatres. *Good level of support and equipment for unseen disabilities.*
Crime: Some mild vandalism comes a cropper of CCTV.

FINANCE:
• Ave debt per year: £3,611
• Access fund ave payment: £100-2,000
Support: There's an emergency loan of £150 available when things get tight. Also bridging loans of £200 and opportunity bursaries for undergrads with low-income families of up to £2,000.

Northumbria University

• *Formerly Newcastle Polytechnic.*
(1) Northumbria University, Newcastle City Campus, Ellison Place, Newcastle upon Tyne, NE1 8ST Tel: (0191) 227 4000 Email: er.admissions@northumbria.co.uk
Website: www.northumbria.ac.uk
Northumbria University Students' Union, Newcastle City Campus, 2 Sandyford Road, Newcastle upon Tyne, NE1 8SB Tel: (0191) 227 4757 Website: www.mynsu.co.uk
(2) University of Northumbria, Coach Lane Campus, Coach Lane, Benton, Newcastle upon Tyne, NE7 7XA Tel: (0191) 215 6000
Email: su.president@unn.ac.uk Website: www.mynsu.co.uk

GENERAL

Newcastle's newer university started from humble beginnings as the city's little poly, *but there's no denying it's now a hefty player*. The main campus, plop in the middle of the city, is the study centre for most courses, with around 15,700 students knocking around at any given time. It's a *distressing muddle* of 1880s municipal buildings, such as the original redbrick Sutherland Building, and 60s concrete architecture, *made easier on the eye by some charming* 19th-century buildings in Ellison Place. *Being just a continuation of buildings and no greenery, it's difficult to tell exactly where the town stops and campus starts, although development of the recently acquired 7-acre site on the edge of campus might make the boundaries clearer cut.*

Sex ratio (M:F): 41:59	Founded: 1969
Full-time u'grads: 14,375	Part-time: 5,330
Postgrads: 1,735	Non-degree: 5,000
Ave course: 3yrs	Ethnic: 13%
State:private school: 91:9	Flunk rate: 14%
Mature: 42%	International: 15%
Disabled: 358	Local: 59%

ATMOSPHERE:
Newcastle's glittering social scene more than compensates for any shortcomings in the University's dreary aesthetic. Many of the students are mature, but neither this, nor the gloomy architecture, dampens their enthusiasm. Unsurprisingly, relations with the community are good since more than half the students come from the local area – but things can still get a bit hairy on a Friday or Saturday night. Like many universities in a thriving city, the campus itself can empty pretty quickly after lectures as everybody scarpers off to the city's heaving fleshpots. The Union building remains a little more lively than its surroundings – busy if not buzzy.

THE CITY: see Newcastle University

TRAVEL: see Newcastle University

University: The University operates its own *infrequent* bus service between the campuses with a last bus after midnight.

SITES:
Coach Lane: (2,000 – Health, Community & Education Studies) 3 miles from the main site in Benton (*quite a rough suburb*) is the Coach Lane site, a modern and recently expanded campus, *clean and green*, with enough pubs and shops around *not to feel too isolated*.

CAREER PROSPECTS:
• Careers Service • No. of staff: 7 full-time • Unemployed after 6mths: 6%
The careers service has limited outposts at both campuses and *tries to plug gaps with its website*.

FAMOUS ALUMNI:
Emmanuel Bajyewv (Lighthouse Family); Jeff Banks (fashion designer/former Clothes Show presenter); Steve Bell (cartoonist); Sarah Blackwood (Dubstar); Steve Cram (athlete); Robson Green (actor/singer of '& Jerome' fame); Scott Henshall (fashion designer); Jonathan Ives (inventor of iMac); Vaughan Oliver (artist/designer); Sting (*pompous* pop star & tantra king); Kevin Whately (actor – Inspector Morse).

FURTHER INFO:
• Prospectuses: undergrads; postgrad; all departments; part-time; international; CD-Rom
• Open days

A C A D E M I C

Northumbria prides itself on being a practical, get-stuck-in kind of university and they have links with industries in the area. Many courses offer work placements and students can nab academic credit by acting as ambassadors into local schools.

Entry points: 140-320	Ave points: 200
Applns per place: n/a	Clearing: 33%
No. of terms: 2	Length of terms: 12wks
Staff/student ratio: 1:20	Study addicts: 8%
Teaching: ****	Research: *
Firsts: 10%	2.2s: 35%
2.1s: 41%	3rds: 5%

140-320 ... **POINTS**

ADMISSIONS:

• Apply via UCAS/NMAS for nursing

Fair range of Access schemes for those from non-traditional routes. Disabled applicants and mature students with qualifications from the University of Life are *warmly* welcomed.

SUBJECTS:

Applied Sciences: 7%
Art & Social Sciences: 17%
Built Environment: 9%
Design: 5%
Health Community & Education: 32%

Informatics, Engineering & Technology: 16%
Law: 11%
Newcastle Business School: 21%
Psychology & Sport Sciences: 5%

Best: Art & Design; Building; Business & Management; Dance & Cinematics; Design & Film; Drama; Economics; Education Studies; Electrical & Electronic Engineering; History of Art; Housing Studies; Information & Library Management; Land & Property Management; Maths & Statistics; Modern Languages; Molecular Biosciences; Nursing; Physics; Politics; Psychology; Sociology; Sport Sciences; Subjects allied to Medicine.
Unusual: Computer Forensics; Computer Game Studies.

LIBRARIES:

• 500,000 books • 1,600 study places • 24-hr access

The main library is a brick and concrete structure with small arrow-slit windows on the edge of a quadrangle in the City Campus. With a swipe card, there's 24-hr access to this library but not others.

COMPUTERS:

• 5,900 workstations • 24-hr access

IT facilities at both campuses and every student gets their own hard-disk space to store files. A wireless network covers most of both campuses and some course resources are available with the 'Blackboard' system.

OTHER LEARNING FACILITIES:

The Study Skills Centre assists students with all the *basic but crucial* aspects of student life such as literacy, numeracy, essay writing and IT. At Carlisle, students can get free foreign language tuition and there are rehearsal rooms, a drama studio, a CAD lab and a practice courtroom.

E N T E R T A I N M E N T

THE CITY: see Newcastle University

UNIVERSITY:

• Price of a pint of beer: £1.80 • Glass of wine £2.20
Bars: The Union runs four bars: Reds (the cheapest), the *clubbier* Venue (gig nights), the *pub-style* Bar One and Coach Lane (pool tables and club nights).
Theatre: Open air productions take place when weather and interest permit.
Clubbing: At the Venue, the self-explanatory 'Wiggle' provides pop thrills and, for rock fans, there's 'Get Your Skates On'.
Cinema: No cinema, but free films in Bar One and Reds on a mini-projector.
Music: Feeder, Girls Aloud, Moby and The Coral have all visited the Venue.
Food: The Union runs four eateries, including Reds, offering a *wide range* from filled stotties (aka Geordie baps, *ooh er*) to full breakfasts. The University has a refectory *doling out the usual greasy spoon fare*. Also a food cart on each campus.
Other: Weekly quiz night, *disturbingly* regular karaoke and Christmas, Graduation and departmental balls.

S O C I A L & P O L I T I C A L

NORTHUMBRIA UNIVERSITY STUDENTS' UNION:

• 4 sabbaticals • NUS member
The students aren't the most politically committed, to put it mildly, but the Union organises a frantic diary of social events during Freshers' Week. Its building, situated on the main campus opposite the library, is enormous and facility-stuffed.

SU FACILITIES:

Four bars; a café; two coffee bars; two pool tables; eight meeting rooms; Lloyds/Barclays ATM; photocopier; photo booth; general store; stationery shop; vending and gaming machines; travel agency; late night minibus; bookshop; TV lounge; advice centre.

CLUBS (NON-SPORTING):

Accounting; Biz; Bladerunners; Centrestage; Chinese; Christian Student Action; Cyprus; Duke of Edinburgh; Elam; Gaming & Roleplaying; GLOBE; Grey; History; IGUNA; ISOC; Libyan; NUTS; Pub Crawl; Swiss; Vietnam; World Welfare. **See also Clubs tables.**

OTHER ORGANISATIONS:

The student newspaper had a name change to Insight, *but that was clearly too exciting,* so it returned to the *dazzling originality* of Northumbria Student. A radio station is run jointly with Newcastle University and Rag *pushes the boat out* regularly for healthcare and global charities. A voluntary group co-ordinates community work.

RELIGIOUS:

• 7 chaplains (CofE, RC, URC, Methodist, Quaker, Salvation Army)
The main Christian God *shops* have chaplains and there are links with most religions, including the Catholic Student Society, Chinese Christian Fellowship, Christian Student Action, Islamic Society, Jewish Society and Methodist Student Society.
Religion in Newcastle: see Newcastle University

PAID WORK: see Newcastle University

• Job bureau
20% of the students are registered with Job Shop, which employs two full-time staff and some casual student assistants during term. They pass on CVs to employers looking for *cheap, exploitable – sorry, flexible, enthusiastic –* labour. See Newcastle University for details of the city's *manifold* opportunities.

SPORTS

- BUSA Ranking: 36

SPORTS FACILITIES:

Most outdoor facilities are based at the Bullocksteads Sports Ground. These include: 13 football and rugby pitches; an all-weather pitch. The *freshly kitted* fitness suite at City Campus includes three squash courts and a fitness conditioning centre. The University is in talks with Newcastle City Council to build an eight-lane 50m swimming pool as well, but until then there are discounts at local pools. Student facility membership costs £70 for one year, £190 for three. See Newcastle University for the city's facilities.

SPORTING CLUBS:

Boxing; Clay Pigeon Shooting; Kendo; Kung Fu; Lacrosse; Mountain Biking; OUTAC; Parachuting; Rowing; Snowsports; Surfing; Table Tennis; Ultimate Frisbee. **See also Clubs tables.**

ATTRACTIONS: see Newcastle University

ACCOMMODATION

IN COLLEGE:

- Catered: 3% • Cost: £75-82 (36wks)
- Self-catered: 12% • Cost: £57-87 (36wks) • Insurance premium: £££

Availability: Anyone from outside Tyne & Wear who applies before August is guaranteed a place in halls if they want one. They might want one in *popular* Camden – the newest halls and the nearest to the city centre. The older ones further out *used to have a bad reputation (poorly maintained with dodgy showers) but things are improving*. They all have a residents' manager to whinge at anyway. The *high spec* Old Brewery has 200 single rooms in five, six and seven bed flats, each with a kitchen/living room, bathroom, shower room and two loos. Some are adapted for disabled students. *Limited* parking and a bike store.

Car parking: *Parking isn't too difficult* with a (free) permit.

EXTERNALLY: see Newcastle University

- Ave rent: £50

Housing help: The University runs an accommodation office with *an extremely thorough and detailed* flat-finding guide online. The accreditation scheme recommends landlords who come up to scratch.

WELFARE

SERVICES:

- Lesbian/Gay/Bisexual Society • Women's Society • Mature Students' Society
- Postgrad Society • International Students' Society • Disabilities Officer
- Self-defence classes • Nightline • College counsellors: 4 full-time • Crime rating: !!!

Health: The City and Coach Lane Campus health centres are staffed by nurses, who ship anyone they can't fix off to local doctors.

Childcare: Although there's no crèche, *generous, means-tested* funding is available towards childcare for full-time students with sprogs up to 5yrs.

Disabilities: Wheelchair-adapted housing at Claude Gibb Hall, Lovine Flats, Stephenson and Rothbury. Some rooms designed for students with hearing impairments. Also *comprehensive* facilities and support for sight- and hearing-impaired and dyslexic students.

FINANCE:
• Ave debt per year: £3,577
Fees: Undergrads pay by the academic credit point (£8.33 each to be precise) and can expect to pay just short of a grand for three full-time years. That's at the moment, at any rate – top-up arrangements have yet to be finalised.
Support: Apart from the access fund (*which runs out quickly*) several awards to the lucky few and some scarce loans for those in urgent need, there's *not really enough support to go around*.

University of Northumbria at Newcastle
see Northumbria University

Norwich
see University of East Anglia

University of Nottingham

(1) The University of Nottingham, University Park, Nottingham, NG7 2RD
Tel: (0115) 951 5151 E-mail: undergraduate-enquiries@nottingham.ac.uk Website: www.nottingham.ac.uk
University of Nottingham Union, Portland Building, University Park, Nottingham, NG7 2RD
Tel: (0115) 846 8800 E-mail: studentsunion@nottingham.ac.uk
Website: www.su.nottingham.ac.uk
(2) University of Nottingham, Sutton Bonington, Nr Loughborough, Leicestershire, LE12 5RD
Tel: (0115) 951 5151
(3) The University of Nottingham Malaysia Campus Website: www.nottingham.edu.my

GENERAL

'Robin Hood: Prince of Thieves' would have you believe that Nottingham is about half an hour by horse from Kent, but it is, actually, in the East Midlands. In fact, it's the region's largest city. As with most cities in the Midlands, it's come a long way since the days of the evil sheriff. It grew rich during the Industrial Revolution then got poorer again when that finished. *But Nottingham didn't let a slight change of fortune get it down, not in the same way that, for instance, Birmingham did.* It remained and *still is a busy, cultural, beautiful* city, about *half an hour by horse* from the Peak District. About 3 miles from the city centre is the University Park Campus, 330 *hugely spacious* acres of *charming* views, parkland, lake and a mixture of *majestic* old buildings (such as the main admin centre and the Union) and newer blocks (such as the white concrete *flying saucer* which disguises itself as the Hallward Library). 2 miles away, the brand new Jubilee Campus is built around a man-made lake. 10 miles south, at Sutton Bonington near Loughborough (see Loughborough University for general details), the University has another self-contained campus, a *huger* 400 acres, which will have the UK's first new school of Vetinary Science for half a century.

Sex ratio (M:F): 41:59	**Founded: 1881**
Full-time u'grads: 17,510	**Part-time: 5,480**
Postgrads: 4,140	**Non-degree: 6,701**
Ave course: 3-4yrs	**Ethnic: 10%**
State:private school: 73:20	**Flunk rate: 3%**
Mature: 8%	**International: 22%**
Disabled: 194	**Local: 45%**

ATMOSPHERE:

The buzz and hum on the campus is like a hive of bees on speed. The social life flows with honey and the clubs milk the efforts of almost all students, yet, a staggering number of students still get involved in the successful Rag and Community Action group. Undiluted essence of life is bottled and served in large quantities at centres around the campus and it would take considerable effort to be bored. Relations with locals would be rosy were it not for a few over-exuberant party animals keeping the town's uglier residents from their beauty sleep.

SITES:

Jubilee: (Business, Computing, Education) This new site is on the western edge of the city. Built as a crescent around the lake, it has accommodation and other facilities including a library and a canteen.

Sutton Bonington and Nursing sites at Lincoln, Derby, Mansfield, Grantham, Boston and Nottingham City Centre: (900 students – Agricultural, Nursing) This site has its own Student Guild (funded by the Union) which runs a shop and some social events. There's a bar and some sporty stuff at Sutton Bonington, but nothing formal at the nursing sites. *Sutton Bonington is self-contained and has all the basic necessities for life, but, if it all gets too claustrophobic, escape into Loughborough or Nottingham is easy.*

The University of Nottingham Malaysia Campus: In the centre of Kuala Lumpur, *it's out of the reach of most undergrads – unless you're reading this in Malaysia – a bit like...*

The University of Nottingham China Campus: *which is in China, if you hadn't guessed. The site in Ningbo is a recent notch on the University's bed post.* See www.unnc.edu.cn

NOTTINGHAM:

- Population: 267,000 • City centre: 3 miles • London: 117 miles
- Birmingham: 47 miles • Loughborough: 13 miles
- High temp: 20 • Low temp: 1 • Rainfall: 59

The city's had to cope with a big influx of students over the past few years (see Nottingham Trent University), *which hasn't exactly been welcomed by all locals. However, town–gown relations have stayed surprisingly sweet, with any bad feeling directed at the universities (which do what they can to smooth things over) rather than individual students (except the noisy ones). Nottingham's big enough to have all the amenities a social animal could desire, but small and cosy enough to avoid urban angst. It has its dank and squalid corners,* but the main areas with shops galore and developments like the Victoria Centre are *clean and spacious. The city centre has been rejuvenated with huge cosmopolitan bars.* Areas such as Hockley, among others, offer *trendy little* bars, *trendy little* designer shops and *trendy big* secondhand markets. Some of the *daintiest* features include the Goose Fair every October (the largest temporary fun fair in Europe), the famous old lace market (an old quarter of the city where lace is still sold wholesale), Nottingham Castle (more of a mansion really), Slab Square for sitting amidst pigeons, and 'Ye Olde Trip to Jerusalem' (built into caves) and 'Salutation Inn', two of the country's oldest pubs. Students particularly enjoy 'The Tales of Robin Hood', a heritage centre aimed at kids of all ages.

TRAVEL:

Trains: Nottingham Midland and Beeston stations both offer services all round the country (north and south are simpler than east and west), including London, Birmingham, Manchester and Edinburgh.
Coaches: National Express services to, among other places, London, Birmingham and Glasgow.

Car: Nottingham is 5 mins off the M1 and is also easily reached by the A6, A47, A52 and the A1 (20 miles away). *The M1 and A52 are best for the University.* Parking permit required on campus.

Air: Nottingham East Midlands Airport, 12 miles outside town, has regular and budget flights inland and to Europe.

Hitching: *The M1 is good for wild rovers.*

College: The University runs a free shuttle bus service between the three campuses. Free Hopper bus services also available.

Taxis: *Pretty reasonable rates in the city centre.*

Bicycles: *Flat with a major network of cycle lanes connecting the city centre, University Park and Jubilee campuses. Laxity with locks can leave legs with little to lever.*

CAREER PROSPECTS:

• Careers Service • Unemployed after 6mths: 8%

FAMOUS ALUMNI:

Matthew Bannister (ex-controller, Radio 1); D H Lawrence (writer); Brian Moore (former England rugby player); Sir Robert Phillis (chairman of Guardian Media Group); Tim Robinson (cricketer); Sultan Raja Azlan Shah (King of Malaysia).

SPECIAL FEATURES:

• The University makes a big deal out of the fact that D H Lawrence was a student here and it's the foremost centre for research into his works, *although Lawrence's attitude to the University was, to say the least, ambivalent.*

• Two recent Nobel Prizes (Medicine, Economic Science) *have got the research scientists all giddy.*

FURTHER INFO:

• Prospectuses: undergrad; postgrad; video • Open days

ACADEMIC

31 schools are grouped into six faculties. All courses (bar Medicine, *thankfully*) are modular, meaning students can pick what they want to study. *Within reason.*

240-360		POINTS
Entry points: 240-360	Ave points: 370	
Applns per place: 10	Clearing: 2%	
No. of terms: 2	Length of terms: 14-16wks	
Staff/student ratio: 1:13	Study addicts: 17%	
Teaching: *****	Research: *****	
Year abroad: 4%	Sandwich students: 2%	
Firsts: 15%	2.2s: 19%	
2.1s: 61%	3rds: 3%	

ADMISSIONS:

• Apply via UCAS/NMAS for nursing

SUBJECTS:

Arts: 21%	Medicine & Health Sciences: 10%
Engineering: 12%	Sciences: 28%
Law and Social Sciences: 230%	

Best: Aeronautical & Manufacturing Engineering; Agriculture; American Studies; Anatomy & Physiology; Archaeology; Chemical Engineering; Civil Engineering; Classics & Ancient History; Economics; Education; Electrical & Electronic Engineering; Environmental Science; Food Science; German; History of Art; Materials Technology; Maths; Mechanical Engineering, Theology & Religious Studies; Medicine; Nursing & Midwifery; Physics & Astronomy; Physiotherapy; Psychology; Sociology; Town & Country Planning.

LIBRARIES:

• 1,200,000 books • 3,038 study places • Spend per student: ££££
There's the main Hallward library, a medical library and a library on the Jubilee and Sutton sites. *Very good facilities, although nocturnally-inclined students aren't happy about the 9.45pm closing time.*

COMPUTERS:

• 1,400 workstations • 24-hr access • Spend per student: £
The Cripps Computing Centre is the base of the *excellent* University network, which is steadily moving into pastures wireless.

OTHER LEARNING FACILITIES:

Language lab; audio/TV centre. Autumn 2006 sees the first 100 students walk through the doors of the *gleaming* new School of Veterinary Science – the first in the country for 50 years.

E N T E R T A I N M E N T

NOTTINGHAM:

• Price of a pint of beer: £1.80 • Glass of wine: £1.95 • Can of Red Bull: £2
Cinemas: Nottingham has a 16-screen multiplex as well as three 4-screen cinemas. The Nottingham Film Theatre shows *arty* pics and the Broadway offers student discounts. The Savoy is a rare instance of a cinema you can smoke in and also has double seats and an ice cream lady.
Theatres: The Royal Theatre is Nottingham's largest theatre and shows mainstream stuff, as well as opera and ballet. The Playhouse offers *top rep* and the Lace Market and Co-op Theatres host local am dram and fringe shows.
Pubs: The local brew is Hardy & Hansons. *Pushplugs: The Bag O' Nails, The Old Peacock, The Grove and The Ropewalk (all well-placed and have friendly atmospheres), Old Trip to Jerusalem (the country's oldest pub). Most local pubs are student friendly, though a few boozers in Beeston might be better avoided.*
Clubbing: *For the discerning clubber, Nottingham has many sweaty cattle markets where students can bop their socks off. Pushplugs: student nights at the Isis (sports night, Weds); Jelly Baby at The Works (SU chart night); The Zone at Ocean on Fridays; Karnival at The Works; Stretch at The Bomb (R'n'B and hip hop); Revolver at Obsessions (indie rock).*
Music venues: Rock City is Nottingham's main indie/rock venue. The Royal Concert Hall has classical concerts and more mainstream ents and Sam Fay's stages reggae events. The Nottingham Ice Arena melts down for big gigs. Girls Aloud did Nottingham recently. *Yes, they were rather tired afterwards.*
Eating out: *Plenty to satisfy the most jaded palate, including the usual run of franchises and dodgy kebabberies. Pushplugs: Tequila, Muchacha's (Mexican); Severez, Sapnars (Indian); Mayflower (Chinese); San Rimo's, Antibo's (Italian); Fat Cats (gorgeous potato skins); Baltimore Exchange (for that parental visit); Wok-u-like (bad name, good food).*

UNIVERSITY:

• Price of a pint of beer: £1.60 • Glass of wine: £2.20 • Can of Red Bull: £1.70
Bars: There are well-patronised bars in the halls of residence and the sports centre, but the focal points are the Buttery and D H Lawrence bars. Campus 14 is a tried and tested bar crawl around halls, which still goes on *despite being outlawed by the sheriffs of Nottingham University.* Union-run The Ark has a late licence at weekends.
Theatres: The New Theatre and D H Lawrence Pavilion are used for 12 productions a year (student and professional). The University Arts Centre, Lakeside, hosts a year-round programme of theatre, comedy, dance and exhibitions (www.lakesidearts.co.uk). Three student shows made it to the Edinburgh Fringe last year.
Film: The cinema, Unifilms, screens three films a week – a *nice* balance of independent and mainstream offerings, from Starsky & Hutch to El Crimen del Padre Amaro.
Clubbing: Two club nights a week and the Buttery Bar has been adapted for live music.

Comedy/Cabaret: A fortnightly session in The Ark pulls in the likes of Adam Bloom, Brendhan Lovegrove and Marcus Brigstocke.

Music venues: *The Ark does a decent line in middle-of-the-road bands.* The Summer Party is the *biggun*, though, bringing several thousand punters to the outdoor venue and big names including Trevor Nelson, Liberty-X and Toploader.

Food: The bars do *reasonable* sarnies to soak up the booze. The University-run Lakeside Diner and Food Court have a wider range *but they're a bit pricey.* The Ballroom is a *rather swanky continental-style* cafe and the Portland Dining Room has a *good* veggie variety. The Ark serves up nosh until 2am at weekends.

Other: *A whopping* 80 balls a year including the Graduation extravaganza and the Snowflake Ball for Rag. The University has its own art galleries, art bookshop, museum and a cafeteria (Café Lautrec).

SOCIAL & POLITICAL

UNIVERSITY OF NOTTINGHAM UNION:

• 8 sabbaticals • Turnout at last ballot: 37% • NUS member
It's a very moderate union, concentrating on slickly-run services rather than identifiable political commitment, though demos have been more successful here than elsewhere. Relations between the Union and the University authorities are very good.

SU FACILITIES:

The Portland Building is the centre of operations: bar; travel agent; three shops; advice centre; jobshop; theatre; rehearsal room; print shop and photocopying; record/CD/video library; car and minibus hire; NatWest and HSBC Banks (with cashpoints); games and vending machines; Endsleigh Insurance office; record and CD library; photo booth; pool table; juke box; TV lounge; eight meeting rooms; car parking.

CLUBS (NON-SPORTING):

Action For Earth; AIESEC; American; Arab; Baha'i; Bands; Bassic; Bell Ringing; Blow *(flutes and things, not Johnny Depp high as a kite)*; Bouncy Castle; Chess & Backgammon; Chinese; Chocolate; Classical; Cocktail; Cymsoc (Welsh); Cyprus; Duke of Edinburgh; Feast; Football Supporters; Funk; Gaba (Going Abroad, Being Abroad); Gilbert & Sullivan; Green; Guinness; Hedonizm; Hellenic; High; Hispanic; Indian; Juggling; Kebab; Korean; Latin & Ballroom Dancing; Law; Malaysian & Singapore; Music; Mutant; New Lit; Orchestra; Pakistan; Politics; Role Play; Russian; Scout & Guide; Scribble; Seventies; Sikh; Slavonic; Soul; Star; Taiwan; Thai; Turkish; Wine.

OTHER ORGANISATIONS:

Impact (monthly magazine) and Grapevine (weekly paper) are the press, but it's University Radio Nottingham that wins the awards. Also Karnival, the charity Rag, is one of the country's biggest, raising more than £416,000 last year. The University's *tremendously successful* Community Action group involves nearly 2,000 students in 75 projects *and can claim some responsibility for the excellent student/community relations.*

RELIGIOUS:

• 7 chaplains (CofE, RC, Methodist, International, URC, Quaker)
Chapel and Muslim prayer room in the Portland Building. Local places of worship for most Christian denominations, Muslims, Jews, Sikhs, Hindus and Buddhists.

PAID WORK:

• Job bureau
The Centre for Career Development runs job agency 'Nucleus'. Apart from the usual money scrambles, students have been known to sell themselves as guinea pigs at the medical school.

SPORTS

• Recent successes: rugby, hockey, lacross, rowing • BUSA Ranking: 15
Outstanding facilities. *Top-level sport is strong and there's a concerted effort to spread the exercise bug with inter-hall competitions and taster sessions.*

SPORTS FACILITIES:

Most outdoor facilities are at Grove Farm, a mile from the campus, but some are also on campus. In all, there are 120 acres of playing fields including a floodlit artificial hockey pitch and a croquet lawn/bowling green. There's also the University lake, a 2,000m rowing course near the campus and the University Boathouse on the Trent. The sports centre on University Park campus has the biggest and *most efficient* sports hall in the country, a 25m 8-lane pool, two tennis courts, 12 indoor sports courts, a smaller hall, seven squash courts, a climbing wall, fitness room, table tennis, snooker room, bar and coffee shop. There are bursaries for the best.

SPORTING CLUBS:

10-Pin Bowling; Aikido; American Football; Bat Polo; Boat; Boxing; Canoe; Canoe Polo; Caving; Darts; Exploring; Gliding; Hand Ball; Ice Hockey; Inline Hockey; Ju-Jitsu; Korfball; Kung Fu; Lacrosse; Lifesaving; Mountaineering; Motorsport; Munro; Nin Jutsu; Parachuting; Paragliding; Polo; Rambling; Rifle & Clay; Rugby League; Snooker; Snowsports; Softball; Surfing; Table Tennis; Thai Boxing; Triathlon; Ultimate Frisbee; Water Polo; Water Skiing; Weight Training; Wing Chun. **See also Clubs tables**.

ATTRACTIONS:

In addition to Nottingham Forest and Notts County FCs, the Rugby Club and the County Cricket, there are geegees and woof-woofs racing at Colwick, the ice rink (where Torvill and Dean learned their craft), the National Watersports Centre and one of Europe's largest Lawn Tennis Association Centres.

ACCOMMODATION

IN COLLEGE:

• Catered: 23% • Cost: £105 (31wks)
• Self-catering: 40% • Cost: £71 (44–46wks)
• First years living in: 96% • Insurance premium: ££££
Availability: Every 1st year is offered the chance to live in one of the catered halls or self-catering flats. *Most popular are the University Park campus halls. The community atmosphere's very strong and there's a friendly rivalry with inter-hall competitions and so on.* Four halls are single sex only (two men's, two women's). There are 2,000 self-catering places in flats of five, six or seven students within Broadgate Park, Raleigh Park and St Peter's Court, within 5-25 mins walking radius of the University Park and Jubilee sites. The privately-rented St Peters Court and Raleigh Park *are more expensive and less popular, though they have good bars.* There's some accommodation for married students and disabled students.
Car parking: *Virtually non-existent on campus, okay at self-catering halls.*

EXTERNALLY:

• Ave rent: £60
Availability: *A decent supply of private housing. Lenton and Dunkirk (not that Dunkirk) are good places to look, lying as they do between the campus and the city. Beeston is also a student spot, but slightly further out. Stapleford and Ilkeston are a bit far and Radford is none too safe. Woollaton is an option for the more sedate scholars.*
Housing help: The Accommodation Office has *plenty* of advisers to help with property vetting and contract approval. There's a vacancy list, approved landlord list and a bulletin board.

WELFARE

SERVICES:
- Lesbian/Gay/Bisexual Society • Women's Society • Mature Students' Society
- International Students' Society • Postgrad Society • Disabilities Society
- Late-night minibus • Welfare Officer • Self-defence classes
- Nightline • College counsellors: 4 full/7 part • Crime rating: !!!!!

The Students' Union Student Advice Centre is *its pride and joy*, co-ordinating all its welfare work from advice and help for all to the International Students' Bureau. It also offers Union solicitors for consultation (free for the first session).

Health: Cripps Health Centre has four doctors, an occupational health specialist and nurses, and offers extra care for a £12 annual subscription. Physios at the Sports Centre.

Women: Free attack alarms available from the Union, which also provides occasional self-defence classes. The late-night minibus runs every night.

Crèches/Nursery: Some childcare facilities are available.

Disabilities: Nottingham's been making *steady* efforts in improving access. There are adapted facilities, rooms for personal assistants, an alternative formats service and a disabled students' minibus.

FINANCE:
- Ave debt per year: £3,300

Fees: Postgrad fees are around £3,020. International students have to pay between £8,350 and £11,020.
- Access fund ave payment: £100-3,500

Support: Hardship fund and some scholarships available. There are plans to create some top-up-balancing bursaries.

Nottingham Trent University

- *Formerly Nottingham Polytechnic, Trent Polytechnic.*
(1) The Nottingham Trent University, Burton Street, Nottingham, NG1 4BU
    Tel: (0115) 941 8418 E-mail: marketing@ntu.ac.uk Website: www.ntu.ac.uk
    The Nottingham Trent University Union of Students, Byron House, Shakespeare Street,
    NG1 4GH Tel: (0115) 848 6200 E-mail: empstore@su.ntu.ac.uk
    Website: www.su.ntu.ac.uk
(2) Clifton Campus, Clifton, Nottingham. Contact details as City campus above.
(3) School of Land-based Studies, Brackenhurst, Southwell, Notts, NG25 0QF
    Tel: (01636) 817 000

GENERAL

Once upon a time there was Trent Poly, then it became Nottingham Poly, and now it's in its third incarnation as a university. There are three campuses: the City site in the city centre, the largest site and, *if the truth be known*, the main site; the more modern Clifton site, 4 miles away; and a third site at Brackenhurst 14 miles from the city centre. Over the last few years, money has been thrown at Nottingham Trent, *like it was a stripper at a rugby bash*, so it's got a bundle of modern facilities.

Sex ratio (M:F): 50:50	Founded: 1992
Full-time u'grads: 15,800	Part-time: 2,865
Postgrads: 1,930	Non-degree: 9,280
Ave course: 3yrs	Ethnic: 16%
State:private school: 90:10	Flunk rate: 10%
Mature: 13%	International: 8%
Disabled: 389	Local: 28%

ATMOSPHERE:

It's a right ol' mix of ages and backgrounds. Students are scattered geographically, because most live out and they're spread across two sites. Despite that, they like nothing more than getting together and solemnly discussing the state of the world and the price of chips. Perhaps with a drink or two thrown in, for social lubrication purposes only.

SITES:

City Site: (Art & Design, Business, Environment, Law & Economics) On the edge of the city centre, the University's main campus is a *jumble* of Victorian three- & four-storey houses, slabs of clean concrete and tower blocks (such as the main Newton Building) with *sparse green areas in between. The Union's main centre is in a block designed as a swimming-pool complex. It's an ugly building but with a lively atmosphere that endears it to the regulars.*
Clifton Campus: (5,775 students – Education, Humanities, Science) Set on a hill overlooking the River Trent and its valley, near where D H Lawrence set Sons and Lovers, Clifton is a *small, friendly and modern site with so much to offer that students can get isolated from city life*. It also boasts one of the only Environmental Chambers in the UK – so *eco-boffins can control a little bit of the weather and pretend to be Sean Connery in The Avengers. Only less ridiculous.*
Brackenhurst: (1,342 – Land-based studies) Full of *eager beavers* enjoying catering and sports facilities, library, SU and bar. It's all set in *tranquil* farmland and woods.

NOTTINGHAM: see University of Nottingham

TRAVEL: see University of Nottingham

Local: Nottingham station is a mile from the City site, buses cost between 50-80p (or a quid return) from the City Centre to Clifton with several companies running regular services. There's also an inter-campus bus service which covers late-night antics and a tram service running between the University, the station and elsewhere.

CAREER PROSPECTS:

• Careers Service • No. of staff: 6 full/11 part • Unemployed after 6mths: 6%
The careers service employs a shed-load of people itself and has bulletin boards, library and advice.

FAMOUS ALUMNI:

Jonathen Glazner (director); Paul Kaye (aka Dennis Pennis); Dame Laura Knight (artist); Paul Ratcliffe (Olympic silver medallist, canoeing); Alan Simpson MP (Lab); Steve Trapmore (Olympic gold rower).

FURTHER INFO:

• Prospectuses: undergrad; postgrad; departmental • Open days

ACADEMIC

Along with a *chunky* amount of investment in new facilities the University is *vocationally very aware.* Strong industry links mean extensive opportunities for student placements and a high rate of graduate employment. Nottingham Trent also has a *good* research rep and plenty of *their bizarre* discoveries find their way into the papers, from findings about female Russian suicide bombers to the psychological perils of watching TV news.

160-360 POINTS

Entry points: 160-360	Ave points: 220
Applns per place: 5	Clearing: 15%
No. of terms: 3	Length of terms: 10wks
Staff/student ratio: 1:15	Study addicts: 69%
Teaching: **	Research: ****
Year abroad: n/a	Sandwich students: 37%
Firsts: 7%	2.2s: 38%
2.1s: 48%	3rds: 4%

ADMISSIONS:

• Apply via UCAS

SUBJECTS:

Animal, Rural & Environmental Science: 2.1%	Business School: 19.9%
Art & Design: 10.5%	Computing & Informatics: 3.9%
Arts, Communication and Culture: 9.9%	Education: 7%
Biomedical & Natural Sciences: 6.2%	Law School: 10.7%
Built Environment: 12%	Social Sciences: 17.6%

Best: Art & Design; Building; Business & Management; Chemistry; Economics; Education; Molecular Biosciences; Organismal Biosciences; Other subjects allied to Medicine; Physics; Politics; Psychology; Sport Science.

LIBRARIES:

• 428,000 books • 900 study places • 24-hr access • Spend per student: ££
There are three libraries shared between the campuses, most open 12 hrs a day, spiced up with some limited 24-hr access. *Rather short on books, though.*

COMPUTERS:

• 1,356 workstations • 24-hr access
Each site has its own IT centre, some with 24-hr access. Most terminals have internet access and all halls are wired so students can dial-up to IT facilities.

OTHER LEARNING FACILITIES:

Silly amounts of recent investment: £3m teaching and lab facility at Brackenhurst; £1.2m biomedical science building at Clifton campus; currently developing a bioscience and healthcare innovation centre; a joint Toyota/University-built £3m training centre at Clifton – the only one of its kind in Europe (*which doesn't necessarily make it special, only rare.*)

ENTERTAINMENT

THE CITY: see University of Nottingham

UNIVERSITY:

• Price of a pint of beer: £1.50 • Glass of wine: £1.45
Bars: The Glo Bar at the City site is designed to be like a modern loft, *or an attic or something. It's popular anyway.* Le Metro's downstairs opens out into a night spot, *but closes unexpectedly from time to time.* Clifton has the Point and *is quite happy about that.*
Theatres: One customised theatre and two lecture rooms with stages and drama soc shows at all of them.
Clubbing/Music: Friday is the big Clifton day, while the City site bops twice a week. Shipwrecked washes the faithful to shore with its blend of charty, dancey, techno stuff. Clifton bar does a comedy night once a week as well as club night Pounded (£1 admission/per drink).
Food: The Sports Diner, Sandwich City and Chaucer Late deal with all fast food requirements. *The school dinners at the University's legoland-like refectory pale by comparison.*
Other: Balls are mostly handled by the societies but the SU does the *big* summer bash.

SOCIAL & POLITICAL

NOTTINGHAM TRENT STUDENTS' UNION

• 6 sabbaticals • NUS member • Turnout at last ballot: 19%

NTSU *shuns politics, preferring to stress its position as a commercial organisation.* The prez sits on the board of governors and student reps have a say at faculty board meetings.

SU FACILITIES:

NTSU has facilities at all three sites, in Byron House on the City site and in the Benenson Building at Clifton. Byron's got two bars; café; minibuses; travel agents; photocopying; shop; games and vending machines; pool tables; juke box; HSBC bank; recycling; meeting rooms; insurance office. Clifton has: a bar; coffee shop; shop; bookshop; printing; pool tables; recycling; games machines. Both sites have employment stores and ticket agencies.

CLUBS (NON-SPORTING):

Bad Poets; Breakbeat; Clubbing; Computer Society; Conversation; Cult Fiction; Drama Club; Geography; Gliding; Hiking; IASS; International Students; Karting; Motorcycle; Mountaineering; Rock (music); Tai Kwon Do; Trampolining; Ultimate Frisbee; Wado Ryu Karate; War Games & Role Play; Yawara Ryu. **See also Clubs table.**

OTHER ORGANISATIONS:

Platform, the free Union newspaper, is distributed free fortnightly during term. Fly FM transmits for a month, twice a year. The Student Festival Week raises cash for charity while the SCAG does *noble things in the wider world*.

RELIGIOUS:

• 6 chaplains (CofE, RC, FC)

The Christian Union is extremely forthright and influential. Muslim prayer space also available.

PAID WORK: see University of Nottingham

• Job bureau

The Students in Classrooms scheme lets undergrads earn money while studying. Students are recruited to work in local schools and further education colleges.

SPORTS

• BUSA Ranking: 36

NTSU sorts out anything that may be considered sporty, but they don't call it sport, they call it *recreation, which reveals the University's attitude to all things healthy. It's not the winning that's important, it's the having a laugh, not being obese and, if possible, developing a six-pack.* The annual fee for facilities is a fiver and then there're *smaller additional* charges after that.

SPORTS FACILITIES:

Sports facilities and 30-odd acres of playing fields are spread between two sites.

City: Sports hall; indoor cricket nets; climbing wall; badminton; netball; volleyball court; fitness suites; aerobics studio; two squash courts; gym. *Enthusiasm gets a bit of a slap as access to the pitches is tricky.*

Clifton: Sports hall; two gyms; multigym; two squash courts; playing fields; all-weather pitches; athletics track; cricket pitch.

Brackenhurst: Facilities for cricket, football and netball. Also home to the University's riding club.

SPORTING CLUBS:

American Football; Belgrave Sports Club; KSBO; Women's Football; Women's Rugby. **See also Clubs tables.**

ATTRACTIONS: see University of Nottingham

ACCOMMODATION

IN COLLEGE:
- Self-catered: 21% • Cost: £65 (40wks)
- First years living in: 80% • Insurance premium: ££££

Availability: Most halls are near the city site (or the main road that leads up to it), with another at Clifton. Students *would be wise to apply early*, but those with unconditional offers or international students *need not worry. Perevill's the most popular choice on campus*, with en-suite facilities. Brackenhurst offers *cheap* places with catering and the University runs a head tenancy scheme *for students who can't be bothered to look for their own flat*.

Car parking: Parking permits allow a handful of deserving students to get at the *gold-dust* spaces.

EXTERNALLY: see University of Nottingham
- Ave rent: £50 • Living at home: 14%

Housing help: The University's Accommodation Service keeps an office on each site has a register of the *least-offensive* housing. They help with contracts, run a landlord accreditation scheme. NTSU runs an introduction to house-hunting course for 1st years.

WELFARE

SERVICES:
- Mature Students' Officer • International Students' Officer • Disabilities Officer & Society
- Late-night/Women's minibus • Self-defence classes • Peer Support Group
- College counsellors: 2 full/3 part • Crime rating: !!!!!

The University offers counselling and student support services. Medical centres at the City and Clifton sites have doctors and nurses.

Women: Free attack alarms available.

Crèches/Nursery: Both sites have daily nurseries for 1-5yrs and a holiday play scheme for 5-14yrs.

Disabilities: The self-catering hall in Peel Street has wheelchair-friendly accommodation. Students are advised to contact the University's Disability Support Service to sort out any issues before they happen. *Having said that, access to lots of buildings is pretty dire.*

FINANCE:
- Ave debt per year: £5,012 • Access fund: £1,013,556

Support: As well as the Access fund there are opportunity bursaries, Learning and Skills Council Learner Support Funds, hardship loans and TTA bursaries.

Nottingham Polytechnic
see Nottingham Trent University

The Open University

Oriental Studies see <u>SOAS</u>

University of Oxford
Balliol College, Oxford
Brasenose College, Oxford
Christ Church, Oxford
Corpus Christi College, Oxford
Exeter College, Oxford
Greyfriars Hall, Oxford
Harris Manchester College, Oxford
Hertford College, Oxford
Jesus College, Oxford
Keble College, Oxford
Lady Margaret Hall, Oxford
Lincoln College, Oxford
Magdalen College, Oxford
Mansfield College, Oxford
Merton College, Oxford
New College, Oxford
Oriel College, Oxford
Pembroke College, Oxford
Regent's Park College, Oxford
Somerville College, Oxford
St Anne's College, Oxford
St Catherine's College, Oxford
St Edmund Hall, Oxford
St Hilda's College, Oxford
St Hugh's College, Oxford
St John's College, Oxford
St Peter's College, Oxford
The Queen's College, Oxford
Trinity College, Oxford
University College, Oxford
Wadham College, Oxford
Worcester College, Oxford

Oxford Brookes University

Oxford Poly see <u>Oxford Brookes University</u>

The Open University

The Open University, Walton Hall, Milton Keynes, MK7 6AA
Tel: (01908) 653 231 E-mail: general-enquiries@open.ac.uk Website: www.open.ac.uk
Open University Students' Association, PO Box 397, Walton Hall, Milton Keynes, MK7 6BE
Tel: (01908) 652 026 E-mail: ousa@open.ac.uk Website: www.open.ac.uk/ousa/

Many first come across the OU while surfing through late-night telly. But the times are a-changing, and younger students *who want to avoid major debt*, or feel they're *not quite cut out for a conventional university experience, are attracted in growing numbers*. It's *especially well-suited* to disabled students, who might have access difficulties elsewhere. Courses are run by 'distance-learning', so there are TV and radio programmes (an increasing number produced with the BBC and aired during prime time), audio-lectures and internet tools *to bolster the books*. All degrees are part-time, *and require particular powers of dedication, especially to resist the dubious temptations of Channel 5 in the middle of a lecture*. Some courses require attendance at regional centres or day schools as well as the substantial amount of self-study students need to undertake.

Sex ratio (M:F): 41:59	**Founded: 1969**
Postgrads: 19,239	**Non-degree: 7,600**
Part-time: 141,635	**Flunk rate: n/a**
Ave course: 6yrs	**Ethnic: 12%**
Mature: 97%	**International: 5%**
Disabled: 836	

ATMOSPHERE:
Open University students hit the books wherever they might be. *For some that means living rooms, local libraries or cafés. For others it has meant while 20,000 leagues beneath the sea in a Navy submarine, living homeless on the streets of London, on board a yacht, in the Bosnian war zone, while on kidney dialysis or while banged up at Her Majesty's pleasure. The closest real place the OU could find to reflect the essentially virtual location is* Milton Keynes. *Appropriately enough, the town looks like it was designed and built by correspondence course. From Mars. Of course, most students are lucky enough never to visit.* They make use of official study centres attached to other universities and colleges around the country (most recently the Tremough campus in Cornwall, part of the Combined Universities Initiative and run in conjunction with Exeter and Plymouth – see <u>Exeter University</u> for more details). Most OU students are mature *(in attitude, as well as age) and tend to juggle study with other commitments (kids, jobs, mortgages, prison etc.). However, that's changing with the* drive to recruit younger members. *But, like the man says, 'OU students do it on their own', which means the atmosphere is a totally individual thing.*

CAREER PROSPECTS:
• <u>Careers Service</u> • <u>No. of staff: 2 full</u>
Most OU students already have jobs – often their employers are shelling out for them in the first place. But the University lays on workshops, newsletters and bulletin boards *to keep job-hunters' options open*.

FAMOUS ALUMNI:
Joan Armatrading (singer); Connie Booth (actress/writer); Craig Brown CBE (former Scotland football manager); Brian Burrige (Air Chief Marshal); Julie Christie (actress); Micky Dolenz (ex-Monkee); Jerry Hall (actress, model); Sheila Hancock (actress); Matthew Kelly (TV presenter); Lord Gardiner (former Lord Chancellor); Dave Sexton (football manager); Vikram Solanki (cricketer); Susan Tully (actress); Meles Zenawi (Prime Minister of Ethiopia). Honorary degrees given to Bill Bryson (author), Alan Ayckbourn (playwright) and Heather Mills-McCartney (former model and wife of Sir Paul).

SPECIAL FEATURES:
In March 2000 the OU held the world's first Virtual Degree ceremony. *It sounds like something from The Matrix*, but was actually to award MAs to students in eight different countries who had taken their entire degrees online.

FURTHER INFO:
• <u>Prospectuses: undergrad; postgrad; departmental</u> • <u>Open days</u>
There are student advisers at regional campuses. For further info on courses – many of which are introductory, non-degree or tied in with the BBC – see www.open.ac.uk/courses

ACADEMIC

Unlike most universities, there are no academic qualifications required to study. The OU has a *well-earned* reputation for teaching excellence, *which it shows off by regularly trouncing the Oxbridge upstarts on University Challenge*. Assessment varies from course to course, with a mix of written assignments, oral or practical assessments, exams and dissertations. Tutors are available via phone or e-mail if support is needed. *As always, the emphasis is on the individual* – so it's up to students how, when and where they work. *Sounds like a slacker's paradise, but it takes Herculean commitment and motivation.*

Length of terms: Traditionally the OU academic year has run from February to October, but many courses now offer multiple start dates.

Teaching: ***	**Research: *** **
Staff/student ratio: 1:19	**2.2s: 31%**
Firsts: 18%	**3rds: 10%**
2.1s: 41%	

ADMISSIONS:

• Apply direct

No formal qualifications are necessary, though the OU will advise students on what level of course is best suited. Younger students are being actively recruited; even prisoners can apply. 1,250 places should be available by 2006.

SUBJECTS:

Arts: 16%	Math & Computing: 11%
Business School: 6%	(Modern) Languages: 4%
Centre of Widening Participation: 6%	Sciences: 14%
Education: 6%	Social Sciences: 17%
Health & Social Welfare: 8%	

Best: Art History; Biology; Business & Management Studies; Chemistry; Classical Studies; Economics; Education; General Engineering; Health Studies; Maths; Philosophy; Physics; Politics; Psychology; Religious Studies; Sociology.

LIBRARIES:

• 200,000+ books • 150 study places

There's a 200,000 volume central library in Milton Keynes, although most students are more likely to use OU regional study centres. Students can also use several thousand e-books, as well as many local and other institution libraries.

COMPUTERS:

More and more courses are conducted on the net, and in many cases the courses actually demand computer access. Electronic resources *are excellent*. An online library contains core text books and more than 4,000 others as well as a conference system that allows students in 150 courses to join in discussion forums. It's up to students to make the practical arrangements, though, either privately or through local colleges and libraries.

SOCIAL & POLITICAL

OPEN UNIVERSITY STUDENTS' ASSOCIATION (OUSA)

OUSA isn't a political organisation, and it concentrates fairly exclusively on academic and welfare issues. 19 part-time officers run OUSA (not affiliated to the NUS) and the minority of students apply for membership.

SU FACILITIES:

No central facilities, although OUSA do sell stationery and products by mail order, co-ordinate some societies and organise occasional ents at summer schools.

College: OUSU runs a nightbus.

Taxis: *Black cabs and minicabs aplenty, but they're happy to charge a small fortune for a smaller journey.*

Bicycles: Oxford's *flat*, some roads are closed to cars and most colleges have sheds. *A few words of warning: (i) a good lock and a cheap bike is the safest defence against theft and (ii) pedestrians – watch out for two-wheeled lunatics.*

CAREER PROSPECTS:

• Careers Service • No. of staff: 16 full • Unemployed after 6mths: 8%

Forget any romantic notions of being headhunted straight out of Oxford into the City, the BBC or the Foreign Office. Oxford grads have to scrap it out with the rabble nowadays. So it's a good job the careers service has vacancy lists, careers library, talks and counselling.

FAMOUS ALUMNI:

See individual colleges.

SPECIAL FEATURES:

• Oxford's *full of ritual*, especially when it comes to exams. Students have to dress in subfusc (formal clothes) and *look like batman on the way to the Oscars*. It's a well-known myth that once a student turned up for his final exams and demanded a glass of sherry in accordance with an ancient rite. After the exam, he was fined a shilling by his college authorities for not wearing his sword during his exam – another forgotten statute. *Rites like these seem positively sane compared with some of the continuing traditions.*

• Speaking of which, it's worth pointing out that while the official HESA figures show a high number of part-time students, it includes those on continuing education and graduate courses – you can't actually apply to do a part-time undergrad degree at Oxford. *What do you think this is, the* Open University?

FURTHER INFO:

• Prospectuses: undergrad; postgrad; deptartmental • Open days • Video

Most colleges produce their own prospectuses and some JCRs also have alternative guides.

ACADEMIC

Workloads are *tough* compared to *the mere mortal unis*, but facilities are *a world apart*. Terms are *short* (eight weeks), although most students stay longer, boning up for exams with *weird and wonderful* titles like 'mods', 'collections', 'prelims' and, er, 'finals'. The newer parts of the Uni include the Begbroke Business and Science Park and the *impressive* glass-fronted Said Business School.

Entry points: 340-360	Ave points: n/a
Applns per place: 4	Clearing: 0
No. of terms: 3	Length of terms: 8wks
Staff/student ratio: 1:8	Study addicts: 36%
Teaching: *****	Research: *****
Year abroad: 5	Sandwich students: 0
Firsts: 24%	2.2s: 10%
2.1s: 66%	3rds: 0%

ADMISSIONS:

• Apply via UCAS

SUBJECTS:

Arts/Humanities: 35.5%   Sciences: 37.4%
Medical Sciences: 6.9%   Social Sciences: 20.2%

Best: Archaeology; Biochemistry; Biological Sciences/Forestry; Classics/Ancient History; Economics; Engineering; Fine Art; Materials; Maths; Medicine/Physiology; Modern Languages; Oriental Studies; Philosophy; Physics; Politics; Psychology.

LIBRARIES:

• 6,000,000 books • 2,500 study places • 24-hr access

The famous Bodleian Library is the collective title given to the University's main research libraries (including the Radcliffe Science Library, Bodleian Law Library and Indian Institute Library, mainly housed in the Old and the New Library Buildings, and all the *marvellous* others). It is one of the country's five copyright libraries which means that it can demand a copy of any book published in the UK and, as a consequence, it has over six million books (*including The Push Guides*). 948,000 of these – *yup, a mere 948,000* – are on open shelves and most of them can't be borrowed, though students can view them *if they ask nicely*. In fact, Oxford students don't have the right to use the Bodleian until they've undergone one of the University's many *bizarre* initiation rituals. This one involves swearing *oddly practical* oaths such as agreeing not to set fire to the buildings. *Nude dancing and sacrificing virgin goats is not usually an essential part of this ceremony.* Each college and most University departments also have their own libraries, most of which lend books.

COMPUTERS:

• 2,500 workstations • 24-hr access

Most colleges have *woken up to the idea of an IT revolution* and upgraded from their clapped-out Amstrads. The Computer Teaching Centre has 100 networked terminals and the Computer Service which provides support for students' research when their departments fall short. 24-hr access during term-time.

ENTERTAINMENT

THE CITY:

• Price of a pint of beer: £2.50 • Glass of wine: £2.60 • Can of Red Bull: £2.50

Cinemas: For standard blockbusters there are two ABC Cinemas (three screens at one, one at the other) *and for the slightly higher brow*, The Phoenix (two screens) in Jericho and the Ultimate Picture Palace in Cowley.

Theatres: The New Theatre has *standard* family fare with pantos at Xmas and summer specials after the end of term. It also hosts the occasional concert. The Playhouse tends towards *brainier* offerings, including a few big student productions. The Pegasus Theatre's *on the fringe in every sense* with experimental productions and a bit of a trek to get there and also shows student productions. The *recently tarted-up* Old Fire Station also hosts student stuff.

Pubs: The old-school charm of many of Oxford's pubs comes at *premium price*. As a result, they aren't too popular with *pocket-conscious* students. *Pushplugs: The King's Arms ('The KA' as it's affectionately known); The Turf; The Bullingdon Arms; The Lamb & Flag (now owned by* St John's*); The Eagle and Child (C S Lewis and Tolkien used to quaff there). The Jolly Farmers is the main gay haunt.*

Clubbing: *Ungracious dogholes in the main. The Bridge is the best of the bunch. Other slightly more dubious, but still popular options are Po Na Na, the Purple Turtle and the Coven.*

Music venues: The music scene's booming, with *loads* of local bands dreaming of *doing a Radiohead*. *Pushplugs: The New Theatre (big, mainstream); The Pub Oxford; The Zodiac (indie).*

Eating out: Various kebab vans open *till they run out of domestic animals or 3am – whichever is sooner*. Cowley Rd in general is *good* for cheap eats. *Pushplugs: Brown's (perfect parent parlour); Jamal's (Indian); Queen's Lane Coffee House; George and Davis (ice cream); Radcliffe Arms (pub grub); La Cappanina (Italian, Supergrass ate here).*

UNIVERSITY:

Bars: Each college has a bar, some of which only serve their own students. The Union (debating society) has a bar, but it's *closed to the riff-raff*: Members Only.

Theatres: The Old Fire Station, the Burton-Taylor Theatre (above The Playhouse) and the larger Newman Rooms host student stuff. In summer there are outdoor productions in many College gardens.

Music venues: Student bands play in any room large enough – bars usually – and the Sheldonian Theatre and Holywell Music rooms host classical concerts. However, because the University has no single big venue, *it doesn't often attract big names*, except for at ball-time.

Clubbing: Most colleges have weekly, fortnightly or termly 'bops' – *sweaty and intensive pissups that often serve as hotbeds for college scandal.*

Comedy/Cabaret: The Oxford Revue (student comedy group which pursues a healthy rivalry with Cambridge's Footlights) performs stand-up and improv at the Comedy Cellar at the Union and does other special shows.

Food: Oxford tends to go for formal meals in a big way, although the frequency, quality and number of gongs and Latin grace-readings *differs* from college to college. There are cafeterias, often known (*predictably obscurely*) as butteries. There are few University facilities – no central refectory, although some faculties have caffs.

Balls: Most colleges have an annual ball where everyone *dons their dapperest* and *thrills* to the strains of live bands, discos, cabarets, casinos, hypnotists, karaoke, in fact *anything that becomes a lot more fun when completely wrecked. Some love them; others resent shelling out £80 for a spruced-up night out in college. Either way, balls are an Oxbridge institution.* Some colleges have a cheaper alternative called an event, which usually doesn't involve the get-up or the grub and costs nearer £20.

SOCIAL & POLITICAL

OXFORD UNIVERSITY STUDENTS' UNION:
• 6 sabbaticals • Turnout at last ballot: 33%

OUSU doesn't have a union building, as there are 39 other common rooms for students to *hang around shooting pool and dodging lectures* in. The main role of OUSU is to *make a lot of noise* campaigning and representing students at University level. Each college has a Junior Common Room (JCR), which is usually a committee as well as a building. They're all affiliated to OUSU, and although OUSU isn't affiliated to the NUS, some JCRs are. *Keeping up?* Anyway, OUSU co-ordinates a *swamp* of societies and prints alternative prospectuses, freshers' guides and so forth. *It's generally leftier than the average and run by cracks and hacks on their way up the greasy pole.*

CLUBS (NON-SPORTING):

Acoustic Music; Air Squadron; Alice (Lewis Carroll appreciation); Alternative Classical; Apathy; Arcadian Singers (unaccompanied singing); Archaeological; Architectural; Art; Arthurian; Artificial Intelligence; Arts; Astronomical; Australia; Bach Choir; Ba'hai; Ballroom Dancing; Bell Ringing; Black Caucus; Bonn (Oxford's German twin town); Book-Lovers; Bow Group (Conservative ideology); Brazilian; Buddhist; Caledonian (Scottish dancing); Friends of Cambodia; Campaign for an Independent Europe (anti-EU); Canadian; Central America Support; Ceroc (French-style jive dancing); Chamber Choir; Champagne Socialists; Choice (teacher & pupil support); Christian Aid; Student Christian Movement; Christian Science; Classical; Classical Drama; Colombian; Comedy Cellar; Comic Books; Community Church; Computing; Contemporary Music; Cranmer (Anglican Christian); Creative Writing; Cribbage; C S Lewis Appreciation; Cypriot; Dangerous Sports; Diplomatic (tactical board games); Dr Who; Douglas Adams (Hitch Hiker's Guide to the Galaxy); Early Music; East Asian Research; Educational Exchange (studying abroad); English-Speaking Union; Enterprise; Esperanto; European Community; Exploration; Film Foundation; Alternative Film; Food & Wine; Freedom (dance music); French; Gamelan (Javanese percussion); German; Gilbert & Sullivan; Go (oriental game); Greek; Guitar; History; History Alive!; Homeless Action; Hong Kong; Humanist; Hunt Sabs; Indie Music; Inner Temple (Law); International Political Economy; Investment; Israel; Italian; Japanese; Juggling; Kites; Laissez-Faire Dining (individual freedoms & food); Latin American; Law; L'Chaim (Jewish cultural); Legal Aid; Light Entertainment; Links (St John Ambulance); Literary Society; Living Marxism; La Maison Française (French cultural); Malaysia- Singapore; Malaysian; Middle-East; Middle Temple (Law); Monty Python Appreciation; Motor Drivers; Natural History; Natural Philosophy; New Testament; Numismatic (Coins); Ockham (philosophical); Opera; Ornithology; Pacific Rim; Past & Present Historical; Pastorate (Christian); Peripheral Vision (film/Third World issues); Club de Pétanque (French game); Philharmonia; Plough (bio-environmental); Poetry; Polish & Central European; Politics; Pooh Sticks (A A Milne appreciation); Practical Arts; Psychology; Railway; Reformed Church; Role-Playing Games; Russian; Save the Children; Schola Cantoram (chamber choir); Scientific; Scottish Dance; Scout & Guide; Sherlock Holmes; Sinfonietta (chamber orchestra); Soul Appreciation; Soviet Jewry Campaign; Space Exploration; Spanish; Star Trek; Strategic Studies; Tawney (discussion); Theatre-Going; Tolkein; Tory Reform; Turf (horse-racing & gambling); UNICEF; Upfront (soul/hip-hop/house disco); Vedic (Indian); Vegetarian; Visual Productions (film/video); Wagner (appreciation); Wargaming; Welsh; John Wesley (Christian); Wheatsheaf (pub philosophy); Wind Orchestra; Wine; WWF; Wychwood Warriors (dark ages); Yank (Americans). **See also Clubs tables.**

OTHER ORGANISATIONS:

Students who spend their days at Oxford doing nothing but their degrees are *made to feel like David Beckham at a Mensa meeting*. There are plenty of fields of endeavour to choose from including various sports, OUSU and college JCRs as well as the following:

The Oxford Union Society: Not to be confused with OUSU (the Students' Union), the Union is Oxford's *world famous* debating society. Ted Heath, Edwina Currie and Benazir Bhutto are among its ex-presidents. Its *high profile* has attracted some of the world's most famous speakers to take part in debates and discussions, from Yasser Arafat to Vinny Jones, JFK to Kermit the Frog. The Union is also the name of the HQ building which offers a social scene, a bar, restaurant, the Comedy Cellar, a library and all the paraphernalia of traditional gentlemen's clubs, but women can join too. *That's the good news. The bad news is that it costs £100 and the Union is a nest for some of the University's most arrogant and obnoxious knob-ends.*

Oxford University Dramatic Society (OUDS): Almost every day of every term, the population of Oxford is faced with a choice of several student theatrical performances. Thesps visit each other's productions and thus the shows go on. The standard often reaches a *thoroughly professional* level, but sometimes, *well, it doesn't*, and the selection is as diverse as any *legal* experience in a theatre can get. Whether the star of Spielberg's last pic or the third sheep in the primary school nativity effort, new talent is welcomed to auditions with *open arms, kisses on both cheeks and the words 'lovely, daaahling'*. The post-audition reception is *more discriminating* and *bitter cries of 'Clique!' have echoes of truth*, although drama at Oxford is so *widespread* that even the *most wooden pretenders* get a chance to try their board-treading technique. Meanwhile, there are *just as many* opportunities to play the non-singing part of unsung hero backstage. OUDS is the organisational body which co-ordinates and supports this plague of plays and runs the Cuppers drama competition.

Media: Magazines come and go *as fast as the tourists* in Oxford but there are several long-standing publications with *excellent* reputations. *Primarily*, there's Cherwell, Oxford's award-winning weekly student newspaper. *Last of the newspapers and least*, is OUSU's Oxford Student. For magazines, there's Isis, the students' answer to Vogue *and verbosity*, and various others such as International Review, Amazon (women's), Phoenix (termly magazine of student writing, both poetry and prose) and a *recycling binful* of college gossip/scandal rags and societies' newsletters.

Rag: With its own sabbatical co-ordinator, Rag raises over £50,000 a year with all the standard pranks, stunts and events.

Student Volunteer Action: The relationship between students and locals *can't be described as nasty – they just tend to misunderstand or ignore each other*. Volunteer Action links students up with nearly 40 help groups both in the University and the local community, *going some way to improve matters in the process*. All sorts of other activities incude KEEN which works with kids and young adults with special needs.

RELIGIOUS:

Put any group of self-consciously intellectual people together – such as Oxford students – and within minutes they'll have established as many different religious groups as they can invent and then some. Many of the colleges owe their existence to funding from Christian sinners in fear of hell. *There's not so much quaking at impending damnation any more. but the fervour for activity amongst Oxford students extends to religion as much as anything else.*

Christianity: Students at Christ Church who say they're popping down to the college chapel are talking about Oxford's Anglican cathedral. The other colleges have less high-church chapels and most have at least one chaplain. Other Christian denominations are also catered for around town: Catholics, Baptists, Evangelicals, Methodists, URC, Seventh-Day Adventists, Christian Scientists, Pentecostals, Unitarians, Quakers, Orthodox, *Cliff Richard Fan Club* and so on. The Inter-Collegiate Christian Union (OICCU) brings these Christian groups together.

Islam: Mosque and prayer room at the Islamic Studies centre.

Jews: Local synagogue and large Jewish student population.

PAID WORK:

• Job bureau

Students are banned from working during term-time (*not that most of them would be able to find time*). That's not to say that no-one does and Oxford has *plenty* of shops and bars around to take students on. The Careers Service has a vacation employment service, and a wide range of jobs and internships are available.

SPORTS

- Recent successes: rowing, rugby • BUSA Ranking: 5

One of the highest accolades in University sport (apart from being able to drink a pint of beer in under three seconds) is an Oxbridge blue. To earn one, you've got to be selected for one of the University's major sports teams. These teams often compete on a first class level, *which doesn't necessarily mean that they're better than all the other University teams, just that they're highly respected and they expect great things.* The *biggest* grudge is the Oxbridge rivalry, Oxford *generally having the edge over Cambridge in football and rugby in recent years. A more cynical observer than Push might say the University admissions procedure becomes a whole lot more flexible if you have an international sporting reputation. Push would (for legal reasons) like to distance itself from any suggestion of the sort.* Suffice it to say that the University places emphasis and funding on its *impressive* record in sports both minor and major. Sport at a college level is *more geared to fun and fitness* and is *very welcoming,* even to students who aren't quite Olympians.

SPORTS FACILITIES:

All colleges have their own facilities to *varying degrees* and the University has an *excellent* range of central amenities: floodlit all-weather hockey pitch; playing fields; sports halls; swimming pool; squash courts; athletics field; bowls and croquet in the quads; tennis courts; gym (with multi-gym); and, of course, the Rivers Isis and Cherwell. The town also has a golf course, ice rink and two swimming pools.

SPORTING CLUBS:

Aerobics; Aikido; American Football; Board Sailing; Boxing; Bridge; Croquet; Gliding; Gymnastics; Hang Gliding; Ice Hockey; Kayak; Korfball; Lacrosse; Mountain Bike; Pentathlon; Pistol; Polo; Rambling & Hill-walking; Real Tennis; Rifle; Rowing; Rugby League; Shoringo Kempo; Squash; Sul Ki Do; Table Football; Tiddlywinks; Triathlon; Water Polo; Yachting. **See also Clubs tables.**

ATTRACTIONS:

The Combined Oxford Universities Cricket team is a joint effort with <u>Oxford Brookes</u>. Oxford United FC are the *lowly* local team and the city also has its own ice hockey side.

ACCOMMODATION

IN COLLEGE:

- Catered: 87% • First years living in: 100%
- Insurance premium: £

Availability: *One of the best* features of the Oxford colleges is that accommodation is guaranteed in college rooms (*often of an excellent standard*) for all 1st years. Most colleges also provide for finalists and so, if they want, students can usually stay in college for all but one of their years – though some can even stay in for their whole University career. What's more, rooms are cleaned, beds are made and sleeping partners are embarrassed by 'scouts' in most colleges. Each college has its own quirks and quiddities – details can be found in the entries following. Centrally, the University has no accommodation other than a few flats – about 390 places – for families, couples and single graduates, *but you can offer to snog the Chancellor to get them and it still won't help.*

Car parking: Oxford city council have done their very best to make it *nigh-on impossible* to park in the city centre and most colleges won't let students bring cars without a very, very good reason.

EXTERNALLY:

- Ave rent: £62.50–100

Availability: Housing in Oxford *rivals London* for costliness, *although there's more to be had for the money.* Cowley Road and Jericho are the most *popular* locations.

Housing help: The *best* way of finding a house is to get friendly with someone who's got one the year before you need it. You can also turn to agencies who'll charge a supplement, or to ads on notice boards around the colleges. The University-run Accommodation Office with four full-time staff, a vacancies list and bulletin board *usually points students in the right direction*. The local Housing Rights Centre is much frequented by students, but, like OUSU, they can only offer free advice and don't have any vacancies to dish out.

WELFARE

SERVICES:
• Lesbian/Gay/Bisexual Society • Women's Officer • Late-night minibus
• Nightline • Crime rating: !!!
The OUSU Welfare Officer can advise and refer students with most problems. Law students give free advice at OUSU two days a week.
Women: St Hilda's is the last all-female college. *Life in the male-dominated colleges can often be just that.* A nightwalk service accompanies women walking alone at night and there's a women-only bus.
Crèches/Nursery: Two nurseries with 94 places for 5mths-5yrs.
Disabilities: Access is *gradually improving* and efforts include OUSU's disabled access guide, a disability co-ordinator and Taylor House, an accommodation block with special facilities. Some colleges have Braille machines etc.

FINANCE:
• Ave debt per year: £3,356
• Access fund: £1,500,000 • Ave payment: £100-3,000
Support: Bursaries available to anyone who's exempt from paying tuition fees. The University pays £4,000 in the 1st year and £3,000 in the 2nd and 3rd years.

Balliol College, Oxford

• ***This College is part of the University of Oxford and students are entitled to use its facilities.***
Balliol College, Oxford, OX1 3BJ Tel: (01865) 277 748 E-mail: admissions@balliol.ox.ac.uk
Website: www.balliol.ox.ac.uk
Balliol College JCR, Oxford, OX1 3BJ
Tel: (01865) 277 744 E-mail: jcr.admissions@balliol.ox.ac.uk Website: www.ballioljcr.org

Balliol's one of the oldest, largest, *famous-est and central-est* colleges, just 350 metres from the Carfax chippy. *Academic standards are high, yet the atmosphere remains relatively relaxed, with a cosmopolitan flavour lent by the proportion of international students. Looks-wise, buildings range from idiosyncratically Gothic through silly Disney to unpleasant and stripey.*

Sex ratio (M:F): 59:41	**Founded: 1263**
Full-time u'grads: 405	**Part-time: 0**
Postgrads: 253	**Mature: <1%**
State:private school: 35:65	**Disabled: 16**
Academic ranking: 3	**International: 25%**

Two bars; two or three *sweaty* bops per term in The Lindsay Bar (cap 250); May Event (not Ball) has a big-name band, but no penguin suits. Music Soc recitals in dining hall (cap 450); choral groups. JCR Arts festival with drama, poetry, film and photography; theatre (Michael Pilch Studio); John de Balliol weekly news-sheet in loos. TV room; secondhand book sale service. Picture loans for room decoration. Anglican chapel. Library (100,000 modern books, 10,000 pre-1800); 35 computers, 24-hr access. *Good* sports facilities and *does okay in a variety of sports*; sports fields 5 mins away. All students live in except 55% of 2nd years; pay-as-you-eat self-service; *legendary* JCR pantry. Hardship funds, living-out grants; doctor, nurse. Welfare reps for postgrads, international students, ethnic minorities and disabled students, LGB support group, taxi fund, free condoms, rape alarms and tampons; crèche with 16 places for 3mths-5yrs; morning nursery for 18mths-4yrs, £10 a day.

FAMOUS ALUMNI:

Rabbi Lionel Blue (writer, broadcaster); Richard Dawkins (scientist); Graham Greene (writer); King Harald of Norway; Sir Edward Heath (former Con PM); Aldous Huxley (author); Gerard Manley Hopkins (poet); Lord Jenkins (Oxford University Chancellor); Boris Johnson MP (editor of the Spectator); Howard Marks (dope evangelist); King Olaf V of Norway; Chris Patten (last governor of Hong Kong); Adam Smith (economist); Algernon Swinburne (*perverse* poet); Stephen Twigg MP (Lab, *Portillo-slayer*); Hugo Young (The Guardian).

Brasenose College, Oxford

• **This College is part of the <u>University of Oxford</u> and students are entitled to use its facilities.**
Brasenose College, Radcliffe Square, Oxford, OX1 4AJ
Tel: (01865) 277 510 E-mail: admissions@bnc.ox.ac.uk Website: www.bnc.ox.ac.uk
Brasenose JCR, contact details as above
E-mail: jcr.president@bnc.ox.ac.uk Website: www.bnc-jcr.co.uk

Brasenose College is named after its brass door knocker (made in 1279 and now hanging over the high table) which is shaped like an animal's face with a pronounced snout (the *famous* brazen nose). *The College is ideally situated at the heart of the University in Radcliffe Square and 300 metres from Carfax. There's an emerging arty side (Law, PPE, History and English)* and provides the University with a steady stream of journalists for Cherwell and so on.

Sex ratio (M:F): 60:40	**Founded: 1509**
Full-time u'grads: 360	**Part-time: n/a**
Postgrads: 120	**Mature: 1%**
State:private school: 47:53	**Disabled: 4**
Academic ranking: 24	**International: 15%**

The best bar in Oxford (cap 120). Student bands in the dining hall (200); cabaret and cocktails jazz nights; JCR (100); digital TV with Sky, Playstation; vending & quiz machines; basement room (100); bops three times per term; quizzes and karaoke; annual drama and arts mini-festival; biennial ball. Termly newspaper, Sanesober. CofE chapel. Two libraries (60,000 books); 20 computers, 24-hrs. Nearly all undergrads live in; wide variety of accommodation; few cooking facilities but microwaves ago-go. CCTV, entry-phones; doctor, nurse; attack alarms issued. Disabled access to JCR. LGB, Women's, Men's, Disabilities, Ethnic Minorities and International Welfare Officers.

FAMOUS ALUMNI:

Lord Jeffrey Archer (briefly, *so he claims*); Colin Cowdrey (cricketer); Stephen Dorrell MP (Con); William Golding (writer); Field Marshall Earl Haig (WW1); Michael Palin (Monty Python, global traveller); Lord Runcie (late Archbishop of Canterbury); Lord Saville (Law Lord); Andrew Linsay (Olympic gold medallist).

Christ Church, Oxford

• **This College is part of the <u>University of Oxford</u> and students are entitled to use its facilities.**
Christ Church, St Aldgate's, Oxford, OX1 1DP Tel: (01865) 276 150
E-mail: tutor.admissions@chch.ox.ac.uk Website: www.chch.ox.ac.uk
Christ Church JCR, St Algate's, Oxford, OX1 1DP Tel: (01865) 276 166
E-mail: president@chchjcr.org Website: www.chchjcr.org

Whoever first linked the words 'dreaming spires' with Oxford was looking at Christ Church's pointy bits when they did it. 'The House', as it's known, is 200 metres from Carfax and is the closest college to the river. It's also home to the city's sumptuous Anglican cathedral. It's a stunning place, with idyllic gardens and gorgeous, almost intimidating architecture – the living embodiment of romantic dreams of Oxford (something the Harry Potter filmmakers realised

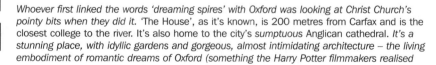

when they chose it as the setting for Hogwarts). The College – largest in the University – is burdened with champagne-quaffing toff stereotypes but, while it's still possible to see tuxedoed undergrads downing bottles of bubbly in Tom's Quad, most students prefer the relaxed and more down-to-earth environs of the bar. Known for serious academia, the natives still find time for high levels of involvement in University-wide arty, sporty and musical activities – especially the latter; the cathedral resonates with choral song on a daily basis.

Sex ratio (M:F): 55:45	Founded: 1525
Full-time u'grads: 424	Part-time: n/a
Postgrads: 261	Mature: 2%
State:private school: 55:45	Disabled: 8
Academic ranking: 20	International: 6%

Lovely stone-floored Undercroft bar with pool, table football and jukebox; *active* drama society, garden shows; own picture gallery with works by Michelangelo and Raphael; internationally renowned choir and long musical tradition; frequent recitals, jazz evenings, gigs and bops; annual ball. Two libraries (one 16th-century, one for Law), main library open till midnight – *among the finest College facilities in Oxford*; reading rooms; 16 24-hr computers; art room; Chit Chat newsletter; *apolitical JCR good on charity work*. Anglican chaplain (*comes free with breathtaking cathedral*). *Almighty Boat Club, also good in tennis and football*; excellent sports facilities 5 mins away. Nearly everyone lives in (£84/28wks); *decent rooms, poor kitchen facilities*; keypad entry; *very* formal dinner every night in what many will recognise as the Hogwarts dining hall; *nightmare parking*. LGB, postgrad, women's and international officers; nurse, doctor and counsellor; attack alarms; *old building poor for access but being improved*; specialised accommodation available. *Generous* financial help: entrance bursaries (£1,000), hardship funds, interest-free 5-yr loans (£1,000), travel and book grants, academic prizes.

FAMOUS ALUMNI:

W H Auden (poet); Lewis Carroll (author and don); Alan Clark (late *raunchy* MP and diarist); David Dimbleby (broadcaster); 13 prime ministers (including Gladstone); John Mortimer (barrister, author and playwright); Richard Curtis (screenwriter, *reason Hugh Grant has a career*); Lord Hailsham (late Lord Chancellor); Lord Nigel Lawson (*slimming guru* and ex-Chancellor); Anna Pasternak ('Di & Hewitt' hack); Auberon Waugh (late *controversialist*); Einstein (*briefly*).

Corpus Christi College, Oxford

• **This College is part of the <u>University of Oxford</u> and students are entitled to use its facilities.**
Corpus Christi College, Oxford, OX1 4FJ Tel: (01865) 276 737
E-mail: college.office@ccc.ox.ac.uk Website: www.ccc.ox.ac.uk
Corpus Christi College JCR, Oxford, OX1 4FJ Tel: (01865) 276 693
Website: www.corpusjcr.org

Tucked away down Merton Street, overlooking Dead Man's Walk, Corpus is one of Oxford's smallest colleges. It's an *unstuffy* sort of place (despite a *strong* academic rep), with the *famous* Pelican sundial at the front of the College. An elegant Tudor building borders the main quad, in which grows the tree that inspired Alice's Cheshire cat.

Sex ratio (M:F): 55:45	Founded: 1517
Full-time u'grads: 225	Part-time: 2
Postgrads: 112	Mature: 1%
State:private school: 45:45	Disabled: 2
Academic ranking: 14	International: 11%

The Beer Cellar Bar (cap 150, closed Sat nights); 'bops' fortnightly; theme nights and gigs in the bar, concerts in New Music room; annual 'Mayhem' event; Burns night with haggis and pipes. 16th-century library (80,000 books); reading rooms; 6 computers, 24-hrs; internet access in all rooms. Smallprint mag and weekly newsletter; music and drama *increasingly popular*; annual tortoise race with <u>Balliol</u> for charity. Playing fields (5 acres) 15 mins walk; shares a boathouse; *emphasis on participation and fun rather than sporting honours but football is strong*. Everyone can live in college in *pretty good* rooms on site; phone/internet points in all rooms; *excellent* food, veggie option. Doctors and nurse; dentist; *excellent* welfare.

FAMOUS ALUMNI:

Dr Arnold (of Rugby fame); Sir Isaiah Berlin (writer); Robert Bridges (Poet Laureate); Lord Fisher (Archbishop of Canterbury – 1906); Brough Scott (racing commentator); Vikram Seth (novelist); William Waldegrave MP (Con).

Exeter College, Oxford

• **The College is part of <u>University of Oxford</u> and students are entitled to use its facilities.**
Exeter College, Oxford, Exeter College, Oxford, OX1 3DP
Tel: (01865) 279 648 E-mail: academic.administrator@exeter.ox.ac.uk
Website: www.exeter.ox.ac.uk
The Stapledone Society, Exeter JCR, Oxford, OX13DP
Tel: (01865) 279 635

Oxford's fourth oldest college, Exeter is slap bang in the middle of the academic heart of Oxford on semi-pedestrianised Turl Street right next door to the Bodleian Library and 250 metres from Carfax. The buildings span five centuries *and afford a magnificent view from the garden*. Access to the high walls makes it possible to snipe from on high at tourists below. *The location and compact layout make it ideal for students allergic to walking.*

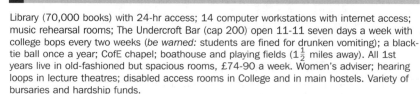

45%	**Sex ratio (M:F): 55:45**	**Founded: 1314**
	Full-time u'grads: 316	**Part-time: 0**
	Postgrads: 154	**Mature: 1%**
	State:private school: 57:43	**Disabled: 3**
55%	**Academic ranking: 13**	**International: 9%**

Library (70,000 books) with 24-hr access; 14 computer workstations with internet access; music rehearsal rooms; The Undercroft Bar (cap 200) open 11-11 seven days a week with college bops every two weeks (*be warned:* students are fined for drunken vomiting); a black-tie ball once a year; CofE chapel; boathouse and playing fields ($1\frac{1}{2}$ miles away). All 1st years live in old-fashioned but spacious rooms, £74-90 a week. Women's adviser; hearing loops in lecture theatres; disabled access rooms in College and in main hostels. Variety of bursaries and hardship funds.

FAMOUS ALUMNI:

Sir Roger Bannister (First runner to run the 4-minute mile); Willliam Morris (designer and social pioneer); Ned Sherrin (broadcaster); Imogen Stubbs (actress); J R R Tolkien, Martin Amis, Alan Bennett, Will Self (writers).

Greyfriars Hall, Oxford

• **This College is part of the <u>University of Oxford</u> and students are entitled to use its facilities.**
Greyfriars Hall, Iffley Road, Oxford, OX4 1SB Tel: (01865) 243 694
Website: www.greyfriars.ox.ac.uk
Greyfriars Hall JCR, Greyfriars Hall, Iffley Road, Oxford, OX4 1SB
Tel: (01865) 246 665 Website: www.greyfriars.ox.ac.uk/jcr

The *beautiful and serene* Greyfriars Hall is one of Oxford's smallest colleges. *Very small – the entire population could take a double-decker together.* It's home to 50 undergrads and seven Franciscan Friars and maintains a strong tradition of Catholicism and the teachings of St Francis of Assisi in particular (hence the Friars). However, students' own spiritual preferences reflect a bigger smorgasbord of world religions. Women have been admitted since 1992 and make up half the student body. The college is *some way* from the centre of town, on the Iffley Road.

Sex ratio (M:F): 50:50	**Founded:** 1224	
Full-time u'grads: 50	**Part-time:** 0	
Postgrads: 5	**Mature:** 2%	
State:private school: 50:50	**International:** 20%	
Disabled: 5	**Ethnic:** 10%	

No bar, just a drinks shelf in the kitchen and free Pimm's at the summer garden parties; one bop per year; regular parties in the basement. *Strongly involved in drama and politics; getting more into journalism and media recently.* Recent sporting successes in rugby, karate and rowing, for which students join the balliol banner (where they currently dominate the women's first boat). Pool table, Sky TV, weights room. Catholic church. *Well-equipped* specialist library (10,000 volumes, 25 study spaces); 3 PCs; 24-hrs; JCR IT officer; all rooms have ethernet access. Just over half the students live in, including all 1st years. Meals are included in catered cost (£80/week), but rebates provided for non-attendance. 8 self-catered bedrooms (£60). Smart formal dinner every evening – students and friars take turns to serve. Strong on student media; successes in football and rowing. Bike lock-ups, limited car parking. LGB and women's officer and free attack alarms; self-defence classes. Scholarships for academic excellence, drama, sport, journalism, charity, 1st and 3rd years. Most arts subjects can be accommodated; no sciences or medicine.

FAMOUS ALUMNI:
Roger Bacon (scholar and polymath); Robert Grosseteste (13th-century Bishop of Lincoln); William of Ockham (of 'Ockham's Razor' fame); John Duns Scotus (theologian).

Harris Manchester College, Oxford
• *This College is part of the <u>University of Oxford</u> and students are entitled to use its facilities.*
Harris Manchester College, Mansfield Road, Oxford, OX1 3TD
Tel: (01865) 271 009 E-mail: college.office@hmc.ox.ac.uk Website: www.hmc.ox.ac.uk
Harris Manchester College JCR, Mansfield Road, Oxford, OX1 3TD
Tel: (01865) 271 006 Website: www.hmc.ox.ac.uk/societies/jcr

Harris Manchester only admits mature students. As a result atmosphere can be *more cardigan and slippers than drinking competitions and meat-market bops*. The buildings are late Victorian Gothic (there's some *lovely Pre-Raphaelite stained glass window* in the chapel) as the college has only been in them since its move from Manchester in 1889. *Push was disappointed to learn that the college takes its name not from Rolf, Chopper or even Bomber; but from Lord Harris of Peckham.*

Sex ratio (M:F): 55:45	**Founded:** 1786	
Full-time u'grads: 89	**Part-time:** 0	
Postgrads: 41	**Mature:** 100%	
State:private school: n/a	**Disabled:** 3	
Academic ranking: 28	**International:** 18%	

Small bar; film club; ball every 3 yrs. Three libraries (40,000 books); six computers, 24-hrs; *cordial* staff/student relations. Unitarian chaplain. Recent emergence in University football and cricket. All 1st years and finalists can live in; *excellent* food, veggie option; two formals a week. *Poor* wheelchair access; CCTV; doctor; hardship fund; Women's and LGB Officers, chaplain.

Hertford College, Oxford
• *This College is part of the <u>University of Oxford</u> and students are entitled to use its facilities.*
Hertford College, Oxford, OX1 3BW Tel: (01865) 279 400
E-mail: admissions@hertford.ox.ac.uk Website: www.hertford.ox.ac.uk
Hertford College JCR, Oxford, OX1 3BW Website: http://jcrweb.hertford.ox.ac.uk/main

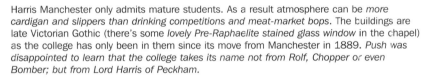

Lady Margaret Hall, Oxford

• *This College is part of the <u>University of Oxford</u> and students are entitled to use its facilities.*
Lady Margaret Hall, Oxford, Lady Margaret Hall, Oxford, OX2 6QA
Tel: (01865) 274 310 E-mail: academic.officer@lmh.ox.ac.uk Website: www.lmh.ox.ac.uk
Lady Margaret Hall JCR, Lady Margaret Hall, Oxford, OX3 6QA
Tel: (01865) 274 277 Website: www.lmh.ox.ac.uk

Lady Margaret Hall is a 19th-century redbrick river college set in extensive gardens. Two purpose-built five-floor residential blocks *slightly damage the idyllic setting and the handsome architecture, but they're really popular with them inside.* Being 1,200 metres from Oxford's centre *doesn't put a dampener on University-level involvement. They're pretty informal and down-to-earth as Oxford goes.*

Sex ratio (M:F): 50:50	Founded: 1878
Full-time u'grads: 440	Part-time: n/a
Postgrads: 182	Mature: 4%
State:private school: 50:50	Disabled: n/a
Academic ranking: 27	International: 5%

Bar (cap 200). Two libraries (one for Law, 70,000 books total); 35 computers, 24-hrs. Anglican chapel. *Strong* drama at the Beaufort Literary Society founded by actor Sam West. Sports facilities a mile away (multigym and squash on-site); *strong on netball, hockey and rowing.* 1st years, finalists and most 2nd years live in; dining hall with fixed payments for meals (whether eaten or not) or pay-as-you-eat. *Better disabled access than most Oxford colleges.* Doctor/nurse; first year, welfare and women's officers; free tampons and condoms.

FAMOUS ALUMNI:

Benazir Bhutto (ex-President, Pakistan); Caryl Churchill (writer); Lady Antonia Fraser (historian); Eglantyne Jebb (founder, Save the Children); Nigella Lawson (domestic goddess); Barbara Mills (Director of Public Prosecutions); Diana Quick (actress); Matthew Taylor MP (Lib Dem); Lady Warnock (educationalist); Sam West (actor); Anne Widdecombe MP (Con).

Lincoln College, Oxford

• *This College is part of the <u>University of Oxford</u> and students are entitled to use its facilities.*
Lincoln College, Oxford, OX1 3DR Tel: (01865) 279 800
E-mail: admissions@lincoln.ox.ac.uk Website: www.lincoln.ox.ac.uk
Lincoln College JCR, Lincoln College, Oxford, OX1 3DR
Tel: (01865) 240094 Website: www-jcr.linc.ox.ac.uk

200 metres from Carfax is Lincoln, *a miniature version of a picture-book Oxford college, though they consider themselves to be 'forward-looking'. If Ikea decided to make a range of 'dreamy, dreaming spires' it might look a bit like the recently sand-blasted stone quad. Students tend to stick to college affairs and this helps to maintain the impressive academic standard.*

Sex ratio (M:F): 56:44	Founded: 1427
Full-time u'grads: 319	Part-time: n/a
Postgrads: 230	Mature: 0%
State:private school: 55:45	Disabled: 13
Academic ranking: 16	International: 7%

Quizzes, bops, karaoke, pool, cabaret in Deep Hall Bar (cap 200); biennial ball. Imperative newsletter twice a term. Music society recitals, opera. Library (40,000); 20 computers, 24-hrs. CofE chapel. *Rowing and croquet are popular;* sports fields 10 mins b ke ride away; winners of Ice Hockey cuppers 2003/4; new gym ready April 2005. Everyone lives in and eats at formal and/or informal dinners; *best food in Oxford; self-catering limited*. Nurse; women's tutor; harassment support; access fund payments of up to £1,000; Oxford Bursaries up to £1,000; scholarships and college prizes.

FAMOUS ALUMNI:

John le Carré (writer); Bill Cash MP (Con, *Europhobe*); Manfred von Richtofen (the Red Baron); Dr Seuss (writer); Edward Thomas (poet); John Wesley (founder of Methodism).

Magdalen College, Oxford

• **This College is part of the _University of Oxford_ and students are entitled to use its facilities.**
Magdalen College, Oxford, OX1 4AU Tel: (01865) 276 063
E-mail: admissions@magd.ox.ac.uk Website: www.magd.ox.ac.uk
Magdalen College JCR, Magdalen College, Oxford, OX1 4AU
Tel: (01865) 276 001 E-mail: president@jcr.magd.ox.ac.uk Website: www.jcr.magd.ox.ac.uk

Magdalen (pronounced 'Maudlin') is one of Oxford's biggest, *richest* colleges. Its *superb* buildings, 800 metres from Carfax, are set in 100 acres of grounds, which include over a mile of riverside walks and a deer park. The surroundings attract a *plague* of tourists and plenty of film crews. The *old-fashioned* bar (crossed oars etc.) overlooks the river. The Magdalen May Morning celebration *is especially enchanting,* coming to a climax when the choir welcomes summer from the top of Magdalen Tower. *The students are a tolerant and friendly bunch, hard-working but not overly so.*

Sex ratio (M:F): 54:46	**Founded: 1458**
Full-time u'grads: 390	**Part-time: 0**
Postgrads: 219	**Ethnic: 17%**
State:private school: 50:50	**Mature: 1%**
Academic ranking: 5	**Disabled: 12**
International: 5%	

Bar used for student bands, pool, quizzes, bops and snacks; tea-parties; punting trips; classical concerts in the chapel; fortnightly bops and cocktail parties; music auditorium; only college with an on-site wine shop; Commemoration Ball every 3 yrs, *one of the biggies*. Five libraries including a special Law Library and a rare books library (120,000 books in total, 100 study places, 24-hr); 28 computers, open 24-hrs. CofE chapel. Weekly student mag Bogsheet. Largest DVD collection in Oxford. Great sports fields 10 mins walk; three squash courts in College; excellent gym; *women's squash strong, as are rounders and cricket.* Almost everyone lives in; very spacious, modern rooms, all with network points; 27 kitchens for undergrads, *lousy food – better in the bar but bring your garibaldi biscuits, anyway.* International Students, Women's and Ethnic Minorities Officers. *College is responsive to students' problems.* Free attack alarms provided. Hardship funds, scholarships, book and travel grants. Wheelchairs hampered by cobbles, no disabilities rep. Motivated Rag and charities reps.

FAMOUS ALUMNI:

John Betjeman (poet, sent down); Edward Gibbon (historian); Darius Guppy (*fraudster*); William Hague MP (ex-Con Leader); Ian Hislop (editor, Private Eye); C S Lewis (writer); Dudley Moore (comedian/actor/pianist); Desmond Morris (socioanthropologist); John Redwood MP (Con); David Rendel MP (LibDem); A J P Taylor (historian); Oscar Wilde (*writer*); Cardinal Wolsey.

Mansfield College, Oxford

• *This College is part of the <u>University of Oxford</u> and students are entitled to use its facilities.*
Mansfield College, Mansfield Road, Oxford, OX1 3TF
Tel: (01865) 282 920 E-mail: admissions@mansfield.ox.ac.uk
Website: www.mansfield.ox.ac.uk
Junior Common Room, Mansfield College, Mansfield Road, Oxford, OX1 3TF
Tel: (01865) 270 889

The main Victorian buildings are set around the huge circular lawn. Outside it *looks inspiring and spacious. Rowing's popular* and the College has its own boathouse – Mansfield was the home of Donald McDonald, the rower made famous(ish) by the film 'True Blue'; most sports amenities are run jointly with <u>Merton College</u>. Mansfield was once a Free Church centre *and prides itself on a tradition of being the source of many a minister. The atmosphere's friendly and down-to-earth and there's a strong tradition of supplying hacks to the SU and journos to Cherwell. Mansfield's turning more of an admiring eye to applicants from FE colleges.*

47%	Sex ratio (M:F): 53:47	Founded: 1886
	Full-time u'grads: 203	Part-time: 0
	Postgrads: 57	Mature: 1%
	State:private school: 60:30	Disabled: 4
53%	Academic ranking: 29	International: 10%

Black Bottle bar, packed at the weekend; two or three bops termly and bands in the JCR (cap 225); cabaret; Sky TV; pool tables; games machines. Weekly newspaper Bogsheet. Two libraries (35,000 volumes, 72 study places including specialist law and theology library); 20 networked PCs for u'grads, 24-hrs; internet access in all rooms on campus; specialist science software packages. URC chapel. Sport: rugby, hockey, cricket, tennis courts, basketball court. *Varied* accommodation for all 1st and 3rd years/finalists. Students eat in college dining halls except Sundays. CCTV, computerised entry. Ramps available; one room for a wheelchair user; College nurse; counselling team; Women's and LGB Officers. Bursaries; scholarships for Law, English, Geography and other subjects.

FAMOUS ALUMNI:

Paul Crossley (concert pianist); C H Dodd, Albert Schweitzer (theologians); Philip Franks (actor); Donald McDonald (mutinous rower); Adam von Trott (tried to kill Hitler).

Merton College, Oxford

• *This College is part of the <u>University of Oxford</u> and students are entitled to use its facilities.*
Merton College, Merton Street, Oxford, OX1 4JD
Tel: (01865) 276 310 E-mail: undergraduates@admin.merton.ox.ac.uk
Website: www.merton.ox.ac.uk
Junior Common Room, Merton College, Merton Street, Oxford, OX1 4JD
Website: http://jcr.merton.ox.ac.uk

Merton's *one of Oxford's oldest and prettiest colleges*, 600 metres from Carfax, with *magical* gardens (where Tolkien wrote Lord of the Rings), a *beautiful* chapel and *bizarre* gargoyles. The Mob Quad is the oldest quad in Oxford and home of the library (the oldest in England), which is supposedly haunted and contains Chaucer's Astrolabe. *The atmosphere's laid-back but academically stellar students have made their mark in University journalism, drama and music. Token archaic traditions include walking backwards around the quad drinking port for an hour when the clocks go back. Like you do.*

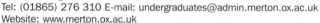

Sex ratio (M:F): 62:38	Founded: 1264
Full-time u'grads: 321	Part-time: 0
Postgrads: 190	Mature: 0
State:private school: 57:43	Disabled: 3%
Academic ranking: 1	International: 7%

Large bar with fortnightly bops *good for pre-town quaffing*; drama in the gardens in May Week; Xmas Ball; *big lung-ed* Choral Society; weekly Merton Newspaper. Library housing 70,000 volumes and a *cramped* 88 study places. 30-workstation 24-hr computer room. Ethernet connections in 85% of rooms. Two tennis courts and sports grounds 10 mins away shared with <u>Mansfield College</u> – *there's more of an emphasis on having a go than on thinking you're hard enough*. More or less everyone can live in *high quality* catered accommodation for 25 weeks of the year (£73/wk); *some very elegant rooms*; daily formals with *tasty chow*. Entry phones and night porters; doctor and shared nurse; LGBT Officer; *narrow doorways and paths make wheelchair access tricky*. Access bursaries (£1,000 in the 1st year, £500 in successive years); scholarships, grants towards books and overseas work and travel.

FAMOUS ALUMNI:

Roger Bannister (athlete); Max Beerbohm (caricaturist and writer); Frank Bough (broadcaster); Howard Davies (deputy Governor, Bank of England); T S Eliot (poet); Mark Haddon (author); William Harvey (discoverer of circulatory system); Kris Kristofferson (singer/songwriter); Robert Morley (actor); Crown Prince Naruhito (Japanese heir apparent); Sir Andrew Wiles (mathematician); John Wycliffe (religious reformer).

New College, Oxford

• **This College is part of the <u>University of Oxford</u> and students are entitled to use its facilities.**
New College, University of Oxford, Holywell Street, Oxford, OX1 3BN
Tel: (01865) 279 555 E-mail: admissions@new.ox.ac.uk Website: www.new.ox.ac.uk
New College JCR, Holywell Street, Oxford, OX1 3BN
Tel: (01865) 279 577 Website: www.newcollegejcr.org.uk

New College, *ironically* one of the oldest colleges (*those crazy jokers*), is *so prettily Gothic that it wouldn't look out of place in Disneyland*, with the city wall running through its *pleasant* grounds. The College is 600 metres from Carfax, but it's hidden to a certain extent from the swarms of tourists. The social scene rotates around the Beer Cellar, a refurbished medieval cave attracting students from all over Oxford.

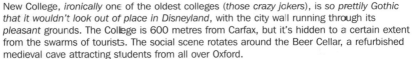

Sex ratio (M:F): 50:50	Founded: 1379
Full-time u'grads: 430	Part-time: 170
Postgrads: 172	Mature: 1%
State:private school: 48:52	Disabled: 4
Academic ranking: 11	International: 10%

Bar (cap 200); classical music in Anglican chapel. Biggest entz budget in the University; themed bops ('100 Greatest Musicals' etc.), jazz and student bands in the Long Room (200); student DJ nights *popular*, open to non-college members. *Strong music and theatre; famous choir.* Music rehearsal rooms. Library (100,000 books, including 30,000 antiquarian); 45 computers, 24-hrs. 8 acres of playing fields nearby. Most can be housed in college; art gallery – students can borrow paintings for their rooms. All students eat in hall; daily formal dinner; self-catering in new buildings. Doctor; nurse; LGB, Women's and Welfare Officers – *good welfare*.

FAMOUS ALUMNI:

Tony Benn (former Lab MP); Angus Deayton (TV presenter); John Fowles, John Galsworthy (writers); Hugh Grant (*er*, actor); Bryan Johnston (late *effusive* cricket commentator, after whom the pavilion is named); Naomi Woolf (feminist writer).

Oriel College, Oxford

• *This College is part of the <u>University of Oxford</u> and students are entitled to use its facilities.*
Oriel College, Oxford, OX1 4EW Tel: (01865) 286 548
E-mail: admissions@oriel.ox.ac.uk Website: www.oriel.ox.ac.uk
JCR, Oriel College, Oxford, OX1 4EW Tel: (01865) 276 587
E-mail: jcr.president@oriel.ox.ac.uk Website: www.orieljcr.org

One of the oldest and smallest colleges, the *beautiful* College of Oriel is 300 metres from Carfax. *It remains fairly conservative and was the last Oxford College to go co-educational (only in 1985). Its quiet, closed quads and tight, friendly communal spirit can be alternately inspiring or suffocating. The sporting reputation it prides itself on has been dwindling in recent years – although the celebratory drinking sessions persist with aplomb (and considerable rowdiness).*

Sex ratio (M:F): 57:43	Founded: 1326
Full-time u'grads: 305	Part-time: n/a
Postgrads: 100	Mature: 1%
State:private school: 50:50	Disabled: 12
Academic ranking: 18	International: 10%

Humming bar with pool table, dartboard, table football and games machines, *unsettlingly popular karaoke; varied* weekly recitals and film screenings; *respected* chapel choir; regular cabaret; ball every 3 years. Well-funded library (100,000 books, 74 study places) split into Junior and Senior sections, Junior Library open 24-hrs; 21 networked computers in two suites; 95% of rooms have ethernet. Anglican chapel with termly RC masses; TV room (*sorry, 'Noam Chomsky Entertainment Wing'*) with video and Sky TV, arcade and pinball machines. *Left-wing JCR,* currently withholding subscription from OUSU (students are still technically members though). Squash courts, multigym, $6\frac{1}{2}$ acres of playing fields a mile away; ideally positioned for the river; *rowers by tradition, darts and rugby also doing well.* All students can live in (£71-105/24wks), either on-site or at James Mellon Hall a mile away; mainly en-suite; *quality mixed but improving;* some entry phones; students eat in hall; formals six days a week; *moderate* food but all-you-can-eat breakfasts. LGB, Postgrad, International and Male and Female Welfare Officers, welfare-organised self-defence classes; nurse available five mornings a week, free condoms, cheap attack alarms. *Older bits bad for access,* adapted rooms at JMH. Range of scholarships, prizes and bursaries (£500-1,200). Oxford Opportunity bursaries for u'grads.

FAMOUS ALUMNI:

Matthew Arnold (poet); Beau Brummel (dandy); Sir Thomas More (executed by Henry VIII); Cardinal Newman (Oxford Movement); Sir Walter Ralegh (potatoes and general swash buckling); Cecil Rhodes (*dodgy imperialist*); A J P Taylor (historian).

Pembroke College, Oxford

• *This College is part of the <u>University of Oxford</u> and students are entitled to use its facilities.*
Pembroke College, Oxford, OX1 1DW Tel: (01865) 276 411
E-mail: admissions@pmb.ox.ac.uk Website: www.pmb.ox.ac.uk
Pembroke College JCR, Oxford, OX1 1DW Website: www.pembrokejcr.com

Pembroke's quads, 300 metres from Carfax, range from *medieval marvels to modern misdemeanours,* but even Alan Titchmarsh could get some tips from their gardens. *They're known for sporting prowess – despite their wussy pink colours – but academic achievement hovers around the adequate mark (in Oxford terms). One of their more deranged traditions is the 'burning of the boats' after rowing victories – with the crew still on board – leaving a 60-metre scorch mark on the North Quad for most of the year. The College has been the butt of some jokes about its financial well being (or lack of it) in recent years – not helped by the word 'broke' in its name. Still, as long as there's beer flowing, students are a happy bunch.*

Sex ratio (M:F): 59:41	Founded: 1624
Full-time u'grads: 406	Part-time: 0
Postgrads: 90	Mature: 1%
State:private school: 50:50	Disabled: 60
Academic ranking: 22	International: 7%

College bar (bops, quizzes, theme nights, pool table and video games) and private bar for postgrads; ball every two-three years; regular *muckraking* Bogsheet; *raucous* Yearbook. Modern library (40,000 books, 64 study places), open till midnight during term, laptop network points (£10 a year). Updated computer suite; printing 3p a sheet; web access in all rooms (£25 a year). Interdenominational chapel with CofE chaplain. Claims to have best-attended JCR meetings in Oxford – *not big on out-of-college issues though*; common room with pool, arcade games; TV room with DVD player. *Hugely sporty:* nominated for Sporting College of the Year Award and made Oxford rowing history in 2004 when both men's and women's 1st VIIIs won the Headship in the annual Summer eights competition. All 1st years and most others live in; *relatively high quality* rooms (£84-132 for 26wks); *Modern Geoffrey Arthur Building most sought after – mainly finalists; Macmillan Building is obligatory 60s carbuncle, but buzzing inside;* no sharing; three formal dinners a week – *pretty much compulsory for 1st years*; decent food complemented by JCR pantry (8am-5pm); *limited* parking, only available at GAB. Postgrad Officer and soc; LGB Officer and soc; Women's Officer and soc; free attack alarms, condoms, sanitary towels, pregnancy tests; doctor; nurse on-site 2hrs a day. Limited hardship fund; bursaries; £200 scholarships for 1st-achievers, £100 to those who come close; assortment of prizes.

FAMOUS ALUMNI:

William Blackstone (lawyer); Denzil Davies MP (Lab); Michael Heseltine (former MP, Con); Samuel Johnson (wrote the 1st English dictionary); John Pym (socialist/historian/revolutionary); Roger Bannister (4-min mile runner) is a former Master of the College.

....

Regent's Park College, Oxford

• **This College is part of the <u>University of Oxford</u> and students are entitled to use its facilities.**
Regent's Park College, Pusey Street, Oxford, OX1 2LB Tel: (01865) 288 120
Website: www.rpc.ox.ac.uk

Regent's Park Junior Common Room, Regent's Park College, Pusey Street, Oxford, OX1 2LB
Tel: (01865) 288 120 Email: info@regentsjcr.org.uk Website: www.regentsjcr.org.uk

Through an *unassuming* little door off the *beautiful* boulevard of St Giles' is the *unassuming* little College of Regent's Park, one of Oxford's smallest. It began its life as a London training institution for Baptist ministers and missionaries and although it's long since been absorbed into <u>Oxford University</u> and opened its door to different denominations (becoming thoroughly ecumenical), it's still got a *heavy* theological slant – it's the national Centre for Baptist History and Heritage. *It remains relatively unknown in the Oxbridge scheme of things, although involvement in the University SU is improving. While many other colleges struggle with the pressures of celebrity, snobbery and the old boy's network, the small number of Arts & Humanities students based here (technoboffins beware) are happy to simply get on with things, whilst maintaining a high level of involvement with University-wide activities. The College doesn't require faith committments from students, welcomes families and has a quietly homely atmosphere that warms the cockles other colleges can't reach.*

Sex ratio (M:F): 45:55	Founded: 1810
Full-time u'grads: 85	Part-time: 20
Postgrads: 40	Ethnic: 1%
State:private school: 60:40	Mature: 30%
International: 10%	Disabled: 4

Tiny bar, but drinking space in the JCR; karaoke, gameshow nights; *fairly strong* dramatic activity, usually at least one major production a year; two discos/bops a term; annual 'Final Fling' mini ball; ad hoc ents; strawberries and Pimm's summer outings, punting trips; London theatre trips. *Very involved JCR, keen on charity work*; common room with newspapers, VCR/DVD/Sky TV. Two libraries (40,000 books, 50 study places), including Angus Library of early Baptist Documents – *good for theology, philosophy and English*. Six 24-hr computers; intranet/internet in all rooms (free). Ecumenical chapel. *Football, netball and rowing doing well*; snooker, table football and table tennis table; no playing fields. Most live in; flats for couples/single sex; no en-suite (£108/24wks). Meals provided weekdays but kitchen facilities are *good*, laundry facilities; no parking. CCTV; free attack alarms; Postgrad, Women's, Men's, LGBT, Harrassment and Welfare Officers; doctor; disabled access *needs improvement*. Various bursaries.

FAMOUS ALUMNI:
Paul Fiddes, Henry Wheeler Robinson (theologians); The bloke who directed Spiceworld – *his name can't be given to protect his own safety*; Maltus Wells (explorer).

....

Somerville College, Oxford

• *This College is part of the* <u>University of Oxford</u> *and students are entitled to use its facilities.*
Somerville College, Woodstock Road, Oxford, OX2 6HD
Tel: (01865) 270 600 E-mail: admissions@somerville.ox.ac.uk
Website: www.somerville.ox.ac.uk
Junior Common Room, Somerville College, Woodstock Road, Oxford, OX2 6HD
Tel: (01865) 270 593 E-mail: jcr.president@somerville.ox.ac.uk
Website: http://student.some.ox.ac.uk/jcr

Somerville's 800 metres from the town centre, near the *trendy* area of Jericho. It's a *relaxed, peaceful college* of *mixed, rather institutional* architecture and *gorgeous* gardens. The small bar, *with its merry happy hours, bonds the bits other bars can't reach*. Men are a controversial recent addition (1994) *but the atmosphere hasn't become as blokey as some hoped/feared. Informality and tolerance is the rule and Somervillians opt out of some of Oxford's dafter traditions, although its political folk are ubiquitous in positions of authority across OUSU and the debating Union. Clearly the college of choice for would-be baronesses.*

51% / 49%		
Sex ratio (M:F): 49:51	Academic ranking: 15	
Full-time u'grads: 392	Founded: 1879	
Postgrads: 100	Part-time: n/a	
State:private school: 63:37	Mature: 1%	
International: 15%	Disabled: 4	

Bar next to digital TV room – also near *legendary* Duke of Cambridge happy hour and Brown's restaurant (*not near much else; students need a bike*); Flora Anderson Hall for bands; *active* drama, JCR drama rep; *busy* music soc; summer Event; ball every 3 years. *Good* Library (100,000 books); 20 computers, all rooms have ethernet; music rehearsal rooms. Non-denominational chapel, Catholic church next door. JCR produces The Siren monthly; *lots* of charity projects; *gallant* JCR *valiantly* fighting against increasing rents. *Some sporting talent, especially in football, netball, rugby and rowing*; gym, shared fields with <u>Wadham</u>. All 1st years live in, all finalists can if they wish; *varied but generally spacious* rooms; JCR Equalisation scheme (£80/ term) helps 2nd years with costs of living out. *Parking impossible.* LGB, Postgrad, Women's, International and Ethnic Minorities Officers; doctor, nurse; crèche with 16 places; *not bad access*; adapted rooms for disabled students; means-tested awards (£5-500), travel and sports grants from JCR, scholarships, book prizes, well-endowed hardship fund. Alternative prospectus online.

FAMOUS ALUMNI:

Sunethra Bandaranaike (Sri Lanka's former PM); Indira Ghandi (India's former PM); Dorothy Hodgkin (Nobel Prize winner); Iris Murdoch (writer); Baroness Park (spymaster); Esther Rantzen (*toothy* TV celeb); Dorothy L Sayers (crime writer – wrote about the College in Gaudy Night); Baroness Margaret Thatcher (former PM); Baroness Shirley Williams.

St Anne's College, Oxford

• *This College is part of the* <u>*University of Oxford*</u> *and students are entitled to use its facilities.*
St Anne's College, Woodstock Road, Oxford, OX2 6HS
Tel: (01865) 274 800 E-mail: enquiries@st-annes.ox.ac.uk Website: www.st-annes.ox.ac.uk
Junior Common Room, St Anne's College, Woodstock Road, Oxford, OX2 6HS
Tel: (01865) 274 870 Website: www.stannesjcr.org

St Anne's is 10 mins walk from the city centre and *gets a fair bit of stick* for being 'miles' away as a result. It was initially a women-only affair, linked to the rise of education for Oxford women in 1878. It became an affiliated college in 1952, and let the boys in to play in 1979. Because of its past it maintains a strict halfway balance of men and women both in the student body and the teaching staff. The main building is made of *warm* Cotswold stone with a battlement top and was built in the 30s. Most of the others were constructed *with more slapdash aesthetics* in the 50s and 60s and the newest building appeared in 1992. *The modern style doesn't sit well with the prestige of some other colleges and architectural snobs occasionally turn up noses. The students are a no-nonsense bunch – not much petty student politicking. They prefer to put their energies into charity Rag events, the wealth of drama societies or a sociable bevy now and then. St Anne's trumpets equality from the rooftops, has appointed its first male principal, claims to be particularly open to applications from minorities and its students are reputed to be 'normal'. Which is comforting.*

Sex ratio (M:F): 50:50	Founded: 1952	
Full-time u'grads: 445	Part-time: 0	
Postgrads: 140	Mature: 0	
State:private school: 50:50	Disabled: 0	
Academic ranking: 17	International: 10%	

Bar with pub quizzes, darts and bar Olympics on offer; *active* drama society (the St Anne's Players), comedy soc; large lecture theatre with screen and collapsible stage; bands in JCR and *whopping bops*; yearly arts festival with drama, comedy, music, photos and all things arty. A *spacious* library, 100,000 books, growing by 2,000 every year; 16 networked computers and ethernet access in most rooms. There's a scheme for students to buy computers off the college, paying in instalments. Double Standards and Agent Orange are the JCR mags – the Bogsheet is for gossip-mongers. *Strong on women's football*; sports facilities are shared with <u>St John's</u> 800 metres away. All except some postgrads live in but *there are grumbles a-rumblin' over the rent* (£100/wk) – the JCR is struggling *for reductions. Rooms fairly standard, though sexy new pads are being built. Catering arrangements a bit restrictive; plenty of formal dinners.* Some parking. LGB, Ethnic Minorities' and Women's Officers; doctor, nurse, student counsellor; *reasonable wheelchair access.* Travel grants, book allowances, scholarships to study in Japan available.

FAMOUS ALUMNI:

Maria Aitken (actress); Edwina Currie (ex-MP, romance novelist and John Major's *bit of stuff*); Penelope Lively, Iris Murdoch, Zoe Heller, Jenny Uglow (writers); Libby Purves (journalist); Sir Simon Rattle (conductor); Baroness Young (MP).

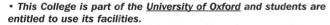

St Catherine's College, Oxford

• *This College is part of the* <u>University of Oxford</u> *and students are entitled to use its facilities.*
St Catherine's College, Manor Road, Oxford, OX1 3UJ Tel: (01865) 271 700
E-mail: admissions@stcatz.ox.ac.uk Website: www.stcatz.ox.ac.uk
The Junior Common Room, St Catherine's College, Manor Road, Oxford, OX1 3UJ
Website: www.stcatz.ox.ac.uk/jcrweb

Catz, as St Catherine's is affectionately known, *far from the typical sandy-stoned Oxford College,* is a modernist concoction of glass and concrete a mile from Carfax, and *the relatively progressive architecture reflects the forward-looking, unstuffy atmosphere inside.* It's a large college and has all the mod cons: warm rooms, showers, kitchens, purpose-built bar, even a grassy amphitheatre and water gardens. *There are plenty of ents and they are keen on maintaining their up-for-it ambience, so for students who want to go to Oxford for the academic kudos, but want to steer clear of the Ivory Tower mentality of the more traditional settings, Catz's a good bet. Students are proud to be here, but even concrete can't quite stave off that inimitable Oxford smugness. It still has that one big happy family feel, mainly because of its comparatively detached setting.*

Sex ratio (M:F): 60:40	Founded: 1962
Full-time u'grads: 437	Part-time: 0
Postgrads: 210	Ethnic: 4%
State:private school: 44:56	Mature: 1%
Academic ranking: 6	Disabled: 4
International: 14%	

Lively all-day bar – but the *famous* Turf Tavern is 5 mins away. *Mightily Theatrical*: JCR and Bernard Sunley Theatres; Music House used for bands; May Ball; *very popular* weekly bops in JCR and MCR; library (57,000 books); 40 networked PCs, 24-hrs. JCR with 18 e-mail stations, shop, snack bar, photocopier. *Not half bad at rowing*; football & cricket pitches, squash court, gym; the rest 15 mins away. All 1st, 3rd and most 2nd years live in (£89/24wks); new accommodation block with Seminar rooms; *large* car park behind college, around £8.50 for 3 meals/day; formal dining hall in the evenings; Pete's Caff for snack meals; buttery. LGB, postgrad and women's officers and socs; college doctor, nurse; *good disabled access.*

FAMOUS ALUMNI:

John Birt (former DG, BBC); Phil De Glanville (former England rugby captain); Joseph Heller (writer, Catch-22); Richard Herring (of Lee & Herring *fame*); Peter Mandelson MP (Lab); A A Milne (writer, Winnie-the-Pooh); Matthew Pinsent (four-time Olympic gold – rowing); Sara Ramsden (controller of Sky One); Jeanette Winterson (writer).

St Edmund Hall, Oxford

• *This College is part of the* <u>University of Oxford</u> *and students are entitled to use its facilities.*
St Edmund Hall, Queens Lane, Oxford, OX1 4AR Tel: (01865) 279,000
E-mail: admissions@seh.ox.ac.uk Website: www.seh.ox.ac.uk
Junior Common Room, St Edmund Hall, Queens Lane, Oxford, OX1 4AR
Website: http//jcr.seh.ox.ac.uk

Small, cute and cuddly, Teddy Hall, as its undergrads know it, is a mixture of ancient and modern buildings set 650 metres from Carfax. Although St Edmund's has only been a college in the strictest sense since 1957, its academic and architectural roots stretch back to the 13th century and it has a legitimate claim to being the first institution ever to educate undergrads anywhere. The buildings include a Norman church (now the library) and its attached graveyard and crypt. *The students are a friendly, confident lot radiating freedom of spirit and intimacy and they definitely know how to party. They're strong in journalism, drama and, especially, sport – indeed, there was a time when it seemed like the College only accepted talented athletes, but now even those who are rubbish at sport are in with a chance – provided they can at least down a pint with the lads after the big games.*

Sex ratio (M:F): 53:47	**Founded: 1263**
Full-time u'grads: 403	**Part-time: 0**
Postgrads: 129	**Mature: 2%**
State:private school: 30:52	**Disabled: 20**
Academic ranking: 9	**International: 12%**

Dinky buttery bar with *legendary* fortnightly bops in Wolfson Hall; ancient dining hall; two JCR party rooms. *Dramatically keen – plenty of theatre trips arranged*; annual black tie Summer Event; two *sumptuous* black tie dinners a term; choral concerts and recitals. Library open till 1am, some parts 24-hrs; over 50,000 books, 85 study places. 20 computers, 18 with web access; all rooms have ethernet, College helps fund net access for rooms that don't; photography darkroom. *Excellent* College paper, the Insider, two JCR news Bogsheets a term. CofE chapel and chaplain. *Small* JCR with games and pool machines, Sky TV and, *most importantly*, free condoms. *Dedicated JCR committee.* Sports facilities 5 mins from site, multigym, *bit of a sporty reputation*. 1st and most 3rd years live in, most 2nd years live out, new accommodation due to open; *wide variety* of rooms available, *most are spacious and well-fitted* (£110/25wks); students eat in *ancient* dining hall – *pricey food* (£50/wk); optional Sunday formal dinner. *Unique* JCR butler serves 'Chaps Tea' of toasted teacakes and other *goodies* every weekday in the coffee bar; self-catering provisions vary. LGB Officer; JCR Welfare Officer; doctor, nurse; one adapted bedroom for wheelchair-users; *access not brilliant*; organ and choral scholarships; £4,000 of travel grants; £2,000 of vacation study grants; annual journalism prize; College hardship fund. Alternative prospectus from http://alt.seh.ox.ac.uk

FAMOUS ALUMNI:
Sir Robin Day (broadcaster); Nicholas Evans (author of The Horse Whisperer); Terry Jones (Monty Python); Graham Kentfield (former chief cashier, Bank of England); John Oldham (17th-century poet).

St Hilda's College, Oxford

• *This College is part of the University of Oxford and students are entitled to use its facilities.*
St Hilda's College, Oxford, OX4 1DY Tel: (01865) 276 884
E-mail: college.office@st-hildas.oxford.ac.uk Website: www.st-hildas.ox.ac.uk
Junior Common Room, St Hilda's College, Oxford, OX4 1DY Tel: (01865) 276 846

St Hilda's College, almost a mile from Carfax, is the last all-female college in Oxford and they plan to keep it that way. Men did to try to *crowbar* their way in in 2004 but the motion was *swiftly* overturned by the JCR. *Despite the strong sense of sisterhood, this is no nunnery – most students are drawn to an environment where macho attitudes don't impinge on academic life, but they don't object to associating with blokes after hours – after all, the only ones around have beer hand picked. The large population of international students lends a cosmopolitan tinge to college social life. A 'sister' programme means each fresher 'Hildabeast' is assigned to a student on the same course in the year above.*

Sex ratio (M:F): 0:100	**Founded: 1893**
Full-time u'grads: 418	**Part-time: 0**
Postgrads: 114	**Mature: <1%**
State:private school: 56:44	**Disabled: 0**
Academic ranking: 30	**International: 25%**

Buttery bar with snacks and juke box, dining room; JCR for student bands and jazz nights; *cheapest* May Ball in town; annual arts festival week. Termly Hilda Guardian mag and weekly Loo News. Two libraries (one for Law), 24-hrs, 60,000 books and 120 study places; 24 computers – free printing and extended facilities – and ethernet in all rooms. Music rehearsal rooms in the Jacqueline du Pré building – *one of Oxford's best concert venues. Competent JCR with high level of student involvement.* Non-denominational chapel. Near Iffley Road Sports Centre; punts, boathouse and tennis court on-site and swimming pool next door. *Very strong on rowing.* A third lives out – accommodation office lists vacancies; all 1st years and most 3rds live in (170 catered places, 287 self-catered with meal tickets, £82-91/wk). *Spacious modern rooms* and new accommodation block. Formal dinners at weekends – *damn good food.* CCTV; night porter; doctor; nurse; no JCR access for wheelchair users; two adapted bedrooms; ramps; disability adviser; adaptations as required; hardship fund; travel grants; £200 music bursary. Alternative prospectus available on web.

FAMOUS ALUMNI:

Zeinab Badawi (newscaster); Helen Jackson MP (Lab); Susan Kramer (London mayoral candidate, Lib Dem); Rosalind Miles (writer); Kate Millett (writer); Barbara Pym (writer); Gillian Shephard MP (Con). Jacqueline du Pré (cellist) was an Honorary Fellow, the music building is named after her.

....

St Hugh's College, Oxford

• **This College is part of the <u>University of Oxford</u> and students are entitled to use its facilities.**

St Hugh's College, St Margaret's Road, Oxford, OX2 6LE
Tel: (01865) 274 900 E-mail: admissions@st-hughs.ox.ac.uk
Website: www.st-hughs.ox.ac.uk
JCR, St Hugh's College, St Margaret's Road, Oxford, OX2 6LE
Tel: (01865) 274 425 Website: www.hughsjcr.com

St Hugh's *spacious but unglamorous juxtaposition* of redbrick, Edwardian, art deco and *brutal* 60s buildings are a mile from Carfax. The College was founded *almost by accident* by Elizabeth Wordsworth, for women's education. *It's known for its unstuffy, creative vibe. Having survived for a century without them, St Hugh's admitted men in 1986. This apparently resulted in an increase of rugby songs and associated lewdness in the bar – though the women's football team give as good as they get* – and the college is welcoming with a tight-knit community atmosphere. Hugh's students plague almost every activity at a University level.

Sex ratio (M:F): 50:50		**Founded: 1886**
Full-time u'grads: 419		**Part-time: 0**
Postgrads: 230		**Mature: 10%**
State:private school: 55:45		**Disabled: 8**
Academic ranking: 19		**International: 15%**

Lancaster University owns a peahen and a peacock which wander around the campus

Bar: Wordsworth Room and Lee House (functions); Morden Hall Theatre, *lots of musicals*; frequent *popular* bops in JCR; opera and jazz trips. Two libraries (88,503 books – *good on suffragette movement*); four computer rooms (20 workstations), 24-hr access. *Sporadic* Hugh's News; *charitable JCR with strong environmental concerns*; interdenominational chapel. *Fairly sporty*; two basketball courts, lawns for croquet, tennis and frisbee; other shared facilities with <u>Wadham</u> 800 metres away. All can live in; buttery for *good* food; weekly formal meal in dining hall. Two Welfare, International, Ethnic, Women's and Disability Officers; visiting doctor, nurse. Access fund varies between £100-500 a pop. Alternative prospectus online.

FAMOUS ALUMNI:

Baroness Barbara Castle (late Lab MP); Emily Davidson (suffragette heroine); Ruth Lawrence (mathematical prodigy); Mary Renault (historical novelist); Aung San Suu Kyi (Burmese Nobel Peace Prize winner); Joanna Trollope (*Aga saga* writer).

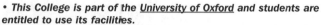

St John's College, Oxford

• *This College is part of the <u>University of Oxford</u> and students are entitled to use its facilities.*
St John's College, Oxford, OX1 3JP Tel: (01865) 277 318
E-mail: college.office@sjc.ox.ac.uk Website: www.sjc.ox.ac.uk
Junior Common Room, St John's College, Oxford, OX1 3JP
Tel: (01865) 277 422 Email: jcr-president@sjr.ox.ac.uk Website: www.sjc-jcr.org.uk

St John's, one of the oldest and *most minted* colleges in Oxford, is 800 metres from Carfax. Its *gorgeous* 15th-, 17th- and 18th-century buildings are arranged around six quads for the public gaze, *and the largest garden in Oxford. Meanwhile – like poor relations or pornographic tattoos – the modern additions are kept wisely out of sight. The only sounds during the day are the pen-jotting, page-flicking or pencil-chewing of diligent students. At night, though, students remove their thinking caps, let their hair down and get down to the bar, already full of the women rowers (The Sirens). Its reputation as an academically snooty workhouse isn't entirely justified – Tony Blair's short-lived rock career began here, after all.*

Sex ratio (M:F): 56:44	**Founded: 1555**
Full-time u'grads: 398	**Part-time: 0**
Postgrads: 200	**Mature: 1%**
State:private school: 69:31	**Disabled: 4**
Academic ranking: 2	**International: 6%**

Largest bar is The Sirens' top venue; others in the Larkin Room, the Prestwich Room and the *post-modern* Basement band venue; auditorium used by St John's Mummers drama group; four bops a term; ball every 3 years; two libraries (one for law) with 75,000 books; 40 computers, 24-hrs; internet in all rooms. Fortnightly TW magazine; Anglican chapel with Sunday choir service. *Active JCR with strong anti-top-up sentiments*; reading room; TV and games room; juke box; vending machine and photocopier. 10 acres of sports fields a mile away; two tennis courts and netball court. *Women's rowing doing well – as usual; tiddlywinks also popular, but there you go.* All live in catered halls (£67-76/24wks); 10% en-suite; 5-8 share kitchens with oven; *very respectable quality rooms* ranging from 16th-century to 90s style; daily formal halls. LGB, Ethnic Minorities', Women's and Disabilities Officers. Doctor, nurse, counsellor. Free condoms and cheap attack alarms for women; *better access than most*; £30,000 access fund; scholarships, grad studentships and hardship funds available.

FAMOUS ALUMNI:

Sir Kingsley Amis, Robert Graves, Philip Larkin, John Wain (all writers/poets); Tony Blair (PM).

St Peter's College, Oxford

• *This College is part of the <u>University of Oxford</u> and students are entitled to use its facilities.*
St Peter's College, New Inn Hall Street, Oxford, OX1 2DL Tel: (01865) 278 863
E-mail: admissions@spc.ox.ac.uk Website: www.spc.ox.ac.uk
St Peter's College JCR, New Inn Hall Street, Oxford, OX1 2DL
Tel: (01865) 278 900 Website: www.spcjcr.co.uk

The *small and cosy* St Peter's College is 800 metres from Carfax, just off Oxford's main High Street. Originally founded by a *disgruntled Liverpudlian* Bishop in hope of offering university education to those who might not be otherwise able to afford it, it became affiliated to <u>Oxford University</u> in 1961 and *the poor Bishop's plans went out the window (although it still maintains a strong open access policy)*. Its buildings are a *low-key* collection of Georgian, Victorian and *nasty* 70s affairs arranged around four grass quads. *St Peter's is a friendly and relaxed college,* noted for its strengths in sport, art and music, and drama.

Sex ratio (M:F): 54:46	Founded: 1929
Full-time u'grads: 396	Part-time: 0
Postgrads: 123	Mature: 2%
State:private school: 50:50	Disabled: 12
Academic ranking: 10	International: 18%

Bar with adjacent games room – *more students drink in town; strong* drama; student bands and four bops a term in the JCR; occasional club events in town; black tie dinner each term, ball every other year; two libraries – one law, (40,000 books in total) open 24-hrs; 15 PCs; ethernet in most rooms. Anglican chapel. Fortnightly mag; JCR does snacks. *Sporty* – rugby champions; darts club; shares sports fields with <u>Exeter</u> and <u>Hertford Colleges</u> (football, rugby, squash, hockey, cricket, tennis, gym). All 1st and most 3rd years live in (£70-84/25-38wks), few 2nd years; accommodation split between main site, college annexes and self-catered college houses in town; college aims to accommodate all undergrads by autumn 2006; rooms *small but pleasant* (23% en-suite); *better kitchen facilities off-main site;* optional formal dinners; termly fixed meal charge (£90-261 depending on housing); parking *next to impossible*. LGB Officer and soc, Postgrad Officer and soc, Women's Officer, *disabled access okay except in library*. Access fund: £500-1,500 a time; means-tested bursary scheme.

FAMOUS ALUMNI:

Edward Akufo Addo (ex-President of Ghana); Carl Albert (former speaker, US House of representatives); Revd W Awdry (author, Thomas the Tank Engine); Simon Beaufoy (screenwriter, The Full Monty); Lord Condon (former Met Police Commissioner); Ken Loach (film director); Sir Paul Reeves (former Governor General of New Zealand); Peter Wright (author, Spycatcher).

The Queen's College, Oxford

• *This College is part of the <u>University of Oxford</u> and students are entitled to use its facilities.*
The Queen's College, High Street, Oxford, OX1 4AW Tel: (01865) 279 167
E-mail: admission@queens.ox.ac.uk Website: www.queens.ox.ac.uk
Junior Common Room, The Queens College, High Street, Oxford, OX1 4AW
Website: www.queens.ox.ac.uk/jcr

Queen's is *steeped* in history and tradition, *but laid-back nonetheless*. Technically, students can still order servants into the cellar to fetch them beer, but now prefer to go themselves – because it's a pub. Its *superb* buildings, 600 metres from Carfax, *dominate* the High Street, and Queen's quad and cupola (designed by Hawksmoor) are *impressive*. More northern students are attracted to Queen's than most colleges *and the atmosphere is refreshingly unpretentious*. Students do a lot of their socialising on campus.

Sex ratio (M:F): 55:45	Founded: 1341
Full-time u'grads: 300	Part-time: 0
Postgrads: 100	Mature: 0
State:private school: 54:46	Disabled: 6
Academic ranking: 26	International: 12%

Bar – the Beer Cellar (cap 150) – with *friendly staff* and *slap-up* dinners preceded by fanfare and afternoon teas. Queen's Hall (cap 350) and JCR (75) used for ents and bands; ball every three years; 40% turn-out last ballot; library (200,000 books), 12 computers, 24-hrs; Anglican chapel. *Queen's students' sport of choice is darts*; sports courts and pitches; gym; track; multigym; squash courts; bowling green. Everyone lives in College halls or flats, some self-catering; dining hall; LGB group; LGB, Minorities, Welfare, Men's and Women's Officers; academic and food reps; doctor and nurse; bursaries, scholarships and hardship funds, *oh my*.

FAMOUS ALUMNI:

Rowan Atkinson (comedian); Jeremy Bentham (philosopher); Tim Berners-Lee (invented the WWW); Edmund Halley (*named after some comet*); Henry V (king); Gerald Kaufman MP (Lab); Oliver Sacks (writer, psychiatrist); Brian Walden (journalist).

Trinity College, Oxford

• *This College is part of the* <u>*University of Oxford*</u> *and students are entitled to use its facilities.*
Trinity College, Broad Street, Oxford, OX1 3BH
Tel: (01865) 279 900 Website: www.trinity.ox.ac.uk
Junior Common Room, Trinity College, Broad Street, OX1 3BH
E-mail: jcr@trinity.ox.ac.uk Website: www.trinity.ox.ac.uk/jcr

Originally Trinity students had to take holy orders, lead monastic lifestyles of study and contemplation and never marry. *Entry requirements have relaxed – now students just have to be clever.* Trinity college sits *very prettily* in extensive gardens, 400 metres from Carfax and within walking distance of the University's main facilities. The College's generally moderate (in size, sporting/political activity and cost) and though it maintains *a keenly academic tilt*, has plenty of journos, politicos and thespos too.

Sex ratio (M:F): 52:48	Founded: 1555
Full-time u'grads: 295	Part-time: n/a
Postgrads: 124	Mature: n/a
State:private school: 50:50	Disabled: 3
Academic ranking: 23	International: 3%

Bar; student bands; three clubbing nights a term in Beer Cellar (cap 150); small weekly ents events; ball every 3 years. Arts week. Library (86,000 books), 24-hrs; 21 computers. 60% turn out for ballots; internet access in all rooms. Soundproof practice room. 5 acres of shared sports fields $1\frac{1}{2}$ miles away (*a bit discouraging for students but strong in fencing, football and athletics*). All students live in college accommodation and eat in the dining hall or Beer Cellar; *good veggie options*; one kitchen for self-catering; night porter; CCTV; doctor; nurse; counsellor; Anglican chapel; ents rep; Ethnic Minorities, Men's and Women's Officers; bursaries; travel funds; scholarships; hardship fund.

FAMOUS ALUMNI:

Richard Burton (explorer); Sir Kenneth Clark (art historian); Cardinal Newman (theologian); William Pitt, Lord North (ex-PMs); Terrance Rattigan (playwright).

University College, Oxford

• *This College is part of the <u>University of Oxford</u> and students are entitled to use its facilities.*
University College, Oxford, OX1 4BH
Tel: (01865) 276 602 E-mail: college.office@univ.ox.ac.uk Website: www.univ.ox.ac.uk
University College JCR, University College, Oxford, OX1 4BH
Tel: (01865) 276 606 E-mail: jcr.president@univ.ox.ac.uk

Though they freely admit claims that King Alfred established it in the 9th century are hokum, University College is still the oldest in Oxford. It presents an *imposing* facade to the High Street but is *pleasantly habitable inside*, with a massive marble memorial to Shelley (who actually got expelled) lurking down one of its quieter corridors. *The college has been a bit insular in the past but now the environment's relaxed and friendly enough, so students aren't easily tempted to stray in search of fun. A good level of things sporty and dramatic complement the excellent academic record.*

Sex ratio (M:F): 63:37	**Founded: 1249**
Full-time u'grads: 430	**Part-time: 0**
Postgrads: 112	**Mature: 1%**
State:private school: 22:53	**Disabled: 22**
Academic ranking: 25	**International: 11%**

Bar (cap 150); three bops a term; jazz evenings; regular dramatic and musical offerings; weekly recitals. JCR paper News & Screws. Formal ball every 3 years. Two libraries (50,000 books), 24-hrs; 35 computers; internet access. One reverend; inter-denominational chapel. 50% turn out at ballots; *strong in sports, especially women's*; $7\frac{1}{2}$ acres of sports pitches; boat house $1\frac{1}{2}$ miles away; tennis; gym; darts; badminton. All 1st/2nd and 70% of 3rd years live in; night porter; CCTV. LGB, Minorities and Women's Officers; nurse; *keen to adapt things for disabled students*; advice; access fund; book fund; travel fund; vacation study grants; bursaries; graduate scholarships.

FAMOUS ALUMNI:

Clement Atlee (ex-PM); Bill Clinton (ex-US Prez and cigar smoker); Bob Hawke (ex-Australian PM); Stephen Hawking (cosmologist); Richard Ingrams (founder, Private Eye); Armando Ianucci (comedian, writer); C S Lewis (author); Andrew Motion (Poet Laureate); Festus Mogae (Botswana's Prez); V S Naipaul (writer); P B Shelley (poet); Peter Snow (BBC presenter); Harold Wilson (ex-PM); Prince Youssoupov (killed Rasputin).

Wadham College, Oxford

• *This College is part of the <u>University of Oxford</u> and students are entitled to use its facilities.*
Wadham College, Parks Road, Oxford, OX1 3PN Tel: (01865) 277 900
E-mail: admissions@wadham.oxford.ac.uk Website: www.wadham.ox.ac.uk
Wadham College SU, Parks Road, Oxford, OX1 3PN Tel: (01865) 277 969
E-mail: su.president@wadh.oxford.ac.uk Website: http://su.wadham.ox.ac.uk

Opposite the Bod (Bodleian Library), 300 metres from Carfax, are the golden stones of Wadham. Founded by a woman (Dorothy Wadham) and one of the first to admit women, *Wadham's a progressive and diverse college*. The old main buildings centre around a grassy Jacobean quad and, along with the newer library, SU and halls, are set amongst *neat* lawns and gardens. *The SU plays an important part of Wadham life, the college is liberal, politically active (but not party political) and its ents are known and feared throughout the University.*

52% 48%		
Sex ratio (M:F): 48:52	Founded: 1610
Full-time u'grads: 450	Part-time: 0
Postgrads: 150	Ethnic: 33%
State:private school: 67:33	Mature: 5%
Academic ranking: 8	Disabled: 23
International: 20%	

Bar; theatre; am dram; classical concerts in Holywell Music Room (cap 150); fortnightly *top* bops, cabaret in JCR (200) including Queer Bop and Wadham Music Festival. Library (40,000 books), 24-hrs; 24 computers. Chapel. 6 acres of playing fields $1\frac{1}{2}$ miles away; tennis and squash courts; gym; *strong in men and women's rowing and cricket*. All 1st years, 98% of finalists and 35% of 2nd years live in; *good self-catering facilities; not great food in cafeteria; rare formal dinners.* LGB, Minorities and Women's groups and Officers; surgery; counselling; lots of spiral staircases – disabled ramps available. Wardens exhibition fund; hardship fund; travel grants; bursaries.

FAMOUS ALUMNI:

Melvyn Bragg (broadcaster); Alan Coren (columnist); Cecil Day-Lewis (poet); Earl of Rochester (poet); Michael Foot (Labour leader 1980-83); C B Fry (cricketer); Rosamund Pike (actress); Rowan Williams (Archbishop of Canterbury); John Wilkins (scientist); Christopher Wren (architect).

Worcester College, Oxford

• *This College is part of the University of Oxford and students are entitled to use its facilities.*

Worcester College, Walton Street, Oxford, OX1 2HB Tel: (01865) 278 300
E-mail: enquiries.academic@worcester.ox.ac.uk Website: www.worcester.ox.ac.uk
Worcester College Junior Common Room, Walton Street, Oxford, OX1 2HB
Tel: (01865) 278 380

Worcester's a *beautiful* college with both medieval and modern buildings and surrounded by 26 acres of *stunning* gardens, complete with a lake and ducks. Institutions of earning have been on the site since the 13th century, but the current incarnation dates back to 1714. *Students are friendly and welcoming. Politics are forgotten in the college's enthusiasm for sport* (one of the few colleges to have most facilities on-site), *dedication to music and devotion to having a good time whilst learning.*

50% 50%		
Sex ratio (M:F): 50:50	Founded: 1714
Full-time u'grads: 408	Part-time: 0
Postgrads: 188	Mature: 2%
State:private school: 47:53	Disabled: 12
Academic ranking: 12	International: 4%

Cellar Bar (cap 100). For bops: hall (150); JCR (100); Morley Fletcher Room (100). Soundproof room; ball every 3 years; lots of live music; choir; weekly recitals; termly boat club cocktail party. Drama soc. Newsletter the Worcester Source. Three libraries (100,000 books); 22 computers. 65% turn-out last ballot. CofE Chapel. 12 acres of sports field on-site; boathouse; gym; tennis and squash courts; *renowned women's football*. All 1st and 2nd years live in, 7.5% of finalists; ethernet in all rooms; most eat in hall; optional formal dinners; *limited* self-catering; CCTV. Surgery; LGB and Women's Officers; *limited but improving* disabled access; book allowance; travel grants; bursaries; hardship funds.

FAMOUS ALUMNI:

Richard Adams (writer, Watership Down); Sir Alistair Burnett (newscaster); Rupert Murdoch (media mogul); John Sainsbury (founder, Sainsbury's).

Oxford Brookes University

- *Formerly Oxford Polytechnic.*
(1) Oxford Brookes University, Headington Campus, Oxford, OX3 0BP
   Tel: (01865) 484848 E-mail: query@brookes.ac.uk Website: www.brookes.ac.uk
   Oxford Brookes University Students' Union, Helena Kennedy Student Centre, Headington
   Hill Campus, Oxford, OX3 0BP Tel: (01865) 484750 E-mail: obsu@brookes.ac.uk
   Website: www.thesu.com
(2) Oxford Brookes University, Harcourt Hill Campus, Oxford, OX2 9AT
(3) Oxford Brookes University, Wheatley Campus, Wheatley, Oxford, OX33 1HX

GENERAL

Oxford Brookes is unlike its famous neighbour in many ways. Despite being in the same city
of ivory towers and dreaming spires, Oxford Brookes dodges any of the dusty stuffiness of
the <u>University of Oxford</u>. The students, however, are just as partial to punting, falling in the
river and strolling through Christchurch meadows. It has four campuses as well as a site
based at the John Radcliffe Hospital. Two of the campuses (Gipsy Lane and Headington Hill)
are basically the same site (*even the University is inconsistent about the distinctions*),
consisting of 25 acres of *modern, pretty functional, if slightly schooly, buildings* (*not as bad
as it sounds*), spread along either side of Headington Road, a mile outside Oxford's centre
in the suburbs, *away from that hazy churn of academic ritual*. Headington's leafy and green,
but it doesn't have much to offer the discerning shopoer, diner or party-goer. There are a
couple of smaller sites at Harcourt Hill (5 miles west) and Wheatley (5 miles east).

Sex ratio (M:F): 41:59	**Founded: 1865**
Full-time u'grads: 9,695	**Part-time: 2,690**
Postgrads: 1,975	**Non-degree: 399**
Ave course: 3yrs	**Ethnic: 14%**
State:private school: 74:26	**Flunk rate: 18%**
Mature: 62%	**International: 24%**
Disabled: 405	**Local: 21%**

ATMOSPHERE:
Brookes attracts a higher proportion of Home Counties trendies than most of the former
polys, probably drawn by the Oxford name-tag (without such demanding entrance
requirements). *That said, there are plenty of mature students and others who don't
necessarily fit the mould and everyone is included in the sporty, boozy lifestyle.*

SITES:
Headington Campus: The main campus is divided into two: Headington Hill, 15 acres that
used to belong to the Captain Dodgy himself, Robert Maxwell, on the north side of
Headington Road; and Gipsy Lane, 11 *more cramped* acres on the south side.
Harcourt Hill: The newest site is a *spacious and green* 95 acres, on the outskirts of the
other side of Oxford, about 2 miles from the city centre, housing the Institute of Education
and some halls.
Wheatley: The Wheatley site houses the business courses and a hall of residence on its 65
acres, 5 miles further out east into the countryside.

OXFORD: see University of Oxford
- City centre: 1 mile

TRAVEL: see University of Oxford
College: OBSU's late night minibus runs from 9pm-3am anywhere within the ringroad for a £1 donation. Also a University bus runs around the various sites. A pass costs £150 and is automatically included in Halls fees. *Some students are less than overjoyed at this, particularly those in the halls right next to the campus.*

CAREER PROSPECTS:
- Careers Service • No. of staff: 3 full/5 part • Unemployed after 6mths: 7%
The careers service provides bulletin boards, job fairs, careers library and interview training.

SPECIAL FEATURES:
- There's a no-smoking rule in all areas of the University, except the SU Bars.
- The University's Chancellor is Jon Snow (Channel 4 News Presenter).

FAMOUS ALUMNI:
Jonathan Djangoly MP (Con); Andy Gomersall (World Cup winning England rugby player); Oliver Heath (designer); John Pilkington (BBC); Adrian Reynard (motorsport entrepeneur); Tim Rodber (rugby player); Debra Shipley MP (Lab); Richard Younger-Ross MP (LibDem).

FURTHER INFO:
- Prospectuses: undergrad; postgrad • Open days

ACADEMIC

In terms of traditional academic pursuits, Brookes isn't a patch on its famous neighbour, but it offers something different and its reputation is far from tatty, especially in business and traditional techie subjects.

80-320		POINTS
Entry points: 80-320	**Ave points: 168**	
Applns per place: n/a	**Clearing: 13%**	
No. of terms: 2	**Length of terms: 15wks**	
Staff/student ratio: 1:12	**Study addicts: n/a%**	
Teaching: ****	**Research: ***	

ADMISSIONS:
- Apply via UCAS

SUBJECTS:

Arts, Humanities, Languages: 15%
Biological & Environmental Sciences: 5%
Built Environment: 10
Business & Hospitality Management: 18%

Education, Sport, Philosophy, Religion: 25%
Engineering, Computing, Maths: 9%
Health & Social Care: 11%
Social Sciences & Law: 9%

Best: Biology, Building, Business & Management, Economics, Environmental Sciences, Fine Art, French, History of Art, Hotel & Restaurant Management, Italian, Mathematical Sciences, Politics, Psychology, Real Estate Management, Religious Studies, Spanish, Theology, Town Planning.

LIBRARIES:
- 450,000 books • 1,100 study places
The main library at the Gipsy Hill campus in Headington is the biggest, but there are smaller collections at Wheatley, Harcourt Hill and Dorset House (further out of town on Headington Road).

COMPUTERS:

• 724 workstations • 24-hr access

All halls have internet points and college intranet access, *but even with 24-hr access, it's not enough computers.*

ENTERTAINMENT

OXFORD: see University of Oxford

UNIVERSITY:

• Price of a pint of beer: £1.80 • Glass of wine: £2 • Can of Red Bull: £2

Bars: Morals Cafe bar at Morrell Hall is the bar (cap 550) and it doubles as a club venue. Hart's Lounge Bar (350) – so-called because it was opened by Tony Hart – and the Mezzanine Bar at Headington Hill are *also buzzy.*

Theatres: The two drama societies are *pretty popular,* with at least one show usually going to the Edinburgh Fringe Festival each year.

Music venues: Brookes pulls in *the biggest names in Oxford.* Recent visits from Feeder, Ash, The Thrills and Spiritualised.

Clubbing: Playground (*cheap and cheerful*); Pleasuredome (£3) is so popular that it put the local Zodiac Club's Wednesday club night out of business. Fabio, Goldie and Grooverider have all appeared recently.

Food: The University's refectory, contracted out to an external caterer, refects at lunchtime and early evenings.

Other: A summer ball every year.

SOCIAL & POLITICAL

OXFORD BROOKES STUDENTS' UNION:

• 6 sabbaticals • Turnout at last ballot: 15% • NUS member

OBSU is a *busy, enthusiastic, high-profile* organisation, which does a *rather good job* of looking after its students and railing against the University suits *whenever the opportunity presents itself.* Most facilities are in the Helena Kennedy Student Centre at Headington.

SU FACILITIES:

Ents venue; four bars; canteen; coffee bar; minibus hire; shops; juke boxes; pool table; vending and games machines; pool tables; photocopying; minibus; TV room; insurance agent; dentist; travel agents.

CLUBS (NON-SPORTING):

8 Dragons; Accounting; Alpha; Anthropology; Anything but Garage; Arab; Arab Culture; Bahai; Beans (nutrition society); Board Game; Brazilian; Business & Retail; CHAOS; Chinese; CIS; Computer Gaming; Engineering; English; European Business; Extreme; Fine Art; Fishes and Wishes; French; Friends of Falun Gong; Geography; German; Greasepaint; Hacky Sac (kicking beanbags around); Health & Social Care; Hellenic; Hollow Way (halls society); International Affairs; Intercultural Society; Italian; Japanese; Jazz; Korfball Appreciation; Krishna Consciousness; Law; LISP (Life Improvement Service Providers – minibus drivers); Lunar; Malaysian; Mandarin; Marshalling; Mixed Futures; Musicals Appreciation; Obsession Radio; Officer Training Corps; OBLX (laser game); Persian; Politics; Psychological; RAG; Real Estate; Religion & Philosophy; Salsa; Shotgun Not (*work-shy* student staff boozing club); Sikh; Sleep; Smoke Free; T-T (T-shirt and tie); Turf; UNA (United Nations); Urban design; Wargames; Wheatley Appreciation Society (halls social). **See also Clubs tables.**

OTHER ORGANISATIONS:

Monthly newspaper OBScene is the main SU vehicle for rants against the University authorities. There are usually *lots of strange and wonderful* charity events – one recent stunt was a 72-hr bus tour of Britain's other student unions. Community action group STAX works with local youths on film and art projects.

RELIGIOUS:
• 9 chaplains (CofE, RC, Methodist, Baptist, Russian Orthodox)
Prayer provisions in the University for Christians and Muslims.

PAID WORK:

• Job bureau
The SU runs a jobshop with specialist staff filling over 1,500 vacancies a year. Unlike their Oxford University counterparts, Brookes students are allowed to take part-time jobs and lots of them do.

• Recent successes: hockey, football, rugby • BUSA Ranking: 30
Sport is one of the few things that can drag Brookes students out of the bar. *They live to put one over on the Oxford University teams* and recently toasted a *glorious victory* on the rugby field. *Unusually*, the SU isn't involved in running sports – the University sports centre manages it all.

SPORTS FACILITIES:

Five football pitches; rugby, hockey, cricket and all-weather pitches. Squash, tennis, basketball and netball courts; swimming pool; gym; aerobics studio; sauna; climbing wall; golf course and river. See also University of Oxford

SPORTING CLUBS:

American Football; Lacrosse; Korfball; Polo; Outdoor Pursuits. **See also Clubs tables.**

ATTRACTIONS: see University of Oxford

IN COLLEGE:
• Catered: 8% • Cost: £74 (42wks)
• Self-catering: 27% • Cost: £57 (42wks) • Insurance premium: £
Availability: A recent spate of refurbs has *smartened the halls up a bit*, but it can be hard to get a place, as the Oxford catchment area for denying applications includes most of London. In all there are 11 halls, housing about 2,500 students. *Cheney and Morrells (great Saturday night club ents)* are the most popular. *Wheatley is really grim, although those unlucky enough to get stuck there often develop an obstinate devotion to the place.*
Car parking: The University clamps cars anywhere near halls. Students have to agree not to bring a car to Oxford.

EXTERNALLY: see University of Oxford
• Ave rent: £75

SERVICES:
• Lesbian/Gay/Bisexual Officer & Society • Ethnic Minorities Officer • Women's Officer
• Men's Officer • International Students' Officer • Eating Disorders Support Group
• Late-night minibus (9pm-3am) • College counsellors: 6 full/8 part • Crime rating: !!
Health: On-campus health centre (four GPs and nurses) and dentist *causing scary drilling sounds.*
Women: Attack alarms provided and priority on the safety bus.
Crèches/Nursery: A crèche looks after young children.
Disabilities: *Better in the new buildings than the old.* Access *isn't great*, although there's a system of improvement underway to try and sort it out.

FINANCE:
* Ave debt per year: £3,003
* Access fund: £255,000 • Successful applications/yr: 445

Support: John Henry Brookes bursary scheme is a limited fund to provide bursaries for hardship cases.

Oxford Poly

see Oxford Brookes University

Paisley University
University Campus Ayr
Crichton University Campus

Paisley College see <u>Paisley University</u>

Polytechnic of Central London (PCL) see <u>Westminster University</u>

Pharmacy see <u>School of Pharmacy, University of London</u>

University of Plymouth

Polytechnic South West see <u>University of Plymouth</u>

Polytechnic of East London see <u>University of East London</u>

Polytechnic of North London (PNL) see <u>London Metropolitan University</u>

Polytechnic of West London see <u>Thames Valley University</u>

University of Portsmouth

Portsmouth Polytechnic see <u>University of Portsmouth</u>

Preston Polytechnic see <u>University of Central Lancashire</u>

Printing see <u>University of the Arts, London</u>

Paisley University

• *Formerly Paisley College.*
University of Paisley, High Street, Paisley, PA1 2BE
Tel: (0141) 848 3000 E-mail: uni-direct@paisley.ac.uk Website: www.paisley.ac.uk
Paisley University Students' Association, Paisley Campus Union, Storie Street, Paisley, PA1 2HB
Tel: (0141) 849 4157 Email: president@upsa@org.uk Website: www.upsa.org.uk
See below for details of other sites.

GENERAL

Paisley made its name flogging the eponymous patterned cloth to proto-golfer types in the 19th century. These days it's not quite so well-off, but despite its proximity to Glasgow, it could be described as a smaller, more run-down version of Edinburgh. There are the same leg-testing hills and the Edwardian and Victorian architecture balanced by some of its rougher elements. To the south there's beautiful countryside in the shape of Glennifer Braes County Park and to the north there's the somewhat less beautiful Glasgow International Airport. With the inexplicably cheap prices offered by budget airlines, you could probably fly here for less than the price of a hamburger. The fact that most students don't (80% are from the local area) does mean that the University has a relatively insular feel but with Scotland's biggest beer festival here every April there's no reason why that shouldn't change. There are also sites in Dumfries and Ayr. **See below for details of each site.**

64%	
Sex ratio (M:F): 36:64	**Founded: 1897**
Full-time u'grads: 6,025	**Part-time: 3,025**
Postgrads: 585	**Non-degree: 1,785**
Ave course: 3-4yrs	**Ethnic: 7%**
State:private school: 98:2	**Flunk rate: 20%**
Mature: 46%	**International: 7%**
Disabled: 150	**Local: 80%**

ATMOSPHERE:

Students don't go to Paisley for the party scene. In fact you could hardly say most of them 'go' here at all – they grew up here, their parents grew up here and, very probably, their great-great-grandparents grew up here too. On the plus side, this does mean that the University's far more integrated with the town than many institutions and the lack of anything approaching a social whirl (more of a gentle social waltz, really) means you might actually get some work done. There is, however, a bit of a townie (or as they say in these part, 'neddy') culture which gets a bit inyerface sometimes.

PAISLEY:

• Population: 176,970 • Town centre: 0 miles • London: 412 miles
• Edinburgh: 56 miles • Glasgow: 10 miles
• High temp: 19 • Low temp: 1 • Rainfall: 96

You can't spend centuries making psychedelic swirling shapes without a fair amount of artiness rubbing off on you. Right opposite the University is the town's museum and art gallery. Along with shops and the like, there's Paisley Abbey (parts of which date back to the 12th century), the Coats Observatory and the Weaver's Cottage, *but Paisley isn't one of Scotland's bigger tourist destinations,* despite it being voted the '29th Most Romantic Place in Scotland' apparently.

OTHER SITES:

See below for details of University Campus Ayr (in Ayr) and Crichton University Campus (in Dumfries).

TRAVEL:

Trains: The nearest mainline station is 5 mins walk from Gilmour Street. Regular direct services to Glasgow (£2.60 rtn) with the last train at night at 11.46pm, and London (£50.80).
Coaches: Served nationally by Scottish Citylink, via Glasgow. London (£27); Glasgow (£1.70).
Car: M8's a mile from the town, also the A737 and A726. The large car park beside the Union has been voted 'Scotland's Best Car Park' – *presumably by the same people behind the romantic poll (see above)* – but parking on campus is still very difficult, nevertheless.
Taxis: Relatively cheap. There's a huge rank by the station.
Hitching: *Generally not recommended due to the local, heroin-fuelled crime problem.*
Local: *Buses allow easy, short hops*: the 85p single fare to Glasgow's cheaper than the train and runs till 3am.
Bicycles: The hills and the fact that there's nowhere to store bikes on campus doesn't stop some students giving it a go. *Bikes shouldn't be left in the town without landmines and electric fencing however.*

CAREER PROSPECTS:

• Careers Service • No. of staff: 4 full/2 part • Unemployed after 6mths: 13%
As well as student/grad job facilities there's help with writing CVs and coping with psychometric testing (*those personality tests popular with firms not confident of spotting lunatics at interviews*). They've also had guest lectures from the likes of John McCormick (BBC controller), former Scotland football manager Craig Brown and Travis star Fran Healy.

FAMOUS ALUMNI:

Gavin Hastings (ex-Scottish rugby union captain); Graeme Obree (cyclist).

FURTHER INFO:

• Prospectuses: undergrad; postgrad; all departments; international • Open Days

A C A D E M I C

People come to Paisley, not for wishy-washy ideas about bettering themselves, but because they want to get a good, solid job when they finish, and the courses reflect this. All degrees provide work experience and the University has links with VW, Shell and Scottish Power. The Media Studies courses also emphasise practical skills – students have been placed with the BBC and Channel Four among others.

Entry points: 144-240	**Ave points: 168**
Applns per place: n/a	**Clearing: 14%**
No. of terms: 2	**Length of terms: 15wks**
Staff/student ratio: 1:20	**Study addicts: n/a**
Teaching: **	**Research: ******

(Left margin: **144-240**) (Right margin: **POINTS**)

ADMISSIONS:

• Apply via UCAS/CATCH (nursing)/direct (postgrad, part-time)

A *flexible* admissions policy. A wide range of qualifications, including the Scottish Wider Access Programme, are accepted.

SUBJECTS:

Business: 13%
Centre for Life Long Learning: 16%
Cultural & Creative Industries: 10%
Engineering & Science: 11%

Health: 29%
ICT: 10%
Social Sciences: 7%

Best: Accountancy & Economics.
Unusual: Commercial Music; Complementary Therapies; Events Management; Forensic Sciences; Music Technology; Performance for Stage & Screen; Sports Injury Rehabilitation; MA Scottish Creative & Cultural Industries.

LIBRARIES:

• 340,000 books • 1,145 study places • Spend per student: £

There are three library sites – Paisley, Ayr and Alexandra Hospital. The main one is the (deep breath) Robertson Trust Library and Learning Resource Centre. *Despite the severe sounding name this is a great place to work. The desks are big enough so that you can spread your books out without them falling on the floor and it's bright, airy and dotted with pot-plants (that's plants in pots, not ... oh never mind).* Students at Ayr and Dumfries *can suffer from IBS (Inadequate Books Syndrome)* but they have the option of ordering books from Paisley. *It's quicker on the train, however.*

COMPUTERS:

• 305 workstations • 24-hr access

The Paisley campus has a new internet café with 30 computers as well as facilities planned for students to connect wirelessly via their laptops. *Again, Ayr and Dumfries are a tad under-facilitied and await a computer boost.*

ENTERTAINMENT

THE TOWN:

• <u>Price of a pint of beer: £2.30</u> • <u>Glass of wine: £2.50</u> • <u>Can of Red Bull: £2</u>

Cinemas: The CAC has two screens (£3.50), the Arts Centre also has regular screenings (£2).

Theatres: Paisley Arts Centre hosts popular touring companies.

Pubs: *Pushplugs: Café Borgia; Cellar Bar (very close to University); Fiddlers Green; O'Neill's and Paddy Malarkey's (Irish); Vodka Wodka (Scotland's first vodka bar).*

Clubbing: The subtly titled *Shag at Furry Murry's, Toledo* and *Utopia* are all popular.

Music venues: *The Arts Centre is the only hot-spot. Well, more of a luke-warm spot, really.*

Eating out: *Pub lunches are a reliable source of sustenance. Other Pushplugs: Café Borgia in the Arts Centre; A Taste of Europe (bargain lunches); Kaldi's Coffee House; Vodka Wodka (excellent value at £2 for 2 colossal courses).*

UNIVERSITY:

• <u>Price of a pint of beer: £1.80</u> • <u>Glass of wine: £2</u> • <u>Can of Red Bull: £1.50</u>

Bars: *The Big Bar isn't ironically named. With its space age seats and vast windows it puts you in mind of an airport. That spaciousness can be detrimental to the atmosphere, except on the major party nights. It's not the sort of place where you find yourself chatting to the person next to you purely because their elbow's in your beer.*

Films: A film a week on art house and world cinema lines. The cinema at Ayr campus is used for teaching media students as well as screening their work.

Clubbing: Friday night is the Big Cheese chart-dance night in the Big Bar, which keeps at it till 3am.

Music: *Speedway played here recently. Who? Exactly. For anything beyond local and tribute bands Paisleyites go to Glasgow.*

Food: *The refectory fare is so-so. Nosh from the SU is cheap and cheerful. There's also a Starbucks. Woo-hooh.*

Comedy: There are comedy nights every couple of months at the Big Bar and the likes of Phil Kay, Jerry Sadowitz and Lee Evans have appeared.

Others: One formal ball a year and a big bash at a nightclub in Glasgow once a term. Major sports events every week in the SA.

SOCIAL & POLITICAL

PAISLEY UNIVERSITY STUDENTS' ASSOCIATION:

• <u>3 sabbaticals</u> • <u>Turnout at last ballot: 6%</u> • <u>NUS member</u>

The Student Association, based in a run-down building, is hardly rabidly political. The last big campaign was for Wednesdays off for people playing sport but this is contested by lecturers who don't see kicking a ball around as important. The SA has also joined the campaign against tuition fees. *The low turnout for elections reflects the fact that so many of the students are part-time and don't really care.*

SA FACILITIES:

Two bars; café; shop; Bank of Scotland ATM; eight pool tables; photocopiers; games and vending machines; juke box; TV lounge; two meeting rooms; advice centre; general store; stationery shop; new & secondhand bookshops; customised night club; launderette.

CLUBS (NON-SPORTING):

Earth Science; Hellenic; Hobbit's Armpit (role play); International Students. **See also Clubs tables.**

OTHER ORGANISATIONS:

Weekly paper, The Banter, *is hardly broadsheet journalism, but is worth its weight in giggles.* UCA Radio broadcasts locally.

RELIGIOUS:

• <u>4 chaplains (RC, CofS, Baptist, Episcopal)</u>
The multi-faith chaplaincy at the Thomas Coats Memorial Church has provisions for the above plus a Muslim prayer room, Episcopalian and lay preachers and links with the local rabbi and Muslim leaders.

PAID WORK:

• <u>Job bureau</u>
The Student Advisory Service lists vacation vacancies and potential term-time jobs in local pubs and restaurants. The SA also recruits staff early on each year.

SPORTS

• <u>Recent successes: none</u> • <u>BUSA Ranking: 48</u>
Sport isn't a major obsession, but the Robertson Trust Sports Centre gets a few people dragging their Green Flash out of the closet.

SPORTS FACILITIES:

The Sports Centre, 2 miles from campus, includes rugby and football pitches, a sports hall and a fitness room. *Extensive* local facilities and reciprocal agreements with other educational establishments nearby mean students have access to a lake, swimming pool, golf course, squash and tennis courts, croquet lawn, sauna/solarium and ice rink.

SPORTING CLUBS:

Aikido; Gaelic Athletics; Mountaineering; Mountain Biking; Snowboarding. **See also Clubs tables.**

ATTRACTIONS:

The local football heroes are St Mirren.

ACCOMMODATION

IN COLLEGE:

• <u>First years living in: 35%</u> • <u>Self-catered: 13%</u> • <u>Cost: £46 (31 wks)</u>
• <u>Insurance premium: £</u>
Availability: The University has 940 places in halls but 16% of new students won't get a place even if they want one. Around 120 2nd years live in, with numbers decreasing in subsequent years. Most places are within 10 mins of the campus, such as Underwood Residence, which has 171 places (165 single rooms). *Thornly Park, about 2 miles from the Paisley campus, is sociable and desirable, as is the modern hall at Christie Street.* Underwood's *less popular.*
Parking: Some accommodation sites have on-site parking.

EXTERNALLY (PAISLEY):

• <u>Ave rent: £55</u>
Availability: 94% of students live outside University accommodation but *it's reasonably easy to find places in Paisley and the standard's okay. West End Park should be avoided on safety grounds and Ladylane and Storie Street are best left alone too, not because they're rough, but because houses have a propensity for growing mould. Many students live in the East End of Glasgow.*
Housing help: The Residential Accommodation Unit employs three full-time staff, offering residential places when available, a register of local private accommodation and gas safety checks.

Edwina Currie is an honorary member of Liverpool Guild of Students.

WELFARE

SERVICES:

- Lesbian/Gay/Bisexual Officer & Society • Ethnic Minorities Officer & Society
- Women's Officer & Society • Mature Students' Officer & Society
- International Students' Officer & Society • Postgrad Officer & Society
- Disabilities Officer & Society • Late-night minibus • Nightline
- College counsellors: 3 full-time • Crime rating: !

Various help organisations: the Student Advisory Service employs four counsellors; Student Welfare Association; the Student Health Service with nurse; another counsellor and a full-time welfare adviser in the SA. They also provide Copeline on (0800) 056 8181 – a freephone service to help with issues like anxiety, depression and relationship problems. A free party bus takes students home to Thornly Park and Underwood every night.

Crèches/Nursery: Ten places for 2-yr-olds and 24 places for 2-5-yr-olds at the Paisley Campus.

Disabilities: Ramps are in place for wheelchair users. A Special Needs service to help students with specific problems with exams.

Drugs/Crime: Paisley is one of the hard drug blackspots of the UK *but problems haven't really filtered into the University.*

FINANCE:

- Ave debt per year: £1,846

Fees: The powers of Paisley have gone on record as saying they have no intention of charging top-up fees. *They may need reminding of that.*

- Successful applications/yr: 627 • Ave payment: £100-2,500

Support: Bursary system and hardship fund (£10,000) from Student Welfare for those who can't get other help. Loans from the access fund available in as little as 48hrs – there's £185,000 to draw from, with mature students able to apply for parts of a £400,000 pot as well as help with childcare and housing. The Welfare Service can refer students to external trusts and scholarships such as Renfrewshire Educational Trust, Carnegie Trust, Elizabeth Nuffield Educational Fund and so on.

University Campus Ayr

University Campus Ayr, University of Paisley, Beech Grove, Ayr, KA8 0SR Tel: (01387) 702 060
University of Paisley Students' Association, Ayr, KA8 0SR Tel: (0141) 849 4169

In marked contrast to the *earnest* business and techie types at Paisley, Ayr's 2,500 students are a *creative bunch*. The half studying Media or Music *add an arty sparkle to the close-knit atmosphere and mix well with the (predominantly female) Education and Nursing students.* It's set in 20 acres of parkland bordering the River Ayr, *but the building itself looks and feels rather like a high school.*

AYR:

- Population 69,378 • City centre: 1.2 miles • London: 409 miles • Edinburgh: 83 miles
- Glasgow: 38 miles

At the heart of South Ayrshire, the land of Robert Burns, Ayr is an 800-yr-old *pedestrian* town by the coast. The 18th-century Culzean Castle is reckoned to be the National Trust of Scotland's top visitor attraction.

Travel: Trains and regular express coaches to Glasgow, an hour's drive away. The M77 links Ayr to the UK's motorway network. There's an international airport at Prestwick, 2 miles away. Students at Ayr have no academic reason to travel to the University's other sites, other than hunting obscure books at Paisley's library.

ACADEMIC

The campus holds the departments of Education, Cultural & Creative Industries and Health and there are some Business School students (mainly 3rd-year). The recently-refurbished library has all the requisite facilities, *but on a smaller scale than at Paisley*. There are just 30 computers and study space is in *short supply*. *Ayr's strong point is its excellent specialist media facilities*: two TV studios; four radio suites; editing suite; two art studios; two computer studios; three recording studios; one of the UK's largest facilities for Pro-Tools, the industry standard digital-recording studio equipment. The *under-used* Careers Service is geared towards the subjects offered on-site and the Paisley-based Careers Adviser visits weekly.

ENTERTAINMENT:

Ayr: *Pushplugs: The Meridian Pub (pricey wine bar); Treehouse; Harley's; Powerhouse, Madisons (clubs); Cecchini's (Italian)*.
Site: The social centre is Fresh Ayr, the SU building, *which is small, cosy and frequently mobbed*. Events throughout the week keep things moving until 12.30 or 1am: karaoke (Mon); quiz night (Tue); live music (Wed); alternate music eg. hip hop, rock (Thurs); TFI and Playstation competitions (Fri). Commercial music students also *treat* their peers to regular live events. The SU bar dishes up *cheap* snacks and lunches, or peckish peeps can eat *school dinneresque fare* or *slightly more palatable* sandwiches and coffee at the University refectory.

SOCIAL & POLITICAL:

The SU building has a bar/diner, events area, games room and a student shop. There's also a *tiny* bookshop. Ayr has its own SU sabbatical officer, Christian Union, Lesbian/Gay/Bisexual Society, radio station (UCA Radio), student handbook (Ayrmail), bar and Rag, which does good deeds fundraising and working with underprivileged children.

SPORTS:

For teaching purposes, there's a gym. Ayr has its own football and hockey teams.

ACCOMMODATION:

On site: • Self-catered cost: £45
Self-catering halls on campus have space for 112 in single or shared study bedrooms with communal facilities. Standards are *pretty basic, but demand for places is increasing*.

WELFARE:

The Student Advisory Service has a welfare adviser, two chaplains (Epicostal, CofS) and a special needs counsellor. A health and safety service has various leaflets on breast cancer, meningitis, flu and Copeline numbers. *Disabled access is easy as the campus is on one level.*
Finance: Lots of tourists mean part-time work is *easy to come by* in the hotels of Ayr. The Careers Service works with the JobCentre to help students find ways to pull in the pennies.

Crichton University Campus

Crichton University Campus, University of Paisley, Maxwell House, Dumfries, DG1 4UQ
Tel: (0800) 027 1000 E-mail: info@crichton.ac.uk Website: www.crichton.ac.uk

Set in Dumfries, this *resolutely local campus* works with local colleges to act as a learning hub for the people of Dumfries and Galloway. Close to the town centre, it's set in 80 acres of parkland and woods in the former Crichton Royal Hospital and overlooks the River Nith and the Galloway Hills.

DUMFRIES:

• Population: 8,000 • Town centre: 1.4 miles
• London: 336 miles • Edinburgh: 81 miles • Glasgow: 78 miles

Dumfries has city-like facilities – high street and independent shops, pubs, clubs, restaurants, cinemas, health clubs – but it's a small place. For culture vultures, there are stunning castles and arty towns in the local area and the nearby countryside has Britain's largest forest park and mountain-biking opportunities aplenty.

Travel: The campus is a quick stroll, drive or bus ride away from the town centre. Public transport runs to the other University sites.

ACADEMIC:

Business and ICT courses are the main areas of study at Crichton. Childhood Studies and Health Studies are also on campus. To encourage local learners, programmes tend to be flexible with opportunities for part-time, evening or daytime study. A lot of students come from Dumfries and Galloway College to top up HNCs and HNDs into a full- or part-time degree. The library is in the Rutherford McCowan Building and has a *peaceful* study area and IT resources.

ENTERTAINMENT:

Dumfries: *What the nightlife lacks in scale is made up for by the cheap prices.*
Site: Students rub shoulders with locals (*who, after all, are usually one and the same*) at Ay-Jay's, a non-Union pub on campus. It has a café/bar and restaurant.

SOCIAL & POLITICAL:

As well as Ay-Jay's, there's an advisory service, student association office, bookshop and games room.

SPORTS:

Football pitch and 9-hole golf course.

ACCOMMODATION:

Not a bed on-site. Lists of private accommodation are available from the residential accommodation unit.

Paisley College

see Paisley University

Polytechnic of Central London (PCL)

see Westminster University

Pharmacy School

see School of Pharmacy, University of London

University of Plymouth

• **Formerly Polytechnic South West.**
(1) University of Plymouth, Drake Circus, Plymouth, PL4 8AA
   Tel: (01752) 232 232 E-mail: prospectus@su.plymouth.ac.uk
   Website: www.plymouth.ac.uk
   University of Plymouth Students' Union, University of Plymouth, Drake Circus, Plymouth, PL4 8AA Tel: (01752) 238 500 E-mail: presplymouth@plymouth.ac.uk
   Website: www.upsu.com

(2) University of Plymouth, Faculty of Arts & Education (Exeter Campus), Earl Richards Road North, Exeter, EX2 6AS Tel: (01392) 475 010
(3) University of Plymouth, Faculty of Arts & Education (Exmouth Campus), Douglas Avenue, Exmouth, EX8 2AT Tel: (01395) 355 522

GENERAL

If Plymouth were any further south-west, it would be Cornwall. If it were any further south it'd be in the English Channel. As it is, it's a port around the Plymouth Sound (the bay) on the south coast of Devon near *wild and windy* Dartmoor. Plymouth has a claim to founding the USA – the Pilgrim Fathers set off in the Mayflower from Plymouth Harbour *(arriving Stateside in Plymouth Harbour – what are the chances?)*. It was also from here that Sir Francis Drake sailed to whip the Spanish Armada's arse. According to the myth, Frankie psyched himself up by playing bowls on the Hoe, a patch of greenery by the sea – *not a giant Elizabethan prostitute*. Drake's Hoe is still touting for custom near the city centre and not far from the main site of the University. The University's old name, Polytechnic South West, was more accurate geographically, because the University actually has five sites spread around the south: Plymouth, Exeter, Exmouth, Taunton and Poole (the latter two for social work). The former Agriculture site of Seale-Hayne in Newton Abbot has been *judiciously* disposed of and its students and possessions have been hoovered up by the Plymouth campus. *To be fair, Plymouth is the focal point for the University that bears its name*, though the other campuses have their own facilities.

Sex ratio (M:F): 39:61	**Founded: 1970**
Full-time u'grads: 15,960	**Part-time: 6,535**
Postgrads: 955	**Non-degree: 3,723**
Ave course: 3yrs	**Ethnic: 2%**
State:private school: 92:8	**Flunk rate: 13%**
Mature: 43%	**International: 8%**
Disabled: 974	**Local: n/a**

ATMOSPHERE:
The south-west as a whole is a pretty mellow place and although Plymouth students are largely laidback, they are capable of perking up when it comes to work (there's lots of careerist zeal) and drinking unfeasible quantities of beer. The smaller sites have their own quirks, but the main Plymouth campus is a haven for surfer dudes and dudettes – why else would anyone wear Bermuda shorts in March? Loads of voluntary projects help bridge town/gown divides.

OTHER SITES:
Each campus has its own SU president and team of Union Officers.
Exeter: (Art) A redbrick campus 2 miles from the city centre, next to the hilly countryside that surrounds Exeter. It was purpose-built as Exeter Art College. For a more detailed low-down on the ups and downs of Exeter, see <u>Exeter University</u>, which, *for students who are willing to mix with the Sloanes, is a social life-saver.* The Branch of the Plymouth SU based here has its own *cosy bar with sofas and pool tables*, as well as a refectory. Being art-based, the campus houses *a fairly artsy crowd* of under 1,000 students – *a good many with imaginatively coloured hair. Skateboards are the de rigeur mode de transport.*
Exmouth: (Education) 50 miles from Plymouth, the town of Exmouth is, unsurprisingly, at the mouth of the River Exe on the east bank of the wide estuary. *This is a small town (but the largest seaside resort in Devon), a bit of a baby brother to Exeter 8 miles upstream.* Exmouth *thumps above its weight for* live music scene and has a theatre and the Pavilion on the seafront, which stage a variety of entertainments. *Samantha's, Matrix and Q club are preferred night-time destinations. 2 miles of golden sands make it a cute little place but Exeter is a vital standby for students who want more from life than pretty sea views.* The campus is a *tasteful* combination of old, new and recently refurbished, giving an academic home to around 3,000 students, *who are generally more than averagely good-looking – it*

must be the surfer thing. The Exmouth branch of the Union is a warm and bustling place that maintains a 1am bar licence on Saturdays and holds regular events and theme nights. Rolle-up is the little but busy site magazine. A new accommodation block provides rooms for over 200 students.

PLYMOUTH:

- Population: 241,000 • City centre: 0 miles • London: 200 miles
- Exeter: 37 miles • Bristol: 106 miles
- High temp: 19 • Low temp: 4 • Rainfall: 76

Apart from a few buildings dating back to the days of Drake, most of Plymouth was *hastily thrown back together* after WWII bombing raids. *As a result, it's got next to no chance in a beauty pageant with other rural West Country towns and the tourists that do spend the night tend to regret it in the morning.* It's a functional but feisty new city with amenities serving a wide catchment area. *That being said, it's got a pleasant enough harbour area and the Hoe and the Barbican are really quite lovely if you ignore the surrounding drabbery and squint a little. Unlike Bournemouth and Eastbourne, it's not a waiting room for the afterlife – there's a healthy mix of young and old and all social classes are represented in the population.* Articles of interest include the *quaint* red and white lighthouse, Smeaton's Tower, the City Museum & Art Gallery and the National Aquarium with its shark theatre and deep reef tank.

TRAVEL:

Trains: Plymouth's the nearest station to the main site, about 5 mins away. Services to London, Bristol etc. Most stop at Exeter (on the same line).
Coaches: National Express and Western National services from Plymouth's Bretonside Bus Station (10 mins from campus) to London and beyond.
Car: The A38 links Plymouth with Exeter. The M5, M4 and A303 are also useful. *There's no student parking, however, and the city centre multi-storeys can only hold so many.*
Air: Flights inland and to Ireland from Plymouth Airport, roughly 6 miles away.
Hitching: *Okay along the A38 for he (and she) that waits, except up the Cornwall end.*
Local: No. 7 is the *most useful* route, going from the popular student area of Mutley to the city centre (£1.10).
Taxis: Plymouth has its fair share of black cabs and minicabs, *but students only really use them for the ride home after a night out (about £3.20 from town to Mutley).*
Bicycles: *Plymouth's a bit hilly for the lazier cyclist, but the more energetic can find wheeled exploration pleasant on a summer's day. The University has secure bike stores.*

CAREER PROSPECTS:

- Careers Service • No. of staff: 12 full/6 part • Unemployed after 6mths: 9%

Plymouth Careers Service does the usual rounds of job fairs, vacancy bulletins and interview training, plus some *sexy cyber-resources* like career databases and aptitude tests.

FAMOUS ALUMNI:

David Braine (BBC weather); Jules Leaver (founded Fat Face clothing company); Clare Nasir (GMTV weather); Didi Osman (Sleeper bassist); Pam St Clement (Eastenders' Pat); Michael Underwood (BBC children's TV presenter); Peter Winterbottom (rugby player).

FURTHER INFO:

- Prospectuses: undergrad; postgrad; departmental • Open days

Prospectuses can be ordered from the *rather labyrinthine* website, or there's an edited version online.

ACADEMIC

Plymouth's interested in what they call student-centric learning – which probably explains some of the crazier courses on offer. The academic structure's undergone some hefty rejiggery recently as they attempt to integrate the six dispersed faculties into some kind of spiritual whole. This means new computer labs, a Faculty of Arts building with exhibition and gallery space and beefed-up library provision. Plymouth has a *highly successful* network of partner colleges around the Southeast (including the Peninsula Medical School).

Entry points: 180-300	Ave points: n/a
Applns per place: n/a	Clearing: 18%
No. of terms: 3	Length of terms: 12wks
Staff/student ratio: n/a	Study addicts: n/a
Teaching: **	Research: ***

ADMISSIONS:

• Apply via UCAS/NMAS for nursing/GTTR for teaching
'Proper' qualifications are the norm, but enthusiasm and commitment also get applicants a look-in. Deferred entry is possible, *if not quite encouraged*.

SUBJECTS:

Best: Building; Civil Engineering; Dance, Drama & Cinematics; Education; Food & Agriculture; History of Art; Hospitality, Leisure, Recreation & Tourism; Media Studies; Nursing; Organismal & Molecular Biology; Politics; Psychology.
Unusual: Brewing & Licensed Trade Management; Cruise Operations Management; Equine Studies; Media Make-up; Plant Discovery & Exploitation; Popular Music; Robotics; Surf Science & Technology (which has been franchised to Australia).

LIBRARIES:

• 518,212 books • 982 study places • Spend per student: £
Figures above are for all three campuses, although the *recently extended* main library at Plymouth has around half the total resources. *The Marine Biology section is one of the best in the country.*

OTHER LEARNING FACILITIES:

In addition to the drama studio, open-access language labs, IT training, rehearsal rooms and audio/TV centre, Plymouth has a planetarium for *ground-bound Major Toms* and is also the only university in the UK to have a *state-of-the-art* diving centre, mainly used by Marine Biologists and, um, Civil Engineers.

E N T E R T A I N M E N T

PLYMOUTH:

• Price of a pint of beer: £2.10 • Glass of wine: £1.45
Cinemas: *The 15-screen Vue cinema comes straight out of the generic multiplex box. The three-screen ABC is similar, but on a smaller scale. The Plymouth Arts Centre may only have one screen but it's got a proper bohemian ethos, with a veggie restaurant to prove it. All have student discounts.*
Theatres: *It may be a seaside town, but theatre is far from limited to Blackpool trademark end-of-the-pier musical rubbish. The Theatre Royal has all the big touring shows (and the blood-curdling musicals). The Barbican shows a more unusual blend of drama, comedy and dance. The Drum Theatre is for cutting-edge contemporary and classics, while the Plymouth Athenaeum shows quirky amateur efforts.*
Pubs: *Flagonfuls of pubs along the Barbican and in and around the major student areas. Pushplugs: The Skiving Scholar (a very literal title); The Fresher (ditto); The Professor (ditto, with a VW Beetle on its roof); Bar 38; Varsity.*
Clubbing: *Most of the nightspots the city has to offer are on Union Street with some smaller clubs on the Barbican. Pushplugs: Boogie Nights at C103 (indie, hip hop, old skool; R&B – SU venue of choice); Varsity on Mondays.*
Music venues: *Classical at the Theatre Royal and the Guildhall; pop and comedy at the Plymouth Pavilions, and a mix of orchestral and big name events at Powderham Castle – recently made victim to Busted. Try The Cooperage for local bands.*

Other: The Plymouth Festival in July is a city-wide funkathon of all kinds of music and fun from international and regional artists.

Eating out: Apart from the usual chain restaurants, *Pushplugs: the milkshakes at the Joint Internet Café; the fresher and the Professor pubs; Jake's (fast food); Veggie Perrins (veggie Indian – bonus points for naming the TV series it's punning on).*

UNIVERSITY:

• Price of a pint of beer: £1.70 • Glass of wine: £1.15

Bars: The SU has four bars (Illusion and Fishbowl) set in an open-ish complex in the SU basement *that's always bustling with drinkers and loungers-around.* There are arcade games around the bars and the Fishbowl has a pool table and air hockey. A new glass roof has finally let some light in. The beer garden, at least, is only dark at night.

Film: Films are shown every other Tuesday in the Union.

Music venues: Ignition gets a few DJs in – Emma B and Scott Mills have dropped by with the Radio 1 Roadshow crew and Electric Six have played.

Clubbing: SU events held Thu, Fri and Sat – *it's the town clubs on other nights.* Ignition does party tunes and guitar-thwanging at Illusion (Fridays). Thursday is Stock Exchange night, when the bars get turned into mini stock markets – the more you buy, the more expensive it gets and vice versa – *anyone for Special Brew, then?*

Comedy/Cabaret: The Union hosts up-and-coming comics on alternate Tuesdays.

Food: Seven eateries in all. The Union Café's *simple, cheap and edible. Loafers Two's queues stretch out the door for lunchtime sarnies. The Babbage Refectory has lovely food and lovely views.* There's also the Cookworthy, Hoe Centre, Portland and Pilgrim's Cafés.

Other: *Big fat daddy of a Summer Ball.*

SOCIAL & POLITICAL

UNIVERSITY OF PLYMOUTH STUDENTS' UNION:

• 7 sabbaticals • Turnout at last ballot: 30% • NUS member

The SU has facilities on all sites, usually in buildings shared with the University. *They may not yet be out to change the world but political activity is on the up.*

SU FACILITIES:

Night club; four bars at Plymouth; one at Exeter and Exmouth; canteen; cafés; fast food outlet; advice centre at all sites; six pool tables; meeting room; six minibuses for hire; car/van hire; Endsleigh Insurance office; HSBC bank and ATMs; photocopying; fax and printing service; photo booth; payphones; juke boxes; gaming and vending machines; general store; launderette.

CLUBS (NON-SPORTING):

DJ; Juggling; Little Goblins; Motorcycle; Terminal. **See also Clubs tables.**

OTHER ORGANISATIONS:

The SU produces Fly magazine, monthly. Charity Rag and Student Community Action Group with links to many other organisations (eg. The Big Issue) and international projects (eg. building work in Africa).

RELIGIOUS:

• 7 chaplains (Ecumenical, CofE, RC, Orthodox, URC, Baptist, Methodist, New Frontiers)

There are chaplaincies at all campuses. Plymouth's has a chapel, lounge and quiet room. Locally there are worship centres for most spiritual needs.

PAID WORK:

• Job bureau

Apart from the usual bar work and all that, there are a few tourist and maritime-based jobs in Plymouth. *The SU's employment register can be fruitful, as can hopping over the Tamar to Cornwall in the summer.*

SPORTS

• Recent successes: football, surfing, general watersports • BUSA Ranking: 41
Okay, they may have an unfair advantage, but Plymouth has the best surf team in the country. Things were looking bleak for a while, with the closure of the Exmouth playing fields (the sports facilities at the smaller campuses are still fairly cruddy) but the University threw over £70,000 at new sailing boats and has a number of sports scholarships for national and international athletes. On the whole: pretty good, but only for those based at the Plymouth campus.

SPORTS FACILITIES:

Plymouth: Fitness room; squash courts; sports hall; aerobics studio; playing fields; all-weather pitch; 7-hole golf course; swimming pool; sailing boats; watersports centre. The city provides facilities for watersports, a bowling green, a baseball diamond, swimming pools and ski slope and ice skating.
Exmouth: Rolle Fitness Suite.
Exeter: Facilities are mainly hired playing fields.

SPORTING CLUBS:

Aikido; Boxercise; Caving; Flying; Ju-Jitsu; Kick-boxing; Life-saving; Mountain Bike; Octopush; Paintball; Shooting; Sky Diving; Snowriders; Surf; Ultimate Frisbee; Waterpolo; Water-Skiing; Windsurfing. **See also Clubs tables.**

ATTRACTIONS:

Plymouth Argyle for footie. Plymouth is one of the UK's big surf spots and ain't a bad choice for regattas and sailing events neither.

ACCOMMODATION

IN COLLEGE:

• Self-catering: 9% • Cost: £60-125 (39wks) • First years living in: 35%
• Insurance premium: £
Availability: Only special needs and non-EU students are guaranteed places in halls, for the rest it's the luck of the draw. No one lives in after the 1st year. At Plymouth halls are within 2 miles of the campus and are integrated into a *lively student village with cute little streets running through it. The buildings are all well maintained and attractive, but Robbins with its kitchen balconies is a top choice, as are cheap, sociable Gilwall and modern Pilgrim.* 60% of rooms are en-suite, most kitchens have internal telephones, most halls have laundry rooms. Exeter runs a head tenancy scheme and Exmouth has benefited from some new rooms – more housing developments are planned in Plymouth. *CCTV records prowlers and streakers.*
Car parking: For Plymouth: *No, no, and once again, no.*

EXTERNALLY

• Ave rent: £48-55
Availability in Plymouth: *There's just about enough for those who are quick off the mark, but students who bend down to tie their laces or check the mirror for zits may look round to find they've missed the boat. Recommended areas include: Mutley, Greenbank, Stoke, Peverell and St Judes. All are reasonably nearby.*
Housing help: The University runs a *well-staffed* accommodation service on each campus offering vacancy lists, property vetting, contract approval and annual property inspections.

WELFARE

SERVICES:

- Lesbian/Gay/Bisexual Officer • Postgrad Students' Officer • Ethnic Minorities Officer
- Women's Officer • Mature Students' Officer • International Students' Officer & Society
- Disabilities Officer • Self-defence classes • Nightline • Taxi fund
- College counsellors: 2 full/10 part • Crime rating: !!

Health: GP facilities at each site. Plymouth has two NHS practices rotating ten doctors and two nurses, as well as a family planning unit.

Crèches/Nursery: The Plymouth crèche has 50 places for 0-5yrs.

Disabilities: *Access could be better at Plymouth but they're trying their best.* There are disabled toilets and ramps, portable hearing loops in the libraries, induction loops in some lecture theatres, tape/Braille transcription facilities and text/minicom phones. Students with unseen disabilities are offered study skills support, a taping service in exams and specialist equipment.

FINANCE:
- Ave debt per year: £6,077 • Access fund: £1,200,000
- Successful applications/yr: 1,300 • Ave payment: £300-700

Support: Mature students have a better chance of scooping large sums from the access fund. There are some small loans available and start-up awards for widening participation students.

Polytechnic South West

see University of Plymouth

Polytechnic of East London

see University of East London

Polytechnic of North London (PNL)

see London Metropolitan University

Polytechnic of West London

see Thames Valley University

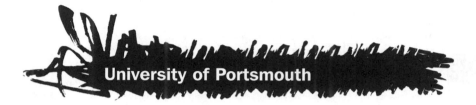

University of Portsmouth

- *Formerly Portsmouth Polytechnic.*
University of Portsmouth, University House, Winston Churchill Avenue, Portsmouth, PO1 2UP
Tel: (02392) 848484 E-mail: admissions@port.ac.uk Website: www.port.ac.uk
University of Portsmouth Students' Union, The Student Centre, Cambridge Road,
Portsmouth, PO1 2EF Tel: (02392) 843640 Website: www.upsu.net

GENERAL

Flanked by the ocean and speared by the Solent, Portsmouth sits within rowing distance of the Isle of Wight. For 400 years it was one of Britain's foremost naval ports *and the nautical influence is still inescapable*. The city, built on Portsea Island (a peninsular rather than a real island), is one of Europe's most densely populated – *it's a small place that can't grow without getting wet*. The University's main site in the city centre has benefited from a £6.2m Union building – with *very swanky* glass wall and reception desk – that now forms the social centre of student life. The satellite campus at Langstone is gradually dwindling except as a sporting and residential centre.

Sex ratio (M:F): 58:42	**Founded: 1992**
Full-time u'grads: 12,320	**Part-time: 2,750**
Postgrads: 1,620	**Non-degree: 500**
Ave course: 3yrs	**Ethnic: 23%**
State:private school: 92:8	**Flunk rate: 16%**
Mature: 30%	**International: 12%**
Disabled: 366	**Local: n/a**

ATMOSPHERE:

Portsmouth has enjoyed a relatively smooth and hassle-free growth recently and is now consolidating its powers on the main Guildhall site, which provides a busy working environment for the relaxed and down-to-earth student crowd. They really do like to be beside the seaside here – summertime brings books to the beaches and students lounge around the University gardens topping up tans. Relations with locals are mild and unthreatening, helped by the fact that most halls aren't in residential areas and Southsea's bars are distinctly student-angled.

SITES:

The Guildhall campus in the city centre is decidedly the focus of university life. The Langstone campus just outside the city is now mainly halls of residence and sports facilities with very little academia or party action going down.

PORTSMOUTH:

• Population: 186,900 • City centre: 0 miles • London: 70 miles
• Southampton: 20 miles
• High temp: 22 • Low temp: 2 • Rainfall: 66
Portsmouth is a *compact if not pocket-sized* place, easily explored on foot. The *lovely, leafy seafront makes for pleasant strolling and there are shiploads of maritime marvels on display*. HMS Victory, the Mary Rose, the Warrior and the Royal Marines are all *intriguing and impressive titbits of Britain's military history* while Southsea House – pied á terre of Henry VIII – and Charles Dickens's birthplace provide tickboxes on the tourist's checklist. The Cascades shopping centre, by contrast, *may not turn as many heads (except away from it)* but it's stuffed with most major stores and chains. All the essentials are available somewhere in Portsmouth. Gunwharf Quays boasts over 70 factory outlets from Ralph Lauren to Levi's. Those who prefer leeks to labels will want to try the daily fruit and veg market. *Although there's little eyebrow-raising architecture or stunning scenery in the city centre,* the stepped and columned Guildhall – with its *rideable* stone lions – provides an *attractive and inspiring* graduation venue.

TRAVEL:

Trains: Portsmouth and Southsea station runs connections to London Waterloo,
Coaches: National Express services travel around the country from the coach station – a mile from Guildhall.

Car: The A27, which runs along the south coast, becomes the M27 between Portsmouth and Southampton. The A3 connects the city with London. *Plentiful Portsmouth parking provision*, but use of University spaces (around 850 at each site) costs £25 a year.
Air: Southampton International Airport is 15 miles away with *cheap* flights from Skybus, flyBe and ScotAirways.
Ferries: Regular ferries to the Isle of Wight, Spain and France (St Malo, Cherbourg, Caen, Le Havre) and the Isle of Wight hovercraft.
Hitching: *Langstone is too far out of town to be any good for thumbing it. Guildhall is a slightly better idea, but not many are prepared to stop on the busy roads.*
Local: Buses and local trains are *reliable* – around £2 for either – *but, since most distances are walkable, students tend to get by on foot.*
College: A free shuttle bus service runs between Langstone halls and Guildhall between 7.30am and 11pm.
Taxis: *Cabs are cheap enough for most students to use semi-regularly, particularly those in the studentish area of Southsea (£2). Those going from the campus to Langstone are less lucky.*
Bicycles: *Plenty of cycle routes and obliging topography make pedalling a pleasure.* Despite this, most students don't bother with bikes *as walking is as good a means as getting around as any*. The University provides lockable sheds (£20 a year) and stacks of racks.

CAREER PROSPECTS:

• <u>Careers Service</u> • <u>No. of staff: 10 full/3 part</u> • <u>Unemployed after 6mths: 9%</u>
The careers service offers loads of online resources like vacancy bulletins, personality and career guidance, and downloadable info leaflets and a cool pink sofa. *Luddites might be more comfy with* the one-on-one discussion sessions, CV surgeries, job fairs and the careers library.

FAMOUS ALUMNI:

Grayson Perry (2003 Turner Prize winning transvestite); David Chidgey MP (LibDem); Shirley Conran (writer); Ron Davies MP (Lab); Ben Fogle (Castaway chap and TV presenter); Nicky Wire (Manic Street Preachers) dropped out because he was 'having a thoroughly miserable time'.

FURTHER INFO:

• <u>Prospectuses: undergrad; postgrad; some departments; international</u> • <u>Open days</u>
The University runs regular Preview Days for anyone interested in applying and there are also invitation-only departmental open days for more specific academic info. Prospectuses can be ordered online.

ACADEMIC

The 25 departments are spread between five faculties and provide lots of vocational courses *and a few woollier ones*. Special mention goes to Engineering, Business and Science-based subjects – *all pretty hot*. Final degree class is based on the 'best of three' idea: whatever's best out of the 2nd year marks, 3rd year marks or the overall grade is what the student walks out with.

160-300 POINTS		
Entry points: 160-300	Ave points: n/a	
Applns per place: 5	Clearing: 4%	
No. of terms: 2	Length of terms: 15wks	
Staff/student ratio: 1:20	Study addicts: 12%	
Teaching: **	Research: ***	
Year abroad: n/a	Sandwich students: 9%	
Firsts: 6%	2.2s: 46%	
2.1s: 40%	3rds: 8%	

ADMISSIONS:

• Apply via UCAS/direct for postgrad

Direct application forms for postgrad study and courses not covered by UCAS. Forms can be downloaded from the website.

SUBJECTS:

Environment: 16%	Science: 21%
Humanities & Social Sciences: 25%	Technology: 18%
Portsmouth Business School: 20%	

Best: Art, Design & Media; Biosciences; Civil Engineering; Economics; Education; Electrical & Electronic Engineering; French; German; Italian; Land & Property Management; Maths & Statistics; Nursing; Other Subjects Allied to Medicine; Pharmacy; Physics; Politics; Psychology; Sociology; Sports Science.
Unusual: Computer Animation; Criminology & Criminal Justice; E-Business; Real Estate Management.

LIBRARIES:

• 600,000 books • 650 study places • Spend per student: £££

The main Frewen Library is *mostly* open till midnight and is due for a *hefty* makeover and extension in 2006. There are a host of smaller departmental libraries, including the Faculty of Environment's Portland LRC which has books, audio-visual materials, IT suites, reprographics facilities *(ie. photocopiers)* and an art shop.

COMPUTERS:

• 1,700 workstations • Spend per student: ££££

The campus is getting more and more wireless as time goes on. Broadband is available in all rooms in halls.

OTHER LEARNING FACILITIES:

Portsmouth has been darned busy of late, chucking up facilities like last night's pizza (but, prettier, naturally). Business students have been shifted into the the purpose-built £12m Richmond Building, right in the centre of the campus. Dentists *are thrilled to the drills about the new* School of Professionals Complementary to Dentistry *(a name so unwieldy even Prince wouldn't think of it)*, with radiography suite and treatment clinic. *But it doesn't stop there, oh no,* there's a new Marine Biology Centre at Eastney Waterfront too, a drama studio, some music rooms, open-access language labs, a design lab and a media centre.

ENTERTAINMENT

THE CITY:

• Price of a pint of beer: £2 • Glass of wine: £3.50 • Can of Red Bull: £2

Cinemas: Three mainstream cinemas in the city (UCI, Warner Village, Odeon) and the Carlton Cinema and No.6 in the dockyard *for adventures in artier celluloid.* The Third Floor Arts Centre holds film festivals from time to time.

Theatres: The King's Theatre is a *decent mainstream thespitoreum – although the jury is out on whether it can be pardoned for showing Ken Dodd.* The historic Theatre Royal is sexier since its refurb. Both offer *considerable* student discounts.

Pubs: *The waterholes around the University have cottoned on to the profit possibilities of the student market* and have a parade of discounts and promos, particularly earlier in the week. Old Portsmouth and *increasingly trendy* Southsea are sure bets for a good night out. *Wetherspoons may be evil, but the one in Guildhall Walk lures in plenty of students for cheap food and beer.* Push also plugs: *Bar Me (good atmosphere and throbbing dance floor); The Pitcher & Piano; Vanilla (funky food and dance music); Walkabout; The Old Vic (straightfriendly gay pub).*

The murals in the Sivell's Bar at Aberdeen University were originally nudes, but they were thought a bit racy for the 1930s, so clothes were added.

Clubbing: *Portsmouth has as many clubs as a Canadian seal-culling expedition, especially around Southsea and the Guildhall area. Pushplugs: Monday's Student Life at Time & Envy for R'n'B, chart, £1 drinks and free VKs before 11pm; Funky Fridays at Po Na Na; VS1 at Po Na Na for free Tuesday cheese; Its Ya Birthday at Time & Envy (commercial dance).*

Music venues: The Guildhall is Portsmouth's premier venue, mixing pop, rock, classical and comedy. There are a handful of other places.

Other: Portsmouth is on the coast so there's piers, candyfloss, whelks, the beach and all the fun of the fair.

Eating out: Loads of cheap deals in the pubs around Guildhall and Southsea, as well as some swankier restaurants, curry houses and pizza parlours. *Fish-lovers will be happy (that's if they love to eat fish – nothing to do with indulging bizarre eel fetishes) thanks to the ocean harvest.*

UNIVERSITY:

• Price of a pint of beer: £1.60 • Glass of wine: £2 • Can of Red Bull: £1.50

Bars: *The Waterhole is the big daddy bar – always busy thanks to its late licence (2am), pool tables, games machines and big screen sport. CO2 next to Lux is for chilling out. There's also the small Embassy Bar for quieter, less frenetic drinking.*

Theatres: *Despite the Musical Theatre society, boards remain thoroughly untrodden.*

Clubbing/Music venues: The 1,600-capacity Lux nightclub has regular events, largely devoted to cheesy beats and dirt-cheap drink, although Saturday's Alchemy night is more hardcore dance-wise.

Food: *Students visit The Pitstop by the Waterhole for a late-night greasing. The Refectory is good for a cheap lunch and there are a number of snacktastic café-style places around.*

Other: Several balls – not usually formal – including the annual Fresher's and Summer events. The Graduation Ball can pull in 3,000+ punters and punteresses.

SOCIAL & POLITICAL

UNIVERSITY OF PORTSMOUTH STUDENTS' UNION:

• 7 sabbaticals • NUS member

UPSUss strongest strengths are sporty and social – although Portsmouth's boys and girls haven't been afraid to throw in their lot with the futile fight against fees. Some of the sabbs have been up to London to lobby Parliament about the quality of student housing. Relations with the University continue to be cosier than cocoa and candy, with students represented on most committees and having a say in most decisions.

SU FACILITIES:

The Student Centre contains the three bars, the Lux club, café, canteen, the Pitstop, Endsleigh Insurance office, stationery shop, pool tables, juke boxes, gaming and vending machines, ATMs advice centre and a 24-hr Blockbuster video and DVD rental machine. Also: fax and printing service; payphones; photocopiers; new bookshop; general store.

CLUBS (NON-SPORTING):

Chinese; Computing; Dramatical Musical; Drum & Bass; Duke of Edinburgh; Entrepreneurs; Finno-Scandinavian; GeoSoc; Hindu; Hong Kong; Malaysian; Music Society; Pagan & Wiccan; Trading Ops; Xylophone Appreciation. **See also Clubs tables.**

OTHER ORGANISATIONS:

Pugwash – *which apparently means something unspeakably rude in Australia* – is the UPSU paper that came top in the Guardian Student Media Awards 2000 and runner-up in 2003. The Union's sports and societies newsletter, Purple Wednesdays, comes out weekly. Radio station Pure broadcasts daily in the Student Centre and on the net, having repeatedly failed to get an FM licence. The Portsmouth Rag – with sabbatical officer – gives everyone a chance to make tits out of themselves for charity with pub-crawls, slave auctions and the rest. Up For It is a volunteer group that runs sports, arts and enterprise activities with local youngsters.

RELIGIOUS:

• 5 chaplains (CofE, RC, Baptist, FC)

On campus there's a chaplaincy meeting room and Muslim prayer room. Most religions are served in the city, which has synagogues, mosques, Hindu and Sikh temples, a Buddhist Monastery *and enough churches of various colours to guarantee a place in heaven*.

PAID WORK:

• Job bureau

The job shop in the Union does its bit to help cash-hunters and with all the bars, ferries, shops and tourists in and around Southsea, chances of finding work are above average.

• Recent successes: football, netball, golf, squash • BUSA Ranking: 48

The Athletics Union does a jolly good job of organising sporting events and keeping the jocks happy. Portsmouth's teams have made quite a name for themselves in the leagues of late and although 'sports for all' is the theory, bursaries for some suggest the University is keen to maintain and improve its sporting rep.

SPORTS FACILITIES:

On the main site, there's the Nuffield Sports Centre with cricket bays, a gym, two weights rooms with multigym, two squash courts, two dance studios and four multi-purpose courts. It hosts 42 fitness classes every week, ranging from boxercise to pilates. St Paul's has a sports hall and four floors of free weights, resistance and cardiovascular gym gear. Near the halls, the 4 acres of sports fields by Langstone Harbour include four soccer pitches, two mini-football fields, two rugby fields, lacrosse pitch and a full-size artificial pitch. The University also has a host of facilities to be used on the Solent, *a flood of fun for those who get wet for water sports*. Annual membership of the sports centres costs £97 a year and the gym costs £3 a time. Locally there are sports centres, tennis courts, golf courses, a swimming complex, and sailing and windsurfing in the Solent.

SPORTING CLUBS:

10-Pin Bowling; Boxing; Caving; Kick Boxing & Kung Fu; Lacrosse; Mixed Martial Arts; Mountain Bike; Offshore Racing; Octopush; Paintball; Roller Hockey; Rowing; Sky Diving; Softball; Surf; Table Tennis; Ultimate Frisbee; Waterpolo; Zen Shorin Do. **See also Clubs tables.**

ATTRACTIONS:

This is decidedly Portsmouth FC's territory, but there's also the greyhound racing track and Hampshire Cricket Club's second ground.

IN COLLEGE:

• Catered: 6% • Cost: £89 (36wks)
• Self-catering: 13% • Cost: £81 (36wks)
• First years living in: 80% • Insurance premium: £

Availability: Although international students are guaranteed places and a large proportion of rooms are reserved for 1st years, 10% of each year's intake gets left out in the cold. James Watson is the newest hall, housing 726 students in *relative* en suite *luxury* in three tower blocks, D, N and A (*geddit?*). Most of the halls are within 10 mins of Guildhall or Langstone campus, but *Langstone can be a drag because of its distance from the city centre and the main student scene. Rooms tend to be of decent quality and neutral décor –* 84% are en-suite *– although some of the older halls, like Bateson at Langstone, are a bit poky and ugly lookin'. The most popular are Trafalgar Hall and the studio flats opposite the Guildhall buildings – these are the most modern and comfortable. Rees Hall may be the furthest away of the city centre halls but its spectacular sea views and Edwardian*

appearance make it a favourite for the wealthier students. Those living catered get between five and 14 meals a week (depends how much they pay) and a microwave for packaged snacks. Self-catered students share kitchens with three to eight people. All halls have laundry rooms, satellite TV lounges and games rooms. *Single-sex flats are available if you ask the Housing Office nicely. Night security patrols shoot bogeymen on sight.*
Car parking: Only available at the halls around Langstone – with permit.

EXTERNALLY:
• Ave rent: £53
Availability: *All students will find something given time, but some graduate first. The most appropriate places are in the large Victorian houses which have been split into tenement flats and bedsits,* usually shared by two to four people. *The best places are Southsea, Fratton and North End. Eastney, Somerstown and Paulsgrove are too rough to be worth it.*
Housing help: The Student Housing Office publishes regular bulletins and keeps a list of respectable digs. 'Find a Home' days at the beginning of each year help match students with potential housemates, *ie. non-kleptomaniacs who don't bottle their own urine.*

WELFARE

SERVICES:
• Lesbian/Gay/Bisexual Officer • Mature Students' Officer & Society
• International Students' Officer & Society • Postgrad Officer & Society
• Disabilities Officer & Society • Late-night minibus • Self-defence classes
• College counsellors: 4 full/2 part • SU counsellors: 1 full/3 part • Crime rating: !!!
In addition to University and Union counsellors, there are up to eight trainee associate counsellors on call to soothe student woes, as well as a Mental Health Adviser on secondment from the Health Authority. The SU Officer for Academic Affairs is available to help with study-related angst and legal advisers make weekly visits to the campus. The late night bus service deposits *boozy* folk on their doorstep for 50p.
Health: NHS practices on both Langstone and Guildhall campuses with three GPs and nurses.
Crèches/Nursery: 38 places for precious things aged 6mths-5yrs.
Disabilities: *Access is good in the newer bits and improving in the older ones.* There are wheelchair ramps and lifts in most buildings and specialised rooms available in almost all halls. Induction loops are fitted in lecture theatres and dyslexia screening and support is available from the Disability Advice Centre.

FINANCE:
• Ave debt per year: £6,077
Fees: International students can pay between £7,250 and £8,350 depending on their course. Postgrads pay £3,010.
• Access fund: £880,417 • Successful applications/yr: 1,150 • Ave payment: £766
Support: The Union's Student Finance Centre dishes out advice, while the University doles out the occasional bursary cash-bucket.

Portsmouth Polytechnic
see University of Portsmouth

Preston Polytechnic
see University of Central Lancashire

Printing
see University of the Arts, London

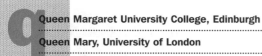

Queen Margaret University College, Edinburgh

Queen Mary, University of London

Queen Mary & Westfield College see Queen Mary, University of London

Queen's College, Glasgow see Glasgow Caledonian University

Queen's University of Belfast

Queen Margaret University College, Edinburgh

(1) Queen Margaret University College, Clerwood Terrace, Edinburgh, EH12 8TS
Tel: (0131) 317 3000 E-mail: admissions@qmuc.ac.uk Website: www.qmuc.ac.uk
Queen Margaret University College Students' Union, Clerwood Terrace, Edinburgh,
EH12 8TS Tel: (0131) 317 3400 E-mail: su-staff@qmuc.ac.uk
Website: www.qmucsu.org.uk
(2) Leith Campus, Duke Street, Leith, Edinburgh, EH6 8HF
Tel: (0131) 317 3353
(3) The Gateway, Gateway Theatre, Leith Walk, Edinburgh, EH7 4AH
Tel: (0131) 317 3900

GENERAL

Made of three campuses dotted around the *beautiful and culturally vibrant* city of Edinburgh
(see University of Edinburgh for more info), QMUC is a *pleasantly mixed bag*. The main site
is in the Corstorphine area, 4 miles from the city centre, in a residential area, neighbouring
a nature reserve, and itself surrounded by mature gardens on a 24-acre greenfield site.
Unfortunately half the buildings look like 60s comprehensive schools. The next is 7 miles
away in Leith, a mile from the Edinburgh's East End. The other is The Gateway on Leith
Walk, 5 mins from town, with its own theatre. By 2007, The Gateway will be the only one
left, as the other two close and a new campus in Musselburgh opens with, we're promised,
fab facilities.

Sex ratio (M:F): 21:79	Founded: 1875
Full-time u'grads: 2,900	Part-time: 775
Postgrads: 440	Non-degree: 316
Ave course: 4yrs	Ethnic: n/a
State:private school: 93:7	Flunk rate: 15%
Mature: 40%	International: 10%
Disabled: 44%	Local: 68%

ATMOSPHERE:
*Friendly and intimate with perky and enthusiastic students. There's a bit of a hefty female
ratio, which can be terrific or torture for either sex depending on their mood and how horny
they're likely to get.*

SITES:

Corstorphine: (3,000 students) The main campus and the heart of admin, academic and SU services.

Leith Campus: (600 students) The Health Studies site, where students study Podiatry, Radiography, Physiotherapy, Occupational Therapy and Art Therapy. *Leith's a nice area by the water* with a shopping centre and the Royal Yacht Britannia. While the *facilities don't rock*, there are pubs, restaurants and clubs enough to satisfy most entertainment urges. The *ethos is more work-orientated though.* **The Gateway:** (200 students – Drama) The Gateway is located in the New Town area of Edinburgh. Despite its name, New Town has some beatiful old buildings and is very close to the city centre. Houses *excellent* facilities for students of production, drama and performance.

EDINBURGH: see University of Edinburgh

• City centre: 4 miles

TRAVEL: see University of Edinburgh

CAREER PROSPECTS:

• Careers Service • Unemployed after 6mths: 4%

QMUC job shop offers interview training, bulletin boards and help with applications and CVs.

FAMOUS ALUMNI:

Dougie Anderson (TV presenter); Matt Baker (Blue Peter); Edith Bowman (MTV and radio DJ); Jimmy Chisholm (actor, Braveheart); Angel Coulby (actress); David Crystal (linguistics guru); Andy Gray (actor); Sally Gray (TV presenter); Simone Lahbib (actress); Brian Marjoribanks (ex-footballer and presenter); Kevin McKidd (actor, Trainspotting); Lloyd Quinan (Scottish weatherman).

FURTHER INFO:

• Prospectuses: undergrad; postgrad • Open days

A C A D E M I C

The College specialises in Business, Theatre and Healthcare subjects and quite a few students end up in work placements of one sort or another. *Its small size makes for cosy class sizes, which is good because it means lecturers will always know your name, and bad … for precisely the same reason.* At the moment, QMUC is building a 'virtual' campus, *an online excuse for students to study in bed.*

156-360		POINTS
Entry points: 156-360	Ave points: 289	
Applns per place: n/a	Clearing: 15%	
No. of terms: 2	Length of terms: 15wks	
Staff/student ratio: 1:18	Study addicts: 96%	
Teaching: *	Research: *	
Firsts: 10%	2.2s: 30%	
2.1s: 56%	3rds: 4%	

ADMISSIONS:

• Apply via UCAS

SUBJECTS:

Creative Arts & Hospitality: 21%
Humanities & Business: 22%
Professions Allied to Health: 44%
Science: 13%

Unusual: Logopaedics (*that's studying speech defects to the rest of us*).

LIBRARIES:

• 135,900 books • 269 study places • Spend per student: £
The library is *well-equipped, except that it doesn't actually have all that many books. It also doesn't open very late.*

COMPUTERS:

• 320 workstations • Spend per student: £££££
Computers are scattered around the campuses, fewest in Gateway. *There aren't enough to go round, which stings at peak times.* Hall bedrooms come with internet points though.

OTHER LEARNING FACILITIES:

Movement studios; voice studios; rehearsal rooms; TV and radio studios; wardrobe and design facility; theatre; training restaurant; photographic studio; dark room; video conferencing; CAD lab.

THE CITY: see University of Edinburgh

COLLEGE:

• Price of a pint of beer: £1.20 • Glass of wine: £1.50 • Can of Red Bull: £2
Anything involving the stage is mighty, everything else sucks slightly, but with the variety of Edinburgh just outside, someone must have thought 'Why bother?'. Students go off-campus to find most entertainment.
Bars/Music/Clubbing: The Union Bar (cap 350), the only place on campus where smoking is allowed. Popular on a Wednesday and during the day. Open late.
Theatres: Teeming with drama and stage management students, the Gateway Theatre houses various productions and QMUC doubles as a Fringe venue during the Festival in the summer. All students are encouraged to get stuck into the theatre.
Film: The film soc is involved in screening films from the arty to the ones where everything explodes at the end. Occasional theme nights.
Comedy/Cabaret: Rarely anything on-site but Edinburgh's comedy and stand-up clubs *keep faces smiling.*
Food: Two dining halls and a fast food bar *gum up students' arteries.*
Other: Christmas and Summer balls.

QUEEN MARGARET UNIVERSITY COLLEGE STUDENTS' UNION

• 2 sabbaticals • Turnout at last ballot: 20% • NUS member
Picking up political pace since the tuition fees brouhaha, students are willing to demonstrate and walk out of lectures for a worthy cause. Internally, the SU enjoys a productive relationship with College and students, and has recently established a student parliament – the first student representation system of its kind in the UK.

SU FACILITIES:

Nothing fancy: bar; canteen; photocopier; stationers; pool table; meeting room; payphone; juke box; TV lounge; games machines.

CLUBS (NON-SPORTING):

Comedy Club; Dance; Fairtrade; Film Society; Glam; Musical Society; Networking Society. **See also Clubs tables.**

OTHER ORGANISATIONS:

The new monthly paper is the Echo. Community relations are discussed with local representatives twice a year. *Rag is small but effective.*

RELIGIOUS:

A meeting room is supplied for anyone feeling all spiritual.

PAID WORK: see University of Edinburgh

• Job bureau

JobShop helps students find part-time and vacation work as well as vocational employment related to their degree. There's a good amount of these jobs around Festival time, but that's during the summer break.

SPORTS

• Recent successes: rugby, fencing, women's hockey • BUSA Ranking: 48

If treading the boards counted as sport, QMUC would have its eye on the Olympics but, alas, sports provisions are limited. Even so, QMUC passes muster at rugby and football.

SPORTS FACILITIES:

QMUC has an all-weather playing field, tennis, netball and basketball courts, swimming pool, sauna and a fitness suite. Students are charged a small fee to use them.

SPORTING CLUBS:

10-Pin Bowling; Martial Arts; Mountaineering. **See also Clubs tables.**

ATTRACTIONS: see University of Edinburgh

ACCOMMODATION

IN COLLEGE:

• Catered: 5% • Cost: £85 (38wks)

• Self-catering: 12% • Cost: £63 (38wks) • Insurance premium: ££

Availability: Corstorphine Campus has three halls: Guthrie Wright Hall (151 catered single rooms), Stevenson Hall (153 self-catered singles) and Grainger Stewart Hall (139 self-contained flats). Leith and Gateway have Halmyre Street flats as off-site accommodation. Catered halls comes in both full-board and B&B flavours, prices reflects this. About 25-30% of students in halls of residence are international students. Others opt to stay at home or get private flats in the city centre.

EXTERNALLY: see University of Edinburgh

• Ave rent: £58

Availability: *Students tend to prefer living in Haymarket, Leith, Dalry and Corstorphine. Leith is the most popular, being cheaper, more plentiful, modern and down by the water.*

Housing help: The Accommodation Office is *helpful,* having an approved list of landlords and some directly leased properties owned by the College.

WELFARE

SERVICES:

• Lesbian/Gay/Bisexual Society • Women's Society • Mature Students' Society

• Postgrad Society • Disabilities Society • College counsellors: 1 full • Crime rating: !

The medical centre at Corstorphine offers family planning, emergency contraception, general health checks and vaccinations. Also a registered nurse, GP and a full-time counsellor.

Crèches/Nursery: The Corstorphine campus has a nursery with some free, part-time places available.

Disabilities: *Access isn't helped by the split sites, which are based in the city or in areas with lots of stairs.* The College has started to provide special disabled accommodation and improved disabled sports facilities, particularly for visually impaired people.

FINANCE:

- Ave debt per year: £1,953
- Access fund: £233,500 • Successful applications/yr: 220 • Ave payment: £150-2,000

Support: The College has £16,000 to hand out each year in hardship loans as well as £86,372 for hardship grants and £71,873 worth of mature students' bursaries.

Queen Mary, University of London

- *Formerly Queen Mary & Westfield College, London.*
- *The College is part of University of London and students are entitled to use its facilities.*

(1) Queen Mary, University of London, Mile End Road, London, E1 4NS Tel: (020) 7882 5555 E-mail: admissions@qmul.ac.uk Website: www.qmul.ac.uk
Queen Mary Students' Union, Mile End Site, 432 Bancroft Road, London, E1 4DH Tel: (020) 7882 5390 E-mail: su-genoff@qmul.ac.uk Website: www.qmsu.org

(2) Barts & the London School of Medicine & Dentisty, Turner Street, London E1 2AD Tel: (020) 7377 7611 E-mail: medicaladmissions@qmul.ac.uk.
Barts & the London Students' Association, Stepney Way, London, E1 2JJ Tel: (020) 7377 7640 E-mail: su-vpassociation@qmul.ac.uk

GENERAL

Situated in East London, close to Canary Wharf and the Docklands and a hair's breadth away from the city, Queen Mary is the only campus college in the University of London. A mish-mash of different buildings, from the *fine old* Queen's building (complete with clock tower) to some 50s art deco and 60s *eyesores*, and strangely, a Jewish cemetery. With 19th-century origins, it was set up to educate East-Enders, while Westfield (now dropped from the name) was a pioneering college for women. Near Regent's Canal and East London's greenbelt as well as having a variety of bustling markets and boozers nearby, Queen Mary shows the best the East End has to offer and is only 15 mins tube journey from Trafalgar Square. **For general information on London: see University of London.**

Sex ratio (M:F): 52:48	**Founded: 1887**
Full-time u'grads: 7,275	**Part-time: 275**
Postgrads: 1,580	**Non-degree: 611**
Ave course: 3yrs	**Ethnic: 52%**
State:private school: 73:27	**Flunk rate: 9%**
Mature: 25%	**International: 21%**
Disabled: 44	**Local: n/a**

ATMOSPHERE:

Multi-racial, multi-national, the cultural gumbo that is QM mirrors the vibrant diversity of the local community, making for a learning experience in itself. It rubs off on the students who mix with each other and the locals with relish. The University spirit loves serious study as much as a proper social life. Early on Friday afternoon the bars fill up, but the study areas also get rammed. Commitment to local volunteering and a general enthusiasm about the area suggest an easy relationship with surrounding East London.

SITES:

The Medical School: Barts and The London School of Medicine and Dentistry is located on two sites in Whitechapel and the City. Students are allowed to use all the main site's facilities, if they have the time.

Whitechapel: (170 students) *Friendly and approachable (at least in comparison with some other medical schools)*, the Royal London Hospital is right opposite Whitechapel tube in an *impressive* brick edifice, 800 metres from the main QM site.

West Smithfield: (730 students) Bart's Hospital is housed in a *lovely* Georgian-fronted building near Smithfield Meat Market (*don't bother, they've heard all the jokes about where the corpses end up*). It's located a mile from QM's main campus.

There are also sites in Charthouse Square and Chislehurst as well as Mile End.

LONDON: see University of London

TRAVEL: see University of London

Trains: Liverpool Street and Stratford are 5 mins by tube or a 20-min walk.
Buses: Numbers 339, 25, 106 and night buses N25, N8 and N15.
Car: City and Tower Hamlets councils have quite strict restrictions and there are the usual traffic/parking concerns.
Underground: Mile End (Central, District, Hammersmith & City lines) and Stepney Green (District, Hammersmith & City lines, peak times only). Whitechapel (District, East London Line, Hammersmith & City) for the London Hospital, St Paul's or Barbican for Bart's.
Bicycles: There's a bicycle users' group (BUG) run by the SU and plenty of cycle racks in the student village and on campus.

CAREER PROSPECTS:

• Careers Service • No. of staff: 5 full • Unemployed after 6mths: 5%
Library, interview training, bulletin boards, job fairs.

FAMOUS ALUMNI:

Dr Barnardo (liked kids); Malcolm Bradury, Eva Figes, Ruth Prawer Jhabvala, Andrea Newman (writers); Bernard Butler (indie guitar *deity*); Graham Chapman (Monty Python); Bruce Dickinson (ex-Iron Maiden); Peter Hain MP (Lab); Sir Roy Strong (former director, V&A museum); David Sullivan (ex-footballer, porn baron); Frederick Treves (treated the elephant man).

FURTHER INFO:

• Prospectuses: undergrad; postgrad; departmental • Open days

A C A D E M I C

Not just a great big medical love-in but also training and research in Science, Engineering, Medicine, Law, Arts, Linguistics and Politics. Students can also learn a language and computing skills if they fancy it.

Entry points: 200-340	**Ave points: 314**
No. of terms: 3	**Length of terms: 12wks**
Staff/student ratio: 1:8	**Study addicts: n/a**
Teaching: ***	**Research: ******

ADMISSIONS:

• Apply via UCAS

LIBRARIES:

• 570,000 books • 1,444 study places

The Law and Medical libraries are quietly impressive, the general one is okay too, having won awards in the past, though they certainly weren't for opening hours.

COMPUTERS:

• 700 workstations

Not enough computers or opening hours.

OTHER LEARNING FACILITIES:

Language lab; drama studio; audio/TV centre.

ENTERTAINMENT

THE CITY: see University of London

• Price of a pint of beer: £2.40 • Glass of wine: £2.60 • Can of Red Bull: £2.25

The New Globe, Hayfield and Coborn pubs are popular as they do special student promos – the Hayfield gets a special student thumbs up. The six-screen Odean cinema does student prices (£3) and there's a local comedy club for when practising autopsies on dead bodies just isn't funny any more.

COLLEGE:

• Price of a pint of beer: £1.70 • Glass of wine: £2 • Can of Red Bull: £1.60

Hard-working students need to blow off steam and take some of the weight off their wallets so they can get to lectures quickly in the morning. College ents lose some of their novelty after the first year and students start pounding the wider stomping ground of the Big Smoke.
Bars: The SU runs four bars. The e1 Venue Bar, remarkably, is at it's best when it's being a venue for QM's *wide range* of ents. The Drapers Arms (cap 350) is the bop shop, Whitechapel has its Association Bar and Smithfield has Bart's Bar. Others are the Forest Bar (popular with staff and postgrads) and the non-smoking Balcony Bar.
Theatres: *Like a drama ninja.* 25 productions were put on last year and shows are regularly taken to the Fringe. *Hai-ya!*
Clubbing/Music: Fizz (themed, Sat) goes down well, as do hip-hop, R'n'B and Bhangra nights. The e1 in its nightclub guise hosts the likes of Dreem Team, DJ Luck and Morcheeba.
Comedy/Cabaret: Top mirth merchants peddle their donkeys once a month at e1. Recent sightings of Paul Tomkinson, Adam Bloom and Junior Simpson.
Food: The refectory spreads over three floors, *quality and value are pretty good*. Bar Med and Global Village have lunch menus. Infusion in the SU does coffees and pastries. For general groceries there's the village shop in the Student Village.
Other: Beer festivals, annual Valentine's Ball and a gallery in the college with local artists' work.

SOCIAL & POLITICAL

QUEEN MARY STUDENTS' UNION:

• 5 sabbaticals • Turnout at last ballot: 13% • NUS member

The SU does well on the ents front with more time channelled into these than political causes. Big picture campaigns don't do so well as ones with immediate relevance to QM students, though they're starting to come around with the high-profilers, like tuition fees and Iraq.

SU FACILITIES:

Five bars; two eateries; two retail outlets; pool tables; meeting room; minibus; car hire; insurance; bank; ATMs; photocopier; fax; printing; photobooth; payphone; advice; TV lounge; juke box; vending machines; bookshops.

CLUBS (NON-SPORTING):
See Clubs tables.

OTHER ORGANISATIONS:
CUB and MaD are the monthly student papers, CUB was short listed for the Guardian Student Newspaper of the Year not so long ago. The community action group is the biggest in London and Rag is huge at Bart's.

RELIGIOUS:
One full- and two part-time chaplains, and Muslim prayer rooms.

PAID WORK: see University of London
• Job bureau • Paid work: term-time 35%: hols 50%
QMSU and the College run job shops advertising opportunities for students. There's a part-time work website, notice boards and workshops. Lots of opportunity to make cash within the SU.

SPORTS

• Recent successes: rowing, women's football, fencing • BUSA Ranking: 41
Sport, like entertainment, acts as a uniting force for QM's disparate colleges and someone's generally being successful at something (for an inner-city institution at any rate), though exactly what varies from year to year.

SPORTS FACILITIES:
Football, rugby, (two) cricket, all-weather and hockey pitches; four tennis, two squash, two basketball and two netball courts; gym; climbing wall; sports hall; multigym; sauna; river.

SPORTING CLUBS:
See Clubs tables.

ATTRACTIONS: see University of London
West Ham and Leyton Orient are the local football sides and there's a dog track, an indoor climbing wall and an ice rink.

ACCOMMODATION

IN COLLEGE:
• Catered: 15% • Cost: £69 (38wks) • Self-catering: 20% • Cost: £79-106 (38wks)
• First years living in: 35% • Insurance premium: £££
Availability: The College's own accommodation has around 2,305 self-catered places. Another 142 find a roof in the University's inter-collegiate halls. All 1st years who apply in time can live in (5% have to share), as can 22% of finalists. The new student village at Mile End is *good-looking with a view of the Regent's Canal though that doesn't go for all sites. It's expensive, even for London (some can be as much as £106 a week).*
Car parking: Students can't park on campus before 4pm.

EXTERNALLY: see University of London
Availability: It's *fairly easy* to get hold of accommodation in the local area (Mile End), and affordable stuff is out there. *The East End is fun but quality can be variable and not all parts are safe.*
Housing help: The College accommodation office has approved landlord and vacancy lists, property vetting and local papers for perusal.

WELFARE

SERVICES:
- Lesbian/Gay/Bisexual Officer & Society • Women's Officer & Society
- Mature Students' Officer & Society • International Students' Officer & Society
- Postgrad Officer & Society • Late-night/Women's minibus • Nightline
- College counsellors: 3 full • Crime rating: !!!!!

The SU runs the Matthew Spencer Support Centre, but when Matthew Spencer doesn't need support it looks after students. There is a welfare suite, counsellors, welfare officers, a health centre with two doctors, a senior nurse and a visiting psychiatrist. All of the different groups, LGB, women's and so on, regularly meet and arrange support groups and advice within their remits.

Disabilities: *Access in college accommodation is okay but is variable in other buildings.* There's a part-time dyslexia support worker and induction loops in all lecture halls.

FINANCE:
- Ave debt per year: £2,390 • Access fund: £260,000
- Successful applications/yr: 641

Support: Undergraduate bursaries of £1,500 per anum *for a lucky few.*

Queen Mary & Westfield College

see Queen Mary, University of London

Queen's College, Glasgow

see Glasgow Caledonian University

Queen's University of Belfast

(1) The Queen's University of Belfast, University Road, Belfast, BT7 1PE
Tel: (028) 9024 5133 E-mail: studentsunion@qub.ac.uk Website: www.qub.ac.uk
Queen's University of Belfast Students' Union, University Road, Belfast, BT7 1PE
Tel: (028) 9097 3106 Website: www.qubsu.org
(2) Queen's University Armagh, 39 Abbey Street, Armagh, BT61 7EB Tel: (028) 3751 0678
E-mail: qua@qub.ac.uk Website: www.armagh.qub.ac.uk

> One of the entrances to Loughborough University is nicknamed
> 'The Bastard Gates' because they were presented by Sir William
> Bastard, a former chairman of the University governors.

GENERAL

On the River Lagan, where the Lough (the bay) opens out into the Irish Sea, lies the largest city in Northern Ireland. The Queen of Queen's University was the *unamused* Victoria – the *tasteful* University buildings date mostly from her time. The University has taken over much of the prosperous surrounding Belfast suburb, so that the houses of the nearby Victorian terraces are more likely to contain one of the University's facilities (or schools) than any Victorians. Given the surrounding greenery – many parks and the nearby botanical gardens – it can be hard to believe that Belfast City Centre is only 800 metres away and the Shankill and Falls Roads 800 metres beyond that.

Sex ratio (M:F): 40:60	Founded: 1845
Full-time u'grads: 12,400	Part-time: 5,355
Postgrads: 1,965	Non-degree: 4,300
Ave course: 3yrs	Ethnic: 3%
State:private school: 99:1	Flunk rate: 9%
Mature: 8%	International: 7%
Disabled: 192	Local: n/a

ATMOSPHERE:
Most students are down to earth with a broad range of social backgrounds (though lots are local and some Northern Ireland state schools are a bit public-like). Belfast is a politically and socially active university, with plenty of entertainment and close to town centre so there's no oppressive small campus feeling. Relations with locals are very good, especially with local businesses. The University is largely untouched by the ever-changing Northern Ireland situation, apart from vigorous debate. The worst of the troubles has passed it by, especially since it's in a prosperous suburb of South Belfast, away from the profoundly sectarian parts, so most of the tension on campus is reserved for essays and exams. The rest is reserved for being rude about University of Ulster, and hardcore drinking.

BELFAST:
• Population: 350,000 • City centre: 1,200 metres • London: 364 miles
• Dublin: 105 miles • Derry: 75 miles
• High temp: 18 • Low temp: 2 • Rainfall: 71
The first impression of Belfast is of a collection of *earthy* Victorian civic buildings and a *monstrously* modern shopping centre. The city is *blossoming* under recent investment, making it quite a happening place, with more tourists than ever. Lying in an *attractive* bay ringed by mountains, when the rain clears (*once or twice a year*) it's possible to enjoy the city's gifts of shopping malls, supermarkets, bookshops, museums, all served up with a *ruthless, tourist-trapping portion of blarney. The debris of the troubles, like murals and protection rackets, lingers on but the locals are a friendly bunch and Belfast is fun-on-a-stick with pubs and clubs doing a roaring trade.*

TRAVEL:

Trains: All of Ireland's main cities and towns, north and south, are just a train journey away, including Derry (£7.20) and Coleraine. A *nippy* train service, the Enterprise (boldly going where it went yesterday), does Dublin for £21.
Coaches: Translink serves most destinations in Northern Ireland and the Republic, but a direct coach from Britain is difficult to catch (what with the Irish Sea and all). National Express runs a service to London (£53).
Car: *The centre of Belfast's a pain for driving in, though parking's easy enough.*
Air: Regular flights from all over Britain and Europe go to Belfast. Competition between budget airlines have reduced the costs of flights to Belfast and prices vary.
Ferries: Services to Stranraer, Holyhead and Liverpool, and a fast Sea Cat service.
Hitching: *Better than most places in the UK, especially heading south or west, but not to the ports or airport.*

Local: Frequent buses provide a 10-min journey into the city centre for around 50p.
Taxis: Loads of the buggers, minimum fare £2.50.
Bicycles: *Theft's not a problem, the rain is.*

CAREER PROSPECTS:

• Careers Service • No. of staff: 12 full • Unemployed after 6mths: 5%
A mixture of full-time staff and student assistants offer advice, services and work
placements.

FAMOUS ALUMNI:

John Alderdice (former Alliance Party leader); Simon Callow, Liam Neeson, Stephen Rea
(actors); Seamus Heaney (Nobel prize-winning poet); Lord Hutton; Patrick Kielty (comedian);
Mary McAleese (President of Rep. of Ireland); Ian Paisley Jnr; Nick Ross (TV presenter);
Dawson Stelfox (mountaineer); David Trimble MP.

FURTHER INFO:

• Prospectuses: undergrad; postgrad; departmental • Open days

A C A D E M I C

Excellent research record especially in science and humanities with great opportunities to
stay on and get involved. Good links to industry means help in getting a placement
especially in science subjects. Learning is structured with an emphasis on teaching,
especially tutorials, lectures and seminars, with some aided application and laboratory work.

Entry points: 200-360	**Ave points: n/a**
Applns per place: n/a	**Clearing: 3%**
No. of terms: 2	**Length of terms: 15wks**
Staff/student ratio: 1:7	**Study addicts: 36%**
Teaching: *****	**Research: ******
Firsts: 9%	**2.2s: 32%**
2.1s: 48%	**3rds: 4%**

ADMISSIONS:

• Apply via UCAS
Following the University's emphasis on mature and adult studies, the number of adult and
older students has been steadily increasing over the past few years.

LIBRARIES:

• 1,200,000 books • 2,530 study places • 24-hr access • Spend per student: ££
*Despite five libraries and vast quantities of books students get a little narky about limited
book availability.* 24-hr access during exam time. A £40m library is slated for 2008/09.

COMPUTERS:

• 2,000 workstations • 24-hr access • Spend per student: £
Lots of (*ageing*) computers. *Printing's a bit of a lottery* and 24-hr access is again just during
exam time, otherwise it's 9-11.

ENTERTAINMENT

THE CITY:

• Price of a pint of beer: £2.30 • Glass of wine: £1.80 • Can of Red Bull: £1

Most Belfast nightlife happens in the Golden Mile that stretches from Queen's to the city centre. *What with the students, the tourist industry and the, frankly silly, amounts of money pumped into Belfast nightlife since the 90s, it's pretty good.*

Cinemas: *The UCG and the Movie House show the Hollywood fodder where Tom Cruise simply never dies, while the Queen's Film Theatre shows those films where everyone dies, in Czech with subtitles.*

Theatres: *You can't throw a stone without it hitting a theatre, and bouncing off another one.* There's seven in all, including the Waterfront, the Lyric Theatre and the *legendary* Belfast Grand Opera House, and visits from touring companies like the Royal Shakespeare or An Culturlann, an innovative Irish language company.

Pubs: *Stout strong enough to stand pencils in, drunken blarney-merchants called Jon arguing with strangers about military tactics, chrome-plated trend pits with a lifespan of three days, Belfast has a pub for all tastes (and some with no taste). Pushplugs: Botanic; Lavery's Gin Palace; The Fly. The main gay venue is the Crow's Nest.*

Clubbing: *Belfast's developing quite a reputation as a clubber's paradise. Pushplugs: Limelight (indie, retro, jazz nights); The Brunswick (soul and hardcore, four separate floors); Network Club (dance/hip hop); M Club (student nights); Thompson's Garage (house); the New Storm.*

Music/Comedy: Ulster Hall for big names, Empire Music Hall for medium-sized and comedy nights, Waterfront Hall for pretty much anything and *innumerable small-scale gigs anywhere they can find space.*

Eating out: Lisburn Road, close to the campus, has a lot of *decent* cafés, patisseries and Chinese and Indian takeaways. *Pushplugs: Bishops (chippie); Speranza's (pizzas, a student institution); the Other Place (bring your own booze); Oasis (cheap); the Mad Hatter; Which Sandwich; many of the pubs do nice nosh too.*

UNIVERSITY:

• Price of a pint of beer: £1.50 • Glass of wine: £2

Wine, women and song are the name of the day along with men and lashings of beer. The city plugs any theatrical holes.

Bars: The Union's two main bars, the Bunatee Bar (cap 300) and the Speakeasy (550) are packed by 7pm.

Film: The University has its own cinema, which hosts regular film festivals and the annual Belfast Film Festival Season.

Music venues: Faithless, Bruce Dickinson and Black Rebel Motor Cycle Club have all recently performed in Belfast's 1,400 capacity music venue, Mandela Hall.

Clubbing: Mandela Hall, with a sound system to go deaf for, stomps to a bunch of different beats, one of the best being Shine (Saturday) which attracts guest DJs and big acts like moths.

Comedy/Cabaret: National Comedy Network shows, fortnightly.

Food: *The Speakeasy is as cheap as chips but has about as much range as a dead archer. The Beech Room and the Cloisters also whore their culinary abilities.*

Other: *Queen's students like their balls and there are up to seven a year, including Freshers', Rag and St Paddy's. Most facilities have some kind of formal too.* The Annual Belfast Festival held at Queen's is up there with Edinburgh, with ballet, theatre, comedy and pretty much anything that might conceivably be entertaining chucked on stage.

SOCIAL & POLITICAL

THE QUEEN'S UNIVERSITY OF BELFAST STUDENTS' UNION:
• 5 sabbaticals • Turnout at last ballot: 14% • NUS member
Most strands of political thought are tangled up in the machinations of the SU, though nationalist are in the majority. The incestuous nature of SU politics has alienated some students but the majority, of course, just regard the SU as a convenient source of booze and opportunities to get laid.

SU FACILITIES:
Bars; canteens; advice centre; Bank of Ireland bank/ATM; launderette; showers; supermarket; writing room; secondhand bookshops; sports shop; insurance office; travel centre; computer shop; hairdresser; snooker room; games room; vending and games machines; photocopier; function rooms; photo booth; crèche; women's room; shop; payphones; jukebox; printing.

CLUBS (NON-SPORTING):
Accounting; Biological; Bridge; Celtic Supporters Club; Chess; Chinese; C S Lewis; Dragon Slayers; Economics; English; European; Finance; French; Hare Krishna; Hispanic; Historical; Internet; Juggling; Law; Malaysian; Republican; SDLP; Sociology; Skipping; Ulster; Wine; Yoga. **See also Clubs tables.**

OTHER ORGANISATIONS:
Gown and the Craic are the student newspapers. Rag is *particularly effective* and the Community Workshop does its things for local relations.

RELIGIOUS:
• 4 chaplains
There are four assigned chaplaincy centres covering 14 different flavours of faith, there's even a church for deaf people. Belfast fills in the blanks.

PAID WORK:
• Job bureau
250 bar jobs provided by the University every year. Plenty of part-time work available in town. 10-wk work placements are a part of many courses and the careers service can also set students up with companies for part-time work, work experience, a year out etc.

SPORTS

• BUSA ranking: 48
Rugby, soccer and hockey are all pretty strong in both men and women's varieties and *sport in general is a popular pastime.* Facilities are *extensive* and students who make the University look good at anything are awarded Blues (which is like being capped), like at Oxbridge colleges.

SPORTS FACILITIES:
13 football/rugby, two hockey, one cricket and two all-weather pitches; 10 squash, one tennis and four basketball courts; two sports halls; two netball courts; athletics track. There's a £6.1m plan to improve the facilities, *perhaps so every student can have their own football pitch.*

SPORTING CLUBS:
Caving; Gaelic Football; Handball; Ju-Jitsu; Kung Fu; Motorcycle; Parachute; Racquet Ball; Road Bowls (a traditional Irish sport); Snooker; Surf; Table Tennis; Waterpolo; Waterski. **See also Clubs tables.**

ATTRACTIONS:
The local ice hockey team is the Belfast Giants. Rugby team Ulster play in local Ravenhill. Northern Ireland play in Windsor Park which is also local, not to mention various Gaelic teams, and football teams, like Glentoran and Linfield.

ACCOMMODATION

IN COLLEGE:
• Catered: 3% • Cost: £62 (32wks)
• Self-catering: 10% • Cost: £64 (50wks) • Insurance premium: £
Availability: About half of all 1st years live in, but they all could if they wanted to. Half of them share, mainly in ten-storey blocks 800 metres from campus (due to be replaced by a student village in the future). *Rooms in halls are pretty adequate, a bit 60s-like but students find them good fun and social places. Riddell is all female, Queen's Elm is groovy and there are a few places in associated halls (with religious links) and flats for married couples.*
Car parking: Plentiful but *costly*.

EXTERNALLY:
• Ave rent: £45 • Living at home: 45%
Availability: Many students are locals. Those who start searching in early summer shouldn't have problems, last-minuters might have difficulties. An area called the Holy Lands (Jerusalem Street, Palestine Street etc.) is the *most popular* as it's close to the University, the Union, the Golden Mile and the gym. *The houses are also the best prices for students. Also popular are Stranmillis, Malone Road and Lisburn Road. Ormeau Road used to be dodgy but is improving – and is dirt cheap.*
Housing help: Several housing associations look after the students, as do the Union welfare office and the University accommodation office.

WELFARE

SERVICES:
• Women's Officer • Mature Students' Society
• International Students' Society • Postgrad Society • Late-night/Women's minibus
• Self-defence classes • Nightline • Taxi fund • Crime rating: !!!
The Union's small counselling service meets most need for troubled souls, while troubled bodies are mended by the Health Centre. The legally troubled can see a solicitor who visits four times a week.
Health: Free NHS treatment in the clinics including regular check-ups. There's a sports injury clinic for those needing the deep heat treatment.
Women: Rape alarms from the SU welfare service. Also a free-phone taxi service, self-defence classes and Shrewd magazine.
Crèches/Nursery: 48-wk crèche with 84 places.
Disabilities: Lots of large, old 60s-style buildings but all with lifts. The University is spread throughout 250 buildings in the Belfast area so it can take a while to get around. All have ramps, lifts, specialist books, accommodation and audio equipment. Deaf students are particularly well cared for by Joint Universities Deaf Education (JUDE).
Drugs: *Apart from the standard dangers, the drugs trade has paramilitary connections, so tread carefully.*

FINANCE:
• Ave debt per year: £1,111 • Access fund: £762,250 • Successful applications/yr: 901
Support: Various scholarships including the Guinness sports bursaries.

University of Reading

....

Richmond see Roehampton University

....

Robert Gordon University

....

Robert Gordon Institute of Technology see Robert Gordon University

....

Roehampton University

....

Royal Academy of Music

....

Royal Agricultural College

....

Royal College of Music

....

Royal Holloway, London

....

Royal Scottish Academy of Music and Drama

....

Royal Veterinary College, London

....

University of Reading

(1) University of Reading, Whiteknights, PO Box 217, Reading, RG6 6AH
Tel: (0118) 378 6586 E-mail: schools.liaison@reading.ac.uk
Website: www.reading.ac.uk
Reading University Students' Union, Whiteknights, University of Reading, PO Box 230,
Reading, RG6 6AZ Tel: (0118) 986 0222 E-mail: rusu@rusu.co.uk
Website: www.rusu.co.uk
(2) Bulmershe Campus, Bulmershe Court, Early, Reading, RG6 1HY Tel: (0118) 987 5123
Reading University Students' Union, address as campus Tel: (0118) 378 8693

GENERAL

*Reading is commuter-belt country and suspiciously close to Staines. It's not the most
inspiring part of Britain*, although some of the *ultra-wealthy* Thames-side commuter villages
in the area are *gently pretty*. The University is based on the large Whiteknights campus,
under 2 miles from the town centre and set in 320 acres of parkland, lake and wood. The
buildings vary from Victorian to very modern, *all managing to be ugly in their own little way*.
There's a second campus about $1\frac{1}{2}$ miles away at Bulmershe, where about 2,000 other
students are holed up.

Sex ratio (M:F): 44:56	Founded: 1892
Full-time u'grads: 7,885	Part-time: 2,560
Postgrads: 2,315	Non-degree: 5,000
Mature: 12%	Flunk rate: 11%
State:private school: 79:18	International: 22%
Ave course: 3/4 yrs	
Disabled: 121	

56% ♀ ♀ ♀ ♀ ♀ ♂ ♂ ♂ ♂ ♂ ♂ 44%

ATMOSPHERE:

Whiteknights is a *cosy* campus given a sense of *friendly community* by the *large* number who live there. The atmosphere *is middle-class and middle-England*, although there are *more than enough exceptions to test the rule*. *Sport's high on the agenda, possibly because most students are in training to high-tail it at the weekend, when the campus drains of life and human activity*.

SITES:

Bulmershe Campus: 2,000 students – Institute of Education, School of Health & Social Care, Film Theatre & TV

READING:

- Population: 143,200 • City centre: 1.5 miles miles • London: 40 miles
- Oxford: 25 miles • Bristol: 74 miles
- High temp: 22 • Low temp: 1 • Rainfall: 48

Although it's dominated by office blocks and *doesn't have beauty on its side*, Reading has a *good* shopping centre and a *vast array* of supermarkets, bookshops, restaurants, bars and a cinema. The modernised city centre has quaint touches, the river and smaller arcades.

TRAVEL:

Trains: Station is about $1\frac{1}{2}$ miles from the main campus. Trains go direct to London Paddington, Oxford and *pretty much anywhere* to the west.
Coaches: National Express lead their magical mystery (*guess how late the bus will arrive*) tours all over the UK. Reading Transport operates a £7 return to London.
Car: M4/A4 for London and M1 via the M25/M40. *Parking in town can be tricky.*
Air: Heathrow is 45 mins by coach.
Local: Buses connect town to campus, £1 each way.
College: The SU runs a free night bus service to the halls every day during term time (except Sundays) until 15 mins after the last bar on campus closes.
Taxis: Campus to town costs £5-6.
Bicycles: *Reading is as flat as a starched and ironed pancake – perfect for pedal power.*

CAREER PROSPECTS:

- Careers Service • No. of staff: 18 full/2 part • Unemployed after 6mths: 8%

FAMOUS ALUMNI:

Suzanne Charlton (BBC weatherperson, daughter of Sir Bobby); Jamie Cullum (jazz-*lite* megastar); Nigel de Gruchy (general secretary, ASUWT); Glynn Ford MEP (Lab); Andy McKay (Roxy Music saxophonist). Gustav Holst (composer) lectured here; Sir Steve Redgrave (rower) holds an honorary degree.

FURTHER INFO:

- Prospectuses: undergrad; postgrad; departmental • Open days • Video

A handbook for students with special needs is available. This and more from www.rdg.ac.uk

 A C A D E M I C

A flexible 1st-year course with the option to take modules from other faculties, but it's *demanding* and capped by *tough* exams. After that *bitter pill* there's the *honey-sweet knowledge* that there's no crossing swords with another exam paper until finals.

160–360		POINTS
Entry points: 160–360	**Ave points:** 339	
Applns per place: 8-28	**Clearing:** 4%	
No. of terms: 3	**Length of terms:** 10wks	
Staff/student ratio: 1:15	**Study addicts:** 17%	
Teaching: ****	**Research:** ***	

ADMISSIONS:

• Apply via UCAS

SUBJECTS:

Arts/Humanities: 42%   Life Sciences: 11%
Economic & Social Sciences: 20%   Sciences: 23%
Institute of Education: 3%
Best: Agriculture; Applied Statistics Archaeology; Biological Sciences; Construction Management; Classics;
Electrical & Electronic Engineering; Film & Drama; Food Science & Technology; French; History of Art; Maths;
Philosophy; Physics; Plant Sciences; Psychology.
Unusual: The UK's only single honours degree in Meteorology.

LIBRARIES:

• 1,000,000 books • 400 study places • 24-hr access
Main library is at Whiteknights. Belmershe and other faculties have their own smaller
libraries.

COMPUTERS:

• 600 workstations

OTHER LEARNING FACILITIES:

Three museums attached to the University – zoology, archaeology and the Museum of
English Rural Life. All students can dabble in foreign tongues if they wish.

E N T E R T A I N M E N T

THE TOWN:

• Price of a pint of beer: £2.60 • Glass of wine: £2.50 • Can of Red Bull: £2.50
Cinemas: *More screens than a film buff could poke an overpriced hot dog at.* Two
multiplexes and a more off-the-wall programme at the Reading Film Theatre.
Theatres: The Hexagon stages *high-profile mainstream stuff*, including snooker and ballet.
Alternative drama at the Progress Theatre.
Pubs: *Commuters have brought London prices with them. Boozing costs and not all of the
town's pubs are happy to rub shoulders with students.* Pushplugs: *Rising Sun (tiny bar, but
fantabulous events); Monk's Retreat; Pavlov's Dog; Newt and Cucumber; College Arms;
Queen's Head.*
Clubbing: *Provincial clubs mean bad sound rigs and sticky carpets.* Purple Turtle and RGI do
the chart/dance bit, Level 1 weighs in with the student nights.
Music venues: *Reading's August festival has long been (after Glasto) the highlight of the
summer.* The Rising Sun *showcases local bands/poetry/crafts/weirdos.* Pushplugs: *Alleycat
Live (indie) and the Rivermead Centre (bigger names).*
Eating out: *Chain restaurants by the stack, with a few grub-pubs to make up numbers.*
Pushplugs: *Cyberspice (order takeaway curry online); Cafe Iguana (veggie); Global Cafe
(hippy); Dalle Vita, Chillies and Back of Beyond (budget-happy).*

UNIVERSITY:

• Price of a pint of beer: £1.50 • Glass of wine: £1.50 • Can of Red Bull: £2.50
Bars: Mojo's is the *main* joint, sports themed with a late licence and a double-life as a
small band venue. The *centre of social gravity* at Bulmershe is Legends Bar.
Theatres: The *thriving* thesp scene churns out an *impressive* array of plays, mainly
Shakespeare and musicals.
Film: The film society shows three or four films a week, *usually on the indie side of
mainstream* (eg. Memento, Mystic River, Spirited Away).
Music venues: 3Sixty's the main University club and pulls some *big* names. Recent visitors
include Ms Dynamite, Supergrass, Athlete and the *lesser-spotted* Minogue (Dannii).
Clubbing: NUS has rated 3Sixty one of the best student clubs in the land for its *sleek
modern design and lively atmosphere.* It crams in almost 2,000 punters at a time for three
big club nights a week.

Comedy/Cabaret: Regular 3Sixty comedy nights feature names like Daniel Kitson, Nina Conti and Paul Tonkinson.

Food: There are six tucker huts on campus, including those serving food healthy (Fresh Start), hot (Mojo's Munchies) or on the hop (Mondial coffee and pastries).

Other: Three balls a year: Freshers, Grand Summer and the Sport Federation's.

SOCIAL & POLITICAL

READING UNIVERSITY STUDENTS' UNION (RUSU):

• <u>6 sabbaticals</u> • <u>Turnout at last ballot: 11%</u> • <u>NUS member</u>

Top-notch facilities provide the centre of daily life. RUSU is very active, running loads of clubs and societies. There's a growing campaigning ethic with volunteer groups pushing lots of worthy causes.

SU FACILITIES:

Travel shop; welfare office; three bars; purpose built club/music/comedy venue; stationery shop; bookshop; general/wholefood shop; Endsleigh Insurance office; Lloyds TSB bank and ATM; other services such as photocopying and vending machines; launderette.

CLUBS (NON-SPORTING):

Agriculture; Arabic; Art; Brazilian & Portuguese; Chess; CSSA (Chinese Students & Scholars Association); Circus Skills; Cyprus; Engineering Social; English; Gospel Choir; Hellenic; Latin American & Spanish; Law; Millennium Volunteers; Music; Photography; Real Ale & Cider; Sci-Fi & Horror; Systems Engineering. **See also Clubs tables.**

OTHER ORGANISATIONS:

Weekly student paper Spark is *trumped* by the award-winning radio station Junction 11. Rag is *very busy* and holds an annual fundraising week.

RELIGIOUS:

Chaplaincy centres and prayer rooms for Christians and Muslims. Prayer places in town for Muslims, Hindus, Sikhs, Jews.

PAID WORK:

• <u>Job bureau</u>

Jobshop advertises vacancies of no more than 16 hours a week – *study comes first, children. Many find work* in local shops.

SPORTS

• <u>BUSA ranking: 20</u>

The University has *plenty* of places to work up a sweat and this patch of the Thames is *excellent* for canoeing and rowing.

SPORTS FACILITIES:

Wolfenden Sports Centre has badminton, archery, basketball, cricket, fencing, 5-a-side football, hockey, martial arts, netball, table tennis, trampolines, tennis courts, gym and a brand new Astroturf pitch. There's also a squash centre, gym and weights room at Bulmershe. Outdoors: athletics pavilion; playing fields for cricket, football and rugby; an all-weather surface and running track. The town adds numerous swimming pools and rowing and sailing on the river.

SPORTING CLUBS:

See also Clubs tables.

ATTRACTIONS:
Reading FC's *not much cop* but the local racing (in boats at Henley Regatta and on nags at Ascot, Windsor and Newbury) is *first rate.*

ACCOMMODATION

IN COLLEGE:
• Catered: 32% • Cost: £94-125 (30wks)
• Self-catered: 19% • Cost: £52-83 (30/39wks)
• First years living in: 96% • Others living in: 18% • Insurance premium: ££
Availability: 1st years applying by June (ie. not via clearing) are guaranteed University accommodation, most will be offered catered housing. Those with Reading as their first choice can take their pick of halls, most of which are within a mile of Whiteknights. Rooms are single with shared kitchens (although there are 45 flats for married couples with or without children).
Car parking: A limited number of halls parking permits are available for 2nd/3rd years and postgrads (£10).

EXTERNALLY:
• Ave rent: £65
Availability: *It's no big deal to find a place to call home in town, although quality varies from luxurious to last-turkey-in-the-shop. Donnington Gardens, Aodington Road and Wokingham Road are all hits. London/Oxford Roads are misses.*
Housing help: The Accommodation Office (five staff) provides vacancy lists. Landlords are vetted by the local council. *Many of the best* digs are found on the RUSU notice board, handed down from previous tenants.

WELFARE

SERVICES:
• Lesbian/Gay/Bisexual Officer • Ethnic Minorities Officer
• Women's Officer • Mature Students' Officer & Society
• International Students' Officer & Society • Postgrad Officer
• Disabilities Officer • Late-night minibus
• Nightline • College counsellors: 6 full/5 part • Crime rating: !!!!
Advice and help from tutors or the Welfare Office.
Health: The Health Centre has five doctors, two dentists, a physiotherapist and various nurses. Annual registration charge, but students are entitled to reduced rates for vaccinations and medical examinations.
Women: Women have priority on the nightbus. RUSU provide free attack alarms.
Crèches/Nursery: 40 places (3mths-5yrs).
Disabilities: A special needs co-ordinator looks after particular requirements including notetaking, sign language, English language support and personal care. The University makes an effort to adapt buildings for access and there are dedicated rooms with disabled facilities in halls.

FINANCE:
• Ave debt per year: £2,694
Fees: *Top-up fees as far as the eye can see.*
• Access fund: £400,000 • Successful applications/yr: 600
• Ave payment: £100-3,500
Support: Food Science scholarships and chemistry bursaries. Other *small* academic bursaries for freshers include an English book award for A Level work and three full scholarships for International Baccalaureate holders.

RICHMOND: see Roehampton University

Robert Gordon University

- *Formerly Robert Gordon Institute of Technology.*
Robert Gordon University, Schoolhill, Aberdeen, AB10 1FR
Tel: (01224) 262 728 E-mail: admissions@rgu.ac.uk Website: www.rgu.ac.uk
Robert Gordon University Students' Association, 60 Schoolhill, Aberdeen, AB10 1JQ
Tel: (01224) 262 262 E-mail: rgusa@rgu.ac.uk Website: www.rgunion.co.uk

GENERAL

Bonny Bobbie Gordon's been around for over 200 years, but 1992's cull of polytechnics saw it awarding university degrees for the first time. Aberdeen is dribbling with students (see University of Aberdeen) and *those from RGU mix well with all the others – just as well, perhaps, since RGU's own Students' Association building doesn't exactly deliver fun in a box. Perhaps the integration comes from the fact that RGU is based on* two sites spread across the city, *covering quite a bit of ground.* The city centre campus (where few students, but the SA and University admin are based) huddles around an original 1729 site at Schoolhill. The *larger* Garthdee campus is 2 miles away, to the south-west of the city.

Sex ratio (M:F): 37:63	Founded: 1750
Full-time u'grads: 6,495	Part-time: 2,345
Postgrads: 960	Non-degree: 237
Ave course: 4yrs	Ethnic: 11%
State:private school: 94:6	Flunk rate: 17%
Mature: 24%	International: 20%
Disabled: 110	Local: 47%

ATMOSPHERE:

RGU students are a friendly, practical bunch who are clearly cut out for careers in helpful and/or useful industries like nursing, engineering and science. Many are from the area, which means that they tend to hang out in the city itself rather than the SA a lot of the time.

SITES:

Garthdee Campus: (Aberdeen Business School, Gray's School of Art, the Scott Sutherland School, Faculty of Health and Social Care) *More attractive than its city centre sibling,* Garthdee is based around a large mansion overlooking the River Dee, surrounded by rolling parkland. *The site is less convenient, but peaceful and conducive to contemplative study.*
Schoolhill campus: (Schools of Engineering, Pharmacy, Life Sciences and Computing) Around a quarter of RGU's students are based here.

ABERDEEN: see University of Aberdeen

TRAVEL: see University of Aberdeen
University: A free shuttle bus between the Garthdee and City Centre sites runs every 15 mins – *if it's on time.*

CAREER PROSPECTS:

• Careers Service • No. of staff: 6 full-time • Unemployed after 6mths: 4%
The Careers Service *does a good job* of shifting students into industry, offering CV workshops, interview preparation, career fairs and a library.

FAMOUS ALUMNI:

Ena Baxter (of the soups); Calum Innes (artist, Turner Prize nominee); Donnie Munro (Runrig singer).

FURTHER INFO:

• Prospectuses: undegrad; postgrad; international; video • Open days
Individual course brochures and an Access prospectus are also available from the admissions office.

 A C A D E M I C

The University's *strong* in Health Sciences, Art & Design, Architecture & Engineering – especially renewable and sustainable energy *(which must go down well in a city built on oil profits)*. Applied learning is the order of the day *and students enjoy knowing they're learning something useful for post-study life.*

Entry points: 144-276	Ave points: n/a
Applns per place: n/a	Clearing: 15%
No. of terms: 3	Length of terms: 18wks
Staff/student ratio: 1:17	Study addicts: 98%
Teaching: ***	Research: *
Year abroad: n/a	Sandwich students: 60%
Firsts: 12%	2.2s: 34%
2.1s: 47%	3rds: 7%

ADMISSIONS:

• Apply via UCAS/CATCH for nursing
Alternative qualifications include Access courses run by the University, equivalent overseas qualifications and SQA, NVQs and BTEC.

SUBJECTS:

Art & Design: 17%	Medical Sciences: 30%
Business/Management: 26%	Sciences: 6%
Computing: 7%	Social Sciences: 5%
Engineering: 8%	

LIBRARIES:

• 255,877 books • 24-hr access

COMPUTERS:

• 1,300 workstations • Spend per student: £££

OTHER LEARNING FACILITIES:

Language labs; CAD lab; practice courtroom.

ENTERTAINMENT

THE CITY: see University of Aberdeen

UNIVERSITY:

• Price of a pint of beer: £1.50 • Glass of wine: £1
Many students hardly ever visit the Union, preferring the increasingly bright lights of the town or leeching off Aberdeen University's social scene.
Bars: Two bars, U-Bar (*pool-playing DJ-hut*) and Blue Iguana (*chilled-out*, food-serving, *DJ-loving*, Wednesday sports fest). Both bars give away prizes like cinema tickets and travel vouchers to keep the punters coming in.

SOCIAL & POLITICAL

ROBERT GORDON UNIVERSITY STUDENTS' ASSOCIATION:

• NUS member • Turnout at last ballot: 5%

SA FACILITIES:

The four-floor Union building at Schoolhill has: two meeting rooms; Information Centre; Clydesdale Bank; general store; stationery shop; vending and games machines; launderette.

CLUBS (NON-SPORTING):

European Exchange; GAP (Gray's Art in Places); Malaysian. **See also Clubs tables.**

OTHER ORGANISATIONS:

Cogno ('knowledge' in Latin) is the monthly Union tabloid.

RELIGIOUS:

• 2 chaplains (CofS, Scottish Episcopal)
No places of worship on campus but Aberdeen has something for most religious palates – churches, chapels, mosques, synagogue and a Hindu cultural centre. See University of Aberdeen for more.

PAID WORK: see University of Aberdeen
• Job bureau

SPORTS

• BUSA Ranking: 48

SPORTS FACILITIES:

The *newish* Robert Gordon Sports Centre has: gym; climbing wall; swimming pool; indoor hockey/basketball/football/tennis hall; sports injury clinic; sports shop. Beyond that, we're talking city facilities – see University of Aberdeen

SPORTING CLUBS:

Bowling; Boxing; Canoe; Fitness; Gaelic Football; In-Line Hockey; Ju-Jitsu; Mountaineering; Rifle; Shinty; Ski & Snowboard; Waterpolo. **See also Clubs tables.**

ATTRACTIONS: see University of Aberdeen

'Spice', the Cardiff SU Dance night, was closed down when all the sweaty bodies set off the fire alarms and nobody paid any attention because they thought it was a techno record.

IN COLLEGE:

• Self-catered 18% • Cost: £59-68 (35wks) • Insurance premium: £
Availability: All 1st years who live 15 or more miles away are guaranteed a place in halls.
Most prefer to live in the city centre rather than at the mercy of the Garthdee shuttle bus.
All halls have communal areas, launderettes and TV rooms and *are kept* safe by CCTV, night porters and entry phones. A small proportion of rooms have en-suite facilities and even fewer are available for families.
Car parking: *Limited, but two-wheeled, motorless car equivalents (as the kids are calling bikes nowadays) can be locked up securely.*

EXTERNALLY: see University of Aberdeen

Housing help: The RGU accommodation service keeps lists of vacancies and approved landlords.

SERVICES:

• Lesbian/Gay/Bisexual Society • International Students' Society
• Disabilities Officer & Society • Self-defence classes
• College counsellors: 3 full-time • Crime rating: !!
Health: Health practice with two GPs and a nurse.
Crèches/Nursery: 90 places for precious ones aged 0-5yrs.
Disabilities: The Centre for Student Access (CenSA) provides advice and support for mobility-impaired, dyslexic and other disabled students.

FINANCE:

• Ave debt per year: £1,510
Support: Hardship/mature student funds, a number of bursaries, a disabled students allowance and dependent's grants are available.

Robert Gordon Institute of Technology

see Robert Gordon University

Roehampton University

• *Formerly Roehampton Institute.*
(1) Roehampton University, Froebel College, Roehampton Lane, London, SW15 5PJ
    Tel. (020) 8392 3470 E-mail: enquiries@roehampton.ac.uk Website: www.roehampton.ac.uk
    Roehampton Student Union, Froebel College, Roehampton Lane, London, SW15 5PJ
    Tel (020) 8392 3221 E-mail: info@roehamptonstudent.com
    Website: www.roehamptonstudent.com
(2) Digby Stuart College, Roehampton Lane, London, SW15 5PH Tel. (020) 8392 3213
(3) Southlands College, 80 Roehampton Lane, London, SW15 5SL Tel. (020) 8392 3400
(4) Whitelands College, Holybourne Avenue, London, SW15 4JD Tel. (020) 8392 3500

An Anglican, a Catholic, a Methodist and an agnostic walked into a bar … well, it wasn't a bar it was a London borough, and the upshot of it was they decided to join their respective colleges together and form a fully-fledged university. Roehampton University officially came into the world in late 2004 and represents the *holy communion* of four neighbouring Victorian teacher training institutes. *The campus itself is located in one of the few pockets of London that isn't crowded by bricky, urban mess* but by *attractive* parkland. Within reach of the West End and only a brief stroll from Richmond Park, *Roehampton is well-placed to enjoy both suburban serenity and the bright lights of the big city.* **For general information on London: see <u>University of London</u>.**

Sex ratio (M:F): 34:66	**Founded: 1841**
Full-time u'grads: 6,912	**Part-time: 786**
Postgrads: 1,719	**Non-degree: n/a**
Ave course: 3yrs	**Ethnic: n/a**
State:private school: n/a	**Flunk rate: 21%**
Mature: 27%	**International: 10%**
Disabled: 330	**Local: n/a**

66%
34%

ATMOSPHERE:

Roehampton's four colleges are pleasant, picturesque places and those qualities seem to be reflected by the students that inhabit them. Like Londoners in general, they're a diverse, metropolitan crowd, and though there are differences in atmosphere from one college to another, everyone's on the same wavelength and the University-wide sense of community is strong. Nevertheless, a little intercollegiate sporting/drinking rivalry never hurt anyone, did it?

COLLEGES:

Roehampton is a collegiate institution, meaning that its student body is divided into four roughly equal chunks – each living, socialising and loitering at a different college. Though the Colleges are self-contained in those respects, teaching is done at a university-wide level, thus students can find themselves travelling between College sites to utilise different facilities. Applicants can specify a particular college upon application, but there's *no enormous distinction to be made between them,* except in terms of architecture, facilities and religious background. All Colleges have their own bar, halls and canteen.

Froebel: (Early Childhood Research Centre, the Education Studies Centre, the Roehampton Education Development Centre) Named after the inventor of the kindergarten and surrounded by 4 acres of *jaw-dropping* landscaped gardens, the College centres on the Grade II listed Grove House, *which looks a lot like the stately home of some minor royal.* It was founded in 1892 as a centre for educational reform and is the only College without a historical religious bias.

Digby Stuart: Founded in 1872 as a teacher training college for women by a nun from the Society of the Sacred Heart, 'Digby' is *a friendly and relaxed* place with strong Catholic roots. Roehampton's main library facility is based here, but *more importantly,* the Belfry Bar has an off-licence.

Southlands: *Like some sort of wandering Methodist minstrel,* Southlands was a latecomer to Roehampton, entering the world in 1872 and passing through Westminster, Battersea and Wimbledon in various incarnations before joining the other three Colleges in 1975. It too began as training ground for women teachers but has been offering non-educational degree programmes since 1905. Southlands has only been wearing its present buildings since 1997 and so has the most contemprary look and feel of the four. *It's a sleek and attractive place, but given architectural shelf life, will probably be called hideous in 20 years.*

Whitelands: (School of Human & Life Sciences) Founded in 1841, it's the oldest of the colleges and is in the process of relocating closer to its three brethren. The new campus centres around an 18th-century Palladian villa that was once home to poet Gerard *'Not all that'* Manly Hopkins. Whitelands was also a women's teacher training college, this time with

Anglican leanings. It boasts a stained glass window by Pre-Raphaelite painter, Edward Burne-Jones, as well as William Morris-designed altar screens.

LONDON: see University of London
• City centre: 6 miles

TRAVEL: see University of London

Cars: The A3 and A205 swing *handily by but, as everywhere in London, prospective students should think twice, weigh up the pros and cons and consult a palmist before bringing a car to the city.*
College: An hourly bus service shuttles between the colleges.
Local: Buses 72, 265, 493. 33 and 337 are useful for getting around – fares hover around £1.20. For those who prefer rail, Barnes is the local overland service and there's a tram service from Wimbledon.
Underground: Hammersmith (Hammersmith & City line) and Putney (District line) stations are the most accessible Tube stops.
Bicycles: Bikes are *generally safe* on campus and there are cycle lanes and paths throughout the borough.

CAREER PROSPECTS:
• Careers Service • No. of staff: 6 full/4 part • Unemployed after 6mths: 5%

FAMOUS ALUMNI:
Toby Anstis (Heart 106.2); Alice Beer (TV presenter); Enid Blyton (children's author, *of lashings of gollywogs infamy*); Naomi Rowe (radio presenter); Darren Shan (children's author).

SPECIAL FEATURES:
Whitelands College holds an annual May Day beauty pageant. It's the legacy of art critic, *latent paedophile and pubic-hair-phobe,* John Ruskin, who in 1881 decided that students should elect 'the nicest and likeablest' girl to be the May Queen, who would then be inaugurated by a visiting bishop. It still goes on, but in these less rampantly misogynous times, students elect a 'May Monarch' of either sex. *Ruskin must be writhing in his grave.*

FURTHER INFO:
• Prospectuses: undergrad; postgrad; some departmental; international • Open days

ACADEMIC

Roehampton's reputation rests on its teaching and education-orientated courses, but it does offer a range of other subjects and, now it's got a proper university hat on, is likely to expand its empire in the coming years. Degree structures are flexible, with over 1,500 module combinations possible and students are encouraged to take 12-week foreign language evening classes, which contribute academic credits to their degrees.

120-260	POINTS
Entry points: 120-260	Ave points: n/a
Appplns per place: n/a	Clearing: 8%
No. of terms: 2	Length of terms: 12wks
Teaching: n/a	Research: n/a
Year abroad: n/a	Sandwich students: 0
Firsts: 5%	2.2s: 5%
2.1s: 46%	3rds: 4%

ADMISSIONS:
• Apply via UCAS
Roehampton also deals with the CAT (Credit Accumulation and Transfer) scheme.

LIBRARIES:

• 420,000 books • 600 study places

The Digby Learning Resource Centre is six floors *of hot library action, although its opening hours aren't quite so spicy* (till 9pm/7pm Fridays). Weekend opening *makes up for it.*

COMPUTERS:

• 200 workstations • 24-hr access

There are IT suites in the halls of residence.

OTHER LEARNING FACILITIES:

The University has an Educational Development Centre (RED) which provides study skill, literacy and numeracy and English language support. Also: language labs; drama studio; rehearsal rooms; CAD lab; and the TV Roehampton video recording and editing suite.

ENTERTAINMENT

THE CITY: see University of London

Putney and the other areas near the University have a flavour of night life *all their own*. For everything from stadium bands to cutting-edge rock chic, there's the Shepherd's Bush Empire, the Hammersmith Apollo and the Half Moon. There are cinemas nearby, plus the Putney Arts Centre and the Richmond Theatre, and *plenty* of pubs to sup, quaff or chug in.

UNIVERSITY:

• Price of a pint of beer: £1.50 • Glass of wine: £2 • Red Bull: £1.50

Bars: Each college has its own bar, all with pool tables and occasional late licences. Digby's Belfry Bar has bands nights on Thursdays.

Theatres: A *wide* array of regular productions are put on in the dance and theatre studios, as well as Montfiore Hall.

Film: The film society arranges double bills every Sunday evening (£2 for two *mainstream* films).

Music venues: Montfiore Hall and the bar at Digby get some *small* bands – *we're not talking musical midgets* – and Jason Donovan-sized acts.

Clubbing: Froebel College has a weekly Friday bop that attempts to cater for all music tastes – *barring silly ones, like Country & Western.*

Food: Each college has a canteen serving food until 8pm, as well as a café and hot & cold food vending machines.

Other: Annual ball.

SOCIAL & POLITICAL

ROEHAMPTON STUDENT UNION:

• 4 sabbaticals • NUS member • Turnout at last ballot: 20%

RSU has over 40 elected officers – *which looks a lot like overkill, given the mid-size student body and lack of political activism beyond a stringent recycling policy but in fact reflects the diverse needs of students. Good on welfare and services.*

SU FACILITIES:

In the Hirst Union Building at Froebel: meeting rooms; Endsleigh Insurance; photo booth; advice centre; launderette.

CLUBS (NON-SPORTING):

Alpha; Anthropological; Anti-repression; Hellenic; Human Rights; Japanese; Junglist Mashup; Krishna; Music & Gaming; Persian; Philosophy; Psychology; Rock, Indie & Alternative; Self-defence; Unicef. **See also Clubs tables.**

OTHER ORGANISATIONS:.

Tabloid-style Fresh comes out on the first Monday of every month, followed hot on the heels by Funsize Fresh, its diminutive e-mail equivalent. *The Rag committee isn't going to make a million any time soon but it's good to know they're around and working their socks off for charidee, mate.*

RELIGIOUS:

• 6 chaplains (CofE, RC, Methodist), rabbi
Roehampton's strong religious heritage is reflected in Digby Stuart, Whitelands and Southlands own chaplaincies, each reflecting the College's denominational background. There's also a Jewish Resource Centre and two Muslim prayer rooms. For religion in London: see University of London

PAID WORK: see University of London
• Job bureau
The Employment and Careers Service posts part-time local vacancies and helps students find jobs relevant to their field of study.

• BUSA Ranking: 48
At Roehampton it's less 'sports for all' than 'sports for none' – campus facilities are sparser than rainforests in the desert. Although there's an admirably low-key attitude to the recreational end of the sports pitch, those involved in the competitive side are mainly in it for the drinking. Both Union and University are hankering after more cash, so extra goodies should be on the horizon.

SPORTS FACILITIES:

Football pitch, two tennis courts and a netball court. Students are obliged to use local facilities, which include: a sports hall; swimming pool; golf course; more tennis courts.

SPORTING CLUBS:

Aerobics; Kick-boxing. **See also Clubs tables.**

ATTRACTIONS:

Fulham FC and Rosslyn Park RFC are the local teams. Putney Bridge is the starting point for the *irresistible anachronism that is the* Oxbridge Boat Race. See also University of London

IN COLLEGE:

• Self-catered: 18% • Cost: £72-107 (38wks) • Insurance premium: £££
Availability: Livers-in are spread between the four colleges (Froebel holds the most). There's a wide variation in facilities and standards – reflected in rents – but *there's nothing to be scared of.* The newer halls are *particularly well-kitted out* and are mainly en-suite. IT suites are accessible in halls throughout the night (and day, for that matter) and there are laundry facilities. Only pillows are provided, so students should bring their own bedding. Women-only accomodation available in Montfiore at Froebel.
Car parking: *Pigs will be soaring through the frozen underworld eating their own headwear before a student parks on campus without a very good excuse.*

EXTERNALLY:

• Ave rent: £75-00
Availability: see University of London
Housing help: An off-campus accommodation service publishes vacancies and offers a mediation service.

WELFARE

SERVICES:
- Lesbian/Gay/Bisexual/Transgender Officer & Society • Mature Students' Officer
- International Students' Officer & Society • Ethnic Minorities' Officer
- Disabilities Officer • Self-defence classes
- College counsellors: 1 full

Health: There's an NHS medical practice unit on-site, but *if you're really broken,* Queen Mary's Hospital is just over the road.

Crèches/Nursery: The University runs a crèche service at special events.

Disabilities: *Buildings are old and access limited.* The fact Roehampton's on a slope doesn't help either. *They do make an effort, however,* and hearing loops, ramps, adapted accommodation and a special education support unit make things a little easier.

FINANCE:

Fees: International students hand over £6,950 for an undergraduate course. Part-timers can take 10 credit modules for £96 each.

Support: Colleges have their own scholarships. University hardship fund also available.

Royal Academy of Music

• **The College is part of the _University of London_ and students are entitled to use its facilities.**
Royal Academy of Music, Marylebone Road, London, NW1 5HT
Tel: (020) 7873 7393 E-mail: registry@ram.ac.uk Website: www.ram.ac.uk
Royal Academy of Music Students Union, Marylebone Road, London, NW1 5HT
Tel: (020) 7837 7337 Email: su@ram.ac.uk

GENERAL

South of Regent's Park, along Marylebone Road from Madame Tussaud's, stands the *striking Edwardian edifice* that houses the Royal Academy of Music (or RAM, *if slightly confusing acronyms are your gig). It's one of the pre-eminent music schools in the country, possibly the world, with the notes of budding geniuses harmonising with the echoes of past greats.* The place is steeped in history and music tradition and *is unashamedly* elitist with it. RAM is *too posh to be small, but too hardworking and vocational (with students as poor as the next) to be petite,* so Push would call it *cosy.* **For general information about London: see University of London.**

Sex ratio (M:F): 44:56	**Founded: 1822**	
Full-time u'grads: 315	**Part-time: 0**	
Postgrads: 310	**Non-degree: 33**	
Ave course: 4yrs	**Ethnic: 23%**	
State: private school: 75:25	**Flunk rate: 15%**	
Mature: 10%	**International: 43%**	
Disabled: 50	**Local: n/a**	

56%
44%

ATMOSPHERE:

Like a classically educated kung-fu midget, it's small and frenetic with a well-spoken student body. People are friendly with it too, but make no mistake, this isn't an artsy institution but a training ground for the cut-throat classical music biz. Okay, it's a bit artsy. But in a cut-throat sort of way.

LONDON: see University of London

TRAVEL: see University of London

CAREER PROSPECTS:

• Careers Service • No. of staff: 1 full • Unemployed after 6mths: 6%
RAM has the Career Surgery, tutor advice, newsletters and support for graduates, including fellowships for the promising. Many go on to be freelance musicians, which *means work levels varying from none to world-famous concert stardom.*

FAMOUS ALUMNI:

Sir John Barbirolli (conductor); Johnny Dankworth (jazz musician); Lesley Garrett (opera singer); Evelyn Glennie (percussionist); Dame Myra Hess (pianist); Sir Elton John (*wig-wearer extraordinaire*); Graham Johnson (pianist); Aled Jones (former chorister, *grans loved him*); Annie Lennox (pop diva); Sir Arthur Sullivan (Gilbert and ...); Mark Wigglesworth (conductor).

FURTHER INFO:

• Prospectuses: undergrad; postgrad; alternative • Open days

A C A D E M I C

Weekly lessons and tutorials. Teaching veers more towards the *academic than the practical* which doesn't sit too well with everyone. Entrance is by audition.

Applns per place: 7	Clearing: 0
No. of terms: 3	Length of terms: 10wks
Staff/student ratio: 1:8	Study addicts: n/a
Teaching: *****	Research: ****
Year abroad: 0	Sandwich students: 0
Firsts: 49%	2.2s: 3%
2.1s: 47%	3rds: 1%

ADMISSIONS:

• Apply direct

SUBJECTS:

Music 100%.

LIBRARIES:

• 125,000 books • 26 study places • Spend per student: £

COMPUTERS:

• 60 workstations
RAM's got two IT centres and facilities in the library.

THE CITY: see University of London

UNIVERSITY:

• Price of a pint of beer: £1.80 • Glass of wine: £1.60 • Can of Red Bull: £1.40
The Academy has only the one bar, see University of London for other entertainment needs.
Bars: The RAM bar (250 cap) is open 5-11 during the week and hosts a variety of music nights and other events.
Theatres: The Sir Jack Lyon Theatre hosts a few student productions.
Music venues: Students do their own music (recitals etc.).
Clubbing: Scrub Up at The Ministry of Sound, organised by the Association of London Colleges of Music, is a chance for mass collegiate fraternisation.
Comedy/Cabaret: There are regular nights, to take student minds off trumpets and French horns.
Food: The canteen, open 8.30am-6pm Mon-Fri does *cheap* food.

SOCIAL & POLITICAL

RAMSU (THE ROYAL ACADEMY OF MUSIC STUDENTS' UNION):

• 1 sabbatical • Turnout at last ballot: 40% • NUS member
RAM students are apolitical, preferring to wave batons rather than banners.

SU FACILITIES:

A *comfy* lounge with a pool table, Sky TV; bar; cafeteria; meeting room; photocopier, printing and fax services; vending machines; ATM.

RELIGIOUS:

• 1 chaplain (CofE)

Religion in London: See University of London

PAID WORK:

• Job bureau • Paid work: term-time 75%: hols 90%
There's regular opera and concert stewarding and occasional admin work to be fought over.

SPORTS

• Recent successes: 5-a-side football
No RAM-specific facilities (see University of London) but there's Regents Park just behind the Academy for the odd game of footie.

SPORTING CLUBS:
T'ai Chi; Yoga. **See also Clubs tables.**

ATTRACTIONS: see University of London

IN COLLEGE:
• Self-catering: 6%: • Cost: £150 (43wks) • First years living in: 10%
• Insurance premium: £££
Availability: *Tricky.* Many 1st years are not able to be housed by the college, though for what's available they and international students get priority. No 2nd or 3rd years live in. Housing is a mixture of flats and halls. The flats are closer to college and recently refurbished; halls are *less popular* as they involve sharing.
Car parking: Central London – *say no more.*

EXTERNALLY: see University of London
• Average rent: £70–200 • Living at home: 2%
Availability: With RAM located slap in the middle of the tourist trail, very local (and affordable) housing is *hard to come by.* Students look further afield.
Housing help: The accomodation office has a full-time employee with a full-time bulletin board.

SERVICES:
• International Students' Society • Postgrad Officer • Disabilities Officer
• Crime rating: !!!!!
Those in need of help or advice can see the Welfare Officer, the full-time counsellor or their tutors. The health centre is 15 mins away and for self-defence students can learn t'ai chi – *presumably the nasty variety or they're in trouble.*

FINANCE:
• Ave debt per year: £3,613
• Access fund: £35,000 • Successful applications/yr: 41 • Ave payment: £1,000
Fees: *RAM is very much a top-up champion, but bursaries should help soak up any resentment.*
Support: A *whopping* 250 different bursaries to be seized, ranging from £20 to £10,000.

Royal Agricultural College

Royal Agricultural College, Stroud Road, Cirencester, Gloucestershire, GL7 6JS
Tel: (01285) 652 531 E-mail: admissions@rac.ac.uk Website: www.rac.ac.uk
RAC Students' Union, Stroud Road, Cirencester, Gloucestershire, GL7 6JS
Tel: (01285) 652 531

When, in 1868, Charles Dickens visited the UK's oldest agricultural college, about a mile outside the Cotswold town of Cirencester, he wrote: 'That part of the holding of a farmer or landowner that pays best for cultivation is the small estate within the ring fence of his skull'

or in less roundabout English, 'Farmers need brains'. This is where they go to get them. Just outside the Roman town of Cirencester, the RAC – *great at farming, useless when your car breaks down* – occupies some *truly treasurable Oxbridge-esque* buildings – the ancient farmhouse and 16th-century tithe barn are *complemented* by the surrounding Victorian Gothic architecture. In Dickens's day, and until 2001, the College was a private institution. In 1995 it became the first agricultural college to award its own degrees and now receives public funding too. Nonetheless, the College's alumni are said to own, manage or administer over 80% of the UK between them. *Conspiracy-theorist heaven or what?*

39%	
Sex ratio (M:F): 61:39	Founded: 1845
Full-time u'grads: 445	Part-time: 15
Postgrads: 140	Non-degree: 65
Ave course: 3yrs	Ethnic: 2%
State:private school: 40:60	Flunk rate: n/a
Mature: 25%	International: 22%
61% Disabled: 4	Local: 20%

ATMOSPHERE:

At Tithe Barn, one of the halls of residence, there's a flyer put up by students that reads, 'Please remove your muddy boots before going up the stairs.' That tells you something about the different atmosphere here. There's a community feel to the place that comes from being (a) in the middle of nowhere and (b) completely unlike anywhere else.

CIRENCESTER:

• Population: 8,400 • Town centre: $1\frac{1}{4}$ miles • London: 95 miles
• Cheltenham: 16 miles • Bristol: 40 miles
• High temp: 22 • Low temp: 1 • Rainfall: 60
Cirencester was founded by the Romans and with its castle and genteel buildings it doesn't seem to have changed much since then. Cheltenham (see University of Gloucestershire) *is relatively more sophisticated and fashionable, but the many tourists stopping off here on their way through the beautiful Cotswolds haven't come for fashion.* Students who want that will probably end up heading for Bristol, but in its own way Cirencester's a *quiet, charming* place.

TRAVEL:

Trains: Kemble Train Station is 3 miles away. Great Western rail services from London Paddington to Kemble, via Swindon, take 1 hr 16 mins (£16.15). From Kemble trains also go to Cheltenham (50 mins, £8.85) and Bristol ($1\frac{1}{2}$ hrs, £9).
Coaches: From Cirencester to Cheltenham Spa (40 mins, £4.50); Bristol ($1\frac{3}{4}$ hrs, £10.25). National Express coach services (every 2 hrs) connect London Victoria Station with Heathrow and Cirencester ($2\frac{1}{4}$ hrs, £17.25).
Cars: The M4 from the south, the M5 from the north, leading to the A433 which gets you to Cirencester. Parking's easy.
Hitching: *Can be a useful means of getting about for the carless and out of pocket.* The best pick-ups are on Stroud Road, usually from sixth form college students – *which is a bit demeaning, really.*
Air: Approximately $1\frac{1}{2}$-hr drive from Heathrow, Birmingham and Bristol airports, all of which have international and budget airlines.
College: Cirencester is a 15-min walk from the College, so feet or cars are convenient. A bus service is being planned between the college, the Business Park and local area for £1 a go.
Taxis: From Kemble Station to the College (3 miles) cost £9.

CAREER PROSPECTS:

• Careers Service • No. of staff: 1 full/1 part • Unemployed after 6mths: 16%
The Careers Service do all the usual stuff in terms of advice, but an extra advantage for RAC students is that they can put you in touch with the old boy (and occasional girl) network scattered around the globe. A networking organisation called 'The 100 Club' also puts students in touch with the big names in agribusiness.

FAMOUS ALUMNI:

Euan Cameron (former President of the Country Landowners' Association); Henry Cecil (racehorse trainer); Geoffrey Clifton-Brown (MP); Jonathan Dimbleby (broadcaster).

FURTHER INFO:

• Prospectuses: undergrad; postgrad; all departments • Open days
Two open days a year, which should be booked in advance. Also two-day taster courses.

ACADEMIC

As well as agriculture, the College runs industry-specific courses in land management, property and a *horse course* (or 'equine degree' as they call it). All Agriculture and Business students take on a six-month work placement in the second year. Learning is hands-on throughout.

Entry points: 40-220	Ave points: 210
Applns per place: 3	Clearing: 1%
No. of terms: 3	Length of terms: 12wks
Staff/student ratio: 1:13	Study addicts: 2%
Teaching: n/a	Research: ***
Year abroad: 2%	Sandwich students: 65%
Firsts: 2%	2.2s: 33%
2.1s: 54%	3rds: 11%

40-220 / **POINTS**

ADMISSIONS:

• Apply via UCAS
All applicants are interviewed – international students are encouraged to visit before making a decision. Disabled applicants are welcomed, but should declare their disability upon application. Students with fewer than 160 UCAS points can do a four-year course at the College that includes a foundation year.

SUBJECTS:

Agriculture: 47% Rural Economy & Land Management: 43%
Business: 10%

LIBRARIES:

• 32,600 books • 160 study places
The *spacious* Garner Building library is open till 12.30am during term and contains a dedicated IT wing.

COMPUTERS:

• 56 workstations • 24-hr access • Spend per student: ££££

OTHER LEARNING FACILITIES:

The RAC farm (2,200 arable acres) has a 300-cow dairy herd and 1,500 breeding ewes. They also have language labs and a media centre.

ENTERTAINMENT

CHELTENHAM: see University of Gloucestershire

CIRENCESTER:

• Price of a pint of beer: £2 • Glass of wine: £2.40 • Can of Red Bull: £1.40
Pubs: *The Tunnel, Crown and the Wild Duck are all popular. Push doesn't plug: The Bear.*

Cinemas: There are UGCs in Bristol, Swindon and Gloucester and an Odeon in Cheltenham, all of which are good for *popcorn fodder flicks*.

Clubbing: The Rock has a *poppy* £4 student night on Wednesdays.

Eating out: Local pubs, *but that's about it*.

COLLEGE:

• Price of a pint of beer: £2 • Glass of wine: £2 • Can of Red Bull: £1.50

Given it's a small college, this is reflected in types of ents.

Bars: The Tithe Bar is run jointly by the SU and College and opens lunchtimes and evenings.

Film: Occasional screenings in The Tithe Barn on Saturday nights.

Clubbing: Occasional rock nights and a disco till 2am on Fridays.

Food: The College diner ladles out three meals a day and serves free coffee. The College shop does sandwiches.

Other: Five black-tie balls a year, including the Hunt Ball. Recent highlights have included: dancing to the Blueshounds, a horn-blowing competition, a fundraising raffle and fairground rides. There's also the Freshers' Ball, Christmas Ball, Rag Ball and the Beagle Ball in May.

S O C I A L   &   P O L I T I C A L

ROYAL AGRICULTURAL COLLEGE STUDENTS UNION:

• Turnout at last ballot: 50%

The Union isn't affiliated to NUS – it's run by the College, but students are involved in managing its facilities.

SU FACILITIES:

The Tithe Barn Union facilities include: bar; canteen; coffee bar; TV lounge; pool table; meeting rooms. Plus, run by the College: photocopier; general store; printing service; launderette; advice centre; secondhand bookshop.

CLUBS (NON-SPORTING):

See Clubs tables.

OTHER ORGANISATIONS:

The monthly student newspaper is Oracle. *Rag is accustomed to raising impressive sums (twenty grand last year), considering RAC's titchiness.*

RELIGIOUS:

• 4 chaplains (CofE, Methodist, RC, Baptist)

Chapel on campus.

PAID WORK:

• Job bureau • Paid work: term-time 20%; hols 30%

Very difficult to find work during term, but during holidays there's always lambing and harvesting, and bar and conference waiter work. Vacancy boards keep the students updated.

S P O R T S

• Recent successes: rugby, clay pigeon shooting, polo, equestrianism • BUSA Ranking: 48

The College clay pigeon shooting club is the largest in the country; they stock their own guns for students to borrow.

SPORTS FACILITIES:
Football pitch; two hockey pitches; a cricket pitch; four tennis courts; one netball court; three rugby pitches; an all-weather pitch; three squash courts; and a clay pigeon shooting range. Membership of the gym costs students £10 and all clubs have subscription fees. Cirencester has a sports hall, swimming pool, ice rink, bowling green, golf course and lakes nearby. See University of Gloucestershire for facilities in Cheltenham.

SPORTING CLUBS:
Beagles; Clay Pigeon Shooting; Lacrosse; Polo. **See also Clubs tables**.

ATTRACTIONS: See University of Gloucestershire

ACCOMMODATION

IN COLLEGE:
• Catered: 58% • Cost: £70-150 (30wks)
• First years living in: 95% • Insurance premium: £
Availability: Nearly all 1st years can live in , but if there's unexpected demand those living locally already may not get a place. Normally, though, there's room enough for a little over 10% of the 2nd and 3rd years and over half of all postgrads. The rooms are *fine* and those in Coad Court or Woodland Lodge have *calming* country views. West Lodge *isn't awful* but it's old, without en-suite, and the views are a bit *uninspiring.* The three newest halls all have en-suite rooms, net access, phone points and TV aerial sockets. Women are not housed on the ground floor wherever possible – *just to give them more exercise.* Rents are reduced for students living in during holidays. A £500 deposit (£300 for sharers) is required before moving into halls *in case students trash the place.*
Car parking: Parking cost is included in hall fees. The Stroud Road car park has room for 500 cars.

EXTERNALLY:
• Ave rent: £60 • Living at home: 10%
Availability: *Cheap, high quality* housing is available in Cirencester.
Housing help: The accomodation service approves landlords, posts vacancies and offers property vetting and contract approval services.

WELFARE

SERVICES:
• International Society • Disabilities Officer
• College counsellors: 1 ful • Crime rating: !
The College motto may be 'Avorum Cultus Percorumque' (or 'Caring for the fields and the beasts'), but they do give some thought to their students in the old welfare department too.
Health: GP surgery four days a week.
Disabilities: Around 17% of the students have some form of dyslexia and extra tuition and they get extra time in exams. *All courses claim to be accessible with ramps etc., but some buildings are just too damn old to be practical.*

FINANCE:
• Ave debt per year: £3,113
• Access fund: £90,000 • Successful applications/yr: 40
Support: In addition to the access fund, a *generous* £40,000 a year is available. This includes hardship awards, international students' bursaries, sports scholarships and Outstanding Achiever Scholarships (for high-flyers or those who've overcome adversity – *slaying dragons and so forth*).

Royal College of Music

Royal College of Music, Prince Consort Road, London, SW7 2BS
Tel: (020) 7589 3643 E-mail: info@rcm.ac.uk Website: www.rcm.ac.uk
The Students Association, Royal College of Music, Prince Consort Road, London, SW7 2BS
Tel: (020) 7591 4350

GENERAL

Right next to the Albert Hall, over the road from Kensington Gardens (where Peter Pan lives, honest) is the *imposing* Victorian edifice of the Royal College of Music. It was founded by the Prince of Wales who went on to become the chubby, popular Timothy West lookalike Edward VII. He also had it off with numerous actresses, *but we're drifting from the point.* We're talking music, not drama here. *The RCM has a worldwide reputation, especially for chamber music, and a growing rep for opera. Things are quite laid-back (although the workload isn't) and the college all-but shuts down at weekends.* The nearest tubes are South Kensington, Gloucester Road and Knightsbridge and the nearest rail station is Paddington. **For general information about London: see University of London**.

Sex ratio (M:F): 47:53	Founded: 1882
Full-time u'grads: 375	Part-time: 5
Postgrads: 200	Non-degree: 230
Ave course: 4 yrs	Ethnic: 16%
State:private school: 50:50	Flunk rate: 4%
Mature: 5%	International: 35%
Disabled: 3	Local: n/a

ATMOSPHERE:
Small with a friendly and supportive atmosphere. Students here are approachable, bright and united by an enthusiasm for music. They can sometimes be found practising with their vocal chords in and around campus. *A very high work ethic and competitive environment. It's like 'Fame' in tweed.*

LONDON: see University of London

TRAVEL: see University of London
It's a 5-min *amble* to South Kensington tube. Number 52, 9 and 10 buses all serve the site.

CAREER PROSPECTS:
• Unemployed after 6 mths: 2%
The Woodhouse Centre does the advice/work-experience/bulletin board thing.

FAMOUS ALUMNI:
Janet Baker, Peter Pears, Joan Sutherland, Jonathan Lemalu (singers); Julian Bream (guitarist); Benjamin Britten, Gustav Holst, Michael Tippet, Mark Anthony Turnage, Julian Anderson, Ralph Vaughan Williams, Andrew Lloyd Webber (composers); Colin Davis, Neville Marriner (conductors); Barry Douglas (pianist); James Galway (flautist); Belcea Quartet (string quartet).

FURTHER INFO:
• Prospectus • Open days

ACADEMIC

RCM does music, and does it very hard, very well and very intensely. Exchange schemes are in place with the Universities of California and Western Ontario. There are Alexander Technique classes and visits from leading musicians (*not the Cheeky Girls, then?*).

No. of terms: 3	Length of terms: 10wks
Teaching: *****	Research: ***
Year abroad: 2%	Sandwich students: 0
Firsts: 16%	2.2s: 27%
2.1s: 54%	3rds: 2%

ADMISSIONS:
• Apply via CUKAS
All applicants are auditioned. *Spoon players need not apply.* You can apply to CUKAS (the Conservatoires UK Admissions Service) online – see www.cukas.ac.uk.

SUBJECTS:
Music: 100%.
Unusual: Physics and Music (run jointly with Imperial College).

LIBRARIES:
• 300,000 books • 29 study places
Students can also use Imperial College library and public music libraries in Kensington and Westminster. *Unsurprisingly, there's a world-class music collection.*

COMPUTERS:
• 50 workstations • 24-hr access
Includes internet café, stations in the library and 20 access terminals in halls.

OTHER LEARNING FACILITIES:
Custom-built opera house; rehearsal rooms; recording studio.

ENTERTAINMENT

THE CITY: see University of London

COLLEGE
• Price of a pint of beer: £1.80 • Glass of wine: £1.50 • Can of Red Bull: £1
The students, being entertainers themselves, sometimes spontaneously erupt into music. Disconcerting for other tube travellers.
Bars: SA bar, most often used after concerts and for parties and *sporadic but packed* events on a Friday evening. It closes at 8pm otherwise, and many students head over to the Union at Imperial College.
Theatres: The theatre is mostly used for musical, rather than dramatic, offerings.
Music venues: *The whole College is essentially built out of potential music venues, but the Concert Hall and the Britten Theatre are the biggest.* Recent appearances from All Day Breakfast (funk soul) and All Jigged Out (folky).
Clubbing: Themed parties and live jazz on campus roughly fortnightly.
Food: The bar does snacks and the canteen provides *cheap, heavenly, made-to-order* sandwiches, *but Kensington's got more variety, if you've got the money.*
Other: Summer Ball in June and a *pretty epic Freshers' Week.*

SOCIAL & POLITICAL

ROYAL COLLEGE OF MUSIC STUDENTS' ASSOCIATION:
• 1 sabbatical • Turnout at last ballot: 40%
If more politicians announced their policies in the style of a Gilbert & Sullivan musical, RCM students might take more interest. They did manage a canteen boycott that lowered food prices, though. The *small* SA has games machines; pool tables; TV lounge; bar and meeting rooms. There's also a College photocopier; Upbeat termly mag; Rag association and Rag week; Catholic chaplain and Christian Union.

PAID WORK:
• Job bureau • Paid work: term-time 90%; hols 90%
The Woodhouse Centre finds paid performances, stewarding and admin work and teaching spotty school-kids and adults *(we don't know if they're spotty too)*.

SPORTS

All sports facilities are shared with Imperial College, London. Football, salsa, netball and yoga are the main physical activities.

ACCOMMODATION

IN COLLEGE:
• Self-catering: 45% • Cost: £50-87 (30wks)
• First years living in: 95% • Insurance premium: ££
Availability: 1st years are housed in College Hall (a converted bank) in Hammersmith – nearest tube Ravenscourt Park – where there are common rooms, shared kitchens, gardens, practice rooms and a resident cat and dog. *Some students don't appreciate how far away it is.*
Car parking: *Difficult, although there are some of the world's most expensive parking meters right outside the College.*

EXTERNALLY: see University of London
• Ave rent: £70-150 • Living at home: 10%
Availability: Houses and flats to be had all over London – most RCM students live in the west. Also hostels and inter-collegiate lodgings.
Housing help: Advice and a list of suitable housing (landlords who don't mind a bit of noise). RCM students can also use Imperial College's services.

WELFARE

SERVICES:
• College counsellors: 1 part • Crime rating: !!!!!
The Welfare team offers advice and support and refers students elsewhere
if in need of further help. *The welfare's good, largely because students can also use Imperial College's facilities,* which include counselling and psychotherapeutic services. *Disabled access is variable – a case of old-building syndrome –* but lifts and ramps have been installed.

FINANCE:
- Ave debt per year: £1,757 • Access fund: £30,000
- Successful applications/yr: 48 • Ave payment: £150-2,000

Support: Scholarships, study support grants, instrument loan fund, hardship money available ranging from £150 to £1,500. *On the whole, quite a soft cushion relatively.*

Royal Holloway, London

• **The College is part of the <u>University of London</u> and students are entitled to use its facilities.**

(1) Royal Holloway, Egham Hill, Egham, Surrey, TW20 8BL
    Tel: (01784) 477 003 E-mail: Liaison-office@rhul.ac.uk Website: www.rhul.ac.uk
    Royal Holloway Students' Union, Egham Hill, Egham, Surrey, TW20 0EX
    Tel: (01784) 443 979 E-mail: reception@su.rhul.ac.uk Website: www.su.rhbnc.ac.uk
(2) Bedford Square, 2 Gower Street, London Tel: (020) 7307 8600

GENERAL

Royal Holloway's part of the <u>University of London</u>, despite being 20 miles away from the capital, and a mile from Egham in Surrey, near Thorpe Park and Windsor. It is sometimes called London's country campus – *it's certainly as green as the University gets, even if it is all manicured and tamed splendour.* The extensive park grounds on a steep hill on the fringe of Windsor Park set off the College's *astoundingly beautiful* Founder's Building, an ornate red brick and stone structure, based on the Château Chambord in the Loire Valley in France. It's arranged as a square around grass courtyards with turrets, domes and ornamental carvings all over. *Fancy, eh?* **For general information about London: see <u>University of London</u>.**

Sex ratio (M:F): 40:60	**Founded: 1886**
Full-time u'grads: 4,215	**Part-time: 640**
Postgrads: 1,010	**Non-degree: 250**
Ave course: 3yrs	**Ethnic: 31%**
State:private school: n/a	**Flunk rate: 5%**
Mature: 7%	**International: 26%**
Disabled: 23	**Local: n/a**

ATMOSPHERE:

Royal Holloway's starting to shrug off its right-wing past and become much more open and multi-cultural, with a high proportion of mature students. It's just the right size and location (small but not claustrophobic, close to London but still green) for fun and friendship and most of the students seem glad to be here. It's a campus university rather than part of the metropolis – those after a central London experience may feel isolated.

SITES:

Bedford Square: (History, Health & Social Care, Media, Arts, Music) A *small* building (four floors) 45 mins from the main site in the relative bustle near Tottenham Court Road.

Facilities are sparse – a communal kitchen and common room – but it's a good place for students to meet and socialise in central London. There's just one student flat, usually filled with postgrads.

LONDON: see University of London

EGHAM: The closest town to the campus is Egham, about a mile away. *It's a typically small, suburban, commutery-type place which can't truthfully be described as either groovy or student-oriented. Staines is nearby too, which is where Ali G's posse hangs.*

TRAVEL: see University of London

Trains: Trains to Waterloo from Egham every 15 mins.
Coaches: *Infrequent and expensive* but there's a College service every 15 mins or so and an SU bus late at night.
Car: Egham's just outside the M25 London ring road, north of where the M3 crosses it on the way south-west. The A30 goes right through the town. *A car is obviously handier than at other London sites but parking's tricky on campus.*
Bicycles: *If cycling up the slight hill doesn't put students off, bikes are useful.*

CAREER PROSPECTS:

• Careers Service • No. of staff: 3 full/2 part • Unemployed after 6mths: 5%
Services are open to students and recent graduates and are run by the University of London.

FAMOUS ALUMNI:

David Bellamy (naturalist); Richmal Crompton (writer, Just William); Emma Freud (broadcaster and Mrs Richard Curtis); Felicity Lott, Susan Bullock (opera singers); Francis Wheen (journalist).

FURTHER INFO:

• Prospectuses: undergrad; postgrad; departmental • Open days • Video
SU handbook, guide for mature students.

ACADEMIC

26 departments in three faculties. *Arts & Humanities, Geography, Music, French, German and Drama are strong.* Compulsory lectures in all subjects; some degrees may include workshops (drama), seminars, computer sessions (maths) and video conferencing (classics). Most degrees have one-to-one or small group tutorial sessions with a personal tutor once or twice a week. Shared teaching with the Royal College of Music is available for the best music students. The language centre has online access to self-study resources including satellite TV. Foundation or core courses in the 1st year give way to more options in later years. Assessment's usually through exams and essays, though different subjects vary (especially drama). 1st year marks don't count towards final degree; 2nd and 3rd year marks usually count for 30% and 70% respectively.

Entry points: 240-340	Ave points: n/a
Applns per place: n/a	Clearing: 14%
No. of terms: 3	Length of semesters: 12wks
Staff/student ratio: 1:15	Study addicts: n/a
Teaching: ****	Research: ****
Firsts: 12%	2.2s: 27%
2.1s: 54%	3rds: 6%

240-340   POINTS

ADMISSIONS:

• Apply via UCAS/direct for postgrads

Most departments invite potential undergrads to visit, meet current students and staff and generally *have a bit of a nose around*. The college has a high proportion of mature students and some postgraduate courses can be undertaken part-time by distance learning.

SUBJECTS:

Biology: 5.9%	History: 8.0%
Classics: 2.5%	Italian: 2.0%
Computer Science: 5.3%	Management: 15.2%
Drama: 5.6%	Maths: 3.6%
Economics: 8.4%	Media Arts: 4.5%
English: 7.8%	Music: 2.7%
European Studies: 2.3%	Physics: 1.5%
French: 3.5%	Psychology: 5.8%
Geography: 4.9%	Spanish: 2.1%
Geology: 2.6%	SPS: 4.0%
German: 1.3%	

Best: Biochemistry; Biology; Classics; Drama; Economics; French; Geography; Italian; Management; Maths; Media Arts; Physics; Psychology; Social & Political Sciences; Sociology.

LIBRARIES:

• 548,815 books • 634 study places

There are three libraries, Bedford, Founders and Music. *Facilities are pretty good but there's still room for improvement.*

COMPUTERS:

• 580 workstations • 24-hr computer access with a swipe card

OTHER LEARNING FACILITIES:

Language lab; drama studio/theatre; computer-aided design lab; music rehearsal rooms.

E N T E R T A I N M E N T

THE CITY: see University of London

• Price of a pint of beer: £1.80 • Glass of wine: £2.30 • Can of Red Bull: £1.55

Egham's about as lively as a flattened hedgehog, although there's no shortage of places to get a drink. Students looking for the high life go into London instead.

Cinemas: The ten-screen Vue in Staines is 5 mins away from the College. Cine World in Eltham is slightly further afield.

Theatres: The Orange Tree Theatre in Richmond (20 mins by train) does discounted tickets. A few seats every Tuesday are available on a pay-as-much-as-you-like basis, *which sounds pretty good to Push.* The National Theatre lays on free events for students.

Pubs: No shortage of watering holes. The Monkey's Forehead, opposite the college, is *popular.*

Music venues: Try the newish Exchange.

Eating out: There are student deals to be munched at local pizza, Indian, Italian, Chinese, Seafood and Fish & Chip places. *Pushplugs: Perfect Pizza (buy one, get one free); Red Rose for Indian (10% discount); Jacks for Fish & Chips.*

UNIVERSITY:

• Price of a pint of beer: £1.70 • Glass of wine: £1.20 • Can of Red Bull: £1

Bars: There are six bars in all (*it's rumoured that the Queen Mum once had a sneaky pint in one of them*). The busiest drink-spot is the recently refurbished Tommy's (*perhaps because*

According to York University regulations' students can be chucked out if they eat the ducks that live on the campus lake.

it's on the ground floor of the SU and not such an effort to reach); there's also Stumble Inn and the Union Bar. Holloway's is *popular with the sporty set.*

Theatres: Two including a Japanese one are used for student and professional productions. The drama and musical theatre socs put on regular plays and productions in London.

Film: The SU shows a film Sat and Sun, *usually mainstream.*

Music venues: Raghav played recently.

Clubbing: *Something for everyone. Cheap and cheerful cheese and R'n'B nights are popular. For the more discerning clubber*, the Union attracts names like Trevor Nelson, Shorty Blitz and Tim Westwood, and arranges group nights to Po Na Na and Ministry of Sound.

Comedy/Cabaret: The Stumble Inn attracts the likes of Tony Hall and John Maloney every three weeks.

Food: The SU-run TWZO's offers *the best range (including a decent vegetarian selection) but some find it a bit pricey. Students who live on campus tend to prefer the University dining halls.* Cafe Jules provides chic and sophisticated dishes.

Other: *More balls than a snooker table*: society, sports, Christmas and summer black tie events. The fashion show in March is a *massive* three-day event.

SOCIAL & POLITICAL

ROYAL HOLLOWAY STUDENTS' UNION:

• 4 sabbaticals • Turnout at last ballot: 12% • NUS member

The SU has good reason to smile. It's finally lost the right-wing tag that dogged it for so many years and is now considered a very fair and democratic union by many. Socially, it excels, with a rapidly-expanding roster of clubs and societies to cater for every taste. It even enjoys massive student support, something that most SU's would trade their grannies for.

SU FACILITIES:

Nightclub; music venue; bars; coffee bar; cafeteria; fast food outlet; 15 pool/snooker tables; photo booth; photocopier; fax service; printing service; payphones; advice centre; TV lounge; three minibuses; games machines; vending machines; NatWest bank on campus; shop; ticket agency; launderette.

CLUBS (NON-SPORTING):

Cinema. **See also Clubs tables.**

OTHER ORGANISATIONS:

The Orbital mag is published by the SU three times a year. The Radio-One-award-winning student radio station 1287 AM Insanity broadcasts full-time in the Union. There's a Community Action Group and Rag's *on the increase*, with all the societies and sports clubs getting in on the charity act.

RELIGIOUS:

Chapels and a Muslim prayer room can be found in College or nearby.

PAID WORK: see University of London

• Job bureau

Plenty of job opportunities on campus or locally *for those in need of an extra bob or two.* The College and the SU provide vacancy boards, and there's a job file and two members of staff *to make job-hunting that bit easier.*

SPORTS

• BUSA Ranking: 26

The Royal Holloway's been declared London's best sporting college by the University of London Union (ULU) and there's a good smattering of facilities on campus and locally.

SPORTS FACILITIES:
Tennis, basketball, squash and netball courts; five football pitches; rugby and cricket fields; multigym; aerobics studio; sports hall. The nearby Thames and Datchet Reservoirs provide sailing and watersport opportunities.

SPORTING CLUBS:
See also Clubs table.

ATTRACTIONS: see University of London
Wentworth Golf Course is nearby.

ACCOMMODATION

IN COLLEGE:
- Catered: 15% • Cost: £60-85 (30-38wks)
- Self-catering: 33% • Cost: £60-85 (30-50wks)
- First years living in: 51% • Insurance premium: £
Availability: Half of all 1st years and one in five finalists live in. Big and modern halls or, for *spacious rooms and kudos*, there are rooms in the Founder's Building. 3% have to share, some single-sex accommodation. 1st years *bed down* in Founders and Kingswood, *although the latter's less popular because of distance from the main campus. Two swanky* new places, Gowar and Wedderburn, opened at the end of 2004.
Car parking: Parking is by permit only and *very limited*.

EXTERNALLY: see University of London
- Ave rent: £55-£70
Availability: Privately rented houses are *easy enough* to find. *Englefield Green is the most convenient area but many prefer Staines (one train stop away) for the better social life it offers – better than Egham, that is.*
Housing help: The College Accommodation Service provides vacancy sheets and standard contracts.

WELFARE

SERVICES:
- Disabilities Officer & Society • Late-night/Women's minibus
- Self-defence classes • Nightline • College counsellors: 4 full-time • Crime rating: !
Decent welfare provisions. Four counsellors are employed by the College and the SU has a Welfare Officer. Other services include an alcohol awareness programme and Nightline.
Health: There's an on-campus health centre with two GPs and a part-time dentist.
Women: The SU lays on self-defence classes and a late-night minibus.
Disabilities: *Access is pretty bad in the older parts of the campus. Receipt of a major grant has improved things a bit with, for example, more ramps being installed. Potential applicants should contact the Educational Support Officer. There's accommodation for disabled students and facilities for the hearing-impaired.*

FINANCE:
- Ave debt per year: £5,800
Fees: International undergrads have to stump up between £7,975 and £11,750 a year.
- Access fund: £217,344 • Successful applications/yr: 335 • Ave payment: £630
Support: There are a few extra bursaries on offer *for the crème de la crème*. Bedford Entrance Scholarships give £1,000 and guaranteed accommodation to *the cleverest undergrads*. Bioscience Entrance Scholarships dish up *the same goodies* to students of that subject. Choral, Organ and Instrumental Scholarships give guaranteed accommodation and between £100-300 to the musically gifted. Sporty students who compete at national or international level may get up to £750, guaranteed accommodation, discounted physio and

free access to local sports centres under the Student Talented Athlete Recognition Scheme (STARS). Separate scholarships are available for international students, particularly those from India.

Royal Scottish Academy of Music and Drama

The Royal Scottish Academy of Music and Drama, 100 Renfrew Street, Glasgow, G2 3DB
Tel: (0141) 332 4101 E-mail: registry@rsamd.ac.uk Website: www.rsamd.ac.uk
RSAMD Students Union, 100 Renfrew Street, Glasgow, G2 3DB
Tel: (0141) 270 8296 E-mail: supresident@rsamd.ac.uk Website: www.rsamd-su.org.uk

GENERAL

The heart of a Scottish city renowned for its industrial past may not appear to be the ideal spot to establish a community of artists and performers, but for the past 150 years RSAMD has been churning out *some of the best musicians in the world and some of the UK's most respected actors*. Right in the middle of the busiest part of Glasgow, near the Glasgow Film Theatre, the Theatre Royal and the Scottish TV Centre, the Academy has now enjoyed ten years in its new, *attractively modern*, purpose-built home. The campus – *or rather, the building* – is more of a cluster of performance spaces than a conventional college. Its *state-of-the-art* concert halls, auditoria and theatre spaces offer a continuous and *wide-ranging* programme of music, drama and opera to paying punters – performed by both students and visiting professionals. *As an arts venue, even the most thesp-hating cynic would be reduced to tears and flower-throwing*. As a university college, it's a totally unique place to study – *its prestigious atmosphere is generated and justified by the portraits of famous alumni and celeb glitterati that line the walls.*

Sex ratio (M:F): 33:67	Founded: 1847
Full-time u'grads: 570	Part-time: 0
Postgrads: 107	Non-degree: n/a
Ave course: 4yrs	Ethnic: n/a
State:private school: n/a	Flunk rate: 11%
Mature: 16	International: 14%
Disabled: 30	Local: n/a

ATMOSPHERE:
Constant public performances and continuous assessment creates a vibrant, humming atmosphere. The Academy never stands still and the students are as busy and on the go as rabbits at an orgy – leaving them with little time to pursue extra-curricular activities. It goes without saying that they're an artsy bunch, determined to take their first steps into professional arts careers. No prima donnas though – the small size of the College makes for a tight-knit and welcoming family atmosphere and the students enjoy close relationships with, and undivided attention from, their tutors.

GLASGOW: see University of Glasgow

TRAVEL: see University of Glasgow

Car: The M8 is the best road for getting to RSAMD and there's a car park around the corner. *Parking elsewhere in Glasgow is a major bitch*, however, and not many students keep cars.
Local: Bus routes 40, 41 and 61 are handy for halls. Fares average out at £1.15.
Bicycles: *Navigating the busy roads can get a bit lairy at times but cycling is generally an easy way to travel to and from the Academy.* There are spaces to chain up bikes with cameras overlooking the area.

CAREER PROSPECTS:

• Unemployed after 6 mths: 1%
There's no specific careers service like in most institutions – *but then, RSAMD isn't like most institutions, is it?* Students have the option of using the University of Glasgow's careers resources *but most don't need to*. RSAMD receives regular visits from professionals (BBC, Scottish Symphony Orchestra etc.), who offer advice on performance, business planning and self-promotion. Students get practical help with career management, including assistance with CVs, headshot photos and auditions and a yearly job fair and careers day. *Students have every chance to learn the tricks of the trade, rub shoulders with the pros and butter up any potential employers.* Actors, for example, receive guidance from casting directors in their final year and an Acting Showcase invites agents and directors to check out the talent, *browsing over student profiles like hawks in a hamster farm*. Final year students in the School of Drama are assigned a graduate mentor who offers personal advice on career choices and auditions, as well as introducing them to professional contacts.
For those not satisfied with all that there's also a university careers service.

FAMOUS ALUMNI:

Billy Boyd (hobbit); Robert Carlyle (Trainspotting, The Full Monty); Tom Conti (actor); Alan Cumming (The High Life, Goldeneye); Sheena Easton (For Your Eyes Only); Hannah Gordon (Watercolour Challenge); John Hannah (Four Weddings and a Funeral, Sliding Doors); James Macpherson (Taggart); Lisa Milne (soprano); Marina Nadiradze (pianist); Ruby Wax (*mouthy presenter*). *More or less any orchestra worth its strings will have a graduate of RSAMD's music school sat in its ranks.*

SPECIAL FEATURES:

The Academy has close relationships with similar conservatoires across the globe, often sending students to Norway, Warsaw, California and Paris among other places. Contemporary Theatre Practice students do professional placements with companies in Glasgow and Edinburgh and often do secondments in other cities and countries.

FURTHER INFO:

• Prospectuses: undergrad; postgrad; departmental; audio • Open days
All prospectuses, including the audio version, are available from the general office. Book in advance for open days.

A C A D E M I C

RSAMD is a conservatoire – *not a French sun lounge*, but rather an institution dedicated to training musicians, actors and production technicians to professional levels of ability. As such, studying here is a vocational affair (*or rather a matter of personal 'calling'*) and Academy students benefit from *highly specialised* facilities, *tight* links with relevant industries and an intensely focused environment. Most degree courses are largely practical (recitals, workshops, rehearsals etc.) with theoretical elements thrown into the mix in the form of essays and written exams. *Studying here is a 9-to-5 job – there's time to relax, but the pressure of regular public performance can make life both exciting and stressful.*

Applns per place: n/a	Clearing: 0
No. of terms: 3	Length of terms: 12wks
Staff/student ratio: 1:1	Study addicts: 25%
Teaching: n/a	Research: *
Year abroad: <1%	Sandwich students: 0

ADMISSIONS:

• Apply via CUKAS
Applications should be made at www.cukas.ac.uk, except for BEd Music, for which students should apply via UCAS to the University of Glasgow. All applicants are interviewed and/or auditioned – if not in person, then by video submission – and *it's performing ability that cuts mustard more than academic qualifications*. Wannabe actors are required to perform two speeches. RSAMD will accept anyone they think is talented enough, regardless of background, although anyone over 30 is normally considered past it – although younger mature students with professional musical experience still stand a chance. The Academy is part of the GOALS scheme, which pulls in pupils from schools in West Scotland that don't send many on to higher education.

SUBJECTS:

School of Drama: 36%   School of Music: 64%
Unusual: All courses are unique among universities, particularly Digital Film & Theatre, Musical Theatre and Technical & Production courses.

LIBRARIES:

• 90,000 books • 32 study places
The Whittaker Library is home to one of the UK's most extensive collections of musical and dramatic performance materials, *including enough CDs, vids and DVDs to keep a dodgy market stall in business for millennia. The place is a tiny thespian Tardis and although there aren't that many study places or books in total, with such a large component of the courses being practical, there don't need to be.*

COMPUTERS:

• 30 workstations
The IT provision in the Ainslie Millar Room *is a bit limp compared to most universities*, but, again, the facilities are entirely tailored to music and drama students. Computer training available. *Fifteen* IT stations are dotted around campus so students can check e-mail on the go.

OTHER LEARNING FACILITIES:

Countless rehearsal rooms for music and other performances, as well as *the indescribably fancy* Groves Studio offering digital film and TV-making facilities and editing suites. And, of course, loads of performance spaces.

E N T E R T A I N M E N T

THE CITY: see University of Glasgow

ACADEMY:

• Price of a pint of beer: £1.80 • Glass of wine: £2 • Can of Red Bull: £1.50
Bars: *The single Café Bar is not a bar in the usual lager-soaked sense, but more of a back-slapping social centre for after performances. It's relaxed and friendly, lined with pictures of the celebs that studied and drank here, but the booze stops flowing at 5pm unless there's a show on.*
Theatres: Over $\frac{1}{3}$ of the students study drama, so the Academy wouldn't get far without its two theatres – the Athenaeum and the Chandler, both constantly in use. There are too many plays to count and acting students also tread a large number of local boards, including the Edinburgh Fringe. Performances are directed by professionals *so there's little risk of school nativity-style dramatic catastrophes*. Several students have been up for Olivier awards in recent years.
Film: Free movies (with free popcorn) chosen by website vote.
Music venues: Four concert venues showcase a variety of student and visiting musicians. Academy musicians are frequently booked to perform at other venues in Glasgow and further afield.

Food: Snacks are available in the Café Bar but it's the *cute* Aramark Canteen that rules the roast. It sells three meals worth of substantial, healthy food, snacks and drinks.

Other: *Special events tend to be highbrow and high profile (the BBC Young Musician of the Year semi-final in 2004) including art exhibitions and special concerts. The Summer Ball is the biggest annual event and there's a spattering of comedy nights.*

SOCIAL & POLITICAL

ROYAL SCOTTISH ACADEMY OF MUSIC AND DRAMA STUDENTS' UNION:

• 1 sabbatical • NUS member

It's such a tiny place, with such cosy ties between students and staff, that the Union has very little to do. The SU is consulted on most issues relating to the College and receives strong support from the authorities. *There's little time for political rallying or armchair revolutions, but they give a nod to most NUS campaigns.*

SU FACILITIES:

Minimal but adequate. The College runs the bar, canteen, meeting rooms, photocopying, payphones, printing and fax service, vending machines and advice centre. The SU takes charge of the common rooms, jukebox and pool table.

CLUBS (NON-SPORTING):

Many students join societies at neighbouring universities. **See also Clubs tables.**

RELIGIOUS:

The Christian Union runs a Bible study group, morning prayer sesh and the odd lecture.
Religion in Glasgow: see University of Glasgow

PAID WORK: see University of Glasgow

• Job bureau

Despite hectic schedules, most students work during and out of term. The Union keeps notice boards of vacancies, mainly relating to the arts, but with the odd wallet-top-up job in sales or call centres. Ushering work is available in the Academy, there's also an informal musicians agency, for more enterprising students.

SPORTS

Maybe it's nature, maybe it's nurture, but the fact is that artistic people have never been much into sport. RSAMD has no sweat-generating facilities, but students can use the University of Glasgow's, Glasgow Caledonian's and Strathclyde's and join their sports clubs. The SU sports officer arranges football tournaments.

SPORTING CLUBS:

Contemporary Dance; Yoga. **See also Clubs tables.**

ATTRACTIONS: see University of Glasgow

ACCOMMODATION

IN COLLEGE:

• Self-catering: 78% • Cost: £80 (35-50wks) • First years living in: 90%
• Insurance premium: ££££
Availability: Although priority is given to 1st years coming from outside Glasgow, 10% don't get a place to crash. Academy accommodation is grouped with the independent Glasgow Student Village on Queen Street. Rooms are either in self-catering hostels or self-contained flats – 1st years and internationals tend to get the former. There's also with 24-hr security,

en-suite rooms, fitted kitchens with dining areas, TV aerial points and internet access –
subject to a fee. *Students aren't exactly satisfied, however.*
Car parking: *None at residences.*

EXTERNALLY: see University of Glasgow
• Ave rent: £60 • Living at home: 25%
Housing help: One Academy counsellor has *very limited* information to dole out and keeps
a bulletin board. Home-seekers should try the online Private Accommodation Database.

WELFARE

SERVICES:
• Equal Opportunities Officer
• College counsellors: 1 full • Crime rating: !!
*The Academy Counsellor and Welfare Adviser is in charge of all things it's possible to make
leaflets about* and readily offers an ear to students with troublesome personal issues. Most
teaching staff are keen to offer help and support. The SU's Equal Opportunities Officer is
responsible for women, international students, students with disabilities and LGBs.
Health: The Woodside Health Centre is nearest. The Dental Hospital is 5 mins away. There's
an on-site Alexander Technique specialist.
Disabilities: *Access is good,* with lifts, ramps and toilets in the Academy building. The Fife
lecture theatre and all auditoria are fitted with hearing loops and have wheelchair spaces.
Note-takers and scribes are available. Many RSAMD students are dyslexic, *so support is
particularly good.*
Crime: *The area around Sauchiehall Street is known as a bit dodgy, so students should take
care. But then, they should take care everywhere really.*

FINANCE:
• Ave debt per year: £2,199 • Home student fees: £1,150
Fees: Costs vary widely, depending on the size of the course's practical element, but
international undergrad fees start at £9,975.
Support: Some bursaries are available for new students and married students over 25 can
be eligible for a Mature Student's Bursary, mainly for childcare. Entrance scholarships
ranging from £100-1,000 are awarded on the basis of admittance auditions. Plus loads of
other awards and scholarships, most of them aimed at promoting exceptional talent.

Royal Veterinary College, London

• ***The College is part of the University of London and students are entitled to use its
facilities.***
(1) The Royal Veterinary College, Royal College Street, London, NW1 0TU
    Tel: (020) 7468 5000 E-mail: registry@rvc.ac.uk Website: www.rvc.ac.uk
(2) Hawkshead, Hawkshead Lane, North Mimms, Hatfield, Herts, AL9 7TA
    Tel: (01707) 652 090
    The Royal Veterinary College Students' Union Society, Hawkshead Campus,
    Hawkshead Lane, North Mimms, Hatfield, Herts, AL9 7TA Tel: (01707) 666 310
    E-mail: sucommunications@rvc.ac.uk

GENERAL

You won't be surprised to learn that RVC (as its chums call it) mostly teaches students how to be vets. It's all to do with training people to make the sort of decisions that send Rolf Harris into floods of tears, *so if those who can't hack five years of that should stop reading now*. The College's main site is $1\frac{1}{4}$ miles from Trafalgar Square, in Camden, which has a reputation as *one of the trendiest, buzziest areas of London, but is getting a bit saggy and complacent nowadays*. Students spend two years at the redbrick Camden site, *falling over minor indie bands every time they go down the pub*, and then move out to the *almost tediously tranquil* countryside of Hawkshead to do their clinical study. The Hawkshead campus, a couple of miles from Hatfield, is an extensive, self-contained *and green* arrangement, set in *relaxed, commuter belt* countryside (see University of Hertfordshire).
For general information about London: see University of London.

Sex ratio (M:F): 24:76	**Founded: 1791**
Full-time u'grads: 805	**Part-time: 15**
Postgrads: 130	**Non-degree: 0**
Ave course: 5yrs	**Ethnic: 8%**
State:private school: 47:32	**Flunk rate: 1%**
Mature: 16%	**International: 21%**
Disabled: 3	**Local: 7%**

ATMOSPHERE:
Despite the fact they're ludicrously busy learning how to tell if an elephant's got cystitis or a budgerigar's got scrofula, students still find time to have fun. There's a closer relationship between students and staff than in many universities, with tutor-tutee socials taking place on a regular basis. Bonds are bound to form in an atmosphere this fast-paced and close-knit, and graduating students often take a post-finals holiday together.

SITES:
Hawkshead: (500 students) *There's even more of an atmosphere of frantic work than there is at Camden, because by the time students move here they're well on the way to becoming vets. The College keeps its own farm here and there are few nicer places to finish off a degree (or stick your hand up a cow's rectum, if you must).*

LONDON: see University of London

TRAVEL:
London: see University of London
Hawkshead: see University of Hertfordshire

CAREER PROSPECTS:
• Unemployed after 6mths: 5%
Students (in London, at least) can use the University of London facilities.

FURTHER INFO:
• Prospectuses undergrad: postgrad • Open days

ACADEMIC

Teaching's mostly based in small groups and on practical experience (*bring the longest, thickest pair of rubber gloves imaginable*). The final year may be lecture-free, *but it's also more intense than Christopher Walken in a staring competition.*

Entry points: 290-360	**Ave points: n/a**
Applns per place: 5	**Clearing: 16%**
No. of terms: 3	**Length of terms: 11wks**
Staff/student ratio: 1:2	**Study addicts: 0**
Teaching: ***	**Research: **** **

ADMISSIONS:

• Apply via UCAS

The College runs a summer school for Year 11 pupils interested in veterinary degrees.

SUBJECTS:

Veterinary Medicine: 100%.

LIBRARIES:

• 30,000 books • 178 study places

There are libraries at both Camden and Hawkshead. *Early closing* (8pm) *raises a few hackles.*

COMPUTERS:

• 180 workstations

The College Intranet service has a number of *useful* resources online (lecture notes, databases and the ilk).

OTHER LEARNING FACILITIES:

Farm; language labs; drama studio; media centre. The Museum of Veterinary History is stuated on the Camden campus.

E N T E R T A I N M E N T

LONDON: see University of London

Obviously there's a lot more going on near Camden than Hawkshead, but prices are higher. The famous Camden weekend market's still pretty cool, especially for young, slightly alternative Japanese tourists. If you're not one, it can get a bit samey. Pushplugged pubs at Hawkshead: the Bridge; the Maypole; avoid Williots. In Camden: Prince Alfred; Lord John Russell. Castle's is a popular Pie & Mash shop near the college.

UNIVERSITY:

• Price of a pint of beer: £1.30

Bars: The bars on each campus are as popular with staff as with students and *the two groups mix well.*

Theatre: Hawkshead has a *small* theatre production company which puts on an annual production.

Clubbing: A boogie bus runs from the Hawkshead site stopping at several pubs and a club in Enfield or Hatfield. *Serious* clubbers at the Camden site head into town or the West End. ULU facilities are open to RVC students.

Food: Both Hawkshead and Camden have refectories open from 10.30am to 2.30pm – *good quality and choice, but expensive.*

Other: An *infamous* 12-hr ball every year.

S O C I A L & P O L I T I C A L

THe ROYAL VETERINARY COLLEGE STUDENTS' UNION SOCIETY:

• NUS member

SU FACILITIES:
Welfare services; shop; vending machine; travel agency; pool table; minibus.

CLUBS (NON-SPORTING):
Clinical Science; Zoological. **See also Clubs tables.**

OTHER ORGANISATIONS:
Rag pops into existence for *enthusiastic* one charity-packed week a year.

RELIGIOUS:
• 1 chaplain (CofE)
For religious advice the sole reverend is willing to help worshippers of any persuasion with matters ecumenical or snooker-related (apparently he's quite good).

RELIGION IN LONDON: see University of London

RELIGION IN HATFIELD: see University of Hertfordshire

PAID WORK: see University of London
• Job bureau
There's a jobs board but students are expected to spend time on animal placements (eg. lambing) so there isn't much time for other work.

• Recent successes: rowing, women's rugby • BUSA Ranking: 48
Rather sporty. Being a vet keeps you fit and a liking for the great outdoors is second nature. However, grimy Camden isn't very conducive to exercise, so all of the sports facilities bar the gym are based in Hawkshead. There are also the facilities at ULU.

SPORTS FACILITIES:
Football, rugby, hockey and cricket pitches; tennis and netball courts; swimming pool; gym; squash courts. See University of London and University of Herfordshire for local facilities.

SPORTING CLUBS:
Polo; Rowing; Water Polo. **See also Clubs table.**

ATTRACTIONS: see University of London

IN COLLEGE:
• Catered: 9% • Cost: £82 (50wks)
• Self-catered cost: £64-72 (46wks)
• First years living in: 63% • Insurance premium: £££
Availability: Camden students stay in halls next to campus or, more likely, University of London accommodation for 2 years. Hawkshead has several self-catering halls on campus – all rooms have network points. All accommodation is in single rooms. There are new-ish houses 2 mins from college and some rooms suitable for wheelchair users at both campuses.
Car parking: *A real problem in Camden. In Hawkshead it's free and there's plenty of it.*

EXTERNALLY: see University of London
• Ave rent: £95 • Living at home: 5%
Camden: *Most Camden students live in Kentish Town which is a bit cheaper than Camden.* The College and SU keep details of housing and run lectures on the pitfalls of renting.

Hawkshead: *Potter's Bar is the best place to look but there's competition from University of Hertfordshire students.*

W E L F A R E

SERVICES:
- Lesbian, Gay & Bisexual Society • International Students' Officer
- Postgrad Officer & Society • Crime rating: !!!!!

Not many welfare provisions but students can use the extensive University of London facilities.

Disabilities: *The physically demanding nature of the course could make it difficult for some students. Both sites have accessible toilets, lifts and induction loops in the main lecture theatre. There's a residential unit adapted for wheelchair users at both campuses. See www.rcvs.org.uk for disability guidelines for vets.*

Health: Occupational health service available.

FINANCE:

Fees: International undergrads pay around £15,000 for courses.
Support: Academic achievement prizes and hardship funds are available.

Salford University

School of Oriental & African Studies see SOAS

The School of Pharmacy, University of London

School of Slavonic & East European Studies see University College London

Scottish College of Textiles see Heriot-Watt University

University of Sheffield

Sheffield Hallam University

Sheffield City Poly see Sheffield Hallam University

Sheffield City Polytechnic see Sheffield Hallam University

SOAS

Solent see Southampton Institute

South Bank University

South Bank Polytechnic see South Bank University

Southampton Institute

University of Southampton

South West Polytechnic see University of Plymouth

University of St Andrews

St David's College see Lampeter University

St George's Hospital Medical School, London

St Martin's College of Art see University of the Arts, London

St Martin's College, Lancaster see Lancaster University

St Mary's Hospital see Imperial College London

St Thomas's Hospital see King's College London

Staffordshire University

Staffordshire Polytechnic see Staffordshire University

Stirling University

Stockton see Durham University

University of Strathclyde

Sunderland University

Sunderland Polytechnic see Sunderland University

Surrey Institute of Art & Design

Surrey University

University of Sussex

Swansea, University of Wales

Salford University

The University of Salford, The Crescent, Salford, Greater Manchester, M5 4WT
Tel: (0161) 295 5000 E-mail: course-enquiries@salford.ac.uk Website: www.salford.ac.uk
University of Salford Students' Union, University House, The Crescent, Salford, M5 4WT
Tel: (0161) 736 7811 E-mail: students-union@salford.ac.uk
Website: www.salfordstudents.com

GENERAL

At the western end of Manchester (just 2 miles from the centre) is the city of Salford, *but screw up your eyes and you can't see the join. Salford isn't magically different, nor is it sufficiently far away to make it properly distinct and so everything we say about Manchester* (see University of Manchester) *applies equally to Salford. It's kind of like Canada's relationship with America, though, in that a lot of famous Mancs are actually Salfordians in disguise. Even uber-Mancunians The Smiths were famously pictured in front of Salford Lads Club on the cover of their The Queen Is Dead album. Salford's certainly not the posh end of Manchester*, but the 34-acre site of the University is quite green *and less hideous than many modern campuses*. With a few redbrick exceptions, the buildings have all been built in the last 20 years and *it'll be a good ten years more before they're officially declared ugly.*

Sex ratio (M:F): 45:55	Founded: 1896
Full-time u'grads: 12,695	Part-time: 2,965
Postgrads: 1,470	Non-degree: 68
Ave course: 3-4yrs	Ethnic: 17%
State:private school: 97:3	Flunk rate: 20%
Mature: 32%	International: 16%
Disabled: 344	Local: n/a

ATMOSPHERE:

Many of the students are local – *part of the community rather than apart from it – and they'd laugh off the suggestion that Salford is a dangerous place to be. Try Moss Side for that sort of thing. But Salford is a more down-to-earth area than Manchester proper (which isn't exactly an airy-fairy place itself). So it's wise to avoid activity that screams 'student' – or 'Southern pansy'. The campus is fairly quiet because many students either go home or head for the bright lights outside hours. It's the best of both worlds: a campus university in a small neighbourhood town with the metropolitan high life of Manchester just around the corner, although the latter tends to overshadow any specifically Salfordian local colour.*

SITES:

Peel Park, Frederick Road and Adelphi: The majority of students are based at these three campuses, all within 10 mins walk of each other. There's also Irwell Valley, a further 10 mins from Frederick Road, near the Castle Irwell Student Village.
Eccles and Bury: Nursing and midwifery are taught at Eccles, 3 miles from the main site.

MANCHESTER: see University of Manchester

SALFORD:

- Population: 392,900
- High temp: 20 • Low temp: 1 • Rainfall: 68

Salford has its own small and friendly community. Occasionally, it looks somewhat like a Lowry painting, full of matchstick men and matchstick cats and dogs, factory gates and the rest of it. Not surprising really, since this is Lowry's home town. There's a *spectacular* gallery to show off his work. *Occasionally, Salford also looks like a scene from Coronation Street.* Again, no surprise, chuck, as this is where it's set. But far more often, it is the rebuilt Salford that shows its face. The docklands have been developed and right in the heart of the North are all sorts of new constructions: high rise blocks, shopping malls and supermarkets, libraries, bookshops, banks *and everything else a growing boy needs,* including three museums, an 'urban heritage park' and its own nightlife.

TRAVEL: see University of Manchester

Local: Salford is covered by Manchester's bus and train networks which are *reliable, comprehensive and generally cheap.* Salford Crescent station is actually on the campus, although for national services it may be necessary to change at one of Manchester's stations (trains every 15 mins). Buses go to Manchester city centre every 3 mins.

CAREER PROSPECTS:

- Careers Service • No. of staff: 15 full-time • Unemployed after 6mths: 7%

As well as the usual rigmarole of finding a job, the careers service provides graduates with help starting their own business as well as placements in local industry.

FAMOUS ALUMNI:

Emma Atkins (Emmerdale actress); Bill Beaumont (ex-England rugby captain); John Cooper Clarke (poet); Christopher Eccleston (latest Dr Who); Euan Evans (rugby); Peter Kay (Phoenix Nights creator); L S Lowry (artist); Jonathan Morris (actor); Norman Whiteside (ex-Man Utd footballer).

FURTHER INFO:

- Prospectuses: undergrad; postgrad; some departments; international; alternative
- Open days

Campus tours are conducted every Wednesday – call (0161) 295 5762 to book. Individual departments arrange open days throughout the year.

 A C A D E M I C

The media courses are all heavily over-subscribed, especially the likes of Performance, TV and Radio Technology. *Salford is big on making sure degrees count in the job market and they're very chummy with local industry, organising placements,* some of which count towards final degree marks.

Entry points: 80-300	Ave points: n/a
Applns per place: n/a	Clearing: 10%
No. of terms: 2	Length of terms: 19wks
Staff/student ratio: 1:6	Study addicts: n/a
Teaching: **	Research: ***
Firsts: 9%	2.2s: 35%
2.1s: 41%	Others: 15%

ADMISSIONS:

- Apply via UCAS/NMAS for nursing

The Admissions Office takes work and experience into account for applicants with no formal qualifications.

SUBJECTS:

Unusual: Aircraft Engineering with Pilot Studies; Aviation Technology with Pilot Studies; Physics with Space Technology.

LIBRARIES:

• 629,000 books • 1,557 study places • 24-hr access

Salford's seven libraries make up (what they claim to be) the second largest university library facility in the country. *The weekend opening hours are pretty weak though* – 3 hours on Saturday, 6 on Sunday.

COMPUTERS:

• 845 workstations • 24-hr access

OTHER LEARNING FACILITIES:

Language labs; drama studio; rehearsal rooms; media centre;TV and radio studio.

E N T E R T A I N M E N T

MANCHESTER: see University of Manchester

SALFORD:

• Price of a pint of beer: £2.20 • Glass of wine: £2.40

Manchester's the Daddy when it comes to nightlife round here but Salford isn't without larks of its own.

Cinemas: Even Mancunians leave their more local cinemas to come to the eight-screen multiplex at Salford Quays.

Pubs: The real Coronation Street has been demolished long since, *but the spirit of the Rover's Return continues in many a local, although many are quite rough and you don't get Betty's hotpots. Pushplugs: the Old Pint Pot; the Crescent; the Black Horse; Wallness Tavern.*

Food: *Pushplugs: Hanrahan's; Frankie & Benny's at Salford Quays; Punter's Bistro.*

UNIVERSITY:

• Price of a pint of beer: £1.35 • Glass of wine: £2 • Can of Red Bull: £1.65

Bars: The main bars are the Lowry, *which is packed at lunchtimes and which the great man would undoubtedly have turned into a heart-warming picture of matchstick men playing the fruities,* or *home-from-home* the Pavilion ('Pav'), which has *value grub,* free Playstation, pool tables, big screen sport, occasional films and a 2am licence. Also the Sub Club on Frederick Road for lunch.

Theatres: Most dramatic posturing happens in and around the Robert Powell Theatre on campus.

Film: Four films a week, usually of the 'modern classic' variety (Withnail & I, Donnie Darko etc).

Food: What with a restaurant, six cafeterias, two sandwich bars and various bar snacks, the campus has 24-hr munchability. Try the Sub Club, the Adelphi Cafeteria or Milliways.

Clubbing/Music venues: The Pav is the Union's customised club venue with regular club nights: Tuesday's Flair; Thursday's Destiny and Friday's Top Banana. Live music tends to be local and/or cover bands but Atomic Kitten and Chesney Hawkes have played recently.

Other: Regular quiz nights, talent spots and live football in the Pav. Also there's a gallery, sometimes exhibiting student work and a campus pottery. Five balls a year.

S O C I A L & P O L I T I C A L

University of salford Students' union:

• 4 sabbaticals • Turnout at last ballot: 7% • NUS member

We're talking more beer than barricades here. The Union's main thrust is its professionally handled services and entertainments. It even has its own company, SUPER Services, which runs the student pub among other things.

SU FACILITIES:

At University House: three bars; eight cafés; four pool tables; eight meeting rooms; Endsleigh Insurance; various ATMs; fax & printing service; advice centre; late-night minibus; TV lounge; women's room; gaming machines; stationery shop; post office; new and secondhand bookshops; travel agent; ticket agency.

CLUBS (NON-SPORTING):

Almost Famous; Angry Dragons; Asian Cultural; Buddhism; CAMRA; Chinese; Circus & Juggling; Cyprus; Fight Racism, Fight Imperialism; Hindu; Indian Fun; Libyan; Linux; Rock; Singapore; United Against Facism; Wargames. **See also Clubs tables.**

OTHER ORGANISATIONS:

The weekly newspaper, Student Direct, is part of University of Manchester's paper (with an added Salford section) and s Europe's widest circulating student publication. Channel M is the University's television station and there's also a radio station (www.shockradio.co.uk) that broadcasts on FM for 12 weeks a year throughout the city. The Community Services Group involves *a healthy* 200 or so students in a range of local projects.

RELIGIOUS:

• 4 chaplains (CofE, RC, Methodist, URC)
The various Christian denominations have a prayer room and there's an on-site mosque and a visiting local rabbi.
Religion in Manchester: see University of Manchester

PAID WORK:

See University of Manchester
The careers service also runs the jobshop in the Union building.

SPORTS

• BUSA Ranking: 48
While Salford may not be nationally toasted for its sporting record, enthusiasm and facilities are at least worth an admiring nod.

SPORTS FACILITIES:

The University has got over 50 acres for students to run, jump, kick balls and throw things across. There are 18 floodlit football pitches, four cricket pitches, a running track, a croquet and bowling lawn and six rugby pitches as well as facilities for hockey, tennis, netball, squash and basketball. There's also a leisure centre right next to the Union building with a multigym, swimming pool sauna and climbing wall. Gym/Swim membership, giving year-long access to the pool, spa, sauna and fitness rooms, costs £95. A discount card is available for other facilities. See University of Manchester for facilities in the local area.

SPORTING CLUBS:

Breakdancing; Canoe & Kayak; Cheerleading; Diving; Hiking; Kung Fu; Motor; Mountaineering; Parachute; Rifle; Ski & Snowboard; Wing Chun. **See also Clubs tables.**

ATTRACTIONS: see University of Manchester

ACCOMMODATION

IN COLLEGE:

• Catered: 2% • Cost: £75-84 (33wks)
• Self-catering: 30% • Cost: £41-53 (39/50wks) • Insurance premium: £££££
Availability: 1st years are guaranteed a place in halls if they apply before 1st September. On campus there are the Horlock and Constantine Halls. Then, about 10 mins away, there's Castle. Near the Adelphi site is Eddie Colman and John Lester. Rosehill and Churchill are *handy for Salford Shopping Centre* although Churchill's a 60s tower-block *and a touch*

prison-esque. On average there's eight to ten students per kitchen in the self-catering blocks and kitchens on all floors. Some rooms available for couples.
Car parking: Parking's *not a problem* so long as students have applied for a (free) permit.

EXTERNALLY:
• Ave rent: £40-55
See University of Manchester

WELFARE

SERVICES:
• Lesbian/Gay/Bisexual/Transgender Officer & Society • Mature Students Officer & Society
• Postgrad Officer & Society • International Students Society
• Ethnic Minorities Officer & Society • Women's Officer & Society
• Disabilities Officer & Society • Late-night minibus • Self-defence classes
• University counsellors: 3 full • SU counsellors: 1 • Crime rating: !!!!
The Union runs its own advice centre with a visiting solicitor every Thursday. Overseas students can turn to the Overseas Student Secretary or the University's Overseas Students Counsellor.
Health: Nurses at the campus health centre on the 3rd floor of the Maxwell building will see students without an appointment.
Crèches/Nursery: 104 places for children aged 6mths-4yrs.
Disabilities: All the newer buildings have ramps and *wheelchair access is generally good and the Equality & Diversity Office is particularly helpful*.

FINANCE:
• Ave debt per year: £3,545

School of Oriental & African Studies
see SOAS

The School of Pharmacy, University of London

• *The College is part of the* University of London *and students are entitled to use its facilities.*
The School of Pharmacy, University of London, 29-39 Brunswick Square, London, WC1N 1AX
Tel: (020) 7753 5831 E-mail: registry@ulsop.ac.uk Website: www.ulsop.ac.uk
The School of Pharmacy Students' Union, 29-39 Brunswick Square, London, WC1N 1AX
Tel: (020) 7753 5809 E-mail: student.union@lisa.ulsop.ac.uk

GENERAL

Don't be fooled by the location. Russell Square may be crash-bang in central London, *but there's not a lot else crash-bang about it*. The Bloomsbury locale is a *quiet, leafy island* between King's Cross and Holborn, home to a *few* plush hotels and *a lot of very rich people*. The School of Pharmacy's *easy on the eye*, with *huge* windows and *an art deco entrance*.

Sex ratio (M:F): 37:63	Founded: 1842
Full-time u'grads: 655	Postgrads: 115
Ave course: 4yrs	Ethnic: 85%
State:private school: 70:30	Flunk rate: 3%
Mature: 20%	International: 25%
Disabled: 4	

63%
37%

ATMOSPHERE:

The School of Pharmacy only runs one course (*no prizes for guessing what*), so it attracts the *career-headed and studious. It feels very much like a school, rather than a university, and is full of class swots who at the age of 18 thought 'I'm going to be a pharmacist – yes!'. Any rogue party fiends have to make their way to UCL or ULU for the action.*

LONDON: see University of London
• City centre: 1,200m
Bloomsbury's *quiet and refined*, but nearby King's Cross is *squalid, noisy and until the redevelopers move them on, swarming with hookers and junkies.* On the other side, Covent Garden and Leicester Square are by turns *exhilaratingly busy and just plain busy.*

TRAVEL: see University of London
Trains: King's Cross and Euston both *within walking distance*, connections to the Midlands, East Anglia and the North.
Buses: 17, 45, 46, 68, 168 swing past.
Car: *Cataclysmically costly* to park, even if there's a space to be snapped up. Right in the middle of the congestion zone.
Underground: Russell Square (Picadilly line); King's Cross (Northern line, Victoria, Circle, Hammersmith & City and Metropolitan lines); Euston (Northern & Victoria).
Bicycles: Bikes can be secured on railings across the road from the school.

CAREER PROSPECTS:
• Careers Service • Unemployed after 6mths: 0

FURTHER INFO:
• Prospectuses: undergrad; postgrad

A C A D E M I C

Everything's geared towards the MPharm and students are expected to put in about 40 hours a week of study.

Applns per place: 6	Clearing: 1%
No. of terms: 2	Length of terms: 15wks
Staff/student ratio: 1:13	Study addicts: 99%
Teaching: *****	Research: *****
Firsts: 8%	2.2s: 36%
2.1s: 54%	3rds: 2%

ADMISSIONS:
• Apply via UCAS

SUBJECTS:
Medical sciences: 100%.
Best: (MPharm).

LIBRARIES:
- 65,000 books • 70 study places • Spend per student: £
Irritatingly closed at weekends, though students have full borrowing rights at the UCL library to carry them through Sat-Sun.

COMPUTERS:
- 88 workstations • 24-hr access • Spend per student: £

OTHER LEARNING FACILITIES:
The practice pharmacy is *a trainee chemist's playroom*.

THE CITY: see University of London
- Price of a pint of beer: £2.30 • Glass of wine: £2 • Can of Red Bull: £2.25
Cinemas: Leicester Square for the *biggest, priciest* screens around.
Theatres: The West End is *as good as theatre gets*.
Pubs: The Goose is a *popular* joint, as is the Lord Russell.
Clubs/Discos: La Scala in King's Cross is *one of the best in London. Just don't hang around outside unless you're looking for crack.*
Eating out: The Hare and Tortoise noodle bar *fulfils the cravings* for Chinese, Deepak Tandoori for Indian and The Piazza and Valtores *also get the thumbs up.*

UNIVERSITY:
- Price of a pint of beer: £1 • Glass of wine: £1.50 • Can of Red Bull: £1.10
Bars: The bar is only open a *dismal* three nights a week and is shut on Saturdays.
Film: The Renoir, an arthouse screen next door to the school, shows arty and foreign films.
Food: The Refectory has limited opening hours and serves *cheap, school-dinner* fare.

SCHOOL OF PHARMACY STUDENTS' UNION:
- Turnout at last ballot: 30%

SU FACILITIES:
Bar; cafeteria; juke box; meeting rooms; photocopier; pool table; vending machine.

CLUBS (NON-SPORTING):
Chinese; Hindu; Krishna Consciousness; Sikh. **See also Clubs tables.**

OTHER ORGANISATIONS:
An unusually active Rag raises stacks of cash for good causes.

PAID WORK: see University of London
Students are expected to take work placements during vacations.

- Recent successes: none
Sport's virtually dropped off the bottom of the agenda. This is bookworm country.

SPORTING CLUBS:
See Clubs tables.

ATTRACTIONS: see University of London
The local footie teams are Arsenal, Spurs and, er, Barnet.

ACCOMMODATION

IN COLLEGE:
- Catered: 13% • Cost: £1C5-110 (38wks)
- First years living in: 50%
- Insurance premium: £££

Availability: Accommodation is in UoL intercollegiate halls. Places only available to non-Londoners. All halls have wheelchair access.

Car parking: The few spaces that exist are mostly reserved for staff.

EXTERNALLY: see University of London
- Ave rent: £120 • Living at home: 50%

Availability: Housing *isn't too hard to come by, but will blow a hole in the budget.* Angel, Camden and Holloway are all *popular* choices.

Housing help: Run through the UoL accommodation office.

WELFARE

SERVICES:
- International Students' Officer • Postgrad Officer & Society
- Disabilities Officer • Crime rating: !!!!!

The college *leans* on UoL and ULU welfare facilites.

Disabilities: *Wheelchair access is difficult – the college building is stair crazy.*

FINANCE:
- Ave debt per year: £3,405 • Access fund: £42,000
- Successful applications/yr: 70 • Ave payment: £100-1,000

School of Slavonic & East European Studies

see University College London

Scottish College of Textiles

see Heriot-Watt University

University of Sheffield

University of Sheffield, 8 Palmerston Road, Sheffield, S10 2TE
Tel: (0114) 222 8031 E-mail: study@sheffield.ac.uk Website: www.shef.ac.uk/asksheffield
The University of Sheffield Union of Students, Western Bank, Sheffield, S10 2TG
Tel: (0114) 222 8500 E-mail: union@sheffield.ac.uk Website: www.sheffieldunion.com

GENERAL

Sheffield, England's fourth largest city, just north-east of the Derbyshire Peak District and equidistant from Leeds and Manchester, is also one of the furthest places from the coast in the whole of Britain. *Most people immediately connect it with the steel industry, which is what made the place famous* and, to the east, there's still a *stark* reminder of industrial demise. Now the city is a *busy, bustling but friendly place* with a modern centre and compact Victorian suburbs. The University's 15 mins walk west from the city centre on a campus extending over about a mile, with buildings *smeared* into the surrounding urban setting. Almost all of them are less than a century old *and have been carefully constructed rather than thrown up as required.* Mostly they're *attractive* redbrick buildings, although there are a few more modern structures – the arts tower and library, which are Grade II listed, are *quite appealing* glass high-rises.

57%			
Sex ratio (M:F): 43:57		**Founded: 1905**	
Full-time u'grads: 16,005		**Part-time: 2,645**	
Postgrads: 4,305		**Non-degree: 0**	
Ave course: 3/4yrs		**Ethnic: n/a**	
State:private school: 83:17		**Flunk rate: 7%**	
Mature: 8%		**International: 17%**	
Disabled: 268		**Local: n/a**	

ATMOSPHERE:

The University buzzes with activity especially around the Union, which is the social and political centrepiece. That's not to say it's a student bubble – they're well integrated into the community (after the 1st year most live out), and a campus spread across the city centre means there's a relaxed and fun town/gown atmosphere, especially in local pubs. The University's closely involved with community issues and representatives from it and the SU sit on community forums. Sport, politics and insane party action all have prominent places in student life – though the libraries and study areas can get as crowded as the bars when they need to. Many students stay in the city after graduation – which can't be a bad thing.

SHEFFIELD:

• Population: 513,100 • City centre: 1 mile • London: 169 miles
• Leeds: 35 miles • Manchester: 37 miles
• High temp: 21 • Low temp: 1 • Rainfall: 48

A sign on the city outskirts reads 'Welcome to Sheffield, the home of British cutlery' but *honestly, it's got platefuls of stuff going for it. The popular image of Sheffield as a gritty northern town populated by ex-steelworkers stripping for cash isn't complete gibberish, but it's a fairly narrow view nowadays.* The old industrial area has been redeveloped (*the outskirts are still rather grim*) and Sheffield is *well set for leisure and sports facilities.* The suburbs in the south-west, where the University accommodation is based, are *greenish and pretty.* Amenities: *local luxuries* like late-night shops; 52 parks; street markets; museums; galleries (the City Museum, the Mappin Art Gallery and now the Winter Garden and Millennium Galleries). *The vast Meadowhall Shopping Centre is one of Europe's largest. It's known as Meadow-hell to some, but its sheer range and size is both crude and astonishing.*

TRAVEL:

Trains: Sheffield Station, less than a mile from the University, offers services to London (£32.35), Birmingham (£18.60), Edinburgh (£47.15) and more.
Coaches: The Sheffield Interchange, also less than a mile, runs National Express and Stagecoach Express services. A trip to London costs £16.50
Car: 10 mins off the M1, also A57, A61, A616 and A631. 20 mins off the end of the M18. Parking's *fairly easy* in the city centre and there are plenty of park & ride spots in the outskirts. University *parking is a different story* – permits needed (£78.60) are not generally available to undergrads.

Air: Manchester or Leeds/Bradford (home of Jet2).
Hitching: *A bus trip to the M1 is the first step. An imploring look and an outstretched thumb is the second.*
Local: Local buses run all day and all night and are *frequent, reliable and quite cheap. Local minibuses are even better because they go everywhere. The Supertram is best of all, though, 'cause it's fun and cheap* (£1.90 all-day pass, Megarider 7-day pass £6.30). The University is on the tram route's Yellow Lines.
College: The SU provides the Union Safety Bus for women (runs at night till 2.15am, SU to halls, £1).
Taxis: *Taxi ranks are common as muck* and are indicated on University maps. Taxi companies are informed of Union events so there's enough on hand at fall-out time. Black cabs *circle like vultures* around Glossop Road and Western Bank, *but private companies offer a cheaper deal.*
Bicycles: The University is keen on bikes and positively bribes its students to use them – free soup and rolls for cyclists are dished out on certain days. *Bumpy geography* puts some off but there are *comprehensive* cycle lanes and routes in the city centre. The police stamp postcodes on students' bikes in Freshers' week – *as if that makes a difference.*

CAREER PROSPECTS:

• <u>Careers Service</u> • <u>No. of staff: 20 full/7 part</u> • <u>Unemployed after 6mths: 6%</u>
The *extensive* service includes a careers library, interview training, job fairs, employer presentations and graduate workshops. The Student Directions website is *stuffed with helpful advice and job-hunting aids.* OpUS is a subdivision that focuses on finding work experience opportunities and promotes work-based learning in academic departments.

FAMOUS ALUMNI:

Carol Barnes (newsreader); David Blunkett MP (Lab); Stephen Daldry (theatre and film director); David Davies (Football Association); Eddie Izzard (*action transvestite*/comedian); Amy Johnson (pioneer airwoman); Harry Kroto (Nobel prize-winning scientist); Sir Peter Middleton (Chairman, Barclays Bank); Jack Rosenthal (late writer); Richard Roberts (another Nobel prize-winning scientist); Helen Sharman (Britain's 1st astronaut); Linda Smith (comedian); Ann Taylor MP (Lab); Dave Weatherall (footballer); Phil Wheatley (Director General of the Prison Service).

FURTHER INFO:

• <u>Prospectuses: undergrad; postgrad; international, departmental</u> • <u>Open days</u> DVD also available.

A C A D E M I C

Strong on Law and subjects that need calculators, a fair dose of Sheffield's courses are modular – students take around 18 for a full degree (*that's six a year to those not mathematically inclined*). Specialisation follows in the 2nd year and the 3rd year usually involves a dissertation. *Other subjects vary, of course.*

260-360		**POINTS**
Entry points: 260-360	Ave points: n/a	
Applns per place: 7	Clearing: 4%	
No. of terms: 2	Length of terms: 15wks	
Staff/student ratio: 1:14	Study addicts: n/a	
Teaching: *****	Research: ****	
Year abroad: 5%	Sandwich students: n/a	
Firsts: 14%	2.2s: 25%	
2.1s: 52%	3rds: 3%	

ADMISSIONS:

• Apply via UCAS/NMAS for Nursing & Midwifery

'Academic suitability' is Sheffield's only *vague criterion* for admissions. They don't always demand the standard three A Levels and are happy to consider other qualifications or experience, particularly in the case of mature students (who account for over a third of the student body).

SUBJECTS:

Architecture: 4%	Medical Sciences: 10%
Art & Design: 15 %	Nursing: 16%
Engineering: 9%	Sciences: 15%
Law: 7%	Social Sciences: 22%

Best: Animal & Plant Sciences; Archaeology; Architecture; Biblical Studies; Engineering; English Literature; Geography; History; Information Studies; Law; Molecular Biosciences; Music; Philosophy; Politics; Russian & Slavonic Studies; Sociological Studies.

LIBRARIES:

• 1,400,000 books • 2,230 study places • Spend per student: ££££

The main library and the St Georges Library both open till 21.30 Mon-Thu, closing earlier at the weekend. There are also nine or ten smaller, departmental libraries. A new LRC is due for October 2006, with 100,000 books and 900 study places, most with computer provision.

COMPUTERS:

• 1,200 workstations • 24-hr access • Spend per student: £

Wireless access across campus

OTHER LEARNING FACILITIES:

The academic arsenal includes language labs, a drama studio, rehearsal rooms, CAD lab and an audio/TV centre.

ENTERTAINMENT

SHEFFIELD:

• Price of a pint of beer: £1.75 • Glass of wine: £1.85

Cinemas: Three mainstream multiplexes (Vue, Odeon, UGC) and the Showroom in the centre for wobbly cameras and subtitles – student tickets £2.50 on Mon/Thur.

Theatres: The Union box office flogs tickets for shows at the Crucible Theatre (of World Snooker Championships fame) and its alternative-leaning studio, the Lyceum and the Studio – student discounts often available *if you ask nicely*. Also smaller community theatres and arts centres around the city.

Pubs: *You'd have to be pretty darned picky not to find a wateringhole in Sheffield that suits your style – hundreds of pubs ranging from nasty chain bars with no atmosphere to crumbling locals. Irish pubs are particularly big business around here.* Pushplugs: Varsity (two meals for £5); Cavendish (discounts, pool and big screen sport); The Place; Revolution. *Students are welcome pretty much everywhere in the city centre. Further out the unpleasantness and accusations of sheep-tampering start.*

Clubbing: *The legendary Gatecrasher breaks into Republic once a month and is one of the North's best nights. The Leadmill holds a weekly student night and the popular Disco Heaven (two rooms of retro tat). Hot Pants at City Hall on Saturdays is another biggie (another two rooms of retro tat). Kingdom holds what may be the best-named gay night around (Fairy Liquid). If there really is nothing on the Sheffield groovy train to take you up where you belong then Leeds and Manchester are a six-pack and train ride away.*

Music venues: Sheffield Arena and Don Valley Stadium deal with the sort of acts *punters are happy to watch through binoculars*, ranging from top touring bands to wrestling and show jumping. *City Hall copes with the smaller-scale mainstream.* The Leadmill, the Roundhouse and Hallamshire Hotel are the major indie venues.

Eating out: If animal grease and BSE aren't up your street – *they're up most of Sheffield's* – *then there's plenty of tastier options, mainly focused around Division Street and Devonshire Green. Lots of choice but tapas is the current student favourite. Pushplugs: BB's (cheap BYOB Italian); Varsity; Cavendish.*

UNIVERSITY:

• Price of a pint of beer: £1.69 • Glass of wine: £1.89
Sheffield SU has its many fingers in many pies – most of them lavishly flavoured with student entertainment. The extent of its involvement in music, club nights, pubbing and food is both staggering and profitable. Nice one.
Bars: *Bar One is one of the* liveliest and longest-running, and crammed with promos, competitions, big-screen sport, DJs and quizzes. Interval is the official Tuesday pre-club bar and is a little more laidback, boasting an international selection of beer and wine and hosting its own exclusive nights: Funktion, Housekeeping, Lost in Musique and Sabroso. The SU also has the keys to two pubs: the beer-gardened Fox & Duck in Broomhill and The Rising Sun in Fulwood.
Theatres: The Drama Studio is an old converted church *and its inhabitants are a busy bunch*, putting on stageloads of plays and organising the odd jaunt up to the Edinburgh fringe.
Film: The Auditorium is a cinema-space and shows several films a week (new release, classics) and is kitted out with hearing loops, Dolby surround sound and wheelchair access. A year's pass costs £30.
Music venues: The Octagon (cap 1,375) hosts quality crooners including The Fun Lovin' Criminals, The Darkness, Motorhead and The Super Furry Animals. The Fusion & Foundary host gigs, while acoustic sets can be heard in Interval and Coffee Revolution.
Clubbing: Five nights a week including the *brazenly naff, astonishingly popular* Pop Tarts retro night, the *renowned* Tuesday Club, which has featured Mr Scruff, Fabio & Grooverider, Coldcut & The Beatnuts, Juice (cheesy chart), plus *cutting edge indie* at the Fuzz Club. There's also a gang of monthly nights, including gay-friendly Climax and R'n'B fuelled Lickerish. Tickets go on sale the morning of the event and *invariably sell out.*
Comedy/Cabaret: *The downside of such strong club culture means comedic tastes are only sporadically catered for. Anyway students seem to have more musical tastes.*
Food: *Many* outlets. One to Go, for scrumptious junk. Interval offers *classier* snackable fare. Loxley's Food Court has a *magnificent* breakfast bar and Coffee Revolution (fair trade paninis) is one of the Union's major money-spinners. Legions of other snack kiosks and coffee stops too.
Other: End of Year Carnival, Freshers, Sports and departmental balls.

SOCIAL & POLITICAL

THE UNIVERSITY OF SHEFFIELD UNION OF STUDENTS:

• 8 sabbaticals • Turnout at last ballot: 25% • NUS member
Sheffield's Union is nearly one of the most powerful forces in the universe. Well, in Sheffield at least. Communication between the Union and the University is a particular plus point – the SU pays students to represent Union issues to University departments and acts as a first point of contact for fellow students, exactly like trade union representatives. The 'Union Links' scheme keeps things sweet between the SU and the authorities. Union politics hovers to the left, with strong 'grants not fees' and anti-racism concerns.

SU FACILITIES:

Two purpose-built nightclubs; two bars; two pubs; four snack bars; three cafeterias; fast food joint; ten pool tables; seven meeting rooms; Endsleigh Insurance office; Oxfam and Natwest banks, five major bank ATMs; general store; stationery shop; new bookshop; quiet room; mature students' lounge; nursery; women's room; photocopier; fax and printing services; payphones; photo booth; advice centre; gaming and vending machines; travel agency; ticket box office; launderette.

CLUBS (NON-SPORTING):

Anime Anonymous; Assassins Guild; Ballroom & Latin American; Bond; Bouncy Castle Appreciation; Catholic; Chess; Comedy; Debating; Everton Supporters; Hindu; Iranian; Italian; Korean; Malaysian; Mileage Marathon; Medieval; Music; North American; Pagan; Portuguese Speaking; Radio; Real Ale; Sound; Sri Lankan; Star Trek; Stocks & Shares; Turkish; Wargames; and many others. **See also Clubs tables.**

OTHER ORGANISATIONS:

Student-run newspaper the Steel Press is published fortnightly, accompanied by a weekly What's On? Event listings, the Union magazine, Stainless, a Nursing & Midwifery newsletter and SheffieldBase.com. Radio station Sure broadcasts on the web but is angling for an AM licence. Sheffield Rag is *alive and kicking*, arranging a *clustered calendar of cash-creating stunts*: pub-crawls; slave auctions. Sheffield Volunteering is *highly active* working with schools, refugees, special needs kids, the homeless and the elderly.

RELIGIOUS:

• 9 chaplains (CofE, URC, Pentecostal, Unitarian, Jewish, Muslim, Hindu, Sikh, Buddhist, Baha'i)
As well as the multifaith chaplaincy centre there are several Muslim prayer rooms on campus. The Chaplaincy produces a guide to religious provision around the town (churches, mosques, synagogues, temples and two cathedrals – RC and CofE).

PAID WORK:

• Job bureau
Potential in bars and shops on campus and in town. Also some departmental envelope-stuffing type daywork and the OpUS section of the Careers Service acts as a job shop for voluntary, vacation and part-time vacancies.

S P O R T S

• Recent successes: orienteering, swimming, water polo, basketball • BUSA Ranking: 22
The sporting amenities are among the best in the country. It's not all about winning though: beginners and casual participants are encouraged to give it a go and even the most dedicated, crisp-encrusted couch potato will find something to do.

SPORTS FACILITIES:

45 acres of sports grounds, including: four football, four rugby, three synthetic (hockey) and two cricket pitches; four squash, four tennis and two netball/basketball/volleyball courts; sports hall; swimming pool; gym; aerobics studio; multigym; sauna and climbing wall. Everything except the gym can be used on a pay & play basis, with discounts at off-peak hours. Sheffield caters for everything its University doesn't. Ponds Forge, Sheffield Arena and The Don Valley Stadium are all world-class sports centres, the city has two ice rinks, and the River Don and the Ogston reservoir are there for watersports. The *glorious* Peak District provides nature's own sports centre for ramblers, cavers, mountaineers, hang gliders and other outdoor types. Sheffield's also home to Europe's largest artificial ski resort.

SPORTING CLUBS:

Pretty much all of them. Here's a few: 10-Pin bowling; Diving; Gymnastics; Hang Gliding; High Peaks; Ju-Jitsu; Korfball; Ladies' Cricket; Mountaineering; Rowing; Scuba-diving; Skydiving; Walking; Windsurfing. **See also Clubs tables.**

ATTRACTIONS:

Sheffield Wednesday and United FCs; Sheffield Eagles (rugby); Steelers (ice hockey); Sharks (basketball); speedway at Owlerton Stadium.

ACCOMMODATION

IN COLLEGE:

- Catered: 18% • Cost: £79-£114 (30-37wks)
- Self-catering: 12% • Cost: £58-£77 (38wks)
- First years living in: 85% • Insurance premium: ££

Availability: Most first years guaranteed University accommodation – either in halls or in one of the many University-owned houses. These range from *cutesy* terrace cottages and Victorian town houses closer to campus to large, brick-heavy halls 20 mins away. *Many opt for Ranmoor, the largest hall, or Stephenson, for its sense of community. Sorby is avoided like an ugly 60s tower block. Because it is one. Facilities and furnishings are generally decent, but it's a bit like booking a hotel – if you want a minibar and trouser press, you have to shell out a bit more. Note: minibars and trouser presses are not available in University accommodation.*

Car parking: *Problematic.* Permits are only given to the most needy *(or argumentative).*

EXTERNALLY:

- Ave rent: £48

Availability: Those living externally find it fairly easy to get hold of reasonable homes in proximity of the campus. Broomhill, Crookes and Walkley are *popular* areas because they're nearby, have plenty of pubs and a large student population.

Housing help: The University accommodation office runs a website with house-finding database. The advice centre provides a recommended contract for tenants. *Most students use word of mouth, notice boards in the Union and ads in shops.*

WELFARE

S

SERVICES:

- Lesbian/Gay/Bisexual Society • Ethnic Minorities Society • Women's Officer & Society
- Mature Students' Society • International Students' Officer & Society
- Postgrad Society • Disabilities Society • Late-night women's minibus
- Self-defence classes • Nightline • Taxi fund
- College counsellors: 3 full/3 part • Crime rating: !!

The sabbatical welfare officer operates an open door policy. One officer sits on postgrad and mature students meetings but has no special responsibility for either. Halls have resident tutors and each student is assigned a personal tutor, *so there are always plenty of people to turn to – the biggest problem is deciding which one.*

Health: The University Health Service has nice doctors, five nurses, in-patient facilities and a website.

Women: Late-night minibus (till 2.15am) between SU-halls/houses, £1, Woman's pack (from Women's Officer) contains magazine, alarm, welfare handbook and contacts list.

Crèches/Nursery: SU nursery has 64 places, to 5yrs.

Disabilities: Town's awkward for wheelchairs. University is trying to improve access, but some buildings are effectively out-of-bounds – but there's *pretty good* support to seen/unseen disabilities in general. Some specially adapted accommodation is available for those with limited mobility or hearing. The SU has good access and there are provisions for the dyslexic and visually/hearing-impaired.

FINANCE:

- Ave debt per year: £3,433

Fees: Postgrads' research degrees are charged at £2,940. International fees vary enormously: £7,650-18,800.

- Access fund: £730,287 • Successful applications/yr: 1,031

Support: Some hardship funds and support to cover childcare. There's up to twelve grand of bursaries for those on 4-year courses, dependent on household income and A Level grades, among other factors.

Sheffield Hallam University

• *Formerly Sheffield City Polytechnic*
Sheffield Hallam University, City Campus, Howard Street, Sheffield, S1 1WB
Tel: (0114) 225 5555 E-mail: enquiries@shu.ac.uk Website: www.shu.ac.uk
Sheffield Hallam University Union of Students, The HUBs, Paternoster Row,
Sheffield, S1 2QQ Tel: (0114) 255 4111 E-mail: hallam-union@shu.ac.uk
Website: www.hallamunion.com

GENERAL

Sheffield Hallam's spread across three campuses in town, with the main site built around a *big, glass atrium*. Each site houses a different department. There's not a lot of site-hopping to be done, but even if there were, *it's not too difficult*. Nonetheless, *applicants should check on which site their course would be based*.

Sex ratio (M:F): 51:49	**Founded: 1969**
Full-time u'grads: 16,030	**Part-time: 4,160**
Postgrads: 1,850	**Non-degree: n/a**
Ave course: 3yrs	**Ethnic: 15%**
State:private school: 95:5	**Flunk rate: 13%**
Mature: 68%	**International: 11%**
Disabled: 496	**Local: 33%**

ATMOSPHERE:

Hallam's high on postgrads and part-timers. Chuck in the fact that lots of students are local, and the spread-out location, and it's no surprise the University gets on well with the town. In fact, it can be hard to lay hand on a student, as they blend seamlessly into the background. The whole place feels like home – mainly because, for most people, it is.

SHEFFIELD: see University of Sheffield
• City centre: 0 miles

SITES:

City campus: (most subjects and SU) Main city centre site, at Pond Street.
Collegiate crescent: (Health, Education – 3,500 students) *Lots* of green space and a *mix* of buildings. SU-run shop, *a few* sports facilities, halls and student houses.
Psalter Lane: (Cultural Studies, Art, Design, Film) *Eclectic, arty* territory 3 miles from the City campus. It's got a Union bar and *a few other facilities to call its own*.

TRAVEL: see University of Sheffield

Car: A lot of local students drive to University, although the time saved on the journey is *usually eaten up going round in circles looking for somewhere to park*.
Local: Good public transport links make getting around University *a doddle*.

CAREER PROSPECTS:
• Careers Service • No. of staff: 13 full • Unemployed after 6mths: 7%

FAMOUS ALUMNI:

Richard Caborn (Minister for Sport); David Kohler (footballer); Bruce Oldfield (fashion designer); Nick Park (animator, Wallace & Gromit big cheese); Howard Wilkinson (football manager with *whatever the opposite of the Midas touch is*).

FURTHER INFO:

• Prospectuses: undergrads; postgrad; departmental • Open days • Video

ACADEMIC

There's a *hands-on, pragmatic* approach to learning with the emphasis on *getting out there and doing something*. There are more sandwich courses *than a student could poke a BLT at* (more than anywhere else in the UK, in fact) and a lot of courses include a year abroad. The degrees offered are *mostly vocational and a bit techie*.

Entry points: 140-280	Ave points: 220
Applns per place: n/a	Clearing: 25%
No. of terms: 2	Length of terms: 14wks
Staff/student ratio: 1:20	Study addicts: 12%
Teaching: ***	Research: ***
Firsts: 5%	2.2s: 39%
2.1s: 40%	3rds: 6%

ADMISSIONS:

• Apply via UCAS
Mature students can be assessed on work experience rather than qualification.

SUBJECTS:

Best: Biomedical Sciences; Business & Technology; Maths; Sport & Leisure Management.

LIBRARIES:

• 518,058 books • 4,011 study places • 24-hr access
There's a library on each campus and a 'learning centre' (Adsetts) at City campus. As well as winning design awards (*apparently it looks like a seagull, go figure*) it includes mobile phone tolerant zones and chillout rooms. The ALL (Access to all Libraries for Learning) scheme means students have reading rights in all the town libraries, including those at University of Sheffield.

COMPUTERS:

• 1,600 workstations • 24-hr access
An online learning system *suits the nocturnal or the just plain shy*.

Six of the MPs elected in Labour's 1997 landslide were former presidents of the National Union of Students.

ENTERTAINMENT

THE CITY: see <u>University of Sheffield</u>

UNIVERSITY:

• <u>Price of a pint of beer: £1.70</u> • <u>Glass of wine: £1.95</u> • <u>Can of Red Bull: £1</u>
As Push went to press, Hallam was putting the finishing touches to a whopping great SU at the site of the old National Centre for Popular Music. Goodies including a public bar serving hot food and snacks, an SU-managed shop, a student bar, areas for live bands and meeting rooms for clubs and societies.
Bars: The Phoenix is the main bar, *aided and abetted* by The Cooler Bar (*not necessarily cooler, but definitely more relaxed*), The Furnace (comedy nights and small ents) and the Forgers Bar on Collegiate campus.
Theatres: Not a *buzzing* drama scene, but definitely a *burgeoning* one. The drama society has *plenty of enthusiastic members*.
Film: Regular film nights in the Hub.
Music venues: The Works (cap 1,000) has recently entertained the crowds with the Bluetones, Big Brovas, Malibu Stacey, The Nolans and *pert-buttocked Romanian novelty act* the Cheeky Girls. New Music Backlash is a mothly showcase for local talent.
Clubbing: The Works hosts Stardust (disco), Sheff1 (chart/dance, indie) and a Wednesday night cheese antidote of rock and indie.
Food: Hub Grub is pub grub. It does soups, nachos, *tasty* sandwiches and pizza. There are three other cafes: The Cutting Edge (continental); The Heartspace Bar (healthy); and Tappers Snack Bar (salads).
Other: Regular black tie bashes.

SOCIAL & POLITICAL

SHEFFIELD HALLAM UNIVERSITY UNION OF STUDENTS:
• <u>5 sabbaticals</u> • <u>Turnout at last ballot: 6%</u> • <u>NUS member</u>
The SU *knows its place* and busies itself supporting *whatever kind of activity* students want to get involved with, so setting up new societies is *dead easy. Not much* politicking goes on, except when a big issue like fees rears its head. University and Union are *pretty pally*.

SU FACILITIES:

Four bars; one cafeteria; three snack bars; photo booth; shop; Endsleigh Insurance office; Nationwide bank; travel agency; disco; gay room; ticket office; video games; minibus hire; vending machines; photocopier; function rooms.

CLUBS (NON-SPORTING):

Breakers (break dancing); Hip Hop; Law; SLAGS (Spirits, Liquor, Ale & Gin Society); Stockbroking. **See also Clubs tables.**

OTHER ORGANISATIONS:

Stage Service is a hands-on techie training group that works the rigs at SU ents. S Press student magazine is pretty *irregular*. Rush radio is the fledgling six-day-a-week station. Rag and Hallam Volunteering do *whatever it takes* to part students from cash for good causes.

RELIGIOUS:

• <u>1 chaplain (multi-faith)</u>
A multi-faith chaplaincy caters for most religious persuasions.

PAID WORK: see <u>University of Sheffield</u>

• <u>Job bureau</u> • <u>Paid work: term-time 62%</u>
Network job fairs help circulate CVs to prospective employers.

SPORTS

- Recent successes: volleyball, cricket, women's basketball • BUSA Ranking: 22
Sports Hallam oversees *decent* facilities and supports budding athletes.

SPORTS FACILITIES:
The University hires a lot of local amenities (see Sheffield University) but it also has a fair few facilities of its own: Club Hallam (*state-of-the-art* gym); three fitness suites; two fitness studios; swimming pool; squash courts; tennis; Astroturf pitch; 23 acres of playing fields; three sports halls; sports injury clinic. Costs range from £40-110 a year, non-members can pay-as-they-go. Coaching badges and qualifications can also be studied.

SPORTING CLUBS:
American Football; Boxing; FMC (running); Gaelic Football; Gymnastics; Kickboxing; Korfball; Rifle; Skydiving; Snowboard; Surf; Thai Boxing. **See also Clubs tables.**

ATTRACTIONS: see University of Sheffield

ACCOMMODATION

IN COLLEGE:
- Catered: 3% • Cost: £74-77 (39wks)
- Self-catering: 6% • Cost: £51-58 (39wks)
- First years living in: 80% • Insurance premium: £
Availability: Most 1st years can be housed. Rooms are *pretty well furnished* and well within hiking range of the campuses. Self-catered accommodation has shared kitchens and there are some single-sex flats. Security is *nice and tight*, with CCTV, swipe cards and night patrols.
Car parking: Permit-parking is available at some halls.

EXTERNALLY: see University of Sheffield
- Ave rent: £48
Availability: The house-hunting season before term is a good time to find the right place to hole up in. *Eccleshall Road is a popular area.*
Housing help: The Housing and Accommodation Centre provides lists of registered accommodation and a database called Online House Search, which allows students to trawl through options according to area, amenities, street name, number of rooms and so on.

WELFARE

SERVICES:
- Lesbian/Gay/Bisexual Society • Part-time Students' Committee • Women's Officer
- Mature Students' Committee • International Students' Society • Postgrad Committee
- Disabilities Committee • Late-night minibus • Ethnic Minorities Society
- Self-defence classes • College counsellors: 15 full • SU counsellors: 3 full/1 part
- Crime rating: !!
The Union Advice Centre has drop-in sessions every afternoon.
Health: Independent practice on City Campus (GPs, nurses) and a purpose-built surgery near the Collegiate Crescent campus. 24-hr GP service for emergencies.
Women: Hallam Union Women's Unit offers free attack alarms.
Crèches/Nursery: 74 places (6mths-5yrs).
Disabilities: Access varies between campuses. It's *best* at City campus and there's disabled parking at all sites. Dyslexia support is *excellent*.

FINANCE:
• Ave debt per year: £2,829 • Access fund: £1,250,000
• Successful applications/yr: 1,691
Support: Hillsborough Trust memorial bursaries, a international prize, scholarships and hardship funds. A loan of £50 cash or food vouchers is available in *extreme emergencies*.

Sheffield City Poly
see Sheffield Hallam University

Sheffield City Polytechnic
see Sheffield Hallam University

• *The College is part of the* University of London *and students are entitled to use its facilities.*
(1) School of Oriental & African Studies (SOAS), Thornhaugh Street, Russell Square, London, WC1H 0XG Tel: (020) 7898 4034 E-mail: study@soas.ac.uk
Website: www.soas.ac.uk
SOAS Students' Union, Thornhaugh Street, Russell Square, London, WC1H 0XG
Tel: (020) 7637 2388 E-mail: study@soas.ac.uk Website: www.soasunion.org
(2) Vernon Square Campus, Vernon Square, Penton Rise, London, WC1X 9EL
Tel: (020) 7074 5100

GENERAL

With students from over 100 nations and the occasional foreign royalty, SOAS is *a diverse and highly respected institution*. It's part of the central complex of the University of London in Bloomsbury, *which makes it convenient for students wanting to wallow in the luxury of University of London Union's (ULU's) services*. Directly over the road is the University's Senate House and Birkbeck College is just round the corner. The whole caboodle is on the streets parallel to Tottenham Court Road, bang in the middle of London and less than a mile north of Trafalgar Square. SOAS itself is a 30s brick building, *depressingly uniform* and overshadowed by the vast Brunei Gallery (a gift from the Sultan) opposite. Originally a training ground for people about to go off and look after the empire, *the tone is now decidedly post-imperial and right on, though not as much as some students would like.*
For general information on London: see University of London.

Sex ratio (M:F): 42:58	Founded: 1916
Full-time u'grads: 1,970	Part-time: 25
Postgrads: 1,095	Non-degree: 170
Ave course: 3-4yrs	Ethnic: 50%
State:private school: 69:31	Flunk rate: 17%
Mature: 36%	International: 54%
Disabled: 10	Local: n/a

58%
42%

ATMOSPHERE:

SOAS is small enough for everyone to know everyone else, by sight at least. There's a wide mix of religious and ethnic backgrounds, a fascinating example of multi-culturalism. ULU offers an escape from the potential pressure cooker of academic life, as well as being the main source of extra-curricular activity.

SITES:

Vernon Square Campus: Between Kings Cross and Islington, 15 mins from the main site, Vernon Square is *more a few extra square metres for the School to play with rather than a true campus*. It's right next door to some of the School's accommodation and has some administrative departments (including the Registry) and an internet café. Many undergrads have classes in the new teaching rooms here.

LONDON: see University of London

TRAVEL: see University of London

CAREER PROSPECTS:

• Careers Service • No. of staff: 1 full/2 part • Unemployed after 6mths: 8%
SOAS's 'Grad Club' is run by the University's of London's Careers Service. It has a careers library, bulletin boards, interview training and weekly seminars.

FAMOUS ALUMNI:

Zeinab Badawi (newsreader); Dom Joly (Trigger Happy comedian); Jomo Kenyatta (ex-president of Kenya); Enoch Powell (*unmourned* MP); Paul Robeson (singer); Princess Sir-indhorn of Thailand.

FURTHER INFO:

• Prospectuses: undergrad; postgrad; departmental • Open days

ACADEMIC

As the name suggests, SOAS specialises in any course even remotely related to Asia or Africa and, perhaps less obviously, the Middle East. In recent years, there's been a bit of a shift from final exams to coursework.

240-340 POINTS

Entry points: 240-340	**Ave points: n/a**
Applns per place: 8	**Clearing: 4.8%**
No. of terms: 3	**Length of terms: 11wks**
Staff/student ratio: 1:11	**Study addicts: 28%**
Teaching: ****	**Research: ******
Year abroad: 24%	**Sandwich students: 46%**
Firsts: 15%	**2.2s: 22%**
2.1s: 62%	**3rds: 21%**

ADMISSIONS:

• Apply via UCAS
Access courses are run for mature students without the usual qualifications.

SUBJECTS:

Arts/Humanites: 27%
Law & Social Sciences: 39%
Languages & Culture: 34%

Best: Anthropology; Art & Archaeology; Development Studies; Economics; History; Language & Cultures of East Asia/South Asia/South-East Asia/Near & Middle East/Africa/China & Inner Asia/Japan & Korea; Law; Linguistics; Music; Politics & International Studies; Study of Religions.

LIBRARIES:

• 1,500,000+ books • 650 study places

The main library is *impressive* with *a shelf-busting* selection on African and Oriental music and around 4,000 languages represented overall. *Undergrads have complained about the lack of books for them (but they haven't got a strong case) and about the general organisation and opening hours – the planned expansion and computer overhaul should calm them down a bit.* Many departments have their own little libraries.

COMPUTERS:

• 300 workstations • Spend per student: £££

Not as many computers as the students need, but what's there is all sufficiently 21st-century. There's internet access on all lab computers, all computers are multilingual, they all have statistics and economic software and there are network points for laptop users. SOAS was one of the pioneer VLE (Virtual Learning Environment) institutions, meaning students have access to online resources, assessment and academic forums.

OTHER LEARNING FACILITIES:

Five language labs; music rehearsal rooms; recording studio for audio/video tapes; and the Brunei Gallery. The new research centre provides four floors of, um ... research for postgrads and profs.

ENTERTAINMENT

THE CITY: see University of London

Situated in Central London, *local entertainments range from chopsticks in Chinatown to mummy-mooning in the British Library. Not for the faint of wallet however.*

SCHOOL:

• Price of a pint of beer: £1.80

Multi-cultural entertainment is at the heart of SOAS's supply of fun, with visiting acts and troupes from many different nations and traditions. *Drinking and clubbing play a half-hearted second-fiddle.*

Bars: *During the day, the bar is relaxed and informal and provides a good melting pot for the School's cultural combo. Evenings are a dead loss as the bar shuts by 8.30pm, but luckily everywhere outside is just waking up.*

Film: The film society does its stuff once a week.

Music venues: Many bands perform – the majority of them are Asian and African, though other nationalities get a look in. Scala, the Palestinian Society, hosts Arabic parties, but *hardcore clubbers go elsewhere for a fix (often The Elbow Room in Islington).*

Food: *The JCR Snack Bar is the best value* but there's also a refectory. Another snack bar and *posh* café are to be found in the Brunei Gallery. The Vernon Square Campus has an internet café.

Other: Many of the international clubs provide ents that attract many people from outside the School. There have been Indonesian Gamelan recitals, Laotian dancing, African groups, Capoeira demonstrations, Ghanian drumming, food and music evenings among other stuff. SOAS also has two balls a year.

SOCIAL & POLITICAL

SOAS STUDENTS' UNION:

• 2 sabbaticals • NUS member • Turnout at last ballot: 28%

The SU has students assigned to watch every aspect of School life, but has had its bust-ups with the authorities, including a bout of wrist-slapping which ended in the SU having its bar taken away. Campaigns, when they happen, stir the masses, Stop the War being a recent biggie.

SU FACILITIES:

A shop; snack bar; newsagents; crèche; jukebox; pool tables; games machines.

CLUBS (NON-SPORTING):

Aikido Society; Anime; Boat Club, Global Image Society, Japanese; Nippon Kempo; Palestine Society; Roots; Stop the War; T'ai Chi & Meditation. **See also Clubs tables.**

OTHER ORGANISATIONS:

The New Spirit is published independently and monthly.

RELIGIOUS:

• 3 chaplains (RC, CofE, FC)
Muslim prayer room on campus and pretty much everything else around the city.

PAID WORK: see University of London

• Job bureau • Paid work: term-time 25%: hols 50%
Students use the University's of London's facilities. *In any case, London's a fiesta of part-time work opportunities.*

• BUSA Ranking: 48
The budget goes elsewhere and the School's facilities don't stretch past squash courts and a gym. Students do have access to the ULU's *fancy* facilities when the sporting bug grabs them. For most SOAS students, *sports are for relaxation rather than rivalry.*

SPORTING CLUBS:

See Clubs tables.

ATTRACTIONS: see University of London

ACCOMMODATION

IN COLLEGE:

• Self-catering: 27% • Cost: £95-108 (30/50wks)
• Insurance premium: £££
Availability: SOAS uses 11 different residences of varying quality for students to rest their heads. It sounds a lot but only two, right next to the Vernon Square Campus (20 mins walk from the main site), actually belong to the School. Two others are run by a private outfit and the rest are the University's of London's intercollegiate halls, which are shared by colleges all over London (and which include an all-female hall). New students get priority, *but there are no guarantees. Accommodation can seem prison-like sometimes, but not as cheap* (and there's a £200 deposit for the School's halls).
Car parking: *Hahaha, that's a good one.*

EXTERNALLY: see University of London

• Ave rent: £125
Housing help: The Student Accommodation Adviser and ULU provide a *respectable* amount of help getting those hard-to-find places to hang one's hat.

SERVICES:
- Lesbian/Gay/Bisexual Society • Mature Students' Society • International Students' Society
- Postgrad Society • Disabilities Officer • College counsellors: 2 part
- SU counsellors: 1 full • Crime rating: !!!!!

Students solve health quandaries via the University of London Hospital. There's a crèche on campus and advice to be had from tutors. For mobility-impaired students, *access is okay, but there are still many annoying little oversights*. CCTV and undercover police have been attempting to do something about soft drugs (*stopping them, that is, not procuring them*).

FINANCE:
- Ave debt per year: £2,444

Fees: Postgrads pay £6,530 at present. Full-time fees for international students are £9,500.
- Access fund: £141,000 • Successful applications/yr: 181 • Ave payment: £6,000

Support: There are a number of funds, such as the hardship fund for EU/overseas students, and bursaries, such as those from the Zoroastrian Studies Fund and Opportunity Bursaries for disadvantaged UK undergrads. Access funds are available *if students' pennies are feeling the pinch*.

Solent

see Southampton Institute

South Bank University

- *Formerly South Bank Polytechnic.*
(1) London South Bank University, 103 Borough Road, London, SE1 0AA
   Tel: (020) 7928 8989 Website: www.lsbu.ac.uk
   London South Bank University Students' Union, Keyworth Street, London, SE1 6NG
   Tel: (020) 7815 6060 E-mail: su.general.@lsbu.ac.uk Website: www.lsbu.org
(2) East London Campus, Faculty of Health, Whipps Cross Hospital, Leytonstone, London, E11 1NR Tel: (020) 7815 4747
(3) Essex Campus, Faculty of Health and Social Care, Harold Wood Road Hospital, Gubbins Lane, Romford, Essex, RN3 0BE Student Council, as above
   Tel: (020) 7815 5908

The South Bank is one of London's most *vibrant, exciting, beautiful* and *culturally sophisticated* areas. LSBU's main campus is $\frac{1}{2}$ mile away in Elephant & Castle. The immediate surroundings are *drab and depressing*. The *worst* is the *lurid* crimson Elephant & Castle Shopping Centre, voted by the London Design Festival as the 5th Ugliest Landmark In London. *It can feel cheated of the top spot.* A £1.5bn regeneration of the area has been announced – *all very exciting, but unlikely to have any effect beyond builders and roadworks before 2010*. For the time being, LBSU is made up of a number of buildings, *jostling for space and including humungous* new Keyworth Centre, which is *massively impressive*.

Sex ratio (M:F): 39:61	**Founded: 1892**
Full-time u'grads: 8,830	**Part-time: 6,565**
Postgrads: 1,655	**Non-degree: 4,720**
Ave course: 3yrs	**Ethnic: 48%**
State:private school: 96:4	**Flunk rate: 20%**
Mature: 21%	**International: 18%**
Disabled: 425	**Local: 70%**

61%
39%

ATMOSPHERE:

LSBU is a serious university, full of a diverse range of students from all sorts of weird and wonderful backgrounds. They've been out in the real world and, more so than anywhere else, they really are here to study. The flip side of this is that, in the kindest way possible, there's not much atmosphere at all. To most ends, it's not much more than an eductional facility for students who generally commute from all over town.

SITES:

Part of the Faculty of Health & Social Care is spread across four sites – Erlang House (Southwark), East London Campus, Stanmore and Essex Campus.

LONDON: see University of London
• City centre: $1\frac{1}{2}$ miles
Elephant & Castle: The South Bank is *great*, but the rest of Southwark, while starting to feel some of the knock-on regeneration, is still *pretty grim and grotty*. On the other hand, it's *cheaper than norf London and not quite so packed with media types with silly haircuts and too much money.*

TRAVEL: see University of London
Trains: Mainline trains from Waterloo or London Bridge, both within 10 mins walk or local trains from Elephant & Castle station.
Car: *There are cars everywhere in the Elephant, most of them hurtling around the notorious gyratory system with the scantest of regard for pedestrians. They tend not to hang around, mainly because there's nowhere to park.* Add the fact that the Elephant borders the Congestion Zone and it should be *pretty clear that it's best to leave the motor at home.*
Local: Zone 1 on the Tube: the Bakerloo and Northern Lines pass through Elephant & Castle station (100m from the Southwark Campus) and Thameslink trains serve the train station. Buses: 1, 2, 2A, 12, 45, 53, 63, 168, 133, 148, 171, 176, 188, 199, 344, 355, C10, P3.
Bicycles: The students union encourages bikes and there's a bike shed, *although convenient railings around campus are apparently more popular. London's trademark smog makes two-wheel take-up scarce.*

CAREER PROSPECTS:
• Careers Service • No. of staff: 7 full/3 part • Unemployed after 6mths: 9%
The Job Shop arranges placements and keeps students posted of vacancies.

FAMOUS ALUMNI:
Simone Callender (Commonwealth gold medallist for judo); Jimeoin (comedian); Nick Leslau (property developer); Norma Major (former PM's wife); Bridget Prentice MP (Lab); Greg Searle (Olympic oarsman); Phil Spencer (Location, Location, Location); Jerszy Seymore (Milan-based fashion designer).

FURTHER INFO:
• Prospectuses: undergrad; postgrad; international; courses • Open days • Video
For more admissions info see www.apply.lsbu.ac.uk

ACADEMIC

The University has *carved its niche* in teaching vocational and techie courses to mature and local students. That said, it covers *a broad base* of subjects and is *strongest* on education and nursing.

Entry points: 140-240	Ave points: 140
Applns per place: n/a	Clearing: 30%
No. of terms: 2	Length of terms: 15wks
Staff/student ratio: 1:20	Study addicts: n/a
Teaching: *	Research: ***
Year abroad: n/a	Sandwich students: 10%
Firsts: 11%	2.2s: 39%
2.1s: 39%	3rds: 9%

140-240 ... **POINTS**

ADMISSIONS:

• Apply via UCAS/GTTR for Teaching/NMAS for Nursing

A Widening Participation Programme is aimed at mature students without formal qualifications. A summer school gets students up to speed if they need it and a Credit Prior to Learning scheme (APL) turns work or other life experience into academic points.

SUBJECTS:

Arts & Human Sciences: 15%
Business, Computing & Information Management: 25%
Engineering, Science & Built Environment: 22%
Health & Social Care: 38%
Best: Anatomy & Physiology; Business & Management; Civil Engineering; Economics; Education; French, German, Iberian Studies; Health Studies; Hospitality; Media Studies; Molecular/Organismal Bioscience; Nursing; Politics; Psychology; Town Planning.

LIBRARIES:

• 450,000 books • 1,500 study places • Spend per student: ££

The Perry Library in Southwark is open seven days a week; the one on Essex campus is open six days.

COMPUTERS:

• 1,750 workstations

The Learning Resource Centre at the main campus runs IT courses available to all students. Almost all students' rooms have internet access, too.

OTHER LEARNING FACILITIES:

Language labs, a CAD lab. A new arts and media centre (including recording studios) are pencilled in for the Elephant and Castle re-development.

ENTERTAINMENT

THE CITY: see University of London

• Price of a pint of beer: £2.20 • Glass of wine: £2.60 • Can of Red Bull: £1.80

Cinemas/Theatres/Music: There's the IMAX cinema, the NFT and all the other attractions of the South Bank arts complex, including the National Theatre and Royal Festival Hall.

Pubs: *There's no real division between students and locals, so there aren't really any studenty or towny pubs. The most popular are the closest (except the Elephant & Castle). Pushplugs: the Ship and the George on Borough Road; Bridge House, Zanzibar and The Flowers of the Forest.*

Clubbing: Despite being *well past the peak of its popularity*, the Ministry of Sound is on the doorstep, with the *more happening* the Fridge, the popular gay club Heaven, Chunnel Club, The Arches and Cloud 9 all near enough.

Music venues: Brixton Academy is down the road a way, or a couple of stops on the tube. *It may not have the best sound system in the world, but it pulls some big names.*
Eating out: For an *artery-clogging pick-me-up*, students head to Terry's on Suffolk Street, while the *classier* students head to Luperella's on Borough Road or Pizzeria Castello on the other side of the Elephant roundabout. The Nest on London Road is a *popular* caff and Castle Sandwich bar by the station provides *overwhelmingly* filled takeaway baps.

UNIVERSITY:
• Price of a pint of beer: £1.60 • Glass of wine: £2.50 • Can of Red Bull: £1.50
Bars: The Isobar is *as studenty as student bars come*, with bar food, music vids on the telly, a stage area and pool tables. The Tavern is a *more traditional* pub.
Theatres: There'll be a new theatre in place by 2006, but there's no drama society to use it.
Film: The Mushroom Film Society puts on popular flicks *as and when they feel like it*.
Clubs/Discos: Oblivion is the Isobar's classic Wednesday night cheese-fest. Raise the Roof is a garage-themed monthly *spectacular*. Recently spotted on the wheels of steel: Lisa Pin-Up, Drez, Renegade, Iron Mike, DJ Neo.
Food: Canteens and snack bars all over. Both bars do fast food and there's the European Coffee Lounge in Borough Road. *The best bet for actual sustenance is the refectory.*
Other: The Summer Ball and the Athletics Union Ball are the two posh-frock/penguin-suit *blow-outs*.

SOCIAL & POLITICAL

SOUTH BANK UNIVERSITY STUDENTS UNION:
• 5 sabbaticals • Turnout at last ballot: 10% • NUS member
The University and Union are *tucked up nicely together*. The Union is more welfare-based than political.

SU FACILITIES:
Two bars (Isobar doubles as a nightclub); two canteens/coffee bars; five pool tables; meeting room; minibus hire; Endsleigh Insurance; HSBC on site branch and ATM; photocopying/faxing/ printing services; crèche; juke boxes; video games; general store; stationery shop; vending machines; new and secondhand bookshop.

CLUBS (NON-SPORTING):
Arabic; Believers (Evangelical Christians); Chinese; Mauritanian Paradise; Mushoom Film; Pan-African; Rock Central; Special Effects; Sikh; Tamil & Lankan (united, *oddly when you think about it*); Urban Music; Young Socialist. **See also Clubs tables**.

OTHER ORGANISATIONS:
Free monthly Union mag (Scratch).

RELIGIOUS:
• 2 chaplains (RC, CofE) • 2 prayer rooms and a Buddhist temple nearby

PAID WORK: see University of London
• Job bureau • Paid work: term-time 60%; hols 75%
Vacancy lists are published in the Union and at the Job Shop.

SPORTS

• Recent successes: rugby; table tennis; women's volleyball; men's badminton
• BUSA Ranking: 46
Despite a low ranking in the BUSA championship there's been a recent haul of medals and a BUSA award for 'Most Improved University for Sport'. They know there's a fair marathon ahead before they become the 'Loughborough of the south' but have shown willing by investing in the almost Stalinist-sounding Academy of Sport, Physical Activity & Well-being to oversee all things sweaty. *Well, most things.*

SPORTS FACILITIES:

25 acres of sports fields, including: seven football pitches; hockey and rugby pitches; three cricket pitches; four tennis courts; netball and basketball courts; sports hall; gym; aerobics studio. There's a £30 annual fee to use the facilities and sport clubs charge £5 yearly subs. There's a swimming pool in the Elephant & Castle sports centre, but most students would rather take a plunge in the Thames.

SPORTING CLUBS:

Aikido; Ju-Jitsu; Table Tennis; Wu-Shu-Kwan (Chinese boxing). **See also Clubs tables.**

ATTRACTIONS: see University of London

The Oval, home of Surrey CCC, is about 10 mins walk away.

A C C O M M O D A T I O N

IN COLLEGE:
- Self-catering: 16% • Cost: £71-89 (40wks)
- First years living in: 45% • Others living in: <1% • Insurance premium: ££££

Availability: All four halls (1,400 places) are *in walking range* of the campus. Rooms are arranged in flats with pay-as-you-talk phones, internet access and some en-suite facilites. There are *only* six specially adapted rooms for disabled students though. Despite being the oldest, smallest and cheapest, the New Kent Road hall is *prided* for its community feel, pool tables and BBQ veranda. However, some of the newer ones, such as McLaren Hall (600 en-suite rooms, *conveniently placed* between the campus and Waterloo) are *quite swish*.
Car parking: No spaces, only drop-off points.

EXTERNALLY: see University of London
- Ave rent: £55-80

Availability: South London is cheaper than north, but the Elephant itself *isn't the best place to live*, although some *grin and bear* it. Camberwell, Kennington and Oval are the most popular.
Housing help: Staff at the Accommodation Office dole out leaflets and keep an approved landlord list.

W E L F A R E

SERVICES:
- Lesbian/Gay/Bisexual Society • Women's Officer
- International Students' Officer • Disabilities Officer
- Self-defence classes • Nightline • Taxi fund
- College counsellors: 4 full/2 part • Crime rating: !!!!

Welfare support from the Personal Development Advice Unit.
Health: A doctor's surgery opposite Southwark campus.
Crèches/Nursery: 52 places for ankle-biters, 6mths-5yrs, for £135 per week.
Disabilities: Newer buildings are fully adapted for access, although in the older parts of campus it *can be a bit of a struggle*. Two dyslexia officers are available.

FINANCE:
- Ave debt per year: £1,703 • Access fund: £1,000,000 • Ave payment: £250-400

Support: LSBU has one of the largest Access funds in the UK, but, with lots of students from backgrounds not exactly typical of more middle-class universities, *it needs it*. There are also lots of sports scholarships (£3,000), the Governers Charitable Fund, the Lawrence Burrow Scholarship (£1,000 grants for ten Asian/West Indian students) and the Minerva Scholarship (£20,000 for Built Enviroment Students).

South Bank Polytechnic

see South Bank University

Southampton Insitutute

Southampton Institute, East Park Terrace, Southampton, SO14 0YN
Tel: (023) 8031 9039 E-mail: enquiries@solent.ac.uk Website: www.solent.ac.uk
Southampton Institute Students' Union, Students Union Building, East Park Terrace,
Southampton, SO14 0YN Tel: (023) 8023 2154 E-mail: suadmin@solent.ac.uk
Website: www.sisuonline.co.uk

GENERAL

Southampton is the *wizened old sea dog* of the south coast. It's *salty, not particularly pretty and it's even got the scars* to prove it tangled with the Luftwaffe during World War II. There's *lots to see* in the surrounding countryside – the Isle of Wight to the south; to the west lies the ancient, 145 sq-mile New Forest; beyond the forest is Bournemouth, which is the *closest to Miami that England does (not very close at all, but there's a beach and a few bars)*; to the north lie the ancient cathedral towns of Salisbury and Winchester; and to the east lies Southampton's *fearsome rival*, Portsmouth. The Institute's located at a *modern* campus in the middle of Southampton, set apart from the very centre of town by *big* gardens – *perfect for chilling out in the summer*. The second site, which does merchant navy training, is 9 miles up the coast at Warsash.

The institute's been given the go-ahead to call itself a university but as yet hasn't decided on a name. *No, they probably won't appreciate answers on a postcard.*

Sex ratio (M:F): 59:41	**Founded: 1984**
Full-time u'grads: 8,525	**Part-time: 1,740**
Postgrads: 260	**Non-degree: 2,066**
Ave course: 3yrs	**Ethnic: 12%**
State:private school: 96:4	**Flunk rate: 15%**
Mature: 24%	**International: 12%**
Disabled: 329	**Local: 25%**

(41% / 59%)

ATMOSPHERE:

Southampton's a *gentle, pleasant* enough place to live, *but the fun doesn't come neatly packaged and left by the front door.* Fortunately, for students who go looking for it, there's the *best part* of 30,000 *partners in crime* (including the University population) and the locals have learned to put up with the droves of students. The Institute campus is *busy, although not necessarily with* academic work – watersporters are particularly noticeable, *taking full advantage* of the Solent. There's a *tight* community feel and *everyone knows everyone else's business. The campus is less twitchy at weekends.*

SITES:

Warsash Maritime Centre: A merchant navy training centre, with practical and watersports facilities.

Southampton: see University of Southampton
• City centre: 400m

TRAVEL: see University of Southampton

Being closer to the city centre than the University the institute is handy for local bus and train stations.
College: A coach service run by the Institute connects the main campus with Warsash.
Taxis: Several ranks close to Institute. Typical journey, city centre to the 'burbs costs £5-7.
Bicycles: *Good* bike facilities on campus and bike sheds at halls. Cycle routes through city and parks. The city centre around the Institute is *generally fairly flat*.

CAREER PROSPECTS:

• Careers Service • No. of staff: 3 full/6 part • Unemployed after 6mths: 9%

FAMOUS ALUMNI:

Ed Dubois (yacht designer); Peter Long (CEO, First Choice holidays); Jenny Packham (fashion designer); David Quayle (the Q in B&Q).

FURTHER INFO:

• Prospectuses: undergrad; postgrad • Open days

A C A D E M I C

The Institute specialises in vocational courses. Its specialities include business, technology, media arts and maritime courses.

Entry points: 100-260	Ave points: n/a
Applns per place: 3	Clearing: 13%
No. of terms: 3	Length of terms: 13wks
Staff/student ratio: 1:22	Study addicts: 8%
Teaching: *	Research: *
Year abroad: 1%	Sandwich students: 9%
Firsts: 4%	2.2s: 36%
2.1s: 50%	3rds: 8%

ADMISSIONS:

• Apply via UCAS

A widening participation programme is in place.

SUBJECTS:

Faculty of Media, Arts & Society: 33%   Southampton Business School: 36%
Faculty of Technology: 31%
Best: Building, Land & Property Management; Business Management; Civil Engineering & Construction; Film; Fine Art Valuation; Leisure; Sport & Tourism;
Unusual: Computer & Video Games; Fine Arts Valuation; Football Studies; Watersports Studies & Management; Yacht & Powercraft Design.

Sussex University has the sunniest campus in Britain.

LIBRARIES:

• 232,000 books • 836 study places • Spend per student: ££

The Mountbatten libraries are on the city campus. *Students' demand is a touch higher than the libraries' ability to supply.*

COMPUTERS:

• 1,100 workstations • Spend per student: ££££

Lots of IT facilities throughout the campus (although only 36 workstations at Warash). Data network and internet points in all student rooms.

OTHER LEARNING FACILITIES:

Language lab with multimedia facilities, towing tank for testing hull designs and, at Warsash, navigational and bridge simulation equipment.

E N T E R T A I N M E N T

THE CITY: see University of Southampton

UNIVERSITY:

• Price of a pint of beer: £1.75 • Glass of wine: £1.75 • Can of Red Bull: £1.50

Bars: *Inventive naming ahoy.* There's the Top Bar (*pubby* and *busy* most days, especially for happy hour), the Bottom Bar (café-style bar/*sociable loitering centre* with hot and cold meals and trendy seating) and, *guess what*, the Middle Bar (chilled-out function room and *pissed-up* sports teams).

Theatres: Central Hall just down the road is also used by Performing Arts students.

Music venues: The occasional local or student band plays the Top Bar.

Clubbing: The Phonic sessions showcase student DJ talent; Unleashed's the Friday night dose of US house and garage.

Comedy/Cabaret: Weekly visits from the Jongleurs comedy club.

Food: Lots of options, from snacky, greasy burgery treats at the Bottom Bar, pizza/pasta/panini from the Works food court and sandwiches from Delice Express. Other cafés do snacks on the hop

Other: Three balls every year (freshers, summer and grad), *and the SU pulls a few more big events out of its hat whenever it gets the urge/cash. The SU ent monkeys are currently scheming to take over Butlins for the Summer Ball this year.*

S O C I A L & P O L I T I C A L

SOUTHAMPTON INSTITUTE STUDENTS' UNION:

• 4 sabbaticals • Turnout at last ballot: 16% • NUS member

SU FACILITIES:

City: three bars; four minibuses for hire; advice centre; two shops (books, stationery, sweets); ATMs (Barclays, NatWest); photo booth; games and vending machines; pool tables; juke boxes; two meeting rooms; satellite TV; dry cleaning. Warsash: shop; bar; refectory.

CLUBS (NON-SPORTING):

Circus; Fine Art; Graphic; Hindu; Journalism; Maritime; Marketing Pool; Officer Training Corps; Socia-Mare (Maritime); Rock; Roleplay. **See also Clubs tables.**

OTHER ORGANISATIONS:

HAVIT's the monthly paper; SIN radio broadcasts across the city every day and SISU student volunteers *muck in* with a load of charitable schemes and causes. The Union has a full-time volunteer co-ordinator. Rag has just been reborn after an absence of several years and *is just getting off the ground.*

RELIGIOUS:
• 3 chaplains (CofE, RC, International)
There's also a multi-faith quiet room.

PAID WORK:
• Job bureau • Paid work: term-time 65%: hols 75%
The SU street team employs students to do promos for the Union. The Jobshop e-mails and advertises vacancies to students after a job. **For work prospects in Southampton: see University of Southampton.**

 S P O R T S

• Recent successes: basketball, boxing, trampolining, yachting • BUSA Ranking: 48
Sport at the Institute falls into the in-tray of Team Solent, a partnership between College and Union: the Institute owns and runs the sports centre, playing fields and watersports centre and provides facilities, the SU runs the clubs and teams. There's a sports scholarship scheme and all sorts of coaching and instructing courses. Sailing is the *big thing* at the Institute, *which regularly trounces* all comers, whether national or international.

SPORTS FACILITIES:

Main site: sports hall; health suite; sailing facilities; two fitness centres (including teaching lab); multigym; circuit training; 12 acres of playing fields 3 miles away; use of squash and tennis courts. Warsash: small sports hall; multigym; sailing/water sports on the Hamble and Itchen. The Institute has links with local sports centres who provide concessionary deals at golf courses, climbing wall, athletics facilities, riding stables, artificial ski-slope and boxing ring.

SPORTING CLUBS:

American Football; Boxing; Capoeira; Cheerleading; Ju Jitsu; Kickboxing; Kung Fu; Racquet Sports; Roller Hockey; Snowboarding; Surf; Triathlon; Wakeboarding & Waterskiing. **See also Clubs tables.**

ATTRACTIONS: see University of Southampton

The Scummers (fans know them as Saints, neutrals as plain old Southampton) play Premiership football *and occasionally hold vicious fights* with arch-rival Portsmouth fans.

 A C C O M M O D A T I O N

IN COLLEGE:
• Self-catering: 27% • Cost: £46-88 (40/48wks)
• First years living in: 60% • Insurance premium: ££
Availability: The *modern* accommodation is dished out to those *who stick their hands up first*, but there's enough to cope with 1st-year demand. Most students reckon it's *a bit pricey*, but they appreciate *tight* security, *cushy* facilities and the proximity to college. Most rooms are en-suite and there are specially adapted disabled flats.
Car parking: A few parking spaces at each hall, far more bike-sheds for pedal pushers.

EXTERNALLY: see University of Southampton
• Ave rent: £45-75
Housing help: The Accommodation Office supplies an accredited housing list, shared with the University.

SERVICES:

- Lesbian/Gay/Bisexual Society • Equal Opps Manager • Women's Officer
- Mature Students' Society • International Students' Society • Late-night minibus
- Self-defence classes • College counsellors: 2 full/3 part • Crime rating: !!!

The Student Support Network co-ordinates helpdesks throughout college, SU, finance and accommodation offices. It brands them all 'Students 1st' centres, *although whether that's a good excuse to queue-jump is uncertain*. The Student Advice Centre is now known as the Source *to funky up welfare awareness*. Newsletter for disabled students, work placements and mentoring scheme for ethnic minorities.

Health: Close links with St Mary's Surgery nearby, which runs *regular* surgeries at halls.
Women: Free personal attack alarms from the Union advice centre.
Disabilities: Wheelchair access to most teaching areas, but some remain inaccessible. The campus is quite compact, which a lot of disabled students find helps. Specialist help with dyslexia and other impairments.
Crime: The Police Liaison Officer helps keep an eye on campus wrongdoing.

FINANCE:

- Ave debt per year: £5,667 • Access fund: £566,763
- Successful applications/yr: 850 • Ave payment: £100-3,500

Support: *A wide range of financial safety nets.* Opportunity bursaries, bridging loans, emergency loans (£50), part-time fee waivers, postgrad bursaries and start-up bursaries. Also scholarships for business, media, arts and society students (£1,000 a year). Sports scholarships help with equipment, training etc.

University of Southampton

(1) University of Southampton, Highfield, Southampton, SO17 1BJ
Tel: (02380) 595 000 E-mail: prospenq@soton.ac.uk Website: www.soton.ac.uk
Southampton University Students' Union, Highfield, Southampton, SO17 1BJ
Tel: (02380) 595 233 E-mail: susu@soton.ac.uk Website: www.susu.org
(2) University of Southampton, Boldrewood Campus, Biomedical Sciences Building, Bassett Crescent East, Southampton, SO16 7PX
(3) University of Southampton, Avenue Campus, Highfield Road, as Highfield campus
(4) National Oceanography Centre, Southampton, University of Southampton, Waterfront Campus,
European Way, Southampton, SO14 3ZH Tel: (02380) 596 666
(5) Southampton General Hospital, Tremona Road, Southampton, SO16 6YD
Tel: (02380) 777 222
(6) Winchester School of Art, Park Avenue, Winchester, SO23 8DL Tel: (02380) 596 900
Winchester School of Art Students' Union, Park Avenue, Winchester, SO23 8DL
Tel: (01962) 840 772

Southampton's the wizened old sea dog of the south coast. It's salty, not particularly pretty and it's even got the scars to prove it tangled with the Luftwaffe during World War II. There *lots to see* in the surrounding countryside – the Isle of Wight to the south; to the west lies the ancient, 145 sq-mile New Forest; beyond the forest is Bournemouth, *which is the closest to Miami that England does (not very close at all, but there's a beach and a few bars)*; to the north lie the cathedral cities of Salisbury and Winchester, and to the east lies Southampton's *fearsome* rival, Portsmouth. The University – *typical of the rest of the city* – has redbrick buildings that survived the war, along with post-war geometric blocks that won awards in the 60s and look *pretty hideous* now, mostly on a landscaped campus, 2 miles from the city centre. The main site is dotted with sculptures including some by Barbara Hepworth.

Sex ratio (M:F): 39:61	**Founded: 1952**
Full-time u'grads: 13,045	**Part-time: 3,305**
Postgrads: 2,900	**Non-degree: n/a**
Ave course: 3/4yrs	**Ethnic: 8%**
State:private school: 81:19	**Flunk rate: 5%**
Mature: 16%	**International: 16%**
Disabled: 446	**Local: 16%**

61%
39%

ATMOSPHERE:
On arrival at Southampton, students tend to turn into unpretentious, vaguely scruffy types no matter what their background. Most of them were white and middle class to begin with, but there's not much attitude about the place.

SITES:
Boldrewood Campus: (1,000 students – Biomedical Sciences) Less than a mile from the main campus is this *large, squat Lego-box* building. Even though it's within *easy* walking distance it's a separate community where the student medics make their own entertainment.
Avenue Campus: (3,000 students – English, History, Philosophy, School of Modern Languages, Archaeology) A short walk from the main campus, served by the University's bus service, housing most arts students, except musicians and artists.
National Oceanography Centre: (600 students – School of Ocean & Earth Science) A purpose-built site taking advantage of Southampton's natural environment. It's 3 miles from the main campus but there's a *regular* shuttle bus service.
Winchester School of Art: (1,000 students – Art) This member of the Southampton family merged with the University in 1996. It's in the *historic* city of Winchester (12 miles from Southampton), maintains a separate identity and is creative and *predominantly* female.

SOUTHAMPTON:
- Population: 217,600 • City centre: 2 miles • London: 74 miles
- Portsmouth: 16 miles • Winchester: 12 miles
- High temp: 22 • Low temp: 3 • Rainfall: 66

Southampton's a gentle, pleasant enough place to live, but the fun doesn't come neatly packaged and left by the front door. Fortunately, for students who go looking for it, there's *the best part* of 30,000 student partners in crime (including the Southampton Institute population). The locals have learned to put up with the droves of students.

TRAVEL:
Trains: Southampton Central offers services to London (£15.45), Bristol (£19.80), Manchester (£38.60) and others.
Coaches: National Express services all over the country, including London (£9.50), Manchester (£26.50) and all points beyond.

Car: The A27 splits for a brief spell into the M27 and the continuing A27 around Southampton. There's also the A31, A33, A36 and A336 and the M3. Parking's *tough in town* and a University permit (£126) *hard to come by*.

Air: Flights inland, to Europe, Ireland and the Channel Islands from Southampton Airport.

Local: Buses are *cheap* and *reliable*, but *infrequent*. Local trains are *regular* with connections all over Hampshire and there are seven stations around the city, *but it's not the cheapest or most practical way of getting around*.

College: Uni-link links the city and the campuses (£1 single/£2 all-day pass). The Union runs a safety bus every evening.

Taxis: *Not a bad way to get around, if you can afford it.* Typical journey, city centre to the 'burbs – £5-7.

Bicycles: *Good* bike facilities on campus and bike sheds at halls. Cycle routes through city and parks. The city centre around the University is *generally fairly flat*.

CAREER PROSPECTS:

• Careers Service • No. of staff: 14 • Unemployed after 6mths: 7%
Careers fairs, vacancy lists, psychometric tests and various others.

FAMOUS ALUMNI:

Laura Bailey (model); Miriam and Guin Batten (Olympic rowers); Roger Black (athlete turned BBC athletics commentator); John Denham MP (Lab, ex-SU President); Jeremy Hardy (comic); John Inverdale (BBC sports presenter); Dominic Mohan (the Sun); Chris Packham (Really Wild Show); John Sopel (BBC correspondent); Lord Tonypandy (former speaker of House of Commons).

FURTHER INFO:

• Prospectuses: undergrad; postgrad; some depts • Open days

A C A D E M I C

Good academic credentials, even with the *young upstart* Southampton Institute hot on the University's heels. *Lots of support* for budding young entrepreneurs.

180-390		POINTS
Entry points: 180-390	**Ave points: 389**	
Applns per place: 7	**Clearing: 9%**	
No. of terms: 2	**Length of terms: 16wks**	
Staff/student ratio: 1:14	**Study addicts: 25%**	
Teaching: *****	**Research: ******	
Firsts: 17%	**2.2s: 24%**	
2.1s: 50%	**3rds: 5%**	

ADMISSIONS:

• Apply via UCAS/NMAS for nursing/GTTR for teaching

SUBJECTS:

Business/Management: 3%	Law: 3%
Chemistry: 1%	Mathematics: 2%
Civil Engineering & the Environment: 2%	Medicine: 6%
Education: 1%	Nursing & Midwifery: 20%
Electronics & Computer Science: 6%	Ocean & Earth Science: 3%
Engineering Sciences: 4%	Physics & Astronomy: 1%
Geography: 2%	Social Sciences: 9%
Healthy Professions & Rehabilitation Sciences: 4%	Winchester School of Art: 4%

Best: Archaeology; Architecture & Design; Art & Design; Business & Management; Civil Engineering; Civil & Environmental Engineering; Economics; Education; Electrical & Electronic Engineering; Electronics & Computer Science; General Engineering; Materials Technology; Maths & Social Statistics; Mechanical, Aeronautical & Manufacturing Engineering; Medicine; Modern Languages; Molecular & Organismal Biosciences; Nursing; Ship Science.

Unusual: Electrical Engineering; Sport Management & Leadership.

LIBRARIES:

• 1,000,000 books • 1,921 sudy places • Spend per student: £

Seven libraries – the main one is the Hartley Library in the centre of the campus. Facilities are *fair to middling*, with *good* opening hours.

COMPUTERS:

• 1,500 workstations • 24-hr access

ENTERTAINMENT

THE CITY:

• Price of a pint of beer: £2.20 • Glass of wine: £2.10 • Can of Red Bull: £2.40

Cinemas: A seven-screen multiplex at Ocean Village. 14-screen multiplex at Leisure World. Harbour Lights is an arthouse/mainstream cinema also in the Ocean Village area. Also has a fortnightly film quiz in the bar.

Theatres: The Nuffield specialises in modern drama, the Mayflower in the touring blockbusters.

Pubs: A *wide* selection, many with extended opening. *Pushplugs: Goblets; the Crown; Gordon Arms; Talking Heads; the Hogshead; the Lizard Lounge; Varsity; the Giddy Bridge. The Crown & Sceptre and the Gate are best avoided.*

Clubbing: *Plenty of sweat-pits, including a few student faves. Pushplugs: Rhino Club (disco/ indie nights); Lennons (rock/indie); Nexus (hip hop, drum 'n bass, alternative nights); Kaos (pop/chart); Frog and Frigate (cheesey classics).* The Hobbit is *legendary* for its massive beer garden and relaxed atmosphere.

Music venues: The Joiners for *middling* indie, the Mayflower and the Guildhall for bigger names (Supergrass, The Vines, Jamelia, Motorhead).

Eating out: *Cheap meal deals at pubs, but loads of other snack-shacks to choose from, particularly around Oxford Street. Pushplugs: Poppadom Express; Goodies Diner (film-themed); Cook House (sarnies, coffee bar); Chutneys (Indian).*

UNIVERSITY:

• Price of a pint of beer: £1.80 • Glass of wine: £1.20 • Can of Red Bull: £1.50

Bars: The Stag's Head (main Union Bar, cap 400) is *fairly pubby.* There's also a sports bar with board games and Twister *for those who need to flex their competitive instincts.* The bar at the School of Art at Winchester has recently been refurbished.

Theatres: A couple of societies put on musicals and mainstream theatre. There's a *once-a-year glitzy extravaganza* at the Nuffield, a professional theatre on the Highfield Campus. There are regular trips to Edinburgh.

Film: The film society puts on three flicks every week, *from mainstream favourites to strange leftfield arthouse numbers.* Membership's £12 a year.

Music venues: The West Refectory receives touring bands with 800 *sets of open arms.* Recent shows from The Thrills, Athlete, Spiritualized and the Wildhearts.

Clubbing: *Big* nights at the Cube (cap 1,800) with rock, urban and *the ubiquitous cheesefests* during the week. Occasional DJ sets from *national names* (eg. Grooverider ShyFX, Judge Jules, Scratch Perverts).

Comedy/Cabaret: Weekly comedy nights at the Bridge *with ribs tickled* by John Ryan, Sarah Kendall, Craig Campbell and more.

Food: Hot/cold fodder and *the best hot chocolate for miles* at the SUSU café. Bar snacks at the Bridge and school dinners at Piazza. *More choice around the campuses than a gastronome could shake Michael Winner at.*

Other: Graduation ball and faculty balls throughout the year.

SOCIAL & POLITICAL

SOUTHAMPTON UNIVERSITY STUDENTS' UNION:
• 5 sabbaticals • Turnout at last ballot: 10%
The *left-leaning*, NUS-shunning Union Council tries to rouse some political interest and *stretches the net a little wider* than moping about top-up fees. *They don't seem to be able to whip up a righteous fervour for the ballot box, though.*

SU FACILITIES:
Dry cleaners; hairdressers; guarded cloakroom; lockers; photo booth; pottery studio; minibus; two bars; café; cheap driving school; showers and baths; launderette; market stalls each Monday; sports equipment and hire service; Barclays, HSBC, Lloyds and Natwest banks/ATMs; TV rooms; Interflora; darkroom; meeting rooms; customised disco; ballroom; retail centre with a shop; travel agency; and sports shop.

CLUBS (NON-SPORTING):
Well over 100 including: AIESEC; Archaeology; Art; Asian; Astronomical; Buddhist; Concert Band; Hellenic; Hindu; Juggling; Lodge; Malaysian; Massage; Radio; Singapore; Students Against NUS; Students For NUS; Wessex Films; Wine; Women's Safety. **See also Clubs tables.**

OTHER ORGANISATIONS:
The SU mag Wessex Scene comes out every 3 weeks. Surge radio broadcasts on AM and the web. SUSU rag does the fundraising number and SCA (community action) make an effort in the local community.

RELIGIOUS:
• 3 chaplains (CofE, FC, RC)
There are many faiths represented in Southampton, with a mosque, Hindu temple, Gurdwara and Christian places of worship for most denominations.

PAID WORK:
• Job bureau • Paid work: term-time 60%; hols 70%
As well as *the usual gamut* of bar and shop slog, students can *rake in the cash* at the boat show in the summer. The job shop, Openings, matches students to taskmasters.

SPORTS

• Recent successes: windsurfing, sailing, rifle, fencing, equestrianism • BUSA Ranking: 16
The Athletic Union funds 74 flavours of sporting society, making use of *decent* facilities in the area. A SportRec card (£45) gives year-long sporting access.

SPORTS FACILITIES:
On campus there's a large sports hall, six squash courts, climbing wall (outdoors), judo room, table tennis, aerobics room, tennis courts, snooker room and, after all that, an injuries clinic. New indoor sports centre with swimming pool, badminton court and gym. Off campus there are 90 acres of playing fields, a rifle range and a boatyard. The city adds a golf course, dry ski slope, bowling green and a cycle track.

SPORTING CLUBS:
10-Pin Bowling; American Football; Baseball; Caving; Fives; Gliding; Hang-gliding; Kickboxing; Kite Surfing; Lacrosse; Lifesaving; Rifle Club; Sky Diving; Snooker; Snowboarding; Surfing; Triathlon; Water Polo; Waterskiing; Windsurfing. **See also Clubs tables.**

ATTRACTIONS:
The Scummers (*as rivals Portsmouth know them – fans know them as Saints, neutrals as plain old Southampton*) play Premiership football *and occasionally hold vicious fights with arch-rival Portsmouth fans.* Hampshire CCC play at the Rose Bowl, and Cowes Week sees *rich folk swan around* the Solent in boats.

ACCOMMODATION

IN COLLEGE:

- Catered: 6% • Cost: £75-119 (32wks)
- Self-catering: 44% • Cost: £49-£125 (39-51wks)
- First years living in: 85% • Insurance premium: ££

Availability: All 1st years who get the forms back on time are guaranteed a place in halls for their troubles. *Most of the halls are liveable-in, although some more so than others.* Glen Eyre student village is close to the campuses and *good craic*. Connaught Halls *also get a thumbs up*.

Car parking: Permit needed, 1st years aren't allowed cars.

EXTERNALLY:

- Ave rent: £55 • Living at home: 7%

Availability: It's *very easy* to find accommodation – *two days' search max to find somewhere (though if it takes longer, don't come crying to Push)*. There's *some good housing* about, particularly around Portswood, Highfield and Bevois Valley, *within staggering distance* of the *best* student pubs. Avoid some parts of Swaythling, Bassett Green and Bitterne *which are about as welcoming as a Strangeways reception committee. Students should also avoid letting anyone convince them to sort it out too long in advance.* Landlords shove up prices and charge for renting over the summer. *It takes guts, but this is the time to wait and hold on till the landlords are a little more anxious to fill their places.*

Housing help: The University accommodation office in Winchester is developing a full private rented sector property service. In Southampton all landlords are asked to produce safety certificates before they can have their property advertised. The Union has a vacancies board.

WELFARE

SERVICES:

- Lesbian/Gay/Bisexual Society • Women's Officer
- Mature Students' Society • International Students' Society
- Postgrad Society • Late-night minibus • Self-defence classes • Nightline (8pm-8am)
- College counsellors: 7 full • Crime rating: !!!

Health: Two health centres. The University health service at Highfield has five GPs and three nurses.

Crèches/Nursery: 108 places for ages 2-5yrs.

Disabilities: *Reasonable* access and residences for students who need care assistance. The Learning Differences Clinic looks out for dyslexics, dyspraxics and anyone else who needs extra help.

FINANCE:

- Ave debt per year: 4,360 • Access fund: £672,000 • Successful applications/yr: 1,458

Support: In addition to the access fund, the University runs a hardship fund for people whose circumstances change mid-course. SUSU also gives short-term emergency loans.

South West Polytechnic

see University of Plymouth

University of St Andrews

University of St Andrews, Education Liaison Office, Admissions Reception, Butts Wynd,
St Andrews, Fife, KY16 9AJ Tel: (01334) 462 245
E-mail: ed-liaison@st-andrews.ac.uk Website: www.st-andrews.ac.uk
The University of St Andrews Students' Association, St Mary's Place, St Andrews, Fife,
KY16 9UZ Tel: (01334) 462 700 E-mail: union@st-andrews.ac.uk
Website: www.yourunion.net

GENERAL

The *postcard-perfect vista* of the Scottish east coast is home to St Andrews, oldest
university in Scotland and beaten only to the same title in England by Oxford and
Cambridge. The University buildings – which occupy a large amount of town-space – reflect
the heritage, spreading from the 15th century to the modern day to some *classic* 16- and
17th-century architecture. Just as a large part of the town is university, a large number of
inhabitants are students, accounting for a third of the population. *The town is so small that
it's more like one big campus. St Andrews has been unfairly classed as a dumping ground
for Oxbridge rejects – both the town and the University may be pint-size, but they're
certainly not featherweight.*

Sex ratio (M:F): 41:59	Founded: 1413
Full-time u'grads: 5,940	Part-time: 465
Postgrads: 1,005	Non-degree: 1,000
Ave course: 4yrs	Ethnic: 14%
State:private school: 67:33	Flunk rate: 14%
Mature: 23%	International: 31%
Disabled: 150	Local: n/a

(59% ♀ / 41% ♂)

ATMOSPHERE:
*Tradition oozes from every crack in the stonework. Student life is peppered with ritual,
ceremony and a healthy drizzle of custom dating back to the darkest recesses of history.
The town itself is a small, quiet place, and the University follows suit. It's easygoing, laid-
back, with none of the frenetic urban pace of Glasgow or Edinburgh. There's little hostility
between locals and students, mainly because the University is the major local employer.
Many students work alongside locals in the town, which is difficult to cross without bumping
into a familiar face. All in all, it's as cosy as cocoa.*

ST ANDREWS:
• Population: 18,000 • City centre: 1 mile • London: 371 miles
• Dundee: 13 miles • Edinburgh: 55 miles
• High temp: 19 • Low temp: 0 • Rainfall: 55
*Mix golf and history and you've either got the most boring lesson ever, or something like St
Andrews. With six courses, including the oldest in the world, the town attracts Rupert Bear
look-alikes like students to a traffic cone. The history part is what brings the tourists in,
flocking over to soak up the tradition that drenches the place, and to enjoy the magnificent
scenery and architecture. The cathedral and the castle are the most photogenic chunks and*

although shops and tea rooms are geared toward the tourist trade decent clothing stores and internet caffs are beginning to crop up too. It's a three-street urban oasis flanked by sandy beaches, rocky coast and countryside. Oh, and golf courses.

TRAVEL:

Public transport is thin on the ground *so it can feel cut off from the outside world.*
Trains: Leuchars station is 5 miles from the main University buildings with direct lines to London (£53.45), Dundee and Edinburgh. For other services, passengers (*sorry, customers*) must change at Edinburgh or Dundee.
Coaches: National Express coaches run from Dundee, 13 miles away, to London (£32), Glasgow (£11) and beyond.
Car: A915 south, A91 west to M90 (to Edinburgh).
Hitching: *Difficult to get from St Andrews to anywhere. Better from Edinburgh (A1) or Dundee if thumbsters can get there.*
Local: Buses every half hour but rarer at night, *although they're quite cheap* (£1.40). *St Andrews is generally small enough to walk everywhere.*
University: Late night minibus (Friday till 1.40am).
Taxis: *A taxi ride into Leuchars is expensive at £8;* some firms offer student discounts.
Bicycles: *The best way to get around short of a chauffeur-driven limo. St Andrews is small and quite flat with limited traffic.*

CAREER PROSPECTS:

• Careers Service • No. of staff: 8 full • Unemployed after 6mths: 9%
Careers library, bulletin boards and interview practice programme. Also a regular newsletter and a bundle of online resources.

FAMOUS ALUMNI:

Sir James Black (Nobel Prize scientist); Crispin Bonham-Carter (*drippy* BBC period drama actor); Hazel Irvine (sports presenter); Edward Jenner (discovered smallpox vaccination); John McAllion (MP for Dundee); Madsen Pirie (Adam Smith Institute); Siobhan Redmond (actress); Alex Salmond MP (SNP); Fay Weldon (writer and feminist). Former Rectors (elected by students) include Rudyard Kipling and John Cleese, who advised students not to let their degrees get in the way of their education. HRH William, the pin-up prince, will soon be leaving these hallowed halls.

SPECIAL FEATURES:

Donning an undergrad gown gets students free entry to the castle. *Surely some kind of ID card would be easier?*

FURTHER INFO:

• Prospectuses: undergrad; postgrad; departmental; alternative • Open days • Video

A C A D E M I C

Like other Scottish universities, 1st years study more than one subject (usually three), and streamline their study in the 2nd or, for arts students, 3rd year.

140-360		POINTS
Entry points: 140-360	Ave points: 320	
Applns per place: 8	Clearing: <1%	
No. of terms: 2	Length of terms: 15wks	
Staff/student ratio: 1:10	Study addicts: 43%	
Teaching: ****	Research: ****	
Year abroad: n/a	Sandwich students: 1%	
Firsts: 14%	2.2s: 13%	
2.1s: 58%	3rds: 2%	

ADMISSIONS:

• Apply via UCAS

Andy's is trying to pull in more locals and international students.

SUBJECTS:

Arts: 65%   Medical Science: 5%
Divinity: 1%   Science: 26%
Best: Cellular & Molecular Biology; Chemistry; Economics; European Languages; Geography; History; Maths &
Statistics; Organismal Biology; Physics; Psychology.
Unusual: Astrophysics; Social Anthropology.

LIBRARIES:

• 951,599 books • 1,046 study places • Spend per student: £££££

Five libraries (two departmental) ensure there's always a place to go to learn stuff. Not at
night, mind you – they close around 10pm weekdays. *The sheer quantity of books is very
impressive for a relative tiddler of a university.*

COMPUTERS:

• 675 workstations • 24-hr access • Spend per student: £££

Rooms have network points and phone lines as standard (requires a *small* annual surcharge
to activate).

OTHER LEARNING FACILITIES:

Language labs, rehearsal rooms, a computer design lab and a debating chamber are all
present and correct for student use.

E N T E R T A I N M E N T

TOWN:

• Price of a pint of beer: £2.20 • Glass of wine: £2.50 • Can of Red Bull: £2
*Even though it's a teeny town, there are a fair few pens to play in. The upside is that big
chains (McDonald's, Starbucks) haven't yet hit the streets. Yet.*
Cinemas: The New Picture House's three screens juggle mainstream releases and culty,
studenty classics (no discounts).
Theatres: Two tiny stages: the Byre Theatre and the Crawford Arts Centre, with occasional
back up from the castle itself.
Pubs: *More pubs drain tourists' wallets than students', but Raisin is cheap and sporty, with
the more upmarket Lizard also a popular haunt. Ma Bell's is generally given a miss by those
trying to avoid the future king and his courtiers. Bet there's a sizeable gaggle of ladies
loitering outside, though.*
Clubbing: *The only swinging clubs here are on the golf course.*
Music venues: Jazzy goings-on at Younger Hall and the Vic Café, which also hosts blues
and folk music. The Gin House has live bands every Thursday.
Eating out: *A wide selection of ethnic eateries (Indian, Mexican, Thai et al). Pubs are often
good bet. Pushplugs: Balaka (Bangladeshi); Vine Leaf (for romantic liaisons à deux); Ziggys
(decent burgers and pizza); North Point (tea shop); Coffee House (15 blends and hotly
tipped bacon sarnies); The Doll's House.*

UNIVERSITY:

• Price of a pint of beer: £1.50 • Glass of wine: £2 • Can of Red Bull: £1.70
Bars: The Union Bar is *the biggie* with the latest licence in town. A new bar for the newly
developed halls is in the offing.
Theatres: *Thesparama.* Dramatoids tread the boards at the local theatres as well as the
campus's Venue 1. Scores of shows make the short trip to the Edinburgh fringe each year
and every student is automatically a member of the Mermaids drama soc.
Film: Three film clubs show a range of flicks from arty to mainstream and Manga. Free to
members.

Music venues: The Union Theatre doubles as a gig venue, and has hosted the likes of Toploader, Mull Historical Society and Snow Patrol.

Clubbing: Three weekly club nights compose the night scene of the whole city, with *popular cheesy Fridays* and other events pulling in the locals. Judge Jules, Toby Anstis and the ever-ready Pat Sharpe have itched and scratched here.

Comedy/Cabaret: Fortnightly comedy gigs have drawn Al Pitcher, Andy Zaltsman and John Oliver to perform. *It's a textbook touring talent stop.*

Food: The Main Bar includes a restaurant which *doles out everything from snacks to full feasts that can only be described as canteen style.* The Old Union coffee bar also deals in nibbles.

Other: *Black tie events are as common as wombles. Between them, socs, halls and faculties hold about one a week.*

SOCIAL & POLITICAL

UNIVERSITY OF ST ANDREWS STUDENTS' ASSOCIATION:

• 4 sabbaticals • Turnout at last ballot: 27%

The SASA is made of two parts: the Student Representative Council (SRC), which does all the shouting, and the Students' Services Council (the Union), which dishes out services. *The SRC ditched the NUS in 1979 and has been going solo ever since.*

SU FACILITIES:

The Union building has three floors of facilities and more dotted across campus: three bars; cafeteria; fast food joint; snack bar; travel agency; general shop; Royal Bank of Scotland ATM; TV lounge; launderette; photocopying; photo booth; payphones; fax service; printing service; two minibuses for hire; sexual health clinic; games & vending machines; six pool tables; snooker table; juke box; five meeting rooms; two conference halls; parking.

CLUBS (NON-SPORTING):

American; Amnesty; Archaeological; Astronomy; Ballroom Dancing; Breakaway Hill Walking; Catholic; Charities Campaign; Chinese; Cocktail; Comedy; Christian Music & Drama; Conservative Unionist; Drinking; French; Gilbert & Sullivan; Hispanic; Hindu; Islamic; Italian; Internet; James Bond; Jazz; Left Wing; Live Music; Marxist Alliance; Medical; Mermaids (drama); Middle Eastern; Model UN; Musical Theatre; One World; Pagan; Project Anime; Real Ale; Rocksoc; Scottish Hellenic; Student Nationalist; Tree & Frog; War-games; Welsh; Whisky; Wired; Women in Art; Wine. **See also Clubs tables.**

OTHER ORGANISATIONS:

The award-laden Saint is the 50p bi-weekly independent paper competing for attention with union-run The Vine, which is churned out once a month. There's the *very active* Student Voluntary Service (SVS) and the Rag, Scotland's *most successful*, raises at least £35,000 every year. There's also the Kate Kennedy Club (named after the niece of the University's founder), a *strangely* all-male charitable group.

RELIGIOUS:

• 8 chaplains (CofS, CofE, Episcopalian, Eden Fellowship, RC, Baptist)

The University chaplaincy, city churches, meetinghouses, and cathedral cater for most types of Christianity. An Orthodox rabbi is also available and there's a Muslim prayer room.

PAID WORK:

• Job bureau

Advertises local vacancies – *mainly involving gimping for golfers (caddying) and other tourist-related hotel and bar work.*

• Recent successes: golf, lacrosse, rugby, squash, hockey • BUSA Ranking: 48
Excellent facilities (especially for golf). Participation and enthusiasm are strong (especially for golf).

SPORTS FACILITIES:

42 acres of sports fields with eight football pitches; three rugby pitches; three all-weather pitches; three squash courts; hockey pitch; cricket wicket; three tennis courts; basketball court; two sports halls; four jogging trails; shinty pitch; ultimate frisbee pitch; multigymn; climbing wall; aerobics studio; running track and golf course, natch. Facilities have small charges per usage. Watersports, climbing, skiing and riding are all catered for in the nearby area.

SPORTING CLUBS:

Canoe; Gaelic Football; Parachute; Polo; Rifle; Shinty; Soaring; Windsurfing. **See also Clubs tables.**

ATTRACTIONS:

What part of 'six golf courses' don't you understand? Students and locals pay the same rates.

IN COLLEGE:

• Catered: 26% • Cost: £49-117(31-50wks)
• Self-catering: 19% • Cost: £29-75 (36-50wks)
• First years living in: 100% • Insurance premium: £
Availability: The gaggle of 13 halls at St Andrews is dispersed across the *weeny town* so are all within walking distance of everything else. All 1st years are guaranteed walls, floors and ceilings if they meet the housing deadline. Around 20% of the rooms are shared, *so better leave the Celine Dion albums and The Great Mould Experiment at home.* Most accommodation is catered, although *the food could do with a few culinary tweaks.* The gender divide is made literal in a few places, with male/female only wings and floors. *The gorgeous St Salvator's halls are highly in demand because of their lurvely old architecture and central location. CCTV is everywhere, so put your pants back on.* Rents are on a gradual rise but the University has promised no private sector sell-outs for at least 20 years.
Car parking: *Lousy in town.* Permits are dished out only to staff, and the campus area *is usually too damned busy to park.*

EXTERNALLY:

• Ave rent: £77 • Living at home: 7%
Availability: Rentable housing is fairly easy to come by in the town although the lack of parking makes pushes some nests further afield in nearby villages. Prices can get *unpleasant* but there are bargains to be had too.
Housing help: Student Accommodation Service with five full-timers provides vacancy lists, bulletin board, and legal help. The SA and local estate agents are also happy to give a nudge in the right direction.

York University hasn't had a central music venue since the Boomtown Rats (Bob Geldof's old band) played in 1979. The fans danced so hard the building began to slip into the lake.

SERVICES:
- Lesbian/Gay/Bisexual Officer & Society • Ethnic Minorities Officer & Society
- Mature Students' Officer • International Students' Officer • Postgrad Officer & Society
- Disabilities Officer • Late-night minibus • Self-defence classes • Nightline
- University counsellors: 15 full/30 part • Crime rating: !

The Director of Representation is the sabbatical officer to turn to in times of personal or academic cataclysm whereas legal worries can be addressed at a free weekly solicitor's clinic. Student Support Services and the SA Welfare Adviser are also available to tackle students' concerns. Upon arrival, undergraduates can aquire 'student families' who offer academic guidance. *And alcohol, if you're lucky.*

Health: Local health centre with dedicated student practice.

Women: Free attack alarms are available as necessary, *but with the lack of any women's welfare representative, that's pretty much it. Women are in the majority, but Girl Power hasn't landed yet.*

Crèches/Nursery: There is a crèche facility with 60 places for kids aged 3mths-12yrs.

Disabilities: *Access is good in the more modern buildings but pretty hopeless in the listed ones. Residences are better.* Dyslexia sufferers can get extra exam time, one-to-one proof reading, scribes and special computers. There are 52 adapted rooms with wheelchair computer desks and other specialised furniture available.

FINANCE:
- Ave debt per year: £2,681

Fees: International undergrads are looking at upwards of £9,000 in fees. UK or EU postgrads need to cough up around £2,940. No top-up plans.

- Access fund: £180,000 • Successful applications/yr: 522 • Ave payment: £350-500

Support: In addition to the access fund, bursaries and scholarships, the University can provide interest-free loans in extreme cases through the Director of Student Support Services. Mature students have a stab at special bursaries and there's an emergency grant or two for internationals.

St David's College

see Lampeter University

St George's Hospital Medical School, London

- **The College is part of the *University of London* and students are entitled to use its facilities.**

St George's Hospital Medical School, University of London, Cranmer Terrace, Tooting, London, SW17 ORE Tel: (020) 8672 9944 E-mail: medicine@sghms.ac.uk
Website: www.sghms.ac.uk

The School Club, St George's Hospital Medical School, Cranmer Terrace, Tooting, London, SW17 ORE Tel: (020) 8725 5201 E-mail: stuuni@sghms.ac.uk
Website: www.students.sghms.ac.uk

GENERAL

Six miles from Nelson's Column sits one of the few self-contained teaching hospital campuses in London. St George's Hospital Medical School is the only independent medical school in the UK, although it's part of the University of London. Tooting (odds-on favourite for the silliest London district name) hasn't much to distinguish it from anywhere else in the capital other than its Victorian streetlights and the 70s redbrick campus which houses the working hospital and all attendant teaching facilities.

Sex ratio (M:F): 28:72	**Founded: 1752**
Full-time u'grads: 1,620	**Part-time: 1,245**
Postgrads: 30	**Non-degree: 16**
Ave course: 5yrs	**Ethnic: 40%**
State:private school: 67:33	**Flunk rate: 5%**
Mature: 37%	**International: 8%**
Disabled: 181	**Local: 50%**

ATMOSPHERE:

Being at St George's can feel more like being in a hospital than a university, mainly because it is one. The corridors bustle with healthcare professionals, patients, visitors and students and the unique eau de hospital aroma fills the air. But for all the bustle, students are relaxed and approachable with a bar-side manner seemingly at odds with the hectic and debt-crippled lifestyle they're compelled to lead for five or more years. The informal atmosphere (rare in other med schools) and inter-year mixing are missed when students are carted off to other teaching hospitals. As far as town/gown relations go – no one likes students but everyone likes doctors. So Tooting residents don't know what to think.

LONDON: see University of London

TRAVEL: see University of London
Trains: Tooting is the closest station, *though it's not hugely useful*.
Buses: Nos 155, 280, G1 for the main site. 44, 70D, 77, N44, 270, 280 for the nearest Tube.
Underground: Tooting Broadway (Northern).
Car: Outside the Congestion Charging Zone, but very limited parking on or around campus.
Bicycles: Most students live within 10 mins of the hospital, so pushbikes *are particularly popular*.

CAREER PROSPECTS:

It's a vocational institution, so a careers service *is largely unnecessary*, although facilities are accessible at the University of London. A med school employee is on hand for vocational advice.

FAMOUS ALUMNI:

Henry Gray (of Gray's Anatomy fame); Harry Hill (*neckless* comic); Edward Jenner (smallpox vaccine inventor); Mike Stroud (Antarctic explorer); Edward Wilson (accompanied Scott to death in the Antarctic).

SPECIAL FEATURES:

1st years are welcomed in with a mammoth 'Fresher's Fortnight' as opposed to the standard week. *If they can survive such extended alcohol intake, they'll presumably do well as medics.*

FURTHER INFO:

• Prospectuses: undergrad, postgrad • Open days
The SU website has admissions info, as does the University site.

George's is the only med school in London that offers a full range of healthcare education on a single site. Teaching is a combination of classroom and clinic and assessment is based both on written exam and clinical performance. Problem Based and Case Based Learning are an academic focus – students frequently have to 'treat' hypothetical patients, usually other students – *anyone fancy a sponge bath?* Assignments to other teaching hospitals are common. Terms are 10-11 weeks in length – but some can stretch to 15.

Entry points: 220-390	**Ave points: 305**
Applns per place: 29	**Clearing: 9%**
No. of terms: 3	**Length of terms: 10/11wks**
Staff/student ratio: 1:7	**Year abroad: 0**
Teaching: ***	**Research: ******

ADMISSIONS:

• Apply via UCAS

SUBJECTS:

Medical Sciences: 100%
Best: Medicine; Radiography.

LIBRARIES:

• 41,000 books • 650 study places • Spend per student: £££££
The Med school library is open till 10 most nights but closed on Sundays.

COMPUTERS:

• 200 workstations • 24-hr access • Spend per student: £££££
George's halls of residence have computer rooms with web access.

OTHER LEARNING FACILITIES:

There's an audio/TV centre for media buffs as well as Clinical Skills Labs.

LONDON: see University of London

UNIVERSITY:

• Price of a pint of beer: £1.55 • Glass of wine: £1.50 • Can of Red Bull: £1.25
The School Club knows how to throw a party and St George's social life gravitates around the bar. Those who like to go out head to Po Na Na's in Wimbledon or The Works in Wandsworth. Tooting is close to being the curry house capital of London. The Trafalgar Arms is there for students craving stodgy hangover fare.
Bars: The ONLU bar can quench 600 thirsts in one sitting. It's non-smoking, but there's a *cancer veranda* on an adjoining balcony.
Theatres: The Monkton Theatre puts on *scriptloads* of shows each year.
Film: Flicks with faint medical undertones tend to be shown in the bar every so often. Admission: £1.
Clubbing/Music venues: The bar gives stage-room to local and student bands and hosts a bundle of late-licence club nights with the usual cheesy themes.
Comedy/Cabaret: The Georges Medics – *a very popular student review and Edinburgh favourite* – steal the stage at Monkton on a monthly basis.
Food: Peabodies café has recently opened beside the bar offering *a good gossip spot for latte addicts. The NHS canteen is a cut-price favourite.*

Other: A recent reduction in balls because students ran out of tuxedo-money has led to one big event each term, usually at the London Hotel. *The difference is made up by sports and societies dinners though.*

SOCIAL & POLITICAL

THE SCHOOL CLUB:

• 3 sabbaticals • Turnout at last ballot: 30% • NUS member
The SU may have previously been as political as a pencil sharpener and primarily concerned with welfare and facilities but the top-up debate is turning a few hard-hit medical heads.

SU FACILITIES:

Bar; four pool/snooker tables; café; three meeting rooms; two minibuses; gaming machines; juke box; new and secondhand bookshops are run by the Union. The hospital offers a canteen; photocopier; fax service; printing service; payphones; advice centre; general store; stationery shop and vending machines. There's a NatWest on campus.

CLUBS (NON-SPORTING):

Adventure Sports; Curry; Duke of Edinburgh; Hindu; Parachuting; Modern Languages; Real Ale; Revue; Refugee Action; Salsa; Wilderness Medicine. **See also Clubs tables.**

OTHER ORGANISATIONS:

The aptly named Sharp is the *tasteless* bimonthly Union paper. Rag is a big money spinner – Rag Week last year raised £108,000 *just by being daft.* Eight community action groups are managed by a sabbatical officer, who ensures students do their bit for the good of humanity *as well as healing the sick.*

RELIGIOUS:

No chaplain yet. There's a multi-faith prayer room in the hospital and a mosque nearby.

PAID WORK: see University of London

• Paid work: term-time 33%: hols 50%
Advice, suggestions and vacancies are posted on the School Club notice board.

SPORTS

• Recent successes: rugby • BUSA Ranking: 48
Teams have a tendency to linger at the bottom of intercollegiate leagues, although they did bring home the Gutteridge cup – London's premier (and only) Medical School Rugby Tournament.

SPORTS FACILITIES:

Five football pitches; rugby pitch; two cricket wickets; three squash courts; four tennis courts; basketball court; sports hall; gym; aerobics studio; multigym; climbing wall. The fields are found in Cobham, with smaller scale facilities on-site in the Robert Lowe Sports Centre. Oarsmen can wield their blades on the Thames at Chiswick. Sailors can hornpipe their way to Burnham-on-Crouch.

SPORTING CLUBS:

Gaelic Football; Paintball; Rowing. **See also Clubs tables.**

ATTRACTIONS: see University of London

ACCOMMODATION

IN COLLEGE:
- Catered: 2% • Cost: £97 (39wks) • Self-catering: 16% • Cost: £59 (40wks)
- First years living in: 50% • Others living in: 13% • Insurance premium: £££

Availability: 1st year students are guaranteed rooms, either catered in Friendship House or in one of the 13 self-catering University houses on the self-contained St George's Grove Estate (15 mins walk). *It's in need to a lick of paint and a splash of elbow grease (planned) but it's decent enough.* Kitchens are usually shared with 10-20 other people *so plenty of sticky labels wouldn't go amiss.* The site has a *nominally priced* launderette and 24-hr security. Three rooms are set aside for international students.
Car parking: Free permits for those mad enough to want to bring a car. No parking at the hospital. Locked garages are available for bikes.

EXTERNALLY: see University of London
- Ave rent: £65-100

Availability: *Rents around the hospital are reasonable. For London.*
Housing help: see University of London

WELFARE

SERVICES:
- Lesbian/Gay/Bisexual Officer • Mature Students' Officer • International Students' Officer
- Disabilities Officer • Self-defence classes • Nightline • Taxi fund
- College counsellors: 3 full • Crime rating: !!!

Health: *It's a hospital. Go figure.*
Women: Women-only minibus for large Union events.
Disabilities: Facilities are a strong point. *Vocationally speaking, it's advisable to check with the assistant registrar to see if some disabilities are compatible with certain specialities.*

FINANCE:
- Ave debt per year: £4,753

Fees: International students can expect £10,825 in fees.
- Access fund: £90,000 • Successful applications/yr: 51 • Ave payment: £,1500

Support: Bursaries and scholarships available, some from the NHS, plus a fistful of prizes and awards.

St Martin's College of Art

see University of the Arts, London

St Martin's College, Lancaster

see Lancaster University

St Mary's Hospital

see Imperial College London

St Thomas's Hospital

see King's College London

Staffordshire University

* *Formerly Staffordshire Polytechnic.*
(1) Staffordshire University, College Road, Stoke-on-Trent, ST4 2DE
Tel: (01782) 294 000 E-mail: admissions@staffs.ac.uk Website: www.staffs.ac.uk
Staffordshire University Students' Union, Staffordshire University, College Road,
Stoke-on-Trent, ST4 2DE Tel: (01782) 294 629 E-mail: theunion@staffs.ac.uk
Website: www.staffsunion.com
(2) Staffordshire University, Beaconside Campus, Stafford, ST18 0AD Tel: (01785) 353 253
Staffordshire University SU, Beaconside Campus, Stafford, ST18 0AD
Tel: (01785) 353 311

GENERAL

Staffordshire is a fairly gentle part of the north-west Midlands. One site is on the outskirts of
Stafford, a *small and pretty* country town. It's a greenfield campus with some *seriously
uninspiring* 60s buildings, reminding everyone that it used to be a technical college. The
Stoke bit of the University is split over two sites at College Road and Leek Road in the city
centre of Stoke-on-Trent. Leek Road has more of the feeling of a *self-contained* campus
with playing fields and accommodation on site.

Sex ratio (M:F): 51:49	**Founded: 1970**
Full-time u'grads: 9,715	**Part-time: 3,395**
Postgrads: 640	**Non-degree: 2,900**
Ave course: 3yrs	**Ethnic: 12%**
State:private school: 98:2	**Flunk rate: 19%**
Mature: 56%	**International: 13%**
Disabled: 159	**Local: n/a**

49%
51%

ATMOSPHERE:

*The Stoke campus is friendly, artsy and has a warm community feel about it, even in
relations with the locals. A lot of students are on part-time or professional courses.*

SITES:

Staffordshire University Beaconside campus: (5,000 students – Engineering, Business,
Computing, School of Health) *The Stafford site might unkindly be descibed as rather geeky,
although the techies who make up the student population would probably point to a lively
drinking culture to dispute that.*

STOKE-ON-TRENT:

* Population: 240,400 • City centre: $1\frac{1}{2}$ miles • London: 165 miles
* Birmingham: 44 miles • Manchester: 38 miles
* High temp: 20 • Low temp: 0 • Rainfall: 56

STOKE:

Stoke *didn't come out well* from a couple of decades of urban decline. Robbie Williams may
have lived here once, *but he's a lot better off in his mansion in LA.* In Hanley there's a
shopping centre and Festival Park, once the site of the National Garden Festival, an

excellent swimming pool and various other attractions. Like many more run-down places, it breeds *a defiant sort of love* among the students who live there, *but then love is blind. Stoke is the original 'good personality, shame about the legs' town.*

STAFFORD:

Inside every twisted nightmare of urban planning there's a pleasant market town wishing they'd left it alone. Stafford's *no different.* There's a market, *obviously* (although the days of herding livestock are long gone) and a modest shopping centre. *Little to set the heart aflutter, though.*

TRAVEL:

Trains: Stafford and Stoke both connect to London on the Merseyside and Manchester services (£19.45). The main Stoke site is about 500 metres from the station.
Coaches: National Express, including Manchester, Liverpool, Birmingham and London.
Car: The M6 and A34 connect the two towns. Stafford is also served by the A518 and A513.
The A50 provides handy links to Derby and Nottingham. A parking permit is a tenner a term.
Air: MyTravel and BMI fly out of Manchester International.
Hitching: *There's the nearby ringroad at Stoke. The M6 is good for both towns.*
Local: Local buses go to both towns for around a quid.
College: An inter-site bus between Stoke and Stafford campus is free for students, *but most of them wouldn't dream of visiting the other side.*
Taxis: *Loads on offer in both towns.* Grab a cab from the station in Stoke.
Bicycles: This is a *flat* part of the world, so bikes are *popular.*

CAREER PROSPECTS:

• Careers Service • No. of staff: 4 full/10 part • Unemployed after 6mths: 11%

FAMOUS ALUMNI:

Jim Davies (aka a Chemical Brother).

SPECIAL FEATURES:

• Applicants under 21 and resident in Staffordshire, Shropshire or Cheshire are guaranteed an offer depending on the usual entry requirements.
• Staffordshire recently became the UK's first university to open an Art Gallery in New York.

FURTHER INFO:

• Prospectuses: undergrad; postgrad; part-time; departmental • Open days • Video

ACADEMIC

Staffordshire has *flung itself into the millennium with real vigour.* There are all sorts of modern learning facilities, and the teaching is *decent* across a range of *unusual* subjects.

200-300		POINTS
Entry points: 200-300	Ave points: 211	
Applns per place: 5	Clearing: 22%	
No. of terms: 2	Length of terms: 12wks	
Staff/student ratio: 1:20	Study addicts: n/a	
Teaching: **	Research: *	
Firsts 8%	2.2s: 42%	
2.1s 39%	3rds: 11%	

ADMISSIONS:

• Apply via UCAS

SUBJECTS:

Arts, Media & Design: 20%   Computing, Engineering & Technology: 24%
Business & Law: 26%   Health & Sciences: 30%
Best: Art & Design; Economics; Hospitality; Molecular Biosciences; Nursing; Other subjects allied to Medicine;
Philosphy; Psychology; Recreation; Sport & Tourism.
Unusual: Football Technology; Forensic Science.

LIBRARIES:

• 314,811 books • 1,331 study places • Spend per student: £££
The libraries on both sites are open until 3am throughout the week, although *there aren't*
quite enough books to keep students occupied until the wee hours. Online journals take up
the slack.

COMPUTERS:

• 2,420 workstations • Spend per student: ££
IT facilities are excellent and up-to-date.

OTHER LEARNING FACILITIES:

The forensic science department has its own crime house, *nicknamed the House of Horror.*
There's also an *incredible* virtual reality room.

E N T E R T A I N M E N T

THE TOWNS:

• Price of a pint of beer: £1 80 • Glass of wine: £2.75 • Can of Red Bull: £2.50
Cinemas: An Odeon in each town (although the one in Stafford only has three screens) and
a Warner to boot in Stoke. All do student discounts.
Theatres: The Royal in Hanley, the Stoke Repertory Theatre, the New Vic in Newcastle
under Lyme near Stoke and the Gatehouse in Stafford.
Pubs: Most pubs are *student-friendly*, especially those closest to college. *Stoke Pushplugs:*
the Terrace; the Roebuck. Stafford: Bird in Hand; HogsHead; Telegraph; Wagon & Horses;
Potterhouse.
Clubbing: *Pushplugs: Sugarmill, Vodka Nation at Creation.* On the whole, the University-
scene is a better bet.
Music venues: The Darkness have played Sugarmill. *There's not much in Stafford.*
Other: Alton Towers is *just down the road.*
Eating out: *Typical* chain pub offerings. Two meals for a fiver deals are *predictably popular*.

UNIVERSITY:

• Price of a pint of beer: £1.45 • Glass of wine: £1.80 • Can of Red Bull: £1.50
Bars: The Ember Lounge is a *chilled-out*, newly refurbished venue at the College Road
campus. Leek Road has the Leek Road Venue, with a bar and live music due for a refurb
over 05–06. In Stafford there's Legends (nightclub bar), which has a day guise as Sleepers
(coffee bar).
Theatres: The drama and theatre students *entertain the masses* with a couple of
productions per semester.
Music venues: The Leek Road Venue holds the most gigs. Recent visitors include Electric
6, Shed 7 and Kosheen (8?).
Clubbing: *Loads* of club nights at the various bars including Gobble (cheese) and Cheeky
(chart) at LRV. BSE (cheese, rather than beef on the bone) at Legends/Sleepers. Leek Road
has Super Friday and Retrospective.
Comedy/Cabaret: A *hugely popular* comedy night at the Leek Road. It features the likes
of Brendon Burns, Mitch Ben and Toby Foster.
Food: The Terrace (Stafford) and LRV (Stoke) are *the best* eateries, but there are smaller
snack bars around both sites, including Ember Lounge.
Other: A summer ball *finishes each year off in style.*

S O C I A L & P O L I T I C A L

STAFFORDSHIRE UNIVERSITY STUDENTS' UNION:
• 5 sabbaticals • Turnout at last ballot: 15% • NUS member
The SU's responsible for representing, entertaining and looking out for the student body at large. It gets on *very well* with the University and students seem to be *pretty happy* with the job it does.

SU FACILITIES:
Three bars/clubs/venues; three cafés/snack bars; two pool tables; meeting rooms; minibus; Endsleigh Insurance; Lloyds TSB, NatWest and Co-op banks/ATMs (not NatWest).

CLUBS (NON-SPORTING):
Chinese; Myth & Role-play; Radio DJ; Roadtrip; Vampire. **See also Clubs tables.**

OTHER ORGANISATIONS:
Get Knotted is the *high-profile* student paper with a history of pushing for The Guardian awards. GK radio broadcasts every day over the intranet. A community action group helps out in the local area.

RELIGIOUS:
The University has a CofE chaplaincy with several other part-time chaplains. Both towns have churches for all the main denominations. A Muslim prayer room is available at Stafford and there are places of worship in Stoke for Jews, Muslims, Hindus and Sikhs.

PAID WORK:
• Job bureau
Bar and shop work is available in both towns and a University workbank to *help students find it*.

S P O R T S

• Recent successes: hockey, swimming, women's football • BUSA Ranking: 40
There's a wide participation in sports; *some clubs have a higher standard than others, though*. With a football technology degree, sport's on the syllabus as well as off it.

SPORTS FACILITIES:
Stoke: 40 acres of fields; three floodlit synthetic pitches; sports hall; activities studio; fitness suite.
Stafford: 30 acres of fields; two synthetic pitches; sports hall; squash court; fitness suite.

SPORTING CLUBS:
See Clubs tables.

A C C O M M O D A T I O N

IN COLLEGE:
• Self-catering: 2% • Cost: £51-64 (38wks)
• First years living in: 60% • Insurance premium: £££
Availability: Rooms is halls are *fairly plush*. Most are en-suite and *decent* sizes. All are *relatively close* to campus and much accommodation in both towns has been rebuilt in the last 3 years. The newer rooms are disabled-adapted. There's 24-hr security and launderette services too.
Car parking: Parking's *not a problem* at most of the halls.

EXTERNALLY:

• Ave rent: £37-43 • Living at home: 40%
Availability: *Lots* of housing, some of it through the University's private landlord scheme. Shelton (Stoke) is a *student ghetto* near the campuses. Highfields is a *good bet* at Stafford.
Housing help: The accommodation office keeps a register of landlords.

WELFARE

SERVICES:

• Lesbian/Gay/Bisexual Society • Women's Officer
• Mature Students' Society • International Students' Society
• Postgrad Society • Disabilities Officer
• College counsellors: 14 full/1 part
• SU counsellors: 1 full/2 part • Crime rating: !!!
Students are *very impressed* with the welfare provisions. The SU, university tutors and counsellors and a legal clinic help out with all sorts of problems. On-site cop shop (community copper).
Health: Medical centres on both campuses with trained health staff.
Women: Subsidised attack alarms from SU shops.
Crèches/Nursery: Nursery places are available for children up to 5yrs.
Disabilities: *No real problems with access as most of the college buildings are modern or newly renovated.*

FINANCE:

• Ave debt per year: £3,898
• Access fund: £75,000 • Successful applications/yr: 1,385 • Ave payment: £634
Support: Up to 30 Ashley scholarships are awarded to local applicants who face particular difficult circumstances in going to university (financial/social/physical). Hardship loans available.

Staffordshire Polytechnic

see Staffordshire University

Stirling University

(1) University of Stirling, Stirling, FK9 4LA Tel: (01786) 467046
E-mail: recruitment@stir.ac.uk Website: www.stir.ac.uk
Stirling University Students' Association, SUSA Office, The Robbins Centre, University of Stirling, Stirling, FK9 4LA Tel: (01786) 467 166
E-mail: susa@stir.ac.uk Website: www.susaonline.org.uk

(2) Highland Campus, University of Stirling, Department of Nursing and Midwifery, Raigmore Hospital, Old Perth Road, Inverness, IV2 3SG Tel: (01463) 704 315

(3) Western Isles Campus, University of Stirling, Department of Nursing and Midwifery, Western Isles Hospital, Macaulay Road, Stornaway, Isle of Lewis, HS1 2AF
Tel: (01851) 704 704

GENERAL

Stirling is tucked away in the heart of Scotland, surrounded by the *picturesque* scenery of the Southern Highlands and Trossachs. The castle, on a cliff face, *dominates* the landscape and was the royal home in Scotland until 1600. Much of the historic architecture survives in the Old Town. The University is 2 miles out of the city just before you get to the small town of Bridge of Allan *and, like Stirling itself, it's small*. The students, who account for one in five of the local population, have a campus reputed for its beauty and set in 310 acres of landscaped grounds, complete with the 18th-century Airthrey Castle, a golf course and a loch with a bridge, separating the residences from the academic buildings and providing a home for wild fowl *and a fun feature for wild students. Apart from the castle*, which houses departments and offices, *the University's other buildings are less impressive than the setting*. Most (for now) are grey or white flat-topped oblongs, usually three or four floors high, but, shaded with trees, *they blend in somehow*. Meanwhile, the towering Wallace Monument (dedicated to William 'Braveheart' Wallace) presides over the goings on.

Sex ratio (M:F): 36:64	Founded: 1967
Full-time u'grads: 5,950	Part-time: 1,145
Postgrads: 850	Non-degree: 0
Ave course: 4yrs	Ethnic: 3%
State:private school: 91:9	Flunk rate: 13%
Mature: 11%	International: 13%
Disabled: 295	Local: 14%

ATMOSPHERE:

There's a lively feel to Stirling, as if everyone knows exactly where they're going, although they're always prepared to take a detour for a coffee and a chat. Many of the students are sporty – and dress the part in hoodies, jogging bottoms, trainers and baseball caps. The international students (from over 80 countries at any one time) add to the general feeling of laidback, but energetic and cosmopolitan campus life. There's plenty of space to study and relax, especially after the dark Scottish winter passes and students make the most of the natural setting through the summer months. The campus is self-sufficient and many students rarely feel the need to leave – though those that do move out after the first year get on just dandily with the local residents. More than two-thirds of them are Scottish themselves.

SITES:

There are two other sites which are both part of the Department of Nursing and Midwifery.
Highland Campus: (370 students) On the outskirts of Inverness (which can be reached on the regular bus) in the grounds of Raigmore Hospital is the medical school.
Western Isles Campus: (60 students) Accessible only by boat, this part of Lewis Hospital in Stornoway on the island of Lewis is *probably the UK's most remote university site*. Almost all the students are drawn from the local population.

STIRLING:

- Population: 85,220 • City centre: 2 miles • London: 378 miles
- Glasgow: 27 miles • Edinburgh: 33 miles
- High temp: 19 • Low temp: 0 • Rainfall: 79

Up 246 steps, from the top of the Wallace Monument, *the surrounding natural beauty provides some of Scotland's finest views.* But Stirling itself is one of the UK's newest cities, having been upgraded from a town as part of Her Maj's jubilee bash in 2002 – *but it's still a small town by most standards.* Also the newness doesn't apply to the mostly 17th- and 18th-century architecture or *the quaint and traditional* shops selling antiques and crafts. Meanwhile, The Thistle Centre, the city's major shopping area, does the normal high street brands with a few independent outlets too – especially around the Arcade and King Street where there are specialist music shops, bookstores and toy shops.

TRAVEL:

Trains: Stirling Station, 2 miles from campus, has half-hourly direct services to London (£62.35) and the main cities in Scotland, including Glasgow (£5.55) and Edinburgh (£6.30) in under an hour.
Coaches: National Express services to major cities in Scotland and England.
Car: A9 and M9.
Air: It's 1hr 20 mins to Glasgow Airport and 45 mins to Edinburgh Airport, both with flights all over the place, including budget operators such as easyJet and Britannia Direct.
Hitching: *Fairly easy to Edinburgh if you start from the outskirts of town.*
Local: First Buses (Nos 52, 53, 54, 58, 62, 63) operate between campus and the town centre and cost 75p to £1.20. Ferguson Coaches scoot along to the train station and students can hire them for a 20% discount.
Taxis: Taxis are *easy to find* and cost £2.50 to £3 from town to campus. A late night trip in the other direction costs up to a fiver.
Bicycles: *Despite the winter wind and rain, the cheap, green option is increasingly popular on campus.*

CAREER PROSPECTS:

• Careers Service • No. of staff: 13 full/2 part • Unemployed after 6mths: 9%
The *busy* Careers Advisory Service does the business from pre-university, through student life on into graduate careers. Services range from long-range advice to a jobshop for part-time and vacation work. Apart from the usual newsletters and bulletin boards, they do CV clinics, aptitude tests and even a four-day course about what a career in management is all about. *All this attracts quite a few employers to visit to sniff out the talent as graduation approaches.*

FAMOUS ALUMNI:

Iain Banks (writer); Mark Daly (journalist); Catriana Matthew (golfer); Jack McConnell MSP (Scottish First Minister); John Reid MP (Health Secretary); Gordon Sherry (golfer).
The current Chancellor is ex-Avenger Dame Diana Rigg (aka Emma Peel).

FURTHER INFO:

• Prospectuses: undergrad; postgrad; international; some departments; CD-Rom
• Open Days
Open evenings, adult learners evenings and applicants' days can be booked on (01786) 467 046.

A C A D E M I C

Over the years Stirling has been quite cutting edge in its approach to courses. The Film and Media Studies course, for example, just turned 25, making it one of the oldest in Britain. It was the first University in the UK to have two 15-week semesters a year rather than three terms and most courses are modular which means students get to try different things before committing to their main subject. They also use lots of continuous assessment – *good for those who hate exams, bad for those who prefer their efforts to be seasonal.* Some of the latest innovations include the option of starting a degree in February or studying in the evenings. *It also has a good track record for widening access.*

Entry points: 100-340	Ave points: n/a
Applns per place: 11	Clearing: 6%
No. of terms: 2	Length of terms: 15wks
Staff/student ratio: 1:18	Study addicts: 16%
Teaching: ***	Research: ****
Year abroad: 5%	Sandwich students: n/a
Firsts: 7%	2.2s: 41%
2.1s: 20%	3rds: 4%

100-340 **POINTS**

ADMISSIONS:

• Apply via UCAS/CATCH for nursing
DAICE (Division of Academic Innovation and Continuing Education) helps students who've just missed the required grades to bring them up to par and for part-timers and adult learners. *There's also strong links with local schools and colleges.*

SUBJECTS:

Arts: 31%	Management: 36%
DAICE: 2%	Natural Sciences: 8%
Human Sciences: 23%	

Best: Administration & Social Work; Earth & Environmental Studies; Economics; European Languages; History; Politics & International Relations; Social Policy.
Unusual: Criminology; European Film & Media; Freshwater Science.

LIBRARIES:

• 505,000 books • 900 study places
The main University Library, which houses four computing libraries, has *decent opening hours. Unfortunately, the same can't be said for its décor* (soon to be refurbed). There are other little libraries for student teachers and language students and at the Highland and Western Isles sites.

COMPUTERS:

• 950 workstations • 24-hr access
Students can plug into the net from their bedrooms in Murray Hall and Geddes Court (more network points are planned) or surf from their own laptop in the library. There are four IT labs accessible to students (most 24-hr), and the library information centre provides guidance on using University systems.

OTHER LEARNING FACILITIES:

Language lab; state-of-the-art Film & Media Studies newsroom with design and audio-visual editing software and equipment.

ENTERTAINMENT

THE CITY:

• Price of a pint of beer: £1.50 • Glass of wine: £1.80 • Can of Red Bull: £1.20
Before you judge too harshly, remember Edinburgh and Glasgow are less than an hour away. An hour's an hour, though.
Cinemas: The Carlton (Allan Park) has two screens, *but it's not up to much*.
Theatres: The Tollbooth and the Cowane Centre offer stuff from panto to Pinter. Student discounts available at both.
Pubs: *Quite a few are tolerant of, even friendly to, students, but some, such as the Rob Roy and the Caperceilidh, deserve a wide berth.* Pushplugs: The Meadow Park Hotel, aka 'The Med', situated at the bottom of the campus; Hog's Head (for good pub grub); Courtyard; Hydes; The Westerton Arms (in Bridge of Allan). The Whistlebinkies pub is a snug place for a winter warmer.
Clubbing: A couple of *tacky* clubs in town. *The FU Bar and Rocks have student nights on Thursdays.* Beat is Stirling's latest club, offering 3 for 2 drinks and 2 for 1 meals.
Music venues: *Stirling Council have finally realised that castles can be fun.* Stirling Castle now hosts open air concerts, recently Ocean Colour Scene, with more planned. Several pubs have folk nights and the Albert Bar hosts jazz.

> The grounds of Heriot-Watt University contain a disused ticket office, all that remains of Edinburgh's proposed underground train system.

Eating out: *The best food in town is probably to be found in the pubs* but there's the standard range of Indian, Italian and fast food feeders as well. *Pushplugs: Pacos; Smilin' Jack's (both Mexican); Littlejohns (American); Riverhouse (classy joint owned by Carol Smiley's husband); The Bistro.* The Clive Ramsay delicatessen in Bridge of Allan has a café attached. *For fish and chips, the Allan Water Cafe cannot be beaten.*
Other: 10-pin bowling in Stirling at AMF Bowling (Riverside). Hillbillies and Frames provide pool and snooker tables respectively.

UNIVERSITY:

• Price of a pint of beer: £1.50 • Glass of wine: £1.10 • Can of Red Bull: £1.50
Bars: As well as the Robbins Student Centre (the Union building), Stirling's got five other bars. Studio is the newest and largest with a full menu available till 8pm. During the day, its deck is *packed with chompers, chatterers and those just taking in the great view. Inside, the plasma screens, sofas and movie memorabilia, make it popular after dark too.* Tuesdays are 'Karaoke Idol' night and Sunday brings the pub quiz. The club venue Glow has three bars: the Long Bar (*packed at night*), the Cocktail Bar (with, er, cocktails) and the Glow Bar itself. The Gannochy Sports Bar next to the Sports Centre shows big screen sports fixtures and hosts regular film and rock nights to boot.
Theatres: The Drama Society (SUDS) struts the boards of the local Tollbooth Theatre or, occasionally, the MacRobert Arts Centre (equipped with both a 466-seat theatre and 140-seat studio), which also feature touring thesps.
Film: The MacRobert Arts Centre is also *film central* with 20-30 movies a week and a late bar with *top snacks.* It's just £3 a movie for anything from blockbusters to *arty farty* fare.
Music venues: In recent times, Shola Ama, Sophie Ellis Bextor, Wheatus, Idlewild and Shed Seven have performed at the SU's Robbins Student Centre, which has also played host to *less illustrious* local and student bands. Head down to the MacRobert for jazz, funk and classical.
Clubbing: *Glow is the place on campus for dancing, prancing and falling over.* Most nights have a different theme: hip hop, cheese and rock'n'pop from the 60s to 90s. Also, big club names such as Ministry of Sound and Artful Dodger turn up from time to time. The Sports Union nights on Wednesdays and Saturdays, with a soundtrack of cheese and R&B, *gets particularly cramped.* Admission from free to £4.

Comedy/Cabaret: Every few weeks, the MacRobert hosts comedy and cabaret.
Food: Haldanes and The Pathfoot Dining Room are the two main scoff stops, *both good value.* Oscars Snack bar sells *simple* snacks and main meals. Meanwhile, in the Andrew Miller Building, Roberto's serves fast food (pizzas, chips and baked potatoes at £2.50 for a meal deal) and Stir C@fé does *posh but pricey* coffees and sandwiches. The MacRobert Bar sells paninis, snacks and sandwiches, with specials on lunch and pre-theatre menus.
Similar snack fare is available from The Long Bar in the Union (*good smoothies*) and Studio (*busy throughout the day*). Students can buy their grub in bulk at the beginning of each semester by topping up their smart card which also gives them *serious* discounts.
Other: Three balls a year and the *anarchic* 'Final Fling'.

SOCIAL & POLITICAL

STIRLING UNIVERSITY STUDENTS' ASSOCIATION (SUSA):

• 4 sabbaticals • Turnout at last ballot: 15% • NUS member
SUSA has a good record of doing the ents stuff, nabbing a Best Students' Union in Scotland award back in '03, and relations with the University remain just fine.

SU FACILITIES:

As well as the *top notch* bars, clubs and catering facilities (see above), SUSA provides a general shop, print room, photo booth, two meeting rooms, five pool/snooker tables and a bunch of web-based stuff. Royal Bank of Scotland is on campus (with cash machine).

CLUBS (NON-SPORTING):

Chinese; Fairtrade; Hellenic; International; Roleplaying; Scottish Socialist Students; Spanish; Strategy Games, Tenteleni Society (recruits students to work in Africa in the summer); Urban Music; Wildwatchers. **See also Clubs tables.**

OTHER ORGANISATIONS:

'Brig' is Stirling's long-running and award-winning free monthly student paper. Air3 1350 sends out sounds across campus from 11am to 11pm daily. Meanwhile Air TV does pictures too, but only a few times a week in the campus cinema. Stirling RAG's recent readies-raising events have included a bean-eating competition.

RELIGIOUS:

• 6 chaplains (Baptist, RC, CofE, Methodist, Congregationalist, CofS)
The campus chaplaincy is basically Christian, but tries to put others in touch with other faith groups and there's a Muslim prayer room.

PAID WORK:

• Job Bureau • Paid work: term-time 40%; hols 90%
The jobshop is part of the careers service and it finds jobs for quite a few students on campus or in the pubs and restaurants in Bridge of Allan and Stirling. *But local employment is a bit scarce on the ground and so time and money may be needed to heigh-ho it off to Glasgow or Edinburgh.*

SPORTS

• Recent successes: golf, swimming, rugby, football, American football • BUSA Ranking: 3
The successful sports bursary scheme has done the University proud. Apart from notable triumphs in international sports competitions for students, in recent years Stirling has spawned four Olympians, a Paralympian swimming double silver medallist and 11 Commonwealth Games athletes. It's also recently become home to the HQ of the Scottish Institute of Sport.

SPORTS FACILITIES:

23 acres of playing fields including artificial pitches, football pitch, rugby pitch, hockey pitch and all-weather pitch; sports hall; squash courts; two basketball courts; athletics field and running track; loch (for angling, sailing, canoeing *and the occasional skinny dip*); croquet lawn/bowling green; Olympic swimming pool; the Scottish National Tennis Centre; all-weather pitch; multigym; running track; sauna and solarium. In addition to a 9-hole golf course, there's a new Golf Centre with a short game practice area and three target greens. Jogging routes are situated around the campus. The town adds a curling and skating rink, 10-pin bowling and the River Forth. Skiing facilities are close by.

SPORTING CLUBS:

American Football; Cheerleading; Gaelic Football; Kayak; Lacrosse; Ladies' Gaelic Football; Mountaineering; Octopush (underwater hockey); Rowing; Se-No-Kai; Table Tennis; Tenshikan; Ultimate Frisbee; Water Polo. **See also Clubs tables.**

ATTRACTIONS:

Stirling County (rugby), Stirling Albion (football) and a greyhound track.

ACCOMMODATION

IN COLLEGE:

• Self-catering: 52% • Cost: £56-70 (30-50wks)
• Insurance premium: £
Availability: There are 33 chalet bungalows on camplus as well as two off-campus halls (favoured by 1st years and postgrads). There are a further four on-campus halls, which

provide cooking and laundry facilities, TV rooms, games rooms, public telephones and common rooms. *The rooms are basic*, equipped with *standard* furniture and wash basins, *although an ongoing sprucing-up programme is gradually making them all more habitable. Andrew Stuart Hall and Geddes Court are the most lively and popular among 1st years.* Half the 3rd years and postgrads can be housed as well, but 2nd years generally fend for themselves. International students can live in for their whole course. 2% of students have to share. A small number of married couples can be housed, mainly in the 130 *sought-after* off-campus flats maintained by the University. There's a women-only flat, specially adapted facilities for disabled students and 24-hr campus security from what are known as the 'Green Meanies'. After 11pm on campus, students must show their student ID and 1st-year guests have signing in times.

Car parking: No spaces for 1st years, but for others *a permit costs a whopping £65 a year.*

EXTERNALLY:

• Ave rent: £55 • Living at home: 30%

Availability: *Stirling is small and finding a comfy rented pad isn't always easy. Quality varies dramatically. Bridge of Allan, the local friendly town, is most popular. Raploch, Caperceilidh and Cornton less so.*

Housing help: The Union website has an accommodation search facility and the University has seven full- and three part-time home-hunt helpers. Services include an approved landlord list, property vetting, legal advice and a bulletin board.

WELFARE

SERVICES:

• Lesbian/Gay/Bisexual Officer & Society • Women's Officer & Society
• Mature Students' Officer & Society • International Students' Officer & Society
• Postgraduate Officer • Disabilities Officer & Society
• Nightline • College counsellors: 1 full/2 part
• SU counsellors: 3 • Crime rating: !

SUSA provides an Advice & Support Centre which doles out advice as well as condoms and attack alarms. Welfare volunteers help with academic, accommodation and mental health concerns.

Health: The on-campus NHS and Dental Practice has four full-time GPs and one other doctor one day a week and offers sexual health surgeries.

Crèches/Nursery: The Bright Beginnings Nursery is next-door to the University and looks after kids from 6wks-5yrs, where, with help from the Council, some spaces are subsidised. The Psychology Department also runs a playgroup for children from just under 3-5yrs.

Disabilities: *The campus designers have really given access some serious thought.* Rooms and facilities have been adapted, lifts have been installed and doorways have been widened. Lecture theatres have induction loops and help is available for students with dyslexia. The Disabilities Officer is there to iron out other creases. Stirling has been nationally recognised for spot-on IT provisions to assist disabled students.

Crime: *Almost none – safe as houses.*

FINANCE:

• Ave debt per year: £1,990

Fees: International full-timers pay £7,660 for class-based courses or £9,500 lab-based.

• Access fund: £139,900 per year • Successful applications/yr: 370
• Ave payment: £200-500

Support: The University distributes hardship loans or non-repayable bursaries to students who have received their full loan but are still finding it difficult to make ends meet. These are administered by SISS (the Student Information and Support Service) which also provides financial advice. Among other scholarships for international, local and UK/EU students, The Stirling Minds Fund bails out students with the brains but not the bucks.

Stockton

see Durham University

University of Strathclyde

(1) University of Strathclyde, 16 Richmond Street, Glasgow, G1 1XQ
    Tel: (0141) 552 4400 E-mail: scls@mis.strath.ac.uk Website: www.strath.ac.uk
    University of Strathclyde Students' Association, 90 John Street, Glasgow, G1 1JH
    Tel: (0141) 567 5000 E-mail: admin@theunion.strath.ac.uk
    Website: www.strathstudents.com
(2) Jordanhill Campus, University of Strathclyde, 76 Southbrae Drive, Glasgow, G13 1PP
    University of Strathclyde Students' Association, Jordanhill Campus, 76 Southbrae Drive,
    Glasgow, G13 1PP Tel: (0141) 950 3256

GENERAL

Strathclyde University is situated on a number of hills slap in the middle of Glasgow and right in the city's central business district. The campus is modern *and fairly brutal, having hit a few branches of the ugly tree on the way out of the architect's office, but it blends inconspicuously with the rest of this part of the city.* The original University building, an *out-of-place redbrick construction, is quite lost* among more modern post-60s structures. The *compact* campus consists of *large* department buildings and tower blocks and is being rapidly developed and re-developed. The 'merger' with Jordanhill College created a second site housing the Faculty of Education.

Sex ratio (M:F): 44:56	**Founded: 1796**
Full-time u'grads: 11,530	**Part-time: 2,510**
Postgrads: 2,875	**Non-degree: 0**
Ave course: 4yrs	**Ethnic: 10%**
State:private school: 90:10	**Flunk rate: 15%**
Mature: 16%	**International: 17%**
Disabled: 179	**Local: 70%**

ATMOSPHERE:

For every student of Glasgow University taking an artsy non-vocational course, there are about ten at Strathclyde intent on gathering CV points and winding up richer than their parents. The vast majority are from the West of Scotland, *blend seamlessly into the Glaswegian backdrop and don't look at university life in the same way as international or English students might – for them it's a case of turn up, tune in, get out.* Many get here and are reunited with school friends, so there's a ready-made social life to drop into. The Union fosters new friendships with many screamingly drunken nights on the schedule, and an emphasis on getting involved in extra-curricular activity. *Music and club nights are relentlessly arranged, although the lactose-intolerant would do well to be wary of all that cheese.*

SITES:

Jordanhill Campus: (2,000 students – Applied Arts, Education, Social Work, Speech & Language Therapy) Formerly Jordanhill College, the *green and leafy* site is 5 miles from the main John Anderson campus in Glasgow's largely residential West End. It has *good* sports facilities mainly used for teaching, a bar, library, computer rooms and the new Crawford Auditorium, which doubles as a multimedia performance space. There's a high proportion of mature and female students. *In theory Jordanhill is completely integrated with the main campus, but in practice it functions almost autonomously.* There's not much need for students to travel between campuses, but there's a free bus for those who want to – *presumably more out of curiosity than anything else.*

GLASGOW: see University of Glasgow

TRAVEL: see University of Glasgow
Trains: Queen's Street and Central Stations are the mainline stations and run regular services to London, Edinburgh, Birmingham and other major cities.
College: The shuttle bus links John Anderson Campus and Jordanhill eight times a day till 5pm.
Bicycles: Steep hills and good local transport links make bikes unnecessary at John Andersen campus, though the University is keen to encourage cycling. *Jordanhill isn't half as mountainous as both bits of its name sound.*

CAREER PROSPECTS:

• Careers Service • No. of staff: 5 full/3 part • Unemployed after 6mths: 7%
A Government Charter mark for the past 5 years commends facilities: 24-hr online help; website; special needs services as well as for international, disabled and mature students. Several job fairs offer permanent/summer positions, plus the *enormous* annual Work Fair. The service opens 1-5pm Tue-Fri.

FAMOUS ALUMNI:

Belle & Sebastian (posterchildren of lo-fi pop); Craig Brown (former Scotland football coach); Malcom Bruce MP (Lib Dem); Michael Connarty; Ian Davidson; Dougie Donnelly (sports commentator); Maria Fyfe; Tom Hunter (founder of Sports Connection); James Kelman (Booker-winning author); Helena Kennedy QC; Paul Laverty (Cannes-winning screenwriter); John Logie Baird (inventor of TV and *picnic-stealing friend of Bubu*); John McFall, Jim Murphy (Labour MPs); Yvonne Murray (Olympic runner); Andrew O'Hagan (author); Lord Reith (BBC founder); Elaine Smith (actress); Tartan Amaebas (band); Teenage Fanclub.

SPECIAL FEATURES:

The Hunter Centre for Enrepreneurship unique to Strathclyde allows students to combine entrepreneurial studies with any degree.

FURTHER INFO:

• Prospectuses: undergrad; postgrad; departmental; international • Open days • Video
See online for prospectuses, e-mail scls@mis.strath.ac.uk for open day info. The Arts and Social Sciences departments run faculty afternoons (*baby open days*). The alternative prospectus is available in cassette form, call (0141) 548 2814.

A C A D E M I C

Strathclyde employs every teaching method you could shake a stick at, and then some. The University has embraced the potential of cyberspace as a learning environment alongside more traditional classroom teaching. Courses are directed towards employability – hence the small number of graduates who don't find careers quickly. The Hunter Centre, founded on the premise that having ideas generates money, has kick-started many a student business. Recent departmental mergers have been making waves, with concerns that students may suffer from a lack of teaching staff.

160-360 | **POINTS**

Entry points: 160-360	Ave points: n/a
Applns per place: n/a	Clearing: 10%
No. of terms: 3	Length of terms: 12wks
Staff/student ratio: 1:17	Study addicts: 20%
Teaching: ***	Research: ****

ADMISSIONS:

• Apply via UCAS
Strathclyde is big on widening access to those who might not consider university. Representatives also go off to exhibitions around the world to net more international students. Entry requirements are *highly flexible* for mature students – there's a Mature Student Guide with details.

SUBJECTS:

Arts & Social Science: 18.5%   Engineering: 19.5%
Business: 25%   Science: 22%
Education: 15%
Best: Politics.
Unusual: Elective classes in Entrepreneurship; Highly specialised Education courses; Undergrad-level Journalism; Forensic Biology; Prosthetics; Orthotics.

LIBRARIES:

• 900,000 books • 2,260 study places
In addition to the main Andersonian library, there are some smaller departmental ones and the one at Jordanhill (the biggest education library in Scotland). *The main library is starting to look a bit raggy* but the large number of laptop plug-in points, extended opening hours in exam periods and the *psychedelically decorated* Orbit Café *more than make up for any aesthetic issues.* The Royal Scottish Geographical Society keeps a collection of rare books and manuscripts here.

COMPUTERS:

• 750 workstations
Networked PCs are dotted all over the various departments *but there aren't really enough to go around.* Business School students are eligible for free laptop loans *to help them look the part when sat on the train.* All student bedrooms are networked. The University flirted with 24-hr access for a while, *but most students slept through it.*

OTHER LEARNING FACILITIES:

Language labs are open to all. There's also a design lab, rehearsal rooms and a film and TV studio. Drama students get the *magnificent* Ramshorn Theatre to frolic in. Strathclyde's not afraid of technology when it comes to learning methods, pioneering the Personal Response System (PRS), where as many as 350 students in one lecture can express their views through personal handsets – *just like on Who Wants to be a Millionaire?* The Centre for Academic Practice offers study skill seminars and workshops.

ENTERTAINMENT

THE CITY: see University of Glasgow

UNIVERSITY:

• Price of a pint of beer: £1.50 • Glass of wine: £1.25 • Can of Red Bull: £1.50
When they're not out and about in fun-crammed Glasgow (especially in the nearby Ark pub), Strathclyders have so much going on in the Union it's amazing they don't die of liver failure.
Bars: *Thank the heavens for Scottish licensing laws. The vast Union's six bars keep the pumps pumping till 3am most nights. Sunday closing in many gives students a chance to calm down and dry out.* The Barony is *pubby and popular – not least on account of DJ Phil's infamous TFI Friday.* The newly refurbished Gameszone is really a pool hall with beer

but the 26 tables draw in a *huge* daytime crowd. There's also: Darkroom (*baguettes by day, bops by night*); Bubble Lounge (*baguettes by day, chill-out zone by night*); The Priory (*beer by day, more beer by night*, non-smoking) and the University-run Lord Todd. Toby's Bar at Jordanhill has theme nights almost every evening and *serves a wicked breakfast*.

Theatres: The Ramshorn Theatre hosts productions from the award-winning Strathclyde Theatre Group as well as well as a range of touring, professional and student productions. Trips to the Edinburgh Fringe are regular events.

Film: The *passionate* Film Society shows *a huge variety of films from blockbusters to art house* as well as films made by its members. Classic movies are also shown in the debating chamber.

Music venues: The Union has a *good reputation*, especially for giving a kick-start to local bands and it's also hosted the likes of East 17, The Bluetones, Travis, Wheatus and The Cheeky Girls. Every bar in the Union building is equipped for big sounds from big names, and Vertigo in particular is a conference suite moonlighting as a mosh-pit.

Clubbing: At least three club nights a week, spread between the Barony, the Darkroom and Vertigo. I Love 1970 is the Darkroom's Friday night retro-fest and the Barony's Thursday cheese platter *is pretty appetising too*.

Comedy/Cabaret: Fortnightly comedy in the Bubble Lounge has included visits from Phil Kaye, the Reverend Obediah Stepperwolf and Hugh Lennon and his Hypnodog.

Food: The food courts in the Darkroom and the Bubble Lounge offer traditional stodge and curries, while Delice de France does *healthy* baguettes. *Burgery junk* is to be had in the Gameszone, while the Lord Todd serves a range of traditional, veggie and international cuisine till 2pm.

Other: The Sports Ball is the biggest and most regular; many departments have their own dos. Freshers week is also pretty social. Christmas all-nighters (8pm-8am) aren't unknown. Jordanhill has its own May Ball on campus.

SOCIAL & POLITICAL

UNIVERSITY OF STRATHCLYDE STUDENTS' ASSOCIATION:

• 6 sabbaticals • Turnout at last ballot: 13% • NUS member

The SA's *tightly organised and intimately involved* with the concerns of the student body. It offers a phenomenal number of commercial services and is good in student development (like the National Student Learning Programme). It's in no way party political, but that's not to say it isn't strongly concerned with ethical and democratic issues – there's been a recent ban on smoking in The Priory Bar and an embargo on Nestlé products in the SA building. The Deputy President is based at Jordanhill and spearheads a committee responsible for issues at that campus.

SA FACILITIES:

The Association's ten-floor building houses: six bars; nightclub/music venue; café; fast food outlet; pool tables; six meeting rooms (including LGB and women's rooms); minibus and car hire service; Endsleigh Insurance office; NatWest bank with three ATMs; payphones; photocopier; photo booth; fax and printing service; advice centre; gaming and vending machines; jukeboxes; travel agency; general and stationery shops; secondhand bookshop; conference suite. Jordanhill has: bar; coffee shop; tea bar; welfare office; USSA office and campus shop.

CLUBS (NON-SPORTING):

007; Accounts; Basil Brush; Beer; Business & IT; Chemical; Chemical Engineering; Chinese; Chocoholics Unanimous; Computer Science; Debates; Electronic & Mechanical Engineering; Hellenic; History; Historical Combat; International Business & Modern Languages; Irn Bru Appreciation; Laser Combat; Law; Malaysian; Marketing; Orgasm (Organisation of Goths and Student Metallers); Pharmacy; Politics; Product Design; Prosthetics & Orthotics; Role Playing; Singaporean; Scottish National Party; Scottish Hotel School; Tennant's Lager Appreciation; Turkish; Web-Soc; Winnie-the-Pooh; Welcome Team. **See also Clubs tables.**

OTHER ORGANISATIONS:

The SA's Strathclyde Telegraph comes out every three weeks and has a circulation of around 5,000. It's an *impressive* publication and was awarded the Herald Student Newspaper of the Year award a few years ago. Fusion radio station survives on an intermittent FM licence and broadcasts on the internet. The sabbatical-run charity Rag is *very active*, generating £56,850 of philanthropic cash last year. They organise a range of events, from urban abseiling to battle of the bands. Cactus is a Community Action Group that specialises in working with single parent kids.

RELIGIOUS:

• 8 chaplains (Scottish Episcopal, CofE, URC, RC, FC, Methodist, Baptist), rabbi
The Chaplaincy service (St Paul's building) has a chapel, library, common room and ARK café and caters for most flavours of biblical faith, plus Muslim and Jewish students. A number of International Student Chaplains work at the centre also. *It's a pro-active service with* a busy calendar of speakers, art exhibitions, ceilidhs and films. See also University of Glasgow

PAID WORK: see University of Glasgow

• Job bureau
The careers service has a database of part-time and vacation opportunities. There are several jobs going in the University doing bar work and the like. The Union keeps its own vacancy board.

• Recent successes: women's athletics, cross country, badminton, men's rugby, sailing, curling • BUSA Ranking: 30
Sport at Strathclyde is as much a social activity as a competitive one but they still have their fair share of almighty victories. A University member took home an Olympic gold medal in curling in 2002. In November 2003 Strathclyde scooped all the trophies for sailing they had going at the Student Yachting World Championships. There are 42 sporting clubs and counting.

SPORTS FACILITIES:

45 acres of playing fields; sports centre with gym and multigym; six squash courts; swimming pool; aerobics studio. Jordanhill's facilities include: astroturf and grass pitches; six badminton courts; swimming pool; fitness suite and weights room. Membership of the USSA is a one-off £20 fork-out that includes accident insurance. Nature's gifts to the University include a lake and the River Clyde for watersports.

SPORTING CLUBS:

Aikido; Boxing; Handball; Kickboxing; Parachuting; Rowing; Shinty; Snowsports; Surfing/Windsurfing; Tukido; Xtreme Street Sports (BMX and skateboards); Zhuan Shu Kuan. **See also Clubs tables.**

ATTRACTIONS: see University of Glasgow

IN COLLEGE:

• Catered: 4% • Cost: £50 (37-50wks)
• Self-catering: 12% • Cost: £47-73 (37wks) • Insurance premium: ££££
Availability: Accommodation is limited to full-time students coming from over 25 miles away. 1st years who meet these criteria are guaranteed a room *but not necessarily a nice one*. 40% of 2nd years can also live in. Most halls are in the campus village with shop and launderettes in the city centre, another 400 students are placed within walking distance of the Merchant City area. The University has two flats in the city for married couples – *families aren't so lucky and have a lengthy wait on their hands before any of the few three-bed flats 14 miles away become available.* Halls are divided into flats shared between four and eight people, 20% with en-suite study bedrooms. *The flat system can be a barrier to social*

mingling and those living in James Goold Hall have to quickly become fans of the bagpipes if August is to be endurable.
Car parking: Patrick Thomas Court has 12 spaces, allocated on a first come, first parked basis. 45 spaces are available at Andrew Ure. Permits not required.

EXTERNALLY: see University of Glasgow
• Ave rent: £55
Housing help: The University helps find private housing and there is a Glasgow-wide student housing website.

WELFARE

SERVICES:
• Lesbian/Gay/Bisexual Officer & Society • Women's Officer & Society
• Mature Students' Officer & Society • International Students' Officer & Society
• Postgrad Officer & Society • Disabilities Officer & Society
• Late-night/Women's minibus • Self-defence classes • Nightline
• College counsellors: 2 full/5 part • Crime rating: !!
The ASK4 service in the Union has two student advisers to help with personal, academic, housing and financial problems.
Health: The Student and Occupational Health Service runs a daily clinic and weekly family planning clinic. Glasgow Royal Infirmary is a block away and the Dental Hospital 15 mins walk.
Women: Attack alarms sold for £1.
Crèches/Nursery: The SA crèche on the John Anderson campus is free of charge for students' children aged 3-5yrs. Kidcare Ltd runs a custom-built nursery facility for pre-school children on a paying basis.
Disabilities: The hills around John Anderson make access tricky and those with mobility problems *should visit before applying.* Disabled students are guaranteed University accommodation and rooms can be specially adapted according to individual needs. Six of the Union building's ten floors have wheelchair access, though there are some rooms in various buildings which still present problems. For the partially sighted/dyslexics the Special Needs Service's Technology Support Officer assists in getting and using specialist software and equipment. There are speaking lifts with Braille buttons.
Crime: The arrival of CCTV has *heavily reduced* crime in the campus village but there are still regular incidents of theft from student rooms, mainly because of open windows.

FINANCE:
• Ave debt per year: £3,372
Fees: Scottish students have £2,000 to pay, but not till they graduate, thanks to the Scottish Graduate Endowment Fund. International and postgraduate fees vary from school to school.
• Access fund: £8,000 • Successful applications/yr: 1,000 • Ave payment: £400
Support: Sports bursaries of up to £1,000 are available from the University (with Glasgow City Council). The Royal and Ancient Golf Club awards £1,500 bursaries to the rising stars of golf. The Mature Student's Bursary fund helps with childcare costs. Also other hardship funds and short-term loans available.

Sunderland University

- *Formerly Sunderland Polytechnic.*
(1) The University of Sunderland, Edinburgh Building, Chester Road, Sunderland, SR1 3SD
Tel: (0191) 515 3000 E-mail: student-helpline@sunderland.ac.uk
Website: www.sunderland.ac.uk
University of Sunderland Students' Union, Wearmouth Hall, Chester Road, Sunderland,
SR1 3SD Tel: (0191) 514 5512 E-mail: sac@sunderland.ac.uk
Website: www.sunderlandsu.ac.uk
(2) St Peter's Campus, Chester Road, Sunderland Tel: (0191) 515 3000

GENERAL

Way up on the map, just south of Newcastle, on the north-east coast of Blighty sits the city
of Sunderland, a *sprawling* industrial port that forms part of the Tyne & Wear conurbation.
Or so it was. It's still a port and hasn't moved, but it has had *a face-lift, getting the botox
treatment* from such attractions as the Stadium of Light, the National Glass Centre,
Sunderland Marina, Riverside Regeneration, Winter Gardens, the Metro and Crowtree
Leisure Centre. Most of the rest of the city centre was shoved up in the 60s *and looks like
it.* It is, however, close to the Northumbrian coast, the moors and two of Europe's biggest
shopping complexes, Gateshead's Metro Centre and Newcastle's Eldon Square (see
Newcastle University). Sunderland University itself is scattered across the city like someone
dropped it, across three areas that you might call campuses with other splinters all over the
city – more than 40 buildings in all. The Chester Road campus in the city centre is
composed of early 60s tower blocks *which match most of the city's architecture in style and
complete lack of aesthetic appeal.* The St Peter's campus, by the river, *is more attractive.
Like the city itself, the University is investing, building and starting to look smarter.*

Sex ratio (M:F): 44:56	Founded: 1901
Full-time u'grads: 7,570	Part-time: 6,230
Postgrads: 1,560	Non-degree: 5,227
Ave course: 3yrs	Ethnic: 38%
State:private school: 97:3	Flunk rate: 27%
Mature: 47%	International: 20%
Disabled: 16	Local: 61%

ATMOSPHERE:
*The University makes a specific point of attracting local students and for many in this once
deprived corner of the country, it can be a life-changing experience. Neither the city nor the
Uni will win any beauty contests (they've won architecture awards, but that's something
different altogether) but they make up for it in friendliness, enthusiasm and perky hedonism.*

SITES:
St Peter's Campus: (7,000 students – Business, IT and Media) This is the *more attractive*
campus, a recently expanded cluster of five buildings, some of which actually won the
Sunday Times Buildings of the Year award back in 1995.

SUNDERLAND:

- Population: 280,800 • City centre: 200m • London: 257 miles
- Newcastle: 10 miles • Durham: 13 miles
- High temp: 19 • Low temp: 0 • Rainfall: 54

No one would claim this is an architecturally appealing city – unless they were an architect – but as we've said, it's on the up. There are two museums, some *interesting* bridges and, a little way inland, the Penshaw Monument, *a big folly that looks like a Greek temple and can be seen for miles around.* As can the Angel of the North a bit further away outside Gateshead.

TRAVEL:

Trains: Sunderland station is 10 mins walk from the Chester Road campus. There are direct trains to Newcastle, Middlesbrough (£3.95) and London (£47.50) and connections to the rest of the country.

Coaches: Blueline and National Express services to many destinations including London (£25.50) and Manchester (£17.50).

Car: 8 miles off the A1(M) on the A123, A19 and A690.

Air: Newcastle International and Teesside Airports are both under an hour's drive away.

Hitching: *Good prospects once out of Sunderland, particularly on the A1 heading north or south.*

Local: The Newcastle Metro Link now runs to Sunderland (and back again) taking in Gateshead on the way. *It's punctual, clean and has proved a godsend for easing traffic.* A return journey costs around £4 and there are several stops around Sunderland itself including 'University Park'. *Buses are cheap* (fares from 20p) *and quite reliable*.

College: A free campus bus service runs between all key University buildings and halls of residence.

Taxis: *Sunderland is small, so taxi fares are pretty cheap.* The Union has struck a deal with Station Taxis where if you hand over your Union card to the driver, the Union is billed the next day. Pay back your fare and get your Union card back.

Bicycles: There are bike lanes between Consett and the coast and between Sunderland and Whitehaven in Cumbria. *Problems with theft are decreasing, but there aren't many secure places to leave bikes in town.*

Ferries: From Newcastle and Hull, serving Europe and Scandinavia.

CAREER PROSPECTS:

- Careers Service • No. of staff: 4 full/2 part • Unemployed after 6mths: 6%

FAMOUS ALUMNI:

Alan Ahlberg (children's writer); Terry Deary (author of the Horrible Histories); Tony Scott (movie mogul).

SPECIAL FEATURES:

(Lord) David Puttnam is the University Chancellor, which means he shakes hands and doles out degrees once a year.

FURTHER INFO:

- Prospectuses: undergrad; postgrad • Open days

ACADEMIC

Having so many local students, Sunderland has strong links with local industry, particularly Nissan who churn out Micras nearby. So the Automotive Engineering course is strong, as are Pharmacy/Pharmacology and, partly thanks to £20m spent recently on the new media arts centre at St Peter's Campus, so is Media Studies.

140-300

Entry points: 140-300	Ave points: 159
No. of terms: 3	Length of terms: 10wks
Staff/student ratio: 1:18	Study addicts: n/a
Teaching: *	Research: **
Year abroad: 0	Sandwich students: 8%
Firsts: 9%	2.2s: 39%
2.1s: 42%	3rds: 6%

POINTS

ADMISSIONS:

• Apply via UCAS

At interview, personality and suitability count for just as much as official points and there's clearly a fondness for locals.

SUBJECTS:

Art & Design: 7%
Arts/Humanities: 3%
Business/Management: 15%
Computing/Digital Media: 11%
Education: 12%
Health & Environment: 5%

Law: 2%
Life Long Learning: 10%
Media: 13%
Psychology: 3%
Sport & Leisure: 4%

Best: Anatomy & Physiology; Art & Design; Media Studies; Molecular Bio-sciences; Nursing; Pharmacology/Pharmacy.

LIBRARIES:

• 500,000 books • 1,900 study places
• 24-hr access

The main libraries are on the Chester Road and St Peter's Campus and there are further departmental libraries.

COMPUTERS:

• 1,250 workstations • 24-hr access

OTHER LEARNING FACILITIES:

The 'media centre' concentrates on TV and radio, with facilities provided by Sony. It was opened by Estelle Morris in September 2003. *Cutting edge and very impressive. The centre, not Estelle Morris.*

ENTERTAINMENT

THE TOWN:

• Price of a pint of beer: £2.10 • Glass of wine: £2 • Can of Red Bull: £1.80

Newcastle is like Sunderland's flashier big brother, but don't under-estimate the little guy, he's got some moves:

Cinemas: A three-screen mainstream house and a 12-screen Virgin cinema 10 miles out of town.

Theatres: The Empire shows mainstream plays, pantos and concerts and the Royalty has local offerings. The Seaburn Centre also hosts visits from the RSC.

Pubs: *Cheap, cheerful and mostly friendly.* Pushplugs: Fitzgerald's; Baroque, a huge Gothic style pub; Royalty Museum Vaults; Ivy House (very student friendly); The Windsor Castle is a cool gay hang-out; Varsity is popular; Lampton Worm is a cheap Weatherspoons. New posh bars include Ttonic, Berlins, Lunar and Chase.

Clubs/Discos: Newcomers include Beach, Liquid, Privilege and the indie-based Que Club. *Old favourites* are Annabel's (dance/retro) and the recently refurbished Pzazz (Britpop). Live jazz jives at the Ground Floor Café.

Music venues: *Sunderland is mainly a local bands town* with the Ropery, Royalty, Greens and Bar 36 all hosting live music. Once a month, the Blue Velvet Caberet at the Mowbray Park Hotel oozes live music, comedy, poetry and art.

Eating out: *All-you-can-eat Chinese is very very popular.* The Tavistock Chain provides two restaurants with *classy* meals and Joe Rigatonis and Capanella (NUS discount) are two of the many *cheap and cheerful* Italian joints. Otherwise, pick from the normal array of kebab and burger joints.

UNIVERSITY:
• Price of a pint of beer: £1.80 • Glass of wine: £1.60 • Can of Red Bull: £1.50
Bars: By day, students frequent The Roker Bar, waiting for somewhere else to open or wishing they'd gone to the *chirpier* Wearmouth Bar on Chester Road. By night, they go to a converted warehouse called The Bonded Warehouse or cram themselves into the varied and the SU's major nightspot, the *popular* Manor Quay.
Theatres: An enthusiastic arts presence at the Bede Theatre and occasional stints at The Sunderland Empire.
Film: Recent films are shown in the Sony Media Centre's cinema at the St Peter's Campus.
Music venues: *Though The Bonded Warehouse makes some effort, Newcastle is generally considered the place to go for music,* as the University limits band appearances to the freshers' fairs and balls. Recent sightings of music celebs include Girls Aloud, Mark Owen and Sinead Quinn.
Clubbing: Manor Quay offers a variety of nights out, from cheesey to serious funk, plus drinks promotions. Let's not forget The Bonded Warehouse which flaunts its late licence on a Friday and Saturday and is a venue for local live bands.
Comedy/Cabaret: A few local comedians on about once a month but Wearmouth's Sunday night quiz is *the big draw.*
Food: The University provides foodstops at all sites, the Bonded Warehouse does *decent* hot food (*Sunday lunches are* excellent and cheap) and the Bonded Bistro now delivers burger and pizza fodder to the local halls at Panns Bank and surrounding student houses.
Other: A Wet T-Shirt competition at Manor Quay recently. *Now that's classy.*

SOCIAL & POLITICAL

UNIVERSITY OF SUNDERLAND STUDENTS' UNION:
• 5 sabbaticals • Turnout at last ballot: 5%
Not the place to start your revolution from with the dismal 5% turnout last ballot. The students are almost aggressively uninterested in all things political. The SU isn't even affiliated to NUS. *Instead, they try to snuggle up to local businesses for cheap prices and special deals for students.*

SU FACILITIES:
Only the bare essentials: three bars which serve food, two small shops, print shop, gaming lounge and a photocopier.

CLUBS (NON-SPORTING):
Hong Kong; Indian; Salsa Dancing. **See also Clubs tables.**

OTHER ORGANISATIONS:
Degrees North is a *pretty pukka* student paper and has a sabbatical editor. Meanwhile, Utopia FM won three gongs at the BBC-backed Student Radio Awards.

RELIGIOUS:
• 1 chaplain (CofE)
Muslim prayer room.

The new offices of Nottingham Trent SU were opened in 1995 by Torvill and Dean but the plaque spelled their names wrong.

PAID WORK:

• Job bureau

The Union bars all employ students but the local area *isn't exactly a job hotbed*. The *wellstaffed* jobshop (combined with the careers service) will help find what there is.

SPORTS

• Recent successes: none • BUSA Ranking: 48

The University recently employed a director of sport – *more a sign of how little there was rather than how much there now is*. They've got their sights on improving four areas: watersports, football, basketball and swimming. *We're not holding our breath*.

SPORTS FACILITIES:

The sports centre on Chester Road has a 25m pool, sports hall and two gyms. St George's House has a dance studio and training room. At Seaburn and Hendon, there are 10 acres of playing fields and the University is finalising a deal with Sunderland FC so students can have a crack at their facilities.

SPORTING CLUBS:

American Football; Equestrian; Gaelic Football; Kite Sports; Martial Arts; Mountain Biking; Parachuting; Rowing; Surf Club. **See also Clubs tables.**

ATTRACTIONS:

Sunderland has squash, badminton and basketball courts, a dry ski-slope, football, rugby and cricket pitches. The local Crowtree Centre also has a pool, ice skating and hockey and boxing facilities. Silksworth outdoor complex has a tennis centre, dry ski-slope, running track, lake and orienteering courses. Sunderland Marina for water sports, the coast for surfing.

ACCOMMODATION

IN COLLEGE:

• Self-catering: 23% • Cost: £56 (50wks)
• First years living in: 35% • Others living in: 30% • Insurance premium: £££££

Availability: 1st years who want to live in, can do so, but only a third want to (most are local, anyway). Nearly a third of other undergrads *should also be in luck*. No one has to share. The facilities range from purpose-built halls to *ageing* tower blocks, from *swish* self-catering flats with en-suite facilities to 450 places under a head tenancy scheme. Security is *good* with 24-hr watch on all sites, CCTV, swipe card entry systems and mobile and foot patrols.

Car parking: *Mostly easy* although not at St Peter's.

EXTERNALLY:

• Ave rent: £45 • Living at home: 51%

Availability: *Wise students bide their time and don't jump at the first pad that comes along. It's not hard to find good, cheap, safe, but, well, studenty housing near the University or University-linked Metro station. Students who can't aren't looking hard enough. Avoid Hendon and Pennywell. Students only ever go there in heavily-armed groups of 30 or more and are still never seen again.*

Housing help: The University-run accommodation service *is small and doesn't need to do much*.

SERVICES:
- Lesbian/Gay/Bisexual Officer & Society
- Women's Officer & Society• Crime rating: !!

Crèches/Nursery: In conjunction with Ofsted, the University has two nurseries on the go, offering places to children as old as 12.

Disabilities: Most buildings, particularly at St Peter's, which is purpose built, have good access. The major problems come with old Langham Tower, which is *so bad* that its services are slowly being relocated and, we guess, the Tower will eventually be melted down and made into disability ramps. A *small* disabled support team and help for dyslexics.

FINANCE:
- Ave debt per year: £3,215

Sunderland Polytechnic

see Sunderland University

Surrey Institute of Art & Design

- *Formerly West Surrey College of Art & Design.*
(1) The Surrey Institute of Art & Design University College, Farnham Campus, Falkner Road, Farnham, Surrey, GU9 7DS Tel: (01252) 722 441 E-mail: registry@surrart.ac.uk
    Website: www.surrart.ac.uk
    Students' Union, Farnham Campus, Falkner Road, Farnham, Surrey, GU9 7DS
    Tel: (01252) 710 263 E-mail: su@surrart.ac.uk
(2) The Surrey Institute of Art & Design University College, Epsom Campus, Ashley Road, Epsom, Surrey, KT18 5BE Tel: (01372) 728 811
    Students' Union, Epsom Campus, Ashley Road, Epsom, Surrey, KT18 5BE

Farnham, on the home counties trail from London to Southampton, is an old rural market town *full of quaint shops and beige jackets*. However, many residents are commuters, so the town has more of a suburban than a village feel. Epsom, 32 miles away, *is eerily similar, at first glance*. *Achingly hip* Design and Arts & Media students are based at the Farnham site, which is on a small, redbrick prefabricated campus with a village on one side and gently rolling hills on the other. The Epsom building was designed by the same bloke and is home to the faculty of Fashion & Communication.

Sex ratio (M:F): 42:58	Founded: 1866
Full-time u'grads: 2,810	Part-time: 80
Postgrads: 50	Non-degree: 710
Ave course: 3yrs	Ethnic: 15%
State:private school: 99:1	Flunk rate: 8%
Mature: 22%	International: 12%
Disabled: 260	Local: 23%

58%
42%

ATMOSPHERE:

Both campuses provide peaceful environments where students can work and rabidly pursue fashion trends. Despite purple hair, piercings and carefully outrageous dress-sense, students are down-to-earth, work-minded and cheerful. Reactions amongst the local rugged, rich folk (whose idea of crazy is orange wellies) are mixed, but don't really stray past grumbling disapproval. Being a bit out-of-the-way, some students could feel cut off from ents. Not that there are that many, moreover public transport can wind down from 6pm.

SITES:

Epsom: (Faculty of Fashion & Communication) Home of the famous racecourse, Epsom's a *little more suburban* than Farnham. There are *oodles* of pubs, bars and restaurants, as well as a theatre and leisure centre with a *top* swimming pool (student rates). A bit more happens in Epsom than Farnham and it's only 17 miles from London's entertainment scene.

FARNHAM:

- Population: 115,600 • Town centre: 450m • London: 42 miles
- Reading: 19 miles • Southampton: 31 miles
- High temp: 22 • Low temp: 1 • Rainfall: 54

Farnham's a small, Georgian leafy townlet with quaint shops and boutiques lining narrow streets and cobbled lanes. It's dominated more by upper class locals than pub-crawling students and is home to the Maltings Centre, with music, arts, theatrical and entertainment events. It also has a castle dating back to the 12th century. They should get a new one.

TRAVEL:

Trains: Farnham station is less than a mile from the College, on the line to London (£6.65) and Guildford. Epsom station is 5 mins walk from the Institute site – a return trip to London costs a *mere* £3.05.

Coaches: Services to London (£8.50), Birmingham (£20.75) and Manchester (£27.50), among others.

Car: *Both towns are bedevilled by one-way systems.* Farnham's best approached from the A325, Epsom from the A24.

Air: Heathrow and Gatwick both less than 30 miles.

Hitching: *No one's going anywhere useful even if they do pick up.*

Local: *Local buses in Farnham are fairly regular. Epsom, being closer to London, has more co-ordinated services.*

Bicycles: No hills, lots of places to leave bikes *and little theft.*

CAREER PROSPECTS:

- Careers Service • No. of staff: 2 full/2 part • Unemployed after 6mths: 11%

Staff and services are split equally between sites. Services include: instructional videos on loan; guidance interviews; CV checking/advice; library; workshops and seminars.

FAMOUS ALUMNI:

Linda Barker (interior designer/*gurning Curry's gimpette*); Michael Dudok de Wit, Daniel Greaves (Oscar-winning animators); Owen Gaster, Gharani Strok (fashion designers); Suzie Templeton (BAFTA winner).

FURTHER INFO:

- Prospectuses: undergrad; postgrad; departmental • Open days

Info available online.

ACADEMIC

All courses offer direct professional training. Work's done in groups and independent projects. The emphasis is more on workshops, *which means fewer lectures to sleep through.*

180-240

Entry points: 180-240
Applns per place: 4.1
No. of terms: 2
Staff/student ratio: 1:27
Teaching: n/a
Firsts: 16%
2.1s: 32%

Ave points: 220
Clearing: 1%
Length of terms: 15wks
Study addicts: 7%
Research: ***
2.2s: 47%
3rds: 5%

POINTS

ADMISSIONS:

• Apply via UCAS

SUBJECTS:

Art & Design: 95%   Arts/Humanities: 5%
Unusual: Animation; Design Management; Digital Screen Arts; Product Design; Sustainable Futures.

LIBRARIES:

• 86,000 books • 400 study places • Spend per student: £££
There are libraries at Farnham and Epsom specific to the faculties on each campus. The library at Farnham's in the award-winning Library & Learning Resource Centre (LLRC). Both libraries are open all week *but not very late.*

COMPUTERS:

• 423 workstations • Spend per student: £££
Extensive IT resources are in IT Centres on each campus. Open access computers for independent study are based in both LLRCs and can be booked.

OTHER LEARNING FACILITIES:

The Foyer and the James Hockey Galleries are open throughout the year and open to the public too.

ENTERTAINMENT

THE TOWN:

• Price of a pint of beer: £2.10 • Glass of wine: £1.80 • Can of Red Bull: £2
Farnham's as dead as disco. Guildford, 11 miles away, has a bunch of clubs, a smattering of pubs, a dollop of cinema and a leisure centre (see University of Surrey). London's pretty close, especially for the Epsom crowd.
Cinemas/Theatre: A cinema in Farnham shows weekly new releases. The Odeon in Guildford, on the banks of the River Wey, is within easy walking distance of the main station. The Maltings Centre in Farnham has film events and theatre, while Epsom's Playhouse does comedy, films, concerts and decidedly *low brow* plays.
Pubs: *There are lots of pubs, but not all welcome students. Pushplugs: the Glasshouse; the Plough; the Hogs Head (Farnham); the Rising Sun (Epsom).*
Clubbing/Music: The Maltings and Chicago Rock Café in Epsom field local musical talent. *For clubbing, Guildford is the only real local option. Elsewhere clubbing only happens to students if they stray on to the wrong farmer's land. Oh, and there's London.*
Eating out: Epsom has *the Rising Sun, a Pierre Victoire* and little else. Farnham has many locations for a *dignified* scoff. *Pushplugs: Pizza Express; Cafe Uno; Vienna (bit posh) Bistro; Lion & Lamb; Goldsmith's pub.*

UNIVERSITY:

• Price of a pint of beer: £1.55 • Glass of wine: £1.20 • Can of Red Bull: £1.60
Bars: Farnham's the Glasshouse is the centre of social activity, with many theme nights and cheap drinks promotions. Epsom's the Retreat, as the name suggests, is a little more intimate.
Film: With several film societies and a handy lecture theatre on hand, film fun is on the menu. £1 entry fee allows access to recent films and classics.

Music/Clubbing: The Glasshouse has housed chart-topping acts such as Goldie, Artful Dodger, Big Brovaz and Cleo and Keith from The Prodigy. Also three dance nights a week, a regular Drum 'n' Bass night and whatever other nights the Union fancies arranging. Buses are laid on between sites when events kick off.

Comedy/Cabaret: Monthly giggles at the Glasshouse from the likes of Jim Tavare, Nina Conte and Mitch Benn.

Food: The Time Out Food Court and the Farnham Canteen *serve up a delicious lack of variety until 5pm.*

Other: Three balls a year, a leavers' event, Rag week, Freshers' Fortnight.

SOCIAL & POLITICAL

SURREY INSTITUTE OF ART & DESIGN STUDENTS' UNION:

• 3 sabbaticals • Turnout at last ballot: 10% • NUS member

The SU *avoids big politics unless it can't help it and concentrates on student services.* When campaigning kicks off though it gets involved and students are *enthusiastic*. Recent campaigns have included MP petitions and awareness for top-up fees, drink spiking and ongoing accommodation price grumblings.

SU FACILITIES:

Two bars; canteen; three snack shops; pool tables; meeting rooms; minibus hire; photocopier; vending machines; fax; payphone; late night minibus; juke boxes; advice; games machines; launderette.

CLUBS (NON-SPORTING):

Amsterdam Trips; Games; International Society; Life Drawing; Rock; T'ai Chi; Yoga. **See also Clubs tables.**

OTHER ORGANISATIONS:

Sketch, the student newspaper, comes out three times a year. Rag's enthusiastic, but *doesn't raise vast sums*. They've promised to improve.

RELIGIOUS:

• 2 chaplains

Local CofE and Baptist churches.

PAID WORK:

• Job bureau

The jobshop has a regularly updated notice board. Supermarket, pub and bar work are the best bets. The Institute also employs students as cleaners and security staff and at the SU for bar work.

SPORTS

• Recent successes: football

It's a fearsome thing to behold when art students start getting sporty, but it's happening here. The Institute's football team is the holder of the Surrey County Cup for the first time. It's even more worrying to know the Institute has no real facilities of its own and has to rent local ones. We're scared too.

SPORTS FACILITIES:

Local facilities are: sports centre; swimming pool; bowling green; ice rink; golf course; tennis court; dry ski slope; squash courts; Farnham Sports Complex (with golf course and sports pitches).

SPORTING CLUBS:

Aerobics; Kick-boxing; Kung Fu. **See also Clubs tables.**

ATTRACTIONS:
Local rugby team. Epsom has a racecourse.

ACCOMMODATION

IN COLLEGE:
- Self-catering: 18% • Cost: £59 (39wks)
- First years living in: 70% (Farnham); 32% (Epsom) • Insurance premium: £
Availability: 420 students can be housed at Farnham, 88 at Epsom. Prices *vary considerably*: £42-94 at Farnham and around £81 at Epsom. 1st years are not guaranteed a place; accommodation is provided according to distance and mobility. *The student village has won awards but Bridge House is a bit scummy.*
Car parking: Parking is *difficult*. Few bring cars anyway.

EXTERNALLY:
- Ave rent: £62
Availability: *Suitable, cheap accommodation may prove hard to find. Wrecclesham, Upper Hale, Dollis Drive and Tilford Road are all convenient. Some move out as far as Aldershot where accommodation is in more abundant supply and cheaper, but comes with a dodgy reputation.*
Housing help: Housing help, based at both sites, runs vacancy lists and a bulletin board.

WELFARE

SERVICES:
- Lesbian/Gay/Bisexual Society • Women's Officer • Mature Students' Officer & Society
- International Students' Officer & Society • Postgrad Officer
- Disabilities Officer • Late-night/Women's minibus • College counsellors: 3 full/2 part
- Crime rating: !

Health: The Institute doctors and nursing staff are available on campus at specific times, or at their own practices nearby. At Farnham on-site surgeries are offered three times a week through a local medical practice; a nurse is available once a week.
Disabilities: Wheelchair access is *generally adequate at best, although all Student Services are accessible to wheelchair users*. Hearing loops are installed in key areas and the learning and teaching co-ordinator manages a team of ten dyslexia support tutors.

FINANCE:
- Ave debt per year: £3,668
- Access fund: £130,000 • Successful applications/yr: 366
Support: Hardship Loans of up to £500 for students in trouble and part-timers under 55. The Institute offers a small number of bursaries and research studentships for postgrads, to be used as a contribution to fees.

Surrey University

University of Surrey, Guildford, Surrey, GU2 7XH
Tel: (01483) 300 800 E-mail: information@surrey.ac.uk Website: www.surrey.ac.uk
University of Surrey Students' Union, Union House, University of Surrey, Guildford, Surrey,
GU2 7XH Tel: (01483) 689 223 E-mail: comms@ussu.co.uk Website: www.ussu.co.uk

GENERAL

Think of Surrey and the *first (and probably only) thing that comes to mind is serious,
stockbroker money tucked into the big houses* of the commuter belt around London. *Some
of this cash seems to have fallen into the pockets of the University, too.* In the last few
years they've *garnished* the centre of their home town of Guildford with several *swanky
modern buildings – a vast improvement* on the older parts of the campus, *some of which
look like Lego dipped in porridge. The University stands on a hill at the western end of town,
near the glum, postwar cathedral where Gregory Peck famously came to a sticky end in 'The
Omen'. Bored Civil Engineering students have put it about that the whole campus is slowly
sliding down hill (probably something to do with Damien) but the newer buildings and the
air of prosperous industriousness suggests a University very much on the up.*

Sex ratio (M:F): 35:65	Founded: 1966
Full-time u'grads: 6,375	Part-time: 3,450
Postgrads: 2,785	Non-degree: 743
Ave course: 4yrs	Ethnic: 23%
State:private school: 88:12	Flunk rate: 9%
Mature: 14%	International: 34%
Disabled: 44	Local: 10%

ATMOSPHERE:
*Students come to Surrey University because they want to do well and doing well, in this
context, means getting a good job and making lots of money. Not that this means they
spend all day swotting. There's plenty of creative, extra-curricular activity going on, it's just
that you get the feeling that if there's not a prize, an award or some other kind of CV-
boosting kudos attached to it, they don't want to know. The atmosphere is 'posh and proud
of it' but for career-minded students there are few better places to go and, in the evenings,
it livens up considerably.*

GUILDFORD:
• Population: 113,000 • Town centre: 800m • London: 35 miles
• High temp: 22 • Low temp: 1 • Rainfall: 54
*Guildford's done well to maintain its own character in the face of the relentless pressure to
be nothing more than a dormitory for London. The centre's still a quaint old place with its
cobbled main street, narrow lanes and rustic atmosphere. There's also the ruined Norman
castle built by William the Conqueror (although it wasn't a ruin when he built it), and a
museum dedicated to Lewis Carroll of 'Alice In Wonderland' fame. Despite the historical
attractions the centre's got all the obligatory chain stores and chain pubs.*

TRAVEL:

Trains: Guildford's on the main London (Waterloo) to Portsmouth line, with a *good* service. Fast trains to Waterloo take 32 mins. There's an alternative line with a slower service, via Cobham (£5.55 sgl).

Coaches: National Express coach No. 030 runs between Victoria Coach Station and Guildford Park Barn every 2 hrs from 09.00 to 19.00 (60 mins, £8.50 rtn).

Car: If approaching from London (A3) or the M25 (Junction 10), remain on A3 until the exit signed to Cathedral and University – don't take the exit signed to Guildford.

Air: Via Heathrow: coaches from Terminal 4 for Woking Station 07.20-23.10, picking up from Terminals 2, 3 and 1 (£6 sgl). Via Gatwick: hourly trains for Guildford between 05.28 and 23.18 weekdays, 05.31 and 23.18 weekends (38 mins, £5.30 sgl).

Local: Arriva bus numbers 17 (hourly), 27 (every 20 mins/hourly Sunday) and 37 run from the Friary Bus Station to the campus (50p sgl, £100 yearly travelcard, £50 3-mth travelcard).

College: A free bus runs between the Varsity sports centre, campus and halls of residence.

CAREER PROSPECTS:

• Careers Service • No. of staff: 5 full/2 part • Unemployed after 6mths: 4%

FAMOUS ALUMNI:

Kirsten Lawton (world No. 1 trampolinist); Alan Parker (MD, Whitbread plc); David Varney (Executive Chairman, HM Revenue & Customs).

FURTHER INFO:

• Prospectuses: undergrad; postgrad; departmental • Open days

A C A D E M I C

Although it's *rigorously academic* Surrey courses are also *very practical*. The University's home to one *of the most successful Research Parks in Europe* and to Surrey Satellite Technology Ltd – the only company in the country designing, building and launching satellites into space.

220-300	POINTS
Entry points: 220-300	**Ave points: 280**
Applns per place: 5	**Clearing: 13%**
No. of terms: 2	**Length of terms: 15wks**
Staff/student ratio: 1:15	**Study addicts: 14%**
Teaching: ***	**Research: *******
Year abroad: 20%	**Sandwich students: 74%**
Firsts: 11%	**2.2s: 45%**
2.1s: 33%	**3rds: 8%**

ADMISSIONS:

• Apply via UCAS/NMAS for nursing

Mature applications are *encouraged*, even where standard qualifications aren't in hand. There are links with local colleges and those on access courses also get a look-in.

SUBJECTS:

Art & Design: 4%
Business/Management: 20%
Mathematical Sciences, IT & Computing: 9%
Medical Sciences: 18%
Sciences: 19%
Social Sciences: 18%

Best: Biomedical Sciences; Chemical Engineering; Economics; Education; Electronic Engineering; Management; Maths; Music; Nursing/Midwifery; Physics; Psychology; Sociology.

LIBRARIES:

• 450,000 books • 900 study places • Spend per student: £££££

There's a European documentation centre with everything you need to know about the EU. There's also a laptop corner on the 2nd floor.

COMPUTERS:
- No. of workstations 725
- 24-hr access • Spend per student: £

OTHER LEARNING FACILITIES:
The Language Centre gives foreign students a hand with essay writing, technical writing and grammar revision, *as well as introducing them to the delicate delights of British humour* and other aspects of British culture. There are 12 music practice rooms, mostly with pianos and a well-stocked audio room with scores, CDs etc.

ENTERTAINMENT

THE CITY:
- Price of a pint of beer: £1.89 • Glass of wine: £1.85 • Can of Red Bull: £1.45

Cinemas: The nine-screen Odeon does a 10% student discount.

Theatres: The Electric Theatre's used for occasional student productions and local amateur theatre. The Yvonne Arnaud Theatre is *one of the UK's top regional theatres* and is home to pre-West End plays, opera and ballet. The New Victoria in nearby Woking is the South East's largest auditorium with West End shows (after London, *natch*).

Pubs: Guildford's home to many a chain pub but locals tend to drink in more traditional places, students stick to JD Wetherspoon and other bars on Bridge Street such as Bar Med and Edward's.

Clubbing: The Drink, Pulse, the Loft and Time are *all popular*.

Music venues: The Powerhouse and RSVP hold open mic nights. The *cherished* Guildford Civic will return with a facelift in 2006.

Eating out: *The well-heeled* might like to pop along to Albert Roux's or one of the many other French restaurants in the town. Or there's Ken Hom's Chinese. Or, *for those who can bear to eat food cooked by someone who hasn't been on TV*, there're loads of Italians and Café Rouge, Café de Paris, Café Nero, Café Uno – *you get the idea*.

UNIVERSITY:
- Price of a pint of beer: £1.80 • Glass of wine: £3 • Can of Red Bull: £2

Bars: The main bar and restaurant Chancellors ('Channies') is so *popular* that students want signs giving the queuing time so they don't keep missing lectures. Other bars are the Varsity, which is *popular with sports clubs*; Helyn Rose, which competes with 'Channies' for *fine* breakfasts; the SU bar (actually five bars, cap 1,600); Roots café (*faster* service than Channies and *nice, booth-style sofas*); and Hari's, which is open in the afternoons.

Film: The film society show screenings on Sunday nights.

Music venues: A *nice* mix of up-and-coming acts like Reuben and Martin Grech have been through the SU Bar, as well as *old-stagers* like Boney M.

Clubbing: Mondays' Sparkle, Wednesdays' Citrus and Friday Night Out are all *popular*. *Surrey's a major point on the superstar DJ circuit*: Carl Cox, Paul Oakenfold, Judge Jules and Seb Fontaine have all *scratched their way* through. *Loads* of themed nights – everything from school disco to drag.

Comedy/Cabaret: Comedy evenings fortnightly in the Helyn Rose bar.

Food: As well as Channies and the other Union bars the University has Pizzaman, Rushes (for quick snacks), Seasons (for *serious* lunches), the Ivy Room (does private bookings) and Wates House which is a bar, function room and self-service restaurant. *With their never-ending yen for innovation and modernity* the University have even provided an online baguette ordering service from Rushes and Seasons – no delivery though.

Other: Three formal balls a year.

SOCIAL & POLITICAL

UNIVERSITY OF SURREY STUDENTS' UNION:

• 6 sabbaticals • Turnout at last ballot: 12% • NUS member

The *huge* 30-strong Union executive have won awards for campaigns against fees and for greater safety measures on the fringes of campus.

SU FACILITIES:

Bar/nightclub; music venue; two bars; canteen; snack bar; fast food place; three pool tables; meeting room; five minibuses and van for hire; Endsleigh Insurance office; NatWest Bank; NatWest and Barclays ATMs; fax and printing service; payphones; advice centre; TV lounge; games machines; general store; stationery shop; new and secondhand bookshops.

CLUBS (NON-SPORTING):

Arabic; Asian; Ballroom Dancing; Big Band; Breakdance; Change Ringing; Chinese Asian; Cyprus; Chinese Student & Scholar Association; Economics; Electronics & Amateur Radio Society (EARS); European; Game; GU2; Hellenic; Iranian; Korean; La Latina; Live Music Society; MadSoc; Magick & Pagan; Malaysian Students; Mauritian; Meditation; Meditation; Music – Dance; Music– No Wave; Music – Presha; Orthodox; Oscar Film Unit (OFU); Paintball; Pakistan; Poker; Photography; Raising and Giving (RAG); Singapore; St. John LINKS; Stage Crew; Surrey Dance Squad; Surrey Gurners; Switchgear; Taiwanese; Tamil; Thai; Turkish Speakers; University of Surrey Society of Russia (USSR); 'V' Scheme; Wind Band; West Country. **See also Clubs tables.**

OTHER ORGANISATIONS:

Free weekly student newspaper, Barefacts, has a 4,000 print-run. The Student Radio station GU2 1350AM runs 24-hrs during the academic year and won Student Radio Station of the Year a few years back.

RELIGIOUS:

• 3 chaplains (RC, FC, CofE)

PAID WORK:

• Job bureau

The University has links with various local stores (Tesco, Debenham's, House of Fraser) and there's *plenty* of bar work in the area.

SPORTS

• Recent successes: squash, golf • BUSA Ranking: 48

In sport, *as in everything else they do*, SurreySport play to win and usually score well in the BUSA league. For £70 a year students can use all of the facilities listed below.

SPORTS FACILITIES:

Football, rugby, all-weather, cricket and hockey pitches; five squash courts; nine tennis courts, netball court; athletics field; croquet lawn and bowling green; gym; aerobics studio; multigym; climbing wall; two indoor practice golf bays; martial arts rooms. Locally there's a leisure centre, swimming pool and athletics track.

SPORTING CLUBS:

10-Pin Bowling; Aerobics; Aikido; American Football; Cheerleading; Gliding; Ju-Jitsu; Kendo; Lacrosse; Rifle; Tai Jitsu; Ultimate Frisbee; Waterpolo; Windsurfing; Yoga. **See also Clubs tables.**

ATTRACTIONS:

The nearby Spectrum Leisure Centre's home to local ice-hockey team the Guildford Flames.

ACCOMMODATION

IN COLLEGE:
- Self-catering: 61% • Cost: £39-77 (28-53wks)
- First years living in: 80% • Insurance premium: £

Availability: All 1st years who want to can live in. Most rooms are *well furnished*: desk, reading-lamp, wardrobe, bookshelves. The *most popular* are at the *expensive* Twyford and University Courts. *More reasonable* rents are at Battersea and Surrey Courts right in the middle of campus. *Less desirable* is Bellerby Court, about 500 metres from campus or Hazel Court, about 3 miles away. Guildford Court is *old, small, and may be knocked down if it doesn't fall down first*.

Car parking: *Not easy.* The required permits cost £68 but *with plenty of dosh sloshing around at Surrey, there are also plenty of cars and relatively few parking spaces.*

EXTERNALLY:
- Ave rent: £62

Availability: Guildford's a commuter town so *cheap housing's in short supply*. Most students live near the train station at Guildford Park or north of the University in *posh* Bellfields. Park Barn to the west is *a bit rough but less painful on the pocket*.

Housing help: Bulletin boards and help with contracts.

WELFARE

SERVICES:
- Lesbian/Gay/Bisexual Officer & Society • Ethnic Minorities Officer & Society
- Women's Officer & Society • Mature Students' Officer & Society
- International Students' Officer & Society • Postgrad Officer & Society
- Disabilities Officer & Society • Late-night/Women's minibus
- Self-defence classes • Nightline • Taxi fund
- College counsellors: 2 full/5 part • Crime rating: !

Health: 24-hr sick bay and health centre staffed by a doctor and nurses.

Disabilities: The University's on a hill but most areas can be accessed in a wheelchair. The Assistive Technology Centre has workstations with software for dyslexic students.

FINANCE:
- Ave debt per year: £2,665
- Access fund: £233,850 • Successful applications/yr: 715 • Ave payment: £1,000

Support: Scholarships of up to £1,500, sports bursaries, various departmental There's also a choral and organ scholarship at the cathedral.

University of Sussex

University of Sussex, Sussex House, Falmer, BN1 9RH
Tel: (01273) 678 416 E-mail: ug.admissions@sussex.ac.uk Website: www.sussex.ac.uk
University of Sussex Students' Union, Falmer House, Falmer, BN1 9RH
Tel: (01273) 678 152 E-mail: ussu-coms@sussex.ac.uk Website: www.ussu.info

GENERAL

$3\frac{1}{2}$ miles inland from Brighton, just before the *stunning* South Downs roll into the landscape, sprawls the 200-acre campus of Sussex University, just beside the *quiet* village of Falmer. *Swathes of gentle greenery* provide the foundation for the *thoroughly modern* Basil Spence University buildings – all arches, courtyards, concrete pillars and redbrick. *It's not ugly, although some might use the word 'interesting' through gritted teeth.* Some of the buildings were designed to look like certain objects from the air, Falmer House is a camera, the arts building is an insect – *all very well, but passing pilots probably feel like they're tripping.* The new Medical School – a joint venture with the University of Brighton, which has a site nearby – *is a more attractive construction, inside and out. It's certainly close to nature, occasionally too close, as drunken students have fallen foul of (or rather 'over') the many badgers with whom they share their environment.*

Sex ratio (M:F): 39:61	**Founded: 1961**
Full-time u'grads: 6,565	**Part-time: 2,810**
Postgrads: 1,720	**Non-degree: 1,640**
Ave course: 3yrs	**Ethnic: 11.5%**
State:private school: 85:15	**Flunk rate: 14%**
Mature: 22%	**International: 22%**
Disabled: 283	**Local: 30%**

ATMOSPHERE:

Sussex students are a friendly bunch with a tendency to lie back and let education and fun wash over them, but far more proactive on politics. The bars and cafes fill up at lunchtimes and evenings – chatting is a major pastime here. The campus quietens down at the weekend as many students go off to nearby Brighton, playground of the funky.

BRIGHTON: see University of Brighton
• City centre: $3\frac{1}{2}$ miles

TRAVEL: see University of Brighton

Trains: Falmer station is 200 metres away from the campus, from where connections to Brighton (£1.50) – and therefore the rest of the country (*£lots*) – are possible.
Car: The A27 links Sussex with the A23. There are car parks around campus, *but not enough space for everyone. Permits cost £300 a year or £1 a day. The University's trying to get car-sharing going.*
Local: *Buses are reliable both when it comes to turning up on time and in taking convoluted routes.* Weekly passes cost £10.
Taxis: There are no cabs around campus. Catching one in Brighton to campus costs about a tenner.
Bicycles: *The University's attempts to coax people into cycling pale somewhat in comparison with the mind-numbing terror of weaving in and out of busy main roads filled with manic drivers, and the exhausting prospect of uphill pedalling.*

CAREER PROSPECTS:

• Careers Service • No. of staff: 7 full/16 part • Unemployed after 6mths: 6%
The Careers Development & Employment Centre hosts career workshops, interview training, job fairs and employer presentations.

FAMOUS ALUMNI:

Alun Anderson (editor, New Scientist); Rob Bonnet (BBC news reporter); Simon Fanshawe (comedian); Brendan Foster (athletic commentator); Peter Hain MP (Lab); Hattie Hayridge (female Holly on 'Red Dwarf'); Billy Idol (*bleached 80s rocker*); Simon Jenkins (journalist);

Thabo Mbeki (President of South Africa); Ian McEwan (writer); Bob Mortimer (Vic Reeves's *gaunt* friend); Andrew Morton (biographer/Diana interviewer); Dermot Murnaghan (ITN reporter); Nigel Planer (Neil from 'The Young Ones'); Gail Rebuck (chief exec of Random House); Alexandra Shulman (editor, Vogue UK); Julia Somerville (newsreader); Virginia Wade (last female Briton to win a Wimbledon singles title). Honorary awards: Paul McCartney (Beatle); Henry Moore (curve-happy sculptor); Anita Roddick (founder of Body Shop); Tom Stoppard (playwright);

FURTHER INFO:

• Prospectuses: undergrad; postgrad; some departments; international • Open days • Video
Open days in autumn and summer, campus tours for schools run every week.

ACADEMIC

Sussex has a range of vocational and non-vocational courses and a strong research basis. *The latest stripe on its shoulder's* the new Medical School, opened in partnership with the University of Brighton. The Psychology course *is a national favourite.*

Entry points: 290-360	Ave points: 345
Applns per place: 7	Clearing: 2%
No. of terms: 3	Length of terms: 10wks
Staff/student ratio: 1:13	Study addicts: 22%
Teaching: ***	Research: *****
Year abroad: 12%	Sandwich students: 1%
Firsts: 13%	2.2s: 23%
2.1s: 56%	3rds: 5%

ADMISSIONS:

• Apply via UCAS
Part-timers and postgrads can apply direct.

SUBJECTS:

Humanities: 24%
Life Sciences: 22%
Science & Technology: 20%

Social Sciences & Cultural Studies: 26%
Sussex Institute: 8%

Best: American Studies; Economics; Education; Electrical & Electronic Engineering; French; History of Art; Linguistics; Maths & Statistics; Media Studies; Molecular Biosciences; Organismal Biosciences; Philosophy; Physics & Astronomy; Politics & International Relations; Sociology.
Unusual: Artificial Intelligence; Landscape Studies.

LIBRARIES:

• 786,000 books • 1,000 study places • Spend per student: £££££
In addition to the two libraries, there's the Geography Resource Centre, which holds over 80,000 maps. The electronic library gives access to a number of databases and online publications.

COMPUTERS:

• 483 workstations • 24-hr access • Spend per student: £££
There are a few Macs and Unix systems as well as the PCs kept in all-night computer clusters around campus/in the libraries. The wireless service lets laptops connect to the network in most academic buildings.

When Mastermind was filmed at Ulster University, students kidnapped the Black Chair. When the BBC refused to pay the ransom, they pushed it into the River Bann.

OTHER LEARNING FACILITIES:
The language labs are open to students who fancy speaking in tongues. The Media Centre's equipped with a TV studio, sound studio and digital editing suite – it isn't exclusively the domain of media students; anyone can have a go. There's also a design lab, rehearsal rooms and a drama studio.

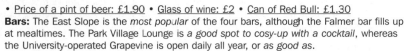

ENTERTAINMENT

BRIGHTON: see University of Brighton

UNIVERSITY:
• Price of a pint of beer: £1.90 • Glass of wine: £2 • Can of Red Bull: £1.30
Bars: The East Slope is the *most popular* of the four bars, although the Falmer bar fills up at mealtimes. The Park Village Lounge is *a good spot to cosy-up with a cocktail*, whereas the University-operated Grapevine is open daily all year, or *as good as*.
Theatres: The Gardner Arts Centre hosts student productions and touring shows, and displays art exhibitions. Sussex's drama and musical theatre societies are *far from inert*.
Film: Three films of the *mildly artsy* breed are shown a week, £2.
Music venues: Mandela Hall is the largest and has showcased Amy Winehouse recently. Smaller bands and student musos twang away in the bars.
Clubbing: The Hothouse churns the tunes and hosts regular nights run by various clubs and socs, or by Brighton promoters. Saturday night's Yoof Club *is the most happening with a retro selection of the finest cheese to emerge from the last three decades*.
Food: Laines Restaurant leads the way with large-scale refectory fodder. There's an assortment of café-style snack stops, including the fair trade Dhaba and the new Doctor's Orders café at the Medical School.
Other: The Summer and Fresher's Balls are *massive* but not formal annual events. There's the Sports Federation Ball and the Clubs & Societies Oscars, where awards are dished out – *American High School Prom style*, plus smaller events like the Halloween Ball and Valentine's Party.

SOCIAL & POLITICAL

UNIVERSITY OF SUSSEX STUDENTS' UNION:
• 6 sabbaticals • Turnout at last ballot: 15% • NUS member
USSU has a stubborn streak and some very pointy teeth when it comes to politics. Relentlessly left-wing, they're committed to greening up the University and have passed a number of eco-friendly policies. Imperialist American politics stick in SU teeth and anti-war organisations spit a lot of bile. The Vice-Chancellor has his work cut out trying to get along with them – SU passed a vote of no confidence in him for failing to retract his pro top-up stance in the face of massive student opposition. But then, relations with the University have never been peachy – the Union reckons it's being charged over the odds for rent on Falmer House and isn't afraid to say so. There is a Student Rep Scheme intended to ease liaison with Sussex authorities, but it ain't up to much – in a recent survey, the vast majority didn't know it existed.

SU FACILITIES:
Across campus: four bars; nightclub; cafeteria; four coffee bars; pool tables; meeting rooms; three minibuses for hire; Endsleigh Insurance office; Barclays and HSBC banks with ATMs; photocopiers; fax and printing services; payphones; photo booth; advice centre; general and stationery stores; post office; travel agency; bookshop; gaming and vending machines; launderette.

CLUBS (NON-SPORTING):

Africa Forum; Autonomous Student (political anarchy); Ballroom Dancing; Buddhist Meditation; Choir; Circus; Colombian; Comedy; Culture Move; Exchange of Language for All; Fair-trade; Go; Human Scientists; Japanese; Legal Observers; Life Drawing; Marxist Leninist Study; Massage; Mexican; Model UN; Open Mic; Q-Soc (physics & astronomy); Red Cross; Socialist Alliance; Sussex Loud & Ugly Tunes Society (SLUTS); Music Appreciation; St John Ambulance; Stop AIDS Campaign; Student Action for Refugees; Student Meditation; Anti War; Sussex Free Education; Sussex Students for a Free Tibet; Pro-Life; Surrealist; SWARM (role playing & war games); Writers. **See also Clubs tables.**

OTHER ORGANISATIONS:

The Badger's the weekly SU newspaper, backed up by The Guardian award-winning termly mag Pulse. URF (University Radio Falmer) broadcasts daily around campus with an intermittent FM licence. The Charity Rag gets up to the usual silly things for money: pubcrawls; slave auctions; blind dates. Project V *isn't an attempt to revive that dodgy 70s sci-fi show*, but rather a group aiming to get the locals and the students working together on community projects.

RELIGIOUS:

• 6 chaplains (CofE, RC, Methodist, Baptist, Evangelical), rabbi
An Interdenominational Meeting House holds the Chaplaincy and quiet rooms. There's a Muslim Student Centre and Baha'i faith group operating on campus.
Religion in Brighton: see University of Brighton

PAID WORK: see University of Brighton
• Job bureau • Paid work: term-time 40%; hols 70%
The Careers Service dredges through the local employment scene and points students in the direction of part-time or vacation work.

• Recent successes: basketball, fencing • BUSA Ranking: 46
Despite the top-notch facilities and the range of classes on offer (yoga, dance, martial arts and so on), sport doesn't change lives at Sussex. There are some bursaries available for talented sports people but national victories aren't regular features of University life.

SPORTS FACILITIES:

The University owns two sports centres. The Falmer Sports Complex contains: two-floor fitness suite with Sky TV; three squash and six tennis courts; floodlit artificial pitch; cricket nets; playing fields; café bar. Sportcentre has: two sports halls; four squash courts; dance and martial arts studio; Lifestyles studio; solarium; sports shop. £18.50 gets annual membership but then there are some *sneaky* sessional charges on top of that (eg. £1.40 for a squash court).

SPORTING CLUBS:

American Football; Football; Mountain Bike; Rowing; Squash; Surf; S-Xtreme (extreme sports); Triathlon; Ultimate Frisbee. **See also Clubs tables.**

ATTRACTIONS: see University of Brighton

IN COLLEGE:

• Self-catering: 46% • Cost: £44-76 (31-42wks)
• First years living in: 95% • Insurance premium: £
Availability: Self-catered accommodation is available to the majority of 1st years, but 5% still choose to go out on their own and relatively few students from other years get a look in. Sussex's no issues about giving local students rooms – *no one should be forced to live with*

parents any longer than they have to. Accommodation comprises halls, houses and self-contained flats on campus or in Brighton (20%), with a scattering of students in head tenancy schemes nearby. *Quality kitchens are divided between 5-12 students and there are a few en-suite rooms.* Several flats are available to families and married couples (both must be studying at Sussex). Single sex housing comes in female and female Muslim-only. *Most halls are of decent-ish standards, the glaring exception East Slope attempting gradual structural suicide.*

Car parking: Students resident on campus aren't allowed cars except for some disabled students and residential advisors (the guys who live on-site and look after new students).

EXTERNALLY: see University of Brighton

• Ave rent: £60

Availability: *The house hunt is as easy as shooting fish in a barrel. From a great distance. With a bent peashooter.* Most students find something a mile or two away.

Housing help: The University Housing Office – *more a man with a pile of classifieds* – runs workshops in how to find a house, produces vacancy lists and manages an online database.

WELFARE

SERVICES:
• Lesbian/Gay/Bisexual Society • Women's Society • Mature Students' Society
• Postgrad Officer & Society • College counsellors: 9 part • SU counsellors: 3 full
• Crime rating: !!

There's a welfare sabbatical and a *huge* number of part-time support group exec officers. USSU runs a daily drop-in centre at Falmer House where students can unload their troubles.

Health: The NHS runs the University Health Service with four GPs, nurses, dentist and chemist.

Crèches/Nursery: 44 places available for children from 4mths and up.

Disabilities: *Wheelchair access is okay, though there are lots of slopes on campus and some difficult buildings.* There are specialist units for dyslexia and mental health, and adapted accommodation is reserved for students with mobility difficulties. Ramps and hearing loops are abundant.

FINANCE:
• Ave debt per year: £1,806

Fees: A definite decision's yet to be made on top-up fees, *but it doesn't take a psychic to see a few strikes and protests on the horizon.*
• Access fund: £455,000 • Successful applications/yr: 877 • Ave payment: £200-3,000

Support: Sports bursaries, ten postgrad bursaries of £2,000 and a hardship fund.

Swansea, University of Wales

• *Part of the University of Wales.*
University of Wales, Swansea. Singleton Park, Swansea, SA2 8PP
Tel: (01792) 205 678 E-mail: admissions@swansea.ac.uk Website: www.swansea.ac.uk
Swansea Students' Union, Singleton Park, Swansea, SA2 8PP
Tel: (01792) 295 466 E-mail: generaloffice@swansea-union.co.uk
Website: www.swansea-union.co.uk

GENERAL

Swansea sits on the arm of the Gower Peninsula, a *landscape artist's wet dream*, covered in beaches, forests and general green bits on the south coast of Wales. The peninsula was the first place in Britain to be officially designated an Area of Outstanding Natural Beauty. About 2 miles out of town, past the cricket ground, following the coast road, is the campus of Swansea University. Made of rolling mini-hills, redbrick and concrete, the University has the beach on its doorstep and parkland around it. The *little* city of Swansea itself is in turn *modern, attractive, run-down and comedically non-descript*, depending on where wandering feet lead.

Sex ratio (M:F): 39:61	**Founded: 1920**
Full-time u'grads: 7,465	**Part-time: 3,035**
Postgrads: 1,275	**Non-degree: 970**
Ave course: 3yrs	**Ethnic: 9%**
State:private school: 92:8	**Flunk rate: 10%**
Mature: 16%	**International: 9%**
Disabled: 202	**Local: 28%**

ATMOSPHERE:

Laid-back and pleasant, Swansea students enjoy taking in the view – the effects of the vast stretch of beach just outside eventually rub off on them. With the Gower having some of the best surf in Britain, the University has its fair share of surfer types swanning around too. Students have a good life and get on well with local residents. The work ethic is quietly studious.

SWANSEA:

- Population: 223,200 • City centre: $2\frac{1}{2}$ miles • London: 160 miles
- Cardiff: 40 miles • Bristol: 60 miles
- High temp: 20 • Low temp: 2 • Rainfall: 105

Dylan Thomas described Swansea as 'the graveyard of ambition' because once discovered, no one wants to leave (Dylan, of course, left). *Perhaps more accurately*, he also called it his 'ugly, lovely town'. It's a *strange mix of beauty and grime*, gleaming pubs and streets half boarded up. In the summer, the surrounding countryside and beaches are *extraordinarily* scenic and the town becomes a pit stop for tourists. Most locals are *cheerful and always willing to have a chat (or, more likely, an epic conversation)*, one or two aren't. While small, Swansea has most amenities, high street shops and banks, as well as the opportunity to try lavabread (*like fishy spinach made from seaweed*).

TRAVEL:

Trains: Direct trains from Swansea station, 3 miles from campus, to Cardiff (£9.05) and London (£23.70); book at least a week early to avoid the price doubling.
Coaches: Services to London (£22.75), Cardiff (£5.50), Manchester (£27.50); again, book early.
Car: A465, A48 and 5 miles off the M4. Parking is limited in residential areas around the campus, but there are a couple of car parks 5 mins amble from Singleton.
Air: Nearest *useful* airport is Cardiff.
Local: Frequent public services pootle between University sites and the city centre.
Taxis: Free phone on campus for students with flammable cash. *Not as expensive as in some towns.*
Bicycles: Bikes are *perfect* between campus and town and *the ecologically-minded University is a real pedal pusher*. The local hills and scenery are *gorgeous* in the right weather and *full of bikeable* trails.

CAREER PROSPECTS:

• Careers Service • No. of staff: 25 full/6 part • Unemployed after 6mths: 6%
A *well-organised and friendly job shop*. They do interview training, jobs fairs, workshops, lectures and job placements and have an *extensive* range of online services.

FAMOUS ALUMNI:

Donald Anderson MP (Lab); Ian Bone (founder of Class War); Daniel Caines (Olympic runner); Andrew Davies AM (Welsh Assembly Government Minister); Richey Edwards, Nicky Wire (Manics); Nigel Evans MP (Con); Dr Hwyel Francis MP; Steve James, Adrian Dale (England cricketers); Jason Mohammed, Mavis Nicolson (TV presenters); Prof. Colin Pillinger (boffin behind bungled Beagle II space probe); Paul Thorburn, Robert Howley, Adedayo Adebayo, Dafydd James, Dwayne Peel, Richie Pugh (rugby players); Two Hats (Goldie Lookin' Chain); Julia Wheeler (BBC Gulf correspondent); Alan Williams MP.

SPECIAL FEATURES:

• Campus includes the Egypt Centre, containing a *considerable* collection of artefacts and curios. The University is already home to the Multidisciplinary Nanotechnology Centre (*a big name for the study of very little things*) and is currently developing the £50m Institute of Life Science, which will include a 'visualisation centre' that could be good news for healthcare and medical innovations.

FURTHER INFO:

• Prospectuses: undergrad; postgrad; all departments; international, video • Open days

The virtual campus (Blackboard) is being put to *quite a lot of use* backing-up normal teaching methods (ie. seminars and workshops), with over 400 modules supported on it. All subjects are modular and some modules are more optional than others. Students can submit exams or projects in Welsh. *Engineering, the Clinical School and Arts & Humanities are considered pretty perky.*

Entry points: 300-360	**Ave points: 284**
Applns per place: 4	**Clearing: 18%**
No. of terms: 3	**Length of terms: 12/10/7wks**
Staff/student ratio: 1:13	**Study addicts: n/a**
Teaching: n/a	**Research: *****
Year abroad: 10%	**Sandwich students: 2%**
Firsts: 9%	**2.2s: 35%**
2.1s: 48%	**3rds: 8%**

ADMISSIONS:

• Apply via UCAS/direct for postgrads and international applicants

SUBJECTS:

Arts, Languages & Social Studies: 36%   Medical Sciences: 18%
Business Studies, Economics & Law: 16%   Sciences: 21%
Engineering: 9%
Best: Biological Sciences; Chemical Engineering; Civic Engineering; Classics; Computer Science; Electrical & Electronic Engineering; Geography; German; Hispanic Studies; History; Italian; Materials Engineering; Physics; Psychology.
Unusual: Egyptology.

LIBRARIES:

• 838,000 books • 1,298 study places • Spend per student: £££££
Swansea's got four different libraries, *none of them too far away*. At least one is open all week, though only till 8pm Sundays. There are 454 PCs for student use in the main Library and Information Centre.

COMPUTERS:

- <u>1,808 workstations</u> • <u>Spend per student: £££</u>

Most of the computer workstations are in the main Library and Information Centre, disguised as study places. There are six students to every computer, *which is good as long as they don't all use it at once.* A cross-campus wireless network gives broadband net access to anyone with a clever enough laptop.

OTHER LEARNING FACILITIES:

Language laboratory; rehearsal rooms; CAD lab; media centre; drama studio; practice court room.

ENTERTAINMENT

THE CITY:

- <u>Price of a pint of beer: £1.95</u> • <u>Glass of wine: £1.20</u> • <u>Can of Red Bull: £1.75</u>

Swansea's *best* for liquid entertainment, being *full* of pubs and clubs. The Kingsway, where most of the clubs hide, teems with revellers at the weekend. The Mumbles Mile, a pub crawl along the seafront, is known as far away as America (*perhaps where someone woke up after trying it*).

Cinemas: Ten-screen multiplex for mainstream films and the Dylan Thomas arts centre for *films in need of York Notes.*

Theatres: The Grand theatre is *popular and successful, but tends to excel more at panto than Pinter.*

Pubs: Mumbles, the Uplands and Wine Street are *popular* for sheer variety and quality of pub. Some pubs on the outskirts should be approached with caution. *Pushplugs: Smoking Dog; Indigo; Ice Bar; Fineleg & Firkin; Rhydding's; Rasputins; Walkabouts; SA1.*

Clubbing: Swansea boasts some *fine* clubs; people come from miles around to visit (*because there's very little elsewhere*). *Pushplugs: Escape (top DJs and indie hangout at weekends); Time (broke the largest student night record when 3,000 freshers turned up); Jumpin' Jacks; Uropa (Drum 'n' Bass); Quids (cheese).*

Music venues: Dozens of pubs are hosts to live music, especially in the Uplands area.

Eating out: *The range, quality and price of Indian restaurants, especially on St Helen's Road, beggars rational belief.* Night nibbles are available till at least 2am and deliveries till midnight, but only till 10 in the Mumbles. *Pushplugs: Café Mambo (Mexican); Mozart's (Austrian); Viceroy (Indian); Slow Boat (Chinese); Angellettos (Italian).*

UNIVERSITY:

- <u>Price of a pint of beer: £1.40</u> • <u>Glass of wine: £1.20</u>

The Taliesin Arts Centre is the crown of the campus with a host of entertainment facilities (from exhibitions to film and music) and *makes up for the city's musical and arty limitations.* In October it's the focus of the Swansea Fringe Festival (the second biggest in Britain after Edinburgh).

Bars: Diva's (cap 450) and Idols (400) are the main bars, putting on a bunch of different nights throughout the year. The Taliesin also has a bar.

Theatres: Swansea students *love* their drama and like to put on a production or twelve in the Taliesin's theatre (cap 350) when the major touring companies aren't using it.

Film: The film society shows two or three a week, usually arthouse or foreign. There's also a gay film season. The Taliesin shows a bit of everything.

Music venues: When a big band's in Swansea, *it's probably lost, but if it's meant to be there,* it'll be in The Refectory (cap 800). Recently it's seen the likes of Snowpatrol and 22-20s. Brangwyn Hall sometimes gets a look in too.

Clubbing: Swansea student craziness revolves around Diva's, more stuff's in town and the SU have been known to hire out popular clubs for the night.

Food: *The Refectory is cheap and has a nice selection, including fodder for the veggie trough. Diva's looks like a chippie with delusions of grandeur.* There's also the free internet café Impressions, Le Café, Café West and Coffee Culture (*they're keen on coffee, y'see*). *Raging carnivores enjoy the bloody pleasures of the Bayview Carvery at lunchtimes.*

Other: Lots of balls. The grand finale is the summer ball *with thumping bass that keeps grannies awake for miles around.* Goldie Lookin' Chain and Kosheen featured at the 05 bash.

SOCIAL & POLITICAL

SWANSEA STUDENTS' UNION:
• 5 sabbaticals • NUS member • Turnout at last ballot: 9%
The college administration are regularly accosted by the SU for various discussions in the name of Swansea students. *As a rule, the student body doesn't let politics interfere with their lack of politics, but they do care about the issues that influence them (fees, racism etc.).* Facilities are *adequate enough to discourage the laidback learners from kicking up a fuss.*

SU FACILITIES:
Three bars; canteen; two fast food outlets; advice; crèche; printing; stationers; travel agent; media centre; TV lounge; insurance shop; pool tables; laundry; video and vending machines; phones; ATMs; photo booth. Hendrefoilan Student Village has: a general shop; bar; licensed diner; vending machines; laundry; payphones.

CLUBS (NON-SPORTING):
Community Action Group; Rag Appeal. **See also Clubs tables.**

OTHER ORGANISATIONS:
Waterfront is the rather *good* newspaper, Xtreme 963 is the rather *loud* radio station and SSCA (Swansea Students' Community Action) is the rather *large* charity dooda running 24 projects a week for the needy.

RELIGIOUS:
• 3 chaplains (CofE, RC, URC), rabbi
Campus has a chapel and a mosque and Swansea is well stocked for places of worship.

PAID WORK:
• Job bureau • Paid work: term-time 50%; hols 85%
Worklink's services include: cuty careers advice sessions; specialist follow-up sessions; CV and application workshops; skills workshops; psychometric testing workshops; employer talks programme; careers fair; six dedicated jobs and placements advisers. Swansea is part of the GO Wales programme so summer jobs in tourism *are not hard to come by. In addition to SU and University opportunities on campus, several employers in the vicinity are sensitive to student situations and offer flexible hours.*

SPORTS

• BUSA Ranking: 41
No shortage of facilities, and the healthy sea air has furnished students with success on a national level in the past and given them something to do when not studying.

SPORTS FACILITIES:
Swansea's *impressive* collection of facilities include: the Swansea Sports Village, consisting of an athletics track, two all-weather pitches and an indoor training centre. There's: 28 acres of playing fields for football, rugby, cricket and hockey; six tennis, one netball, six squash and two basketball courts; swimming pool; indoor and outdoor running tracks; climbing wall; martial arts dojos; golf course; sports hall; river; lake; gym; multigym; athletics field; and, *when all that sport gets too strenuous, a physiotherapy room.* Gym visits cost £2 a time; everything else is £1. Students can also purchase passes (term's gym use: £50, Annual: £140, Annual Activity Pass: £65 plus 50p court booking fee).

SPORTING CLUBS:

Athletics; Badminton; Basketball; Climbing; Cricket; Fencing; Football; Hockey; Netball; Rugby; Sailing; Squash; Swimming; Tennis; Trampolining; Volleyball. **See also Clubs tables.**

ATTRACTIONS:

Swansea's got the sea, with all its sailing, surfing and other such soggy stuff, a dry-ski slope, the Vetch to watch the Swans' *latest defeat* and St Helens to watch the rugby. Wales National Pool is a *bit snazzy* – a 50m pool in a £11m complex, and they're tacking on bits to the outside like the floodlit athletics track. It's a joint University and City/County councils initiative.

IN COLLEGE:

• Catered: 9% • Cost: £65-80 (31wks)
• Self-catering: 30% • Cost: £40-72 (40-51wks)
• First years living in: 99% • Insurance premium: £
Availability: Almost all 1st years get accommodation, as do a handful of others; *only local clearing students are unlucky*. Catered students get seven meals a week. Self-catered costs vary enormously, depending on facilities, but fuel costs are included. The Clyne Halls, just out of town, are *cosy and popular*. The student village in Hendrefoilan is a *little gem*, quite far from campus, but featuring a *cute* cluster of purpose-built housing (with shop). *Clyne and Hendrefoilan are self-contained communities with their own facilities and organisations.* 5% share (no mixed sex) and some rooms and flats are available to couples and families. Students in tower block accomodation have to sign in and out because of fire regulations. Phones in all rooms.
Car parking: *There's no student parking at Singleton but spacious* suburban areas around Clyne and Hendrefoilan mean parking's *easy*. Permits are issued free to those wishing to stow the motor at Hendrefoilan.

EXTERNALLY:

• Ave rent: £44
Availability: Swansea is student-friendly and there's little difficulty finding a relatively nice house in a relatively good area. Good places include Brynmill, Uplands and Sketty. Bad places include Townhill and Bonymaen.
Housing help: Accommodation Office offers sharing lists, advice leaflets, general advice and a bulletin board. The SU provides its own handbook to help avoid unscupulous landlords and a local accreditation scheme allows trustworthy landlords to advertise at slightly higher rates.

SERVICES:

• Lesbian/Gay/Bisexual Officer & Society • Ethnic Minorities Officer & Society
• Women's Officer & Society • Interntaional Student's Officer & Society
• Mature Students' Officer & Society • Postgrad Officer & Society
• Disabilities Officer & Society • Late-night/Women's minibus • Nightline
• College counsellors: 5 full/7 part • Crime rating: !!!
2004 saw the opening of the central Student Support Services Department. There's now also an on-campus police officer.
Health: The University runs a health centre with Mental Health Co-ordinator and counselling services. The NHS practice on campus has four GPs, two nurses and a dentist.
Women: Free attack alarms and advice are offered to women – *who should avoid Singleton Park behind the University at night if they don't like being flashed at.*
Crèches/Nursery: 32 places for munchkins aged 3mths-7yrs.

Disabilities: *The Welsh hills make for difficult times for wheelchair users, though most buildings have access.* There are tactile pathways and a centre for blind students as well as weekly classes by a dyslexia tutor. The Disability Office provides note-takers and co-ordinates a Voluntary Support Worker Scheme that offers non-medical human support. Its Assessment and Training Centre offers academic support, including alternative examination provisions, IT training and equipment loan. Several adapted rooms are available.

FINANCE:

• Ave debt per year: £1,523

Fees: The Welsh Assembly has ruled out top-up fees before 2007.

• Access fund: £545,545 • Successful applications/yr: 950 • Ave payment: £300-3,500

Support: A *wide* range of cashpots, including scholarships worth £1,000 a year and bursaries worth £350 a year, are offered to students outstanding in sport or the arts. Awards of £1,000 are available to cover the cost of tuition fees for students with disabilities, special needs, those of outstanding academic ability and mature students. International students have access to a £22,000 hardship fund and international disabled students can obtain an additional £5,000. 16 bundles of £750 are available for accommodation help.

Staffordshire University has pioneered the use of sewage for making bricks and floor tiles.

University of Teesside
....

Teesside Polytechnic see University of Teesside
....

Textiles see Heriot-Watt University
....

Thames Poly see Greenwich University
....

Thames Valley University
....

Trent University see Nottingham Trent University
....

Trent Polytechnic see Nottingham Trent University
....

Trinity & All Saints see Leeds University
....

University of Teesside

• *Formerly Teesside Polytechnic.*
University of Teesside, Middlesbrough, Tees Valley, TS1 3BA
Tel: (01642) 218 121 E-mail: recruit@tees.ac.uk Website: www.tees.ac.uk
University of Teesside Students' Union, Middlesbrough, TS1 3BA
Tel: (01642) 342 234 E-mail: enquiry@utsu.org.uk Website: www.utsu.org.uk

GENERAL

Middlesbrough is *a crouton in the sprawling industrialised urban soup* that used to go by the name of Cleveland. Over a million Teessiders (that's local folk, not students) are squeezed into Middlesbrough, Stockton, Redcar and Hartlepool. There's been *broad* regeneration in recent years and the University is *part and educational parcel* of it all. There's also a *mammoth* new shopping centre and a leisure complex, both built in the last couple of years. *And should the urban existence start to jar, the Swampy centre (more properly known as Nature's World) is on hand to provide mud, grass and all other things rural.*

58%		
Sex ratio (M:F): 42:58	Founded: 1992
Full-time u'grads: 7,755	Part-time: 9,850
Postgrads: 615	Non-degree: 10,434
Ave course: 3yrs	Ethnic: 8%
State:private school: 97:3	Flunk rate: 21%
Mature: 35%	International: 9%
Disabled: 212	Local: 49%
42%		

ATMOSPHERE:
Like one of Big Daddy's skimpier leotards, the Teesside campus is straining at the seams, with loads of modern facilities and a welcoming, friendly body of students that draws heavily from the local population. It's a clean, green kind of campus and the most recent buildings really are impressive.

MIDDLESBROUGH:

- Population: 134,800 • City centre: 500m • London: 256 miles • York: 49 miles
- Newcastle: 39 miles
- High temp: 19 • Low temp: 0 • Rainfall: 51

Middlesbrough's *not a million miles away from the Corrie end credits – military lines* of Victorian terraces and *plenty* of hills (*although the days of bluff northern chaps doffing their flat caps are long past*). There's still an *active* docking industry though many of the older manufacturing industries are just *shadows of former glories*. There's a *rich seam of shops to be mined*, including bookshops and four *massive* shopping centres. The Tees Valley runs alongside the North York Moors so those who like to go out and about can, um … go out and about.

TRAVEL:

Trains: Middlesbrough Station offers direct links to Newcastle (£5.15), Manchester (£18.15) and other major interchanges. For London (£42.25) change at Darlington.
Coaches: Coach services courtesy of Blue Line, City Link, Swiftline and National Express to London (£21), Manchester (£11.75) and all over.
Car: The A19 south to York and north to Newcastle runs straight past Middlesbrough. There's the A66 cross country to the lakes, and the A1 runs past Darlington, 15 miles to the west.
Air: Teesside Airport's 12 miles away: domestic flights and to Europe and Scandinavia.
Local: Buses are *cheap* (50p max) and *fairly regular* (until 11pm). Trains run all over the Teesside conurbation.
Taxis: *Reasonably* priced (£2 across town) and *readily* available.
Bicycles: The town is flat, *but small enough to render pedalling purely recreational*.

CAREER PROSPECTS:

- Careers Service • No. of staff: 6 full-time • Unemployed after 6mths: 7%

The careers service ticks all the right boxes, providing students with bulletin boards, a careers library, job fairs, individual guidance, employer presentations and psychometric testing. There are good links with *national companies* and graduates' careers are kick-started through Knowledge Transfer Partnerships – *the modern equivalent of having an uncle on the board of directors*.

FAMOUS ALUMNI:

David Bowe, Steve Hughes (MEPs); Paul Marsden (MP); Chris Newton (Olympic bronze medallist, Sydney 2000); Skin (singer, once of Skunk Anansie). Honorary grads: Elizabeth Estensen (Emmerdale's Woolpack landlady); Andrew Lomas (Computer graphics *whizz* on Matrix Revolutions etc.)

SPECIAL FEATURES:

- Teesside's Hemispherium is the world's only virtual reality auditorium.
- *Technotronic* Teesside hosts Animex each year – a major international animation and computer games festival that attracts designers, animators and general *geeks* from around the world. The Animex Student Animation Awards are held and judged here.

FURTHER INFO:

- Prospectuses: undergrads; postgrads; departmental; video; CD-Rom • Open days

ACADEMIC

Toasty hot on media-related subjects, *particularly where computers are involved*. The CAD course makes use of the Hemispherium, *which might otherwise just be used for re-runs of Gladiator*. Also strong for Health and Sport Studies.

Entry points: 120-280
Applns per place: 4
No. of terms: 3
Staff/student ratio: 1:12
Teaching: *
Year abroad: n/a
Firsts: 8%
2.1s: 37%

Ave points: 236
Clearing: 9%
Length of terms: 12wks
Study addicts: 31%
Research: *
Sandwich students: 28%
2.2s: 43%
3rds: 11%

ADMISSIONS:

- Apply via UCAS/NMAS for nursing

SUBJECTS:

Arts& Media: 16%
Business School: 13%
Computing: 24%

Health & Social Care: 14%
Science & Technology: 10%
Social Sciences & Law: 23%

Best: Allied Health Professions; Art & Design; Electrical & Electronic Engineering; History; Nursing & Midwifery; Psychology; Social Work; Sport & Exercise.
Unusual: Computing, Animation & Games Design; Crime Science; Criminology; Forensic Science; Fraud Science; Policing.

LIBRARIES:

- 381,000 books • 1,304 study places • Spend per student: £££

The new Learning Resource Centre is visually and technologically *impressive, but students complain that there just aren't enough books to go round.*

COMPUTERS:

- 1,719 workstations

University accommodation should come with free internet access by September 2005.

OTHER LEARNING FACILITIES:

Plenty of added bonuses, including: language labs open to all; the *elaborate* Crime Scene House Laboratory; the nanotechnology centre; a Vehicle Examination Centre *(for rozzers in training);* and sports testing labs. There are whispers about the forthcoming Institute of Digital Innovation, which will coincide with the development of a DigitalCity in Middlesbrough, and be a research centre for digital design, film and sound.

ENTERTAINMENT

THE TOWN:

- Price of a pint of beer: £2.05 • Glass of wine: £2 • Can of Red Bull: £1.60

Cinemas: Two new multiplexes. The UCG does a discount for students.
Theatres: The *unadventurously named* Middlesbrough Theatre and Little Theatre show *mainstream* performances with the Arc doing the *diversity bit.*
Pubs: Linthorpe Road is a *spanking* new stretch of boozers and bars. *Pushplugs: Dickens Inn; Cornerhouse; The Crown; Scruffy Murphy's; Star & Garter.*
Clubbing: *Pushplugs: Monday night at Jumpin Jaks; Liquid; Empire. Best of a borderline bunch.*
Music venues: The Town Hall hosts *big-to-middling* names. Recent visitors include Black Rebel Motorcycle Club and The Libertines.
Eating out: Curry houses *galore can't overshadow the student institution that is* Roy's Cafe. Roy's an honorary lifetime SU member. *Pushplugs: Jo Rigatonies (Italian); The Purple Onion; Royal Palace; Khans (Indian).*

UNIVERSITY:

• Price of a pint of beer: £1.70 • Glass of wine: £1.45 • Can of Red Bull: £1.50
Bars: The Terrace Bar has had an *essential* chrome and wood panelling facelift. More to the point, it's open for *hard boozing* seven days a week.
Film: The film society shows four a week, from *classics* (Brighton Rock) to *mainstream favourites* (Pirates of the Caribbean) and latest releases.
Music venues: *Stiff competition* from the Town Hall has *beaten the Terrace Bar into a poor second, consigned to hosting* the likes of the Pet Shop Boys.
Clubbing: Club One is the *favourite*, with DJ sets from circuit names like DJ Lotti and Mixi Moto.
Comedy/Cabaret: The Joke Joint (twice monthly at the Terrace) features *minor* names. The Phoenix Nights cast pitch up *now and again*.
Food: *Unspectacular but edible* at the Terrace Bar and the Gallery.
Other: Black tie and ballgowns at the ready for the Freshers' and Graduation balls.

SOCIAL & POLITICAL

UNIVERSITY OF TEESSIDE STUDENTS UNION:

• 4 sabbaticals • Turnout at last ballot: 8% • NUS member
The award-winning SU is *known for putting extra effort into ents*.

SU FACILITIES:

Two bars; one cafeteria; general shop; cash machine (HSBC); Endsleigh Insurance; advice centre; new activities and skills centre; pool tables; vending machines; market stalls; and other general services such as phones, photocopiers and photo booths.

CLUBS (NON-SPORTING):

Anime; Coffee; Cultural; First Aid; Hellenic; Irish; Mystical; Photography; Rock; Role Playing & Wargaming; Wine.
See also Clubs tables.

OTHER ORGANISATIONS:

Monthly publication Cup of Tees is published by the SU. *Rag's place in heaven is secure – it scrapes together a few grand every year for charity.*

RELIGIOUS:

• 2 chaplains (CofE, RC)
Churches, mosques and synagogues are all available in Middlesbrough.

PAID WORK:

• Job bureau
The Student Job Centre helps students find part-time work and the SU employs more than 150 students every year.

SPORTS

• Recent successes: none • BUSA Ranking: 48
The SU did win a Sport England VIP recognition award, but sporting successes are *thin on the ground* – shocking, given the mighty state of the ground (a *frankly awesome* £6.5m two-storey building, which houses *every sporting facility imaginable). The University is aware of all this wasted potential and has a 'try it, you might like it' attitude.* Wednesday afternoons are left free for mucking about on the pitch.

SPORTS FACILITIES:

Saltersgill Sports Ground has 65 acres of playing fields for football, rugby and hockey – including one all-weather; netball court; two squash courts; basketball court; two sports halls; gym; climbing wall; watersports centre; *bizarre and extravagant* temperature-controlled environment centre which can simulate any climate in the world. *No, really.* With a sports card (£40), almost everything is free. Locally: leisure centre; golf course; watersports lake; ski slope; swimming pool.

SPORTING CLUBS:
10-Pin Bowling, Gaelic Football, Rowing and various Martial Arts. **See also Clubs tables.**

ATTRACTIONS:
Middlesbrough FC recently won their first trophy for 127 years; West Hartlepool rugby union; horse racing at Redcar; speedway at Stockton. Tees Barrage is an 11-mile stretch of world-class white water for rafting and canoeing.

A C C O M M O D A T I O N

IN COLLEGE:
• Self-catering: 17% • Cost: £40 (38wks)
• Head tenancy: 7% • Cost: £32-36 (37wks)
• First years living in: 40% • Insurance premium: £££££
Availability: All 1st years firmly accepting a place are now being guaranteed a bed. Accommodation ranges from *positively plush to pretty poor* but is all *close to college – so close that it can get a bit claustrophobic.* King Edward's Square and Parkside Flats *get the thumbs up.* Parkside Hall (shared study bedrooms) and Woodlands (*pricey* rooms) *get a thumbs down. But, on the other hand, it's as cheap as David Dickinson's fake tan.*
Car parking: £63 buys a year-long parking pass for college and halls.

EXTERNALLY:
• Ave rent: £35
Availability: *Good value at twice the price* and all the student neighbourhoods are in *spitting distance* of campus. Accommodation is *ridiculously easy* to find, and, since the North York Moors and the North Sea Coast are on the doostep, *the view's always pretty.*
Housing help: Five full-time staff are on hand at the University Accommodation Service.

W E L F A R E

SERVICES:
• Lesbian/Gay/Bisexual Officer & Society • Ethnic Minorities' Officer & Society
• Women's Officer & Society • Mature Students' Officer & Society
• International Students' Officer & Society • Disabilities Officer & Society
• Late-night minibus • Self-defence classes
• College counsellors: 3 full/2 part • Crime rating: !!!!
Welfare provision at the University Advice Centre is *top dollar*, and the SU/University collaborate *to keep things that way.* The late-night minibus operates in a 3-mile radius of college and costs 50p a trip.
Health: *Loads* of medical practices in the town centre.
Crèches/Nursery: 66 places for children aged 6wks-5yrs.
Disabilities: The low-level, ramped-up campus is *big* on access. The Learning Resource Centre has a reading edge scanner, large-screen PC, braille machine and tactile diagram facility. Hearing loops are installed around the campus. The University provides specialist dyslexia support and a mental health co-ordinator.

FINANCE:
• Ave debt per year: £3,938
• Access fund: £870,353 • Successful applications/yr: 1,253 • Ave payment: £50-£3,500
Support: Bursaries are available to cover a range of circumstances, including sports funds and short-term emergency loans. *Incredibly*, all UK and EU students receive a £500 welcome grant, just for showing up.

Teesside Polytechnic

see University of Teesside

Textiles

see Heriot-Watt University

Thames Poly

see Greenwich University

Thames Valley University

- **Formerly Polytechnic of West London.**
(1) Thames Valley University, St Mary's Road, Ealing, London, W5 5RF
Tel: (0800) 036 8888 E-mail: learning.advice@tvu.ac.uk Website: www.tvu.ac.uk
Thames Valley Students' Union, Thames Valley University, St Mary's Road, Ealing, London,
W5 5RF Tel: (020) 8231 2573 E-mail: student.services@tvu.ac.uk
Website: www.tvu.ac.uk/student-services
(2) Thames Valley University, Wellington Street, Slough, Berkshire, SL1 1YG
Tel: (01753) 534585
(3) Thames Valley University, King's Road, Reading, Berkshire, RG1 4HJ
Tel: (0118) 967 5000

GENERAL

Thames Valley University is made up of three sites, following the winding path of the Thames through Reading, Slough and Ealing. In 1991, Thames Valley College Slough merged with London College of Music which merged with Queen Charlotte's College of Healthcare Study to form the Polytechnic of West London. A year later it became Thames Valley University. In January 2004, Reading College was sucked into the mix. *It also tried to merge with a passing milkman, but he was having none of it. The University has a strong commitment to the local area and encouraging entry through non-traditional routes.* Most students are at the main Ealing site, in the suburban west of London, 10 miles from Trafalgar Square. **For general information about London see University of London.**

Sex ratio (M:F): 34:66	Founded: 1992
Full-time u'grads: 7,335	Part-time: 7,355
Postgrads: 410	Non-degree: 13,218
Ave course: 3yrs	Ethnic: 58%
State:private school: 87:1	Flunk rate: 25%
Mature: 91%	International: 13%
Disabled: 70	Local: 70%

ATMOSPHERE:

Diverse and then some, TVU takes in large numbers of students who are mature, international or from the ethnically diverse local community. There are also many students on part-time, day-release and evening courses and far from all are studying for degrees.

There's also quite a chunk who've rolled in off the roulette wheel of clearing. This all means TVU is about as far as you can get from the stereotypical university (20-year-old white males with posh voices, reading poetry in college scarves). The main campus at Ealing is quiet and away from the main, gritty urban splat of London. Students are always in a hurry – as if they're worried that if they stand still the University will try to merge with them.

SITES:

Slough Campus: (Hotel & Catering, Science, Computing, Accounting, Business & Finance, Nursing & Healthcare) The train station's right opposite which is dead handy, more space and free facilities than Ealing, it's got a gym and an expanded range of courses *but, of course, it's in Slough,* 13 m les from Ealing. *A heroically unimpressive commuter satellite town, with a name like a groinal infection in sheep, Slough is perhaps best described by John Betjeman 'Come friendly bombs and fall on Slough. It's no fit for humans now'. So it's just as well £4m has been slated for rejuvenating the town centre.*
Reading College: (Fine Art, Fashion, Chemical Science, Building Studies) Still further west out of London (Ealing, 25 miles; Slough, 21 miles). *There's fierce rivalry with Slough in the dullness stakes, but Oxford (20 miles) is easy to get to from Reading for more aesthetic pleasures. Trains to Paddington are fairly regular and speedy (30 mins), so a night out in the West End is doable (you don't want to stay out too late).*

LONDON: see University of London

EALING:

Ealing is an *easily accessible* part of West London *and mostly affluent* with *posh* shops flogging stuff alongside the budget. *South Ealing has things a bit harder.* The main campus is halfway between the two. The area is known as a haunt for would-be celebs – Ealing Studies is opposite the University. Situated by a private estate, local noise-related friction has caused sparks in the past, ably sorted out by the University wading in and threatening to ban ents and bars.

TRAVEL: see University of London
Underground: Ealing Broadway, Ealing Common and South Ealing are all under a mile away.
Trains: Nearest station is Ealing Broadway, 800m away.
Buses: Buses serving Ealing are 65, 207, 83 E1, E2, E7, E8, E9, E10, E11, PR1, 297, 607 and night buses too. *Enough, already.*
Coaches: Nearest stop is Hammersmith, 10 mins by Tube.
Car: There are short-term parking meters throughout central Ealing. The University has limited parking for students at £5 per day. Also a number of council-run car parks in the area.
College: A free bus service connects the Ealing and Slough campuses running hourly in term time between 7 and 7.
Bicycles: Bikes are *a popular option*, with sheds at all buildings and sites. *Although Ealing has no cycle lanes, there a large number of parks, which makes for peaceful cycling.*

CAREER PROSPECTS:

• Careers Service • No. of staff: 8 full/2 part • Unemployed after 6mths: 10%
A well-stocked careers service, with career planning and management, appointments, workshops, student-employer meetings and employer presentations.

FAMOUS ALUMNI:

Emma Anderson (musician); John Bird (Big Issue founder); Sergey Ivanov (Russian defence minister); James Larlett (ex British hockey captain); Alan Lee (illustrator); Freddie Mercury (Queen, *RIP*); Robert Rankin (writer); Pete Townshend (the Who); Ron Wood (Rolling Stones). Honorary Awards have gone to David Frost, Neil Kinnock and Alexi Sayle and recently Gary Rhodes and Brian Turner.

FURTHER INFO:

• Prospectuses: undergrad; postgrad; departmental • Open days • Video

The big idea is to provide education from FE (A Levels etc.) right the way through to postgrad, and *it shows TVU is always willing to make the most of what they've got and give new things a bash (especially if they're cheap)*. For starters, 'Blackboard', a virtual campus, is in place, designed to help distance learning. There's also a 'credit accumulation scheme', where students can take a break from study, change the structure of their course or obtain a certificate for the work they've done if they quit. Workshops, group work, case studies, lectures and seminars are the norm with assessment concentrated on the 3rd year. *Many students think it's all a bit disorganised, partly due to the recent Reading merger.*

Entry points: 40-280	Ave points: n/a
Applns per place: n/a	Clearing: 34%
No. of terms: 4	Length of terms: 10wks
Staff/student ratio: n/a	Study addicts: 20%
Teaching: *	Research: *
Year abroad: n/a	Sandwich students: 1%
Firsts: 10%	2.2s: 33%
2.1s: 39%	3rds: 8%

ADMISSIONS:
• Apply via UCAS

SUBJECTS:

Art & Design: 27%	Medical Sciences: 28%
Arts/Humanities: 1%	(Modern) Languages: 1%
Business/Management: 36%	Sciences: 1%
Engineering: 1%	Social Sciences: 5%

Best: Nursing; Psychology; Tourism, Hospitality & Leisure.
Unusual: Acupuncture.

LIBRARIES:
• 350,000 books • 900 study places • Spend per student: £££
TVU has five libraries, the two main ones being at Ealing and at Slough in the *fancy* Paul Hamlyn Resource Centre (*which looks like a train station*). *The opening hours are uninspiring, the latest being 10pm.*

COMPUTERS:
• 1,200 workstations • 24-hr access
• Spend per student: £££
Three different labs, with both Macs and PCs and special provision for disabled students. Ealing has 700 terminals with 24-hr access.

OTHER LEARNING FACILITIES:
Audio, TV and video studio, CAD lab, language laboratory and photography studio.

THE CITY: see University of London
• Price of a pint of beer: £2.40 • Glass of wine: £1.75 • Can of Red Bull: £2
With a better than average selection of bars and restaurants, Ealing has enough to mean treks into central London can be kept for occasions worth the extra hassle and expense.
Theatre & cinema: Ealing UGL is the flick-pit of choice. There are more further out. Ealing has the small Questors with fringe performances, but the *top-notch* Lyric Hammersmith and Riverside ain't far away and *usually have an innovative programme*. Watermans Arts Centre is 10 mins by bus and does arthouse cinema, exhibitions etc.

Pubs: *Most local pubs have the feel of a middle-class family day out, but are still fun with the right crowd. There are a couple of chain pubs about too. Pushplugs: The Better Half; Ha Ha; The Townhouse; Old Orleans; The Green; ONeill's.*
Clubbing/Music: The Broadway Boulevard is Ealing's *classiest* venue, with a student night on Tuesdays. Live music is mainly pub-based but the Labatts Apollo (Hammersmith) and the Shepherds Bush Empire are within easy reach.
Eating out: All sorts of multi-cultural scoff shops. *Pushplugs: Pizza on the Green (Italian); Tandoori Villa; Café Grove (Polish); Red Lion (British, but with outdoor eating). Monty's does cult Indian eating.*

UNIVERSITY:
• Price of a pint of beer: £1.50 • Glass of wine: £1
Plenty of space club-wise, but this isn't exactly TVU's forte. Variety lacks, so students have adventures off-campus in search of the missing fun.
Bars: The Union Bar and Cheeky Monkeys, plus two bars in Slough.
Music/Clubbing: Lawrence Hall (cap 800) hosts a bunch of club nights and gigs. Tribute bands turn up a lot and *inexplicably* aren't chased away.
Other: Societies stage cultural events at the SU throughout the year. Each site has its own annual ball: welcome balls, the black tie sports awards and the 10-hr extravaganza that is the Annual May Ball.

SOCIAL & POLITICAL

THAMES VALLEY STUDENTS' UNION:
• 4 sabbaticals • NUS member • Turnout at last ballot: 8%
All campuses are united in not giving a flying fig about politics. Good relations exist between the University and the SU. Students sit on the governing and academic boards and get to hear and have a say in most things that go on.

SU FACILITIES:
The main SU is a converted Victorian Grammar School with a bar, minibuses, coffee shop, photocopying, printing, snack shop, vending and games machines.

CLUBS (NON-SPORTING):
High Society (for creative types); Law; Sikh. **See also Clubs tables.**

OTHER ORGANISATIONS:
Monthly student newspaper, the Valley; on-air and online radio station the Tube.

RELIGIOUS:
• 2 chaplains (CofE, RC), rabbi
World Faith Room in the North Building.

PAID WORK: see University of London
• Job bureau • Paid work: term-time 96%; hols 97%
The Careers & Employment Service has various opportunities including bar work, marketing, IT support, office admin, retail, translation, marketing and charity work.

UCL has removed the preserved head of philosopher Jeremy Bentham from its display case after a group of King's College students 'borrowed' it for a game of football.

• BUSA Ranking: n/a
*The students have been developing a keen interest in sports, despite the lack of facilities,
which they pay £20 a year for.*

SPORTS FACILITIES:

Football, hockey, cricket and rugby pitches; basketball and squash courts, sports hall; gym;
multigym.

SPORTING CLUBS:

Boxing; Capoiera; Ju-Jitsu; Yoga. **See also Clubs tables.**

ATTRACTIONS: see University of London

IN COLLEGE:

• Self-catering cost: £70-90 (43-52wks) • Catered cost: £85-99 (43-52wks)
• Insurance premium: £££
Availability: TVU has no accommodation of its own, *but does its best to locate living spaces
for its students in the local area.*

EXTERNALLY:

• Ave rent: £85
Availability: *South Ealing, Hanwell and Acton are popular and cheapish, though Acton is a
bit dull. The rest of Ealing is avoided because it's costly. Slough: the last thoughts of many
a victim of horrible deaths are probably 'Oh well, at least I don't live in Slough'. Windsor is
near, but very expensive.*
Housing help: The Administration Department runs an *excellent* housing help service,
probably because they have to. They have approved housing lists, vetted properties, advice
and so on.

SERVICES:

• Women's Officer • International Students' Officer • Disabilities Society
• Self-defence classes • Minibus • College counsellors: 3 full
• SU counsellors: 2 • Crime rating: !!!
TVU's student advice team, personal tutors and counsellors supply general help and
wisdom, alongside the SU's case workers (available by appointment only).
Health: Nursing staff are available at Ealing and Slough and a GP visits the Ealing campus
four times a week.
Women: Self-defence classes are run through the sports department.
Disabled: *Wheelchair access is excellent* and there are induction loops, dyslexia support,
talking lifts and an assistive technology suite with computers that have Jaws, Kurswell 3000
and Texthelp.

FINANCE:
- Ave debt per year: £5,009
- Access fund: £1,000,000
- Successful applications/yr: 596 • Ave payment: £100-3,500

Support: Various trusts and charitable donations can be had and scholarships are available through the faculties (aka academic departments).

Trent University

see Nottingham Trent University

Trent Polytechnic

see Nottingham Trent University

Trinity & All Saints

see Leeds University

UCE
see University of Central England

UCL
see University College, London

UEA
see University of East Anglia

UEL
see University of East London

University of Ulster

(1) University of Ulster, Cromore Road, Coleraine, Co. Londonderry, BT52 1SA
Tel: (08700) 400 700 E-mail: online@ulster.ac.uk Website: www.ulster.ac.uk
UUSU, University of Ulster, Cromore Rd, Coleraine, Co. Londonderry, BT52 1SA
Tel: (028) 7032 4323 E-mail: info@uusu.org Website: www.uusu.org
(2) The University of Ulster, Jordanstown, Shore Road, Newtonabbey, Co. Antrim, BT37 0QB
Tel: (028) 9036 5131
(3) The University of Ulster, York Street, Belfast, BT15 1ED Tel: (028) 9032 8515
(4) The University of Ulster, Magee College, Northland Road, Londonderry, BT48 7JL
Tel: (028) 7137 1371

GENERAL

Once upon a time, there was a university and a polytechnic in Northern Ireland. Then, in 1984, they merged and became one large university with four distinct sites, *thinly* spread across three of the six counties. The largest is Jordanstown, the former poly site on the hills above Belfast overlooking the Lough (bay), and the smallest (housing Art & Design) is in Belfast city centre. The University HQ is on the outskirts of Coleraine, nearly 60 miles north of Belfast on the *beautiful* Antrim coast. 30 miles to the west of that is the fourth site, Magee College in (London)Derry. Each site may be part of the same institution, but *geography will be geography and no grand integration plan is going to prevent them from maintaining their own separate and unique atmnospheres. Indeed, all that Jordanstown and Coleraine have in common are a beautiful, isolated setting and unlovable modern concrete buildings.*

Sex ratio (M:F): 38:62	**Founded: 1968**
Full-time u'grads: 15,010	**Part-time: 4,010**
Postgrads: 2,175	**Non-degree: 6,791**
Ave course: 3yrs	**Ethnic: 1%**
State:private school: 99:1	**Flunk rate: 16%**
Mature: 21%	**International: 16%**
Disabled: 290	**Local: n/a**

ATMOSPHERE:
We're talking about four different sites here which, despite the University's best efforts towards integration and certain similarities in the make-up of the student body (a strong sense of community thanks to so many being local), still stubbornly remain up to 80 miles apart. Failing divine intervention, they'll remain geographically separate, so that's how we'll treat them.

SITES:
Jordanstown: (13,893 students) The largest site swallows the vast majority of the student population and is still *greedily* expanding. Belfast, 7 miles away, is the nearest town of any size. *There is a slight degree of isolation though the campus is well-connected and the attractive grounds, buildings and views over the bay provide some compensation. Most of the students go home every weekend, so there's no room for claustrophobia. Relaxed and occasionally a bit vacant.*
Coleraine: (5,687 students) The original site of the University and its current administrative HQ. The campus is on the edge of the *small, quiet and nearly-but-not-quite-happening* market town of Coleraine, and less than 5 miles from the coastal resorts of Portrush and Portstewart, where most students live. The neighbouring towns make up 'the Triangle' – not an apocalyptic cult, but an *amiable threesome* of seaside tourist spots. The campus is surrounded by green countryside and nearby the Giant's Causeway reaches out across the Irish sea towards Scotland. *It's a peaceful place – sometimes a tad too peaceful. Every night at 6pm the campus sputters to a halt. This is true for weekends too (so if you're after a blinding Saturday night, better be inventive).* There is grooving to be had, though, in the pubs and clubs in Portrush and Portstewart.
Magee: (3,451 students) An *attractive* campus on the River Foyle, just north of the old city of (London)Derry. The £3m centre for Dramatic Arts has *increased the pulse somewhat*.
Belfast: (1,213 students) Art & Design students are housed on York Street, just a mile away from Queen's University of Belfast, *whose facilities they share and which is the focus of their social life*. A £30m redevelopment programme is underway, *which should make it something to stop and gawp at while in Belfast*.

TOWNS:
Belfast: see Queen's University of Belfast
Coleraine/Portrush/Portstewart: The three towns form a triangle with the two ports to the north providing accommodation, jobs and *sporadic* nightlife, and Coleraine at the south tip providing what could only be called amenities. A town of 20,000 give or take a few, Coleraine has *a fair sprinkling of cheapy* supermarkets, Irish and UK banks and bookshops. It's an *isolated, parochial, coastal and touristy outpost*.

(London)Derry: An ancient and *scenic* city and Northern Ireland's second biggest. The huge stone walls betray the city's turbulent history. *People's lives aren't ruled by terrorism though, but by the normal, mundane concerns. (Okay, the London prefix thing: saying 'Londonderry' marks a person as pro-Unionist, saying Derry ruffles the feathers the other way. Either way, students are stuffed. No wonder most come from Northern Ireland – at least they understand the questions, even if they don't know the answers.)*

TRAVEL: see Queen's University of Belfast
Trains: Direct lines from Coleraine to Belfast and (London)Derry only on Northern Ireland Railways. Trains are frequent and *frequently dirty*. Trains for Dublin can also be picked up from Belfast.
Coaches: Goldline Express and Ulsterbus link Belfast, (London)Derry and Coleraine.
Car: The M2 and the A26 provide *a fast route between Jordanstown and Coleraine.*
Air: Flights to the UK and mainland Europe from Belfast International. Other flights go to the UK from Belfast City Airport and Derry airport in the north-west.
Hitching: *Good between Coleraine and the ports, otherwise only with the greatest care.*
Local: *Comprehensive and expensive local bus routes,* but half-price for students around Coleraine. Ulsterbus does an all-day rambler ticket for a fiver.
Taxis: *Readily available and cheap if shared.*
Bicycles: *With the hills and inclement weather, cycling's only for the hardy, but bike theft's not too much of a worry.*

CAREER PROSPECTS:

• Careers Service • No. of staff: 4 full • Unemployed after 6mths: 6%
The Jordanstown, Coleraine and Magee sites all have their own services. Coleraine's looks after students up to two years after graduation.

FAMOUS ALUMNI:

Gerry Anderson (radio personality); Brian Friel (playwright); Kate Hoey MP (Lab); Brian Keenan (ex-hostage); Brian Robinson (Irish rugby). Honorary graduates include: Amanda Burton (TV actress); James Nesbitt (Cold Feet); Ewan McGregor (actor).

SPECIAL FEATURES:

• *It's rare to have to travel between the sites, rarer still because of* a video conferencing facility. *It's not for chats about the weather, though.*

FURTHER INFO:

• Prospectuses: undergrad; postgrad; departmental

A C A D E M I C

Ulster's a busy and rampantly progressive institution. Public speaking and debating are encouraged because they're seen as being useful in the workplace. *Students have a good deal of independence in their own learning, something the University encourages.*

Entry points: 120-360	**Ave points: 256**
Applns per place: 6	**Clearing: 10%**
No. of terms: 3	**Length of terms: 12wks**
Staff/student ratio: 1:18	**Study addicts: 20%**
Teaching: *****	**Research: *******
Year abroad: 22%	**Sandwich students: 47%**
Firsts: 9%	**2.2s: 34%**
2.1s: 54%	**3rds: 3%**

ADMISSIONS:

• Apply via UCAS
Admissions are taken on academic ability only. If the points are met, the student's in.

SUBJECTS:

Art & Design: 14%   Life & Health Sciences: 27%
Business/Management: 22%   Social Sciences: 14%
Best: Business & Management; Celtic Studies; Economics; Education; Hospitality, Leisure, Sport & Tourism; Maths, Statistics & Operational Research; Nursing; Other Subjects Allied to Medicine; Philosophy; Politics; Psychology.
Unusual: Dance; Postgrad diplomas in: Belfast: The Social & Cultural History of a Changing City; Coastal Zone Management; Dementia Studies; Disaster Relief; Peace & Conflict Studies.

LIBRARIES:

• 650,000 books • 2,831 study places • Spend per student: £££
University libraries are sprinkled across the campuses. In Coleraine it's considered *adequate*, Belfast has the arts books, Magee the Irish ones *(so Push wonders where students of Irish Art go)*. *It's tricky to travel to some of the other campuses to work, but the ambitious* virtual campus (www.campusione.ulster.ac.uk) attempts to link everyone cybernetically, at least.

COMPUTERS:

• 1,500 workstations • 24-hr access
Each facility has its own computers and there are up to four IT centres on each campus. There are ports for laptops, including net access but with extra charges for printing.

ENTERTAINMENT

THE CITY: see Queen's University of Belfast

COLERAINE:

• Price of a pint of beer: £1.80 • Glass of wine: £2.20 • Can of Red Bull: £1.20
Coleraine's *far from the beating heart of the fun monster and what there is can be jealously guarded by a hulking, tattooed section of the local population. Any nightlife is found in Portrush and Portstewart.*
Cinemas: Coleraine has the Jet Centre, *a little more dynamic-sounding than it really is.* Portrush has the Playhouse, a student fave that shows all sorts of *quality* flicks.
Pubs: Burberry's is the only pub of note in Coleraine itself, but the Derry and Harbour Inn at Portrush and the Anchor and O'Hara's in Portstewart are pretty *pro-student money*. The Bushmill's distillery is nearby and does guided tours.
Clubbing: Trax (Portrush) is the *student meat market* on a Monday.
Music venues: *Loads of the bars and clubs host bands, some are less impressive than others such as* Snappers in Portstewart. Pushplugs: O'Hara's in Portstewart (traditional music).
Eating out: *The ports have all the chips and candyfloss a fat kid could ever want, but only during the summer season.* Pushplugs: Morelli's in Portstewart (for ice cream).

UNIVERSITY

• Price of a pint of beer: £1.50 • Glass of wine: £1.20 • Can of Red Bull: £0.80
Not entertainmentsville by a long shot; students actually prefer to seek out the local hotspots.
Bars: Jordanstown has three bars including the popular Arthur's. There's also Club Bar at Coleraine; Bunker Bar at Magee; and Conor Hall at Belfast.
Theatres: *The jewel in the crown is* the Riverside Theatre, the third-largest professional theatre in Northern Ireland. The Riverside programme incorporates drama, music recitals, rock bands, contemporary dance, ballet, opera, variety, children's shows, pantomimes and recordings for TV and radio.
Music venues: *Jordanstown comes out best with its* Assembly Hall, *though* Coleraine's Biko Hall *ain't bad either and the* Riverside *occasionally pulls something out of the hat.*
Clubbing: *The most popular night out is* Kelly's in Portrush. The Saturday night raves at Conor Hall in Belfast *are popular too and can attract big DJs.* Most campuses will have something quietly rocking along most nights.
Food: All sites except Belfast have *cheap but basic* canteens run by the SU. Belfast has no catering facilities. Banside canteen at Coleraine *may be best avoided*.
Other: Freshers ball every year and various others. The Hallowe'en festival in Derry is like a mini Mardi Gras.

SOCIAL & POLITICAL

THE UNIVERSITY OF ULSTER STUDENTS' UNION (UUSU):
• 9 sabbaticals • Turnout at last ballot: 8% • NUS member
Coherent political identity is a tall order at the best of times, but when everything's so spread out it's almost impossible. Technically speaking, the SU co-ordinates ents and facilities across all sites but is distant and unapproachable and has difficulty achieving any kind of global view. Most students think the SU is just a bar.

SU FACILITIES:
All sites have bars and snack bars or cafeteria facilities as well as music venues. In the South Building at Coleraine: general shop; ATM; pool tables; crèche; travel agents; hairdresser; launderette; printing facilities; vending machines; jukebox. At Jordanstown: shop; travel agents; ATM; insurance office; secondhand bookshop; car and van hire; photocopying. At Belfast: art shop; games room; free shuttle after SU ents. Magee: general shop; photocopier; photo booth.

CLUBS (NON-SPORTING):
Coleraine: An Cumman Gaelach; Bahai'I; Nutrition. Jordanstown: An Cumman Eirannach; Chinese; Duke of Edinburgh. Magee: Sinn Fein. Belfast: Art & Craft Appreciation; Divine Enlightenment; Silversmith. **See also Clubs tables.**

OTHER ORGANISATIONS:
Each site has its own publication and there's an all-site publication called – *wait for it* – Foursite, as well as the Coleraine-based publication Ufouria. The combined Rag raises money every year with *wacky stunts and zany antics and student groups do good work – sorry about this – 'fourging' links with their respective local communities.*

RELIGIOUS:
• 2 chaplains (CofE, RC)
Non-denominational prayer rooms are available. *Non-Christians will be a bit pushed to find a handy worship stop.*

PAID WORK: see Queen's University of Belfast
• Job bureau
The SU employs around 100 people throughout the year. There's plenty of part-time/vacation work to be had in local bars, cafés and other tourist traps.

SPORTS

• BUSA Ranking: 48
Sport's an enthusiasm on a campus-wide rather than a University-wide basis. *The best facilities are inevitably centred on Jordanstown and Coleraine, but the nearby coast offers a host of opportunities for hydrophiliacs.*

SPORTS FACILITIES:
Coleraine and Jordanstown have over 40 acres of playing fields (collectively); sports centres; athletics tracks; steam rooms; squash and tennis courts. Coleraine has floodlit hockey and soccer pitches; fitness suite; netball; multigym and gym.

SPORTING CLUBS:
Coleraine: Aikido; Canoe; Camogie; Gaelic Football; Hurling; Shotokan Karate; Surf. Jordanstown: Camogie; Canoe; Gaelic Football; Hurling; Ju Jitsu; Shotokan Karate; Snooker; Swimming & Waterpolo. Magee: Gaelic Football; Hurling. **See also Clubs tables.**

ATTRACTIONS: see Queen's University of Belfast
The Antrim coast provides *some of the best* surfing, wind surfing and swimming conditions in the British Isles, *though it can be ferocious at times.* Fishing is popular too, as is rock climbing, mountaineering, parachuting and rowing. Irish games such as hurling, camogie and Gaelic football should be experienced, and the rugby teams are in the highest Irish leagues.

ACCOMMODATION

IN COLLEGE:
• Self-catering: 6% • Cost: £38-45 (37wks)
• First years living in: 65% • Insurance premium: £
Availability: All 1st years can be housed, as can international students if they meet the 1st August deadline. Jordanstown has six-bedroom houses and flats, Coleraine offers four lots of halls and flats and Magee has three blocks and a student village. Belfast art students need to find their own pads, though there's a head tenancy scheme to help them.
Car parking: Car parking is *easy* and without the hassle of needing a permit.

EXTERNALLY: see Queen's University of Belfast
• Ave rent: £46 • Living at home: 35%
Availability: *Pretty easy to find.* Most students at Coleraine live in the port towns, *where housing is exceptionally cheap* and more affluent students fork out a bit more for a single flat. The University's renting scheme shares houses at the ports that are given up to tourists during the summer. *Most are more than happy with a comfortable room in a shared house. Cars make life simpler at Coleraine and parking is not problem.*
Housing help: Both the SU and the accommodation office dispense advice.

WELFARE

SERVICES:
• Lesbian/Gay/Bisexual Society • Women's Officer
• International Students' Society • Disabilities Officer
• Self-defence classes • College counsellors: 5 full/2 part • Crime rating: !!!
There's a parent support group and the University is proud of its child-care provision with *well-run* crèches at all sites. It employs several counsellors under the supervision of the Head of Welfare Services, also a trained counsellor. The SU adds three welfare officers. The SU solicitor's on hand once a week with legal advice. The chaplaincy runs a non-alcoholic bar at Jordanstown.
Health: Health and welfare facilities are *less comprehensive* on the Coleraine campus. The University of Ulster has health clinics in Jordanstown, Magee and Belfast.
Disabilities: Sites have ramps, parking, special accommodation, automatic doors, talking lifts, Braille signs, toilet facilities and dropped kerbs. Also there's the Coalition for Disability Awareness and the Joint Universities Deaf Education. *A significant effort is being made to improve things.*

FINANCE:
• Ave debt per year: £528 • Access fund: £1,045,500
• Successful applications/yr: 2,070 • Ave payment: £100-3,500
Support: Several kinds of financial aid are available, including a support fund for home students, the *amusingly named* Visa Card Royalty Fund, the Royal & Ancient Golf Bursary Scheme of £1,500 a year for outstanding golfers. Fee waivers are available for *impoverished but capable* students. Most of these involve an interview with the Student Funding Adviser.

The United Medical and Dental Schools (UMDS)

see King's College, London

UMIST

see University of Manchester

> The Queen's College, Oxford, is allowed to shut down the High Street for archery practice.

University College, London

• *The College is part of the __University of London__ and students are entitled to use its facilities.*
University College London, Gower Street, London, WC1E 6BT
Tel: (020) 7679 3000 E-mail: degree-info@ucl.ac.uk Website: www.ucl.ac.uk
University College London Union, 25 Gordon Street, London, WC1H OAY
Tel: (020) 7387 3611 E-mail: uclu-personnel@ucl.ac.uk Website: www.uclunion.org

GENERAL

University College London (UCL) is the largest college in the University of London and *big enough to be a whopper university on its own.* Faculties and accommodation are concentrated in Bloomsbury, *so UCL's the nearest thing the University of London has to a campus in the city.* It was founded by a group of worthies influenced by the ideas of Jeremy Bentham, the famous Utilitarian philosopher, to promote equality and the crossing of class barriers. It had no religious leanings – which was unique in those days – and was also the first university college to admit women.

The main building is *beautiful* with steps leading to an *impressive* portico at the main entrance. The library dome can be seen behind it. Three stone cloisters edge a big grass lawn. It's all a bit like an inner city stately home. *Unfortunately, the other buildings, humdrum brick, aren't all like that.* **For general information on London: see __University of London__.**

Sex ratio (M:F): 48:52	**Founded: 1826**	
Full-time u'grads: 11,480	**Part-time: 340**	
Postgrads: 4,540	**Non-degree: 581**	
Ave course: 3yrs	**Ethnic: 30%**	
State:private school: 70:30	**Flunk rate: 7%**	
Mature: 13%	**International: 29%**	
Disabled: 154	**Local: n/a**	

ATMOSPHERE:

Most applicants think they're going to like being a student at UCL, and the University rarely disappoints. The increasingly middle-class student body are a fairly laid-back bunch – the atmosphere is one of drinking beer, contemplating navels and putting off that library stint for another hour. The size of the college and its proximity to all the temptations of the West End combine to dilute any specific college spirit, but it's not an unfriendly place.

SITES:

Royal Free and University College Medical School: the Royal Free Hospital site (about 4 miles away in Hampstead), and the Whittington Hospital site (at Archway). The Royal Free Hospital, an early 70s concrete building, is based in the *very upmarket and trendily wealthy London district of Hampstead. It's a relaxed environment and students demonstrate a team spirit which is usually put into practice on the sports field.* The School of Slavonic and East European Studies (SSEES) merged with UCL in 1999 and is based in Bloomsbury. Space science and astronomy students have access to sites in Mill Hill (London) and Dorking (Surrey) with specialist observatories and equipment.

LONDON: see University of London

TRAVEL: see University of London
Trains: Nearest tube to Senate House/ULU Building is Goodge Street (Northern Line).
Car: The University's slapbang in the middle of London, which means the congestion charge applies to vehicles on the roads around it. On-campus parking is *non-existent*.

CAREER PROSPECTS:

• Careers Service • No. of staff: 11 full • Unemployed after 6mths: 5%
UCL has its own careers service, complete with job fairs, careers library and interview training.

FAMOUS ALUMNI:

Brett Anderson (Suede); Rabbi Lionel Blue (writer/broadcaster); Raymond Briggs (writer/illustrator); A S Byatt (novelist); Tom Courtney (actor); Jonathan Dimbleby (broadcaster); Ken Follet (writer); Sir Norman Foster (architect); Justine Frischmann (Elastica); Hugh Gaitskell (late former Labour leader); Mahatma Gandhi; David Gower (cricketer); Margaret Hodge MP (Lab); Derek Jarman (film director); Dr Hilary Jones (TV doctor); Jonathan Miller (writer/ director); Sir Eduardo Paolozzi (artist/sculptor); Raj Persaud (celebrity shrink); Dr Mark Porter (another TV doctor); Stanley Spencer (artist); Marie Stopes (birth control pioneer); all of Coldplay.

SPECIAL FEATURES:

• UCL includes the Slade School of Fine Art – *dead prestigious and nothing to do with a cuppa-soup-loving yob-rock quartet from Wolverhampton*.

FURTHER INFO:

• Prospectuses: undergrad; postgrad; some departments • Open days

A C A D E M I C

Entry points: 240-360	Ave points: n/a
Applns per place: n/a	Clearing: 9%
No. of terms: 3	Length of terms: 10-11wks
Staff/student ratio: 1:3	Study addicts: n/a
Teaching: *****	Research: *****

240-360 POINTS

ADMISSIONS:

• Apply via UCAS

LIBRARIES:

• 1,500,000 books • 1,514 study places
Apart from the Main and Science libraries there are 12 specialist book barns and another at the Royal Free.

COMPUTERS:

• 781 workstations
Advance booking for computers available, and some 24-hr access.

OTHER LEARNING FACILITIES:

Language lab; drama facilities and music rehearsal rooms at Bloomsbury Theatre; limited audio/TV centre at the Slade.

ENTERTAINMENT

THE CITY: see <u>University of London</u>

UNIVERSITY:

• <u>Price of a pint of beer: £1.80</u> • <u>Glass of wine: £1.80</u>
Bars: There are eight bars around the campus and in its halls of residence, the central one being the *pub-like* Phineas. Others include the *sporty* 2nd floor Bar, the vast Windeyer and Gordon's Café Bar. Another three bars are at the Royal Free site – the Doctors', Students' and Hospital Bars.
Theatres: The Bloomsbury Theatre hosts student and professional productions. There's also a smaller theatre, the Garage, *where fringe stuff gets to see the light of day.*
Film: There's a cinema in the Union and a film society.
Music venues: Occasional theme nights (eg. salsa) with live bands. Royal Free has the New JCR (cap 200) for live bands and the Peter Samuel Hall for classical music.
Clubbing: There's something of the dance variety every night, major events being the Thursday Cocktails night and the Windeyer Bar, with guest DJs. The SU at the Royal Free throws a *cheesy* party every 2-3 weeks (but no crackers).
Comedy/Cabaret: Shows at the Bloomsbury Theatre.
Food: There are three University refectories *but students tend to prefer the SU facilities,* which include snack and sandwich bars and food served in six of the bars as well as cafés in some departments. There's also the hospital canteen, bars and a servery at the Royal Free.
Other: Three black tie balls a year *for those who can't resist the lure of the penguin suit.*

SOCIAL & POLITICAL

UNIVERSITY COLLEGE LONDON UNION:

• <u>6 sabbaticals</u> • <u>Turnout at last ballot: 14%</u> • <u>NUS member</u>
UCLU's not renowned for political activity, although things are warming up. It's very close to ULU, so those desperate for a soap box or frantic for fantastic facilities don't have far to go. The Union at the Royal Free site has merged with UCL.

SU FACILITIES:

In UCLU's main building: four bars; fast food and sandwich bars; two shops including a general shop; print shop; travel agency; advice centre; HSBC ATM; hairdresser; games machines and pool tables. There's a shop; various games; pool table; Lloyds ATM and satellite TV at the Royal Free site.

CLUBS (NON-SPORTING):

Arabic; Bangla; Bloomsbury TV; Chess; Chinese; Debating; Hindu; Human Powered Flight; Japan; Jazz; Music; Pakistani; Photographic; Stage Crew; Singapore Students; Spectrum (helping special-needs children); Taiwanese.
See also Clubs tables.

OTHER ORGANISATIONS:

PI is the official monthly rag. The award-winning television station BTV can be seen occasionally at Union venues. Rare FM (www.rarefm.co.uk) has been the most-listened-to online student radio station and does an *old-style* FM broadcast one month a year. Union Volunteers organises voluntary placements in the local community. At the Royal Free there's Spectrum community action group and a Rag week.

RELIGIOUS:

Despite UCL's *godless foundations,* the Christian Union is one of London's largest. In the Union there's a multi-purpose meditation room and the University's church (the Church of Christ the King) is in Byng Place.

PAID WORK: see University of London
• Job bureau
This being London, many students need to earn a bit of extra cash. Luckily, the capital has no shortage of opportunities for bar and shop work and the Union-run Workstation is invaluable in finding flexible, part-time work. A bunch of student entrepreneurs make money from their IT skills, running website companies and the like.

SPORTS

• BUSA Ranking: 47
All faculties keep Wednesday afternoons free for sports, although facilities are not so free – there's an annual charge for the Bloomsbury Fitness Centre. *Royal Free has a strong sporting reputation among the London medical schools.*

SPORTS FACILITIES:

In the Bloomsbury Fitness Centre (also open to the public) there are: squash courts; aerobics, fencing and dance halls; weights gym. The sports centre at Somers Town is 10 mins walk from campus. The UCLU sports grounds at Shenley in Hertfordshire provide good facilities and is also Watford FC's training ground.

SPORTING CLUBS:

See Clubs tables.

ATTRACTIONS: see University of London
There is no end to London's sporting attractions: from tennis and strawberries at Wimbledon to football and fighting at Millwall; from cricket at Lords to croquet at Hurlingham; from athletics at Crystal Palace to rugby at Twickers; from ... *well, as we said, there's no end.*

ACCOMMODATION

IN COLLEGE:

• Catered: 12% • Cost: £99 (38wks) • Self-catering: 20% • Cost: £88 (38wks)
• Insurance premium: £££
Availability: All 1st years who apply in time get college accommodation, 15% of them sharing. 2nd years are almost certainly on their own, but a few finalists come back. Those who do get housed will be in one of UCL's halls of residence or in the University's intercollegiate accommodation. There's also accommodation at the Royal Free. Catered halls provide breakfast and evening meals every day, except Ifor Evans which doesn't at weekends and has cooking facilities instead. *The food has a poor reputation though.* Self-catering halls have *good big* kitchens with a couple of cookers and fridges between ten people. Parking's only available at Max Rayne, Ifor Evans and Langton Close.
Car parking: Parking is by permit only and *permits are like gold dust. This is London, after all.*

EXTERNALLY: see University of London
Availability: Many UCL students live in Stoke Newington (the number 73 bus runs to UCL) and the Finsbury Park/Manor House ghetto or Camden *if they're feeling flush. The areas around the Royal Free are more expensive.*
Housing help: UCL keeps information on private and College accommodation and publishes a regular bulletin.

 WELFARE

SERVICES:

- Lesbian/Gay/Bisexual Officer & Support Group • Women's Officer & Society
- Postgrad Sabbatical Officer & Society • Disabilities Officer • Self-defence classes
- Nightline • College counsellors: 7 full • Crime rating: !!!!!

Students' welfare needs *are well-tended*. The University provides counsellors and personal tutors, while the SU lays on *a host of advisers*.

Health: The Gower Street Health Centre has three GPs, dentists and a practice nurse.

Women: The SU has two advisers for female students. Subsidised attack alarms *can be picked up* from the Union shop.

Crèches/Nursery: 38 places are available for kiddies aged between 3mths-5yrs.

FINANCE:

- Ave debt per year: £2,866

Support: Hard-up students have been able to get up to £1,320 from the access fund. Cash from other funds, eg. the Friend's Trust, is occasionally available – notices are posted by the Registry department.

University College Stockton

see University of Durham

Uxbridge

see Brunel University

University of Wales

Wales College of Medicine see Cardiff University

Wales Poly see Glamorgan University

University of Warwick

University of the West of England see Bristol, University of the West of England

West London Poly see Thames Valley University

West Surrey College of Art and Design see Surrey Institute of Art and Design

Westfield see Queen Mary, University of London

University of Westminster

Winchester College of Art see University of Southampton

University of Wolverhampton

University College Worcester

Writtle College see University of Essex

Wye College see Imperial College, London

University of Wales

University of Wales, King Edward VII Avenue, Cathays Park, Cardiff, CF10 3NS
Tel: (02920) 382 656 E-mail: uniwales@wales.ac.uk Website: www.wales.ac.uk

GENERAL

The University of Wales is the third largest in the country after Open University and University of London, and like these, it's rather unusual. It's a federal university, a collection of colleges which operate almost entirely independently of each other. *Many students in Wales don't even realise that their colleges aren't, technically, fully fledged universities.* Interested students shouldn't start writing off to the University of Wales for its prospectus or wondering why they can't find the campus on the map. Try investigating instead the individual colleges, which are, of course, included elsewhere in *Push*, as follows:
Aberystwyth, University of Wales
Bangor, University of Wales
Cardiff Institute
Lampeter, University of Wales
Newport, University of Wales
Swansea, University of Wales
UCAS applications are made to the individual colleges.

Wales College of Medicine

see Cardiff University

Wales Poly

see Glamorgan University

University of Warwick

University of Warwick, Coventry, Warwickshire, CV4 7AL
Tel: (02476) 523 523 E-mail: ugoffice@warwick.ac.uk Website: www.warwick.ac.uk
Students' Union, University of Warwick, Coventry, Warwickshire, CV4 7AL
Tel: (02476) 572 777 E-mail: sunion@sunion.warwick.ac.uk
Website: www.sunion.warwick.ac.uk

GENERAL

Warwick Castle is in Warwick. Warwick University isn't. This 500-acre piece of civic lost property has been left somewhere in the hinterland between Coventry and Leamington Spa. Coventry already has a university and Leamington Spa *is too weedy to deserve one, so, short of calling it the University of Somewhere-In-The-South-East-Midlands, 'Warwick University' is probably the best option. The hilly surroundings can make it seem deceptively remote*, although it's only 3 miles to the centre of Coventry and 25 to Birmingham's. The campus is *a crazed and colourful creation: smeared with sculptures, kid's play-block buildings* and three artificial lakes. Built in the 60s, *when 'bland' was the standard architectural blueprint, Warwick stands out as being not as depressingly dull as some universities' token monoliths. But there sure is a lot of white around.*

Sex ratio (M:F): 42:58	**Founded: 1964**
Full-time u'grads: 9,625	**Part-time: 9,165**
Postgrads: 3,040	**Non-degree: 16,932**
Ave course: 3-4yrs	**Ethnic: 19%**
State:private school: 76:24	**Flunk rate: 5%**
Mature: 6%	**International: 33%**
Disabled: 82	**Local: 36%**

ATMOSPHERE:
Although it attracts a sizeable middle-class contingent and a fair few Oxbridge rejects, the campus is buzzing, cosmopolitan and enormous. Situated far from the city centre, it's almost entirely self-sufficient. Indeed, most 1st year students who live there never actually need to leave. It's been called a 'bubble' or a 'holiday camp' in the past and it can all get a bit 'Prisoner' from time to time. Campus fever can be relieved by jaunts into Leamington or Coventry, where students are tolerated fairly well.

COVENTRY: see Coventry University

LEAMINGTON SPA:

More Warwick students live in Leamington Spa than in Coventry, and it's a pretty, park-filled place that still pulls in quite a few tourists. As far as shops and night activities go, *they're limited but respectable*, with two student-angled clubs, plenty of posh eateries (tourists) and coffee shops. *The town is basically divided into the good and the ugly. Past the railway bridge into South Leamington, the picturesque stops and the cheap, rough area begins. This means many takeaways and no pretty houses. Overall, a quaintly cheerful little town with an unprecedented number of skater kids and good music stores. Birmingham and Coventry are better bets for bigger fun, though.*

TRAVEL: see Coventry University
Trains: The main station is 2 miles away in Coventry but there's a line running through Leamington Spa and Warwick.
Car: *It's in the middle of nowhere and the University likes to keep it that way.* There's room for 1,000 cars on campus but permits are the order of the day. The M6 is *handy* for drivers.
Air: 10 miles to Birmingham International.
Local: From the bus stops on campus, the numbers 12, 12A and 112 run into Coventry centre via the train station every 10 mins until 11pm (80p-£1). There are similar services to Leamington and Kenilworth. Late-night services during term-time.
Taxis: *It's almost inevitable that students will get trapped on campus in the witching hour at some point. That's where the on-site taxi rank comes in handy.* Fares to Coventry vary around £6, while Leamington can cost over a tenner.
Bicycles: *Helpful for getting around campus, but no one fancies 7 miles to Leamington twice a day unless they want really big calves.* Bike racks and cycle lanes dotted around the site.

CAREER PROSPECTS:

• Careers Service • No. of staff: 11 full/8 part • Unemployed after 6mths: 6%
Newsletters, bulletin boards, a full careers library, job fairs and interview prep.

FAMOUS ALUMNI:

Baroness Amos (Leader of the House of Lords); Jenny Bond (BBC correspondent and 'I'm a Celebrity *Give Me a Lethal Injection*' starlet); David Davis MP (senior Tory); A L Kennedy, Hari Kunzru (authors); Timmy Mallett (hammer-wielding TV *prat*); Simon Mayo (DJ); Sheila McKechnie (late campaigner); Stephen Merchant (The Office co-writer); Dave Nellist (Militant ex-MP); Stephen Pile (writer); Jeff Rooker MP (Lab); Frank Skinner (comedian); Gary Sinyor and Vadim Jean (film makers); Sting (for a term).

Special features:

• The campus has the biggest *and most active* university Arts Centre outside London.
• There's a roaring trade in conferences, which means there are some *excellent* facilities and accommodation is better whilst *being relatively cheap. It also means students can feel like they're an inconvenience stuck between the real business of travelling salesmen's piss-ups and dandruff-dripping, navel-gazing academics reading logarithms to each other.*

FURTHER INFO:

• Prospectuses: undergrad; postgrad; alternative; some departmental • Open days • Video
The SU issues an alternative prospectus.

A C A D E M I C

Grades for some courses are dependent on 2nd- and 3rd-year performance, *making the 1st year a test merely to determine whether students stay on. Meanwhile*, some science courses count 1st year grades as up to 20% of the final degree mark. Optional/compulsory modules for each course are detailed on the University website.

280-360 **POINTS**

Entry points: 280-360
Applns per place: 9.4
No. of terms: 3
Staff/student ratio: 1:12
Teaching: *****
Year abroad: 2%
Firsts: 16%
2.1s: 10%

Ave points: 340
Clearing: 1%
Length of terms: 10/11wks
Study addicts: 17%
Research: *****
Sandwich students: <1%
2.2s: 60%
3rds: <1%

ADMISSIONS:

• Apply via UCAS/GTTR for PGCE

Warwick is *weak at the knees* for widening participation (access schemes and so on) and accepts postgrad applications directly through its online system.

SUBJECTS:

Arts/Humanities: 19%   Sciences: 42%
Medical Sciences: 1%   Social Sciences: 34%
Unusual: Women & Gender. MORSE (Maths, Operational Research, Statistics & Economics) is unique to Warwick.

LIBRARIES:

• 1,000,000 books • 1,890 study places • 24-hr access • Spend per student: £££££

In addition to the main library (open till midnight), there are various smaller departmental libraries. The Resource Centre has 10,000 'core texts' stuffed onto its shelves. The new Learning Grid group study facility is proving *popular – not a place for peaceful, reflective learning.*

COMPUTERS:

• 1,000 workstations • 24-hr access

Internal correspondence is becoming increasingly dependent on e-mail. All campus bedrooms come complete with broadband portal – *no need for brown paper bags for porn, then.*

OTHER LEARNING FACILITIES:

Language labs, drama studio, rehearsal rooms and audio/TV centre.

E N T E R T A I N M E N T

COVENTRY: see Coventry University

LEAMINGTON:

• Price of a pint of beer: £1.70 • Glass of wine: £1.40 • Can of Red Bull: £1.50

Excellent facilities on campus compensate for Leamington's deficiencies.

Pubs: *Pushplugs: Benjamin Satchwell's; Jug & Jester; Varsity (cheap on Thursdays), Robin's Well and Scholars (made for students). Don't win on the bandit in The Guardsman – it upsets the locals.*

Cinemas: Two with seven screens between them. *The Rubin Cinema is a bit artier than the Apollo.*

Theatre: The Royal Spa is a *standard* regional rep house but Leamington is on a direct rail route to the *bard-licious* Stratford-upon-Avon.

Clubbing/Music venues: Sugar is the new club on the scene; Mirage has a Thursday student night; Brown's Cow attracts bands and DJs from out of town.

Eating out: *Again, not a huge deal, although, this being the Midlands, there's a number of excellent value Balti houses. Pushplugs: Mongolian Wok Bar in Coventry (£7.50 buffet lunch); Ali Baba (Balti).* Spun End Balti does deliveries to campus.

UNIVERSITY:

• Price of a pint of beer: £1.80 • Glass of wine: £2 • Can of Red Bull: £1.70

Bars: The principal bars are Cholo and the Cooler *(actually rather warm)* which doubles as a club. Others include, *pubby* Grumpy John's, two Bottles & Shots bars and two newer places: Xananas, a café bar, and The Bar (University-run; formerly Airport Lounge). There are also supping stops at the Arts Centre and in the Sports Pavilion.

Arts Centre: *The Arts Centre on campus is fantastic in every respect – it looks as though it's sprung from some futuristic fantasy and has facilities to dream about:* two theatres; conference hall; film theatre; art gallery; sculpture court; concert hall; music centre and bookshop. *250,000 people a year flock to bathe in its glory.*

Theatres: In the Arts Centre, the main theatre attracts touring companies (drama, dance, opera etc.), as well as big student shows. The studio theatre lends itself to smaller scale productions. *Students enter into the dramatic fray with thespian gusto.*

Cinemas: The Cinema Society shows classics and blockbusters for around £2, while the Arts Centre provides *a less commercial counterbalance* at higher prices, *ironically enough.*

Clubbing: Six events a week, everything from acid jazz to Quench which takes over the Market Place with its blend of trance and dance sounds. *Soul Nation is aspiring to become the biggest club night in the Midlands. It will probably succeed.* Guest DJs have included Carl Cox, Paul Oakenfold, Fabio and Tim Westwood.

Music venues: The Union's Market Place is the biggest, recently featuring Jamelia, Big Brovaz and Space. *Massive* Butterworth Hall in the Arts Centre features a variety of music, mostly classical, and attracts top international performers. The University Chorus and orchestra perform here *between Wembley Stadium gigs.*

Comedy/Cabaret: Fortnightly comedy spurts from various venues. *Past masters* include Bill Bailey, Stewart Lee and Ross Noble.

Food: Grub served at Xananas (baguettes and meals), Kaleidoscope, Viva (Pret-a-Manger-like), Eat (*expensive*), Rootes, Battered (fish'n'chips), Bar Food (junk) and the Cooler – *if you can't find what you want in there, you never will. If all else fails there's always the Costcutter supermarket.*

Other: Several varyingly sized balls a year as well as the February Real Ale and One World Week Festivals.

SOCIAL & POLITICAL

UNIVERSITY OF WARWICK STUDENTS' UNION (UWSU):

• 7 sabbaticals • Turnout at last ballot: 19% • NUS member

The Union building is the biggest in Europe. The SU juggles *a varied and unfaltering social calendar* with serious representation: they managed to kill off the threat of compulsory student laptops a while back. *The Club & Socs list at Warwick is longer than a supermarket sweep receipt – even the most eccentric student should find enough like-minded weirdos to feel cosy.*

SU FACILITIES:

In and around the Union building: nightclub; nine bars; cafeteria; two coffee bars; fast food joint; five meeting rooms; four banks with ATMs; Endsleigh Insurance branch; Costcutter; stationery shop; computers for sale; fax and printing services; photo booth; photocopiers; payphones; travel agency; launderette; opticians; hairdressers; pool and snooker tables; juke boxes; gaming and vending machines; late-night campus bus; advice centre; DTP suite; darkroom; three minibuses and a car for hire; TV lounges.

CLUBS (NON-SPORTING):

More than any other Union in the country: Academy; Accounting; AIESEC; Almost Teachers; Americas; Animal Rights; Anime & Manga; Anti-sexism; Arabic; Art; Art of Living; Atomic; Asian; Baha'; Band; Bangladeshi; Banking & Finance; Baobab; Beatdown; Bell Ringing; Bhangra; Big Band; Biker; Biology; Bizcom; Blues, Jazz, Soul; Bollywood; BORDER; Brass; Break Dancing; Bridge; Buddhist; BUNAC; Café; Carribean Heat; Caribean Riddims; Catalan & Basque; Ceilidh; CELTE; Centre for Alternative Culture; Chamber Music; Cheema; Cheese & Chocolate; Chill Out; China in Question; Chinese; Chinese Chess; Chorus; CIS in Focus; Classical & Modern Dance; Classics; Clublands; Codpiece; Comedy; Computing; Conceptual Art Performance; Curry; Cypriot; Dancasianal; Dance Mat; Darts; Deck Masters; Decriminalise Cannabis; Diversity; Duke of Edinburgh; Dutch; Dynamics of Alcoholic Fluids Team; Eastern

European Central Asian; Eastern Food; E-commerce; Economics; English Literature; Engineers; Enterprise; Envision; ERASMUS; European; European Law Students Association; European School; Expedition; Fashion Show; Football Fans; Francophone; Free Spirits; French; Friends of Palastine; German; Get Decked; G-Force; Global Development; Globalise Resistance; Go; Goffbeat; Hack; Hellenic; Hindu; History; Hong Kong; Horror; Human Rights Debating; Indian; Indonesian; Intelligent; International Business Consulting; International Current Affairs; Italian; Jailbreak; Japanese; Jubilee; Juggling; Kernow; Knitting & Craft; Korean; Krishna Consciousness; Laser Quest; Latin American; Law; Law & Business; Leicester Warwick Medical Society; Linguistic Improvement & Practice; Link Africa; Live Action Roleplay; Love; Mah Jong; Malaysian; Manufacturing; Maths; Mauritian; Medsin; Morse; Music Festival; Music Theatre; New Writing; Nordic; Noise; Offbeat; Off Broadway; One; Opera Projects; Operations Management Society; Orchestra; Pagan; Paintball; Pakistan; Persian; Philosophy & Literature; Physics; Piano; Poker; Politics; Polonia; Portugese Speaking; Pottery; Pride; Psychology; Quiz; Real Ale; Revelation Rock Gospel; RIP (Research In Production); ROAR; Rock; Russian Speaking; Scout & Guide; Scottish; Sikh; Silk Urban Music; Singapore; SIS; Socialist Students; Sociology; Spanish; Speak; S.Punk; Sri Lankan; St John Ambulance; Stop the War Coalition; Street Vibe; String Orchestra; Stunt, Power & Traction Kite; Symphony Orchestra; Table Football; Taiwan; Tap Dancing; Taste; Tech Crew; Thai; The Hookah; Tibet Support; Touring Band; Travel; Turkish; Ultimate Jenga; Underground; United Nations; United World Colleges; Vietnamese; Welsh; WERL Records; Wine & Whisky Appreciation; Young Jains; WUDS. **See also Clubs tables.**

OTHER ORGANISATIONS:

The award-hogging Boar newspaper is *in no way as dull as it sounds*. Union mag The Word comes out every couple of weeks. Radio station RaW pulses *relentlessly* through local radio waves. Newly created WTV broadcasts around the Union and campus halls. Rag *rakes it in* – recently staging the world's largest pillow fight with over 300 combatants beating each other with soft feathery clubs – and *is so cocky* it has its own website (www.warwickrag.co.uk). Warwick Volunteers gets students involved in local help projects.

RELIGIOUS:

• 3 chaplains (CofE, RC, FC), rabbi
Multi-faith chaplaincy and a Muslim prayer room. Coventry and around is *intensely multi-cultural with according religious provision*.

PAID WORK: see Coventry University
• Job bureau
Unitemps on campus gives advice and posts vacancies. With such a conference-heavy vacation agenda, there's always plenty of work to be had looking after visitors. The SU itself employs 300 students.

SPORTS

• BUSA Ranking: 19
Sport plays as much a part of life as academia, with a £3m shell-out on a *gleaming* new facility. *The ethos is not only 'sport for all', but 'all sport for all' with a baffling range on offer, although Warwick's jocks take great pride in trashing the* Coventry University *whenever they can.* Most facilities are based on campus.

SPORTS FACILITIES:

Bucketloads: eight football pitches; three rugby; three all-weather; two cricket wickets; three sports halls with seven squash courts; three basketball; 12 tennis; five netball; running track; athletics field; croquet lawn/bowling green; sauna/steam room; multigym; gym; aerobics studio; swimming pool; sportable river and climbing wall – which has hosted the British Climbing Championships.

SPORTING CLUBS:

10-Pin Bowling; Aerobics; Aikido; American Football; Snooker; Skydiving; Submission Wrestling; Surfing; Water Polo; Table Tennis; Canoe; Canoe Polo; Taekwondo; Thai Boxing; Croquet; Eskrima; Triathlon; Ultimate Frisbee; 5-a-Side; Water Skiing; Weight Training; Gliding; T'ai Chi; Inline Skating; Baseball; Windsurfing; Yoga; Zhuan Shu Kuan; Ice Hockey; Kempo Ju Jitsu; Samurai Ju Jitsu; Lacrosse; Lifesaving; Motorsports; Polo; Pool; Rifle; Roller-hockey; Snowsports; Rowing. **See also Clubs tables.**

ATTRACTIONS: see Coventry University
Birmingham NEC and any Midland team are within chanting distance.

ACCOMMODATION

IN COLLEGE:
• Catered: 9% • Cost: £86 (30wks) • Self-catered: 60% • Cost: £50-78 (30-39wks)
• First years living in: 95% • Insurance premium: ££££
Availability: *Although some of the rooms are small hobbit dwellings, others are fairly plush (around a third en-suite) and some border on luxurious – primarily to attract conference-goers, which means as well as paying more, those in better rooms are at risk of temporary eviction when the vacations begin.* Guaranteed broadband access is a bonus as are the beefy security measures: CCTV, entry phones and 24-hr porters. *The head tenancy scheme plonks some 2,000 students in shared houses off-campus. The cleaners are a thorough bunch,* laundering linen, hoovering rooms and swabbing the kitchen.
Car parking: *Permits (£250) are required, but 1st years aren't allowed cars on campus anyhow.* Some pay & display available.

EXTERNALLY: see Coventry University
• Ave rent: £60
Availability: *Coventry is getting to be more and more at the cheaper end, but Leamington is still the most popular. Earlsdon ain't a bad bag either.*
Housing help: The Accommodation Office has 14 staff who post and approve vacancies, help negotiate contracts and offer legal help.

WELFARE

SERVICES:
• Lesbian/Gay/Bisexual Officer & Society • Ethnic Minorities Officer & Society
• Women's Officer & Society • Mature Students' Officer & Society
• International Students' Officer & Society • Postgrad Officer & Society
• Disabilities Officer & Society • Late-night minibus • Nightline
• College counsellors: 4 part • Crime rating: !!!
The SU runs an Advice & Welfare Centre with four staff and a sabbatical officer. Each hall has a resident tutor who *doesn't 'tute' anything but* will help with personal problems if Nightline seems too impersonal.
Health: A fully staffed health centre with several GPs *helps clear your nose and soothe your throat.*
Women: Free personal alarms and late-night minibus around campus (not just for women).
Crèches/Nursery: Facilities for children aged 3mths-4yrs.
Disabilities: *Wheelchair access is among the best in the country* with ramps, lifts and specialised rooms. Hearing loops, specialist learning facilities and Braille signs on some buildings.
Crime: *Campus is largely safe and security heavy. Coventry's no ghetto either.*
Drugs: *Bongfuls of middle-class arts students have given Warwick a bit of a rep for cannabis culture,* but the University claims to come down hard on users.

FINANCE:
• Ave debt per year: £3,473
• Access fund: £350,000 • Successful applications/yr: 500 • Ave payment: up to £2,000
Support: There are 50 or so Graduate Association bursaries each year worth about £2,000 each, plus music scholarships and a hardship fund.

West London Poly

see Thames Valley University

West Surrey College of Art and Design
see Surrey Institute of Art and Design

Westfield
see Queen Mary, University of London

University of Westminster

* **Formerly Polytechnic of Central London.**
University of Westminster, 309 Regents Street, London, W1B 2UW
Tel: (020) 7911 5000 E-mail: Admissions@wmin.ac.uk Website: www.wmin.ac.uk
University of Westminster Students' Union, 32-38 Wells Street, London, W1T 3UW
Tel: (020) 7911 5738 E-mail: supresi@wmin.ac.uk Website: www.uwsu.com

GENERAL

Originally founded as the Royal Polytechnic Institute in order to educate the public on engineering and all matters scientific, Westminster has gone through all manner of changes and expansions since Victorian times. This has resulted in a tapestry of different architectural styles, from the *handsome* pre-war headquarters building on Regent Street to the more modern constructions at Harrow. *Three sites are close enough to Trafalgar Square to offer students the West End on a big, glitzy over-priced plate,* while the Harrow site *nudges the suburbs and is lovingly smudged* with greenery. **For general information about London: see University of London**.

Sex ratio (M:F): 46:54	Founded: 1838
Full-time u'grads: 10,790	Part-time: 6,735
Postgrads: 3,045	Non-degree: 4,211
Ave course: 3yrs	Ethnic: 62%
State:private school: 94:6	Flunk rate: 19%
Mature: 32%	International: 28%
Disabled: 230	Local: n/a

ATMOSPHERE:

Undergrads are a diverse bunch with a big ethnic mix and a high proportion of mature students. Although most campuses are relatively close together inhabitants tend to stick like glue to their own site's bars and facilities so there's little sense of one big cohesive family. Still, with all the fun of the West End on their doorsteps there's no excuse to be bored. Jimmy 'The Solo' Hendrix played here, and Cherie 'The Lips' Blair taught at the law school.

SITES:

Regents: (School of Law, School of Social Sciences, Humanities & Languages, Diplomatic Academy of London Health & Fitness Centre) The admin centre for both University and SU. *For fans of fancy stonework:* the historic Headquarters building holds an *elegant* 1911 marble foyer.

Cavendish: (Biosciences, Integrated Health, Computer Science, Educational Initiative Centre) Cavendish has two sub-sites: New Cavendish Street and Euston Centre, 10 mins walk apart. A £35m campus facelift has just been completed.

Harrow: (Formerly Harrow College of Higher Education, 5,000 students – Arts & Design, Business School, Computer Science, Media) 12 miles – *or 20 mins on a good Tube day* – from the Central London campuses, Harrow houses the *prestigious* Media School (which has garnered top BBC awards), as well as some *swanky* computer labs, photography and music studios thanks to open purse strings in recent years.

Marylebone: Home to the *fabtastic* careers service (CaSe), plus the Counselling and Housing services, the Educational Initiative Centre, Architecture & the Built Environment courses and Westminster Business School. Not forgetting Marylebone Books.

LONDON: see University of London

TRAVEL: see University of London
Trains: Euston is closest at 20 mins stroll away.
Car: *Driving in London is naturally a dumb idea*, but there are pay & displays at the Harrow campus – which, together with the Marylebone site, is outside the Congestion Charge Zone.
Underground: For Cavendish: Warren Street (Northern, Victoria); for Marylebone: Baker Street (Bakerloo, Circle, Jubilee, Metropolitan, Hammersmith & City); for Regent: Oxford Circus (Bakerloo, Central, Victoria); for Harrow: Northwick Park (Metropolitan) and Kenton (Bakerloo).

CAREER PROSPECTS:

• Careers Service • No. of staff: 9 full/11 part • Unemployed after 6mths: 10%
CaSE covers all aspects of employment during and after study: everything from job fairs to CV advice – *the whole 9 yards*. See www.wmin.ac.uk/careers for online resources.

FAMOUS ALUMNI:

Sir Anthony Caro (sculptor); Baroness Chalker (Tory peer); the Emmanuels (Di's wedding dress designers); Trisha Goddard (TV presenter); Lisa I'Anson and Annie Nightingale (Radio 1 DJs); Michael Jackson (C4 chief exec, not Wacko); Nico Ladenis (restaurateur); Markus Lupfer (fashion designer); Julian Metcalfe and Sinclair Beecham (creators of Pret à Manger); Lord Puttnam and Anand Tucker (directors); Ian Ritchie (architect); Jon Ronson (journo); Philip Sycamore (ex-Law Society president); Timothy West (actor); Vivienne Westwood (fashion designer).

SPECIAL FEATURES:

Marylebone campus building hosted the first International Business & Development Conference.

FURTHER INFO:

• Prospectuses: undergrad; postgrad; departmental; international • Open days
Several campus open days and course presentations throughout the year.

A C A D E M I C

Many courses are of a vocational nature, with relevant industries closely involved in the development of course programmes, *ensuring that teaching is up to date as well as up to scratch. There has been a ripple of discontent in the student body, however, who feel that some courses are heavy on the academic side with not enough on the practical.*

Entry points: 40-340	Ave points: 108
Applns per place: 4	Clearing: 30%
No. of terms: 2	Length of terms: 12wks
Staff/student ratio: 1:15	Study addicts: 18%
Teaching: **	Research: ***
Year abroad: 1%	Sandwich students: 9%
Firsts: 11%	2.2s: 33%
2.1s: 53%	3rds: 2%

40-340 ... **POINTS**

ADMISSIONS:

• Apply via UCAS
Contact the Admissions and Marketing Offices directly for part-time courses and postgrad degrees.

SUBJECTS:

Architecture & Built Environment: 8.3%
Biosciences: 4.5%
Business School (Harrow): 4%
Business School (Westminster): 14.6%
Communication & Creative Industries: 11.2%

Computer Science : 8.7%
Educational Initiative Centre: 0.2%
Integrated Health: 3.2%
Law: 7%
Social Sciences, Humanities & Languages: 23%

Best: Arabic; Building; Chinese; French; Housing & Surveying; Media & Communications; Other Subjects allied to Medicine; Psychology; Tourism.
Unusual: Complementary Therapies; Urban Redevelopment.

LIBRARIES:

• 410,000 books • 1,900 study places
Four libraries are distributed around the campuses, including a Learning Resource Centre (*which is the same thing really*) at Harrow. Its 2nd floor is devoted to special needs learning resources, including books software and AV material.

COMPUTERS:

• 1,700 workstations
Each site has a number of computer labs, most open till 9pm. Many courses employ the Blackboard system, an online learning facility with e-journals, past papers etc.

OTHER LEARNING FACILITIES:

Cavendish has a self-access language centre, open to all. Harrow has music rehearsal rooms and broadcast-quality TV and radio studios. Marylebone boasts a CAD lab. There's also a museum of period instruments, an internationally renowned portrait collection and historical performance paraphernalia.

E N T E R T A I N M E N T

LONDON: see University of London

UNIVERSITY:

• Price of a pint of beer: £2.10 • Glass of wine: £1.70 • Can of Red Bull: £1.50
When they're not rampaging through the West End, swanning through Bloomsbury pubs or drinking neighbouring Imperial College's bar dry, Westminster students enjoy a limited but lavish range of domestic entertainments.

Bars: The Dragon Bar on Wells Street is *fairly funkadelic*, with pool tables, Playstation 2 and an Xbox. The Undercroft at Harrow is *a little less alcoholically intimidating*, and has a wide range of *cheapish* beers. Thursday nights are society events; Fridays is acoustic night. A posh new bar is due for Marylebone next year.

Theatres: Two or three *fairly mundane* productions a year in Lecture Theatre 2.

Film: There's a big screen at Harrow. Student-made films are shown occasionally *and Manga flicks are pretty popular.*

Clubbing/Music venues: Area 51 at Harrow hosts a weekly mix of club nights and gigs, with frequent acoustic sets from those on the contemporary music course. Trevor Nelson and Norman Jay have spun a groove or two here.

Food: There are University-run outlets at each site, with student *complaints about the cost if not taste.* Bars dish out snackage as well.

Other: Annual May Ball and some large-scale Freshers' events.

SOCIAL & POLITICAL

UNIVERSITY OF WESTMINSTER STUDENTS UNION:
• 4 sabbaticals • Turnout at last ballot: 6% • NUS member
The hardworking exec is prepared to stand up to the administration but the students don't seem to know or care what's going on. There's now a member of staff whose job it is to obtain feedback from the student body – *which goes some way to showing how distanced relations have become. They have been trying to drum up anti-tuition fee support and organise political protests, but enthusiasm and interest remain rather reserved.* UWSU's HQ building on Wells Street *has seen better days and is need of extension and refurbishment – likely to happen when it moves to a new site in Marylebone.*

SU FACILITIES:
Two bars; purpose-built nightclub; four cafeterias; two snack/coffee bars; fast food outlet; four pool tables; table football; jukeboxes; minibus for hire; Barclays ATMs; photocopiers; fax and printing services; photo booth; payphones; advice centre; TV lounge; gaming and vending machines; general store and stationery shop; art supply store at Harrow; new and secondhand bookshops.

CLUBS (NON-SPORTING):
Ahlul Bayt; Believers Loveworld; Chinese; Comparative Ideologies; CPE; Drum & Bass; Electronic Dance Music; Fashion; Fight Against Aids; Flying Circus (Architecture); Frontline; Gaming; Integrated Medicine; International Human Rights; International Student; Japanese; Korean; Literature & Culture; Live Music; Mothers; Muslim Women; Performers & Songwriters; Punjabi; Radio; Russian; Service for Peace; Sikh; Soul Train; Stop the war on Coalition; Students on Tour; Tamil; Urban Music; Uzbekistan Awareness; Wi Fi. **See also Clubs tables**.

OTHER ORGANISATIONS:
Monthly the Smoke is the *well-worth thumbing* student paper. Smoke radio *wafts* across the Harrow campus via the internet. Community volunteering is on the up, but *after a bit of a kerfuffle*, there's still no Rag.

RELIGIOUS:
• 3 chaplains (CofE, RC, Methodist)
Prayer rooms available on each campus. See University of London for wider religious provisions.

PAID WORK: see University of London
• Job bureau
Along with CaSE, the SU runs a job shop (external jobs and employment within the SU).

SPORTS

• Recent successes: rugby • BUSA ranking: 46
Bearing in mind the urban location and the lack of cohesion between sites, sporting success is nowhere near as lame as might be expected. The men's rugby team have a good record in the SESSA league, and though there are relatively few sporting teams, those that exist are buff enough to kick ass when they have to.

SPORTS FACILITIES:
The Regent Street site has badminton and snooker facilities, a gym, a sauna, solarium and multigym. At Harrow there's a fitness centre and a sports hall. There's a sports ground at Chiswick, complete with running track, boathouse, bar and 55 acres of pitches. There's also a gym and all-weather pitches.

SPORTING CLUBS:
Ju-Jitsu; Tae Kwon Do. **See also Clubs tables.**

ATTRACTIONS: see University of London

A C C O M M O D A T I O N

IN COLLEGE:
• Self-catering: 10% • Cost: £76-90 (38wks)
• First years living in: 26%
• Insurance premium: £
Availability: Limited: a quarter of 1st years looking for a room aren't going to find one, with priority going to those coming from the 'wrong' side of the M25. In most of the five halls, kitchens and bathrooms are shared by 6-12 people. In Harrow's *pricey* on-site flats, however, some rooms have en-suite facilities and no more than six share kitchen facilities. Students from the Central London campuses have half an hour on public transport to get from bed to study – *Harrovians are luckier*. Most halls have TV common rooms and launderettes. Single sex accommodation is available upon request and mixed sex couples can share.
Car parking: *No sir.*

EXTERNALLY: see University of London
• Ave rent: £87
Housing help: The University-run Student Housing Service at the Marylebone and Harrow sites provides a notice board, approval scheme and advice. Temporary accommodation available in September during house-hunting season.

W E L F A R E

SERVICES:
• Lesbian/Gay/Bisexual Officer & Society • Muslim Women's Society
• Mature Students' Officer & Society • International Students' Officer & Society
• Disabilities Officer & Society • Late-night/Women's minibus • Nightline
• College counsellors: 4 full/5 part • Crime rating: !!!!!
Health: A University nurse deals with most complaints and administrates a GP referral service. There are a number of advice clinics on travel vaccines and contraception etc., and several trained first-aiders to hand. The University pays for psychiatric referrals when necessary.
Crèches/Nursery: There's a 20-place nursery at Marylebone and a playgroup at Harrow. Both take 2-5-yr-olds.
Disabilities: The Central London campuses and location aren't wheelchair-friendly. Harrow is a lot better, with full access and converted accommodation on-site. Two disability advisers are there to help.

FINANCE:
• Ave debt per year: £2,537
Fees: International undergraduates pay £7,735-8,110 depending on course.
• Access fund: £924,000 • Successful applications/yr: 902 • Ave payment: £1,000
Support: All students are assessed for scholarships on arrival. There are also opportunity bursaries and hardship funds.

Winchester College of Art

see <u>University of Southampton</u>

University of Wolverhampton

- *Formerly Wolverhampton Polytechnic.*

University of Wolverhampton, Wulfruna Street, Wolverhampton, WV1 1SB
Tel: (01902) 322 222 E-mail: enquiries@wlv.ac.uk Website: www.wlv.ac.uk
University of Wolverhampton Students' Union, Wulfruna Street, Wolverhampton, WV1 1LY
Tel: (01902) 322 021 E-mail: UWSU@wlv.ac.uk Website: www.wolvesunion.org

GENERAL

Wolverhampton may be part of the Birmingham *urban spill* but it has *an identity of its own –
woe betide anyone who mixes the two up*. The 13 miles to the centre of Brum are taken up
with Dudley, West Bromwich and Walsall and each has its *own distinctive feel*. Wolves is *far
more residential* than Brum and moves at a *much slower pace*. But the differences shouldn't
disguise the fact that all the towns in the conurbation are part of the same family, *which is
just as well*, as Wolves Uni squats across all of them *without a definitive centre of gravity*.
Education is taught at Walsall, while *right out in the sticks* and split between the *almost rural*
towns of Telford and Compton, is the Business School.

Sex ratio (M:F): 43:57	**Founded: 1983**
Full-time u'grads: 12,835	**Part-time: 6,295**
Postgrads: 945	**Non-degree: 4,701**
Ave course: 3yrs	**Ethnic: 32%**
State:private school: 99:1	**Flunk rate: 24%**
Mature: 67%	**International: 20%**
Disabled: 152	**Local: 72%**

ATMOSPHERE:

*This part of the Midlands is still struggling to convince the rest of the UK that it's not just
smoggy, clogged up and thoroughly short on glam. After years of jibes and bad Black
Country impressions, it's a thankless task, but locals know the truth. As a result, there's a
large body of local students, which smoothes town/gown relations and gives airs, graces and
pretensions short shrift.*

SITES:

City Campus: The modern main campus is about $1\frac{1}{2}$ miles from the city centre. The main
building is *scrubbed to a clinical gleam*, although it's actually a bit *disconcertingly
institutional – like going to college in a hospital*. It's *slap in the centre of Wolves, handy for
the hub of social life* that is the 24-hr Asda.
Compton Park Campus: (Business Studies) A smart, new campus about $1\frac{1}{2}$ miles from the
centre of town. Students get *the best of both worlds*: a close community and easy links to
town on the University shuttle bus.

Walsall Campus: (Education, Sport, Performing Arts, Health) Walsall can feel a bit *isolated*, but the social life is *more than enough to make up for that*. It's a *sporty* sort of place with *recently refurbished* halls and facilities, and's *very popular* with residents.
Telford: (Business, Engineering, Social Work) Telford's *very definitely a campus unto itself*. It's 16 miles from Wolves, almost into the Shropshire countryside. Like Compton, it's a *pleasant enough* place to be, *but the intensity of community spirit borders on cabin fever*.

BIRMINGHAM: see University of Birmingham

TRAVEL: see University of Birmingham
Trains: Wolverhampton Station's 10 mins from the City campus. It's a piece of cake to get to London (from £8.50), Edinburgh (from £15.50), Manchester (from £6.50), Reading (from £7.50) and all over.
Coaches: National Express does London (£18.50 rtn), Manchester, Edinburgh etc.
Car: M5, M54, M6 for Wolves and Walsall, A41, M54 for Telford.
Local: The supertram Metro links Wolves to Brum. £2.30 to Brum on the train, or the everpopular night special, £1.40 rtn (last train 3am). There's also a 50p night bus from Brum to Walsall.
College: Shuttle buses (free with NUS ID) ferry between lectures on different sites. They're *reliable*, but some take *the closest thing that Wolves has to a scenic route*. There's a late-night safety bus that does doorstep drop-offs within a 3-mile radius of college events. Women get first dibs.
Bicycles: *Not the best idea, unless heavy sweating and crippling thigh pain is the goal.*

CAREER PROSPECTS:
• Careers Service • No. of staff: 22 full • Unemployed after 6mths: 10%
Comprehensive service with newsletters, bulletin boards, library, job fairs, interview coaching, psychometric testing and vacancy database.

FAMOUS ALUMNI:
Z-lists ahoy: Trevor Beattie (advertising guru); Sir Terence Beckett (deputy chairman, CEGB); Jenny Jones, Michael Foster (MPs); Mark O'Shea (TV snake expert); Suzi Perry (TV presenter); Vernie (Eternal).

FURTHER INFO:
• Prospectuses: undergrad; postgrad; some depts • Open days
Get online for more info, including the SU website for alternative *bumf*.

A C A D E M I C

Wolves is a *typical* 'new' university with lots of vocational courses, a *healthy dose* of mature and local students and some *off-the-wall* degree subjects: Complementary Therapies, Virtual Reality, E-commerce and a totally online degree (Business Administration).

Entry points: 60-300	Ave points: n/a
No. of terms: 2	Length of terms: 17wks
Staff/student ratio: 1:28	Study addicts: 23.6%
Teaching: **	Research: *
Year abroad: 7%	Sandwich students: 36%
Firsts: 6%	2.2s: 41%
2.1s: 47%	3rds: 2%

60-300 | POINTS

ADMISSIONS:
• Apply via UCAS

SUBJECTS:

Applied Sciences: 7.7%
Art & Design: 8.5 %
Business/Management: 12.2%
Computing & Information Technology: 7.6%
Engineering & Built Environment: 7%

Humanities, Languages & Social Sciences: 10.8%
Legal Studies: 12.3%
Sport, Performing Arts & Leisure: 5.1%
School of Education: 12.2%
School of Health: 16.6%

Best: Art & Design; Business & Management; Economics; Education; Hospitality, Leisure & Sport Tourism; Maths, Statistics & Operational Research; Molecular & Organismal Bio-sciences; Nursing; Other subjects allied to Medicine; Philosophy; Politics; Psychology; Theology.
Unusual: Popular Music.

LIBRARIES:

• 300,000 books • 900,000 study places • 24-hr access
There's a library on each site and a modern Learning Centre, *which has everything except enough books to go around*. The most popular ones are now on 4-hr loan, *which means that everyone can get them, but no one has time to read them*.

COMPUTERS:

• 2,000 workstations • 24-hr access
The Learning Centre has around 750 machines; *unfortunately* only about 450 of them actually work. Laptops can be borrowed.

ENTERTAINMENT

THE CITY: see University of Birmingham
• Price of a pint of beer: £1.85 • Glass of wine: £2 • Can of Red Bull: £2
Cinemas: The 12-screen Cineworld's a *short* bus or taxi-ride from the City campus.
Theatres: The Grand Theatre takes *pride of place* in Wolves and there's a lefty sort of arts place on campus.
Pubs: *Perfect student territory: lots of cheap beer deals in student-happy chain pubs. Pushplugs: Scream; Tube; Revolution; Bank; Edwards; The Wanderer. There are also some hard, tattooed and aggressively towny venues (the Feathers, for instance).*
Clubbing: Wolves *used to have a good scene but* the the University scene is *King of the Castle in that respect now.* Blast Off (indie) at the civic hall is *the only half-decent one left.*
Music venues: *Best to make a break for Brum to catch really top live music*, although The Civic has a few names, and the Quadrant Lounge has a *reasonable low key* scene.

Other: The zoo and castle in Dudley are *worth a peek*, as is the West Midlands Safari Park and the Black Country Living Museum. Wolverhampton and Walsall have art galleries; Walsall even has a leather museum.
Eating out: Lots of choices, most of them the *typical Midlands ethnic jumble. Pushplugs: Bilash Tandoori; Imperial (Chinese); Dilshad Tandoori; Gepetto's (Italian); Moon Under Water; John Balti; J's Cafe.*

UNIVERSITY:

• Price of a pint of beer: £1.65 • Glass of wine: £1.70 • Can of Red Bull: £1.50
All campuses have their own SU buildings and bars.
Bars: Fat Mick's (City campus) is the *main* hang-out, with quiz nights, promos and giveaways *galore*. Seasoned boozers pick up a £1 discount card, which knocks about 10% off the price of the next 20 drinks.
Theatres: The Arena Theatre puts on *well-received contemporary drama* (about 80 productions a year) and sends *loads* to the Edinburgh Fringe.
Film: Cult and mainstream films *brighten up dreary Sunday nights* for a fiver (includes drink and popcorn).
Clubbing: There's *some kind of groove* to find every night, but the *most popular* are Double Vision and Quids In. Emma B, Howard Donald and Tim Westwood have all stopped by recently.
Comedy/Cabaret: There's comedy, *but not as Push knows it*. Recent acts are Timmy Mallett, Keith Harris & Orville and – *wait for it* – Bubble from Big Brother 2. The Walsall campus *count themselves lucky* to have Tilly, resident drag queen.
Food: A *pricey* University refectory or pre-packed sarnies in the Union.
Other: Graduation balls are organised by departments. There's a *huge* end of year ball for all and sundry.

SOCIAL & POLITICAL

UNIVERSITY OF WOLVERHAMPTON STUDENTS' UNION:

• 6 sabbaticals • Turnout at last ballot: 7% • NUS member
Woefully apolitical – only 40 of 22,000 turned up to a recent anti-fees demo – but the SU's *central* to student life in *more practical ways* (social ents and welfare).

SU FACILITIES:

SU building on each campus; nightclub/music venue; five bars; four canteens; seven pool tables; meeting rooms; seven minibuses; people carrier; Endsleigh Insurance; ATMs; photocopying, fax, printing services; photo booth; payphones; crèche; late-night minibus; juke boxes; video games; general store; stationery shop; vending machines; new and secondhand bookshop; launderette; printing and graphics shop; hairdressers; optician.

CLUBS (NON-SPORTING):

Advocacy at the Bar; Anime; Chinese; Computer Games; Dances @ Wolves; Equestrian; Hunt Sabs; Irish; Lesbian, Gay, Bisexual, Transgender; LINKS; Malaysian; Mauritian Society; Sign Language Society; Students 4 Change; Vegan & Vegetarian. **See also Clubs tables.**

OTHER ORGANISATIONS:

An *enthusiastically edited* student paper, Cry Wolf, comes out every six weeks. Rag do Ann Summers and Valentines events (*not necessarily at the same time*).

RELIGIOUS:

• 4 chaplains (CofE, RC, FC)
There's a multi-faith chaplaincy and a Muslim prayer room.

PAID WORK: see University of Birmingham
• Job bureau • Paid work: term-time 75%: hols 80%
Wolves work is *easy to come by*, with loads of pubs, bars and restaurants in town. The University Job Shop can also help.

SPORTS

• BUSA Ranking: 36
Walsall's the site for sports courses and the new national judo centre has just opened there. It's part of a new sports centre development with 12 indoor courts, a full-size all-weather pitch and an athletics track.

SPORTS FACILITIES:

Five football pitches; three rugby pitches; two hockey pitches; two all-weather pitches; two squash courts; nine tennis courts; nine multi-purpose courts; 12 netball courts; four sports halls; swimming pool; running track; athletics field; gym; aerobics studio. The local area has a leisure centre; running track; squash courts; swimming pool; ice rink; croquet lawn; golf course. Of course, *then there are the delights* of Brum.

SPORTING CLUBS:

5-a-side; Aerobics; Aikido; Dualthlon; Ju-Jitsu; Kickboxing; Self Defence; T'ai Chi; Yoga. **See also Clubs tables.**

ATTRACTIONS: see University of Birmingham

Wolves *hover* between Premiership and First Division status. The University's practically on top of the Molineux stadium and there's also Birmingham City, Aston Villa, West Brom and Walsall.

 ACCOMMODATION

IN COLLEGE:
- Self-catering: 16% • Cost: £45-62 (37wks) • Insurance premium: ££££

Availability: Students need to live more than 15 miles from town to qualify for halls. *Even then, they're dished out to the first takers*; only disabled students are guaranteed accommodation. Most housing's single sex, though there are mixed flats at Telford and North Road Halls. Halls are *generally pretty habitable* – most are en-suite at Telford and City. *Despite their ghastly appearance*, Randall Lines are *popular, sociable and cheap*. Walsall *used to be the pits*, but new buildings have changed that.
Car parking: Telford is the easiest campus for parking. Finding a spot at City or Walsall *is no joke*.

EXTERNALLY: see University of Birmingham

Availability: *Easy to find and even easier on the pocket*. Whitmore Reans and Penfield are student strongholds. Heath Town's *so grotty* that the housing service won't even advertise properties there.
Housing help: The accommodation office has online vacancy lists, property vetting, landlord blacklists and housing checks.

WELFARE

SERVICES:
- Lesbian/Gay/Bisexual Society • Ethnic Minorities Society • Mature Students' Society
- International Students' Society • Postgrad Society • Disabilities Society
- Late-night minibus • Self-defence classes • College counsellors: 3 full/1 part
- SU counsellors: 5 full • Crime rating: !!!

The SU Advisory team is at City campus, with a once-weekly service at Telford and Walsall. They deal with everything from health and housing to debt.
Health: The SU deals with sexual health and there's an opticians on-site. *But if it's not eyes or genitals causing the problem, look to town*.
Women: Attack alarms are available from the Union.
Crèches/Nursery: Limited places for 2-5-yr-olds.
Disabilities: Best in Telford (hearing loops, ramps, adapted rooms) and *okay* in City, particularly for wheelchair access. Building work at Walsall means *access is pretty poor*. There's a dyslexia unit and adviser.

FINANCE:
- Ave debt per year: £4,268
- Access fund: £3m • Ave payment: £50-1,000

Support: University hardship loans and bursaries and there's a fund for black South African students.

Loughborough University has warned its students that they could face 7 years' imprisonment for stealing traffic cones.

University College Worcester

University College Worcester, Henwick Grove, Worcester, WR2 6AJ
Tel. (01904) 855 000 3000 E-mail: study@worc.ac.uk Website: www.worc.ac.uk
Worcester Students' Union, University College Worcester, Henwick Grove, Worcester, WR2 6AJ
Tel. (01904) 740 800 Website: www.worcsu.com

GENERAL

Just south of Birmingham, the historic city of Worcester is, *predictably enough*, the county town of Worcestershire – the River Severn's last stop on its way into Wales. Just south of its banks, in a *greenish* suburb of this *pretty* city, the compact campus *quietly* and *leafily minds its own business*. Built on the site of an old RAF base, the buildings are a collection of *nice* modern buildings, *slightly marred* by the *stubborn vestiges* of 70s architecture and *what are essentially a few run-down shacks*. Overall, however, the effect is one of *unassuming charm*.

Sex ratio (M:F): 25:75	Founded: 1947
Full-time u'grads: 4,919	Part-time: 2,191
Postgrads: 700	Non-degree: 1,432
Ave course: 3yrs	Ethnic: 5%
State:private school: n/a	Flunk rate: 18%
Mature: 58%	International: 2%
Disabled: 6%	Local: 50%

ATMOSPHERE:

You could scarcely call it an academic powerhouse, but while Worcester's students are as keen for a drink and a knees-up (in the bar or on the sports field) as much as anyone else, they're by no means slackers – timetables for their predominantly vocational courses can get pretty packed. They're a relaxed lot, with a pleasant, welcoming and strongly communal attitude – since everything's effectively on the doorstep, the campus functions as a small village within the city. Many courses, like teaching and nursing, rely heavily on work placements in the wider community, which is quite fond of its students in return. Finally, male students might like to note the gender ratio – three girls to every bloke should appeal to anyone who fancies a touch of Worcester sauce...

WORCESTER:

• Population: 93,000 • City centre: 1,200m • London: 115 miles • Birmingham: 52 miles
• Leeds: 190 miles
• High temp: 22 • Low temp: 1 • Rainfall: 60

People have been living in and around Worcester for thousands of years. The Romans came and went. Those great gifts to English spelling, the Saxons, knew it affectionately and unpronounceably as 'Weagornoceaster', and the Middle Ages saw it grow into a prosperous town heavily involved with the cloth industry and its famous porcelain. Its rich history is reflected in its current appearance – contemporary buildings share space with Tudor houses and medieval churches. The skyline is pierced with spires – *not quite dreaming like Oxford, but at least twitching in their sleep*. Reasons to visit include the ancient and *impressive* cathedral with its 200-metre tower and medieval cloisters, the birthplace of composer Edward Elgar and the reputed tomb of the *villified* King John. Reasons to stay include an *adequate* variety of pubs, shops and restaurants, a *surprisingly lively* nightlife, and the *beautiful* surrounding countryside. *Okay, so it's not a throbbing metropolis, but that's what Birmingham – less than an hour away – is for.*

TRAVEL:

Trains: Both Worcester's mainline stations – Forgate Street and Shrub Hill – are within a mile of the University and have frequent connections all over the country (Birmingham: £9.70 sgl).
Coaches: National Express services stop in the city centre.
Car: The M5, A443, A44 and A38 are some of Worcester's *favourite* roads. *Parking isn't much of an issue* as there are *plenty* of pay & displays around and 500 spaces on campus (£1.20/day, 60p after 6pm). Permits cost £25 a term – but conditions apply.
Air: Birmingham International 45 mins away serves both national and international destinations.
Local: *Handy* bus 31 goes in and out of town for £1.20.
College: Free minibuses are laid on for certain nursing and education classes.
Taxis: *Reliable* but *unhailable* services. Several firms have an understanding with the University and are always around at peak times.
Bicycles: *Cycle fever hasn't really hit Worcester the town or Worcester the University*, but campus storage facilities are *more than adequate* in any case.

CAREER PROSPECTS:

• Careers Service • No. of staff: 2 full • Unemployed after 6mths: 3%
Newsletters, bulletin boards, interview training, job fairs and a careers library. The Careers Service itself used to be a RAF morgue and still has the sloping floors. *No jokes about 'dead-end jobs' please – that'd be tasteless.*

FAMOUS ALUMNI:

Matt Beechey (rower); Jacqui Smith MP (Minister for Industry and the Regions); Andy Train (Olympic canoeist); Jo Yapp (England Women's Rugby captain).

FURTHER INFO:

• Prospectuses: undergrad; postgrad; international • Open days

 ACADEMIC

 Traditionally a training ground for nurses and teachers, Worcester's *rapidly becoming a rising star* in the fields of digital arts and sports science. All undergrad courses are modular, allowing students to tackle various subjects in varying depth over their course of study.

Entry points: 80-200	Ave points: 200
No. of terms: 2	Length of terms: 19wks
Clearing: 10%	Study addicts: 17%
Teaching: *	Research: n/a
Year abroad: n/a	Sandwich students: 1%

ADMISSIONS:

• Apply via UCAS/NMAS for nursing/GTTR for PGCE
Mature students without formal qualifications can be admitted via interview and essay assessment.

SUBJECTS:

Art & Design: 3%	IT: 5%
Arts/Humanities: 9%	Science & Sport: 14%
Business/Management: 9%	Nursing: 19%
Education: 33%	Social Sciences: 8%

Best: Art & Design; Biology; Business; Education; Nursing; Psychology; Sociology; Sport.

LIBRARIES:

• 150,000 books • 480 study places • Spend per student: £££
Perks include the collection housed on behalf of the Worcestershire Archaelogical Society and *a treasure trove* of kids' lit.

COMPUTERS:

• <u>444 workstations</u> • <u>Spend per student: ££</u>
Computer provision isn't Worcester's strongest point – only one of the three accomodation blocks is networked – but there is wireless access across campus and the other two halls should be jacked up in 2006.

OTHER LEARNING FACILITIES:

In addition to the drama studio-cum-theatre, language labs and recording studio, there's a *particularly sexy* digital arts centre containing a video production studio. *Even fancier,* however, is MARRC – the Motion Analysis Research and Rehabilitation Centre which uses cameras, sensors and animation to create 3D computer models. The English polo and cricket teams have been using it recently. *Sports Science has never tasted so good.* The nursing department has two simulation hospital wards.

E N T E R T A I N M E N T

THE CITY:

• <u>Price of a pint of beer: £2.20</u> • <u>Glass of wine: £2.50</u> • <u>Can of Red Bull: £1.20</u>
Cinemas: The six-screen Odeon and ten-screen Vue (free popcorn deal on Tuesdays) do NUS discounts.
Theatres: The Swan Theatre and Huntingdon Hall are *small* venues nearby, but *if all the world's a stage, Worcester ain't included.* Stratford-Upon-Avon and the Royal Shakespeare Company is 30 mins away by car if you fancy a bit of thesp-action.
Pubs: *Worcester has plenty to offer the discerning student beer fiend, from traditional pubs to wine bars to alternative joints and all the winding, staggering way back again. Local establishments have embraced the College with open arms and* the sports team-sponsoring Crown & Anchor begins each term by hoisting its *notorious* 'Drinking Term commences soon. Enrol today' banner. The Garibaldi and the Bedwardine have their share of live-outers as regulars. *The only bar Push wouldn't prop up is the Brewers Arms, since it seems peculiarly keen on elderly men.*

Clubbing: *Nothing particularly diverse or alternative, but if good, wholesome chart dance gets your party started,* Le Mangos (2 rooms – retro & mainstream) and Tramps (R&B, cheese, dance) should do the trick.
Music venues: *Birmingham gets the stars of the stadium. Worcester makes do with* live pub sessions at places like the Marrs Bar, Keystones and Drummonds.
Eating out: *A fair range of reasonable eateries. Most Worcesterites are happy with the kebabulous Shakeey's after a night out, but since Push is way too classy for that, a plug goes to the cheap and sizeable portions at Keystones.*

UNIVERSITY:

• <u>Price of a pint of beer: £1.55</u> • <u>Glass of wine: £2</u> • <u>Can of Red Bull: £1.50</u>
Bars: The *unashamedly named* Dive is the only bar on campus and probably the only student bar to be made out of an old RAF aircraft hangar. *Apparently, the spirits of long dead pilots still turn up for a pint.* It's busy *most of the time, luring* students in with pool tables, Sky TV and *enough promo deals to floor a bull elephant.*
Theatres: Two societies perform *irregularly* in the drama studio, *which masquerades as a theatre.*
Film: New DVD releases get shown on Sunday evenings.
Music venues: The Dive has a small stage for bands: mostly tributes and Chesney.
Clubbing: The SU is *willing* but the venue is *weak,* at least until they get their licensing sorted. The Dive has a DJ booth and dance floor, *and the atmosphere often buzzes in a clubby way,* but there are no bona fide club nights.
Comedy/Cabaret: An open mic comedy night is planned.
Food: Snak Attack *can't spell but they can cook* – usually artery-clogging fare, but a pasta option exists for health-freaks. The Food Court canteen is the lunch venue of choice, with an *extensive* selection and vegetarian options. Café Connections and Ritazza make the kind of food you eat with coffee.
Other: The Colours Ball is an awards night/*piss-up* for sportsfolk.

SOCIAL & POLITICAL

WORCESTER STUDENTS' UNION:

• 3 sabbaticals • NUS member • Turnout at last ballot: 9%
'Politically ferocious lobbying machine' is not a phrase you'll ever see used in conjunction with Worcester's Union (except here) because representation and service matters are their main hobby horse, although to be fair, they knocked together some banners and dusted off some surly expressions for the anti top-up demos. Relations with the University itself are comfily co-operative.

SU FACILITIES:

Bar; music venue; two cafés; canteen; five pool/snooker tables; meeting room; Alliance & Leicester ATM; photo booth; fax & printing service; payphones; women's room; games & vending machines; juke box; general store; Waterstone's books; stationery shop.

CLUBS (NON-SPORTING):

Alternative Music; Archaeology. **See also Clubs tables.**

OTHER ORGANISATIONS:

SU newspaper, the Voice, is hot off the press twice termly or so. *Small but warm-hearted* Rag releases its own yearly magazine and arranges a Rag Week and various events throughout the year.

RELIGIOUS:

• 1 chaplain (CofE)
There's a multi-faith chaplaincy and prayer room on campus but, *for those who like their places of worship a touch more bespoke,* the city offers a variety of Christian churches and a mosque.

PAID WORK:

• Paid work: term-time 65%; hols 90%
Worcester is the UK's first University to introduce a Job Pod scheme, where students can search for part-time or temporary work via a touch-screen databank, all without having to leave the SU. A free phone connects straight through to local and national Job Centres. Worcester has a few bar and shop jobs kicking around and the campus employs tour guides, note-takers for disabled students and other SU workers.

SPORTS

• Recent successes: basketball • BUSA Ranking: 48
Worcester seems to be more successful at dealing with injuries than opposing teams, thanks to its Sports Performance Labs and BUPA clinic on campus, *but they're by no means afraid to roll around in the mud with the best of them.* The basketball squad recently *trounced the mighty Loughborough* – with a little help from their friend, the Worcester Wolves' team coach – and are the UK champions in BUSA's basketball league.

SPORTS FACILITIES:

There are a couple of *scrappy* pitches and some Astroturf on campus, but most of the sporting larks happen off-site on the three competition pitches. There's also: a floodlit *but tatty* tennis court; two training and one full-size basketball court; two netball courts; Sports hall; gym; multigym; aerobics studio, and the river nearby. Students pay £25 a term for access to the fitness suite; everything else is free. Members of the public can use the Sports Hall and gym *at the extortionate prices that members of the public deserve.* The city adds various other leisure facilities, including a golf course, a running track and, fairly nearby, outdoor adventure activities areas. The county cricket ground is in pebble-hurling distance of campus.

SPORTING CLUBS:

Jiu Jitsu. **See also Clubs tables.**

ATTRACTIONS:

If it weren't for the fact they knocked Liverpool out of the FA Cup in 1959, *footie pub bores would never have heard of* Worcester City FC. Worcester's Zurich Premiership Rugby Union team dangle over relegation, while the *not-quite-brilliant* Worcester Wolves basketball boys bounce about in Division One.

ACCOMMODATION

IN COLLEGE:

• Self-catered:10% • Cost: £45-64 (37+wks) • Insurance premium: £
Availability: College accommodation – *and there isn't much of it* – is allocated on a first-come, first-housed basis and only students from Worcestershire are exempt from applying. *Miraculously*, only 1% of 1st years go away disappointed. Halls are composed of flats for four or six people, sharing large kitchens and communal areas which *add to the homey feel (in both the domestic and gangsta sense of the word)*. All halls are either on or within a mile of campus and most are new, *attractive blocks – Worcester Halls being the newest and attractivest.* Security patrols, CCTV and entry phones *keep the outside out whilst, on the inside, 3rd year hall wardens keep their power-crazed eyes on the inmates within.* All halls are non-smoking.
Car parking: £25-permits are only available to teaching students or those on work placements.

EXTERNALLY:

• Ave rent: £53
Availability: The St John's area is *easily meanderable* from campus and has a *wide* range of *affordable* options.
Housing help: The SU and Student Services jointly pen the anuual Housing List each March. Landlords are approved or blacklisted *according to their relative moral status,* vacancy lists and bulletin boards are maintained and legal help is offered.

WELFARE

SERVICES:

• Lesbian/Gay/Bisexual Society • Women's Officer • Mature Students' Officer
• International Students' Officer • Postgrad Officer & Society • Disabilities Officer
• Nightline • College counsellors: 1 full/ 1 part
Health: The Health Centre on campus is staffed by a medical attendant and several trained staff. An NHS practice is available locally.
Crèches/Nursery: The University nursery has 36 places for student's spawn 3mths-5yrs.
Disabilities: A College-wide overhaul has added ramps, sliding and automatic doors and a disabled lift *(no, that doesn't mean it's been turned off)*. Some of the older areas *present obstacles to access* – especially on the door front. Four rooms have been adapted for wheelchair users and adjacent rooms for carers are also available. Assistant Disability Co-ordinators have responsibility for visually- and hearing-impaired students and there are several adapted rooms, support tutors, hearing loops, vibrating pagers, a Braille embosser and specialised computer software available. Dyslexics benefit from sensitive marking and software support.
Drugs: *All sorts of unpleasent things are done to campus drug users.*

FINANCE:

Support: Some sports scholarships are available to athletic supermen and women, and there's an emergency hardship fund. As far as fees go there are £700 bursaries for those on the maintenance grant – £500 for everyone else.

Writtle College

see University of Essex

Wye College

see Imperial College, London

University of York

University of York, Heslington, York, North Yorkshire, YO10 5DD
Tel: (01904) 430 000/433 533 E-mail: admissions@york.ac.uk Website: www.york.ac.uk
York University Students' Union, The Daw Suu Centre, Goodricke College, Heslington, York,
North Yorkshire, YO10 5DD Tel: (01904) 433 724 E-mail: su-enquiries@york.ac.uk Website:
www.yusu.org

GENERAL

For some reason, all civil wars seem to occur between North and South. York (or 'Jorvik',
for the more Viking-minded) didn't come out of the War of the Roses too well, by all
accounts, but a few centuries and several judicious beheadings later, *York is now a scenic,
peaceful city, pulsing with an intense cultural and historical atmosphere.* Half the hike from
London to Edinburgh, a seagull's throw from the coast and within puking distance of Leeds
– major transport node of the north-east, it's thoroughly accessible by land, sea or air. The
University itself is a relative spring-chicken at just over 40 years old. Rather than sharing
the *glorious architecture* of the Minster, the off-city campus was designed in the days when
meaning something was more important than looking sexy, so the landscaped concrete
'concept' campus *may not be to all tastes,* although the 200 acres of surrounding parkland
and the central lake are *undeniably pretty.* The concept itself is 'discovery around every
corner' – that's not to say you're likely to stumble over copulating couples behind every
department, *but that the architects were trying to imbue the very buildings with the
essence of learning.* They didn't do a bad job – York has *one of the best academic
reputations of any concrete university.*

Sex ratio (M:F): 42:58	Founded: 1963
Full-time u'grads: 6,555	Part-time: 1,400
Postgrads: 2,230	Non-degree: 1,629
Ave course: 3yrs	Ethnic: 6%
State:private school: 80:20	Flunk rate: 5%
Mature: 12%	International: 19%
Disabled: 111	Local: 10%

58%
42%

ATMOSPHERE:

*York, like Oxbridge, is a collegiate university, although the resemblance ends there. There
are eight colleges with roughly 1,000-odd students stashed away in each. The system is
more a convenient means of breaking the student body into manageable chunks than
brewing up true collegiate spirit. You can ask for a specific college though requests aren't
guaranteed. The large Heslington campus (in a wee village 1½ miles south-east of the
famous city walls) isn't exactly a frenetic hub of activity (especially at the weekend, when the
silence of death pervades), but there is a quiet sense of community all around – even if it's
just among the ubiquitous waterfowl. Relations between students and locals are largely
amicable, although University plans for campus extension have been getting up residents'*

noses a bit. Local input, however, has been encouraged at every stage of planning, so it looks as though the magic of compromise will keep everyone happy.

YORK:

• Population: 181,300 • City centre: $1\frac{1}{2}$ miles • London: 205 miles • Leeds: 23 miles • High temp: 21 • Low temp: 2 • Rainfall: 53

From the moment the *striking* city walls come into view, it's clear that York has a lot to offer the cultural historian or flash-happy tourist (that's photography, not indecent exposure). It's the top British tourist lure after London, what with the Minster, the castle, the oldest street in the country and *the intentionally musty* Jorvik Viking Centre. York is a melting pot of *intriguing* architecture: Viking huts, Roman affairs and a host of *elegant* Georgian buildings. Abounding in pubs and all the high-street trimmings, *the city's full of diversions for the dedicated party player as well as those more interested in tinkly-dangly crafty shops.*

TRAVEL:

Trains: York Station is right next to the city centre, about 2 miles from the campus. Connections are available to most destinations, although many journeys will involve travelling via Leeds.

Coaches: National Express runs coaches to most destinations from the rail station.

Car: The A64, A1, A19, M1 and M62 are all accessible from York. *Parking in the city can be tricky,* however, as the city council's green transport policy has resulted in parking restrictions. The University will only issue parking permits in exceptional circumstances (free to disabled students, £18 to others). There are four pay & display car parks on campus, which *aren't too evilly priced.* Most students opt for bikes instead of cars, which are generally only used for out-of-city travel.

Air: Leeds Bradford Airport is 24 miles away (40 mins by car) and has a few budget airlines on offer (Ryanair, BMI, Jet2, British European). Direct train link to Manchester Airport.

Hitching: *Prospects are uncertain, but the M1 and A1 are busy enough to ensure a trip somewhere.*

Local: Bus No. 4 goes from campus to the city centre in about 10 mins and costs £1.25 one way or £2.20 for a day ticket.

College: The SU runs a free minibus service from the city centre to the campus, and from there to student homes off-campus, so everyone can get home *unscathed.* Donations appreciated, but aren't obligatory.

Taxis: Local services are *reasonably priced and popular with students.* A journey from the large rank outside the station to the Heslington campus costs around a fiver.

Bicycles: *Flat York is best navigated by bicycle, making the campus seem like the aftermath of an explosion in a bike shop. It's often quicker and more efficient than a car, and the campus is well provisioned for the two-wheeled wonders with numerous bike sheds dotted around the campus for storage or playground canoodling purposes, and the city itself is blessed with extensive cycle routes.*

CAREER PROSPECTS:

• Careers Service • No. of staff: 8 full/4 part • Unemployed after 6mths: 7%

The Careers Service boasts bulletin boards, interview practice, a careers library and a programme of employer presentations to start students off in the big bad world of work.

FAMOUS ALUMNI:

Tony Banks MP, Robin Cook MP; Jung Chang (writer); Greg Dyke (the ex-Director-General of the BBC and the University's Chancellor); Harry Enfield (comedian); Harriet Harman MP, Oona King MP; Peter Lord (of Aardman Animations, the cartoon boffins behind Wallace & Gromit); Victor Lewis-Smith (comedian/journalist); Denise O'Donohue (HatTrick TV); Genista McIntosh (theatre director); Dominic Muldowney (composer); John Witherow (editor, Sunday Times).

FURTHER INFO:

• Prospectuses: undergrad; postgrad • Open days • Video
All info from the Admissions and Schools Liaison by phone on (01904) 433 196 or online at www.york.ac.uk/admissions. The SU flogs an alternative prospectus at £1 a pop.

ACADEMIC

York is heavy on research, with glowing teaching standards across the board. All courses are credit-based, with students taking 120 credits a year, divided across an assortment of compulsory and optional modules. Assessment is very much course dependent, with some departments shunning end of year exams altogether.

Entry points: 280-340	**Ave points: 421**
Applns per place: 9	**Clearing: 5%**
No. of terms: 3	**Length of terms: 10wks**
Staff/student ratio: 1:16	**Study addicts: 28%**
Teaching: *****	**Research: *******
Year abroad: 8%	**Sandwich students: 4%**

ADMISSIONS:

• Apply via UCAS/NMAS for nursing/GTTR for PGCE
York's trying to bump up its mature and international student numbers.

SUBJECTS:

Arts/Humanities: 25%   Modern Languages: 3%
Business/Management: 1%   Sciences: 51%
Best: Archaeology; Biochemistry; Biology; Chemistry; Computer Science; Economics; Education; Electronics; English; Environment; History; History of Art; Language & Linguistic Science; Maths; Management; Music; Nursing; Philosophy; Physics; Politics; Psychology; Sociology; Social Policy; Social Work.

LIBRARIES:

• 800,000 books • 750 study places • Spend per student: ££££
The Raymond Burton library for humanities has freed up shelf space in the main J B Morrell library, *which is lovely and modern inside, but ugly concrete externally.* It stays open till 10pm on weekdays in term and you can issue books yourself *so you don't always have to deal with unnecessary librarians.*

COMPUTERS:

• 1,387 workstations
Open access computer rooms in seven of the colleges as well as the libraries, all with networked, internet-enabled PCs. High-speed connection points are available in all on-campus student rooms, which they can hook up to for £20 a term.

OTHER LEARNING FACILITIES:

York's Language For All (LFA) programme has 14 languages to pick from, at all levels of competence. Students can learn a foreign language in addition to their course, night-school style. In-coming students can also take a basic research and IT course named Information Literacy in all Departments (or ILIAD – *someone worked hard for that acronym*) which introduces useful skills for studying. There's even a certificate. *Wow.* Other facilities include: language labs, music rehearsal rooms (for music students and the Music Society), a drama studio (for drama students) and media centre (the University's TV station's base).

ENTERTAINMENT

THE CITY:

• Price of a pint of beer: £2 • Glass of wine: £2.50 • Can of Red Bull: £1.60

Cinemas: Three to choose from, including the usual Odeon and Warner Village (Vue) multiplexes, and City Screen – a baby three-screener, with a classic/cult bias and regular stand-up comedy nights. And, *most importantly*, a bar. All offer student discounts.

Theatres: The Theatre Royal is the largest venue for mainstream plays and comedy.

Pubs: York is *dribbling* with traditional olde worlde British pubs like the Old White Swan, Punch Bowl and the Royal Oak, which boast proper northern ales. There are a few *more lively and swanky* establishments, including Harker's, Fiesta Mehicana, Ha!Ha! Bar and the Gallery. For retro boozage: Flares (dedicated to 1970s) and Reflex (where the 80s never ends. *The horror, the horror*).

Clubbing: *Although a bit naff and meat-markety, there's fun to be had in the York club scene. Monday through to Wednesday there's at least one student night on at Ikon, Diva, Toffs or the Gallery, which fills three rooms with mainstream, pop and dance, indie and acid, jazz and chill out vibes. And students, of course. The more reliable hardcore club scene lingers alluringly in Leeds.*

Music venues: York has a *middleweight* music scene, with many pubs presenting regular live n' local music nights. Fibbers (200 cap) reels in the bigger fish, like Badly Drawn Boy and Franz Ferdinand. Around a fiver to get in and it's friendly and sweaty. *Yum.*

Eating out: *Nothing too special, but a good range of cheap eats, including some quality curry houses. Pushplugs: Oscar's wine bar; Caesar's and Fellini's for Italian; the Cello for coffee and edible coffee accessories; and the Willow – a Chinese that, much like Cinderella, becomes a cheesy disco at midnight. There's a new Wetherspoon's in town with very cheap food and criminally inexpensive drink. Oh, and any visit to York is incomplete without a stop in Betty's Tea Rooms, where cake looks, tastes and is priced like a work of art.*

UNIVERSITY:

• Price of a pint of beer: £1.50 • Glass of wine: £1.75 • Can of Red Bull: £1.70

Bars: Seven college-run bars ensure a wide variety of surroundings to lose bodily control in. Henry's (at Alcuin College) is a *trendy city-style* café bar; Café Sol (Derwent) has a Mediterranean theme. Hoggies (Langwith) is more central *and traditional*, while Vanbrugh bar is *the show house of the York Brewery* and, along with Goodricke bar, is *pretty popular*. Kasbah (Wentworth) is *a popular postgrad haunt with a sophisticated continental style* and JJ's (Halifax) is the place to be for big screen premiership matches and cocktail pitchers. Hours are pretty standard, although weekend drinking doesn't usually start until the evening.

Theatres: *Drama is strong* with several drama societies and three theatres on the go. The Drama Barn, Jack Lyons Concert Hall and Central Hall stage numerous student productions.

Film: The University-built cinema shows four current mainstream titles per week and the odd bit of arthouse for £2.50 admission. By contrast, the Word Cinema Society picks out independent celluloid to screen each week.

Music venues: There are no purpose-built music venues on campus, but the SU sets up the four large dining halls as gig-holes when the need arises. Visitors have included the Bluetones, Pat Sharpe and the Vengaboys, *but don't let that put you off*. The SU runs a yearly Battle of the Bands and a 'Woodstock' festival competition to showcase local and student talent. Or lack of it.

Clubbing: Various ents are held regularly at various colleges, such as 'Langwith Large', 'GSpot' and 'Club D'. 'Planet V' at Vanbrugh is the latest pop fest. 'Breakz' is an alternative dance night, spotlighting techno, house, D&B and breakbeat. On top of these Platinum Society runs hip hop nights. The Indie soc does, er, Indie nights.

Comedy/Cabaret: Wentworth College hosts three comedy nights a term.

Food: Most of the college bars offer snacks or more substantial edibles, as well as dining halls. JJ's, for example, offers free pizza delivery to all houses in Halifax college and all porters' lodges. Royston's at Langwith is a giant (300+) Fish'n'Chip emporium. Roger Kirk's Galleria restaurant serves all kinds of quick food. Several departments and a library have their own cafeteria or snack bar too, so students are never far from a meal. Until after 7.30pm, that is. Then it's Costcutter or *starvation*.

Other: Different colleges and societies run a number of black tie balls, totalling around 15 every year. The biggest is the £60 Graduation Ball, sometimes held at York Race Course, which includes a three-course meal and top acts headlining.

SOCIAL & POLITICAL

YORK UNIVERSITY STUDENTS' UNION (YUSU):

• 6 sabbaticals • Turnout at last ballot: 14% • NUS member

YUSU has survived many years without a centralised union building and still lacks its own bar/music venue. *It's only real problem with the University authorities has been the repeated rejection of proposals to get one. The collegiate system can work against Union-awareness on campus, so YUSU has had to work particularly hard to combat this,* implementing an electronic voting system so that students can have their say on union issues online, without having to leave their room. One recent change to union policy is that societies can now be started with just three members instead of the usual 40, allowing more new societies with greater diversity. *It's not as radical an institution as it once was, but good support was shown in the struggle against top-up fees.*

SU FACILITIES:

Student facilities, not all in the SU: seven bars; seven canteens, two snack bars; 11 pool tables; meeting room; six minibuses for hire; Endsleigh Insurance; ATMs: Link and NatWest; photocopier; fax service; printing service; photo booth; payphones; advice centre; crèche; late night minibus; TV lounge; juke box; video machines; general store; stationery shop; vending machine; secondhand bookshop; video gaming machines.

CLUBS (NON-SPORTING):

Anime; Astronomy; Ballroom & Latin American Dancing; Ballet; Biochemistry; Book Group; Boris Johnson Appreciation; Breakz; Bridge; Campus Bands; Christian Focus; Christis; Chinese Students; Choral; Cinematography; City; Concert; Conservative/Unionist; Debating; Digital Art & Music; Douglas Adams; Duke of Edinburgh; Finance; Football Supporters; French; Friends of Antara; Fusion; German; Gilbert & Sullivan; Gin & Tonic; Hellenic; History; Indie; Japanese; Jazz & Blues; Juggling; LAN gaming; Lunatic Fringe; Links; Medieval Re-enactment; Malaysian; Namaskar; Oriental Dream Studio (Asian Design); Outdoor; Pants; Physics; Platinum; Poker; Quiet; Radio; Railway; Recreation; Singapore; Socialist; Student Action for Palestine; Student Stop AIDS; Taiwanese; Tea; Turkish; UN; World Cinema; York Glee Singers; York Students Against the War; York Unity. **See also Clubs tables.**

OTHER ORGANISATIONS:

Vision and Nouse are the two free titles published by independent bodies regularly each term – Vision has been a Guardian Student Newspaper of the year in the past. There's also a free SU magazine containing articles on student life and union events. University Radio was one of the first student stations in the country, and hits the campus airwaves 24 hrs a day. YSTV (the student-run TV station) is shown in campus bars and JCRs for 5 hrs or so each day. Plans are afoot to feed the signal into all student bedrooms. *The York Rag is a busy little bee,* arranging campus events, sponsored life-endangerment and students escape into Europe with a bucket to jangle. The Community Action Group *is equally active,* with a large number of local and international welfare projects, including drama in prisons, AIDS awareness campaigns in Africa and conservation and education work.

RELIGIOUS:

• 3 full-time chaplains (CofE, Methodist, RC); visiting chaplains of other denominations

For Anglicans, the Minster, home to one of England's two archbishops, *has an inspiring influence, which has rubbed off on other Christian denominations.* Following an incident involving a Jewish massacre nearly 1,000 years ago, there's no synagogue in York, but there are meetings, prayers and accommodation for four people at the Jewish Centre on campus.

In 1994 students at Portsmouth were housed temporarily in a naval barracks and subjected to naval discipline.

The nearest synagogue is *awkwardly* 20 mins away in Leeds. There are churches of most denominations in York and a mosque very close to campus.

PAID WORK:

• Job bureau

The thriving tourist industry ensures job opportunities for students in the high seasons. Museum, tearoom, restaurant and pub work is easy to get to fill the piggy bank. The University operates a job centre and Unijobs, a *helpful* agency that links students up with local businesses. Target assists 1st and 2nd years in finding vacation or gap-year work in all corners of the globe.

SPORTS

• BUSA ranking:41

York has something of a communist attitude to sporting activity: a firmly held 'sports for all' credo, whether at college or university level. The Athletics Union co-ordinates all sporting events on the *well-equipped* campus. Membership includes personal accident insurance, discounts in sports stores and the chance to join any one of York's 56 athletics clubs. *The bitter taste of history returns at* the annual Roses Tournament with Lancaster University, the largest intervarsity event in the country. *Beheadings are blessedly rare.*

SPORTS FACILITIES:

40-acre sports area; eight football/rugby pitches; hockey pitch; all-weather pitch; two cricket pitches; four squash courts; six tennis courts; one basketball/netball court; two sports halls; running track; athletics field; croquet/bowling green; aerobics studio; climbing wall; seven badminton courts. Locally: a swimming pool, golf course and opportunities for mountaineering, potholing or mucking about on the river. Another sports hall is perhaps in the offing, with plans to incorporate a fitness suite, aerobic studio, glass-backed squash courts and social area.

SPORTING CLUBS

Aerobics; Aikido; Ben Lairig (walking & mountaineering); Boxing; Brazilian Jiu Jitsu; Canoe; Canoe Polo; Cave & Pothole; Chess; Croquet; Danceport; Futsal (similar to 5-a-side football, but with non-bouncing ball); Gliding; Jiu Jitsu; Karting; Lacrosse; Paintball; Parachute; Pole Exercise; Polo; Pool; Skateboarding; Street Hockey; Surf; Table Tennis; Thai Boxing; Ultimate Frisbee. **See also Clubs tables.**

ATTRACTIONS:

York Race Course is nearby, for *big-hatted gambling* types.

ACCOMMODATION

IN COLLEGE:

• Self-catering cost: £56-72 per week (33/34 or 38wks)
• First years living in: 100% • Insurance premium: £

Availability: Barring exceptional circumstances (eg. getting the form in late), all 1st year students are guaranteed a room and a few finalists can be safely tucked up in college accommodation. Students who are *very deeply in lurve* have a stab at obtaining one of the five double rooms in Holgates Hall, while students with families on their backs have some limited accommodation available to them. *The halls of residence themselves are fairly similar (being no more than 40 years old), although some of the newer accommodation blocks can seem a smidge antisocial, since tight security limits mixing between corridors.* Rooms are divided into four price bands (or 'luxury bands' technically), ranging from economy to superior en-suite. The price range differs by just over a tenner a week. *There are a few rooms that are ready to be taken out to the barn and shot, but overall, York accommodation is good value for money.*

Car parking: Parking is restricted to those with disabilities or exceptional requirements (a permit costs £18), so *unless the car can be easily disguised as modern sculpture, forget it.* Lockable bike sheds are available at most colleges, though.

EXTERNALLY:
• Ave rent: £55 • Living at home: 4%
Availability: Around 60% of undergraduates live out and no one has so far been unable to find a spot to crash in. *Recently, however, the house hunt has been getting trickier and more competitive. Nearby Heslington Rd is the first choice for living out, but Bishopthorpe Rd and South Bank are also getting quite popular. Fulford prices tend to be prohibitive.* Luckily, no real dodgy areas since York is relatively free from crime. *Relatively.*
Housing help: The Accommodation Office holds a list of properties that comply with guidelines. It also posts vacancies on its bulletin board and blacklists iffy landlords.

WELFARE

SERVICES:
• Lesbian/Gay/Bisexual Officer & Support Group • Racial Equality Officer
• Women's Officer & Society • Mature Students' Association
• Overseas Students' Association • Graduate Students Association
• Disabilities Officer & Society • Late-night/Women's minibus
• Nightline • Taxi fund • University counsellors: 5 part • Crime rating: !!!
The University provides trained counsellors, a legal support service and personal tutors responsible for pastoral care (*no sheep involved*).
Health: Students have the option of registering with the University Health Centre on campus or any York GP.
Women: There are weekly women's committee meetings and a frequently updated notice board. The Well Women service on campus can provide breast examination and cervical smear testing. There's a women's bookshop and women have priority on the late-night minibus. YUSU provides free attack alarms and pregnancy tests.
Crèches/Nursery: University facilities for 30 children aged 2-5yrs and nine children aged 3mths-2yrs.
Disabilities: The equal opps policy should mean full access to all facilities and activities. *There's a good record of admitting and supporting disabled students* and there are lifts in almost every building, plenty of ramps, adapted accommodation and hearing induction loops. The dyslexia support centre offers diagnosis and advice and those with unseen disabilities receive support from the Disability Services Office.

FINANCE:
• Ave debt per year: £2,474
Fees: Fees for non-EU nationals vary between £8,154 and £10,765 depending on the course. For postgrads, we're talking between £3,010 and £10,765 a year.
• Access fund: £500,000
Support: The SU can provide a hardship loan of £100 on the spot. There are some bursaries and sponsorships available, particularly for international or mature students.

Push, of course

How to use 'Push, of course'

On the next few pages are listed the courses available at each of the universities in the UK. If you know what you want to study, find it in the list (or the closest thing to it) and below you'll find the names of the universities where you can study it. But not so fast, speedy. There's a few things it may be handy to know.

First off, the **course names**. Because there are nearly 20,000 individual courses, we've simplified the names and grouped them together. So, 'English Literature' and 'Literature in English' have been bundled in under 'English' (along with 'English Studies', 'Studies in English', 'Twentieth Century English Fiction' and, quite probably, 'Nursery Rhyme Studies'). And English is grouped together with 'Literature, Linguistics, Classics, etc'. Some of these groups may seem a little odd at first, but blame UCAS (where we got our information from) and they can blame the universities (where they got it). We've added cross-references which should make it pretty straightforward.

That means if you want to study Guatemalan History, try thinking a bit wider: in this instance, 'History, specialising in a specific country or area'. But be warned, the universities listed there may not offer Guatemalan History per se, but they will offer the closest thing possible. **Check with the university in question for the exact range of courses on offer.**

Next up: the order that the universities are listed indicates the **entrance requirements** needed to get in. The first ones only accept students with the highest grades and the last listed may not expect you to have much more than a bronze swimming certificate. (Those requiring the same grades are listed alphabetically.)

Bear in mind that some courses are harder to get into than others: they don't let people with half an A Level and a scout's badge study Medicine, for instance. **Again, check with the university itself for the exact grades they'd want from you.**

The courses listed are often available in **combinations** – just occasionally, they're only available jointly with other subjects. Yet again, the university itself will have the latest details.

This list – with loads more detail and search and sort facilities – is also available in the members' area of **Push Online (www.push.co.uk)** and UCAS's own website (www.ucas.com) has its own version. Once you've found which universities offer your chosen course, check out their profiles to see whether you like the place and what else they have to offer.

CHOOSING A COURSE

For every different student, there's probably a different way to choose a course. Many take one look at the list of courses available and run screaming into the night. Others stick to their 'best' subject at A Level, without giving a thought to the fact that maths at A Level and maths as a degree can be about as similar as watching a Formula 1 car racing and standing in front of one.

Others pick a degree based on the career they want to follow. This is usually sound but don't forget that you can get a career in the media without a media studies degree and not all accountants studied accountancy at university.

The safest bet is always to pick a course you'll enjoy. If you enjoy it, it'll be worthwhile and you'll do better. You'll also be qualified for jobs you might enjoy.

Check out a university you like the sound of. Visit or phone the relevant departments of the subjects you're considering. Then talk to the students who're studying it and the tutors who teach it to find out what it's all about.

Choose carefully – you can sometimes change your course once you've started it, but at some universities it's about as difficult, exhausting and painful as listening to Britney Spears's views on politics.

Courses

JOINT HONOURS COURSES

Forget any notion of lazy, hazy Sunday afternoons – these are degrees where you study two subjects instead of just the one, usually in two separate departments of the university.

Most universities offer combinations of courses. Obvious ones are language courses (eg. French and German), but more adventurous bods may want to tackle something less likely – physics and music, anyone?

Don't presume, however, that just because two separate subjects are available at one institution that you can do both together. Check with the prospectus and/or in the UCAS listings.

How the courses are combined also varies. Some are 'interdisciplinary' (meaning you do a course which combines stuff from both subjects) and some are independent of each other – in effect you're doing two separate half-courses.

Just to confuse you even more, some mix 50% of each course and others offer the option of picking one subject as a 'major' (though you usually don't have to decide which until after your first year).

Some students find the workload on joint courses is heavier than on single honours equivalents and that communication levels between departments seem to pre-date the telephone. As a result, the students' organisational skills need to be as watertight as a lilo in a shark-infested paddling pool. But at the end of it all you should have a wider range of skills, be less likely to be fed up with your subjects and have had the chance to make loads more friends.

For those who really like to live on the edge (or who can't make up their minds and pick just one course), there are combined honours courses where you study not one, not two, but three subjects.

MODULAR COURSES

Most universities now offer modular courses. This means you can pick and choose a range of options across the academic spectrum.

You go through university life successfully completing (hopefully) individual 'modules' in different subject areas and collecting credits. When you've got enough credits, you can trade them in for a degree – like collecting tokens off the back of cereal packets.

This system is particularly good for students with outside commitments, since you can often accumulate credits, go back to full-time work for a year and then pick up again where you left off. It's also great for people who don't know at the time of application what sort of subjects will interest them.

LENGTH OF COURSE

Most full-time degrees are three years in length while some – eg. Engineering, most languages – tend to take a wee while longer, being four years. That's not to say that all Engineering and language courses take four years nor that all other courses are only three. *Push* probes where others fear to smell, but we all have limits, so contact the college or university in question to find out the exact length of the course you're interested in.

The difference often depends on the letters at the beginning of the course name – BA/BSc will usually be three years of hard and fruitful graft and make you a 'bachelor' of your subject. Meanwhile MA/MSc/MEng/etc. will be a four-year course (if not five) and mean you're a 'master' ('... but only a master of evil, Darth').

Most undergraduate courses in England and Wales are bachelor courses, but in Scotland, they usually head to masters degrees and so take an extra year.

For added relish, 'sandwich' courses are four years in length, but get you a bachelor degree. A sandwich course contains some time (usually a year, but often in more than one bit) doing a work placement (and getting paid for it) or studying abroad, usually betwen your second and final year, in a country, industry or bed, as appropriate to your degree.

Medicine, Dentistry and Veterinary Science are just far too long for all but the mad, dedicated, perverted or rich, being a whacking five or six years of studenthood. But don't let *Push* stop you. We want dentists to have all the training they can get before anyone starts drilling *our* teeth, thank you.

Accountancy: *see* **Business, Management & Administration.**

Agriculture, Veterinary Sciences, etc.

Pre-clinical veterinary medicine: Liverpool, Bristol, Cambridge, Edinburgh, Royal Veterinary College, Glasgow, Middlesex.

Clinical veterinary medicine & dentistry: UWE Bristol, Glamorgan.

Animal science: Bristol, Imperial, Reading, Newcastle, Nottingham, Queen's Belfast, Aberdeen, Lincoln, Oxford Brookes, Canterbury Christ Church, Napier, Plymouth, Nottingham Trent, UWE Bristol, Anglia Poly, Bath, Bournemouth, Brighton, De Monfort, Aberystwyth, Bangor, Buckinghamshire Chilterns, Wolverhampton, Central Lancashire, Harper Adams, Kent, Northampton, Worcester.

Agriculture: Bristol, Imperial, Leeds, Bangor, Nottingham, Reading, Newcastle, Stirling, Aberdeen, Queen's Belfast, Salford, Lincoln, Manchester Metropolitan, Sheffield Hallam, Gloucestershire, Plymouth, Royal Agricultural College, Southampton Institute, South Bank, Wolverhampton, Bolton, Derby, Nottingham Trent, Anglia Poly, Bath, Bournemouth, Canterbury Christ Church, Glamorgan, UWE Bristol, Aberystwyth, Buckinghamshire Chilterns, Central Lancashire, Harper Adams, Northampton, Greenwich.

Forestry: Bangor, Aberdeen, Brighton, Sunderland, Central Lancashire, Northampton.

Food & beverages: Imperial, Queen's Belfast, Leeds, Nottingham, Reading, Wolverhampton, Bournemouth, Abertay Dundee, Glasgow Caledonian, Huddersfield, Nottingham Trent, Sheffield Hallam, Bath Spa, Middlesex, Plymouth, Liverpool John Moores, Manchester Metropolitan, Derby, Salford, Harper Adams, Cardiff Institute, Thames Valley, Ulster.

Agricultural sciences: Imperial, Queen's Belfast, Aberdeen, Royal Agricultural College, Anglia Poly, Brighton, Wolverhampton, Worcester, Harper Adams.

Other similar & related: Liverpool, Worcester.

American Studies: *see* **Languages & Literature, Eastern, Asian, African, etc.**

Ancient History: *see* **History, Philosophy, etc. & Literature, Linguistics, Classics, etc.**

Ancient Languages: *see* **Literature, Linguistics, Classics, etc.**

Anthropology: *see* **Social Studies.**

Archaeology: *see* **History, Philosophy, etc.**

Architecture, Building & Planning

Architecture: Bath, Cambridge, Cardiff, Nottingham, Liverpool, Sheffield, Birmingham, Edinburgh, Manchester, Newcastle, Plymouth, UCL, Brighton, Central England, Queen's Belfast, Strathclyde, Ulster, Dundee, Kingston, Manchester Metropolitan, Northumbria, De Montfort, Greenwich, Huddersfield, Liverpool John Moores, London Metropolitan, Oxford Brookes, Portsmouth, Robert Gordon, Anglia Poly, Sheffield Hallam, Lincoln, Heriot-Watt, Westminster, Nottingham Trent, UWE Bristol, Derby, East London, Leeds Metropolitan, South

Bank, Cardiff Institute, Southampton Institute, Bournemouth, Bolton, Buckinghamshire Chilterns.

Building: Manchester, Nottingham, Loughborough, Reading, Strathclyde, Kingston, Aston, UCL, Central England, Napier, Central Lancashire, Heriot-Watt, Robert Gordon, Ulster, Westminster, Glasgow Caledonian, Brighton, Nottingham Trent, UWE Bristol, Derby, Oxford Brookes, Portsmouth, Northumbria, Anglia Poly, Wolverhampton, Coventry, Sheffield Hallam, Glamorgan, Leeds Metropolitan, Liverpool John Moores, Plymouth, Salford, Teesside, Cardiff Institute, Bolton, Newport, Northampton, Southampton Institute, South Bank, Greenwich, Lincoln.

Landscape design: Central England, Kingston, Sheffield, Dundee, Greenwich, Manchester Metropolitan, Nottingham Trent, Leeds Metropolitan, Bournemouth, Brighton, Central Lancashire, Derby, Glamorgan, Gloucestershire, Harper Adams, Buckinghamshire Chilterns.

Planning (urban, rural & regional): Cambridge, Reading, Birmingham, Liverpool, Newcastle, Queen's Belfast, UCL, Cardiff, Heriot-Watt, Manchester, Salford, Sheffield, Kingston, Aberdeen, Aston, Bradford, Brighton, Dundee, Glamorgan, Kent, Ulster, Central Lancashire, Nottingham Trent, UWE Bristol, Anglia Poly, Central England, Greenwich, East London, Gloucestershire, Liverpool John Moores, Middlesex, Portsmouth, South Bank, Wolverhampton, Cardiff Institute, Northumbria, Southampton Institute, Derby, Harper Adams, Leeds Metropolitan, Sheffield Hallam, Glasgow Caledonian, Westminster.

Other similar & related: Birmingham, South Bank, Gloucestershire, Robert Gordon, Derby, Glamorgan.

Arts & Design

Fine Art: Oxford, Edinburgh, Lancaster, Aberystwyth, Central England, De Montfort, Leeds, Newcastle, Nottingham Trent, UCL, Loughborough, Dundee, Lincoln, Northumbria, Oxford Brookes, Plymouth, Sheffield Hallam, Central Lancashire, Coventry, Greenwich, Derby, East London, Gloucestershire, Huddersfield, Liverpool John Moores, Northampton, Salford, Surrey Institute, Bolton, Sunderland, Southampton Institute, Staffordshire, Anglia Poly, Bath Spa, Brighton, East London, Kent, Leeds Metropolitan, Manchester Metropolitan, Portsmouth, Reading, UWI Cardiff, UWE Bristol, Wolverhampton, London Metropolitan, Southampton, Arts, Buckinghamshire Chilterns, Canterbury Christ Church, Goldsmiths, Hertfordshire, Kingston, Liverpool Hope, London Metropolitan, Middlesex, Worcester.

Design: Goldsmiths, Leeds, Brunel, Manchester, Reading, Central England, Dundee, Greenwich, Northumbria, Nottingham Trent, Strathclyde, Loughborough, Bradford, Liverpool, Plymouth, Sheffield Hallam, Surrey Institute, Westminster, Central Lancashire, Coventry, Hull, Napier, Paisley, Plymouth, East London, Gloucestershire, Heriot-Watt, Huddersfield, Liverpool John Moores, Luton, Manchester Metropolitan, Middlesex, Newport, Portsmouth, Robert Gordon, Teesside, Ulster, Bolton, Sunderland, Thames Valley, Southampton Institute, Salford, Staffordshire, Anglia Poly, Bath Spa, Bournemouth, Brighton, De Montfort, Derby, East London, Lincoln, UWE Bristol, Leeds Metropolitan, London Metropolitan, UWI Cardiff, Wolverhampton, Chichester, Northampton, Southampton, Abertay Dundee, Arts, Buckinghamshire Chilterns, Glamorgan, Glasgow Caledonian, Hertfordshire, Kingston, Liverpool Hope, Worcester.

Music: Royal College of Music, Royal Academy of Music, Royal Scottish Academy of Music & Drama, Southampton, Cambridge, King's, Manchester, Nottingham, Oxford, Birmingham, Bristol, Newcastle, York, Durham, Edinburgh, Goldsmiths, Huddersfield, Leeds, Liverpool, Royal Holloway, Sheffield, Sussex, Brunel, Cardiff, Glasgow, Lancaster, Queen's Belfast, Surrey, Bangor, City, Exeter, Keele, Reading, SOAS, UEA, Ulster, Hertfordshire, Hull, Plymouth, Southampton Institute, Central England, De Montfort, Staffordshire, UWE Bristol, Glamorgan, Manchester Metropolitan, Oxford Brookes, Liverpool John Moores, Napier, Anglia Poly, Bath Spa, Canterbury Christ Church, Central Lancashire, Derby, East London, Kent, Kingston, Leeds Metropolitan, Paisley, Salford, Strathclyde, Wolverhampton, Bolton,

Coventry, Brighton, Buckinghamshire Chilterns, Thames Valley, Bournemouth, Middlesex, Northampton, Aberdeen, Liverpool Hope, Roehampton, Sunderland, Westminster.

Drama: Royal Scottish Academy of Music & Drama, Cambridge, Birmingham, Royal Holloway, Sussex, Goldsmiths, Hull, Lancaster, Loughborough, Manchester, Queen Mary, UEA, Warwick, Brunel, Exeter, Glasgow, Queen Margaret, Queen's Belfast, UWE Bristol, Aberystwyth, Bristol, Leeds, Northumbria, Central England, Kingston, Nottingham Trent, Ulster, Lincoln, Middlesex, Southampton Institute, Staffordshire, Central Lancashire, De Montfort, Derby, Liverpool John Moores, Paisley, Plymouth, Anglia Poly, Bath Spa, Greenwich, Kent, London Metropolitan, Luton, Reading, South Bank, Thames Valley, Salford, Huddersfield, Bournemouth, East London, Essex, Manchester Metropolitan, Teesside, Buckinghamshire Chilterns, Wolverhampton, Hertfordshire, Newport, Northampton, UWI Cardiff, Arts, Coventry, Glamorgan, Liverpool Hope, Oxford Brookes, Sunderland, Roehampton, Worcester.

Dance: Surrey, Leeds, Ulster, Manchester Metropolitan, Middlesex, UWI Cardiff, De Montfort, Bath Spa, Coventry, Northampton, Wolverhampton, Derby, Salford, East London, London Metropolitan, Plymouth, Brighton, Liverpool Hope, Northumbria, Roehampton, Sunderland.

Film studies & photography: Southampton, UEA, Warwick, Exeter, Glasgow, Royal Holloway, Queen's Belfast, Reading, Aberystwyth, Brunel, Essex, Sheffield Hallam, Aberdeen, Bradford, Central England, Nottingham Trent, Kingston, Lincoln, Northumbria, Southampton Institute, Staffordshire, De Montfort, Huddersfield, Liverpool John Moores, Manchester Metropolitan, Surrey Institute, Anglia Poly, Canterbury Christ Church, Lampeter, Napier, Napier, Paisley, Portsmouth, Central Lancashire, East London, Gloucestershire, Middlesex, Newport, South Bank, Westminster, Bolton, Sunderland, Thames Valley, Bournemouth, Derby, Teesside, Buckinghamshire Chilterns, Plymouth, Wolverhampton, Kent, Leeds Metropolitan, Northampton, Arts, Brighton, Dundee, Glamorgan, Hertfordshire, Roehampton, Birkbeck.

Crafts: Loughborough, Lincoln, Manchester Metropolitan, Sheffield Hallam, Surrey Institute, East London, Huddersfield, Northampton, Central England, Staffordshire, Brighton, Plymouth, London Metropolitan, Buckinghamshire Chilterns, Coventry, Dundee, Hertfordshire, Westminster.

Creative Writing: UEA, Essex, Aberystwyth, Bradford, Glamorgan, Leeds, Kingston, Manchester Metropolitan, Anglia Poly, Derby, East London, Gloucestershire, Greenwich, Liverpool John Moores, London Metropolitan, Luton, Liverpool Hope, Middlesex, Roehampton, Wolverhampton, Bolton, Buckinghamshire Chilterns.

Other similar & related: Lancaster, Leeds, Portsmouth, De Montfort, Middlesex, Southampton Institute, Liverpool John Moores, Strathclyde, Coventry, Glamorgan, London Metropolitan, Newport, South Bank, Thames Valley, Westminster, Sunderland, Bath Spa, Manchester Metropolitan, Derby, Greenwich, Birkbeck, Liverpool Hope, Roehampton, Worcester, Open.

Asian languages: see **Languages & Literature, Eastern, Asian, African, etc.**

Biology, etc.

Biology: Oxford, Cambridge, Bath, Durham, Imperial, Nottingham, UCL, Bristol, Cardiff, Edinburgh, Leicester, Reading, Sheffield, Warwick, York, Aston, Birmingham, Exeter, Leeds, Liverpool, Manchester, Newcastle, Southampton, St Andrews, Sussex, Swansea, Queen's Belfast, Royal Holloway, UEA, Ulster, Bangor, Brunel, Essex, Glasgow, Kent, Lancaster, Northumbria, Queen Mary, Strathclyde, Aberystwyth, Dundee, Keele, Sheffield Hallam, Stirling, Aberdeen, Anglia Poly, Glamorgan, Hull, Plymouth, Portsmouth, Salford, Coventry, Heriot-Watt, Oxford Brookes, Queen Margaret, UWE Bristol, Bath Spa, Canterbury Christ Church, Central Lancashire, Harper Adams, Huddersfield, Kingston, Liverpool John Moores, Manchester Metropolitan, Middlesex, Northampton, Nottingham Trent, Staffordshire, Bolton, Derby, Napier, Robert Gordon, Teesside, Abertay Dundee, East London, London Metropolitan, Paisley, Gloucestershire, Westminster, Wolverhampton, Brighton, Greenwich,

Hertfordshire, Roehampton, South Bank, Worcester, Cardiff Institute, Buckinghamshire Chilterns, Birkbeck.

Botany/plant science: Durham, Bristol, Edinburgh, Sheffield, Birmingham, Manchester, Southampton, Imperial, Reading, UEA, Bangor, Glasgow, Nottingham, Aberystwyth, Aberdeen, Plymouth, Canterbury Christ Church, Wolverhampton, Worcester.

Zoology: Durham, Imperial, Nottingham, UCL, Bristol, Cardiff, Edinburgh, Leicester, Reading, Sheffield, Birmingham, Leeds, Liverpool, Manchester, Newcastle, Southampton, St Andrews, Swansea, Queen's Belfast, Royal Holloway, Bangor, Glasgow, Queen Mary, Aberystwyth, Dundee, Stirling, Aberdeen, Anglia Poly, Portsmouth, Liverpool John Moores, Derby, East London, Hull, Roehampton, Worcester.

Genetics: Sheffield, UCL, Cardiff, Edinburgh, King's, Leicester, Nottingham, York, Birmingham, Brunel, Leeds, Liverpool, Manchester, Newcastle, Sussex, Swansea, Queen's Belfast, Royal Holloway, Essex, Glasgow, Queen Mary, Aberystwyth, Dundee, Wolverhampton, Aberdeen, Anglia Poly, Portsmouth, UWE Bristol, Huddersfield, Westminster.

Microbiology: Imperial, UCL, Bristol, Cardiff, Edinburgh, Leicester, Nottingham, Reading, Warwick, Birmingham, King's, Leeds, Liverpool, Manchester, Newcastle, Strathclyde, Bradford, Queen's Belfast, Surrey, UEA, Aston, Essex, Glasgow, Kent, Aberystwyth, Dundee, Aberdeen, Anglia Poly, Glamorgan, Portsmouth, Glasgow Caledonian, Heriot-Watt, Hertfordshire, UWE Bristol, Huddersfield, Manchester Metropolitan, Middlesex, Nottingham Trent, South Bank, Westminster, Wolverhampton, Napier, Teesside, Liverpool John Moores, London Metropolitan.

Sports science: Sheffield, Exeter, Leeds, Queen Mary, Ulster, Brighton, Leeds Metropolitan, Loughborough, Sheffield Hallam, Bangor, Bournemouth, Brunel, Edinburgh, Hertfordshire, Liverpool John Moores, Northumbria, Stirling, Aberystwyth, Birmingham, Essex, Glasgow, Heriot-Watt, Hull, Oxford Brookes, Portsmouth, Robert Gordon, Salford, Sunderland, De Montfort, Dundee, Aberdeen, Abertay Dundee, Coventry, Huddersfield, Lincoln, Manchester Metropolitan, Napier, Nottingham Trent, Strathclyde, Kingston, Staffordshire, Thames Valley, Canterbury Christ Church, Gloucestershire, London Metropolitan, Luton, Newport, South Bank, Westminster, Bolton, Kent, Southampton Institute, Anglia Poly, Bath, Buckinghamshire Chilterns, East London, Central Lancashire, Glamorgan, Cardiff Institute, UWE Bristol, Derby, Middlesex, Plymouth, Wolverhampton, Anglia Poly, Greenwich, Liverpool Hope, Northampton, Roehampton, Swansea, Teesside, Worcester.

Molecular biology, biophysics & biochemistry: Bath, Bristol, Oxford, Durham, Imperial, Leeds, Sheffield, UCL, York, Birmingham, Cardiff, Edinburgh, Leicester, Nottingham, Reading, Warwick, King's, Lancaster, Liverpool, Manchester, Newcastle, Southampton, St Andrews, Strathclyde, Sussex, Swansea, Bradford, Brunel, Exeter, Queen's Belfast, Royal Holloway, Surrey, UEA, Ulster, Aston, Bangor, Essex, Glasgow, Hull, Keele, Kent, Queen Mary, Staffordshire, Aberystwyth, Dundee, Sheffield Hallam, Aberdeen, Anglia Poly, Glamorgan, Portsmouth, Salford, Coventry, Glasgow Caledonian, Greenwich, Heriot-Watt, Hertfordshire, Kingston, Canterbury Christ Church, Central Lancashire, Huddersfield, Manchester Metropolitan, Middlesex, South Bank, UWE Bristol, Westminster, Leeds Metropolitan, East London, Liverpool John Moores, London Metropolitan, Roehampton, Wolverhampton, Worcester, Birkbeck.

Psychology: Warwick, Bath, Southampton, Bristol, Cardiff, Exeter, Newcastle, Oxford, Sheffield, UCL, Birmingham, Durham, Lancaster, Leeds, Liverpool, Loughborough, Manchester, Nottingham, Reading, Royal Holloway, St Andrews, Surrey, York, Aston, Brighton, City, Edinburgh, Essex, Kent, Leicester, Portsmouth, Queen's Belfast, Sussex, Swansea, UEA, Goldsmiths, Hertfordshire, Northumbria, Nottingham Trent, Ulster, Bangor, Brunel, Hull, Kingston, Sheffield Hallam, Anglia Poly, Bradford, Central Lancashire, Coventry, Glasgow, Glasgow Caledonian, Heriot-Watt, Leeds Metropolitan, Liverpool John Moores, Manchester Metropolitan, Queen Margaret, Stirling, Thames Valley, Wolverhampton, Derby, Dundee, Glamorgan, Huddersfield, Lincoln, Oxford Brookes, Salford, Southampton Institute, Aberdeen, Abertay Dundee, Buckingham, Central England, Greenwich, Cardiff Institute, UWE Bristol, Bolton, Bournemouth, De Montfort, East London, Northampton, Sunderland, Teesside, Bath Spa, Canterbury Christ Church, Gloucestershire, London Metropolitan, Luton,

Middlesex, Napier, South Bank, Staffordshire, Westminster, Buckinghamshire Chilterns, Paisley, Keele, Liverpool Hope, Plymouth, Roehampton, Worcester, Birkbeck, Open.

Other similar & related: Edinburgh, Sussex, York, Strathclyde, UEA, Bradford, Kent, Kingston, Royal Holloway, Bangor, Glasgow, Keele, Abertay Dundee, Anglia Poly, Heriot-Watt, Lincoln, Manchester, Oxford Brookes, UWE Bristol, Liverpool John Moores, Manchester Metropolitan, Bolton, Derby, Robert Gordon, Brighton, Aberystwyth, Liverpool, Roehampton, Sheffield Hallam, Bournemouth, Birkbeck, Open.

Business, Management & Administration

Business: Newcastle, Warwick, Aston, Birmingham, City, Manchester, Northumbria, Nottingham, Reading, Sussex, Cardiff, Edinburgh, Hull, Lancaster, Liverpool, Loughborough, Strathclyde, Brunel, De Montfort, Kingston, Leeds, Queen Mary, Surrey, Swansea, Bournemouth, Essex, Stirling, Westminster, Bangor, Brighton, Coventry, Dundee, Nottingham Trent, Plymouth, Salford, Sheffield Hallam, Abertay Dundee, Aberystwyth, Buckingham, Huddersfield, Bradford, Central England, Heriot-Watt, Hertfordshire, Napier, Portsmouth, Ulster, UWE Bristol, Central Lancashire, Derby, Glamorgan, Greenwich, Liverpool John Moores, Anglia Poly, Bath Spa, Canterbury Christ Church, Glasgow Caledonian, Gloucestershire, Kent, Lincoln, London Metropolitan, Luton, Paisley, Queen Margaret, South Bank, Southampton Institute, Thames Valley, Wolverhampton, Bolton, Teesside, Leeds Metropolitan, Manchester Metropolitan, Bath, East London, Newport, Sunderland, Cardiff Institute, Middlesex, Staffordshire, Northampton, Aston, Buckinghamshire Chilterns, Oxford Brookes, Liverpool Hope, Roehampton, Worcester, Open.

Management: Southampton, Nottingham Trent, Manchester, Warwick, Birmingham, City, King's, Lancaster, Leeds, Newcastle, Nottingham, Royal Holloway, Sheffield, St Andrews, Surrey, York, Cardiff, Exeter, Hull, Leicester, Loughborough, LSE, Queen's Belfast, Reading, Brunel, Durham, Essex, Glasgow, SOAS, Swansea, UEA, Edinburgh, Heriot-Watt, Keele, Stirling, Aberdeen, Bradford, Queen Mary, Ulster, Westminster, Buckingham, Hertfordshire, Napier, Royal Agricultural College, UWE Bristol, Glamorgan, Lampeter, Staffordshire, Strathclyde, Bournemouth, Brighton, Canterbury Christ Church, Glasgow Caledonian, Liverpool John Moores, Luton, Northampton, Paisley, Queen Margaret, Sunderland, Harper Adams, Coventry, Buckinghamshire Chilterns, De Montfort, Leeds Metropolitan, London Metropolitan, Manchester Metropolitan, Middlesex, Anglia Poly, Central Lancashire, East London, Gloucestershire, Huddersfield, Kingston, Lincoln, Plymouth, Portsmouth, Sheffield Hallam, Southampton Institute, Thames Valley, Bangor, Derby, Salford, Cardiff Institute, Wolverhampton, Bolton, Central England, Chichester, Kent, Oxford Brookes, South Bank, Teesside, Abertay Dundee, Arts, Bath, Greenwich, Northumbria, Robert Gordon, Roehampton, Worcester, Birkbeck.

Finance: LSE, Warwick, City, Manchester, Nottingham, Queen's Belfast, Reading, Birmingham, Cardiff, Kent, Lancaster, Loughborough, Surrey, Essex, Northumbria, Brunel, Heriot-Watt, Keele, Aberdeen, Bangor, Coventry, Dundee, Nottingham Trent, Sheffield Hallam, Stirling, Ulster, Aberystwyth, Bournemouth, Brighton, Buckingham, Lincoln, Portsmouth, Greenwich, Staffordshire, Anglia Poly, Glasgow Caledonian, Liverpool John Moores, Luton, Middlesex, Northampton, South Bank, Teesside, Southampton Institute, London Metropolitan, Derby, East London, Gloucestershire, Salford, Cardiff Institute, Thames Valley.

Accounting: Southampton, Queen's Belfast, Aston, Birmingham, Manchester, Cardiff, Exeter, Glasgow, Hull, Lancaster, Leeds, Liverpool, Newcastle, Northumbria, Reading, Sheffield, Strathclyde, Ulster, Bristol, Durham, Essex, UEA, Oxford Brookes, Aberdeen, Abertay Dundee, Bangor, Bournemouth, Bradford, De Montfort, Dundee, Kingston, Manchester Metropolitan, Nottingham Trent, Sheffield Hallam, Stirling, Aberystwyth, Brighton, Buckingham, Central England, Glamorgan, Leeds Metropolitan, Robert Gordon, Hertfordshire, Huddersfield, Napier, Portsmouth, UWE Bristol, Central Lancashire, Derby, Glasgow Caledonian, Greenwich, Kent, Staffordshire, Sunderland, Cardiff Institute, Anglia Poly, Coventry, East London, Gloucestershire, Lincoln, Liverpool John Moores, Luton,

Middlesex, Newport, Paisley, Thames Valley, Wolverhampton, Bolton, Southampton Institute, Teesside, London Metropolitan, Salford, Plymouth, Northampton South Bank.

Marketing: Aston, Newcastle, Northumbria, Bournemouth, Hull, Lancaster, Liverpool, Ulster, Oxford Brookes, Keele, Plymouth, Stirling, Bangor, Bradford, Brighton, Coventry, De Montfort, Kingston, Nottingham Trent, Sheffield Hallam, Aberystwyth, Buckingham, Central England, Huddersfield, Hertfordshire, Napier, Portsmouth, Surrey Institute, UWE Bristol, Central Lancashire, Derby, Glamorgan, Greenwich, Anglia Poly, Canterbury Christ Church, Glasgow Caledonian, Lincoln, Luton, Middlesex, Northampton, Paisley, Queen Margaret, South Bank, Sunderland, Thames Valley, Wolverhampton, Bolton, Newport, Teesside, Buckinghamshire Chilterns, Southampton Institute, Leeds Metropolitan, London Metropolitan, Manchester Metropolitan, East London, Gloucestershire, Liverpool Hope, Roehampton, Salford, Cardiff Institute, Arts.

Human resource management: Manchester, Aston, Hull, Lancaster, Leeds, Liverpool, Ulster, Northumbria, Keele, Kent, Stirling, Coventry, De Montfort, Kingston, Nottingham Trent, Plymouth, Hertfordshire, Huddersfield, Manchester Metropolitan, Napier, Portsmouth, Central Lancashire, Derby, Greenwich, Staffordshire, Anglia Poly, Lincoln, London Metropolitan, Luton, Middlesex, Northampton, Paisley, Sunderland, Wolverhampton, Bolton, Buckinghamshire Chilterns, Southampton Institute, East London, Glamorgan, Gloucestershire, Roehampton, Salford, Teesside.

Office skills: Bangor, Central Lancashire, Northampton, Worcester.

Tourism, transport & travel: Glasgow, Northumbria, Oxford Brookes, Ulster, Bournemouth, Coventry, Hull, Robert Gordon, Stirling, Aberystwyth, Napier, UWE Bristol, Sheffield Hallam, Staffordshire, Bath Spa, East London, Glasgow Caledonian, Gloucestershire, Huddersfield, Lincoln, Liverpool John Moores, Luton, Middlesex, Paisley, Plymouth, Queen Margaret, South Bank, Sunderland, Wolverhampton, Bolton, Leeds Metropolitan, Manchester Metropolitan, Cardiff Institute, Anglia Poly, Brighton, Glamorgan, London Metropolitan, Southampton Institute, Thames Valley, Buckinghamshire Chilterns, Derby, Harper Adams, Salford, Central Lancashire, Hertfordshire, Kent, Northampton, Teesside, Abertay Dundee, Arts, Bangor, Bath, Canterbury Christ Church, Greenwich, Liverpool Hope, Westminster, Worcester.

Other similar & related: Birmingham, Loughborough, Keele, Westminster, Aston, Brighton, Ulster, Coventry, Manchester Metropolitan, Greenwich, Huddersfield, Southampton Institute, Gloucestershire, Queen Margaret, Derby, Liverpool John Moores, Teesside, Cardiff Institute, Buckinghamshire Chilterns, Leeds Metropolitan, Liverpool Hope, Northumbria, Roehampton, Worcester.

Celtic: see **Literature, Linguistics, Classics, etc.**

Chemistry: see **Physical Sciences.**

Chinese: see **Languages & Literature, Eastern, Asian, African, etc.**

Classics: see **Literature, Linguistics, Classics etc.**

Communications & Media

Information & library services: Loughborough, Sheffield, UCL, Brighton, Lincoln, Robert Gordon, Aberystwyth, Leeds Metropolitan, Manchester Metropolitan, Paisley, Wolverhampton, Abertay Dundee, Liverpool Hope, Northumbria, Worcester.

Publicity, PR, etc.: Bournemouth, Westminster, Swansea, Sunderland, Ulster, Queen Margaret, Central Lancashire, Central England, Southampton Institute, London Metropolitan, Leeds Metropolitan, Lincoln, Luton, Thames Valley, Wolverhampton, Buckinghamshire Chilterns.

Media studies: King's, Sussex, Birmingham, Glasgow, Goldsmiths, Leeds, Exeter, Lancaster, Manchester, Queen Mary, Queen's Belfast, Sheffield Hallam, Stirling, Westminster, Aberystwyth, De Montfort, Essex, Keele, Leicester, Sunderland, Surrey, Ulster, Brighton, Central Lancashire, City, Kingston, Lincoln, Portsmouth, Queen Margaret, Swansea, Bangor,

Glamorgan, Hertfordshire, Northumbria, Nottingham Trent, Southampton Institute, Liverpool John Moores, Oxford Brookes, UWE Bristol, Lampeter, Paisley, Anglia Poly, Canterbury Christ Church, Coventry, Derby, East London, Gloucestershire, Greenwich, Huddersfield, London Metropolitan, Luton, Wolverhampton, Bolton, Teesside, Central England, Staffordshire, Bath, Buckinghamshire Chilterns, Leeds Metropolitan, Thames Valley, Liverpool Hope, Manchester Metropolitan, Middlesex, Northampton, Arts, Glasgow Caledonian, Roehampton, Worcester.

Publishing: Goldsmiths, Loughborough, Oxford Brookes, Robert Gordon, Napier, Middlesex, East London.

Journalism: Nottingham Trent, Cardiff, Bournemouth, Brighton, Central Lancashire, Leeds, Queen Mary, Sheffield, Liverpool John Moores, Salford, Staffordshire, Stirling, Strathclyde, Southampton Institute, Sunderland, Glamorgan, Lincoln, Surrey Institute, Ulster, Kingston, Napier, Paisley, East London, Glasgow Caledonian, Gloucestershire, Luton, Middlesex, South Bank, Thames Valley, Teesside, Wolverhampton, Northampton, Arts, London Metropolitan.

Other similar & related: UCL, Leeds, Leicester, Loughborough, Bournemouth, Cardiff, Central England, King's, Lancaster, Newcastle, Brunel, Glasgow Caledonian, Liverpool, Ulster, Brighton, Glamorgan, Nottingham Trent, Oxford Brookes, Queen Margaret, Sheffield Hallam, Bangor, Lincoln, Robert Gordon, Napier, Coventry, UWE Bristol, Anglia Poly, Canterbury Christ Church, East London, Huddersfield, London Metropolitan, Middlesex, Thames Valley, Westminster, Wolverhampton, Bath Spa, Liverpool Hope, Manchester, Metropolitan, Roehampton, Worcester.

Eastern European languages: see **Languages & Literature, European.**

Economics: see **Social Studies.**

Education

Training teachers: Cambridge, Essex, Leeds, Northumbria, Durham, Nottingham Trent, Brighton, Edinburgh, Glasgow, Liverpool John Moores, Loughborough, Manchester Metropolitan, Oxford Brookes, Aberdeen, Anglia Poly, Hull, Sheffield Hallam, Bangor, Derby, Dundee, Strathclyde, UWE Bristol, De Montfort, Leeds Metropolitan, Northampton, Reading, Sunderland, Wolverhampton, Bath Spa, Canterbury Christ Church, Central England, Gloucestershire, Goldsmiths, Greenwich, Middlesex, Newport, Paisley, Plymouth, Cardiff Institute, Bradford, London Metropolitan, Buckinghamshire Chilterns, Hertfordshire, Huddersfield, Kingston, Liverpool Hope, Roehampton, Teesside, Worcester.

Research & study skills in education: East London, Liverpool Hope, Teesside.

Academic studies in education: Warwick, Edinburgh, Leeds, Liverpool, Cardiff, Exeter, Lancaster, York, Aberystwyth, Bangor, Brighton, Leeds Metropolitan, Northumbria, De Montfort, Manchester Metropolitan, Nottingham Trent, Liverpool John Moores, Sheffield Hallam, Anglia Poly, East London, Goldsmiths, Greenwich, Hull, London Metropolitan, Luton, Middlesex, Northampton, Strathclyde, Cardiff Institute, Wolverhampton, Dundee, Newport, Sunderland, UWE Bristol, Bolton, Gloucestershire, Plymouth, Central Lancashire, Derby, Bath Spa, Canterbury Christ Church, Central England, Lincoln, Oxford Brookes, Roehampton, Sussex, Worcester.

Other similar & related: De Montfort, Central Lancashire, Derby, Glamorgan, City, Liverpool Hope, London Metropolitan, Roehampton, Worcester, Open.

Engineering

General engineering: Cambridge, Oxford, Bristol, Durham, Bath, Edinburgh, Nottingham, Reading, Strathclyde, Ulster, Liverpool, Sheffield, UCL, Glasgow Caledonian, Lancaster, Newcastle, Queen's Belfast, Birmingham, Cardiff, Exeter, Hertfordshire, Leicester, Northumbria, Nottingham Trent, Surrey, Warwick, Aberdeen, Heriot-Watt, Hull, Leeds, Queen Mary, Robert Gordon, Staffordshire, Aston, Swansea, Greenwich, Sunderland, Bournemouth, Brunel, De Montfort, Glasgow, London Metropolitan, Loughborough, Salford, Bolton, Oxford

Courses

Brookes, UWE Bristol, Bradford, Buckinghamshire Chilterns, Central England, Coventry, Wolverhampton, Brighton, Central Lancashire, Portsmouth, Harper Adams, Huddersfield, Kingston, Napier, Sheffield Hallam, Teesside, Anglia Poly, Liverpool John Moores, Manchester Metropolitan, Newport, Northampton, Plymouth, South Bank, Southampton Institute, Manchester, Paisley, Open.

Civil engineering: Southampton, Oxford, Bath, Durham, Brighton, Bristol, Brunel, Edinburgh, Imperial, Sheffield, Nottingham, UCL, Birmingham, Liverpool, Liverpool John Moores, Manchester, Newcastle, Nottingham Trent, Queen's Belfast, Strathclyde, Swansea, Ulster, Cardiff, Dundee, Exeter, Glasgow, Leeds, Loughborough, Reading, Salford, Surrey, Warwick, City, Aberdeen, Bradford, Abertay Dundee, Heriot-Watt, UWE Bristol, Glasgow Caledonian, Sheffield Hallam, South Bank, Huddersfield, Robert Gordon, Napier, Northumbria, Paisley, Anglia Poly, Wolverhampton, East London, Greenwich, Leeds Metropolitan, Plymouth, Portsmouth, Coventry, Glamorgan, Kingston, Teesside, Bolton, Central Lancashire, Newport, Southampton Institute.

Mechanical engineering: Southampton, Bath, Imperial, Oxford, Sheffield, Bristol, Durham, Brunel, Edinburgh, Leeds, Manchester, Nottingham, Strathclyde, Birmingham, Cardiff, King's, Liverpool, Sussex, UCL, Coventry, Lancaster, Loughborough, Newcastle, Queen's Belfast, Reading, Swansea, Aston, Exeter, Glasgow, Hertfordshire, Kingston, Leicester, Manchester Metropolitan, Northumbria, Plymouth, Portsmouth, Queen Mary, Salford, Surrey, Warwick, Aberdeen, Central England, City, Dundee, Hull, Robert Gordon, Staffordshire, Ulster, Bradford, Central Lancashire, Heriot-Watt, Glasgow Caledonian, Sunderland, UWE Bristol, De Montfort, South Bank, Liverpool John Moores, Napier, Paisley, Brighton, Derby, Greenwich, Huddersfield, Wolverhampton, Anglia Poly, Bangor, Harper Adams, Middlesex, Sheffield Hallam, Teesside, Bolton, Chichester, Kent, Newport, Oxford Brookes, Southampton Institute, Glamorgan.

Aerospace engineering: Southampton, Bath, Bristol, Imperial, Leeds, Brunel, Durham, Sheffield, Hertfordshire, Liverpool, Loughborough, Manchester, Queen Mary, Strathclyde, Glasgow, Queen's Belfast, Surrey, Swansea, City, Staffordshire, De Montfort, London Metropolitan, UWE Bristol, Coventry, Kingston, Salford, Bolton, Buckinghamshire Chilterns, Glamorgan.

Naval architecture: Southampton, Newcastle, Strathclyde, UCL, Southampton Institute.

Electronic & electrical engineering: Southampton, Bristol, Imperial, Oxford, Cardiff, Durham, Liverpool, Newcastle, Sheffield, UCL, Bangor, Birmingham, Edinburgh, Exeter, King's, Lancaster, Leeds, Robert Gordon, Sussex, Swansea, Abertay Dundee, Surrey, Brunel, Essex, Glasgow, Manchester, Nottingham, Queen Mary, Queen's Belfast, Sunderland, Aston, City, Dundee, Hertfordshire, Leicester, Loughborough, Northumbria, Oxford Brookes, Strathclyde, Warwick, UWE Bristol, Central England, De Montfort, East London, Hull, Nottingham Trent, Bradford, Heriot-Watt, Napier, Reading, Bournemouth, Coventry, Derby, Kingston, Middlesex, Northampton, Portsmouth, Thames Valley, Westminster, Glasgow Caledonian, Liverpool John Moores, Teesside, Aberdeen, Buckinghamshire Chilterns, London Metropolitan, Staffordshire, Anglia Poly, Bolton, Brighton, Central Lancashire, Leeds Metropolitan, Manchester Metropolitan, Cardiff Institute, Glamorgan, Huddersfield, Paisley, Plymouth, Salford, Sheffield Hallam, Chichester, Greenwich, Kent, Newport, South Bank, Southampton Institute, Bath, York.

Production & manufacturing engineering: Southampton, Bath, Durham, Newcastle, Exeter, Leeds, Queen Mary, King's, Sheffield, Sussex, Brunel, Loughborough, Nottingham, Queen's Belfast, Swansea, Aston, Cardiff, Greenwich, Hertfordshire, Northumbria, Nottingham Trent, Strathclyde, Warwick, Bradford, Central England, East London, Hull, Liverpool, Ulster, De Montfort, Heriot-Watt, Portsmouth, Salford, Sunderland, Cardiff Institute, UWE Bristol, Leeds Metropolitan, Robert Gordon, South Bank, Staffordshire, Wolverhampton, Anglia Poly, Bolton, Coventry, Derby, Huddersfield, Liverpool John Moores, Napier, Teesside, Paisley, Derby, Glamorgan, Sheffield Hallam, Newport, Southampton Institute, Buckinghamshire Chilterns, Glasgow Caledonian.

Chemical, process & energy engineering: Oxford, Imperial, Bath, Birmingham, Edinburgh, Manchester, Nottingham, Swansea, UCL, Queen's Belfast, Sheffield, Aston, Leeds,

Loughborough, Newcastle, Strathclyde, Surrey, Bradford, Heriot-Watt, Central Lancashire, Paisley, Teesside, South Bank, Glasgow Caledonian.

Other similar & related: Sheffield, UCL, Bradford, Derby.

English: see **Literature, Linguistics, Classics, etc.**

Food & beverages: see **Agriculture.**

French: see **Languages & Literature, European.**

Geology: see **Physical Sciences.**

Geography, physical & environmental: see **Physical Sciences.**

Geography, human & social: see **Social Studies.**

German: see **Languages & Literature, European.**

Greek, classical: see **Literature, Linguistics, Classics, etc.**

History, Philosophy, etc.

History, general or specialising in a specific period: Durham, Exeter, Southampton, Cambridge, Manchester, Oxford, St Andrews, York, Birmingham, Cardiff, King's, LSE, Newcastle, Nottingham, Royal Holloway, Sheffield, UCL, Warwick, Edinburgh, Kent, Lancaster, Leeds, Leicester, Liverpool, Queen Mary, Sussex, Glasgow, Queen's Belfast, Reading, UEA, Bristol, Essex, Goldsmiths, Huddersfield, Hull, Keele, Northumbria, SOAS, Stirling, Aberdeen, Bradford, Brunel, Dundee, Portsmouth, Sheffield Hallam, Swansea, Ulster, UWE Bristol, Westminster, Aberystwyth, Bangor, Central Lancashire, Kingston, Nottingham Trent, Oxford Brookes, Glamorgan, Hertfordshire, Lampeter, Lincoln, Staffordshire, De Montfort, Derby, Leeds Metropolitan, Liverpool John Moores, Manchester Metropolitan, Newport, Plymouth, Salford, Anglia Poly, Bath Spa, Bournemouth, Canterbury Christ Church, Coventry, East London, Gloucestershire, Greenwich, Liverpool Hope, London Metropolitan, Middlesex, Northampton, Sunderland, Cardiff Institute, Wolverhampton, Bolton, Roehampton, Teesside, Worcester, Birkbeck, Open.

History, specialising in a specific country or area: St Andrews, King's, Edinburgh, Birmingham, Glasgow, Manchester, Swansea, UEA, Essex, Keele, Stirling, Aberdeen, Dundee, UCL, Ulster, Aberystwyth, Anglia Poly, Glamorgan, Kent, Surrey.

History, specialising in a specific topic: Cambridge, Oxford, Southampton, LSE, Birmingham, Courtauld, Edinburgh, Kent, St Andrews, Sussex, Glasgow, Lancaster, Leeds, Manchester, Nottingham, Oxford Brookes, Queen's Belfast, UCL, UEA, Warwick, York, Bristol, Essex, Goldsmiths, Huddersfield, Leicester, Liverpool, Reading, Sheffield Hallam, SOAS, Aberdeen, Northumbria, Swansea, Aberystwyth, Brighton, Lincoln, Coventry, Lampeter, Kingston, Manchester Metropolitan, Plymouth, East London, Liverpool John Moores, Middlesex, Northampton, Roehampton, Sunderland, Anglia Poly.

Archaeology: York, Edinburgh, Leicester, Swansea, UCL, Birmingham, Glasgow, King's, Manchester, UEA, Bradford, Bristol, Cardiff, Exeter, Liverpool, Newcastle, Queen's Belfast, Reading, Royal Holloway, SOAS, Southampton, Aberdeen, Nottingham, Bangor, Lampeter, Newport, Bournemouth, Canterbury Christ Church, Plymouth, Worcester.

Philosophy: Exeter, Southampton, Cambridge, LSE, Oxford, Durham, King's, Sheffield, St Andrews, Sussex, UCL, Warwick, York, Birmingham, Edinburgh, Leeds, Liverpool, Manchester, Nottingham, Reading, UEA, Bristol, Cardiff, Glasgow, Hull, Kent, Queen's Belfast, Essex, Keele, Lancaster, Aberdeen, Bradford, Dundee, Heythrop, Oxford Brookes, Stirling, Hertfordshire, Staffordshire, UWE Bristol, Lampeter, Central Lancashire, Glamorgan, Greenwich, Liverpool Hope, London Metropolitan, Manchester Metropolitan, Middlesex, Newport, Northampton, Roehampton, Wolverhampton, Bolton, Anglia Poly, Birkbeck.

Courses

Theology & religious studies: Cambridge, Oxford, Durham, Edinburgh, Manchester, Nottingham, Birmingham, Bristol, Cardiff, Lancaster, Queen's Belfast, Exeter, Hull, Kent, King's, Leeds, Sheffield, SOAS, Aberdeen, Bangor, Heythrop, Oxford Brookes, Stirling, Glasgow, Lampeter, Bath Spa, Canterbury Christ Church, Greenwich, Roehampton, Wolverhampton, St Andrews.

Other similar & related: Edinburgh, Leeds, Manchester, Essex, Aberdeen, Kent, Glamorgan, Bath Spa, Canterbury Christ Church, Kent, Kingston, Wolverhampton.

Italian: see **Languages & Literature, European.**

Japanese: see **Languages & Literature, Eastern, Asian, African, etc.**

Journalism: see **Communications & Media.**

Languages & Literature: Eastern, Asian, African, etc.

Chinese: Oxford, Edinburgh, Sheffield, Leeds, SOAS, Lampeter, Liverpool John Moores, Westminster.

Japanese: Oxford, Edinburgh, Sheffield, Cardiff, Leeds, Oxford Brookes, SOAS, Liverpool John Moores.

South Asian studies: Leeds, Sheffield, SOAS, Central Lancashire, Westminster.

Other Asian studies: Newcastle, Sheffield, SOAS.

African studies: Birmingham, SOAS.

Modern Middle Eastern studies: Oxford, St Andrews, Edinburgh, Exeter, Glasgow, King's, Leeds, SOAS, Manchester, Birmingham, Lampeter, Salford, Westminster.

American studies: Birmingham, King's, Edinburgh, Manchester, Nottingham, Sheffield, Sussex, Warwick, Hull, Keele, Kent, Lancaster, Leicester, Queen's Belfast, UEA, Essex, Liverpool, Reading, Aberdeen, Dundee, Portsmouth, Swansea, Ulster, Aberystwyth, Central Lancashire, Lincoln, Manchester Metropolitan, UWE Bristol, De Montfort, Derby, Lampeter, Plymouth, Canterbury Christ Church, London Metropolitan, Middlesex, Northampton, Sunderland, Wolverhampton, Worcester.

Other similar & related: Cambridge, Oxford, Edinburgh, Liverpool, Newcastle, Nottingham, Sheffield, St Andrews, Sussex, York, Aston, Hull, King's, Queen Mary, SOAS, Leicester, Surrey, UEA, Keele, Salford, Stirling, Aberystwyth, Bangor, Nottingham Trent, Napier, Central Lancashire, Canterbury Christ Church, Open.

Languages & Literature: European

French: Warwick, Southampton, Bath, Edinburgh, Exeter, King's, Manchester, Newcastle, Nottingham, Royal Holloway, St Andrews, York, Aston, Birmingham, Essex, Glasgow, Heriot-Watt, Kent, Lancaster, Leeds, Liverpool, Queen Mary, Queen's Belfast, Sheffield, UCL, UEA, Ulster, Bristol, Cardiff, Essex, Hull, Keele, Leicester, Oxford Brookes, Reading, Aberdeen, Bradford, Brighton, Salford, Stirling, Swansea, Aberystwyth, Bangor, Kingston, Northumbria, Nottingham Trent, Coventry, Portsmouth, Sheffield Hallam, UWE Bristol, Liverpool John Moores, Anglia Poly, Canterbury Christ Church, Central Lancashire, London Metropolitan, Manchester Metropolitan, Middlesex, Northampton, Roehampton, Westminster, Wolverhampton, Birkbeck.

German: Southampton, Bath, Cardiff, Edinburgh, Exeter, Newcastle, Royal Holloway, St Andrews, UEA, Warwick, York, Aston, Birmingham, Essex, Glasgow, Heriot-Watt, King's, Lancaster, Manchester, Nottingham, Queen Mary, Queen's Belfast, Sheffield, UCL, Bristol, Hull, Keele, Kent, Leeds, Leicester, Liverpool, Reading, Aberdeen, Brighton, Oxford Brookes, Salford, Swansea, Ulster, Aberystwyth, Bangor, Northumbria, Nottingham Trent, Coventry,

Portsmouth, Sheffield Hallam, UWE Bristol, Liverpool John Moores, Anglia Poly, Central Lancashire, Northampton, Westminster, Wolverhampton, Manchester Metropolitan, Birkbeck.

Italian: St Andrews, Bath, Edinburgh, Exeter, Royal Holloway, Birmingham, Essex, Glasgow, Hull, Lancaster, Manchester, Warwick, Bristol, Cardiff, Kent, Leeds, Leicester, Reading, UCL, Salford, Swansea, Bangor, Nottingham Trent, Coventry, Liverpool John Moores.

Spanish: Southampton, Bath, Birmingham, Edinburgh, Exeter, Manchester, Newcastle, Royal Holloway, St Andrews, UCL, Aston, Cardiff, Essex, Glasgow, King's, Lancaster, Leeds, Liverpool, Queen's Belfast, Sheffield, UEA, Bristol, Goldsmiths, Kent, Nottingham, Queen Mary, Aberdeen, Bradford, Hull, Salford, Stirling, Swansea, Ulster, Aberystwyth, Bangor, Northumbria, Nottingham Trent, Oxford Brookes, Coventry, Portsmouth, Roehampton, Sheffield Hallam, Liverpool John Moores, UWE Bristol, Anglia Poly, Central Lancashire, London Metropolitan, Manchester Metropolitan, Middlesex, Westminster, Wolverhampton, Derby.

Portuguese: Birmingham, Manchester, Bristol, King's, Leeds, Nottingham, Salford.

Scandinavian: Edinburgh, Newcastle, Glasgow, UCL, UEA.

Russian & East European: Bath, Edinburgh, St Andrews, UCL, Exeter, Glasgow, Birmingham, Bristol, Leeds, Queen Mary, Sheffield, Nottingham, Westminster, Manchester.

Other similar & related: St Andrews, Durham, Southampton, Birmingham, Cardiff, Newcastle, Nottingham, Sussex, UCL, Aston, King's, Lancaster, Leeds, Manchester, Queen's Belfast, Reading, Essex, Goldsmiths, Hull, Leicester, Royal Holloway, Salford, UEA, Aberdeen, Dundee, Stirling, Ulster, Aberystwyth, Bangor, Leeds Metropolitan, Northumbria, Nottingham Trent, Plymouth, Liverpool John Moores, Manchester Metropolitan, Portsmouth, UWE Bristol, Central Lancashire, Kent, Anglia Poly, London Metropolitan, Paisley, Roehampton, Sunderland, Derby, Birkbeck, Open.

Latin: see **Literature, Linguistics, Classics, etc.**

Law

Law, general or specialising in a specific country or area: Southampton, Cambridge, Durham, UCL, Warwick, Birmingham, Bristol, Cardiff, Exeter, King's, Leeds, Leicester, LSE, Manchester, Newcastle, Nottingham, Oxford, Queen's Belfast, Sheffield, SOAS, UEA, City, Essex, Glasgow, Kent, Lancaster, Liverpool, Northumbria, Queen Mary, Reading, Strathclyde, Surrey, Sussex, Aberdeen, Brunel, Dundee, Edinburgh, Hull, Keele, Kingston, Oxford Brookes, Swansea, Central England, De Montfort, Glamorgan, Leeds Metropolitan, Manchester Metropolitan, Nottingham Trent, Ulster, Westminster, Abertay Dundee, Aberystwyth, Bangor, Bournemouth, Central Lancashire, Coventry, Glasgow Caledonian, Robert Gordon, Sheffield Hallam, UWE Bristol, Bradford, Brighton, Buckingham, Derby, Greenwich, Liverpool John Moores, Portsmouth, South Bank, Stirling, Thames Valley, Anglia Poly, Hertfordshire, Sunderland, East London, Lincoln, Middlesex, London Metropolitan, Huddersfield, Northampton, Gloucestershire, Luton, Napier, Paisley, Teesside, Wolverhampton, Bolton, Buckinghamshire Chilterns, Liverpool Hope, Southampton Institute, Staffordshire, Birkbeck, Open.

Law, specialising in a specific topic: Queen's Belfast, Westminster, Kent, De Montfort, Glamorgan, Aberystwyth, Bournemouth, Coventry, Loughborough, Plymouth, Sheffield Hallam, UWE Bristol, Keele, Liverpool John Moores, Stirling, Swansea, Anglia Poly, Bradford, Huddersfield, Kingston, Northumbria, Central England, Manchester Metropolitan, London Metropolitan, Glasgow Caledonian, Middlesex, Canterbury Christ Church, Staffordshire, Sunderland, Wolverhampton, Derby, Newport, Buckinghamshire Chilterns, Southampton Institute, Teesside, Thames Valley.

Other similar & related: Sheffield, Brighton, Leeds, Cardiff, Leicester, Ulster, Aberystwyth, Lancaster, Aberdeen, Bangor, Central Lancashire, Lincoln, Robert Gordon, Abertay Dundee, East London, Greenwich, Liverpool Hope, London Metropolitan, Luton, Northampton, Roehampton, South Bank, Birmingham.

Literature, Linguistics, Classics, etc.

Language/linguistics: Oxford, Southampton, Edinburgh, Manchester, Newcastle, Sussex, York, Birmingham, Essex, Kent, Lancaster, Leeds, Queen Mary, Queen's Belfast, Sheffield, UCL, Cardiff, Reading, SOAS, Surrey, UEA, Aberdeen, Nottingham Trent, Salford, Aberystwyth, Bangor, Glamorgan, Kingston, Ulster, Hertfordshire, Portsmouth, UWE Bristol, Buckingham, Oxford Brookes, Anglia Poly, Central Lancashire, East London, Luton, Sunderland, Cardiff Institute, Westminster, Wolverhampton, Strathclyde, Birkbeck.

Comparative literature: Durham, Warwick, UEA, Glasgow, King's, Liverpool, Northumbria, Essex, Kent, Sheffield Hallam, Stirling, Anglia Poly, Derby, Manchester Metropolitan, East London, Liverpool Hope, Roehampton, Wolverhampton, Buckinghamshire Chilterns.

English: Southampton, Durham, Birmingham, Bristol, Cambridge, Cardiff, Manchester, Newcastle, Oxford, St Andrews, UCL, Warwick, York, Kent, King's, Lancaster, Leeds, Liverpool, Nottingham, Oxford Brookes, Reading, Royal Holloway, Sheffield, Sussex, UEA, Edinburgh, Exeter, Goldsmiths, Leicester, Loughborough, Queen Mary, Brunel, Glasgow, Hull, Kingston, Northumbria, Nottingham Trent, Queen's Belfast, Salford, Sheffield Hallam, Swansea, UWE Bristol, Essex, Keele, SOAS, Stirling, Aberdeen, Aberystwyth, Bradford, Brighton, Dundee, South Bank, Ulster, Bangor, Central Lancashire, Glamorgan, Huddersfield, Leeds Metropolitan, Lincoln, Coventry, De Montfort, Hertfordshire, Lampeter, Newport, Portsmouth, Staffordshire, Anglia Poly, Bath Spa, Buckingham, Canterbury Christ Church, Manchester Metropolitan, Plymouth, Central England, Gloucestershire, Greenwich, Liverpool John Moores, London Metropolitan, Middlesex, Northampton, Paisley, Sunderland, Westminster, Wolverhampton, Bolton, Derby, Teesside, Buckinghamshire Chilterns, East London, Roehampton, Worcester, Birkbeck.

Ancient languages: Oxford, Edinburgh, St Andrews, Leeds, SOAS, UCL, Greenwich.

Celtic studies: Cambridge, Edinburgh, Glasgow, Queen's Belfast, Cardiff, Stirling, Aberdeen, Liverpool, Swansea, Ulster, Aberystwyth, Bangor, Glamorgan, Lampeter.

Latin: Birmingham, Edinburgh, Exeter, Manchester, Reading, St Andrews, UCL, Glasgow, King's, Leeds, Nottingham, Royal Holloway, Swansea, Lampeter.

Classical Greek: Edinburgh, Manchester, St Andrews, UCL, Glasgow, King's, Leeds, Royal Holloway, Swansea, Lampeter.

Classics: Warwick, Cambridge, Oxford, Edinburgh, Exeter, Liverpool, Manchester, Reading, UCL, Birmingham, Bristol, Glasgow, Kent, King's, Newcastle, Queen's Belfast, Sheffield, St Andrews, Leeds, Nottingham, Royal Holloway, Swansea, Lampeter, Roehampton, Birkbeck.

Other similar & related: Southampton, Cambridge, Oxford, Cardiff, St Andrews, SOAS, Swansea, Aberystwyth, Anglia Poly, Lampeter, London Metropolitan, Middlesex, Roehampton, Westminster, City.

Marketing: see **Business, Management & Administration**.

Maths & Computing

Mathematics: Southampton, Bath, Bristol, Cambridge, Durham, Imperial, LSE, Nottingham, Oxford, Warwick, King's, Manchester, Sheffield, St Andrews, UCL, UEA, York, Birmingham, Cardiff, Edinburgh, Exeter, Hull, Lancaster, Leeds, Leicester, Liverpool, Newcastle, Reading, Surrey, Sussex, Aston, Brunel, Kent, Loughborough, Queen Mary, Royal Holloway, Swansea, City, Essex, Northumbria, Nottingham Trent, Queen's Belfast, Strathclyde, Aberdeen, Aberystwyth, Bangor, Brighton, Coventry, Dundee, Glasgow, Central Lancashire, Glamorgan, Keele, Stirling, Anglia Poly, Greenwich, Heriot-Watt, Kingston, Manchester Metropolitan,

Plymouth, Portsmouth, Sheffield Hallam, UWE Bristol, Glasgow Caledonian, Hertfordshire, Staffordshire, Derby, Liverpool John Moores, Napier, Northampton, Westminster, Wolverhampton, Bolton, Oxford Brookes, Liverpool Hope, London Metropolitan, Paisley, De Montfort, Middlesex, Open.

Operational research: Lancaster, Reading, Hertfordshire, Greenwich, Paisley.

Statistics: Bath, Imperial, Leeds, Manchester, St Andrews, UCL, Hull, Lancaster, Liverpool, Newcastle, Sussex, Glasgow, Queen Mary, Swansea, Reading, Strathclyde, Aberystwyth, Brighton, Heriot-Watt, Salford, Anglia Poly, Coventry, Hertfordshire, Kingston, Oxford Brookes, Plymouth, UWE Bristol, Middlesex, Northampton, Wolverhampton, City, Greenwich.

Computer science: Southampton, Bristol, Cambridge, Imperial, Oxford, UCL, Warwick, York, City, King's, Leeds, Manchester, Strathclyde, Birmingham, Brunel, Edinburgh, Leicester, Newcastle, Reading, Royal Holloway, Sheffield, Sussex, Cardiff, Durham, Exeter, Lancaster, Loughborough, Nottingham, Queen Mary, St Andrews, Surrey, Swansea, UEA, Ulster, Aston, Essex, Goldsmiths, Liverpool, Nottingham Trent, Bangor, Bradford, Dundee, Glasgow, Hull, Oxford Brookes, Sunderland, Abertay Dundee, Heriot-Watt, Keele, Salford, Stirling, Aberdeen, Napier, UWE Bristol, Aberystwyth, Central Lancashire, Derby, Westminster, Canterbury Christ Church, De Montfort, Glasgow Caledonian, Luton, Paisley, Robert Gordon, Brighton, Kingston, Leeds Metropolitan, Coventry, Greenwich, Huddersfield, Liverpool John Moores, Sheffield Hallam, Staffordshire, Anglia Poly, Bath, Bolton, Bournemouth, Central England, East London, Gloucestershire, Hertfordshire, Lincoln, London Metropolitan, Manchester Metropolitan, Northumbria, Portsmouth, Thames Valley, Wolverhampton, Buckinghamshire Chilterns, Glamorgan, Plymouth, Cardiff Institute, Chichester, Kent, Liverpool Hope, Middlesex, Newport, Northampton, Roehampton, South Bank, Southampton Institute, Teesside, Queen's Belfast, Open.

Information systems: Imperial, Bath, City, Leeds, Strathclyde, Manchester, Queen Mary, Queen's Belfast, Reading, St Andrews, Sussex, Loughborough, Newcastle, Sheffield, Southampton, Surrey, Swansea, UEA, Essex, Goldsmiths, Lancaster, Liverpool, Nottingham Trent, Ulster, Bradford, Glasgow, Hertfordshire, Oxford Brookes, Portsmouth, Heriot-Watt, Hull, Salford, Stirling, Aberdeen, Bournemouth, Buckingham, Napier, Abertay Dundee, Derby, Greenwich, Lampeter, UWE Bristol, Westminster, Brunel, Canterbury Christ Church, East London, Luton, Middlesex, Paisley, Robert Gordon, Glasgow Caledonian, Kingston, Liverpool John Moores, London Metropolitan, Brighton, Leeds Metropolitan, Coventry, Huddersfield, Staffordshire, Sunderland, Central England, De Montfort, East London, Glamorgan, Gloucestershire, Keele, Lincoln, Manchester Metropolitan, Thames Valley, Wolverhampton, Buckinghamshire Chilterns, Plymouth, Sheffield Hallam, Bolton, Central Lancashire, Newport, Northampton, South Bank, Southampton Institute, Teesside, Cardiff Institute, Anglia Poly, Liverpool Hope, Northumbria, Roehampton, Worcester, Birkbeck.

Software engineering: Southampton, Imperial, Bath, City, Strathclyde, Birmingham, Edinburgh, Manchester, Newcastle, Sheffield, Durham, Ulster, Essex, Liverpool, Nottingham Trent, Aberystwyth, Bournemouth, Bradford, Glasgow, Hull, Kingston, Leicester, Oxford Brookes, Sunderland, Heriot-Watt, Stirling, Anglia Poly, Hertfordshire, Napier, Sheffield Hallam, UWE Bristol, Derby, Leeds Metropolitan, Liverpool John Moores, Westminster, Bolton, Coventry, De Montfort, East London, Gloucestershire, Luton, Northampton, Paisley, Plymouth, Wolverhampton, Brighton, Southampton Institute, Huddersfield, Staffordshire, Central England, Central Lancashire, Glamorgan, Liverpool Hope, Manchester Metropolitan, Portsmouth, Roehampton, South Bank, Teesside, Greenwich.

Artificial intelligence: Imperial, Leeds, Manchester, Bristol, Sheffield, Sussex, Birmingham, Essex, Liverpool, Reading, Hertfordshire, Heriot-Watt, Manchester Metropolitan, Staffordshire, Bradford, Oxford Brookes, UWE Bristol, Sunderland, Liverpool Hope, Luton, Robert Gordon, Westminster.

Other similar & related: Cardiff, Exeter, Ulster, Hertfordshire, Oxford Brookes, Stirling, Portsmouth, Sheffield Hallam, UWE Bristol, Canterbury Christ Church, Derby, East London, Greenwich, Coventry, Liverpool Hope, London Metropolitan, Roehampton, Worcester, Open.

Media: see **Communications & Media.**

Medicine & Health

Medicine: Cardiff, Cambridge, Oxford, Queen's Belfast, Southampton, Birmingham, Edinburgh, Glasgow, Imperial, Keele, King's, Leeds, Leicester, Liverpool, Manchester, Nottingham, Queen Mary, UCL, UEA, Aberdeen, Dundee, Sheffield, St Andrews, Bristol, Newcastle, St George's Hospital, Swansea, Warwick.

Dentistry: Liverpool, Queen's Belfast, Queen Mary, Birmingham, Bristol, Cardiff, Dundee, Glasgow, King's, Leeds, Manchester, Newcastle, Sheffield.

Anatomy, physiology & pathology: Oxford, Bath, Sheffield, Ulster, Birmingham, Leicester, Queen Margaret, Brighton, Bristol, Edinburgh, Nottingham, Plymouth, Reading, Robert Gordon, Sheffield Hallam, St George's Hospital, Sussex, UCL, Aston, Brunel, Cardiff, Coventry, East London, King's, Manchester, Newcastle, Southampton, St Andrews, UWE Bristol, Bradford, Liverpool, Loughborough, Glasgow, Queen's Belfast, Swansea, Dundee, Northumbria, Wolverhampton, Aberdeen, Abertay Dundee, Salford, Glasgow Caledonian, Greenwich, Hertfordshire, Oxford Brookes, Central Lancashire, Gloucestershire, Huddersfield, Leeds, Leeds Metropolitan, Luton, Manchester Metropolitan, Northampton, Nottingham Trent, Roehampton, South Bank, Staffordshire, Sunderland, Westminster, Teesside, London Metropolitan, Keele, Worcester.

Pharmacology, toxicology & pharmacy: Queen's Belfast, Bath, Reading, Bristol, Edinburgh, Nottingham, Robert Gordon, School of Pharmacy, Strathclyde, UCL, UEA, Ulster, Cardiff, King's, Manchester, Newcastle, Southampton. Bradford, De Montfort, Keele, Leeds, Liverpool, Glasgow, Sunderland, Brighton, Dundee, Sheffield Hallam, Aberdeen, Central Lancashire, Middlesex, Portsmouth, Coventry, Hertfordshire, Queen Margaret, UWE Bristol, Huddersfield, Kingston, Nottingham Trent, Westminster, Wolverhampton, Napier, East London, London Metropolitan, Greenwich, Liverpool John Moores, Aston.

Complementary medicine: Glamorgan, Central Lancashire, Salford, Derby, East London, Lincoln, Middlesex, Napier, Teesside, Cardiff Institute, Westminster, Wolverhampton, London Metropolitan, Brighton, Anglia Poly, Thames Valley.

Nutrition: King's, Newcastle, Southampton, Surrey, Coventry, Glasgow, Ulster, Northumbria, Nottingham, Plymouth, Kingston, Cardiff Institute, Abertay Dundee, Greenwich, Huddersfield, Liverpool John Moores, Oxford Brookes, Queen Margaret, Sheffield Hallam, Glasgow Caledonian, Leeds Metropolitan, Robert Gordon, South Bank, Westminster, London Metropolitan, Teesside, Bournemouth, Liverpool Hope, Manchester Metropolitan, Roehampton.

Ophthalmics: Aston, Cardiff, Ulster, Bradford, City, Manchester, Anglia Poly, Sheffield, Liverpool, Wolverhampton, Glasgow Caledonian.

Ear, nose & throat (aural & oral): Ulster, Southampton, Newcastle, Sheffield, City, Manchester Metropolitan, Queen Margaret, Reading, Strathclyde, UEA, Cardiff Institute, Aston, Bristol, Central England, Manchester, UCL, De Montfort, Leeds Metropolitan, Swansea, Central Lancashire, Leeds, Middlesex, Wolverhampton.

Nursing: Southampton, Edinburgh, De Montfort, Lancaster, Liverpool, Manchester, Nottingham, Surrey, UEA, Ulster, Bangor, Birmingham, Bradford, Cardiff, Coventry, Glamorgan, Glasgow, Hull, King's, Leeds, Northumbria, Oxford Brookes, Swansea, Brighton, City, Robert Gordon, Kingston, Abertay Dundee, Central England, Liverpool John Moores, Middlesex, Queen Margaret, Staffordshire, Teesside, Wolverhampton, Northampton, Sheffield Hallam, Anglia Poly, Bournemouth, Canterbury Christ Church, Glasgow Caledonian, Gloucestershire, Hertfordshire, Huddersfield, Keele, Leeds Metropolitan, Luton, Portsmouth, Salford, South Bank, UWE Bristol, Kent, Buckinghamshire Chilterns, Central Lancashire, Greenwich, Plymouth, Reading, Stirling, Sunderland.

Courses

Medical technology: Imperial, Nottingham, Ulster, Manchester, Sheffield, Bradford, Exeter, Liverpool, Teesside, Bangor, Cardiff, St George's Hospital, Staffordshire, Salford, Derby, Queen Margaret, Canterbury Christ Church, Central England, City, Glasgow Caledonian, Hertfordshire, Leeds, Robert Gordon, Sheffield Hallam, South Bank, UWE Bristol, Cardiff Institute, Manchester Metropolitan, Portsmouth.

Other similar & related: King's, Sheffield, Bradford, Imperial, UCL, Warwick, Birmingham, Brunel, Liverpool, Manchester, Newcastle, Queen Mary, Southampton, Surrey, Swansea, Ulster, Durham, Lancaster, Queen's Belfast, St George's Hospital, Coventry, Essex, Glasgow, Kent, Oxford Brookes, Robert Gordon, Salford, Strathclyde, Sunderland, Teesside, UEA, Aberdeen, Aberystwyth, Northumbria, Nottingham Trent, Anglia Poly, Hull, Manchester Metropolitan, Portsmouth, Abertay Dundee, De Montfort, Hertfordshire, Kingston, Queen Margaret, UWE Bristol, Bath Spa, Canterbury Christ Church, Cardiff, Central England, Central Lancashire, Glasgow Caledonian, Gloucestershire, Leeds Metropolitan, Lincoln, Liverpool John Moores, Luton, Middlesex, Northampton, Plymouth, Staffordshire, Thames Valley, Westminster, Napier, Bournemouth, East London, Huddersfield, London Metropolitan, Brighton, City, Wolverhampton, Derby, Sheffield Hallam, Glamorgan, Cardiff Institute, Arts, Greenwich, Liverpool Hope, Paisley, Roehampton, Worcester, Open.

Middle Eastern studies and languages: see **Languages & Literature, Eastern, Asian, African, etc.**

Nursing: see **Medicine & Health.**

Philosophy: see **History, Philosophy, etc.**

Physical Sciences

Chemistry: Oxford, Imperial, Southampton, Warwick, Durham, UEA, Bath, Leeds, Manchester, Sussex, York, Birmingham, Bradford, Bristol, Cardiff. Edinburgh, Heriot-Watt, Kent, Newcastle, Northumbria, Nottingham, Reading, Sheffield, St Andrews, Strathclyde, Surrey, UCL, Aston, Exeter, Glasgow, Hull, Leicester, Liverpool, Queen's Belfast, Bangor, Dundee, Keele, Lancaster, Loughborough, Aberdeen, Brighton, Nottingham Trent, Portsmouth, Plymouth, South Bank, Staffordshire, Wolverhampton, Kingston, Robert Gordon, Teesside, Anglia Poly, Liverpool John Moores, London Metropolitan, Paisley, Greenwich, Sunderland, Coventry, Glamorgan, Manchester Metropolitan, Derby, Central Lancashire, Huddersfield, Birkbeck.

Materials science: Oxford, Sheffield, Liverpool, St Andrews, Queen Mary, Manchester Metropolitan.

Physics: Oxford, Imperial, Southampton, Bristol, Durham, Warwick, Bath, Birmingham, Edinburgh, King's, Manchester, Newcastle, Nottingham, Sheffield, St Andrews, UCL, UEA, York, Exeter, Lancaster, Leeds, Leicester, Liverpool, Loughborough, Reading, Strathclyde, Sussex, Cardiff, Kent, Liverpool John Moores, Royal Holloway, Surrey, Swansea, Aberystwyth, Glasgow, Hull, Queen Mary, Queen's Belfast, Central Lancashire, Dundee, Keele, Nottingham Trent, Aberdeen, Salford, Heriot-Watt, Hertfordshire, Paisley, Birkbeck.

Forensic & archaeological science: Strathclyde, Durham, Edinburgh, UCL, Anglia Poly, Sheffield, Bradford, Cardiff, Dundee, Exeter, Kent, Leicester, Northumbria, Reading, Abertay Dundee, Bangor, Central Lancashire, Nottingham Trent, Robert Gordon, Huddersfield, Lampeter, Lincoln, Portsmouth, Coventry, Kingston, Liverpool John Moores, Sheffield Hallam, UWE Bristol, Canterbury Christ Church, Glasgow Caledonian, South Bank, Staffordshire, Westminster, Derby, Teesside, East London, London Metropolitan, Paisley, Bournemouth, Keele, Wolverhampton, Glamorgan, De Montfort.

Astronomy: Durham, Leeds, Sheffield, Cardiff, Edinburgh, Liverpool, St Andrews, UCL, Kent, Liverpool John Moores, Royal Holloway, Sussex, Aberystwyth, Glasgow, Keele, Queen Mary, Central Lancashire, Glamorgan, Hertfordshire.

Geology: Oxford, Imperial, Bristol, Cardiff, Durham, Leeds, Liverpool, Southampton, St Andrews, UEA, Aberystwyth, Birmingham, Edinburgh, Lancaster, Leicester, Manchester, Reading, UCL, Brighton, Glasgow, Royal Holloway, Bangor, Greenwich, Keele, Kingston, Aberdeen, Glamorgan, Plymouth, Huddersfield, Portsmouth, Bath Spa, Northampton, Staffordshire, Wolverhampton, Derby, Liverpool John Moores, Paisley, Exeter, Birkbeck, Open.

Ocean sciences: Southampton, Liverpool, UEA, Ulster, Aberdeen, Bangor, Heriot-Watt, Plymouth, Glamorgan.

Physical geography & environment: Southampton, Durham, Nottingham, Bristol, Manchester, Newcastle, Birmingham, Edinburgh, Leeds, LSE, Reading, Sheffield, St Andrews, Sussex, UCL, Cardiff, Glasgow Caledonian, Lancaster, Liverpool, Loughborough, Plymouth, Royal Holloway, UEA, Aberystwyth, Exeter, King's, Leicester, Queen's Belfast, Swansea, Ulster, Aston, Bangor, Brighton, Coventry, Glasgow, Hull, Northumbria, Portsmouth, Queen Mary, Strathclyde, Bradford, Dundee, Greenwich, Kingston, Oxford Brookes, Sheffield Hallam, Stirling, Aberdeen, Manchester Metropolitan, Central Lancashire, Hertfordshire, Nottingham Trent, Salford, UWE Bristol, Anglia Poly, Bath Spa, Bournemouth, Canterbury Christ Church, East London, Gloucestershire, Huddersfield, Liverpool John Moores, Newport, Northampton, Southampton Institute, Staffordshire, Sunderland, Wolverhampton, Derby, Cardiff Institute, Glamorgan, Keele, Liverpool Hope, Worcester, Birkbeck, Open.

Other similar & related: Southampton, Edinburgh, LSE, Birmingham, Glasgow, Liverpool, Sheffield, Sussex, UEA, Aberystwyth, Aston, Exeter, Imperial, Lancaster, Leeds, Nottingham, York, Bangor, Kent, Northumbria, Queen Mary, Bradford, Brighton, Greenwich, Stirling, Ulster, Aberdeen, Heriot-Watt, Hull, Oxford Brookes, Central Lancashire, Coventry, Glamorgan, Hertfordshire, Kingston, Lampeter, Manchester Metropolitan, Nottingham Trent, Portsmouth, Sheffield Hallam, UWE Bristol, Anglia Poly, Bath Spa, East London, Huddersfield, Liverpool John Moores, Southampton Institute, Staffordshire, Bolton, Derby, Teesside, Gloucestershire, Keele, Reading, Wolverhampton, Salford, Cardiff Institute, Liverpool Hope, Newport, Birkbeck, Open.

Politics: *see* **Social Studies.**

Portuguese: *see* **Languages & Literature, European.**

Psychology: *see* **Biology, etc.**

Religious Studies: *see* **History, Philosophy, etc.**

Russian: *see* **Languages & Literature, European.**

Scandinavian languages: *see* **Languages & Literature, European.**

Social Studies

Economics: LSE, Nottingham, UCL, Southampton, Bath, Cambridge, Oxford, Warwick, York, Aston, Bristol, Durham, Lancaster, St Andrews, Birmingham, Cardiff, Edinburgh, Exeter, Hull, Leeds, Leicester, Manchester, Newcastle, Queen's Belfast, Reading, Royal Holloway, SOAS, Sussex, Essex, Glasgow, Kent, Liverpool, Loughborough, Queen Mary, Sheffield, Swansea, UEA, Brunel, City, Goldsmiths, Keele, Northumbria, Surrey, Aberdeen, Bangor, Coventry, De Montfort, Dundee, Heriot-Watt, Kingston, Manchester Metropolitan, Oxford Brookes, Salford, Stirling, Ulster, Aberystwyth, Leeds Metropolitan, Nottingham Trent, Bradford, Buckingham, Hertfordshire, London Metropolitan, Napier, Plymouth, Portsmouth, UWE Bristol, Abertay Dundee, Central England, Liverpool John Moores, Staffordshire, Sunderland, Anglia Poly, Central Lancashire, East London, Glasgow Caledonian, Greenwich, Middlesex, Northampton, Paisley, Teesside, Robert Gordon, Birkbeck.

Politics: Durham, Oxford, St Andrews, Southampton, Bath, Exeter, King's, LSE, Manchester, Nottingham, Sheffield, Warwick, York, Birmingham, Cardiff, Edinburgh, Leeds, Newcastle, Surrey, Sussex, UCL, Bradford, Bristol, Essex, Glasgow, Leicester, Queen Mary, Queen's Belfast, Reading, Royal Holloway, SOAS, UEA, Aston, Goldsmiths, Hull, Lancaster, Liverpool,

Aberdeen, Aberystwyth, Brunel, Dundee, Keele, Loughborough, Salford, Stirling, Swansea, Ulster, Westminster, Northumbria, Nottingham Trent, Anglia Poly, Coventry, Kingston, Oxford Brookes, Plymouth, Portsmouth, UWE Bristol, De Montfort, Derby, Huddersfield, Kent, Liverpool John Moores, Canterbury Christ Church, Central Lancashire, East London, Glamorgan, Gloucestershire, Greenwich, Leeds Metropolitan, Lincoln, London Metropolitan, Manchester Metropolitan, Middlesex, Northampton, South Bank, Sunderland, Cardiff Institute, Liverpool Hope, Wolverhampton, Robert Gordon, Roehampton.

Sociology: Cambridge, Exeter, Southampton, Birmingham, Bristol, Edinburgh, LSE, Manchester, Nottingham, Sussex, Brighton, Cardiff, Durham, Essex, Glasgow, Lancaster, Leeds, Newcastle, Queen's Belfast, Reading, Royal Holloway, Sheffield, UEA, Warwick, York, Aston, Bath, Brunel, Goldsmiths, Keele, Leicester, Liverpool, Loughborough, Queen Mary, Stirling, Aberdeen, Bradford, City, Hull, Nottingham Trent, Queen Margaret, Sheffield Hallam, Surrey, Swansea, Ulster, Westminster, Bangor, Glasgow Caledonian, Kingston, Abertay Dundee, Central England, De Montfort, Northumbria, Oxford Brookes, Plymouth, Portsmouth, Salford, Staffordshire, UWE Bristol, Central Lancashire, Derby, Leeds Metropolitan, Liverpool John Moores, Bath Spa, Canterbury Christ Church, Coventry, East London, Glamorgan, Gloucestershire, Greenwich, Huddersfield, Kent, London Metropolitan, Luton, Manchester Metropolitan, Middlesex, Northampton, South Bank, Sunderland, Thames Valley, Cardiff Institute, Wolverhampton, Bolton, Lincoln, Liverpool Hope, Napier, Paisley, Robert Gordon, Roehampton, Buckinghamshire Chilterns, Teesside, Worcester.

Social policy: Southampton, LSE, Manchester, Nottingham, Brighton, Essex, Glasgow, Queen's Belfast, Sheffield, UEA, York, Aston, Bath, Birmingham, Cardiff, Leeds, Reading, Stirling, Bristol, Brunel, Hull, Sheffield Hallam, Swansea, Bangor, Bradford, Northumbria, Ulster, Central England, Portsmouth, Salford, Canterbury Christ Church, Coventry, East London, Gloucestershire, Huddersfield, Leeds Metropolitan, Lincoln, London Metropolitan, Luton, Manchester Metropolitan, Middlesex, Newport, Northampton, South Bank, Teesside, Wolverhampton, Anglia Poly, Buckinghamshire Chilterns, De Montfort, Thames Valley, Bath Spa, Central Lancashire, City, Kent, Derby, Glamorgan, Roehampton, Worcester, Open.

Social work: Edinburgh, Queen's Belfast, Sussex, Ulster, Brighton, Glasgow, Goldsmiths, Leeds, Reading, Southampton, Strathclyde, York, Bath, Bradford, Bristol, Exeter, Hull, Keele, Lancaster, Manchester, Royal Holloway, Sheffield, Stirling, Brunel, Northumbria, Nottingham Trent, Robert Gordon, South Bank, Swansea, Bangor, Dundee, Huddersfield, Kingston, De Montfort, Liverpool John Moores, Middlesex, Plymouth, Staffordshire, Abertay Dundee, Birmingham, Bournemouth, Canterbury Christ Church, Central England, Central Lancashire, Coventry, East London, Glasgow Caledonian, Gloucestershire, Hertfordshire, Lincoln, London Metropolitan, Luton, Northampton, Portsmouth, Sheffield Hallam, Thames Valley, UWE Bristol, Westminster, Wolverhampton, Manchester Metropolitan, Oxford Brookes, Paisley, Southampton Institute, Buckinghamshire Chilterns, Greenwich, Newport, Salford, Teesside, Bolton, Derby, Cardiff Institute, Anglia Poly, Durham, Glamorgan, Kent, Leeds Metropolitan, Sunderland, Worcester.

Anthropology: Cambridge, Oxford, Manchester, SOAS, St Andrews, Birmingham, Edinburgh, LSE, Sussex, UCL, Glasgow, Goldsmiths, Kent, Lancaster, Queen's Belfast, UEA, Brunel, Durham, Hull, Aberdeen, Nottingham Trent, Anglia Poly, Brighton, Oxford Brookes, Staffordshire, UWE Bristol, Lampeter, East London, Liverpool John Moores, Middlesex, Roehampton.

Human & social geography: Cambridge, Durham, Nottingham, Oxford, Southampton, Bristol, Leeds, Manchester, Newcastle, St Andrews, Birmingham, Cardiff, Edinburgh, Loughborough, LSE, Reading, Sheffield, Sussex, UCL, UEA, Exeter, Glasgow, Lancaster, Liverpool, Plymouth, SOAS, Aberystwyth, King's, Leicester, Queen Mary, Queen's Belfast, Royal Holloway, Swansea, Aberdeen, Bangor, Brighton, Coventry, Dundee, Hull, Keele, Northumbria, Portsmouth, Westminster, Sheffield Hallam, Bradford, Greenwich, Kingston, Nottingham Trent, Manchester Metropolitan, Oxford Brookes, UWE Bristol, Central England, Central Lancashire, Huddersfield, Liverpool John Moores, Anglia Poly, Canterbury Christ Church, East London, Gloucestershire, Leeds Metropolitan, Liverpool Hope, Northampton, Southampton Institute, Staffordshire, Sunderland, Wolverhampton, Worcester, Glamorgan, Newport, Open.

Other similar & related: Cardiff, King's, Manchester, SOAS, UEA, Bradford, Leeds, Liverpool, Hull, Lancaster, Buckingham, Leeds Metropolitan, Central Lancashire, East London, Manchester Metropolitan, Middlesex, Newport, Sunderland, Wolverhampton, Derby, Brighton, Plymouth, Roehampton, Teesside, Open.

Spanish: *see* **Languages & Literature, European.**

Sports: *see* **Biology, etc.**

Technologies

Minerals technology: Exeter, Leeds, Nottingham, Glamorgan.

Metallurgy: Sheffield, Liverpool, Birmingham, Manchester.

Ceramics & glasses: Sheffield, Canterbury Christ Church.

Polymers & textiles: Sheffield, Manchester, Queen Mary, Loughborough, Nottingham Trent, Portsmouth, Heriot-Watt, East London, Glasgow Caledonian, Northampton, Bolton, Napier, London Metropolitan, De Montfort, Manchester Metropolitan, Arts.

Technology relating to other materials: Sheffield, Liverpool, Birmingham, Imperial, Manchester, Queen Mary, Leeds, Loughborough, Plymouth, Swansea, Manchester Metropolitan, Wolverhampton, London Metropolitan, Arts.

Maritime technology: Southampton, Southampton Institute, Plymouth, Portsmouth, Strathclyde, Liverpool John Moores, Bournemouth.

Industrial biotechnology: Imperial, Cardiff, Edinburgh, Leeds, Birmingham, Northumbria, Reading, Aberdeen, Portsmouth, Hertfordshire, Oxford Brookes, Westminster, Liverpool John Moores, Wolverhampton, Paisley.

Other similar & related: Birmingham, Loughborough, City, Keele, Queen's Belfast, Surrey, Manchester, Aston, Huddersfield, Hull, Central England, Nottingham Trent, Staffordshire, Ulster, Anglia Poly, Bradford, Coventry, Lincoln, Salford, Bath Spa, Glasgow, De Montfort, Derby, Leeds Metropolitan, London Metropolitan, Portsmouth, Southampton Institute, Oxford Brookes, Teesside, Thames Valley, Glamorgan, Plymouth, Central Lancashire, Arts, Glasgow Caledonian, Newport.

Theology: *see* **History, Philosophy, etc.**

Tourism: *see* **Business, Management & Administration.**

Veterinary Science: *see* **Agriculture.**

Zoology: *see* **Biology, etc.**

Entrance requirements

However much you might like to choose from every university in this book, not every one will have you. The best way of knowing in advance which ones would welcome you with open arms and which would give you the finger is to check out the entrance requirements.

Who they'll accept is usually based largely on points that students collect by passing exams and qualifications. A Levels, obviously, but also Highers, AS Levels, NVQs and any one of the new bits of paper that pass for proof of intelligence.

Each grade in each qualification is worth a different number of points and, in theory, once you've got enough points for a particular course, you should stand a good chance of being accepted. The 'UCAS points tariff' looks like this...

A Levels		Highers		Advanced Highers		Vocational A Levels		AS Levels		Key Skills	
Grade	Pts	Grade	Pts	Grade	Pts	Grade	Pts	Grade	Pts	Level	Pts
A	120	A	72	A	120	AA	240	A	60	4	30
B	100	B	60	B	100	BB	200	B	50	3	20
C	80	C	48	C	80	CC	160	C	40	2	10
D	60					DD	120	D	30		
E	40					EE	80	E	20		

However, it's not that simple. (Is it ever?) All points are supposed to be equal, but some are a lot more equal than others.

First off, it matters what qualifications you've got. Whatever the points score says, some universities don't take AS Levels or vocational A Levels quite as seriously as an equal number of points at A Level.

Then there's the subject you've studied. In practice, points gained in a relevant subject count for more than points in something completely unrelated. For example, if you want to do a science degree, but all you've got is arts A Levels, only universities desperate for students aren't going to look at your application and snigger.

The whole system of points is more than a bit dubious at the edges, not least because many mature students will be accepted without traditional qualifications and the set-up of modular courses throws a spanner in the works. Besides, come Clearing, universities with vacancies to fill will throw their list of requirements out the window and take what they can get.

Heed that huge health warning and the additional advice that it's best to check with the actual department you're applying to for what grades they'd be likely to want from you, given the subjects and qualifications you're taking.

Having said that, here's *Push*'s exclusive guide to grades.

Have a look at the points table on the following pages, which is a quick reference to help you narrow down where to study, depending entirely on what points you already have or expect to get. It's a good tool for seeing the range of points required to get in where you want.

In the past, UK students took an average of three or four A Levels. Now you're more likely to sit four AS exams in the first year and three A2 exams in the second year of A Level studies, giving you up a maximum of 420 UCAS points. But, as Push likes to keep it simple, for now we've shown the maximum points as 360, which is what most universities are still dealing with.

Some universities offer a narrow range of points. For example, Cambridge and Oxford expect you to have a minimum of 340 points (AAB) for most courses. With anything from 240 to 340 (CCC to AAB), Manchester's courses span a wider range of abilities and at Hull, the spread is even wider – from just 40 up to 300 (from a D to BBB).

Of course, remember that these are the minimum requirements for their various courses. Whether you've a penchant for Portuguese at Paisley or a hankering for Higher Maths at Heriot-Watt, when *Push* comes to shove you'll need to check with the department involved exactly what they want from you before you apply.

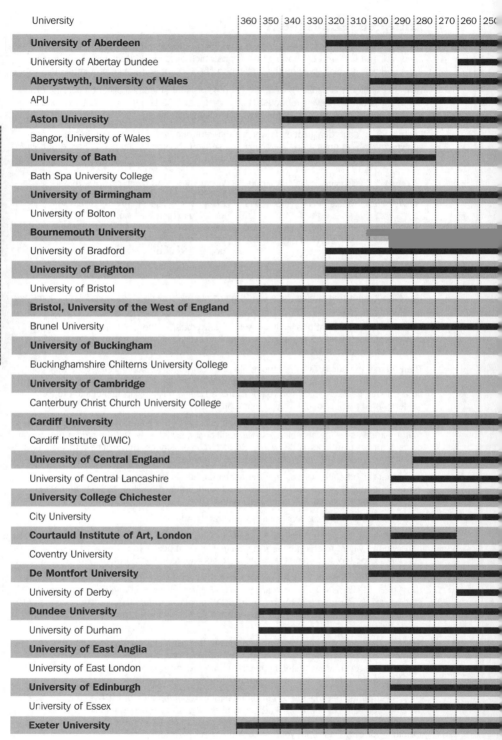

University	360	350	340	330	320	310	300	290	280	270	260	250
University of Aberdeen					■	■	■	■	■	■	■	■
University of Abertay Dundee										■	■	
Aberystwyth, University of Wales				■	■	■	■	■	■	■	■	■
APU					■	■	■	■	■	■	■	■
Aston University			■	■	■	■	■	■	■	■	■	■
Bangor, University of Wales				■	■	■	■	■	■	■	■	■
University of Bath	■	■	■	■	■	■	■	■				
Bath Spa University College												
University of Birmingham	■	■	■	■	■	■	■	■	■	■	■	■
University of Bolton												
Bournemouth University								■	■	■	■	■
University of Bradford					■	■	■	■	■	■	■	■
University of Brighton					■	■	■	■	■	■	■	■
University of Bristol	■	■	■	■	■	■	■	■	■	■	■	■
Bristol, University of the West of England												
Brunel University					■	■	■	■	■	■	■	■
University of Buckingham												
Buckinghamshire Chilterns University College												
University of Cambridge	■	■	■									
Canterbury Christ Church University College												
Cardiff University	■	■	■	■	■	■	■	■	■	■	■	■
Cardiff Institute (UWIC)												
University of Central England								■	■	■	■	■
University of Central Lancashire									■	■	■	■
University College Chichester							■	■	■	■	■	■
City University					■	■	■	■	■	■	■	■
Courtauld Institute of Art, London							■	■	■	■		
Coventry University							■	■	■	■	■	■
De Montfort University							■	■	■	■	■	■
University of Derby											■	■
Dundee University		■	■	■	■	■	■	■	■	■	■	■
University of Durham		■	■	■	■	■	■	■	■	■	■	■
University of East Anglia	■	■	■	■	■	■	■	■	■	■	■	■
University of East London							■	■	■	■	■	■
University of Edinburgh	■	■	■	■	■	■	■	■	■	■	■	■
University of Essex			■	■	■	■	■	■	■	■	■	■
Exeter University	■	■	■	■	■	■	■	■	■	■	■	■

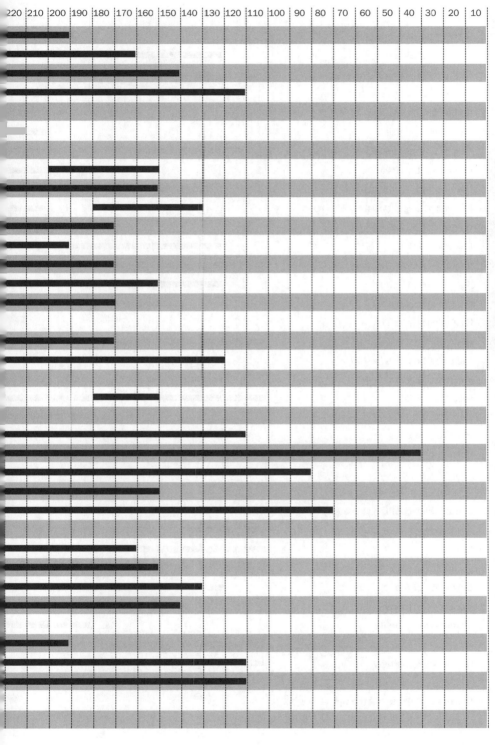

points

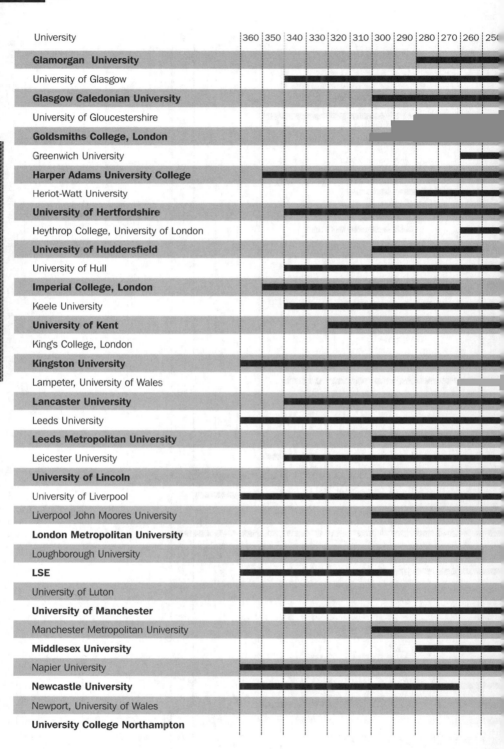

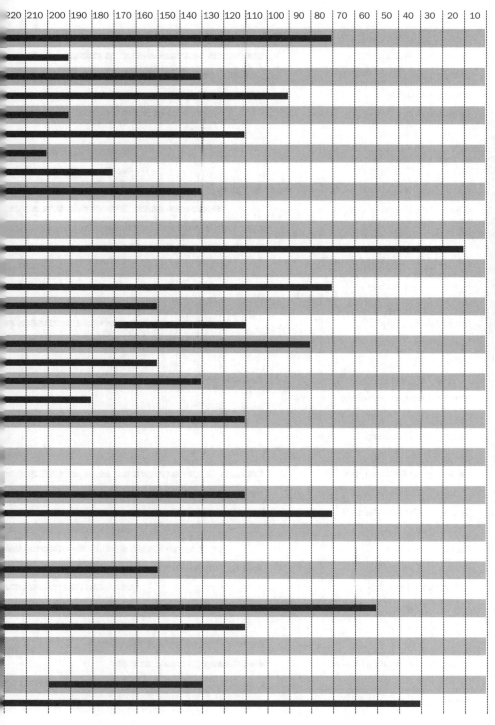

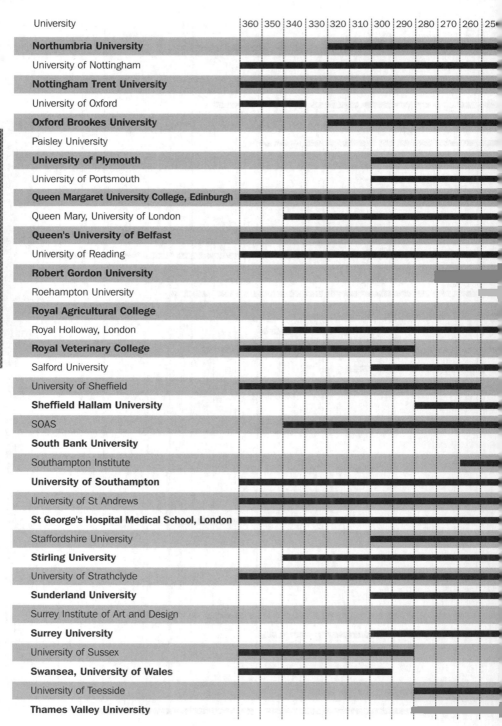

University	360	350	340	330	320	310	300	290	280	270	260	250
Northumbria University					▓	▓	▓	▓	▓	▓	▓	▓
University of Nottingham	▓	▓	▓	▓	▓	▓	▓	▓	▓	▓	▓	▓
Nottingham Trent University	▓	▓	▓	▓	▓	▓	▓	▓	▓	▓	▓	▓
University of Oxford	▓	▓	▓									
Oxford Brookes University					▓	▓	▓	▓	▓	▓	▓	▓
Paisley University												
University of Plymouth								▓	▓	▓	▓	▓
University of Portsmouth							▓	▓	▓	▓	▓	▓
Queen Margaret University College, Edinburgh	▓	▓	▓	▓	▓	▓	▓	▓	▓	▓	▓	▓
Queen Mary, University of London			▓	▓	▓	▓	▓	▓	▓	▓	▓	▓
Queen's University of Belfast	▓	▓	▓	▓	▓	▓	▓	▓	▓	▓	▓	▓
University of Reading	▓	▓	▓	▓	▓	▓	▓	▓	▓	▓	▓	▓
Robert Gordon University												
Roehampton University												
Royal Agricultural College												
Royal Holloway, London				▓	▓	▓	▓	▓	▓	▓	▓	▓
Royal Veterinary College	▓	▓	▓	▓	▓	▓	▓	▓	▓	▓	▓	▓
Salford University								▓	▓	▓	▓	▓
University of Sheffield	▓	▓	▓	▓	▓	▓	▓	▓	▓	▓	▓	▓
Sheffield Hallam University									▓	▓	▓	▓
SOAS				▓	▓	▓	▓	▓	▓	▓	▓	▓
South Bank University												
Southampton Institute											▓	▓
University of Southampton	▓	▓	▓	▓	▓	▓	▓	▓	▓	▓	▓	▓
University of St Andrews	▓	▓	▓	▓	▓	▓	▓	▓	▓	▓	▓	▓
St George's Hospital Medical School, London	▓	▓	▓	▓	▓	▓	▓	▓	▓	▓	▓	▓
Staffordshire University								▓	▓	▓	▓	▓
Stirling University			▓	▓	▓	▓	▓	▓	▓	▓	▓	▓
University of Strathclyde	▓	▓	▓	▓	▓	▓	▓	▓	▓	▓	▓	▓
Sunderland University								▓	▓	▓	▓	▓
Surrey Institute of Art and Design												
Surrey University								▓	▓	▓	▓	▓
University of Sussex	▓	▓	▓	▓	▓	▓	▓	▓				
Swansea, University of Wales	▓	▓	▓	▓	▓	▓						
University of Teesside										▓	▓	▓
Thames Valley University									▓	▓	▓	

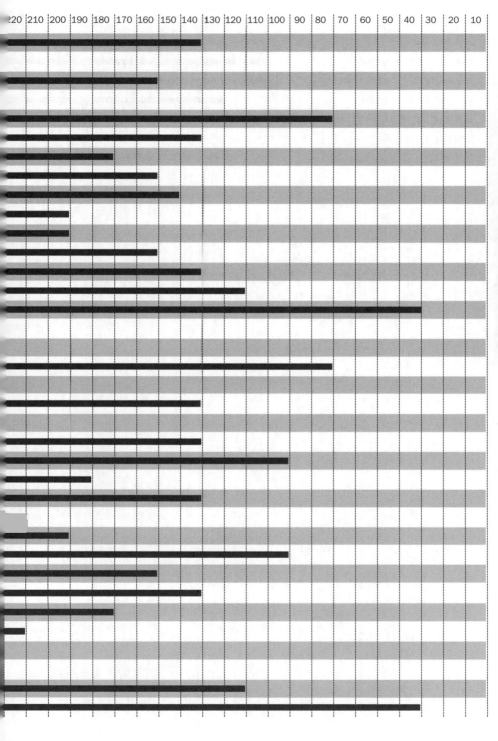

points

University	360	350	340	330	320	310	300	290	280	270	260	250
University of Ulster	■	■	■	■	■	■	■	■	■	■	■	■
University College, London	■	■										■
University of Warwick	■	■	■	■	■	■	■	■	■			
University of Westminster			■	■	■	■	■	■	■	■	■	■
University of Wolverhampton									■	■	■	■
University College Worcester												
University of York			■	■	■	■	■	■				

220	210	200	190	180	170	160	150	140	130	120	110	100	90	80	70	60	50	40	30	20	10

Push tables

Where would education be without tables? There's a great tradition from the Periodic Table, times tables and time-tables to the governments own league tables. And of course school desks, which are tables. Sort of.

Never one to buck a trend, *Push* introduces the tables to end all tables – the crucial guides to clubs and sports and the controversial reality of hard facts.

CLUBS

Some clubs and societies are available at most institutions. So, rather than bore you rigid listing them in every university profile, Push has detailed them in the following pages so you can see if there's rock at Reading or karate at Keele.

VITAL STATISTICS

What you want to do is get those universities up against the wall and see how they look side by side. So on the following pages *Push* has distilled the finest facts and charted them: the sex ratio; founding year; student numbers; the level of care; the numbers of those who enter through clearing; the numbers who flunk; cost and availability of housing; the cost of booze (average of a pint of beer, glass of wine and a Red Bull); employment prospects; and the average yearly student debt (including student loans).

For a fuller explanation of *Push*'s statistical data, please see 'How to use *Push*' (page viii).

TOP 10S

Top 10s are eye candy – found everywhere from Top of the Pops to Viz, recording everything from the biggest-selling records to the world's fastest slugs. They're also an easy way to decode information without having to do much at all apart from raise the occasional eyebrow.

Push's Top 10s shouldn't be taken too seriously. Anyone choosing a university solely on the basis that it tops the charts for cheap beer has maybe not made a full and rounded decision. But all else being equal, it's as good a clincher as any.

Furthermore, taken together our Top 10s tell you quite a bit. Every university has its good and bad points and we help you pinpoint the strongest strengths and weakest weaknesses. (It also provides a quick guide to cheap rent, top totty and bargain beer.)

Clubs

	ABERDEEN	ABERTAY DUNDEE	ABERYSTWYTH	THE ARTS, LONDON	APU	ASTON	BANGOR	BATH	BATH SPA	BIRKBECK, LONDON	BIRMINGHAM	BOLTON	BOURNEMOUTH	BRADFORD	BRIGHTON	BRISTOL	BRISTOL, WEST OF ENGLAND	BRUNEL	BUCKINGHAM	BUCKINGHAMSHIRE CHILTERNS	CAMBRIDGE
NON-SPORTING																					
African-Caribbean	•		•			•	•		•		•		•		•	•	•		•	•	
Amnesty	•		•	•		•					•				•		•	•		•	•
Animal Rights			•			•					•										•
Anti-Racist/Anti-Nazi						•					•					•					•
Asian	•	•			•		•	•			•					•	•	•	•		•
BUNAC											•					•					•
Catholic	•		•				•	•			•				•	•	•	•			
Chess				•							•				•	•	•	•			•
Christian Union	•	•		•	•	•	•		•		•	•	•		•		•	•	•	•	•
Cinema Club		•	•								•				•						
Conservation	•		•					•		•	•				•						•
Conservative	•		•					•	•		•		•		•			•			•
Dance				•			•				•				•						•
Debating		•	•								•		•		•						
Drama				•		•					•				•	•			•	•	•
Film Making			•		•			•			•				•						•
Green/Environment											•										•
Industrial Society																					•
Irish							•						•					•			
Islamic	•	•		•		•	•				•	•	•	•	•	•	•	•	•	•	•
Jewish				•			•		•	•	•		•	•	•	•	•				•
Labour	•	•	•								•				•						•
Lesbian/Gay/Bisexual		•		•	•			•			•				•	•	•	•			•
Lib Dem		•					•				•				•						•
Orchestra(s)																					•
People & Planet	•		•	•	•		•		•		•				•		•				•
Photography		•					•			•	•		•				•		•	•	
Rock/Indie Music		•					•				•				•	•	•	•			
SF & Fantasy	•	•	•				•		•		•				•						
Socialist Worker	•	•					•			•					•		•		•		•
SPORTING																					
Archery	•		•			•		•			•				•		•				•
Athletics		•					•	•			•				•	•	•	•	•	•	
Badminton	•		•	•		•	•	•			•	•			•	•	•	•	•	•	•
Basketball	•	•	•	•	•	•	•				•	•			•	•	•	•	•	•	•
Canoeing	•		•			•	•	•						•	•	•	•				
Climbing		•				•	•	•			•	•	•	•		•	•		•		
Cricket	•		•	•		•	•	•			•	•			•	•	•			•	•
Cross Country											•										
Cycling											•										
Fencing	•		•				•	•							•		•	•	•	•	•
Football	•	•	•	•	•	•	•	•	•	•	•	•			•		•	•	•	•	•
Golf	•	•	•			•	•	•							•		•	•		•	•
Hill Walking							•										•				•
Hockey	•	•	•	•		•	•	•	•		•	•			•	•	•	•		•	•
Horse Riding						•	•	•	•					•	•	•	•			•	•
Judo	•	•	•			•	•		•		•				•		•				
Karate	•	•	•			•		•			•				•	•	•		•	•	
Netball	•	•	•	•	•	•		•	•		•	•			•	•	•	•		•	
Orienteering	•										•										•
Rugby	•	•	•			•	•	•	•		•	•			•	•	•	•	•	•	
Sailing	•		•	•			•	•			•			•	•	•	•				
Skiing	•		•		•	•	•	•	•			•			•	•	•				•
Squash	•		•			•	•	•							•		•		•	•	•
Sub-Aqua	•		•			•	•	•							•	•	•		•	•	
Swimming	•		•		•	•	•				•				•	•	•	•	•		
Tae Kwon Do	•	•	•			•		•			•				•	•	•	•	•		•
Tennis	•		•	•		•	•	•			•				•	•	•	•		•	•
Trampolining	•						•	•							•	•	•	•	•	•	
Volleyball	•	•	•				•	•							•	•	•	•	•	•	

Clubs

	Canterbury Christ Church	Cardiff	Cardiff Institute	Central England	Central Lancashire	College Chichester	City	Courtauld Institute of Art	Coventry	De Montfort	Derby	Dundee	Durham	East Anglia	East London	Edinburgh	Essex	Exeter	Glamorgan	Glasgow	Glasgow Caledonian
NON-SPORTING																					
African-Caribbean	•			•	•		•		•		•	•	•	•							
Amnesty		•				•			•			•	•		•	•	•		•	•	
Animal Rights											•										
Anti-Racist/Anti-Nazi																					
Asian		•		•			•					•		•		•		•			
BUNAC												•				•		•			
Catholic		•			•				•			•	•			•					
Chess			•			•										•	•	•			
Christian Union	•	•	•	•	•	•	•	•	•	•	•		•		•	•	•	•	•	•	•
Cinema Club		•		•	•							•				•	•				
Conservation												•	•	•	•	•	•	•			
Conservative		•							•			•	•			•	•	•	•		
Dance		•		•		•	•			•	•	•				•	•		•		
Debating	•	•				•	•	•			•	•		•			•	•	•		
Drama	•		•	•	•							•	•						•		
Film Making			•								•					•		•			
Green/Environment		•	•						•			•	•		•	•	•	•			
Industrial Society												•									
Irish		•										•									
Islamic		•		•	•				•	•	•	•	•		•	•	•	•	•		
Jewish		•	•			•	•					•	•		•	•	•	•			
Labour		•										•	•	•		•	•	•	•		
Lesbian/Gay/Bisexual	•	•	•	•	•		•					•	•		•	•	•	•	•	•	•
Lib Dem		•										•	•			•	•	•			
Orchestra(s)		•		•								•				•		•	•		
People & Planet	•	•		•						•	•	•				•			•		
Photography		•								•	•	•	•			•	•		•		
Rock/Indie Music	•	•		•		•			•			•	•				•	•			
SF & Fantasy				•								•	•			•		•	•		
Socialist Worker		•		•	•							•	•		•		•	•			
SPORTING																					
Archery												•	•			•		•			
Athletics		•	•	•	•				•			•	•	•		•	•		•	•	•
Badminton	•	•	•	•	•		•		•	•	•	•	•	•		•	•		•	•	•
Basketball	•	•	•	•	•		•			•	•	•		•		•	•		•	•	•
Canoeing		•	•		•	•				•	•	•	•	•		•			•	•	•
Climbing	•	•		•	•		•		•	•	•	•	•	•		•	•	•	•		•
Cricket	•	•	•				•		•	•	•	•	•	•	•	•	•		•	•	•
Cross Country		•		•										•							
Cycling		•		•	•									•		•	•				
Fencing		•		•		•				•		•	•	•		•	•		•		
Football	•	•		•	•	•	•		•	•	•	•	•	•		•	•		•	•	•
Golf		•	•	•						•		•	•	•		•			•		•
Hill Walking		•		•		•						•	•	•		•					•
Hockey	•	•		•			•		•	•	•	•	•	•	•	•	•		•	•	•
Horse Riding	•	•		•						•		•	•			•	•				
Judo			•	•								•	•			•			•		•
Karate	•	•		•			•		•			•		•		•	•	•	•	•	
Netball	•	•		•	•		•		•	•	•	•		•		•	•		•	•	•
Orienteering												•	•			•			•		
Rugby	•	•	•	•	•	•	•		•	•	•	•	•	•	•	•	•		•	•	•
Sailing		•			•	•						•	•	•		•	•		•		
Skiing	•		•	•			•		•			•	•	•			•	•	•	•	•
Squash		•	•	•			•		•			•	•	•		•	•		•		•
ub-Aqua		•							•			•	•	•	•	•	•		•		•
Swimming		•		•					•			•	•	•		•	•		•	•	•
Tae Kwon Do	•			•			•		•	•	•	•		•		•	•				•
Tennis	•	•		•			•		•	•	•	•	•	•		•			•	•	•
Trampolining	•	•	•	•			•		•			•	•	•		•			•	•	•
Volleyball	•	•	•		•		•		•		•	•	•	•		•	•		•	•	•

clubs

	GLOUCESTERSHIRE	GOLDSMITHS COLLEGE	GREENWICH	HARPER ADAMS	HERIOT-WATT	HERTFORDSHIRE	HEYTHROP COLLEGE	HUDDERSFIELD	IMPERIAL COLLEGE, LONDON	HULL	KEELE	KENT	KING'S COLLEGE, LONDON	KINGSTON	LAMPETER, UNIVERSITY OF WALES	LANCASTER	LEEDS	LEEDS METROPOLITAN	LEICESTER	LINCOLN	LIVERPOOL
NON-SPORTING																					
African-Caribbean	•	•	•		•	•			•	•	•		•		•		•		•	•	
Amnesty					•				•	•			•	•		•	•	•		•	•
Animal Rights																	•				
Anti-Racist/Anti-Nazi		•																			•
Asian		•	•						•		•	•	•			•	•	•	•		•
BUNAC																			•	•	
Catholic									•		•	•	•			•	•		•		•
Chess					•			•		•	•		•	•			•				
Christian Union	•	•	•	•		•	•	•	•	•	•	•	•	•			•	•	•	•	•
Cinema Club	•	•							•	•				•		•	•	•			
Conservation				•												•	•				
Conservative	•								•	•	•	•	•	•	•		•			•	
Dance	•	•							•	•	•		•			•	•	•	•		•
Debating	•									•						•	•	•	•		•
Drama	•	•	•			•			•	•	•	•				•			•	•	•
Film Making													•			•					•
Green/Environment		•				•			•	•	•										•
Industrial Society																					
Irish		•							•												
Islamic	•	•			•	•		•	•	•	•	•	•	•		•	•	•	•		•
Jewish		•							•	•	•					•	•	•	•		
Labour					•				•	•						•					
Lesbian/Gay/Bisexual	•	•	•			•		•			•	•	•			•	•			•	•
Lib Dem													•			•		•	•	
Orchestra(s)			•						•	•			•	•	•	•	•	•	•	•
People & Planet						•					•				•					
Photography		•			•				•				•							
Rock/Indie Music					•				•	•	•	•	•	•	•	•	•	•	•
SF & Fantasy	•								•	•			•						
Socialist Worker		•									•					•	•	•	•
SPORTING																					
Archery					•				•	•			•			•	•			•
Athletics	•				•			•		•			•			•	•	•	•	•	•
Badminton	•	•	•		•	•		•	•	•	•	•	•	•	•	•	•	•	•	•	•
Basketball	•	•	•		•	•		•	•	•	•	•	•	•	•	•	•	•	•	•	•
Canoeing					•	•		•	•	•	•	•		•	•	•	•	•	•	•
Climbing	•					•		•	•	•	•	•		•	•	•	•	•	•	•
Cricket		•	•	•	•				•	•	•	•	•	•	•	•	•	•	•	•
Cross Country									•	•	•		•			•	•			
Cycling								•	•	•						•	•			•
Fencing					•	•			•	•	•	•	•	•	•	•	•			•
Football	•	•	•	•	•		•	•	•	•	•	•	•	•	•	•	•	•	•	•	•
Golf	•				•	•			•	•	•	•	•	•		•	•	•	•	•	•
Hill Walking					•	•									•	•	•	•	•	•
Hockey	•	•	•	•	•	•		•	•	•	•	•	•	•	•	•	•	•	•	•	•
Horse Riding	•			•		•						•				•	•	•	•	•
Judo					•				•	•	•		•			•	•		•	•
Karate		•			•	•			•	•	•	•	•	•		•	•		•	•
Netball	•	•	•		•	•	•	•	•	•	•		•	•	•	•	•	•	•	•
Orienteering										•							•			
Rugby	•	•	•	•	•			•	•	•	•	•	•	•	•	•	•	•	•	•	•
Sailing			•		•					•	•	•		•		•	•	•		•
Skiing	•	•	•		•			•	•	•	•			•		•	•	•		
Squash		•	•	•	•	•		•	•	•	•	•		•		•	•	•	•	•
Sub-Aqua					•				•	•	•		•	•		•	•	•	
Swimming	•				•	•			•	•	•	•	•	•		•	•	•	•	•
Tae Kwon Do					•					•		•	•	•		•	•		•	•
Tennis	•		•	•	•			•	•	•	•	•	•	•		•	•	•	•	•	•
Trampolining								•			•	•		•		•	•		•	•
Volleyball	•	•	•	•	•			•	•	•	•	•	•	•		•	•	•	•	•	•

Clubs

	Liverpool Hope	Liverpool John Moores	London Metropolitan	London South Bank	Loughborough	LSE	Luton	Manchester	Manchester Metropolitan	Middlesex	Napier	Newcastle	Newport	College Northampton	Northumbria	Nottingham	Nottingham Trent	Oxford	Oxford Brookes	Paisley	Plymouth
NON-SPORTING																					
African-Caribbean	●	●	●	●		●	●	●	●			●		●		●	●	●	●	●	●
Amnesty			●			●		●		●		●	●			●		●	●		
Animal Rights													●			●		●			
Anti-Racist/Anti-Nazi											●							●			
Asian	●	●	●		●		●	●				●	●			●		●	●		
BUNAC					●											●		●			
Catholic	●	●			●	●					●			●	●	●		●	●		
Chess		●				●	●	●							●						
Christian Union	●	●	●	●	●	●	●	●	●	●	●	●	●	●	●	●	●	●	●		●
Cinema Club	●		●		●		●	●		●	●		●				●	●			
Conservation												●			●		●	●			●
Conservative				●		●		●	●							●		●	●		
Dance	●				●	●	●	●	●			●	●	●	●	●		●	●		●
Debating				●	●	●		●	●			●			●	●		●	●		●
Drama	●	●	●		●		●	●	●		●			●		●	●	●	●		●
Film Making	●				●							●	●			●		●	●	●	●
Green/Environment		●										●	●			●		●			
Industrial Society														●							
Irish	●		●		●				●					●							
Islamic		●	●	●	●	●	●	●	●	●		●		●		●	●	●	●		●
Jewish		●	●		●			●	●	●						●	●	●	●		
Labour					●						●	●				●		●	●		
Lesbian/Gay/Bisexual	●	●	●			●	●	●	●		●	●	●	●	●	●	●	●	●		●
Lib Dem					●							●				●		●	●		
Orchestra(s)		●				●	●	●		●	●					●		●	●		
People & Planet				●	●		●					●	●	●		●	●	●	●		●
Photography				●	●		●					●	●			●					
Rock/Indie Music		●			●	●		●				●	●		●	●	●	●	●		●
SF & Fantasy					●	●	●	●								●				●	
Socialist Worker		●			●		●	●	●	●			●	●	●			●		●	
SPORTING																					
Archery		●			●							●				●	●	●			●
Athletics	●	●	●				●	●	●			●	●		●	●	●	●	●		●
Badminton	●	●			●	●	●	●	●			●			●	●			●		●
Basketball	●	●	●	●	●	●	●	●	●		●	●	●	●		●	●		●		●
Canoeing					●		●	●				●	●		●	●	●	●			●
Climbing		●			●		●	●				●	●		●	●	●	●	●		
Cricket	●	●	●	●	●	●	●	●		●		●	●	●		●	●	●			●
Cross Country					●		●	●				●				●	●	●			
Cycling		●			●		●	●				●			●	●	●	●			●
Fencing					●		●	●	●			●	●		●	●	●	●			●
Football	●	●	●	●	●	●	●	●	●	●	●	●	●	●	●	●	●		●		●
Golf		●			●	●	●	●				●		●	●	●	●	●			●
Hill Walking					●	●						●				●	●			●	
Hockey	●	●	●	●	●	●	●	●	●	●	●	●	●	●	●	●	●	●	●	●	●
Horse Riding					●		●	●	●			●				●	●				●
Judo	●	●	●	●	●							●				●	●				●
Karate		●					●	●	●			●	●		●	●		●			●
Netball	●	●	●	●		●	●	●	●	●	●	●	●	●	●	●	●	●	●		●
Orienteering												●				●					
Rugby	●	●	●	●	●		●	●	●	●	●	●	●	●	●	●	●	●	●		●
Sailing					●				●	●		●			●	●	●	●			●
Skiing		●			●		●	●	●		●	●			●	●	●	●	●		●
Squash					●	●	●	●	●		●	●			●	●	●	●	●		●
Sub-Aqua					●			●	●			●				●	●				●
Swimming		●	●		●	●	●	●	●	●		●			●	●	●	●			●
Tae Kwon Do		●			●	●	●					●			●	●	●		●		●
Tennis		●	●	●	●	●	●	●	●	●		●			●	●	●	●	●		●
Trampolining					●			●	●			●				●	●	●			●
Volleyball	●	●	●	●	●	●	●	●	●	●	●	●			●	●	●	●			●

Clubs

	Portsmouth	Queen Margaret, Edinburgh	Queen Mary, London	Queen's, Belfast	Reading	Robert Gordon	Roehampton	Royal Academy of Music	Royal Agricultural College	Royal College of Music	Royal Holloway, London	Royal Veterinary College	RSAMD	The School of Pharmacy	Salford	Sheffield Hallam	Sheffield	Southampton	SOAS	Southampton Institute	St Andrews
NON-SPORTING																					
African-Caribbean	●				●		●				●				●	●			●	●	
Amnesty					●		●				●					●		●	●	●	●
Animal Rights					●										●	●		●			
Anti-Racist/Anti-Nazi															●						
Asian			●		●						●				●	●			●	●	●
BUNAC																●			●	●	
Catholic	●		●	●												●	●		●		
Chess				●												●			●		
Christian Union	●	●	●	●	●	●	●	●		●	●	●	●	●	●	●	●	●	●	●	●
Cinema Club			●	●	●		●									●	●	●			
Conservation											●				●	●		●	●	●	
Conservative											●				●	●					●
Dance		●	●								●		●		●	●					●
Debating			●								●				●	●					●
Drama	●	●	●	●	●						●	●			●	●		●	●		●
Film Making																●		●		●	●
Green/Environment			●	●			●								●	●			●		●
Industrial Society																●					
Irish											●				●	●					
Islamic	●		●	●			●				●				●	●	●	●	●	●	
Jewish			●	●	●		●				●				●	●					
Labour			●													●		●	●	●	●
Lesbian/Gay/Bisexual	●		●	●		●	●	●			●	●	●		●	●			●		●
Lib Dem	●															●					●
Orchestra(s)			●													●					
People & Planet	●		●	●	●		●				●					●		●	●	●	
Photography			●	●							●				●	●	●	●	●		
Rock/Indie Music	●	●	●	●	●						●				●	●	●		●	●	●
SF & Fantasy	●			●	●						●					●		●			
Socialist Worker	●		●	●							●				●	●	●				
SPORTING																					
Archery							●									●	●	●			●
Athletics	●		●	●	●						●					●	●	●		●	●
Badminton	●		●	●	●	●	●				●					●	●	●	●	●	●
Basketball	●	●	●	●	●	●	●				●				●	●	●	●	●	●	●
Canoeing	●		●	●	●										●	●	●		●		●
Climbing	●		●		●						●	●	●				●	●	●	●	●
Cricket	●		●	●	●						●	●	●	●	●	●	●	●	●	●	●
Cross Country			●																		●
Cycling					●											●	●	●		●	
Fencing	●		●	●	●	●									●	●		●		●	
Football			●	●	●	●	●	●	●	●	●	●	●	●	●	●		●	●	●	●
Golf	●		●	●	●	●			●		●						●			●	
Hill Walking			●				●				●	●			●	●		●			
Hockey	●	●	●	●	●	●						●	●	●	●		●		●	●	●
Horse Riding	●		●	●								●	●	●	●				●	●	●
Judo			●	●	●											●		●	●		
Karate	●	●	●	●	●	●	●				●						●	●		●	●
Netball	●	●	●	●	●	●	●		●		●	●	●		●	●	●	●	●	●	
Orienteering			●												●		●	●			●
Rugby	●	●	●	●	●	●			●		●	●	●		●	●	●	●	●	●	●
Sailing	●				●	●					●					●	●	●			●
Skiing	●		●		●	●			●		●	●	●	●		●		●			
Squash	●		●	●					●		●	●	●							●	●
Sub-Aqua	●		●	●												●	●	●		●	●
Swimming	●		●	●	●						●	●				●		●			●
Tae Kwon Do	●		●	●	●									●	●		●		●	●	●
Tennis	●		●	●	●	●	●				●	●	●				●	●			
Trampolining	●		●	●							●					●		●	●	●	●
Volleyball	●		●	●							●					●	●	●	●	●	●

	St George's Hospital Medical School	Staffordshire	Stirling	Strathclyde	Sunderland	Surrey	Surrey Institute	Sussex	Swansea	Teesside	Thames Valley	Ulster	University College, London	Warwick	Westminster	Wolverhampton	Worcester	York
NON-SPORTING																		
African-Caribbean		•			•		•	•	•	•			•	•	•			•
Amnesty	•					•		•	•		•	•	•					•
Animal Rights							•						•		•			
Anti-Racist/Anti-Nazi				•									•					
Asian		•		•	•	•		•	•			•	•	•				
BUNAC		•		•									•					
Catholic						•			•									
Chess								•		•			•					•
Christian Union	•	•		•	•	•		•	•	•		•	•	•	•	•	•	•
Cinema Club	•	•			•		•	•					•	•	•			•
Conservation		•	•			•		•	•				•					•
Conservative			•			•		•				•	•					•
Dance		•		•	•	•			•	•			•					•
Debating		•				•		•	•			•	•	•	•			
Drama	•	•	•	•	•	•		•	•				•		•		•	•
Film Making	•		•			•		•	•			•	•		•			•
Green/Environment			•	•		•		•				•	•	•				
Industrial Society			•										•					
Irish			•						•				•		•			
Islamic	•	•		•		•		•	•			•	•		•			•
Jewish	•							•				•	•	•	•			
Labour		•	•	•					•				•					•
Lesbian/Gay/Bisexual		•	•	•	•	•	•	•	•			•	•		•	•		•
Lib Dem			•	•				•	•				•		•			•
Orchestra(s)	•		•			•		•					•		•			•
People & Planet			•	•		•		•	•				•		•			•
Photography	•		•			•		•					•					
Rock/Indie Music				•			•	•		•			•		•	•		
SF & Fantasy				•		•					•		•					•
Socialist Worker			•	•				•	•				•		•			•
SPORTING																		
Archery				•		•		•					•		•			•
Athletics	•	•	•	•	•	•			•	•		•	•		•	•		•
Badminton	•	•	•	•	•	•	•	•	•	•	•	•	•	•	•	•	•	•
Basketball			•	•	•	•		•	•	•			•		•	•		•
Canoeing			•	•	•	•		•	•	•			•		•	•		•
Climbing			•	•	•	•		•	•	•			•		•	•		•
Cricket	•		•	•	•	•	•	•	•	•	•		•		•	•		•
Cross Country			•	•									•		•	•		
Cycling					•			•	•				•		•	•		•
Fencing			•	•	•	•		•	•		•		•		•	•		•
Football	•		•	•		•		•	•		•	•	•	•	•	•		•
Golf			•			•		•	•		•		•		•	•		•
Hill Walking				•	•	•		•					•		•	•		•
Hockey		•	•	•	•	•		•	•	•		•	•	•	•	•		•
Horse Riding			•			•		•	•		•		•		•	•		•
Judo				•					•		•		•		•	•		•
Karate		•	•	•		•	•	•	•		•		•		•	•		•
Netball		•	•		•	•		•	•	•	•	•	•	•	•	•		•
Orienteering				•									•		•	•		•
Rugby	•	•	•	•	•	•	•	•	•	•	•	•	•	•	•	•	•	•
Sailing	•		•	•	•	•		•	•				•					•
Skiing			•			•		•	•				•		•			•
Squash	•	•	•	•		•		•	•	•		•	•		•			•
Sub-Aqua			•	•		•		•			•		•		•			•
Swimming		•	•	•	•	•		•	•		•		•		•	•		•
Tae Kwon Do				•		•		•			•	•	•	•				•
Tennis	•	•	•		•	•		•	•			•	•	•		•		•
Trampolining		•	•		•			•		•	•		•			•		•
Volleyball	•		•		•		•	•	•		•	•	•		•	•		•

Stats

	SEX RATIO M:F	STAFF: STUDENT RATIO	FOUNDED	NUMBER OF UNDERGRADUATES	NUMBER OF PART-TIME STUDENTS	NUMBER OF POSTGRADS	% IN THROUGH CLEARING
University of Aberdeen	46:54	n/a	1495	9,200	1,060	1,460	9
University of Abertay Dundee	54:46	1:20	1888	3,485	330	365	3
Aberystwyth, University of Wales	45:55	1:24	1872	6,070	2,355	895	7
APU	35:65	1:29	1989	9,985	11,755	710	15
University of the Arts, London	40:60	1:17	1989	9,175	590	1,035	5
Aston University	49:51	1:15	1895	5,260	160	595	8
Bangor, University of Wales	36:64	1:14	1884	5,430	1,995	1,185	8
University of Bath	51:49	1:14	1966	7,155	2,425	1,330	2
Bath Spa University College	34:66	1:23	1983	3,220	270	630	7
Birkbeck, University of London	35:65	n/a	1823	15	17,920	860	n/a
University of Birmingham	43:57	1:15	1900	15,975	4,280	5,140	3
University of Bolton	54:46	1:5	1982	3,190	2,630	500	n/a
Bournemouth University	42:58	1:18	1976	9,045	3,455	1,285	13
University of Bradford	43:57	1:12	1966	6,670	1,705	1,020	18
University of Brighton	37:63	1:22	1976	10,705	4,460	1,170	10
University of Bristol	47:53	1:13	1876	10,575	3,895	2,615	1
Bristol, University of the West of England	41:59	1:20	1992	15,940	4,995	1,540	9
Brunel University	52:48	1:19	1966	9,715	1,050	1,625	23
University of Buckingham	45:55	1:10	1974	426	43	105	38
Buckinghamshire Chilterns University College	43:57	1:10	1893	6,020	3,140	140	19
University of Cambridge	46:54	1:12	1209	11,955	4,595	5,210	0
Canterbury Christ Church University College	26:74	n/a	1962	5,755	4,125	870	10
Cardiff University	43:57	1:6	1883	13,035	4,005	3,845	3
Cardiff Institute (UWIC)	47:53	1:15	1976	6,080	1,420	715	10
University of Central England	39:61	1:15	1971	11,915	6,660	1,540	10
University of Central Lancashire	42:58	1:18	1828	15,490	10,010	680	21
University College Chichester	30:70	1:20	1839	2,435	735	240	<1
City University	37:63	1:18	1894	6,200	6,955	3,045	n/a
Courtauld Institute of Art, London	35:65	1:5	1932	115	0	210	n/a
Coventry University	50:50	1:15	1843	10,920	4,605	1,235	n/a
De Montfort University	42:58	1:19	1969	13,910	4,280	1,205	17
University of Derby	46:54	1:22	1851	8,360	2,505	490	n/a
Dundee University	32:68	1:10	1967	8,685	3,650	940	10

Stats

% OF MATURE STUDENTS	% OF OVERSEAS STUDENTS	NUMBER OF DISABLED STUDENTS	STATE:PRIVATE STUDENTS	AVERAGE ENTRY POINTS	AVERAGE ACCOMMODATION PER WEEK	% IN COLLEGE ACCOMMODATION	BOOZE INDEX	% OF GRADS UNEMPLOYED AFTER 6 MONTHS	NUMBER OF STUDENTS PER COUNSELLOR	FLUNK RATE (%)	AVERAGE DEBT PER YEAR
19	18	142	85:15	n/a	£66.43	26	£1.76	6	3,730	13	£1,065
32	15	79	87:13	n/a	£45.63	21	£1.69	10	2,008	30	£2,440
13	14	236	94:6	303	£60.14	61	£1.80	7	2,326	10	£2,728
60	13	107	95:5	207	£56.56	9	£2.21	7	3,315	17	£5,898
65	33	91	98:2	n/a	£89.95	15	£2.34	9	2,830	13	£2,321
8	19	74	89:11	312	£52.71	40	£1.73	8	1,079	10	£2,771
30	10	268	94:6	280	£47.22	12	£1.81	10	3,806	14	£4,221
10	14	179	80:20	315	£65.08	42	£2.08	7	2,771	3	£7,471
32	5	181	80:20	180	£62.08	20	£2.09	5	2,657	12	£5,528
99	5	37	n/a	n/a	£92.50	0	£2.50	n/a	3,519	n/a	£125
11	25	240	80:20	300	£59.16	36	£1.74	6	3,578	7	£3,482
86	15	45	96:4	140	£42.37	34	£1.68	15	1,251	36	£3,435
18	13	380	93:7	239	£65.50	25	£2.06	8	3,014	14	£6,945
33	32	155	93:7	268	£43.46	27	£1.88	7	949	15	£5,895
40	17	356	92:8	240	£70.11	15	£2.54	8	1,659	14	£2,114
10	21	193	61:39	280	£52.83	32	£1.73	6	1,892	3	£5,767
24	8	201	84:16	250	£63.33	23	£1.92	7	2,103	21	£5,215
24	17	187	79:8	260	£69.73	27	£2.30	11	2,157	11	£2,866
30	79	n/a	n/a	220	£99.12	7	£1.97	12	79	n/a	£5,270
30	13	208	n/a	n/a	£52.60	19	£2.33	10	1,288	12	£4,164
6	28	42	55:45	n/a	£66.67	n/a	£1.59	6	1,854	1	£1,488
61	6	151	96:4	180	£70.68	20	£2.06	4	1,086	14	£3,733
18	20	296	n/a	350	£50.98	36	£1.63	5	1,259	8	£2,079
17	9	407	95:5	140	£40.70	6	£1.62	6	3,753	14	£3,061
37	10	309	97:3	n/a	£54.93	46	£1.64	13	5,595	20	£3,720
21	15	427	96:4	220	£57.76	9	£1.84	6	4,235	26	£5,187
46	6	116	87:2	217	£66.49	19	£2.03	6	507	14	£4,015
29	35	15	72:28	r/a	£84.45	21	£2.27	6	3,181	13	£1,683
10	37	3	40:60	n/a	£85.00	0	£2.50	5	320	n/a	£2,728
21	19	306	96:4	n/a	£53.97	23	£1.70	8	4,819	15	£3,372
28	9	319	96:4	232	£64.33	18	£2.08	9	4,930	18	£2,726
51	8	239	97:3	n/a	£53.07	28	£2.03	7	4,041	21	£3,272
23	20	139	n/a	330	£56.44	10	£1.78	6	3,817	17	£3,482

Stats

	SEX RATIO M:F	STAFF: STUDENT RATIO	FOUNDED	NUMBER OF UNDERGRADUATES	NUMBER OF PART-TIME STUDENTS	NUMBER OF POSTGRADS	% IN THROUGH CLEARING
University of Durham	**45:55**	**1:19**	**1832**	**10,380**	**385**	**2,190**	**7**
University of East Anglia	35:65	1:12	1963	6,905	3,805	2,010	14
University of East London	**45:55**	**1:19**	**1970**	**7,540**	**2,625**	**1,410**	**46**
University of Edinburgh	44:56	n/a	1582	15,095	1,055	3,275	5
University of Essex	**48:52**	**1:13**	**1964**	**5,480**	**1,815**	**1,840**	**19**
Exeter University	47:53	1:14	1955	7,715	1,655	2,010	5
Glamorgan University	**48:52**	**1:20**	**1913**	**9,380**	**7,240**	**845**	**20**
University of Glasgow	42:58	1:13	1451	14,815	4,565	2,510	2
Glasgow Caledonian University	**39:61**	**1:10**	**1875**	**10,610**	**2,305**	**905**	**n/a**
University of Gloucestershire	46:54	1:19	1834	5,815	1,865	525	6
Goldsmiths College	**34:66**	**1:15**	**1891**	**3,560**	**1,255**	**1,375**	**17**
Greenwich University	46:54	1:15	1890	10,605	4,070	2,285	38
Harper Adams University College	**65:35**	**1:14**	**1901**	**1,340**	**100**	**70**	**21**
Heriot-Watt University	61:39	1:14	1821	4,905	225	1,200	7
University of Hertfordshire	**45:55**	**1:18**	**1952**	**13,465**	**3,545**	**1,655**	**15**
Heythrop College, University of London	40:60	1:20	1614	184	0	438	8
University of Huddersfield	**43:57**	**1:19**	**1992**	**9,600**	**5,150**	**1,030**	**20**
University of Hull	40:60	1:15	1927	9,615	8,110	1,775	20
Imperial College, London	**63:37**	**1:9**	**1907**	**7,365**	**0**	**3,165**	**3**
Keele University	34:66	1:11	1962	4,905	4,795	1,055	14
University of Kent	**45:55**	**1:10**	**1965**	**8,165**	**3,370**	**1,075**	**n/a**
King's College, London	35:65	1:9	1829	11,915	2,430	2,910	16
Kingston University	**49:51**	**1:9**	**1971**	**12,675**	**1,880**	**1,215**	**n/a**
Lampeter, University of Wales	36:64	1:8	1822	875	5,185	180	8
Lancaster University	**41:59**	**1:9**	**1964**	**7,510**	**6,005**	**1,510**	**4**
Leeds University	43:57	1:15	1904	21,130	4,555	5,920	5
Leeds Metropolitan University	**47:53**	**1:18**	**1970**	**14,280**	**8,180**	**1,195**	**15**
Leicester University	47:53	1:9	1921	7,575	1,635	1,870	5
University of Lincoln	**43:57**	**1:18**	**1861**	**7,875**	**5,235**	**985**	**5**
University of Liverpool	45:55	1:15	1881	12,500	4,265	2,225	n/a
Liverpool Hope University College	**30:70**	**n/a**	**1844**	**4,250**	**1,395**	**755**	**n/a**
Liverpool John Moores University	45:55	1:22	1970	13,500	4,160	1,170	15
London Metropolitan University	**46:54**	**1:10**	**2002**	**16,460**	**8,565**	**2,430**	**28**

% OF MATURE STUDENTS	% OF OVERSEAS STUDENTS	NUMBER OF DISABLED STUDENTS	STATE:PRIVATE STUDENTS	AVERAGE ENTRY POINTS	AVERAGE ACCOMMODATION PER WEEK	% IN COLLEGE ACCOMMODATION	BOOZE INDEX	% OF GRADS UNEMPLOYED AFTER 6 MONTHS	NUMBER OF STUDENTS PER COUNSELLOR	FLUNK RATE (%)	AVERAGE DEBT PER YEAR
8	15	61	61:33	382	£89.22	53	£1.76	7	1,501	2	£2,722
30	16	34	90:10	300	£50.36	45	£1.86	8	3,091	7	£2,407
75	25	442	96:2	210	£63.03	7	£1.83	17	1,710	28	£4,443
13	18	374	n/a	240	£56.94	38	£1.99	8	2,700	7	£3,360
18	45	102	96:4	99	£57.20	44	£1.70	9	633	15	£3,395
7	15	261	71:29	360	£63.14	50	£1.82	7	3,518	5	£3,988
53	13	280	97:3	200	£42.84	40	£1.75	6	1,731	25	£4,568
11	11	188	86:14	n/a	£61.48	22	£1.91	7	2,801	15	£3,330
38	6	105	96:4	n/a	£51.24	6	£2.03	10	1,583	18	£2,518
30	5	220	94:6	200	£55.10	20	£1.95	8	2,078	22	£4,015
62	21	77	91:9	287	£75.39	30	£2.28	7	1,854	14	£3,652
83	23	253	95:5	n/a	£81.21	20	£2.30	12	4,975	23	£2,565
16	10	97	15:85	n/a	£65.98	33	£1.66	4	2,920	17	£1,173
21	26	96	61:8	n/a	£56.35	18	£2.08	10	6,218	18	£4,355
55	19	281	95:5	220	£64.88	21	£2.11	9	1,689	16	£4,970
20	6	6	80:20	250	£100.00	26	£2.50	8	622	17	£3,681
55	8	113	97:3	n/a	£48.46	15	£1.76	10	2,032	21	£4,175
52	21	362	93:7	253	£48.23	29	£1.82	6	3,432	13	£3,917
13	33	23	59:41	341	£91.09	46	£2.06	9	4,212	4	£5,582
11	12	92	83:9	240	£57.56	65	£1.62	5	2,786	4	£4,653
16	24	119	88:12	n/a	£69.70	43	£1.82	5	2,428	12	£3,608
29	22	120	71:21	n/a	£76.16	26	£2.21	5	944	7	£4,703
38	15	197	92:8	200	£78.54	26	£2.07	11	1,854	19	£3,457
45	18	92	60:40	200	£44.96	53	£1.77	9	1,216	10	£2,608
11	19	142	85:15	n/a	£53.22	83	£1.50	6	1,093	6	£3,920
19	18	462	73:27	202	£61.39	25	£1.91	5	2,550	6	£4,188
19	13	428	93:7	128	£44.50	18	£2.05	9	3,261	17	£4,339
11	29	212	88:12	371	£62.63	62	£1.75	6	2,053	8	£3,747
40	24	289	97:3	240	£59.51	17	£1.82	12	3,826	22	£4,157
18	16	121	93:7	n/a	£64.13	57	£1.35	8	4,816	9	£3,583
n/a	n/a	239	n/a	n/a	£59.94	28	£1.36	7	n/a	24	n/a
46	11	40	95:5	n/a	£44.81	20	£1.58	8	1,861	22	£3,225
53	25	203	95:5	n/a	£93.69	18	£1.93	17	3,565	28	£4,475

Stats

Stats

	SEX RATIO M:F	STAFF: STUDENT RATIO	FOUNDED	NUMBER OF UNDERGRADUATES	NUMBER OF PART-TIME STUDENTS	NUMBER OF POSTGRADS	% IN THROUGH CLEARING
Loughborough University	62:38	1:18	1908	10,165	185	2,375	5
LSE	54:46	1:8	1895	3,405	130	3,585	0
University of Luton	37:63	1:20	1993	6,225	3,620	1,015	30
University of Manchester	39:61	n/a	1824	17,795	2,385	4,065	8
Manchester Metropolitan University	43:57	1:21	1970	20,725	4,060	2,275	n/a
Middlesex University	41:59	1:18	1973	13,625	4,490	2,605	30
Napier University	44:56	1:15	1992	8,635	2,110	1,095	15
Newcastle University	48:52	1:7	1834	11,680	1,170	3,770	6
Newport, University of Wales	44:56	1:10	1841	2,535	4,770	365	20
University College Northampton	37:63	1:17	1999	7,230	2,625	275	10
Northumbria University	41:59	1:20	1969	14,375	5,330	1,735	33
University of Nottingham	41:59	1:13	1881	17,510	5,480	4,140	2
Nottingham Trent University	50:50	1:15	1992	15,800	2,865	1,930	15
The Open University	42:58	1:19	1969	0	141,635	465	n/a
University of Oxford	49:51	1:8	1150	11,455	4,580	5,040	0
Oxford Brookes University	41:59	1:12	1865	9,695	2,690	1,975	13
Paisley University	36:64	1:20	1897	6,025	3,025	585	14
University of Plymouth	39:61	n/a	1970	15,960	6,535	955	18
University of Portsmouth	58:42	1:20	1992	12,320	2,750	1,620	4
Queen Margaret University College, Edinburgh	21:79	1:18	1875	2,900	775	440	15
Queen Mary, University of London	52:48	1:8	1887	7,275	275	1,580	n/a
Queen's University of Belfast	40:60	1:7	1845	12,400	5,355	1,965	3
University of Reading	44:56	1:15	1892	7,885	2,560	2,315	4
Robert Gordon University	37:63	1:17	1750	6,495	2,345	960	15
Roehampton University	23:77	n/a	1841	5,575	820	1,020	n/a
Royal Academy of Music	44:56	1:8	1822	315	0	310	0
Royal Agricultural College	61:39	1:13	1845	445	15	140	1
Royal College of Music	47:53	n/a	1882	375	5	200	n/a
Royal Holloway, London	40:60	1:15	1886	4,215	640	1,010	14
Royal Scottish Academy of Music and Drama	33:67	1:1	1847	555	0	100	0
Royal Veterinary College, London	24:76	1:2	1791	805	15	130	16

% OF MATURE STUDENTS	% OF OVERSEAS STUDENTS	NUMBER OF DISABLED STUDENTS	STATE:PRIVATE STUDENTS	AVERAGE ENTRY POINTS	AVERAGE ACCOMMODATION PER WEEK	% IN COLLEGE ACCOMMODATION	BOOZE INDEX	% OF GRADS UNEMPLOYED AFTER 6 MONTHS	NUMBER OF STUDENTS PER COUNSELLOR	FLUNK RATE (%)	AVERAGE DEBT PER YEAR
7	17	166	86:14	310	£69.62	47	£1.89	7	2,105	7	£3,767
10	72	49	64:36	340	£90.64	51	£1.78	5	1,411	3	£2,763
45	37	82	99:1	n/a	£49.58	26	£1.94	12	1,508	25	£4,127
7	19	451	48:52	404	£62.49	35	£1.91	7	2,561	7	£1,454
45	7	380	95:5	n/a	£48.90	14	£1.96	8	8,343	17	£3,654
45	27	309	80:20	220	£67.38	14	£2.40	13	3,695	27	£4,193
53	17	31	86:5	200	£69.47	11	£2.18	11	7,190	37	£1,040
11	22	379	67:33	n/a	£57.79	32	£1.97	4	3,207	7	£1,362
41	6	32	99:1	180	£50.51	26	£1.85	14	5,285	22	£4,362
29	7	220	98:2	210	£46.00	23	£1.87	6	2,939	25	£3,611
42	14	358	91:9	200	£48.75	12	£2.12	6	2,682	14	£3,577
8	22	194	73:20	370	£72.08	40	£1.88	8	3,252	3	£3,300
13	8	389	90:10	220	£53.30	21	£2.04	6	5,475	10	£5,012
97	5	836	n/a	n/a	n/a	n/a	n/a	n/a	n/a	n/a	n/a
6	10.5	62	52:48	n/a	n/a	n/a	£1.58	8	5,574	2	£3,357
62	24	405	74:26	168	£69.99	36	£2.32	7	1,302	18	£3,003
46	7	150	98:2	168	£53.89	13	£2.20	13	2,708	20	£1,846
43	8	974	92:8	n/a	n/a	9	£1.74	9	2,883	13	£6,077
33	12	366	92:8	n/a	£59.40	18	£2.36	9	1,178	16	£3,533
40	18	81	93:7	289	£59.62	19	£2.13	4	3,728	15	£1,953
25	21	44	73:27	314	n/a	35	£2.19	5	2,998	9	£2,390
8	7	192	99:1	n/a	£47.91	12	£1.56	5	2,840	9	£1,111
12	22	121	79:18	339	£79.65	49	£2.19	8	1,351	11	£2,694
24	20	110	94:6	n/a	£64.67	18	£1.73	4	2,876	17	£1,510
27	10	330	n/a	n/a	£88.08	29	£2.26	6	n/a	21	n/a
10	43	50	75:25	n/a	£134.02	6	£2.45	6	625	15	£3,613
25	22	4	40:60	210	£89.21	59	£1.87	16	593	0	£3,113
5	35	3	50:50	n/a	£91.19	45	£1.75	2	231	4	£1,757
7	26	23	n/a	n/a	£68.01	59	£2.14	5	1,386	5	£5,800
16	14	30	n/a	n/a	£69.54	78	£1.83	1	655	11	£2,199
16	21	3	47:32	n/a	£93.45	9	£2.39	5	291	1	n/a

Stats

Stats

	SEX RATIO M:F	STAFF: STUDENT RATIO	FOUNDED	NUMBER OF UNDERGRADUATES	NUMBER OF PART-TIME STUDENTS	NUMBER OF POSTGRADS	% IN THROUGH CLEARING
Salford University	**45:55**	**1:16**	**1896**	**12,695**	**2,965**	**1,470**	**10**
The School of Pharmacy, University of London	37:63	1:13	1842	655	0	115	1
University of Sheffield	**43:57**	**1:14**	**1905**	**16,005**	**2,645**	**4,305**	**4**
Sheffield Hallam University	51:49	1:20	1969	16,030	4,160	1,850	25
SOAS	**42:58**	**1:11**	**1916**	**1,970**	**25**	**1,095**	**4.8**
South Bank University	39:61	1:20	1892	8,830	6,565	1,655	30
Southampton Institute	**59:41**	**1:22**	**1984**	**8,525**	**1,740**	**260**	**13**
University of Southampton	39:61	1:14	1952	13,045	3,305	2,900	9
University of St Andrews	**41:59**	**1:10**	**1413**	**5,940**	**465**	**1,005**	**<1**
St George's Hospital Medical School, London	28:72	1:7	1752	1,620	1,245	30	9
Staffordshire University	**51:49**	**1:20**	**1970**	**9,715**	**3,395**	**640**	**22**
Stirling University	36:64	1:18	1967	5,950	1,145	850	6
University of Strathclyde	**44:56**	**1:17**	**1796**	**11,530**	**2,510**	**2,875**	**10**
Sunderland University	44:56	1:18	1901	7,570	6,230	1,560	n/a
Surrey Institute of Art and Design	**42:58**	**1:27**	**1866**	**2,810**	**80**	**50**	**1**
Surrey University	35:65	1:15	1966	6,375	3,450	2,785	13
University of Sussex	**39:61**	**1:13**	**1961**	**6,565**	**2,810**	**1,720**	**2**
Swansea, University of Wales	39:61	1:13	1920	7,465	3,035	1,275	18
University of Teesside	**42:58**	**1:12**	**1992**	**7,755**	**9,850**	**615**	**9**
Thames Valley University	34:66	n/a	1992	7,335	7,355	410	34
University of Ulster	**38:62**	**1:18**	**1968**	**15,010**	**4,010**	**2,175**	**10**
University College, London	48:52	1:3	1826	11,480	340	4,540	9
University of Warwick	**42:58**	**1:12**	**1964**	**9,625**	**9,165**	**3,040**	**1**
University of Westminster	46:54	1:15	1838	10,790	6,735	3,045	30
University of Wolverhampton	**43:57**	**1:28**	**1983**	**12,835**	**6,295**	**945**	**n/a**
University College Worcester	23:77	n/a	1947	3,430	2,635	300	10
University of York	**42:58**	**1:16**	**1963**	**6,555**	**1,400**	**2,230**	**5**
Averages	43:57	1:15	-	8,408	4,357	1,558	13

% OF MATURE STUDENTS	% OF OVERSEAS STUDENTS	NUMBER OF DISABLED STUDENTS	STATE:PRIVATE STUDENTS	AVERAGE ENTRY POINTS	AVERAGE ACCOMMODATION PER WEEK	% IN COLLEGE ACCOMMODATION	BOOZE INDEX	% OF GRADS UNEMPLOYED AFTER 6 MONTHS	NUMBER OF STUDENTS PER COUNSELLOR	FLUNK RATE (%)	AVERAGE DEBT PER YEAR
32	16	344	97:3	n/a	£48.02	30	£2.11	7	5,216	20	£3,545
20	25	4	70:30	n/a	£118.16	75	£1.45	0	821	3	£3,405
8	17	268	83:17	n/a	£61.92	30	£1.80	6	2,704	7	£3,433
68	11	496	95:5	220	£49.16	8	£1.78	7	1,079	13	£2,829
36	54	10	69:31	n/a	£118.69	27	£2.31	8	2,052	17	£2,444
21	18	425	96:4	140	£69.48	16	£2.06	9	2,754	20	£1,703
24	12	329	96:4	n/a	£61.21	27	£2.08	9	2,759	15	£5,667
16	16	446	81:19	389	£75.80	49	£1.87	7	5,028	5	£4,360
23	31	150	67:33	320	£74.84	19	£2.14	9	359	14	£2,681
37	8	0	67:33	305	£78.93	18	£2.31	n/a	758	5	£4,753
56	13	159	98:2	211	£38.70	2	£2.33	11	3,444	19	£3,898
11	13	121	91:9	n/a	£59.50	52	£1.43	9	1,475	13	£1,990
16	17	179	90:10	n/a	£55.40	16	£2.10	7	3,480	15	£3,372
47	20	16	97:3	159	£47.54	23	£1.89	6	2,723	27	£3,215
22	12	260	99:1	220	£61.38	18	£1.88	11	725	8	£3,668
14	34	44	88:12	280	£59.88	61	£2.06	4	2,419	9	£2,665
22	22	283	85:15	345	£59.87	46	£2.24	6	2,153	14	£1,806
16	9	202	92:8	284	£50.79	38	£1.51	6	1,207	10	£1,523
35	9	212	97:3	236	£35.86	17	£1.83	7	3,324	21	£3,938
91	13	70	87:1	n/a	£85.00	0	£2.05	10	2,285	25	£5,009
21	16	290	99:1	256	£44.88	6	£1.70	6	3,198	16	£528
13	29	154	70:30	n/a	£92.35	32	£2.28	5	2,313	7	£2,866
6	33	82	76:24	340	£68.01	20	£1.59	6	8,624	5	£3,473
32	28	230	94:6	108	£87.24	10	£2.43	10	2,647	19	£2,537
67	20	152	99:1	n/a	£40.15	16	£1.90	10	1,991	24	£4,269
58	2	133	n/a	n/a	£52.84	17	£1.92	6	3,365	18	n/a
12	19	111	80:20	421	£57.40	53	£1.83	7	3,794	5	£2,474
36	18	282	86:13		£62	24	£1.94	7	3,032	14	£3,477

stats

top ten

TOP 10 — Cheapest Campus Pint

- Abertay Dundee
- Bradford
- Bolton Institute
- Roehampton
- Bournemouth
- Worcester
- Aston
- Aberdeen
- Bangor
- Aberystwyth

TOP 10 — Highest male sex ratio

- Harper Adams
- Imperial
- Loughborough
- Heriot-Watt
- Royal Agricultural College
- Southampton Institute
- Abertay Dundee
- Bolton Institute
- LSE
- Brunel

TOP 10 — Cheapest college accommodation

- Ulster
- Teesside
- Paisley
- Bolton
- Abertay Dundee
- Lampeter
- Leeds Metropolitan
- East Anglia
- Wolverhampton
- Worcester

TOP 10 — Lowest external rent

- Teesside
- Lampeter
- Bradford
- Keele
- Kent
- Wolverhampton
- Leicester
- Liverpool John Moores
- Staffordshire
- Bangor

TOP 10 — Highest female sex ratio

- Roehampton
- Worcester
- Royal Veterinary College
- Canterbury Christ Church
- St George's Hospital Medical School
- University College Chichester
- Liverpool Hope
- London
- Bath Spa
- Goldsmith's

top ten

TOP 10

Lowest unemployment after 6 months

School of Pharmacy
Royal Scottish Academy of Music & Drama
Royal College of Music
Harper Adams
Canterbury Christ Church
Robert Gordon
Newcastle
Surrey University
Queen Margaret, Edinburgh
Queen's University, Belfast

TOP 10

Highest proportion living in

Lancaster
RSAMD
School of Pharmacy
Keele
Leicester
Surrey
Aberystwyth
UEA
Royal Holloway
Royal Agricultural College

TOP 10

Best at student sport

Loughborough
Bath
Stirling
Oxford
Leeds
Cambridge
Durham
Birmingham
Bristol
London
Manchester

TOP 10

Highest private:state school ratio

Harper Adams
Courtauld Institute
Royal Agricultural College
London
Manchester
Royal College of Music
Oxford
Cambridge
Imperial
Bristol

TOP 10

Highest proportion living out

Open University
Birkbeck
Courtauld Institute
Thames Valley
Glasgow Caledonian
Paisley
Sheffield Hallam
Plymouth
APU
Dundee

GLOSSARY

GLOSSARY

In the world of higher education, there's a whole language of weird words and interminable terminology. Ever true to our no-nonsense, cut-the-brown-smelly-stuff approach, *The Push Guide* takes you on a ramble through the jargon jungle, explaining all the terms to help anyone pass themselves off as a student. We've even highlighted some of the more confusing course terms that don't tend to crop up in pre-university education – they're the ones in italics.

A Levels: A Levels are the exams most students take at the end of school or college (further education) in England, Wales and Northern Ireland. Usually, students heading for university take three or four A Levels (or the equivalent, such as through AS Levels split over the two years). Those equivalents include Highers in Scotland, the International Baccalaureate in other countries or new qualifications such as vocational A Levels.

Accountancy/Accounting: Not a professional qualification, just a background course giving prospective accountants the necessary insight into finance, investment, tax, management and business.

Admissions: The admissions office of any university or college handles the applications and enrolments. That's the department to ask for when you phone up to talk about getting in.

Alumni: 'Old boys' and 'old girls', ie. former students. Singular: alumnus. Feminine singular: alumna. Feminine plural: alumnae. Neuter ablative plural: go ask a Latin student.

American Studies: Often dismissed as a doss subject (eg. 'you just watch films and listen to old jazz records') this is a multi-disciplinary subject, covering the culture (?), history and current affairs of the US. Usually includes a period spent in the States – a big draw for people who like Oreo cookies, country music and drive-by shootings.

Archaeology: You might think 3 years risking the wrath of disturbed Egyptian mummies is a cool way to spend a degree course, but archaeology courses are more 'Time Team' than 'Indiana Jones', using a combination of history, science, languages and other disciplines, as well as practical fieldwork.

Architecture: Architecture requires a combination of technical knowledge of forms and structures (sciencey) with creative and aesthetic talents (arty), as well as history, economics and environmental studies.

Art(s): Arts subjects include pretty much anything creative. You know, painting, drama, music and all that. It often overlaps with humanities.

Athletics Union/Sports Union: The student organisation that runs student sports clubs and sometimes sports facilities. They're usually hot-beds of sexism, alcohol abuse and hairy chests ... and that's just the women.

Awards: Most students get awards, but unfortunately there's no big Oscars-style ceremony because these awards are basically the new version of what used to be called grants. Students get awards from their local education authority or equivalent to pay towards their university tuition costs.

Bachelor: of ... Arts, Science, Education, Engineering, etc. At English, Welsh and Northern Irish universities, this is the degree most undergraduate students are heading for. When you get it, you can put BA, BSc, BEd, BEng or whatever else is appropriate at the end of your name, but if you feel you have to boast about it like that, most people will think you're a nob.

Balls: Big black-tie and posh frock parties, of course. Why? What did you think it meant? Many student balls include not only a slap-up dinner and much drinking, but also bands (often including quite big has-been names), discos, casinos, fun-fairs, cabaret acts, fortune-tellers, snogging and vomiting. Hardy ball-goers often party all night and occasionally the event is rounded off with a champagne breakfast and 'survivors' photo' (not a pretty sight).

Bops: A dance night more in the school disco style than a hardcore club night.

Botany: The plant bit of Biology.

Business Studies: The study of business, obviously, but it also includes maths and economics and, less predictably, bits of psychology and sociology. And what with Europe and all that stuff, languages are becoming increasingly unavoidable.

Campaign for Free Education: Unlike the NUS, whose policy commits them to trying to get rid of tuition fees (but in practice, they've accepted it now), these guys still campaign to get grants restored.

Campus: The area of land on which a collection of college buildings are built. So, a campus university is one built entirely or mainly on a single campus. A civic campus is a campus in a town. And a greenfield campus is not. Just to confuse things, some universities use 'campus' as a synonym for 'site' and vice versa, so it could mean anything from a single building to an almost entirely separate college.

Convocation: a fancypants term for graduation – the formal ceremony when you receive your degree.

Court: The Cambridge term for a quad.

Chaplain: Chaplains hang around universities offering religious guidance and support to those who want it. They usually come in a variety of religious flavours.

Clearing: Each year after the A Level results are published, many students find they haven't got the place they wanted and many universities find they haven't filled their courses. Having participated in a sophisticated applications and admissions process up to then, the universities and students throw caution to the wind and often try to shove square pegs into round holes. Clearing tends not to result in the best possible matches. There's more about making the most of clearing without making a meal of it at *Push Online* (www.push.co.uk).

College: A vague word that could mean (a) a sixth form college where students do A Levels, (b) a semi-self-contained unit in a collegiate university, (c) an institution of higher education that isn't allowed to call itself a university or (d) any university, college of higher education, its buildings and/or its administrative authorites.

Combined honours: An undergraduate degree course that involves several subject areas – usually three – in approximately equal parts (to start with at any rate).

Degree: A higher education qualification of a certain level. They're split into undergraduate degrees or first degrees which are usually Bachelorships and various postgraduate degrees (masters, doctorates, PGCEs and so on). A university isn't a university if it doesn't teach degrees although some do other higher education qualifications too like Higher National Diplomas (HNDs).

Department: Most universities break down different subject areas into departments and students 'belong' to whichever department teaches their course. It gets more complicated if they study more than one subject, because they may end up in several departments. Some universities don't have departments, they have schools or faculties instead (or even as well), but they're basically the same thing.

Desmond: Slang for a lower-second class honours degree, ie. a Desmond Tutu (two-two. Geddit?). For the record, a first is known as 'a Geoff' (Hurst), a 2.i is 'an Attila' (the Hun) and a third is 'a turd'. Don't blame *Push if* you get a third – we didn't invent the rules of Cocker-nee rhyming slang.

Dons: Dons are Mafia bosses, but in the context of universities, particularly Oxbridge, they're more likely to be lecturers, tutors or other academics who do teaching.

Economics: Economists will tell you that their subject is 'the study of the allocation of scarce resources'. In fact, they mean it's about the way money changes hands, affecting society (and managing never to reach you and me).

Education: A Bachelor of Education degree trains teachers to teach, within a specialised field at any rate (usually determined by age group, academic subject, or both). Some take a

'normal' first degree (BA, BSc, etc.) instead and study for a further year to get a Postgraduate Certificate of Education (PGCE). Either way, after four years of being a student, they know how to work for low pay and look moth-eaten.

Engineering: Engineering is the study of how to create things that make people's lives easier/ healthier/safer/better. There are sub-divisions such as: Chemical Engineering (studying how materials change); Civil Engineering (transport, sewage, public buildings, etc.); Electrical Engineering and so on. Engineers usually work phenomenally hard, play 'Doom' for hours, and tell you that their subject is 'really interesting, actually'.

Ents: Short for entertainments, which are usually run by the students' union and include such larks as gigs, hypnotists and, if you're unlucky, karaoke.

Environmental Studies: A relatively new discipline that takes bits of biology, chemistry, geology and social sciences and investigates how environmental problems occur, how to prevent them and how to chain yourself to a bulldozer.

European Studies: French, Spanish and Italian aren't just languages, nowadays there are courses which combine learning how to talk with learning something to talk about. A French course might include bits about French culture, business, law, history and Thierry Henry's tackling techniques.

Faculty: Old lecturers never die, they just lose their faculties. Universities are usually divided into departments (see above). Just in case these departments feel lonely, they're allowed to club together into faculties. So, the physicists join their chemistry and biology chums in a Science Faculty and the musicians get together with the drama luvvies in an Arts Faculty and everybody's happy. Except the lawyers, who usually have a faculty on their own. Maybe they smell.

Finals/Finalists: Finals are the exams in the final year of study that decide whether or not the last 3 or 4 years have been worth living in abject poverty for. Hence, finalists are students in their final year with their heads on the exam block.

First: Not something to do with when you don't drink enough water, but the top-scoring honours degree.

Flunking: To flunk is to drop out of university or fail. Hence the proportion of students who do it is the flunk rate.

Formals: Posh universities and colleges (the Oxbridge ones, for a start) sometimes have formal dinners where students are supposed to dress up sometimes in black tie, sometimes in suits or sometimes in gowns over their combats and T-shirts. Such formals may be compulsory or voluntary or they may be so popular that students have to sign up to attend (especially if the formals are followed by ents of some sort). Some places have formals every night, some have them only once a term.

Foundation degree: A relative newbie – they've been on offer since 2001 – these are employment-related courses studied over two years (if taken full-time, but part of the lure is the flexible approach). While a university might offer a foundation degree, its content could be planned and even taught by employers.

Freshers: Freshers are first year students in their first few weeks – when the pace is faster than curry through a dog with diarrhoea and the main topics of conversation are home towns, A Level grades and UCAS codes. During students' time as freshers, they are likely to spend 99% of their student loan, join student clubs whose events they never attend and get staggeringly drunk most nights. After three weeks of this, they are hungover, broke and wiser – ie. fully-fledged students.

Freshers' Week: Also known as Week One, Orientation Week, Intro Week and 'Cyril' for all we know, this is the first week of the first term of the first year of a student's university career. It's packed with events and ents designed to help students settle in, make friends and to tell them everything they need to know about how the university and students' union work. In the process, they tend to both drink and spend too much, but have a damn good time. See Freshers, above.

Further education (FE): Further education is what comes after primary and secondary education. In other words it's usually what 16- to 18-year-olds do. In yet other words, it's A Levels, Highers and the like. And in other, other, other words, it's what you have to do to be qualified to go on to higher education (universities and the like).

Gap year: Many students decide to take a year off – or a gap year – after school or college and before going to university. This is best not spent in front of the TV, but getting work experience, earning money, travelling or doing something exciting or mind-expanding. Or a mixture of all of the above. See 'Pushing the Boat Out' at the front of the book.

Geology: Geologists study the structure of the earth and the rocks, fossils, minerals and all the general gunk that's in it.

Graduand: A student in the few months between finishing their course and being awarded their degree.

Graduate: Someone who's successfully completed a degree. A graduate student is a glutton for punishment who's embarking on another degree, usually a postgraduate degree.

Graduation: Also known as convocation. When you're officially awarded your degree.

Grants: Once upon a time, students used to get grants which paid for their tuition and grants which paid towards their living costs. They still exist in Scotland for Scottish students only, but otherwise they are the stuff of myth and legend. Now students get far less generous 'awards'.

Guild of Students/Students' Guild: Another name for a students' union.

Hack: Not the sound of a bad cough or a lozenge to cure it, but a person who is utterly committed to their extra-curricular activities. Usually refers to those involved in SUs or student journalism. You can tell a hack because they're the ones claiming everyone else is apathetic.

Halls: At most colleges, when students talk about halls, they mean 'halls of residence', the accommodation blocks, which traditionally provide catered meals (but increasingly are becoming self-catered), cleaners, heat, light and electricity and a variety of amenities such as launderettes, common rooms and TV lounges. Oxbridge, of course, has to be different. At Oxford or Cambridge, halls are the formal dining rooms.

Head tenancy scheme: Rather than handing out cardboard boxes or have students cluttering up the gym floor, some colleges have started to do the house-hunting themselves. They get a group of landlords together, rent all their brick boxes that pretend to be homes and then sublet them to students, often at cheaper rates or on better terms.

Higher education (HE): After primary school, there's secondary school, then further education and, finally, higher education which takes place at universities, colleges of higher education and so on. HE includes undergraduate and postgraduate degrees, higher national diplomas (HNDs) and a few other things like certain vocational qualifications (such as LCPs for lawyers, for instance).

Highers: In Scotland, students take Highers as the equivalent of A Levels.

HND: The Higher National Diploma is based on vocational studies and is generally aimed at prepping students for a particular career or industry. It can lead to or count towards a degree course.

Honours degree: When people boast about having an *honours* degree, don't be too impressed. Most degrees are honours degrees and, depending on how you do in your exams or coursework, are split into: first class honours (or <u>firsts</u>), upper second class or 2.i (pronounced 'two-one'), lower-second class or 2.ii (a 'two-two', more commonly called a <u>Desmond</u>) and third class honours, or a third. If a student does badly, but not quite badly enough to fail, that's when they might not get an honours degree, but an ordinary degree instead.

Humanities: The study of human creative endeavour, whether it's literature, art, music or whatever. 'Richard & Judy' probably doesn't count. Humanities aren't quite the same as actually doing the creative bit, ie. The <u>Arts</u> (which includes almost anything likely to get Lottery funding).

Intro Week: Another name for <u>Freshers' Week</u>.

Jobshop: A student employment agency usually run by the students' union. Apart from advertising vacancies, jobshops are sometimes more proactive and actually look for appropriate paid work for students. They also sometimes check that the employer's not a crooked slave-driver and doesn't impose minimum pay and conditions. Unlike most job agencies, they usually don't take a cut and often students get work in the jobshop or students' union itself.

Joint Honours: Not an honours degree in cooking big roasts or rolling spliffs, but, like a <u>combined honours</u> degree, a course involving more than one subject. In this case, two subjects.

Junior Common Room (JCR): Another name for a <u>students' union</u>, but usually quite a modest affair such as in an <u>Oxbridge</u> college or a hall of residence. It's also usually a real common room too for undergrad students.

Law: An LLB course will not qualify a student to don a silly wig and act like Kavanagh QC. In theory, it teaches the workings of the legal system (usually the English one) and how laws are applied. It also includes the skills and methods that the legal profession requires, such as learning to shout 'you can't handle the truth!'. Not all degrees are qualifying law degrees – meaning you'll still need to sit the Common Professional Examination (CPE). Even with an undergrad law degree under your belt you'll need to do further vocational training to become a barrister or solicitor.

LEA: Your friendly, neighbourhood Local Education Authority. They're the nice people you hope will give you money towards tuition fees and living expenses. Slowly being superseded by Your Parents.

Learning Resources Centre (LRC): In the old days (when there were Tories in Scotland) universities used to have libraries (which had books in them) and computer rooms (which had computers). Now they're just as likely to have LRCs which are vast buildings with books and computers.

Lecture: Someone once defined a lecture as the process of transferring words from the notes of the lecturer to the student without passing through the brain of either. Lectures are one of the main teaching mechanisms of universities. They tend to be larger than a regular school class and less interactive. (Seminars are closer to school classes.) Usually attendance is not compulsory, but missing them isn't likely to help your studies.

Lecturer: Apart from the obvious – ie. someone who gives a lecture – lecturers are academics at a certain level in the hierarchy well above postgraduates but below professors and deans.

Mature students: It is not necessarily true that mature students behave any more maturely than conventional ones. Nor are they necessarily old fogeys – some are as young as 21 – but, generally, they are older than most other students and are probably returning to education rather than being fresh out of school. (Having a year out counts as being fresh, having 10 years out living in a brothel doesn't.)

Means-testing: Local Education Authorities (<u>LEAs</u>) assess how much money students have at their disposal before handing out any money for their tuition fees. Similarly student loans are based on a means test. However it may seem, they're not called that because they're trying to see how mean they can be.

Media Studies: A heavily over-subscribed course, often by students who think (i) it'll get them straight into the BBC or Hollywood or (ii) it's a doss course. Both are wrong. Media courses usually cover practical and theoretical training in all areas of mass communication and while the experience and contacts might give students an edge in pursuit of a glittering career full of men with pony-tails, unfortunately, life-membership of the Groucho Club is not automatic and there are many other routes to media infamy.

Middle Common Room (MCR): Like a <u>Junior Common Room</u>, but for postgrads only.

Modular courses: A sort of pick'n'mix course comprising a number of components (modules), either within just one department or across a range of subjects.

Nightline: All students have times when the skin on the cup of cocoa of life is just a bit too thick and Nightline services, available in most colleges worth their salt, are there for those times. They are telephone counselling services, a bit like the Samaritans, run (usually) by students for students.

Non-completion/non-progression rate: A politer term for what we at *Push* call the flunk rate (see <u>flunking</u>).

NUS: The National Union of Students, run by students who never grew up, provides research, welfare information and services to SUs which are affiliated. NUS is also the national body which represents and campaigns on behalf of students. At a day-to-day level you'll deal with your <u>students' union</u>.

NUS card: You'll get your NUS card from your <u>students' union</u>. Guard it with your life: it can get you into nightclubs and museums for free or money off very useful things like undies, train tickets, books or even (most importantly) booze.

NVQ: The National Vocational Qualification is usually taken when you've already got a job (or work experience) and, basically, it's a bit like your boss sending you off to study, but only the bits she really wants you to know about. They're taught at an industry-agreed standard, so employers in those industries can be keen if you've got one on your CV.

Open days: An opportunity for prospective students to be shown around the university. Beware only being shown the good parts and take the opportunity to talk to the inmates, er, students.

Ordinary degree: An 'ordinary degree' is somewhat less than ordinary, because most students get an <u>honours</u> degree. You only get an ordinary degree if either you decide to aim lower for some reasons or you fail an honours degree, but don't fail so badly you get nothing.

Oxbridge: The collective name for the two oldest universities in the country, Oxford and Cambridge, both collegiate, both traditional, both highly respected (not least by themselves). It's strange that Camford never caught on.

Personal tutors/Moral tutors: At many, if not most, universities, students are assigned to a personal tutor who is charged with responsibilities beyond the purely academic. The extent of their remit and of their usefulness varies enormously. Some have regular meetings to discuss everything from exams to sex, others introduce themselves to their tutees at the beginning of their college career with some Le Piat d'Or and limp cheese and don't see them again till graduation day. Sometimes they're called moral tutors, but expecting academics to give moral guidance is like asking a fish to run a marathon.

Philosophy: 'What is philosophy?' is a philosophical question, but, ever ready to ponder even the deepest mysteries, *Push*'s definition is that it's about asking the complex questions behind other subjects. Without necessarily expecting an answer. So, when philosophers ask 'Does God exist?', they're more interested in the ideas and arguments involved, than His fax number (for that you want <u>theology</u>).

PGCE: A Postgraduate Certificate in Education is a one-year postgraduate course that graduates can take and which qualifies them to become teachers. At the moment, most students get six grand just for doing the course and might get their student loan paid off too if they go on to become a teacher in a subject where there's a shortage. A PGCE's not the only way to become a teacher – you can also do a four-year Bachelor of Education undergrad degree.

Politics: Of course, nobody with the intelligence and decency to read *The Push Guide* would want to become anything as vile as a politician, but you might wish to study how these creatures operate. Politics (aka Political Studies, Government, etc.) uses elements of history, economics, statistics and more to investigate how people govern themselves and each other and whether Gordon Brown will ever smile.

Polytechnic: Once upon a time there was something called 'the binary divide' which distinguished between universities and polytechnics. It never meant much anyway and now it means nothing at all. Polytechnics tended to have a slant towards vocational courses and an often unfair reputation for lower academic standards than universities. Now they've all become universities themselves, but the old poly prejudices seem to linger about like last week's dirty socks, again somewhat unfairly.

Postgraduate/postgrad: A student doing a postgraduate degree. ie. they've already got one degree and now they're doing another higher one such as a masters degree, a doctorate (PhD) or a postgraduate certificate in education (PGCE).

Practical: A form of teaching, or probably more accurately, of learning, usually used in sciencey type subjects. It involves doing experiments and the like.

Professor: A big cheese in an academic department – often the head – but, at any rate, someone who has climbed the brain hierarchy.

Psychology: If, at university, you ever get pestered by students wielding clipboards and asking intimate questions about sexuality and your favourite colour, chances are they're either chatting you up or they're psychologists (or both). Psychology is the study of the way people think and behave, using elements of biology, sociology, maths and other disciplines. And sometimes they make cute little mazes for rats to run around in. Aw.

Quad: A square surrounded by buildings, usually covered in grass and commonly found in Oxbridge colleges. Only at Cambridge they call them courts, just to be difficult.

Rag: Rag (from 'Raise and Give') is an excuse to dress up in stupid clothing and get up to wacky, irresponsible and sometimes illegal antics – and all in the name of charity. Collectively, student charity Rags raise millions of pounds with stunts like parachute jumps, sponsored hitch-hikes and so-called Rag raids where students (usually dressed as rabbits, the Cheeky Girls, characters from Rocky Horror, etc.) accost strangers in the street and try to sell them 'Rag magazines'. Rag mags are tackily printed joke books, which usually fulfil one of two conditions: either, they are not very funny, or they're in appalling bad taste, or both.

Redbrick: A redbrick building or campus does not necessarily have to have a single red brick. Instead, it refers to a style of building, or a period from around the turn of the century through to the Second World War. What redbrick means is not very precise, but what it doesn't mean is easier to explain. A campus is described as redbrick if it isn't an Oxbridge rip-off or a modern concrete monstrosity.

Sabbatical: Every year at most colleges, a few students either take a year off their studies or hang around after them because they've got nothing better to do. In the meantime they are employed (sub-peanut wages) by various student bodies in official roles, such as in SUs, Rags, newspapers, athletics unions and so on. Not just anyone can do this though – they almost always have to be elected by the other students, who then spend the rest of the sabbatical's year of office wondering why they ever voted for them. Just like real politics.

Sandwich course: Not a catering course (although, come to think of it, you could do a sandwich course in catering), but a course that involves vocational experience. So, the bread in a sandwich course is academic study and the filling is a work placement usually in business or industry. Usually it takes a year to fill a sandwich (as a result, most last 4 years), but there are thin and thick versions that involve different amounts of filling dispersed between different thicknesses of bread. *Push* eagerly awaits the introduction of toasted and club sandwich courses.

Semester: A semester is the American word for a term and is used in Britain to describe American-style college terms that are longer (usually about 15 weeks) than British ones (between 8-11 weeks). Generally speaking, universities have either two semesters or three terms.

Seminar: A teaching class, overseen by a lecturer, in which anything from half a dozen to about 35 students discuss and maybe even do exercises. Sound familiar? They're rather similar but larger than tutorials.

Senior Common Room (SCR): Like a Junior or Middle Common Room, but this is for the fully qualified academics and the emphasis is exclusively on the room itself and a few clubby activities rather than any kind of students' union or representative role.

Single honours: An undergraduate degree involving one main subject.

Social science: A social science is any subject which uses scientific methods to study human society, rather than the natural world. Originally regarded as a soft option, some social scientists can now earn big wads by going on the telly and talking lots.

Sociology: The study of how people operate within social groups (eg. families, schools, football crowds). Sociologists have to use a variety of skills, such as dealing with data and statistics. Sociology still has an undeserved reputation as a dumping ground for left-wing under-achievers, but it's as intellectually rigorous (and attractive to employers) as any other social science subject.

Socs: Short for 'societies', these are the student clubs which range from serious political battlegrounds to sporting teams, from cultural groups to seriously silly socs, such as the Rolf Harris Appreciation Club and Up Shit Creek Without A Paddle Soc – both genuine.

Students' Association (SA): Just another name for a students' union really. Common in Scotland.

Students' Union (SU): Almost all colleges have a students' union and students are usually automatically members, though they can opt out if they wish. As a rule, an SU is usually a services and representative organisation run by students for students or the building in which such services are housed.

Students' Representative Council/Committee (SRC): Yet another name for a students' union or part of one, especially the part that focuses on representation.

SU: A students' union.

Subsidiary course: A course that acts as a side dish to the main course, usually in a single honours course.

Tariff: The list of points you score for each of your further education qualifications. Collect enough points and you might have enough to get into a particular degree at a particular university. As it happens, the tariff is almost complete fiction because most universities tend to rely on your whole application, not just your grades.

Theology: The study of God, gods and religion.

Thesp: An arty-farty acting type.

Top-up fees: The tuition fees that universities are now allowed to directly charge students in most parts of the UK – before, your LEA would usually stump up. What you have to pay varies at each university and on how much you or your parents earn, though they're currently capped at 3 grand. See 'Hard *Pushed*' at the front of the book for details on the whole fees shebang.

Town/Gown: An expression which describes the relationship between locals and the student and academic staff community. People say 'town/gown' even though students these days are more at home in a GAP T-shirt and a pair of scuffed Skechers than a gown and mortar board. Come Graduation Day, though, students are geared up in 'subfusc', as the outfit is called, and photos are taken of them. Embarrassment guaranteed.

Tutee: A student whose work (and/or well-being) is overseen by a particular tutor. It's pronounced more like 'chew tea' than like 'tutty'.

Tutor: An academic who oversees or supervises the work of individual students (tutees).

Tutorial: A small group of students – definitely no more then five otherwise it's a seminar whatever they claim – who meet up with a tutor and discuss their studies. If they're lucky, students get one-to-one tutorials which are a great opportunity to discuss individual ideas, thoughts and problems with work.

UCAS: The Universities & Colleges Admissions Service is the organisation that handles most university applications. Prospective students fill out a form online (or on paper) and submit it to UCAS who send it to the universities the student wants to apply to. After the decision process and interviews the student either gets accepted or not, and UCAS oversees the process to check no one finds themselves with more than one place and to try to match students with vacancies as efficiently as possible.

Undergraduate: A student doing their first degree.

Union: Usually this is just another name for a students' union or the building in which the students' union and/or its facilities and services are based. As such, it's often the students' main hang-out on campus. However, at Oxbridge (and various other universities that just have to be awkward), the Union might also be the Union Society, a debating club with some highly exclusive (even elitist) facilities attached.

University: Not nearly as easy to define as you might have thought, although officially a UK university has to be founded by Parliamentary Statute. There are plenty of places like certain university colleges and places like King's College London (and other colleges of London University) that deserve the name as much as many of the places that have it. The long and the short of it is that a university is a place to get a higher education.

University College: Officially, a college that has the power to award its own degrees, but isn't a fully-fledged university, or a college run by a fully-fledged university. HE colleges which are independent, but whose degrees are rubber-stamped by a university, aren't allowed to use the 'University' bit, but to the student on the ground they're pretty much the same thing.

Vice-Chancellor: Aka principals, wardens, masters etc. These are the big cheeses – the Stilton amongst the Dairyleas of academia. Students rarely get to meet them, but basically they run the place. Where there are vice-chancellors, there are also chancellors, who are the token heads of the institutions and usually B-list celebs but usually don't do much more than shake students' hands at the graduation ceremony. The allegations that vice-chancellors have anything to do with vice are entirely unfounded.

Vocational course: Any course that is intended at least to train students for a particular profession, career or job. They often involve practical experience in a work environment, such as placements, or doing projects similar to what goes on in real world jobs.

Women's Studies (aka Gender Studies): A multi-disciplinary subject that studies how women (and men) are treated in fields as diverse as law, history and health and the reasons for gender differences in behaviour, communication, pay and more. Oh, and men are allowed to apply.

Zoology: The animal bit of biology.

Short, sharp *Push*

The abbreviations used in *Push*:

AU:	Athletics Union
BUNAC:	British Universities North American Club
BUSA:	British Universities Sports Association
cap:	capacity
CATS:	Credit Accumulation and Transfer Scheme
CDL:	Career Development Loan
CofE:	Church of England
CofS:	Church of Scotland
CUKAS:	Conservatoires UK Admissions Service
DfES:	Department for Education and Skills
ents:	entertainments
FC:	Free Church
GTTR:	Graduate Teacher Training Registry
HND:	Higher National Diploma
HE:	higher education (ie. degree/HND-level or above)
HESA:	Higher Education Statistics Agency
HEFCE:	Higher Education Funding Council for England
JCR:	Junior Common/Combination Room (usually Oxbridge)
LEA:	Local Education Authority
LGB:	Lesbian, Gay, Bisexual
LRC:	Learning Resources Centre
NHS:	National Health Service
NMAS:	Nursing and Midwifery Admissions Service
NUS:	National Union of Students
Poly:	polytechnic
postgrads:	postgraduates
RC:	Roman Catholic
SA:	Students' Association (usually Scotland)
sabb:	sabbatical officer
SCR:	Senior Common Room
SLC:	Student Loans Company
SNP:	Scottish National Party
soc:	society or club
SRC:	Student Representative Council
SU:	Students' Union
SWSS:	Socialist Workers' Student Society
u'grads:	undergraduates
UCAS:	The Universities and Colleges Admissions Service
ULU:	University of London Union
URC:	United Reform Church

*Push*ing on

Where to go from here. A guide to useful publications, websites and other resources:

GENERAL

Push **Online** (www.push.co.uk) has loads of information for anyone thinking about going to university, links to university and college websites (plus a fair few student unions and student papers) and is just generally fab (though we probably would say that).

The *Push* Guide to Choosing a University, Ruth Bushi, Dan Jones and Anthony Leyton; Nelson Thornes, £15.95, ISBN: 0748790276. E-mail: editor@push.co.uk

Everything You Need to Know About Going to University, Sally Longson; Kogan Page, £9.99, ISBN: 07494339858

Choosing Your Degree Course and University 2004, Brian Heap; Trotman, £21.99, ISBN: 0856609455

The UCAS website (www.ucas.com) has details of the application procedure, order forms for books, forms and resources and a course search facility for finding which universities do the course you're after. To apply online, see www.ucas.com/apply The UCAS directory and Big Book list details about course and university codes, which is not only a thrilling read but stuff you actually need to know when applying. Your careers library will have these, or you can get the info or buy it online.

Clearing the Way: Getting into University and College through the UCAS Clearing System, Tony Higgins; UCAS, £8.99, ISBN: 0856602280. A practical guide to the Clearing system.

Student Life – A Survival Guide, Natasha Roe; Lifetime Careers, £10.99, ISBN: 1902876369

TAKING A YEAR OFF/TRAVELLING

Taking a Year Off, Margaret Flynn; Trotman, £11.99, ISBN: 0856608505

The Gap Year Guide Book, Susannah Hecht; Peridot Press, £11.95, ISBN: 0901577936

Taking a Gap Year, Susan Griffith; Trotman, £11.95, ISBN: 1854582941

Planning Your Gap Year, Nick Vandome; How To Books, £9.99, ISBN: 1845280105

Work Your Way Around the World 2003, Susan Griffith; Trotman, £12.95, ISBN: 1854582747

Working Holidays Abroad, Mark Hempshall; Trotman, £9.99, ISBN: 1857332660

The Virgin Travellers' Handbook 2002, Tom Griffiths; Trotman, £14.99, ISBN: 0753506335

Let's Go Guides: Web: www.letsgo.com

Lonely Planet Guides: Web: www.lonelyplanet.com

Rough Guides: many of their guide books are available at www.roughguides.co.uk

www.gapwork.com: guide to working holidays and current vacancies

www.gap-year.com: provides good information on taking a year out

Working Holidays (Central Bureau of Educational Visits and Exchanges). If you can't find a copy in your local library, contact the Bureau on (020) 7725 9402.

A Year Out (UCAS brochure, £2) and **A Year Off ... A Year On** (UCAS book, £10.50). To order, contact UCAS Distribution on (01242) 544 610.

The Year in Industry Scheme. E-mail: enquiries@yini.org.uk Tel: (0161) 2754 396. www.yini.org.uk

There's a full list of year-out organisations at www.yearoutgroup.org/organisations.htm, including:

Africa and Asia Venture: 4- and 5-month schemes offering great scope for cultural and interpersonal development in Kenya, Tanzania, Uganda, Malawi, Zimbabwe, India and Nepal. Mainly unpaid teaching work, with extensive travel and safari opportunities. E-mail: av@aventure.co.uk. Web: www.aventure.co.uk Tel: (01380) 729 009. Address: 10 Market Place, Devizes, Wiltshire SN10 1HT

BUNAC (British Universities North America Club): offers an extensive range of work/travel programmes worldwide, varying from a few months to a whole year, depending on destination and programme. Web: www.bunac.org Tel: (020) 7251 3472

Community Service Volunteers (CSV): full-time voluntary placements throughout the UK for people between 16 and 35. Allowance, accommodation and food provided. Web: www.csv.org.uk Freephone (0800) 374 991

Gap Activity Projects Ltd (GAP): an independent educational charity founded in 1972, which organises voluntary work overseas in 30 different countries. E-mail: volunteer@gap.org.uk. Web: www.gap.org.uk Tel: (0118) 9594 914

Gap Challenge/World Challenge Expeditions: varied schemes for students 18-25, from voluntary conservation projects to paid hotel work in many different countries. E-mail: welcome@world-challenge.co.uk. Web: www.world-challenge.co.uk Tel: (020) 8961 1551

Raleigh International: a charity-run scheme giving young people the opportunity to go on 3-month expeditions all over the world for varied project work. Over 20,000 young people (including Prince William) have taken part in a total of 168 expeditions in 35 countries since 1984. Web www.raleigh.org.uk Tel: (020) 7371 8585

If you fancy **working on a kibbutz**, contact: Kibbutz Representatives, 1a Accommodation Road, London NW11 8ED. Web: www.kibbutz.org.il (in Hebrew and English) Tel: (020) 8458 9235. Plus, try Project 67, also based in London: E-mail: project67@aol.com Tel: (020) 7831 7626

Students Partnership Worldwide: challenging and rewarding 4-9 month projects in developing countries. Web: www.spw.org Tel: (020) 7222 0138

Teaching & Projects Abroad: foreign travel and experience in teaching English, conservation work, medicine and journalism among others. Countries include China, Ghana, India, Thailand, Mexico and South Africa. Web: www.teaching-abroad.co.uk Tel: (01903) 708 300

UKSA: gap year meets radical sports – windsurfing, kayaking, sailing, professional crew and skipper training. Web: www.uk-sail.org.uk Tel: (01983) 294 941

For **teaching opportunities** (no formal training needed to take up a temporary position), contact: Gabbitas Educational Consultants, Carrington House, 126-130 Regent Street, London W1R 6EE Tel: (020) 7734 0161

Voluntary Service Organisation (VSO): runs special overseas youth programmes for under 25s. Contact: VSO Enquiries: (020) 8780 7200, or E-mail: infoservices@vso.org.uk You can apply online at www.vso.org.uk

www.volunteerafrica.org: information on voluntary opportunities in Africa. E-mail: support@volunteerafrica.org

ACADEMIC GUIDES & APPLICATIONS PROCEDURE

Individual colleges publish prospectuses for admissions and many students' unions produce alternative prospectuses. To get hold of a copy, use the contact details in the *Push* entries or see your careers adviser/library. For top tips on completing your application form and personal statement, have a look also at *Push Online*.

The Big Guide (University and College Entrance: The Official Guide), UCAS, £32.50. Includes the StudyLink CD-Rom

The UCAS/Universities Scotland Entrance Guide to Higher Education in Scotland 2005 Entry, UCAS, £8.95

How to Complete Your UCAS Form, 2006 Entry; Trotman, £11.99, ISBN: 1844550060

Choosing Your Degree Course and University, Brian Heap; Trotman, £21.99, ISBN: 1844550052

Degree Course Offers 2005, Brian Heap; Trotman, £26.99, ISBN: 0856608815

You want to study what?! vol 1, Dianah Ellis; Trotman, £14.99, ISBN: 0856608939

You want to study what?! vol 2, Dianah Ellis; Trotman, £14.99, ISBN: 0856608947

The UCAS/Trotman Complete Guides Series: individual guides for various subject areas from Engineering to Performing Arts. £17.99 each

The Directory of University and College Entry 2005/6; Butterworth-Heinemann, £39.99, ISBN: 0856609536

UK Course Discover, ECCTIS+, subscription CD and website (www.ecctis.co.uk), covering over 100,000 courses at universities and colleges in the UK. Available at schools, colleges, careers offices and training access points (TAP).

UCAS/Universities Scotland Entrance Guide to Higher Education in Scotland 2005 Entry, UCAS, £8.95, ISBN: 184361006X. Focuses solely on full-time degrees and diplomas at Scottish institutions.

For Scottish Students: **Student Awards Agency for Scotland (SAAS):**
E-mail: saas.geu@scotland.gsi.gov.uk. Web: www.saas.gov.uk. Tel: (0845) 1111 711 (24 hours), also (0131) 4768 212
Address: Gyleview House, 3 Redheughs Rigg, Edinburgh EH12 9HH
Student Support in Scotland: a guide for undergraduate students. Published annually, can be obtained from SAAS.

British Vocational Qualifications; Kogan Page, £40.00, ISBN: 0749441976

NVQs and How to Get Them, Hazel Dakers; Kogan Page, £9.99, ISBN: 0749437111

Getting into Business & Management Courses 2003; Trotman, £9.99, ISBN: 0856608610

Getting into Dental School, James Burnett; Trotman, £11.99, ISBN: 1844550214

Getting into Law 2004, Justina Burnett; Trotman, £11.99, ISBN: 085660948X

Getting into Mathematics, Richard Skerrett (ed.); Trotman in association with UCAS, £8.99, ISBN: 0856603597

Getting into Medical School 2006, Joe Ruston and James Burnett; Trotman, £11.99, ISBN: 1844550303

Getting into Psychology, James Burnett; Trotman, £11.99, ISBN: 0856609501

Getting into Veterinary School, Mario di Clemente; Trotman, £11.99, ISBN: 1844550206

Getting into Oxford & Cambridge; Trotman, £9.99, ISBN: 0856608696

Q & A Studying Art & Design; Trotman, £4.99, ISBN: 0856605700

Q & A Studying Business & Management 2000; Trotman, £4.99, ISBN: 0856605719

Q & A Studying Chemical Engineering 2000; Trotman, £4.99, ISBN: 0856605778

Q & A Studying Computer Science 2000; Trotman, £4.99, ISBN: 0856605727

Q & A Studying Drama 2000; Trotman, £4.99, ISBN: 0856605735

Q & A Studying English 2000; Trotman, £4.99, ISBN: 0856605743

Q & A Studying Law 2000; Trotman, £4.99, ISBN: 0856605751

Q & A Studying Media 2000; Trotman, £4.99, ISBN: 085660576X

Q & A Studying Psychology 2000; Trotman, £4.99, ISBN: 056605786

Q & A Studying Sports Science 2000; Trotman, £4.99, ISBN: 0856605794

Complete Guide to Art & Design Courses 2005; Trotman, £17.99, ISBN: 0856609587

Complete Guide to Business Courses 2005; Trotman, £17.99, ISBN: 0856609609

Complete Guide to Computer Science Courses 2005; Trotman, £17.99, ISBN: 0856609617

Complete Guide to Engineering Courses 2005; Trotman, £17.99, ISBN: 0856609560

Complete Guide to Healthcare Professions Courses 2005; Trotman, £17.99, ISBN: 0856609579

Complete Guide to Performing Arts Courses 2005; Trotman, £17.99, ISBN: 0856609595

Complete Guide to Physical Science Courses 2005; Trotman, £17.99, ISBN: 0856609625

STUDY ABROAD

For Australian universities: www.australian-universities.com

For European universities: www.eua.be/eua (European University Association)

Getting Into American Universities 2004, James Burnett; Trotman, £11.99, ISBN: 0856609781

For international students or UK students studying overseas:
www2.britishcouncil.org/learning.htm – info about UK courses and qualifications available and also those in the home country of international students.

Europe, Hobsons/Trotman, £9.99, ISBN: 1904638228

ERASMUS: E-mail: info@erasmus.ac.uk Web: www.erasmus.ac.uk Tel: (01227) 762 712. Address: UK Socrates-Erasmus Council, University of Kent, R 7 D Building, Canterbury CT2 7PD

UK NARIC: E-mail: info@naric.org.uk Web: www.naric.org.uk Tel: 0870 9904088. Address: ECCTIS Ltd, Oriel House, Oriel Road, Cheltenham, Gloucestershire GL50 1XP

British Council: E-mail: general.enquiries@britishcouncil.org Web: www.britcoun.org Tel: (020) 7930 8466
Address: 10 Spring Gardens, London SW1A 2BN
Also, **Comenius action 2.2, Leonardo da Vinci**, Central Bureau for International Educational Education and Training, in the British Council.

Commission of the European Communities: Web: www.cec.org.uk Tel: (020) 7973 1992 Address (London office): 8 Storey's Gate, London SW1P 3AT

Experience Erasmus 2006; Trotman, £15.95, ISBN: 0003800278

www.student.com: site on college life in the USA

FINANCE, GRANTS AND SPONSORSHIP

The *Push* Guide to Money 2005: Student Survival, Johnny Rich and Alice Tarleton; Nelson Thornes, £9.95, ISBN: 0748790284. Money advice is also available at www.push.co.uk

For information on student loans: **Student Loans Company:** Web: www.slc.co.uk
Help Line: (0800) 405 010 General Enquiries: (0870) 6060 704
Address: 100 Bothwell Street, Glasgow G2 7JD

Department for Education and Skills (DfES): Tel: 0870 000 2288
Address: Publications Centre, PO Box 5050, Annesley, Nottingham NG15 0DL
The DfES's riveting missives on student funding are also available on their website
(www.dfes.gov.uk).

University Scholarships and Awards 2004, Brian Heap; Trotman, £19.99, ISBN:
0856609773. All the info you'll need, plus information for overseas students and a list
of charitable and other awards. Each university is broken down with a list of awards
they offer.

The Educational Grants Directory 2004/5, Alan French et al; Directory of Social Change,
£29.95, ISBN: 190399151X. Lists all sources of non-statutory help for students in
financial need.

Students' Money Matters 2005, Gwenda Thomas; Trotman, £14.99, ISBN:
1844550281. This is an excellent reference book with details on just about everything
concerning student finance, plus student case studies and 'thrift tips' throughout.

Balancing Your Books, Josephine Warrior; CRAC, £6.99, ISBN: 0954756517

Leaflet HC11 produced by the **Department of Health** has information about help with
costs for prescriptions, dental and eye care charges. Claims can be made on form HC1,
or directly over the phone – call 08870 610 1198.

Scholarship Search UK (SSUK): Web: www.scholarship-search.org.uk Launched in April
2000, this is a free search facility for all undergraduate students. Constantly updated.
You can search by subject, awarding body or region. Tel: (020) 8600 5300
Address: SSUK, Hotcourses Ltd, 150-152 King Street, London W6 9JG

The **Windsor Fellowship** runs undergraduate personal and professional development
programmes (such as sponsorships, community work and summer placements).
This is primarily for gifted black and Asian students.
E-mail: office@windsor-fellowship.org Web: www.windsor-fellowship.org.
Tel: (020) 7613 0373
Address: The Stables, 138 Kingsland Road, London E2 8DY

Education Grants Advisory Service (EGAS): Web: www.egas-online.org
Tel: (020) 7254 6251
Address: 501-505 Kingsland Road, Dalston, London E8 4AU (Enclose a stamped
addressed envelope with your enquiry letter.)

The Sponsorship and Funding Directory 2003; Hobsons, £8.99, ISBN: 1860179304.
Available in most schools, colleges and public libraries. As above, also lists charities that
offer educational sponsorships.

Engineering Opportunities for Students and Graduates 2004, Institution of Mechanical
Engineers. If you are studying any kind of engineering course, this magazine lists several
sponsors and universities with sponsored courses.
Call (020) 7222 7899 or e-mail: education@imeche.org.uk Web:
www.imeche.org.uk/education

Student Life – A Survival Guide, Natasha Roe and Mark Cripps; Lifetime Careers,
£10.99, ISBN: 1902876369.

www.scraptuitionfees.com: the Liberal Democrats' petition regarding fees.

The **National Union of Students** (NUS) produces a series of information sheets on student
finance. Send an A4 stamped self-addressed envelope with subject details to:
The Welfare Unit, NUS, 461 Holloway Road, London N7 6LJ. Tel: (020) 7272 8900
Web: www.nusonline.co.uk

www.hefce.ac.uk: site of Higher Education Funding Council for England

www.studentuk.com: a general student guide including a good money section

If you're looking for a job, check out **www.studentjobs.org.uk** or **www.hotrecruit.com**.

Also: **www.ncwe.com** (National Council for Work Experience) has excellent info and details of companies who offer student placements.

www.jobpilot.co.uk/content/channel/student is another one to try.

The **Guardian** newspaper has student and graduate opportunities advertised regularly (especially in Saturday editions), or try www.guardian.co.uk/jobs

www.dti.gov.uk/er/pay.htm tells you about the national minimum wage and hours of employment and also has a 'young worker' section.

www.studentswapshop.co.uk: speaks for itself.

Other useful student websites: **www.student123.com, www.interstudent.co.uk** and **www.uni4me.com**

OVERSEAS STUDENTS

British University & College Courses; UCAS/Trotman, £10.95

The **British Council** website (www.britcoun.org.uk) has information on coming to university in Britain and a good 'virtual campus' to introduce you to life at UK universities. EU students (non-UK) should contact: The European Team at the Department for Education and Skills (2F – Area B, Mowden Hall, Staindrop Road, Darlington, Durham DL3 9BG). Call 01325 391199 during office hours or visit www.dfes.gov.uk/studentsupport/eustudents

www.ukcosa.org.uk (The Council for International Education) is a support organisation for international students.

www.prospects.csu.ac.uk: postgraduate advice for international students in the 'International Students in the UK' section.

MATURE STUDENTS

The Mature Students' Directory 2005; Trotman, £19.99, ISBN: 0856609854

The Mature Students' Guide to Higher Education, available free from UCAS

Studying for a Degree: How to Succeed as a Mature Student in Higher Education, Stephen Wade; How to Books, £6.99, ISBN: 1857034155

Coming Back to Learning – A Handbook for Adults, Monica Brand et al; Lifetime Careers, £9.99, ISBN: 1902876881

POSTGRADUATE STUDY

How to Get a PhD 2000, Open University Press, £16.99, ISBN: 033520550X

Directory of Postgraduate Studies, Hobsons, £109.99 (at that price, don't buy it, try the library)

Sources of Funding

The UK Research Councils – Biotechnology and Biological Sciences Research Council (BBSRC):
Web: www.bbsrc.ac.uk Tel: (01793) 413 200
Address: Polaris House, North Star Avenue, Swindon SN2 1UH

Economic and Social Research Council (ESRC): Web: www.esrc.ac.uk
Tel: (01793) 413 000 Address as above (Postcode SN2 1UJ)
Engineering and Physical Sciences Research (EPSRC): Web: www.epsrc.ac.uk
Tel: (01793) 444 000 Address as above (Postcode SN2 1ET)

Natural Environment Research Council (NERC): Web: www.nerc.ac.uk
Tel: (01793) 411 500 Address as above (Postcode SN2 1EU)

Particle Physics and Astronomy Research (PPARC): Web: www.pparc.ac.uk
Tel: (01793) 442 000 Address as above (Postcode SN2 1SZ)

Medical Research Council (MRC): Web: www.mrc.ac.uk Tel: (020) 7636 5422
Address: 20 Park Crescent, London W1B 1AL

The Arts and Humanities Research Board (AHRB): Web: www.ahrb.ac.uk
Tel: (0117) 9876 500 (Postgraduate Awards Division)
Address: Whitefriars, Lewins Mead, Bristol BS1 2AE

Council for the Central Laboratory of the Research Councils (CCLRC):
Web: www.cclrc.ac.uk Tel: 01235 821900
Address: Rutherford Appleton Laboratory, Chilton, Didcot, Oxon, Oxfordshire OX11 0QX

Further Postgraduate Sources

The Association of Graduate Careers Advisory Service (AGCAS): Web:
www.agcas.org.uk Tel: (0161) 2369 816
Address: Armstrong House, Oxford Road, Manchester M1 7ED
They publish a booklet called **Postgraduate Study & Research**, free from your careers
service. Alternatively, it can be purchased from CSU (Publications) at the address above.

Royal Society Research Fellowships: Web: www.royalsoc.ac.uk Tel: (020) 7451 2500
Address: Research Appointments Department, 6-9 Carlton House Terrace, London
SW1Y 5AG

www.prospects.ac.uk: postgraduate section

STUDENTS WITH DISABILITIES

Applying to Higher Education: Guidance for Disabled People, Skill, £2.50 to students

Funding for Disabled Students in Higher Education, Skill, £2.50 to students. This
booklet contains information about social security entitlements.

SKILL: Tel: (020) 7450 0620 Address: Chapter House, 18-20 Crucifix Lane, London
SE1 3JW
Their website (www.skill.org.uk) offers information for students and carers and details of
how to get hold of Skill publications. For disabled students looking for work they have
loads of jobs across all sectors, and your university careers service or students' union will
have their details. For more information, see www.skill.org.uk/info/links/employment.asp
or contact them directly.

The Disabled Students' Guide to University 2005; Trotman, £21.99,
ISBN: 0856609463
Provides information on the financial, practical (eg. accommodation, transport), social
and academic provisions each university has for disabled students.

Action for Blind People: Web: www.afbp.org National Helpline: 0800 915 4666.
Address: Grants Officer, 14-16 Verney Road, London SE16 3DZ

For the DfES leaflet **Bridging the Gap: A Guide to the Disabled Students' Allowances**,
and information about the Disabled Students' Allowances, call the DfES information line
on (0800) 7319 133. Web: www.dfes.gov.uk

Association for Spina Bifida and Hydrocephalus: Web: www.asbah.org
Tel: (01733) 555 988
Address: ASBAH House, 42 Park Road, Peterborough PE1 2UQ
Maximum award £2,000.

The Dyslexia Institute Bursary Fund: Web: www.dyslexia-inst.org.uk
Tel: (01784) 463 851
Address: 133 Gresham Road, Staines, Middlesex TW18 2AJ

Snowdon Award Scheme: Web: www.snowdonawardscheme.org.uk Tel: (01403) 211 252
Address: 22 City Business Centre, 6 Brighton Road, Horsham, West Sussex RH13 5BB
Helps disabled students aged 17-25 in further, higher or adult education.

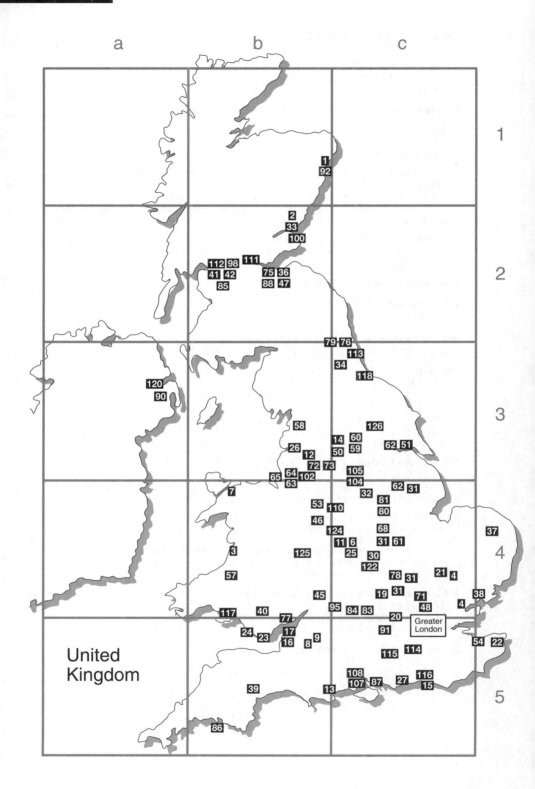

a
b
c

1

2

3

4

5

1
92

2
33
100

112 98 111
41 42
85
75 36
88 47

79 76
113
34
118

120
90

58
126
14 60
50 59
62 51
26
12
72 73
105
65 64 102
104
63
7
62 31
32
53 110
81
80
46
124
68
11 6
31 61
25
30
122
3
125
57
78 31
19 31
21 4
45
71
4 38
95
84 83
20
4
117 40 77
Greater
London
91
54 22
24 23 17
16
8 9
115 114
108 107 87 27 116
39
13
15
86

United
Kingdom

37

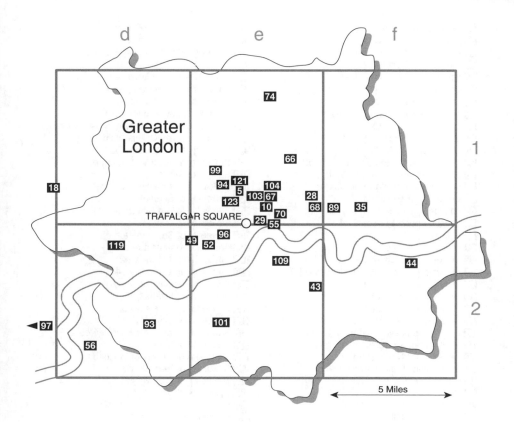

d   e   f

Greater London

74

66

99
94 121
5
123 103 67
10
70
29 55
104
28
68 89 35

TRAFALGAR SQUARE

18

119

49
96
52

109

43

44

97

93

101

56

5 Miles

1 University of Aberdeen *b1*
2 University of Abertay Dundee *b2*
3 Aberystwyth, Unversity of Wales *b4*
4 APU *c4*
5 University of the Arts, London *e1*
6 Aston University *c4*
7 Bangor, University of Wales *b4*
8 University of Bath *b5*
9 Bath Spa Univeristy College *b5*
10 Birkbeck College, London *e1*
11 University of Birmingham *c4*
12 University of Bolton *b3*
13 Bournemouth University *b5*
14 University of Bradford *b3*
15 University of Brighton *c5*
16 University of Bristol *b5*
17 Bristol, UWE *b5*
18 Brunel University *d1*
19 University of Buckingham *c4*
20 Buckinghamshire Chilterns University College *c4*
21 University of Cambridge *c4*
22 Canterbury Christ Church University College *c5*
23 Cardiff University *b5*
24 University Of Wales Institute, Cardiff *b5*
25 University of Central England *c4*
26 University of Central Lancashire *b3*

27 University College Chichester *c5*
28 City University *e1*
29 Courtauld Institute *e1*
30 Coventry University *c4*
31 De Montfort University *c4*
32 University of Derby *c4*
33 Dundee University *b2*
34 University of Durham *c3*
35 University of East London *f1*
36 University of Edinburgh *b2*
37 University of East Anglia *c4*
38 University of Eseex *c4*
39 Exeter University *b5*
40 Glamorgan University *b4*
41 University of Glasgow *b2*
42 Glasgow Caledonian University *b2*
43 Goldsmiths College, London *e2*
44 Greenwich University *f2*
45 University of Gloucestershire *b4*
46 Harper Adams University College *b4*
47 Heriot-Watt University *b2*
48 University of Hertfordshire *c4*
49 Heythrop College, London *e2*
50 University of Huddersfield *c3*
51 University of Hull *c3*
52 Imperial College, London *e2*

53 Keele University *b4*
54 University of Kent *c5*
55 King's College, London *e1*
56 Kingston University *d2*
57 Lampeter, University of Wales *b4*
58 Lancaster University *b3*
59 Leeds University *c3*
60 Leeds Metropolitan University *c3*
61 Leicester University *c4*
62 University of Lincoln *c3, c4*
63 University of Liverpool *b3*
64 Liverpool John Moores University *b3*
65 Liverpool Hope University College
66 London Metropolitan University *e1*
67 University of London *e1*
68 London Guildhall University *e1*
69 Loughborough University *c4*
70 LSE *e1*
71 University of Luton *c4*
72 University of Manchester *b3*
73 Manchester Metropolitan University *b3*
74 Middlesex University *e1*
75 Napier University *b2*
76 Newcastle University *b2*
77 Newport, University of Wales *b4*
78 University College, Northampton *c4*
79 Northumbria University *b2*
80 University of Nottingham *c4*
81 Nottingham Trent University *c4*
82 Open University *not marked on map*
83 University of Oxford *c4*
84 Oxford Brookes University *c4*
85 Paisley University *b2*
86 University of Plymouth *b5*
87 University of Portsmouth *c5*
88 Queen Margaret College, Edinburgh *b2*
89 Queen Mary College, London *f1*

90 Queen's University of Belfast *a3*
91 University of Reading *c5*
92 Robert Gordon University *b1*
93 Roehampton University *d1*
94 Royal Academy of Music *e1*
95 Royal Agricultural College *c4*
96 Royal College of Music *e2*
97 Royal Holloway, London *d2*
98 Royal Scottish Academy of Music & Drama
99 Royal Veterinary College, London *e1*
100 University of St Andrews *b2*
101 St George's Hospital, London *e2*
102 Salford University *b3*
103 School of Pharmacy, London *e1*
104 University of Sheffield *c3*
105 Sheffield Hallam University *c3*
106 SOAS *e1*
107 University of Southampton *c5*
108 Southampton Institute *c5*
109 South Bank University *e2*
110 Staffordshire University *c4*
111 Stirling University *b2*
112 University of Strathclyde *b2*
113 Sunderland University *c3*
114 Surrey University *c5*
115 Surrey Institute of Art & Design *c5*
116 University of Sussex *c5*
117 Swansea, University of Wales *b4*
118 University of Teesside *c3*
119 Thames Valley University *d2*
120 University of Ulster *a3*
121 University College London *e1*
122 University of Warwick *c4*
123 University of Westminster *e1*
124 University of Wolverhampton *b4*
125 University College Worcester *b4*
126 University of York *c3*

Index

GUIDE TO SYMBOLS

Academic

excellent   average   poor

Entertainment

cheap   average   expensive

Social & Political

hot, hot, hot   lukewarm   frozen stiff

Sports

triumphant   average   slobbish

Accommodation

cheap   average   expensive

Welfare

pampering   passable   poor

Push knows that thumbs don't tell the whole story.
So do yourself a favour and read the profile for the bigger picture.

Entries are arranged in alphabetical order (ignoring the words 'University' or 'University of')

Words in *italic* type are Push's point of view – take it or leave it

For more information on how to use Push see '*Push*over', page viii.

Push craves feedback – if you have any thoughts or suggestions, please contact:

The Push Guides, Nelson Thornes, Delta Place,
27 Bath Road, Cheltenham, Gloucestershire GL53 7TH
Tel: (01242) 267 943

e-mail: editor@push.co.uk

Push online: www.nelsonthornes.com/push